C000115723

1 MONTH OF FREE READING

at

www.ForgottenBooks.com

By purchasing this book you are eligible for one month membership to ForgottenBooks.com, giving you unlimited access to our entire collection of over 1,000,000 titles via our web site and mobile apps.

To claim your free month visit:
www.forgottenbooks.com/free601170

ISBN 978-0-483-31959-2
PIBN 10601170

SOUTHERN REBELLION.

BOSTON: SAMUEL WALKER, 3 TREMONT ROW.
NEW YORK: THOMAS FARRELL & SON, 107 FULTON STREET.

THE

SOUTHERN REBELLION:

BEING

A HISTORY OF THE UNITED STATES

FROM THE

COMMENCEMENT OF PRESIDENT BUCHANAN'S ADMINISTRATION THROUGH THE WAR
FOR THE SUPPRESSION OF THE REBELLION.

CONTAINING

A RECORD OF POLITICAL EVENTS, MILITARY MOVEMENTS, CAMPAIGNS, EXPEDITIONS,
BATTLES, SKIRMISHES, ETC.

PREPARED FROM OFFICIAL DOCUMENTS AND OTHER AUTHENTIC SOURCES.

BY W. A. CRAFTS.

ILLUSTRATED WITH ELEGANT STEEL ENGRAVINGS,
FROM ORIGINAL DESIGNS AND PHOTOGRAPHS, EXECUTED EXPRESSLY FOR THE WORK.

BOSTON:
PUBLISHED BY SAMUEL WALKER.
1862.

TO THE

DEFENDERS OF THE UNION,

ON THE LAND AND ON THE SEA,

THIS WORK IS RESPECTFULLY INSCRIBED.

THE Southern Rebellion

INTRODUCTION

THE history of the great Southern Rebellion should, perhaps, commence many years before the actual breaking out into open resistance in 1861. After the suppression of nullification in South Carolina, in 1832, General Jackson wrote, in effect, that there was a settled determination on the part of the leaders of that movement to establish a "southern confederacy" — that the tariff was then made the pretext for their resistance to the authority of the United States, but that the next pretext would be the slavery question. There are various evidences that the keen observation of President Jackson was not at fault. The language of the aiders and abettors in the nullification movement indicated that there was a fixed purpose in some quarters to bring about a division of the United States, and to establish a separate government at the south, under which the material, political, and social interests of that section should be promoted, better than they could be by association with the different interests of the north. The secret history of the movement has not been written, but occasional glimpses have been had through all the period, from 1831 to the final breaking out of rebellion in 1861, which revealed the purposes of the leaders of the ultra southern party, while a consideration of the public history of the country, in relation to those matters having a bearing upon the interests, or supposed interests, of the south, confirm the observer in the belief that this purpose of separation has been, to some extent, constantly entertained, and that the action of certain parties has tended constantly and consistently to such a result.

The structure of southern society is such as might naturally lead to the desire for the establishment of a government on a different theory from that of the United States, as interpreted by the more democratic society of the north. A privileged class, accustomed to lead and control in social life, and having such a community of interest as makes it expedient and necessary for them to act together in their local politics, and withal based upon an institution which at once magnifies their importance, both social and political, and renders them jealous of their privileges, could hardly be expected to be content with the control of their own local politics, or with their social superiority in their own community, if beyond these they had other political relations, and were part of a larger community. Such a privileged class are the southern planters and slaveholders — an aristocracy without titles, but with as much power, socially and politically, and with as many privileges, practically and legally, in their own states and communities, as, perhaps, any nobility of the old world. They have all the influence which wealth can give; all the distinction which freedom from labor, and the absolute control over the great laboring class, can afford; all the power which common interest and united purpose can secure by means of wealth, leisure, ability, and social influence. The local governments are theirs, the local laws are especially for them and their property, and the whole political system hinges upon their rights and interests.

These things are facts, entirely independent of any moral or political question in relation to slavery. Such is the class which has neces-

sarily grown up at the south under the influence of institutions and ideas constantly extending in that one direction, and which so rules as to give the tone and character to that portion of the country. At home, in their own community and states, their power and their position have been sufficiently established, their interests sufficiently protected. But in the United States — the whole country — they were not paramount and absolute. By the constitution southern institutions were recognized; but ever since the establishment of the government, and especially since the culture of cotton has given increased importance to the landholder and slaveholder of the south, there has been a contest between the north and the south respecting the extent to which this recognition was intended to be carried in the constitution, and how it was to be carried out by the laws and practices, and assent, of the whole country; and almost as continually there have also been other contests, of a more temporary character, in relation to policy affecting more or less the interests of the privileged class at the south. A review of the history of the country will show that in a majority of these contests, and for a long time, the south ultimately prevailed, or secured some substantial gain, if not all that it desired.

It is not to be inferred from this that the privileged class of the south were always united and contending against a united natural opposition at the north. Parties were divided, both at the north and the south, on other great questions and measures, and partly on the traditional distinctions of the early days of the republic. The questions before the whole country which affected the interests of the dominant power at the south were for a long time incidental or temporary, and such as might naturally be viewed differently among themselves. But that power, for the most part, affiliated with the party at the north which most nearly supported its interests and ideas.

By degrees, in the lapse of time, old issues disappeared, and every new question that arose, or was forced upon the country, involved more and more the interests or privileges of the institution on which the southern power was based. As these interests and privileges came directly in question, the power of the ruling class among its own people became manifest, by the union of the greater part of the southern voters. In former years, and under the old issues, their efforts had been mainly not to lose any advantages. But as the social and political institutions of the south became more compact and firmly established, and the privileges and power of the aristocratic part of the community consequently increased, the efforts were not simply defensive or protective, but were directed to the control of the general government. In these efforts they succeeded until the last election, because in the more democratic north parties are not so easily consolidated, and the interests involved in such contests, being too remote to be personally felt, as at the south, were in part controlled or modified by other and local interests. Thus the southern party have always found at the north a party which acted with them, partly from traditional associations, and partly from the various motives of interest, feeling, sympathy, and opposition to other men, parties, or measures. And thus they gained an influence in the general government, and gradually brought it, or sought to bring it, into a position, with regard to their social institutions, as near as possible to that of their local governments, and in opposition to the principles and institutions of the north.

This was the policy of the more extreme party at the south; that party which, from its positive character and determined course, shaped the policy of that section. There were others, a majority of whom were probably not so deeply interested in the peculiar institutions of the south, who were disposed to a more moderate policy. But in the course of time the latter class grew smaller or less influential, while the extreme party gained, as every such party must, when its leaders are composed of the ablest men, its measures are positive, and its success is probable. Northern opposition to slavery, especially to the extension of slavery into new states, served also to consolidate the south.

As before remarked, the efforts of the southern party had at first been not to lose any advantages, and they succeeded in maintaining an equal power in the national senate by the admission of a new slave state whenever a new free state was admitted. But the rapid increase of the free states in population with each decade reduced the direct influence of the south in the popular branch of Congress. So long, however, as the people of the north were divided, and a considerable portion of them and their representatives could, by interest or sympathy, be attached to the ruling party of the south, it could still control the government. But the Missouri compromise secured to the north a larger territory for new free states than was open to the south for new slave states; and the rapid settlement of that territory indicated that the free states would soon predominate in the senate. Such a result was dreaded by the extreme southern party, for by it they saw the sceptre would pass from their hands. And it was no less plain to the more far-seeing that the institution on which their social and political superiority was based could flourish only by expansion in the cotton and sugar-growing regions. The annexation of Texas was then accomplished; and though that measure was brought about by the aid of the north, it was a southern measure, and for the strengthening of the south and its institutions. The Mexican war followed, with its conquest of vast additional territories. It was hoped that this territory, adjoining the slave states and the territory conceded to slavery, would secure the continued equality, if not preponderance, of the slave states. But the rapid settlement of California, in consequence of the discoveries of gold, by a population of working men, mostly from the free states, disappointed the hope. Then came the agitation in 1849–50, consequent upon this result in California and other questions connected with the settlement of the condition of the conquered territory. Power was passing from the hands of the south. The extreme party talked of secession, and demanded new guaranties for slavery as a condition for remaining in the Union. At that time, there is reason to believe, the doctrine of secession was widely spread among the ruling class of the slave states. Social meetings and associations peculiar to them gave it many advocates and supporters. The doctrine of " state rights," which had always been one of the pillars of their political faith, and the more so because it was a protection to their cherished institution, was asserted more strenuously than since the period of nullification, and to the extent of justifying secession. But the storm passed then. Through the efforts of some of the ablest men of both sections the compromise measures were adopted, some new guaranties were conceded to slavery, the country acquiesced, and peace was restored for a time.

But the compromise measures were not satisfactory to the extreme southern party. They saw that the power of the south was not secured in the future, and could only wane under the existing condition of the territories and the comparative growth of the two sections of the country. New schemes were originated for extending slavery and its consequent political power. The conquest and ultimate annexation of Central America were projected by some of the wildest spirits, and signally failed. The next movement was the abrogation of the Missouri compromise, advocated by the south with a view of opening to slavery territory from which it was excluded by that act, and by a portion of the north as a settlement of the whole question on general principles. Then came another agitation, both at the south and at the north. The evident purpose of the southern party excited a counter purpose at the north, and the north, after a long contest, triumphed, by securing Kansas as a free state.

It is at about this period — the commencement of Mr. Buchanan's administration — that the present volume opens, thus forming a continuation of the History of the United States from the time at which it was left in a former work. Besides the advantage of thus giving a continuous history of the country, there is a propriety in commencing the narrative of the Rebellion with the administration during which the scheme of secession was matured and finally carried into effect. The record of that administration in its ordinary phase, occupied with other cares, or unwittingly — on the part of some of its members — aiding the secret movements for secession, which it proved too weak to oppose, will show how suddenly the apparent calm was disturbed by the storm. Giving, therefore, as in a previous volume, the history of events as they occurred, the writer will enter upon the narrative of the rebellion in due course, believing that the events so presented will give a more faithful picture of the times.

BUCHANAN'S ADMINISTRATION.

BOOK I.

CHAPTER I.

JAMES BUCHANAN, the fifteenth president, was born at Stony Batter, in Franklin County, Pennsylvania, April 22, 1791. He graduated at Dickinson College, in 1809, and was admitted to the bar in 1812, at the age of twenty-one. He was very successful in his practice, and was enabled to retire from the profession at the age of forty. He entered public life, as a member of the Pennsylvania legislature, at an early age. Although a Federalist, he advocated a vigorous prosecution of the war with England in 1812, and enlisted as a private in a company of volunteers. Mr. Buchanan entered Congress in 1820, where he took a high position as a debater and statesman. In 1828 he advocated the election of General Jackson to the presidency, and was a zealous supporter of the administration of that president, who, in 1831, selected him as minister at the Russian court. Upon his return from Russia, in 1833, he was elected to the

senate, when he was again the stanch supporter of General Jackson's administration. At this time he strenuously opposed the slavery agitation, then in its infancy, and advocated stringent measures to suppress it. Mr. Van Buren's administration also found in Mr. Buchanan a firm supporter, and he earnestly advocated the great measure of that administration, the independent treasury. The annexation of Texas was warmly supported by Mr. Buchanan, when that measure came up under the administration of President Tyler. Mr. Buchanan's senatorial career closed with the inauguration of President Polk, who appointed him secretary of state, and while he held this position, the northwestern boundary, between the United States and the British possessions, was settled. At the close of Mr. Polk's administration, Mr. Buchanan retired to private life; but upon the accession of President Pierce he was appointed minister to England, where he remained until April, 1856, when he returned, to be elected president.

The inauguration of Mr. Buchanan was attended by a large concourse of people, gathered from all parts of the country, many from

(1)

a desire to witness the simple ceremonies of the occasion, but more from a desire to pay court to the new administration and those having influence with it, — courtiership being as diligently followed, though under different forms, in our republic, as in some of the monarchies of the old world. From the eastern portico of the Capitol, which usage has assigned for this purpose, before taking the oath of office, Mr. Buchanan delivered his inaugural address. About him were the judges of the Supreme Court, the members of Congress, the diplomatic corps, and high military and civil officers; before him were the people, representing the immense constituency by whom he had been chosen. He addressed them as follows : —

"Fellow-Citizens: I appear before you this day to take the solemn oath that I will faithfully execute the office of president of the United States, and will, to the best of my ability, preserve, protect, and defend the constitution of the United States. In entering upon this great office, I most humbly invoke the God of our fathers for wisdom and firmness to execute its high and responsible duties in such a manner as to restore harmony and the ancient friendship among the people of the several states, and to preserve our free institutions throughout many generations. Convinced that I owe my election to the inherent love for the constitution and the Union which still animates the hearts of the American people, let me earnestly ask their powerful support in sustaining all just measures · calculated to perpetuate these, the richest political blessings which Heaven has ever bestowed upon any nation. Having determined not to become a candidate for reëlection, I shall have no motive to influence my conduct in administering the government, except the desire ably and faithfully to serve my country, and to live in the grateful memory of my countrymen.

"We have recently passed through a presidential contest in which the passions of our fellow-citizens were excited to the highest degree by questions of deep and vital importance; but when the people proclaimed their will, the tempest at once subsided, and all was calm. The voice of the majority, speaking in the manner prescribed by the constitution, was heard, and instant submission followed. Our own country could alone have exhibited so grand and striking a spectacle of the capacity of man for self-government. What a happy conception, then, was it for Congress to apply this simple rule, that the will of the majority shall govern to the settlement of the question of domestic slavery in the territories! Congress is neither to legislate slavery into any territory or state, nor to exclude it therefrom, but to leave the people thereof perfectly free to form and regulate their domestic institutions in their own way, subject only to the constitution of the United States as a natural consequence. Congress has also prescribed, that when the territory of Kansas shall be admitted as a state, it shall be received into the Union with or without slavery, as their constitution may prescribe at the time of their admission. A difference of opinion has arisen in regard to the time when the people of a territory shall decide this question for themselves. This is, happily, a matter of but little practical importance; and besides, it is a judicial question, which legitimately belongs to the Supreme Court of the United States, before whom it is now pending, and will, it is understood, be speedily and finally settled. To their decision, in common with all good citizens, I shall cheerfully submit, whatever this may be, though it has been my individual opinion that, under the Nebraska-Kansas act, the appropriate period will be when the number of actual residents in the territories shall justify the formation of a constitution with a view to its admission as a state into the Union. But, be this as it may, it is the imperative and indispensable duty of the government of the United States to secure to every resident inhabitant the free and independent expression of his opinion by his vote. This sacred right of each individual must be preserved. This being accomplished, nothing can be fairer than to leave the people of a territory free from all foreign interference, to decide their own destiny for themselves, subject only to the constitution of the United States. The whole territorial question being thus settled upon the principle of popular sovereignty, — a principle as ancient as free government itself, — every thing of a practical nature has been decided, and no other question remains for adjustment, because all agree that, under the constitution, slavery in the states is beyond the reach of any human power, except that of the respective states themselves wherein it exists. May we not, then, hope that the long agitation on this subject is approaching its end, and that the geographical parties to which it has given birth, so much dreaded by the father of his country, will speedily become extinct? Most happy will it be for the country when the public mind shall be diverted from this question to others of more pressing and practical importance.

"Throughout the whole progress of this agitation, which has scarcely known any intermission for more than twenty years, while it has been productive of no positive good to any human being, it has been the prolific source of great evils to the master, to the slave, and to the whole country; it has alienated and estranged the people of the sister states from each other, and has even seriously endangered the very existence of the Union. Nor has the danger yet entirely ceased. Under our system there is a remedy for all mere political evils in the sound sense and sober judgment of the people. Time is a great corrective. The political subjects which, but a few years ago, exasperated the public mind, have passed away, and are now nearly forgotten; but this question of domestic slavery is of far greater importance than any mere political question, because, should the agitation continue, it may eventually endanger the personal safety of a large portion of our countrymen where the institution exists. In that event, no form of government, however productive of material benefits, can compensate for the loss of peace and domestic security around the family altar. Let every Union-loving man, therefore, exert his best influence to suppress this agitation, which, since the recent legislation of Congress, is without any legitimate object.

"It is an evil of the times, that men have undertaken to calculate the mere material value of the Union. Reasoned estimates have been presented of the pecuniary profits and local advantages which would result to different states and sections from its dissolution, and of the comparative injuries which such an event would inflict on other states and sections. Even descending to this low and narrow view of the mighty question, all such calculations are at fault. The bare reference to a single consideration will be conclusive on this point.

"We at present enjoy a free trade throughout our extensive and expansive country, such as the world never witnessed. This trade is conducted on railroads and canals, on noble rivers and arms of the sea, which bind together the north and the south, the east and the west of our confederacy. Annihilate this trade, arrest its free progress by the geographical lines of jealous and hostile states, and you destroy the prosperity and onward march of the whole and every part, and involve all in one common ruin.

"But such considerations, important as they are in themselves, sink into insignificance when we reflect on the terrific evils which would result from disunion to every portion of the confederacy — to the north not more than to the south, to the east not more than to the west. These I shall not attempt to portray, because I feel a humble confidence that the kind Providence which inspired our fathers with wisdom to frame the most perfect form of government and union ever devised by man, will not suffer it to perish until it shall have been peacefully instrumental, by its example, in the extension of civil and religious liberty throughout the world.

"Next in importance to the maintenance of the constitution and the Union, is the duty of preserving the government free from the taint, or even the suspicion, of corruption. Public virtue is the vital spirit of republics; and history proves that when this has decayed, and the love of money has usurped its place, although the forms of free government may remain for a season, the substance has departed forever. Our present financial condition is without a parallel in history. No nation has ever before been embarrassed from too large a surplus in the treasury. This almost necessarily gives birth to extravagant legislation. It produces wild schemes of expenditures, and begets a race of speculators and jobbers, whose ingenuity is exerted in contriving and promoting expedients to obtain the public money. The party, through its official agents, whether rightfully or wrongfully, is suspected, and the character of the government suffers in the estimation of the people. This is, in itself, a very great evil. The natural mode of relief from this embarrassment is to appropriate the surplus in the treasury to great national objects, for which a clear warrant can be found in the constitution. Among these, I might mention the extinguishment of the public debt, a reasonable increase of the navy, which is at present inadequate to the protection of our vast tonnage afloat, — now greater than that of any other nation, — as well as the defence of our extended sea coast. It is, beyond all question, the true principle, that no more revenue ought to be collected from the people than the amount necessary to defray the expenses of a wise, economical, and efficient administration of the government. To reach this point, it was necessary to resort to a modification of the tariff; and this has been accomplished in such a manner as to do as little injury as may have been practicable to our domestic manufactures, especially those necessary for the defence of the country. Any discrimination against a particular branch, for the purpose of benefiting favored corporations, individuals, or interests, would have been unjust to the rest of the community, and inconsistent with that spirit of fairness and equality which ought to govern in the adjustment of a revenue tariff; but the squandering of the public money sinks into comparative insignificance, as a temptation to corruption, when compared with the squandering of the public lands.

"No nation in the tide of time has ever been blessed with so rich and noble an inheritance as we enjoy in the public lands. In administering this important trust, while it may be wise to grant portions of them for the improvement of the remainder, yet we should never forget, that it is our cardinal policy to reserve these lands as much as may be for actual settlers, and this at moderate prices. We shall thus not only best promote the prosperity of the new states, by furnishing them a hardy and independent race of honest and industrious citizens, but shall secure homes for our children and our children's children, as well as for those exiles from foreign shores who may seek in this country to improve their condition, and to enjoy the blessings of civil and religious liberty. Such emigrants have done much to promote the growth and prosperity of the country. They have proved faithful, both in peace and in war. After becoming citizens, they are entitled, under the constitution and laws, to be placed on perfect equality with native-born citizens, and in this character they should ever be kindly recognized.

"The federal constitution is a grant from

the states to Congress of certain specific powers, and the question whether this grant shall be liberally or strictly construed, has, more or less, divided political parties from the beginning. Without entering into the argument, I desire to state at the commencement of my administration, that long experience and observation have convinced me, that a strict construction of the powers of the government is the only true, as well as the only safe, theory of the constitution. Whenever, in our past history, doubtful powers have been exercised by Congress, they have never failed to produce injurious and unhappy consequences. Many such instances might be adduced if this were the proper occasion. Neither is it necessary for the public service to strain the language of the constitution, because all the great and useful powers required for a successful administration of the government, both in peace and in war, have been granted, either in express terms or by the plainest implication. While deeply convinced of these truths, I yet consider it clear that, under the war-making power, Congress may appropriate money towards the construction of a military road, when this is absolutely necessary for the defence of any state or territory of the Union against foreign invasion. Under the constitution, Congress has power to declare war, to raise and support armies, to provide and maintain a navy, and to call forth the militia to repel invasion. Thus, endowed in an ample manner with the war-making power, the corresponding duty is required, that the United States shall protect each of them (the states) against invasion. How is it possible to afford this protection to California and our Pacific possessions, except by means of a military road through the territory of the United States, over which men and munitions of war may be speedily transported from the Atlantic states to meet and repel the invader? In case of a war with a naval power much stronger than our own, we should then have no other available access to the Pacific coast, because such a power would instantly close the route across the Isthmus of Central America. It is impossible to conceive, that while the constitution has expressly required Congress to defend all the states, it should yet deny to them, by any fair construction, the only possible means by which one of these states can be defended. Besides, the government, ever since its origin, has been in the constant practice of constructing military roads. It might also be wise to consider whether the love for the Union, which now animates our fellow-citizens on the Pacific coast, may not be impaired by our neglect or refusal to provide for them, in their remote and isolated condition, the only means by which the power of the states on this side of the Rocky Mountains can reach them in sufficient time to protect them against invasion.

"I forbear, for the present, from expressing an opinion as to the wisest and most economical mode in which the government can lend its aid in accomplishing this great and necessary work. I believe that many difficulties in the way, which now appear formidable, will, in a great degree, vanish as soon as the nearest and best route shall have been satisfactorily ascertained.

"It may be right that, on this occasion, I should make some brief remarks as to our rights and duties as a member of the great family of nations. In our intercourse with them, there are some plain principles, approved by our own experience, from which we should never depart. We ought to cultivate peace, commerce, and friendship with all nations, and this not merely as the best means of promoting our own national interest, but in a spirit of Christian benevolence towards our fellow-men, wherever their lot may be cast. Our diplomacy should be direct and frank, neither seeking to obtain more nor accepting less than is our due. We ought to cherish a sacred regard for the independence of all nations, and never attempt to interfere in the domestic concerns of any, unless this shall be imperatively required by the great law of self-preservation. To avoid entangling alliances has been a maxim of our policy ever since the days of Washington, and its wisdom no one will attempt to dispute. In short, we ought to do justice, in a kindly spirit, to all nations, and require justice from them in return. It is our glory, that while other nations have extended their dominions by the sword, we have never acquired any territory, except by fair purchase, or, as in the case of Texas, by the voluntary determination of a brave, kindred, and independent people to blend their destinies with our own. Even our acquisitions from Mexico form no exception. Unwilling to take advantage of the fortune of war against a sister republic, we purchased these possessions, under the treaty of peace, for a sum which was considered at the time a fair equivalent. Our past history forbids that we shall in the future acquire territory unless this be sanctioned by the laws of justice and honor. Acting on this principle, no nation will have a right to interfere or to complain if, in the progress of events, we shall still further extend our possessions. Hitherto, in all our acquisitions, the people, under the protection of the American flag, have enjoyed civil and religious liberty, as well as equal and just laws, and have been contented, prosperous, and happy. Their trade with the rest of the world has rapidly increased, and thus every commercial nation has shared largely in their successful progress. I shall now proceed to take the oath prescribed by the constitution, while humbly invoking the blessing of divine Providence on this great people."

Having delivered his inaugural address, the oath of office was administered by Chief Justice Taney, and the simple ceremony was over. James Buchanan was the chief magistrate of the country, and invested with all the powers pertaining to that high office — powers equal to, and in some respects greater than, the powers of some of the sovereign rulers of Europe.

President Buchanan soon sent to the senate the nominations for the members of his cabinet, which were all confirmed without opposition, as usual in such cases. The cabinet thus appointed consisted of the following gentlemen : —

Secretary of State,	Lewis Cass, of Michigan.
" " the Treasury,	Howell Cobb, of Georgia.
" " the Interior,	Jacob Thompson, of Miss.
" " War,	John B. Floyd, of Virginia.
" " the Navy,	Isaac Toucey, of Conn.
Postmaster-General,	Aaron V. Brown, of Tenn.
Attorney-General,	Jeremiah S. Black, of Penn.

It was soon after the organization of the new administration that the opinion in the Dred Scott case was pronounced by the Supreme Court. The president alluded incidentally, in his inaugural address, to an expected decision on one or more of the points involved in the Kansas issue, that decision being in the Dred Scott case, and it would appear to have been looked forward to as a judicial sanction of the principles and policy of the party of the administration. We have given place to this subject under the administration of President Pierce, because the inception of the case, and its trial, had taken place under that administration, and, in its political aspect, was the result of the previous progress of the power behind the administration.

The policy which the new administration would adopt with regard to Kansas, was one of the earliest subjects of interest to the public. Affairs in that territory, though greatly improved over their condition of the year preceding, were still in an unsettled state. The election held in October, 1856, mentioned in our last allusion to this subject, was not attended by the free state settlers, who had adopted a general resolution not to participate in elections under the laws of the legislature, whose power they deemed illegal. Mr. Whitfield was therefore elected delegate to Congress without opposition, and he had by a close vote been admitted to a seat in that body at its last session.

The territorial legislature assembled in January, and Governor Geary sent in a long message, setting forth the condition of the territory, and the measures he had adopted to secure tranquillity. He urged the legislature to permit all doubtful questions to remain in abeyance until the formation of a state constitution, the question of slavery especially. He recommended also the immediate repeal of all the objectionable laws which had been passed by the first legislature, and called the attention of the legislature to various public measures to promote the interests of the territory. The legislature adopted some of the governor's recommendations, and modified the objectionable laws. They also passed an act providing for a convention to frame a state constitution. This bill was objectionable in some of its features, and it was vetoed by Governor Geary on the ground that it did not provide for submitting the proposed constitution to the vote of the people for acceptance or rejection, and because he thought the time had not yet arrived for such a movement. The legislature, however,— the members of which had no great regard for a governor who did not sympathize with them,— passed the bill, notwithstanding his veto, by a unanimous vote, and it became a law.

In the mean time the state legislature under the Topeka constitution assembled at Topeka. Governor Robinson had previously resigned the post of governor under that constitution, being convinced that he could better serve the free state cause in a private capacity. The lieutenant-governor also declined to attend. Upon assembling, writs were served upon the principal members, and they were arrested. This was probably expected, and was, perhaps, desired by some of the free state men, as a movement which would advance their cause. In March a free state convention was held, which passed resolutions denouncing the legislative assembly and the act providing for a constitutional convention; declaring that the people could not participate in the election of delegates to this convention without compromising their rights as American citizens, sacrificing the best interests of Kansas, and jeoparding the public peace. They also declared that the state constitution framed by the Topeka convention was a choice of a majority of the people of the territory, and that it ought to be acknowledged by Congress.

On the day of the inauguration of Mr. Buchanan, Governor Geary resigned his post as governor of Kansas. A failure of his health was the cause assigned, and the governor had, indeed, injured his health by his attention to the duties of his place under such difficult circumstances. It is not improbable, too, that he was weary of the cares and the annoyances of the office. By his direct course he had come in conflict not only with individuals who thought they had a claim upon him on party grounds, but with certain officials whose less straightforward views did not agree with his. Judge Lecompte and Marshal Donelson were among those who did not like the governor, and whom the governor had no reason to regard with much favor; and they were removed by President Peirce. After resigning his office, Governor Geary wrote the following farewell address to the people of Kansas:—

Farewell Address of Governor Geary to the People of Kansas Territory.

"Having determined to resign the executive office, and retire again to the quiet scenes of private life and the enjoyment of those domestic comforts of which I have so long been deprived, I deem it proper to address you on the occasion of my departure.

"The office from which I now voluntarily withdraw was unsought by me, and at the time of its acceptance was by no means desirable. This was quite evident from the deplorable moral, civil, and political condition of the territory; the discord, contention, and deadly strife which then and there prevailed; and the painful anxiety with which it was regarded by patriotic citizens in every portion of the American Union. To attempt to govern Kansas at such a period, and under such circumstances, was to assume no ordinary responsibilities. Few men could have desired to undertake the task, and none would have been so presumptuous, without serious forebodings as to the result. That I should have hesitated is no matter of astonishment to those acquainted with the facts; but that I accepted the appointment was a well-grounded source of regret to many of my well-tried friends, who looked upon the enterprise as one that could terminate in nothing but disaster to myself. It was not supposed possible that order could be brought, in any reasonable space of time, and with the means at my command, from the then existing chaos.

"Without descanting upon the feelings, principles, and motives which prompted me, suffice it to say that I accepted of the president's tender of the office of governor. In doing so, I sacrificed the comforts of a home endeared by the strongest earthly ties and most sacred associations, to embark in an undertaking which presented at the best but a dark and unsatisfactory prospect. I reached Kansas, and entered upon the discharge of my official duties, in the most gloomy hour of her history. Desolation and ruin reigned on every hand; homes and firesides were deserted; the smoke of burning dwellings darkened the atmosphere; women and children, driven from their habitations, wandered over the prairies and among the woodlands, or sought refuge and protection even among the Indian tribes. The highways were infested with numerous predatory bands, and the towns were fortified and garrisoned by armies of conflicting partisans, each excited almost to frenzy, and determined upon mutual extermination. Such was, without exaggeration, the condition of the territory at the period of my arrival. Her treasury was bankrupt; there were no pecuniary resources within herself to meet the exigencies of the time; the congressional appropriations, intended to defray the expenses of a year, were insufficient to meet the demands of a fortnight; the laws were null, the courts virtually suspended, and the civil arm of the government almost entirely powerless. Action — prompt, decisive, energetic action — was necessary. I at once saw what was needed, and without hesitation gave myself to the work. For six months I have labored with unceasing industry. The accustomed needed hours for sleep have been employed in the public service. Night and day have official duties demanded unremitting attention I have had no proper leisure moments for rest or recreation. My health has failed under the pressure. Nor is this all. To my own private purse, without assurance of reimbursement, have I resorted, in every emergency, for the required funds. Whether these arduous services and willing sacrifices have been beneficial to Kansas and my country you are abundantly qualified to determine.

"That I have met with opposition, and even bitter vituperation and vindictive malice, is no matter for astonishment. No man has ever yet held an important or responsible post, in our own or any other country, and escaped censure. I should have been weak and foolish, indeed, had I expected to pass through the fiery ordeal entirely unscathed, especially as I was required, if not to come in conflict with, at least to thwart, evil machinations, and hold in restraint wicked passions, or rid the territory of many lawless, reckless, and desperate men. Besides, it were impossible to come in contact with the conflicting interests which governed the conduct of many well-disposed persons without becoming an object of mistrust and abuse. While from others, whose sole object was notoriously personal advancement at any sacrifice of the general good and at every hazard, it would have been ridiculous to anticipate the meed of praise for disinterested action; and hence, however palpable might have been my patriotism, however just my official conduct, or however beneficial, in its results, I do not marvel that my motives have been impugned and my integrity maligned. It is, however, so well known that I need scarcely record the fact, that those who have attributed my labors to a desire for gubernatorial or senatorial honors were, and are, themselves the aspirants for those high trusts and powers, and foolishly imagined that I stood between them and the consummation of their ambitious desires and high, towering hopes.

"But whatever may be thought or said of my motives or desires, I have the proud consciousness of leaving this scene of my severe and anxious toil with clean hands, and the satisfactory conviction that He who can penetrate the inmost recesses of the heart, and read its secret thoughts, will approve my purposes and acts. In the discharge of my executive functions I have invariably sought to do equal and exact justice to all men, however humble or exalted. I have eschewed all sectional disputations, kept aloof from all party affiliations, and have alike scorned numerous threats of personal injury and violence and the most flattering promises of advancement and reward. And I ask and claim nothing more for the part I have acted than the simple merit of having endeavored to perform my duty. This I have done at all times, and upon every occasion, regardless of the opinions of men, and utterly fearless of consequences. Occasionally I have been forced to assume great responsibilities, and depend solely upon my own resources to accomplish important ends; but in all such instances I have carefully examined surrounding circumstances, weighed well the probable results, and acted upon my own deliberate judgment; and in now reviewing them, I am so well satisfied with the policy uniformly pursued, that were it to be done over again it should not be changed in the slightest particular.

"In parting with you I can do no less than give you a few words of kindly advice, and even of friendly warning. You are well aware that most of the troubles which lately agitated the territory were occasioned by men who had no special interest in its welfare. Many of them were not even residents; whilst it is quite evident that others were influenced altogether in the part they took in the disturbances by mercenary or other personal considerations. The great body of the actual citizens are conservative, law-abiding, peace-loving men, disposed rather to make sacrifices for conciliation and consequent peace, than to insist for their entire rights should the general good thereby be caused to suffer. Some of them, under the influence of the prevailing excitement and misguided opinions, were led to the commission of grievous mistakes, but not with the deliberate intention of doing wrong.

"A very few men, resolved upon mischief, may keep in a state of unhealthy excitement, and involve in fearful strife, an entire community. This was demonstrated during the civil commotions with which the territory was convulsed. While the people generally were anxious to pursue their peaceful callings, small combinations of crafty, scheming, and designing men succeeded, from purely selfish motives, in bringing upon them a series of most lamentable and destructive difficulties. Nor are they satisfied with the mischief already done. They never desired that the present peace should be effected; nor do they intend that it shall continue if they have the power to prevent it. In the constant croakings of disaffected individuals, in various sections, you hear only the expressions of evil desires and intentions. Watch, then, with a special jealous and suspicious eye those who are continually indulging surmises of renewed hostilities. They are not the friends of Kansas, and there is reason to fear that some of them are not only the enemies of this territory, but of the Union itself Its dissolution is their ardent wish, and Kansas has been selected as a fit place to commence the accomplishment of a most nefarious design. The scheme has thus far been frustrated; but it has not been abandoned. You are intrusted not only with the guardianship of this territory, but the peace of the Union, which depends upon you in a greater degree than you may at present suppose.

"You should, therefore, frown down every effort to foment discord, and especially to array settlers from different sections of the Union in hostility against each other. All true patriots, whether from the north or south, the east or west, should unite together for that which is and must be regarded as a common cause — the preservation of the Union; and he who shall whisper a desire for its dissolution, no matter what may be his pretensions, or to what faction or party he claims to belong, is unworthy of your confidence, deserves your strongest reprobation, and should be branded as a traitor to his country. There is a voice crying from the grave of one whose memory is dearly cherished in every patriotic heart, and let it not cry in vain. It tells you that this attempt at dissolution is no new thing; but that even as early as the days of our first president it was agitated by ambitious aspirants for place and power. And if the appeal of a still more recent hero and patriot was needed in his time, how much more applicable is it now and in this territory!

"'The possible dissolution of the Union,' he says, 'has at length become an ordinary and familiar subject of discussion. Has the warning voice of Washington been forgotten? or have designs already been formed to sever the Union? Let it not be supposed that I impute to all of those who have taken an active part in these unwise and unprofitable discussions a want of patriotism or of public virtue. The honorable feelings of state pride and local attachments find a place in the bosoms of the most enlightened and pure. But while such men are conscious of their own integrity and honesty of purpose, they ought never to forget that the citizens of other states are their political brethren; and that, however mistaken they may be in their views, the great body of them are equally honest and upright with themselves. Mutual suspicions and reproaches may, in time, create mutual hostility, and artful and designing men will always be found who are ready to foment these fatal divisions, and to inflame the natural jealousies of different sections of the country. The history of the world is full of such examples, and especially the history of republics.'

"When I look upon the present condition of the territory, and contrast it with what it was when I first entered it, I feel satisfied that my administration has not been prejudicial to its interests. On every hand I now perceive unmistakable indications of welfare and prosperity. The honest settler occupies his quiet dwelling, with his wife and children clustering around him, unmolested and fearless of danger. The solitary traveller pursues his way unharmed over every public thoroughfare. The torch of the incendiary has been extinguished, and the cabins which by it were destroyed have been replaced with more substantial buildings. Hordes of banditti no longer lie in wait in every ravine for plunder and assassination. Invasions of hostile arms have ceased, and infuriated partisans living in our midst have emphatically turned their swords into ploughshares and their spears into pruning hooks. Laborers are every where at work, farms undergoing rapid improvements, merchants are driving a thriving trade, and mechanics pursuing with profit their various occupations. Real estate, in town and country, has increased in value almost without precedent, until in some places it is commanding prices that never could have been anticipated. Whether this healthy and happy change is the result solely of my executive labors or not, it certainly has occurred during my administration. Upon yourselves must mainly depend the preservation and perpetuity of the present prosperous condition of affairs. Guard it with unceasing vigilance, and protect it as you would your lives. Keep down that party spirit which, if permitted to obtain the mastery, must lead to desolation. Watch closely, and condemn in its infancy, every insidious movement that can possibly tend to discord and disunion. Suffer no local prejudices to disturb the prevailing harmony. To every appeal to these turn a deaf ear, as did the Saviour of men to the promptings of the deceiver. Act as a united band of brothers, bound together by one common tie. Your interests are the same, and by this course alone can · they be maintained. Follow this, and your hearts and homes will be made light and happy by the richest blessings of a kind and munificent Providence.

" To you, the peaceable citizens of Kansas, I owe my grateful acknowledgments for the aid and comfort your kind assurances and hearty coöperation have afforded in many dark and trying hours. You have my sincerest thanks and my earnest prayers that you may be abundantly rewarded of Heaven.

" To the ladies of the territory — the wives, mothers, sisters, and daughters of the honest settlers — I am also under a weight of obliga-

tion. Their pious prayers have not been raised in vain, nor their numerous assurances of confidence in the policy of my administration failed to exert a salutary influence.

" And last, though not the least, I must not be unmindful of the noble men who form the military department of the west. To General Persifer F. Smith and the officers acting under his command, I return my thanks for many valuable services. Although from different parts of the Union, and naturally imbued with sectional prejudices, I know of no instance in which such prejudices have been permitted to stand in the way of a faithful, ready, cheerful, and energetic discharge of duty. Their conduct in this respect is worthy of universal commendation. and presents a bright example for those executing the civil power. The good behavior of all the soldiers who were called upon to assist me is, in fact, deserving of especial notice. Many of these troops, officers and men, had served with me on the fields of Mexico against a foreign foe, and it is a source of no little satisfaction to know that the laurels there won have been further adorned by the praiseworthy alacrity with which they aided to allay a destructive fratricidal strife at home.

" With a firm reliance in the protecting care and overruling providence of that great Being who holds in his hands the destinies alike of men and of nations, I bid farewell to Kansas and her people, trusting that whatever events may hereafter befall them, they will, in the exercise of his wisdom, goodness, and power, be so directed as to promote their own best interest, and that of the beloved country of which they are destined to form a most important part.

" JOHN W. GEARY.

" LECOMPTON, March 12, 1857."

CHAPTER II.

New Governor of Kansas, R. J. Walker. — His Instructions. — His Address to the People of Kansas. — Action of the Free State Men. — Constitutional Convention at Lecompton. — The Constitution, and Mode of Submission to the People.—Election of Territorial Legislature. — Frauds. — Result. — Purpose of the Convention. — Governor Walker leaves the Territory. — Course of Secretary Stanton. — His Removal. — Resignation of Governor Walker. — Letter to Mr. Cass, and Reply.

PRESIDENT BUCHANAN showed that he considered the post of governor of Kansas of no little consequence, by his appointment of the successor of Governor Geary. That successor was Robert J. Walker, of Mississippi, and formerly secretary of the treasury. After some hesitation Mr. Walker accepted the appointment. Mr. F. P. Stanton, of Tennessee, was at the same time appointed secretary of the territory, and went immediately to assume the duties of acting governor until the arrival of Governor Walker. In his instructions to Governor Walker the secretary of state, General Cass, says, —

"There are two great objects connected with the present excitement growing out of the affairs of Kansas, and the attainment of which will bring it to a speedy termination. These were clearly and succinctly stated in the president's recent inaugural address, and I embody the paragraphs in this communication, asking your special attention to them. It is declared in that instrument to be 'the imperative and indispensable duty of the government of the United States to secure to every resident inhabitant the free and independent expression of his opinion by his vote. This sacred right of each individual must be preserved;' and, 'that being accomplished, nothing can be fairer than to leave the people of a territory free from all foreign interference to decide their own destiny for themselves, subject only to the constitution of the United States.'

"Upon these great rights of individual action and of public decision rests the foundation of American institutions, and if they are faithfully secured to the people of Kansas, the political condition of the country will soon become quiet and satisfactory. The institutions of Kansas should be established by the votes of the people of Kansas, unawed and uninterrupted by force or fraud. And foreign voters must be excluded, come whence they may, and every attempt to overawe or interrupt the free exercise of the right of voting must be promptly repelled and punished. Freedom and safety for the legal voter, and exclusion and punishment for the illegal one — these should be great principles of your administration.

"The regular legislature of the territory having authorized the assembling of a convention to frame a constitution to be accepted or rejected by Congress under the provisions of the federal constitution, the people of Kansas have the right to be protected in the peaceful election of delegates for such a purpose, under such authority, and the convention itself has a right to similar protection in the opportunity for tranquil and undisturbed deliberation. When such a constitution shall be submitted to the people of the territory, they must be protected in the exercise of their right of voting for or against that instrument, and the fair expression of the popular will must not be interrupted by fraud or violence."

Upon arriving in the territory Mr. Stanton found the people "peaceable and quiet, and exhibiting every disposition to remain so." In order to encourage this good disposition, he recommended the discontinuance of all the prosecutions growing out of the political disturbances. He advised this course in his despatches, and in his address to the people of Kansas he announced it as his deliberate judgment and wish that such a course should be adopted. This, with the assurances that all the power of the territorial executive should be exerted to prevent fraud, and "to secure to every resident inhabitant the free and independent expression of his opinion by his vote," gave to the people of the territory a better feeling of security.

Governor Walker reached the territory in the latter part of May. He published an inaugural address to the people, from which we make the following extracts:—

"Fellow-Citizens of Kansas: At the earnest request of the president of the United States, I have accepted the position of governor of the territory of Kansas. The president, with the cordial concurrence of all his cabinet, expressed to me the conviction that the condition of Kansas was fraught with imminent peril to the Union, and asked me to undertake the settlement of that momentous question, which has introduced discord and civil war throughout your borders, and threatens to involve you and our country in the same common ruin. This was a duty thus presented, the performance of which I could not decline consistently with my view of the sacred obligations which every citizen owes to his country.

"The mode of adjustment is provided in the act organizing your territory, namely, by the people of Kansas, who, by a majority of their own votes, must decide this question for themselves in forming their state constitution.

"Under our practice, the preliminary act of framing a state constitution is uniformly performed through the instrumentality of a convention of delegates chosen by the people themselves. That convention is now about to be elected by you under the call of the territorial legislature, created and still recognized by the authority of Congress, and clothed by it, in the comprehensive language of the organic law, with full power to make such an enactment. The territorial legislature, then, in assembling this convention, were fully sustained by the act of Congress, and the authority of the convention is distinctly recognized in my instructions from the president of the United States. Those who oppose this course cannot

aver the alleged irregularity of the territorial legislature, whose laws in town and city elections, in corporate franchises, and on all other subjects but slavery, they acknowledge by their votes and acquiescence. If that legislature was invalid, then are we without law or order in Kansas — without town, city, or county organization; all legal and judicial transactions are void, all titles null, and anarchy reigns throughout our borders.

"It is my duty, in seeing that all constitutional laws are fairly executed, to take care, as far as practicable, that this election of delegates to the convention shall be free from fraud and violence, and that they shall be protected in their deliberations.

"The people of Kansas, then, are invited by the highest authority known to the constitution to participate freely and fairly in the election of delegates to frame a constitution and state government. The law has performed its entire appropriate function when it extends to the people the right of suffrage, but it cannot compel the performance of that duty. Throughout our whole Union, however, and wherever free government prevails, those who abstain from the exercise of the right of suffrage authorize those who do vote to act for them in that contingency, and the absentees are as much bound under the law and constitution, where there is no fraud or violence, by the act of the majority of those who do vote, as if all had participated in the election. Otherwise, as voting must be voluntary, self-government would be impracticable, and monarchy or despotism would remain as the only alternative.

"You should not console yourselves, my fellow-citizens, with the reflection that you may, by a subsequent vote, defeat the ratification of the constitution. Although most anxious to secure to you the exercise of that great constitutional right, and believing that the convention is the servant, and not the master, of the people, yet I have no power to dictate the proceedings of that body. I cannot doubt, however, the course they will adopt on this subject. But why incur the hazard of the preliminary formation of a constitution by a minority, as alleged by you, when a majority, by their own votes, could control the forming of that instrument?

"But it is said that the convention is not legally called, and that the election will not be freely and fairly conducted. The territorial legislature is the power ordained for this purpose by the Congress of the United States; and in opposing it, you resist the authority of the federal government. That legislature was called into being by the Congress of 1854, and is recognized in the very latest congressional legislation. It is recognized by the present chief magistrate of the Union, just chosen by the American people, and many of its acts are now in operation here by universal assent. As the governor of the territory of Kansas, I must support the laws and the constitution; and I have no other alternative under my oath, but to see that all constitutional laws are fully and fairly executed.

"I see in this act calling the convention no improper or unconstitutional restrictions upon the right of suffrage. I see in it no test oath or other similar provisions objected to in relation to previous laws, but clearly repealed as repugnant to the provisions of this act, so far as regards the election of delegates to this convention. It is said that a fair and full vote will not be taken. Who can safely predict such a result? Nor is it just for a majority, as they allege, to throw the power into the hands of a minority, from a mere apprehension — I trust entirely unfounded — that they will not be permitted to exercise the right of suffrage. If, by fraud or violence, a majority should not be permitted to vote, there is a remedy, it is hoped, in the wisdom and justice of the convention itself, acting under the obligations of an oath, and a proper responsibility to the tribunal of public opinion. There is a remedy, also, if such facts can be demonstrated, in the refusal of Congress to admit a state into the Union under a constitution imposed by a minority upon a majority by fraud or violence. Indeed, I cannot doubt that the convention, after having framed a state constitution, will submit it for ratification or rejection, by a majority of the then actual *bona fide* resident settlers of Kansas.

"With these views, well known to the president and cabinet, and approved by them, I accepted the appointment of governor of Kansas. My instructions from the president, through the secretary of state, under date of the 30th of March last, sustain 'the regular legislature of the territory' in 'assembling a convention to form a constitution,' and they express the opinion of the president, that 'when such a constitution shall be submitted to the people of the territory, they must be protected in the exercise of their right of voting for or against that instrument; and the fair expression of the popular will must not be interrupted by fraud or violence.'

"I repeat, then, as my clear conviction, that unless the convention submit the constitution to the vote of all the actual resident settlers of Kansas, and the election be fairly and justly conducted, the constitution will be, and ought to be, rejected by Congress.

"There are other important reasons why you should participate in the election of delegates to this convention. Kansas is to become a new state, created out of the public domain, and will designate her boundaries in the fundamental law. To most of the land within her limits the Indian title, unfortunately, is not yet extinguished, and this land is exempt from settlement, to the grievous injury of the people of the state. Having passed many years of my life in a new state, and represented it for a long period in the senate of the United States, I know the serious encumbrance arising from large bodies of lands within a state to which the Indian title is not extinguished. Upon this subject the convention may act by such just and constitutional provisions as will accelerate the extinguishment of Indian title.

" There is, furthermore, the question of railroad grants made by Congress to all the new states but one, (where the routes could not be agreed upon,) and, within a few months past, to the flourishing territory of Minnesota. This munificent grant of four millions and a half of acres was made to Minnesota, even in advance of her becoming a state, and will enable our sister state of the north-west, under the auspices of her present distinguished executive, speedily to unite her railroad system with ours.

"Kansas is undoubtedly entitled to grants similar to those just made to Minnesota, and upon this question the convention may take important action.

" These, recollect, are grants by Congress, not to companies, but to states. Now, if Kansas, like the state of Illinois, in granting hereafter these lands to companies to build these roads, should reserve, at least, the seven per cent. of their gross annual receipts, it is quite certain that so soon as these roads are constructed, such will be the large payments into the treasury of our state, that there will be no necessity to impose in Kansas any state tax whatever, especially if the constitution should contain wise provisions against the creation of state debts.   *   *   *

" There is a law more powerful than the legislation of man, more potent than passion or prejudice, that must ultimately determine the location of slavery in this country ; it is the isothermal line, it is the law of the thermometer, of latitude or altitude, regulating climate, labor, and productions, and, as a consequence, profit and loss. Thus even upon the mountain heights of the tropics slavery can no more exist than in northern latitudes, because it is unprofitable, being unsuited to the constitution of that sable race transplanted here from the

equatorial heats of Africa. Why is it that in the Union slavery recedes from the north and progresses south ? It is this same great climatic law now operating for or against slavery in Kansas. If, on the elevated plains of Kansas, stretching to the base of our American Alps, — the Rocky Mountains, — and including their eastern crest, crowned with perpetual snow, from which sweep over her open prairies those chilling blasts, reducing the average range of the thermometer here to a temperature nearly as low as that of New England, should render slavery unprofitable here, because unsuited to the tropical constitution of the negro race, the law above referred to must ultimately determine that question here, and can no more be controlled by the legislation of man than any other moral or physical law of the Almighty. Especially must this law operate with irresistible force in this country, where the number of slaves is limited, and cannot be increased by importation — where many millions of acres of sugar and cotton lands are still uncultivated, and, from the ever-augmenting demand, exceeding the supply, the price of those great staples has nearly doubled, demanding vastly more slave labor for their production.

"If, from the operation of these causes, slavery should not exist here, I trust it by no means follows that Kansas should become a state controlled by the treason and fanaticism of abolition. She has, in any event, certain constitutional duties to perform to her sister states, and especially to her immediate neighbor, the slaveholding state of Missouri. Through that great state, by rivers and railroads, must flow, to a great extent, our trade and intercourse, our imports and exports. Our entire eastern front is upon her border ; from Missouri come a great number of her citizens ; even the farms of the two states are cut by the line of state boundary — part in Kansas, part in Missouri ; her citizens meet us in daily intercourse ; and that Kansas should become hostile to

Missouri, an asylum for her fugitive slaves, or a propagandist of abolition treason, would be alike inexpedient and unjust, and fatal to the continuance of the American Union. In any event, then, I trust that the constitution of Kansas will contain such clauses as will forever secure to the state of Missouri the faithful performance of all constitutional guarantees, not only by federal, but by state authority, and the supremacy within our limits of the authority of the Supreme Court of the United States on all constitutional questions be firmly established.   *   *   *

"Our country and the world are regarding with profound interest the struggle now impending in Kansas. Whether we are competent to self-government; whether we can decide this controversy peacefully for ourselves by our own votes, without fraud or violence; whether the great principles of self-government and state sovereignty can be carried here into successful operation, are the questions now to be determined; and upon the plains of Kansas may now be fought the last great and decisive battle, involving the fate of the Union, of state sovereignty, of self-government, and the liberties of the world. If, my fellow-citizens, you could, even for a brief period, soften or extinguish sectional passions or prejudice, and lift yourselves to the full realization of the momentous issues intrusted to your decision, you would feel that no greater responsibility was ever devolved on any people. It is not merely, shall slavery exist in or disappear from Kansas, but shall the great principles of self-government and state sovereignty be maintained or subverted. State sovereignty is mainly a practical principle in so far as it is illustrated by the great sovereign right of the majority of the people, in forming a state government, to adopt their own social institutions; and this principle is disregarded whenever such decision is subverted by Congress, or overthrown by external intrusion, or by domestic fraud or vio-

lence. All those who oppose this principle are the enemies of state rights, of self-government, of the constitution and the Union. Do you love slavery so much, or hate it so intensely, that you would endeavor to establish or exclude it by fraud or violence against the will of the majority of the people? What is Kansas, with or without slavery, if she should destroy the rights and union of the states? Where would be her schools, her free academies, her colleges and university, her towns and cities, her railroads, farms, and villages, without the Union, and the principles of self-government? Where would be her peace and prosperity, and what the value of her lands and property? Who can decide this question for Kansas, if not the people themselves? and if they cannot, nothing but the sword can become the arbiter.

"On the one hand, if you can and will decide peacefully this question yourselves, I see for Kansas an immediate career of power, progress, and prosperity unsurpassed in the history of the world. I see the peaceful establishment of our state constitution, its ratification by the people, and our immediate admission into the Union; the rapid extinguishment of Indian title, and the occupancy of those lands by settlers and cultivators; the diffusion of universal education; preëmptions for the actual settlers; the state rapidly intersected by a network of railroads; our churches, schools, colleges, and university, carrying westward the progress of law, religion, liberty, and civilization; our towns, cities, and villages prosperous and progressing; our farms teeming with abundant products, and greatly appreciated in value; and peace, happiness, and prosperity smiling throughout our borders. With proper clauses in our constitution, and the peaceful arbitrament of this question, Kansas may become the model state of the American Union. She may bring down upon us from north to south, from east to west, the praises and blessings of every patriotic American, and of every friend of self-government throughout the world; she may record her name on the proudest page of the history of our country and of the world, and as the youngest and last-born child of the American Union, all will hail and regard her with respect and affection.

"On the other hand, if you cannot thus peacefully decide this question, fraud, violence, and injustice will reign supreme throughout our borders, and we will have achieved the undying infamy of having destroyed the liberty of our country and of the world. We will become a byword of reproach and obloquy, and all history will record the fact that Kansas was the grave of the American Union. Never was so momentous a question submitted to the decision of any people, and we cannot avoid the alternatives now placed before us of glory or of shame.

"May that overruling Providence who brought our forefathers in safety to Jamestown and Plymouth; who watched over our colonial pupilage; who convened our ancestors in harmonious councils on the birthday of American independence; who gave us Washington, and carried us successfully through the struggles and perils of the revolution; who assembled, in 1787, that noble band of patriots and statesmen from north and south who framed the federal constitution; who has augmented our numbers from three millions to thirty millions; has carried us from the eastern slope of the Alleghanies, through the great valleys of the Ohio, Mississippi, and Missouri, and now salutes our standard on the shores of the Pacific,—rouse in our hearts a love of the whole Union, and a patriotic devotion to the whole country; may it extinguish or control all sectional passions and prejudice, and enable us to conduct to a successful conclusion the great experiment of self-government now being made within our boundaries.

"Is it not infinitely better that slavery should be abolished or established in Kansas, rather than that we should become slaves, and not permitted to govern ourselves? Is the absence or existence of slavery in Kansas paramount to the great questions of state sovereignty, of self-government, and of the Union? Is the sable African alone entitled to your sympathy and consideration, even if he were happier as a freeman than as a slave, either here, or in St. Domingo, or the British West Indies, or Spanish American, where the emancipated slave has receded to barbarism, and approaches the lowest point in the descending scale of moral, physical, and intellectual degradation? Have our white brethren of the great American and European race no claims upon our attention? Have they no rights or interests entitled to regard and protection? Shall the destiny of the African in Kansas exclude all considerations connected with our own happiness and prosperity? And is it for the handful of that race now in Kansas, or that may be hereafter introduced, that we should subvert the Union and the great principles of self-government and state sovereignty, and imbrue our hands in the blood of our countrymen? Important as this African question may be in Kansas, and which it is your solemn right to determine, it sinks into insignificance compared with the perpetuity of the Union and the final successful establishment of the principles of state sovereignty and free government. If patriotism, if devotion to the constitution, and love of the Union, should not induce the minority to yield to the majority on this question, let them reflect that in no event can the minority successfully determine this question permanently, and that in no contingency will Congress admit Kansas as a slave or free state, unless a majority of the people of Kansas shall first have fairly and freely decided this question for themselves by a direct vote on the adoption of the constitution, excluding all fraud or violence. The minority, in resisting the will of the majority,

3

may involve Kansas again in civil war; they may bring upon her reproach and obloquy, and destroy her progress and prosperity; they may keep her for years out of the Union, and, in the whirlwind of agitation, sweep away the government itself But Kansas never can be brought into the Union, with or without slavery, except by a previous solemn decision, fully, freely, and fairly made, by a majority of her people, in voting for or against the adoption of her state constitution. Why, then, should this just, peaceful, and constitutional mode of settlement meet with opposition from any quarter? Is Kansas willing to destroy her own hopes of prosperity merely that she may afford political capital to any party, and perpetuate the agitation of slavery throughout the Union? Is she to become a mere theme for agitators in other states — the theatre on which they shall perform the bloody drama of treason and disunion? Does she want to see the solemn acts of Congress, the decision of the people of the Union in the recent election, the legislative, executive, and judicial authorities of the country, all overthrown; and revolution and civil war inaugurated throughout her limits? Does she want to be 'bleeding Kansas' for the benefit of political agitators within or out of her limits? or does she prefer the peaceful and quiet arbitrament of this question for herself? What benefit will the great body of the people of Kansas derive from these agitations? They may, for a brief period, give consequence and power to political leaders and agitators; but it is at the expense of the happiness and welfare of the great body of the people of this territory.

"Those who oppose slavery in Kansas do not base their opposition upon any philanthropic principles or any sympathy for the African race. For in their so-called constitution, framed at Topeka, they deem that entire race so inferior and degraded as to exclude them all forever from Kansas, whether they be bond or free, thus depriving them of all rights here, and denying even that they can be citizens of the United States; for, if they are citizens, they could not, constitutionally, be exiled or excluded from Kansas. Yet such a clause, inserted in the Topeka constitution, was submitted by that convention for the vote of the people, and ratified here by an overwhelming majority of the anti-slavery party. This party here, therefore, has, in the most positive manner, affirmed the constitutionality of that portion of the recent decision of the Supreme Court of the United States declaring that Africans are not citizens of the United States.

"This is the more important, inasmuch as this Topeka constitution was ratified, with this clause inserted, by the entire republican party in Congress, thus distinctly affirming the recent decision of the Supreme Court of the Union that Africans are not citizens of the United States; for, if citizens, they may be elected to all offices, state and national, including the presidency itself; they must be placed upon a basis of perfect equality with the whites, serve with them in the militia, on the bench, the legislature, the jury box, vote in all elections, meet us in social intercourse, and intermarry freely with the whites. This doctrine of the perfect equality of the white with the black in all respects whatsoever, social and political, clearly follows from the position that Africans are citizens of the United States. Nor is the Supreme Court of the Union less clearly vindicated by the position now assumed here by the published creed of this party, that the people of Kansas, in forming their state constitution, (and not Congress,) must decide this question of slavery for themselves. Having thus sustained the court on both the controverted points decided by that tribunal, it is hoped they will not approve the anarchical and revolutionary proceedings in other states, expunging the Supreme Court from our system by depriving it of the great power for which it was created — of expounding the constitution. If that be done, we can have, in fact, no unity of government or fundamental law, but just as many ever-varying constitutions as passion, prejudice, and local interests may, from time to time, prescribe in the thirty-one states of the Union.

"I have endeavored heretofore faintly to foreshadow the wonderful prosperity which would follow at once in Kansas the peaceful and final settlement of this question. But if it should be in the power of agitators to prevent such a result, nothing but ruin will pervade our territory. Confidence will expire, and law and order will be subverted. Anarchy and civil war will be reinaugurated among us. All property will greatly depreciate in value. Even the best farms will become almost worthless. Our towns and cities will sink into decay. Emigration into our territory will cease. A mournful train of returning settlers, with ruined hopes and blasted fortunes, will leave our borders. All who have purchased property at present prices will be sacrificed, and Kansas will be marked by universal ruin and desolation.

"Nor will the mischief be arrested here. It will extend into every other state. Despots will exult over the failure here of the great principles of self-government and the approaching downfall of our confederacy. The pillars of the Union will rock upon their base, and we may close the next presidential conflict amid the scattered fragments of the constitution of our once happy and united people. The banner of the stars and stripes, the emblem of our country's glory, will be rent by contending factions. We shall no longer have a country. The friends of human liberty in other realms will shrink despairing from the conflict. Despotic power will resume its sway throughout the world, and man will have tried in vain the last experiment of self-government. The architects of our country's ruin, the assassins of her peace and prosperity, will share the same common ruin of all our race. They will

meet, whilst living, the bitter curses of a ruined people, whilst history will record as their only epitaph, 'These were the destroyers of the American Union, of the liberties of their country and of the world.'

"But I do not despair of the republic. My hope is in the patriotism and intelligence of the people; in their love of country, of liberty, and of the Union. Especially is my confidence unbounded in the hardy pioneers and settlers of the west. It was such settlers of a new state, devoted to the constitution and the Union, whom I long represented in the senate of the United States, and whose rights and interests it was my pride and pleasure there, as well as in the treasury department, to protect and advocate. It was men like these whose rifles drove back the invader from the plains of Orleans, and planted the stars and stripes upon the victorious fields of Mexico. These are the men whom gold cannot corrupt, nor foes intimidate. From their towns and villages, from their farms and cottages, spread over the beautiful prairies of Kansas, they will come forward now in defence of the constitution and the Union. These are the glorious legacy they received from our fathers, and they will transmit to their children the priceless heritage. Before the peaceful power of their suffrage this dangerous sectional agitation will disappear, and peace and prosperity once more reign throughout our borders. In the hearts of this noble band of patriotic settlers the love of their country and of the Union is inextinguishable. It leaves them not in death, but follows them into that higher realm, where, with Washington and Franklin and their noble compatriots, they look down with undying affection upon their country, and offer up their fervent prayers that the Union and the constitution may be perpetual. For, recollect, my fellow-citizens, that it is the constitution that makes the Union; and unless that immortal instrument, bearing the name of the father of his country, shall be maintained entire in all its wise provisions and sacred guarantees, our free institutions must perish.

"My reliance also is unshaken upon the same overruling Providence who has carried us triumphantly through so many perils and conflicts; who has lifted us to a height of power and prosperity unexampled in history, and, if we shall maintain the constitution and the Union, points us to a future more glorious and sublime than mind can conceive or pen describe. The march of our country's destiny, like that of His first chosen people, is marked by the footprints of the steps of God. The constitution and the Union are 'the cloud by day and the pillar of fire by night,' which will carry us safely, under his guidance, through the wilderness and bitter waters, into the promised and ever-extending fields of our country's glory. It is his hand which beckons us onward in the pathway of peaceful progress and expansion, of power and renown, until our continent, in the distant future, shall be covered by the folds of the American banner; and instructed by our example, all the nations of the world, through many trials and sacrifices, shall establish the great principles of our constitutional confederacy of free and sovereign states."

In his first despatch to Washington, Governor Walker writes thus:—

"My inaugural was extremely well received by the people here, and, so far as I can learn, it seems quite probable that it will be approved by a very large majority of the people of this territory. On one point the sentiment of the people is almost unanimous — that the constitution must be submitted, for ratification or rejection, to a vote of the people who shall be *bona fide* residents of the territory next fall. The difficulties in this territory are not yet adjusted, and without the submission of the constitution to the people a peaceful settlement is entirely impracticable."

The governor also stated that where disturbances or resistance to the territorial laws were threatened, it was his purpose to address the people, and endeavor by a persuasive course to correct the evil, rather than resort to force. This course he followed in several cases, and addressed several assemblies of free state men with alleged good effect. He visited various parts of the territory, and by his addresses and intercourse with the people brought about a better feeling.

The free state voters in Kansas adhered to their resolution not to participate in the election of delegates to the constitutional convention, and the pro-slavery party elected nearly or quite the whole body. They also still supported the Topeka constitution, and in June the state legislature under that constitution again met. Mr. Robinson, who had been persuaded to continue to hold the office of governor of this prospective government, sent a message to the legislature recommending a thorough organization of the state government, and acts were passed providing for taking a state census, and appointing an election to be held in August for state officers and a representative to Congress. Governor Walker was at Topeka at the time, and addressed a convention of the free state men, being listened to with attention, and some of its more ultra proceedings being abandoned in consequence of his advice and conciliatory language; but no movement was made by him to interfere with the legislature. Some of the free state men were dissatisfied with the moderation of the legislature, and were disposed to organize an opposition to the territorial laws — usually termed by them the "bogus laws." Among the measures undertaken by the free state men was the establishment of a city charter for Lawrence, by the people of that town. This step was regarded by the federal authorities as an insurgent act, and it was feared, probably without cause, that this was the beginning of other similar acts designed to resist by an organized movement the territorial laws and authority. But the free state men contended that it was only a municipal organization, designed to promote the safety of the citizens by proper police and health regulations. It was, however, with the organization of the militia among the free state men, considered good cause for calling upon the military to support the civil authorities of the territory, and a large body of dragoons was ordered into the vicinity of Lawrence. After a brief season it was found that there was no occasion for calling the military into requisition; and this force, which had already been ordered to Utah, was withdrawn and proceeded towards that territory.

The constitutional convention provided for by the act of the territorial legislature met at Lecompton in September, and proceeded to form a constitution for a state government. This constitution recognized slavery indirectly in its provisions, and also had a provision prohibiting the legislature from ever passing a law for the emancipation of slaves. It was evidently the intention of the pro-slavery party that the constitution should not be submitted to the people, notwithstanding Governor Walker and Secretary Stanton had constantly declared, in conformity with the views and instructions of the president, that such a constitution must and should be fully and fairly submitted to the people for their ratification or rejection. The position taken by the governor on this point, and by many of the opponents of the free state party also, was so strong, that the convention at last made a show of submitting the constitution to the people. But it must be acknowledged by every candid mind that the provision adopted was a mere sham. By this provision the constitution was to be submitted to the people, and they were to vote in this form : " Constitution with slavery;" or " Constitution without slavery." In either case they must have the constitution with whatever objectionable features there might be in it; and there were many such features, which satisfied the free state men that with that constitution freedom could not for years be established as the ruling principle in Kansas. Nor did this proposition meet the views of Governor Walker or Secretary Stanton. It was not in conformity with their own express promises, or their conviction, nor was it in conformity with the declarations of the president and his instructions to these officers. But this question will occur in another part of our narrative.

While the convention was in session the election of a territorial legislature and delegate to Congress took place, in October. Governor Walker had made urgent appeals to the people to vote in this election, assuring them that they should have a fair election, and should be protected from any invasion of parties out of the territory. The free state men by degrees had been persuaded that this course would be the wisest, if the governor would carry out his promises, and they had confidence that he would. They therefore prepared for the election, and the qualifications of voters having been modified by an act of the territorial legislature, they participated in it by a general, though it is said not a full, vote of the free state party. The result of this election was the choice of Mr. Parrott, the free state candidate for delegate to Congress; and by the correct returns it also appeared that the same party had control of both branches of the legislature. In some of the voting precincts gross frauds were perpetrated in favor of the pro-slavery candidates. These frauds were too evident and too gross to pass without observation, and Governor Walker, after inquiring into the facts, rejected the returns, and thus gave the legislature into the hands of the free state party. In one of the counties where these spurious returns were made, the pro-slavery candidates, who were, by such rejection, refused certificates, applied to Judge Cato, who issued a writ of mandamus to the governor and secretary, commanding them to give certificates to the claimants. The governor and secretary, however, denied the authority of the judge in the premises, and refused to comply.

The result of this election was a source of great joy to the free state men in Kansas, and to their friends in the states. It served to conciliate and pacify many of those who, through wrong and oppression, had been disposed to resist to the utmost the territorial laws. The laws were now within their own power for repeal or modification, and this was accomplished in a way against which no objection could be raised by the federal authorities. Quiet was therefore restored among the free state settlers. By the pro-slavery party it was received with less satisfaction. The unscrupulous among them had determined, if they could not have the aid of votes from Missouri, that they would have the benefit of spurious votes; and hence the fraudulent returns. The constitutional convention had adjourned until after the election, and they then proceeded with their work, but evidently with a determination that the free state majority, which had just been ascertained, should not have the opportunity of rejecting the constitution they should frame. This purpose soon became evident, and excited the indignation of the free state men. And when the work was finally done, and the mode of submitting it, with slavery or without slavery, as already mentioned, the territory was again in a ferment.

Before the convention had arrived at the conclusion of its work, and before it had determined how it should be submitted to the people, Governor Walker had obtained leave of absence from the territory for a season, and left it fully assured that the declared wishes of the president, and his own repeated pledges of a fair submission of the whole instrument to the vote of the people, would be adopted. Secretary Stanton was now acting governor.

In the excitement prevailing in consequence of the action of the convention, both in regard to the manner of submitting the question to the popular vote, and in regard to the appointment of judges of elections, and other details relating to the reception of votes and returns, the acting governor was requested to convene the territorial legislature at an earlier day than that appointed for its regular meeting. Vigilance committees had been organized by the free state party, who were again aroused to take decisive measures rather than suffer a constitution so obnoxious to be forced upon them. It was hoped that a meeting of the legislature might avert these troubles by providing by law for the submission of the constitution to a fair vote. Such a measure Mr. Stanton suggested in his message to the legislature when it assembled. That message is characterized by a spirit of fairness and a desire to meet the popular will, which, it would seem, was entitled to commendation except from those who were disposed only to carry out the will of the convention and the minority which it represented.

When, however, it was known at Washington that Mr. Stanton had convened the legislature in such a manner and for such a purpose, it was deemed by the president and his advisers a cause for immediate removal. James W. Denver, commissioner of Indian affairs, was appointed in his place, and ordered to proceed forthwith to Kansas to assume the duties of secretary and acting governor. Governor Walker was still absent from the territory, in Washington. The views of the president on Kansas affairs as expressed in his annual message, and the removal of Secretary Stanton for his endeavor to pacify the majority of the people of Kansas by securing to them in a legal way their rights, and thus redeeming the pledges of the governor and the administration, indicated a change in the policy of the government. Governor Walker, pledged to the policy which the acting governor was endeavoring to carry out, was not disposed to adopt any other course ; and a few days after the removal of Mr. Stanton he resigned his post as governor of the territory. In tendering his resignation he addressed the following letter to the secretary of state, reviewing the affairs of Kansas from the time of his connection with the territory, and the policy which he had pursued :—

"WASHINGTON, *December* 15, 1857.

"SIR : I resign the office of governor of the territory of Kansas. I have been most reluctantly forced to this conclusion after anxious and careful consideration of my duty to the country, to the people of Kansas, to the president of the United States, and to myself.

"The grounds assumed by the president in his late message to Congress, and in recent instructions in connection with the events now transpiring here and in Kansas, admonish me that, as governor of that territory, it will no longer be in my power to preserve the peace or promote the public welfare.

"At the earnest solicitation of the president, after repeated refusals, the last being in writing, I finally accepted this office upon his letter showing the dangers and difficulties of the Kansas question, and the necessity of my undertaking the task of adjustment. Under these circumstances, notwithstanding the great sacrifices to me, (personal, political, and pecuniary,) I felt that I could no more refuse such a call from my country, through her chief magistrate, than the soldier in battle who is ordered to command a forlorn hope.

"I accepted, however, on the express condition that I should advocate the submission of the constitution to the vote of the people for ratification or rejection. These views were clearly understood by the president and all his cabinet. They were distinctly set forth in my letter of acceptance of this office of the 26th of March last, and reiterated in my inaugural address of the 27th of May last, as follows :—

"'Indeed, I cannot doubt that the convention, after having framed a state constitution, will submit it for ratification or rejection by a majority of the then actual *bona fide* resident settlers of Kansas. With these views, well known to the president and cabinet, and approved by them, I accepted the appointment of governor of Kansas. My instructions from the president, through the secretary of state, under date of the 30th of March last, sustain "the regular legislature of the territory" in "assembling a convention to form a constitution," and they express the opinion of the president that "when such a constitution shall be submitted to the people of the territory, they must be protected in the exercise of their *right* of voting *for* or *against* that instrument ; and the fair expression of the popular will must not be interrupted by fraud or violence." I repeat, then, as my clear conviction, that unless the convention submit the constitution to the vote of all the actual resident settlers of Kansas, and the election be fairly and justly conducted, the constitution will be, and ought to be, rejected by Congress.'

"This inaugural most distinctly asserted that it was not the question of slavery merely, (which I believed to be of little practical importance then in its application to Kansas,) but the entire constitution which should be submitted to the people for ratification or rejection. These were my words on that subject in my inaugural : 'It is not merely, shall slavery exist in or disappear from Kansas, but shall the great principles of self-government and state sovereignty be maintained or subverted.' In that inaugural I proceed further to say that the people 'may by a subsequent vote defeat the ratification of the constitution.' I designate this as a 'great *constitutional* right,' and add, that 'the convention is the servant, and not the master, of the people.'

"In my official despatch to you of 2d June last, a copy of that inaugural address was transmitted to you for the further information of the president and his cabinet. No exception was ever taken to any portion of that address; on the contrary, it is distinctly admitted by the president in his message, with commendable frankness, that my instructions in favor of the submission of the constitution to the vote of the people were 'general and unqualified.' By that inaugural and subsequent addresses I was pledged to the people of Kansas to oppose by all 'lawful means' the adoption of any constitution which was not fairly and fully submitted to their vote for ratification or rejection. These pledges I cannot recall or violate without personal dishonor and the abandonment of fundamental principles, and therefore it is impossible for me to support what is called the Lecompton constitution, because it is not submitted to a vote of the people for ratification or rejection.

"I have ever uniformly maintained the principle that sovereignty is vested exclusively in the people of each state, and that it performs its first and highest function in forming a state government and state constitution. This highest act of sovereignty, in my judgment, can only be performed by the people themselves and cannot be delegated to conventions or other intermediate bodies. Indeed, the whole doctrine of the sovereignty of conventions, as distinct from that of the people,— of conventional or delegated sovereignty, as contradistinguished from state or popular sovereignty,— has ever been discarded by me, and was never heard of, to my knowledge, during the great canvass of 1856. This is the great principle of state rights and state sovereignty maintained in the Virginia and Kentucky resolutions of 1798–'99, sustained by the people in the great political revolution of 1800, and embraced in that amendment to the federal constitution, adopted under the auspices of Mr. Jefferson, declaring that 'the powers not delegated to the United States by the constitution, nor prohibited by it to the states, are reserved to the states respectively or to the people.'

"The reservation to 'the states' is as separate states, in exercising the powers granted by their state constitutions, and the reservation to 'the people' is to the people of the several states, admitted or inchoate, in exercising their sovereign right of framing or amending their state constitution. This view was set forth in my printed address delivered at Natchez, Mississippi, in January, 1833, against nullification, which speech received the complimentary sanction of the great and good Madison, the principal founder of our constitution, as shown by the letter of the Hon. Charles J. Ingersoll, of Philadelphia, as published in the Globe, at Washington, in 1836. What adds much more force to this opinion is the statement then made by Mr. Madison, that these were also the views of Mr. Jefferson. By this clause of the federal constitution the sovereignty of the people of each state is clearly reserved, and especially their own exclusive sovereign right to form in all its entirety their own state constitution.

"I shall not enter fully into the argument of this question at this period, but will merely state that this is the position I have ever occupied; and my reasons for entertaining this opinion are clearly and distinctly set forth in a printed pamphlet, published over my signature on the 13th June, 1856, and then extensively circulated, from which I quote as follows:—

"'Under our confederate system sovereignty is that highest political power which, at its pleasure, creates governments and delegates authority to them. Sovereignty grants powers, but not sovereign powers; otherwise it might extinguish itself by making the creature of its will the equal or superior of its creator. Sovereignty makes constitutions, and through them establishes governments. It delegates certain powers to these governments, distributing the exercise of the granted powers among the

Robert Anderson

legislative, executive, and judicial departments. The constitution is not sovereign, because it is created by sovereignty. The government is not sovereign for the same reason, much less any department of that government. Having defined sovereignty, we must not confound the power with its source or exercise; that is, sovereignty is one thing, where it resides or how to be exercised is another. Under the system of European despotisms, sovereignty was claimed to reside in kings and emperors, under the sacrilegious idea of the "divine right of kings;" and the blasphemous doctrine was, that sovereigns in legitimate succession, although stained with crimes and blackened with infamy, were clothed by Deity with absolute power to rule their subjects, who held nothing but privileges granted by the crown. Such were the absurd and impious dogmas to which the people of Europe, with few exceptions, have been compelled to submit by the bayonet, sustained by the more potent authority of ignorance and superstition. Under this theory the people were mere ciphers, and crowned heads sub-deities — the sole representatives on earth of the governing power of the Almighty.' 'Our doctrine is just the reverse, making the people the only source of sovereign power. But what people? With us sovereignty rests exclusively with the people of each state.' By the revolution, each colony, acting for itself alone, separated from Great Britain, and sanctioned the Declaration of Independence. 'Each colony, having thus become a state, and each adopting for itself its separate state government, acted for itself alone under the old Continental Congress. Each state acted for itself alone in acceding to the Articles of Confederation in 1778, and each state acted for itself alone in framing and ratifying, each for itself, the constitution of the United States. Sovereignty, then, with us rests exclusively with the people of each state. The constitution of the United States is not sovereign, for

4

it was created by states, each exercising for itself the highest political power called sovereignty. For the same reason the government of the United States is not sovereign, nor does it exercise any sovereign powers. It exercises only "delegated powers," as declared by the constitution, and those powers only which are granted by that instrument. Delegated powers are not sovereign powers, but are powers granted by sovereignty. Sovereignty, being this highest political power, cannot be delegated; it is indivisible; it is a unit, incapable of partition. Hence the great error of supposing that sovereignty is divided between the states and the United States.

"'The constitution of the United States is the "supreme law," and obligatory as such; but a law is not sovereignty, but an act of sovereignty. All laws imply law-makers; and, in this case, those who framed and ratified this "supreme law" were those sovereignties called the states, each acting exclusively for itself, uncontrolled by any sister state, except by the moral force of its influence and example. The government of the United States possessing, as we have shown, no sovereignty, but only delegated powers, to them alone it must look for the exercise of all constitutional authority in territories as well as states, for there is not a single power granted by the constitution to this government in a territory which is not granted in a state, except the power to admit new states into the Union, which, as shown by the Madison Papers, the framers of the constitution (as first demonstrated in my Texas letter) refused to limit to our then existing territories. In the territories, then, as well as the states, Congress possesses no sovereignty, and can exercise only the powers delegated by the constitution; and all the powers not thus granted are dormant or reserved powers, belonging, in common territory, to all the states, as coequal joint tenants there of that highest political power called sovereignty.'

"It will be perceived that this doctrine, that 'sovereignty makes constitutions,' that 'sovereignty rests exclusively with the people of each state,' that 'sovereignty cannot be delegated,' that 'it is inalienable, indivisible,' 'a unit incapable of partition,' are doctrines ever regarded by me as fundamental principles of public liberty and of the federal constitution. It will be seen that these views, which I have ever entertained, were not framed to suit any emergency in Kansas, but were my life-long principles, and were published and promulgated by me, in an elaborate argument over my own signature, twelve months before my departure to that territory, and when I never thought of going to Kansas. These rights I have ever regarded as fully secured to the people of 'all the territories' in adopting their state constitution by the Kansas and Nebraska bill. Such is the construction given to that act by Congress in passing the Minnesota bill, so justly applauded by the president. Such is the construction of this Kansas act by its distinguished author, not only in his late most able argument, but in addresses made and published by him long antecedent to that date; showing that this sovereign power of the people in acting upon a state constitution is not confined to the question of slavery, but includes all other subjects embraced in such an instrument. Indeed, I believe the Kansas and Nebraska bill would have violated the rights of sovereignty reserved to the people of each state by the federal constitution if it had deprived them, or Congress should now deprive them, of the right of voting for or against their state constitution. The president, in his message, thinks that the rights secured by this bill to the people in acting upon their state constitution are confined to the slavery question; but I think, as shown in my address before quoted, that 'sovereignty is the power that makes constitutions and governments,' and that not only the slavery clause in a state constitution, but all others, must be submitted. The president thinks that sovereignty can be delegated, at least in part. I think sovereignty cannot be delegated at all. The president believes that sovereignty is divisible between conventions and the people, to be exercised by the former on all subjects but slavery, and by the latter only on that question; whereas I think that sovereignty is 'inalienable,' 'indivisible,' 'a unit incapable of partition,' and that 'it cannot be delegated,' in whole or in part.

"It will not be denied that sovereignty is the only power that can make a state constitution, and that it rests exclusively with the people; and if it is inalienable, and cannot be delegated, as I have shown, then it can only be exercised by the people themselves. Under our government we know no sovereigns but the people. Conventions are composed of 'delegates.' They are mere agents or trustees, exercising not a sovereign, but a delegated power, and the people are the principals. The power delegated to such conventions can properly only extend to the framing of the constitution; but its ratification or rejection can only be performed by the power where sovereignty alone rests, namely, the people themselves. We must not confound sovereign with delegated powers. The provisional authority of a convention to frame a constitution and submit it to the people is a delegated power; but sovereignty alone, which rests exclusively with the people, can ratify and put in force that constitution.

"And this is the true doctrine of popular sovereignty; and I know of no such thing, nor does the federal constitution recognize it, as delegated or conventional sovereignty. The president, in a very lucid passage of his able message, gives unanswerable reasons why the people, and not conventions, should decide the question of slavery in framing a state constitution. He says, very truly, that, from the necessary division of the inchoate state into districts, a majority of the delegates may think one way and the people another, and that the delegates (as was the case in Kansas) may violate their pledges or fail to execute the will of the people. And why does not this reasoning apply with equal force to all other great questions embodied in a state constitution? and why should the question of slavery alone override and extinguish the doctrine of popular sovereignty and the right of self-government? Most fortunately this is no sectional question, for it belongs alike to the states admitted or inchoate, of the south as of the north. It is not a question of slavery, but of state rights and of state and popular sovereignty, and my objections to the Lecompton constitution are equally strong, whether Kansas under its provisions should be made a free or a slave state. My objections are based upon a violation of the right of self-government and of state and popular sovereignty, and of forcing any constitution upon the people against their will, whether it recognized freedom or slavery. Indeed, the first question which the people ought to decide in forming a government for an inchoate state is, whether they will change, or not, from a territorial to a state government. Now, as no one who, with me, denies federal or territorial sovereignty, will contend that a territorial legislature is sovereign, or represents sovereignty, or that such legislature (a mere creation of Congress) can transfer sovereignty, which it does not possess, to a territorial convention, this change from a territorial to a state government can only be made by the power where sovereignty rests; namely, the people. Yet a state government is forced upon the people of Kansas by the Lecompton constitution whether they will it or not; for they can only vote for the constitution, and not against it. But, besides the change from a territorial to a state government, which the people alone have a right to make in framing a state constitution, there are many other momentous questions included in

that instrument. It involves all the powers of state government. There is the bill of rights, the *magna charta* of the liberties of a free people; the legislative, executive, and judicial functions; the taxing power; the elective franchise; the great question of education; the sacred relations of husband and wife, parent and child, guardian and ward; and all the rights affecting life, liberty, and property. There is also the question of state debts, of banks and paper money, and whether they shall be permitted or prohibited. As all free government, as stated by Mr. Jefferson in the Declaration of Independence, depends upon the 'consent of the governed,' how can it be known whether the people would assent to the constitution unless it is submitted to their vote for ratification or rejection? But if acquiescence can be presumed in any case, surely it cannot be in that of Kansas, where so many of the delegates violated their pledge to submit the constitution itself to a vote of the people, where the delegates who signed the constitution represented scarcely one tenth of the people, and where nearly one half the counties of the territory were disfranchised, and (by no fault of theirs) did not, and could not, give a single vote at the election for delegates to the convention.

"I have heretofore discussed this subject mainly on the question that conventions are not sovereign, and cannot rightfully make a state constitution without submission to the vote of the people for ratification or rejection; yet surely even those who differ with me on this point must concede, especially under the Kansas-Nebraska bill, it is only such conventions can be called sovereign as have been truly elected by the people and represent their will. On reference, however to my address of the 16th September last on the tax-qualification question,—a copy of which was immediately transmitted to you for the information of the president and cabinet,—it is evident that the Lecompton convention was not such a body.

That convention had vital, not technical, de-feets in the very substance of its organization under the territorial law, which could only be cured, in my judgment, as set forth in my in-augural and other addresses, by the submission of the constitution for ratification or rejection by the people. On reference to the territorial law under which the convention was assembled, thirty-four regularly organized counties were named as election districts for delegates to the convention. In each and all of these counties it was required by law that a census should be taken and the voters registered; and when this was completed the delegates to the convention should be apportioned accordingly. In nine-teen of these counties there was no census, and therefore there could be no such apportion-ment there of delegates based upon such cen-sus. And in fifteen of these counties there was no registry of voters. These fifteen counties, including many of the oldest organized coun-ties of the territory, were entirely disfranchised, and did not give, and (by no fault of their own) could not give, a solitary vote for delegates to the convention. This result was superinduced by the fact that the territorial legislature ap-pointed all the sheriffs and probate judges in all these counties, to whom was assigned the duty by law of making this census and registry. These officers were political partisans, dissent-ing from the views and opinions of the people of these counties, as proved by the election in October last. These officers, from want of funds, as they allege, neglected or refused to take any census or make any registry in these counties; and therefore they were entirely dis-franchised, and could not, and did not, give a single vote at the election for delegates to the constitutional convention. And here I wish to call attention to the distinction, which will ap-pear in my inaugural address, in reference to those counties where the voters were fairly registered and did not vote. In such counties, where a full and free opportunity was given to register and vote, and they did not choose to exercise that privilege, the question is very dif-ferent from those counties where there was no census or registry, and no vote was given, or could be given, however anxious the people might be to participate in the election of dele-gates to the convention. Nor could it be said these counties acquiesced; for wherever they endeavored, by a subsequent census or registry of their own, to supply this defect, occasioned by the previous neglect of the territorial offi-cers, the delegates thus chosen were rejected by the convention. I repeat, that in nineteen counties out of thirty-four there was no census. In fifteen counties out of thirty-four there was no registry, and not a solitary vote was given, or could be given, for delegates to the conven-tion in any one of these counties. Surely then, it cannot be said that such a convention, chosen by scarcely more than one tenth of the present voters of Kansas, represented the peo-ple of that territory, and could rightfully impose a constitution upon them without their consent. These nineteen counties in which there was no census constituted a *majority* of the counties of the territory, and these fifteen counties in which there was no registry gave a much larger vote at the October election, even with the six months' qualification, than the whole vote given to the delegates who signed the Lecomp-ton constitution on the 7th November last. If, then, sovereignty can be delegated, and con-ventions, as such, are sovereign, which I deny surely it must be only in such cases as when such conventions are chosen by the people, which we have seen was not the case as regards the late Lecompton convention. It was for this, among other reasons, that in my inaugu-ral and other addresses I insisted that the con-stitution should be submitted to the people by the convention, as the only means of curing this vital defect in its organization. It was, therefore, among other reasons, when, as you know, the organization of the so-called Topeka state government, and as a consequence an inevitable civil war and conflict with the troops must have ensued, these results were prevented by my assuring, not the abolitionists, as has been erroneously stated, — for my address was not to them, but the people of Kansas, — that in my judgment the constitution would be submitted fairly and freely for ratification or rejection by their vote, and that if this was not done, I would unite with them, the people, as I now do, in 'lawful opposition' to such a procedure.

"The power and responsibility being devolved exclusively upon me by the president of using the federal army in Kansas to suppress insurrection, the alternative was distinctly presented to me by the question propounded at Topeka of arresting revolution by the slaughter of the people, or of preventing it, together with that civil war which must have extended throughout the Union, by the solemn assurance then given that the right of the people to frame their own government, so far as my power extended, should be maintained. But for this assurance, it is a conceded fact that the Topeka state government, then assembled in legislative session, would have been put into immediate actual operation, and that a sanguinary collision with the federal army and civil war must have ensued, extending, it is feared, throughout the Union.

"Indeed, the whole idea of an inaugural address originated in the alarming intelligence which had reached Washington city of the perilous and incipient rebellion in Kansas. This insurrection was rendered still more formidable, on my reaching the territory, by the near approach of the assembling of the revolutionary state legislature, and the very numerous mass conventions by which it was sustained. In truth, I had to choose between arresting that insurrection, at whatever cost of American blood, by the federal army, or to prevent the terrible catastrophe, as I did, by

my pledges to the people of the exertion of all my power to obtain a fair election, and the submission of the constitution to the vote of the people for ratification or rejection.

"My inaugural and other addresses were, therefore, really in the nature of proclamations, (so often issued by presidents and governors,) with a view to prevent, as they did in this case, civil war and insurrection.

"Now, by my oath of office, I was sworn to support the constitution of the United States, which I have shown, in my judgment, required the submission of the constitution to the vote of the people. I was sworn also to 'take care' that the Kansas and Nebraska bill 'should be faithfully executed,' which bill, in my judgment, as heretofore stated, required that the constitution should be submitted to the vote of the people; and I was therefore only performing a solemn duty when, as governor of the territory, to whose people my first obligations were due, I endeavored to secure to them these results. The idea entertained by some that I should see the federal constitution and the Kansas-Nebraska bill overthrown and disregarded, and that, playing the part of a mute in a pantomime of ruin, I should acquiesce by my silence in such a result, especially where such acquiescence involved, as an immediate consequence, a disastrous and sanguinary civil war, seems to me most preposterous. Not a drop of blood has been shed by the federal troops in Kansas during my administration. But insurrection and civil war, extending, I fear, throughout the country, were alone prevented by the course pursued by me on those occasions, and the whole people, abandoning revolutionary violence, were induced by me to go, for the first time, into a general and peaceful election.

"These important results constitute a sufficient consolation for all the unjust assaults made upon me on this subject. I do not understand that these assaults have ever received the slightest countenance from the president; on the contrary, his message clearly indicates an approval of my course up to the present most unfortunate difference about the so-called Lecompton constitution. Inasmuch, however, as this difference is upon a vital question, involving practical results and new instructions, it is certainly much more respectful to the president, on my part, to resign the office of governor, and give him an opportunity of filling it, as his right under the constitution, with one who concurs with him in his present opinions, rather than go to Kansas and force him to remove me by disobedience to his instructions. This latter course, in my judgment, would be incompatible with proper respect for the chief magistrate of the Union, inconsistent with the rules of moral rectitude or propriety, and could be adopted with no other view than to force the president to remove me from office. Such a course, it is alleged, would present me to the public as a political martyr in the defence of the great principle of self-government; but to go to Kansas with any such purpose, or with a certain knowledge that such a result must follow, would be alike unjust and improper. My only alternative, then, is that of a respectful resignation, in the hope that Kansas and our beloved country may be shielded from that civil war with which I fear both are threatened, by any attempt to force the so-called Lecompton constitution upon the people of Kansas.

"I state it as a fact, based on a long and intimate association with the people of Kansas, that an overwhelming majority of that people are opposed to that instrument, and my letters state that but one out of twenty of the press of Kansas sustains it. Some oppose it because so many counties were disfranchised and unrepresented in the convention. Some, who are opposed to paper money, because it authorizes a bank of enormous capital for Kansas, nearly unlimited in its issues and in the denomination of its notes, from one dollar up and down. Some because of what they consider a know-nothing clause, by requiring that the governor shall have been twenty years a citizen of the United States. Some, because the elective franchise is not free, as they cannot vote against the constitution, but only on the single issue, whether any more slaves may be imported, and then only upon that issue by voting for the constitution to which they are opposed. They regard this as but a mockery of the elective franchise, and a perilous sporting with the sacred rights of the people. Some oppose because the constitution distinctly recognizes and adopts the Oxford fraud in apportioning legislative members from Johnson county upon the fraudulent and fictitious *returns*, falsely so called, from that precinct, which recognition of that fraud in the constitution is abhorrent to the moral sense of the people. Others oppose it because, although in other cases presidents of conventions have been authorized to issue writs of election to the regular territorial or state officers with the usual judges, with the established precincts and adjudication of returns, in this case unprecedented and vice-regal powers are given to the president of the convention to make the precincts, the judges, and to decide finally upon the returns. From the grant of these unusual and enormous powers, and from other reasons connected with the fraudulent returns of Oxford and McGee, an overwhelming majority of the people of Kansas have no faith in the validity of these returns, and therefore will not vote. Indeed, disguise it as we may to ourselves, under the influence of the present excitement, the facts will demonstrate that any attempt by Congress to force this constitution upon the people of Kansas will be an effort to substitute the will of a small minority for that of an overwhelming majority of the people of Kansas; that it will not settle the Kansas question or localize the issue; that it will, I fear, be attended by civil war, extending, perhaps, throughout the Union; thus bringing this question back again upon Congress and before the people in its most dangerous and alarming aspect.

"The president takes a different view of the subject in his message; and, from the events occurring in Kansas as well as here, it is evident that the question is passing from theories into practice; and that, as governor of Kansas, I should be compelled to carry out new instructions, differing on a vital question from those received at the date of my appointment. Such instructions I could not execute consistently with my views of the federal constitution, of the Kansas and Nebraska bill, or with my pledges to the people of Kansas. Under these circumstances, no alternative is left me but to resign the office of governor of the territory of Kansas. No one can more deeply regret than myself this necessity; but it arises from no change of opinion on my part. On the contrary, I should most cheerfully have returned to Kansas to carry out my original instructions, and thus preserve the peace of the territory, and finally settle the Kansas question by redeeming my pledges to the people.

"It is not my intention to discuss, at this time, the peculiar circumstances and unexpected events which have modified the opinions of the president upon a point so vital as the submission of the constitution for ratification or rejection by the vote of the people; much less do I desire any controversy with the president on this subject; yet, however widely my views may differ from those entertained by him on this question, — views which I have held all my life, and which, as involving fundamental principles of public liberty and of the constitution, are unchangeable, — yet, as regards all those great Democratic measures which, I trust, will constitute the policy of his administration in other respects, it will give me pleasure, as a private citizen, to yield my cordial support.

"I have said that the slavery question, as a practical issue, had disappeared from Kansas long before my arrival there, and the question of self-government had been substituted in its place. On some future occasion I shall dissipate the delusion which has prevailed upon this subject, and show that, after three years' experiment, when I arrived in Kansas there were less than three hundred slaves there, and the number constantly diminishing; that, as proved by the official records of Congress, published and authenticated by those distinguished southern statesmen, John C. Calhoun and Jefferson Davis, the winter climate even of Eastern Kansas is colder than that of New England, and that the pro-slavery territorial convention of Kansas, consolidated with the pro-slavery territorial legislature on the 4th of January, 1857, nearly five months before my arrival there, did distinctly abandon the slavery issue, because as set forth by one of their number, 'the pro slavery party was in a small and admitted minority,' 'and the coöperation of the free state Democrats was invited as the only hope of success, not to make Kansas a slave state, which was conceded to be impossible, but to make it a conservative Democratic free state.' Even as late as the 3d of July, 1857, when a Democratic territorial convention assembled at Lecompton, in consequence of the laws of climate and the well-known will of the people, none contended that slavery could be established there. Nor was it until my southern opponents interfered in the affairs of Kansas, and, by denunciation, menace, and otherwise, aided at a critical period by several federal office-holders of Kansas, including the surveyor-general, (the president of the convention,) with his immense patronage, embracing many hundred *employés*, intervened, and, as I believe, without the knowledge or approbation of the president of the United States, produced the extraordinary paper called the Lecompton constitution. Yet this act of intervention by federal officers to defeat the will of the people seems to be sustained by my opponents; whilst my intervention, as it is called, in obedience to my duty and oath of office to support the federal constitution, and to take care that our organic law should be fairly executed, by endeavoring to secure to the people of Kansas their rights under that act, is denounced and calumniated. It is still more extraordinary that the hypothetical remarks made by me as regards climate in its connection with its influence upon the question of slavery in Kansas, after that issue had been abandoned there, which views were consolidating the union between conservative, free state, and pro-slavery Democrats, so as to prevent the confiscation of the small number of slaves then held in Kansas, have been denounced by many distinguished southern senators, who, when the Kansas and Nebraska bill was pending in Congress, and when such remarks from them, if ever, might affect southern emigration, were then loudest in proclaiming that, because of its climate, Kansas could never become a slave state. Indeed, it seems that all persons in and out of Kansas, whether in public or in private life, may publish what opinions they please in regard to these questions, except the governor of that territory, who has so little power and no patronage.

"And now be pleased to express to the president my deep regret as regards our unfortunate difference of opinion in relation to the Lecompton constitution, and to say to him, that, as infallibility does not belong to man, however exalted in intellect, purity of intention, or position, yet, if he has committed any errors in this respect, may they be overruled by a superintending Providence for the perpetuation of our Union and the advancement of the honor and interest of our beloved country.

"In now dissolving my official connection with your department, I beg leave to tender to you my thanks for your constant courtesy and kindness.

"Most respectfully, your obedient servant,
"R. J. WALKER.
Hon. LEWIS CASS, *Secretary of State.*"

To this letter Mr. Cass sent the following reply: —

"DEPARTMENT OF STATE,
WASHINGTON, *December* 18, 1857.}

"SIR: On Wednesday last I received your communication of the 15th instant, tendering your resignation as governor of Kansas. This resignation is accompanied by a long argument on the affairs of that territory generally, to which you are well aware it would be improper for the department to reply. If every officer of the government, who feels himself constrained to refuse obedience to the instructions of the president, should pursue this unusual course, and thus place on the files of the appropriate department a criticism on the policy of the administration, no person knows better than yourself to what consequences this might lead. The department must either cause charges and arguments against the president to be filed among the public archives of the country, without contradiction or reply, or it must spend the time which ought to be devoted to the public service in controversies with subordinate officers who may disapprove the president's policy. Whilst duty, therefore, forbids me to enter into a controversial discussion with you on the various topics embraced by your argument, it is proper I should make a remark upon a single point.

"You state that the president has changed his policy in regard to Kansas. And why this allegation? Simply because the convention of Kansas having, in the exercise of the right belonging to them, decided that they would not submit the whole constitution to the people, although they have submitted the all-important and dangerous question of slavery, which threatened to convulse the Union, and was alone prominent in the minds of the people throughout every state, he had not treated the submission of this momentous question as a mere nullity. Under these circumstances it was his imperative duty, and this in strict conformity with previous instructions, to take care that a fair election should be held on this vital question, and thus give peace to the Union. Had he acted in any other manner, merely because he preferred the submission of the constitution generally to the people, his responsibility would have been of the gravest character.

" He never entertained or expressed the opinion, that the convention were bound to submit any portion of the constitution to the people, except the question of slavery, much less that the other portions of the constitution would be invalid without such a submission. Had he entertained such an opinion, this would have been in opposition to the numerous precedents which have occurred since the adoption of the federal constitution by the different states.

" The question of slavery was the all-absorbing question, and you were sent to Kansas with the full confidence of the president to carry out the principles of the Kansas-Nebraska act. With the question, whether Kansas was to be a free or slave state, you were not to interfere. You were to secure to the people of Kansas a free and fair election, to decide this question for themselves. The president was, therefore, happy to learn from your despatch to this department of the 15th July last, that in all your speeches you had refrained from expressing any opinion as to whether Kansas should be a slave or a free state.

" I am instructed to inform you that your resignation of the office of governor of Kansas has been accepted.

" I am, sir, your obedient servant,

" LEWIS CASS.

' Hon. ROBERT J. WALKER, *Washington*."

5

CHAPTER III.

Utah. — Rebellious Disposition of the Mormons. — New Governor appointed. — An Army to support the Civil Authorities. — Progress of the Expedition. — Hardships. — Character of the Cabinet. — Death of Members of President Pierce's Cabinet. — Indian Troubles. — Monetary Pressure of 1857. — Results.

AT this point it is necessary to leave the subject of Kansas for a time, in order to make mention of other matters, which, during the period we have passed over, received a share of attention from the government and the public.

Early in the year affairs in Utah, which had for some time been in an unpromising condition, threatened to result in serious disturbances. The Mormons were disposed to resist the authority of the United States, if it was again attempted to send officers not of their faith to the territory, in place of those who had been obliged to leave. They denied the right of the federal government to appoint territorial officers over them, and affirmed that polygamy is a purely local institution, concerning nobody out of Utah. The militia were organized and trained, and the preachers urged the "Saints," as the Mormons call themselves, to prepare for resistance. The chief justice of the territory, Mr. Drummond, who resigned his position at this time, revealed to the government a state of affairs in Utah which demanded immediate attention if the territory was still to be held by the United States. After recounting the offences of which the Mormons had been guilty, including certain murders committed by them or by the Indians at their instigation, Mr. Drummond said, that if a governor were sent to the territory who was not a Mormon, and were supported by a sufficient military force, something might be done to reform the abuses and to punish the crimes complained of; but otherwise it would be madness to attempt to administer the laws in the territory.

Acting upon these representations, and other

testimony to the same effect, the administration took measures to send out a governor and other civil officers, supported by a military force which should secure respect and obedience. Brigham Young, the head of the Mormon church, had been governor of the territory since the administration of Mr. Fillmore. It was determined to remove him, — and there were abundant reasons for so doing, — and after some difficulty in finding a proper person for his successor who would accept the post, Mr. Alfred Cumming, of Missouri, was appointed. Other civil officers were appointed, and a force of twenty-five hundred men was concentrated for the purpose of marching to Utah, to maintain the authority of the federal government. In the mean time matters grew worse in that territory, and all the federal officers, with the exception of the Indian agent, had been obliged to leave. It was late in the season before the forces, under the command of Colonel Johnstone, an old and experienced officer, commenced their long and difficult journey across the plains and through the mountain passes. The transportation of supplies was effected at an enormous expense and at great loss, by the death of cattle and mules, and the attacks of the Indians, the long trains not being sufficiently protected. The expedition suffered great hardships by the approach of winter before they reached the valley of the Great Salt Lake. Scarcity of provisions threatened them in the midst of the severities of the winter, and, as it were, almost in a desert, and Captain Marcy was sent to the settlements in New Mexico, a distance of seven hundred miles, with a small force of volunteers, to procure cattle. This was a severe and perilous undertaking; but after great hardships Captain Marcy accomplished his journey, and brought back a small supply of cattle. In the mean time the expedition was encamped, or quartered in huts, on the banks of Henry's Fork, within two hundred miles of Salt Lake City, and suffered not a little

from the hardships of such a winter campaign. There they waited for the opening of spring in order to enter the valley. Governor Cumming declared the territory to be in a state of rebellion, and Judge Eckels organized a district court, in which were tried offences originating about the camp; and the grand jury found bills against the Mormon leaders for treason. The Mormons, in the mean time, threatened resistance, and made some show of it, though they kept at a distance from the main body of the army.

Thus did Mr. Buchanan, at the onset, have two serious and important territorial *imbroglios* bequeathed to him by his predecessor, and his administration was taxed with the management of these affairs before he had an opportunity of meeting Congress, to explain his policy or receive their support and assistance. Of long experience in public life himself, he had the aid of a man of equal experience and prominence in the state department, while the other members of the cabinet, though less known, were men of some ability, and probably more devoted supporters of what was now the policy of the Democratic party. In point of ability, perhaps, the new cabinet was not so strong as that of Mr. Pierce, but it appeared in the course of events that they were quite as devoted to the policy under which the country was growing, and, in spite of all obstacles, flourishing.

We may here mention that two members of President Pierce's cabinet died in the summer of 1857, but a few months after their release from the arduous duties of their departments. William L. Marcy, the late secretary of state, died at Ballston, New York, very suddenly, on the 4th of July, at the age of seventy-two years. He was born in Massachusetts, but settled in New York in early life. He entered public life at the age of thirty, and from that time he was almost constantly in the public service. He held many important state offices, and was three times elected governor. He had also served in Congress, and was secretary of war during the administration of Mr. Polk, having charge of that department during the Mexican war, and discharging the duties with industry and ability. As secretary of state, under Mr. Pierce, he exhibited great ability as a diplomatist; and had the representatives of the United States abroad been what they should have been, the foreign relations of the country might have done more credit to his department. He was a man who was highly respected both in public and private life. Mr. Marcy's colleague in office, as secretary of the navy, John C. Dobbin, died a month later, August 4th, at Fayetteville, North Carolina.*

In addition to the expedition to Utah, and the repression of disturbances in Kansas, the administration had a further unusual demand for troops to act against the Indians, who had become very troublesome and hostile all along the western and north-western frontier. They had committed outrages in Minnesota and on the borders of Iowa, as well as in Nebraska, besides attacking the supply trains which were going forward for the Utah expedition. They had taken many lives, and had carried off a number of women. All the available troops were sent to punish these savages, but little has ever been accomplished by this sort of warfare.

In the summer of 1857 the country began to suffer from an unusual monetary pressure. The first indications were a remarkable fall in the price of stocks; failures of unsound corporations followed, and a panic seized upon the commercial community, the doubt and distrust arising therefrom adding not a little to the misfortunes which the mercantile community suffered. The contraction of loans by the

banks of the principal commercial cities caused great distress among those who had done a large business on the credit system, and many of the houses reputed to be the wealthiest were the greatest sufferers in this crisis. As the troubles increased and commercial credit seemed to be so questionable, the panic extended to all classes of society. The next thing was a suspicion of the solvency of the banks, and there was, consequently, a demand on the banks for specie in redemption of their notes. This demand increased with the panic, and the panic was increased by the rush for specie, until at last the banks of the principal cities were obliged, for their own safety and for the welfare of the business public, to suspend specie payments; and the banks throughout the country soon followed. This measure enabled them to increase their loans, while it also brought the panic among the poorer classes to an abrupt end. After a time the severity of the storm abated, the crisis was passed, but many a merchant was wrecked, and the distress was widely extended. The industry of the country, too, received a severe blow. Manufacturing establishments were among those which had suffered most, and a total or partial suspension of their operations was necessary, thus throwing numerous persons out of employment, and extending the distress, step by step, through all the branches of industry. Nor was the government exempt from the pressure, although at the outset there were twenty millions of dollars in the treasury. For the relief of the public the government had purchased its own securities when offered, thus paying out several millions of specie, which otherwise would have remained in its vaults. But in the mean time, by the commercial distress and the new tariff, the receipts into the treasury were greatly diminished, and the surplus, which for several years had remained on hand at the close of the fiscal years, was likely to be changed to a deficit.

* Thomas J. Rusk, United States senator from Texas, not long after this, committed suicide, while laboring under great depression of spirits. He was one of the ablest members of the Democratic party, and was mentioned as a probable candidate for the presidency.

CHAPTER IV.

Thirty-fifth Congress. — Organization. — President's Message.

Such was the state of affairs when the thirty-fifth Congress commenced its first session. The elections which had occurred in the several states at the time of the presidential election, and afterwards, had resulted more favorably for the Democratic party than had been the case in the previous Congress. The administration still having the senate, though by a diminished majority, had also a very decisive majority in the house of representatives. The latter was organized at once by the choice of J. L. Orr, of South Carolina, as speaker, by one hundred and twenty-eight votes to eighty-four for Mr. Grow, the Republican candidate.

The president's message was communicated to Congress the next day, December 8th. From that document we make the following extracts in relation to some of the more important subjects which were before the country. After referring to the prosperity of the several great interests of the people, the president proceeds: —

"We have possessed all the elements of material wealth in rich abundance, and yet, notwithstanding all these advantages, our country, in its monetary interests, is at the present moment in a deplorable condition. In the midst of unsurpassed plenty in all the productions of agriculture, and in all the elements of national wealth, we find our manufactures suspended, our public works retarded, our private enterprises of different kinds abandoned, and thousands of useful laborers thrown out of employment and reduced to want. The revenue of the government, which is chiefly derived from duties on imports from abroad, has been greatly reduced, whilst the appropriations made by Congress, at its last session, for the current fiscal year, are very large in amount.

"Under these circumstances a loan may be required before the close of your present session; but this, although deeply to be regretted, would prove to be only a slight misfortune when compared with the suffering and distress prevailing among the people. With this the government cannot fail deeply to sympathize, though it may be without the power to extend relief

"It is our duty to inquire what has produced such unfortunate results, and whether their recurrence can be prevented. In all former revulsions the blame might have been fairly attributed to a variety of coöperating causes; but not so upon the present occasion. It is apparent that our existing misfortunes have proceeded solely from our extravagant and vicious system of paper currency and bank credits, exciting the people to wild speculations and gambling in stocks. These revulsions must continue to recur at successive intervals so long as the amount of the paper currency and bank loans and discounts of the country shall be left to the discretion of fourteen hundred irresponsible banking institutions, which, from the very law of their nature, will consult the interest of their stockholders rather than the public welfare.

"The framers of the constitution, when they gave to Congress the power 'to coin money and to regulate the value thereof,' and prohibited the states from coining money, emitting bills of credit, or making any thing but gold and silver coin a tender in payment of debts, supposed they had protected the people against the evils of an excessive and irredeemable paper currency. They are not responsible for the existing anomaly that a government endowed with the sovereign attribute of coining money and regulating the value thereof should have no power to prevent others from driving this coin out of the country, and filling up the channels of circulation with paper which does not represent gold and silver.

"It is one of the highest and most responsible duties of government to insure to the people a sound circulating medium, the amount of which ought to be adapted with the utmost possible wisdom and skill to the wants of internal trade and foreign exchanges. If this be either greatly above or greatly below the proper standard, the marketable value of every man's property is increased or diminished in the same proportion, and injustice to individuals, as well as incalulable evils to the community, are the consequence.

"Unfortunately, under the construction of the federal constitution, which has now prevailed too long to be changed, this important and delicate duty has been dissevered from the coining power, and virtually transferred to more than fourteen hundred state banks, acting independently of each other, and regulating their paper issues almost exclusively by a regard to the present interest of their stockholders. Exercising the sovereign power of providing a paper currency instead of coin for the country, the first duty which these banks owe to the public is to keep in their vaults a sufficient amount of gold and silver to insure the convertibility of their notes into coin at all times and under all circumstances. No bank ought ever to be chartered without such restrictions on its business as to secure this result. All other restrictions are comparatively vain. This is the only true touchstone, the only efficient regulator of a paper currency — the only one which can guard the public against over-issues and bank suspensions. As a collateral and eventual security, it is doubtless wise, and in all cases ought to be required, that banks shall hold an amount of United States or state securities equal to their notes in circulation, and pledged for their redemption. This, however, furnishes no adequate security against over-issues. On the contrary, it may be perverted to inflate the currency. Indeed, it is possible by this means to convert all the debts of the United States and state governments into bank notes, without reference to the specie required to redeem them. However valuable these securities may be in themselves, they cannot be converted into gold and silver at the moment of pressure, as our experience teaches, in sufficient time to prevent bank suspensions and the depreciation of bank notes. In England, which is to a considerable extent a paper-money country, though vastly behind our own in this respect, it was deemed advisable, anterior to the act of Parliament of 1844, which wisely separated the issue of notes from the banking department, for the Bank of England always to keep on hand gold and silver equal to one third of its combined circulation and deposits. If this proportion was no more than sufficient to secure the convertibility of its notes, with the whole of Great Britain, and to some extent the continent of Europe, as a field for its circulation, rendering it almost impossible that a sudden and immediate run to a dangerous amount should be made upon it, the same proportion would certainly be insufficient under our banking system. Each of our fourteen hundred banks has but a limited circumference for its circulation, and in the course of a very few days the depositors and note-holders might demand from such a bank a sufficient amount in specie to compel it to suspend, even although it had coin in its vaults equal to one third of its immediate liabilities. And yet I am not aware, with the exception of the banks of Louisiana, that any state bank throughout the Union has been required by its charter to keep this or any other proportion of gold and silver compared with the amount of its combined circulation and deposits. What has been the consequence? In a recent report made by the treasury department on the condition of the banks throughout the different states, according to returns dated nearest to January, 1857, the aggregate amount of actual specie in their vaults is fifty-eight million three hundred and forty-nine thousand eight hundred and thirty-eight dollars; of their circulation, two hundred and fourteen million seven hundred and seventy-eight thousand eight hundred and twenty-two dollars; and of their deposits, two hundred and thirty million three hundred and fifty-one thousand three hundred and fifty-two dollars. Thus it appears that these banks, in the aggregate, have considerably less than one dollar in seven of gold and silver compared with their circulation and deposits. It was palpable, therefore, that the very first pressure must drive them to suspension, and deprive the people of a convertible currency with all its disastrous consequences. It is truly wonderful that they should have so long continued to preserve their credit, when a demand for the payment of one seventh of their immediate liabilities would have driven them into insolvency. And this is the condition of the banks, notwithstanding that four hundred millions of gold from California have flowed in upon us within the last eight years, and the tide still continues to flow. Indeed, such has been the extravagance of bank credits that the banks now hold a considerably less amount of specie, either in proportion to their capital or to their circulation and deposits combined, than they did before the discovery of gold in California. Whilst in the year 1848 their specie, in proportion to their capital, was more than equal to one dollar for four and a half, in 1857 it does not amount to one dollar for every six dollars and thirty-three cents of their capital. In the year 1848 the specie was equal, within a very small fraction, to one dollar in five of their circulation and deposits; in 1857 it is not equal to one dollar in seven and a half of their circulation and deposits.

"From this statement it is easy to account for our financial history for the last forty years. It has been a history of extravagant expansions in the business of the country, followed by ruinous contractions. At successive intervals the best and most enterprising men have been tempted to their ruin by excessive bank loans of mere paper credit, exciting them to extravagant importations of foreign goods, wild speculations, and ruinous and demoralizing stock gambling. When the crisis arrives, as arrive it must, the banks can extend no relief to the people. In a vain struggle to redeem their liabilities in specie, they are compelled to contract their loans and their issues; and, at last, in the hour of distress, when their assistance is most needed, they and their debtors together sink into insolvency.

"It is this paper system of extravagant expansion, raising the nominal price of every article far beyond its real value, when compared with the cost of similar articles in countries whose circulation is wisely regulated, which has prevented us from competing in our own markets with foreign manufacturers, has produced extravagant importations, and has counteracted the effect of the large incidental protection afforded to our domestic manufactures by the present revenue tariff. But for this, the branches of our manufactures composed of raw materials, the production of our own country, — such as cotton, iron, and woollen fabrics, — would not only have acquired almost exclusive possession of the home market, but would have created for themselves a foreign market throughout the world.

"Deplorable, however, as may be our present financial condition, we may yet indulge in bright hopes for the future. No other nation has ever existed which could have endured such violent expansions and contractions of paper credits without lasting injury; yet the buoyancy of youth, the energies of our population, and the spirit which never quails before difficulties, will enable us soon to recover from our present financial embarrassment, and may even occasion us speedily to forget the lesson which they have taught.

"In the mean time it is the duty of the government, by all proper means within its power, to aid in alleviating the sufferings of the people occasioned by the suspension of the banks, and to provide against a recurrence of the same calamity. Unfortunately, in either aspect of the case, it can do but little. Thanks to the independent treasury, the government has not suspended payment, as it was compelled to do by the failure of the banks in 1837. It will continue to discharge its liabilities to the people in gold and silver. Its disbursements in coin will pass into circulation, and materially assist in restoring a sound currency. From its high credit, should we be compelled to make a temporary loan, it can be effected on advantageous terms. This, however, shall, if possible, be avoided; but, if not, then the amount shall be limited to the lowest practicable sum.

"I have therefore determined, that whilst no useful government works already in progress shall be suspended, new works which are not already commenced will be postponed, if this can be done without injury to the country. Those necessary for its defence shall proceed as though there had been no crisis in our monetary affairs.

"But the federal government cannot do much to provide against a recurrence of existing evils. Even if insurmountable constitutional objections did not exist against the creation of a national bank, this would furnish no adequate preventive security. The history of the last Bank of the United States abundantly proves the truth of this assertion. Such a bank could not, if it would, regulate the issues and credits of fourteen hundred state banks in such a manner as to prevent the ruinous expansions and contractions in our currency which afflicted the country throughout the existence of the late bank, or secure us against future suspensions. In 1825 an effort was made by the Bank of England to curtail the issues of the country banks, under the most favorable circumstances. The paper currency had been expanded to a ruinous extent, and the bank put forth all its power to contract it in order to reduce prices and restore the equilibrium of the foreign exchanges. It accordingly commenced a system of curtailment of its loans and issues, in the vain hope that the joint-stock and private banks of the kingdom would be compelled to follow its example. It found, however, that as it contracted they expanded, and at the end of the process, to employ the language of a very high official authority, 'whatever reduction of the paper circulation was effected by the Bank of England (in 1825) was more than made up by the issues of the country banks.'

"But a Bank of the United States would not, if it could, restrain the issues and loans of the state banks, because its duty as a regulator of the currency must often be in direct conflict with the immediate interest of its stockholders. If we expect one agent to restrain or control another, their interests must, at least in some degree, be antagonistic. But the directors of a Bank of the United States would feel the same interest and the same inclination with the directors of the state banks to expand the currency, to accommodate their favorites and friends with loans, and to declare large dividends. Such has been our experience in regard to the last bank.

"After all, we must mainly rely upon the patriotism and wisdom of the states for the prevention and redress of the evil. If they will afford us a real specie basis for our paper circulation by increasing the denomination of bank notes, first to twenty, and afterwards to fifty dollars; if they will require that the banks shall at all times keep on hand at least one dollar of gold and silver for every three dollars of their circulation and deposits; and if they will provide by a self-executing enactment, which nothing can arrest, that the moment they suspend they shall go into liquidation, I believe that such provisions, with a weekly publication by each bank of a statement of its condition, would go far to secure us against future suspensions of specie payments.

"Congress, in my opinion, possess the power to pass a uniform bankrupt law applicable to all banking institutions throughout the United States, and I strongly recommend its exercise. This would make it the irreversible organic law of each bank's existence, that a suspension of specie payments shall produce its civil death. The instinct of self-preservation would then compel it to perform its duties in such a manner as to escape the penalty and preserve its life.

"The existence of banks and the circulation of bank paper are so identified with the habits of our people, that they cannot, at this day, be suddenly abolished without much immediate injury to the country. If we could confine them to their appropriate sphere, and prevent them from administering to the spirit of wild and reckless speculation by extravagant loans and issues, they might be continued with advantage to the public.

"But this I say, after long and much reflection: If experience shall prove it to be impossible to enjoy the facilities which well-regulated banks might afford, without at the same time suffering the calamities which the excesses of the banks have hitherto inflicted upon the country, it would then be far the lesser evil to deprive them altogether of the power to issue a paper currency, and confine them to the functions of banks of deposit and discount."

Of the relations between the United States and Great Britain the president spoke at some length, explaining the position of the Central American question, as follows : —

"The diplomatic difficulties which existed between the government of the United States and that of Great Britain at the adjournment of the last Congress have been happily terminated by the appointment of a British minister to this country, who has been cordially received.

"Whilst it is greatly to the interest, as I am convinced it is the sincere desire, of the governments and people of the two countries to be on terms of intimate friendship with each other, it has been our misfortune almost always to have had some irritating, if not dangerous, outstanding question with Great Britain.

"Since the origin of the government we have been employed in negotiating treaties with that power, and afterwards in discussing their true intent and meaning. In this respect, the convention of April 19, 1850, commouly called the Clayton and Bulwer treaty has been the most unfortunate of all; because the two governments place directly opposite and contradictory instructions upon its first and most important article. Whilst, in the United States, we believed that this treaty would place both powers upon an exact equality by the stipulation that neither will ever 'occupy, or fortify, or colonize, or assume or exercise any dominion' over, any part of Central America, it is contended by the British government that the true construction of this language has left them in the rightful possession of all that portion of Central America which was in their occupancy at the date of the treaty ; in fact, that the treaty is a virtual recognition on the part of the United States of the right of Great Britain, either as owner or protector, to the whole extensive coast of Central America, sweeping round from the Rio Hondo to the port and harbor of San Juan de Nicaragua, together with the adjacent Bay Islands, except the comparatively small portion of this between the Sarstoon and Cape Honduras. According to their construction, the treaty does no more than simply prohibit them from extending their possessions in Central America beyond the present limits. It is not too much to assert, that if in the United States the treaty had been considered susceptible of such a construction, it never would have been negotiated under the authority of the president, nor would it have received the approbation of the senate. The universal conviction in the United States was, that when our government consented to violate its traditional and time-honored policy, and to stipulate with a foreign government never to occupy or acquire territory in the Central American portion of our own continent, the consideration for this sacrifice was, that Great Britain should, in this respect at least, be placed in the same position with ourselves. Whilst we have no right to doubt the sincerity of the British government in their construction of the treaty, it is at the same time my deliberate conviction that this construction is in opposition both to its letter and its spirit.

"Under the late administration negotiations were instituted between the two governments for the purpose, if possible, of removing these difficulties ; and a treaty having this laudable object in view was signed at London on the 17th October, 1856, and was submitted by the president to the senate on the following 10th of December. Whether this treaty, either in its original or amended form, would have accomplished the object intended without giving birth to new and embarrassing complications between the two governments, may perhaps be well questioned. Certain it is, however, it was rendered much less objectionable by the different amendments made to it by the senate. The treaty, as amended, was ratified by me on the 12th March, 1857, and was transmitted to London for ratification by the British government. That government expressed its willingness to concur in all the amendments made by the senate, with the single exception of the clause relating to Ruatan and the other islands in the Bay of Honduras. The article in the original treaty, as submitted to the senate, after reciting that these islands and their inhabitants 'having been, by a convention bearing date the 27th day of August, 1856, between her Britannic majesty and the republic of Honduras, constituted and declared a free territory

6

under the sovereignty of the said republic of Honduras,' stipulated that 'the two contracting parties do hereby mutually engage to recognize and respect in all future time the independence and rights of the said free territory as a part of the republic of Honduras.'

"Upon an examination of this convention between Great Britain and Honduras of the 27th August, 1856, it was found that, whilst declaring the Bay Islands to be 'a free territory under the sovereignty of the republic of Honduras,' it deprived that republic of rights without which its sovereignty over them could scarcely be said to exist. It divided them from the remainder of Honduras, and gave to their inhabitants a separate government of their own, with legislative, executive, and judicial officers, elected by themselves. It deprived the government of Honduras of the taxing power in every form, and exempted the people of the islands from the performance of military duty, except for their own exclusive defence. It also prohibited that republic from erecting fortifications upon them for their protection — thus leaving them open to invasion from any quarter ; and finally it provided 'that slavery shall not at any time hereafter be permitted to exist therein.'

"Had Honduras ratified this convention, she would have ratified the establishment of a state substantially independent within her own limits, and a state at all times subject to British influence and control. Moreover, had the United States ratified the treaty with Great Britain in its original form, we should have been bound 'to recognize and respect in all future time' these stipulations to the prejudice of Honduras. Being in direct opposition to the spirit and meaning of the Clayton and Bulwer treaty as understood in the United States, the senate rejected the entire clause, and substituted in its stead a simple recognition of the sovereign right of Honduras to these islands in the following language : 'The two contracting parties do hereby mutually engage to recognize and respect the islands of Ruatan, Bonaco, Utila, Barbaretta, Helena, and Morat, situate in the Bay of Honduras, and off the coast of the republic of Honduras, as under the sovereignty and as part of the said republic of Honduras.'

"Great Britain rejected this amendment, assigning as the only reason that the ratifications of the convention of the 27th August, 1856, between her and Honduras, had not been 'exchanged, owing to the hesitation of that government.' Had this been done, it is stated that 'her majesty's government would have had little difficulty in agreeing to the modification proposed by the senate, which then would have had in effect the same signification as the original wording.' Whether this would have been the effect — whether the mere circumstance of the exchange of the ratifications of the British convention with Honduras prior in point of time to the ratification of our treaty with Great Britain would, 'in effect,' have had 'the same signification as the original wording,' and thus have nullified the amendment of the senate — may well be doubted. It is, perhaps, fortunate that the question has never arisen.

"The British government, immediately after rejecting the treaty as amended, proposed to enter into a new treaty with the United States, similar in all respects to the treaty which they had just refused to ratify, if the United States would consent to add to the senate's clear and unqualified recognition of the sovereignty of Honduras over the Bay Islands the following conditional stipulation: 'whenever and so soon as the republic of Honduras shall have concluded and ratified a treaty with Great Britain, by which Great Britain shall have ceded, and the republic of Honduras shall have accepted, the said islands, subject to the provisions and conditions contained in such treaty.'

"This proposition was, of course, rejected. After the senate had refused to recognize the British convention with Honduras of the 27th August, 1856, with full knowledge of its contents, it was impossible for me, necessarily ignorant of 'the provisions and conditions' which might be contained in a future convention between the same parties, to sanction them in advance.

"The fact is, that when two nations, like Great Britain and the United States, mutually desirous as they are, and I trust ever may be, of maintaining the most friendly relations with each other, have, unfortunately, concluded a treaty which they understand in senses directly opposite, the wisest course is to abrogate such a treaty by mutual consent, and to commence anew. Had this been done promptly, all difficulties in Central America would most probably ere this have been adjusted to the satisfaction of both parties. The time spent in discussing the meaning of the Clayton and Bulwer treaty would have been devoted to this praiseworthy purpose, and the task would have been the more easily accomplished because the interest of the two countries in Central America is identical, being confined to securing safe transits over all the routes across the isthmus.

"Whilst entertaining these sentiments, I shall, nevertheless, not refuse to contribute to any reasonable adjustment of the Central American questions which is not practically inconsistent with the American interpretation of the treaty. Overtures for this purpose have been recently made by the British government in a friendly spirit, which I cordially reciprocate; but whether this renewed effort will result in success I am not yet prepared to express an opinion. A brief period will determine."

In relation to Spain, the message contained the following: —

"With all other European governments, except that of Spain, our relations are as peaceful as we could desire. I regret to say that no progress whatever has been made, since the adjournment of Congress, towards the settlement of any of the numerous claims of our citizens against the Spanish government. Besides, the outrage committed on our flag by the Spanish war frigate Ferrolana, on the high seas, off the coast of Cuba, in March, 1855, by firing into the American mail steamer El Dorado, and detaining and searching her, remains unacknowledged and unredressed. The general tone and temper of the Spanish government towards that of the United States are much to be regretted. Our present envoy extraordinary and minister plenipotentiary to Madrid has asked to be recalled; and it is my purpose to send out a new minister to Spain, with special instructions on all questions pending between the two governments, and with a determination to have them speedily and amicably adjusted, if this be possible. In the mean time, whenever our minister urges the just claims of our citizens on the notice of the Spanish government, he is met with the objection that Congress has never made the appropriation recommended by President Polk, in his annual message of December, 1847, 'to be paid to the Spanish government for the purpose of distribution among the claimants in the Amistad case.' A similar recommendation was made by my immediate predecessor, in his message of December, 1853; and entirely concurring with both in the opinion that this indemnity is justly due under the treaty with Spain of the 27th of October, 1795, I earnestly recommend such an appropriation to the favorable consideration of Congress."

Upon Central American affairs, independent of Great Britain, the president says, —

"Our difficulties with New Granada, which a short time since bore so threatening an aspect, are, it is to be hoped, in a fair train of settlement in a manner just and honorable to both parties.

"The Isthmus of Central America, including that of Panama, is the great highway between the Atlantic and Pacific, over which a large portion of the commerce of the world is destined to pass. The United States are more deeply interested than any other nation in preserving the freedom and security of all the communications across this isthmus. It is our duty, therefore, to take care that they shall not be interrupted either by invasions from our own country or by wars between the independent states of Central America. Under our treaty with New Granada of the 12th December, 1846, we are bound to guarantee the neutrality of the Isthmus of Panama, through which the Panama Railroad passes, 'as well as the rights of sovereignty and property which New Granada has and possesses over the said territory.' This obligation is founded upon equivalents granted by the treaty to the government and people of the United States.

"Under these circumstances, I recommend to Congress the passage of an act authorizing the president, in case of necessity, to employ the land and naval forces of the United States to carry into effect this guaranty of neutrality and protection. I also recommend similar legislation for the security of any other route across the isthmus in which we may acquire an interest by treaty.

"With the independent republics on this continent it is both our duty and our interest to cultivate the most friendly relations. We can never feel indifferent to their fate, and must always rejoice in their prosperity. Unfortunately, both for them and for us, our example and advice have lost much of their influence in consequence of the lawless expeditions which have been fitted out against some of them within the limits of our country. Nothing is better calculated to retard our steady material progress, or impair our character as a nation, than the toleration of such enterprises in violation of the law of nations.

"It is one of the first and highest duties of any independent state, in its relations with the members of the great family of nations, to restrain its people from acts of hostile aggression against their citizens or subjects. The most eminent writers on public law do not hesitate to denounce such hostile acts as robbery and murder.

" Weak and feeble states, like those of Central America, may not feel themselves able to assert and vindicate their rights. The case would be far different if expeditions were set on foot within our own territories to make private war against a powerful nation. If such expeditions were fitted out from abroad against any portion of our own country, to burn down our cities, murder and plunder our people, and usurp our government, we should call any power on earth to the strictest account for not preventing such enormities.

" Ever since the administration of General Washington, acts of Congress have been in force to punish severely the crime of setting on foot a military expedition within the limits of the United States, to proceed from thence against a nation or state with whom we are at peace. The present neutrality act of April 20, 1818, is but little more than a collection of preëxisting laws. Under this act, the president is empowered to employ the land and naval forces, and the militia, ' for the purpose of preventing the carrying on of any such expedition or enterprise from the territories and jurisdiction of the United States,' and the collectors of customs are authorized and required to detain any vessel in port when there is reason to believe she is about to take part in such lawless enterprises.

" When it was first rendered probable that an attempt would be made to get up another unlawful expedition against Nicaragua, the secretary of state issued instructions to the marshals and district attorneys, which were directed by the secretaries of war and the navy to the appropriate army and navy officers, requiring them to be vigilant, and to use their best exertions in carrying into effect the provisions of the act of 1818. Notwithstanding these precautions, the expedition has escaped from our shores. Such enterprises can do no possible good to the country, but have already inflicted much injury both on its interests and its character. They have prevented peaceful emigration from the United States to the states of Central America, which could not fail to prove highly beneficial to all the parties concerned. In a pecuniary point of view alone, our citizens have sustained heavy losses from the seizure and closing of the transit route by the San Juan between the two oceans.

" The leader of the recent expedition was arrested at New Orleans, but was discharged on giving bail for his appearance in the insufficient sum of two thousand dollars.

" I commend the whole subject to the serious attention of Congress, believing that our duty and our interest, as well as our national character, require that we should adopt such measures as will be effectual in restraining our citizens from committing such outrages."

The message then proceeds, in relation to difficulties with Paraguay : —

" I regret to inform you that the president of Paraguay has refused to ratify the treaty between the United States and that state as amended by the senate, the signature of which was mentioned in the message of my predecessor to Congress at the opening of its session in December, 1853. The reasons assigned for this refusal will appear in the correspondence herewith submitted.

" It being desirable to ascertain the fitness of the River La Plata and its tributaries for navigation by steam, the United States steamer Water Witch was sent thither for that purpose, in 1853. This enterprise was successfully carried on until February, 1855, when, whilst in the peaceful prosecution of her voyage up the Parana River, the steamer was fired upon by a Paraguayan fort. The fire was returned ; but as the Water Witch was of small force, and not designed for offensive operations, she retired from the conflict. The pretext upon which the attack was made was a decree of the president of Paraguay of October, 1854, prohibiting foreign vessels of war from navigating the rivers of that state. As Paraguay, however, was the owner of but one bank of the river of that name, the other belonging to Corientes, a state of the Argentine Confederation, the right of its government to expect that such a decree would be obeyed cannot be acknowledged. But the Water Witch was not, properly speaking, a vessel of war. She was a small steamer engaged in a scientific enterprise intended for the advantage of commercial states generally. Under these circumstances, I am constrained to consider the attack upon her as unjustifiable, and as calling for satisfaction from the Paraguayan government.

"Citizens of the United States, also, who were established in business in Paraguay, have had their property seized and taken from them, and have otherwise been treated by the authorities in an insulting and arbitrary manner, which requires redress.

"A demand for these purposes will be made in a firm but conciliatory spirit. This will the more probably be granted if the executive shall have authority to use other means in the event of a refusal. This is accordingly recommended."

Of Kansas affairs and the troubles in Utah the president spoke at length, as follows:—

"It is unnecessary to state in detail the alarming condition of the territory of Kansas at the time of my inauguration. The opposing parties then stood in hostile array against each other, and any accident might have relighted the flames of civil war. Besides, at this critical moment, Kansas was left without a governor by the resignation of Governor Geary.

"On the 19th of February previous, the territorial legislature had passed a law providing for the election of delegates, on the third Mon-

day of June, to a convention to meet on the first Monday of September, for the purpose of framing a constitution preparatory to admission into the Union. This law was in the main fair and just; and it is. to be regretted that all the qualified electors had not registered themselves and voted under its provisions.

"At the time of the election for delegates, an extensive organization existed in the territory, whose avowed object it was, if need be, to put down the lawful government by force, and to establish a government of their own, under the so-called Topeka constitution. The persons attached to this revolutionary organization abstained from taking any part in the election.

"The act of the territorial legislature had omitted to provide for submitting to the people the constitution which might be framed by the convention; and in the excited state of public feeling throughout Kansas, an apprehension extensively prevailed that a design existed to force upon them a constitution, in relation to slavery, against their will. In this emergency it became my duty, as it was my unquestionable right, having in view the union of all good citizens in support of the territorial laws, to express an opinion on the true construction of the provisions concerning slavery contained in the organic act of Congress of the 30th May, 1854. Congress declared it to be 'the true intent and meaning of this act, not to legislate slavery into any territory or state, nor to exclude it therefrom, but to leave the people thereof perfectly free to form and regulate their domestic institutions in their own way.' Under it Kansas, 'when admitted as a state,' was to 'be received into the Union with or without slavery, as their constitution may prescribe at the time of their admission.'

"Did Congress mean by this language that the delegates elected to frame a constitution should have authority finally to decide the question of slavery, or did they intend, by leaving it to the people, that the people of Kansas themselves should decide this question by a direct vote? On this subject I confess I had never entertained a serious doubt, and, therefore, in my instructions to Governor Walker of the 28th March last, I merely said that when 'a constitution shall be submitted to the people of the territory, they must be protected in the exercise of their right of voting for or against that instrument, and the fair expression of the popular will must not be interrupted by fraud or violence.'

"In expressing this opinion it was far from my intention to interfere with the decision of the people of Kansas, either for or against slavery. From this I have always carefully abstained. Intrusted with the duty of taking 'care that the laws be faithfully executed,' my only desire was, that the people of Kansas should furnish to Congress the evidence required by the organic act, whether for or against slavery; and in this manner smooth their passage into the Union. In emerging from the condition of territorial dependence into that of a sovereign state, it was their duty, in my opinion, to make known their will by the votes of the majority, on the direct question, whether this important domestic institution should or should not continue to exist. Indeed, this was the only possible mode in which their will could be authentically ascertained.

"The election of delegates to a convention must necessarily take place in separate districts. From this cause it may readily happen, as has often been the case, that a majority of the people of a state or territory are on one side of a question, whilst a majority of the representatives from the several districts into which it is divided may be upon the other side. This arises from the fact that in some districts delegates may be elected by small majorities, whilst in others those of different sentiments may receive majorities sufficiently great not only to overcome the votes given for the former, but to leave a large majority of the whole people

in direct opposition to a majority of the delegates. Besides, our history proves that influences may be brought to bear on the representative sufficiently powerful to induce him to disregard the will of his constituents. The truth is, that no other authentic and satisfactory mode exists of ascertaining the will of a majority of the people of any state or territory on an important and exciting question, like that of slavery in Kansas, except by leaving it to a direct vote. How wise, then, was it for Congress to pass over all subordinate and intermediate agencies, and proceed directly to the source of all legitimate power under our institutions!

"How vain would any other principle prove in practice! This may be illustrated by the case of Kansas. Should she be admitted into the Union with a constitution either maintaining or abolishing slavery, against the sentiment of the people, this could have no other effect than to continue and to exasperate the existing agitation during the brief period required to make the constitution conform to the irresistible will of the majority.

"The friends and supporters of the Nebraska and Kansas act, when struggling on a recent occasion to sustain its wise provisions before the great tribunal of the American people, never differed about its true meaning on this subject. Every where throughout the Union they publicly pledged their faith and their honor that they would cheerfully submit the question of slavery to the decision of the bona fide people of Kansas, without any restriction or qualification whatever. All were cordially united upon the great doctrine of popular sovereignty, which is the vital principle of our free institutions. Had it, then, been insinuated from any quarter that it would be a sufficient compliance with the requisitions of the organic law for the members of a convention, thereafter to be elected, to withhold the question of slavery from the people, and to substitute their own will for that of a legally-ascertained majority of all their constituents, this would have been instantly rejected. Every where they remained true to the resolution adopted on a celebrated occasion recognizing 'the right of the people of all the territories — including Kansas and Nebraska, acting through the legally and fairly expressed will of a majority of actual residents, and whenever the number of their inhabitants justifies it — to form a constitution with or without slavery, and be admitted into the Union upon terms of perfect equality with the other states.'

"The convention to frame a constitution for Kansas met on the first Monday of September last. They were called together by virtue of an act of the territorial legislature, whose lawful existence had been recognized by Congress in different forms and by different enactments. A large proportion of the citizens of Kansas did not think proper to register their names and to vote at the election for delegates; but an opportunity to do this having been fairly afforded, their refusal to avail themselves of their right could in no manner affect the legality of the convention.

"This convention proceeded to frame a constitution for Kansas, and finally adjourned on the 7th day of November. But little difficulty occurred in the convention, except on the subject of slavery. The truth is, that the general provisions of our recent state constitutions are so similar, and, I may add, so excellent, that the difference between them is not essential. Under the earlier practice of the government, no constitution framed by the convention of a territory preparatory to its admission into the Union as a state had been submitted to the people. I trust, however, the example set by the last Congress, requiring that the constitution of Minnesota 'should be subject to the approval and ratification of the people of the proposed state,' may be followed on future occasions. I took it for granted that the convention of Kansas would act in accordance with this example, founded, as it is, on correct principles; and hence my instructions to Governor Walker, in favor of submitting the constitution to the people, were expressed in general and unqualified terms.

"In the Kansas-Nebraska act, however, this requirement, as applicable to the whole constitution, had not been inserted, and the convention were not bound by its terms to submit any other portion of the instrument to an election, except that which relates to the 'domestic institution' of slavery. This will be rendered clear by a simple reference to its language. It was 'not to legislate slavery into any territory or state, nor to exclude it therefrom, but to leave the people thereof perfectly free to form and regulate their domestic institutions in their own way.' According to the plain construction of the sentence, the words 'domestic institutions' have a direct, as they have an appropriate, reference to slavery. 'Domestic institutions' are limited to the family. The relation between master and slave and a few others are 'domestic institutions,' and are entirely distinct from institutions of a political character. Besides, there was no question then before Congress, nor indeed has there since been any serious question before the people of Kansas or the country, except that which relates to the 'domestic institution' of slavery.

"The convention, after an angry and excited debate, finally determined, by a majority of only two, to submit the question of slavery to the people, though at the last forty-three of the fifty delegates present affixed their signatures to the constitution.

"A large majority of the convention were in favor of establishing slavery in Kansas. They accordingly inserted an article in the constitution for this purpose similar in form to those which had been adopted by other territorial conventions. In the schedule, however, providing for the transition from a territorial

to a state government, the question has been fairly and explicitly referred to the people, whether they will have a constitution 'with or without slavery.' It declares that, before the constitution adopted by the convention 'shall be sent to Congress for admission into the Union as a state,' an election shall be held to decide this question, at which all the white male inhabitants of the territory above the age of twenty-one are entitled to vote. They are to vote by ballot; and 'the ballots cast at said election shall be indorsed "constitution with slavery," and "constitution with no slavery." ' If there be a majority in favor of the 'constitution with slavery,' then it is to be transmitted to Congress by the president of the convention in its original form. If, on the contrary, there shall be a majority in favor of the 'constitution with no slavery,' 'then the article providing for slavery shall be stricken from the constitution by the president of this convention;' and it is expressly declared that 'no slavery shall exist in the state of Kansas, except that the right of property in slaves now in the territory shall in no manner be interfered with;' and in that event it is made his duty to have the constitution thus ratified transmitted to the Congress of the United States for the admission of the state into the Union.

"At this election every citizen will have an opportunity of expressing his opinion by his vote 'whether Kansas shall be received into the Union with or without slavery;' and thus this exciting question may be peacefully settled in the very mode required by the organic law. The election will be held under legitimate authority, and if any portion of the inhabitants shall refuse to vote, a fair opportunity to do so having been presented, this will be their own voluntary act, and they alone will be responsible for the consequences.

"Whether Kansas shall be a free or a slave state, must eventually, under some authority, be decided by an election; and the question can never be more clearly or distinctly presented to the people than it is at the present moment. Should this opportunity be rejected, she may be involved for years in domestic discord, and possibly in civil war, before she can again make up the issue now so fortunately tendered, and again reach the point she has already attained.

"Kansas has for some years occupied too much of the public attention. It is high time this should be directed to far more important objects. When once admitted into the Union, whether with or without slavery, the excitement beyond her own limits will speedily pass away, and she will then, for the first time, be left, as she ought to have been long since, to manage her own affairs in her own way. If her constitution on the subject of slavery, or on any other subject, be displeasing to a majority of the people, no human power can prevent them from changing it within a brief period. Under these circumstances it may well be questioned whether the peace and quiet of the whole country are not of greater importance than the mere temporary triumph of either of the political parties in Kansas.

"Should the constitution without slavery be adopted by the votes of the majority, the rights of property in slaves now in the territory are reserved. The number of these is very small; but if it were greater the provision would be equally just and reasonable. The slaves were brought into the territory under the constitution of the United States, and are now the property of their masters. This point has at length been finally decided by the highest judicial tribunal of the country — and this upon the plain principle that when a confederacy of sovereign states acquire a new territory at their joint expense, both equality and justice demand that the citizens of one and all of them shall have the right to take into it whatsoever is recognized as property by the common constitution. To have summarily confiscated the property in slaves already in the territory, would have been an act of gross injustice, and contrary to the practice of the older states of the Union which have abolished slavery.

"A territorial government was established for Utah by act of Congress approved the 9th September, 1850, and the constitution and laws of the United States were thereby extended over it 'so far as the same, or any provisions thereof, may be applicable.' This act provided for the appointment by the president, by and with the advice and consent of the senate, of a governor, who was to be ex officio superintendent of Indian affairs, a secretary, three judges of the Supreme Court, a marshal, and a district attorney. Subsequent acts provided for the appointment of the officers necessary to extend our land and our Indian system over the territory. Brigham Young was appointed the first governor on the 20th September, 1850, and has held the office ever since. Whilst Governor Young has been both governor and superintendent of Indian affairs throughout this period, he has been at the same time the head of the church called the Latter-Day Saints, and professes to govern its members and dispose of their property by direct inspiration and authority from the Almighty. His power has been, therefore, absolute over both church and state.

"The people of Utah, almost exclusively, belong to this church, and believing, with a fanatical spirit, that he is governor of the territory by divine appointment, they obey his commands as if these were direct revelations from Heaven. If, therefore, he chooses that his government shall come into collision with the government of the United States, the members of the Mormon church will yield implicit obedience to his will. Unfortunately, existing facts leave but little doubt that such is his determination. Without entering upon a minute history of occurrences, it is sufficient to say

7

that all the officers of the United States, judicial and executive, with the single exception of two Indian agents, have found it necessary for their own personal safety to withdraw from the territory; and there no longer remains any government in Utah but the despotism of Brigham Young. This being the condition of affairs in the territory, I could not mistake the path of duty. As chief executive magistrate, I was bound to restore the supremacy of the constitution and laws within its limits. In order to effect this purpose, I appointed a new governor and other federal officers for Utah, and sent with them a military force for their protection, and to aid as a *posse comitatus*, in case of need, in the execution of the laws.

"With the religious opinions of the Mormons, as long as they remained mere opinions, however deplorable in themselves and revolting to the moral and religious sentiments of all Christendom, I had no right to interfere. Actions alone, when in violation of the constitution and laws of the United States, become the legitimate subjects for the jurisdiction of the civil magistrate. My instructions to Governor Cumming have therefore been framed in strict accordance with these principles. At their date a hope was indulged that no necessity might exist for employing the military in restoring and maintaining the authority of the law; but this hope has now vanished. Governor Young has, by proclamation, declared his determination to maintain his power by force, and has already committed acts of hostility against the United States. Unless he should retrace his steps, the territory of Utah will be in a state of open rebellion. He has committed these acts of hostility notwithstanding Major Van Vliet, an officer of the army, sent to Utah by the commanding general to purchase provisions for the troops, had given him the strongest assurances of the peaceful intentions of the government, and that the troops would only be employed as a *posse comitatus* when called on by the civil authority to aid in the execution of the laws.

"There is reason to believe that Governor Young has long contemplated this result. He knows that the continuance of his despotic power depends upon the exclusion of all settlers from the territory, except those who will acknowledge his divine mission and implicitly obey his will; and that an enlightened public opinion there would soon prostrate institutions at war with the laws both of God and man. He has, therefore, for several years, in order to maintain his independence, been industriously employed in collecting and fabricating arms and munitions of war, and in disciplining the Mormons for military service. As superintendent of Indian affairs he has had an opportunity of tampering with the Indian tribes, and exciting their hostile feelings against the United States. This, according to our information, he has accomplished in regard to some of these tribes, while others have remained true to their allegiance, and have communicated his intrigues to our Indian agents. He has laid in a store of provisions for three years, which, in case of necessity, as he informed Major Van Vliet, he will conceal, 'and then take to the mountains, and bid defiance to all the powers of the government.'

"A great part of all this may be idle boasting; but yet no wise government will lightly estimate the efforts which may be inspired by such frenzied fanaticism as exists among the Mormans in Utah. This is the first rebellion which has existed in our territories; and humanity itself requires that we should put it down in such a manner that it shall be the last. To trifle with it would be to encourage it and to render it formidable. We ought to go there with such an imposing force as to convince these deluded people that resistance would be vain, and thus spare the effusion of blood. We can in this manner best convince them that we are their friends, not their ene-

mies. In order to accomplish this object, it will be necessary, according to the estimate of the war department, to raise four additional regiments; and this I earnestly recommend to Congress. At the present moment of depression in the revenues of the country I am sorry to be obliged to recommend such a measure; but I feel confident of the support of Congress, cost what it may, in suppressing the insurrection and in restoring and maintaining the sovereignty of the constitution and laws over the territory of Utah."

In relation to the finances of the country it appeared that the surplus on hand at the commencement of the fiscal year, July 1, 1857 was seventeen millions seven hundred and ten thousand one hundred and fourteen dollars. The receipts for the first quarter from that date were twenty millions nine hundred and twenty-nine thousand eight hundred and nineteen dollars, and the estimated receipts for the remaining three quarters, thirty-six millions seven hundred and fifty thousand dollars; making, with the surplus, seventy-five millions three hundred and eighty-nine thousand nine hundred and thirty-three dollars. The estimated expenditures reached about this sum, while it was added that they might be increased so that it would be desirable that the secretary of the treasury should have power to meet any temporary deficiency by the issue of treasury notes.

The president recommended the Pacific Railroad to the consideration of Congress, the raising of four additional regiments for the army, the construction of ten war steamers of light draught, and other matters of less general interest, as submitted by the several departments. The message concluded as follows:—

"The late disastrous monetary revulsion may have one good effect, should it cause both the government and the people to return to the practice of a wise and judicious economy both in public and private expenditures.

"An overflowing treasury has led to habits of prodigality and extravagance in our legislation. It has induced Congress to make large appropriations to objects for which they never would have provided had it been necessary to raise the amount of revenue required to meet them by increased taxation or by loans. We are now compelled to pause in our career, and to scrutinize our expenditures with the utmost vigilance; and in performing this duty, I pledge my coöperation to the extent of my constitutional competency.

"It ought to be observed, at the same time, that true public economy does not consist in withholding the means necessary to accomplish important national objects intrusted to us by the constitution, and especially such as may be necessary for the common defence. In the present crisis of the country it is our duty to confine our appropriations to objects of this character, unless in cases where justice to individuals may demand a different course. In all cases care ought to be taken that the money granted by Congress shall be faithfully and economically applied.

"Under the federal constitution, 'every bill which shall have passed the house of representatives and the senate shall, before it becomes a law,' be approved and signed by the president; and, if not approved, he shall return it with his objections to that house in which it originated.' In order to perform this high and responsible duty, sufficient time must be allowed the president to read and examine every bill presented to him for approval. Unless this be afforded, the constitution becomes a dead letter in this particular; and even worse, it becomes a means of deception. Our constituents, seeing the president's approval and signature attached to each act of Congress, are induced to believe that he has actually performed this duty, when, in truth, nothing is, in many cases, more unfounded.

"From the practice of Congress, such an examination of each bill as the constitution requires has been rendered impossible. The most important business of each session is generally crowded into its last hours, and the alternative presented to the president is either to violate the constitutional duty which he owes to the people, and approve bills which, for want of time, it is impossible he should have examined, or, by his refusal to do this, subject the country and individuals to great loss and inconvenience.

"Besides, a practice has grown up of late years to legislate in appropriation bills, at the last hours of the session, on new and important subjects. This practice constrains the president either to suffer measures to become laws which he does not approve, or to incur the risk of stopping the wheels of the government by vetoing an appropriation bill. Formerly, such bills were confined to specific appropriations for carrying into effect existing laws and the well-established policy of the country, and little time was then required by the president for their examination.

"For my own part, I have deliberately determined that I shall approve no bill which I have not examined, and it will be a case of extreme and most urgent necessity which shall ever induce me to depart from this rule. I therefore respectfully, but earnestly, recommend that the two houses would allow the president at least two days previous to the adjournment of each session, within which no new bill shall be presented to him for approval. Under the existing joint rule one day is allowed; but this rule has been hitherto so constantly suspended in practice, that important bills continue to be presented to him up till the very last moments of the session. In a large majority of cases no great public inconvenience can arise from the want of time to examine their provisions, because the constitution has declared that if a bill be presented to the president within the last ten days of the session, he is not required to return it, either with an approval or with a veto, 'in which case it shall not be a law.' It may then lie over, and be taken up and passed at the next session. Great inconvenience would only be experienced in regard to appropriation bills; but fortunately, under the late excellent law allowing a salary, instead of a *per diem*, to members of Congress, the expense and inconvenience of a called session will be greatly reduced.

"I cannot conclude without commending tc your favorable consideration the interest of the people of this district. Without a representative on the floor of Congress, they have for this very reason peculiar claims upon our just regard. To this I know, from my long acquaintance with them, they are eminently entitled."

CHAPTER V.

Kansas. — Territorial Legislature. — Submission of the Lecompton Constitution to the People — Two Elections. — The Vote of each. — Election of State Officers. — Frauds. — Constitution " with Slavery " sent to Washington. — Communicated to Congress by the President. — Action of Congress. — Position of Mr. Douglas. — Reports in the House. — Debates. — Mr. Montgomery's Proposition. — The Vote. — Disagreement of the Senate. — Conference Committee — Their Report. — The Result.

To the affairs of Kansas, which still attracted much attention, not only from the president in his message, but in Congress and through the country, we are compelled again to return. The territorial legislature convened for a special session by Mr. Stanton, the acting governor, on the 7th of December, organized by the choice of free state officers, and then proceeded to act upon the business for which it met. A bill was passed providing for the submission of the Lecompton constitution to the people, at an election to be held on the 4th of January, 1858, the ballots to be in three forms: " Constitution with slavery," " Constitution without slavery," and " No Lecompton constitution."

The legislature also passed a bill organizing a territorial militia, which was vetoed by the acting governor, but was passed by a two thirds vote over his veto.

In the mean time the election provided for by the constitutional convention was held on the 21st of December, when the Lecompton constitution was submitted to the people, in the two forms mentioned above, with and without slavery. The free state men, who were opposed to that constitution on other grounds as well as that of slavery, abstained from voting; and the consequence was, that the " Constitution with slavery" was adopted by a large majority, five thousand one hundred and forty-three, to five hundred and sixty-nine for the " Constitution without slavery." This result, although a matter of course, was the cause of new excitement between the parties, one of which was triumphant and assuming, and the other indignant. But on the 4th of January this apparent decision of the people of the territory was reversed, the vote against the constitution, in any shape, being about eleven thousand; for the constitution with slavery one hundred and fifty, and for the constitution without slavery twenty-four. At the same time, the election for officers under the state constitution as adopted at the election of December 21st took place. This election resulted in the choice of the free state candidates for the state officers, George W. Smith being elected governor. The legislature was for a long time in doubt, owing to the manner in which the returns were made to the president of the convention and declared by him. It appeared evident to the president of the council and the speaker of the house, free state men, who had examined the returns of the votes on the constitution given December 21st, that a large majority of the votes given on that day were returned from certain counties where the population was very sparse, and could not have afforded the vote returned. The returns were probably false, and there was reason to believe that the returns of the election of state officers, on January 4th, which were made to Mr. Calhoun, the president of the convention, alone, were also false and fraudulent. Upon investigation such proved to be the case. Gross frauds in the returns had been made, in some cases if not in all, after they had left the hands of the judges of elections, and were sent to Mr. Calhoun. These and other facts were elicited by the investigations made by or for a committee of the house of representatives in Congress. Throwing out such false returns, the state legislature would be strongly free state.

But the Lecompton constitution having been adopted with slavery, according to the vote of December 21st, it was sent to Washington, and was communicated to Congress by President Buchanan, who, in a long message, urged the admission of Kansas as a state, under that constitution. The president's arguments were, that the slavery question was the only one at issue in the territory; that the free state men, if they had voted and really were in the majority, might have defeated slavery; that they subsequently voted for state officers under the Lecompton constitution; that the people of Kansas, having thus framed a constitution and elected officers under it, should be admitted to the Union; that they have a right to alter their constitution when they will; that the admission of Kansas would localize the question of slavery, leaving it for the people of Kansas to settle; that the admission would bring quiet to the whole country, and then the troops might be withdrawn from that territory for other purposes.

This question created much feeling in Congress. It was warmly discussed on both sides, and gave rise to some complications in the administration party, several of its most prominent men taking strong grounds against the validity of the Lecompton constitution. In reviewing the case it seems strange that a

statesman of Mr. Buchanan's antecedents and experience, especially after his instructions to Governor Walker, in which he had declared that when "a constitution shall be submitted to the people of the territory, they must be protected in the exercise of their right of voting *for or against that instrument*, and the fair expression of the popular will must not be interrupted by fraud or violence," should not be found acting with those of his party who still claimed that this principle was essential to the validity of the constitution. But the president now asserted that the only question at issue between the parties in Kansas was the slavery question, — which statement is hardly sustained by the well-known facts, — and totally ignored the large majority against the constitution in any shape, by a vote legally taken by authority of the territorial legislature. It seems impossible, except from a pro-slavery point of view, that the president should, in face of the clearly-expressed will of the people of Kansas, and of the frauds then alleged and afterwards proved, thus have urged Congress to recognize this constitution.

In the senate the message was referred to the committee on territories, and a motion instructing the committee to inquire into the number and legality of the votes given in Kansas was rejected. In the house it was referred, after a long and exciting contest, to a select committee of fifteen, with instructions to inquire into all the facts connected with the formation of the constitution and its accordance with the wishes of the people of Kansas. This was on the motion of an administration member, Mr. Harris, of Illinois. He was opposed to the constitution as invalid, and not approved by the people of Kansas. In this view he was sustained by Mr. Douglas, senator from the same state, who took a similar stand in the senate.

In the committee of the house, which was constituted so as to show eight in favor of the constitution and seven against it, the minority made repeated and persistent steps to obey the instructions of the house by investigating the facts required; but in every instance they were opposed by the majority, who would only go into some merely technical and formal inquiries, and the object of the committee was thus in a measure defeated.

Three reports were made in each branch. In the senate, the majority report, presented by Mr. Green, of Missouri, adopted essentially the arguments of the president, and recommended a bill for the admission of Kansas under this constitution. A minority report by Mr. Collamer, of Vermont, and Mr. Wade, of Ohio, opposed the constitution mainly on the grounds urged against it by the free state men of Kansas, that the territorial government was formed by the usurpation of a foreign force; that the Lecompton constitution is the result of this usurpation, and is also contrary to the will of the people legally expressed. A third report, by Mr. Douglas, took the ground that there is no evidence that the Lecompton constitution was the act of the people of Kansas, or embodied their will; that the convention had no power to establish the constitution, but only to frame one to be presented to Congress, with a memorial for admission, which should be granted or denied according as the constitution embodied the will of the people. This report is a very elaborate one, and Mr. Douglas denied at length, and with force, some of the statements and arguments of the president and of the majority report. The position of Mr. Douglas on this question was a strong one, and acting as he did against his party, it may be looked upon as giving nothing more than simple justice to the people of Kansas.

In the house, the majority presented a report which fully indorsed the views of the president, and was accompanied by a bill for the admission of Kansas. A minority report, signed by five Republican members, after referring to the course of the majority of the committee in refusing to investigate the facts connected with the subject, argued, upon such evidence as they had, that the Lecompton constitution was not the will of the people; that it had not been submitted to the vote of all the actual settlers of Kansas, at an election fairly and justly conducted, according to the repeated and emphatic pledges of Governor Walker, approved by the administration, except by the vote authorized by the territorial legislature, which vote was ignored by the president and the majority. The report ably reviewed the whole subject, exposing the frauds that had been perpetrated, and controverting the arguments offered in favor of the proposed constitution. Another minority report, signed by Mr. Harris, of Illinois, and Mr. Adrain, of Pennsylvania, took much the same ground as that of Mr. Douglas in the senate. The report concludes as follows: —

"In conclusion of this subject, we will only add that, being fully convinced that this Lecompton constitution is neither acceptable nor satisfactory to any considerable number of the people of Kansas, much less to a majority of them; that it is not their act; that it neither speaks their sentiments nor embodies their will; that it is the offspring of fraud, corruption, and villainy; that the laws under which it was originated and the proceedings connected with its prosecution have been informal, irregular, and unjust; that the instrument bears upon its own face and in its own composition ample evidence of its base origin and deceitful pretensions, — we think it would be highly improper to admit Kansas into the Union as a state under this constitution, and that such act would not only be unjust to the people of that territory, but it would be dangerous to the peace and welfare of the whole country."

These reports occasioned long and earnest debates, in which there were frequent asperities, and some ill feeling. The bills were amended, and many amendments were rejected. In the senate one amendment, recognizing the right of the people to amend or alter their constitution at pleasure, was adopted, notwithstanding its futility was shown, as the provision could not alter the terms of the constitution, which itself prohibited any change before the year 1864. This amendment being adopted, the bill passed the senate on the 23d of March, by yeas thirty-three, nays twenty-five.

In the house the 1st of April was finally fixed for the vote; and on that day, other propositions being rejected, one proposed by Mr. Montgomery, of Pennsylvania, was adopted. This proposition was to strike out all the senate bill after the enacting clause, and substitute a bill admitting Kansas to the Union upon the condition that the constitution shall be submitted to the vote of the people, and if it be assented to, the president to make proclamation to that effect; and if not assented to, authorizing the people of Kansas to hold a convention to frame another constitution. This was passed by yeas one hundred and twenty, nays one hundred and twelve. This was a defeat of the administration in the house, although its own party had a large majority. The bill thus passed in the house was sent to the senate; which body disagreed, and the house adhered. The subject was then referred to conference committees, the house acceding to the request of the senate by one hundred and eight to one hundred and eight, the speaker giving a casting vote in favor of the reference. The committee of the senate consisted of Messrs. Green, Hunter, and Seward; that of the house, of Messrs. English, Stephens, and Howard. After prolonged conference the majority of the committee — Messrs. Seward and Howard dissenting — reported a proposition altogether different from any previous one. This was a bill to admit Kansas, but on the condition precedent,

that certain propositions to be submitted to them shall be accepted by the people. These propositions were grants to Kansas, from the public domain, of two sections of land in every township, for the use of schools; seventy-two sections for the support of a university; ten sections for the erection of public buildings; salt springs, not exceeding twelve in number, with six sections of land contiguous to each; and five per centum of the net proceeds of the sales of all public lands within the state. These propositions were to be submitted to the people, who should vote by ballot, "Proposition accepted," or, "Proposition rejected." If a majority of votes should be cast for "Proposition accepted," the admission of Kansas was to be complete without further proceedings; but if a majority should be cast for "Proposition rejected," Kansas was not to be admitted; but, when the population of the territory equalled the ratio of representation required for a member of the house of representatives, and not before, the people may determine by vote whether they wish to form a state for admission into the Union, and if they so desire, may elect delegates to a convention to form a constitution.

This bill passed the senate on the 30th of April, by a vote of thirty yeas to twenty-two nays, ten members being absent. The result in the house was more uncertain, but it was soon ascertained that some of the administration members, who had voted for the bill of Mr. Montgomery, would now change their position. The bill finally passed by yeas one hundred and eleven, nays one hundred and two, the absentees being equally divided. And thus the exciting topic passed from Congress for a time.

But the people of Kansas were not to be tempted into the Union, with a constitution which they considered so obnoxious, by the bounty thus held out to them, nor coerced into it by any threat of being obliged to wait for a large increase of population. The question proposed by Congress was duly submitted to them in the manner provided, at an election held for the purpose in July. The result was, that the proposition was rejected. The vote was, "to accept the proposition," one thousand seven hundred and eighty-eight; "to reject the proposition," eleven thousand and three hundred; showing a majority against the Lecompton constitution, and the bounty offered with it, of nine thousand five hundred and twelve votes.

CHAPTER VI.

Fillibuster Expedition to Nicaragua. — Capture by Commodore Paulding. — Opinions in the Senate. — Expedition to Paraguay. — Proposed Increase of the Army defeated. — Deficiency of Revenue. — Admission of Minnesota. — " Speck of War " with England. — Search of Vessels by British Cruisers. — Action of the Government. — Friendly Relations restored. — Adjournment of Congress.

EARLY in the session of this Congress information was received that another fillibuster expedition to Nicaragua, under General William Walker, who had before been engaged in such schemes, had been broken up, and the parties concerned taken prisoners by the naval forces of the United States, on the coast of Central America. The expedition of Walker was fitted out in the United States, in violation of the neutrality laws, and had escaped the vigilance of the civil officers. The expedition had arrived at Nicaragua, and the men had been landed, when Commodore Paulding, acting in conformity with the spirit of his instructions to arrest such parties, landed a sufficient force, and captured Walker and his associates. This transaction was not received with much favor by those disposed to encourage these lawless expeditions; but it was considered by others as a wise and just proceeding, and one likely to prevent much mischief, and to produce some positive good.

When this event was known in Congress,

the president, as usual, was called upon for information, which he promptly transmitted. In his message he says, —

"In capturing General Walker and his command, after they had landed on the soil of Nicaragua, Commodore Paulding has, in my opinion, committed a grave error. It is quite evident, however, from the communications herewith transmitted, that this was done from pure and patriotic motives, and in the sincere conviction that he was promoting the interest, and vindicating the honor, of his country. In regard to Nicaragua, she has sustained no injury by the act of Commodore Paulding. This has enured to her benefit, and relieved her from a dreaded invasion. She alone would have any right to complain of the violation of her territory; and it is quite certain she will never exercise this right. It unquestionably does not lie in the mouth of her invaders to complain in her name that she has been rescued by Commodore Paulding from their assaults."

The president severely condemns the expedition of Walker, and in conclusion thus speaks of the future of Central America : —

"It is, beyond question, the destiny of our race to spread themselves over the continent of North America, and this at no distant day, should events be permitted to take their natural course. The tide of emigrants will flow to the south, and nothing can eventually arrest its progress. If permitted to go there peacefully, Central America will soon contain an American population which will confer blessings and benefits, as well upon the natives as their respective governments. Liberty under the restraint of law will preserve domestic peace, whilst the different transit routes across the isthmus, in which we are so deeply interested, will have assured protection.

"Nothing has retarded this happy condition of affairs so much as the unlawful expeditions which have been fitted out in the United States to make war upon the Central American states. Had one half the number of American citizens who have miserably perished in the first disastrous expedition of General Walker settled in Nicaragua as peaceful emigrants, the object which we all desire would ere this have been in a great degree accomplished. These expeditions have caused the people of the Central American states to regard us with dread and suspicion. It is our true policy to remove this apprehension, and to convince them that we intend to do them good, and not evil. We desire, as the leading power on this continent, to open, and, if need be, to protect every transit route across the isthmus, not only for our own benefit, but that of the world, and thus open a free access to Central America, and through it to our Pacific possessions. This policy was commenced under favorable auspices, when the expedition under the command of General Walker escaped from our territories and proceeded to Punta Arenas. Should another expedition, of a similar character, again evade the vigilance of our officers, and proceed to Nicaragua, this would be fatal, at least for a season, to the peaceful settlement of these countries, and to the policy of American progress. The truth is, that no administration can successfully conduct the foreign affairs of the country in Central America, or any where else, if it is to be interfered with at every step by lawless military expeditions, 'set on foot' in the United States."

In the senate some warm speeches were made on this subject, and several senators of the administration party condemned not only the action of Commodore Paulding, but the views of the president in relation to such expeditions. At the south Walker was received, after his release from arrest, with great favor and sympathy. He there avowed — how truly cannot be said — that his expedition had virtually been sanctioned by the government of the United States; that a member of the cabinet

had advised him where to land, and assured him that American vessels of war would proteet him from the English; that subsequently he was informed that the president had changed his views, and suggested that he should offer his services to the president of Mexico, with a view to bring about a war with Spain and a descent upon Cuba! He refused this because Cuba, if annexed to Mexico, would become a free state. Whether this statement contains any truth or not, the spirit in which the filibuster expeditions have been fitted out is made apparent by it.

In accordance with the suggestion of the president, provision was made, though not without opposition, for an expedition to the South American republic of Paraguay, to settle the difficulties with its government. These difficulties are set forth in the president's message, which we have quoted. Much delay attended the preparation of this expedition, from the want of small steamers, and other vessels of light draught, which could ascend the river to this interior country. After a time, however, several such vessels were purchased and chartered for the expedition, and when they were prepared, they sailed at different times for their destination. A commissioner, Mr. J. B. Bowlin, was appointed to negotiate with President Lopez, of Paraguay, the naval force being held in reserve to support the negotiations if they faltered. Only a part of the squadron ascended the river, and it appeared that they were not required. The difficulty was speedily settled, the government of Paraguay remunerating the family of a sailor who was killed on board of the Water Witch, and also providing for an indemnity to certain American merchants, who had suffered by the acts of Lopez. A treaty of amity and commerce was also negotiated.*

---

* We have anticipated events somewhat in this case, in order to complete the brief narrative. Commissioner Bowlin arrived home in April, 1859, with the treaty.

8

Another recommendation of the president was less favorably received. A bill for the increase of the army by the addition of four regiments, in accordance with the president's suggestion, gave rise to some sharp debate, and met with the strongest opposition from some of the Republican members, in view of the use which the government had made of the troops in Kansas, when they were intended for the Utah expedition. Senator Seward, however, spoke and voted in favor of the administration, while several administration senators opposed the measure, on various grounds. The bill was defeated; but subsequently a bill was passed authorizing the president to receive the services of volunteers to protect the frontier from Indian depredations.

It was early found that it would be necessary to provide additional means to meet the expenses of the government, the surplus of the preceding year and the receipts being entirely inadequate. A deficiency bill of ten millions of dollars, to pay, chiefly, the expenses of the army and navy, was passed; and in order to meet the expenses, ordinary and extraordinary, the secretary of the treasury was authorized to negotiate a loan of fifteen millions of dollars. A single half year had wrought a great change in the condition of the treasury. From a large surplus it had been reduced to borrowing. This, however, was on account of an increase of expenses by the Utah affair, and a great diminution of the receipts. Near the close of the session it was found that this would not be sufficient, and an additional loan of twenty millions of dollars was authorized.

A new state, Minnesota, was admitted to the Union at this session of Congress. Opposition was made to the admission of Minnesota on account of some irregularities in framing the constitution, and because the constitution extended the right of suffrage to aliens. Extraneous matters caused some opposition. In the case of Oregon, which was also an applicant for admission, objections were made by some of the Republican members, because the constitution prohibited free negroes and Chinese from coming into the state to reside. The bill for the admission of Oregon passed the senate, but was not acted upon in the house.

In the spring of 1858 another "speck of war" arose between the United States and England. The British government, with a view of more successfully operating for the suppression of the slave trade, had increased its cruisers in the West Indies, and the prize money accruing to officers and men from the capture of a slaver induced them to keep a very sharp lookout. The officers on that station, therefore, stopped and boarded all the vessels which they fell in with approaching or leaving the coast of Cuba. Many American vessels were thus interfered with, some of them in an unwarrantable manner, while pursuing their voyages in a legal traffic. This created a great deal of indignation throughout the country, and it appeared that the nation was disposed to go into a war with Great Britain rather than submit to the indignity and outrage of such visitation and stoppage on the high seas. In Congress some very warlike speeches were made, though it appeared afterwards that some of the stories of outrages, which had caused the excitement, were greatly exaggerated, and some of them were but little better than inventions. The government brought the subject to the immediate attention of the British government, demanding a discontinuance of any such visitation as had been practised. The British government replied that they had not given any new or special instructions to their officers, and that their proceedings were disapproved of. A steamer was also despatched by that government to intercept their cruisers in the Gulf of Mexico, directing them to abstain from any such visitation of American vessels. In the mean time the government of the United States had ordered several additional vessels to the Gulf, and measures had been proposed in Congress which looked to more decisive action to repel the invasion of American rights. Fortunately such measures were unnecessary, and the friendly relations between the two countries were soon restored by the prompt and considerate action of the English government. The general feeling, however, and the unanimity of all parties, when the national honor was assailed, were evidences of a hearty patriotism still existing in the United States, which internal strife seemed in no degree to have quenched.

After the transaction of much business of importance, in addition to that which we have mentioned, Congress adjourned on the 14th of June.*

CHAPTER VII.

Utah. — Action of the Mormons. — Army Movements. — Temporizing Policy of the Mormons. — Course of Governor Cumming. — Judge Eckels. — Court and Grand Jury. — Governor Cumming at Salt Lake City. — Remarkable Exodus of Mormons. — The Governor's Opinion. — Disagreement of the Civil and Military Officers. — Peace Commissioners. — Their Arrival in the Territory. — Negotiations. — Entrance of the Army into the Valley. — Peace.

WE must now recur to the expedition to Utah. In the winter of 1857-8 the territorial legislature met, and Brigham Young, still assuming the office of governor, addressed to them the customary annual message. No allusions were made in that document to the declarations of independence which had previously been reiterated by the Mormons, high and low; but the president was charged with treason in his action towards the Mormons, and the federal officers were reviled as depraved and abandoned men, while the army was called a mob.

Utah was lauded, at the same time, as "the most loyal territory known since the days of the revolution." "Popular sovereignty" was the basis of all the argument, and the president was accused of inconsistency in his application of the doctrine. The legislature passed a series of resolutions, pledging it to sustain "Governor Young" in every act he might perform or dictate for the protection of the people of the territory, and joining with him in denouncing the president for oppression in "forcing profane, drunken, and otherwise corrupt officials upon Utah at the point of the bayonet." And they further resolved "to resist any attempt of the administration to bring the people into a state of vassalage, by appointing, contrary to the constitution, officers whom the people have neither voice nor vote in electing." Acts were passed by this legislature to disorganize the county of Green River, where the army was encamped, and to attach it to Great Salt Lake county; giving the authority to license the manufacture of ardent spirits to the "President of the Church of Jesus Christ of Latter-day Saints," instead of the governor, who had previously had that power; and granting large tracts of the public domain to private persons, contrary to the provisions of the organic law of the territory. A memorial was also adopted and sent to Congress, complaining of grievances, and claiming a recognition of their rights.

In the mean time Colonel Johnston, — who had now been made brigadier general by brevet, — although he was not in want of provisions, was anxious that his supplies should be seasonably forwarded in the spring; and in midwinter he despatched a small party to the east to communicate his anxieties at head quarters. The war department was not idle, and provisions were made to hasten on the supplies, even before the messengers, who had suffered terribly on the journey, arrived. Reenforcements — three thousand strong — were also

* During the session two members of the senate had died, Josiah J. Evans, of South Carolina, on the 2d of May, and James P. Henderson, on the 4th of June.

making preparations to march across the plains as soon as the season should permit. The business of supplying this force, in addition to that already on the borders of Utah, for an expedition to such a distance in a desert country, was one of great magnitude, and involved large expenditures. The trains to be organized for this purpose were estimated to require forty-five hundred wagons, more than fifty thousand oxen, four thousand mules, and five thousand teamsters and other *employés*. At one time it was contemplated to operate against the Mormons from California also; but this project was abandoned, and all the operations were to be conducted from the Missouri side.

While the army was anxiously waiting the return of Captain Marcy from New Mexico, and some intelligence to govern their future course, a Mr. Kane, who had gone to the Mormons from California, on some mission, — whether official, or semi-official, or private, did not distinctly appear, — came into the camp and commenced negotiations with Governor Cumming, keeping aloof, however, from General Johnston. Mr. Kane acted in the capacity of a mediator, being duly authorized by Brigham Young; and it appeared that the Mormon leaders, knowing the folly of resisting the United States forces, desired to secure from Governor Cumming indemnity for past offences, in consideration of recognizing his authority. Mr. Kane apparently made good progress with the governor in a plan for temporizing; but he confided none of his business to the general or to Judge Eckels, neither of whom was probably disposed to any such course.

Early in April, Governor Cumming started, with Mr. Kane, for Salt Lake City — an event for which those who knew what had been going on were not unprepared. On the same day, the District Court commenced its spring term at Fort Bridger, where the army was now encamped. Judge Eckels, in his charge to the grand jury, instructed them, in relation to polygamy, that,

as there was no statute of the territory legalizing that social practice, nor any affixing a punishment for it, either the rule of the old Spanish law or the common law was the basis of jurisprudence in such cases, and both of those laws recognized marriage as the union of one man with one woman, and defined adultery as the cohabitation of either the man or the woman with a third party. And as the territorial laws affixed a punishment to adultery, it was, therefore, the duty of the grand jury to return indictment in such cases. No indictments, however, were found, as there could be no evidence offered there to sustain them. Nor were any further proceedings had under the indictments for treason which had been previously found.

Upon arriving in Salt Lake City, Governor Cumming was waited upon by Brigham Young and other ecclesiastical dignitaries, who tendered to him the territorial seal, and acknowledged his authority as governor of the territory. He remained several weeks in the city, examining the public property and informing himself with regard to the state of affairs in the territory. A large number of persons signified to him their desire to leave the territory; but it was represented, and probably with truth, that they would not be permitted to do so by the Mormon leaders: the governor, therefore, issued a proclamation, promising protection to all such parties. The names of these persons were registered, and, according to Governor Cumming, leading men among the Mormons had promised to assist them; but it is, perhaps, a question, whether the purpose of these leading men was not to destroy, if it were in their power, all who were thus ready to apostatize.

The governor attended, during his stay in the city, a meeting in the "Tabernacle," where three or four thousand persons were present. He was introduced by Brigham Young as governor of Utah, and proceeded to address the assembly, telling them that he had come to vindicate the national sovereignty, and to secure the supremacy of the constitution and laws. The governor stated, in his letter to the state department giving an account of his proceedings, that "the whole manner of the people was calm, betokening no consciousness of having done wrong, but indicating a conviction that they had done their duty to their religion and their country." After Governor Cumming had concluded, several of the Mormons addressed the assembly, dwelling upon the wrongs which they had suffered, and charging the federal government with oppression. The people were greatly excited at the allusions to the presence of the troops, and the governor felt himself called upon to state that it was not his intention to station the army in immediate contact with their settlements, and that the military *posse* would not be resorted to except when other means of arrest had failed. The excitement, however, was not quieted until Brigham Young exerted his power, when all was still.

While the governor was still in the city a remarkable exodus of the faithful took place. They went southward from all the northern settlements, including Salt Lake City, — men, women, and children, carrying their household goods and driving their flocks. Men of property, as well as the poorer sort, left their lands and houses, and joined with their brethren in this strange emigration. The destination of these people was not known to the governor; but they always declared that they were "going south." It was also asserted that the torch would be applied to the vacated dwellings upon the entrance of the troops into the settlement. There is reason to believe that this emigration was by the orders of the ecclesiastical authorities, whose power over their followers is unbounded; and it is a question whether it was intended to be a *bona fide* emigration, or was a piece of deception practised upon both

the federal authorities and the deluded followers of the Mormon hierarchy.

Whatever was the object of this movement, it was a most extraordinary one. Coming from the scattered settlements, the people gathered on the western shore of Lake Utah, in the neighborhood of Provo, fifty miles south of Salt Lake City, to the number of more than thirty thousand. There, in utter poverty, living in tents, wagons, and the meanest of cabins, a large portion of this number suffered the greatest hardships, showing by their endurance of distress how strong a hold their church and its rulers had upon them. This endurance can only be accounted for on the supposition that the Mormon leaders had impressed upon these people, most of whom were very ignorant and credulous, that they were suffering persecution on account of their religion.

The result of Governor Cumming's sojourn in Salt Lake City was, that he was convinced that the Mormons were peaceably disposed, that they had, indeed, been deeply injured, and that they would submit to the federal authority if the troops should not be quartered among them. It is a little mysterious how he should have been brought to such a conviction, in view of the testimony of all the federal officers who had been in the territory, and of what he says he himself saw and heard among the Mormons. Peace and quiet, however, appeared to be in a degree restored by his actions and his concessions; the federal authority was acknowledged; the Mormons laid aside their arms; the roads were free for the mails and passengers. In this aspect of affairs the governor returned to General Johnston's camp. His principal trouble was, that the people of the territory he had been sent out to govern were leaving him but deserted houses and barren fields. To prevent this departure from the territory, the governor was satisfied that the only way would be, to quash the indictments for treason which had been found against the

Mormon leaders, and to .nsure them against contact with the military forces. The governor had no power over the courts, although he might advise such a course in relation to these prosecutions. Over the movements of the troops he assumed to have control, and had given assurances to the Mormons on that assumption. But General Johnston differed from the governor on this point, and the civil and military authorities, who, since Mr. Kane's visit, had not been very cordial in their intercourse, were now decidedly at variance.

In the mean time, according to the repeated suggestion of members of Congress and of the press, the president appointed two peace commissioners, Mr. L. W. Powell, of Kentucky, and Major Ben. M'Culloch, of Texas, with instructions to proceed to Utah, bearing the president's proclamation, offering a free and full pardon to all the people of the territory who should submit themselves to the federal government. A large force was concentrating at Fort Leavenworth to proceed to Utah, and to General Persifer F. Smith was assigned the command of this army and the forces already in Utah. The peace commissioners proceeded in advance of this force, and reached the army under General Johnston about the first of June. The announcement of the president's proclamation there was not received with much favor, for the officers and men naturally felt that they had been sent on this expedition and had endured hardships for no purpose whatever, since the offer of pardon was sent before the president was aware of the state of affairs in the territory. This leniency towards the men who had long rebelled against the government, and who were with good reason suspected of heinous crimes, was naturally contrasted with the unyielding determination to force submission on the people of Kansas. It is still a question whether this leniency was not extended too far when it included the leaders of the Mormons.

The peace commissioners remained a few days in the camp, and then proceeded with Governor Cumming to Salt Lake City. There were some indications that the governor feared that the commissioners would not entirely coincide with his views for the pacification of the territory, and it appeared that he was doubtful of his own success. Besides this, the commissioners urged General Johnston not to delay his march to the city beyond the time when he should be ready to advance. On reaching the city they found it deserted and quiet. The houses were closed and tenantless; the doors and windows were boarded over; some dwellings had been partially demolished, and others had been burned. A small body of the Mormon militia was there, and workmen were engaged in demolishing the roofs of buildings in the enclosure of the Temple; these, with a few persons who were removing their property, were the only inhabitants of the city. In a day or two afterwards, the proclamation having been announced, Young and other Mormon leaders came from Provo, and a conference commenced. The commissioners offered only the presidential pardon, and gave no pledges; but it was said that the governor satisfied the Mormons in their demands, and promised that the army should not be quartered near the city, and that efforts should be made to remove Judge Eckels, whose charge against polygamy was altogether distasteful to the Mormons. After several days and long discussions, affairs were arranged, and the commissioners proceeded to Provo to proclaim the pardon, the leaders having made the required capitulation and submission to the federal authority. They addressed large audiences, exhorting the people to return to their homes, assuring them that the troubles were over, and that they need not fear any molestation of person or property. After a time the people followed this advice, and most of them returned.

While the negotiations were going on the army moved slowly forward into the valley

When they entered the city the streets were deserted, the few inhabitants who had been permitted to come up from Lake Utah being forced into their houses by the Mormon guard, before the army arrived. It had the appearance of a conquered city, and the inhabitants wore the demeanor of a conquered people. After a few days' stay in the city General Johnston proceeded with the army to the place selected by him for his permanent camp. This was in Cedar Valley, on the western side of Lake Utah, and about equidistant from Provo and Salt Lake City; and it was selected without regard to any understanding which might have existed between the Mormons and Governor Cumming. On their march no person or property was molested, and not a field was encroached upon.

Governor Cumming's despatch, announcing the success of his first visit to Salt Lake City, reached Washington a few days before the adjournment of Congress, and on the 10th of June the president communicated the intelligence to the two houses, and announced that there would be no necessity for making appropriations for the volunteers already authorized. Subsequently the reënforcements * which had not marched for Utah were otherwise disposed of, and it was evident that the "Mormon war" was ended. But whether all the troubles in Utah were ended was by no means certain. Subsequent accounts showed a disagreement between Governor Cumming and Judge Eckels as well as General Johnston. How nearly the Mormons had been associated with this misunderstanding was not known, and what complications might arise therefrom time only could reveal.

---

* General Persifer F. Smith, who had been ordered to the command of the Utah army, died at Fort Leavenworth on the 17th of May, 1858, on the way to the scene of his duties. He was sixty years of age, and had entered the regular army in 1846. He served with distinction in the Mexican war, and was promoted to the rank of major-general for those services.

CHAPTER VIII.

AN event which contrasted strongly with the troubles and warlike demonstrations in the interior of the country, was the successful laying of an electric telegraph cable across the Atlantic, which was accomplished by the United States steam frigate Niagara and the British steam frigate Agamemnon, in July, 1858. An attempt was made to lay the cable the preceding year; but after laying down between three and four hundred miles, and at a distance of about two hundred and forty miles from the Irish coast, the cable parted, and the work was abandoned for that year. The proprietors, however, were not discouraged, and with improved machinery for "paying out" the cable, and such additional precautionary measures as experience suggested, a new attempt was made in the month of June, 1858, the two governments again granting the use of the national vessels for the purpose. In the previous attempt it was proposed to lay the cable in one stretch, commencing at the Irish coast. It was now proposed to splice the cable in mid-ocean, and that the two ships should then part, one for the coast of Newfoundland and the other for the coast of Ireland. The cable manufactured was composed of seven copper wires closely connected or twined together, and protected by an exterior of three coats of gutta percha. Outside this, again, were six strands of yarn, and finally an external coating of wire, making the cable eleven sixteenths of an inch in diameter. Its flexibility was so great as to allow of its being tied around the arm without injury, and its strength such, that, if suspended vertically in water, it will bear six miles of its own length before breaking. This cable w: coiled in such a manner as to be easily paid out as required, — one half on board the Niagara and one half on board the Agamemnon. The two frigates, with an attendant steamer for each, sailed from Plymouth Sound, England, on the 10th of June, for the rendezvous in mid-ocean. They met with some very tempestuous weather, and the Agamemnon, which was heavily laden, was in imminent danger of being lost; but on the 26th of June they succeeded in uniting the ends of the cable, and commenced the work. When forty miles had been laid the cable broke, and the vessels returned for another beginning. After two or three breaks, before they had fairly got under way, the cable was again spliced, and the vessels separated for the second time. They were fairly under way, and encouraged by their success thus far, when the cable again parted, the vessels being two hundred and ninety miles apart. According to previous arrangements the vessels then sailed for Queenstown, Ireland. These failures were very discouraging, and confirmed the doubts very generally entertained of the practicability of laying the cable. The proprietors, however, were determined not to abandon the attempt, and as the remaining cable was considered amply sufficient, the vessels were again despatched on their errand. On the 29th of July the splice was successfully made in mid-ocean; and under the most favorable auspices with regard to the weather and the smoothness of the sea, they separated, the Niagara taking her course for Newfoundland, and the Agamemnon proceeding to Ireland. This time no break occurred; and on the 4th of August the Niagara arrived at Trinity Bay, the place selected for the landing of the cable at Newfoundland, and at about the same time the Agamemnon arrived at the Bay of Valentia, the appointed place in Ireland.

In the mean time, although there was a profound interest felt by the people of England and America in the undertaking, there was a general conviction that this attempt would fail, like the others. It was, therefore, a somewhat startling announcement which the telegraph from Newfoundland conveyed to the Atlantic cities, that the cable was successfully laid. The story was scarcely believed; but when it was by repeated despatches confirmed, the event was hailed with the greatest enthusiasm wherever the electric telegraph carried the news. It was celebrated at once by salutes, ringing of bells, illuminations, and in various ways by which the gratification of the public could be expressed; and more formal celebrations were afterwards made of this event, which seemed to bind together the two countries by the closest ties. The achievement of this important work is to be credited, in a great measure, to the energy and indomitable perseverance of Cyrus W. Field, a native of Massachusetts and a citizen of New York, who, as manager of the enterprise and one of the vice-presidents of the company, had devoted his fortune and his whole study and labor to the work.

The ocean cable having been connected with the "shore ends," and the instruments set up in the stations, it was found that the communication was perfect, and that messages could be transmitted, though not as rapidly as over the wires on land. The first words transmitted after the arrangements were complete, were, "Glory to God in the highest; on earth peace; good will towards men." A despatch from the queen of Great Britain to the president of the United States was then transmitted, and the president's reply was returned. These messages were as follows: —

The Queen's Despatch.

"To the President of the United States, Washington.

"The Queen desires to congratulate the President upon the successful completion of this great international work, in which the Queen has taken the deepest interest.

"The Queen is convinced that the President will join with her in fervently hoping that the electric cable, which now connects Great Britain with the United States, will prove an additional link between the nations, whose friendship is founded upon their common interest and reciprocal esteem.

"The Queen has much pleasure in thus communicating with the President, and renewing to him her wishes for the prosperity of the United States."

The President's Reply.

"WASHINGTON CITY, *August* 16, 1858.

"TO HER MAJESTY VICTORIA, THE QUEEN OF GREAT BRITAIN.

"The President cordially reciprocates the congratulations of her majesty the Queen on the success of the great international enterprise accomplished by the science, skill, and indomitable energy of the two countries.

"It is a triumph more glorious, because far more useful to mankind, than was ever won by conqueror on the field of battle.

"May the Atlantic telegraph, under the blessing of Heaven, prove to be a bond of perpetual peace and friendship between the kindred nations, and an instrument destined by divine Providence to diffuse religion, civilization, liberty, and law throughout the world.

"In this view, will not all nations of Christendom spontaneously unite in the declaration that it shall be forever neutral, and that its communications shall be held sacred in passing to their places of destination, even in the midst of hostilities?

"JAMES BUCHANAN."

The fact that the cable had been laid, and messages transmitted, however, did not insure a continuance of the successful use of the ocean telegraph. The public were anticipating great results, and the effects of daily communication between Europe and America were being discussed, when it was announced that the telegraph had ceased to work. It appeared that a very few days after the cable was laid there were signs of defective insulation in some part of the cable, so that the electric currents, although still passing through the cable, were not sufficiently strong to operate the instruments for any practical purposes. The electricians were at fault, and various causes were suggested, and experiments tried. But it was found impossible to restore communication, and further measures were accordingly postponed till another year. The successful laying down of this cable, however, and the transmission of messages through it, have proved the practicability of such a work, and in time it must be accomplished. When it is so accomplished it will be a bond of peace between the nations.[*]

The troubles with the remnant of the Seminole Indians in Florida, who had been at war with the whites, from time to time, for many years, were finally ended in the spring of 1858. The celebrated chief, known by the not very high sounding name of Billy Bowlegs, consented, with his followers, and their women and children, to leave the state and accept lands in the Indian Reservation beyond the Mississippi. One aged chief, more than a hundred years old, and a few followers, are all the Indians now remaining in Florida.

The Indians of New Mexico and Utah had, for some time, made many hostile demonstrations, those of the latter territory having been

[*] The Niagara, which had performed her peaceful work so well, was afterwards commissioned for another service, not in accordance with the purpose for which she was constructed. A slaver having been captured by the United States brig Dolphin, in the Gulf of Mexico, with three hundred and eighteen slaves on board, was brought into the port of Charleston, and, according to law, the slaves were sent back to Africa. The Niagara was ordered to this service, and the unfortunate captives were thus returned as safely and comfortably as they could be. The duty of the officers was a trying and unpleasant one, but it was faithfully and humanely performed.

9

incited thereto, as it was supposed, by the Mormons. The large force which was sent to Utah proved to be of much use in punishing the offending Indians, and securing from them more peaceful conduct towards the trains of the government, and of traders and emigrants. In Oregon, too, the Indians had, for some time, exhibited a warlike disposition, and had committed many outrages and murders upon the settlers. Colonel Stepto, with a small force, while operating against these Indians, was obliged to yield to overwhelming numbers, and suffered a defeat. This success had encouraged the Indians to greater aggressions. A stronger force of the regular army, with the militia of the territory, were sent against them, and they were compelled to retire from their positions near the settlements. Additional forces were sent from California by the general government, and a detachment of the Utah army was ordered to the same service, and the war was carried on so effectively against the savages that they were finally compelled to sue for peace.

It is worthy of mention that, early in the year, (1858,) after some trouble and delay, negotiations were concluded by which Mr. John A. Washington, the proprietor of Mount Vernon, agreed to convey to the "Ladies Mount Vernon Association," incorporated by the state of Virginia, two hundred acres of the estate, in which are included the mansion of Mount Vernon, the landing place, and the tomb of Washington. The price was two hundred thousand dollars, to be paid in instalments. It was long a matter of regret, and was, indeed, a disgrace to the country, that the home and the tomb of Washington was not in the possession of the government, or in some way dedicated to the public, and preserved with proper respect and care. Efforts had been made to have the estate purchased by Congress, but unfortunately without success. A proposition for the state of Virginia to purchase it was also rejected by the legislature of that state. There were fears that it might fall into the hands of parties who would speculate upon its sacred associations and desecrate the place. Even in the hands of one of the family of Washington it was not wholly exempt from such desecration, while it was fast going to waste and ruin, and the proprietor declared that he was not able to maintain it, place of public resort as it was. At this stage it was proposed that the women of the country should purchase it, and make provision for maintaining it as one of the most hallowed spots in the land, to be visited in all coming time by citizen and stranger, and sacred always to the memory of Washington. Accordingly an association of the ladies of Virginia was incorporated, with agents in each of the other states. Negotiations were entered into with the proprietor, which resulted in the purchase, as above stated. Active measures were taken to obtain the required sum, and with such success as to enable them to anticipate some of the payments. Among those who labored to secure the accomplishment of this sacred purpose was Hon. Edward Everett, who in all parts of the country delivered an able and eloquent oration on Washington, attracting large numbers who thus aided in the purchase. Nearly or quite half of the sum required was thus obtained through the devoted labors of Mr. Everett.

Walker, whose illegal and piratical expedition to Nicaragua had been suddenly and very effectually ended by the action of Commodore Paulding, was not disposed to let his efforts stop at that point. When set at liberty in the United States he immediately began his plans for another similar expedition, being determined, if possible, to reinstate himself in Nicaragua, where he had at first been so successful. It was, of course, a work of time to get up such an expedition, and to procure the necessary funds for so doing; but at last, Walker thought that he had prepared the preliminaries, and, in the autumn of 1858, publicly announced that such an expedition was in preparation. The president, therefore, deemed it necessary to issue a proclamation, in which he stated that, "One of the leaders of a former illegal expedition, who has been already twice expelled from Nicaragua, has invited, through the public newspapers, American citizens to emigrate to that republic, and has designated Mobile as the place of rendezvous and departure, and San Juan del Norte as the port to which they are bound. This person, who has renounced his allegiance to the United States, and claims to be president of Nicaragua, has given notice to the collector of the port of Mobile that two or three hundred of these emigrants will be prepared to embark from that port about the middle of November. For these and other good reasons, and for the purpose of saving American citizens who may have been honestly deluded into the belief that they are about to proceed to Nicaragua as peaceful emigrants, — if any such there be, — I, James Buchanan, President of the United States, have thought fit to issue this my proclamation, enjoining upon all officers of the government, civil and military, in their respective spheres, to be vigilant, active, and faithful in suppressing these illegal enterprises." *

The policy of the administration, as time had developed it, especially in relation to the affairs of Kansas, had not strengthened it with the people. In the thirty-fifth Congress there was a strong majority of the administration party in both houses. But the Kansas question had caused a division in the party both in

Congress and out of it, and more especially in Pennsylvania, the president's own state. In Congress Mr. Douglas was the leader of the disaffected members of the party, and the ardent supporters of the administration attacked him with great bitterness. It appeared for a time that he must abandon the Democratic party or be driven out of it. Mr. Douglas, however, was not disposed either to withdraw or to be forced out of the party. He took his position boldly, and maintained it with skill and ability, appealing to the people of his state to support him. There he was opposed by the administration Democrats and by the Republicans. The former, however, dwindled away as the election approached, and fell into the ranks of the supporters of Mr. Douglas. After a most exciting and hard-fought canvass, the friends of Mr. Douglas succeeded in electing a majority of the legislature, and thus secured his reëlection to the senate.

In many of the other states where elections for members of Congress took place, in the autumn of 1858, the administration suffered losses. In Pennsylvania, where the Democrats who opposed the president's Kansas policy had taken a more decided position than elsewhere, under the lead of Mr. Forney, formerly one of the most earnest friends of the president, the opposition elected a large majority of the members of Congress, besides carrying the state government. The defeat of the administration in these elections showed the unpopularity of the policy of the administration among its own friends in the free states. The fall elections indicated an opposition majority in the house of representatives of the next Congress, if not an actual Republican majority; the senate remaining nearly the same as before.

---

* Walker persisted in his scheme, and with a small number of followers proceeded to Nicaragua, where he was taken prisoner and shot. Most of his followers were released.

THE second session of the thirty-fifth Congress commenced on the 6th of December, 1858. The President's message was communicated to the two houses without delay. It contained the usual summary of the domestic condition and the foreign relations of the country. There was no topic of absorbing interest to occupy the attention of the public. The Kansas question had been settled for the time being, and the Utah affair was so far disposed of as to excite but little interest. The president in his message reviewed these matters at some length, and congratulated the country upon their settlement. But, as if to have some question to occupy the attention of the country, he again suggests the acquisition of Cuba, and under certain contingencies the occupation of Mexican territory by an armed force, as a means of securing redress for injuries, and the settlement of claims due to our citizens.

In relation to Cuba, after complaining of the wrongs and injuries suffered at the hands of Spanish officials, and the difficulty of obtaining redress, the president used the following language: —

"The truth is, that Cuba, in its existing colonial condition, is a constant source of injury and annoyance to the American people. It is the only spot in the civilized where the African slave trade is tolerated; and we are bound by treaty with Great Britain to maintain a naval force on the coast of Africa, at much expense both of life and treasure, solely for the purpose of arresting slavers bound to that island. The late serious difficulties between the United States and Great Britain respecting the right of search, now so happily terminated, could never have arisen if Cuba had not afforded a market for slaves. As long as this market shall remain open, there can be no hope for the civilization of benighted Africa. Whilst the demand for slaves continues in Cuba, wars will be waged among the petty and barbarous chiefs in Africa for the purpose of seizing subjects to supply this trade. In such a condition of affairs, it is impossible that the light of civilization and religion can ever penetrate these dark abodes.

"It has been made known to the world by my predecessors that the United States have, on several occasions, endeavored to acquire Cuba from Spain by honorable negotiation. If this were accomplished, the last relic of the African slave trade would instantly disappear. We would not, if we could, acquire Cuba in any other manner. This is due to our national character. All the territory which we have acquired since the origin of the government has been by fair purchase from France, Spain, and Mexico, or by the free and voluntary act of the independent state of Texas in blending her destinies with our own. This course we shall ever pursue, unless circumstances should occur, which we do not now anticipate, rendering a departure from it clearly justifiable, under the imperative and overruling law of self-preservation.

"The Island of Cuba, from its geographical position, commands the mouth of the Mississippi, and the immense and annually increasing trade, foreign and coastwise, from the valley of that noble river, now embracing half the sovereign states of the Union. With that island under the dominion of a distant foreign power, this trade, of vital importance to these states, is exposed to the danger of being destroyed in time of war, and it has hitherto been subjected to perpetual injury and annoyance in time of peace. Our relations with Spain, which ought to be of the most friendly character, must always be placed in jeopardy, whilst the existing colonial government over the island shall remain in its present condition.

"Whilst the possession of the island would be of vast importance to the United States, its value to Spain is, comparatively, unimportant. Such was the relative situation of the parties when the great Napoleon transferred Louisiana to the United States. Jealous, as he ever was, of the national honor and interests of France, no person throughout the world has imputed blame to him for accepting a pecuniary equivalent for this cession.

"The publicity which has been given to our former negotiations upon this subject, and the large appropriation which may be required to effect the purpose, render it expedient, before making another attempt to renew the negotiation, that I should lay the whole subject before Congress. This is especially necessary, as it may become indispensable to success, that I should be intrusted with the means of making an advance to the Spanish government immediately after the signing of the treaty, without awaiting the ratification of it by the senate. I am encouraged to make this suggestion by the example of Mr. Jefferson, previous to the purchase of Louisiana from France, and by that of Mr. Polk, in view of the acquisition of territory from Mexico. I refer the whole subject to Congress, and commend it to their careful consideration."

On affairs in Mexico, after a brief review of the chronic unhappy condition of that country, and of the claims of American citizens against its government, the message proceeds:—

"Our late minister was furnished with ample powers and instructions for the adjustment of all pending questions with the central government of Mexico, and he performed his duty with zeal and ability. The claims of our citizens, some of them arising out of the violation of an express provision of the treaty of Guadalupe Hidalgo, and others from gross injuries to persons as well as property, have remained unredressed, and even unnoticed. Remonstrances against these grievances have been addressed, without effect, to that government. Meantime, in various parts of the republic, instances have been numerous of the murder, imprisonment, and plunder of our citizens by different parties claiming and exercising a local jurisdiction; but the central government, although repeatedly urged thereto, have made no effort either to punish the authors of these outrages or to prevent their recurrence. No American citizen can now visit Mexico on lawful business without imminent danger to his person and property. There is no adequate protection to either; and in this respect our treaty with that republic is almost a dead letter.

"This state of affairs was brought to a crisis in May last by the promulgation of a decree levying a contribution *pro rata* upon all the capital in the republic, between certain specified amounts, whether held by Mexicans or foreigners. Mr. Forsyth, regarding this decree in the light of a 'forced loan,' formally protested against its application to his countrymen, and advised them not to pay the contribution, but to suffer it to be forcibly exacted. Acting upon this advice, an American citizen refused to pay the contribution, and his property was seized by armed men to satisfy the amount. Not content with this, the government proceeded still farther, and issued a decree banishing him from the country. Our minister immediately notified them that, if this decree should be carried into execution, he would feel it to be his duty to adopt 'the most decided measures that belong to the powers and obligations of the representative office.' Notwithstanding this warning, the banishment was enforced, and Mr. Forsyth promptly announced to the government the suspension of the political relations of his legation with them, until the pleasure of his own government should be ascertained.

"This government did not regard the contribution imposed by the decree of the 15th May last to be in strictness a 'forced loan,' and as such prohibited by the 10th article of the treaty of 1826 between Great Britain and Mexico, to the benefits of which American citizens are entitled by treaty; yet the imposition of the contribution upon foreigners was considered an unjust and oppressive measure. Besides, internal factions in other parts of the republic were at the same time levying similar exactions upon the property of our citizens and interrupting their commerce. There had been an entire failure on the part of our minister to secure redress for the wrongs which our citizens had endured, notwithstanding his persevering efforts. And from the temper manifested by the Mexican government he had repeatedly assured us that no favorable change could be expected until the United States should 'give striking evidence of their will and power to protect their citizens,' and that 'severe chastening is the only earthly remedy for our grievances.' From this statement of facts, it would have been worse than idle to direct Mr. Forsyth to retrace his steps and resume diplomatic relations with that government; and it was therefore deemed proper to sanction his withdrawal of the legation from the city of Mexico.

"Abundant cause now undoubtedly exists for a resort to hostilities against the government still holding possession of the capital. Should they succeed in subduing the constitutional forces, all reasonable hope will then have expired of a peaceful settlement of our difficulties.

"On the other hand, should the constitutional party prevail, and their authority be established over the republic, there is reason to hope that they will be animated by a less unfriendly spirit, and may grant that redress to American citizens which justice requires, so far as they may possess the means. But for this expectation I should at once have recommended to Congress to grant the necessary power to the president to take possession of a sufficient portion of the remote and unsettled territory of Mexico, to be held in pledge until our injuries shall be redressed and our just demands be satisfied. We have already exhausted every milder means of obtaining justice. In such a case this remedy of reprisals is recognized by the law of nations, not only as just in itself, but as a means of preventing actual war.

"But there is another view of our relations with Mexico, arising from the unhappy condition of affairs along our south-western frontier, which demands immediate action. In that remote region, where there are but few white inhabitants, large bands of hostile and predatory Indians roam promiscuously over the Mexican states of Chihuahua and Sonora, and our adjoining territories. The local governments of these states are perfectly helpless, and are kept in a state of constant alarm by the Indians. They have not the power, if they possessed the will, even to restrain lawless Mexicans from passing the border and committing depredations on our remote settlers. A state of anarchy and violence prevails throughout that distant frontier. The laws are a dead letter, and life and property wholly insecure. For this reason the settlement of Arizona is arrested, whilst it is of great importance that a chain of inhabitants should extend all along its southern border, sufficient for their own protection, and that of the United States mail passing to and from California. Well-founded apprehensions are now entertained, that the Indians, and wandering Mexicans equally lawless, may break up the important stage and postal communication recently established between our Atlantic and Pacific possessions. This passes very near to the Mexican boundary throughout the whole length of Arizona. I can imagine no possible remedy for these evils, and no mode of restoring law and order on that remote and unsettled frontier, but for the government of the United States to assume a temporary protectorate over the northern portions of Chihuahua and Sonora, and to establish military posts within the same;

and this I earnestly recommend to Congress. This protection may be withdrawn as soon as local governments shall be established in these Mexican States, capable of performing their duties to the United States, restraining the lawless, and preserving peace along the border.

"I do not doubt that this measure will be viewed in a friendly spirit by the governments and people of Chihuahua and Sonora, as it will prove equally effectual for the protection of their citizens on that remote and lawless frontier, as for citizens of the United States."

Troubles in Central America were also spoken of at some length, as requiring attention. Of these the president thus spoke : —

"The political condition of the narrow isthmus of Central America, through which transit routes pass between the Atlantic and Pacific oceans, presents a subject of deep interest to all commercial nations. It is over these transits that a large proportion of the trade and travel between the European and Asiatic continents is destined to pass. To the United States these routes are of incalculable importance as a means of communication between their Atlantic and Pacific possessions. The latter now extend throughout seventeen degrees of latitude on the Pacific coast, embracing the important state of California and the flourishing territories of Oregon and Washington. All commercial nations, therefore, have a deep and direct interest that these communications shall be rendered secure from interruption. If an arm of the sea connecting the two oceans penetrated through Nicaragua and Costa Rica, it could not be pretended that these states would have the right to arrest or retard its navigation, to the injury of other nations. The transit by land over this narrow isthmus occupies nearly the same position. It is a highway in which they themselves have little interest when compared with the vast interests of the rest of the world. Whilst their rights of sovereignty ought to be respected, it is the duty of other nations to require that this important passage shall not be interrupted by the civil wars and revolutionary outbreaks which have so frequently occurred in that region. The stake is too important to be left at the mercy of rival companies claiming to hold conflicting contracts with Nicaragua. The commerce of other nations is not to stand still and await the adjustment of such petty controversies. The government of the United States expect no more than this, and they will not be satisfied with less. They would not, if they could, derive any advantage from the Nicaragua transit not common to the rest of the world. Its neutrality and protection for the common use of all nations is their only object. They have no objection that Nicaragua shall demand and receive a fair compensation from the companies and individuals who may traverse the route; but they insist that it shall never hereafter be closed by an arbitrary decree of that government. If disputes arise between it and those with whom they may have entered into contracts, these must be adjusted by some fair tribunal provided for the purpose, and the route must not be closed pending the controversy. This is our whole policy, and it cannot fail to be acceptable to other nations.

"All these difficulties might be avoided, if, consistently with the good faith of Nicaragua, the use of this transit could be thrown open to general competition; providing at the same time for the payment of a reasonable rate to the Nicaraguan government on passengers and freight.

"In August, 1852, the Accessory Transit Company made its first interoceanic trip over the Nicaragua route, and continued in successful operation, with great advantage to the public, until the 18th February, 1856, when it was closed, and the grant to this company, as well as its charter, was summarily and arbitrarily revoked by the government of President Rivas. Previous to this date, however, in 1854, serious disputes concerning the settlement of their accounts had arisen between the company and the government, threatening the interruption of the route at any moment. These the United States in vain endeavored to compose. It would be useless to narrate the various proceedings which took place between the parties up till the time when the transit was discontinued. Suffice it to say that, since February, 1856, it has remained · closed, greatly to the prejudice of citizens of the United States. Since that time the competition has ceased between the rival routes of Panama and Nicaragua, and in consequence thereof, an unjust and unreasonable amount has been exacted from our citizens for their passage to and from California.

"A treaty was signed on the 16th day of November, 1857, by the secretary of state and minister of Nicaragua, under the stipulations of which the use and protection of the transit route would have been secured not only to the United States, but equally to all other nations. How and on what pretext this treaty has failed to receive the ratification of the Nicaraguan government, will appear by the papers herewith communicated from the state department. The principal objection seems to have been to the provision authorizing the United States to employ force to keep the route open, in case Nicaragua should fail to perform her duty in this respect. From the feebleness of that republic, its frequent changes of government, and its constant internal dissensions, this had become a most important stipulation, and one essentially necessary, not only for the security of the route, but for the safety of American citizens passing and repassing to and from our Pacific possessions. Were such a stipulation embraced in a treaty between the United States and Nicaragua, the knowledge of this fact would of itself most probably prevent hostile parties from committing aggressions on the route, and render our actual interference for its protection unnecessary.

"The executive government of this country,

in its intercourse with foreign nations, is limited to the employment of diplomacy alone. When this fails it can proceed no farther. It cannot legitimately resort to force without the direct authority of Congress, except in resisting and repelling hostile attacks. It would have no authority to enter the territories of Nicaragua, even to prevent the destruction of the transit, and protect the lives and property of our own citizens on their passage. It is true, that on a sudden emergency of this character, the president would direct any armed force in the vicinity to march to their relief; but in doing this he would act upon his own responsibility.

"Under these circumstances, I earnestly recommend to Congress the passage of an act authorizing the president, under such restrictions as they may deem proper, to employ the land and naval forces of the United States in preventing the transit from being obstructed or closed by lawless violence, and in protecting the lives and property of American citizens travelling thereupon, requiring at the same time that these forces shall be withdrawn the moment the danger shall have passed away. Without such a provision our citizens will be constantly exposed to interruption in their progress, and to lawless violence.

"A similar necessity exists for the passage of such an act for the protection of the Panama and Tehuantepec routes.   *   *   *

"The injuries which have been inflicted upon our citizens in Costa Rica and Nicaragua, during the last two or three years, have received the prompt attention of this government. Some of these injuries were of the most aggravated character. The transaction at Virgin Bay, in April, 1856, when a company of unarmed Americans, who were in no way connected with any belligerent conduct or party, were fired upon by the troops of Costa Rica, and numbers of them killed and wounded, was brought to the knowledge of Congress by my predecessor soon after its occurrence, and was also presented to the government of Costa Rica for that immediate investigation and redress which the nature of the case demanded. A similar course was pursued with reference to other outrages in these countries, some of which were hardly less aggravated in their character than the transaction at Virgin Bay. At the time, however, when our present minister to Nicaragua was appointed, in December, 1857, no redress had been obtained for any of these wrongs, and no reply even had been received to the demands which had been made by this government upon that of Costa Rica more than a year before. Our minister was instructed, therefore, to lose no time in expressing to those governments the deep regret with which the president had witnessed this inattention to the just claims of the United States, and in demanding their prompt and satisfactory adjustment. Unless this demand shall be complied with at an early day, it will only remain for this government to adopt such other measures as may be necessary, in order to obtain for itself that justice which it has in vain attempted to secure by peaceful means from the governments of Nicaragua and Costa Rica. While it has shown, and will continue to show, the most sincere regard for the rights and honor of these republics, it cannot permit this regard to be met by an utter neglect, on their part, of what is due to the government and citizens of the United States."

In this review of the relations of the United States with the countries lying immediately south, and the proposed means of settling difficulties, one cannot but feel that while we may have been unfortunate in our neighbors in that particular direction, there were a desire and a policy on the part of some of our people and the government to take advantage of such complaints to extend our territory. The acquisition of Cuba, a part or the whole of Mexico, and eventually of Central America, would certainly secure to the south that preponderance

which the former increase of territory had failed to realize for it.

The financial crisis of 1857 was noticed at some length in the message, and some suggestions were made with a view to guard against panics in the commercial world. The state of the finances of the country was not very flattering, the public debt having increased to nearly fifty-five millions, and the treasury at the close of the fiscal year showing a deficit, notwithstanding the issue of twenty millions of treasury notes.

The other matters discussed in the message were of little interest, except the Pacific Railroad, the construction of which by private capital, or companies incorporated by states, with the aid of government, was advocated as a measure of importance.

The construction of this railroad was early in the session the subject of interesting debates in the senate, most of the leading members taking a part in them. The expediency, and even necessity, of such a road were generally admitted, but there was a diversity of opinion as to the route to be adopted, and by whom it should be constructed. Southern men demanded a southern route; northern men desired a northern or a central route; and there were some who favored two or more lines, which should satisfy the desires of both sections.

Mr. Seward, among others, made an able and elaborate speech, in which he advocated the construction of a railroad from the western borders of Missouri, by the most direct and feasible route, to San Francisco, adopting a line which would be a continuation of the route of our great north-western emigration. He urged the immediate construction of the road, on the grounds of public policy, by the government itself. His own plan would be to discard all employment of companies and grants of public lands, and to build the road as a military, postal, and national highway, with the money and credit of the federal government, giving the lands along the route to actual settlers. The road was wanted for political and military purposes; commerce was a mere adjunct. If such means of communication were not provided, the Atlantic and Pacific states would not always remain united; and the action of Congress would determine whether Washington should remain the capital of the whole United States, or only of the United States of the Atlantic, while the city of Mexico should become the capital of the United States of the Pacific.

Mr. Iverson, of Georgia, desired that the committee should be instructed to report two routes, a northern and a southern one. *He believed the dissolution of the Union to be at hand,* and was unwilling to vote money and lands for a road which was sure to be located outside of the south; but he wished to have a route which should aid that section while in the Union, and belong to it when out.

Mr. Bigler advocated the construction of the road as a military measure, and preferred a central route. Were a war to break out with a great maritime power, without this means of concentrating our forces, California would speedily be cut off from communication with the Atlantic states. Six months of such a war might cost more than such a railroad. With this road, what power would be strong enough to meet us on the Pacific? Without it, what power would be too weak to annoy us there? He could see little difference between the construction of such a work and the erection of forts to defend the commercial cities of the seaboard. Three or four hundred millions of dollars would, if required, be voted for the purchase of Cuba, and why should not a grant of public lands be made for the protection of California, Washington, and Oregon?

Many other members of the senate advocated the construction of such a railroad, but the great diversity of opinion as to the line to be taken, and the policy to be adopted for its construction, and the numerous projects, differing in detail, which were proposed, prevented Congress from arriving at any conclusion upon this important measure, the necessity for which is each year demonstrated. After a long discussion, the only result was the passage of a resolution that the secretary of the interior be authorized to advertise for proposals for building the road upon three lines — the northern, central, and southern. The bill for the construction of the road was thus defeated, and the measure wholly failed.

On the subject of the acquisition of Cuba, Mr. Slidell presented an elaborate report, setting forth the reasons for such acquisition, among which were the increase of our national security, the practical abolition of the slave trade, and the consequent relief from maintaining a squadron on the coast of Africa, the suppression of the cooly trade, so far as the West Indies were concerned, and the commercial advantages to be derived from the possession of the island. The mode of acquisition proposed was by purchase, and the sum estimated as sufficient for the purpose was one hundred and twenty millions of dollars. Accompanying the report was a bill, which, after setting forth in a preamble the reasons therefor, provided " that thirty millions of dollars be placed in the president's hands for expenditure, either from cash in the treasury, or to be borrowed on five per cent. bonds of one thousand dollars each, redeemable in from twelve to twenty years." This bill, with the various amendments and substitutes which were proposed, occupied the attention of the senate for some time; but it being evident that the measure could not become a law at that session of Congress, a test vote was had on laying the bill on the table, when it appeared that thirty senators sustained the measure, and seventeen opposed it. Mr. Broderick,* of Cali-

---

* During the recess of Congress, and after the election in California, Mr. Broderick was killed in a duel with Judge Terry, of that state. Mr. Broderick's political course had created many enemies in his own party, and it was quite generally asserted

fornia, was the only Democratic senator who voted with the Republicans to lay the bill on the table. The session was so near its close that the bill could not be acted upon in the house, and it was withdrawn.

The 4th of March came before Congress had passed upon the various subjects before them, and with the exception of the principal appropriation bills, and the admission of Oregon as a state, little had been done. The latter measure had passed the senate at the previous session, and, after considerable opposition in the house, was agreed to in that branch. On the last day of the session the president sent a message to Congress appealing to them to preserve the public credit by making some provision for the deficit in the treasury, for which nothing had yet been done. To provide for this exigency at the last moment, a provision was attached to one of the appropriation bills for the issue of treasury notes to the amount of twenty millions of dollars. The credit of the government was thus saved by increasing the public debt.

Among the measures which failed was the appropriation for the post office department. This was the result of a disagreement between the two houses, which had not been settled when the session terminated. It threatened to derange and materially to curtail the mail facilities of the country. There was a large deficiency, which should have been provided for, and was constantly increasing; and this, it was feared, might bring the department to a stand in some of its arrangements. A special session of Congress was contemplated, but this was finally avoided. The postmaster-general, Aaron Vail Brown, died on the 8th of March, and he

that there was a concerted plan to force him into one or more duels for the purpose of killing him. The canvass in California was very bitter, and this duel was the consequence of language used in it. It was also said that Mr. Broderick, when he left Washington, was impressed with the idea that he should never be permitted by his enemies to return.

was succeeded by Joseph Holt, of Kentucky, previously commissioner of patents. Mr. Holt was a man of ability, energy, and great administrative talent, and he determined to carry on the department without the necessary provision as far as he was able.

Of the other measures of importance which failed, were a bill granting pensions to those engaged in the war of 1812, and a bill granting homesteads to actual settlers on the public domain, which, having passed the house, were lost in the senate. A bill giving large quantities of the public lands to the several states and territories for the purpose of establishing agricultural colleges, was vetoed by the president.

It is worthy of mention that the extension of the Capitol, which had been in progress for some years, was sufficiently advanced for Congress to occupy the new halls intended for their use. Upon taking leave of the old senate chamber, interesting speeches were made, recalling the scenes of former years, and recollections of the illustrious men who had rendered the place sacred by their eloquence.

CHAPTER X.

State of Political Feeling. — Policy of the Opposition or Republican Party. — Northern Sentiments. — Southern Sentiments. — Reopening of the African Slave Trade. — Protest of the Grand Jury at Savannah against the Law for the Punishment of Parties engaged in the Slave Trade. — Speech of A. H. Stephens. — R. Barnwell Rhett. — Jefferson Davis. — Issues for the Presidential Election. — Mr. Douglas.

AFTER the adjournment of Congress there was little of political importance to occupy the attention of the country. Great issues were in abeyance for a time, there being no practical question or measure, in which they were involved, immediately before the public. Affairs in Europe were assuming such an aspect, too, and threatened so serious and general a war, that our domestic concerns absorbed less of attention. But as it was the year preceding the next presidential canvass, the hopes and expectations of some were naturally turned in that direction, and there were some indications of the issues which would be shaped by the policy of the contending parties, and by the progress of public opinion. A glance at some of these may aid in a better appreciation of succeeding events.

The policy of the opposition, or Republican party, was well defined on the great issue which had brought it into existence. It was simply political organization against the further extension of slavery, and the power and influence of slavery in the federal government, with a general advocacy of the interests of free labor in its various branches of agriculture, manufactures, and commerce. It was not an aggressive policy, for the origin of the party itself was defensive. During this year, as in the preceding autumn, the Republicans succeeded in electing their candidates in many of the northern states, and in the canvass the policy and principles of their party appear to have been distinctly and quite uniformly stated. Governor Goodwin, of New Hampshire, who was elected by this party, in his message to the legislature, used language which is an index of the feeling of the party at that time, and of the repeated declarations of its public men in all the northern states. " New Hampshire," he said, " yields to no state in her adherence to the Federal Union and the constitution, and her people will never tolerate the doctrines of nullification, or the idea of a dissolution of this confederacy; but while she allows to all other states their rights, she will maintain hers. She will never meddle with the domestic institutions of her sister states, but is bound to prevent the extension of slavery over territory now free." Similar opinions were expressed by the governors of other northern states, and were reaffirmed at the conventions of the Republican party.

On the other hand the sentiments and policy of the south were declared with equal freedom, and the issues for the coming national contest were there being more definitely shaped. The further recognition and protection of slavery under the federal government, both in the territories and in relations between the states, were insisted upon as a right; and the reopening of the slave trade, which had been discussed for some years, now found more numerous advocates. One or more ship loads of slaves had been brought from Africa and landed on the southern coast. One vessel was seized and condemned after having landed its load of slaves; but the officers and owners were not brought to punishment under the law, because of the sentiment which prevailed at the south, in opposition to a statute that condemned the slave trade as piracy, if not absolutely in favor of the trade itself. The grand jury at Savannah found bills against the parties charged with the offence, as by their oaths they were bound to do, but they at the same time protested against being compelled to do so.

This protest exhibits the change which southern sentiment had undergone in respect to this subject, and the new demands which were to be made upon Congress to remove the stigma which had been attached to the African slave trade. " We feel humbled," it states, " as men, in the consciousness that we are freemen but in name, and that we are living, during the existence of such laws, under a tyranny as supreme as that of the despotic governments of the old world. Heretofore the people of the south, firm in their consciousness of right and strength, have failed to place the stamp of condemnation upon such laws as reflect upon the institution of slavery, but have permitted, unrebuked, the influence of foreign opinion to prevail in their support. Longer to yield to a sickly sentiment of pretended philanthropy and diseased mental aberration of ' higher law ' fanatics, the tendency of which is to debase us in the estimation of civilized nations, is weak and unwise. Regarding all such laws as tending to encourage such results, and consequently as baneful in their effects, we unhesitatingly advocate the repeal of all laws which directly or indirectly condemn this institution, and those who have inherited or maintain it, and think it the duty of the southern people to require their legislators to unite their efforts for the accomplishment of this object."

About the same time the "Southern Commercial Convention," which from time to time had met to discuss the policy which should promote the commercial interests of the south, assembled at Vicksburg, and after some opposition, but by a very decisive vote, adopted a resolution to the effect that "all laws, state or federal, prohibiting the African slave trade, ought to be abolished."

Alexander H. Stephens, of Georgia, who had been one of the more conservative statesmen of the south, in an address to his constituents, upon retiring from Congress, showed that even men of his class were taking stronger ground in favor of slavery. He declared that the question whether the south should expand and enlarge, by the people of that section going into the territories with their slaves, protected by the constitution, had been settled fully up to the demands of the south. These measures, however, did not go as far as he wished. He would have Congress give protection to slave property in the public domain so long as it remained in a territorial condition. But he had finally yielded to the doctrine of non-intervention because it was not aggressive, and because it secured all that the south had demanded. Mr. Stephens also, while he did not appear to advocate openly the renewal of the African slave trade, argued that the south could not expand by the settlement of the territories unless the number of the African stock is increased. "States cannot be made without people," said he; "rivers and mountains do not make them; and slave states cannot be made without Africans." He believed, however, that slavery was stronger than ever before, and would continue to increase in strength whether in the Union or out of it. He looked forward to the acquisition of Cuba, and considered Mexico and Central America as open to the south.

Mr. Stephens represented the more moderate but rapidly diminishing class of southern statesmen and politicians. The more aggressive and increasing class were represented by R. Barnwell Rhett, of South Carolina, who considered that the doctrines of Calhoun, McDuffie, and Hayne had practically fallen to the earth. He looked to the formation of a southern confederacy as the salvation of southern institutions, and he congratulated his auditors (the people of the seventh congressional district of South Carolina) that they had "elected representatives to a southern Congress, with a view to a southern confederacy." Mr. Rhett lamented that the question was not met at the time of the admission of Missouri. "The contest," he said, "would have ended in one of three ways: The rights of the south would have been conceded; the constitution would have been amended; or the Union would have been dissolved. But the evil genius of concession ruled our councils. On the very eve of victory the leaders of the south surrendered our rights in a compromise. They yielded to Congress the power of excluding us from the territories. The sectional majority of the north grows stronger and more resolute every day. They have the power of controlling the legislation of Congress. They failed in controlling the executive in the last presidential election only by a few votes. They expect to succeed in the next presidential election. Having mastered these two great departments of government, they openly declare their determination to command the third — the judiciary of the United States." The result of this success would be, that high tariffs would be imposed; railroads and other national improvements would be undertaken by the government; land would be given to the landless, by which means northern and immigrant population would take possession of the common territory, and make free states of it; squatter sovereignty would be established; no new slave state would be admitted; and finally slavery would be abolished in the south. He then urged that the south, in order to have a free government, *must control it*, and he advised the south to go into the presidential election prepared to meet the one issue, and to let no question not immediately connected with this divide them. "Our first great duty," he said, "is to place the south *above* or *beyond* the power of the north. First make our property safe under our own control; before we divide as to measures for its increase or extension. After our safety is accomplished, it will be time enough for the south to determine on measures most expedient to promote her agricultural interests or advance her general prosperity. If our rights are victorious in the next presidential election, we may consider it as a kind augury of a more auspicious future. If they are overthrown, let this be the last contest between the north and the south, and the long weary night of our dishonor and humiliation be dispersed at last by the glorious dayspring of a southern confederacy."

Mr. Rhett was among the most extreme and aggressive of the southern politicians; but his sentiments were echoed from the press and the platform, and were rapidly extending from South Carolina, where they were already quite generally entertained, to the other southern states.

Jefferson Davis, of Mississippi, also delivered an elaborate address before the Democratic convention of that state, in which he discussed the whole question of slavery, in more moderate and statesmanlike language than that of Mr. Rhett, but advocated the rights and claims of the south with as much strength and apparently with the same ulterior views. He did not directly advocate the reopening of the African slave trade, but he denounced the law of 1820, which branded "as infamous the source from which the chief part of the laboring population of the south is derived," and urged the repeal of that law and all other national laws upon the subject, leaving it entirely to the respective states. Mr. Davis also argued that slavery should be protected in the territories by the enactment of laws by Congress for that purpose. He advocated the acquisition of Cuba as advantageous to the Union, and as especially necessary in the event of the formation of a southern confederacy; and he concluded by expressing a wish for the dissolution of the Union in case a president is elected on the platform of Mr. Seward's Rochester speech.*

These speeches, and many similar ones, by some of the leading men of the south, together with the articles of some of the most influential newspapers and periodicals, indicated the sentiments which were to prevail there, and the policy upon which it was determined to enter into the presidential contest. The issues which were thus suggested, if not distinctly offered, were direct legislation for the protection of slavery in the territories; the repeal of laws against the African slave trade; the acquisition of Cuba, and, if necessary, of portions of Mexico and Central America; and by some were demanded new guaranties for the safety of slavery even in the free states. If the south failed in securing such demands by the election of a president favorable to them, secession and a southern confederacy were held up as the alternative and remedy.

It is but just to say, however, that at this time the public sentiment of the south was not

* The speech of Mr. Seward, which was used much at the south for the purpose of replying to its arguments as there stated, was not a partisan speech, nor did it indicate or advocate political action beyond the limitations of the constitution. It was rather a philosophical or politico-economical statement of an "irrepressible conflict" or incompatibility between the systems of free labor and slave labor in the same territory, and argued that whenever the conflict arose, one or the other would eventually go to the wall.

altogether in favor of this policy. There were many who were opposed especially to the re-opening of the slave trade. Among those who most strongly declared their opposition were Henry A. Wise, of Virginia, and Samuel Houston, of Texas, the latter of whom was elected governor of his state after his declarations against the reopening of the slave trade, and appeared thus to be indorsed in those views by the people of that state. But it was evident that those who were now shaping the opinions and actions of the people of the Southern States were such as maintained substantially the views expressed above. And that such was understood — not only by Republicans, but by a portion of the Democratic party of the north — to be the policy of the southern leaders, may be seen by the reply of Mr. Douglas to a letter of inquiry whether his friends might use his name as a candidate for the presidency in the National Democratic Convention which was to be held at Charleston. In his reply Mr. Douglas remarks that before the question can be finally determined, it will be necessary to understand distinctly upon what issues the canvass is to be conducted; and after presenting briefly the principles of the Democratic party as before maintained, and upon which he would be a candidate, he says, " If, on the contrary, it shall become the policy of the Democratic party — which I cannot anticipate — to repudiate these their time-honored principles, on which we have achieved so many patriotic triumphs; and if, in lieu of them, the convention shall interpolate into the creed of the party such new issues as the revival of the African slave trade, or a congressional slave code for the territories, or the doctrine that the constitution of the United States either establishes or prohibits slavery in the territories beyond the power of the people legally to control it as other property, — it is due to candor to say that, in such an event, I could not accept the nomination if tendered to me."

CHAPTER XI.

DURING this year (1859) the relations between the United States and England were disturbed by occurrences at the Island of San Juan, one of a group of small islands lying between Vancouver's Island and Washington territory, the sovereignty of which was not definitely settled by the treaty which established the northwestern boundary. The British government claimed that the channel between these islands and the continent is the main channel indicated by the treaty; while the United States government contended that the channel between these islands and Vancouver's Island is both wider and deeper through its whole length, and should therefore be considered the main channel, and rested its claim also on the general rule of international law, that the jurisdiction of an island belongs to the adjacent main land, rather than to a neighboring island. The British had resorted to the island for fishing, and the Hudson Bay Company had an establishment for raising sheep there; but there was no permanent British settlement, while the Americans had a settlement there, and Port Townsend had been made a port of entry. A difficulty having arisen between an *employé* of the Hudson Bay Company and an American settler, the factor of that company went to the island in a British sloop of war, and threatened to arrest the American and take him to Victoria for trial. This raised the question of jurisdiction, and at the request of the American settlers the island was immediately occupied by a small force of United States soldiers by order of General

Harney. The question was then referred to the home governments. As the affair threatened to assume a somewhat serious aspect, General Scott, who had, by his former services on occasions of border troubles, received the name of the "great pacificator," was sent there to take charge of the interests of the United States. It appeared that the reason for the military occupancy of the island had not been well founded; but as the question of jurisdiction had been raised, the troops remained until that question could be settled, and it was agreed that until such settlement the British should occupy another part of the island in a similar manner. General Scott, having brought matters to an amicable understanding, returned.

This affair, however, did not take hold of the public attention very seriously, and the country was looking forward to the next year as a more eventful one, while the issues of the presidential contest were being framed, as indicated in the last chapter. But towards the close of the year, an event occurred in Virginia which created an excitement throughout the country, and served to increase the bitterness of the south, and to confirm the political leaders of that section in the policy which they advocated, and the remedy which they contemplated. This was a singular and insane, though at first successful, attempt to seize Harper's Ferry armory and village, made by a small party of men, only twenty-two in all, under the lead of John Brown, a native of New York, and of the Kansas free state settlers. Brown was a stern opponent of the pro-slavery party in Kansas, and, during the troubles there, lost two of his sons. He thus imbibed a bitter hatred against slavery in all its phases. After quiet was restored to Kansas, he organized a wild scheme for running off slaves from their masters, in which he sought to enlist all the prominent abolitionists and some of the leading Republicans; but he was regarded as a monomaniac, and received little encouragement from them. He, however, succeeded in organizing in Canada a project for carrying into effect his wishes, and notwithstanding it was a very quixotic project, he enlisted a small number of men, white and black, to aid him. With two of his sons he rented a small farm in Maryland, near Harper's Ferry. Here he collected a quantity of arms and ammunition, and when he was prepared he was joined by seventeen white men and five negroes, and on the night of October 16th he made a descent upon the town of Harper's Ferry, a village of five thousand inhabitants, and containing the United States armory, in which there were upwards of one hundred thousand stand of arms. The party took possession of the unguarded buildings, and then quietly arrested and confined a number of the leading citizens of the place and vicinity. In the morning the persons connected with the armory, not having heard of the events of the night, went to their business in the several buildings, and were also taken prisoners.

The alarm soon spread, and the most exaggerated reports of the numbers and acts of the insurgents were sent through the neighborhood and to distant parts of the country. Some desultory firing occurred early in the morning, and several lives were lost. After a time military companies arrived from some of the larger towns in the vicinity, and the insurgents were gradually driven within the armory grounds, two of their number having been captured. Occasional shots were fired, one of which, discharged by one of Brown's sons, killed the mayor of the town. Brown and his associates, with some of their most important prisoners, retired to an engine house, a small brick building, where they kept the military and the attendant crowd at bay for a long time; the danger of killing their friends, who were held as prisoners, deterring the besiegers from an attack with artillery. The doors were finally battered down by the forces outside, and the survivors of the party — Brown, who was severely wounded, one other white man, and two negroes — were captured. Thirteen of Brown's party had been killed, including one who had previously been taken, and was dragged out of his place of confinement and shot; one was mortally wounded, and two had gone off with fugitive slaves, but were subsequently captured in Pennsylvania, and returned to Virginia.

The grand jury of the county being in session at the time, bills of indictment were found against the prisoners forthwith, for inciting slaves to insurrection, for treason, and murder. The trials followed immediately after, and, the prisoners demanding to be tried separately, Brown was selected for the first trial. He was badly wounded and unable to sit up, and he therefore requested delay; but it was refused, and he went through the trial lying upon a mattress in court. A verdict of guilty on all the counts was rendered; and Brown, being asked if he had any thing to say, responded in a characteristic speech, in which he justified his action, and declared his only purpose was to aid in freeing slaves, not to incite them to insurrection or murder. He was then sentenced to be executed on the 2d of December. Four of his associates were subsequently tried, found guilty, and sentenced to be hanged on the 16th of December. One was reserved for trial by the United States court, it being supposed that Brown had had confederates or accomplices in the free states, and the witnesses residing in those states, by whom it was expected to implicate other parties, could only be compelled to attend by United States authority. This intention was subsequently abandoned, and this man was also tried by the state court, found guilty, and condemned like the others.

Great excitement prevailed in Virginia, and the most unusual precautions were taken, at the time of Brown's execution, to prevent any attempt at rescue. Such precautions were entirely unnecessary, for there was not the slightest indication of any such attempt. Brown's insane raid was condemned by all men at the north, except by a very few radical abolitionists, possibly, and there was no good reason to expect that any organized attempt at a rescue would be made. But the fears of the Virginia authorities were excited, and the approach of all strangers to Charlestown, the place of execution, was prevented; and there, under the guard of a considerable body of military, the sentence was carried into effect. Previous to his execution Brown's conduct was dignified and firm, showing a conviction of having acted aright, and with fidelity to his principles. The other parties were executed at the time appointed, under similar circumstances.

These events occurred so shortly before the assembling of Congress, that that body shared in some degree the excitement which was felt by the people of the slave states. It was early made the subject of debate in the senate, and, so far as could be previous to organization, — which was long delayed, — in the house. It was also made the subject of investigation, with a view of discovering the extent of the plot, many of the southern members apparently being impressed with the belief, or desiring to make it appear, that John Brown was aided and abetted, or at least encouraged, in his scheme by prominent men of anti-slavery sentiments at the north. The committee being authorized to send for persons and papers, many parties, who were supposed to sympathize with such movements as this in Virginia, were summoned before it, and were examined at length. Among those thus summoned was Mr. Thaddeus Hyatt, of New York, who refused to answer the questions put to him, and was consequently imprisoned for contempt. Mr. F. B. Sanborn, of Concord, Mass., who was supposed to be implicated with John Brown, and had refused to appear before the committee, was arrested at his residence at night, by parties acting as the deputies of the sergeant at arms of the senate. A crowd of citizens prevented the officers from taking him away until a writ of habeas corpus

11

could be procured, and upon this he was discharged by the Supreme Court of Massachusetts, on the ground that the sergeant at arms could not depute his authority for such a purpose to another person. The investigation was protracted to a great length, but it failed to show any complicity with John Brown's scheme on the part of any prominent men, and the Republican members condemned the Harper's Ferry raid as strongly as those of the administration party. But this did not prevent some very acrimonious debates, and charges against the Republicans and their alleged policy, the whole question of slavery being discussed on the one side and on the other. In these debates it is to be observed that the Republicans, while they condemned the system of slavery, and its influence on the general government, expressly and uniformly declared that they did not claim for the federal government any right to interfere with the institutions of the states, but that the party was formed to prevent the extension of slavery into new territories and states. On the other hand it was averred that the question of slavery in the territories was settled by the opinion of the Supreme Court; the institution of slavery was defended and praised as the basis of the truest civilization; the Republicans were still persistently charged with seeking to assail the institution even in the states; and while the dissolution of the Union was deprecated, the formation of a southern confederacy was dwelt upon as the happy result of such a dissolution. The frequent reference to a southern confederacy indicated that the project was quite generally discussed among the southern politicians, and was probably even then strenuously advocated by some, contingent, perhaps, upon the result of the presidential election.

The president, in his message, spoke of the Harper's Ferry affair, taking occasion to urge mutual forbearance between the north and south, but suggesting gloomy forebodings, which he professed he did not entertain, and thus, perhaps, doing little to allay the feelings which he deprecated. "I shall not refer," he said, "in detail, to the recent sad and bloody occurrences at Harper's Ferry. Still, it is proper to observe that these events, however bad and cruel in themselves, derive their chief importance from the apprehension that they are but symptoms of an incurable disease in the public mind, which may break out in still more dangerous outrages, and terminate, at last, in an open war by the north to abolish slavery in the south.

"Whilst, for myself, I entertain no such apprehension, they ought to afford a solemn warning to us all to beware of the approach of danger. Our Union is a stake of such inestimable value as to demand our constant and watchful vigilance for its preservation. In this view let me implore my countrymen, north and south, to cultivate the ancient feelings of mutual forbearance and good will towards each other, and strive to allay the demon-spirit of sectional hatred and strife now alive in the land. This advice proceeds from the heart of an old public functionary whose service commenced in the last generation, among the wise and conservative statesmen of that day, now nearly all passed away, and whose first and dearest earthly wish is to leave his country tranquil, prosperous, united, and powerful.

"We ought to reflect that in this age, and especially in this country, there is an incessant flux and reflux of public opinion. Questions which in their day assumed a most threatening aspect have now nearly gone from the memory of men. They are 'volcanoes burned out, and on the lava, and ashes, and squalid scoria of old eruptions grow the peaceful olive, the cheering vine, and the sustaining corn.' Such, in my opinion, will prove to be the fate of the present sectional excitement, should those who wisely seek to apply the remedy continue always to confine their efforts within the pale of the constitution. If this course be pursued, the existing agitation on the subject of domestic slavery;

like every thing human, will have its day, and give place to other and less threatening controversies. Public opinion in this country is all powerful, and when it reaches a dangerous excess upon any question, the good sense of the people will furnish the corrective, and bring it back within safe limits. Still, to hasten this auspicious result at the present crisis, we ought to remember that every rational creature must be presumed to intend the natural consequences of his own teachings. Those who announce abstract doctrines subversive of the constitution and the Union must not be surprised should their heated partisans advance one step farther, and attempt by violence to carry these doctrines into practical effect. In this view of the subject it ought never to be forgotten that however great may have been the political advantages resulting from the Union to every portion of our common country, these would all prove to be as nothing should the time ever arrive when they cannot be enjoyed without serious danger to the personal safety of the people of fifteen members of the confederacy. If the peace of the domestic fireside throughout these states should ever be invaded, — if the mothers of families within this extensive region should not be able to retire to rest at night without suffering dreadful apprehensions of what may be their own fate and that of their children before the morning, — it would be vain to recount to such a people the political benefits which result to them from the Union. Self-preservation is the first instinct of nature; and therefore any state of society in which the sword is all the time suspended over the heads of the people must at last become intolerable. But I indulge in no such gloomy forebodings. On the contrary, I firmly believe that the events at Harper's Ferry, by causing the people to pause and reflect upon the possible peril to their cherished institutions, will be the means, under Providence, of allaying the existing excitement and preventing further outbreaks of a similar

character. They will resolve that the constitution and the Union shall not be endangered by rash counsels, knowing that should ' the silver cord be loosed or the golden bowl be broken ... at the fountain,' human power could never reunite the scattered and hostile fragments."

CHAPTER XII.

Thirty-sixth Congress. — Delay in organizing the House. — Ballots for Speaker. — "The Impending Crisis." — Debates. — The Candidates. — Withdrawal of Mr. Sherman. — Election of Mr. Pennington. — Character of Opposition to Mr. Sherman. — President's Message. — Political Discussions. — Party Principles and Policy. — Democratic Resolutions. — Speech of Mr. Seward. — Measures before Congress. — Homestead Bill. — Covode Investigating Committee. — Protest of the President. — Discovery of an important Letter. — Further Results. — The Japanese Embassy.

THE thirty-sixth Congress assembled on the 5th of December, 1859; but the parties were so nearly balanced in the house that it was many weeks before that branch was organized. On the first ballot for speaker Mr. Bocock, Democrat, of Virginia, received eighty-six votes; Mr. Sherman, Republican, of Ohio, sixty-six; Mr. Grow, Republican, of Pennsylvania, forty-three; Mr. Boteler, American, of Virginia, fourteen; and the remaining twenty-one votes were divided among ten candidates. As one hundred and sixteen were necessary for a choice, there was no election. Mr. Grow then withdrew his name. Mr. Clark, of Missouri, introduced a resolution to the effect that the sentiments of a book called "The Impending Crisis at the South,"* the circulation of which had been recommended by many persons at the north, were incendiary and hostile to the peace and tranquillity of the country, and that no person

---

* Mr. Helper, the author of this book, was a native of North Carolina, and was long a resident of the south. The work contained statistics concerning slavery, and its economical value, together with the views of the fathers of the republic upon the institution, and other matter which was considered objectionable by the friends of that system of labor.

who recommended or indorsed it was fit to be speaker of the house. This resolution was aimed at Mr. Sherman, who, among many others, had given the book some sort of a recommendation. A long debate arose upon this resolution, and was continued from time to time during the contest for the election of speaker, the question furnishing occasion for numerous speeches upon slavery and general political issues which might be involved in the approaching presidential election. After Mr. Grow had withdrawn his name, the Republican vote was concentrated upon Mr. Sherman, and continued to be thrown for him through many ballots, in which he lacked from two to six votes of the number required for a choice. The American vote, which was composed principally of the southern opposition, with a few members from the northern states, was given at different times to Mr. Gilmer and Mr. Smith, of North Carolina, Mr. Boteler and Mr. Millson, of Virginia, the latter of whom also received at one ballot a large part of the Democratic vote. The Democrats took a number of candidates at different times, and on several ballots supported Mr. Smith, who on one occasion lacked but three votes of an election. At this point Mr. Sherman, who had been uniformly supported by the Republicans, withdrew his name, and urged his friends to vote for a gentleman who could receive a larger number of votes than himself, saying that he should regard it as a national calamity that any supporter of the administration, or any one who had expressed disunion sentiments, should be chosen speaker. The Republicans and two or three others then voted for Mr. Pennington, of New Jersey, and on the succeeding ballot Mr. Pennington was elected.

The election was effected on the 1st of February, 1860, the house having been in session about two months. During this time but forty-four ballots were had, most of the time being consumed in speeches, the greater part of which were made by the administration men of the south, the Republicans generally taking but little part in the debates. During the discussion strong disunion sentiments were avowed by some of the southern members, and a southern confederacy was freely spoken of. It also appeared that an agreement was entered into among some of these members to employ parliamentary tactics to prevent the choice of a speaker during the whole session, rather than to permit the election of Mr. Sherman.

The president, after waiting three weeks, and finding little prospect of the immediate organization of the house, sent his message to Congress on the 27th of December. The views of the president on the Harper's Ferry affair, with which the message commenced, have been given in the preceding chapter. The other subjects which were mentioned most at length, were the African slave trade and Mexican affairs. The message opposed the revival of the slave trade as injurious to both the master and the native-born slave, and as likely to retard the civilization of Africa. Of Mexican affairs the president spoke at some length, and after recounting our unsatisfactory relations with that country and its unhappy condition, he again urged upon Congress to authorize him to employ a military force for the purpose of obtaining redress for grievances and security against future injuries, and also on the ground that without foreign interference that country will be given up to anarchy and ruin. The president also pressed upon the attention of Congress, again, the acquisition of Cuba. The other topics treated of in the message were matters of less interest.

The organization of the house, while it enabled Congress to pass some necessary appropriation bills, as that for the post office department, for which the previous Congress had failed to make provision, did not materially advance the general legislation. The time was occupied too much with debates, or rather with set speeches, upon the issues which were to be settled by the presidential election. It has repeatedly been charged upon Congress that its sessions, especially in the year of the national election, have been devoted almost wholly to president-making. The thirty-sixth Congress was probably as open to this charge as its predecessors, while the issues involved were discussed with more than usual rancor, and disgraceful scenes were not infrequent.

The Democratic party, in caucus, adopted certain resolutions declaring the principles and policy on which they would have the government administered, and they were submitted to the senate by Mr. Davis, of Mississippi. These resolutions declared that in the adoption of the federal constitution the states acted as sovereigns, — otherwise, asserted the state rights doctrine, — the whole of them maintaining the inviolability of slavery in the states where it exists, its recognition by the constitution, and the right of the slaveholder to be protected in his property in the territories. They affirmed that neither Congress nor a territorial legislature possesses the power, directly or indirectly, to impair the right of any citizen to take his slaves into any territory, and to hold them while the territorial condition remains; and that if at any time experience should prove that the judiciary and executive authority do not possess the means to secure protection to constitutional rights in a territory, and if the territorial governments should fail to provide the necessary remedies, it will be the duty of Congress to supply the deficiency. But even this did not satisfy some of the southern members, who thought that Congress ought to legislate without delay for the protection of slavery in the territories.

The Republicans did not formally offer any declaration of their principles, but speeches were made by some of their most prominent men which showed the position occupied by the party. Among these was the speech of Mr. Seward on presenting the memorial of the legislature of Kansas for admission to the Union, in which he discussed at length the merits of free and slave labor. In the slave states, he said, the laborer is regarded not as a person, but as capital; in the free states he was invested with the rights of personality, and generally of citizenship. In the one case capital invested in slaves becomes a great political force; in the other, labor, thus enfranchised and ennobled, becomes the dominating political power. Hence he called the one "labor states," and the other "capital states." He then reviewed the history of the national legislation and compromises between the labor and capital states down to 1850, when the compromise of that year, collated with the ordinance of 1787, the Missouri prohibitory law of 1820, and the articles of Texas annexation, disposed by law of slavery in the territories, and was considered a final and absolute settlement of all disputes concerning it under the federal authority. But hardly had this adjustment been accepted before it was stricken down by the assumption that the compromise abrogated the Missouri prohibition. The Democratic party adopted this view, and the Whig representatives of the capital (or slave) states concurred. The Whig party went down, never to rise again, and the Republican party was formed. Between the principles of this and the Democratic party was now the only choice of the nation. The Democratic party now held the principle that both territorial governments and Congress were incompetent to legislate against slavery in the territories, while they are not only competent, but obliged, when it is necessary, to legislate for its protection there.

Of the Republican party Mr. Seward said that he knew of but one policy which it had adopted or avowed in relation to this subject, namely, the saving of the territories of the United States, if possible, by constitutional and lawful means, from being homes for slavery and polygamy. He defended the Republican party from being sectional, contending that it was no more so than the Democratic party, and much less intolerant and proscriptive. He denied that the Republican party proposed to introduce the equality of the negro and the whites at the south, and said, "We are excluded justly, wisely, and contentedly from all political power and responsibility in the capital states. You are sovereigns on the subject of slavery within your own borders, as we are on the same subject within our borders." Mr. Seward also condemned the attempt of John Brown as an act of sedition and treason.

As Mr. Seward was looked upon at that time as the probable candidate for the presidency on the part of the Republicans, and as his anti-slavery sentiments were quite as extreme as those of a great portion of his party, his views, thus deliberately expressed, and his statement of the policy and principles of the party, were well entitled to be considered as authoritative. What there was in this policy and declaration of political principles to excite the rancor of southern politicians, and to lead to threats of disunion, the reader in future years will be at a loss to understand.

While the discussion of such questions ocen-pied the greater part of the time in both houses of Congress, a few of the important measures before them were from time to time acted upon. A homestead bill, giving lands from the public domain to actual settlers who were heads of families, after some differences between the two houses, was passed by both, but was vetoed by the president. A bill for the admission of Kansas under the Wyandot constitution, framed by a convention held the preceding autumn, and adopted by the people by a large vote, was passed in the house, but was not acted upon in the senate. The Pacific Railroad, the tariff, and other matters of importance also failed to be acted upon; and indeed little of general interest beyond the necessary appropri-ation bills was finally acted on in both houses;

and of these, the post office appropriation for the current year failed, through disagreement between the senate and the house.

One measure of importance and interest was the appointment of a committee, of which Mr. Covode, of Pennsylvania, was the chairman, for the purpose of investigating whether the pres-ident or any officer of the government had sought to influence the passage of any law ap-pertaining to the rights of any state or terri-tory; or had attempted to defeat the execution of any law; or had failed or refused to compel the execution of any law. Against this com-mittee the president earnestly protested in a message to the house, in which he character-ized this action of that body as a violation of the rights of the executive, and subversive of its constitutional independence.

The committee, however, proceeded with the work assigned them, and among other matters of interest which were revealed was the letter of instructions, written in July, 1857, by Mr. Buchanan to Mr. R. J. Walker, then appointed governor of Kansas. In this letter the presi-dent wrote, "The point on which your and our success depends is the submission of the consti-tution to the people; and by the people I mean, and I have no doubt you mean, the actual *bona fide* residents, who have been long enough in the territory to identify themselves with its fate. *   *   *

"On the question of submitting the con-stitution to the *bona fide* resident settlers of Kansas I am willing to stand or fall. It is the principle of the Kansas-Nebraska bill, the prin-ciple of popular sovereignty, and the principle at the foundation of all popular government. The more it is discussed, the stronger it will become. Should the convention of Kansas adopt this principle, all will be settled harmo-niously, and you will return triumphantly from your arduous, important, and responsible mis-sion. The strictures of the Georgia and Missis-sippi conventions will then pass away, to be speedily forgotten. * * * Should you answer the resolution of the latter, I would advise you to make the great principle of the submission of the constitution to the *bona fide* residents of Kansas conspicuously prominent. On this you will be irresistible."

Mr. Walker, as observed in preceding pages, acted up to the principle so strongly urged in this letter; but, as has also been seen, Mr. Buchanan's administration did not support him in his policy, and he consequently left the territory and resigned his office. The policy adopted by the convention which framed the Lecompton constitution was very different from that proposed in Mr. Buchanan's letter; but its advocates maintained that it was in accordance with the wishes of the administration, and the course of the administration in relation to Kansas proved that they had reason for so saying. The existence of this letter, which Mr. Walker had alluded to in some of his correspondence, was positively denied by members of the administration; but after making some objections, Mr. Walker laid it before the committee of investigation. He took occasion to say, however, that while he believed the scheme of the Lecompton constitution was framed by members of the administration, he was convinced that it was done without the approval of the president. Among those who had denied the existence of the letter was Mr. Black, the attorney-general; and Mr. Walker, construing this denial as a charge of falsehood, sent a challenge to Mr. Black, which the latter refused to accept.

The committee of investigation discovered, also, gross frauds and abuses connected with the public printing, and that not only had a great amount beyond the value of the work been paid, but that large sums had been given to the partisan press and to others for political purposes. The report of the committee reflected severely upon the conduct of the administration in relation to the matters above mentioned, and to contracts, and contained a great amount of evidence in support of the charges. When this report was made, the president again protested against the action of the committee, and of the house in appointing it. The house, however, subsequently adopted resolutions condemning the course of the administration in relation to certain contracts for the navy, the distribution of patronage to members of Congress, and the award of contracts according to the party relations of the bidders.

Before entering upon the record of the presidential contest and the succeeding eventful period, it may be proper to mention an event which served for a time to distract public attention from the political discussions of Congress and the excitement of the opening campaign. This was the visit of ambassadors from the emperor of Japan. They were brought in a national vessel to Panama, and, having crossed the isthmus, were transferred to another national vessel, which took them to New York, and thence directly to Washington. The embassy was a happy result of the treaty negotiated with the government of Japan by Mr. Harris, the United States commissioner. It consisted of two principal ambassadors, princes of high rank, and two assistant ambassadors of inferior rank, together with a large retinue of officers, artists, interpreters, and servants. They were received with all due respect and solemnity, and entertained in a liberal manner by the government, great pains being taken to impress them with the wealth, power, and civilization of the country. The ambassadors were observant, and their artists and historian were constantly taking pictures and notes of much that they saw. After being entertained by the government at Washington, the embassy proceeded to Baltimore, Philadelphia, and New York, where they were lavishly entertained in a manner characteristic of the metropolis. The journey of the ambassadors terminated at New York, and they were soon after conveyed to their own country in the United States steamer Niagara. As the first embassy from Japan to the "barbarians" of the west, this visit was a matter of great interest; but in its results it appears to have been of less account than was at first anticipated.

CHAPTER XIII.

Nominations for the Presidency. — Democratic Convention. — "Platforms." — Majority and Minority Reports. — Adoption of Minority Platform. — Secession of Delegates. — Unsuccessful Ballots. — Adjournment. — Convention of Seceding Delegates. — Convention at Baltimore. — More Troubles. — Another Secession. — Nomination of Mr. Douglas. — Convention of Seceders. — Platform. — Nomination of Mr. Breckinridge. — Constitutional Union Convention. — Platform. — Nomination of Messrs. Bell and Everett. — Republican Convention. — Resolutions. — Ballots. — Nomination of Mr. Lincoln. — The Campaign opened. — Its Features. — The Election. — Results.

BEFORE the session of Congress terminated, the political contest which had occupied so much of its time was transferred to the people themselves. Public attention was turned towards the national conventions of the several parties which were to nominate the candidates and organize for the canvass, and the delegates to which, since the commencement of the year, had been chosen from time to time in the several states.

The first convention held was that of the Democratic party, which assembled at Charleston, S. C., on the 23d of April. Every state in the Union was fully represented, and from New York there were two sets of delegates, the one, headed by Dean Richmond, representing that section of the party known in New York as the "softs," and the other, headed by Fernando Wood, representing the section known as the "hards." Of these the "soft" delegation was admitted to the convention after an exciting examination of the claims of the rival parties. Caleb Cushing, of Massachusetts, was chosen president of the convention. At the outset it was resolved that the convention would not ballot for candidates until a declaration of principles or "platform" had been adopted. For a long time there had been warm discussion in the Democratic meetings and in the press upon this subject, the question being whether the "Cincinnati platform," adopted by the Democratic convention of 1856, should remain, without alteration, as the platform of the party in the canvass of 1860. Most of the northern press and politicians were disposed to adhere to that declaration of principles, while at the south new declarations were demanded, looking to a guaranty of their rights and claims as now set forth. It was anticipated, therefore, that the convention would experience some difficulty in settling this point. A committee of thirty-three, one member from each state, was appointed to prepare the platform. After refusing to report the "Cincinnati platform" unaltered, the committee found much difficulty in agreeing upon the additions to be reported, and occupied several days in wrangling over the matter. At last seventeen of the thirty-three, being the delegates from the fifteen slave states, with those from California and Oregon, agreed to the following resolutions: —

"*Resolved*, That the platform adopted at Cincinnati be affirmed, with the following resolutions: —

"That the Democracy of the United States hold these cardinal principles on the subject of slavery in the territories: first, that Congress has no power to abolish slavery in the territories; second, that the territorial legislature has no power to abolish slavery in any territory, nor to prohibit the introduction of slaves therein, nor any power to exclude slavery therefrom, nor any power to destroy or impair the right of property in slaves by any legislation whatever.

"*Resolved*, That the enactments of state legislatures to defeat the faithful execution of the fugitive slave law are hostile in character,

subversive of the constitution, and revolutionary in their effect.

"*Resolved*, That it is the duty of the federal government to protect, when necessary, the rights of person and property on the high seas, in the territories, or wherever else its constitutional authority extends.

"*Resolved*, That the Democracy of the nation recognize it as the imperative duty of this government to protect the naturalized citizen in all his rights, whether at home or in foreign lands, to the same extent as its native-born citizens.

"*Resolved*, That the National Democracy earnestly recommend the acquisition of the Island of Cuba at the earliest practicable period.

"*Whereas*, One of the greatest necessities of the age, in a political, commercial, postal, and military point of view, is a speedy communication between the Pacific and Atlantic coasts, — therefore be it

"*Resolved*, That the National Democratic party do hereby pledge themselves to use every means in their power to secure the passage of some bill for the construction of a Pacific Railroad, from the Mississippi River to the Pacific Ocean, at the earliest practicable moment."

A minority series of resolutions agreed to by delegates from twelve states, was presented, as follows : —

"*Resolved*, That we, the Democracy of the Union, in convention assembled, hereby declare our affirmance of the resolutions unanimously adopted, and declared as a platform of principles by the Democratic Convention at Cincinnati, in the year 1856, believing that Democratic principles are unchangeable in their nature when applied to the same subject matters; and we recommend as our only further resolutions the following : —

"Inasmuch as differences of opinion exist in the Democratic party as to the nature and extent of the powers of a territorial legislature, and as to the powers and duties of Congress, under the

constitution of the United States, over the institution of slavery within the territories, —

"*Resolved*, That the Democratic party will abide by the decisions of the Supreme Court of the United States on the questions of constitutional law.

"*Resolved*, That it is the duty of the United States to afford ample and complete protection to all its citizens, whether at home or abroad, and whether native or foreign.

"*Resolved*, That one of the necessities of the age, in a military, commercial, and postal point of view, is speedy communication between the Atlantic and Pacific states ; and the Democratic party pledge such constitutional government aid as will insure the construction of a railroad to the Pacific coast at the earliest practical' period.

"*Resolved*, That the Democratic party are in favor of the acquisition of the Island of Cuba on such terms as shall be honorable to ourselves and just to Spain.

"*Resolved*, That the enactments of state legislatures to defeat the faithful execution of the fugitive slave law are hostile in character, subversive of the constitution, and revolutionary in their effect."

Another minority "platform" was presented by the delegates from Massachusetts, Illinois, Indiana, and Minnesota. This simply reaffirmed the "Cincinnati platform," without alteration or addition. It was voted down by a large majority. The minority resolutions, after long and fierce debate, were substituted for those of the majority by a vote of one hundred and sixty-five to one hundred and thirty-eight. Of those who voted to substitute the minority resolutions, twelve were from the slave states and one hundred and fifty-three were from the free states ; of those who opposed the substitution, one hundred and eight were from the slave states and thirty were from the free states. Most of the southern delegates then declined to vote upon the adoption of the "platform," and the resolutions were adopted separately by large majorities. At this stage of the proceedings the Alabama delegation withdrew from the convention, and were followed in that course by a majority of the delegations from South Carolina, Georgia, Florida, Mississippi, Louisiana, and Arkansas. There was great excitement consequent upon these proceedings, not only in Charleston, but throughout the country where the telegraph announced them. The convention, however, having adopted a "platform," proceeded on the eighth day of its session to ballot for a candidate for the presidency. At an earlier stage of the proceedings a rule had been adopted that two hundred and two votes, or two thirds of the whole number of delegates, should be requisite for a nomination. Notwithstanding some fifty delegates from the states above named had withdrawn from the convention, this rule still remained in force.

On the first ballot Mr. Douglas, of Illinois, received one hundred and forty-five and a half votes; Mr. Hunter, of Virginia, forty-two; Mr. Guthrie, of Kentucky, thirty-six and a half; Andrew Johnson, of Tennessee, twelve; Mr. Dickinson, of New York, seven; Mr. Lane, of Oregon, six; Jefferson Davis, of Mississippi, one. Fifty-seven ballots were taken with little variation in the result. On the last ballot Mr. Douglas received one hundred and fifty-one and a half votes; Mr. Hunter sixteen; Mr. Guthrie sixty-five and a half; Mr. Dickinson two; Mr. Lane sixteen; Mr. Davis one. It was now evident that no nomination could be made, Mr. Douglas, the highest candidate, not receiving the votes of two thirds even of the remaining delegates, while he lacked fifty votes of the number required by the rule. All propositions for a change of the rule were scouted, and there was no possibility of the majority succeeding in the nomination of their favorite,' or uniting upon a compromise candidate who would be stronger. The convention therefore adjourned

to meet at Baltimore on the 18th of June, after adopting a vote requesting that new delegates should be chosen in the place of those who had seceded.

Meanwhile the seceding delegates met in separate convention, — Mr. Bayard, of Delaware, acting as chairman, — and adopted the resolutions reported by the majority of the committee, on account of the rejection of which they had withdrawn from the regular convention. They then adjourned, without making any nominations, to meet at Richmond on the 11th of June, one week preceding the Baltimore convention, inviting all states which approved their "platform" to send delegates to the adjourned meeting.

When the regular convention assembled in Baltimore serious questions arose concerning the admission of delegates from those states whose original delegates had withdrawn. In some of the states new delegates were chosen, and the original delegates also claimed seats in the convention, thus presenting difficulties which must be settled before any nomination could be made. The committee on credentials made two reports, the majority being in favor of admitting the new delegates where the original delegates did not appear, portions of each delegation where there were contestants, and the original delegates where there were no contestants, with special provisions in certain cases. Several of the southern states were wholly or partially unrepresented. The minority of the committee reported in favor of admitting the original delegates in all cases. The minority report was rejected, and that of the majority was accepted. This result brought on another crisis, many of the delegates from the southern states, the entire delegations from California and Oregon, and a few members from other free states, withdrawing from the convention. Among those who thus withdrew was Mr. Cushing, the president of the convention. The remaining delegates, having reorganized, then proceeded to ballot for a candidate for the presidency. On the first ballot two hundred and twelve and a half votes were cast; of which Mr. Douglas received one hundred and seventy-three and a half; Mr. Guthrie nine; Mr. Breckinridge five; four gentlemen received one each, and there were twenty-one blank votes. On the second ballot Mr. Douglas received one hundred and eighty and a half votes out of one hundred and ninety-four and a half, the whole number cast, and he was then by resolution unanimously nominated. Benjamin Fitzpatrick, of Alabama, was nominated for vice-president; but after the adjournment of the convention, Mr. Fitzpatrick declined the nomination, and the ticket was completed by the nomination of Herschel V. Johnson, of Georgia.

The seceding delegates organized as a convention, Mr. Cushing presiding, and after adopting the majority "platform" which the convention at Charleston had rejected, they nominated John C. Breckinridge, of Kentucky, for president, and Joseph Lane, of Oregon, for vice-president. Meanwhile the convention which met at Richmond had adjourned to await the action at Baltimore, and, after the nominations were made, reassembled and adopted the candidates of the seceding convention.

The "Constitutional Union" party, which was composed of the remnants of the old Whig party and of the more recent American party, held a national convention at Baltimore on the 10th of May. The convention did not put forth any formal declaration of principles, but adopted the following resolution: —

"*Whereas*, Experience has shown that all platforms adopted by political parties have the effect to mislead and to cause political divisions by encouraging geographical and sectional parties, — therefore

"*Resolved*, That both patriotism and duty require that we should recognize no policy or principles but those resting on the broad foundation of the constitution of the United States and the enforcement of the laws; and that as representatives of the Constitutional Union party and of the country, we pledge ourselves to maintain, protect, and defend these principles, thus affording security at home and abroad, and securing the blessings of liberty to ourselves and posterity."

The convention then proceeded to ballot for a candidate for the presidency; and John Bell, of Tennessee, was unanimously nominated on the second ballot. Edward Everett, of Massachusetts, was then nominated by acclamation as candidate for the vice-presidency.

The Republican convention was held at Chicago on the 16th of May, in a spacious building which had been erected expressly for the purpose by the Republicans of that city. Twenty-four states were represented, including all the free states, and Delaware, Maryland, Virginia, Kentucky, Missouri, and Texas. The slave states, however, did not all have full delegations. George Ashmun, of Massachusetts, was chosen president of the convention, which proceeded to business without much delay and with great harmony. The "platform," or declaration of principles, was reported without division in the committee appointed to prepare it, and after a slight amendment was adopted by the convention with great unanimity and enthusiasm. It set forth at length the principles and policy of the party, as follows: —

"*Resolved*, That we, the delegated representatives of the Republican electors of the United States, in convention assembled, in the discharge of the duty we owe to our constituents and our country, unite in the following declarations: —

"1. That the history of the nation during the last four years has fully established the propriety and necessity of the organization and perpetuation of the Republican party, and that the causes which called it into existence are permanent in their nature, and now, more than ever before, demand its peaceful and constitutional triumph.

" 2. That the maintenance of the principles promulgated in the Declaration of Independence, and embodied in the Federal Constitution, ' that all men are created equal ; that they are endowed by their Creator with certain inalienable rights ; that among these are life, liberty, and the pursuit of happiness ; that to secure these rights governments are instituted among men, deriving their just powers from the consent of the governed,' is essential to the preservation of our republican institutions ; and that the federal constitution, the rights of the states, and the union of the states, must and shall be preserved.

" 3. That to the union of the states this nation owes its unprecedented increase in population, its surprising development of material resources, its rapid augmentation of wealth, its happiness at home and its honor abroad ; and we hold in abhorrence all schemes for disunion, come from whatever source they may, and we congratulate the country that no Republican member of Congress has uttered or countenanced the threats of disunion so often made by Democratic members of Congress without rebuke, and with applause from their political associates ; and we denounce those threats of disunion, in case of a popular overthrow of their ascendency, as denying the vital principles of a free government, and as an avowal of contemplated treason, which it is the imperative duty of an indignant people sternly to rebuke and forever silence.

" 4. That the maintenance inviolate of the rights of the states, and especially the right of each state to order and control its own domestic institutions according to its own judgment exclusively, is essential to that balance of powers on which the perfection and endurance of our political fabric depend ; and we denounce the lawless invasion by an armed force of any state or territory, no matter under what pretext, as among the gravest of crimes.

" 5. That the present Democratic administra-tion has far exceeded our worst apprehensions in its measureless subserviency to the exactions of a sectional interest, as especially evident in its desperate exertions to force the infamous Lecompton constitution upon the protesting people of Kansas ; in construing the personal relation between master and servant to involve an unqualified property in persons ; in its attempted enforcement every where, on land and sea, through the intervention of Congress and the federal courts, of the extreme pretensions of a purely local interest, and in its general and unvarying abuse of the power intrusted to it by a confiding people.

" 6. That the people justly view with alarm the reckless extravagance which pervades in every department of the federal government ; — that a return to rigid economy and accountability is indispensable to arrest the systematic plunder of the public treasury by favored partisans, while the recent startling developments of fraud and corruption at the federal metropolis show that an entire change of administration is imperatively demanded.

" 7. That the new dogma that the constitution of its own free force carries slavery into any or all of the territories of the United States, is a dangerous political heresy, at variance with the explicit provisions of that instrument itself, with contemporaneous exposition, and with legislative and judicial precedent — is revolutionary in its tendency, and subversive of the peace and harmony of the country.

" 8. That the normal condition of all the territory of the United States is that of freedom ; that as our republican fathers, when they had abolished slavery in all our national territory, ordained that ' no person should be deprived of life, liberty, or property without due process of law,' it becomes our duty, by legislation, whenever such legislation is necessary, to maintain this provision of the constitution against all attempts to violate it ; and we deny the authority of Congress, of a territorial legislature, or of any individuals, to give legal existence to slavery in any territory of the United States.

" 9. That we brand the recent reopening of the African slave trade, under the cover of our national flag, aided by perversions of judicial power, as a crime against humanity, a burning shame to our country and age, and we call upon Congress to take prompt and efficient measures for the total and final suppression of that execrable traffic.

" 10. That in the recent vetoes by their federal governors of the acts of the legislatures of Kansas and Nebraska, prohibiting slavery in those territories, we find a practical illustration of the boasted Democratic principle of non-intervention and popular sovereignty embodied in the Kansas-Nebraska bill, and a denunciation of the deception and fraud involved therein.

" 11. That Kansas should of right be immediately admitted as a state under the constitution recently formed and adopted by her people, and accepted by the house of representatives.

" 12. That, while providing revenue for the support of the general government, by duties upon imports, sound policy requires such an adjustment of these imposts as to encourage the development of the industrial interests of the whole country, and we commend that policy of national exchanges which secures to the working men liberal wages, to agriculture remunerating prices, to mechanics and manufacturers an adequate reward for their skill, labor, and enterprise, and to the nation commercial prosperity and independence.

" 13. That we protest against any sale or alienation to others of the public lands held by actual settlers, and against any view of the free homestead policy which regards the settlers as paupers or suppliants for public bounty, and we demand the passage by Congress of the complete and satisfactory homestead measure which has already passed the house.

" 14. That the Republican party is opposed to any change in our naturalization laws, or any state legislation by which the rights of citizenship, hitherto accorded to immigrants from foreign lands, shall be abridged or impaired; and in favor of giving a full and efficient protection to the rights of all classes of citizens, whether native or naturalized, both at home and abroad.

" 15. That appropriations by Congress for river and harbor improvements of a national character, required for the accommodation and security of an existing commerce, are authorized by the constitution, and justified by the obligation of government to protect the lives and property of its citizens.

" 16. That a railroad to the Pacific Ocean is imperatively demanded by the interests of the whole country; that the federal government ought to render immediate and efficient aid in its construction, and that, as a preliminary thereto, a daily overland mail should be promptly established.

" 17. Finally, having thus set forth our distinctive principles and views, we invite the coöperation of all citizens, however differing on other questions, who substantially agree with us in their affirmance and support."

On the third day the convention proceeded to ballot for a candidate for the presidency. Mr. Seward had been the most prominent candidate previous to the convention, and was supported by ardent and firm friends. But he was also as strenuously opposed by many, chiefly on the grounds of expediency; and there were other gentlemen whose friends pressed their claims to the nomination. On the first ballot the vote stood: for Mr. Seward, of New York, one hundred and seventy-three and a half; for Mr. Lincoln, of Illinois, one hundred and two; for Mr. Cameron, of Pennsylvania, fifty and a half; for Mr. Chase, of Ohio, forty-nine; for Mr. Bates, of Missouri, forty-eight; for Mr. Dayton, of New Jersey, fourteen; for Mr. McLean, of Ohio, twelve; for Mr. Collamer, of Vermont, ten; and six other votes were given for four different gentlemen. On the second ballot several of the candidates were dropped; Mr. Seward's vote was one hundred and eighty-four and a half, and Mr. Lincoln's one hundred and eighty-one. The third ballot, when the delegates had all voted, stood: for Mr. Seward, one hundred and eighty and a half; for Mr. Lincoln, two hundred and thirty-one and a half, the number required for a choice being two hundred and thirty-three. Before the vote was declared, however, the delegates from several states changed their votes, giving to Mr. Lincoln three hundred and fifty-four. Abraham Lincoln, of Illinois, was therefore declared the nominee, and the nomination was then unanimously confirmed. Hannibal Hamlin, of Maine, was subsequently nominated with equal unanimity as candidate for the vice-presidency.

The several nominations being thus made, the campaign was opened, and was carried on with much spirit and some rancor from an early day. The Republican party, though some portions of it were disappointed in the result of the convention, heartily accepted the nomination of Mr. Lincoln, and the canvass was conducted by them, especially at the west, with an earnestness which augured success. The division of the Democratic party rendered it probable that the Republicans would carry the election in all the northern states unless the two factions were united; and attempts were made to bring about a union, but each faction claimed to be the true Democratic party, and was almost as bitterly opposed to the other as both were to the Republicans. In two or three states, however, a partial arrangement was made, by which an electoral ticket composed of members from each party opposed to the Republicans was nominated. But such tickets failed to receive the cordial support of either party.

At the south the campaign was carried on with exceeding bitterness. The success of the Republican party was regarded as an outrage upon their rights; and notwithstanding the declarations of that party justified no such interpretation, it was asserted constantly that it was the purpose of the party to interfere with the institutions of the southern states, and to overthrow slavery. The course pursued by the opponents of the Republicans in the free states was calculated to encourage these feelings. The consequence was, that during the canvass the southern leaders not only declared that they would not submit to the administration of the federal government by a Republican president, but made preparations for resistance and secession. At the north such threats of disunion were generally regarded as a repetition of the empty menaces by which the southern politicians had long sought to accomplish their purposes. But the temper of the south had been growing more violent, and the canvass afforded opportunities for the disunionists to spread their pernicious doctrines. A southern convention was proposed, and other measures were taken to unite the state governments in the policy to be pursued.

As beyond the border slave states there was no Republican organization, the Douglas Democrats met with bitter local opposition, and were professedly regarded with hardly less dislike than the Republicans themselves. The result of the election was of so much doubt that each party expressed confidence of success. The Republicans claimed that they should secure the electoral vote of all the free states, with the possible exception of California and Oregon, and would thus succeed in electing Mr. Lincoln. The friends of Mr. Douglas claimed that he would carry most of the western and southern states, and secure a majority of the electoral votes. The Breckinridge Democrats claimed all the southern states and enough from the middle and western states to carry the election. The Constitutional Union party expected to carry a few states both at the north and at the south, but believed that there would be no election by the electoral colleges, and that the choice of a president would devolve on the house of representatives, in which case they claimed that their candidate would eventually be chosen.

The state elections in Pennsylvania, Indiana, and Ohio, which took place in October, indicated the result of the national election in those states, the first two of which had been considered doubtful; and it seemed almost certain that the Republicans would elect their candidate, unless their opponents, by a hearty union in some of the free states, should succeed in carrying them. A perfect union, however, was impossible, and the result showed that it would have been of no avail. The election was conducted with spirit, and Mr. Lincoln proved more popular than even his friends had hoped.

By means of the electric telegraph the result was early known throughout the country. The doubtful states had gone for Mr. Lincoln by large majorities, even where there had been a "fusion" of all the opposition parties against him; and it was soon ascertained that he was certainly elected, having carried all the free states east of the Rocky Mountains except New Jersey, where four of the electoral votes were for Mr. Lincoln and three for Douglas. When the returns were received from California and Oregon, it appeared that those states had also voted for the Republican candidate, and thus every one of the free states — except New Jersey in part — had given its vote for Abraham Lincoln. Mr. Douglas had received a large vote in most of the free states, — but had carried three electoral votes only, in New Jersey, — and a small vote in the slave states, except Missouri, which alone gave him a majority.* Kentucky, Tennessee, and Virginia (the latter by the non-attendance of six Breckinridge elec-

* The entire vote for Mr. Douglas in the slave states, excluding Missouri, was only about one hundred thousand; less than half of the vote actually given for him in New York — not two thirds of the vote given him either in Illinois or Ohio.

tors at the meeting of the electoral college) gave their electoral vote for Mr. Bell. All the other slave states, with Virginia in part, gave their vote for Mr. Breckinridge, except South Carolina, where the electors are chosen by the legislature, but whose voters were generally in favor of Mr. Breckinridge.

CHAPTER XIV.

Effect of the Presidential Election at the South. — Excitement. — Violent Measures advocated. — South Carolina Legislature.— Message of the Governor. — Secession proposed. — Military Organization. — Convention for Secession called. — Action in other States. — Alabama. — Georgia. — Secession Convention of South Carolina. — Election of Delegates. — Sentiment of People. — Mr. Rhett. — Secession Ordinance. — Its Effect. — Demonstrations of Approval.—Announcement in Congress. — Offers of Military Aid to South Carolina.— Fort Moultrie. — Major Anderson. — Withdrawal to Fort Sumter. — Effect of the Movement. — Return demanded. — Occupation of Fort Moultrie and Castle Pinckney by State Troops. — Seizure of Arsenal. — New Fortifications. — Conduct towards Major Anderson. — Seizure of Forts and Arsenals in other States. — Feeling at the North. — Cannon at Pittsburg for Southern Forts. — Shipment stopped. — Compromise. — Close of the Year.

THE result of the presidential election was hardly ascertained, when the oft-repeated threats of southern politicians assumed a new earnestness, and there were immediate indications that they were about to be carried into effect. The greatest excitement prevailed throughout the south. A portion of the press teemed with articles calling upon the slave states to secede, and the people to resist the authority of a Republican administration. Speeches more violent and bitter than ever were made to excited assemblies, calling for immediate measures to defend the rights of the south and to dissolve the Union. The state authorities, especially in the more southern states, taking counsel from the strongest disunionists, made preparations for military defence, and initiated at once measures for secession, or for combining the slave states in resistance to federal authority.

The legislature of South Carolina, which had

been convened for the purpose of choosing presidential electors, was still in session when the election returns made it certain that Mr. Lincoln must be chosen president. The governor sent them a message recommending that they remain in permanent session and take action to prepare the state for the crisis. He considered secession the only remedy for the threatening evils, and believed that such a step on the part of South Carolina would be followed by the entire south. He recommended military reorganization, that every able-bodied citizen be furnished with the most approved fire-arms, and that ten thousand volunteers be prepared at once for service. The legislature adopted resolutions indorsing the action and views of the governor, and proceeded to carry his advice into effect by legislation. The militia was reorganized, purchases of arms were provided for, and other military preparations " for defence " were made, and a state loan authorized to meet the great expenses. The legislature also passed an act for a convention to dissolve the connection of the state with the Union. They had virtually seceded, or put the state in rebellion, without the aid of a convention ; but it was considered that such a body could with due solemnity and better effect absolve the state from relations which were assumed by similar action. In the mean time, the federal officers, excepting the officers of the customs and postmasters, resigned, and there was no means of enforcing the federal laws in the ordinary way. The governor was in communication with other states who were also expected to secede ; but it was the purpose of the leaders, and evidently the desire of the people of South Carolina, to take separate action, and to leave the formation of a new confederacy for future consideration. The people of that state were, in fact, completely imbued with the spirit of secession. Those who opposed it were so few in number and of so little influence that they were of no account ; and the only form in which opposition dared to show itself was to favor delay and coöperation with all the slaveholding states, rather than immediate and separate action.

Meanwhile the spirit of secession and revolution spread rapidly through the Gulf states, and the leaders of the movement were pressing the state governments to follow the course of South Carolina. In Alabama, the legislature, before the election, had instructed the governor of that state to call a convention immediately upon the election of a Republican president ; and the instruction was obeyed with alacrity. In Georgia, the governor sent a special message to the legislature, opposing immediate secession, and advising that delegates should not be sent to the southern convention, which was then earnestly proposed. He, nevertheless, urged retaliatory measures against the citizens and interests of those states by whose action the citizens of Georgia may have suffered. The legislature, however, were better disposed towards disunion than the governor, and took measures to increase the military resources of the state and to prepare the way for secession. Other states, by their governors, took initiatory steps ; the legislatures were convened, preparations for " arming the states " were quite generally made, commissioners were sent to each of the other slave states to secure a union of action, and conventions were called ; but all seemed to await the action of South Carolina as the leader of the movement.

The election of delegates to the convention in South Carolina took place on the 6th of December, and the result was the choice of a large majority in favor of immediate secession, most of the opponents of that action being " coöperationists " rather than friends of the Union. The feeling which actuated some of the most violent secessionists — and a sentiment of no recent origin — may be measured by the language of Mr. Rhett on the occasion of his election to the convention. In the course of a speech to his constituents he said, —

"Nineteen years have I served as a representative of the people of South Carolina, in her long contest for her rights and liberties. I began in 1828. For thirty-two years have I followed the quarry. Behold it, at last, in sight! A few more bounds, and it falls — the Union falls; and with it falls its faithless oppressions — its insulting agitations — its vulgar .tyrannies and fanaticism. The bugle blast of our victory and redemption is on the wind; and the south will be safe and free."

This was a flourish of rhetoric, indeed, and it is but just to say that a large party, even in South Carolina, were as yet not quite so thorough or so old disunionists; but the popular demonstrations there, under the lead of men like Mr. Rhett, exhibited enthusiastic approval of such sentiments. And it may here be again remarked that the movement for secession and the establishment of a southern confederacy was, to most of its leaders as to Mr. Rhett, an old and settled purpose, for which the recent election was rather the pretext than the cause. In a letter upon the crisis, Mr. Bell, of Tennessee, one of the presidential candidates, wrote upon this point as follows : —

"What gives me the greatest concern at present is the painful conviction that the movement in favor of secession, in Mississippi and other states of the south, is led, for the most part, by men of distinguished ability and influence, with whom the expediency of secession is a foregone conclusion and a settled conviction; men who can be reached by no argument or remonstrance; men who do not want to be convinced of the insufficiency of existing grievances to justify a disruption of the Union; men whose imaginations have been taken possession of, and their judgments led captive, by the dazzling, but, as I think, delusive vision of a new, great, and glorious republican empire, stretching far into the south. The scheme of disunion, as I have reason to believe, has been long cherished by some of these leaders, and

they have only waited a pretext more plausible than any heretofore presented to attempt the accomplishment of it."

The convention assembled on the 17th of December, at Columbia, the capital, but immediately adjourned to Charleston, on account of the prevalence of the small-pox at the former place. A committee was appointed to prepare an ordinance for secession, which was soon reported in the following form : —

"We, the people of the state of South Carolina, in convention assembled, do declare and ordain, and it is hereby declared and ordained, that the ordinance adopted by us in convention on the 23d day of May, in the year of our Lord 1788, whereby the constitution of the United States of America was ratified, and also all acts or parts of acts of the general assembly of this state ratifying the amendments to said constitution, are hereby repealed, and that the union now subsisting between South Carolina and other states under the name of the United States of America is hereby dissolved."

After a brief debate the ordinance was passed, December 20th, by a unanimous vote, and its adoption was followed by the wildest demonstrations of joy, both within the convention and among the people outside, who were awaiting this formal ratification of what was a foregone conclusion. The next day a declaration of the causes justifying secession was adopted and published to the world. The announcement of the passage of the secession ordinance caused general enthusiasm in all the more southern slave states, and was received with unrestrained satisfaction by large numbers in the border slave states. It was announced in the house of representatives at Washington, by Mr. Garnet, of Virginia, in a speech which he was making, as follows : "Why, sir, while your bill is under debate, one of the sovereign states of this confederacy has, by the glorious act of her people, withdrawn, in vindication of her rights, from the Union." And even there

13

the announcement was greeted with applause. In many of the principal towns at the south the event was celebrated with great demonstrations of joy, and every where the excitement occasioned by it was used to press forward the secession cause in the other states.

Offers of aid by military companies in other states had been made to the governor of South Carolina from the commencement of the secession movement. After the secession ordinance had been adopted, these tenders were multiplied, and a new impetus was given to the organization of such companies. Some correspondence and communications between the representatives of South Carolina and the national administration had already taken place in relation to the forts in the harbor of Charleston. A small garrison occupied Fort Moultrie, and repairs were being made on Fort Sumter. The occupation of these forts by the federal government seemed to annoy the secessionists of Charleston. They desired to obtain possession of them, if possible, before any reënforcements could be sent there. They remembered that in the days of "nullification" the strong federal force in the forts had compelled the submission of the nullifiers, and they were somewhat tender upon the subject of the occupation of the forts by a force which might threaten a similar compulsion. They perhaps felt, too, that upon this question would first ˏcome the conflict between the federal government and the state in its assumed independence. From President Buchanan, through Secretary Floyd, they received some assurance that the forts should not be reënforced; at the same time he had declared that he must see that the federal laws were observed and the federal property protected. The position of the federal administration on this point was quite unsatisfactory to the South Carolina leaders, and after the declaration of secession further negotiations or correspondence took place, with a view to secure the release or abandonment of the forts

to the state government without bringing on any conflict. While these negotiations were occasionally going on, there were repeated threats among the people of an attack on the forts so weakly garrisoned, and seizure of the property claimed by the state. A very ill feeling, akin to that entertained by the people of the colonies towards the British soldiers on the eve of the revolutionary struggle, was cherished towards Major Anderson and the garrison under his command. Knowing that such ill feeling was prevailing among that portion of the people who would join in a mob assault, and that policy only prevented the men of character and influence from openly encouraging such an assault, Major Anderson strengthened his position in Fort Moultrie, to be prepared for an attack. Fort Sumter, in Charleston harbor, was a much stronger fortification, though not complete in all respects, nor fully provided with ordnance. Not being garrisoned, it was liable to seizure at any time by the South Carolina military, which was now mustering, or even by the mob, and Fort Moultrie would thus be at the mercy of assailants. Foreseeing the danger which the government at Washington could not or would not notice, on the 26th of December Major Anderson caused his command, with their provisions and ammunition, to be transferred to Fort Sumter, leaving only a few men in Fort Moultrie, who spiked the guns and burned the gun carriages. The night was clear, and the moon shone brightly; but though an armed guard boat of the state authorities passed near the vessels transporting the garrison, the movement was not noticed.

This act of Major Anderson caused great excitement and indignation among the people of · Charleston when discovered. They had, undoubtedly, been assured by the secretary of war, Floyd, that the existing state of things in relation to the forts in Charleston harbor should continue unchanged, and there was a *quasi* promise on their part that no attack should be made;

and when Major Anderson abandoned Moultrie and took possession of Sumter, they declared that it was a "breach of faith" and "an act of war." They were, perhaps, chagrined, too, that they had not acted more promptly in their designs to get possession of the forts. While they were promising to make no assault, they were making every preparation for such an act; but they had been outgeneraled.

Military organization now received a new impulse, and there seemed to be a general call to arms in South Carolina, while a like spirit in other states led to renewed offers of military aid to "repel the invasion of South Carolina."

Having taken the first decisive step, the government of South Carolina seemed now determined to carry their hostile measures to the extreme. They complained bitterly that the promise of the secretary of war was broken; but while demanding that Major Anderson should be ordered back to Fort Moultrie, a military force of the state took possession of that post, and would thus have prevented the return, had it been contemplated. But though Major Anderson had not been authorized to retire from Moultrie to Sumter, the president declined to order him back, and Mr. Floyd made this refusal a pretext for tendering his resignation as secretary of war; while among the secessionists it was proclaimed as a determination on the part of the federal government to "coerce" the state into the Union again. There was a great outcry at this time among the secessionists, and even those who claimed to be Union men at the south, against "coercion." If a state secedes, was the argument, there is no power in the federal government, under the constitution, to *coerce* such state or its people to remain in the Union. Specious arguments against "coercion" were urged north and south, and while the doubtful and the timid were listening to them and weighing them, the work of disunion went on as if there were authority for *that* under the constitution.

F. W. Pickens was now governor of South Carolina, a strong secessionist, and a man who was disposed to carry out the will of the leaders of rebellion. On the 24th of December he issued a proclamation, embodying the final clause of the declaration of the causes for secession, that South Carolina was a free, independent, and sovereign state. By his order the state troops the same day occupied Castle Pinckney (a small fort near the city) and Fort Moultrie, and a day or two afterwards another body of state troops took possession of the United States arsenal in the city, in which were many thousand arms and large quantities of military stores. Every where the "palmetto flag" of South Carolina was raised in the place of the flag of the Union. Immediate measures were taken to repair Fort Moultrie, and for the erection of new fortifications about the harbor of Charleston, with a view of preventing reënforcements to Fort Sumter, and of compelling that stronghold to yield. For a time Major Anderson's communications with the government at Washington were cut off, and he was refused the privilege of purchasing fresh provisions in the city.

The secessionists of other states followed the example of South Carolina, and seized the national forts and arsenals which were undefended. In some instances this was done by the direct authority or sanction of the state governments, and in some by unauthorized acts of mobs or military organizations. In Savannah the revenue cutter was thus seized by a party of secessionists, and was released by the governor of Georgia; but Fort Pulaski was taken possession of by order of the same governor. In North Carolina a similar unauthorized seizure of forts was made, and the governor directed them to be abandoned, but with the declaration that the order was given in the belief that the existing national administration would not resort to coercion.

While these things were going on at the south, they produced a different kind of feeling at the north. There the Union was looked upon as indissoluble, and the right of secession was admitted by scarcely any one. When South Carolina took measures for seceding, and claimed that the federal forts belonged to the state, there was a general feeling that the government ought not to, and could not, permit such proceedings without asserting its authority. Finding that the national administration, through divided counsels, or inefficiency, did not take any steps to maintain the rights of the government and to protect the public property, a feeling of indignation pervaded the community. And when it was found that even in the cabinet there were those who were using all their power and influence to promote the purposes of the secessionists, the northern public were dismayed at the prospect. The doubts which for some time hung over the question of retaining the forts in Charleston harbor created intense anxiety. But when Major Anderson, on his own responsibility, took a step which indicated that the rights of the federal government were not to be pusillanimously abandoned, a feeling of relief and joy followed. The determination of the government not to order Major Anderson to retrace his steps, and thus far, at least, resolving to assert the rights of the Union, reassured the people. The feeling was almost universal in favor of decided steps, except among some of the blind adherents of the administration; and had the president taken such measures he would have been heartily supported.

While the secessionists were arming and seizing the national arsenals, an inquiry naturally arose as to the military stores in the similar establishments at the north; and it was found that for some time arms had been freely sent from the northern arsenals and from the national armories to the south. At Pittsburg, Pennsylvania, a quantity of ordnance belonging to the government had been ordered to be shipped south. A considerable portion of it yet remained to be transported, when the events occurring at the south indicated that it would pass immediately into the hands of the enemies of the Union, if sent as ordered. The people of Pittsburg were consequently determined to resist any further shipment. By their action they prevented it, until at last, when there was a change in the war department, the order for shipment was revoked.

There was a desire on the part of many that some measures might be adopted by Congress, or a national convention, to settle the questions of difference between the north and the south; yet there was, undoubtedly, a large majority of the people of the north who were opposed to any compromise which should in any way recognize secession or simply postpone the crisis. What disposition there was to compromise, however, extended only to those slave states which had not seceded, or taken measures for that end; but towards South Carolina, and those states which were disposed hastily to follow her example, there was generally a feeling of resentment, which looked to the measure so much deprecated at the south — coercion.

Such was the state of affairs at the close of the year 1860; secession, disunion, rebellion, making rapid strides through the southern states; an administration weak through the timidity of some of its members and the disloyalty of others; among the people of the north suspense and anxiety, but withal a determination to maintain the Union, and to assert and defend its rights.

CHAPTER XV.

WHILE the excitement at the south was yet increasing, but before the disunion movement had culminated in secession, the second session of the thirty-sixth Congress commenced. It was hoped and believed by many, both north and south, that through the action of Congress the excitement would be allayed, and the states threatening secession would be content to remain in the Union. There was a desire, too, to know what course would be adopted by southern members of Congress, what demands and what concessions were to be made; and while it was feared that the conflict of opinion between the north and the south on these questions, which entirely engrossed public attention, might for a time be fiercer than ever, it was hoped that a free discussion might eventually lead to some good result.

To this session of Congress President Buchanan transmitted his last annual message. The events transpiring at the south, and the questions arising therefrom, of course demanded from him especial attention, and he presented his views at length in the opening of the message, as follows: —

"Throughout the year since our last meeting, the country has been eminently prosperous in all its material interests. The general health has been excellent, our harvests have been abundant, and plenty smiles throughout the land. Our commerce and manufactures have been prosecuted with energy and industry, and have yielded fair and ample returns. In short, no nation in the tide of time has ever presented a spectacle of greater material prosperity than we have done, until within a very recent period.

"Why is it, then, that discontent now so extensively prevails, and the union of the states, which is the source of all these blessings, is threatened with destruction?

"The long-continued and intemperate interference of the northern people with the question of slavery in the southern states has at length produced its natural effects. The different sections of the Union are now arrayed against each other, and the time has arrived, so much dreaded by the father of his country, when hostile geographical parties have been formed.

"I have long foreseen, and often forewarned, my countrymen of the now impending danger. This does not proceed solely from the claim on the part of Congress or the territorial legislatures to exclude slavery from the territories, nor from the efforts of different states to defeat the execution of the fugitive slave law. All or any of these evils might have been endured by the south, without danger to the Union, (as others have been,) in the hope that time and reflection might apply the remedy. The immediate peril arises not so much from these causes as from the fact, that the incessant and violent agitation of the slavery question throughout the north for the last quarter of a century has at length produced its malign influence on the slaves, and inspired them with vague notions of freedom. Hence a sense of security no longer exists around the family altar. This feeling of peace at home has given place to apprehensions of servile insurrections. Many a matron throughout the south retires at night in dread of what may befall herself and her children before the morning. Should this apprehension of domestic danger, whether real or imaginary, extend and intensify itself, until it shall pervade the masses of the southern people, then disunion will become inevitable. Self-preservation is the first law of nature, and has been implanted in the heart of man by his Creator, for the wisest purpose; and no political union, however fraught with blessings and benefits in all other respects, can long continue, if the necessary consequence be to render the homes and the firesides of nearly half the parties to it habitually and hopelessly insecure. Sooner or later the bonds of such a Union must be severed. It is my conviction that this fatal period has not yet arrived; and my prayer to God is, that he would preserve the constitution and the Union throughout all generations.

"But let us take warning in time, and remove the cause of danger. It cannot be denied that for five and twenty years the agitation at the north against slavery has been incessant. In 1835 pictorial handbills and inflammatory appeals were circulated extensively throughout the south, of a character to excite the passions of the slaves, and, in the language of General Jackson, 'to stimulate them to insurrection, and produce all the horrors of a servile war.' This agitation has ever since been continued by the public press, by the proceedings of state and county conventions, and by abolition sermons and lectures. The time of Congress has been occupied in violent speeches on this never-ending subject; and appeals, in pamphlet and other forms, indorsed by distinguished names, have been sent forth from this central point and spread broadcast over the Union.

"How easy would it be for the American people to settle the slavery question forever, and to restore peace and harmony to this distracted country! They, and they alone, can do it. All that is necessary to accomplish the object, and all for which the slave states have ever contended, is to be let alone and permitted to manage their domestic institutions in their own way. As sovereign states, they, and they alone, are responsible before God and the world for the slavery existing among them. For this the people of the north are not more responsible, and have no more right to interfere, than with similar institutions in Russia or in Brazil.

"Upon their good sense and patriotic forbearance, I confess, I still greatly rely. Without their aid it is beyond the power of any president, no matter what may be his own political proclivities, to restore peace and harmony among the states. Wisely limited and restrained as is his power under our constitution and laws, he alone can accomplish but little for good or for evil on such a momentous question.

"And this brings me to observe, that the election of any one of our fellow-citizens to the office of president does not of itself afford just cause for dissolving the Union. This is more especially true if his election has been effected by a mere plurality, and not a majority, of the people, and has resulted from transient and temporary causes, which may probably never again occur. In order to justify a resort to revolutionary resistance, the federal government must be guilty of 'a deliberate, palpable, and dangerous exercise' of powers not granted by the constitution. The late presidential election, however, has been held in strict conformity with its express provisions. How, then, can the result justify a revolution to destroy this very constitution? Reason, justice, a regard for the constitution, all require that we shall wait for some overt and dangerous act on the part of the president elect, before resorting to such a remedy. It is said, however, that the antecedents of the president elect have been sufficient to justify the fears of the south that he will attempt to invade their constitutional rights. But are such apprehensions of contingent danger in the future sufficient to justify the immediate destruction of the noblest system of government ever devised by mortals?

From the very nature of his office, and its high responsibilities, he must necessarily be conservative. The stern duty of administering the vast and complicated concerns of this government affords in itself a guarantee that he will not attempt any violation of a clear constitutional right.

"After all, he is no more than the chief executive officer of the government. His province is not to make, but to execute, the laws; and it is a remarkable fact in our history that, notwithstanding the repeated efforts of the anti-slavery party, no single act has ever passed Congress, unless we may possibly except the Missouri compromise, impairing in the slightest degree the rights of the south to their property in slaves. And it may also be observed, judging from present indications, that no probability exists of the passage of such an act by a majority of both houses, either in the present or the next Congress. Surely, under these circumstances we ought to be restrained from present action by the precept of Him who spake as man never spoke, that 'sufficient unto the day is the evil thereof.' The day of evil may never come unless we shall rashly bring it upon ourselves.

"It is alleged as one cause for immediate secession, that the southern states are denied equal rights with the other states in the common territories. But by what authority are these denied? Not by Congress, which has never passed, and I believe never will pass, any act to exclude slavery from these territories. And certainly not by the Supreme Court, which has solemnly decided that slaves are property, and, like all other property, their owners have a right to take them into the common territories and hold them there under the protection of the constitution.

"So far then as Congress is concerned, the objection is not to any thing they have already done, but to what they may do hereafter. It will surely be admitted that this apprehension of future danger is no good reason for an immediate dissolution of the Union. It is true that the territorial legislature of Kansas, on the 23d February, 1860, passed in great haste an act over the veto of the governor, declaring that slavery 'is, and shall be forever, prohibited in this territory.' Such an act, however, plainly violating the rights of property secured by the constitution, will surely be declared void by the judiciary, whenever it shall be presented in a legal form.

"Only three days after my inauguration the Supreme Court of the United States solemnly adjudged that this power did not exist in a territorial legislature. Yet such has been the factious temper of the times that the correctness of this decision has been extensively impugned before the people, and the question has given rise to angry political conflicts throughout the country. Those who have appealed from this judgment of our highest constitutional tribunal to popular assemblies, would, if they could, invest a territorial legislature with power to annul the sacred rights of property. This power Congress is expressly forbidden by the federal constitution to exercise. Every state legislature in the Union is forbidden by its own constitution to exercise it. It cannot be exercised in any state except by the people in their highest sovereign capacity when framing or amending their state constitution. In like manner it can only be exercised by the people of a territory, represented in a convention of delegates, for the purpose of framing a constitution preparatory to admission as a state into the Union. Then, and not until then, are they invested with power to decide the question whether slavery shall or shall not exist within their limits. This is an act of sovereign authority, and not of subordinate territorial legislation. Were it otherwise, then indeed would the equality of the states in the territories be destroyed and the rights of property in slaves would depend not upon the guarantees of the constitution, but upon the shifting majorities of an irresponsible territorial legislature. Such a doctrine, from its intrinsic unsoundness, cannot long influence any considerable portion of our people, much less can it afford a good reason for a dissolution of the Union.

"The most palpable violations of constitutional duty which have yet been committed consist in the acts of different state legislatures to defeat the execution of the fugitive slave law. It ought to be remembered, however, that for these acts neither Congress nor any president can justly be held responsible. Having been passed in violation of the federal constitution, they are therefore null and void. All the courts, both state and national, before whom the question has arisen, have, from the beginning, declared the fugitive slave law to be constitutional. The single exception is that of a state court in Wisconsin; and this has not only been reversed by the proper appellate tribunal, but has met with such universal reprobation, that there can be no danger from it as a precedent. The validity of this law has been established over and over again by the Supreme Court of the United States with perfect unanimity. It is founded upon an express provision of the constitution, requiring that fugitive slaves who escape from service in one state to another shall be 'delivered up' to their masters. Without this provision it is a well-known historical fact that the constitution itself could never have been adopted by the convention. In one form or other, under the acts of 1793 and 1850, both being substantially the same, the fugitive slave law has been the law of the land from the days of Washington until the present moment. Here, then, a clear case is presented, in which it will be the duty of the next president, as it has been my own, to act with vigor in executing this supreme law against the conflicting enactments of state legislatures. Should he fail in the performance of this high duty, he will then have manifested a disregard of the constitution and laws, to the great injury of the people of nearly one half of the states of the Union. But are we to presume in advance that he will thus violate his duty? This would be at war with every principle of justice and of Christian charity. Let us wait for the overt act. The fugitive slave law has been carried into execution in every contested case since the commencement of the present administration; though often, it is to be regretted, with great loss and inconvenience to the master, and with considerable expense to the government. Let us trust that the state legislatures will repeal their unconstitutional and obnoxious enactments. Unless this shall be done without unnecessary delay, it is impossible for any human power to save the Union.

"The southern states, standing on the basis of the constitution, have a right to demand this act of justice from the states of the north. Should it be refused, then the constitution, to which all the states are parties, will have been wilfully violated by one portion of them in a provision essential to the domestic security and happiness of the remainder. In that event, the injured states, after having first used all peaceful and constitutional means to obtain redress, would be justified in revolutionary resistance to the government of the Union.

"I have purposely confined my remarks to revolutionary resistance, because it has been claimed within the last few years that any state, whenever this shall be its sovereign will and pleasure, may secede from the Union in accordance with the constitution, and without any violation of the constitutional rights of the other members of the confederacy; that as each became parties to the Union by the vote of its own people assembled in convention, so any one of them may retire from the Union in a similar manner by the vote of such a convention.

"In order to justify secession as a constitutional remedy, it must be on the principle that the federal government is a mere voluntary association of states, to be dissolved at pleasure by any one of the contracting parties. If this be so, the confederacy is a rope of sand, to be penetrated and dissolved by the first adverse wave of public opinion in any of the states. In this manner our thirty-three states may resolve themselves into as many petty, jarring, and hostile republics, each one retiring from the Union without responsibility whenever any sudden excitement might impel them to such a course. By this process a Union might be entirely broken into fragments in a few weeks which cost our forefathers many years of toil, privation, and blood to establish.

"Such a principle is wholly inconsistent with the history as well as the character of the federal constitution. After it was framed with the greatest deliberation and care, it was submitted to conventions of the people of the several states for ratification. Its provisions were discussed at length in these bodies, composed of the first men of the country. Its opponents contended that it conferred powers upon the federal government dangerous to the rights of the states, whilst its advocates maintained that, under a fair construction of the instrument, there was no foundation for such apprehensions. In that mighty struggle between the first intellects of this or any other country, it never occurred to any individual, either among its opponents or advocates, to assert, or even to intimate, that their efforts were all vain labor, because the moment that any state felt herself aggrieved she might secede from the Union. What a crushing argument would this have proved against those who dreaded that the rights of the states would be endangered by the constitution! The truth is, that it was not until many years after the origin of the federal government that such a proposition was first advanced. It was then met and refuted by the conclusive arguments of General Jackson, who, in his message of the 16th January, 1833, trans-

mitting the nullifying ordinance of South Carolina to Congress, employs the following language: 'The right of the people of a single state to absolve themselves at will and without the consent of the other states from their most solemn obligations, and hazard the liberty and happiness of the millions composing this Union, cannot be acknowledged. Such authority is believed to be utterly repugnant both to the principles upon which the general government is constituted, and to the objects which it was expressly formed to attain.'

"It is not pretended that any clause in the constitution gives countenance to such a theory. It is altogether founded upon inference, not from any language contained in the instrument itself, but from the sovereign character of the several states by which it was ratified. But is it beyond the power of a state, like an individual, to yield a portion of its sovereign rights to secure the remainder? In the language of Mr. Madison, who has been called the father of the constitution, 'It was formed by the states — that is, by the people in each of the states, acting in their highest sovereign capacity, and formed consequently by the same authority which formed the state constitutions.' 'Nor is the government of the United States, created by the constitution, less a government, in the strict sense of the term, within the sphere of its powers, than the governments created by the constitutions of the states are within their several spheres. It is, like them, organized into legislative, executive, and judiciary departments. It operates, like them, directly on persons and things; and, like them, it has at command a physical force for executing the powers committed to it.'

"It was intended to be perpetual, and not to be annulled at the pleasure of any one of the contracting parties. The old articles of confederation were entitled, 'Articles of Confederation and Perpetual Union between the States;' and by the thirteenth article it is expressly

14

declared that ' the articles of this confederation shall be inviolably observed by every state, and the union shall be perpetual.' The preamble to the constitution of the United States having express reference to the articles of confederation, recites that it was established ' in order to form a more perfect union.' And yet it is contended that this ' more perfect union ' does not include the essential attribute of perpetuity.

" But that the union was designed to be perpetual, appears conclusively from the nature and extent of the powers conferred by the constitution on the federal government. These powers embrace the very highest attributes of national sovereignty. They place both the sword and the purse under its control. Congress has power to make war and to make peace ; to raise and support armies and navies, and to conclude treaties with foreign governments. It is invested with the power to coin money, and to regulate the value thereof, and to regulate commerce with foreign nations and among the several states. It is not necessary to enumerate the other high powers which have been conferred upon the federal government. In order to carry the enumerated powers into effect, Congress possesses the exclusive right to lay and collect duties on imports, and, in common with the states, to lay and collect all other taxes.

" But the constitution has not only conferred these high powers upon Congress, but it has adopted effectual means to restrain the states from interfering with their exercise. For that purpose it has in strong prohibitory language expressly declared that ' no state shall enter into any treaty, alliance, or confederation ; grant letters of marque and reprisal ; coin money ; emit bills of credit ; make any thing but gold and silver coin a tender in payment of debts ; pass any bill of attainder, *ex post facto* law, or law impairing the obligation of contracts.' Moreover, ' without the consent of Congress no state shall lay any imposts or duties on any imports or ex-

ports, except what may be absolutely necessary for executing its inspection laws,' and if they exceed this amount, the excess shall belong to the United States. And ' no state shall, without the consent of Congress, lay any duty of tonnage, keep troops or ships of war in time of peace, enter into any agreement or compact with another state, or with a foreign power, or engage in war, unless actually invaded or in such imminent danger as will not admit of delay.'

" In order still further to secure the uninterrupted exercise of these high powers against state interposition, it is provided ' that this constitution, and the laws of the United States which shall be made in pursuance thereof, and all treaties made, or which shall be made, under the authority of the United States, shall be the supreme law of the land ; and the judges in every state shall be bound thereby, any thing in the constitution or laws of any state to the contrary notwithstanding.'

" The solemn sanction of religion has been superadded to the obligations of official duty, and all senators and representatives of the United States, all members of state legislatures, and all executive and judicial officers, ' both of the United States and of the several states, shall be bound by oath or affirmation to support this constitution.'

" In order to carry into effect these powers, the constitution has established a perfect government in all its forms, legislative, executive, and judicial ; and this government, to the extent of its powers, acts directly upon the individual citizens of every state, and executes its own decrees by the agency of its own officers. In this respect it differs entirely from the government under the old confederation, which was confined to making requisitions on the states in their sovereign character. This left it in the discretion of each whether to obey or to refuse, and they often declined to comply with such requisitions. It thus became necessary, for the purpose of removing this barrier, and ' in order to form a more perfect union,' to establish a government which could act directly upon the people, and execute its own laws without the intermediate agency of the states. This has been accomplished by the constitution of the United States. In short, the government created by the constitution, and deriving its authority from the sovereign people of each of the several states, has precisely the same right to exercise its power over the people of all these states in the enumerated cases, that each one of them possesses over subjects not delegated to the United States, but 'reserved to the states respectively or to the people.'

"To the extent of the delegated powers the constitution of the United States is as much a part of the constitution of each state, and is as binding upon its people, as though it had been textually inserted therein.

"This government, therefore, is a great and powerful government, invested with all the attributes of sovereignty over the special subjects to which its authority extends. Its framers never intended to implant in its bosom the seeds of its own destruction, nor were they at its creation guilty of the absurdity of providing for its own dissolution. It was not intended by its framers to be the baseless fabric of a vision, which, at the touch of the enchanter, would vanish into thin air, but a substantial and mighty fabric, capable of resisting the slow decay of time, and of defying the storms of ages. Indeed, well may the jealous patriots of that day have indulged fears that a government of such high powers might violate the reserved rights of the states, and wisely did they adopt the rule of a strict construction of these powers to prevent the danger. But they did not fear, nor had they any reason to imagine that the constitution would ever be so interpreted as to enable any state by her own act, and without the consent of her sister states, to discharge her people from all or any of their federal obligations.

"It may be asked, then, Are the people of the states without redress against the tyranny and oppression of the federal government? By no means. The right of resistance on the part of the governed against the oppression of their governments cannot be denied. It exists independently of all constitutions, and has been exercised at all periods of the world's history. Under it old governments have been destroyed, and new ones have taken their place. It is embodied in strong and express language in our own Declaration of Independence. But the distinction must ever be observed that this is revolution against an established government, and not a voluntary secession from it by virtue of an inherent constitutional right. In short, let us look the danger fairly in the face; secession is neither more nor less than revolution. It may or it may not be a justifiable revolution; but still it is revolution.

"What, in the mean time, is the responsibility and true position of the executive? He is bound by solemn oath, before God and the country, 'to take care that the laws be faithfully executed,' and from this obligation he cannot be absolved by any human power. But what if the performance of this duty, in whole or in part, has been rendered impracticable by events over which he could have exercised no control? Such, at the present moment, is the case throughout the state of South Carolina, so far as the laws of the United States to secure the administration of justice by means of the federal judiciary are concerned. All the federal officers within its limits, through whose agency alone these laws can be carried into execution, have already resigned. We no longer have a district judge, a district attorney, or a marshal in South Carolina. In fact, the whole machinery of the federal government necessary for the distribution of remedial justice among the people has been demolished, and it would be difficult, if not impossible, to replace it.

"The only acts of Congress on the statute

book bearing upon this subject are those of the 28th February, 1795, and 3d March, 1807. These authorize the president, after he shall have ascertained that the marshal, with his *posse comitatus*, is unable to execute civil or criminal process in any particular case, to call forth the militia and employ the army and navy to aid him in performing this service, having first by proclamation commanded the insurgents 'to disperse and retire peaceably to their respective abodes within a limited time.' This duty cannot by possibility be performed in a state where no judicial authority exists to issue process, and where there is no marshal to execute it, and where, even if there were such an officer, the entire population would constitute one solid combination to resist him.

"The bare enumeration of these provisions proves how inadequate they are without further legislation to overcome a united opposition in a single state, not to speak of other states who may place themselves in a similar attitude. Congress alone has power to decide whether the present laws can or cannot be amended so as to carry out more effectually the objects of the constitution.

"The same insuperable obstacles do not lie in the way of executing the laws for the collection of the customs. The revenue still continues to be collected, as heretofore, at the custom house in Charleston, and should the collector unfortunately resign, a successor may be appointed to perform this duty.

"Then, in regard to the property of the United States in South Carolina. This has been purchased for a fair equivalent, 'by the consent of the legislature of the state,' 'for the erection of forts, magazines, arsenals,' &c., and over these the authority 'to exercise exclusive legislation' has been expressly granted by the constitution to Congress. It is not believed that any attempt will be made to expel the United States from this property by force; but if in this I should prove to be mistaken, the officer in command of the forts has received orders to act strictly on the defensive. In such a contingency the responsibility for consequences would rightfully rest upon the heads of the assailants.

"Apart from the execution of the laws, so far as this may be practicable, the executive has no authority to decide what shall be the relations between the federal government and South Carolina. He has been invested with no such discretion. He possesses no power to change the relations heretofore existing between them, much less to acknowledge the independence of that state. This would be to invest a mere executive officer with the power of recognizing the dissolution of the confederacy among our thirty-three sovereign states. It bears no resemblance to the recognition of a foreign *de facto* government, involving no such responsibility. Any attempt to do this would, on his part, be a naked act of usurpation. It is, therefore, my duty to submit to Congress the whole question in all its bearings. The course of events is so rapidly hastening forward that the emergency may soon arise when you may be called upon to decide the momentous question whether you possess the power, by force of arms, to compel a state to remain in the Union. I should feel myself recreant to my duty were I not to express an opinion on this important subject.

"The question fairly stated is: Has the constitution delegated to Congress the power to coerce a state into submission which is attempting to withdraw or has actually withdrawn from the confederacy? If answered in the affirmative, it must be on the principle that the power has been conferred upon Congress to declare and to make war against a state. After much serious reflection, I have arrived at the conclusion that no such power has been delegated to Congress or to any other department of the federal government. It is manifest, upon an inspection of the constitution, that this is not among the specific and enumerated powers granted to Congress; and it is equally apparent that its exercise is not 'necessary and proper for carrying into execution' any one of these powers. So far from this power having been delegated to Congress, it was expressly refused by the convention which framed the constitution.

"It appears from the proceedings of that body that on the 31st May, 1787, the clause '*authorizing an exertion of the force of the whole against a delinquent state*' came up for consideration. Mr. Madison opposed it in a brief but powerful speech, from which I shall extract but a single sentence. He observed, 'The use of force against a state would look more like a declaration of war than an infliction of punishment, and would probably be considered by the party attacked as a dissolution of all previous compacts by which it might be bound.' Upon his motion the clause was unanimously postponed, and was never, I believe, again presented. Soon afterwards, on the 8th June, 1787, when incidentally adverting to the subject, he said, 'Any government for the United States, formed on the supposed practicability of using force against the unconstitutional proceedings of the states, would prove as visionary and fallacious as the government of Congress,' evidently meaning the then existing Congress of the old confederation.

"Without descending to particulars, it may be safely asserted that the power to make war against a state is at variance with the whole spirit and intent of the constitution. Suppose such a war should result in the conquest of a state: how are we to govern it afterwards? Shall we hold it as a province and govern it by despotic power? In the nature of things, we could not, by physical force, control the will of the people, and compel them to elect senators and representatives to Congress, and to perform all the other duties depending upon their own volition, and required from the free citizens of a free state as a constituent member of the confederacy.

"But, if we possessed this power, would it be wise to exercise it under existing circumstances? The object would doubtless be to preserve the Union. War would not only present the most effectual means of destroying it, but would banish all hope of its peaceable reconstruction. Besides, in the fraternal conflict a vast amount of blood and treasure would be expended, rendering future reconciliation between the states impossible. In the mean time, who can foretell what would be the sufferings and privations of the people during its existence?

"The fact is, that our Union rests upon public opinion, and can never be cemented by the blood of its citizens shed in civil war. If it cannot live in the affections of the people, it must one day perish. Congress possesses many means of preserving it by conciliation; but the sword was not placed in their hand to preserve it by force.

"But may I be permitted solemnly to invoke my countrymen to pause and deliberate, before they determine to destroy this, the grandest temple which has ever been dedicated to human freedom since the world began. It has been consecrated by the blood of our fathers, by the glories of the past, and by the hopes of the future. The Union has already made us the most prosperous, and ere long will, if preserved, render us the most powerful nation on the face of the earth. In every foreign region of the globe the title of American citizen is held in the highest respect, and when pronounced in a foreign land, it causes the hearts of our countrymen to swell with honest pride. Surely, when we reach the brink of the yawning abyss we shall recoil with horror from the last fatal plunge.

"By such a dread catastrophe, the hopes of the friends of freedom throughout the world would be destroyed, and a long night of leaden despotism would enshroud the nations. Our example for more than eighty years would not only be lost, but it would be quoted as a conclusive proof that man is unfit for self-government.

"It is not every wrong — nay, it is not every grievous wrong — which can justify a resort to such a fearful alternative. This ought to be the last desperate remedy of a despairing people, after every other constitutional means of conciliation had been exhausted. We should reflect that, under this free government, there is an incessant ebb and flow in public opinion. The slavery question, like every thing human, will have its day. I firmly believe that it has reached and passed the culminating point. But if, in the midst of the existing excitement, the Union shall perish, the evil may then become irreparable.

"Congress can contribute much to avert it, by proposing and recommending to the legislatures of the several states the remedy for existing evils which the constitution has itself provided for its own preservation. This has been tried at different critical periods of our history, and always with eminent success. It is to be found in the fifth article, providing for its own amendment. Under this article amendments have been proposed by two thirds of both houses of Congress, and have been 'ratified by the legislatures of three fourths of the several states,' and have consequently become parts of the constitution. To this process the country is indebted for the clause prohibiting Congress from passing any law respecting an establishment of religion, or abridging the freedom of speech or of the press, or of the right of petition. To this we are, also, indebted for the bill of rights, which secures the people against any abuse of power by the federal government. Such were the apprehensions justly entertained by the friends of state rights at that period as to have rendered it extremely doubtful whether the constitution could have long survived without those amendments.

"Again, the constitution was amended by the same process, after the election of President Jefferson by the house of representatives, in February, 1803. This amendment was rendered necessary to prevent a recurrence of the dangers which had seriously threatened the existence of the government during the pendeney of that election. The article for its own amendment was intended to secure the amicable adjustment of conflicting constitutional questions like the present, which might arise between the governments of the states and that of the United States. This appears from contemporaucous history. In this connection, I shall merely call attention to a few sentences in Mr. Madison's justly celebrated report, in 1799, to the legislature of Virginia. In this he ably and conclusively defended the resolutions of the preceding legislature, against the strictures of several other state legislatures. These were mainly founded upon the protest of the Virginia legislature against the 'alien and sedition acts,' as 'palpable and alarming infractions of the constitution.' ·In pointing out the peaceful and constitutional remedies — and he referred to none other — to which the states were authorized to resort on such occasions, he concludes by saying, that 'the legislatures of the states might have made a direct representation to Congress, with a view to obtain a rescinding of the two offensive acts, or they might have represented to their respective senators in Congress their wish that two thirds thereof would propose an explanatory amendment to the constitution, or two thirds of themselves, if such had been their option, might, by an application to Congress, have obtained a convention for the same object.' This is the very course which I earnestly recommend, in order to obtain an 'explanatory amendment' of the constitution on the subject of slavery. This might originate with Congress or the state legislatures, as may be deemed most advisable to attain the object.

"The explanatory amendment might be confined to the final settlement of the true construction of the constitution on three special points : —

" 1. An express recognition of the right of property in slaves in the states where it now exists or may hereafter exist.

" 2. The duty of protecting this right in all the common territories throughout their territorial existence, and until they shall be admitted as states into the Union, with or without slavery, as their constitutions may prescribe.

" 3. A like recognition of the right of the master to have his slave, who has escaped from one state to another, restored and ' delivered up' to him, and of the validity of the fugitive slave. law enacted for this purpose, together with a declaration that all state laws impairing or defeating this right are violations of the constitution, and are consequently null and void. It may be objected that this construction of the constitution has already been settled by the Supreme Court of the United States ; and what more ought to be required ? The answer is, that a very large proportion of the people of the United States still contest the correctness of this decision, and never will cease from agitation and admit its binding force until clearly established by the people of the several states in their sovereign character. Such an explanatory amendment would, it is believed, forever terminate the existing dissensions, and restore peace and harmony among the states.

" It ought not to be doubted that such an appeal to the arbitrament established by the constitution itself would be received with favor by all the states of the confederacy. In any event, it ought to be tried in a spirit of conciliation before any of these states shall separate themselves from the Union."

This portion of the message was referred in the senate to a committee of thirteen, and in the house to a select committee of thirty-three, one member from each state, from whose deliberations it was hoped some measure might result which should prevent secession, or at least con-

fine it to a few of the more southern states, and eventually lead even those to reconsider their action. Some of the southern members declined to vote on this proposition, on the ground that their states had already taken measures for seceding. While, however, it was hoped that conciliation and a purpose to stand by the constitution, on the part of the north, might allay the excitement at the south, and prevent the spread of disunion, there was, nevertheless, a determination not to yield to any arrogant demands, or to concede any new vantage ground to slavery. A president had been elected according to constitutional forms, who would administer the government in a constitutional way, and it was felt that his inauguration and exercise of the duties and privileges of the office were not to be purchased by the abandonment of any constitutional principle on which the people had elected him, or by the permanent and unalterable establishment of the principles and policy of those who had opposed him. It was soon apparent that nothing short of such entire abandonment of principle, or even the relinquishment of the government itself by the Republicans, would satisfy the real secessionists. But there were some true friends of the Union at the south, especially in the border slave states, and some *quasi* Unionists, whose attachment to the Union was qualified by their attachment to the institution of slavery. They desired to enjoy the blessings of the Union, but they wished for additional guaranties for the permanence of that institution. A variety of propositions was submitted to each committee and discussed, but the opinions of members were so various that no conclusion could be readily arrived at. Among those which attracted most attention was one submitted by Mr. Crittenden, of Kentucky, which provided for the practical reëstablishment of the Missouri compromise, prohibited Congress from abolishing slavery in places under its exclusive jurisdiction if in slave states, or in the District of

Columbia, without compensation to owners, so long as slavery exists in Virginia or Maryland, and proposed new guaranties for the faithful execution of the fugitive slave law. This, however, was not altogether satisfactory to many of the southern members, who demanded at least that the right to take slaves into any of the territories should be recognized. The Republicans, on the other hand, were willing to provide for an amendment to the constitution declaring that the federal government should have no power to interfere with slavery in the states, that being in accordance with the spirit of the constitution, but were not disposed to agree to any guaranties for its extension. A proposition was also submitted by a committee of the border states, including New Jersey, Pennsylvania, Ohio, Indiana, and Illinois from the north, and Delaware, Maryland, Virginia, North Carolina, Kentucky, and Missouri from the south, which suggested certain guaranties for the enforcement of the fugitive slave law, and modification of some of its objectionable details, and also provided that no new territory shall be acquired by the United States without the consent of three fourths of the senate.

While these propositions were still before the committees, and the country was awaiting events and some possible solution of difficulties, the spirit of secession was at work at Washington, in Congress, in the cabinet, among the people. The administration, as before observed, either from a division of counsel or from supineness, exhibited an inefficiency which was regarded with dismay among the loyal people at the north. Besides the lack of decision and strong will in the president himself, which were demanded in emergencies like the present, it soon became evident that the secessionists controlled a portion of the cabinet, and that the treason which was plotting disunion in the southern states had aiders and abettors among the advisers and executive officers of the president. Mr. Cobb, secretary of the treasury, re-

signed his office on the 10th of December. In his letter of resignation he stated, that while he differed from the president in some of the views contained in the message, and in the hope, therein expressed, of the preservation of the Union, yet he concurred generally in the policy and measures of the administration. Up· to this time, however, the policy of the administration had been as lenient and forbearing towards secession as could well be desired. It was, confessedly, not on account of any difference with the president, that the resignation was tendered, but because Mr. Cobb was a leading secessionist himself, and, either from ambitious motives or from thorough sympathy with disunion, desired to take part in the active measures for its accomplishment. In an address to the people of Georgia, issued about this time, Mr. Cobb, after reviewing the condition of affairs, said, "I should feel that I had done injustice to my own convictions, and been unfaithful to you, if I did not in conclusion warn you of the dangers of delay, and impress upon you the hopelessness of any remedy for these evils short of secession." He then called upon them to arouse, and take Georgia out of the Union before the 4th of March. The president, notwithstanding Mr. Cobb's position must have been known to him, in accepting the resignation expressed his regret at losing Mr. Cobb from his cabinet, and complimented him upon the fidelity and ability with which he had discharged his duties. Philip F. Thomas, of Maryland, was appointed in the place of Mr. Cobb; but the appointment was such as inspired but little confidence among the loyal people, who rejoiced that the cabinet had been relieved of one secessionist.

Four days after the resignation of Mr. Cobb, another resignation was tendered, which occasioned regret rather than satisfaction among the people of the north, especially as its cause indicated the weakness or inefficiency of the government. This was the resignation of Mr.

Cass, secretary of state, which was tendered on account of the refusal of the president to reënforce the garrison under Major Anderson, then still at Fort Moultrie, and to use his constitutional powers to enforce the laws in South Carolina. The secretary of war, Mr. Floyd, protested against such reënforcement; the president adopted the policy of the secretary of war, and Mr. Cass accordingly resigned a position which he felt he could not hold with honor if such a course was to be pursued. Mr. Black, attorney-general, was appointed as successor to Mr. Cass. The president, it appeared, was firm in his determination not to reënforce Major Anderson, although he had been most earnestly besought to do so by men of influence, and by Major Anderson's wife, as a measure of safety to the officers and men of the garrison. There was without doubt an agreement, express or implied, between the government and the secessionists of South Carolina, that if the garrison at Fort Moultrie was not reënforced, or, as the secessionists asserted, if affairs in Charleston harbor should remain in *statu quo*, no attack should be made during the administration of Mr. Buchanan.

When Major Anderson removed his command from Fort Moultrie to Fort Sumter, Mr. Floyd demanded authority to order him back at once. This the president refused, upon consultation, and Mr. Floyd then resigned his office also, on the 29th of December. This resignation was promptly accepted by the president, and Mr. Holt, postmaster-general, was at once placed in charge of the war department. This change was highly satisfactory to the loyal people; and when Mr. Holt's views and efficiency were more fully realized, as they were shortly after, the country found cause for gratitude.

On the 8th of January, Mr. Thompson, secretary of the interior, resigned for reasons similar to those assigned for Mr. Floyd's resignation. Under the influence of the new members of his cabinet, the president was disposed to adopt

a more decided policy with regard to the forts in Charleston harbor, and Mr. Thompson resigned in consequence. Still another resignation occurred on the 11th of January, when Mr. Thomas also retired from the treasury department, which he had held but a month, because he could not agree with the administration in its policy, as now indicated, towards South Carolina. John A. Dix, of New York, was promptly invited to take the place, and accepted.

Thus within a month five members of Mr. Buchanan's cabinet had resigned. With the exception of that of Mr. Cass, the loyal people rejoiced at these resignations. From the first open acts towards secession some of the cabinet had been looked upon with distrust, for they were known to belong to that political school which was now attempting to destroy the Union. Mr. Cobb's administration of the finances of the country had been such as to reduce the government from an overflowing treasury to a considerable debt, and to weaken it for any emergency like that which was about to arise. Whether he had pursued such a policy to aid disunion or not, he was known to be a secessionist, and the later acts of his administration were perhaps justly considered as being for the benefit of secession. Mr. Floyd, it was found, had illegally issued acceptances for a large amount alleged to be due to certain contractors; and it appeared also in connection with this operation, that $870,000 of the Indian Trust Funds, in charge of the department of the interior, had been abstracted by a clerk of that department, and turned over to these contractors, for a part of which Mr. Floyd's illegal acceptances had been pledged. The secretary of the interior was not implicated in the abstraction of the bonds, nor was Mr. Floyd; but the investigation revealed the unwarranted issue of acceptances by the latter, and his loose and careless methods of business.

It also appeared, from subsequent investiga-

15

tions, that under Mr. Floyd's administration of the war department, a large quantity of arms, many of them of the most approved patterns, had been distributed among the southern states, in excess of the proportion distributed among the northern states. The quota of arms for 1861 had been in some cases distributed in advance, and the order from South Carolina had been filled but a few days previous to the passage of the secession ordinance. The national arsenals at the south had also been replenished in some instances, and heavy ordnance had been sent south for the armament of fortifications, while equally important works at the north had been neglected. Mr. Floyd's course in relation to the garrison at Charleston, and his actions after leaving the cabinet, were sufficient to confirm the general belief that he had been using his office to advance the interests of the south in case of disunion, and that more recently he had been plotting treason by promoting secession. He went forth from the cabinet execrated by all loyal men as a traitor. He was afterwards indicted by the grand jury for maladministration of office, complicity in the abstraction of the Indian bonds, and for conspiracy against the government.

Mr. Thompson, the secretary of the interior, was a man of somewhat different stamp, but of his loyalty there was also some question. He was a coöperationist, desiring that the south should act in concert, and that the states should not secede separately. He visited several states in the early part of the winter, with the alleged purpose of inducing them to join in a southern convention, which should present the demands of the south to the free states, and if they were not acceded to should take measures to form at once a southern confederacy. While he did not openly advocate immediate secession, he represented a large class who were waiting for an opportunity to form a southern confederacy, and needed but a slight pretext to desert the government and join them.

With such counsellors as these Mr. Buchanan needed great self reliance and an iron will to save his administration from the charges of imbecility, and even of leaning towards secession. He seemed most anxious to go through with his administration without collision either in or out of the cabinet, and from the opening events of secession he halted between the desire to perform his duty and the fear of offending somebody. Thus the scheming secessionists held him in such subjection that the people began to feel that they had no government to save their country from speedy destruction. Relieved from the evil influences of secession counsel, however, and prompted by the patriotic energy of such men as Mr. Holt and Mr. Stanton, (who had been appointed attorney-general,) the president pursued a more decided policy, though not so strong and energetic as to secure the hearty approval of the loyal people, and escape the charge of vacillation. At the same time, he urged upon Congress, in a special message, the adoption of some measures of compromise without delay.

Amid the perplexities which surrounded him, and at the time when his cabinet was divided and breaking up, the president issued a recommendation for a national fast, to be observed on the 4th day of January, 1861. The governors of many of the states coöperated with the president's recommendation, and it was generally appropriately observed.

In Congress, more than in the cabinet, the spirit of secession was prevalent. The members of those states which were considered as certain to secede at an early day, acted as if they were already out of the Union, though they continued to occupy their seats, and some of them to express their opinions freely. Even before the secession ordinance was adopted in South Carolina, the senators from that state withdrew from the senate ; and, upon the formal announcement of the secession of the state, the representatives sent to the speaker of the house a communication announcing that "the people of South Carolina have resumed the powers heretofore delegated by them to the federal government of the United States, and have thereby dissolved our connection with the house of representatives."

The formal secession of South Carolina, and the withdrawal of her representatives from Congress, seemed to excite in the other secession members a desire to hasten similar proceedings in their own states, and to prevent any lingering feeling for the Union from influencing the conventions about to be held ; while they made new efforts to spread the poison of secession and treason among the members from the border states, and the public officers of the government. Even before the South Carolina members retired, Mr. Toombs, senator from Georgia, telegraphed an address to the people of his state, in which he stated that there was no hope of a compromise ; that the propositions which he had submitted in the senate committee of thirteen had been treated with derision or contempt; that Mr. Crittenden's resolutions were "voted against unanimously by the Black Republicans;" that the committee of thirty-three in the house was "controlled by the Black Republicans, your enemies, who only seek to amuse you with delusive hope till your election, that you may defeat the friends of secession." The address concluded as follows : "If you are deceived by them it shall not be my fault. I have put the test fairly and frankly. It is decisive against you now. I tell you, upon the faith of a true man, that all further looking to the north for security for your constitutional rights in the Union, ought to be instantly abandoned. It is fraught with nothing but ruin to yourselves and your posterity. Secession by the 4th day of March next should be thundered from the ballot-box by the unanimous vote of Georgia on the 2d day of January next. Such a voice will be your best guaranty for liberty, security, tranquillity, and glory."

This address indicated a fear lest more moderate counsels might prevail with the people of Georgia, and that delay might be dangerous to secession. Perhaps it was a well-grounded fear ; for secession was the fruit of excitement and hasty and intemperate action, and if attachment to the Union could be encouraged by hope till some adjustment could be made, or the south come to a better understanding of the principles of the incoming administration, secession might be doomed. But the people of the south are easily excited, and such addresses as these sent from Washington by a majority of the members of Congress from the states most disaffected, enabled the secessionists to control public opinion, or at least its expression at the ballot-box and in the conventions. The Alabama and Mississippi delegations in Congress held a conference on the 6th of January, and telegraphed to the conventions of their respective states to advise immediate secession ; and a caucus of southern senators agreed to advocate separate and immediate secession. Thus were men who composed in part the government of the United States, and were sworn to maintain it, treasonably laboring for its overthrow.

CHAPTER XVI.

Commissioners from South Carolina at Washington. — Communication to the President. — President's Reply. — Rejoinder of
Commissioners. — Its Insolent Character. — Refusal to receive
it. — Effect in South Carolina. — The Secession Press. — Plans
for capturing Fort Sumter. — Change of Policy by the Administration. — Attempt to reenforce Fort Sumter. — The Star
of the West. — Arrival off Charleston Harbor. — Fired into by
the South Carolina Batteries. — Forced to retire. — Major
Anderson's Letter to Governor Pickens. — He threatens Retaliation. — The Governor's Reply. — The Matter referred to
the Government. — Lieutenant Talbot goes to Washington. —
Effect of these Events at Charleston. — Action of South Carolina Authorities. — A Surrender of Fort Sumter demanded. —
Mr. Hayne sent an Envoy to Washington. — Demand of Governor Pickens on the Government for Surrender of Fort Sumter. — Action of Senators from seceding States. — A Delay in
presenting the Demand. — Mr. Holt's Letter to the Senators.
— Mr. Hayne presents his Demand with Modifications. — Mr.
Holt's Reply. — Return of Lieutenant Talbot. — Instructions
to Major Anderson. — Rumors. — Position of Affairs.

WHEN South Carolina had seceded, one of the
first steps of her authorities was to send commissioners to Washington, duly accredited as
from a foreign state, to negotiate with the federal government. These commissioners, Messrs.
Barnwell, Orr, and Adams, arrived in Washington on the 26th of December; but before they
presented their credentials or opened their negotiations the removal from Fort Moultrie to
Fort Sumter occurred, and they probably then
awaited instructions before acting. In the mean
time they were cordially received by the secession members from the south, and were not
neglected by certain men of the north. On the
29th of December they sent to the president
the following communication : —

"WASHINGTON, *December* 28, 1860.

"SIR: We have the honor to transmit to you
a copy of the full powers from the convention
of the people of South Carolina under which we
are 'authorized and empowered to treat with
the government of the United States for the
delivery of the forts, magazines, lighthouses,
and other real estate, with their appurtenances,
within the limits of South Carolina; and also

for an apportionment of the public debt, and a
division of all other property held by the government of the United States as agent of the
confederated states of which South Carolina was
recently a member; and generally to negotiate
as to all other measures and arrangements
proper to be made and adopted in the existing
relations of the parties, and for the continuance
of peace and amity between this commonwealth
and the government at Washington.'

"In the execution of this trust, it is our duty
to furnish you, as we now do, with an official
copy of the ordinance of secession, by which the
state of South Carolina has resumed the powers
she delegated to the government of the United
States, and has declared her perfect sovereignty
and independence.

"It would also have been our duty to have
informed you that we were ready to negotiate
with you upon all such questions as are necessarily raised by the adoption of this ordinance;
and that we were prepared to enter upon this
negotiation with the earnest desire to avoid all
unnecessary and hostile collision, and so to inaugurate our new relations as to secure mutual
respect, general advantage, and a future of good
will and harmony, beneficial to all parties concerned.

"But the events of the last twenty-four hours
render such an assurance impossible. We came
here the representatives of an authority which
could at any time within the past sixty days
have taken possession of the forts in Charleston
harbor, but which, upon pledges given in a
manner that we cannot doubt, determined to
trust to your honor rather than to its own power. Since our arrival an officer of the United
States, acting, as we are assured, not only without but against your orders, has dismantled one
fort and occupied another, thus altering to a
most important extent the condition of affairs
under which we came.

"Until these circumstances are explained in a
manner which relieves us of all doubt as to the

spirit in which these negotiations shall be conducted, we are forced to suspend all discussion as to any arrangements by which our mutual interests might be amicably adjusted.

"And, in conclusion, we would urge upon you the immediate withdrawal of the troops from the harbor of Charleston. Under present circumstances they are a standing menace, which renders negotiation impossible, and, as our recent experience shows, threatens speedily to bring to a bloody issue questions which ought to be settled with temperance and judgment.

"We have the honor to be, sir, very respectfully, your obedient servants,

"R. W. BARNWELL,
"J. H. ADAMS,
"JAMES L. ORR,
"Commissioners.

"The PRESIDENT OF THE UNITED STATES."

To this letter the president replied as follows: —

"WASHINGTON CITY, December 31, 1860.

"GENTLEMEN: I have had the honor to receive your communication of the 28th instant. * * * In answer to this communication, I have to say that my position as president of the United States was clearly defined in the message to Congress on the 3d instant. In that I stated that 'apart from the execution of the laws, so far as this may be practicable, the executive has no authority to decide what shall be the relations between the federal government and South Carolina. He has been invested with no such discretion. He possesses no power to change the relations heretofore existing between them, much less to acknowledge the independence of that state. This would be to invest a mere executive officer with the power of recognizing the dissolution of the confederacy among our thirty-three sovereign states. It bears no resemblance to the recognition of a foreign de facto government, involving no such responsibility. Any attempt to do this would, on his part, be a naked act of usurpation. It is,

therefore, my duty to submit to Congress the whole question in all its bearings.'

"Such is still my opinion, and I could therefore meet you only as private gentlemen of the highest character, and I was quite willing to communicate to Congress any proposition you might have to make to that body upon the subject. Of this you were well aware.

"It was my earnest desire that such a disposition might be made of the whole subject by Congress, who alone possess the power, as to prevent the inauguration of a civil war between the parties in regard to the possession of the federal forts in the harbor of Charleston; and I therefore deeply regret that, in your opinion, 'the events of the last twenty-four hours render this impossible.' In conclusion, you urge upon me 'the immediate withdrawal of the troops from the harbor of Charleston,' stating that, 'under present circumstances, they are a standing menace which renders negotiation impossible, and, as our recent experience shows, threatens speedily to bring to a bloody issue questions which ought to be settled with temperance and judgment.'

"The reason for this change in your position is, that, since your arrival in Washington, 'an officer of the United States, acting, as we [you] are assured, not only without but against your [my] orders, has dismantled one fort and occupied another, thus altering to a most important extent the condition of affairs under which we [you] came.' You also allege that you came here 'the representatives of an authority which could at any time within the past sixty days have taken possession of the forts in Charleston harbor, but which, upon pledges given in a manner that we [you] cannot doubt, determined to trust to your [my] honor rather than to its own power.'

"This brings me to a consideration of the nature of those alleged pledges, and in what manner they have been observed. In my message of the 3d of December instant, I stated, in regard to the property of the United States in South Carolina, that it 'has been purchased for a fair equivalent "by the consent of the legislature of the state for the erection of forts, magazines, arsenals," &c., and over these the authority "to exercise exclusive legislation" has been expressly granted by the constitution to Congress. It is not believed that any attempt will be made to expel the United States from this property by force; but if in this I should prove to be mistaken, the officer in command of the forts has received orders to act strictly on the defensive. In such a contingency the responsibility for consequences would rightfully rest upon the heads of the assailants.'

"This being the condition of the parties on Saturday, December 8, four of the representatives from South Carolina called upon me and requested an interview. We had an earnest conversation on the subject of these forts and the best means of preventing a collision between the parties, for the purpose of sparing the effusion of blood. I suggested, for prudential reasons, that it would be best to put in writing what they said to me verbally. They did so accordingly, and on Monday morning, the 10th instant, three of them presented to me a paper signed by all the representatives of South Carolina, with a single exception, of which the following is a copy : —

" ' WASHINGTON, December 9, 1860.

" ' In compliance with our statement to you yesterday, we now express to you our strong convictions that neither the constituted authorities nor any body of the people of the state of South Carolina will either attack or molest the United States forts in the harbor of Charleston previously to the action of the convention, and we hope and believe not until an offer has been made through an accredited representative to negotiate for an amicable arrangement of all matters between the state and the federal government, provided that no reënforcements shall be sent into those forts, and their relative military status shall remain as at present.'

"And here I must, in justice to myself, remark that at the time the paper was presented to me I objected to the word 'provided,' as it might be construed into an agreement on my part which I never would make. They said that nothing was further from their intention ; they did not so understand it, and I should not so consider it. It is evident they could enter into no reciprocal agreement with me on the subject.

"They did not profess to have authority to do this, and were acting in their individual character. I considered it as nothing more in effect than the promise of highly-honored gentlemen to exert their influence for the purpose expressed. The event has proven that they have faithfully kept this promise, although I have never since received a line from any one of them, or from the convention, on the subject. It is well known that it was my determination — and this I freely expressed — not to reënforce the forts in the harbor, and thus produce a collision, until they had been actually attacked, or until I had certain evidence that they were about to be attacked. This paper I received most cordially, and considered it as a happy omen that peace might be still preserved, and that time might thus be gained for reflection. This is the whole foundation for the alleged pledge.

"But I acted in the same manner as I would have done had I entered into a positive and formal agreement with parties capable of contracting, although such an agreement would have been on my part, from the nature of my official duties, impossible. The world knows that I have never sent any reënforcements to the forts in Charleston harbor, and I have certainly never authorized any change to be made 'in their relative military status.' Bearing upon this subject, I refer you to an order issued by the secretary of war, on the 11th instant, to

Major Anderson, but not brought to my notice until the 21st instant. It is as follows : —

" 'You are carefully to avoid every act which would needlessly tend to provoke aggression, and for that reason you are not, without evident and imminent necessity, to take up any position which could be construed into the assumption of a hostile attitude ; but you are to hold possession of the forts in this harbor, and if attacked, you are to defend yourself to the last extremity. The smallness of your force will not permit you, perhaps, to occupy more than one of the three forts ; but an attack on or attempt to take possession of either one of them will be regarded as an act of hostility, and you may then put your command into either of them which you may deem most proper to increase its power of resistance. You are also authorized to take similar defensive steps whenever you have tangible evidence of a design to proceed to a hostile act.'

" These were the last instructions transmitted to Major Anderson before his removal to Fort Sumter, with a single exception in regard to a particular which does not in any degree affect the present question. Under these circumstances, it is clear that Major Anderson acted upon his own responsibility and without authority, unless, indeed, he had 'tangible evidence of a design to proceed to a hostile act' on the part of the authorities of South Carolina, which has not yet been alleged. Still he is a brave and honorable officer, and justice requires that he should not be condemned without a fair hearing.

" Be this as it may, when I learned that Major Anderson had left Fort Moultrie and proceeded to Fort Sumter, my first promptings were to command him to return to his former position, and there await the contingencies presented in his instructions. This could only have been done with any degree of safety to the command by the concurrence of the South Carolina authorities. But before any steps could possibly have been taken in this direction, we received information, dated on the 28th instant, that the ' palmetto flag floated out to the breeze at Castle Pinckney, and a large military force went over last night (the 27th) to Fort Moultrie.' Thus the authorities of South Carolina, without waiting or asking for any explanation, and doubtless believing, as you have expressed it, that the officer had acted not only without but against my orders, on the very next day after the night when the movement was made, seized by a military force two of the three federal forts in the harbor of Charleston, and have covered them under their own flag instead of that of the United States. At this gloomy period of our history startling events succeed each other rapidly. On the very day, the 27th instant, that possession of these two forts was taken, the palmetto flag was raised over the federal custom house and post office in Charleston ; and on the same day every officer of the customs — collector, naval officer, surveyor, and appraisers — resigned their offices ; and this although it was well known from the language of my message that, as an executive officer, I felt myself bound to collect the revenue at the port of Charleston under the existing laws.

" In the harbor of Charleston we now find three forts confronting each other, over all of which the federal flag floated only four days ago ; but now over two of them this flag has been supplanted, and the palmetto flag has been substituted in its stead. It is under all these circumstances that I am urged immediately to withdraw the troops from the harbor of Charleston, and am informed that without this negotiation is impossible. This I cannot do ; this I will not do. Such an idea was never thought of by me in any possible contingency. No allusion had ever been made to it in any communication between myself and any human being. But the inference is, that I am bound to withdraw the troops from the only fort remaining in the possession of the United States in the harbor of

Charleston, because the officer there in command of all the forts thought proper, without instructions, to change his position from one of them to another. I cannot admit the justice of any such inference. And at this point of writing I have received information by telegraph from Captain Humphreys, in command of the arsenal at Charleston, that it 'has to-day (Sunday, the 30th) been taken by force of arms.' Comment is needless. It is estimated that the property of the United States in this arsenal was worth half a million of dollars.

"After this information, I have only to add that, whilst it is my duty to defend Fort Sumter, as a portion of the public property of the United States, against hostile attacks, from whatever quarter they may come, by such means as I may possess for this purpose, I do not perceive how such a defence can be construed into a menace against the city of Charleston.

"With great personal regard, I remain, yours,
"Very respectfully,
"JAMES BUCHANAN.
" Hons. R. W. BARNWELL, J. H. ADAMS, J. L. ORR."

The commissioners rejoined in another long communication, in which they attempted to refute, and not in the most courteous or respectful manner, the president's statements in relation to any pledge. They reviewed the history of the matter as they understood it, as follows: —

"Some weeks ago the state of South Carolina declared her intention, in the existing condition of public affairs, to secede from the United States. She called a convention of her people to put her declaration in force. The convention met, and passed the ordinance of secession. All this you anticipated, and your course of action was thoroughly considered in your annual message. You declared you had no right, and would not attempt, to coerce a seceding state, but that you were bound by your constitutional oath, and would defend the property of the United States within the borders of South Carolina, if an attempt was made to take it by force. Seeing very early that this question of property was a difficult and delicate one, you manifested a desire to settle it without collision. You did not reënforce the garrison in the harbor of Charleston. You removed a distinguished and veteran officer from the command of Fort Moultrie because he attempted to increase his supply of ammunition. You refused to send additional troops to the same garrison when applied for by the officer appointed to succeed him. You accepted the resignation of the oldest and most eminent member of your cabinet, rather than allow the garrison to be strengthened. You compelled an officer stationed at Fort Sumter to return immediately to the arsenal forty muskets which he had taken to arm his men. You expressed not to one, but to many of the most distinguished of our public characters, whose testimony will be placed upon the record whenever it is necessary, your anxiety for a peaceful termination of this controversy, and your willingness not to disturb the military status of the forts, if commissioners should be sent to the government, whose communications you promised to submit to Congress. You received and acted on assurances from the highest official authorities of South Carolina, that no attempt would be made to disturb your possession of the forts and property of the United States, if you would not disturb their existing condition until the commissioners had been sent, and the attempt to negotiate had failed. You took from the members of the house of representatives a written memorandum that no such attempt should be made, 'provided that no reënforcements should be sent into those forts, and their relative military status shall remain as at present.' And although you attach no force to the acceptance of such a paper — although you 'considered it as nothing more in effect than the promise of highly

honorable gentlemen' — as an obligation on one side, without corresponding obligation on the other — it must be remembered (if we were rightly informed) that you were pledged, if you ever did send reënforcements, to return it to those from whom you had received it, before you executed your resolution. You sent orders to your officers commanding them strictly to follow a line of conduct in conformity with such an understanding. Besides all this, you had received formal and official notice from the governor of South Carolina that we had been appointed commissioners, and were on our way to Washington. You knew the implied condition under which we came ; our arrival was notified to you, and an hour appointed for an interview. We arrived in Washington on Wednesday at three o'clock, and you appointed an interview with us at one the next day. Early on that day (Thursday) the news was received here of the movement of Major Anderson. That news was communicated to you immediately, and you postponed our meeting until half past two o'clock on Friday, in order that you might consult your cabinet. On Friday we saw you, and we called upon you then to redeem your pledge. You could not deny it. With the facts we have stated, and in the face of the crowning and conclusive fact that your secretary of war had resigned his seat in the cabinet, upon the publicly avowed ground that the action of Major Anderson had violated the pledged faith of the government, and that unless the pledge was instantly redeemed, he was dishonored, denial was impossible; you did not deny it. You do not deny it now, but you seek to escape from its obligation on the grounds, first, that we terminated all negotiation by demanding, as a preliminary, the withdrawal of the United States troops from the harbor of Charleston ; and, second, that the authorities of South Carolina, instead of asking explanation, and giving you the opportunity to vindicate yourself, took possession of other property of the United States. * * *

" In relation to the withdrawal of the troops from the harbor, we are compelled, however, to notice one passage of your letter. Referring to it you say, 'This I cannot do. This I will not do. Such an idea was never thought of by me in any possible contingency. No allusion to it had ever been made in any communication between myself and any human being.'

" In reply to this statement we are compelled to say that your conversation with us left upon our minds the distinct impression that you did seriously contemplate the withdrawal of the troops from Charleston harbor. And in support of this impression we would add that we have the positive assurance of gentlemen of the highest possible public reputation and the most unsullied integrity — men whose name and fame, secured by long service and patriotic achievement, place their testimony beyond cavil — that such suggestions had been made to and urged upon you by them, and had formed the subject of more than one earnest discussion with you. And it was this knowledge that induced us to urge upon you a policy which had to recommend it its own wisdom and the weight of such authority."

The following is the menacing conclusion of this rude and ill-tempered communication : —

" You have decided — you have resolved — to hold by force what was obtained through misplaced confidence, and converted Major Anderson's violation of orders into a legitimate executive order. You have rendered civil war inevitable. Be it so. If you choose to force the issue upon South Carolina, she will accept it, relying upon Him who is the God of justice as well as the God of hosts, and she will endeavor to do her duty bravely and hopefully."

The president properly refused to receive this communication, and it was returned to them with an indorsement to that effect.

16

Finding that the president would receive no further communication from them, the commissioners left Washington for Charleston, considering the abrupt termination of their mission an insult to themselves and their state, and proclaiming it as a declaration of war. But South Carolina, without awaiting the result of this mission, had already ordered new fortifications to be constructed in and around the harbor of Charleston, to resist any attempt to reënforce Fort Sumter, and threatening the safety of that post. Upon the receipt of the intelligence of the failure of the commissioners to accomplish their errand, the attitude of the government was regarded as warlike, and military preparations were pushed with renewed vigor. Fort Moultrie was repaired and strengthened, new batteries were erected on Sullivan's Island and on Morris's Island, and subsequently on Cummings Point. A floating battery was commenced, and one or two steamers and other small vessels were taken possession of and armed. The revenue cutter William Aiken had been previously betrayed into the hands of the state authorities by the commander, Captain Coste, and became a part of the South Carolina navy. The press was very warlike, teeming with falsehood and bombast to keep up the excitement, and anonymous appeals intended to stir up the people to attack Fort Sumter; and the demonstrative portion of the people echoed the voice of the press with manifold variations.

A variety of plans for capturing Fort Sumter was proposed through the newspapers and directly to the government, such as sending down to the fort huge fire rafts to smoke out the garrison; or bribing the men to surrender; or filling bombs with prussic acid or other offensive substance, the explosion of which would suffocate; or sending down a floating battery, constructed of cotton bales, which should coöperate with Fort Moultrie and the other land batteries, and an armed fleet, and thus, with the aid of sharp-shooters to pick off the garrison, man by man, compel the few survivors to capitulate. But with all these schemes to capture an unfinished, partially-armed fortification, garrisoned by about seventy men, and with all the military ardor which manifested itself throughout the state, and the warlike spirit and hatred towards the United States, which was ever ready to threaten such an enterprise, the authorities appeared to be inclined to no such demonstration.

When the changes in the cabinet had infused more vigor into the administration, and the course pursued by the South Carolina commissioners had revealed to the president the character of secession, he consented to a change of his policy in regard to reënforcing the little garrison of Fort Sumter. Accordingly, the merchant steamship Star of the West was chartered to transport troops, stores, and ammunition to that post. This vessel, unarmed, cleared at New York for Havana and New Orleans on the 5th of January, 1861, and quietly taking on board in the bay two hundred artillerists and marines, with the necessary ammunition and provisions, proceeded on her voyage to Charleston. Upon her arrival there the hostile intentions of South Carolina were unequivocally manifested. The Star of the West arrived off Charleston bar in the night, and, the lights having been extinguished, was obliged to await daylight before entering harbor. At daybreak, on the 9th of January, a steamer which had been on the watch — the South Carolina authorities probably being informed of the expedition — burned signal lights and steamed up the harbor. The Star of the West proceeded over the bar and up the channel as soon as it was sufficiently light. When about two miles from Fort Moultrie, and the same distance from Fort Sumter, the new battery on Morris Island opened fire upon her. The American flag was flying at the staff, and another large American flag was now hoisted at the fore, but the battery continued to fire, seconded by Fort Moultrie. Two shots took effect without doing material damage, and several others came near doing serious injury. The vessel being unarmed, and being obliged, in following the channel, to approach Fort Moultrie within easy range of its guns, and as a vessel apparently armed was seen coming down the harbor, towed by a steamer, it was deemed too dangerous to attempt to reach Fort Sumter, and the commander accordingly put the vessel about, and sailed out of the harbor, the Morris Island battery continuing its fire until the shot fell short.

These proceedings were watched with intense interest from Fort Sumter, and the guns fronting Fort Moultrie and Morris Island were run out, but no further demonstration was made. When the Star of the West retreated from the harbor, Major Anderson sent a messenger to Governor Pickens, bearing the following note:—

"To the Governor of South Carolina.

"SIR: Two of your batteries this morning fired on an unarmed vessel bearing the flag of my government. As I have not been notified that war has been declared by South Carolina against the United States, I cannot but think this hostile act was committed without your authority. Under that hope I refrain from opening fire on your batteries. I respectfully ask whether the above-mentioned act — one which I believe *without a parallel in the history of this country or of any other civilized government* — was committed in obedience to your instructions, and notify you that if it is not disclaimed, I shall regard it as an act of war, and shall not, after a reasonable time for the return of my messenger, permit any vessel to pass within the range of the guns of my fort. In order to save as far as in my power the shedding of blood, I beg you will take due notification of my decision, for the good of all concerned;

hoping, however, your answer may justify a further continuance of forbearance on my part.

"I remain, respectfully,

"ROBERT ANDERSON."

To this Governor Pickens replied, after stating the position of South Carolina towards the United States, that any attempt to send government troops to reënforce the forts would be regarded as an act of hostility, and any attempt to reënforce Fort Sumter, or to retake and resume possession of the forts within the waters of South Carolina, which Major Anderson had abandoned, would be regarded as coercive of the state. Special agents had been off the bar to warn vessels with troops for Fort Sumter not to enter the harbor. Special orders had been given the commanders of the forts not to fire into vessels until a shot across their bows should warn them. Under such orders and circumstances the Star of the West was fired into; "and the act," said the governor, "is perfectly justified by me." In response to Major Anderson's threat about vessels in the harbor, he said, "You must be the judge of your own responsibility. Your position in the harbor has been tolerated by the authorities of the state; and, while the act of which you complain is in perfect consistency with the rights and duties of the state, it is not perceived how far the conduct you propose to adopt can find a parallel in the history of any country, or be reconciled with any other purpose than that the government is imposing on South Carolina the condition of a conquered province."

Major Anderson replied to the governor that, upon further consideration, he deemed it proper to refer the whole matter to the government, and would defer the course he indicated in his former note until the arrival of instructions from Washington. Lieutenant Talbot was accordingly despatched to Washington to lay the matter before the government, Major Anderson requesting that the governor would afford every facility for his departure and return.

This affair created great excitement at Charleston, and gave additional impetus to the military preparations. The first gun had been fired ; the attempt to reënforce Fort Sumter was a declaration of war on the part of the federal government; it had been defeated by an appeal to arms, and would not be renewed ; but if it were, the soldiers of South Carolina would only be too glad to repel it. Such was the common sentiment; and the state authorities acted in a similar spirit, the legislature adopting a resolution that any new attempt to reënforce Fort Sumter would be considered a declaration of war. But further measures were forthwith adopted to demand the surrender of the fort, before taking the final hostile step which the excited people demanded.

The governor demanded of Major Anderson a surrender of Fort Sumter ; but that gallant officer declined doing what he had no authority to do. Isaac W. Hayne, attorney-general of South Carolina, was then sent to Washington with the following formal demand on the president to deliver the fort into the possession of South Carolina : —

"STATE OF SOUTH CAROLINA, EXECUTIVE OFFICE,
HEADQUARTERS, CHARLESTON, *January* 12, 1861. }

"SIR: At the time of the separation of the state of South Carolina from the United States, Fort Sumter was, and still is, in possession of troops of the United States, under the command of Major Anderson. I regard that possession as not consistent with the dignity or safety of the state of South Carolina, and have this day addressed to Major Anderson a communication to obtain from him the possession of that fort by the authorities of this state. The reply of Major Anderson informs me that he has no authority to do what I required ; but he desires a reference of the demand to the president of the United States. Under the circumstances now existing, and which need no comment by me, I have determined to send to you the Hon. I. W. Hayne, the attorney-general of the state of South Carolina, and have instructed him to demand the delivery of Fort Sumter, in the harbor of Charleston, to the constituted authorities of the state of South Carolina. The demand I have made of Major Anderson, and which I now make of you, is suggested because of my earnest desire to avoid the bloodshed which a persistence in your attempt to retain possession of that fort will cause, and which will be unavailing to secure to you that possession, but induce a calamity most deeply to be deplored. If consequences so unhappy shall ensue, I will secure for this state, in the demand which I now make, the satisfaction of having exhausted every attempt to avoid it.

"In relation to the public property of the United States within Fort Sumter, the Hon. I. W. Hayne, who will hand you this communication, is authorized to give you the pledge of the state that the valuation of such property will be accounted for by this state upon the adjustment of its relations with the United States, of which it was a part.

"F. W. PICKENS.

"The PRESIDENT OF THE UNITED STATES."

Before presenting this letter to the president, however, ten senators from the seceding states held a correspondence with Mr. Hayne to induce him to delay the delivery of it until after the seceded states had met in convention to form a new confederation, urging that it was due from South Carolina to their states that she should avoid initiating hostilities. Mr. Hayne acceded so far as to submit their proposition to the government of South Carolina, if they had assurances that in the mean time Fort Sumter should not be reënforced. This correspondence was sent to the president by the senators participating in it, and was replied to by Mr. Holt, secretary of war, who in his letter said, —

"In regard to the proposition of Colonel Hayne, 'that no reënforcements will be sent to Fort Sumter in the interval, and that public peace will not be disturbed by any act of hostility towards South Carolina,' it is impossible for me to give you any such assurances. The president has no authority to enter into such an agreement or understanding. As an executive officer, he is simply bound to protect the public property, so far as this may be practicable; and it would be a manifest violation of his duty to place himself under engagements that he would not perform this duty either for an indefinite or a limited period. At the present moment it is not deemed necessary to reënforce Major Anderson, because he makes no such request, and feels quite secure in his position. Should his safety, however, require reënforcements, every effort will be made to supply them. * * *

"I am glad to be assured, from the letter of Colonel Hayne, that 'Major Anderson and his command do *now* obtain all necessary supplies, including fresh meat and vegetables, and, I believe, fuel and water, from the city of Charleston, and do *now* enjoy communication, by post and special messenger, with the president, and will continue to do so, certainly until the door to negotiation has been closed.' I trust that these facilities may still be afforded to Major Anderson. This is as it should be. Major Anderson is not menacing Charleston; and I am convinced that the happiest result which can be obtained is, that both he and the authorities of South Carolina shall remain on their present amicable footing, neither party being bound by any obligations whatever, except the high Christian and moral duty to keep the peace, and to avoid all causes of mutual irritation." .

Mr. Hayne, having referred the proposition to the authorities of his state, received new instructions, showing a disposition on the part of South Carolina not to delay entering upon negotiations, but modifying the character of the demand, as appears by the following reply to Mr. Hayne's letter, made by Mr. Holt: —

"WAR DEPARTMENT, *February 6, 1861.*

"SIR: The president of the United States has received your letter of the 31st ultimo, and has charged me with the duty of replying thereto.

"In the communication addressed to the president by Governor Pickens, under date of the 12th of January, and which accompanies yours now before me, his excellency says, 'I have determined to send to you the Hon. I. W. Hayne, the attorney-general of the state of South Carolina, and have instructed him to demand the surrender of Fort Sumter, in the harbor of Charleston, to the constituted authorities of the state of South Carolina. The demand I have made of Major Anderson, and which I now make of you, is suggested because of my earnest desire to avoid the bloodshed which a persistence in your attempt to retain the possession of that fort will cause, and which will be unavailing to secure to you that possession, but induce a calamity most deeply to be deplored.' The character of the demand thus authorized to be made appears (under the influence, I presume, of the correspondence with the senators to which you refer) to have been modified by subsequent instructions of his excellency, dated the 26th, and received by yourself on the 30th of January, in which he says, 'If it be so that Fort Sumter is held as property, then, as property, the rights, whatever they may be, of the United States can be ascertained, and for the satisfaction of these rights the pledge of the state of South Carolina you are authorized to give.' The full scope and precise purport of your instructions, as thus modified, you have expressed in the following words: 'I do not come as a military man to demand the surrender of a fortress, but as the legal officer of the state — its attorney-general — to claim for the state the exercise of its undoubted right of eminent domain, and to pledge the state to make good all injury to the rights of property which arise from the exercise of the claim.' And lest this explicit language should not sufficiently define your position, you add, 'The proposition now is, that her [South Carolina's] law officer should, under authority of the governor and his council, distinctly pledge the faith of South Carolina to make such compensation, in regard to Fort Sumter and its appurtenances and contents, to the full extent of the money value of the property of the United States delivered over to the authorities of South Carolina by your command.' You then adopt his excellency's train of thought upon the subject, so far as to suggest that the possession of Fort Sumter by the United States, 'if continued long enough, must lead to collision,' and that 'an attack upon it would scarcely improve it as property, whatever the result; and if captured, it would no longer be the subject of account.'

"The proposal, then, now presented to the president, is simply an offer on the part of South Carolina to buy Fort Sumter and contents as property of the United States, sustained by a declaration, in effect, that if she is not permitted to make the purchase she will seize the fort by force of arms. As the initiation of a negotiation for the transfer of property between friendly governments, this proposal impresses the president as having assumed a most unusual form. He has, however, investigated the claim on which it professes to be based, apart from the declaration that accompanies it. And it may be here remarked, that much stress has been laid upon the employment of the words 'property' and 'public property' by the president in his several messages. These

are the most comprehensive terms which can be used in such a connection; and surely, when referring to a fort or any other public establishment, they embrace the entire and undivided interest of the government therein.

"The title of the United States to Fort Sumter is complete and incontestable. Were its interests in this property purely proprietary, in the ordinary acceptation of the term, it might probably be subjected to the exercise of the right of eminent domain; but it has also political relations to it of a much higher and more imposing character than those of mere proprietorship. It has absolute jurisdiction over the fort and the soil on which it stands. This jurisdiction consists in the authority to 'exercise exclusive legislation' over the property referred to, and is therefore clearly incompatible with the claim of eminent domain now insisted upon by South Carolina. This authority was not derived from any questionable revolutionary source, but from the peaceful cession of South Carolina herself, acting through her legislature, under a provision of the constitution of the United States. South Carolina can no more assert the right of eminent domain over Fort Sumter than Maryland can assert it over the District of Columbia. The political and proprietary rights of the United States in either case rest upon precisely the same ground.

"The president, however, is relieved from the necessity of further pursuing this inquiry by the fact that, whatever may be the claim of South Carolina to this fort, he has no constitutional power to cede or surrender it. The property of the United States has been acquired by force of public law, and can only be disposed of under the same solemn sanctions. The president, as the head of the executive branch of the government only, can no more sell and transfer Fort Sumter to South Carolina than he can sell and convey the Capitol of the United States to Maryland or to any other state or individual seeking to possess it. His excellency the governor is too familiar with the constitution of the United States, and with the limitations upon the powers of the chief magistrate of the government it has established, not to appreciate at once the soundness of this legal proposition.

"The question of reënforcing Fort Sumter is so fully disposed of in my letter to Senator Slidell and others, under date of the 22d of January, a copy of which accompanies this, that its discussion will not now be renewed. I then said, 'At the present moment it is not deemed necessary to reënforce Major Anderson, because he makes no such request. Should his safety, however, require reënforcements, every effort will be made to supply them.' I can add nothing to the explicitness of this language, which still applies to the existing status. The right to send forward reënforcements when, in the judgment of the president, the safety of the garrison requires them, rests on the same unquestionable foundation as the right to occupy the fortress itself.

"In the letter of Senator Davis and others to yourself, under date of the 15th ultimo, they say, 'We therefore think it especially due from South Carolina to our states — to say nothing of other slaveholding states — that she should, as far as she can consistently with her honor, avoid initiating hostilities between her and the United States or any other power;' and you now yourself give to the president the gratifying assurance that 'South Carolina has every disposition to preserve the public peace;' and since he is himself sincerely animated by the same desire, it would seem that this common and patriotic object must be of certain attainment. It is difficult, however, to reconcile with this assurance the declaration on your part that 'it is a consideration of her [South Carolina's] own dignity as a sovereign, and the safety of her people, which prompts her to demand that

this property should not longer be used as a military post by a government she no longer acknowledges,' and the thought you so constantly present, that this occupation must lead to a collision of arms and the prevalence of civil war. Fort Sumter is in itself a military post, and nothing else; and it would seem that not so much the fact as the purpose of its use should give to it a hostile or friendly character. This fortress is now held by the government of the United States for the same objects for which it has been held from the completion of its construction. These are national and defensive; and were a public enemy now to attempt the capture of Charleston or the destruction of the commerce of its harbor, the whole force of the batteries of this fortress would be at once exerted for their protection. How the presence of a small garrison, actuated by such a spirit as this, can compromise the dignity or honor of South Carolina, or become a source of irritation to her people, the president is at a loss to understand. The attitude of that garrison, as has been often declared, is neither menacing, nor defiant, nor unfriendly. It is acting under orders to stand strictly on the defensive; and the government and people of South Carolina must well know that they can never receive aught but shelter from its guns, unless, in the absence of all provocation, they should assault it and seek its destruction. The intent with which this fortress is held by the president is truthfully stated by Senator Davis and others in their letter to yourself of the 15th January, in which they say, 'It is not held with any hostile or unfriendly purpose towards your state, but merely as property of the United States, which the president deems it his duty to protect and preserve.'

"If the announcement, so repeatedly made, of the president's pacific purposes in continuing the occupation of Fort Sumter until the question shall have been settled by competent authority, has failed to impress the government of South Carolina, the forbearing conduct of his administration for the last few months should be received as conclusive evidence of his sincerity. And if this forbearance, in view of the circumstances which have so severely tried it, be not accepted as a satisfactory pledge of the peaceful policy of this administration towards South Carolina, then it may be safely affirmed that neither language nor conduct can possibly furnish one. If, with all the multiplied proofs which exist of the president's anxiety for peace, and of the earnestness with which he has pursued it, the authorities of that state shall assault Fort Sumter, and peril the lives of the handful of brave and loyal men shut up within its walls, and thus plunge our common country into the horrors of civil war, then upon them and those they represent must rest the responsibility.

" Very respectfully, your obedient servant,

" J. HOLT, *Secretary of War.*

"Hon. I. W. HAYNE,

" *Attorney-General of the State of South Carolina.*"

Meanwhile Lieutenant Talbot had returned to Fort Sumter with verbal instructions to Major Anderson to hold and defend the fort at all hazards, and to protect vessels bearing the American flag. It was understood, however, to be the policy of the government not to make any further attempt to reënforce the garrison unless an attack was threatened. Rumors alternated between reënforcement and consequent hostilities, and evacuation and a peaceful settlement of difficulties. But while there was a prospect of immediate hostilities, the work proceeded on the batteries which threatened the safety of Fort Sumter, and Major Anderson and his garrison were virtually besieged, though limited facilities were afforded them for obtaining fresh provisions from the city. Matters here continued in this condition through the remainder of Mr. Buchanan's administration.

CHAPTER XVII.

WHEN secession had once begun by the action of South Carolina, it was evident that some of the other " cotton states" would follow the example, if the schemes of the secessionists could accomplish it. In some of the states conventions had already been called, and in others the secession of South Carolina was a signal for calling them. In Alabama, Florida, Mississippi, and Georgia, the conventions assembled early in January, 1861, and proceeded at once not to the discussion of the right or expediency of secession, but to frame ordinances therefor, and to take other measures for carrying that purpose into effect.

The Mississippi convention adopted the ordinance of secession on the 9th of January, with but fifteen votes in opposition; and the influences brought to bear on the dissentients subsequently made the vote unanimous. All efforts to postpone action were unavailing. The action of the convention produced a wild excitement throughout Mississippi, and was received by the secessionists of other states with demonstrations of joy.

Florida and Alabama were the next states to secede, and the convention of each adopted their respective ordinances of secession on the same day, January 11. The vote in the Florida convention was sixty-two to seven, and even the seven opponents were reported to have finally given in their adhesion. In Alabama the plan did not succeed so easily. There was a strong and able opposition to the adoption of the ordinance, and it was finally carried by a vote of sixty-one yeas to thirty-nine nays, thus indicating that there was a large number in that state, chiefly in the northern part, who were opposed to hasty and extreme measures. The Alabama ordinance, after reciting that " the election of Abraham Lincoln and Hannibal Hamlin to the offices of president and vice-president of the United States of America, by a sectional party, avowedly hostile to the domestic institutions and peace and security of the people of the state of Alabama, following upon the heels of many and dangerous infractions of the constitution of the United States, by many of the states and people of the northern section, is a political wrong of so insulting and menacing a character as to justify the people of the state of Alabama in the adoption of prompt and decided measures for their future peace and security," then declared that Alabama withdraws from the Union, and resumes her sovereignty. It also invited the people of all the slave states by their delegates to assemble in convention at Montgomery on the 4th of February, to take measures for organizing a provisional or permanent government upon the principles of the government of the United States. The South Carolina convention had, a few days before, adopted an ordinance embodying this latter proposition, laying the foundations for the southern confederacy.

17

The Georgia convention adopted an ordinance of secession on the 19th of January, by a vote of two hundred and eight to eighty-nine. It was similar in terms to that of South Carolina, Georgia being one of the original thirteen states. A motion to postpone its operation till the 3d of March was lost by about thirty majority.

On the 26th of January Louisiana seceded, the vote for the ordinance in the convention being one hundred and thirteen to seventeen. A resolution was also reported to the convention, recognizing the right of free navigation of the Mississippi River, and of free ingress and egress of the mouths of that river by all friendly states; but it does not appear that it was adopted. This ordinance was submitted to the people for ratification, when it met with more opposition than it had received in the convention, but was ratified by a vote of twenty thousand four hundred and forty-eight against seventeen thousand two hundred and ninety-six.*

In Texas the convention had been chosen in an irregular manner, Governor Houston having refused to convene the legislature to initiate the proceedings. It assembled, however, and on the 1st of February adopted an ordinance of secession, which was submitted to the people on the 23d of the same month, and, being ratified, took effect on the 2d of March.

Thus seven states had declared that they had withdrawn from the Union, and took measures to form a confederacy according to the plan proposed by Alabama, by sending delegates to the convention at Montgomery. The secession party in other southern states labored persistently to add to this number; but while several of them seemed ripe for secession, the scheme was not carried out so promptly as the extreme secessionists desired.

The course to be pursued by the border

---

* There was some question whether the ordinance was actually ratified by the people. Another statement gave a majority of three hundred and twenty in the state against secession.

slave states in the crisis was awaited with anxious interest, both north and south. There was, unquestionably, a desire among the people of these states to preserve the Union; but there was also a warm sympathy between them and the people farther south on account of their common institutions. The most determined efforts were made by the secessionists to carry these states over at once to the side of a southern confederacy, and to stifle or control the Union sentiment there as it was controlled in the states committed to secession. Commissioners were sent from the seceding states to influence the governments of the border states, while there were more private emissaries to affect the opinions of the people.

The commissioners from Mississippi were the first who appeared on this mission in the border states. In Delaware, after hearing an address from one of these envoys, the legislature unanimously " Resolved, that, having. extended to Hon. H. Dickinson, commissioner from Mississippi, the courtesy due to him as a representative of a sovereign state of the confederacy, as well as to the state he represents, we deem it proper and due to ourselves and to the people of Delaware to express our unqualified disapproval of the remedy for the existing difficulties suggested by the resolutions of the legislature of Mississippi."

The people of Delaware, with some exceptions, were loyal, and being a small state, no further direct efforts were made to secure her secession. In Maryland the legislature was not in session, and the governor declined to receive the commissioner from Mississippi, and refused to convene the legislature either to receive this envoy or to take any other steps which might complicate Maryland with secession. Governor Hicks, through all this period, acted with the greatest firmness; and while signifying his sympathy for the more southern states, declared his unalterable attachment to the Union, and his purpose to keep Maryland in it. The

adherence of Maryland to the southern cause was considered of great importance, and within its borders there were many of the most bitter and .persistent secessionists. To the loyalty and firmness of the governor, who was supported by a majority of the people, the preservation of Maryland from secession, and the safety of the national capital, may in a great measure be attributed.

It may be well to observe, in this connection, that the secession publicly advocated before the people of Maryland, and perhaps of other border states, was different from that which South Carolina considered a " final separation," and which was urged upon the extreme southern or cotton states. The Mississippi commissioner, addressing the citizens of Baltimore, said, " Secession is not intended to break up the present government, but to perpetuate it. We do not propose to go out by way of breaking up or destroying the Union as our fathers gave it to us, but we go out for the purpose of getting further guaranties and security for our rights; not by a convention of all the southern states, nor by congressional tricks, which have failed in times past, and will fail again. But our plan is for the southern states to withdraw from the Union, for the present, to allow amendments to the constitution to be made guaranteeing our just rights; and if the northern states will not make those amendments, by which these rights shall be secured to us, then we must secure them the best way we can."

In Virginia the secession envoys met with more favor. Some of the leading men of that state were strong secessionists. The sentiment of the people was divided, but there was, among the people and in the legislature, a majority who were professedly for the Union. Their sympathies were with the south, but the advantages of the Union could not be overlooked; and if there were any way by which the demands of the slave states could be substantially obtained, Virginia was for the Union.

Virginia therefore undertook the character of mediator between the Union and the seceding states; but at the same time she assumed a threatening position — that her people would go with the south if such demands were not conceded in some new compromise; that any attempt on the part of the federal government to coerce a state was not to be admitted, and that if the government undertook to march or transport troops over her soil for such coercion of South Carolina or other southern state, the act would be regarded as invasion, and resisted as such. Western Virginia was for the most part loyal, and true Union men were found in other parts of the state; but the majority were of that character who apologized for secession, or who openly advocated it.

In North Carolina a more certain Union feeling was to be found; but that state assumed substantially the same position as Virginia. Tennessee was also like Virginia in respect to the sentiments of the people. The inhabitants of East Tennessee were for the most part loyal Unionists, but the western and controlling part of the state was favorable to secession; and as the governor of the state sympathized with the movement, it was early considered as one of the states of the proposed confederacy. Neither North Carolina nor Tennessee, however, properly belonged to the " border states."

In Kentucky, whatever were the sympathies of the governor, who was supposed to be inclined to secession, if not committed to it, there was a large majority of the people determined to keep the state in the Union. Yet there were bitter and determined secessionists there, who used all their influence to carry it over to the south. Missouri was similarly situated. With a governor an avowed secessionist, and a large part of the legislature to support him, steps were taken to secure the adoption of secession by a convention; but the people willed otherwise, and the convention eventually proved the safety of the state.

While the border states were yet in this undecided condition, the Virginia legislature adopted resolutions expressing a determination to "make a final effort to restore the Union and the constitution in the spirit in which they were established by the Fathers of the Republic," and inviting all the states, " whether slaveholding or non-slaveholding, who are willing to unite with Virginia in an earnest effort to adjust the present unhappy controversies," to appoint commissioners to meet at Washington on the 4th of February. If these commissioners agreed upon any plan of adjustment, by amending the constitution, they were to report to Congress the proposed amendments, for the purpose of having them submitted to the people in due form. Commissioners were sent to the president, and to South Carolina and the other seceding states, requesting each party to abstain from all acts calculated to produce a collision while this convention was in session. This proposition was communicated to Congress by the president, who hailed it with great satisfaction, and, in commenting on the course of Virginia, said, " I yet cherish the belief that the American people will perpetuate the union of the states on some terms just and honorable for all sections of the country. I trust that the mediation of Virginia may be the destined means, under the providence of God, of accomplishing this inestimable benefit. Glorious are the memories of her past history, such an achievement, both in relation to her own fame and the welfare of the whole country, would surpass them all."

The Virginia proposition being submitted to the several states, most of them sent commissioners to the convention. But the South Carolina legislature unanimously adopted resolutions declaring that " the separation of South Carolina from the federal government is final, and that she has no further interests in the constitution of the United States; and that the only appropriate negotiations between her and the federal government are as to their mutual relations as foreign states;" and that they considered it "unadvisable to initiate negotiations when South Carolina has no desire or intention to promote the ultimate object in view." This action on the part of South Carolina revealed the feelings and purposes of the secessionists, not only of that state, but throughout the south, which was to establish and maintain a southern confederacy, whatever guaranties might be given for the protection of southern interests in the Union.

This convention, which was known as the "peace convention," assembled on the 5th of February. In it were gentlemen of eminent ability, and of the highest character; and whatever respect it commanded was on this account, for it was regarded as an assembly without authority, whose action would be of no avail except through the action of Congress. Ex-President Tyler, of Virginia, presided over its deliberations, which continued till near the close of the month, during which many propositions were discussed. A majority of the convention finally agreed upon a plan combining the essential features of Mr. Crittenden's and the "border state" propositions, and embraced in seven proposed amendments to the constitution. This plan was communicated to the senate, where it came up for action just at the close of the session, and failed.

The convention proposed by Virginia having thus produced no practical result, the position of that state changed gradually from that of a mediator to that of an armed neutral. While the peace congress was in session, Virginia was continuing her military preparations begun some time previous. The legislature had authorized a convention, and other measures were adopted, such as had led in other states to secession. The convention held some of its sessions with closed doors, and with an injunction of secrecy upon its members; true Union men withdrew from it, but evidently under restraint, and a few were in the end actually held as prisoners; the real action of the convention was not known, but all the indications were, that Virginia was ready to join the south whenever there should be a collision between the federal government and the seceding states, remaining in the mean time nominally in the Union; thus pursuing a deceptive policy, scarcely worthy of the "glorious memories of her past history," to which the president had so kindly alluded.

In the seceding states, even before as well as after the ordinances of secession were adopted, the forts, arsenals, and other public property of the United States within their respective limits, where they were unprotected, were seized by the state authorities, or by parties of secessionists, who subsequently turned them over to the states.

Fort Pulaski, below Savannah, was taken possession of by the state troops of Georgia, under orders from the governor, on the 3d of January, although the state did not formally secede until the 19th of the month. On the 24th of the month, after secession, the arsenal at Augusta was compelled to surrender.

The United States arsenal at Mobile, and Fort Morgan, in the harbor of that city, were taken possession of on the 4th of January, the former apparently by an armed mob, and the latter by the state troops of Alabama, who remained in the fort as a garrison. The state did not secede until the 11th of the same month. The Apalachicola arsenal and Fort Marion, at St. Augustine, were seized on the 5th and 7th of January, some days before Florida seceded. The arsenal at Little Rock, Arkansas, was also taken possession of by the authorities of that state, though secession was not yet determined on.

The United States Marine Hospital, below New Orleans, was taken by a party of Louisiana state troops, January 11th, two weeks before the state seceded. Upwards of two hundred patients, sick or disabled seamen, were ordered to be removed; those who were convalescent immediately, and those who were confined to their beds as soon as possible. This cruel action was justified by the authorities on the ground that they wanted the hospital as quarters for their troops. The inhuman and base act was aggravated by the fact that the hospital was not a military or naval establishment, but a charitable institution for the benefit of seamen in the merchant service, and maintained, under the care of the United States, by dues levied on the merchant marine. On the same day, the national arsenal and barracks at Baton Rouge were surrounded by another force of Louisiana troops, and the small force stationed there was obliged to surrender, the officers and men carrying away their arms and equipments, and personal effects.

At Pensacola, on the 12th of January, the day before the adoption of the secession ordinance by the Florida convention, bodies of Florida and Alabama troops, surrounding the navy yard, demanded the surrender of that station. Commodore Armstrong, the commandant of the yard, having no sufficient means of resistance, and finding the assailing forces had possession of the magazine and the entrances to the yard, was compelled to surrender. With a few exceptions, the officers and men employed in the yard sympathized with the secessionists, and some of them were traitors. Nearly all of these, immediately upon the surrender, transferred their allegiance from the United States to the state of Florida. The small marine guard were the only men upon whom could be placed any reliance. A party of "ordinary men" had, the day previous, been sent to Fort Pickens.

The government, upon the accession of Mr. Holt to the war department, and when the purpose to seize United States property was manifested, had sent orders to Pensacola for the protection of the navy yard and the forts which guarded the harbor. These orders,

transmitted by telegraph, were brief and indefinite; but they were made known to the secessionists, and a special messenger who carried more particular orders in writing, was intercepted, and his despatches taken possession of, the navy yard having already surrendered. A small garrison was in Fort Barrancas, under the command of Lieutenant Slemmer. Upon receiving the orders telegraphed, and seeing the indications of an intention to take possession here, as had been done elsewhere, that officer followed the example of Major Anderson, and transferred his garrison, with all the stores and ammunition that he could transport, from Fort Barrancas, which would have proved untenable, to Fort Pickens, on Santa Rosa Island. This fortification was one of the strongest on the whole coast, and was easily accessible by sea, without exposure to the other forts of the harbor. In transferring his force, with ordnance and provisions, Lieutenant Slemmer fortunately had the assistance of two United States vessels, the steamer Wyandotte and storeship Supply, which were at the navy yard, and he was also reënforced by about fifty men from the yard. The intention of the state troops of Florida and Alabama was to have seized Fort Pickens, and forced a surrender of Barrancas, and they were greatly disappointed that Lieutenant Slemmer had been too watchful and too efficient to permit their purposes to be carried out. He was now in a strong position, by which he had command of the harbor, and could easily be reënforced. An immediate attack was proposed, but more prudent counsels prevailed. Fort Barrancas, however, was taken possession of by the state forces, on the same day on which the navy yard was surrendered. Fort Pickens was quietly reënforced by the government, and means were furnished to put it in a more complete state of defence, the work not being entirely finished or supplied with its armament. Before they were reënforced, Lieutenant Slemmer and his garrison labored incessantly to strengthen their position, and suffered much from their watchfulness and labors. The importance of the movement has since been realized and appreciated by the country.

Not only were the forts, arsenals, and other United States property on the land thus taken possession of, but the revenue cutters were, through the treachery of their commanders and the collectors of the customs, transferred to the authorities of the seceding states. The betrayal of the revenue cutter at Charleston has already been mentioned. Similar treachery was practised at Galveston, Mobile, and New Orleans. After the loss of the vessel at Charleston, measures were taken to secure the other cutters stationed at the ports of states proposing to secede. The cutter at Savannah, after being ordered to Baltimore, was seized by a party of secessionists, acting without any state authority, as has been observed in a previous chapter. Being restored by the governor of Georgia, the vessel proceeded on her voyage, and was saved. A special agent was despatched to Mobile and New Orleans to secure the cutters there. The commander of the cutter, McClelland, had been ordered by the collector of New Orleans to proceed with his vessel to that city, with the view of securing it for Louisiana. That officer, it appeared, was very ready to join in the treachery. When the special agent arrived at New Orleans, and gave orders direct from the treasury department for the commander of the cutter to proceed with his vessel immediately to New York, the latter absolutely refused to obey the order. Upon being informed of this refusal, the secretary of the treasury (Mr. Dix, who had been but a few days in office) sent a despatch directing the second officer to assume command of the cutter; if the recusant commander interfered, to arrest him as a mutineer, and to shoot any one who attempted to pull down the American flag. This despatch, however, failed to reach its destination, and the special agent was unable to secure the vessel. Proceeding to Mobile, he found that the cutter there had already been betrayed into the hands of the state authorities by the officer in command.

But the most extensive surrender of United States property was made by General Twiggs, who betrayed, on the demand of the authorities of Texas, all the military posts in that state, together with all the ordnance and commissary stores, and other military property, the value of which was upwards of a million of dollars. Having surrendered these posts, and the property contained in them, the commanding general ordered his subordinates to carry out the treason. There were among the officers not a few secessionists and traitors, but there were some who refused to obey such orders. Some of these were subsequently compelled to surrender, and others on the frontier succeeded in taking their commands out of the state safely. For this treachery to his country General Twiggs was dismissed in disgrace from the service, but his treason was rewarded by a command in the confederate service.

Secession thus seemed to destroy all sense of honor, and even of common honesty, among those who espoused its cause. All these forts, arsenals, military stores, and other public property of the United States were seized as if they were the property of an alien enemy, instead of the government to which these states owed allegiance, and had not yet, in some instances, even declared themselves absolved from it. The voluntary surrender, by military, naval, and revenue officers, of the property which they were sworn to protect, was base treason, and an utter abandonment of that honor which is supposed to be so tenderly guarded by men in such positions.

CHAPTER XVIII.

ONE of the most alarming signs of the progress of secession was the condition of Washington during the winter of 1860–1. In the various departments were many men who were from the south, or were connected with southern families, or were under the influence of southern men ; and a large proportion of these, in view of the changes which a new administration would make among its employés, were disposed to attach themselves to the secessionists, or sympathized with them so heartily that they were in fact enemies of the government which was giving them support. The sympathies of Washington society were also on the side of secession. That society was southern in its characteristics ; its leaders were for the most part southern families sojourning there, or those permanent residents who were allied to southern families, or who, from the very force of fashion, imbibed those sentiments and prejudices which southern society constantly asserted. Besides being opposed to the political sentiments of the northern party which had elected the incoming president, it could not tolerate the elevation to the first place in the republic, and in the capital, of a man of the people — one who did not belong to an aristocratic family, but was self-made, and reputed not to possess many of the graces of polished

society. The feeling among the women who moved prominently in this society — or assumed to do so — was by no means so gentle as elegance and refinement should have made it. It was a bitter prejudice, nourished in part, perhaps, by the probable effect of the change of administration on the interests of their husbands or families, but arising from the aristocratic notions of the degradation of labor, and antipathy to any thing which called in question the institution on which their aristocracy rested. It was but a short step from this feeling to a hearty and demonstrative sympathy with secession, and such a sympathy was soon aiding the disunion cause. Had the administration been from the start vigorously opposed to secession and all kindred action, its influence might have prevented, in some measure, the spread of this social poison. But the families of members of the cabinet, as well as of senators, were alike leaders in the social circle in this evil example. The aid thus received by the secession cause from men and women in the highest society at Washington was not small. It extended wherever the influence of that society extended, among officials in the departments and officers of the army and navy, leading men, whose loyalty would otherwise have been unquestionable, either to forswear their allegiance, or yield to the government only a cold support.

Upon the secession of South Carolina it was apparent that in Washington, and all about it in Maryland and Virginia, there were many disunionists ready to coöperate with secession wherever it might appear. The presence of so many men from the seceding states who still remained in Washington, as well as the influence of society there, as before mentioned, strengthened and increased this class. Loyal men naturally became alarmed, and it was soon found that there was reason for such alarm. Numerous facts came to light which indicated a purpose somewhere, if opportunity should offer, to prevent the inauguration of the president elect, if not to seize the capital itself, and hold it for the further purposes of the secessionists. That such a purpose was contemplated there was good reason to believe; but by whom, to what extent it was organized, and how far it was countenanced by the leading secessionists, it was difficult to ascertain. A special committee of the house was instructed to inquire into the facts, to ascertain if any attempt to seize the public buildings was contemplated. But the inquiries of this committee were such as could hardly be expected to develop the existence of the alleged plot, unless within the knowledge of officials.

There was in Washington a military organization known as the "National Volunteers," which was composed of members of a political association of the recent canvass, devoted to the interests of the Breckinridge party. It was generally believed that this organization, the sympathies of its members being with the secessionists, was designed to take part in any demonstration such as was feared. There were no facts ascertained, however, which showed any purpose or preparation on their part to commit acts of violence. In Maryland and Virginia, too, there were sundry military organizations, some authorized by the state laws, and others formed without legal authority, which were armed and drilled as if in preparation for some service. But it did not appear that any of these had a definite purpose. It was evident, however, from the character of these organizations and the political sentiments of the members, that it would need only a signal from influential disunionists, or some sudden excitement, to call them into active demonstrations for the resistance of the inauguration or the overthrow of the government. Vague rumors of such a purpose were constantly in circulation; secession newspapers contained frequent threats of violence, and advice for forcible resistance to the inaugura-

tion,* and there were conferences at Washington, and other movements among the avowed secessionists of Maryland and Virginia, which indicated a readiness, if not a plot, to carry out the advice and the threats.

It should be remembered that at this time there were large numbers of people at the north, who, through political partisanship or social or business relations, sympathized with the south, and, though they may not have approved of disunion, yet, by sympathy with disunionists in their alleged causes for dissatisfaction, gave the latter reason to suppose that the north would be divided on the question of disunion, as it had been on other questions. The tone of a portion of the northern press † — a

---

* The following from the Richmond (Va.) Examiner of December 17, 1860, a paper of great influence in Virginia, is a specimen of the articles referred to : —

"If any commissioners are appointed by the legislature, they should be sent first to Maryland, to confer with that state upon the plan of resisting the inauguration of Mr. Lincoln. It is the duty of Maryland and Virginia to take earnest and decided steps to prevent the government from going into Republican hands. There is now no hope of preserving the Union, and by the 4th of March there will be little use for any federal government. It would be the greatest folly for Virginia and Maryland to permit the army, navy, and treasury to pass into the hands of those who will use them for the subjugation of those states. Let the first convention, then, be held between Maryland and Virginia, and, these two states agreeing, let them provide sufficient force to seize the city of Washington, and, if coercion is to be attempted, let it begin with subjugating the states of Maryland and Virginia. Thus practical and efficient fighting in the Union will prevent the powers of the Union from falling into the hands of our enemies. We hope Virginia will depute her commissioners to Maryland first, and, providing for the seizure of Washington city, Forts McHenry, Washington, and Old Point, Harper's Ferry and Gosport Navy Yard, present these two states in the attitude of rebels inviting coercion. This was the way Patrick Henry brought about the revolution, and this is the best use that Virginia can make of commissioners of any kind."

† The New York Day Book, a Democratic paper, which had supported Breckinridge, contained the following article, quite sufficient to encourage the secessionists in their schemes : —

"Will Lincoln be inaugurated?—Every intelligent mind in the nation is now revolving this inquiry, and, as day after day passes by, it becomes more and more apparent that Abraham Lincoln will not be inaugurated president of the republic founded by Washington and Jefferson. The white laboring men of New York and other northern cities should rally to a man to prevent a destiny so horrible, a treason so monstrous, a crime so hideous,

small portion, happily — and of the speeches of certain public men, led the secessionists to believe that in case of any collision they would not only receive aid from the northern states, but that civil war, if it came, must arise among the people of those states. A military or political organization here and there, of questionable origin and purpose, gave some color to this supposition, which appears to have entered into the consideration of all the schemes of the secessionists.

The special committee were of opinion that all the rumored designs upon the capital were contingent upon the secession of Maryland or Virginia. In their report they said, —

"Too much diversity of opinion seems to have existed to admit of the adoption of any well-organized plan, until some of the states commenced to reduce their theories of secession to practice. Since then persons thus disaffected seem to have adopted the idea that all resistance to the government, if there is to be any, should have at least the color of state authority. If the purpose was at any time entertained of forming an organization, secret or open, to seize the District of Columbia, attack the Capitol, or prevent the inauguration of Mr. Lincoln, it seems to have been rendered contingent upon

the secession of either Maryland or Virginia, or both, and the sanction of one of those states.

"Certain organizations in this district and in Maryland, that prior to the election seem to have been only political clubs, have since assumed the character of military organizations, are now engaged in drilling, and expect to provide themselves with arms, some from the state authorities, and others from private subscriptions. But so far as the committee were able to learn their purposes, while they sympathized strongly with secession, there is no proof that they intend to attack either the capital or the District, unless the surrender should be demanded by a state to which they profess a high degree of allegiance. Some of these companies in Baltimore profess to be drilling for the sole purpose of preventing other military companies from passing through the state of Maryland. Whether these representations of the purposes of these companies be correct or not, the committee have failed to discover any satisfactory evidence that they have any purpose whatever, as a mere mob, without the sanction of state authority, to attack the Capitol, or any other public property in this District, or to seize the District."

Although the Congressional committee discovered no secret plot, definite and organized, for the seizure of the capital, there was sufficient evidence before the administration of such a purpose, on the part of the secessionists, to lead to the adoption of measures for the defeat of its execution. General Scott was consulted, and by his advice a military force was quietly and gradually brought to Washington and the military posts in the vicinity, and the militia of the District of Columbia was organized. It was found that not a few of the officers of this militia were secessionists, and a new organization was required, which was put under the charge of Captain Charles Stone, an officer of the regular army, who had served with distinction in the Mexican war. Volunteers were also organized for the defence of the city and public property.

---

as that now attempted by the party supporting Lincoln. They should organize as minute-men at once, and declare to the world that they will march at a moment's notice to put down and crush out any man or any party that attempts 'impartial freedom,' or to include negroes in our political system.

"It is a terrible alternative; but self-preservation, as well as self-respect, demands that Maryland and Virginia shall never permit their territory to be occupied by those who vow in advance to revolutionize their society, and establish nigger equality, or 'impartial freedom.' We trust, however, that this will be done with the gravity and the prudence that the occasion demands — that the Virginian and Maryland delegates in Washington will submit resolutions to Congress that shall test perfectly and beyond mistake the true purposes and real policy of the 'anti-slavery' or Republican party. If that party will disavow a free-negro policy, and declare that it will never place the government in conflict with southern society, and that this is a white man's government, in which the negro has no part or parcel whatever, then we should apprehend that no obstacles would be likely to be in the way of Lincoln's inauguration on the 4th of March."

18

138 HISTORY OF THE UNITED STATES.

The preparations made by General Scott were violently condemned by disloyal men, and produced some irritation among that class of the residents of Washington. Each day, however, convinced the loyal that the preparations were wise and prudent, if not absolutely necessary, and would, at least, prevent an outbreak or attempt at violence, which might be invited by a want of preparation and weakness on the part of the government.

It was rumored that one plan of those who conspired to overthrow the constitutional government, was to prevent the formal announcement of the votes of the presidential electors, and the declaration of the election as prescribed by the constitution. But if such a purpose was ever entertained, the preparations made by the officers of Congress at the Capitol, and by General Scott in the city, deterred its authors from any attempt to put into execution a scheme which promised little success. The two houses met in convention, and the certificates of the electors having been examined and announced in due form by a joint committee, Vice-President Breckinridge declared that "Abraham Lincoln, of Illinois, having received a majority of the whole number of electoral votes, is duly elected president of the United States for the four years commencing on the 4th of March, 1861." A similar declaration was made that Hannibal Hamlin, of Maine, was chosen vice-president of the United States for the same term. The threatened danger having been avoided in this case, and another of the constitutional steps safely taken towards the inauguration of a president constitutionally elected, the loyal people experienced a sense of relief — not so much on account of the escape from danger, as the fact that no attempt was made to interrupt the execution of the requirements of the constitution.

The next danger feared was an armed resistance to the inauguration of the president elect. This had been threatened and counselled by one class of men in the border states, whose sympathies were with the extreme southern party, but who were disposed to regard the condition of the country in a party view, the remedy for which was to compel the triumphant party to abandon the government, and submit to the dictation of such amendments to the constitution as the southern party desired; and by another class, who were in favor of disunion, but who would like to obtain possession of the capital, the archives, finances, and all the insignia of government, and thus make the northern states appear the seceders. A successful blow here and at this time, before the Republican administration could be installed, with most of the departments of government in the hands of sympathizers, was one which at first promised as successful a result as had attended the secession movement at the south. But the changes in the cabinet had rendered the chances of success very doubtful, and the determination of the administration and of General Scott to maintain the government and the constitution, probably caused the scheme to be abandoned. General Scott made preparations to meet any such emergency, by the disposal of troops in Washington in a manner to secure its safety except from a force greater than was likely to be brought against it. In doing this he did not always meet with the approval of the president, who was averse to displaying any considerable military force. The president, however, declared his determination that the government should be maintained, and his successor duly inaugurated.

While the proper precautions were taken to guard against any revolutionary attempt, or any riotous proceedings which might lead to serious results, there was reason to believe, from knowledge which came to General Scott and to Mr. Lincoln's friends in Washington, that on his journey to the capital there might be an attempt on his life, either by direct assassination or by throwing the railroad train in which he travelled from the track. The idea of such a plot being conceived and attempted was by most persons, except the very credulous, considered improbable. But there were reasons, known to those then best acquainted with the secret history of secession, for taking unusual precautions along the entire route by which Mr. Lincoln travelled. These precautions were the means of guarding against most serious accident in several instances, the preparation for which was but too surely designed and made for the special train in which the party of the president elect were conveyed. That there was such a plot for accomplishing the death or fatal injury of Mr. Lincoln can now, when the character of secession and its supporters has been realized, be more readily believed. All through the south have been the most wicked and cruel cases of violence and murder for opinion's sake. The remedy thus applied to obnoxious parties would naturally be suggested to certain minds as one to be used in this case, which they believed of so much more serious a nature; and certainly it would be no difficult thing to find among the inhabitants of a great city men who would mature the suggestion and carry it into execution. The suggestion had been repeatedly made in southern papers, and even if no plot had been carefully matured, a riot might afford facilities and provocations for accomplishing a purpose only half determined on, but ardently desired by many who would have scorned to be privy to such a scheme.

Mr. Lincoln had extended his journey to New York, and arrived safely at Philadelphia, having been received with honors due to his position as president elect. He was accompanied by his family and several friends from his own state, and by Colonel Sumner, who had been detailed by order of General Scott to attend him. At Philadelphia he was met by a special messenger from Washington, who bore an urgent request for him to proceed at once, privately, to that city. Having engaged to take part in the ceremony of raising the American flag in Independence Square on the following day, and also

to visit the legislature at Harrisburg, he could not be prevailed upon to break these engagements; but after having fulfilled them, he agreed to proceed at once to Washington, avoiding any delay or public reception at Baltimore. This he did, accompanied by only two or three friends, taking the regular night train from Philadelphia to Washington, where he arrived early in the morning of February 23d, and was met by some friends, who took him to the quarters prepared for him.* His family, and the other members of his party, proceeded in the special train intended for his conveyance. At Baltimore there were some disorderly demonstrations; Mr. Lincoln having already proceeded privately to Washington, and Mrs. Lincoln and family having left the train at a station out of town to partake of the hospitalities of a friend, there was no opportunity, if there had been a disposition, to make any riotous assault upon the party. The committee of Baltimore republicans who had been to meet Mr. Lincoln, and others of the party, received some indignities, but were protected from real harm by the police. The municipal authorities of Baltimore had taken measures to prevent any riotous demonstrations, but subsequent events in that city induce the belief that the protection of its police, on an occasion involving a display of so much bitter feeling, would be very uncertain at least. To the order-loving people of that city, as elsewhere, it was a source of congratulation that Mr. Lincoln was safe in Washington. The only disappointment expressed was on the part of those disposed to riot, and that portion of the press which was most bitterly opposed to the president elect.

This sudden and secret movement of Mr. Lincoln was the subject of much speculation and some condemnation, though the latter was gen-

* The story that Mr. Lincoln travelled in disguise has been pronounced untrue by those who were acquainted with the facts. He wore an ordinary travelling dress.

erally expressed by his political opponents, rather than his friends. The reasons suggested were various. One was, that his friends in Washington considered that his immediate presence there was imperatively demanded. Another was, that there was danger of riotous proceedings in Baltimore, on the occasion of his arrival there according to the published programme of his journey. Still another was, that a plot to assassinate the president elect, on his passage through Baltimore, had been discovered; and it was to evade this that the change had been made. It is probable that both of these latter reasons weighed with the advisers of Mr. Lincoln. A statement subsequently published in a journal* which had facilities for becoming acquainted with the facts, asserted that a conspiracy to assassinate Mr. Lincoln had actually been discovered. It was said that Mr. Lincoln's friends, having heard of such conspiracy, employed a detective of great experience to investigate the matter, and that he, with the aid of other detectives, discovered not only the existence of the plot, but the parties to it, and their plans. These plans, as narrated, were, should Mr. Lincoln pass safely over the railroad to Baltimore, (it being asserted that there was a plot to throw the special train in which he was expected to travel from the track,) that the conspirators should mingle with the crowd that might surround his carriage, and by pretending to be his friends, be enabled to approach his person. At a given signal, some of them were to shoot at Mr. Lincoln with pistols, while others would throw into the carriage hand-grenades similar to those used in an attempt to assassinate the Emperor Louis Napoleon, the assailants expecting to escape in the confusion which would ensue, and be carried to Mobile. This plot, it was stated, was revealed to Mr. Lincoln at Philadelphia, and the revelation induced the change of plans by which the

*Albany Evening Journal.

plot was foiled. It was further stated, that General Scott and Mr. Seward had been apprised, from other sources, that imminent danger threatened Mr. Lincoln if he should publicly pass through Baltimore; and Mr. Seward's son was accordingly despatched to Philadelphia, to urge the president elect to come directly to Washington, in a private manner. It was difficult to believe, that in this country such a conspiracy could be entered into, and such plans laid for assassination; but, as before observed, the events which have since transpired, and the desperate character of many men to be found in a city like Baltimore, render it less incredible now than at that time.

Mr. Lincoln's presence in Washington appeared to have a favorable effect. The country felt relieved that thus far there had been no obstruction to the usual course of events attending a change of administration in the government, and it was hoped that Mr. Lincoln's conservative views would disarm some of the bitter prejudices against him and his party. He was received with the respect due to his position, and was waited upon by the heads of departments, members of Congress, and the "peace convention," which was still in session. Although he did not indicate the policy which he should pursue with regard to secession, yet his general conservative opinions, so far as he expressed them, gave confidence to all who really desired the preservation of the Union, or who were not blinded by political partisanship. Public attention was now in a measure directed to the views and policy of Mr. Lincoln, and the cabinet which he would form. Men seemed to feel assured that the inauguration would take place without any attempt to prevent it, or to disturb the peace. But for this they relied on the preparations which General Scott was known to have made. Meanwhile the friends of secession, encouraged by the action of the "cotton states," were not idle, nor any better disposed towards the president elect. Their schemes, so far as Washington was concerned, may have been changed, in view of the preparations made by the government and the friends of the incoming administration; but they were none the less active in their exertions for the dismemberment of the Union, scouting all idea of a peaceful adjustment of the questions at issue, either through the action of Congress or the peace convention; and ready to avail themselves of any conflict which might arise between the government and the seceded states, to force the border states into the disunion movement.

CHAPTER XIX.

The Confederate Convention at Montgomery. — Framing and adoption of a Constitution for a Provisional Government. — Preamble and Provisions. — Election and Inauguration of Provisional President and Vice-President. — Inaugural Address of Mr. Davis. — Mr. Stephens. — Cabinet Officers. — Further Measures adopted by the Convention. — The Constitution not submitted to the People. — Principles of the Southern Confederacy. — Speech by Mr. Stephens.

THE convention of delegates from the seceded states, which had been agreed to by the several conventions of those states, assembled at Montgomery, Alabama, on the 4th of February. Six of the seceded states were represented. The secession ordinance of Texas had not been voted upon by the people of that state, and it had not yet sent delegates. There were also present commissioners from several of the slave states which had not seceded. The first business was the framing of a constitution for a provisional government of the confederacy of seceding states. For this the constitution of the United States was taken as the basis, and such modifications were made as should adapt it to the purposes of the secessionists. One distinctive feature was embodied in the opening declaration, in which the language indicating a union of the people was carefully avoided, and supplied by that which should distinctly show that their association was what the southern politi-

cians had always maintained the Union to be — simply a confederation of sovereign states.

The title of the instrument was, "The Constitution for the Provisional Government of the Confederate States of America." The introductory declaration was, "We, the deputies of the sovereign, independent states of South Carolina, Georgia, Florida, Alabama, Mississippi, and Louisiana, invoking the favor of the Almighty, hereby, in behalf of the states, ordain and establish this constitution for a provisional government of the same, to continue one year from the inauguration of the president, or until a permanent constitution or confederacy be put into operation." The seventh section provided that "the importation of African negroes from any foreign country other than the slaveholding states of the United States, is hereby forbidden; and Congress is required to pass such laws as shall effectually prevent the same." It also provided that "Congress shall also have power to prohibit the introduction of slaves from any state not a member of this Confederacy." Provision was made for the rendition of fugitive slaves, and for the settlement by the new government "of all matters between the states forming it and their late confederates of the United States, in relation to the public property and public debt, at the time of their withdrawal from them." Most of the other provisions were substantially the same as those in the constitution of the United States. This constitution was unanimously adopted, and was put into operation at once.

The constitution having been adopted, the convention elected Jefferson Davis, of Mississippi, provisional president, and Alexander H. Stephens, of Georgia, provisional vice-president of the Confederacy. These officers were inaugurated on the 18th of February, with much parade and enthusiastic demonstrations on the part of the people. Mr. Davis delivered an inaugural address, of which the following are the most important passages: —

" Our present condition, achieved in a manner unprecedented in the history of nations, illustrates the American idea that governments rest upon the consent of the governed, — and that it is the right of the people to alter and abolish governments whenever they become destructive of the ends for which they were established. The declared compact of the Union from which we have withdrawn was to establish justice, insure domestic tranquillity, provide for the common defence, promote the general welfare, and secure the blessings of liberty to ourselves and our posterity; and when, in the judgment of the sovereign states now composing this Confederacy, it has been perverted from the purposes for which it was ordained, and ceased to answer the ends for which it was established, a peaceful appeal to the ballot-box declared that, so far as they were concerned, the government created by that compact should cease to exist. In this they merely asserted the right which the Declaration of Independence of 1776 defined to be inalienable. Of the time and occasion for the exercise of this right, they, as sovereigns, were the final judges, each for itself The impartial and enlightened verdict of mankind will vindicate the rectitude of our conduct; and He who knows the hearts of men will judge of the sincerity with which we labored to preserve the government of our fathers in its spirit.

"The right of the states solemnly proclaimed at the birth of the United States, and which has been affirmed and reaffirmed in the bills of rights of the states subsequently admitted to the Union of 1789, undeniably recognizes in the people the power to resume the authority delegated for the purposes of government. Thus the sovereign states here represented proceeded to form this Confederacy, and it is by an abuse of language that their act has been denominated revolution. They have formed a new alliance, but within each of the states its government has remained. The rights of per-

son and property have not been disturbed. The agent through which they communicated with foreign nations is changed, but this does not necessarily interrupt their international relations. Sustained by the consciousness that the transition from the former Union to the present Confederacy has not proceeded from a disregard on our part of our just obligations, or any failure to perform every constitutional duty; moved by no interest or passion to invade the rights of others; anxious to cultivate peace and commerce with all nations, — if we may not hope to avoid war, we may at least expect that posterity will acquit us of having needlessly engaged in it. Doubly justified by the absence of wrong on our part, and by wanton aggression on the part of others, there can be no cause for doubt that the courage and patriotism of the people of the Confederate States will be found equal to any measures of defence which soon their security may require.

" An agricultural people, whose chief interest is the export of a commodity required by every manufacturing country, our true policy is peace and the freest trade which our necessities will permit. It is alike our interest and that of all those to whom we would sell, and from whom we would buy, that there should be the fewest possible restrictions upon an interchange of commodities. There can be but little rivalry between ours and any manufacturing or navigating community, such as the north-eastern states of the American Union. It must therefore follow that mutual interests would invite good will and kind offices. If, however, passion or lust of dominion should cloud the judgment or inflame the ambition of those states, we must prepare to meet the emergency and maintain by the final arbitrament of the sword the position which we have assumed among the nations of the earth. We have entered upon a career of independence, which must be inflexibly pursued through many years of controversy with our late associates of the northern states.

We have vainly endeavored to secure tranquillity and obtain respect for the rights to which we were entitled. As a necessity, not a choice, we have resorted to the remedy of a separation, and henceforth our energies must be directed to conduct our own affairs, and promote the perpetuity of the Confederacy we have formed. If a just perception of mutual interests shall permit us peaceably to pursue our separate political career, my most earnest desire will have been fulfilled. But if this be denied us, and the integrity of our territory and jurisdiction be assailed, it will but remain for us with a firm resolve to appeal to arms, and invoke the blessing of Providence upon a just cause.

"As a consequence of our new condition, and with a view to meet anticipated wants, it will be necessary to provide for the speedy and efficient organization of the branches of the executive department having special charge of foreign intercourse, finance, military affairs, and postal service. For purposes of defence, the Confederate States may, under ordinary circumstances, rely mainly upon their militia; but it is deemed advisable, under the present condition of affairs, that there should be a well instructed and disciplined army, more numerous than would usually be required on a peace establishment.

"I also suggest that for the protection of our harbors and commerce on the high seas a navy adapted to those objects will be required. These necessities have doubtless engaged the attention of Congress.   *   *   *

"Actuated solely by a desire to preserve our own rights and promote our own welfare, the separation of the Confederate States has been marked by no aggressions upon others, and has been followed by no domestic convulsions. Our industrial pursuits have received no check; the cultivation of our fields progresses as heretofore, and even should we be involved in a war there would be no considerable diminution of the staples which constitute our exports, and in

which the commercial world has an interest scarcely less than our own. This common interest of producer and consumer can only be intercepted by exterior force which should obstruct its transmission to foreign markets — a course of conduct which would be detrimental to the manufacturing and commercial interests abroad. Should reason guide the action of the government from which we have separated, a policy so detrimental to the civilized world, and the northern states included, would not be followed. But should it be otherwise, a terrible responsibility will rest upon it, and the sufferings of millions will bear testimony to the folly and wickedness of our aggressors. In the mean time there will remain to us besides the ordinary remedies before suggested, well-known sources of retaliation upon the commerce of an enemy."

Mr. Stephens accepted the office to which the convention had elected him with expressions of hearty allegiance to the new confederacy, as calculated to secure more perfectly the peace, prosperity, and domestic tranquillity of the south. The first movements for secession he had strenuously opposed, and in a speech made but three months previous to this election, he had declared that it was his settled conviction that the government of the United States, though not without its defects, "comes nearer the objects of all good government than any other on the face of the earth" — that it was "a model republic, the best that the history of the world gives us any account of;" and he asked, "Where will you go, following the sun in his circuit round the globe, to find a government that better protects the liberties of the people, and secures to them the blessings which we enjoy?"

Mr. Davis, after his inauguration, nominated for his cabinet, Mr. Toombs, of Georgia, secretary of state, Mr. Memminger, of South Carolina, secretary of the treasury, and Mr. L. Pope Walker, of Alabama, secretary of war. These nominations were confirmed, and the new government entered upon the functions assigned to it. The convention proceeded to make further arrangements for the establishment of the provisional government by providing for the election of a Congress and the passage of ordinances and laws immediately necessary for putting their constitution into operation. Among other measures which they adopted was an act declaring the navigation of the Mississippi River free. A flag for the Confederacy was also adopted, consisting of a blue field, with stars representing the number of states, in the upper corner, as in the American flag, and three horizontal stripes, or "bars," of red, white, and red. As the several states had seceded, they had raised their own flags, generally a representation of the state arms; and the Confederate flag was not adopted with universal satisfaction, either because of its similarity to the old flag which had so long waved over them, and to which an unaccountable antipathy had arisen, or because of the notions of state sovereignty which lay at the bottom of secession.

The constitution and government thus established were not submitted to the people for ratification in any way, but were ratified by the conventions or legislatures of the several states interested. This was the occasion of some discontent among those who did not belong to the ultra secession party, but it was in accordance with the principles and plans upon which the scheme of secession was conceived and carried out. Among the leaders there was an apparent distrust of the people, who were to be controlled and governed rather than to be constituents and the origin of power.

The principles upon which this southern Confederacy was established, were set forth and vindicated in a speech made by Mr. Stephens, the vice-president of the confederacy, at Savannah, and which may justly be considered as an authoritative exposition, both because of his position, and because of the comparatively moder-

ate views which he had previously expressed. After specifying certain differences between the constitution of the United States and that adopted by the seceding states, in praising which it may be observed he was by no means consistent with his previous public record, he continued: —

" But not to be tedious in enumerating the numerous changes for the better, allow me to allude to one other — though last, not least: the new constitution has put at rest *forever* all the agitating questions relating to our peculiar institutions — African slavery as it exists among us — the proper *status* of the negro in our form of civilization. This was the immediate cause of the late rupture and present revolution.[*] Jefferson, in his forecast, had anticipated this as the 'rock upon which the old Union would split.' He was right. What was conjecture with him is now a realized fact. But whether he fully comprehended *the great truth upon which that rock stood and stands*, may be doubted. *The prevailing ideas entertained by him and most of the leading statesmen at the time of the formation of the old constitution were, that the enslavement of the African was in violation of the laws of nature; that it was wrong in principle, socially, morally, and politically.* It was an evil they knew not well how to deal with; but the general opinion of the men of that day was, that, somehow or other, in the order of Providence, the institution would be evanescent, and pass away. This idea, though not incorporated in the constitution, was the prevailing idea at the time. The constitution, it is true, secured every essential guaranty to the institution while it should last, and hence no argument can be justly used against the constitutional guaranties thus secured, because of the common sentiment of the day. *Those ideas, however, were fundamentally wrong.* They rested upon the assumption of the equality of the

---

* The secessionists have generally insisted that secession was not revolution, but the simple exercise of reserved rights.

races. This was an error. It was a sandy foundation, and the idea of a government built upon it — when the 'storm came and the wind blew, it *fell.'*

. "*Our new government is founded upon exactly the opposite ideas ; its foundations are laid, its corner-stone rests, upon the great truth that the negro is not equal to the white man ; that slavery, subordination to the superior race, is his natural and normal condition. This, our new government, is the first in the history of the world based upon this great physical, philosophical, and moral truth.* This truth has been slow in the process of its development, like all other truths in the various departments of science. It is so even amongst us. Many who hear me, perhaps, can recollect well that this truth was not generally admitted, even within their day. The errors of the past generation still clung to many as late as twenty years ago.,   *   *   *

"In the conflict thus far, success has been on our side, complete throughout the length and breadth of the Confederate States. It is upon this, as I have stated, our social fabric is firmly planted ; and I cannot permit myself to doubt the ultimate success of a full recognition of this principle throughout the civilized and enlightened world."

CHAPTER XX.

Close of Mr. Buchanan's Administration. — His Policy with regard to Secession and its Effect. — Review of the Condition of the Government. — Finances. — The War Department. — The Army. — The Navy. — Lack of Available Force. — Report of Congressional Committee on the Subject. — The Civil Service. — Foreign Ministers and Secession Emissaries. — Sympathy for Secessionists at the North. — Conclusion.

THUS had the rebellion made rapid progress and attained to the most formidable dimensions before the termination of Mr. Buchanan's administration. Seven states had adopted secession ordinances, and had formed a confederacy in rebellion against the authority of the United States. They had organized military forces, seized forts, arsenals, and other public property of the Union, and were making every preparation that they could to maintain their position by a war. This they had been suffered to do without any adequate action on the part of the government to prevent it. Had the government been prepared, and taken vigorous measures at the outset, to maintain its authority, though it is not probable that the rebellion would have been wholly stayed, it is reasonable to presume that it would not have made such rapid progress. But for more than a month after the first acts of secession and rebellion, the administration did nothing to maintain the authority committed to its charge and to preserve the Union. It was paralyzed by the presence, in its own councils, of secessionists and traitors, and the too great political sympathy with the leaders of the rebellion on the part of those who were not traitors. Nor can it be denied that Mr. Buchanan's annual message itself gave encouragement to the secessionists. Lamenting what he alleges to be the cause of secession, and deprecating the action of the south, he argued away the authority to prevent it which the loyal nation supposed was in the government. Well might the secessionists hurry on their scheme if there was to be no "coercion" to maintain the authority of the Union, and while they knew that their own friends controlled the administration.

When, at last, Mr. Buchanan seemed to be aroused from his apathy by the evident treachery of members of his cabinet, and called new advisers to council, he was fettered by the opinions which he had expressed, and which he still appeared to entertain, though he saw the Union crumbling around him ; and he was not disposed to adopt to any extent the vigorous policy which some of the new members of his cabinet were supposed to advocate. It is true that under better counsels he adopted more decided measures in relation to the protection of the public property ; but his chief desire seemed to be to prevent any collision between the seceding

19

states and the federal government which might lead to war, or at least to postpone such a calamity until his administration had expired. He hoped for a compromise; he asked for concession to the arrogant power which now not only threatened disunion, but was accomplishing it. But it was too late for any compromise. From the first the leaders of secession would be satisfied with nothing but the subjugation of the political and moral sentiments of the north to their will. Rather than any compromise, they preferred secession and a southern confederacy. The measures of congressional committees, of peace conventions, of states or individuals, were unsatisfactory to them; and their efforts, quite as much as those of the most radical anti-slavery men of the north, were directed to the defeat of any compromise based upon such propositions. They knew well that now was the time to carry out their conspiracy, while there was an administration that would not oppose them. Profiting by Mr. Buchanan's anti-coercive policy, they hurried forward their work during the remnant of his term, in order to be prepared for what might follow.

Disappointed in his hopes of compromise and peace, having done little to maintain the authority of the government, and scarcely more in preserving its property, and regarding the Union as severed beyond all remedy, Mr. Buchanan at last saw his administration come to a close, and yielded the government, surrounded with unexampled difficulties, into the hands of his successor.

At this point it is proper to review the condition in which the government was placed when the rebellion in full-grown proportions was sprung upon it, and it was transmitted to a new administration. As observed in a former chapter, there were traitors in the cabinet who had, for a time at least, controlled its counsels after secession had assumed active measures, and who, it was afterwards discovered, had used their offices and their influence for a long time previous to promote the cause of disunion. The finances of the country had been so conducted that from a large surplus in the treasury at the commencement of Mr. Buchanan's administration the government had become burdened with a debt, and its credit was impaired. Nor did it appear that any efforts on the part of Mr. Cobb in the latter part of his administration of the department were directed to any other purpose than to weaken the government financially.

In the war department, as has been seen, a rank secessionist was plotting disunion. When secession commenced, all his efforts were directed to contribute to its success and to the overthrow of the federal power in the seceding states. But previous to this he had been using his position to strengthen the south for the crisis when it should arise. Upwards of a hundred thousand stand of arms were distributed, without any proper order, to the federal. arsenals in South Carolina, Georgia, Alabama, and Louisiana, where they fell into the hands of the secessionists at the commencement of actual secession, and in such a manner that it would appear to have been a part of the preconcerted plan. In addition to these, arms had been distributed to the southern states for the use of the militia in large excess of those distributed to the northern states. Heavy ordnance was ordered south even while disunion was being accomplished, and when there were no forces in the places to which it was sent to protect it. The little federal army was scattered over the distant frontier in an unusual manner. A considerable force was in Oregon and Washington territory, so far away that they could not be readily used in an emergency. There was also a comparatively large force in Texas, under the command of the traitor Twiggs; and these it was probably expected might, with their general and other officers, be carried over to the side of rebellion, or at least might be so disorganized and divided that they could be rendered of no service to the Union

Scarcely a fort at the north, except on the western frontier, was garrisoned. Moreover, efforts had been made, from the commencement of the plot, to undermine the loyalty of the officers of the army. Many of them — an undue proportion — were of southern birth, or connected with southern families, and all such were either but too ready to forswear their allegiance, or were plied with arguments and glittering inducements to adhere to the south against the Union. The exceptions to this widespread disaffection were entitled to all honor, but they were by no means numerous. It was difficult to know upon whom to rely, for while many of the southern officers resigned their commissions, others, of no less disloyal feelings, still held their commands, waiting only for the actual secession of the states to which they belonged as an excuse for deserting their flag. Thus was the government essentially crippled and deprived of the ability to use its legitimate power to suppress rebellion or protect the public property.

As with the army, so was it with the navy. Mr. Toucey, the secretary of the navy, though a northern man, was of that school of politicians which sympathized heartily with the southern Democracy, in whose ranks secession numbered its most zealous friends. Though not in complicity with these men in their disunion plot, he saw the secession movements going on to open rebellion without taking any measures to prepare his department for resistance, or for the protection of forts and dock yards. When, therefore, the crisis came, there was no naval force at the disposal of the government. Forty-eight vessels were in commission in distant parts of the world; twenty-eight were at the navy yards, unfit for service, and in such a condition as to require weeks or months for the necessary repairs, and no orders were given for such repairs; and there were in January 1861, only two vessels that were available, the steamer Brooklyn, of twenty-five guns, and the storeship Re-

lief, of two guns, the former being unable by reason of her draught to enter Charleston harbor, and the latter being under orders to sail for the coast of Africa. Moreover, while the threats of secession and rebellion were rife, and preparations were being made to carry them into execution, in the months of September and October, 1860, several vessels were despatched to join distant squadrons. At the same time there was, as in the army, disaffection among the southern officers of the navy; some resigned, and others only waited for the action of their states on the question of secession to take a similar, if not a more treasonable, step. The secretary accepted these resignations without objection, notwithstanding some of them were tendered under most suspicious circumstances, and in several cases with apparent haste.

A special committee of the house of representatives were, in January, 1861, instructed to inquire into the condition of the navy, and the circumstances attending the resignations of officers. Their investigation developed the facts above stated. In their report the committee reviewed the condition of affairs as follows: —

"From this statement it will appear that the entire naval force available for the defence of the whole Atlantic coast, at the time of the appointment of this committee, consisted of the steamer Brooklyn, twenty-five guns, and the storeship Relief, two guns, while the former was of too great draught to permit her to enter Charleston harbor with safety, except at spring tides, and the latter was under orders to the coast of Africa, with stores for the African squadron. Thus the whole Atlantic seaboard has been, to all intents and purposes, without defence during all the period of civil commotion and lawless violence to which the president has called our attention as 'of such vast and alarming proportions' as to be beyond his power to check or control.

"It further appears that of the vessels which might have been available for protection or defence in case of any sudden emergency arising at home, now at stations in distant seas or on the way thither, on the 13th of October last the Richmond left our coast to join the Mediterranean squadron; the Vandalia left on the 21st of December to join the East India squadron; and about the same time the Saratoga to join the African squadron; and others to join the home squadron, then in the harbor of Vera Cruz, supporting one of the revolutionary governments of Mexico.

"The committee cannot omit to call attention to this extraordinary disposition of the entire naval force of the country, and especially in connection with the present no less extraordinary and critical juncture of public affairs. They cannot call to mind any period in the past history of the country of such profound peace and internal repose as would justify so entire an abandonment of the coast of the country to the chances of fortune. Certainly, since the nation possessed a navy, it has never sent its entire available force into distant seas, and exposed the immense interests at home, of which it is the special guardian, to the dangers from which, even in times of the utmost quiet, prudence and forecast do always shelter them.

"But the committee cannot shut their eyes to the fact that this remarkable state of things has occurred at a period in our history without a parallel for internal commotion, lawless violence, and total disregard of the authority of the constitution and laws, and of the rights of property, public and private — a state of things which the president himself, in the message referred to this committee, denominated a revolution of 'such vast and alarming proportions as to place the subject entirely above and beyond executive control.' During this period combinations have been formed for the avowed purpose of overthrowing the government itself, and have carried forward that purpose in overt acts of violence never before known in the country. The arms of the government have been seized in arsenals, and other places of deposit, by lawless mobs, and placed in the hands of those in open rebellion. Fortifications have been taken possession of, navy yards plundered, and magazines robbed. The guns of the United States upon the battlements of the national defence have been turned upon unarmed vessels of the government, and the flag of the country fired upon by insolent rebels. The revenue service has been betrayed, and its vessels treacherously surrendered to those who defied the authority of the United States by men holding commissions under the very government they were betraying. The public moneys in the national mints have been seized, and naval stores plundered. The commerce of the country, and the lives of its citizens, have been put in peril by the wanton and lawless destruction of buoys erected to warn the mariner of sunken rocks; and the lights on the coast have been put out that the darkness and the tempest might be invoked in aid of the schemes of those resisting the law. Unarmed and unoffending merchant vessels riding peacefully at anchor in the harbors of the nation, and beneath its own flag, have been seized by insurgent forces in retaliation for obstructions thrown in the way of their revolutionary designs. The law has been defied, the constitution thrust aside, and the government itself assaulted.

"Nor has this state of lawless violence and total disregard of public and private rights been a sudden outburst of passion or discontent at some new and unexpected measure of governmental policy, to which resistance had never been threatened and could not have been provided against. But it is in fulfilment of schemes long entertained and frequently threatened in certain quarters of the Union. Indeed, it is resistance to the law and the constitution consequent upon the election of a particular person to the office of chief magistrate of the nation. Of all this, those charged with the execution of the laws and the preservation of the public peace had ample notice. It was for many months apparent to all but the blind that the whole current of events was turned in the direction which was to bring to the test the sincerity of the threats thus uttered. A chief magistrate of one of the states had, more than two years before, publicly confessed a design on his part, if the like contingency had happened at the general election four years ago, to have made the attempt to overthrow the government by seizing the public arms at Harper's Ferry, and marching upon the capital itself. When the legislature of South Carolina assembled in November last to discharge the constitutional obligation of making choice of electors of president and vice-president, the governor of the state, by special message, recommended that measures should be taken to overthrow that constitution if the choice of the majority did not coincide with her own. In fulfilment of these open threats, overt acts of resistance to the government by bands of lawless men followed the announcement that the people, according to the requirements of the constitution, had made selection of a chief magistrate, for the ensuing four years, not the choice of those who had openly avowed resistance if their own preferences should be disregarded by that majority. From that time to the present the public authority has been defied, and the public rights disregarded. Yet during all this time that most important arm of the public defence, the entire navy, has been beyond the reach of orders, however great the emergency.

"To the committee this disposition of the naval force at this critical time seems most extraordinary. The permitting of vessels to depart for distant seas after these unhappy difficulties had broken out at home ; the omission to put in repair and commission, ready for orders, a single one of the twenty-eight ships dismantled and unfit for service in our own ports, and that, too, while six hundred and forty-six thousand six hundred and thirty-nine dollars and seventy-nine cents of the appropriations for repairs in the navy the present year remained unexpended, were, in the opinion of the committee, grave errors in the administration of the navy department, the consequences of which have been manifest in the many acts of lawless violence to which they have called attention. The committee are of opinion that the secretary had it in his power, with the present naval force of the country at his command, and without materially impairing the efficiency of the service abroad, at any time after the settled purpose of overthrowing the government had become manifest, and before that purpose had developed itself in overt acts of violence, to station at anchor, within reach of his own orders, a force equal to the protection of all the property and all the rights of the government and the citizen, as well as the flag of the country from any outrage or insult, at any point on the entire Atlantic seaboard. The failure to do this is without justification or excuse.

"The attention of the committee was also drawn to the resignations which have taken place among the officers in the navy, caused by the political troubles in which the country is now involved, and the course pursued by the navy department in reference thereto. It will appear, from a 'list of resignations' furnished by the department, and which accompanies this report, that since the election twenty-nine officers in the navy, citizens of the southern disaffected states, have tendered their resignations to the secretary, all of which have been forthwith, and without inquiry, accepted by him. The circumstances under which these resignations have been received and accepted, and the effect of that acceptance, deserve especial notice. That these officers have sought to resign, and relieve themselves from the obligation to the government, imposed by their commissions, because of disaffection and a desire to join, and in many instances to lead, insurgent forces against that government, is notorious. One of them, Lieutenant J. R. Hamilton, a citizen of South Carolina, forwarded his resignation from on board the Wyoming at Panama, dated December 1, 1860. It did not reach the department till the 15th of the same month; and, without inquiry into his conduct, his purpose in resigning, his loyalty, or any circumstance connected with so unusual a proceeding at such a time, his resignation was accepted the same day. He immediately, from Charleston, South Carolina, issued a letter addressed to all the officers in the navy from southern states, urging them to resign and join a hostile force against the government, and that those of them in command should bring with them their vessels into southern ports, and surrender them to the traitors already in arms, taking new commissions under their authority, and then turning their guns upon their own flag.

"Such conduct is nothing less than treason, and has no parallel since the attempt of Benedict Arnold to deliver over important military posts to the enemies of his country. Had the secretary declined to accept the resignation thus tendered, this man would have been subject to the trial and punishment of a court-martial, according to the rules which govern the service, and would have met the fate of a traitor. This extraordinary letter was published throughout the United States. After its circulation in the public prints in Washington, V. M. Randolph, a captain in the navy, a citizen of Alabama, who had been excused from active service for two or three years because of alleged ill health, on the 10th of January, 1861, forwarded from Montgomery, Alabama, his resignation to the secretary. Before twelve o'clock at noon of the 12th, and before his resignation had reached Washington, and while he was still a captain in the navy, he appeared at the gates of the Pensacola navy yard, in Florida, at the head of an insurgent force, and demanded its surrender. The

yard, with whatever of force it had, and the United States stores, and other property, to a vast amount, therein, was unconditionally surrendered to him; and he is now its commandant, occupying the quarters of the late commandant, and granting paroles of honor to such of his prisoners of war as have desired to depart, and not serve under him. The despatch from the late commandant, then a prisoner of war, informing the secretary of this ignominious surrender, was received at the department on the evening of the 13th of January; and the resignation of Captain Randolph, who on the 12th was the leader of the insurgents, did not reach the secretary till the 14th, when, without inquiry or delay, it was immediately accepted.

"E. Farrand, commander in the navy, and also a citizen of Alabama, was the second in command at the Pensacola navy yard, the executive officer of the yard. When the attack was made upon the yard, Farrand met the assailants at the gates by previous understanding, admitted them to the yard, and conducted their leader to the commanding officer; participated in the formal capitulation, and immediately engaged in service under the new commandant of the yard. This was done while he still held in his possession his commission as a commander in the navy. On the 13th or 15th of January, (the department does not know which,) Farrand forwarded his resignation to the secretary, but it did not reach him till the 21st of the same month, seven days after official notice of the surrender had been received at the department. Yet this resignation was immediately, and without inquiry, accepted.

"F. B. Renshaw, a lieutenant in the navy, and a citizen of Florida, was the first lieutenant of the yard, and actively engaged in securing its surrender. It was by his order that the flag was hauled down amid the jeers and shouts of a drunken rabble. He immediately enrolled himself under the leader of the insurgents and present commandant of the yard, and from the day of its surrender has continued under him to discharge the duty of first lieutenant, as before under the United States. Yet he continued to hold his commission as a lieutenant in the navy till the 16th of January, and his resignation did not reach the secretary until the 22d, when, like the others, it was, without inquiry or delay, accepted.

"The conduct of these officers plainly comes within the constitutional definition of treason against the United States, viz., 'levying war against them, or in adhering to their enemies, giving them aid and comfort.' And so long as their resignations were unaccepted by the secretary, they could be tried and punished by a court-martial as traitors. From this they have been relieved by the secretary himself To have done this with a knowledge of their acts, would have been to have involved himself in their crime — would have been to have committed treason himself. To have done it without inquiry, and without reason to know that they have committed no offence, shows a want of that solicitude for the honor and efficiency of the service which is indispensable to its just administration. Yet the resignations of Farrand and Renshaw, and also those of the other officers resigning at the Pensacola navy yard, were all received and accepted after the secretary had already been officially informed that they had surrendered to a lawless band of insurgents; and he had detached them to await orders, having 'neither approved nor disapproved of their conduct, and not proposing to do so without full information touching their conduct in the surrender of the yard.' Why, after having been thus warned, and having taken his position, the secretary did not wait for this 'information,' the committee cannot understand.

"Several other resignations of officers who do not appear to have engaged in actual war against the United States before tendering the same, were nevertheless accepted by the secre-tary with an unnecessary haste which neither the purpose of the resignations nor the times would justify or excuse. Some of them were even accepted by telegraph, when it was perfectly apparent that the object of resigning was to relieve themselves as early as possible from embarrassment and the obligation of the oath of office, as well as summary trial and punishment by a court-martial, previous to joining insurgent forces against the constituted authorities of their country. These resignations, thus accepted, have been followed by immediate engagement in a service hostile to the government.   *   *   *

"The course pursued by the secretary, in thus accepting these resignations, appears, under the circumstances, to be most extraordinary. No custom of the department, in ordinary times, could justify it. No want of confidence in the loyalty of these officers can excuse it; for if their previous conduct had justified any such suspicion, it also demanded investigation beforehand, which would, as to some of them, have disclosed to the secretary their complicity in treason, calling for court-martial rather than honorable discharge. A prudent regard for the public safety would, no doubt, have justified, if not imperiously demanded, that some of these officers should have been early removed from delicate and responsible positions of trust by the substitution of others more reliable. But these very considerations appear to the committee to have forbidden the furnishing any such facilities for engaging in hostilities against the government, as the relief from the summary trial and punishment of a court-martial secured by an acceptance of their resignations.

"The course pursued by the secretary has resulted in furnishing those engaged in an attempt to overthrow the government with the skill, experience, and discipline, which education at the expense of the government, and a long service in the navy, have conferred upon our own officers. The committee cannot understand how this course is consistent with a proper discharge of the duties of his office by the secretary in this critical juncture of affairs. It appears to them to have been attended with consequences the most serious to the service and the country."

In the civil service affairs were in even a worse condition. Nearly all the officers in the seceding states, officers of the customs, postmasters, marshals and district attorneys, refused to recognize the federal government, transferred their allegiance to the rebel authorities, and in many cases retained funds belonging to the United States. In the departments at Washington there were numerous officers and clerks who were implicated in the conspiracy, or were of doubtful loyalty,—sympathizers with the rebellion, and spies into the confidential affairs of the government, ready to use their position for the overthrow of the Union from which they derived support.

Abroad there were diplomatic agents, from plenipotentiaries to *attachés* and consuls, who were using all their influence and arts to misrepresent the Union, to prejudice governments and people against it, and to prepare the way for sympathy with, and a recognition of, the southern confederacy. Besides these men who were thus laboring to destroy the government whose honor and interests were intrusted to their hands, there were private emissaries of the secessionists in Europe laboring unscrupulously for the same end. The success with which these secession agents, official and private, labored, was made manifest when the rebellion broke out in aggressive war.

Even at the north there were many men whose political or business associations with the south led them to sympathize with the secessionists at this period. They attributed all the troubles to northern fanatics, and while indulging in bitterness against them, apologized for, and even justified, the course of the secessionists. Northern journals, some of them of wide circulation and influence, if not openly advocating secession, encouraged its friends, preached disunion by suggesting a division of the northern states, and promised the sympathy and coöperation of large numbers in case of aggression upon the south by the incoming administration. One journal even proposed that the western and middle states should adopt the constitution of the southern Confederacy,* leaving the New England states to form a separate government or seek some other alliance.

Such was the condition of the country at the close of Mr. Buchanan's administration, and under such circumstances, which might well awaken the gloomiest forebodings in the minds of loyal men, a new administration was to assume the reins of government. That government, weakened by the uncertain policy of those who had it in charge, and by the treachery of their political associates, was threatened with entire overthrow or a material abridgment of its constitutional authority. It was a critical period for the country, and it was a great and perilous undertaking for untried men to assume the responsibility of saving it. But among the loyal people there was little regret that a change was to be made, and there was much in the character of the man who had been called to the presidency which inspired hope, if not confidence.

---

* This proposition, under the provisions of that constitution involved the extention of slavery over these states.

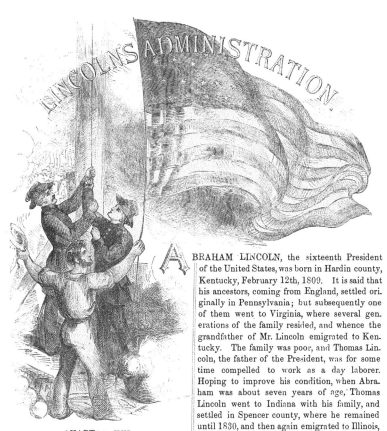

CHAPTER XXI.

ABRAHAM LINCOLN, the sixteenth President of the United States, was born in Hardin county, Kentucky, February 12th, 1809. It is said that his ancestors, coming from England, settled originally in Pennsylvania; but subsequently one of them went to Virginia, where several generations of the family resided, and whence the grandfather of Mr. Lincoln emigrated to Kentucky. The family was poor, and Thomas Lincoln, the father of the President, was for some time compelled to work as a day laborer. Hoping to improve his condition, when Abraham was about seven years of age, Thomas Lincoln went to Indiana with his family, and settled in Spencer county, where he remained until 1830, and then again emigrated to Illinois, whither the rich prairie lands were then inviting numerous settlers.

Quite early in his life, and with no advantages except the encouragement of a good but uneducated mother, young Lincoln had learned to read and write, so that his proficiency was somewhat noted among the illiterate pioneers of the west. With hardly a year's instruction during all his early life, he improved all the leisure time that he could command in acquiring knowledge, with such limited means and few books as came within his reach. But as soon as he was able to assist upon the farm, he was inured to labor, and found but little time for the pursuits of learning; and it was not until mature years that he was enabled to acquire some of the more ordinary branches of a common English education. His early labor, however, served to give him a robust constitution and a large and vigorous frame, if not of altogether comely proportions. In his work he was steady, energetic, and cheerful, showing those solid elements of character which have since, in more important and public duties, commanded the respect, and secured the confidence of so many.

Soon after the removal of the family to Illinois, Mr. Lincoln was employed by a neighbor to assist in taking one of the huge flat-boats of western rivers down the Illinois and the Mississippi to New Orleans. His fidelity in this expedition secured from his employer an appointment as manager of a part of his business. While thus engaged, the "Black Hawk war" assumed such proportions as to require a call for volunteers, and Mr. Lincoln enlisted in a company, of which, much to his surprise and gratification, he was chosen captain. The war was soon ended, and his military career was but of three months duration. He then, in connection with another party, opened a country store, and he was also appointed postmaster. He was not, however, successful in business, and after relinquishing it, for a time he found employment as assistant surveyor. But Mr. Lincoln appears to have had even before this a desire to become a lawyer; and as he found opportunity to pursue the study of the law, he did so, even while engaged in other occupations. Having thus commenced the study, he afterwards pursued it with energy, and was admitted to the bar in 1836. Soon afterwards he went to Springfield, and commenced the practice of the profession, in which he rapidly earned an honorable name and position. He was prudent, thorough, and patient in the discharge of his duty to his clients, skilful in conducting the causes which he tried, and eminent for fidelity and honesty. He thus became distinguished in his profession, and attained to an extensive practice as a counsellor and an advocate.

Mr. Lincoln early took an interest in political affairs, in which he acted with the opponents of the Democratic national administration, who were afterwards consolidated as the Whig party. He was nominated as candidate for the legislature in 1832, but he was then defeated by his Democratic opponent. In 1834 he was more successful, and was elected. Though not inclined to take a prominent part in debate, he discharged his duties as member of the assembly so acceptably to his constituents, that he was several times reëlected, and established a character for political sagacity and integrity which inspired the confidence of his political friends, and won the respect of his opponents. After his service for several years as a member of the legislature, his professional business engrossed his attention; and though taking a deep interest in political affairs, he was not a candidate for office until 1844, when he was nominated as a candidate for presidential elector. In 1846 he was elected a representative in Congress, in which position he maintained the character which he had established as a member of the legislature of his state. He agreed with the large majority of his party in opposition to the extension of slavery, and voted invariably for the Wilmot Proviso. He proposed a plan for abolishing slavery in the District of Columbia, with the consent of a majority of the voters, by compensating the slave owners from the treasury. While he had opposed the annexation of Texas, he voted in favor of all necessary supplies for the war with Mexico, and for the measures for the benefit of the soldiers. He also voted in favor of river and harbor improvements, a tariff which would afford protection to home industry, and the sale of the public domain at the lowest price to actual settlers.

Mr. Lincoln served but one term in Congress; but his influence in the Whig party continued, and in 1848 he took an active part in securing the nomination and election of General Taylor to the Presidency. In 1849 he was a candidate for senator in Congress; but the majority of the legislature was Democratic, and his opponent, General Shields, was elected. He was next called into active political life by the repeal of the Missouri compromise, when, adhering to the principles upon which he had acted in the Whig party, he affiliated with the new Republican party, organized to meet the issues which were then pressed upon the country. In 1856, the Illinois delegation in the Republican national convention presented his name as a candidate for the vice-presidency; but the nomination was determined, in part, upon grounds of locality. Mr. Lincoln, indeed, at that time, was scarcely known beyond his own state; and it was not until 1858, when, as Republican candidate for the United States Senate, he canvassed the state in company with his opponent, Stephen A. Douglas, that he achieved a reputation throughout the free states. Great interest was felt in that remarkable canvass by the people of the whole country. Mr. Douglas was one of the most prominent men of the nation, the strong supporter, if not the author, of the Kansas-Nebraska act; and he also occupied a somewhat peculiar position with regard to the Democratic party, for whose nomination for the Presidency he and his friends were nevertheless hoping. The issues discussed were those arising from the passage of that act — the issues which were before the whole nation. Each candidate exerted himself to maintain the cause in which he was enlisted. Mr. Douglas possessed many advantages over Mr. Lincoln as a debater and an orator, as well as in manner and appearance; but Mr. Lincoln's clear reasoning, good nature, frankness, and honesty, were a match for all the ability and shrewdness that his competitor could command, and his speeches manifested qualities which subsequently led to his selection as a candidate for the Presidency. The election which followed the canvass was a very close one. The vote of the whole state showed a popular majority for the Republican candidates; but owing to the inequality of the districts, a small majority of the legislature was Democratic, and Mr. Douglas was accordingly reëlected. This canvass, in which such an unusual interest was felt beyond the state immediately concerned, served to make Mr. Lincoln better known to the whole country, and at the west, especially, made him one of the most popular of the Republican leaders. In 1860, at the Republican national convention, he was brought forward by the delegates of that section as a candidate for the Presidency; and his popularity in the western states, together with his ability as manifested in his contest with Mr. Douglas, and his solid character, finally led to his nomination and election as President.

With a personal appearance neither attractive nor commanding, and accustomed to the hearty and informal manners of western society, Mr. Lincoln made no pretensions to the polish and dignity which by some people had been considered essential to the high position to which he was called; but there were elements in his character of more value than the refinements born of artificial society. He was honest in his purposes, faithful to his convictions, self-reliant, prudent, sagacious, and just; and he was, withal, accessible, good-humored, kind. These characteristics, however, were not such as commended themselves to the false-hearted society whose sympathies were with secession and rebellion, and they were made the object of gross and malignant attack and misrepresentation, from Mr. Lincoln's first appearance in Washington.

The inauguration of President Lincoln took place with the usual ceremonies. The military escort was composed of the district volunteer soldiery only, the military of the northern states having been requested not to visit Washington on the occasion, for fear of a disturbance there or at Baltimore should they appear. General Scott had the regular troops posted in different parts of the city, where they would be available in case of any outbreak or riot; and the police arrangements were also made with unusual care. There were large numbers of people in the city, those from the north being greatly in excess of those from the south; and many of them were so organized as to assist the authorities, or protect the new President in case of need. But, whether on account of the preparations made to guard against disturbance, or because the secessionists and opponents of the Republican President had no such purpose, the proceedings passed off quietly, and much after the usual manner, though there were fewer demonstrations of enthusiasm, and less civic display, than on some former occasions.

The President elect was accompanied by President Buchanan when escorted from his quarters to the Capitol, and a large civic procession, in addition to the military escort, was in attendance. At the Capitol, the two houses of Congress, the supreme court, foreign ministers, officers of the army and navy, governors of states, and others whose official position entitled them to the privilege, assembled in the Senate chamber, and thence proceeded, in the order established for such occasions, to the east front of the Capitol, in the spacious portico of which the simple inauguration ceremonies have taken place ever since its completion. A vast concourse of people had assembled in the spacious area, anxious to hear the inaugural address of the new President, upon whom now depended the safety and perpetuity of the government, so shaken and threatened when intrusted to his hands. When the parties in the procession had reached the positions assigned to them, Senator Baker, of Oregon, the chairman of the Senate committee of arrangements, introduced the President elect, who at once proceeded to deliver his inaugural address, as follows: —

"FELLOW-CITIZENS OF THE UNITED STATES:

"In compliance with a custom as old as the government itself, I appear before you to address you briefly, and to take in your presence the oath prescribed by the constitution of the United States to be taken by the President ' before he enters on the execution of his office.'

" I do not consider it necessary at present for me to discuss those matters of administration about which there is no special anxiety or excitement.

"Apprehension seems to exist among the people of the southern states that by the accession of a Republican administration their property, and their peace and personal security, are to be endangered. There has never been any reasonable cause for such apprehension. Indeed, the most ample evidence to the contrary has all the while existed and been open to their inspection. It is found in nearly all the published speeches of him who now addresses you. I do but quote from one of those speeches when I declare that ' I have no purpose, directly or indirectly, to interfere with the institution of slavery in the states where it exists. I believe I have no lawful right to do so, and I have no inclination to do so.' Those who nominated and elected me did so with full knowledge that I had made this and many similar declarations, and had never recanted them. And, more than this, they placed in the platform for my acceptance, and as a law to themselves and to me, the clear and emphatic resolution which I now read: —

"'Resolved, That the maintenance inviolate of the rights of the states, and especially the right of each state to order and control its own domestic institutions according to its own judgment exclusively, is essential to that balance of power on which the perfection and endurance of our political fabric depend; and we denounce the lawless invasion by armed force of the soil of any state or territory, no matter under what pretext, as among the gravest of crimes.'

" I now reiterate these sentiments; and in doing so, I only press upon the public attention the most conclusive evidence of which the case is susceptible, that the property, peace, and security of no section are to be in any wise endangered by the now incoming administration. I add, too, that all the protection which, consistently with the constitution and the laws, can be given, will be cheerfully given to all the states when lawfully demanded, for whatever cause — as cheerfully to one section as to another.

"There is much controversy about the delivering up of fugitives from service or labor. The clause I now read is as plainly written in the constitution as any other of its provisions : —

" ' No person held to service or labor in one state, under the laws thereof, escaping into another, shall, in consequence of any law or regulation therein, be discharged from such service or labor, but shall be delivered up on claim of the party to whom such service or labor may be due.'

" It is scarcely questioned that this provision was intended by those who made it for the reclaiming of what we call fugitive slaves; and the intention of the lawgiver is the law. All members of Congress swear their support to the whole constitution — to this provision as much as to any other. To the proposition, then, that slaves, whose cases come within the terms of this clause, ' shall be delivered up,' their oaths are unanimous. Now, if they would make the effort in good temper, could they not, with nearly equal unanimity, frame and pass a law by means of which to keep good that unanimous oath ?

" There is some difference of opinion whether this clause should be enforced by national or by state authority ; but surely that difference is not a very material one. If the slave is to be surrendered, it can be of but little consequence to him, or to others, by which authority it is done. And should any one, in any case, be content that his oath shall go unkept, on a merely unsubstantial controversy as to *how* it shall be kept ?

" Again, in any law upon this subject, ought not all the safeguards of liberty known in civilized and humane jurisprudence to be introduced, so that a free man be not, in any case, surrendered as a slave ? And might it not be well at the same time to provide by law for the enforcement of that clause in the constitution which guarantees that ' the citizen of each state shall be entitled to all privileges and immunities of citizens in the several states ' ?

" I take the official oath to-day with no mental reservations, and with no purpose to construe the constitution or laws by any hypercritical rules. And while I do not choose now to specify particular acts of Congress as proper to be enforced, I do suggest that it will be much safer for all, both in official and private stations, to conform to and abide by all those acts which stand unrepealed, than to violate any of them, trusting to find impunity in having them held to be unconstitutional.

" It is seventy-two years since the first inauguration of a President under our national constitution. During that period fifteen different and greatly-distinguished citizens have, in succession, administered the executive branch of the government. They have conducted it through many perils, and generally with great success. Yet, with all this scope of precedent, I now enter upon the same task for the brief constitutional term of four years under great and peculiar difficulty. A disruption of the federal Union, heretofore only menaced, is now formidably attempted.

" I hold that, in contemplation of universal law, and of the constitution, the Union of these states is perpetual. Perpetuity is implied, if not expressed, in the fundamental law of all national governments. It is safe to assert that no government proper ever had a provision in its organic law for its own termination. Continue to execute all the express provisions of our national constitution, and the Union will endure forever — it being impossible to destroy it except by some action not provided for in the instrument itself

"Again, if the United States be not a government proper, but an association of states in the nature of contract merely, can it, as a contract, be peaceably unmade by less than all the parties who made it? One party to a contract may violate it — break it, so to speak; but does it not require all to lawfully rescind it?

"Descending from these general principles, we find the proposition that, in legal contemplation, the Union is perpetual, confirmed by the history of the Union itself. The Union is much older than the constitution. It was formed, in fact, by the articles of association in 1774. It was matured and continued by the declaration of independence in 1776. It was further matured, and the faith of all the then thirteen states expressly plighted and engaged that it should be perpetual, by the articles of confederation in 1778. And, finally, in 1787, one of the declared objects for ordaining and establishing the constitution was '*to form a more perfect union.*'

"But if destruction of the Union by one, or by a part only, of the states, be lawfully possible, the Union is *less* perfect than before the constitution, having lost the vital element of perpetuity.

"It follows, from these views, that no state, upon its own mere motion, can lawfully get out of the Union; that *resolves* and *ordinances* to that effect are legally void; and that acts of violence, within any state or states, against the authority of the United States, are insurrectionary or revolutionary, according to circumstances.

"I therefore consider, that, in view of the constitution and the laws, the Union is unbroken, and. to the extent of my ability, I shall take care, as the constitution itself expressly enjoins upon me, that the laws of the Union be faithfully executed in all the states. Doing this I deem to be only a simple duty on my part; and I shall perform it, so far as practicable, unless my rightful masters, the American people, shall withhold the requisite means, or, in some authoritative manner, direct the contrary. I trust this will not be regarded as a menace, but only as the declared purpose of the Union that it *will* constitutionally defend and maintain itself

"In doing this there needs to be no bloodshed or violence; and there shall be none, unless it be forced upon the national authority. The power confided to me will be used to hold, occupy, and possess the property and places belonging to the government, and to collect the duties and imposts; but, beyond what may be necessary for these objects, there will be no invasion, no using of force against or among the people any where. Where hostility to the United States, in any interior locality, shall be so great and universal as to prevent competent resident citizens from holding the federal offices, there will be no attempt to force obnoxious strangers among the people for that object. While the strict legal right may exist in the government to enforce the exercise of these offices, the attempt to do so would be so irritating, and so nearly impracticable, withal, that I deem it better to forego, for the time, the uses of such offices.

"The mails, unless repelled, will continue to be furnished in all parts of the Union. So far as possible, the people every where shall have that sense of perfect security which is most favorable to calm thought and reflection. The course here indicated will be followed, unless current events and experience shall show a modification or change to be proper, and in every case and exigency my best discretion will be exercised, according to circumstances actually existing, and with a view and a hope of a peaceful solution of the national troubles, and the restoration of fraternal sympathies and affections.

"That there are persons in one section or another who seek to destroy the Union at all events, and are glad of any pretext to do it, I will neither affirm nor deny; but if there be such, I need address no word to them. To those, however, who really love the Union, may I not speak?

"Before entering upon so grave a matter as the destruction of our national fabric, with all its benefits, its memories, and its hopes, would it not be wise to ascertain precisely why we do it? Will you hazard so desperate a step while there is any possibility that any portion of the ills you fly from have no real existence? Will you, while the certain ills you fly to are greater than all the real ones you fly from — will you risk the commission of so fearful a mistake?

"All profess to be content in the Union, if all constitutional rights can be maintained. Is it true, then, that any right, plainly written in the constitution, has been denied? I think not. Happily, the human mind is so constituted that no party can reach to the audacity of doing this. Think, if you can, of a single instance in which a plainly written provision of the constitution has ever been denied. If, by the mere force of numbers, a majority should deprive a minority of any clearly written constitutional right, it might, in a moral point of view, justify revolution — certainly would, if such right were a vital one. But such is not our case. All the vital rights of minorities and of individuals are so plainly assured to them by affirmations and negations, guarantees and prohibitions, in the constitution, that controversies never arise concerning them. But no organic law can ever be framed with a provision specifically applicable to every question which may occur in practical administration. No foresight can anticipate, nor any document of reasonable length contain, express provisions for all possible questions. Shall fugitives from labor be surrendered by national

or by state authority? The constitution does not expressly say. *May* Congress prohibit slavery in the territories? The constitution does not expressly say. *Must* Congress protect slavery in the territories? The constitution does not expressly say.

"From questions of this class spring all our constitutional controversies, and we divide upon them into majorities and minorities. If the minority will not acquiesce, the majority must, or the government must cease. There is no other alternative; for continuing the government is acquiescence on one side or the other. If a minority in such case will secede rather than acquiesce, they make a precedent which in turn will divide and ruin them; for a minority of their own will secede from them whenever a majority refuses to be controlled by such minority. For instance, why may not any portion of a new confederacy, a year or two hence, arbitrarily secede again, precisely as portions of the present Union now claim to secede from it? All who cherish disunion sentiments are now being educated to the exact temper of doing this.

"Is there such perfect identity of interests among the states to compose a new Union as to produce harmony only, and prevent renewed secession?

"Plainly, the central idea of secession is the essence of anarchy. A majority held in restraint by constitutional checks and limitations, and always changing easily with deliberate changes of popular opinions and sentiments, is the only true sovereign of a free people. Whoever rejects it does, of necessity, fly to anarchy or to despotism. Unanimity is impossible; the rule of a minority, as a permanent arrangement, is wholly inadmissible; so that, rejecting the majority principle, anarchy or despotism, in some form, is all that is left.

"I do not forget the position assumed by some, that constitutional questions are to be decided by the supreme court; nor do I deny that such decisions must be binding, in any case, upon the parties to a suit, as to the object of that suit, while they are also entitled to very high respect and consideration in all parallel cases by all other departments of the government. And while it is obviously possible that such decision may be erroneous in any given case, still the evil effect following it, being limited to that particular case, with the chance that it may be overruled, and never become a precedent for other cases, can better be borne than could be the evils of a different practice. At the same time, the candid citizen must confess that if the policy of the government upon vital questions, affecting the whole people, is to be irrevocably fixed by decisions of the supreme court, the instant they are made, in ordinary litigation between parties in personal actions, the people will have ceased to be their own rulers, having to that extent practically resigned their government into the hands of that eminent tribunal. Nor is there in this view any assault upon the court or the judges. It is a duty from which they may not shrink to decide cases properly brought before them, and it is no fault of theirs if others seek to turn their decisions to political purposes.

" One section of our country believes slavery is *right*, and ought to be extended, while the other believes it is *wrong*, and ought not to be extended. This is the only substantial dispute. The fugitive slave clause of the constitution, and the law for the suppression of the foreign slave trade, are each as well enforced, perhaps, as any law can ever be in a community where the moral sense of the people imperfectly supports the law itself. The great body of the people abide by the dry legal obligation in both cases, and a few break over in each. This, I think, cannot be perfectly cured; and it would be worse in both cases *after* the separation of the sections than before. The foreign slave trade, now imperfectly suppressed, would be ultimately revived without restriction in one section, while fugitive slaves, now only partially surrendered, would not be surrendered at all by the other.

" Physically speaking, we cannot separate. We cannot remove our respective sections from each other, nor build an impassable wall between them. A husband and wife may be divorced, and go out of the presence and beyond the reach of each other; but the different parts of our country cannot do this. They cannot but remain face to face; and intercourse, either amicable or hostile, must continue between them. Is it possible, then, to make that intercourse more advantageous or more satisfactory *after* separation than *before?* Can aliens make treaties easier than friends can make laws? Can treaties be more faithfully enforced between aliens than laws can among friends? Suppose you go to war: you cannot fight always; and when, after much loss on both sides, and no gain on either, you cease fighting, the identical old questions, as to terms of intercourse, are again upon you.

" This country, with its institutions, belongs to the people who inhabit it. Whenever they shall grow weary of the existing government, they can exercise their *constitutional* right of amending it, or their *revolutionary* right to dismember or overthrow it. I cannot be ignorant of the fact that many worthy and patriotic citizens are desirous of having the national constitution amended. While I make no recommendation of amendments, I fully recognize the rightful authority of the people over the whole subject, to be exercised in either of the modes prescribed in the instrument itself; and I should, under existing circumstances, favor rather than oppose a fair opportunity being afforded the people to act upon it. I will venture to add, that to me the convention mode seems preferable, in that it allows amendments to originate with the people themselves, instead of only permitting them to take or reject propositions originated by others, not especially chosen for the purpose, and which might not be precisely such as they would wish to either accept or refuse. I understand a proposed amendment to the constitution — which amendment, however, I have not seen — has passed Congress, to the effect that the federal government shall never interfere with the domestic institutions of the states, including that of persons held to service. To avoid misconstruction of what I have said, I depart from my purpose not to speak of particular amendments so far as to say that, holding such a provision to now be implied constitutional law, I have no objection to its being made express and irrevocable.

"The chief magistrate derives all his authority from the people, and they have conferred none upon him to fix terms for the separation of the states. The people themselves can do this also if they choose; but the executive, as such, has nothing to do with it. His duty is to administer the present government, as it came to his hands, and to transmit it, unimpaired by him, to his successor.

"Why should there not be a patient confidence in the ultimate justice of the people? Is there any better or equal hope in the world? In our present differences is either party without faith of being in the right? If the Almighty Ruler of nations, with his eternal truth and justice, be on your side of the north, or on yours of the south, that truth and that justice will surely prevail by the judgment of this great tribunal of the American people.

"By the frame of the government under which we live, this same people have wisely given their public servants but little power for mischief; and have, with equal wisdom, provided for the return of that little to their own hands at very short intervals. While the people retain their virtue and vigilance, no administration, by any extreme of wickedness or folly, can very seriously injure the government in the short space of four years.

"My countrymen, one and all, think calmly
21

and *well* upon this whole subject. Nothing valuable can be lost by taking time. If there be an object to *hurry* any of you, in hot haste, to a step which you would never take *deliberately*, that object will be frustrated by taking time; but no good object can be frustrated by it. Such of you as are now dissatisfied, still have the old constitution unimpaired, and, on the sensitive point, the laws of your own framing under it; while the new administration will have no immediate power, if it would, to change either. If it were admitted that you who are dissatisfied hold the right side in the dispute, there still is no single good reason for precipitate action. Intelligence, patriotism, Christianity, and a firm reliance on Him who has never yet forsaken this favored land, are still competent to adjust, in the best way, all our present difficulty.

"In *your* hands, my dissatisfied fellow-countrymen, and not in *mine*, is the momentous issue of civil war. The government will not assail *you*. You can have no conflict without being yourselves the aggressors. *You* have no oath registered in heaven to destroy the government, while *I* shall have the most solemn one to 'preserve, protect, and defend it.'

"I am loath to close. We are not enemies, but friends. We must not be enemies. Though passion may have strained, it must not break, our bonds of affection. The mystic chords of memory, stretching from every battle field and patriot grave to every living heart and hearthstone, all over this broad land, will yet swell the chorus of the Union, when again touched, as surely they will be, by the better angels of our nature."

After the delivery of the inaugural address, the oath of office was administered to Mr. Lincoln by Chief Justice Taney,* and Abraham Lincoln was President of the United States.

It was a relief to the loyal people that

---

* Mr. Lincoln was the eighth President to whom Chief Justice Taney had administered the oath of office, having performed that duty from the inauguration of President Van Buren.

another threatened danger was safely passed, and that the new administration was thus duly intrusted with the government that had been nearly wrecked by the treachery and faithlessness which had paralyzed its predecessor.

There were various opinions in regard to the inaugural address; but among the loyal people of the north, including many of the opponents of the President, it was generally considered conservative and conciliatory towards the south. Among the secessionists, however, and those who sympathized with them, it was regarded as warlike and menacing. Its firmness and declared adherence to the obligations of the President to maintain the Union and the federal authority, gave assurance to the nation that the government would not be permitted to fall to pieces without an effort to save and perpetuate it; while, on the other hand, there appeared no purpose of unnecessary aggression.

President Lincoln sent the nominations for his cabinet to the Senate without delay, and they were immediately confirmed. The cabinet was composed as follows: —

Secretary of State,   William H. Seward, of N.Y.
"   " the Treasury, Salmon P. Chase, of Ohio.
"   " War,   Simon Cameron, of Penn.
"   " the Navy,   Gideon Welles, of Conn.
"   " the Interior, Caleb B. Smith, of Indiana.
Postmaster-General,   Montgomery Blair, of Md.
Attorney-General,   Edward Bates, of Missouri.

The new administration, like its predecessors, was besieged by applicants for office, who came from all the states that had not yet seceded, and some even from seceded states. There was, indeed, reason for a change in many offices, the incumbents of which were either secessionists, or so bound by party ties as to sympathize with the south even in its disunion schemes. These matters, therefore, necessarily occupied much of the attention of the administration in the commencement of its term; but in the mean time efforts were quietly directed to ascertain the available strength of the govern-

ment in the army and navy, as well as in the civil service. As may well be imagined, when we consider the state of the country, as described in the last chapter, this was a work of difficulty and embarrassment. But until the government knew its strength, and had rid itself of some of the traitors and uncertain men in public places, it could scarcely attempt to maintain its authority, even where it was not as yet wholly denied. Fortunately the administration found no obstruction to its policy in executive matters in the Senate. By the withdrawal of the senators of seceding states, and the admission of Kansas at the late session of Congress, the Republicans were left in a majority in that body. The president's nominations, therefore, and other executive business that came before the Senate, were acted upon in a friendly spirit.

Among the appointments to foreign embassies the most important were the following: —

To England,   Charles Francis Adams, of Mass.
To France,   William L. Dayton, of New Jersey.
To Russia,   Cassius M. Clay, of Kentucky.
To Austria,   Anson Burlingame,* of Mass.
To Italy,   George P. Marsh, of Vermont.
To Spain,   Carl Schurz, of Wisconsin.
To Prussia,   Norman B. Judd, of Illinois.
To Mexico,   Thomas Corwin, of Ohio.

Though a general outline of the policy to be pursued by the administration was given in the President's inaugural address, no active steps were immediately taken to indicate more definitely what that policy would be when reduced to practice. This delay was very unsatisfactory to the secessionists, who hoped either for a complete abandonment of the federal authority in the seceded states, or some hasty act of coercion which would involve a war

* On account of Mr. Burlingame's efforts in Congress for the recognition of the kingdom of Italy, with its enlarged territory recovered from Austria, the Austrian government declined to receive him. Mr. J. Lothrop Motley, of Massachusetts, was appointed in his stead, and Mr. Burlingame was sent commissioner to China.

while the "Confederacy" was better prepared for it than the United States. It also served to hold in abeyance the secession movement in the border states, where what was called an aggressive or coercive policy was needed, only, to hasten the further dismemberment of the Union. But the administration was ascertaining the real condition of the government, and was using what means were at command to strengthen it, and enable it to carry out its policy with firmness and vigor.

It appeared, however, that it was Mr. Lincoln's purpose, as declared in his inaugural, to pursue a peaceful policy, so far as his obligations to the constitution would enable him; and while he would undertake to exercise the authority of the government, where necessary, in the seceded states, he would not commence any movement which could reasonably be considered as aggressive.

CHAPTER XXII.

Commissioners from the Confederate States Government. — They desire to present their Credentials to the President. — Mr. Seward refuses to recognize them officially. — Reply of the Commissioners. — Policy of the Administration with regard to Fort Sumter. — Difficulty of the Question. — Determination to hold other Forts. — Preparations for Reënforcement. — Evacuation of Fort Sumter a Military Necessity. — The Expediency of indicating a Policy. — The Purpose of the Government. — Determination to provision Fort Sumter. — Messengers to Charleston. — Notice to Governor Pickens of the Intention of the Government. — Major Anderson's Condition. — Fort Sumter and the Besieging Batteries.

WHILE the new administration was thus occupied in reorganizing the various departments of the government, commissioners from the Confedcrate States appeared at Washington, for the purpose of opening negotiations with the government of the United States for the "speedy adjustment of all questions growing out of this political separation, upon such terms of amity and good will as the respective interests, geographical contiguity, and future welfare of the two nations may render necessary." These commissioners were John Forsyth, Martin J. Crawford, and A. B. Roman. They requested Mr. Seward to appoint a time when they might present their credentials to the President; but this was declined by the secretary of state in a note in which he said, —

"The secretary of state frankly confesses that he understands the events which have recently occurred, and the condition of political affairs which actually exists in the part of the Union to which his attention has thus been directed, very differently from the aspect in which they are presented by Messrs. Forsyth and Crawford. He sees in them not a rightful and accomplished revolution and an independent nation, with an established government, but rather a perversion of a temporary and partisan excitement to the inconsiderate purposes of an unjustifiable and unconstitutional aggression upon the rights and the authority vested in the federal government, and hitherto benignly exercised, as from their very nature they always must be exercised, for the maintenance of the Union, the preservation of liberty, and the security, peace, welfare, happiness, and aggrandizement of the American people. The secretary of state, therefore, avows to Messrs. Forsyth and Crawford that he looks patiently, but confidently, for the cure of evils which have resulted from proceedings so unwise, so unusual, and so unnatural, not to irregular negotiations, having in view new and untried relations with agencies unknown to the constitution and laws, but to regular and considerate action of the people in those states, in coöperation with their brethren in other states, through the Congress of the United States, and such extraordinary conventions, if there shall be need thereof, as the federal constitution contemplates and authorizes to be assembled."

"A simple reference to [the inaugural address] will be sufficient to satisfy these gentlemen that the secretary of state, guided by the principles therein announced, is prevented altogether from admitting or assuming that the states referred to by them have, in law or in fact, withdrawn from the federal Union, or that they could do so in the manner described by Messrs. Forsyth and Crawford, or in any other manner than with the consent and concert of the people of the United States, to be given through a national convention, to be assembled in conformity with the provisions of the constitution of the United States. Of course the secretary of state cannot act upon the assumption, or in any way admit that the so-called Confederate States constitute a foreign power, with whom diplomatic relations ought to be established."

Mr. Seward therefore declared " that he has no authority, nor is he at liberty, to recognize them as diplomatic agents, or hold correspondence or other communication with them."

This communication of Mr. Seward was dated March 15th, but it was not delivered to the Confederate commissioners till April 8th. In the mean time Judge Campbell, of the supreme court, had acted as a mediator between the commissioners and the government. To him Mr. Seward had expressed a desire not to be obliged to return an immediate reply to the communication of the commissioners, and had, perhaps, encouraged the belief that Fort Sumter, unless it could be peaceably supplied with provisions, would be evacuated. Such, it appears, was the impression received by Judge Campbell; but it may have been in this case as in the unofficial negotiations between the South Carolina commissioners and Mr. Buchanan, that the parties interested drew inferences beyond the true import of the secretary's language. But it is not improbable that Mr. Seward desired to obtain time for the administration to feel more assured of its position before taking such action as would decide its whole future policy, and perhaps determine the question of peace or

war. And it is also probable that the final action of the government with regard to Fort Sumter was misinterpreted by the commissioners, who believed that deception had been practised upon them.

When at last Mr. Seward's communication was delivered to the commissioners, they replied to it in another, in which they endeavored to fix upon the government the responsibility of bloodshed, which they assumed would be the result of the failure of their mission, and charged the administration with perfidy in pretending that Fort Sumter would be evacuated, while they were preparing an " immense armada " to reënforce it. " Your refusal," they wrote, " to entertain these overtures for a peaceful solution, the active naval and military preparations of this government, and a formal notice to the commanding general of the Confederate forces in the harbor of Charleston, that the president intends to provision Fort Sumter by forcible means if necessary, are viewed by the undersigned, and can only be received by the world, as a declaration of war against the Confederate States ; for the president of the United States knows that Fort Sumter cannot be provisioned without the effusion of blood. The undersigned, in behalf of their government and people, accept the gage of battle thus thrown down to them ; and appealing to God and the judgment of mankind for the righteousness of their cause, the people of the Confederate States will defend their liberties to the last against this flagrant and open attempt at their subjugation to sectional power." Farther on they assert that it is clear " that Mr. Lincoln had determined to appeal to the sword to reduce the people of the Confederate States to the will of *the section or party* whose president he is." And this was because a constitutionally elected president of the United States, from fidelity to his oath and his duty to his country, felt himself under obligation to provision the small garrison of a fort belonging to the United States, by right of property and jurisdiction solemnly ceded by the state of South Carolina.

What should be done in relation to Fort Sumter, was the immediate practical question to be determined by the administration upon assuming the government. It was a question of great importance and difficulty, practically, however simple it might appear in principle. Upon it in a measure depended the whole policy to be pursued towards the seceding states, and the course of events which would follow. To evacuate it upon the demands of South Carolina or the Confederate States, would be yielding to "coercion" on their part, and might be construed into an abandonment of the authority claimed by the United States; while to reënforce it and hold it, would probably lead to bloodshed. The people of the north were by no means inclined to acquiesce in the abandonment of the federal authority over any of the forts or other property of the United States, or to have the government submit to any arrogant demands from disunionists and rebels. But the administration, though determined to perform its duty according to the general policy set forth in the inaugural address, was not disposed to take any action which should lead to hostilities without first trying conciliatory measures. One thing, however, was determined both by the government and the people, and that was, that the other important posts on the southern coast, which had not already been seized by, or betrayed into the hands of, the disunionists, should be reënforced, strengthened, and held at all hazards. Accordingly preparations were made for this purpose. The available vessels belonging to the navy were fitted out with all possible despatch, such small force of the regular army as could be collected was prepared, and several large steam transports were chartered for carrying troops, provisions, and ordnance stores.* These preparations,

though not on a very formidable scale, compared with subsequent expeditions, created some excitement at the south, where it was assumed at once that the destination of the expedition was Charleston harbor.

In the mean time the question concerning Fort Sumter still remained in abeyance. The Congress of the Confederate States had adopted measures for the establishment of an army, and General P. G. T. Beauregard, formerly of the United States army, was sent to Charleston to assume command of the forces there, and direction of the fortifications. The work on these fortifications proceeded; troops from other southern states, as well as South Carolina, were concentrated at Charleston; and the preparations on the part of the seceded states were pressed forward with a determination to reduce the fort unless it was speedily surrendered. And so effectually was it invested by the hostile batteries, that there was little hope of its holding out for any length of time, in its incomplete state, and with its limited number of guns and small garrison.

While, therefore, it was objected to as a political measure, the evacuation of Fort Sumter as a military necessity was regarded with less disfavor by the people, and was assented to by the administration, with the advice of General Scott. Major Anderson, in a despatch sent to the war department at the very commencement of the administration of Mr. Lincoln, had given his opinion as an officer that it would be impossible, in the existing state of affairs, to reënforce him before his provisions should be exhausted, except with a force of at least twenty thousand men. General Scott, after examining the subject, and consulting with other experienced officers, concurred in that opinion. It appeared, therefore, that at this

* The expedition consisted of the steam sloops of war Pawnee and Powhattan, cutter Harriet Lane, the steam transports Atlan-

tic, Baltic, and Illinois, and steam tugs Yankee and Uncle Ben. The ships of war mounted twenty-six guns, and the transports took nearly a thousand troops, with large quantities of ordnance stores and provisions.

juncture, nothing was left for the government to do but to order the evacuation. It was, however, a difficult point to decide, for evacuation would, perhaps, be so misconstrued at home and abroad, and thus lead to new complications, that it was not to be adopted until its necessity was fully demonstrated, and all efforts to supply the little garrison peacefully had failed; nor until the government had indicated by some practical measures that its policy was not to voluntarily abandon the forts which it still held.

It had been the intention of the administration to indicate its policy by reënforcing Fort Pickens, at Pensacola, before the evacuation of Fort Sumter should be rendered necessary by the exhaustion of provisions. Orders were sent to the naval officer commanding on that station to land a force which had been sent out by the last administration in the war steamer Brooklyn. But it appeared that some arrangement or understanding similar to that which palsied the arm of the government in Charleston harbor, had been made by the Buchanan administration, and the order was not carried into execution. When this state of affairs became known at Washington, there remained but a few days before the time when the supplies of Fort Sumter would inevitably be exhausted; and, finding matters thus complicated, and that delay in taking measures to indicate its policy — not of "coercion," but simply of holding the property and maintaining the authority of the United States — might be dangerous, the administration determined to use a part of the expedition which was being fitted out, and which was prepared for such a juncture, to take supplies to the beleaguered fort. The intention, however, was, first to send an unarmed vessel into the harbor, and to resort to force only to repel an attack.

While these measures were under advisement, several special messengers were sent by the government to Charleston, for the purpose of ascertaining the condition of Major Ander-son's command, and consulting in relation to supplies. One of these, Captain Fox, who had been connected with the coast survey, and was familiar with the harbor of Charleston, and understood all the risk to be run, submitted a plan for sending supplies to Fort Sumter; but it was not at once adopted. Colonel Lamon was subsequently sent to Charleston, and communicated with Major Anderson; but the precise object of his mission was not known. On the part of the South Carolina authorities, it was probably supposed at that time, when such rumors were prevalent, that the fort was to be evacuated, and that the mission was to give instructions to that effect to Major Anderson. Lieutenant Talbot, one of Major Anderson's officers, was the next messenger; but he was not allowed to communicate with Fort Sumter, and returned to Washington without accomplishing the whole of his mission. At this time the supplies of fresh provisions, which the garrison had been allowed to purchase in Charleston, were cut off, and immediately afterwards a final messenger gave notice to Governor Pickens that it was the intention of the government to send supplies to the fort. According to the Confederate authorities, this messenger declared that "provisions would be sent to Fort Sumter peaceably, otherwise by force."

In the mean time, Major Anderson had done what he could, with his small force of soldiers and workmen, to put the fort in a better condition to resist bombardment, and to reply to an attack. Surrounded as he was by numerous batteries, mounted with guns of heavy calibre, his provisions nearly exhausted, and his men worn down by work, communication with his government practically cut off, and with no hope of relief, the prospect was gloomy enough for the gallant commander; but he was determined to do his duty to his country, and to stand by his flag to the last, and in this he was seconded by all the officers and men of his command.

The batteries which had been constructed for the reduction of Fort Sumter, the work on which had been suffered to continue for months, while the fort was neither reënforced nor evacuated, nor permitted to stop these hostile preparations, were now quite completed, and were really formidable, both from their position and the calibre of the guns. On Morris's Island were two breaching batteries, one of which was covered with railroad iron, and was skilfully constructed, and two mortar batteries. On James Island was Fort Johnson, the guns of which could not be very effective upon Fort Sumter, and another mortar battery. On Sullivan's Island were two columbiad batteries and two mortar batteries; and a floating battery, concerning which there had been much boasting in the Charleston papers, was anchored off the upper end of the island. Fort Moultrie, and a small mortar battery at Mount Pleasant, completed the beleaguering fortifications. These batteries mounted at least thirty guns and seventeen mortars, most of the guns being of heavy calibre, and one or more being rifled guns. They bore upon Fort Sumter from the north, north-east, south-east, and south-west. The force which was sent to these fortifications, and to repel a land attack, if such were attempted by the expected expedition for the relief of Fort Sumter, was about seven thousand men.

The armament of Fort Sumter, available against these batteries, consisted of twenty-seven barbette guns, and twenty-one casemate guns, the heaviest and most effective being in barbette; but none of them could be considered sufficiently formidable for the defence of such a work. The garrison of the fort consisted of about seventy officers and men; and there were also in it about forty mechanics and laborers, under the direction of the officers of the engineer corps, who had been employed upon the construction of the fort, and most of whom volunteered to do duty in its defence, by working at the guns, or in carrying shot and cartridges; but the whole effective force was less than a hundred men. In preparing for the expected bombardment, it was found that the supply of cartridges was entirely inadequate for a protracted defence, and it was necessary to cut up all the surplus blankets, and extra company clothing, to make cartridge bags. But there were only six needles in the fort, and the work of preparing cartridges was consequently slow. In all the preparations for the defence of the fort, the garrison labored early and late; but their work was not completed when the attack was made.

CHAPTER XXIII.

Bombardment of Fort Sumter. — Beauregard instructed to demand its Evacuation. — The Demand, and Major Anderson's Reply. — Another Proposition. — The Reply unsatisfactory. — Commencement of Hostilities. — Major Anderson's Force. — Want of Cartridges. — Materials used for Supply. — Effect of the Bombardment on the Fort. — Fire from the Fort slackened. — Appearance of United States Vessels off the Bar. — Night. — The last Rice eaten. — Renewal of the Engagement. — Hot Shot thrown by the Rebel Batteries. — The Quarters and Barracks set on Fire. — Powder taken from the Magazine. — Spread of the Flames, and Danger. — Appearance of Mr. Wigfall with a Flag of Truce. — His Representations. — Display of his White Flag at the Embrasure not respected. — Interview with Major Anderson. — Agreement to evacuate on Terms previously proposed. — Other Messengers from Beauregard. — Mr. Wigfall acting without Authority. — Terms arranged. — Evacuation. — Salute to the Flag. — Departure of the Garrison. — Major Anderson's Report.

As soon as the determination of the government to send supplies to Fort Sumter was made known to the authorities of South Carolina and the Confederate States, they made immediate preparations to bombard the fort, without waiting for the appearance of any vessel or fleet to carry out the purposes of the government. General Beauregard telegraphed to the Confederate secretary of war that a messenger from President Lincoln had notified Governor Pickens and himself, " that provisions will be sent to Fort Sumter peaceably, or otherwise by force." The secretary, in reply, directed him to demand the evacuation of the fort, and if this was refused, to reduce it. Accordingly, General Beauregard, on the 11th of April, sent a communication to Major Anderson, in which, after dwelling upon the forbearance of the government of the Confederate States in allowing the United States forces to hold Fort Sumter for so long a period, he wrote, "I am ordered by the government of the Confederate States to demand the evacuation of Fort Sumter. My aids, Colonel Chesnut and Captain Lee, are authorized to make such demand of you. All proper facilities will be afforded for the removal of yourself and command, together with company arms and property, and all private property, to any post in the United States which you may elect. The flag which you have upheld so long and with so much fortitude, under the most trying circumstances, may be saluted by you on taking it down."

To this communication Major Anderson replied: —

"GENERAL: I have the honor to acknowledge the receipt of your communication demanding the evacuation of this fort; and to say, in reply thereto, that it is a demand with which I regret that my sense of honor, and of my obligations to my government, prevents my compliance.

"Thanking you for the fair, manly, and courteous terms proposed, and for the high compliment paid me,

"I am, General, very respectfully,
　　　"Your obedient servant,
　　　　　"ROBERT ANDERSON,
"*Major U. S. Army, Commanding.*"

At the same time, Major Anderson stated, unofficially, to Beauregard's aids, that the garrison was now nearly out of provisions, and that they could not probably hold out longer than the 15th of the month. This statement was referred, with the refusal to evacuate, to the Confederate government, and led to a proposition from General Beauregard that, if Major Anderson would state the time when he

would evacuate the fort, and in the mean time would not use his guns against the Confederate forces unless theirs were employed against the fort, they would abstain from opening fire upon him. In reply to this proposition, Major Anderson said that he would evacuate the fort by noon on the 15th instant, should he not receive, prior to that time, controlling instructions from his government, or additional supplies; and that he would not open fire from the fort unless compelled to do so by some hostile act on the part of General Beauregard's forces against the fort or the United States flag.

This reply, it appeared, was not satisfactory to the Confederate States authorities. They expected that the fleet which had been fitting out at New York would attempt to supply and reënforce Fort Sumter, and they were not disposed to wait for its arrival. The bearers of the proposition were instructed upon this point, and upon receiving Major Anderson's reply, after a brief consultation, without returning to their superior, at half past three, on the morning of the 12th of April, gave notice that their batteries would open fire in one hour from that time.

Major Anderson's command, few in numbers, and worn down by hard labor, and by insufficient food, was entirely inadequate for a full defence of the fort, and to man the guns effectively. But, with a determination to do his duty, even under such discouraging circumstances, he proceeded to make the best disposal that he could of his little band. The command was divided into three reliefs, to serve two hours each, in order to husband the strength of the garrison. The men were ordered at once to the bomb proofs, it being the intention of the major to keep them safe, and not reply to the fire until broad daylight. In the mean time they received their scanty breakfast of rice and pork, the biscuit having been already exhausted.

At half past four, a signal·shell was thrown

from the mortar battery on James Island, and immediately after, fire was opened on the fort from all the batteries simultaneously, and was kept up for two hours and a half before any reply was made from Fort Sumter. At seven o'clock, the first shot was fired from the fort, by one of the guns in charge of Captain Doubleday; and, from that time, the little garrison responded to the fire from each of the batteries making the attack. The shot and shell flew thickly over the fort; and, in order not to expose his few men, Major Anderson did not work his barbette guns, which were larger and more effective than those in the casemates, and the only ones with which he could throw shells. Some of the direct shot from the Cummings Point battery, on Morris Island, especially those from an English rifled gun, took effect upon the upper part of the barracks and quarters, and made some breaches around two or three of the embrasures. Those fired from the other batteries were directed mostly against the barbette guns, one of which was dismounted, and another damaged by the shot. But the most damaging, and the most dangerous, were the shells thrown from the mortar batteries, to which the interior of the fort, on all sides, was exposed. There was a constant explosion of these shells, which several times set fire to the barracks; but the flames were quickly extinguished by the energetic efforts of the officers and men.

At the commencement of the engagement there were but seven hundred cartridges in the fort, and by noon it was found that the supply was so much reduced that Major Anderson was obliged to slacken his fire. The six needles were kept constantly at work, and every thing that could be spared for the purpose — extra clothing, hospital blankets, and coarse paper — was made into cartridges, the men working constantly till midnight in preparing them. While Major Anderson was thus obliged to confine his fire to six guns, he responded to each of the rebel batteries as if in defiance.

The assailants, thinking, perhaps, that the fire of the fort was slackened by damage from their shot and shell, kept up an incessant fire through the day, and continued it frequently through the night, although at dark Major Anderson ceased firing, and closed his ports.

Soon after noon on this day three United States vessels were seen off the bar of the harbor, and were signalled by Fort Sumter. They remained there, however, without any attempt apparently to enter the harbor. Their appearance had been hailed with joy by the little garrison, who expected that some relief and aid had come to them. At night it was hoped that the vessels would attempt to run in, and Major Anderson kept his signal light burning. But the night was dark and stormy, the channel was intricate, and the lights in the lighthouses were extinguished. When the morning came and the garrison arose from their brief rest, the vessels were still off the bar, with no appearance of attempting to come in. The last rice was eaten for breakfast, and the men, disappointed but true, went again to the guns, which were bravely manned and briskly fired, but from their insufficient calibre were not of much avail against the works of the besiegers.

The effect of the fire from the fort on the first day had apparently not been very great. As before observed, the heavy guns, being in barbette, had not been used, and the thirty-two and forty-two pound shot were not of sufficient weight. Fort Moultrie was damaged to some extent, and several guns were dismounted; the houses on Sullivan's Island were riddled with shot; a revenue cutter, which was near the island with the Confederate flag flying, was struck by a shot, and hauling down her flag, moved out of range; the floating battery received some trifling injury, but was so protected behind a breakwater that it could not be hit fairly; while against the iron-clad battery on Cummings Point the shot had scarce-

22

ly any effect, the balls glancing off harmlessly.

The fire from the fort was commenced early on the second day, the assailants having already opened a rapid firing. The contest continued as on the preceding day, the shot and shells more seriously damaging the fort, and wounding several men, the aim of the rebel gunners being better than on the first day. It was soon apparent that the guns of Fort Moultrie were throwing hot shot, and at nine o'clock dense volumes of smoke arose from the officers' quarters, which had just been struck by a shot. From the exposed position of the building it was impossible to extinguish the flames, while there was danger of the fire spreading so as to encircle the magazine. Efforts were immediately directed to the removal of as much powder as possible from the magazine to the casemates; but so rapidly did the flames extend, that it was possible to remove only fifty barrels of the powder before it became necessary to close the doors of the magazine and bank them with earth.

As soon as the smoke and flames burst from the roof of the quarters, the fire of the besieging batteries was redoubled in rapidity, and hot shot was thrown from most of their guns. The whole range of officers' quarters was soon in flames, and the fire was communicated to the roof of the barracks on two sides of the fort. The floors of the barracks were fireproof; but it required all the exertions of the garrison to prevent the fire spreading down the stairways, and by the wood work outside to the east barrack, in which the officers and men had taken their quarters. The flames at last reached the magazines of grenades, which were arranged in the stair towers and implement rooms, when they exploded, completely destroying the stair towers, and otherwise damaging that part of the fort. The casemates were filled with smoke and cinders, so as almost to suffocate the men, and boxes, beds, and other articles belonging to the garrison were set on fire, so that it became unsafe to retain the powder which had been taken from the magazine. For a time efforts were made to save it by covering the casks with wet cloths; but the danger was imminent, and Major Anderson ordered all but five barrels to be thrown out of the embrasures into the water. There were but few cartridges left, and but little powder with which to make them; the men were laboring to prevent the spread of the flames, so that the guns could only be fired occasionally; but they sent at intervals a defiant shot, to show that the fort still held out. The flagstaff had several times been struck by shot, and the lanyards were cut, but the flag did not come down. At last the staff fell; but the flag was secured, and as soon as it could be attached to a temporary staff, it was again raised upon the rampart, in spite of the danger, by Lieutenant Snyder and Sergeant Hart.[*]

At this stage of affairs a man appeared outside of the fort with a white flag tied to his sword, and desired admission. He was allowed to enter through one of the embrasures, and announced himself to the officers there as Mr. Wigfall,[†] an aid to General Beauregard, from whom he came to desire that, inasmuch as the flag of Sumter was shot down, a fire raging in the quarters, and the garrison in a great strait, hostilities should be suspended, and the white flag raised for this object. Lieutenant Davis replied that the flag was again hoisted on the parapet, and that the white flag would not be raised except by order of the commanding officer. Mr. Wigfall then requested that his own white flag might be waved to stop the fire from Sullivan's Island, that from Cummings

---

[*] Hart had formerly been a sergeant in Major Anderson's command, but he was now employed as a carpenter by the engineer officer. He had been very active in trying to extinguish the fire in the barracks, and in endeavoring to secure the flag when the lanyards were shot away. Though exposed to shot and shell, he did not flinch till the flag was securely fixed.

[†] Formerly United States senator from Texas.

Point being already suspended. This was refused; but he was permitted to wave the white flag himself, and got into an embrasure for that purpose. After displaying it a few minutes without effect, a corporal was allowed to take his place; but the fire continuing, and a shot striking very near the embrasure, the corporal jumped inside, and throwing down the flag, declared to Mr. Wigfall that "he would not hold his flag, for it was not respected."

Major Anderson having appeared, Mr. Wigfall repeated the purpose of his visit, and complimenting that officer upon the defence he had made, renewed the request for a suspension of hostilities, in order to arrange terms of evacuation. Upon Major Anderson's inquiring what terms, Mr. Wigfall replied, "Any terms that you may desire; your own terms, the precise nature of which General Beauregard will arrange with you."* Major Anderson assented to the proposition, saying that the terms which he accepted were those proposed by General Beauregard before hostilities commenced, and no others. The white flag was consequently displayed, and the United States flag was lowered.

Shortly afterwards, the firing having ceased, a boat arrived at the fort, bringing three of General Beauregard's aids, who stated that, seeing the white flag raised, the general sent them to inquire what assistance he could lend, in extinguishing the flames or otherwise. Upon being informed of the circumstances under which the white flag was hoisted, these officers declared that Mr. Wigfall had acted entirely without authority, not having seen General Beauregard for two days. Major Anderson, finding that he had been deceived, ordered the United States flag to be again raised; but at the urgent request of the aids, he consented to wait till they could report to their chief and receive his instructions. In the mean time the garrison exerted themselves to extinguish the flames, which were still raging. Messengers from General Beauregard, after some delay, announced that the terms were approved, with the exception of saluting the flag; but Major Anderson insisted upon this, and it was finally acceded to. It was agreed, also, that the garrison, with their effects, should be transported to such port in the United States as the commanding officer should designate. The steamer Isabel was accordingly sent to the fort for that purpose; but communication having been had with the fleet off the bar, it was subsequently determined that the officers and men should be transferred to one of the United States transports.

The evacuation of the fort took place on Sunday, April 14th. A part of the men had gone on board the Isabel the night previous; but a sufficient force remained in the fort to salute the flag† which they had so faithfully defended, and which was lowered at the last discharge amid the cheers of the men. During the firing of the salute, one of the guns burst, killing one man instantly, and wounding several others, one of them fatally. This was the only loss of life that occurred at the fort during those eventful days, and but three or four had been wounded during all the bombardment. There was, probably, as little loss of life among the Confederate forces.‡

---

* Report of J. G. Foster, captain of engineers, afterwards brigadier-general.

† The first raising of this flag by Major Anderson over Fort Sumter, after the transfer of his command thither, was an occasion more impressive than its final lowering, according to the following statement, which is generally believed. Major Anderson, on that occasion, assembled the whole of his little force, and the workmen employed on the fort, around the foot of the flagstaff. The national ensign was attached to the cord, and Major Anderson, holding the lines in his hand, knelt reverently down. The officers and men clustered around, many of them on their knees, and all deeply impressed with the solemnity of the scene. The chaplain made an appropriate and fervent prayer, and as he ceased and the men responded "Amen," Major Anderson drew the flag to the top of the staff, where it was greeted by the whole assembly with loud and exultant cheers, and the national air by the band. Well might those men be true to that flag

‡ There were various reports of numbers being killed and wounded among the rebel forces, including Beauregard himself; but they appeared to be unfounded.

After the evacuation, the Isabel conveyed the little garrison to the transport Baltic, outside the bar, on which they were taken to New York. Fort Sumter was immediately taken possession of by a portion of the Confederate forces.

Upon his arrival at New York, Major Anderson sent the following despatch to the secretary of war: —

"SIR: Having defended Fort Sumter until our quarters were entirely burned, the main gates destroyed by fire, the gorge wall seriously injured, the magazine surrounded by flames, and its door closed from the effects of heat, and three cartridges of powder only being available, and no provisions but pork remaining, — I accepted the terms of evacuation offered by General Beauregard, being the same offered by him on the 11th instant, prior to the commencement of hostilities, and marched out of the fort on Sunday afternoon, 14th instant, with colors flying and drums beating, bringing away my company and our private property, and saluting my flag with fifty guns.

"ROBERT ANDERSON,
"*Major First Artillery*." *

Major Anderson received the thanks of the government for his gallant defence of the fort under such trying circumstances, and was grant-

ed a furlough in consideration of his impaired health. He was also at once promoted to the rank of colonel, and was subsequently appointed brigadier-general of volunteers.

CHAPTER XXIV.

Effect of the Bombardment of Sumter at the North. — Intense Feeling. — Action of the Government. — President's Proclamation. — Requisition for Troops. — Patriotic Response of the People. — Approval of the Action of the Government to vindicate its Authority. — The Press. — Response to the Requisition for Troops. — Promptness of the Free States. — Refusal of Slave States. — Massachusetts, New York, Rhode Island, &c. — Public Meetings. — Action of Banks and Boards of Trade. — The National Flag.

THE bombardment of Fort Sumter, before any attempt was made even to supply it peacefully, was an act of open and flagrant rebellion, and of wanton hostilities, which no longer left a choice of policy on the part of the government, nor any doubt of the purposes of the secessionists. It created an intense feeling among the people of the north; and as the intelligence of the conflict and the final result was announced by telegraph, there arose a common sentiment of indignation against the assailants, and a determination to maintain the authority of the government.

At Washington the feeling was no less in-

---

* In a private narrative of the bombardment, Major Anderson made, among others, the following statements: The batteries kept up the fire on the fort, at intervals, all night, to prevent the men from sleeping; but they failed in their object. He ordered the men to bed, and they slept soundly, while the sentinels alone kept on duty. Although he had been up the night before in the correspondence and conferences with Beauregard's aids, he staid up this night also, thinking that by a bare possibility some small boats from the relief squadron might work their way up to the fort. But they did not; and he was satisfied that relief was an impossibility. It was too late, and he was rejoiced that the fleet did not endanger themselves by the attempt.

The reports that were telegraphed from Charleston to the north, that when his barracks were on fire, relief was proffered him; that when his flag was shot down, another one was tendered; that after the evacuation, he was the guest of Beauregard, — are all equally untrue. When his fort was filled with the smoke of his burning quarters, the hostile batteries redoubled their fire on him. He says that though the Charleston Mercury is now denouncing him for having spoken in condemnation of this at the north, he has the satisfaction of remembering that he spoke of it with equal frankness to the Carolinians. At the evacuation, he said to one of the officers, "If our cases had been reversed, and your quarters had been on fire, I should have stopped firing and offered aid to extinguish the flames. War is a sad business at best, and we should strive to humanize it as much as possible. The officer replied, "We did just right." "Then," said Anderson, "we need have no further conversation, sir."

All the time he was in Sumter he was in a genteel state prison. Visits could only be made to him, even by his sick and anxious wife, by consent of the Carolina authorities: when they chose they would refuse to let him buy any potatoes; and a present of two cases of tobacco from New York, to the soldiers, was kept in Charleston, after being examined, three weeks before they were allowed to taste what was such luxury to them, and of which they had been for so long a time deprived.

tense. The administration, impressed with the magnitude of the responsibility which was forced upon it, and determined to maintain and protect the authority and the trusts committed to its charge, took immediate steps to meet the crisis which had at last arisen. There were long sessions of the cabinet, and earnest consultations with General Scott, while the conflict was still proceeding at Charleston; but almost with the result of that battle the prompt decision of the government was known, and found to accord with the feelings and wishes of the people of the north, and of all who sincerely desired to maintain the Union and the federal authority. Conciliation had failed to accomplish any thing, and all but the wilfully blind could see that the purpose of the disunionists was to establish a southern confederacy, regardless of any efforts to conciliate, or of any compromise, save such as should subject the whole country to their control and the principles on which they founded their confederacy. The people desired in this crisis to realize that there was an administration which recognized its duty and was determined to perform it. However unwelcome, therefore, was the prospect of war, or of the resort to arms even to secure peace, it was a relief to popular anxiety to find the government disposed to be prompt and energetic in the performance of its office, and in maintaining the honor of the Union and the flag which is its symbol.

Fort Sumter was evacuated on Sunday, the 14th of April, the bombardment having ceased the previous afternoon. On the morning of the 15th the President issued the following

PROCLAMATION.

" Whereas the laws of the United States have been for some time past, and now are, opposed, and the execution thereof obstructed, in the states of South Carolina, Georgia, Alabama, Florida, Mississippi, Louisiana, and Texas, by combinations too powerful to be suppressed by the ordinary course of judicial proceedings, or by the powers vested in marshals by law, —

" Now, therefore, I, ABRAHAM LINCOLN, President of the United States, in virtue of the power vested in me by the constitution and the laws, have thought fit to call forth, and hereby do call forth, the militia of the several states of the Union to the aggregate number of seventy-five thousand, in order to suppress said combinations, and to cause the laws to be duly executed. The details for this object will be immediately communicated to the state authorities through the war department.

" I appeal to all loyal citizens to favor, facilitate, and aid this effort to maintain the honor, the integrity, and the existence of our national Union, and the perpetuity of popular government, and to redress the wrongs already long enough endured.

" I deem it proper to say, that the first service assigned to the forces hereby called forth will probably be to repossess the forts, places, and property which have been seized from the Union; and in every event the utmost care will be observed, consistently with the objects aforesaid, to avoid any devastation, any destruction of or interference with property, or any disturbance of peaceful citizens in any part of the country.

" I hereby command the persons composing the combinations aforesaid to disperse and retire peaceably to their respective abodes within twenty days from this date.

" Deeming that the present condition of public affairs presents an extraordinary occasion, I do hereby, in virtue of the power in me vested by the constitution, convene both houses of Congress. The senators and representatives are therefore summoned to assemble at their respective chambers at twelve o'clock, noon, Thursday, the fourth day of July next, then and there to consider and determine such measures as in their wisdom the public safety and interest may seem to demand.

" In witness whereof, I have hereunto set my

hand, and caused the seal of the United States to be affixed.

"Done at the city of Washington, this fifteenth day of April, in the year of our Lord one thousand eight hundred and sixty-one, and of the independence of the United States the eighty-fifth.

"ABRAHAM LINCOLN.

" By the President:

"WILLIAM H. SEWARD, *Secretary of State.*"

At the same time a requisition was sent to the governor of each state, requesting the immediate detail from the militia of his state of the force required therefrom, to serve for a period of three months, unless sooner discharged. The quota for each state was as follows: Maine, New Hampshire, Vermont, Rhode Island, Connecticut, Delaware, Michigan, Iowa, Minnesota, and Wisconsin, one regiment each; Massachusetts and Tennessee, two each; New Jersey, Kentucky, and Missouri, four each; Indiana and Illinois, six each; Pennsylvania, sixteen; New York, seventeen; Arkansas, one regiment; North Carolina, two; Ohio, thirteen; Maryland, four; Virginia, three. It was ordered that each regiment consist of seven hundred and eighty officers and men. The total thus called out was seventy-three thousand three hundred and ninety-one; the troops of the District of Columbia completing the seventy-five thousand.

The quota for some of the free states was increased immediately afterwards, in consequence of the urgent necessity of having a sufficient force promptly in the field.

The unjustifiable bombardment of Sumter, heralding open rebellion and war against the Union and government of the United States, followed by this prompt call for its defence on the part of the administration, aroused the patriotism of the loyal people to an unexpected degree. Party dissensions were abated, save among an unworthy few, and the differences, which had divided the people even so recently as the probable policy of the government had been discussed, were now forgotten, or assumed to be, in a common attachment to the institutions so seriously threatened, which they were called to maintain. Feeling that they had a government which would not crumble in pieces from its own weakness, if they rallied in support of the administration which had it in charge and was faithful in its defence, the people were ready to sustain it with loyal hearts and strong arms. With all their indignation at the dishonor of the national flag, and the certainty of the evils of war and necessity of sacrifices before them, there was a more cheerful and confident feeling than during the long months of uncertainty when rebellion was organizing, and the government was helplessly witnessing the preparations for its own ruin and dissolution.

The press of all parties spoke out in earnest language for the maintenance of the government by vigorous measures, and responded heartily to the proclamation of the President. There were, indeed, some journals, with whom party ties were so strong and whose affiliations with the south were such, that for a time they denounced the administration, and defended the rebels and their cause. The people, however, were little disposed to tolerate any open sympathy with rebellion and treason, and public opinion, or more cogent reasons, soon effected a suppression of such sentiments. The great majority of the journals, as well as a great majority of the people, were loyal and hearty in the support of the government.

The call for troops was responded to with all the despatch that could be expected from the unorganized condition of the military and the want of arms and equipments in most of the states. A few of the states, as New York, Massachusetts, Rhode Island, and a part of Pennsylvania, had a militia force organized, armed, and equipped. There were a few other states that had skeleton organizations, which enabled them to fill up their quota with some promptness, while others, being obliged to organize and equip anew, were necessarily more tardy in responding to the requisition. The governors of all the free states seconded the call of the President, and exerted themselves to supply the requisite force, and in none of these states was there any lack of men or disinclination to serve under this call. In the border slave states, including all the slave states which had not seceded, there was no response to the requisition, the governors of most of those states refusing — some in a most insolent manner — to furnish troops "for the subjugation of the seceding states." They were not backward, however, in calling upon the people to form military organizations for the defence of their states, to maintain "neutrality," or for such action as events might give occasion for.

Massachusetts was the first state to respond to the requisition of the President. Having a volunteer militia, comparatively well organized, armed, equipped, and officered, who were first to be called into service upon an emergency like this, that state was better prepared than most of the others. Governor Andrew issued an order, on the day the President's proclamation was received, for four regiments to assemble forthwith in Boston. These regiments were all in the country, and it was necessary to notify personally the members of the various companies, scattered through many small towns; but the next day these regiments, with full ranks, were at the rendezvous, and ready to be forwarded to their destination. The men had left their ordinary avocations and their homes with the same promptness and patriotism that their fathers had shown in 1776; tarrying not to arrange their business or provide for their families, and scarcely to say farewell. But the patriotism of friends and neighbors bade them God speed, and gave assurance that their families and affairs should be cared for. As some of the companies took their departure from the towns in which they were organized, they were greeted by the entire population, and left amid the cheers and with the prayers and blessings of a loyal people. In Boston the troops were received with much enthusiasm, and their ready response to the call of their country awakened an increased patriotism and pride of country among the people. After being supplied with clothing and new arms and equipments, they were sent forward; three of the regiments on the 17th of April, two days after the issue of the President's proclamation, and the other on the succeeding day. Two — the third and fourth — were sent to Fortress Monroe, and the other two — the sixth and eighth — to Washington, the last being accompanied by Brigadier-General Benjamin F. Butler, as commander of the brigade.

In Rhode Island, Connecticut, New York, Pennsylvania, and other states which were enabled to respond promptly to the call for troops, there were manifested similar patriotism and enthusiasm. In Rhode Island Governor Sprague[*] exerted himself with great spirit to prepare the quota required of that state; and though not the earliest in the field, none of the three months' troops were better equipped, or made a finer appearance. In New York the first troops to march were the seventh regiment of New York city, celebrated throughout the country as the best disciplined and most efficient body of citizen soldiery in the United States. Other regiments soon followed, and the Empire State evinced a promptness and patriotism in furnishing its large quota worthy of its influential position in the Union. Nor was Pennsylvania any less active and efficient. A portion of the troops from that state were among the first to march for Washington, though not supplied with

---

[*] When Governor Sprague was elected, some of the secessionists at the south imagined that, because he was chosen over a Republican opponent, he was in sympathy with them and their treason; and they boasted, perhaps half in jest and half in earnest, of making Newport not only the summer resort of southern fashion, but the great commercial emporium of the Confederacy.

arms and equipments. The other free states, with fewer facilities for organizing military forces, were none the less patriotic and earnest in defending the Union; and troops were raised in a remarkably short time, and ready for service.

The people of the free states manifested their patriotism and loyalty not only by responding to the military call, but by an earnest approval and support of the action of the administration, and by liberal offers of the "sinews of war" to the state and national governments. Meetings were held in large cities and small towns, attended by men of all ages, parties, creeds, and professions, at which the patriotism of all was stirred by the most glowing eloquence, and strengthened by the earnest words of wisdom; measures were taken to sustain the government in all its efforts to put down the rebellion; funds were contributed for the supply of clothing to the soldiers, and support for their families during their absence, and for their more liberal reward than the small wages paid by government. Banks tendered liberal loans to the national and state governments, and gave assurance of continued aid for the suppression of the rebellion. Boards of trade adopted resolutions approving the vigorous action of the administration, and pledging support to all measures which indicated a determination to vindicate the authority of the government. A new regard for the national flag was awakened by the insults and dishonor with which the enemies of the Union had treated it. The flag was every where displayed, on public buildings and private dwellings, and the "Star-Spangled Banner" became more than ever before the national hymn and melody.

Of the feelings thus manifested by the people of the free states, a journal of that time remarked truly, as follows : —

"We do not call that a war fever which now burns in the hearts of all the people of these northern states. It is no vindictive spirit towards any section, no desire for vengeance, no outbreak of long-standing hate. It is simply the blazing out of the suppressed flame of loyalty, which shallow observers have denied to have any existence in our people. It is the spontaneous, unchecked demonstration of the love for a common country, which the shackles of partisan organizations have long hampered and repressed, but never destroyed. We rejoice that in our day it has come to pass that party differences have for once been laid aside in the presence of a general and sacred duty ; that all parties have had occasion to comprehend that there is one higher appeal to be made to the patriot, before which all ties or jealousies of party are alike forgotten.

"The loyal states to-day have all the advantage of being a united people. The Confederate states have claimed this advantage for themselves, and have steadily held to the belief that to the end of the struggle our counsels would be divided. They can see to-day what it is to have provoked a nation to the defence of its government. They can see what it is for a people to unite, for defence as well as for attack. Three days have brought about such a revolution in the attitude of these states as has not been seen since this day 1775.* With all our sanguine belief that the people would stand by their government to the last, we confess that we never conceived of the enthusiasm and unanimity which are now seen. A great people have risen as one man ; the press, with scarcely an important exception, has declared for the hearty support of authority, while the list of exceptions is daily lessened by the pressure of an irresistible public sentiment. Blood and treasure are ready to be poured out like water in defence of the Union. The ancient spirit which once achieved our liberties rises to protect them, unharmed by the dangerous influences of generations of prosperity, peace, and increasing wealth."

* April 19.

CHAPTER XXV.

Urgent Necessity of Troops at Washington. — Movement of Massachusetts Regiments. — The Sixth Regiment departs for Washington. — Demonstrations of the People on the Route. — Danger apprehended at Baltimore. — Arrival at Baltimore. — Passage through the City. — Separation of the Companies. — Safe Transit of a Part in Cars. — Obstructions by the Mob. — The March of Four Companies. — Attack by the Mob — Soldiers killed and wounded. — Fire returned by the Soldiers. — Mayor of Baltimore. — Arrival at the Washington Station. — Continued Riot. — Departure for Washington. — Mob Rule in Baltimore. — Action of Governor and Mayor. — Excitement in Massachusetts. — The Associations of the 19th of April. — The People aroused. — Despatch of Governor Andrew.

UPON the commencement of hostilities at Charleston, the movements and temper of the secessionists in Maryland and Virginia, and the treacherous attitude which the latter state had already assumed, gave reason for the government to suspect that an attack might be made upon Washington, as well as other important places belonging to the United States, within the limits of the states named. There was urgent need, therefore, for the immediate presence of more troops at these points, and especially in Washington. A portion of the small force of regular troops which had been concentrated there had been sent away to reënforce the more distant forts exposed to attack; and the troops remaining there, with the District military, which was not altogether to be depended upon, were inadequate to a defence of the capital should an attack be made by such a force as the secessionists, especially with the coöperation of the Virginia authorities, could certainly bring against it. The governors of those states which could respond immediately to the requisition for troops were requested to forward their forces as soon as practicable.

Massachusetts, as before stated, from the organization of her volunteer militia, was enabled to make the first response to the call. On the 17th of April three regiments, well armed and equipped, left the state in answer to the summons for the defence of the government; two

of them being transported by water to Fortress Monroe, and the other, the sixth, proceeding by land to Washington. Previous to their departure they were addressed in eloquent and feeling words by the governor, who presented to them the colors of the state; and they received the heartiest cheers and blessings of the people, who were alike grateful and proud that Massachusetts should so promptly and efficiently rally to the support of the Union and the government. The sixth regiment met with similar demonstrations all along the route to New York, and in that city they were hailed with great enthusiasm, and abundant hospitalities and kindness were extended to them, the patriotism of the "Old Bay State" receiving the commendation and the gratitude of the loyal people of the metropolis. In New Jersey and at Philadelphia the regiment was also handsomely greeted, so that, thus far at least, their journey towards Washington was a pleasant excursion, at times almost a triumphant ovation, rather than a march to active service and war against rebels who were conspiring to overthrow the government.

At Philadelphia, however, intimations were received that the passage of the regiment through Baltimore would be disputed; and the urgent necessity of being in Washington, if such was the feeling at Baltimore, led Colonel Jones to hurry on. The regiment left Philadelphia at one o'clock in the morning of the 19th of April, and in view of the threatened resistance, ammunition was distributed, and the arms were loaded as they proceeded in the cars, and orders were issued to prevent any collision with the mob by the hasty action of the soldiers. On the journey, at Susquehanna, a number of cars, containing a Pennsylvania regiment, unarmed, also destined for Washington, was added to the train. In rearranging the train upon this addition, without the knowledge of Colonel Jones, the cars containing the band and three or four companies which should have been in

23

the advance, were separated from the remainder of the regiment, and were some distance in the rear. The great length of the train retarded its speed, and it did not arrive at Baltimore until noon, the mob thus having a better opportunity to collect and the excitement to increase. The cars are drawn by horses through the city of Baltimore from the Philadelphia road to the Washington road; and upon the arrival of the train and the detachment of the locomotive, horses were immediately attached to the forward cars, and, with one exception, they were drawn safely through the city, the soldiers being assailed only with insults by the mob. The last car containing this part of the regiment was thrown from the track by some obstruction, and thus became separated from those preceding it. The major of the regiment had received orders to accompany the last or left flank company through the city, and not being aware that any part of the regiment had become separated and was still farther in the rear, he was with the company in this car, which should have formed the rear. The mob grew more noisy and demonstrative when the car ran from the track, but through the determined efforts of Major Watson it was replaced, and continued as far as Pratt Street, where the mob surrounded the car and detached the horses, and at the same time a volley of stones was thrown. Major Watson ordered the soldiers to remain in the car, and by means of threats and a resolute manner compelled the driver to reattach the horses, when, with slight obstructions, but followed by imprecations and missiles, the company reached the Washington station in safety.

In the mean time the companies which had become separated, and were in the rear, met with rougher usage. The mob became more violent with each delay, and upon the passage of the car just mentioned, they seemed determined to prevent the transit of any more soldiers. The track was torn up and the street barricaded, so that it was impossible for the cars to proceed. The troops, consisting of three companies and part of a fourth, under the command of Captains Follansbee, Hart, Pickering, and Dike, with the band, then left the cars, and under the command of Captain Follansbee, the senior officer, formed in order and began their march through the city. Perceiving the small number of troops, which did not exceed two hundred, the mob soon became emboldened, and crowded about the soldiers to obstruct their march, occasionally throwing at them paving stones, bricks, and whatever else they could seize upon. The troops moved at a quickstep at first, but this was soon changed to "double quick;" and the mob, believing this to be evidence of fear, or that the arms were not loaded, assailed them the more fiercely. A shower of missiles was thrown, and numerous shots from guns and pistols were fired at them. Several of the soldiers were wounded, one of them mortally, and two were killed. Until thus furiously assailed the soldiers had kept along steadily and without any attempt to retaliate; but at this stage of the attack neither officers nor men could endure it longer, and the word was given to fire upon the assailants. This was not, however, done in a volley, but scattering shots were fired at those who were most violent among the rioters, as much care as possible being taken not to injure innocent persons. A number of the mob were thus killed and wounded, and the others for a time fell back so as to permit the easier passage of the troops; but they soon renewed the attack with stones and firearms, and many shots were fired from the windows of houses. In the midst of the attack, the mayor of Baltimore, with some of the police, joined the troops. He marched at the head of the column with Captain Follansbee, promising to protect the troops, and begging the officers not to permit their men to fire. But when the assault increased in violence, and a soldier was struck down by his side, the mayor seized a gun and shot one of the rioters. The police also used their revolvers, but the assistance rendered by some of the police was rather questionable. Thus contending with some thousands of desperate rioters, the small force passed through the city. Many of them were wounded, and had been taken into the houses or stores on the street; some were separated from their comrades, and were not able to get through; two were killed, and one was mortally wounded. Upon the arrival of the companies at the station of the Washington Railroad, where the other part of the regiment was awaiting them, it was found that, including the musicians, upwards of a hundred of the command were missing.

Of the passage of this small force through the city against the opposition of the mob, an eye witness wrote as follows: —

"The Massachusetts men formed in line, and wheeled into open column of sections, and marched some distance at quick time, and then at double quick, all the while surrounded by the mob — now swelled to the number of at least ten thousand — yelling and hooting. The military behaved admirably, and still abstained from firing upon their assailants. The mob now began throwing a perfect shower of missiles, occasionally varied by random shots from revolvers or muskets. The soldiers suffered severely from the immense quantity of stones, oysters, brickbats, paving stones, &c. The shots fired also wounded several. When two of the soldiers had been killed, and the wounded had been conveyed to places of safety, the troops at last, exasperated and maddened by the treatment they had received, commenced returning the fire singly, killing several, and wounding a large number of the rioters; but at no one time did a single platoon fire in a volley. The volunteers, after a protracted and severe struggle, at last succeeded in reaching the station, bearing with them in triumph many of the wounded. The calm courage and heroic bearing of the troops spoke volumes for the sons of Massachusetts, who, though marching under a fire of the most embarrassing description, and opposed to overwhelming odds, nevertheless succeeded in accomplishing their purpose, and effected a passage through crowded streets a distance of over a mile and a half — a feat not easily accomplished by so small a body of men when opposed to such terrific odds."*

At the station the mob continued to press about the cars and to attack with stones, and, occasionally, with firearms; but the soldiers were kept within the cars, with the blinds closed, so that retaliation might not lead to greater bloodshed. One citizen, however, was shot here, but not till he was himself seen to throw a missile into one of the cars. An attempt was made to obstruct the track, remove the rails, and otherwise hinder the passage of the train; but the police prevented the accomplishment

* Another person, who was in Baltimore at the time, spoke in the strongest terms of the "inhumanity of the mob and the people of Baltimore. During the fight a soldier was knocked down by a stone. He fell upon his face in the middle of the street, and endeavored to crawl towards the sidewalk. The mob made a rush towards him. One ruffian came with an axe-helve raised, shouting, 'Let me kill him.' A Boston man in the city rushed in, pushed the fellow back, and stood over him, saying, 'No, you shan't; he is a wounded man; let him alone.'

"By his efforts the soldier was protected, the crowd rushing on after the soldiers. The man then tried to get some one to open their house and take in the soldier. He called at nine doors before he could find a person with humanity enough to help the wounded man. The purport of their answers was, 'Let the Yankee die!'

"At ten o'clock at night, a Boston lady, but who for many years has resided in Baltimore, went to the police station to offer her services in aid of the wounded. She was told that they had been taken care of. She begged then, as a privilege, to be admitted to see them. It was twelve hours after the fight; yet she found them in the station house, with only such comforts as could be found at a police station.

"She succeeded in obtaining two of them, Sergeant J. F. Ames, of Lowell, and private Coburn, of Dracut. She had them quietly removed to her house, sent for a surgeon, and had their wounds dressed. She requested the surgeon not to mention the circumstance; but he violated the confidence reposed in him, mentioned it to secessionists, and for a time she had apprehension that she might be subjected to much inconvenience in consequence. The surgeon had not visited his patients for thirty hours, when the writer left the city, and the good lady, whose name will be forever held in remembrance, was obliged not only to nurse them, but to dress their wounds."

of these purposes, and the train at last moved away beyond the limits of the city and the assaults of the mob, and in due time arrived in Washington, much to the relief of the government and citizens, who heartily welcomed this first arrival of troops in answer to the call of the President. In the mean time, the unarmed Pennsylvania troops, finding that it would be almost impossible for them to pass through Baltimore without arms, returned over the railroad to Pennsylvania.

The mob was composed of the "roughs" of the city of Baltimore, which has had an unenviable notoriety for the number and lawless character of this class of society. But it was instigated by parties who claimed a higher position. On the day previous, a large secession meeting had been held, at which the most violent expressions against the national administration were used, and the question was put by one of the speakers, if "the seventy-five thousand minions of Lincoln should pass over the soil of Maryland to subjugate our sisters of the south." To this question there was a fierce answer in the negative, and the first fruits of this meeting was the mob of the 19th of April. For several days the mob ruled the city. Gunshops were broken into and the arms seized, and so great was the excitement that other shops were closed, and business was suspended. Those known to entertain Union sentiments were subject to insult and violence, and a reign of terror seemed to be inaugurated. Under the lead of prominent secessionists, the mob destroyed several bridges on the railroad leading to Philadelphia, and committed other violent and riotous acts, for the purpose of preventing the transportation of troops.

Governor Hicks, though true to the Union, joined with the mayor of Baltimore in requesting the President not to have any more troops pass through the city; asserting that if they did so, they would be obliged to fight their way through. They also adopted a measure of more

questionable loyalty, by requesting the officers of the Baltimore and Ohio Railroad not to transport any more troops. At this time it appeared that the Union men of Baltimore were not entirely faithful to their professions, or were in a hopeless minority. But many of them were timid, and disposed to yield to the rule of the mob, who were led by the enemies of the government, although the very existence of the government might depend upon the prompt support which it should receive from the loyal soldiers of the north. But after the excitement had subsided, a better and more loyal feeling began to assert itself, though not successfully till the military power of the Union was brought there to sustain it, and to overawe the disunionists.

Almost as great an excitement, though of a different character, was aroused in Massachusetts, upon the receipt of intelligence of the riotous attack on the sixth regiment, and the death of three and the wounding of many others of the citizen soldiers of that state, while marching to defend the capital of the Union. The 19th of April was a memorable day in the history of the old commonwealth, as the inauguration of the revolutionary struggle. Upon that day, in 1775, the patriots of Middlesex county had hastily armed to resist British tyranny, and had shed the first blood of the revolution in defence of the liberties of their country. Upon the anniversary of that day, 1861, the descendants and successors of those patriots, the men of Middlesex, while marching to defend the government and institutions secured by the struggle that day commenced, had shed the first blood in resisting the tyranny that would overthrow the blessings transmitted to them. The spirit of the people was aroused in some degree as it had been by the fall of the heroes at Lexington and Concord. There was a determination, rendered more firm and sacred by the associations of the day, to defend the institutions established by their fathers, and to crush out the unholy rebellion that would overthrow and destroy them. Nor was this excitement confined to Massachusetts; it was felt throughout the free states, and the blood shed at Baltimore so quickly after the attack on Fort Sumter awakened a spirit among the loyal people which showed that patriotism was not extinct, and that they were ready to rally around the government for the suppression of the rebellion.

Immediately upon the receipt of the intelligence of the bloody affair at Baltimore, Governor Andrew, of Massachusetts, mindful of the families of the victims, as he had been efficient and patriotic in forwarding troops to sustain the government, telegraphed to the mayor of Baltimore as follows: —

"To His Honor the Mayor.

"I pray you to cause the bodies of our Massachusetts soldiers dead in Baltimore to be immediately laid out, preserved with ice, and tenderly sent forward by express to me. All expenses will be paid by this commonwealth.

"John A. Andrew,
"Governor of Massachusetts."

This request could not be fully complied with at once, owing to the cutting off of communication between Baltimore and the north; but the bodies were taken in charge by the city authorities, and properly prepared for interment, and they were subsequently sent home at the expense of the city of Baltimore.

It may be proper here to anticipate the regular course of our narrative somewhat, in order to do justice to the loyal people of Baltimore and of Maryland. On the following 4th of July a splendid banner was presented to the sixth regiment of Massachusetts, suitably inscribed, and bearing on its folds the words "Pratt Street, April 19, 1861."

Subsequently, when the state of Maryland, after much apparent hesitation on the part of its people, and many misgivings among the people of the north, assumed a position of undoubted loyalty, the legislature elected by the Union majority passed the following act, which, as far as possible, wipes away the stain that rested upon the honor and loyalty of the state: —

"An Act for the relief of the families of those of the Massachusetts sixth regiment of volunteers, who were killed or wounded in the riot of the nineteenth of April, eighteen hundred and sixty-one, at Baltimore.

"Whereas the sixth regiment of Massachusetts volunteers, on their way to defend the national capital, were brutally attacked by a mob in the streets of Baltimore, on the nineteenth day of April, eighteen hundred and sixty-one, and three were killed and eight wounded; and

"Whereas the state of Maryland is anxious to do something to efface that stain from her hitherto untarnished honor; therefore, —

"Section 1. Be it enacted by the General Assembly of Maryland, that the sum of seven thousand dollars be, and the same is hereby, appropriated, and placed at the disposal of His Excellency John A. Andrew, or any one acting as governor of the commonwealth of Massachusetts, who shall disburse the same in the manner and proportion he thinks best for the relief of the families of those belonging to the sixth regiment of Massachusetts volunteers who were killed or disabled by wounds received in the riot of the nineteenth of April, in Baltimore.

"Section 2. And be it enacted, that this act shall take effect from the date of its passage."

This act was passed March 10, 1862, and was transmitted to the Governor of Massachusetts April 19, the anniversary of the sad events for which it was intended to atone.

CHAPTER XXVI.

Danger threatening the Government. — Efforts to forward
Troops from Loyal States. — General Butler and the Massachusetts Eighth Regiment. — New York Seventh. — Choice of
a Route to Washington. — Departure of General Butler and
Massachusetts Troops from Philadelphia. — From Perryville to
Annapolis. — Naval Academy and Frigate Constitution. —
Danger of Seizure. — The Constitution towed from her Sta-
tion. — Difficulties encountered. — Arrival of New York Sev-
enth. — Troops landed. — Fort McHenry reënforced. — United
States Steamer Alleghany. — The Elkridge Railroad. — Repair
of Locomotive. — Tracks relaid. — March to Annapolis Junc-
tion. — Fatigue and Hunger. — Arrival of more Troops. —
Transportation to Washington. — Opposition of People of
Maryland to the Passage of Troops. — Protest by Governor
Hicks. — General Butler's Reply. — Reply of Mr. Seward to
Suggestions of Governor Hicks.

THE reality of the dangers threatening the
government could no longer be doubted, when
on the one side armed forces were threatening
it, and on the other a mob in the interest of
rebellion had cut off communication with its
loyal supporters. The people of the north
were, with reason, alarmed at this state of
affairs, and it seemed for a short time that the
rebels would accomplish a revolution, and seize
upon the government before its defenders could
strike an effective blow for its safety. One
northern regiment had reached the capital, and,
with the small regular force and the district
militia, might afford some protection; but the
position of affairs in Maryland, the interruption
of railway and telegraphic communication, and
the treachery of Virginia, which was just being
revealed, rendered the prospect gloomy enough
for a few days. But the loyal people were not
dismayed, and they felt assured that, though
rebels and traitors by secret and sudden attack
might gain some temporary advantage, when
the power of the loyal people was fully put
forth, rebellion must be overcome. Some prompt
action, however, was necessary, lest any delay
or apparent supineness should increase the
danger. The people of the north and the state
authorities were fully alive to this necessity, and
great efforts were made to hasten the equip-

ment and transportation of troops. Numbers
were already on the way, the vanguard of a
large army of citizen soldiers. But the first
thing required was to open communication with
the national capital; and this was soon accomplished by the energy of a Massachusetts officer
and troops, ably seconded by the seventh regiment of New York.

Brigadier-General Butler, who had been assigned to the command of the several regiments
from Massachusetts, arrived at Philadelphia, with
the eighth regiment of that state, on the evening
after the attack upon the sixth regiment in
Baltimore. Shortly afterwards the New York
seventh regiment arrived. There the intelligence of the events in Baltimore, and the interruption of the travel through that city by a
lawless and armed mob, created intense feeling
among the people, and a determination on the
part of the loyal soldiers to fight their way
through the mob-ruled city, if necessary, in order
to answer the call of the government. It soon
appeared that the Baltimore and Ohio Railroad
Company refused to transport troops, and that
it was not only not expedient, but impracticable,
unless with a great loss of life, to pass that
way to Washington, and it became necessary to
choose some other route. General Butler, accordingly, after examination of the means of
reaching Washington which were at his command, decided to proceed to Annapolis, and
thence, if there were no facilities for transportation, to march to the capital. In this movement he desired the coöperation of the New
York seventh regiment; but Colonel Lefferts,
the commander of that regiment, did not at
first accede to the proposition. General Butler,
therefore, decided to proceed with the Massachusetts regiment; and he left Philadelphia on
the 20th of April, going by railroad to Perryville, at the head of Chesapeake Bay, opposite
Havre de Grace, between which places the railroad passengers were transported by a ferry
boat. Before arriving at Perryville it was ru-

mored that a large armed force was at that place to prevent the passage of troops. It was found, however, that there was only a collection of men who might have resisted the passage of unarmed soldiers, but were not prepared to oppose an armed force, and rapidly dispersed upon the approach of the troops after leaving the cars.

On arriving at Perryville, the large ferry boat, which was fortunately on that side of the bay, was immediately taken possession of, and the troops embarked. In this, with many discomforts, they proceeded down the bay to Annapolis, arriving in the harbor of that city on Sunday morning, April 21. Here General Butler found the frigate Constitution, familiarly known and prized by the people as "Old Ironsides," which was stationed off the United States Naval Academy, in imminent danger of being seized by the secessionists. The officer in command was expecting such an attempt, and, not having crew enough to man the vessel or to make any effectual defence in case of attack, had made preparations to blow her up if necessary, to prevent her falling into the hands of the enemy. The arrival of the Massachusetts regiment at this juncture obviated the necessity of destroying the frigate, and prevented the seizure of the buildings and other property belonging to the school. General Butler put two companies of the troops and a corps organized as sappers and miners on board the Constitution. Many of these soldiers were hardy fishermen from Cape Ann, and were quite familiar with the duties of a sailor. They bent the sails and performed other labors of seamen on board the ship to prepare her for sailing. Meanwhile the ferry boat was used to tow the ship from her station to the mouth of the harbor; but in doing this both vessels got aground, and notwithstanding great efforts were made to float them, they remained aground till the next day; preparations being made in the mean

time to defend them against any attack that might be made.

The next morning a steamer arrived from Philadelphia, bringing the New York seventh regiment. This timely arrival was a relief to General Butler and his troops, confined as they were on board the boat with scarcely any food, except what was supplied from some of the old ship stores found on board the Constitution. An unsuccessful attempt was made at once to tow the ferry boat into deep water; but, finding it impossible to do so, Colonel Lefferts proceeded to the wharf with his steamer, and debarked his troops, and the steamer then took the Massachusetts troops from the ferry boat to the wharf, and subsequently towed the Constitution into deep water.

Thus the northern troops entered upon the soil of Maryland with a determination to reach the national capital in spite of the opposition of the mob of Baltimore and the secessionists of Annapolis, an armed body of whom appeared in the neighborhood. But the passage from this point to Washington was not to be accomplished without much difficulty and some suffering, on account of the want of food, by the Massachusetts troops. One of General Butler's first steps, however, after getting the ferry steamer afloat, was to send one company to Fort McHenry, near Baltimore, to reënforce the small garrison stationed there. A few miles from that fort was the United States steamer Alleghany, without any sufficient crew to prevent capture, and before proceeding to their destination the company took possession of this steamer, and anchored her under the guns of the fort; thus, without doubt, saving the vessel from the hands of the secessionists. The ferry boat was then armed and despatched for supplies, and, with other boats taken possession of by General Butler at Perryville, continued to run between that place and Annapolis, for the transportation of stores and troops.

The next object with the troops who had thus been landed at Annapolis was to reach Washington with the greatest despatch. The Annapolis and Elkridge Railroad, leading from that city to the Washington Railroad, it was found had been seized by the secessionists, the depot yard and buildings securely closed, and the locomotives rendered unfit for use. But such difficulties as these were easily overcome by such men as General Butler had under his command. Having taken possession of the railroad depot, the general called for engineers and machinists, and a number of skilful mechanics at once responded from the ranks of the Massachusetts eighth. They were at once set at work to examine the only locomotive remaining at this station, and in a short time, notwithstanding it was pretty thoroughly taken to pieces, they repaired the engine so that it could be used.* In the mean time a part of the regiment was sent out on the railroad on a scouting expedition, and found the rails torn up and the track obstructed. But there were railroad builders as well as machinists in the ranks of the Massachusetts regiment, who were abundantly able to repair the road.

On the morning of the 24th of April preparations were sufficiently advanced to push forward the column of soldiers towards Washington. By this time several other transports had arrived in the harbor of Annapolis with more troops from New York, Massachusetts, and Rhode Island, so that the "base of operations" could be held against any force likely to be brought against it. Accordingly the Massachusetts eighth and New York seventh regiments commenced their march to the junction of the Annapolis with the Washington Railroad. The howitzers carried by the New York regiment were placed upon a car for offensive or defensive service if necessary, and pushed slowly along, a part of the Massachusetts men removing obstructions and relaying the track as they advanced, while the New York troops performed guard and picket duty, and prevented any attack of armed men or interruption from others. The march was slow and the work laborious, and the advanced party of Massachusetts troops were for a long time without food; but their comrades from New York generously shared their own rations with them. By this and other mutual acts of kindness on the march, the most friendly feelings were established between these two regiments, which, nobly responding to the call of their country, were so very different in the material of which they were composed; the one being chiefly made up of those engaged in mercantile or professional pursuits in the city of New York, many of them men of property, while the other was composed of mechanics, fishermen, and farmers, mostly from the small towns of Essex county, in Massachusetts.

Along the route were seen many horsemen, though never in any considerable numbers together, who watched the proceedings and progress of the troops, apparently with the purpose of conveying intelligence to some more formidable party. The people met with appeared to be secessionists, and to regard the troops as invaders; and there were many indications that they were in hostile territory rather than in one of the still loyal states of the Union. At night it was feared that some considerable force familiar with the country might make an attack upon the column; but the march and the labor was continued through the night by moonlight, although numbers of the soldiers were so weary and worn out with labor that they fell asleep upon the march. But the next morning Annapolis Junction was reached, and the troops sunk to rest with scarcely a guard to prevent a surprise.

In the course of the day the repaired locomotive and a train of cars arrived from Annapolis with the remainder of the regiments. The

---

* One of the men employed on this work discovered in this locomotive a piece of his own work, he having been employed in the construction of it in his own county.

Engraved by J. Rogers

secessionists had again torn up the rails and obstructed the track after the repairs had been made, so that the train moved slowly, and was frequently detained by the necessity of new repairs. But the road was at last opened, and the forces which had now arrived at Annapolis could easily protect it from further serious injury. Trains came up from Washington to the Junction, and the troops were carried forward as rapidly as new regiments arrived to guard the route. Communication between the capital and the loyal north, upon which it depended for safety, was again established by the energy of General Butler and the mechanical skill which was exhibited in such a remarkable manner by the Massachusetts soldiers; and as the troops from the loyal states hurried forward with a common patriotism to support the government of the Union, the people felt a great relief that the capital was safe, and could not again be placed in such peril.

This route for the transportation of troops to the national capital was not opened without the opposition of the people of Annapolis and of Maryland, and the protest of the governor of the state. The idea of the neutrality of the state in the impending contest was cherished by many men, who, though disposed to be loyal, were alarmed at the prospect of further riot and bloodshed, and it was encouraged by the secessionists as a long step towards joining the rebellion, which it certainly was. Governor Hicks was loyal; but he yielded to the wishes of the people who advocated neutrality, and not only sent a protest to General Butler against landing troops at Annapolis, but he advised the President to order them elsewhere, and also that no more be sent through Maryland. At the same time, undoubtedly with an earnest desire to adjust the differences which were involving the country in civil war, he suggested that Lord Lyons be requested to act as a mediator between the contending parties.

To the protest of Governor Hicks General

Butler made a suitable reply, while he did not release the military possession which he had taken of the railroad, or abate his efforts to forward troops. He also offered the services of troops to suppress an insurrection of slaves, which was alleged to be in contemplation. To the suggestions made to the government Mr. Seward replied as follows:—

"DEPARTMENT OF STATE, *April* 22, 1861.

"To THOMAS H. HICKS, GOVERNOR OF MARYLAND.

"SIR: I have had the honor to receive your communication of this morning, in which you have informed me that you have felt it to be your duty to advise the President of the United States to order elsewhere the troops off Annapolis, and also that no more be sent through Maryland, and that you have further suggested that Lord Lyons be requested to act as mediator between the contending parties in our country, to prevent the effusion of blood.

"The President directs me to acknowledge the receipt of that communication, and to assure you that he has weighed the counsels which it contains with the respect which he habitually cherishes for the chief magistrates of the several states, and especially for yourself. He regrets as deeply as any magistrate or citizen of the country can, that demonstrations against the safety of the United States, with very extensive preparations for the effusion of blood, have made it his duty to call out the force to which you allude. The force now sought to be sent through Maryland is intended for nothing but the defence of this capital.

"The President has necessarily confided the choice of the national highway which that force shall take in coming to the city to Lieutenant-General Scott, commanding the army of the United States, who, like his only predecessor, is not less distinguished for his humanity than for his loyalty, patriotism, and distinguished public service.

"The President instructs me to add that the

24

national highway thus selected by the lieuten-ant-general has been chosen by him, upon con-sultation with prominent magistrates and citi-zens of Maryland, as the one which, while a route is absolutely necessary, is farther re-moved from the populous cities of the state, and with the expectation that it would, therefore, be the least objectionable one.

"The President cannot but remember that there has been a time in the history of the American Union when forces designed for the defence of its capital were not unwelcome any where in the state of Maryland, and certainly not at Annapolis — then, as now, the capital of that patriotic state, and then, also, one of the capitals of the Union. If eighty years could have obliterated all other noble sentiments of that age in Maryland, the President would be hopeful, nevertheless, that there is one that would forever remain there and every where. That sentiment is, that no domestic contention whatever that may arise among the parties of this republic, ought, in any case, to be referred to any foreign arbitrament, least of all to the arbitrament of a European monarchy.

"I have the honor to be,

  "With distinguished consideration,

    "Your Excellency's most obedient servant,

        "WILLIAM H. SEWARD."

CHAPTER XXVII.

WHILE the spirit of the loyal north was thus aroused by the attack on Fort Sumter, and the government was taking vigorous measures to maintain the federal authority, the spirit of rebellion seemed to receive a similar impetus from the same events. It appeared as if the secessionists had waited and longed for the commencement of hostilities, and, indifferent whether the first shot was fired on one side or the other, were rejoiced to have the war begin. They were encouraged in this desire for war by the belief that there would be so great a defec-tion at the north as to render the government almost powerless, while with their martial spirit and preparation they would be able to show a power of resistance and of attack which would soon secure terms from a weak government. Besides this, they depended upon hostilities to drive the border slave states at once into seces-sion and rebellion.

The bombardment and surrender of Fort Sumter produced the wildest excitement among the people of the south, and the announcement of the result was received with the greatest satisfaction. The proclamation of President Lincoln calling for troops, which followed im-mediately after the fall of Sumter, aroused at once ridicule and indignation. Great stress was laid upon the alleged unconstitutionality of the President's call for troops; and it really seemed that these people, who were grossly violating the constitution and laboring to over-throw and destroy it, had relied upon northern loyalty to that instrument to aid them in carry-ing out their wicked purposes. In their view the constitution must be strictly and literally observed by the government, while they absolved themselves from all obligation to it, and undertook to overthrow at once both constitution and government. It was also believed that the troops could not be raised, and that while the southern and border slave states would indignantly refuse to furnish their quota, some of the northern states would decline, or find it impossible to respond to the requisition. At the same time new impetus was given to the martial spirit of the south, and increased efforts were made to raise and equip troops; a more bitter feeling against the government and people of the north was encouraged by every sort of misrepresentation and falsehood; and all possible means were used to injure the north through trade and commerce.

The Confederate government, in addition to the army previously authorized and the militia already called into service, issued a requisition for thirty-two thousand volunteers, and most of the states called out large numbers in addition to these. And as a counter-proclamation to that of President Lincoln, Mr. Davis, aiming at what was considered the most vulnerable interest of the north, and one which would soon demand from the federal government a more pacific policy, issued the following proclamation: —

"Whereas Abraham Lincoln, President of the United States, has announced his intention of invading this Confederacy with an armed force, for the purpose of capturing its fortresses and thereby subverting its independence, and subjecting its free people to the dominion of a foreign power; and whereas it has thus become the duty of this government to repel the threatened invasion and defend the rights and liberties of the people by all the means which the laws of nations and the usages of civilized warfare place at its disposal; —

"Now, therefore, I, Jefferson Davis, President of the Confederate States of America, do issue this my proclamation, inviting all those who may desire by service in private armed vessels on the high seas to aid this government in resisting so wanton and wicked an aggression, to make application for commissions or letters of marque and reprisal, to be used under the seal of these Confederate States. * * *

"And I do further specially enjoin upon all persons holding offices, civil and military, under the authority of the Confederate States, that they be vigilant and zealous in the discharge of the duties incident thereto.

"And I do moreover solemnly exhort the good people of the Confederate States, as they love their country, as they prize the blessing of free government, as they feel the wrongs of the past and those now threatened in aggravated form by those whose enmity is more implacable because unprovoked, that they exert themselves in preserving order, in promoting concord, in maintaining the authority and efficiency of the laws, and in supporting and invigorating all the measures which may be adopted for the common defence, and by which, under the blessing of divine Providence, we may hope for a speedy, just, and honorable peace.

"In testimony whereof I have set my hand and seal this 17th day of April.

"By the President.

"ROBERT TOOMBS, *Secretary of State.*"

It was believed, according to the southern journals, that there would be many persons in Europe, and even at the north, who would gladly take out letters of marque for the purpose of preying upon the commerce of the United States. But the result showed that this reliance was altogether unfounded, and the whole scheme accomplished but little.

But the aspect of some of the border slave states at this juncture was the most threatening to the safety of the government. The temper of the people of Maryland has been incidentally noticed in the preceding chapters.

There was a strong secession element in that state, and there were also numbers who were nominally Union men, but were opposed to any decided and vigorous action on the part of the government to maintain the Union or protect itself But there was also a genuine Union sentiment there which was destined in the end to triumph. At this time the Union men were overwhelmed by the more demonstrative action of the secessionists, who, being more thoroughly organized, and composed of the more active and violent classes, would not tolerate any thing but sympathy with the south. But, by degrees, as the power of the federal government was sustained by large armed forces posted in such positions as to command Maryland, the Union sentiment was more boldly asserted, and secession became more cautious.

Governor Hicks convened the legislature of Maryland to take such action as the disturbed condition of the state demanded, and, though a Union man, recommended that Maryland should take a neutral position between the north and the south. The legislature met at Frederick, Annapolis still being occupied by the federal troops. There was some fear that secession might succeed in the legislature ; but better counsels or prudence prevailed, and sundry attempts to bring about secession, directly or indirectly, were voted down. A committee of the legislature visited the President, and declared their opinion that no attempt at secession or resistance to the federal authority would be made, and they therefore asked that the state might be spared the evils of military occupation, or any revengeful chastisement for former transgressions. The character of this address to the President perhaps reveals the reasons why secession had not been more successful. The presence of loyal troops in the state was not favorable to the success of treason. The legislature was, indeed, by no means loyal. They declared the war for the defence of the government unconstitutional, recognized

the southern Confederacy, and desired the government to accept its terms of peace, while they also adopted such measures as would prevent the organization of loyal troops in the state to respond to the call of the President, and thus practically put themselves in opposition to the government. In the mean time the secessionists of the state were doing all in their power to aid the rebellion, by furnishing men and means, evidently hoping, too, that the time would soon come when Maryland should be forced out of the Union. ˙The military power, however, was a great restraint upon their operations, and encouraged the timid still to have confidence in the Union. The prevention of hasty action served to develop and concentrate the Union sentiment, and thus, notwithstanding the efforts of rebels in and out of state, preserved Maryland to the Union without a sanguinary struggle.

On the 14th of May the loyalty of Maryland was so far established that Governor Hicks issued a proclamation calling for four regiments of volunteers for three months, in response to the requisition of the national government, to serve " within the limits of Maryland, or for the defence of the capital of the United States," these conditions having been agreed to by the secretary of war. The regiments were duly raised, and subsequent calls for troops were more promptly responded to.

The course pursued by Virginia was marked alike by treason and duplicity. The Virginia convention had assembled in February, and efforts were then made to carry the state over to the southern Confederacy, but without success. The secessionists, however, among whom were many of the most influential men of the state, were untiring in their efforts to increase the disunion sentiment, and to prepare the public mind, as well as the members of the convention, for secession upon the occurrence of some event which might afford a pretext. Under such counsels Virginia recognized the

Confederate States as an independent government, and herself took the position of an independent sovereignty even before she seceded, and declared that she would not suffer any federal troops to pass over her soil to "invade" the south, and that any attempt at "coercion" in the seceding states would be resisted by her. In the mean time measures were taken to organize and increase a military force in the state. Having thus practically joined the seceded states while professing to remain in the Union, it needed only something which might be called "coercion" to afford the desired pretext for openly joining the cotton states in the rebellion. The reënforcement of Fort Sumter was sufficiently "coercive" to answer the purposes of the secessionists; but the uncertainty and delay of the action of the government in this matter did not bring affairs to a crisis so soon as desired, and for this reason, or in order to have an appearance of deliberation, a committee of the convention was sent to Washington to ascertain what policy the government was about to pursue.

This committee had an interview with the President on the 13th of April, the day on which the attack on Fort Sumter was commenced. The following reply of the President, embracing the resolution under which the committee was appointed, shows the object and character of the mission : —

"To MESSRS. PRESTON, STUART, AND RANDOLPH.

"GENTLEMEN : As a committee of the Virginia convention, now in session, you present me a preamble and resolution as follows : —

'Whereas, in the opinion of this convention, the uncertainty which prevails in the public mind as to the policy which the Federal Executive intends to pursue towards the seceded states is extremely injurious to the industrial and commercial interests of the country, tends to keep up an excitement which is unfavorable to the adjustment of the pending difficulties, and threatens a disturbance of the public peace, therefore,

'Resolved, That a committee of three delegates be appointed to wait on the President of the United States, present to him this preamble, and respectfully ask him to communicate to this convention the policy which the Federal Executive intends to pursue in regard to the Confederate States.'

"In answer, I have to say, that, having at the beginning of my official term expressed my intended policy as plainly as I was able, it is with deep regret and mortification I now learn there is great and injurious uncertainty in the public mind as to what that policy is, and what course I intend to pursue.

"Not having as yet occasion to change, it is my purpose to pursue the course marked out in the inaugural address. I commend a careful consideration of the whole document, as the best expression I can give to my purposes. As I then and therein said, I now repeat : the power confided to me will be used to hold, occupy, and possess property and places belonging to the government, and to collect the duties and imposts; but beyond what is necessary for these objects there will be no invasion, no using of force against or among the people any where.

"By the words 'property and places belonging to the government,' I chiefly allude to the military posts and property which were in possession of the government when it came into my hands. But if, as now appears to be true, in pursuit of a purpose to drive the United States authority from their places, an unprovoked assault has been made upon Fort Sumter, I shall hold myself at liberty to repossess it, if I can, like places which had been seized before the government was devolved upon me, and in any event I shall to the best of my ability repel force by force.

"In case it proves true that Fort Sumter has been assaulted as is reported, I shall perhaps cause the United States mails to be withdrawn from all the states which claim to have seceded, believing that actual war against the government justifies and possibly demands it.

"I scarcely need say that I consider the military posts and property situated within the states which claim to have seceded as yet belonging to the United States government, as much as they did before the supposed secession. Whatever else I may do for the purpose, I shall not attempt to collect the duties and revenues by any armed invasion of any part of the country; not meaning by this, however, that I may not land a force deemed necessary to relieve a fort upon the border of the country. From the fact that I have quoted a part of the inaugural address, it must not be inferred that I repudiate any other part — the whole of which I reaffirm, except so far as what I now say of the mails may be regarded as a modification."

The fall of Fort Sumter and the call for troops by President Lincoln followed immediately the interview of this committee with the President, and probably had more effect upon the convention than the report of the committee. The proclamation of the President was used to excite the people and the members of the convention, and, viewed through the atmosphere that pervaded the Virginia capital, that document assumed the appearance of a threat, to resist which all southern men were called upon. The true friends of the Union were completely overborne in the excitement, and it was intimated that they were subjected to other pressure besides the opinion of a large majority. The convention held secret sessions, and thus determined upon secession. While the ordinance was yet before the convention, further military preparations were made in secret session, and probably measures were adopted for sudden movements to take possession of the United States property within the limits of Virginia, if not for an attack upon Washington itself. The ordinance of secession, which was adopted on the 17th of April, but was not pub-

lished for some days afterwards, was in the following form: —

ORDINANCE

"*To repeal the ratification of the constitution of the United States of America, by the state of Virginia, and to resume all the rights and powers granted under said constitution.*

"The people of Virginia, in their ratification of the constitution of the United States of America adopted by them in convention, on the twenty-fifth day of June, in the year of our Lord one thousand seven hundred and eighty-eight, having declared that the powers granted under the said constitution were derived from the people of the United States, and might be resumed whensoever the same should be perverted to their injury and oppression, and the federal government having perverted said powers, not only to the injury of the people of Virginia, but to the oppression of the southern slaveholding states, —

"Now, therefore, we, the people of Virginia, do declare and ordain, that the ordinance adopted by the people of this state in convention on the twenty-fifth day of June, in the year of our Lord one thousand seven hundred and eighty-eight, whereby the constitution of the United States of America was ratified, and all acts of the General Assembly of this state, ratifying or adopting amendments to said constitution, are hereby repealed and abrogated; that the union between the state of Virginia and the other states under the constitution aforesaid is hereby dissolved, and that the state of Virginia is in the full possession and exercise of all the rights of sovereignty which belong and appertain to a free and independent state. And they do further declare that said constitution of the United States of America is no longer binding on any of the citizens of this state.

"This ordinance shall take effect and be an act of this day, when ratified by a majority of the votes of the people of this state, cast at a poll to be taken thereon, on the fourth Thursday in May next, in pursuance of a schedule hereafter to be enacted.

"Done in convention in the city of Richmond, on the seventeenth day of April, in the year of our Lord one thousand eight hundred and sixty-one, and in the eighty-fifth year of the commonwealth of Virginia.

"A true copy.   JNO. L. EUBANK,
                                        "Secretary of Convention."

On the same day that the ordinance was adopted, Governor Letcher issued a proclamation in reply to that of the President, in which he recognized the independence of the Confederate States, argued that the President had no right under the constitution of the United States to call for an extraordinary force to wage offensive war against a foreign power, repeated the declaration that Virginia would consider the exertion of such force against the seceded states as a virtual declaration of war; and, expressing the belief that "the influence which operates to produce this proclamation against the seceding states will be brought to bear upon Virginia if she should exercise her undoubted right to resume the powers granted by her people, and that it is due to her honor that an improper exercise of force against her people should be repelled," he ordered the military of the state to hold themselves in readiness for immediate orders, and to prepare for efficient service.

At the same time he replied to the requisition from the secretary of war as follows:—

"Your object is to subjugate the southern states, and a requisition made upon me for such an object, in my judgment, is not within the purview of the constitution or of the act of 1795, and will not be complied with. You have chosen to inaugurate civil war, and having done so we will meet it in a spirit as determined as the administration has exhibited towards the south."

By a vote of the people at the time of the election of the members of the convention, the ordinance was required to be submitted to them for ratification. The more zealous secessionists were greatly opposed to this course, considering it a great mistake that the will of the people should be consulted in such a movement. But the time fixed for the popular vote was at a late day, considering the emergency, and the soldiers, who were now every-where assembling, were to have the privilege of voting in their camps, and could easily be (as they in fact were) so disposed as to influence, if not control, the vote of the people, if there were any danger of the ordinance being rejected. Besides this, the state, at the time of the voting, was already practically out of the Union, and coöperating with the southern Confederacy as fully as if it were a member of it. Secession was a foregone conclusion, with which the people had really little to do. Mr. Mason, then recently a senator in Congress, published a letter just before the election, in which he urged that by the ordinance of secession and the convention with the Confederate States the faith of Virginia was pledged to the southern states, and her people were absolved from all obligation to the United States; and he declared, of those who were opposed to secession, that "honor and duty alike require that they should not vote on the question; if they retain such opinions they must leave the state." Under such circumstances and such instructions from the leaders of secession, the ordinance was in form submitted to the popular vote, and, according to the returns, was duly ratified. The vote of Western Virginia, however, was very strong against the ordinance, and in some other portions of the state there was a considerable, though unavailing, opposition vote.

The leaders of secession and rebellion in Virginia did not wait for the ratification of the ordinance, which by its own terms was not to take effect until ratified. They at once took measures to carry out their purpose. On the 25th of April, a full month before the ordinance of secession was to be submitted to the popular vote, the convention passed another ordinance "for the adoption of the constitution of the provisional government of the Confederate States of America." This ordinance adopted and ratified the constitution of the Confederate States at once and absolutely, subject, however, to the proviso that it should be void if the ordinance of secession should be rejected by the people. At the same time the following "convention" between the commonwealth of Virginia and the Confederate States of America was entered into : —

"The commonwealth of Virginia, looking to a speedy union of said commonwealth and the other slave states with the Confederate States of America, according to the provisions of the constitution for the provisional government of said states, enters into the following temporary convention and agreement with said states, for the purpose of meeting pressing exigencies affecting the common rights, interests, and safety of said commonwealth and said Confederacy.

"1. Until the union of said commonwealth with said Confederacy shall be perfected, and said commonwealth shall become a member of said Confederacy, according to the constitutions of both powers, the whole military force and military operations, offensive and defensive, of said commonwealth, in the impending conflict with the United States, shall be under the chief control and direction of the President of said Confederate States, upon the same principles, basis, and footing as if said commonwealth were now, and during the interval, a member of said Confederacy.

"2. The commonwealth of Virginia will, after the consummation of the union contemplated in this convention, and her adoption of the constitution for a permanent government of said Confederate States, and she shall become a member of said Confederacy under said permanent constitution, if the same occur, turn over to said Confederate States all the public property, naval stores, and munitions of war, &c., she may then be in possession of acquired from the United States, on the same terms and in like manner as the other states of said Confederacy have done in like cases.

"3. Whatever expenditures of money, if any, said commonwealth of Virginia shall make before the union, under the provisional government as above contemplated, shall be consummated, shall be met and provided for by said Confederate States.

"This convention entered into and agreed to in the city of Richmond, Virginia, on the twenty-fourth day of April, 1861, by Alexander H. Stephens, the duly authorized commissioner to act in the matter for the said Confederate States, and John Tyler, William Ballard Preston, Samuel McD. Moore, James P. Holcombe, James C. Bruce, and Lewis E. Harvie, parties duly authorized to act in like manner for said commonwealth of Virginia, — the whole subject to the approval and ratification of the proper authorities of both governments respectively.

"In testimony whereof the parties aforesaid have hereto set their hands and seals the day and year aforesaid, and at the place aforesaid, in duplicate originals.

"ALEXANDER H. STEPHENS, [Seal,]
            "Commissioner for Confederate States.
"JOHN TYLER,   [Seal,]
"WM. BALLARD PRESTON, [Seal,]
"S. McD. MOORE,   [Seal,]   Commission-
"JAMES P. HOLCOMBE,   [Seal,]   ers for
"JAMES C. BRUCE,   [Seal,]   Virginia.
"LEWIS E. HARVIE,   [Seal,]

"Approved and ratified by the convention of Virginia, on the 25th of April, 1861.
            "JOHN JANNEY, President.
"JNO. L. EUBANK, Secretary."

Governor Letcher issued his proclamation promulgating this ordinance and convention, and from that time Virginia was considered by its own people (except those of Western Virginia) and by the whole south as one of the Confederate States.

Soon afterwards Governor Letcher issued another proclamation, in which he said that "the sovereignty of the commonwealth of Virginia having been denied, her territorial rights assailed, her soil threatened with invasion by the authorities at Washington, and every artifice employed which could inflame the people of the northern states, it therefore becomes the solemn duty of every citizen in Virginia to prepare for the impending conflict." "To this end, and for these purposes, and with the determination to repel invasion," the commanding general of the military forces was authorized "to call out and cause to be mustered into service, from time to time, as public exigencies may require, such additional volunteers as he may deem necessary." And under this order, before the people had voted upon the question of secession, an army was arrayed in Virginia against the government of the United States.

While the posture of affairs in Maryland and Virginia, from their proximity to the national capital, was regarded with most anxiety, and from these states, especially the latter, the greatest danger threatened the government, the attitude of the other slave states at this juncture was also a matter of great importance. Of these the course of Kentucky was regarded with the deepest interest. There was a strong Union sentiment in that state, and until the surrender of Fort Sumter there seemed to be little doubt that the state would remain true to the Union, notwithstanding the efforts made by influential secessionists. The Union sentiment here, however, was like that which was at first manifested in Maryland, and was in favor of neutrality rather than a firm support of the government. The governor of the state,

Mr. Magoffin, was a secessionist, whose sympathies were all with the seceded states; and so far as his action could effect any thing, it was undoubtedly for the promotion of secession. He was in correspondence with the government of the Confederate States and the governors of the several seceded states, and with the aid of other secessionists in Kentucky and in Tennessee, he might have carried the state over to the side of rebellion but for the determined stand taken by the Union men. The call for troops by the national government, producing, as it did every where at the south, intense feeling, was an occasion which, it was feared, might be used to bring about a crisis in which the state would be committed to secession before the people could prevent it. But this danger was fortunately escaped.

Governor Magoffin peremptorily refused to comply with the requisition for troops, and convened the legislature to take such action as the crisis demanded. That body was not disposed to aid in the secession scheme, but, on the contrary, inquired pretty sharply into the governor's proceedings. There was a determination shown not to go with the rebellious states, nor yet to give the government a firm and vigorous support, but to assume a position of neutrality, and to put the state in a condition to maintain that position. Measures were taken to organize a military force, but not to respond to the requisition of the government; and while the United States forces were desired to keep away from the soil of Kentucky, the Confederate forces were at least equally notified not to enter the state. Neutrality here was not so much in the interest of secession as it appeared to be in some other states, and was honestly and earnestly advocated by some of the ablest men of the state, as Mr. Crittenden, Mr. Guthrie, and others. But among the people there was also a genuine loyalty; and though the state government did not respond to the call for troops, there were many ready to enlist in the defence

25

of the national flag. Several regiments were raised for the defence of the state against any invasion from the seceded states, and to put down any rebellion within its borders. On the other hand, there were many who joined the rebel army, and some who still openly labored and hoped to secure the secession of Kentucky; while others, under the semblance of Union men, really gave all their wishes and efforts for the success of the rebellion.* But Kentucky, like Maryland, having escaped a sudden and hasty plunge into rebellion, grew more loyal, until at last its position of neutrality was in some degree abandoned, and it was ranged with the firm supporters of the government.

Missouri was, perhaps, in a more critical situation than Kentucky. Though there was in some parts of the state a considerable anti-slavery sentiment, there was in a large proportion of it a very strong pro-slavery feeling, as was manifested in the Kansas troubles, and consequently a warm sympathy with the southern movement. A state convention had been called in January, 1861 for the purpose of taking "such action as the condition of the country demanded." The legislature which passed the bill for this convention was supposed to be in favor of secession, and it was the hope of secessionists, undoubtedly, that an ordinance of secession would be adopted. But the Union men made an earnest effort at the polls, and elected a majority of the members of the con-

vention; and when that body assembled, in March, a vote was adopted requiring the members to take an oath to support the constitution of the United States as well as that of Missouri, and subsequently it voted decisively against secession, and adjourned till the following December.

The governor of the state, Mr. Jackson, was a secessionist, who had been in conference with the leaders of the rebellion in the more southern states; and though, influenced by the unmistakable language and action of the convention, he professed fidelity to the Union, and advocated an attitude of neutrality, he showed himself ready to do all that was in his power to unite Missouri with the seceded states. The convention having failed to carry out the scheme of secession, the governor subsequently convened the legislature to put the state " in a proper attitude of defence," by organizing the militia and adopting other military measures. In the mean time he replied to the requisition for troops from the secretary of war as follows: —

"Sir: Your despatch of the 15th instant, making a call on Missouri for four regiments of men for immediate service, has been received. There can be, I apprehend, no doubt but these men are intended to form a part of the President's army to make war upon the people of the seceded states. Your requisition, in my judgment, is illegal, unconstitutional, and revolutionary in its object, inhuman and diabolical, and cannot be complied with. Not one man will the state of Missouri furnish to carry on such an unholy crusade."

In his message to the legislature, Governor Jackson expressed himself in equally strong terms against the government, and justified the action of the seceded states. The legislature, holding secret sessions much of the time, adopted measures for organizing and arming the militia of the state, and to divert the school fund from its legitimate purpose to pay the

* Of the loyal men of Kentucky, Joseph Holt stands among the truest patriots in the country. He gave some character to the administration of Mr. Buchanan in its last days, and saved the government from utter destruction; and he was afterwards the unflinching supporter of the government, whose decision and firmness did much for the preservation of Kentucky among the loyal states. Among the traitors of that state Mr. Breckinridge, because of his former position, was preëminent. He had been Vice-President of the United States, and was now a senator in Congress. But he had been the presidential candidate of those who led the secession movement, and though for a time he held the position of a loyal man and senator in Congress, his sympathies were all on the side of treason and rebellion, and eventually he joined the rebels, and was appointed a general in their army.

military expenses. Other measures were also adopted, which, under the pretence of neutrality in the contest between the national government and the rebel states, were designed to aid the rebel cause. Having thus provided for a military force, the governor soon found occasion to call them out, and General Sterling Price, whose sympathies were also with the rebels, was appointed to organize and command them.

Meanwhile the loyal citizens of the state, chiefly in St. Louis and vicinity, organized as home guards, and were mustered into the service of the United States. And on the other hand the secessionists organized into military forces, seized the United States arsenal at Liberty, and in various parts of the state committed hostile acts and violence against Union citizens. A bitter feeling arose between the loyal citizens and the secessionists, and, encouraged by the state and local authorities, the latter were enabled to bring about collisions which must inevitably lead to such action on the part of the United States authorities, as, it was hoped, would cause an uprising in favor of the "independence of Missouri." To this end the action of the disloyal authorities of Missouri seemed constantly to be directed, until it was at last reached. But though they entailed civil war upon the state, they did not succeed in consummating their purpose. The events to which this action led will be mentioned in another chapter.

The three slave states south of the border slave states found it less difficult to slide into the rebel Confederacy. In North Carolina there had been what was termed a strong Union sentiment, and it had been among the most loyal of the southern states; but there was a disposition among the majority to coöperate with the other slave states, and the excitement created by the opening of hostilities at Charleston and the President's call for troops afforded an opportunity for secessionists to hurry the state into the rebellion. Through misrepresen-

tation of the purposes and views of the federal government, and fierce calls to resist a threatened invasion of their state and their rights, and perhaps through the apathy or alarm of those who were at heart loyal to the Union, the people of North Carolina suffered themselves to be transferred from the Union to the Confederate States. The position taken by Virginia, already committed to the rebel cause, probably had its influence; for North Carolina was thus territorially separated from the Union, and hemmed in by the Confederacy, and would be exposed to dangers to which no other state was subjected.

Governor Ellis had not shown himself a secessionist, though he was carried along with the prevailing current of sympathy for the south. He had not advised secession, and had resisted the unauthorized attempts of secessionists to seize United States property. When the requisition for troops was issued, he refused to comply with it in more courteous terms than were used by some of the slave state governors; but he issued a proclamation for a meeting of the legislature, in which he characterized the call as unconstitutional, " a high-handed and tyrannical outrage," and " a direct step towards the subjugation of the south," and declared that " united action in defence of the sovereignty of North Carolina and of the rights of the south becomes now the duty of all." He next called for volunteers in addition to the militia of the state, and seized the United States arsenal and mint. These steps were preliminary to the final action of the state through a convention which soon assembled, and which, on the 20th of May, adopted an ordinance of secession, and another ratifying and adopting the provisional constitution of the Confederate States.

Tennessee joined the rebel states at an earlier day. Although the state in February had given a large Union majority, the governor, Mr. Harris, and some of its leading politicians, were thorough secessionists, and from the commencement of the movement had been enlisted in it. In the course of time it appeared that a majority of the people in the western part of the state were also really imbued with the spirit of secession and rebellion. In the eastern part of the state there was a strong Union sentiment; but the loyal people there were overwhelmed by the secessionists, and were subjected to the grossest outrages and tyranny on account of their loyalty. The state being substantially under the control of the secessionists, they waited only something which should afford a pretext for going over to the rebellion. The action of the government in taking measures to maintain its authority and to preserve the Union was all that was required. Governor Harris replied to the requisition for troops, "Tennessee will not furnish a single man for coercion, but fifty thousand, if necessary, for the defence of our rights or those of our southern brothers." The seizure of bonds and other property belonging to the United States was next resorted to. Already the rebel army had received considerable additions from this state; and now further military preparations were made both on behalf of the state and of the southern Confederacy, of which it was not yet a member. The method of accomplishing secession was similar to that adopted in Virginia. A convention, or league, authorized by the legislature in secret session, was entered into between the state and the Confederate States, similar to that agreed to by Virginia and the Confederacy, in which it was provided that, until Tennessee became a member of the Confederacy, the "whole military force and military operations, offensive and defensive, of said state, in the impending conflict with the United States, shall be under the chief control and direction of the President of the Confederate States, upon the same basis, principles, and footing, as if said state were now, and during the interval, a member of said Confederacy." And it was also provided that all the public property

"acquired* from the United States" should be transferred to the Confederate States. At the same time a declaration of independence and a secession ordinance were also adopted in secret session, to be submitted to the people for ratification. But as the league had practically carried Tennessee into the rebel confederacy, and the time for voting was put at a distant day, before which there would be further acts to commit the state more irretrievably to rebellion, the vote of the people was of little consequence. Tennessee was, therefore, actually one of the Confederate States from the time of the forming of the league and passing the secession ordinance, which were on the 6th of May.†

In Arkansas there was, probably, some loyalty among the people, but it was of little account in the secession excitement which spread so swiftly through the slave states after the fall of Fort Sumter. Rebellious demonstrations had before been made by the people in different parts of the state, and as early as February the United States arsenal at Little Rock had been surrendered to the state authorities. To the President's call for troops Governor Rector replied, in a letter to the secretary of war, as follows : —

"In answer to your requisition for troops from Arkansas, to subjugate the southern states, I have to say that none will be furnished. The demand is only adding insult to injury. The people of this commonwealth are freemen, not slaves, and will defend to the last extremity their honor, lives, and property against northern mendacity and usurpation."

---

* The rebels used mild terms to express the robbery, plunder, and theft by which they "acquired" the property of the United States.

† Among the loyal men and earnest patriots of Tennessee, who would not join, or in any way consent to, the rebellion, were Andrew Johnson, United States senator, Horace Maynard, representative in Congress, Emerson Etheridge, subsequently clerk of the house of representatives, and Rev. William G. Brownlow, known as Parson Brownlow, of the Knoxville "Union." Among those of whom the country had reason to expect better things than joining in the treason, was John Bell, recently the "Union" candidate for president.

As in some of the other states, the refusal to furnish troops was followed by acts of hostility against the federal government, in the seizure of public property, and organizing forces to resist rather than to aid the Union. A state convention, which had been previously elected, was reassembled, and on the 6th of May adopted an ordinance of secession. On the 17th of the month Arkansas was admitted as a member of the Confederate States by the Congress at Montgomery.

Thus the seceded states were increased to ten, and had reached the limit to which they were likely to extend. One other of the border slave states remains to be mentioned, the little state of Delaware, which alone of the slave states assumed a loyal attitude at the outset, and in which, by the state authority, a force was duly organized in response to the President's requisition, and mustered into the service of the United States.

CHAPTER XXVIII.

Attempts to seize United States Property in Virginia. — Fortress Monroe. — Gosport Navy Yard. — Preparations of the Government for saving Public Vessels and Property. — Negligence of Commander and Treachery of Subordinate Officers. — Report of Secretary of the Navy on the Subject. — Commodore Paulding sent to Norfolk. — His Arrival too late to save the Vessels. — Ships already scuttled. — Preservation of the Cumberland. — The Vessels and Buildings burned. — Loss to the United States. — Harper's Ferry Armory. — Small Force sent for its Protection. — Advance of a Rebel Force to seize it. — Arsenal destroyed by Lieutenant Jones. — Disappointment of the Virginia Rebels. — Seizure of other Posts and Military Property in North Carolina, Tennessee, and Arkansas. — Military Posts in the seceded States still retained by the United States.

WHEN secession had been determined upon in Virginia, and before the ordinance was yet promulgated, preparations were made to seize the public property of the United States within the limits of the state. The most important places belonging to the United States in Virginia, of which treason thus sought to get pos-

session, were Fortress Monroe, in Hampton Roads, Gosport Navy Yard, and the armory at Harper's Ferry; the first an extensive and strong fortification, commanding the entrance to the only good harbors and thriving ports in the state, and the others containing a large quantity of arms and ordnance stores, while at the navy yard were also several valuable vessels of war.

The government was aware of the danger which threatened these important posts, and took measures to save them, or to prevent them from falling into the hands of the rebels. In Fortress Monroe there was a garrison of two or three hundred men, which was not sufficient to hold it against a very large force attacking from the land side, and was entirely inadequate to prevent the rebels from taking strong positions in the immediate vicinity. Two of the Massachusetts regiments, which were the first to respond to the federal requisition, were accordingly sent to that stronghold, and arrived there just as the Virginia rebels were about to put in execution their plans. This timely arrival secured the safety of the fort if an attack or surprise was contemplated, and, in a sudden emergency, was instrumental in destroying some of the public property at the Gosport Navy Yard, in order that it might not be used by the rebels.

But a place much more easily seized, and far more valuable to the rebels, because of the great quantity of ordnance and stores, as well as formidable ships of war which were lying there, was the Gosport Navy Yard.* The measure adopted by the government to preserve the property at this important naval station, and the criminal negligence of some of its officers, and the treachery of others, are recounted in the report of the secretary of the navy as follows: —

---

* Known more generally, perhaps, as the Norfolk Navy Yard, but really on the opposite side of the Elizabeth River, from the more important port of Norfolk.

" The navy yard at Norfolk, protected by no fortress or garrison, has always been a favored depot with the government. It was filled with arms and munitions, and several ships were in the harbor, dismantled and in ordinary, and in no condition to be moved, had there been men to move them. There were, however, no seamen there or on home stations to man these vessels, or even one of them of the larger class, and any attempt to withdraw them, or either of them, without a crew, would, in the then sensitive and disturbed condition of the public mind, have betrayed alarm and distrust, and been likely to cause difficulty.

" Apprehensive, however, that action might be necessary, the commandant of the yard was, early in April, advised of this feeling, and cautioned to extreme vigilance and circumspection. These admonitions were, a few days later, repeated to Commodore McCauley. This commandant, whose patriotism and fidelity were not doubted, was surrounded by officers in whom he placed confidence; but most of them, as events soon proved, were faithless to the flag and the country.

" On the 10th of April, Commodore McCauley was ordered to put the shipping and public property in condition to be moved and placed beyond danger, should it become necessary; but in doing this he was warned to take no steps that could give needless alarm. The steam frigate Merrimac could, it was believed, were her machinery in order, be made available in this emergency, not only to extricate herself, but the other shipping in the harbor. Not knowing, however, who could be confided in to take charge of her, a commander and two engineers were detailed to proceed to Norfolk for that purpose. Two days after, on the 12th of April, the department directed that the Merrimac should be prepared to proceed to Philadelphia with the utmost despatch. It was stated that to repair the engine and put it in working condition would require four weeks.

Discrediting this report, the engineer-in-chief was ordered to proceed forthwith in person, and attend to the necessary preparations.

" On the 16th of April the commandant was directed to lose no time in placing armament on board the Merrimac; to get the Plymouth and Dolphin beyond danger; to have the Germantown in a condition to be towed out, and to put the more valuable public property, ordnance, stores, &c., on shipboard, so that they could, at any moment, be moved beyond danger.

" Such was the energy and despatch of the engineer-in-chief, that on the 16th the department was advised by the commandant of the yard that on the 17th the Merrimac would be ready for temporary service; but when, on the afternoon of that day, the engineer-in-chief reported her ready for steam, Commodore McCauley refused to have her fired up. Fires, were, however, built early the next morning, and at nine o'clock the engines were working, engineers, firemen, &c., on board; but the commandant still refused to permit her to be moved, and in the afternoon gave directions to draw the fires. The cause of this refusal to move the Merrimac has no explanation other than that of misplaced confidence in his junior officers, who opposed it.

" As soon as this fatal error was reported to the department, orders were instantly issued to Commodore Paulding to proceed forthwith to Norfolk, with such officers and marines as could be obtained, and take command of all the vessels afloat on that station; to repel force by force, and prevent the ships and public property, at all hazards, from passing into the hands of the insurrectionists. But when that officer reached Norfolk, on the evening of Saturday the 20th, he found that the powder magazine had already been seized, and that an armed force had commenced throwing up batteries in the vicinity. The commandant of the yard, after refusing to permit the vessels to be moved on Thursday, and omitting it on Friday, ordered them to be scuttled on Saturday evening; and they were sinking when Commodore Paulding, with the force under his command, arrived at Norfolk. This officer, knowing that to sink the ships would be only a temporary deprivation to the insurgents, who would, when in full possession of the place, again have them afloat, ordered the torch to be applied to the sinking ships. Pursuant to instructions, he also destroyed, so far as he was able with his limited force, the public property in the yard before abandoning the place.

"The Cumberland was towed down the river, and passed, after some little delay, over the obstructions that had been sunk in the channel to prevent her removal.

"This unfortunate calamity at Norfolk not only deprived the government of several vessels, but of a large amount of ordnance and stores which had there accumulated. In preventing the shipping and property from passing into the hands of the insurgents, who had gathered in considerable force in that vicinity under General Talliaferro, Commodore Paulding, the officers, and those under them, performed their duty, and carried out, so far as was in their power, the wishes of the government and the instructions of the department."

Commodore Paulding, on his passage to Norfolk in the Pawnee, stopped at Fortress Monroe, and there took on board the third Massachusetts regiment, which had that day arrived from Boston. With this force to aid in the preservation of the public property, or to keep it from the hands of the rebels, he proceeded to Norfolk. There was great excitement at Norfolk and Portsmouth, and the secessionists seemed exceedingly anxious to obtain possession of the yard and the vessels. They had already seized the magazine, and, aided by traitors in the yard, would undoubtedly soon have had possession of the coveted prize but for the timely arrival of the Pawnee. The troops were landed, and the vessel placed in a position to resist any attack. The vessels, however, with the exception of the frigate Cumberland, had already been scuttled, and were sinking. It was impossible to save them and the valuable works in the yard, and every effort was directed to their destruction in order that they might be of no service to the rebels. While a portion of the troops, and a marine force of about sixty men, were posted so as to repel an attack, the other soldiers and a body of seamen were engaged in the work of destruction. All the government papers and other movable property were first secured, however, on board the Pawnee and Cumberland. The costly dry dock was ruined, the guns, of which there were a great number of the largest and most effective belonging to the United States, were spiked, the ship-houses and other buildings were amply supplied with combustibles for the flames, and the more valuable vessels, which were in shoal water, were prepared in like manner. When these preparations were made, as they were in a hurried manner, under the expectation of an attack from the military forces in the vicinity of the yard, the trains were fired, and the Pawnee towed the Cumberland down the river, safely passing the obstructions sunk in the channel by order of Governor Letcher for the purpose of preventing the escape of the coveted vessels.

The fire raged fiercely, and occasional explosions hastened the work of destruction, which was in some parts complete, and in others only partial. The most valuable of the vessels, the steam frigate Merrimac, was but very partially burned before she sunk so as to extinguish the fire; and other property was saved by the Virginia soldiers and people as soon as the departure of the Union force and the fear of explosions allowed them to enter the yard. The vessels thus sacrificed were

the line of battle ships Pennsylvania, Columbus, and New York, the latter still being on
the stocks; the frigates United States, Raritan,
and Columbia; the sloops of war Germantown
and Plymouth; the brig Dolphin; and the
steam frigate Merrimac. Several of the vessels were old and of little value; but the Merrimac and one or two others were a serious loss
to the government. The Virginia rebels had
counted on securing these vessels, and they
were greatly disappointed at the failure of their
plans and enraged at the destruction of property which, with singular notions of proprietorship, they regarded as their own.

They were equally disappointed in their
attempts to seize the armory at Harper's Ferry
and the arms contained in it. This attempt
was made at about the same time as that at
Norfolk, pursuant to the arrangements of the
Virginia authorities when the secession ordinance was adopted. A company of mounted
riflemen, under the command of Lieutenant
Roger Jones, had been sent by the government
to protect the armory; but this was too small
a force to resist any considerable body of men,
such as would probably be sent to take possession of the armory, should the rebels determine upon such a course. Orders were accordingly given for the destruction of the arms and
arsenal, should it be impossible to hold the place.

On the night of April 18, Lieutenant Jones
received information that a force of twenty-
five hundred or three thousand men was
approaching the town, and was within a few
hours' march. The arsenal buildings had already been prepared for the flames, and upon
learning that a portion of the Virginia troops
would reach the armory in a few minutes, Lieutenant Jones ordered the torch to be applied.
These buildings and the carpenter's shop were
soon in flames, but the armory buildings, with
much of their valuable machinery, were not set
on fire. Having thus secured the destruction
of the arms, which it was most important to

keep from the hands of the rebels, the small
federal force was withdrawn, and crossing into
Maryland, proceeded by a forced march to Carlisle Barracks, in Pennsylvania.

Here again the Virginians were baffled. The
arms contained in the arsenal were what they
most desired to obtain; but the greater part of
them were totally destroyed, or rendered unfit
for service. Parts of the valuable machinery
used in the manufacture of the arms, were,
however, not damaged, and the rebels claimed
to have saved a large number of arms also; but
it was the belief of Lieutenant Jones that these
were almost wholly destroyed.

While the rebels were prevented by this
action of the federal troops from obtaining any
immediate material advantage, the destruction
of the arsenal and its contents, and the abandonment of the armory, were a serious loss to the
United States. The arms were much needed,
so many of the best muskets having been distributed by Floyd among the southern states.
The armory at Springfield, Massachusetts, was
the only other national manufactory of small
arms, and that was, of course, inadequate to
supply the number which would soon be required by the forces to be called into the field.
The works at Harper's Ferry were extensive
and valuable, and a very effective arm was made
there. But the small force at the disposal of
the government rendered it impossible to protect them from an attack by large numbers, and
the only alternative was to destroy what would
most aid the insurgents.

The abandonment of the Gosport Navy Yard
and Harper's Ferry left all the national posts
in Virginia, except Fortress Monroe, in the
hands of the rebels. They took possession of
Fort Norfolk, near the city of Norfolk, and other
small fortifications, and the United States arsenal near Richmond, as well as the navy yard and
the armory; and they also posted their military
forces in other important places on the coast,
and erected new fortifications.

The forts, military posts, and other public property of the United States in North Carolina, Tennessee, and Arkansas, which had not already been seized, were taken possession of immediately upon the secession of those states, so that now the United States retained within the seceded states only Fort Pickens, at the entrance of Pensacola Bay, the Tortugas, Key West, and Fortress Monroe, together with the Rip Raps, an unfinished fort at the entrance to Hampton Roads, near Fortress Monroe. Reenforcements had been sent to Fort Pickens, and were landed in safety, a portion on the 12th, and others on the 16th of April, so that this important position could be held notwithstanding the threatened attack of considerable forces which were collected in the vicinity. Fort Jefferson, on the Dry Tortugas, off the coast of Florida, and Key West were also strengthened at this time, and from their position were safe against any attack which the rebels would be able to make. These important posts the government was determined to hold at all hazards, both for the maintenance of its authority within the states in which they were situated, and as bases of future operations in case they should be necessary.

CHAPTER XXIX.

Blockade of Southern Ports. — President's Proclamations. — Action of the Navy Department. — Concentration of available Vessels. — The Blockading Squadrons. — Deficiency of Officers. — Spirit and Action of the seceded States. — Existence of War recognized by the Confederate Congress. — Troops concentrated in Virginia. — Purposes of the Rebels. — Hostile Acts in Texas. — Capture of the Star of the West. — Troops made Prisoners of War. — Measures of the Government to meet this State of Affairs. — Call for Volunteers for Three Years. — Response from the Loyal States. — Excess of Troops offered. — Equipment and Organization of Troops. — Concentration of Federal Troops. — Command of the Forces. — Generals appointed. — Patriotism of the People. — Hearty Support of the Government in extraordinary Measures.

THE government, being forced by the action of the seceded states to assert its authority by
26

force, determined to do so at once, and with such vigor as the means at its command would allow. One of the first steps was to blockade the ports of the seceded states. In order to do this so as to guard against complications with foreign governments, it was deemed proper to announce the purpose of blockading these ports in the usual manner when the ports of another power are to be blockaded. Accordingly, the President issued the following

PROCLAMATION.

" Whereas an insurrection against the government of the United States has broken out in the states of South Carolina, Georgia, Alabama, Florida, Mississippi, Louisiana, and Texas, and the laws of the United States for the collection of the revenue cannot be effectually executed therein conformably to that provision of the constitution which requires duties to be uniform throughout the United States;

" And whereas a combination of persons engaged in such insurrection have threatened to grant pretended letters of marque to authorize the bearers thereof to commit assaults on the lives, vessels, and property of good citizens of the country lawfully engaged in commerce on the high seas, and in waters of the United States ; —

" And whereas an executive proclamation has been already issued, requiring the persons engaged in these disorderly proceedings to desist therefrom, calling out a militia force for the purpose of repressing the same, and convening Congress in extraordinary session to deliberate and determine thereon ; —

" Now, therefore, I, ABRAHAM LINCOLN, President of the United States, with a view to the same purposes before mentioned, and to the protection of the public peace, and the lives and property of quiet and orderly citizens pursuing their lawful occupations, until Congress shall have assembled and deliberated on the said unlawful proceedings, or until the same shall have ceased, have further deemed it advisable to set on foot a blockade of the ports within the states aforesaid, in pursuance of the laws of the United States, and of the law of nations in such case provided. For this purpose a competent force will be posted so as to prevent entrance and exit of vessels from the ports aforesaid. If, therefore, with a view to violate such blockade, a vessel shall approach, or shall attempt to leave, any of the said ports, she will be duly warned by the commander of one of the blockading vessels, who will indorse on her register the fact and date of such warning, and if the same vessel shall again attempt to enter or leave the blockaded port, she will be captured and sent to the nearest convenient port, for such proceedings against her and her cargo as prize as may be deemed advisable.

" And I hereby proclaim and declare that if any person, under the pretended authority of the said states, or under any other pretence, shall molest a vessel of the United States, or the persons or cargo on board of her, such person will be held amenable to the laws of the United States for the prevention and punishment of piracy.

" In witness whereof, I have hereunto set my hand, and caused the seal of the United States to be affixed.

" Done at the city of Washington, this nineteenth day of April, in the year of our Lord one thousand eight hundred and sixty-one, and of the independence of the United States the eighty-fifth.

[L. S.]   " ABRAHAM LINCOLN.
" By the President.
   "WILLIAM H. SEWARD, *Secretary of State.*"

When Virginia and North Carolina had joined in the rebellion, it became necessary to extend the blockade to those states also, and an additional proclamation was issued, as follows : —

" *By the President of the United States.*
    " A PROCLAMATION.

" Whereas, for the reasons assigned in my proclamation of the 19th instant, a blockade of the ports of the states of South Carolina, Georgia, Florida, Alabama, Louisiana, Mississippi, and Texas was ordered to be established ;

" And whereas, since that date, public property of the United States has been seized, the collection of the revenue obstructed, and duly commissioned officers of the United States, while engaged in executing the orders of their superiors, have been arrested and held in custody as prisoners, or have been impeded in the discharge of their official duties without due legal process, by persons claiming to act under authorities of the states of Virginia and North Carolina, an efficient blockade of the ports of those states will also be established.

" In witness whereof, I have hereunto set my hand, and caused the seal of the United States to be affixed.

" Done at the city of Washington, this twenty-seventh day of April, in the year of our Lord one thousand eight hundred and sixty-one, and of the independence of the United States the eighty-fifth.
[L. S.]   " ABRAHAM LINCOLN.
" By the President.
   "WILLIAM H. SEWARD, *Secretary of State.*"

The navy department took prompt and efficient measures, so far as it was able, to enforce the blockade and to maintain the authority of the government. The seaboard of the insurgent states embraced an extent of nearly three thousand miles, along which were numerous ports and harbors of more or less magnitude and importance ; and to institute an effective blockade of such an extensive coast required a very large force. All the available vessels were concentrated as quickly as possible to perform this work ; those in the dockyards were prepared for service with as much despatch as could be commanded, and most of those on foreign stations were recalled. But with all the efforts of the department there were at its disposal, for all purposes at home and abroad, but sixty-two vessels, carrying about one thousand guns and eleven thousand men. But immediate measures were taken to build, with all proper despatch, seven or eight steam sloops of war, which had been authorized by Congress at its late session, and also for the construction of a considerable number of smaller steam-gun-boats, for which there was no authority except the pressing wants of the government. Steamers and sailing vessels were also purchased and chartered, and being furnished with small armaments were rendered serviceable for the blockade and other duties required by the government.

With such vessels as could be collected, two blockading squadrons were formed; one on the Atlantic coast, under command of Flag-officer Stringham, consisting at first of twenty-two vessels with two hundred and ninety-six guns and thirty-three hundred men; and the other in the Gulf of Mexico, under Flag-officer Mervine, consisting of twenty-one vessels, with two hundred and eighty-two guns and thirty-five hundred men. In the mean time, Flag-officer Pendergrast, of the home squadron, with two or three of his vessels, established non-intercourse as far as possible, and gave notice of the blockade to foreigners. It was some time before the blockading squadrons were filled up to the numbers above stated; but as fast as the vessels could be prepared they were despatched to their destination, and the blockade, which at first was confined to only a few of the more important ports, was gradually extended as far as the limited number of vessels would permit.

One difficulty with which the navy department had to contend, in putting into service a large naval force, was a lack of officers.

After the 4th of March there were a great number of resignations, and at the time of organizing the blockading squadrons no less than two hundred and fifty-nine officers had resigned or been dismissed for disloyalty, in addition to those who had previously left the service. To supply the deficiency it was necessary to appoint officers from the merchant marine, though a considerable number of gentlemen who had formerly been connected with the navy, some of them of great ability and experience, tendered their services to sustain the flag and the country.

In making these preparations to meet the emergency in which the country was placed, the navy department, like the war department, was obliged to transcend its authority and the appropriations which had been made for that branch of the public service. But when the existence of the nation was threatened, it was necessary for the government to assume powers for its preservation, and all its acts in this direction were sustained by the common sentiment of the loyal people.

The fierce spirit in which the action of the federal government was regarded at the south, and the great military preparations which were made by the several seceded states and the government of the Confederate States, made it evident that secession was to become a determined rebellion. The Confederate Congress passed an act recognizing the "existence of war between the United States and the Confederate States," and making hostile preparations to carry it on. Troops were at once sent from all the seceded states into Virginia to join the forces of that state, and it was declared by the press and by influential parties, though not avowed by the Confederate authorities, that the army thus collecting was to attack Washington and invade the free states. The leaders of the rebellion undoubtedly had such intentions; contingent, however, upon the secession of Maryland, or such an insurrection there against the federal government as should give promise, with southern coöperation, of the addition of that state to the Confederacy.* And it was, moreover, evident that the disloyal people in Maryland were ready to accomplish secession if possible, or, failing in that, to take up arms in aid of the rebel cause.

In Texas hostile acts of a more decided character were committed. The United States troops in that state, who had been so basely betrayed by General Twiggs, had, in some cases, been surrounded by superior numbers of the state troops, and compelled to surrender. It was declared, at the time General Twiggs betrayed these forces, that the men should be free to go north if they desired it. The transport Star of the West had been despatched to Indianola to bring away a portion of these troops, when both the vessel and the soldiers, although making no hostile demonstrations, were treacherously made captive. At midnight, on the 19th of April, (the memorable day of the riot in Baltimore,) a Texan steamer approached the Star of the West, for the alleged purpose of embarking on board the latter vessel some three hundred United States soldiers. Preparations were accordingly made for their reception; but instead of the United States troops, the steamer had a large number of Texan soldiers, who took possession of the transport, and sent her to New Orleans, retaining the crew as prisoners of war. Shortly afterwards a body of unarmed United States troops, while attempting to leave Indianola in two sailing vessels, were pursued by the Texans in armed steamers, and made prisoners.

Similar hostile demonstrations, wherever the secessionists could make them, especially in Virginia, where, from their proximity to the national capital, they were most threatening, indicated a determination on the part of the

rebels, who so readily acknowledged "the existence of war," to wage it with all their power.

It was apparent, therefore, that the government must prepare for a more formidable struggle, and a longer one, than was anticipated when the call for three months' troops was issued. It was accordingly determined to raise troops for a longer term, and a call for volunteers for three years, or for the war, was issued, as follows: —

" *By the President of the United States.*

"A PROCLAMATION.

"Whereas existing exigencies demand immediate and adequate measures for the protection of the national constitution and the preservation of the national Union, by the suppression of the insurrectionary combinations now existing in several states for opposing the laws of the Union, and obstructing the execution thereof, to which end a military force, in addition to that called forth by my proclamation of the fifteenth day of April of the present year, appears to be indispensably necessary, —

"Now, therefore, I, ABRAHAM LINCOLN, President of the United States, and Commander-in-Chief of the Army and Navy thereof, and of the militia of the several states when called into actual service, do hereby call into the service of the United States forty-two thousand and thirty-four volunteers to serve for a period of three years, unless sooner discharged, and to be mustered into service as infantry and cavalry. The proportion of each arm, and the details of enrolment and organization, will be made known through the department of war.

"And I also direct that the regular army of the United States be increased by the addition of eight regiments of infantry, and one of cavalry, and one regiment of artillery, making, altogether, a maximum aggregate increase of

* The speech of A. H. Stephens, at Atlanta, Georgia, April 30, 1861, acknowledges such a purpose.

twenty-two thousand seven hundred and fourteen officers and enlisted men, the details of which increase will also be made known through the department of war.

"And I further direct the enlistment, for not less than one nor more than three years, of eighteen thousand seamen, in addition to the present force, for the naval service of the United States. The details of the enlistment and organization will be made known through the department of the navy.

"The call for volunteers hereby made, and the direction for the increase of the regular army and for the enlistment of seamen hereby given, together with the plan of organization adopted for the volunteers and for the regular forces hereby authorized, will be submitted to Congress as soon as assembled. In the mean time, I earnestly invoke the coöperation of all good citizens in the measures hereby adopted for the effectual suppression of unlawful violence, for the impartial enforcement of constitutional laws, and for the speediest possible restoration of peace and order, and, with those, of happiness and prosperity throughout our country.

"In testimony whereof I have hereunto set my hand, and caused the seal of the United States to be affixed.

"Done at the city of Washington, this third day of May, in the year of our Lord one thousand eight hundred and sixty-one, and of the independence of the
• United States the eighty-fifth.
"ABRAHAM LINCOLN.
"By the President.
"WILLIAM H. SEWARD, Secretary of State."

The response to this call in the loyal states was prompt and enthusiastic; and so numerous were the offers of troops that the government accepted a much larger number of regiments than were called for. To arm and equip this large number of men taxed the military resources of the government and of the states to the utmost. The supply of the most effective arms was limited, and it was found necessary to make large purchases in Europe. This was done both by the federal government and by some of the states. Fortunately this want of equipments was early foreseen, and orders had been sent to Europe in season to import a part of the requisite supply by the time the troops were organized. The most liberal provisions were made by the state legislatures, municipal authorities, and individuals to raise and equip these troops, and to supply them with comforts. The sums thus appropriated amounted in the aggregate to many millions of dollars, and greatly facilitated the complete equipment of the soldiers. In many of the states, too, liberal aid was given, by public appropriations or by private funds, to the families of volunteers, thus relieving the soldier from anxiety on account of those dependent upon him.

The troops, when organized and equipped, were collected in Washington, in the vicinity of Baltimore, in Cairo, at the junction of the Ohio and Mississippi Rivers, in St. Louis, and at points on the Ohio River from which they could enter Western Virginia; but the larger part were assembled in Washington and vicinity, gradually forming a large army there, to be used either for the protection of the capital or for offensive operations in Virginia, where the rebels were collecting their most formidable forces.

For the command of the large army thus suddenly called into the field a great number of general officers was required, besides the regimental and company officers, who were appointed by the governors of states. The number of experienced officers who could be appointed to these important posts was quite limited. Many officers who had been educated at the West Point Military Academy, and had served in the small army of the United States, were promoted to a rank much above that they had held; and some men in civil life, who were judged to have the requisite qualifications, were also appointed to places of high rank. Among the general officers who were early appointed were George B. McClellan and John C. Fremont, major-generals in the regular army; Benjamin F. Butler, John A. Dix, and Nathaniel P. Banks, major-generals of volunteers; E. V. Sumner, J. R. F. Mansfield, Irvin McDowell, Robert S. Anderson, and William S. Rosecrans, brigadier-generals in the army, and some of them also major-generals of volunteers. Many of the brigadier-generals of volunteers were regular army officers of an inferior grade, and not a few were taken from civil life, though many of these had received a military education, and had formerly served in the army.*

The preparations made by the government to oppose the rebel forces and to put down the rebellion, though on a vast scale, compared with any previous war measures in the history of the country, did not keep pace with the patriotism and ardor of the people in the loyal states. The patriotism of the people was fully aroused, and they were disposed to support the government in the heartiest manner in all its efforts to maintain the Union, giving men and money without stint for a vigorous prosecution of the war against a rebellion so rapidly assuming gigantic proportions. The secretary of the treasury found bankers and capitalists sympathizing with the mass of the people in their desire to furnish the government with all necessary means to secure success; and he was enabled to obtain, on much better terms than in the last months of the previous administration, large loans for the purpose of meeting the enormous expenses to which the country was so suddenly subjected

by the necessity of these vast military and naval preparations.

While the government transcended its powers in the organization of armies and naval forces, and in raising the large sums required for these purposes, it could safely rely on the manifest patriotism of the people that all such action would be ratified by Congress when that body should assemble, as it was at once by the people whom Congress represented. Never, perhaps, was a constitutional government, of limited powers, so thoroughly sustained by the confidence of the people, and its necessary assumption of power so readily acquiesced in. To the nations of Europe it revealed a new phase of republican institutions. They learned that true patriotism is consistent with such institutions; that loyalty to principles and ideas is as true and strong a sentiment as fidelity to a crowned head; and that the obedience of an intelligent, free people to its constituted rulers, even when they transcend their legitimate power for the common good, is more certain, as it is more hearty, than that which is secured by force.

CHAPTER XXX.

THE action of foreign powers, in relation to the internal troubles of the United States and the assumptions of the "Confederate States"

---

* See Appendix.

as an independent and sovereign power, was a subject of great importance, and early received the attention of the government. It was certain that great efforts would be made, and, indeed, had begun in the early stages of secession, to secure a recognition, by some of the great powers of Europe, of the independence of the Confederate States. Emissaries were sent abroad to create a sympathy for the south among influential classes, which should eventually secure the friendly action of the governments. Extraordinary advantages of cheap cotton and free trade were held out to the self-interest and avarice of the nations, as inducements for this recognition; and by the mean misrepresentations of some of the *élite* of southern society, who, under the false pretences of chivalry and social superiority, stooped to deception and falsehood, the poison of secession was infused into aristocratic circles. Even some of the diplomatic agents of the United States were engaged in this treacherous work, while others, less active, promoted the rebel interests by a weak, half-earnest support of the government they represented.

On the 28th of February, Mr. Black, then secretary of state under President Buchanan, addressed a circular to the foreign ministers of the United States, in which he said, —

" It is not improbable that persons claiming to represent the states which have thus attempted to throw off their federal obligations will seek a recognition of their independence by the [Emperor of Russia.*] In the event of such an effort being made, you are expected by the President to use such means as may in your judgment be proper and necessary to prevent its success.

" It must be very evident that it is the right of this government to ask of all foreign powers that the latter shall take no steps which may tend to encourage the revolutionary movement

* The same circular, *mutatis mutandis*, was sent to the representatives at other courts.

of the seceding states, or increase the danger of disaffection in those which still remain loyal. The President feels assured that the government of the Emperor will not do any thing in these affairs inconsistent with the friendship which this government has always heretofore experienced from him and his ancestors. If the independence of the ' Confederate States' should be acknowledged by the great powers of Europe, it would tend to disturb the friendly relations, diplomatic and commercial, now existing between those powers and the United States."

Upon assuming the office of secretary of state under President Lincoln, Mr. Seward addressed a circular to the same ministers, in substance as follows : —

"Sir: My predecessor, in his despatch number 10, addressed to you on the 28th of February last, instructed you to use all proper and necessary measures to prevent the success of efforts which may be made by persons claiming to represent those states of this Union in whose name a provisional· government has been announced to procure a recognition of their independence by the government of Spain.

" I am now instructed by the President of the United States to inform you that, having assumed the administration of the government in pursuance of an unquestioned election and of the directions of the constitution, he renews the injunction which I have mentioned, and relies upon the exercise of the greatest possible diligence and fidelity on your part to counteract and prevent the designs of those who would invoke foreign intervention to embarrass or overthrow the republic.

" When you reflect on the novelty of such designs, their unpatriotic and revolutionary character, and the long train of evils which must follow directly or consequentially from even their partial or temporary success, the President feels assured that you will justly appreciate and cordially approve the caution which prompts this communication.

"I transmit herewith a copy of the address pronounced by the President on taking the constitutional oath of office. It sets forth clearly the errors of the misguided partisans who are seeking to dismember the Union, the grounds on which the conduct of those partisans is disallowed, and also the general policy which the government will pursue with a view to the preservation of domestic peace and order, and the maintenance and preservation of the federal Union.

"You will lose no time in submitting this address to the Spanish minister for foreign affairs, and in assuring him that the President of the United States entertains a full confidence in the speedy restoration of the harmony and unity of the government by a firm, yet just and liberal bearing, coöperating with the deliberate and loyal action of the American people.

"You will truthfully urge upon the Spanish government the consideration that the present disturbances have had their origin only in popular passions, excited under novel circumstances of very transient character, and that while not one person of well-balanced mind has attempted to show that dismemberment of the Union would be permanently conducive to the safety and welfare of even his own state or section, much less of all the states and sections of our country; the people themselves still retain and cherish a profound confidence in our happy constitution, together with a veneration and affection for it such as no other form of government ever received at the hands of those for whom it was established.

"We feel free to assume that it is the general conviction of men, not only here but in all other countries, that this federal Union affords a better system than any other that could be contrived to assure the safety, the peace, the prosperity, the welfare, and the happiness of all the states of which it is composed. The position of these states, and their mining, agricultural, manufacturing, commercial, political,

and social relations and influences, seem to make it permanently the interest of all other nations that our present political system shall be unchanged and undisturbed. Any advantage that any foreign nation might derive from a connection that it might form with any dissatisfied or discontented portion, state, or section, even if not altogether illusory, would be ephemeral, and would be overbalanced by the evils it would suffer from a disseverance of the whole Union, whose manifest policy it must be hereafter, as it has always been heretofore, to maintain peace, liberal commerce, and cordial amity with all other nations, and to favor the establishment of well-ordered government over the whole American continent.

" Nor do we think we exaggerate our national importance when we claim that any political disaster that should befall us, and introduce discord or anarchy among the states that have so long constituted one great, pacific, prosperous nation, under a form of government which has approved itself to the respect and confidence of mankind, might tend by its influence to disturb and unsettle the existing systems of government in other parts of the world, and arrest that progress of improvement and civilization which marks the era in which we live."

But according to the usual custom of the government upon a change of administration, new appointments were early made, as already mentioned,* to the more important foreign missions; and in the present juncture, when some of the ministers were in coöperation with the secession movement, and others, from lack of sympathy with the new administration, were but indifferent representatives of their country, the appointment of new envoys was important and necessary. To the new ministers special instructions were given more in detail, exhibiting, to some extent, the policy of the administration, as far as then developed, with regard

---

* Page 162.

to the rebellion, and its position towards foreign powers. These instructions differed according to the mission, but the general principles and arguments were much the same, and as an example of them, the following, to Mr. Dayton, the minister to France, are explicit and forcible in stating the views of the government respecting the rebellion and concerning the rights of foreign nations : —

Mr. Seward to Mr. Dayton.

"DEPARTMENT OF STATE, WASHINGTON, *April* 22, 1861.

"SIR: You enter a very important foreign mission at a moment when our domestic affairs have reached a crisis which awakens deep solicitude. Throughout a period of eighty years law and order have prevailed, and internal peace and tranquillity have been undisturbed. Five months ago sedition showed itself openly in several of the southern states, and it has acted ever since that time with boldness, skill, and energy. An insurrectionary government, embracing seven members of this Union, has been proclaimed under the name of the Confederate States of America. That pretended authority, by means chiefly of surprise, easily seen here to have been unavoidable, although liable to be misunderstood abroad, has possessed itself of a navy yard, several fortifications and arsenals, and considerable quantities of arms, ordnance, and military stores. On the 12th of April, instant, its forces commenced an attack upon, and ultimately carried, Fort Sumter, against the brave and heroic resistance of a diminutive garrison, which had been, through the neglect of the former administration, left in a condition to prevent supplies and reënforcements.

"Owing to the very peculiar construction of our system, the late administration, Congress, and every other department of the federal government, including the army and the navy, contained agents, abettors, and sympathizers in this insurrection. The federal authorities thus

27

became inefficient, while large portions of the people were bewildered by the suddenness of the appearance of disunion, by apprehension that needless resistance might aggravate and precipitate the movement, and by political affinities with those engaged in it.

"The project of dismembering the Union doubtless has some support in commercial and political ambition. But it is chiefly based upon a local, though widely-extended partisan disappointment in the result of the recent election of President of the United States. It acquired strength for a time from its assumed character of legitimate opposition to a successful party, while, on the other hand, that party could not all at once accept the fact that an administrative political issue had given place to one which involved the very existence of the government and of the Union. These embarrassments are passing away so rapidly as to indicate that far the greater mass of the people remain loyal as heretofore. The President improved the temporary misfortune of the fall of Fort Sumter by calling on the militia of the states to reënforce the federal army, and summoning Congress for its counsel and aid in the emergency. On the other hand, the insurrectionists have met those measures with an invitation to privateers from all lands to come forth and commit depredations on the commerce of the country.

"To take care that the government of his Majesty the Emperor of France do not misunderstand our position, and through that misunderstanding do us some possible wrong, is the chief duty which you will have to perform at Paris.

"It would have been gratifying to the President if the movements to which I have alluded had taken such a course as to leave this government free from the necessity, in any event, of conferring upon them in the presence of foreign powers. In this age of social development, however, isolation even in misfortune is impossible, and every attempt at revolution in one country becomes a subject of discussion in every other. The agitators in this case have, perhaps not unnaturally, carried their bad cause before foreign states by an appeal for recognition of the independence they have proclaimed, and which they are committed to establish by arms. Prudence requires that we oppose that appeal. The President believes that you will be able to do this in such a manner as will at once comport with the high consideration for his Imperial Majesty which this government habitually entertains, and a due sense of the dignity and honor of the American people.

"The Emperor of France has given abundant proofs that he considers the people in every country the rightful source of all authority, and that its only legitimate objects are their safety, freedom, and welfare. He is versed in our constitution, and therefore he will not need demonstration that the system which is established by the constitution is founded strictly on those very principles. You will be at no loss to show also that it is perfectly adapted to the physical condition and the temper, spirit, and habits of the American people. In all its essential features it is the same system which was first built, and has since existed with ever-renewed popular consent in this part of America. The people of this country have always enjoyed the personal rights guaranteed by the great statutes of British freedom, representation concurrent with taxation, jury trial, liberty of conscience, equality before the laws, and popular suffrage. The element of federation or union was early developed while the colonies were under the authority of, and during their revolutionary contest with, the British crown, and was perfected afterwards by the establishment of the constitution of the United States. Practically it has been voluntarily accepted by every state, territory, and individual citizen of the United States. The working of the system has been completely successful, while not one square mile of domain that we at any time had occu-

pied has ever been lost to us. We have extended our jurisdiction from the St. Mary's River to the Rio Grande, on the Gulf of Mexico, and in a wide belt from the Mississippi to the Pacific Ocean. Our population has swollen from four millions to thirty-one millions. The number of our states has increased from thirteen to thirty-four. Our country has risen from insignificance to be the second in the world. Leaving out of view unimportant local instances of conflict, we have had only two foreign wars, and the aggregate duration of them was less than five years. Not one human life has hitherto been forfeited for disloyalty to the government, nor has martial law ever been established, except temporarily in case of invasion. No other people have ever enjoyed so much immunity from the various forms of political casualties and calamities.

"While there is not now, even in the midst of the gathering excitement of civil war, one American who declares his dissent from the principles of the constitution, that great charter of federal authority has won the approbation of the civilized world. Many nations have taken it as a model, and almost every other one has in some degree conformed its institutions to the principles of this constitution. The empire of France, and the new kingdom of Italy especially, are built on the same broad foundation with that of this federal republic, namely, universal suffrage.

"Surely we cannot err in assuming that a system of government which arose out of the free consent of the people of this country, which has been often reconsidered and yet continually upheld in preference to every other throughout a period of two hundred years, which has commanded the acceptance or the approval of all other nations, and to the principles of which even those who attempt to overthrow it adhere in the very heat of insurrection, must be regarded as one which is not only well adapted to the condition and character of the American people, but is even indispensable and inseparable from their national existence.

"Should it be answered that while all this has heretofore seemed true, yet that it is now disproved by the existing insurrection, you may truthfully reply that we must wait for that refutation until we see the end of the insurrection; that the insurrection proves in fact nothing else except that eighty years of peace is as much as human nature has the moderation to endure under circumstances the most conducive to moderation.

"The attempted revolution is simply causeless. It is, indeed, equally without a reason and without an object. Confessedly there is neither reason nor object, unless it be one arising out of the subject of slavery. The practice of slavery has been so long a theme of angry political debate, while it has all the time been, as it yet is, a domestic concern, that I approach it with deep regret in a communication which relates to the action of a representative of this government abroad. I refrain from any observation whatever concerning the morality or the immorality, the economy or the waste, the social or the unsocial aspects of slavery, and confine myself, by direction of the President, strictly to the point that the attempt at revolution on account of it is, as I have already said, without reason and without object. Slavery of persons of African derivation existed practically within all the European colonies which, as states, now constitute the United States of America. The framers of our government accepted that fact, and with it the ideas concerning it which were then gaining ground throughout the civilized world. They expected and desired that it should ultimately cease, and with that view, authorized Congress to prohibit the foreign slave trade after 1808. They did not expect that the practice of African slavery should be abruptly terminated to the prejudice of the peace and the economy of the country. They therefore placed the entire control of slavery,

as it was then existing, beyond the control of the federal authorities, by leaving it to remain subject to the exclusive management and disposition of the several states themselves, and fortified it there with a provision for the return of fugitives from labor and service, and another securing an allowance of three fifths of such persons in fixing the basis of direct taxation and representation. The legislators of that day took notice of the existence of a vast and nearly unoccupied region lying between the western borders of the Atlantic states and the Mississippi River. A few slaves were found in the south-west, and none in the north-west. They left the matter in the south-west to the discretion of the new states to be formed there, and prohibited the practice of slavery in the north-western region forever.

"Economical, moral, and political causes have subsequently modified the sentiments of that age differently in the two sections. Long ago slavery was prohibited by all the northern states, and, on the contrary, the increased production of cotton has resulted in fortifying the institution of slavery in the southern states. The accretions of domain, by purchase from Spain, France, and Mexico, brought regions in which slavery had either a very slight foothold or none at all; and this new domain, as it should come under occupation, was to be constituted into new states, which must be either free states or slave states. The original states divided according to their own divers practices — the free states seeking so to direct federal legislation and action as to result in multiplying free states, and the slave states so to direct them as to multiply slave states. The interest became more intense because the several states have equal representation in the senate of the United States. This controversy soon disclosed itself in the popular elections, and more distinctly than ever before in the recent canvass, which resulted in the accession of the present administration.

"It is now to be observed that, from the earliest agitation of the subject until that last election, the decisions of the people were practically favorable to the interest of the class which favored the extension of slavery; and yet their opponents always acquiesced. Under these circumstances, the executive administration, the national legislature, and the judiciary, were for practical purposes in the hands of that party, and the laws, with the administration and execution of them, conformed to their own policy. The opposite class prevailed in the late election so far as to bring in the President and Vice-President, the citizens they had preferred, but no further — Congress and the judiciary remained under the same bias as before. The new President could not assume his trust until the 4th of March, 1861, and even after that time, as before, the laws and the execution of them must remain unchanged. He could not, without consent of his opponents in Congress, change either, nor appoint a minister, or a ministerial officer, nor draw a dollar from the treasury even for his own defence or support. It was under these circumstances that, on the very day when the election closed and its result became known, four months before the new administration was to come in, the disappointed party took their appeal from the ballot-box to arms, and inaugurated their revolution.

"I need not further elaborate the proposition that the revolution is without a cause; it has not even a pretext.

"It is just as clear that it is without an object. Moral and physical causes have determined inflexibly the character of each one of the territories over which the dispute has arisen, and both parties after the election harmoniously agreed on all the federal laws required for their organization. The territories will remain in all respects the same, whether the revolution shall succeed or shall fail. The condition of slavery in the several states will remain just the same whether it succeed or fail. There is not even

a pretext for the complaint that the disaffected states are to be conquered by the United States if the revolution fail; for the rights of the states, and the condition of every human being in them, will remain subject to exactly the same laws and forms of administration, whether the revolution shall succeed or whether it shall fail. In the one case, the states would be federally connected with the new confederacy; in the other, they would, as now, be members of the United States; but their constitutions and laws, customs, habits, and institutions in either case will remain the same.

"It is hardly necessary to add to this incontestable statement the further fact that the new President, as well as the citizens through whose suffrages he has come into the administration, has always repudiated all designs whatever and wherever imputed to him and them of disturbing the system of slavery as it is existing under the constitution and laws. The case, however, would not be fully presented if I were to omit to say that any such effort on his part would be unconstitutional, and all his actions in that direction would be prevented by the judicial authority, even though they were assented to by Congress and the people.

"This revolution, thus equally destitute of just cause and legitimate object, aims, nevertheless, at the dismemberment of the federal Union, and, if successful, must end in the overthrow of the government of the United States. If it be true, as the consent of mankind authorizes us to assume, that the establishment of this government was the most auspicious political event that has happened in the whole progress of history, its fall must be deemed not merely a national calamity, which a patriotic government ought to try to prevent, but a misfortune to the human race, which should secure for us at least the forbearance of all other nations.

"It cannot be maintained that disunion would leave it still existing in its true character, and for its proper ends, although in two not very unequal and similar parts. Its integrity as a federal government, embracing all of the American independent, contiguous, and homogeneous states, protecting them all against foreign dangers and internal commotions, securing to them all a common property, greatness, dignity, influence, and happiness, is an indispensable feature of its constitution.

"Dismemberment would be less effectually subversive of the character, objects, and purposes of the Union, if the two confederacies, which it is proposed shall succeed it, could severally be expected to exercise its great functions within their respective dominions. But this would be impossible. The several states are now held in union with each other by a confessed obligation of cohesion that only their common consent could dissolve, and that moral law, hitherto acknowledged by all, is substituted for the central military authority, which, in other systems, secures the integrity, as well as the peace and harmony, of states. But if the revolution shall prevail, and dismemberment ensue, the federal obligation in that case will be broken, its moral force spent, and in its place there must come up the principles which are the acknowledged elements of the revolution, namely: first, that in either confederacy each state is at liberty to secede at pleasure; and secondly, the minority in each confederacy, and even in each state, may, whenever the will of the majority is ascertained, take an appeal from the ballot to the sword. It is manifest that the success of this revolution would therefore be not only a practical overthrow of the entire system of government, but the first stage by each confederacy in the road to anarchy, such as so widely prevails in Spanish America. The contest, then, involves nothing less than a failure of the hope to devise a stable system of government upon the principle of the consent of the people, and working through peaceful expressions of their will without de-

pending on military authority. If the President were addressing his countrymen at home on this occasion, instead of one of their representatives going abroad, he would direct me to set forth the consequences which obviously must follow the dissolution of the American Union — the loss of the ambition, which is a needful inspiration to a great people; the loss of the respect of mankind, and the veneration and respect of posterity; the loss of the enterprise and vigor which make us a prosperous nation; and, with the loss of sustained and constant culture, which makes us an intellectual people, the loss of safety, both at home and abroad, which directly involves the greatest calamity of all, the loss of liberty. It is sufficient only to allude to these possible evils on this occasion to afford you the grounds for assuring the government of France that the President regards the revolution as one which in every event must and will be prevented, since it is manifest that the evils which would result from its success would be as incurable as they would be intolerable.

"It is, indeed, an occasion of much regret that it has been found needful to employ force for this purpose. It is contrary to the genius and the habits of the people, as it is repugnant to the sentiments of the government of the country and of mankind. But the President believes that the country will accept that alternative with the less regret because sufficient time has been allowed to try every expedient of conciliatory prevention, and civil war is at last proved to be unavoidable. The responsibility of it must rest with those who have not only inaugurated it, but have done so without cause and without provocation. The world will see that it is an evil that comes upon us not from any necessity growing out of administration, or out of our constitution itself, but from a necessity growing out of our common nature.

"It must not, however, be inferred, that the

reluctance of the government to employ force so long has demoralized the administration, or can demoralize the American people. They are capable of a high, resolute, and vigorous defence of the Union, and they will maintain that defence with only the more firmness and fidelity, because they are animated by no hostile spirit, but, on the contrary, by a friendly and even fraternal one, being satisfied that its benefits will result equally to those who are engaged in overthrowing and those who are engaged in defending the Union.

"I have thus, under the President's direction, placed before you a simple, unexaggerated, and dispassionate statement of the origin, nature, and purposes of the contest in which the United States are now involved. I have done so only for the purpose of deducing from it the arguments you will find it necessary to employ in opposing the application of the so-called Confederate States to the government of his Majesty the Emperor for a recognition of its independence and sovereignty.

"The President neither expects nor desires any intervention, or even any favor, from the government of France, or any other, in this emergency. Whatever else he may consent to do, he will never invoke, nor even admit, foreign interference or influence in this or any other controversy in which the government of the United States may be engaged with any portion of the American people. It has been simply his aim to show that the present controversy furnishes no one ground on which a great and friendly power, like France, can justly lend aid or sympathy to the party engaged in insurrection, and therefore he instructs you to insist on the practice of neutrality by the government of the Emperor, as all our representatives are instructed to insist on the neutrality of the several powers to which they are accredited.

"Not entertaining the least apprehension of the departure from that course by his Majes-ty's government, it is not without some reluctance that the President consents to the suggestion of some considerations affecting France herself, which you may urge in support of it. France is an agricultural and manufacturing country. Her industry depends very largely on a consumption of her productions and fabrics within the United States, and on the receipt, in exchange, of cotton, or other staples, or their equivalent in money, from the United States. The ability of the United States to thus consume and furnish depends on their ability to maintain and preserve peace. War here will in any case be less flagrant, and peace, when broken, will be restored all the more quickly and all the more perfectly if foreign nations shall have the sagacity, not to say the magnanimity, to practise the neutrality we demand.

"Foreign intervention would oblige us to treat those who would yield it as allies of the insurrectionary party, and to carry on the war against them as enemies. The case would not be relieved, but, on the contrary, would only be aggravated, if several European states should combine in that intervention. The President and the people of the United States deem the Union, which would then be at stake, worth all the cost and all the sacrifices of a contest with the world in arms, if such a contest should prove inevitable.

"However other European powers may mistake, his Majesty is the last one of those sovereigns to misapprehend the nature of this controversy. He knows that the revolution of 1775 in this country was a successful contest of the great American idea of free popular government against resisting prejudices and errors. He knows that the conflict awakened the sympathies of mankind, and that ultimately the triumph of that idea has been hailed by all European nations. He knows at what cost European nations resisted for a time the progress of that idea, and perhaps is not unwilling to confess how much France, especially, has profited by it. He will not fail to recognize the presence of that one great idea in the present conflict, nor will he mistake the side on which it will be found. It is, in short, the very principle of universal suffrage, with its claim to obedience to its decrees, on which the government of France is built, that is put in issue by the insurrection here, and is in this emergency to be vindicated, and, more effectually than ever, established by the government of the United States.

"I forbear from treating of questions arising out of the revenue laws of the United States, which lately have been supposed to have some bearing on the subject. They have already passed away before the proclamation of the blockade of ports in the hands of the revolutionary party. Nor could considerations so merely mercenary and ephemeral in any case enter into the counsels of the Emperor of France.

"You will, naturally enough, be asked, What is the President's expectation concerning the progress of the contest and the prospect of its termination? It is, of course, impossible to speculate, with any confidence, upon the course of a revolution, and to fix times and seasons for the occurrence of political events affected by the excitement of popular passions; but there are two things which may be assumed as certain: first, that the union of these states is an object of supreme and undying devotion on the part of the American people, and, therefore, it will be vindicated and maintained; secondly, the American people, notwithstanding any temporary disturbance of their equanimity, are yet a sagacious and practical people, and less experience of evils than any other nation would require will bring them back to their customary and habitual exercise of reason and reflection, and, through that process, to the settlement of the controversy without further devastation and demoralization by needless continuance in a state of civil war.

"The President recognizes, to a certain extent, the European idea of the balance of power. If the principle has any foundation at all, the independence and the stability of these United States, just in their present form, properties, and character, are essential to the preservation of the balance between the nations of the earth as it now exists. It is not easy to see how France, Great Britain, Russia, or even reviving Spain, could hope to suppress wars of ambition which must inevitably break out if this continent of North America, now, after the exclusion of foreign interests for three quarters of a century, is again to become a theatre for the ambition and cupidity of European nations.

"It stands forth now to the glory of France that she contributed to the emancipation of this continent from the control of European states — an emancipation which has rendered only less benefit to those nations than to America itself. The present enlightened monarch of France is too ambitious, in the generous sense of the word, to signalize his reign by an attempt to reverse that great and magnanimous transaction. He is, moreover, too wise not to understand that the safety and advancement of the United States are guaranteed by the necessities, and, therefore, by the sympathies, of mankind.

"I am, sir, respectfully,

"Your obedient servant,

"WILLIAM H. SEWARD.

"HON. WILLIAM L. DAYTON, &c."

In view of the proclamation of Jefferson Davis, proposing to issue letters of marque, and the possibility that under that proposition the sea might swarm with privateers, greatly to the detriment of the commerce of the United States, the government further sought to establish with other maritime powers certain principles of public law for the protection of private property upon the sea. The principles in question had, some years before, been the subject of negotiation among the leading maritime powers of Europe, and the United States had, to some extent, participated in these negotiations, but without becoming a party to any convention or agreement. The history of the negotiations, and the character of the propositions to which the European powers agreed, are shown in the following circular sent by Mr. Seward to the United States ministers at the courts of those powers, for the purpose of now making the United States a party to the international agreement, and thus diminishing the dangers to commerce by stamping privateering as piracy.

" Mr. Seward to Ministers of the United States in Great Britain, France, Russia, Prussia, Austria, Belgium, Italy, and Denmark.

CIRCULAR.

"DEPARTMENT OF STATE, WASHINGTON, *April* 24, 1861.

"SIR: The advocates of benevolence and the believers in human progress, encouraged by the slow though marked meliorations of the barbarities of war which have obtained in modern times, have been, as you are well aware, recently engaged with much assiduity in endeavoring to effect some modifications of the law of nations in regard to the rights of neutrals in maritime war. In the spirit of these movements the President of the United States, in the year 1854, submitted to the several maritime nations two propositions, to which he solicited their assent as permanent principles of international law, which were as follows:

"'1. Free ships make free goods; that is to say, that the effects or goods belonging to subjects or citizens of a power or state at war are free from capture or confiscation when found on board of neutral vessels, with the exception of articles contraband of war.

"'2. That the property of neutrals on board an enemy's vessel is not subject to confiscation unless the same be contraband of war.'

"Several of the governments to which these propositions were submitted expressed their willingness to accept them, while some others, which were in a state of war, intimated a desire to defer acting thereon until the return of peace should present what they thought would be a more auspicious season for such interesting negotiations.

"On the 16th of April, 1856, a congress was in session at Paris. It consisted of several maritime powers, represented by their plenipotentiaries, namely, Great Britain, Austria, France, Russia, Prussia, Sardinia, and Turkey. That congress having taken up the general subject to which allusion has already been made in this letter, on the day before mentioned, came to an agreement, which they adopted in the form of a declaration, to the effect following: namely,—

"'1. Privateering is and remains abolished.

"'2. The neutral flag covers enemy's goods, with the exception of contraband of war.

"'3. Neutral goods, with the exception of contraband of war, are not liable to capture under enemy's flag.

"'4. Blockades, in order to be binding, must be effective; that is to say, maintained by forces sufficient really to prevent access to the coast of the enemy.'

"The agreement pledged the parties constituting the congress to bring the declaration thus made to the knowledge of the states which had not been represented in that body, and to invite them to accede to it. The congress, however, at the same time insisted, in the first place, that the declaration should be binding only on the powers who were or should become parties to it as one whole and indivisible compact; and, secondly, that the parties who had agreed, and those who should afterwards accede to it, should, after the adoption of the same, enter into no arrangement on the application of maritime law in time of war without stipulating for a strict obser-

rance of the four p...
ration.

"The declaration ...
tially recited of cont...
ers which became ...
the two proposit...
submitted to the ...
dent of the Unite...

"The declaration ...
by the governmen...
gress at Paris to the ...
States.

"The President ...
1856, made known ...
unwillingness to acc...
making that annexa...
government, my p...
the attention of ...
points, namely:—

"1st. That the ...
tions, contained in ...
substantially the ...
tions which had le...
maritime states by th...

"2d. That the P...
conditions annexed, ...
United States in the ...
that the governmen...
could not give its a...
tion contained in the ...
'privateering is an ...
though it was will...
amendment which ...
property of in ...
belligerent states fr...
by national vessel ...
that for this reason ...
the declaration viz ...
be taken altogether ...
without modification ...
Third, that the ...
the declaration whil ...
acceding to it sh...

vance of the four points resolved by the declaration.

"The declaration which I have thus substantially recited of course prevented all the powers which became parties to it from accepting the two propositions which had been before submitted to the maritime nations by the President of the United States.

"The declaration was, in due time, submitted by the governments represented in the congress at Paris to the government of the United States.

"The President, about the 14th of July, 1856, made known to the states concerned his unwillingness to accede to the declaration. In making that announcement on behalf of this government, my predecessor, Mr. Marcy, called the attention of those states to the following points, namely : —

"1st. That the second and third propositions, contained in the Paris declaration, are substantially the same with the two propositions which had before been submitted to the maritime states by the President.

"2d. That the Paris declaration, with the conditions annexed, was inadmissible by the United States in three respects; namely, first, that the government of the United States could not give its assent to the first proposition contained in the declaration, namely, that 'privateering is and remains abolished,' although it was willing to accept it with an amendment which should exempt the private property of individuals, though belonging to belligerent states, from seizure or confiscation by national vessels in maritime war. Second, that for this reason the stipulation annexed to the declaration, viz., that the propositions must be taken altogether or rejected altogether, without modification, could not be allowed. Third, that the fourth condition annexed to the declaration, which provided that the parties acceding to it should enter into no negotiation

28

for any modifications of the law of maritime war with nations which should not contain the four points contained in the Paris declaration, seemed inconsistent with a proper regard to the national sovereignty of the United States.

"On the 29th of July, 1856, Mr. Mason, then minister of the United States at Paris, was instructed by the President to propose to the government of France to enter into an arrangement for its adherence, with the United States, to the four principles of the declaration of the congress of Paris, provided the first of them should be amended as specified in Mr. Marcy's note to the Count de Sartiges on the 28th of July, 1856. Mr. Mason accordingly brought the subject to the notice of the imperial government of France, which was disposed to entertain the matter favorably, but which failed to communicate its decision on the subject to him. Similar instructions regarding the matter were addressed by this department to Mr. Dallas, our minister at London, on the 31st day of January, 1857; but the proposition above referred to had not been directly presented to the British government by him when the administration of this government by Franklin Pierce, during whose term these proceedings occurred, came to an end, on the 3d of March, 1857, and was succeeded by that of James Buchanan, who directed the negotiations to be arrested for the purpose of enabling him to examine the questions involved, and they have ever since remained in that state of suspension.

"The President of the United States has now taken the subject into consideration, and he is prepared to communicate his views upon it, with a disposition to bring the negotiation to a speedy and satisfactory conclusion.

"For that purpose you are hereby instructed to seek an early opportunity to call the attention of Her Majesty's government to the subject, and to ascertain whether it is disposed to enter into negotiations for the accession of the government of the United States to the declaration of the Paris congress, with the conditions annexed by that body to the same; and if you shall find that government so disposed, you will then enter into a convention to that effect, substantially in the form of a project for that purpose herewith transmitted to you; the convention to take effect from the time when the due ratifications of the same shall have been exchanged. It is presumed that you will need no special explanation of the sentiments of the President on this subject for the purpose of conducting the necessary conferences with the government to which you are accredited. Its assent is expected on the ground that the proposition is accepted at its suggestion, and in the form it has preferred. For your own information it will be sufficient to say that the President adheres to the opinion expressed by my predecessor, Mr. Marcy, that it would be eminently desirable for the good of all nations that the property and effects of private individuals, not contraband, should be exempt from seizure and confiscation by national vessels in maritime war. If the time and circumstances were propitious to a prosecution of the negotiation with that object in view, he would direct that it should be assiduously pursued. But the right season seems to have passed, at least for the present. Europe seems once more on the verge of quite general wars. On the other hand, a portion of the American people have raised the standard of insurrection, and proclaimed a provisional government, and, through their organs, have taken the bad resolution to invite privateers to prey upon the peaceful commerce of the United States.

"Prudence and humanity combine in persuading the President, under the circumstances, that it is wise to secure the lesser good offered by the Paris congress, without waiting indefi-

nitely in hope to obtain the greater one offered to the maritime nations by the President of the United States.

"I am, sir, respectfully,
"Your obedient servant,
"WILLIAM H. SEWARD."

Various obstacles were thrown in the way of agreeing to such a convention by some of the principal maritime powers, and no immediate advantage was derived from the proposition. The action of the government, however, was of moment to the future interests of lawful commerce, and had an important bearing on questions likely to arise in the course of the war; while the failure to enter into the proposed convention may subsequently have prejudiced the interests of parties, the subjects of European sovereigns, who might have claimed the protection of the neutral flag.

The spirit manifested by some of the principal powers of Europe towards the United States was such as had been hoped for. Russia, with whom the relations of the United States had always been most friendly, expressed a hearty sympathy with the United States, and a hope that the internal troubles would soon be settled. Austria, who naturally had an aversion to insurrection and rebellion against established authority, gave ample assurance that the rebel states would receive no encouragement there. Prussia declared her sympathy with the federal government, and some of the inferior powers expressed their friendship in a similar manner. In England and France, however, with whose people the United States were more intimately connected, there was less cordiality for the federal government than was expected. It was in those countries, especially, that the secessionists had labored most earnestly to poison the public mind, and to secure the interest of the governments. They found there not a few influential presses and individuals who espoused their course openly, or, with secret friendship, indirectly aided them by advocating neutrality on the part of their government, and advising "peaceful separation" as the best and only mode of adjusting the difficulties. Neutrality, indeed, was all that the government and people of the United States demanded, though they hoped for sympathy from nations and governments which had so often avowed their abhorrence of slavery. But it was a genuine neutrality that was asked, of action and of language — a thorough non-intervention on the part both of government and people, and an avoidance of any recognition of the rebellious states that should give them the rights of an independent government, or put them on an equality with the government of the United States, with which these powers had treaties and friendly relations.

It was some time before the English and French governments declared their purposes with regard to the rebellion. It was commonly understood that they would act in concert, as they had in other cases; and there were constant rumors of the course which they had decided to pursue. At last, on the 13th of May, the English government defined its policy by a proclamation of neutrality by the Queen. The substance of this proclamation was as follows: —

"Whereas we are happily at peace with all sovereign powers and states; and whereas hostilities have unhappily commenced between the government of the United States and certain states styling themselves the Confederate States of America; and whereas we, being at peace with the government of the United States, have declared our royal determination to maintain a strict and impartial neutrality in the contest between the said contending parties, — we, therefore, have thought fit, with the advice of privy council, to issue our royal proclamation.

"And we do hereby strictly charge and command all our loving subjects to observe a strict neutrality in and during the aforesaid hostilities, and to abstain from violating or contravening either the laws and statutes of the realm in this behalf, or the law of nations in relation thereto, as they will answer to the contrary at their peril.

"And we hereby further warn all our loving subjects, and all persons whatever entitled to our protection, that if any of them shall presume, in contempt of this royal proclamation, and of our high displeasure, to do any acts in derogation of their duty as subjects of a neutral sovereign in said contest, or in violation or contravention of the law of nations in that behalf, as, for example and more especially, by entering into the military service of either of the contending parties, as commissioned or non-commissioned officers or soldiers; or by serving as officers, sailors, or marines on board any ship or vessel of war, or transport of or in the service of either of the contending parties; or by serving as officers, sailors, or marines on board any privateer bearing letters of marque of or from either of the said contending parties; or by engaging to go or going to any place beyond the seas, with intent to enlist or engage in any such service, or by procuring or attempting to procure within Her Majesty's dominions, at home or abroad, others to do so; or by fitting out, arming, or equipping any ship or vessel to be employed as a ship of war, or privateer, or transport, by either of the said contending parties; or by breaking, or endeavoring to break, any blockade lawfully and actually established by or on behalf of either of the said contending parties; or by carrying officers, soldiers, despatches, arms, military stores or materials, or any article or articles considered and deemed to be contraband of war, according to law or modern usage of nations, for the use or service of either of the said contending parties, — all persons so offending will incur and be liable to the several penalties and penal consequences by said statute, or by the law of nations in that behalf imposed.

"And we do hereby declare that all our subjects, and persons entitled to our protection, who may misconduct themselves in these premises, will do so at their own peril and of their own wrong, and that they will in no wise obtain any protection from us, against any liabilities or penal consequences, but will, on the contrary, incur our high displeasure by such misconduct.

"Given at Richmond Park, May 13."

France soon followed the example of England by declaring neutrality, and the Emperor issued a similar proclamation. These proclamations probably had the effect to deter persons, who otherwise might have been tempted by the offer of Jefferson Davis, from fitting out privateers; but the cupidity of many of the English led them to fit out vessels loaded with articles contraband of war for the purpose of running the blockade. The rebels in this way received much aid and comfort from the English; and while any thing destined for the United States was closely watched, it does not appear that the proceedings intended to aid the rebels were, to any considerable extent, interfered with. In the British North American Provinces and the British West Indies the Queen's proclamation was constantly violated with impunity, and large supplies were thus furnished to the rebels by running the blockade in small vessels and steamers, which, at some point or other on the extended coast of the southern states, were enabled to avoid the blockading cruisers. As the blockading fleet was increased, the difficulties attending this contraband trade were multiplied, and many of the vessels were captured as prizes. The principal depot of the trade was at Nassau, New Providence, to which place large quantities of contraband goods were carried, and were there transferred to smaller and swift vessels, to be carried into some of the southern ports. And while this trade was carried on without any apparent restraint on the part of the British authorities, the cruisers of the United States were not allowed to coal there, or at any other British port in the West Indies; an example which was followed in the Dutch colonies.

Such was the policy of the leading maritime powers towards the "belligerents," as the government and loyal people of the United States, on the one hand, and the traitors and rebels on the other, were termed. The United States government, a leading power among the nations of the world, having treaty relations with all other leading powers, was treated with the coldest forms of strict neutrality; while the rebel Confederacy, not recognized as an independent power by any nation, was nominally subjected to the same neutrality, while practically it received all the benefits of a lax administration on the part of the public authorities, and the hearty sympathy and aid of parties who should have been bound to a close observance of the avowed neutrality. It is to be observed, however, in justice to other foreign nations, that the contraband trade, by which the rebels were supplied with materials of war, and the violation of the blockade, were carried on almost wholly by the English.

It has been necessary to anticipate our narrative a little in thus alluding to the foreign relations of the United States and the policy adopted by other nations with regard to the insurrection; but, as a matter of considerable importance in the history of the rebellion, these affairs could not well be overlooked before continuing the relation of domestic events and the warlike movements of armed forces.

CHAPTER XXXI.

Military Movements. — Position of the Rebels in Virginia. — Federal Troops sent to the Relay House. — Their Position. — Effect of the Movement. — Landing of Troops in Baltimore. — Entrance of Massachusetts Troops into Baltimore. — Possession of Federal Hill. — Route through Baltimore opened for Federal Troops. — Effect of the Presence of Troops in the City. — Sympathy with the Rebellion. — Secession Women. — Seizure of Contraband Articles, and Arrest of Rebel Sympathizers. — Military Movements at the West. — Cairo. — Conspiracy to seize it. — Conferences between General Prentiss and Kentucky Officers. — Organization of State Troops in Missouri. — Removal of Arms from the Arsenal at St. Louis to Illinois. — General Harney. — Home Guards. — Demand of the Police Commissioners of St. Louis. — Camp Jackson. — Evident Purpose of the Encampment of State Troops. — Arms from Louisiana. — Measures adopted by Captain Lyon. — Camp Jackson surrounded. — Surrender of State Troops. — Attack by the Mob on Federal Troops. — The Result. — Proclamation by General Harney. — Gradual Restoration of Quiet and Confidence.

THE events in the history of the rebellion thus far recorded are chiefly preliminary to the actual struggle which was to ensue. Secession had gradually proceeded till it had included eleven states, and assumed the position of a hostile power, organizing forces and making every preparation for resistance to legitimate, constitutional authority, and, indeed, for the overthrow of the free and liberal government under which the United States had become a great power among the nations. To suppress insurrection, to repel assaults upon its authority, and to maintain itself, the integrity of the Union, and the rights of the loyal states, the federal government had called into the field large forces, and had greatly increased its navy. The position of the several states was essentially settled, though the rebels had not abandoned their hopes of securing Maryland, Kentucky, and Missouri; the rebellion had become well defined in territorial extent, though its gigantic proportions were hardly yet realized; and we now enter upon the period when it becomes necessary to record the movements of military and naval forces, and the actual hostilities which it was evident could no longer be

avoided without suffering the government to fall in pieces, and yielding the country to the control of the oligarchy which originated the rebellion.

A considerable force had been collected at Washington by the first of May, and was constantly receiving accessions through Annapolis and by way of the Potomac. But the route through Baltimore was not yet opened, communication by way of the Potomac was threatened with interruption by batteries on the Virginia shore, and the Baltimore and Ohio Railroad was held at Harper's Ferry and at points west of that place by large numbers of the rebels. With such limited means of communication with the loyal states, while a hostile feeling of formidable extent still existed in Maryland, Washington could not be considered out of danger. For, besides the large force which was collecting at Harper's Ferry, an army equal at least to that already concentrated by the federal government was forming at Richmond. It was necessary, therefore, to secure Maryland beyond all danger of being added to the states in rebellion, to open communication through Baltimore, and to prepare for any attempt to throw a rebel force into the rear of Washington from Harper's Ferry. Accordingly one of the first steps taken by the government, after making Washington secure from immediate danger, was to send a force of about three thousand infantry, consisting of two Massachusetts regiments and one from New York, with a Massachusetts battery of artillery, to the Relay House, a short distance from Baltimore, at the junction of the Baltimore and Ohio Railroad with the Washington branch. At the same time the garrison of Fort McHenry, near Baltimore, was reënforced by a battalion of rifles, and a ship of war was stationed in the harbor of that city to assist the garrison in case of necessity.

The movement of troops to the Relay House, which took place on the 5th of May, was under the command of General Butler, and was effected quite suddenly and unexpectedly to the secessionists of Baltimore. The force was so posted as to command the Baltimore and Ohio Railroad and the Washington branch, and a body of troops was constantly stationed at the junction of the railroads to examine the trains for contraband goods which might be forwarded by the secessionists of Baltimore to the rebels in Virginia. These measures had the effect to stop the transit of many contraband articles destined for the rebels, and to suppress, in some degree, the sympathy and aid which the disloyal people of Baltimore were disposed to extend to the rebellion. But the chief purpose of this movement and disposition of troops was probably to prevent any rebel force from moving from Harper's Ferry by railroad to Baltimore, and exciting the disloyal people to join them in holding that city and attacking Washington. Previous to this the rebels might easily have carried out such a movement, and, probably, with success; for most of the managers and employés of the Baltimore and Ohio Railroad were notoriously in sympathy with the rebels, and the insurgents could have been as suddenly and secretly moved as were the troops of General Butler. The slumbering disloyalty of Maryland would thus have been aroused; and in the condition in which the Union men of the state then were, unarmed and disorganized, the rebels would have had every advantage. Fortunately General Scott foresaw the danger before any such attempt was made; and in his action the loyal people of the north saw, with satisfaction, that the government was becoming strong enough to take some more effective measures than simply collecting troops at Washington, though all felt that was the first necessity.

Soon after General Butler went to the Relay House, a considerable force of regular soldiers and Pennsylvania volunteers were landed at "Locust Point," in Baltimore, one of the termini of the Baltimore and Ohio Railroad. They were transported from Perryville in a steamboat, and the steam cutter Harriet Lane stood off the Point with her ports open, ready to fire upon any force of rebels or rioters who should oppose the debarkation. There was no attempt to interfere with the troops. The mayor of Baltimore and a police force were present, and the crowd of spectators appeared to have been attracted by curiosity rather than a purpose to obstruct the passage of troops, so far as their acts indicated. The soldiers, with artillery, horses, and baggage, were transferred from the steamboat to the cars, and carried immediately to Washington.

In the mean time the bridges on the railroads between Pennsylvania and Baltimore were repaired, and were soon after opened for the transportation of troops. On the 13th of May General Butler entered Baltimore with a part of his troops, carrying into effect a prophetic threat which he had made to some of the Baltimore authorities, that Massachusetts troops in the service of the United States must march unmolested over the pavements where Massachusetts blood was shed on the 19th of April. The march into Baltimore was looked upon by the disloyal people there with indignation; but there was no outbreak, for it was well understood that in case of such attack the city would be at the mercy of Fort McHenry, now fully garrisoned, the vessels of war in the harbor, and the United States troops that could at very short notice be brought to quell any rebellious demonstration. On the other hand, the loyal people of Baltimore received the troops with cheers and other demonstrations of welcome. Proceeding to Federal Hill, in the southern part of the city, the artillery was posted so as to be of service in case of necessity, and the forces disposed of to meet any emergency. Troops from the north now arrived on the railroads from Pennsylvania, and marched unmolested through the city. Some attempts were made secretly to destroy the bridges or track of the railroads, but without success, and no riotous obstruction of the passage of the troops was made. The route through Baltimore was opened not to be again closed to the passage of the forces called to the support of the government.

The troops at Federal Hill, after a few days' stay, returned to the Relay House; but the position was held by some of the newly-arrived regiments, and from that time a considerable force was kept in Baltimore to sustain the Union sentiment and to repress secession. General Cadwallader, of Pennsylvania, who came with the troops from that state, was assigned to the command of the forces in the city. General Butler's efficient and unceremonious course had not been very acceptable to the secessionists and semi-disloyal people of Baltimore, and they expressed much satisfaction with the change, though General Butler still had command of the department, his headquarters being at Annapolis. By the genuine loyalists his course was universally approved. General Butler soon after, being now appointed major-general, was ordered to Fortress Monroe, to take command of a considerable force which was being collected at that point.

Though the presence of troops in Baltimore kept the secessionists in subjection, and prevented them from any open demonstrations of sympathy with the rebels, secret aid and comfort were constantly extended to them. Small parties went into Virginia to join the rebel forces, and arms, ammunition, and medical stores, in small quantities, were smuggled away. There were also not infrequent exhibitions of sympathy with the southern cause, and contempt for the federal soldiers, by individuals. The secession women of Baltimore were conspicuous in this conduct, taking great pains to display upon their persons or in their windows miniature flags of the southern Confederacy, and avoiding, or otherwise manifesting their dislike for, the federal officers and soldiers. To such an extent was this conduct carried, that it

became necessary to repress it by military orders; and some of the more reckless female sympathizers with the rebels were justly humiliated by the insulted soldiers.

At the Relay House, as well as in Baltimore, the troops were employed to prevent the passage of men to join the rebels and the transportation of stores for their benefit. The contraband trade was in this way, to some extent, stopped, but it was directed into other channels, and conducted more secretly. Among the seizures made by the troops at the Relay House was that of the Winans steam-gun, a piece of ordnance which was alleged to be a very formidable affair, and about which a great deal had been said. Special pains were taken to secure this gun, and it was finally captured while being transported, in an incomplete state, on a common road. It proved to be of little value; and though its capture was regarded as of some importance, it would probably have been of little use to the rebels. There were also at Baltimore and in the vicinity a number of captures of men and contraband goods on board of steamers and small vessels bound down the bay; and in the city there were several important seizures of arms, evidently intended for the rebels in Virginia, or for the arming of the rebels of Maryland, should they have an opportunity to use them.

While military movements were thus being made at the east, and an army was collecting about Washington, similar movements were made at the west. As before stated, a force was stationed at Cairo, an important position at the junction of the Ohio and Mississippi Rivers, and this point was made the rendezvous of a large part of the volunteers in the western states. This disposition of the volunteers was made by the war department in consequence of evidence being received that a conspiracy existed in Kentucky, Tennessee, and Missouri to seize Cairo as an important strategic point, and to take possession of the southern portion of the Illinois

Central Railroad, and thus cut off communication between that point and the more loyal northern and central part of the state. From time to time the reports continued of military preparations in Kentucky hostile to the United States government, and rumors were frequent of a contemplated attack upon the troops at Cairo. On the other hand, it was more generally stated that the preparations in Kentucky were to prevent any "invasion of the state by either party" according to the policy advocated by some of the leading men of the state at the commencement of the rebellion. Conferences were held at different times between General Prentiss, commanding the forces at Cairo, and several Kentucky officers, among whom were Generals Buckner and Tilghman, afterwards in the rebel army, the result of which was, that there would be no "invasion" of Kentucky, except to attack a rebel force, or to suppress a rebel movement. In this position matters remained for some time, the rebels in the mean time concentrating forces at different points in Western Kentucky, and the loyal people becoming gradually more decided in their adhesion to the government, until they welcomed a movement of federal forces upon their own soil.

In Missouri active military movements were early found necessary. As seen in a previous chapter, Governor Jackson and the legislature were in favor of secession, and their efforts were directed to that end. A large number of the people sympathized with the movement, and it was quite evident that Missouri would be the scene of civil strife sooner than any other state, and, perhaps, of a more malignant character. Armed bands were every where formed for the avowed purpose of aiding the rebellion, and the state troops organized by the governor and General Price, under the acts of the secession legislature, were really designed to aid the same cause. On the other hand, troops designated as the "home guard" were formed by the loyal people, chiefly at St. Louis and some of the more important towns, and some of them were mustered into the service of the United States.

While affairs were in this condition in Missouri, and the activity of the secessionists, with the aid of the state and municipal authorities, seemed to give them the advantage, some solicitude was felt for the United States arsenal at St. Louis. There was a body of regular troops posted there, and the home guards were being organized as rapidly as could be done under the circumstances; but a sudden movement of the state forces and the mob, which for some time gathered in the vicinity of the arsenal, might effect the destruction, if not the capture, of a large quantity of arms. These arms were needed for the equipment of troops in Illinois and Indiana, as well as the home guard of Missouri; and it was deemed desirable to secure and transport them to those states without bringing about any collision. This object was successfully accomplished on the night of the 25th of April, by Captain James H. Stokes, of Illinois.

Having a requisition from the secretary of war for ten thousand muskets for the governor of Illinois, Captain Stokes went to St. Louis, where he found a large mob about the arsenal, watching the movement of the federal soldiers, and ready to obstruct any removal of the public property, and to bring in the state troops, who only awaited such an attempt in order to make a descent upon the arsenal. On the 25th of April, Captain Stokes received information that Governor Jackson had ordered two thousand of the state troops from Jefferson City to St. Louis; and it was considered by the United States officers that such a movement threatened the seizure of the arsenal. Already batteries had been planted in the vicinity of the arsenal, and with the small force which as yet could be depended upon for its defence, the success of an attack by a large body of secessionists was more than probable. An order was telegraphed to Alton, in Illinois, some miles above St. Louis, for a steamer to be sent down to the arsenal landing at midnight. Before the arrival of this boat some five hundred flint-lock muskets, which had been brought to the arsenal from Kentucky for repairs, were sent on board another steamer, for the purpose of covering the real intentions of the officers. A large part of the mob followed these arms, and they were taken possession of by the secessionists. The spies, who still lingered about the arsenal, were put in the guard house, and while the secessionists were rejoicing over their success in preventing the transportation of arms beyond the state, the steamboat from Alton came down to the arsenal landing, and the ten thousand percussion arms, for which Captain Stokes brought a requisition, were quickly placed on board. Having secured them, Captain Stokes entreated Captain Lyon and Major Callender, the officers in charge, to allow him to take the remainder of the valuable arms contained in the arsenal. In view of the danger of the arms falling into the hands of the secessionists if they were retained, these officers yielded to the appeal; and accordingly, about eleven thousand more of effective arms were placed on board the boat, together with ammunition and equipments, leaving but seven or eight thousand guns for arming the home guards. The work of loading being completed, it was found that the steamboat, in consequence of the weight of the load, was fast aground. The danger of an attack under these circumstances was great, should the facts become known to the secessionists; but by shifting the cargo the boat was got afloat, and proceeded safely to Alton. There the citizens were summoned to bring away the arms, or to protect them from attack, should the rebels of St. Louis pursue, as they were likely to do; and the entire load was soon transferred from the boat to cars, and was carried to Springfield, to be placed in loyal

29

hands for the maintenance of the government.

General Harney was commander of the western military department; but at this time he was on his way to Washington. While on the Baltimore and Ohio Railroad at Harper's Ferry, he was taken from the cars by rebel soldiers, and detained as a prisoner. Being sent to Richmond, however, he was immediately released. By some his loyalty was called in question; but he soon after showed himself a hearty supporter of the Union, though it was feared that his social relations might render him less active and stern in his measures against rebellion than the exigencies required.

The home guards organized in St. Louis were quartered in their armories in different parts of the city. The organization and arming of this body of men gave offence to the secessionists, who saw in such a force a serious obstacle to the accomplishment of their purposes. The police commissioners, who were in sympathy with the rebellion, accordingly demanded of Captain Lyon, the commandant of the post in the absence of General Harney, that all forces in the service of the United States, except those in the arsenal, should be removed. The demand was refused, as might have been expected; and the subject was referred by the commissioners to the state government. The secessionists evidently hoped in this way to bring about a collision between the state and the federal government, by which Missouri might be carried out of the Union before a sufficient force should be able to repress the rebellious and sustain the Union sentiment.

A few days after this demand, a "camp of instruction" of the state troops was formed at St. Louis, in obedience to orders from Governor Jackson, and men from the south-western part of the state were sent to it. The camp was styled "Camp Jackson," and was under the command of Brigadier-general Frost, of the

Missouri militia. To arm these or some other portions of the state troops, it was known that some of the arms taken by the Louisiana secessionists from the United States arsenal at Baton Rouge were sent to Missouri. Other camps of the state troops had been formed at the same time in different parts of the state, avowedly for the purpose of instructing the troops for a period of six days. But the well-known sympathies of the governor of the state and of the legislature, as well as of the men enrolled in this militia, made it evident that if they were not assembled for some ulterior and hostile purpose, they might be used in the present condition of affairs to precipitate a collision and secure secession.

Acting from a conviction based on a knowledge of events transpiring in the state, and of the purposes of the leading men in the state government, and also under instructions from Washington, Captain Lyon determined to nip this plan in the bud. Accordingly, on the 10th of May, with the force under his command, numbering some five or six thousand men, including the home guards mustered into the service of the United States, Captain Lyon marched out of the city to Camp Jackson, and posting his troops so as completely to surround it, he summoned the commander of the state troops to surrender. Previous to this, General Frost addressed a note to Captain Lyon, stating that he had received intimations that the latter intended to make an attack on the camp, and denying that any attack was contemplated on the arsenal by the troops under his command. Captain Lyon, however, made no reply to this note, but carried out his plans, feeling assured that it was time, and that it was his duty, to take stringent measures to prevent the success of the secession plot. In his note to General Frost, demanding the surrender, Captain Lyon wrote, —

"Your command is regarded as evidently hostile towards the government of the United States. It is, for the most part, made up of those secessionists who have openly avowed their hostility to the general government, and have been plotting at the seizure of its property and the overthrow of its authority. You are openly in communication with the so-called southern Confederacy, which is now at war with the United States, and you are receiving at your camp, from the said Confederacy and under its flag, large supplies of material of war, most of which is known to be the property of the United States. These extraordinary preparations plainly indicate none other than the well-known purpose of the governor of this state, under whose orders you are acting, and whose purpose, recently communicated to the legislature, has just been responded to by that body in the most unparalleled legislation, having in direct view hostilities to the general government and coöperation with its enemies."

Captain Lyon gave General Frost half an hour to comply with his demand. After a brief consultation with his officers, General Frost agreed to surrender. The state troops were accordingly made prisoners of war, and upon laying down their arms were offered their freedom if they would take an oath of allegiance. This, however, with a few exceptions, they refused to do, and were accordingly taken to the arsenal. The number of prisoners was about one thousand, and a considerable quantity of the arms brought from Louisiana was found in the camp.

When the federal troops, with their prisoners, were returning to the city, an attack was made by some of the mob upon a portion of the troops, and several shots were discharged at them. The soldiers were so fiercely assaulted that they were obliged to defend themselves, and they fired upon their assailants. Unfortunately there was a vast crowd of people present, — men, women, and children, — from the midst of whom the rioters made their assault. Knowing the purpose for which the federal troops marched to the camp, and the danger of some conflict, it was folly for such a crowd to attend from mere curiosity, and it was hardly to be expected that soldiers, wantonly and fiercely assailed, should forbear to defend themselves, or should see the crowd beyond their immediate assailants. Upwards of twenty persons were killed or wounded by the fire of the soldiers, and the crowd, with the rioters, immediately scattered. Great excitement ensued in the city, and the most violent threats against the soldiers and the federal government were uttered. But the display of force made by Captain Lyon, and the determination which he had shown to suppress insurrection in its incipient stages, had a good effect. The Union men were encouraged by the exercise of federal power, and the secessionists found that their plots were to be crushed by force if necessary. The next day another attack was made by a mob upon a body of the home guard who had just been enlisted, and more blood was shed. The repetition of such scenes threw the people of St. Louis into a state of excitement and alarm. To restore confidence, General Harney, who had now returned, issued a proclamation, expressing regret at the existing state of things, and pledging himself to do all he could to preserve the peace and to protect the citizens. A body of regular troops was placed in the city to assist in maintaining order, and after a time quiet and confidence were partially restored, many of the secessionists left the city to join insurrectionary forces in other places, and the Union men grew stronger and more hopeful.

In order to prevent, as far as possible, the arming of insurgent forces, seizures of arms were made at several places in St. Louis, most of which were secreted, and were evidently intended to be used in the rebel cause. These measures, and the continued mustering of the home guards into the service of the United States, kept up a state of excitement in the city among those who sympathized with secession,

while, on the other hand, the continued organization of the state troops created some well-grounded alarm among the Union men. In this state of things an agreement was made between General Harney and General Price, who commanded the state troops, by which it was arranged that these troops should be disbanded; and as this would tend to secure the maintenance of the public peace, General Harney declared that he should have no object, as he had no wish, to make military movements which might create excitement and jealousies. The state troops, however, refused to disband, according to the agreement of General Price, and it was evidently the purpose of their leaders that, under the pretext of maintaining the neutrality and safety of the state, they should be organized to aid the rebellion. General Price, too, issued a proclamation to his subordinate officers, in which, with specious arguments, he enjoined upon them " to see that all citizens, of whatever opinions in politics or religion, be protected in their persons and property " — an injunction evidently designed to bring about a collision with the United States military authorities.

General Harney was, soon after, relieved from the command of this department, and Captain Lyon, now appointed brigadier-general, succeeded him. This appointment was very unsatisfactory to the secessionists, for in his decisive action in capturing the state troops at Camp Jackson they saw reason to suppose that he would not deal leniently with rebellion. Governor Jackson then proposed to disband and disarm the " state guard," if general Lyon would disband the various forces of home guards which had been mustered into the service of the United States. Such a proposition could not, of course, be entertained by General Lyon; and Governor Jackson, finding that his scheme for suffering Missouri to fall into the Confederacy without opposition would fail, issued a proclamation for the purpose of taking it out by force, and joining at once in the rebellion. In it the governor thus stated the position taken by General Lyon and Francis P. Blair, Jr., member of Congress from the St. Louis district, who was associated with him in the conference : "They demanded not only the disorganization and disbanding of the state militia, and the nullification of the military bill, but they refused to disband their own home guard, and insisted that the federal government should enjoy the unrestricted right to move and station its troops throughout the state whenever and wherever it might, in the opinion of its officers, be necessary either for the protection of the loyal subjects of the federal government or for repelling invasion, and they plainly announced that it was the intention of the administration to take military possession, under these pretexts, of the whole state, and to reduce it, as avowed by General Lyon himself, to the exact condition of Maryland." Bent upon making Missouri independent of the federal government, Governor Jackson considered these terms as degrading, and he charged the federal agents with "energetically hastening the execution of their bloody and revolutionary schemes for the inauguration of civil war in your midst, and for the military occupation of your state by armed bands of lawless invaders—for the overthrow of your state government, and for the subversion of those liberties which the government has a right to protect; and they intend to bring their whole power to subjugate you, if possible, to the military despotism which has assumed the powers of the federal government." Inflaming the people with such misrepresentations, he called "the militia of the state, to the number of fifty thousand, into the service of the state, for the purpose of repelling such invasion."

The safety of St. Louis appeared to be secured for the present; but this action of Governor Jackson, and the military preparations in various parts of the state in conse-quence thereof, soon led to open rebellion and civil war, the events of which will be recorded in subsequent pages.

CHAPTER XXXII.

Movements of Confederate Troops to Virginia. — Danger to Washington. —Federal Movements. — Advance of the Army into Virginia. — Entrance into Alexandria. — Colonel Ellsworth's Movements. — He hauls down a Secession Flag. — Assassinated by the Proprietor. — The Assassin killed. — Entrance of other Troops into the City. — Capture of Cavalry. — Success of the Movement. — The Death of Ellsworth. — Sketch of his Life. — Funeral Ceremonies. — Movement of Troops from Fortress Monroe into Virginia. — Another Movement in North-western Virginia. — Effect of the Advance of Federal Troops at the South. — Misrepresentation to excite the Hatred of the People towards the Government and Army. — Beauregard's Proclamation. — Jefferson Davis's Speech. — Proclamations and Orders of Federal Officers. — General McClellan's Proclamation and Orders. — General Patterson's Orders. — Colonel Duryea's Proclamation. — General McDowell's Orders. — Leniency of Federal, and Barbarity of Rebel, Warfare.

As soon as Virginia had been, by its convention, contingently transferred from the Union to the Confederate States, and before the people had acted upon the question of secession, troops from the other seceded states were sent as rapidly as they could be raised and equipped into that state, and were placed under command of General Robert E. Lee,* who had been made commander-in-chief of the Virginia troops. The cry of the south was, "On to Washington;" and from the disposition of the troops such was supposed to be the design of the rebels. On the southern bank of the Potomac, Arlington Heights and adjacent hills commanded the city, and there were constant rumors that the rebels were erecting batteries upon them, or were preparing to do so. There was known to be a body of rebel soldiers in Alexandria. On the Lower Potomac they had certainly appeared,

----

* General Lee had been an officer of the United States army, one of General Scott's staff, and was highly esteemed by that general. He treacherously left the service when the secession of Virginia was probable.

in more or less force, and were erecting batteries, while at Harper's Ferry their numbers were increasing, and they were taking up positions at other points above and below that place, and had indeed taken possession of Maryland Heights, opposite Harper's Ferry. These movements had been made before the secession of Virginia had been consummated by the vote of the people, which was given on the 23d of May.

A federal force had already been ordered forward from Chambersburg, Pennsylvania, to Hagerstown in Maryland, to oppose any advance of the rebels from Harper's Ferry; and a movement of troops into Virginia, to such an extent at least as to secure the safety of Washington, was now determined upon. This movement was delayed, for weighty reasons, till the election in Virginia had passed; but on the night following the election, the necessary preparations were made, and early on the morning of the 24th of May, the troops entered Virginia. The entire force consisted of about thirteen thousand men, and was under the command of General J. K. F. Mansfield, of the United States army.

A portion of this force, of which the District of Columbia volunteers formed the vanguard, crossed the "Long Bridge" over the Potomac, and proceeded towards Alexandria, the advance halting about half a mile from the town for the main body to come up. Another division of the troops proceeded down the river by steamboats. At about the same time, a third division crossed the chain bridge, near Georgetown, and took possession of Arlington Heights and the adjacent hills.

A little before five o'clock in the morning, the commander of the United States steamer Pawnee, which was lying off Alexandria, sent a flag of truce to the rebel forces, giving them one hour within which to withdraw from the town. Soon after, the New York Fire Zouaves, commanded by Colonel Ellsworth, and other troops, arrived at the wharf, and immediately debarked. After detailing a company to destroy the railroad track near by, Colonel Ellsworth formed his regiment, and leaving them to await further orders, proceeded, with two or three officers and a very small guard, to take possession of the telegraph office and to cut the wires.

While on the way, a large secession flag was observed raised over a hotel, called the "Marshall House," and the small party entered the building, Colonel Ellsworth being determined to haul down the flag, which for some time had been waving there in sight of the loyal troops about Washington. Proceeding to the top of the house with his companions, Colonel Ellsworth cut down the flag, and was returning with it, preceded by private Brownell, when, as he had nearly reached the foot of the upper stairs, the proprietor of the house suddenly met them, and, levelling a double-barrelled gun at Colonel Ellsworth, discharged one of the barrels, killing the colonel instantly. Private Brownell had endeavored to turn the gun aside, but ineffectually. No sooner, however, had the man discharged his piece, than Brownell shot him, and thrust his bayonet through him, killing him at once, as he was in the act of discharging the other barrel. The suddenness of this attack, and the loss of their commander, alarmed the small party, who did not know how large a body of men might attack them from the various rooms opening upon the hall in which they were. Posting themselves as guards in the passage-way, and threatening any one who should dare to open a door, they awaited the arrival of a company of the Zouaves, for which Colonel Ellsworth had despatched one of his men upon entering the house. The time seemed long, for the company had missed the street; but it arrived at last, and relieved the party from their unpleasant, and, as they supposed, dangerous position. It appeared, however, that there were no armed men in the house, and that the proprietor, whose name was Jackson, had acted without concert with any other parties.

Meanwhile other troops entered the city, and the first Michigan regiment, with a detachment of regular cavalry and a section of a battery of artillery, proceeding directly to the railroad depot, saw a train just moving off with the principal part of the rebel force which had occupied the city. The artillery, however, captured a small body of cavalry, which was unable to get away. The railroad track was then torn up at different points outside of the town, to prevent the passage of trains with troops, or the transportation of stores from the town. The forces were disposed so as to hold the place against any attack, and to prevent any disturbance or insurrection among the secession inhabitants.

The entire movement was well planned and executed, though no force, as was by some anticipated, disputed possession of the points aimed at. By it the city of Washington was secured from the danger of rebel batteries on the hills of the Virginia side of the Potomac, and the entire line of that bank of the river from Georgetown to Alexandria, was held and could be occupied by a force adequate to repel any rebel attack. The one drawback to the success of the movement was the untimely death of Colonel Ellsworth — an event which caused a deeper and more general sorrow than the fall of any one man during the war. His youth, his ability, his manly and chivalric character, and his patriotism, had endeared him to the people even though they knew him not, and he was universally lamented as one of the first and noblest martyrs in the wicked rebellion. Such a man will live in history; and his memory merits more than the brief record of his death.

Ephraim Elmer Ellsworth was born in Mechanicsville, New York, April 23, 1837. The business misfortunes of his father, when he was quite young, limited his opportunities for more

than a common education, and he was early thrown upon his own resources for support. Proud, sensitive, and generous, he felt the weight of circumstances even in his boyhood, but devoted himself with energy to the pursuits in which he was engaged. While yet quite young he went to Chicago, and associated himself in business with Mr. Devereux,* of Massachusetts. For a time they met with success; but through the acts of another party, they afterwards suffered some losses, and were compelled to give up their business. Ellsworth then commenced the study of law with the energy which characterized all his undertakings, and supported himself by copying during the hours which he could spare from study and sleep. At this time he must have endured great privations and mental suffering. He lived by himself, with very few friends and no amusements. He would not permit himself to accept hospitalities and courtesies which his poverty would not admit of his reciprocating, and generous and genial as his nature was, his pride and sensitiveness must have often caused him severe struggles.

Ellsworth was not a man, however, to waste his strength in morbid suffering. He had an ambition to accomplish something practical, and to do some good for his country. The idea which most occupied his attention from an early period of his manhood, and even of his youth, was a complete and effective organization of the militia of the United States. To this he gave much thought and study; and, deeply impressed with the necessity of such a system of national defence, he undertook to convince the people of the value of his theory of organization and drill by a practical illustration of its worth. He first trained himself in the manual of arms, by severe discipline and practice, and close study of all the movements of the soldier in an anatomical view; and he thus was able to make

* Afterwards lieutenant-colonel of the 19th Massachusetts regiment.

some improvements on the chasseur drill then in use. Having made himself perfect, he organized a company whose movements and drill should be equally exact and perfect. But he was not content with having men who could drill well; he must have them disciplined in all respects, of unimpeached moral character and unquestioned sobriety, and bound together by confidence in each other, a chivalrous sense of honor, and fidelity to the purpose of their organization. With such a company thoroughly organized, he visited, in 1860, the principal cities of the north, challenging competition and winning the admiration of the vast numbers who witnessed the exhibitions of the corps. He thus secured the attention of the public, and one result of his tour was the formation of numerous companies of Zouaves, nominally on the plan of the Chicago Zouaves. He next formed a regiment in Northern Illinois, organized in a manner similar to that of the original company; and, as if foreseeing the coming struggle, tendered the services of his command to the governor of the state.

But Ellsworth's plan embraced the whole militia of the United States; and he hoped, should the presidential election result in the choice of Mr. Lincoln, that he might be enabled to accomplish the work to which he had given so much thought and study. He entered the office of Mr. Lincoln as a law student soon after his return from his military tour, but still engaged most industriously in his favorite study and plans. He enlisted heartily in the canvass, and eloquently advocated before the people the election of Mr. Lincoln. When that desired result was accomplished, he accompanied the President elect, who had become his firm friend, to Washington, trusting that now his hope might be realized by the establishment, in the war department, of a bureau of militia, to be placed under his superintendence. Disgusted with office-seeking as conducted at the capital, and waiting apparently in vain for an appoint-

ment, he abandoned the distasteful contest, and was appointed by the President a lieutenant in the army.

Before entering upon the special service for which it was intended to detail him, the attack on Fort Sumter was made; and Ellsworth, rising from a sick bed, proceeded to New York, where, by the reputation he had acquired as a soldier, and the confidence with which he inspired all who came in contact with him, he speedily raised a regiment of Zouaves, chiefly among the firemen of the city. This regiment, composed of men somewhat rough, unruly, and peculiar, but athletic, active, daring, and accustomed to danger, was well fitted for the Zouave drill and tactics to which Ellsworth had devoted so much attention. He secured discipline among these untamed men by the force of his character, by his personal qualities of head and heart, and by his physical training, strength, and endurance. All these inspired the confidence of his men, and they were ready to obey all his orders and to follow him into any danger. With this regiment, finely equipped by the liberality of citizens of New York, Colonel Ellsworth went to Washington, and when the time came for the movement into Virginia he and his command were ready.

Too rash in his desire to accomplish something, and scarcely realizing, as few did at that time, the malignant and murderous spirit of secession, he met with his untimely death. His fall was lamented throughout the country, for he was every where known as a young, noble, and chivalric soldier. But he was more than a brave soldier; he was a youth of pure and noble character, of high aims, of tender and generous affections. For his parents, whose staff and pride he was, he cherished the truest filial love, and his life and death were colored by the romance of a still more tender tie of betrothed affection. One of his last acts on the night before going to Alexandria was to write a letter to his parents, in which, as if the result were foreshadowed to his mind, he said, "Whatever may happen, cherish the consolation that I was engaged in the performance of a sacred duty; and to-night, thinking over the probabilities of the morrow and the occurrences of the past, I am perfectly content to accept whatever my fortune may be, confident that He who noteth the fall of a sparrow will have some purpose even in the fate of one like me."

The funeral ceremonies over the remains of the gallant Ellsworth took place in Washington, where the body lay in state in the presidential mansion, and every mark of respect to his memory was paid by the President, who was much attached to him, and by the military authorities.

The day preceding the movement of the troops across the Potomac, General Butler, who was now in command at Fortress Monroe, made a reconnoissance with a Vermont regiment, under Colonel Phelps, into Hampton village and vicinity. Some of the inhabitants, observing the approach of the troops, attempted to burn the bridge leading from the fortress to the Hampton side of the bay. The soldiers, however, by a rapid movement, scattered the incendiaries and extinguished the fire before it had caused much damage. The next day, the same when the movement was made from Washington, two or three regiments went over from the fortress and established a permanent camp upon ground near the bridge in Hampton, thus occupying Virginia soil in another quarter.

A few days after, on the 27th of May, a regiment of loyal Virginians, organized at Wheeling, moved towards Grafton, at which point a body of rebels were collected, and two Ohio regiments crossed the river and entered Virginia, one following the Virginia regiment from Wheeling towards Grafton, and the other crossing from Marietta to Parkersburg. A large portion of the people in this part of Virginia were loyal, as will be more particularly noticed in a subsequent chapter; but there were also many secessionists, and small bodies of troops from other parts of the state were collecting at different points, destroying bridges on the Baltimore and Ohio Railroad, and oppressing and annoying the Union families, and the movement of the Union troops was for the protection of these people, and to open communication by the railroad with Washington. This force, and those which soon followed, were under the command of Major-general George B. McClellan, who, on entering upon the soil of Virginia, issued a proclamation to the loyal Virginians, announcing that the purpose of his coming was to aid their own troops, and to enable them to organize for their own defence against the traitors. And he declared that not only would his forces abstain from all interference with slavery, but that they would, with an iron hand, crush any attempt at insurrection on the part of the slaves.

As these troops proceeded they were received with much joy by the Union people, who were largely in the majority in most of the places in the north-western part of the state, the small bodies of rebel soldiers scattered and fled at their approach, and loyal people were relieved from the presence of active rebel sympathizers by their capture or flight.

Thus were the first movements of troops made into territory which was claimed to be no longer under the jurisdiction of the United States government, and the first steps taken by the government to assert its authority against the rebellion. These movements created a great excitement, not only in Virginia, but throughout the seceded states. They were declared to be an invasion of the soil of a sovereign state and of the rights of the south, and the most fiery appeals were made to excite the people to resistance. Every sort of misrepresentation of the purposes of the government was made to inflame the passions and prejudices of men, to force into open and active rebellion all who were yet uncommitted to it or were slow in its support, and even to alarm the slaves with fears for their lives should the northern armies reach them. The martial spirit was more fully aroused, and the rebel authorities made new efforts to hurry forward troops for the defence of Virginia, which was now considered absolutely one of the Confederate States.

General Beauregard, who commanded the forces at Charleston at the time of the bombardment of Fort Sumter, was appointed to the command of the Confederate army collecting in Virginia; and upon assuming that position he issued a proclamation to the people of the counties in the vicinity of Washington, containing the most infamous misrepresentations of the character and purposes of the federal government. This proclamation commenced as follows: —

"A reckless and unprincipled tyrant has invaded your soil. Abraham Lincoln, regardless of all moral, legal, and constitutional restraints, has thrown his abolition hosts among you, who are murdering and imprisoning your citizens, confiscating and destroying your property, and committing other acts of violence and outrage too shocking and revolting to humanity to be enumerated.

"All rules of civilized warfare are abandoned, and they proclaim by their acts, if not on their banners, that their war-cry is 'Beauty and Booty.' All that is dear to man — your honor and that of your wives and daughters, your fortunes and your lives — are involved in this momentous contest."

Jefferson Davis, upon his arrival at Richmond, whither the Confederate government was now removed, in a speech to the people of that city, said, "To the enemy we leave the base acts of the assassin and incendiary; to them we leave it to insult helpless women; to us belongs vengeance upon man."

The proclamations and orders issued by the federal officers sufficiently refute these misrepresentations and falsehoods with which the
30

leaders of the rebellion sought to excite the hatred of the people of the south against the federal government and armies. General McClellan, when his forces entered Virginia, issued a proclamation to the people, setting forth that the troops came as friends, that their houses, homes, families, and property were safe under their protection, and that no interference would be made with their slaves, but, on the contrary, any attempt at insurrection would be crushed. In his orders to his soldiers he said, —

"You are ordered to cross the frontier and enter the soil of Virginia. Your mission is to restore peace and confidence, protect the majesty of the law, and secure our brethren from the grasp of armed traitors. I place under the safeguard of your hands the persons and property of Virginians. I know you will respect their feelings and all their rights, and preserve the strictest discipline. Remember that each one of you holds in his keeping the honor of Ohio and the Union. If you are called upon to overcome an armed opposition, I know your courage is equal to the task. Remember your only foes are armed traitors, and show mercy even to them when in your power, for many of them are misguided. When, under your protection, the loyal men of Western Virginia have been enabled to organize and form, they can protect themselves, and you can then return to your homes with the proud satisfaction of having preserved a gallant people from destruction."

General Patterson, when about to move from Chambersburg towards Harper's Ferry, issued orders to his troops, in which he said, —

"You are going on American soil to sustain the civil power, to relieve the oppressed, and to retake that which is unlawfully held. You must bear in mind you are going for the good of the whole country, and that, while it is your duty to punish sedition, you must protect the loyal, and, should the occasion offer, at once suppress servile insurrection."

Colonel Duryea, who commanded the troops sent from Fortress Monroe to Hampton, issued a proclamation to the inhabitants, telling them that their rights of person and property would be entirely respected, and saying, " Be assured that we are here in no war against you, your liberty, your property, or even your local customs; but to keep on high that flag of which your own great son was the bearer; to sustain those institutions and those laws made by our ancestors, and defended by their common blood."

So, too, General McDowell issued orders for keeping a strict account of all damage done to property by the advance of the army into Virginia. And such was the spirit of the proclamations and orders of other officers of the Union army as they entered the territory occupied by secessionists. These orders were strictly observed; and, as the sequel proved, the Union forces, for the most part, erred on the side of leniency towards people whose sympathies and acts were altogether on the side of rebellion. On the other hand, the barbarities of the rebels towards Union men and women in the seceded states, and towards the federal troops who fell into their hands, as well as their manner of conducting the war in many instances, are a striking commentary on the language of Davis and Beauregard.

CHAPTER XXXIII.

THE federal troops having entered Virginia, new regiments were constantly added to the forces as fast as they could be forwarded, due care being taken to keep a sufficient force in and about Baltimore, and along the Potomac above Washington. Brigadier-general Irwin McDowell, of the United States army, was assigned to the command of the army in Eastern Virginia, except the forces at Fortress Monroe and vicinity, succeeding Major-general Sandford, of the New York militia, who had been first in command. Extensive earthwork fortifications were constructed on the eminences on the south side of the Potomac, opposite Washington and Georgetown, and beyond Alexandria. The troops were advanced a short distance into Virginia, but with the exception of an occasional capture of a few rebel soldiers or disloyal residents, and some picket firing and skirmishing, little of importance transpired. One of the most spirited of these affairs was the dash of Lieutenant Tompkins, with a company of cavalry, numbering about fifty, into the village of Fairfax Court House. With this small force Lieutenant Tompkins entered the village about daylight, taking the rebel force, which numbered several hundred, by surprise. Charging upon a body of Virginia cavalry, he dispersed them, and then dashed again through the village upon some detachments of rebel troops who were just forming, and, taking five prisoners, he withdrew and returned within the Union lines, with a loss of three men missing and three wounded. Captain Marr, of the rebel troops, was the only one known to be killed, though a number were wounded. Two of the missing men were captured by the rebels, and were reported to have been retaken the next night by another bold dash of the same company.

On the 17th of June an engagement occurred unexpectedly near Vienna, on the line of the Alexandria and Loudon Railroad, and about thirteen miles from Alexandria. This railroad had just been repaired and put in a condition for use, and a train was despatched with a force consisting of the first Ohio regiment, under Brigadier-general Schenk, of Ohio, to be posted at important points along the road for its protection. The guards were posted as the train proceeded until the regiment was reduced to only four companies. With this small force the train was approaching Vienna, when, upon turning a curve, it was fired upon by a rebel battery of three guns, so posted as to command the track, and not to be seen till the train was fairly within its range. The fire killed and wounded a number of the men, who were on open cars. The train being stopped, the troops left the cars, and, being formed on either side of the railroad, prepared to resist any further attack. As they did so, the engine driver, instead of retiring slowly, as ordered, detached one car and ran back to Alexandria, leaving the troops and the remainder of the train. The small force, who were under the immediate command of Colonel McCook, stood their ground well; but it was seen that the enemy had a large body of infantry and cavalry to support his artillery, and his force was so much greater that it was deemed prudent to retire. This was done slowly, the dead and wounded being taken along on litters and blankets. The rebels did not follow, nor even make any attack with their infantry or cavalry, with which they might have overwhelmed the small number of federal soldiers. It appeared that they were fearful that a large federal force was at hand, and that the engine had returned to bring up reënforcements. General Schenk fell back slowly through the night, and was met by reënforcements early the next morning; but the enemy abandoned their position, and a large federal force was advanced to Vienna.

Quite a large number of troops were wisely kept in and about Baltimore and at Annapolis. These troops kept the secessionists in subjection, although General ,Cadwallader was more lenient than General Butler had been, and the spirit of secession in Baltimore was more demonstrative than it had dared to be while the latter was in command. Many disloyal persons were arrested and confined in Fort McHenry. Among them were some of the leading and wealthy citizens, whose sympathy with the rebel cause was shown by more than words. Writs of habeas corpus were issued in behalf of some of these prisoners; but under orders from the government, General Cadwallader refused to deliver them up or to answer to the process. Chief Justice Taney, of the Supreme Court, who issued a writ of habeas corpus in one of these cases, sent a protest to the President against the suspension of the writ, which he said the President had no right to suspend, the power being vested only in Congress. The necessity for suspending the writ was so apparent in the condition of affairs in Maryland, that the truly loyal people were ready to sustain the course of the government even if it transcended its powers. But the question of right was an open one, and the argument in favor of the power, as well as the necessity of exercising it, or even assuming it at such a perilous time, was clearly set forth in the President's message at the extra session of Congress, which will be found in a subsequent chapter. General Banks, who soon after succeeded to the command of this department, drew a tighter rein upon secession.

In Western Virginia a considerable force had followed the advance regiments, and gradually occupied many of the most important towns. Small forces of the rebels were scattered at various points; but there was hardly a skirmish, until an attack was made upon a rebel force of about fifteen hundred men at the town of Philippi. The Union troops left Grafton in two columns, composed of parts of several regiments and a battery of artillery, under the command of Colonels Dumont, Kelly, Crittenden, and Lander,* and marched in the night, and through a severe storm, about twenty miles, to the town where the rebels were encamped. Colonel Lander was to attack the enemy in front, while Colonel Kelly was to cut off their retreat by a movement in the rear. But the long and difficult march, and a mistake of a road, prevented Colonel Kelly's force from reaching the position at the appointed time, and Colonel Lander's approach being discovered by the rebels, and his men being impatient for an attack before the rebels could retreat, the latter officer, after waiting as long as he could for Colonel Kelly to reach his position, opened the attack. The cannonading had but just begun, when Colonel Kelly's force appeared on one side of the rebel camp, and moved rapidly towards it. The rebels, however, scarcely offered resistance, but, after firing a single volley, scattered and fled, pursued by the Union troops; but as there was no cavalry to follow them, they could not be overtaken by the infantry, already wearied with a long march. A few prisoners and the camp equipage were captured. The enemy lost also sixteen killed and a large number wounded. The federal loss was but one or two killed and a few wounded; among the latter, Colonel Kelly, who was shot by a rebel whom he was summoning to surrender after the battle, if it could be called such, was over.

The success of this attack relieved the greater part of North-western Virginia from the presence of rebel forces for a season. The loyal inhabitants of this vicinity were greatly rejoiced to return to their usual occupations, and to be rid of the oppression of the rebel forces. The secessionists, who were in a decided minority,

either followed the retreating rebel forces, or prudently kept quiet in their homes.

General Morris, under whose orders the federal forces had moved upon Philippi, soon after issued a proclamation, in which he said, " Western Virginia is free from the enemies of her freedom and peace. In full confidence of your ability and desire to protect yourselves, I now call upon you to come to the support of your constitutional government. I am empowered to muster you into the service of the United States, to serve only in defence of your own soil." To this call the people responded in considerable numbers, and a large body of militia, or home guards, were organized, in addition to the regiments of volunteers raised for the general service of the United States. Holding the ground they thus gained in North-western Virginia, the federal forces continued their advance into the state southward and eastward, for the purpose of opening the Baltimore and Ohio Railroad. But though no large rebel forces were again collected in this part of the state, there were numerous guerrilla parties, who inflicted much damage upon the loyal citizens, destroyed bridges, and waged a petty warfare in various ways against the federal forces and all who sympathized with the Union cause.

Early in June, a force of ten or twelve thousand men, under General Patterson, moved down from Chambersburg, Pennsylvania, towards Harper's Ferry, and another force moved up the north bank of the Potomac from the District of Columbia. There were some unimportant skirmishes, mostly firing across the river by pickets and other small bodies of troops, but no battle or decisive movement on either side. As General Patterson's forces approached Harper's Ferry, the rebels evacuated the Maryland Heights, which they had for some time occupied, and where they had some artillery mounted, and fell back to their main body on the Virginia side of the river.

* F. W. Lander, of Massachusetts, afterwards brigadier-general, who died while in command of a brigade on the Upper Potomac.

The positions held by the rebels at and near Harper's Ferry were naturally strong, and they claimed — what was generally believed — that they had rendered them impregnable. Their confidence in their ability to hold the positions, however, seemed to vanish as the federal forces approached; and after gradually withdrawing their outlying detachments, they finally, on the 14th of June, evacuated their main position at Harper's Ferry, and retreated towards Winchester. Before leaving the place, they destroyed the fine bridge over the Potomac, the government buildings, and other property which they could not remove, as well as their own provisions which they were unable to transport. General Patterson moved his forces to Williamsport, some miles above Harper's Ferry, and also advanced towards the latter place, taking possession of strong positions on the Maryland side. The rebels still remained in some force in the neighborhood, and an advance into Virginia was delayed.

In Eastern Virginia the Union forces were advanced from Hampton to Newport News Point, an important position at the mouth of the James River, where several regiments encamped and erected fortifications. At the first advance of the Union troops into this part of Virginia, most of the secessionists of the vicinity who had not previously left, abandoned their houses and estates, and left many of their slaves to take care of themselves. Large numbers of these sought the protection of the federal troops, and gathered about Fortress Monroe. For the sake of humanity it became necessary to make some provision for these unfortunate people, men, women, and children, of all ages. General Butler had, at the outset, refused to surrender some slaves, fugitives from a known secessionist, and he now adopted the general policy of considering the able-bodied negroes escaping from rebel masters, as "contraband of war," many of such being compelled by the rebels to do service in constructing batteries

and in other hostile work. Upon the question of detaining and protecting such fugitives General Butler had no doubt; but in relation to the children and infirm he would not assume to decide, and submitted the question, with his general policy, to the war department. The secretary of war approved the course of General Butler in the following reply:—

"SIR: Your action in respect to the negroes who came within your lines from the service of the rebels, is approved. The department is sensible of embarrassments which must surround officers conducting military operations in a state by the laws of which slavery is sanctioned. The government cannot recognize the rejection by any state of its federal obligations; nor can it refuse the performance of the federal obligations resting upon itself. Among these federal obligations, however, no one can be more important than that of suppressing and dispersing armed combinations formed for the purpose of overthrowing its whole constitutional authority; while, therefore, you will permit no interference by the persons under your command with the relations of persons held to service under the laws of any state, you will, on the other hand, so long as any state, within which your military operations are conducted, is under the control of such organizations, refrain from surrendering to alleged masters any persons who may come within your lines. You will employ such persons in the services to which they may be best adapted, keeping an account of the labor by them performed, of the value of it, and of the expenses of their maintenance. The question of their final disposition will be reserved for future determination.

"S. CAMERON, *Secretary of War.*
"To MAJOR-GENERAL BUTLER."

Acting under these instructions, large numbers of the slaves, who from this time were quite generally called "contrabands," were employed at Fortress Monroe and in the camps at Hampton and Newport News. In the village of Hampton, which had been almost wholly deserted by the rebel whites, these fugitives formed a large part of the population. Such as could be were employed in various ways by the government officers, receiving rations, and in some cases a tardy compensation, and others raised vegetables and fruit on the deserted grounds of their late masters, for which they found a ready sale. The care of these people required no little time and attention, and was an important department in the administration of affairs at Hampton Roads, though not, at all times, successfully or faithfully managed.

Soon after the occupation of Newport News by the federal forces, the rebels, in more or less force, were found to be posted at points north of this place, on the peninsula formed by the James and York Rivers. The pickets of the enemy occasioned some annoyance, and it was found that fortifications were erected at Great Bethel, a place some nine miles from Hampton, an advance post of their more important position at Yorktown and Williamsburg, from which they sent small forces to impress slaves, arrest Union men, and to attack the federal pickets. General Butler, having determined to drive them back from so close proximity to his lines, sent a force, consisting of the New York regiments of Colonels Townsend, Duryea, and Bendix, and a battalion of Vermont and Massachusetts troops, under Lieutenant-colonel Washburn, with four pieces of artillery, under Lieutenant Grebble, to make the attack. This force, which was commanded by Brigadier-general Pierce, of Massachusetts, numbered about three thousand men, and moved before daylight from Hampton and Newport News, the several regiments moving separately, and with orders to form a junction near Little Bethel, a place between Hampton and Great Bethel, where the rebels had an outpost. A part of the forces had thus united, and the detailed orders of Gen-

eral Butler were being successfully carried out, when, by an unfortunate mistake, Colonel Bendix's regiment, which was left at the cross-roads to guard against an attack in the rear, opened fire upon the command of Colonel Townsend as it approached in column by another road, being mistaken for the enemy, and killed and wounded several men. The fire was returned by some of Colonel Townsend's men, and confusion and excitement followed among the men of these two regiments. The troops which were in advance, hearing the firing in their rear, reversed their march to form a junction with their support. The design had been to surprise the force at Little Bethel, and then to advance quickly upon the force at Great Bethel; but this unfortunate mistake of course gave the alarm to the enemy, and, leaving their camp, they hastily retreated to Great Bethel. Colonel Duryea, however, just before this affair, had succeeded in surprising a small force, and captured thirty prisoners.

The mistake having been discovered, the troops again moved on towards Great Bethel. Here the rebels had constructed fortifications commanding the approaches to the place, and protected on one side by a creek, the bridge over which had been destroyed. From this work the rebels opened a fire with heavy guns upon the federal forces. Lieutenant Grebble replied rapidly with his howitzers, and an attempt was made by a part of the infantry to storm the fortification; but though forced to abandon one of their batteries, the rebels, protected by their intrenchments, finally repulsed their assailants by their fire of musketry and artillery. The federal troops, now for the first time under fire, behaved well and bravely for the most part; but the attack was made without sufficient knowledge of the position of the enemy, and without any well-digested plan. Finding that the place could not be carried by such an attack, and that the ammunition was failing, a retreat was ordered by General Pierce, and his forces fell back in good order. Had there been sufficient ammunition, and had the attack been continued but a short time longer, there is reason to believe that it would have been successful. The federal loss in this contest was sixteen killed, fifty-three wounded, and five missing; of whom two were killed and nineteen were wounded by the mistake made by Colonel Bendix's command.

Among the killed were Lieutenant Grebble, of the regular army, who commanded the artillery, and Major Winthrop, of General Butler's staff. Lieutenant Grebble used his pieces with great skill and bravery, though they were too light to avail much against the intrenchments and the more effective artillery of the rebels. He had fired his last shot, and had just spiked the gun under his immediate charge, lest it should fall into the hands of the enemy before it could be drawn away, when he was killed by a shot from a rifled cannon.

Major Theodore Winthrop had served in the New York seventh regiment in its brief campaign at Washington and on the road thither, and when that regiment returned home he went to Fortress Monroe, and again entered the service as a member of General Butler's staff. A man of brilliant mind and great literary talent, he was as yet almost unknown to the world, though he left some manuscript works which have since been widely read and admired. His ardent patriotism would not permit him to lie idle when his country, and the great principles of freedom involved in this contest, called for his services. He went with the expedition to Great Bethel as a volunteer; but while there he showed the greatest bravery, cheering on the men and advancing the farthest towards the rebel lines. While thus leading a charge he was shot, not by a chance bullet, but by the deliberate aim of a rebel. His body fell so near the rebel lines that the soldiers were unable to bring it away. It was, however, subsequently recovered under a flag of truce. Among those who knew him, Major Winthrop's death was felt as keenly as was Ellsworth's, so many noble traits of character had he, and such genuine ability; and the public have since realized, by the publication of some of his works, how great a loss to the literary world he was.

The rebel force at Great Bethel was supposed to be about two thousand, with ten guns in their batteries. The number may have been exaggerated; but they had the advantage of a strong position and better artillery than that of the federal troops. Their success, however, was not such as to lead them to pursue the retreating forces, except for a short distance, by a body of cavalry which was soon disposed to retire, the column being protected by the howitzers. The news of the repulse had reached Newport News and Fortress Monroe some time before the troops arrived, and had produced great excitement and activity in preparing to resist an attack which it was supposed might be made upon the camp at the former place, in case the rebels should follow in force. The ships of war moved up the roads so as to afford additional protection to the camp, and other measures for defence were taken; but it appeared that the rebels were not disposed to make any attack.

While these movements and skirmishes of the land forces, preliminary to more important movements, were taking place, a gun-boat "flotilla" was organized on the Potomac. It consisted chiefly of small steamers, purchased for the purpose, and carrying a few guns of heavy calibre; and its duty was to keep the river open for navigation, and to prevent the passage of rebel forces or contraband goods between Maryland and Virginia. The rebels had fortified several points on the Virginia side of the river, and the government transports and war vessels had been repeatedly fired upon.

Among other places, batteries had been erected at Acquia Creek, about fifty miles below Washington, the terminus of a railroad from Richmond. These batteries had caused some annoyance and damage to passing vessels, and Captain Ward, who commanded the flotilla, determined to attempt their destruction. On the 31st of May he made an attack with his flag ship, the steamer Freeborn, supported by two steamers of lighter armament. Three batteries erected near the railroad were, after several hours' cannonading, effectually silenced by the heavy fire from the steamers, and the vessels were then hauled off, though another battery on the heights back from the shore still continued its fire. The next day the bombardment was renewed by the Freeborn and the more formidable steamer Pawnee, and was continued for five hours, when it was suspended in consequence of the fatigue of the men. During the night the damage to the batteries near the shore had been repaired, and the guns from the battery on the heights had apparently been transferred to them. The firing on the part of the rebels was not so spirited as on the day previous; but the vessels were slightly damaged, and had the rebel gunners been more skilled, the damage might have been serious. The rapid and heavy firing of the steamers caused a precipitate flight of a part of the rebels, and their batteries were almost entirely silenced when the vessels withdrew. The buildings in the vicinity of the batteries were destroyed, but the fortifications were of such a character that the damage caused by the gun-boats could be easily repaired.

At a later day, June 27, Captain Ward, who had shown himself an active and efficient officer, in the performance of most arduous duties as the commander of the Potomac flotilla, was killed in an engagement at Matthias Point. There had been frequent reports that the rebels had erected batteries at this point, which was a strong position from which to attack the vessels navigating the Potomac; but Captain Ward had himself reconnoitred on the point, and satisfied himself that no permanent batteries had been erected. It appeared, however, that the rebels had visited the place with field artillery, and had thus annoyed the passing vessels. The growth of wood was very thick, and would serve to cover the enemy in his operations there; and Captain Ward had determined to fell and burn the trees and underwood, and thus prevent the enemy from masking his batteries, with the view also of inducing the government to hold the position with a land force. With a detachment of men from the Freeborn and the Pawnee, he effected a landing under the fire of the Freeborn, which threw shot and shell into the woods to drive back any rebel force that might be there. Pickets were at once thrown out, who soon met the pickets of a rebel force; and soon after a body of rebel troops approached, when the naval force was ordered to take to the boats and lie off, while Captain Ward returned to the Freeborn and shelled the woods. A landing was again effected, and the men proceeded to erect a breastwork of sand-bags for protection in future movements. They had nearly completed this work, and covered it with branches, when the signal for their return to the vessel was made. As they were embarking in the boats the rebels opened fire upon them with musketry. Several men were severely wounded; but they all reached the boats, and rowed to the Freeborn safely, though under a heavy fire. On board that vessel it was found that Captain Ward was killed by a musket ball at the time of the attack on the forces on shore, and just as he was sighting his gun to open fire upon the attacking force. This event prevented the protection to the boats' crew, which Captain Ward intended to give them, and the safety of the men was greatly endangered. The expedition thus failed to accomplish what the brave commander had intended, and in the attempt the country lost an able, active, and patriotic officer. The rebels still held the Point, and continued to endanger the navigation of the river, until at a later period it was entirely blockaded by their batteries on the Virginia shore.

CHAPTER XXXIV.

Rebellion in Missouri. — Action of General Lyon. — Movement of Troops from St. Louis to Jefferson City. — Flight of Governor Jackson and his Friends. — The Federal Troops take Possession of the Capital. — Proclamation of General Lyon. — Advance of Federal Troops towards Booneville. — Battle at Booneville. — Flight of the Rebel Forces. — Occupation of Booneville. — Liberation of Prisoners. — Proclamation by General Lyon. — Movement to the South-west.

THE proclamation of Governor Jackson, of Missouri, was the signal for the breaking out of rebellion in that state. The secessionists responded to his call for troops to act against the United States forces, and armed resistance was organized wherever the secessionists predominated. These rebel forces soon began to assemble at Jefferson City, the capital, and at other places in the central and western part of the state, and it was evident that the governor, with other secession leaders, was determined to bring on a conflict which should result in carrying the state speedily into the southern Confederacy. General Lyon, with whom Colonel F. P. Blair coöperated with great activity and zeal, was not the man to wait for the rebellion to become completely organized, and the rebel forces to concentrate into a formidable army, before he took measures to repress it. Knowing the sympathies of the governor and the purposes of the disloyal legislature, he had foreseen to what the course of events led; but when the governor, by his proclamation, committed himself to open rebellion, he at once made preparations to move a part of his forces to Jefferson City, to hold the capital of the state, and, if necessary, to organize a provisional government.

Governor Jackson issued the proclamation spoken of on the 12th of June. On the following day General Lyon's forces left St. Louis for Jefferson City, and troops were sent in other directions westward, to guard the railroads and for future operations. Other troops followed immediately, and Governor Jackson, finding that

the federal authority was to be asserted, left the capital with his secession friends, and the considerable force of state troops which had assembled there, issuing orders for the destruction of the railroads and telegraph lines leading to the east. The federal forces took possession of the city on the 15th. Subsequently, Colonel Bornstein, who was placed in command of the forces there, issued a proclamation to the people, in which he promised protection to all, called upon the civil authorities to continue the legal exercise of their official duties, offering to aid them in the enforcement of the constitutional laws of the country, declared that he would suffer no attempt to destroy the Union and the government, and called upon the friends of the Union to organize for its defence. General Lyon, on leaving St. Louis, issued the following proclamation, which is inserted because it describes the position of affairs in the state : —

"TO THE PEOPLE OF MISSOURI.

"Prior to the proclamation issued by Governor Jackson of June 12, it was well known to you that the governor and legislature sympathized with the rebellion movements now in progress in the country, and had adopted every means in their power to effect the separation of this state from the general government. For this purpose parties of avowed secessionists were organized into military companies throughout the state, with the full knowledge and approval of the governor. The establishment of encampments in this state at this unusual season of the year, and authorized for an indefinite period, could have had no other object than the concentration of a large military force, to be subjected to the provisions of the military law then in contemplation, and subsequently passed — a bill so offensive to all peaceable inhabitants, so palpably unconstitutional, that it would only be accepted by those who are willing to conform to its extraordinary provisions for the purpose of effecting their cherished object, the disruption of the federal government. That bill provides for obligation to the state on the part of all persons enrolled under its provisions, irrespective of any obligation to the United States, when the constitution requires all state officers to take the oath of allegiance to the United States. This of itself is a repudiation of all authority of the general government, whose constitution is the supreme law, on the part of the state government, its officers and such citizens as might choose to adopt the provisions of the bill, and coupled, as it was, on the part of the legislature and governor, with declarations hostile to its authority, and in sympathy with those arrayed in hostility against it, could leave no doubt of its object to carry out the provisions of this extraordinary bill, having in direct view hostilities to the federal government. It was so denounced by General Harney, who characterized it as a secession ordinance in his proclamation of the 14th of May. That proclamation, doubtless, gave rise to the interview between General Harney and General Price, resulting in an agreement which it was hoped would lead to the restoration of tranquillity and good order in your state. That the repudiation of the military bill, and all efforts of the militia of the state under its provisions, was the basis of the agreement, was shown as well by the proclamation of General Harney immediately preceding it, as by the paper submitted to General Price containing the preliminary conditions to an interview with him.

"This agreement failed to define specifically the terms of peace, or how far a suspension of the provisions of the military bill should form a part of it, though, from the express declaration of General Harney at the time of the conference, a suspension of any action under the bill until there could be a judicial determination of its character by some competent tribunal, must, in good faith, be regarded as the fundamental basis of the negotiation. Nevertheless,

immediately after this arrangement, and up to the time of Governor Jackson's proclamation, complaints of attempts to execute the provisions of this bill, by which the most extraordinary hardships have been imposed on peaceful and loyal citizens, coupled with the persecution and proscription of those opposed to its provisions, have been made to me as commander of the United States forces here, and have been carried to Washington, with appeals for relief from Union men of all parties in the state, who have been abused, insulted, and, in some instances, driven from their homes. That relief I conceive it to be the duty of a just government to use every exertion in its power to give.

"Upon this point the policy of the government is set forth in the following communication from the department at Washington, dated May 27, to Brigadier-general W. S. Harney, commanding department of the west, St. Louis : —

"'Sir : The President observes with concern that, notwithstanding the pledge of the state authorities to coöperate in preserving the peace of Missouri, loyal citizens continue to be driven from their homes. It is immaterial whether these outrages continue from inactivity or indisposition on the part of the state authorities to prevent them. It is enough that they continue, and it will devolve on you the duty of putting a stop to them summarily by the force under your command, to be aided by such troops as you may require from Kansas, Iowa, and Illinois. The professions of loyalty to the Union by the state authorities of Missouri are not to be relied upon. They have already falsified their professions too often, and are too far committed to secession to be admitted to your confidence, and you can only be sure of their desisting from their wicked purposes when it is not in their power to prosecute them. You will, therefore, be unceasingly watchful of their movements, and not permit the clamors of their partisans or the opponents of the wise measures already taken, to prevent your check ing any movement against the government, however disguised. The authority of the United States is paramount, and whenever it is apparent that any movement, whether by color of state authority or not, is hostile, you will not hesitate to put it down.

" ' L. THOMAS, *Adjutant-general.'*

" It is my design to carry out these instructions in letter and spirit. Their justice and propriety will be appreciated by any one who takes an enlightened view of the relation of the citizens of Missouri to the general government. Nor can such a policy be construed as at all disparaging to the rights or dignity of Missouri, or infringing upon individual liberty.

" The recent proclamation of Governor Jackson, by which he set at defiance the authority of the United States, and urged you to make war upon them, is but the consummation of his treasonable purposes long indicated by his acts and expressed opinions, and now made manifest. If, in suppressing these treasonable purposes, and carrying out the policy of the government, and maintaining its dignity, as above indicated, hostilities should unfortunately occur, and unhappy consequences should follow, I would hope that all aggravation of those events may be avoided, and that they may be diverted from the innocent, and fall only upon the heads of those by whom they have been provoked.

" In the discharge of these plain but onerous duties, I shall look for the countenance and active coöperation of all good citizens, and shall expect them to discountenance all illegal combinations or organizations, and support and uphold by every lawful means the federal government, upon the maintenance of which depend their liberties and the perfect enjoyment of all their rights.

" N. LYON, *Brigadier-general*
" *U. S. Volunteers, commanding.*"

Leaving a small force under Colonel Bornstein at Jefferson City, General Lyon, with about two thousand men, proceeded up the Missouri River towards Booneville, where it was understood the state troops were posted in considerable force. On the 17th the troops landed near Rocheport, and, learning that the state troops were really at Booneville, and preparing to give battle, General Lyon marched towards that place. After proceeding several miles, the enemy — for such they showed themselves to be — were discovered, posted in a strong position along a lane and about a large brick house, upon some rising ground. On arriving at a suitable position, about three hundred yards from the rebel line, fire was opened by the artillery of General Lyon's force, and the infantry, forming on the right and left, commenced a fire of musketry. The fire was returned with some spirit for a time; but the well-directed fire of the artillery scattered the enemy, and the infantry following up the advantage by effective discharges of musketry, they retired in great haste, but formed again in a neighboring field. They now returned the fire of the federal troops with more spirit, and another portion of their forces commenced an effective fire from a grove on the left of the centre of the Union forces. For a short time there was the appearance of a severe battle; but the enemy soon gave way again, and retreated with more haste than order. Although the ground was well adapted for an obstinate defence, the scattered insurgents did not rally to resist the advance of the federal troops, who took possession of the deserted camp. In the mean time the fire from a howitzer on board one of the steamboats had compelled the enemy to abandon a battery about a mile from the camp, constructed near the bank of the river to oppose the passage of federal steamers. At the camp a considerable quantity of ammunition, camp equipage, and clothing was captured, and a number of prisoners were also taken.

Arriving at Booneville, the scattered insurgents showed some indications of making another stand at the fair-grounds, where a state armory had recently been established; but a few shots from the gun of the steamer prevented them from rallying. They passed on through the town in great disorder, and continued their flight westward. The Union troops entered the town amid many demonstrations of satisfaction on the part of the loyal inhabitants. The state troops collected at this point numbered, probably, about three thousand, but only a part of them were in the engagement; and of the Union troops hardly more than one fourth participated in the action. The loss of the state troops was supposed to be upwards of fifty killed and wounded, and the federal loss was two killed and ten wounded. General Price, who had been in command of the state troops, had gone west before the federal troops arrived, and, according to rebel statements, had given orders for his troops to retreat; but subsequent orders from Governor Jackson led to the engagement. General Lyon's prompt action in attacking this force, which would soon have increased to a formidable rebel army, saved the capital of the state, and relieved the state itself from a secession government holding the insignia of authority and supported by a large armed force.

General Lyon liberated the prisoners whom he had taken, most of whom were quite young, and had " been misled by frauds ingeniously devised and industriously inculcated by designing leaders," upon condition that they should not serve in hostilities against the United States. In proclaiming this act, he declared, —

" I have done this in spite of the well-known fact that the leaders in the present rebellion, having long experienced the mildness of the general government, still feel confident that this mildness cannot be overtaxed even by factious hostilities having in view its overthrow; but lest, as in the case of the late Camp Jackson affair, this clemency shall still be misconstrued, it is proper to give warning that the government cannot always be expected to indulge in it to the compromise of its evident welfare.

" Hearing that those plotting against the government have falsely represented that the government troops intended a forcible and violent invasion of Missouri for purposes of military despotism and tyranny, I hereby give notice to the people of this state that I shall scrupulously avoid all interference with the business, rights, and property of every description recognized by the laws of the state, and belonging to law-abiding citizens. But it is equally my duty to maintain the paramount authority of the United States with such force as I have at my command, which will be retained only so long as opposition makes it necessary, and that it is my wish, and shall be my purpose, to visit any unavoidable rigor arising in this issue upon those only who provoke it."

General Lyon remained at Booneville until early in July, there being indications of a gathering of the rebel forces at some point above that place, on the Missouri River; but it did not assume such proportions as to require the advance of his entire force. In the mean time other Union forces had been moved forward towards the south-western part of the state. To that part of the state Governor Jackson and General Price had gone, and a rebel army was there organized. When it became apparent that the rebellion was to be met in that quarter, General Lyon also marched thither to form a junction with his forces, which had already proceeded in that direction.

CHAPTER XXXV.

Western Virginia. — Opposition to Secession. — Union Convention. — Address to the People. — Convention to organize a Government. — Declaration of Vacancies. — Separation opposed. — State Officers elected. — Inauguration of Governor. — Inaugural Address. — Government recognized by the United States Government. — Legislature. — United States Senators. — Affairs in Maryland. — General Banks. — His Policy. — Arrest of Marshal Kane. — Proclamation of General Banks. — Action of the Police Commissioners. — Discovery of Arms, &c., in the Marshal's Office. — Disloyalty of Police Commissioners. — Their Arrest. — Proclamation by General Banks. — Effect of his Measures.

WE have now reviewed the principal military movements and events which took place previous to the assembling of Congress at the extra session. War had been inaugurated from Eastern Virginia to the western borders of Missouri. The rebels were collecting forces at various points along this whole line and at places on the coast, a considerable army still beleaguering Fort Pickens, at the entrance to Pensacola Bay, and the various fortifications in the seceded states which belonged to the United States being strengthened and garrisoned by troops of the Confederate States. On the other hand, the federal forces, greatly exceeding the number first called for, were also collecting and making the first advance movements against the insurgents. Before entering upon the period when the action of the government was sustained by the authority of Congress, and more important events followed, it is proper to mention certain other events of a political character, and of no little importance in maintaining the federal authority.

The loyalty of the people of North-western Virginia has already been mentioned. They opposed secession from the commencement of its agitation, and a majority of their representatives contended against it in the state convention. When the ordinance of secession was submitted to the popular vote, they gave a large majority of votes against it. On the 13th of May, a Union convention was held at Wheeling, which adopted resolutions declaring "that the Virginia convention, in assuming to change the relations of the state of Virginia to the federal government, have not only acted unwisely and unconstitutionally, but have adopted a policy utterly ruinous to all the material interests of our section, severing all our social ties, and drying up all the channels of our trade and prosperity." Measures were inaugurated for the maintenance of relations to the Union, even by carrying out the doctrine of secession, if necessary, to its logical conclusion. A more formal convention was called, to meet on the 11th of June, to take action upon this subject, and an address was issued by a committee of the convention, which ably discussed the question of secession, denied its constitutionality and propriety, and argued in favor of establishing a new state government, through which the relations of the people to the Union might be preserved. The address concluded as follows: —

"Whilst we have a constitution and code of laws for our state government, and local officers to administer them, the executive and his immediate subordinates have submitted themselves to the government of the Confederate States. They have thrown off their allegiance to the United States, and are now diligently and laboriously preparing themselves to wage war against the government of the Union. We need not characterize, in terms, such conduct; but, as true and loyal citizens of Virginia, we can and must declare that, in our calm and deliberate judgment, it will be the duty of the people of North-western Virginia to provide, in the lawful and constitutional mode, for the exercise of those executive and legislative functions of our state government which have been intrusted to those who are faithless and disloyal, and thus save ourselves from that anarchy which so imminently threatens us. In submitting this grave subject for your consideration, we do so in the earnest faith and hope that you will send to the convention of the 11th of June your best and truest men, that such action may be secured as will best subserve the interests of our state and secure the perpetuity of its union with the United States."

The new convention assembled at the appointed time, about forty counties of the state being represented. It proceeded at once to the important business for which it was convened, and on the 17th the following declaration was adopted, and subsequently signed by the members of the convention: —

"The true purpose of all government is to promote the welfare and provide for the protection and security of the governed; and when any form or organization of government proves inadequate for or subversive of this purpose, it is the right, it is the duty, of the latter to alter or abolish it. The Bill of Rights of Virginia, framed in 1776, reäffirmed in 1830, and again in 1851, expressly reserves this right to the majority of her people, and the existing constitution does not confer upon the General Assembly the power to call a convention to alter its provisions, or to change the relations of the commonwealth, without the previously expressed consent of such majority. The act of the General Assembly calling the convention which assembled at Richmond in February last was therefore usurpation; and the convention thus called has not only abused the powers nominally intrusted to it, but, with the connivance and active aid of the executive, has usurped and exercised other powers, to the manifest injury of the people, which, if permitted, will inevitably subject them to a military despotism.

"The convention, by its pretended ordinances, has required the people of Virginia to separate from and wage war against the government of the United States, and against the citizens of neighboring states with whom they have heretofore maintained friendly, social, and business relations.

"It has attempted to subvert the Union founded by Washington and his compatriots in the purer days of the republic, which has conferred unexampled prosperity upon every class of citizens, and upon every section of the country.

"It has attempted to transfer the allegiance of the people to an illegal confederacy of rebellious states, and required their submission to its pretended edicts and decrees.

"It has attempted to place the whole military force and military operation of the commonwealth under the control and direction of such confederacy, for offensive as well as defensive purposes.

"It has, in conjunction with the state executive, instituted, wherever their usurped power extends, a reign of terror intended to suppress the free expression of the will of the people, making elections a mockery and a fraud.

"The same combination, even before the passage of the pretended ordinance of secession, instituted war by the seizure and appropriation of the property of the federal government, and by organizing and mobilizing armies, with the avowed purpose of capturing or destroying the capital of the Union.

"They have attempted to bring the allegiance of the people of the United States into direct conflict with their subordinate allegiance to the state, thereby making obedience to their pretended ordinance a reason against the former.

"We, therefore, the delegates here assembled in convention to devise such measures and take such action as the safety and welfare of the loyal citizens of Virginia may demand, having mutually considered the premises, and viewing with great concern the deplorable condition to which this once happy commonwealth must be reduced, unless some regular adequate remedy is speedily adopted, and appealing to the Supreme Ruler of the Universe for the rectitude of our intentions, do hereby, in the name and on the behalf of the good people of Virginia, solemnly declare that the preservation of their dearest rights and liberties, and their security in person and property, imperatively demand the reörganization of the government of the commonwealth, and that all acts of said convention and executive, tending to separate this commonwealth from the United States, or to levy and carry on war against them, are without authority and void, and the offices of all who adhere to the said convention and executive, whether legislative, executive, or judicial, are vacated."

A proposition was made for the ultimate separation of the north-western part of the state, and the formation of a new state. But, though this proposition was favored by many of the most earnest of the Union people, it was not deemed expedient to adopt such measures at first; and, accordingly, after the adoption of the foregoing declaration, the convention proceeded to the establishment of a government for the state of Virginia. Hon. Francis H. Pierpont, one of the firmest of the loyal men,* was elected governor, and the various other offices under the state constitution were filled by the election of Union men. The governor elect was inaugurated at once. In his inaugural address he thus stated the position of the loyal people of Virginia: "We have been driven into the position we occupy to-day by the usurpers at the south, who have inaugurated this war upon the soil of Virginia, and have made it the great Crimea of this contest. We, representing the loyal citizens of Virginia, have been bound to assume the position we have assumed to-day for the protection of ourselves, our wives, our children, and our property. We, I repeat, have been driven to assume this position; and now we are but recurring to the great fundamental principle of our fathers, that to the loyal people of a state belongs the law-making power of that state. The loyal people are entitled to the government and governmental authority of the state. And, fellow-citizens, it is the assumption of that authority upon which we are now about to enter. It will be for us, by firmness, and by prudence, by wisdom, by discretion, in all our acts, to inaugurate every step we take for the purpose of restoring law and order to this ancient commonwealth; to mark well our steps, and to implore the divine wisdom and direction of Him that ruleth above, who has every hair of our heads numbered, and who suffereth not a sparrow to fall unnoticed to the ground, and his guidance and direction in enabling us to carry out the great work we have undertaken here, in humility, but with decision and determination."

The convention took further measures to establish the new government in its various departments, and to organize the militia forthwith. These acts of the convention were cordially approved by a large majority of the people in most of the counties represented, and in Wheeling and other towns along the border they were hailed with great demonstrations of satisfaction.

The government thus established, upon applying to the United States government "for aid to suppress rebellion and violence," was at once recognized as the government of Virginia, and from that time coöperated with the federal authorities in the measures to maintain the national cause. A legislature, composed of members from the loyal counties, assembled at Wheeling, on the 2d of July, when, among other acts, it elected two senators in Congress, and provided for the election of representatives; so that Virginia was still an active member of the Union, through her loyal people,

* A loyal journal of Virginia said of Governor Pierpont at this time, "He is more than a mere anti-secessionist. He is an original and devoted friend of progress and liberalism, as it has been especially advocated in Western Virginia. He entertains none of those old, effete, hair-splitting notions of despotism, under the guise of democracy, which have for the last fifty years governed and cursed the great official centre of this commonwealth. He is a live man, of and from the people."

while by her disloyal leaders she had been committed to the fortunes of the Southern Confederacy. In this respect Virginia stood alone, though Tennessee had still two or three loyal members to represent her Union people in the United States Congress.

The maintenance of the federal authority in Maryland, though placed in the hands of the military power, was a matter of political management. A show of force was evidently necessary to keep down the spirit of rebellion; but the condition of affairs was such, and so large a part of the people were loyal, that strict martial law was neither necessary nor expedient. A watchful care was, however, required, to keep the secessionists from actively aiding their friends in arms, and preparing for the much desired opportunity of openly rising in rebellion. As before observed, this class of persons was greatly pleased at the departure of General Butler, and, taking courage from the leniency of General Cadwallader, were gathering strength and confidence, and were showing their sympathy with the rebellion in a more positive way, while they also chafed at the presence of the military force. Such was the state of affairs when General Banks was assigned to the command of this department, and established his headquarters at Baltimore.

General Banks adopted a conciliatory policy towards the mass of the people, but showed a firm purpose of keeping the spirit of rebellion in subjection. He sought to coöperate with the civil authorities in maintaining order and suppressing sedition and rebellion; but he gave those authorities to understand that they must act honestly for the maintenance of the federal government and the Union. It soon appeared, however, that the police authorities of Baltimore were disloyal, and that they not only suffered secessionists to furnish aid and comfort to the rebels, but that the police force, under the lead of its chief, Marshal Kane, contributed to that end. That officer was known to be a secessionist, and, at the time of the riot on the 19th of April, he had taken measures to summon armed men to resist the passage of northern troops to the national capital. The pressure of public opinion, and the failure to accomplish secession in Maryland, subsequently caused him to modify his course; but, while he pretended to be loyal, he was secretly as strong a secessionist as before, and there was good reason to believe that his efforts were directed to the overthrow, rather than the support, of the federal government. General Banks accordingly caused him to be arrested and taken to Fort McHenry, and issued the following proclamation to explain to the people the reason for that act:—

"HEADQUARTERS,
"DEPARTMENT OF ANNAPOLIS, *June* 27, 1861.

"By virtue of the authority vested in me, and in obedience of orders as commanding general of the military department of Annapolis, I have arrested, and do now detain in custody, Mr. George P. Kane, chief of the police of Baltimore.

"I deem it proper at this moment of arrest to make formal public declaration of the motive by which I have been governed in this proceeding. It is not my purpose, neither is it in consonance with my instructions, to interfere in any manner whatever with the legitimate government of the people of Baltimore or Maryland. I desire to support the public authorities in all appropriate duties, in preserving the peace, in protecting property, in obeying and enforcing every municipal regulation and public statute consistent with the constitution and laws of the United States and Maryland. But unlawful combinations organized for resistance to such laws, that provide hidden deposits of arms and ammunition, and encourage contraband traffic with men at war with the government, and while enjoying its protection and privileges, stealthily wait the opportunity to combine their means and

Engraved by H. Wright Smith from a photograph

F. Si.

MAP OF THE BATTLE FIELD AT BULL RUN.

July 21st 1861.

EXPLANATION.

Scale of Miles.

AAA 1 U.S. Camps July 20th
AA 2 Rebel Camps.
U.S. Columns.
Rebel Columns.
Batteries
Rebel Cavalry Charge.

forces with those in rebellion against its authority. These are not among the recognized legal rights of any class of men, and cannot be permitted under any form of government whatever.

"Such combinations are well known to exist in this department. The mass of the citizens of Baltimore and Maryland are loyal to the constitution and the Union, and are neither parties to, nor responsible for, them; but the chief of police is not only cognizant of these facts, but in contravention of his duty, and in violation of the law, he is, by direction or indirection, both a witness and protector to the transactions and parties engaged therein. Under such circumstances, the government cannot regard him otherwise than as the head of an armed force, hostile to its authority, and acting in concert with its avowed enemies. For this reason, superseding his official authority, as well as that of commissioner of police, I have arrested and do now detain him in the custody of the United States; and in further pursuance of my instructions, I have appointed, for the time being, Colonel Kenley, of the first Maryland regiment of volunteers, provost marshal in and for the city of Baltimore, to superintend, and cause to be executed, the police laws provided by the legislature of Maryland, with the aid and assistance of subordinate officers of the police department; and he will be respected accordingly.

"Whenever a loyal citizen shall be otherwise named for the performance of this duty, who will execute the laws impartially and in good faith to the government of the United States, the military force of this department will render to him that instant and willing obedience due from every good citizen to his government.

"NATHANIEL P. BANKS,
"Major-General commanding the
"Department of Annapolis."

This act was exceedingly unpalatable to the disloyal people of Baltimore, and, among others,

to the police commissioners, whose loyalty was not much more certain than that of the marshal. The commissioners protested against the act, and told the officers of the police department to take off their badges and disband, though still held subject to the orders of the commission for some purpose. An examination of the premises occupied by the marshal revealed a quantity of arms and ammunition concealed there, evidently, under the circumstances, intended for no lawful purpose; and, about the same time, several cannon were discovered in another quarter, which were said to have been made some time previously by order of Marshal Kane, and to have been intended for the bombardment of Fort McHenry. The action of the police commissioners, and the consequent excitement among a dangerous class of the population, made it necessary for General Banks to take another step, which was promptly done. Troops were sent to various parts of the city, prepared to suppress any outbreak, and the police commissioners themselves were then quietly arrested, and the fact announced by General Banks, as follows:—

"FORT MCHENRY, *July* 1.

• "In pursuance of orders issued from the headquarters of the army at Washington, for the preservation of the public peace in the department, I have arrested, and now detain in the custody of the United States, the late members of the board of police, Messrs. Charles Howard, William Getchell, Charles Hinks, and John W. Davis. The incidents of the past week afforded a full justification for this order. The headquarters under the charge of the board, when abandoned by the officers, resembled, in some respects, a concealed arsenal. After a public recognition and protest against the suspension of their functions, they continued their sessions daily. Upon a forced and unwarrantable construction of my proclamation of the 28th ult., they declared that the police law was suspended, and the police officers and men put off duty for the present, intending to leave the city without any protection whatever. They refused to recognize the officers and men necessarily selected by the provost marshal for its protection, and hold subject to their orders, now and hereafter, the old police force, a large body of armed men, for some purpose not known to the government, and inconsistent with its peace and security. To anticipate any intentions or orders on their part, I have placed temporarily the force under my command within the city. I disclaim, on the part of the government I represent, all desire, intention, and purpose to interfere in any manner whatever with the ordinary municipal affairs of the city of Baltimore. Whenever a loyal citizen can be named who will execute its police laws with impartiality and in good faith to the United States, the military will be withdrawn from the central parts of the municipality at once. No soldiers will be permitted in the city, except under regulations satisfactory to the marshal; and if any so admitted violate the municipal law, they shall be punished by the civil law through the civil tribunals.

" NATHANIEL P. BANKS,
" *Major-General commanding.*"

Other arrests of private individuals followed, and the secessionists found that the federal authority was to be asserted firmly, though mildly and with reason. A better administration of the police department soon followed, and the disloyal spirit was held in subjection, if not wholly suppressed.

CHAPTER XXXVI.

First Session of the Thirty-seventh Congress. — Organization of the House. — Senators from Virginia. — President's Message. — Reports of the Secretary of War and the Secretary of the Navy. — Sanitary Commission. — Opposition in Congress to Executive Measures. — Hon. Andrew Johnson. — Measures adopted by Congress.

THE thirty-seventh Congress assembled, pursuant to the call of the President, on the 4th of July. The house of representatives was organized by the choice of Hon. Galusha A. Grow, of Pennsylvania, for speaker, and Hon. Emerson Etheridge, one of the patriotic loyalists of Tennessee, for clerk. In the senate, Hon. Andrew Johnson, of Tennessee, one of the boldest and ablest champions of the Union, was the only representative of a seceded state. Not admitting the right of secession, he still held his seat, to represent the loyal people of his state. Two senators elected by the legislature in Western Virginia subsequently took seats in that body as the representatives of that state.

The President's message was transmitted to the two houses the next day. This important document, which reviews the progress of secession and the action of the government, was as follows : —

MESSAGE.

" FELLOW-CITIZENS OF THE SENATE AND
" HOUSE OF REPRESENTATIVES :

" Having been convened on an extraordinary occasion, as authorized by the constitution, your attention is not called to any ordinary subject of legislation.

" At the beginning of the present presidential term, four months ago, the functions of the federal government were found to be generally suspended within the several states of South Carolina, Georgia, Alabama, Mississippi, Louisiana, and Florida, excepting only those of the post office department.

" Within these states all the forts, arsenals, dock yards, custom houses, and the like, including the movable and stationary property in and about them, had been seized, and were held in open hostility to this government, excepting only Forts Pickens, Taylor, and Jefferson, on and near the Florida coast, and Fort Sumter, in Charleston harbor, South Carolina.

The forts thus seized had been put in improved condition; new ones had been built, and armed forces had been organized, and were organizing, all avowedly with the same hostile purpose. " The forts remaining in the possession of the federal government in and near these states were either besieged or menaced by warlike preparations, and especially Fort Sumter was nearly surrounded by well-protected hostile batteries, with guns equal in quality to the best of its own, and outnumbering the latter as perhaps ten to one. A disproportionate share of the federal muskets and rifles had somehow found their way into these states, and had been seized to be used against the government. Accumulations of the public revenue, lying within them, had been seized for the same object. The navy was scattered in distant seas, leaving but a very small part of it within the immediate reach of the government. Officers of the federal army and navy had resigned in great numbers; and of those resigning, a large proportion had taken up arms against the government. Simultaneously, and in connection with all this, the purpose to sever the federal Union was openly avowed. In accordance with this purpose, an ordinance had been adopted in each of these states, declaring the states, respectively, to be separated from the national Union. A formula for instituting a combined government of these states had been promulgated; and this illegal organization, in the character of confederate states, was already invoking recognition, aid, and intervention, from foreign powers.

" Finding this condition of things, and believing it to be an imperative duty upon the incoming Executive to prevent, if possible, the consummation of such attempt to destroy the federal Union, a choice of means to that end became indispensable. This choice was made, and was declared in the inaugural address. The policy chosen looked to the exhaustion of all peaceful measures before a resort to any stronger ones. It sought only to hold the public places and property not already wrested from the government, and to collect the revenue; relying, for the rest, on time, discussion, and the ballot-box. It promised a continuance of the mails, at government expense, to the very people who were resisting the government; and it gave repeated pledges against any disturbance to any of the people, or any of their rights. Of all that which a President might constitutionally and justifiably do, in such a case, every thing was forborne, without which it was believed possible to keep the government on foot.

" On the 5th of March, (the present incumbent's first full day in office,) a letter of Major Anderson, commanding at Fort Sumter, written on the 28th of February, and received at the war department on the 4th of March, was, by that department, placed in his hands. This letter expressed the professional opinion of the writer that reënforcements could not be thrown into that fort within the time for his relief, rendered necessary by the limited supply of provisions, and with a view of holding possession of the same, with a force of less than twenty thousand good and well-disciplined men. This opinion was concurred in by all the officers of his command, and their *memoranda* on the subject were made enclosures of Major Anderson's letter. The whole was immediately laid before Lieutenant-General Scott, who at once concurred with Major Anderson in opinion. On reflection, however, he took full time, consulting with other officers, both of the army and the navy, and, at the end of four days, came reluctantly, but decidedly, to the same conclusion as before. He also stated at the same time that no such sufficient force was then at the control of the government, or could be raised and brought to the ground within the time when the provisions in the fort would be exhausted. In a purely military point of view, this reduced the duty of the administration in the case to the mere matter of getting the garrison safely out of the fort.

"It was believed, however, that to so abandon that position, under the circumstances, would be utterly ruinous; that the *necessity* under which it was to be done would not be fully understood; that by many it would be construed as a part of a *voluntary* policy; that at home it would discourage the friends of the Union, embolden its adversaries, and go far to insure to the latter a recognition abroad; that, in fact, it would be our national destruction consummated. This could not be allowed. Starvation was not yet upon the garrison; and ere it would be reached, *Fort Pickens* might be reënforced. This last would be a clear indication of *policy*, and would better enable the country to accept the evacuation of Fort Sumter as a military *necessity*. An order was at once directed to be sent for the landing of the troops from the steamship Brooklyn, into Fort Pickens. This order could not go by land, but must take the longer and slower route by sea. The first return news from the order was received just one week before the fall of Fort Sumter. The news itself was, that the officer commanding the Sabine, to which vessel the troops had been transferred from the Brooklyn, acting upon some *quasi* armistice of the late administration, (and of the existence of which the present administration, up to the time the order was despatched, had only too vague and uncertain rumors to fix attention,) had refused to land the troops. To now reënforce Fort Pickens, before a crisis would be reached at Fort Sumter, was impossible — rendered so by the near exhaustion of provisions in the latter-named fort. In precaution against such a conjuncture, the government had, a few days before, commenced preparing an expedition, as well adapted as might be, to relieve Fort Sumter, which expedition was intended to be ultimately used, or not, according to circumstances. The strongest anticipated case for using it was now pre-

sented; and it was resolved to send it forward. As had been intended, in this contingency, it was also resolved to notify the governor of South Carolina, that he might expect an attempt would be made to provision the fort; and that, if the attempt should not be resisted, there would be no effort to throw in men, arms, or ammunition, without further notice, or in case of an attack upon the fort. This notice was accordingly given; whereupon the fort was attacked, and bombarded to its fall, without even awaiting the arrival of the provisioning expedition.

"It is thus seen that the assault upon and reduction of Fort Sumter was in no sense a matter of self-defence on the part of the assailants. They well knew that the garrison in the fort could by no possibility commit aggression upon them. They knew — they were expressly notified — that the giving of bread to the few brave and hungry men of the garrison was all which would on that occasion be attempted, unless themselves, by resisting so much, should provoke more. They knew that this government desired to keep the garrison in the fort, not to assail them, but merely to maintain visible possession, and thus to preserve the Union from actual and immediate dissolution — trusting, as herein before stated, to time, discussion, and the ballot-box, for final adjustment; and they assailed, and reduced the fort, for precisely the reverse object — to drive out the visible authority of the federal Union, and thus force it to immediate dissolution. That this was their object the Executive well understood; and having said to them, in the inaugural address, ' You can have no conflict without being yourselves the aggressors,' he took pains, not only to keep this declaration good, but also to keep the case so free from the power of ingenious sophistry, as that the world should not be able to misunderstand it. By the affair at Fort Sumter, with its surrounding circumstances, that point was reached. Then and thereby the assailants of the government began the conflict of arms, without a gun in sight or in expectancy to return their fire, save only the few in the fort, sent to that harbor, years before, for their own protection, and still ready to give that protection in whatever was lawful. In this act, discarding all else, they have forced upon the country the distinct issue: 'Immediate dissolution or blood.'

" And this issue embraces more than the fate of these United States. It presents to the whole family of man the question, whether a constitutional republic or democracy — a government of the people, by the same people — can, or cannot, maintain its territorial integrity against its own domestic foes. It presents the question, whether discontented individuals, too few in numbers to control administration, according to organic law, in any case, can always, upon the pretences made in this case, or on any other pretences, or arbitrarily, without any pretence, break up their government, and thus practically put an end to free government upon the earth. It forces us to ask, 'Is there in all republics this inherent and fatal weakness? ' Must a government of necessity be too *strong* for the liberties of its own people, or too *weak* to maintain its own existence?'

" So viewing the issue, no choice was left but to call out the war power of the government, and so to resist force employed for its destruction by force for its preservation.

"The call was made, and the response of the country was most gratifying, surpassing in unanimity and spirit the most sanguine expectation. -Yet none of the states commonly called slave states, except Delaware, gave a regiment through regular state organization. A few regiments have been' organized within some others of those states by individual enterprise, and received into the government service. Of course, the seceded states, so called, (and to which Texas had been joined about the time of the inauguration,) gave no troops to the cause

of the Union. The border states, so called, were not uniform in their action; some of them being almost *for* the Union, while in others — as Virginia, North Carolina, Tennessee, and Arkansas — the Union sentiment was nearly repressed and silenced. The course taken in Virginia was the most remarkable — perhaps the most important. A convention, elected by the people of that state to consider this very question of disrupting the federal Union, was in session at the capital of Virginia when Fort Sumter fell. To this body the people had chosen a large majority of *professed* Union men. Almost immediately after the fall of Sumter, many members of that majority went over to the original disunion minority, and, with them, adopted an ordinance for withdrawing the state from the Union. Whether this change was wrought by their great approval of the assault upon Sumter, or their great resentment at the government's resistance to that assault, is not definitely known. Although they submitted the ordinance, for ratification, to a vote of the people, to be taken on a day then somewhat more than a month distant, the convention, and the legislature, (which was also in session at the same time and place,) with leading men of the state not members of either, immediately commenced acting as if the state were already out of the Union. They pushed military preparations vigorously forward all over the state. They seized the United States armory at Harper's Ferry, and the navy yard at Gosport, near Norfolk. They received — perhaps invited — into their state large bodies of troops, with their warlike appointments, from the so-called seceded states. They formally entered into a treaty of temporary alliance and coöperation with the so-called 'Confederate States,' and sent members to their congress at Montgomery. And, finally, they permitted the insurrectionary government to be transferred to their capital at Richmond.

" The people of Virginia have thus allowed this giant insurrection to make its nest within her borders; and this government has no choice left but to deal with it *where* it finds it. And it has the less regret, as the loyal citizens have, in due form, claimed its protection. Those loyal citizens this government is bound to recognize and protect, as being Virginia.

" In the border states, so called, — in fact, the middle states, — there are those who favor a policy which they call 'armed neutrality;' that is, an arming of those states to prevent the Union forces passing one way, or the disunion the other, over their soil. This would be disunion completed. Figuratively speaking, it would be the building of an impassable wall along the line of separation — and yet not quite an impassable one; for, under the guise of neutrality, it would tie the hands of the Union men, and freely pass supplies from among them to the insurrectionists, which it could not do as an open enemy. At a stroke, it would take all the trouble off the hands of secession, except only what proceeds from the external blockade. It would do for the disunionists that which, of all things, they most desire — feed them well, and give them disunion without a struggle of their own. It recognizes no fidelity to the constitution, no obligation to maintain the Union; and while very many who have favored it are, doubtless, loyal citizens, it is, nevertheless, very injurious in effect.

" Recurring to the action of the government, it may be stated that, at first, a call was made for seventy-five thousand militia; and rapidly following this, a proclamation was issued for closing the ports of the insurrectionary districts by proceedings in the nature of blockade. So far all was believed to be strictly legal. At this point the insurrectionists announced their purpose to enter upon the practice of privateering.

" Other calls were made for volunteers to serve three years, unless sooner discharged, and also for large additions to the regular army and navy. These measures, whether strictly legal or not, were ventured upon, under what appeared to be a popular demand and a public necessity; trusting then, as now, that Congress would readily ratify them. It is believed that nothing has been done beyond the constitutional competency of Congress.

"Soon after the first call for militia, it was considered a duty to authorize the commanding general, in proper cases, according to his discretion, to suspend the privilege of the writ of habeas corpus, or, in other words, to arrest and detain, without resort to the ordinary processes and forms of law, such individuals as he might deem dangerous to the public safety. This authority has purposely been exercised but very sparingly. Nevertheless, the legality and propriety of what has been done under it are questioned, and the attention of the country has been called to the proposition that one who is sworn to 'take care that the laws be faithfully executed' should not himself violate them. Of course some consideration was given to the questions of power and propriety before this matter was acted upon. The whole of the laws which were required to be faithfully executed were being resisted, and failing of execution in nearly one third of the states. Must they be allowed to finally fail of execution, even had it been perfectly clear, that by the use of the means necessary to their execution, some single law, made in such extreme tenderness of the citizen's liberty, that, practically, it relieves more of the guilty than of the innocent, should, to a very limited extent, be violated? To state the question more directly: are all the laws *but one* to go unexecuted, and the goverment itself go to pieces, lest that one be violated? Even in such a case, would not the official oath be broken, if the government should be overthrown, when it was believed that disregarding the single law would tend to preserve it? But it was not believed that this question was presented. It was not believed that any law was violated. The provision of the constitution, that 'the privilege of the writ of habeas corpus shall not be suspended unless when, in cases of rebellion or invasion, the public safety may require it,' is equivalent to a provision — is a provision — that such privilege may be suspended when, in cases of rebellion or invasion, the public safety *does* require it. It was decided that we have a case of rebellion, and that the public safety does require the qualified suspension of the privilege of the writ which was authorized to be made. Now, it is insisted that Congress, and not the Executive, is vested with this power. But the constitution itself is silent as to which, or who, is to exercise the power; and as the provision was plainly made for a dangerous emergency, it cannot be believed the framers of the instrument intended that in every case the danger should run its course until Congress could be called together, the very assembling of which might be prevented, as was intended in this case by the rebellion.

"No more extended argument is now offered, as an opinion, at some length, will probably be presented by the attorney-general. Whether there shall be any legislation upon the subject, and, if any, what, is submitted entirely to the better judgment of Congress.

"The forbearance of this government had been so extraordinary, and so long continued, as to lead some foreign nations to shape their action as if they supposed the early destruction of our national Union was probable. While this, on discovery, gave the Executive some concern, he is now happy to say that the sovereignty and rights of the United States are now every where practically respected by foreign powers; and a general sympathy with the country is manifested throughout the world.

"The reports of the secretaries of the treasury, war, and the navy, will give the information in detail deemed necessary and convenient for your deliberation and action; while the Executive, and all the departments, will stand ready to supply omissions, or to communicate new facts, considered important for you to know.

"It is now recommended that you give the legal means for making this contest a short and a decisive one; that you place at the control of the government, for the work, at least four hundred thousand men, and four hundred millions of dollars. That number of men is about one tenth of those of proper ages within the regions where, apparently, *all* are willing to engage; and the sum is less than a twenty-third part of the money value owned by the men who seem ready to devote the whole. A debt of six hundred millions of dollars *now* is a less sum per head than was the debt of our revolution when we came out of that struggle; and the money value in the country *now* bears even a greater proportion to what it was *then*, than does the population. Surely each man has as strong a motive *now* to *preserve* our liberties, as each had *then* to *establish* them.

"A right result, at this time, will be worth more to the world than ten times the men and ten times the money. The evidence reaching us from the country leaves no doubt that the material for the work is abundant, and that it needs only the hand of legislation to give it legal sanction, and the hand of the Executive to give it practical shape and efficiency. One of the greatest perplexities of the government is to avoid receiving troops faster than it can provide for them. In a word, the people will save their government, if the government itself will do its part only indifferently well.

"It might seem, at first thought, to be of little difference whether the present movement at the south be called 'secession' or 'rebellion.' The movers, however, well understand the difference. At the beginning, they knew they could never raise their treason to any respectable magnitude by any name which implies *violation* of law. They knew their people possessed as much of moral sense, as much of devotion to law and order, and as much pride in, and reverence for, the history and government of their common country, as any other civilized and patriotic people. They knew they could make no advancement directly in the teeth of these strong and noble sentiments. Accordingly they commenced by an insidious debauching of the public mind. They invented an ingenious sophism, which, if conceded, was followed by perfectly logical steps, through all the incidents, to the complete destruction of the Union. The sophism itself is, that any state of the Union may, *consistently* with the national constitution, and therefore *lawfully* and *peacefully*, withdraw from the Union, without the consent of the Union, or of any other state. The little disguise that the supposed right is to be exercised only for just cause, themselves to be the sole judge of its justice, is too thin to merit any notice.

" With rebellion thus sugar-coated, they have been drugging the public mind of their section for more than thirty years, and until at length they have brought many good men to a willingness to take up arms against the government the day *after* some assemblage of men have enacted the farcical pretence of taking their state out of the Union, who could have been brought to no such thing the day *before.*

" This sophism derives much, perhaps the whole, of its currency from the assumption that there is some omnipotent and sacred supremacy pertaining to a *state* — to each state of our federal Union. Our states have neither more nor less power than that reserved to them, by the constitution — no one of them ever having been a state *out* of the Union. The original ones passed into the Union even *before* they cast off their British colonial dependence; and the new ones each came into the Union directly from a condition of dependence, excepting Texas. And even Texas, in its temporary independence, was never designated a state. The new ones only took the designation of states on coming into the Union, while that name was first adopted for the old ones in and by the Declaration of Independence.

Therein the ' United Colonies' were declared to be ' free and independent states;' but, even then, the object plainly was not to declare their independence of *one another*, or of the *Union*, but directly the contrary, as their mutual pledge, and their mutual action, before, at the time, and afterwards, abundantly show. The express plighting of faith, by each and all of the original thirteen, in the Articles of Confederation, two years later, that the Union shall be perpetual, is most conclusive. Having never been states, either in substance or in name, *outside* of the Union, whence this magical omnipotence of ' state rights,' asserting a claim of power to lawfully destroy the Union itself? Much is said about the ' sovereignty' of the states ; but the word, even, is not in the national constitution ; nor, as is believed, in any of the state constitutions. What is a ' sovereignty,' in the political sense of the term? Would it be far wrong to define it, ' A political community without a political superior ?' Tested by this, no one of our states, except Texas, ever was a sovereignty. And even Texas gave up the character on coming into the Union ; by which act she acknowledged the constitution of the United States, and the laws and treaties of the United States made in pursuance of the constitution, to be, for her, the supreme law of the land. The states have their *status* IN the Union, and they have no other legal *status*. If they break from this, they can only do so against law, and by revolution. The Union, and not themselves separately, procured their independence and their liberty. By conquest or purchase, the Union gave each of them whatever of independence and liberty it has. The Union is older than any of the states, and, in fact, it created them as states. Originally some dependent colonies made the Union, and, in turn, the Union threw off their old dependence for them, and made them states, such as they are. Not one of them ever had a state constitution independent of the Union. Of course, it is not forgotten that all the new states framed their constitutions before they entered the Union; nevertheless, dependent upon, and preparatory to, coming into the Union.

"Unquestionably the states have the powers and rights reserved to them in and by the national constitution; but among these, surely, are not included all conceivable powers, however mischievous or destructive; but, at most, such only as were known in the world, at the time, as governmental powers; and certainly a power to destroy the government itself had never been known as a governmental — as a merely administrative power. This relative matter of national power and state rights, as a principle, is no other than the principle of *generality* and *locality*. Whatever concerns the whole should be confided to the whole — to the general government; while whatever concerns *only* the state should be left exclusively to the state. This is all there is of original principle about it. Whether the national constitution, in defining boundaries between the two, has applied the principle with exact accuracy, is not to be questioned. We are all bound by that defining, without question.

"What is now combated is the position that secession is *consistent* with the constitution — is *lawful* and *peaceful.* It is not contended that there is any express law for it; and nothing should ever be implied as law, which leads to unjust or absurd consequences. The nation purchased with money the countries out of which several of these states were formed. Is it just that they shall go off without leave, and without refunding? The nation paid very large sums (in the aggregate, I believe, nearly a hundred millions) to relieve Florida of the aboriginal tribes. Is it just that she shall now go off without consent, or without making any return? The nation is now in debt for money applied to the benefit of these so-called seceding states, in common with the rest. Is it just, either that creditors shall go unpaid, or the

remaining states pay the whole? A part of the present national debt was contracted to pay the old debts of Texas. Is it just that she shall leave, and pay no part of this herself?

"Again, if one state may secede, so may another; and when all shall have seceded, none is left to pay the debts. Is this quite just to creditors? Did we notify them of this sage view of ours when we borrowed their money? If we now recognize this doctrine by allowing the seceders to go in peace, it is difficult to see what we can do if others choose to go, or to extort terms upon which they will promise to remain.

"The seceders insist that our constitution admits of secession. They have assumed to make a national constitution of their own, in which, of necessity, they have either *discarded* or *retained* the right of secession, as, they insist, it exists in ours. If they have discarded it, they thereby admit that, on principle, it ought not to be in ours. If they have retained it, by their own construction of ours they show that, to be consistent, they must secede from one another, whenever they shall find it the easiest way of settling their debts, or effecting any other selfish or unjust object. The principle itself is one of disintegration, and upon which no government can possibly endure.

"If all the states, save one, should assert the power to *drive* that one out of the Union, it is presumed the whole class of seceder politicians would at once deny the power, and denounce the act as the greatest outrage upon state rights. But suppose that precisely the same act, instead of being called 'driving the one out,' should be called 'the seceding of the others from that one,' it would be exactly what the seceders claim to do; unless, indeed, they make the point, that the one, because it is a minority, may rightfully do what the others, because they are a majority, may not rightfully do. These politicians are subtle and profound on the rights of minorities. They are not

33

partial to that power which made the constitution, and speaks from the preamble, calling itself 'We, the People.'

"It may well be questioned whether there is, to-day, a majority of the legally qualified voters of any state, except perhaps South Carolina, in favor of disunion. There is much reason to believe that the Union men are the majority in many, if not in every other one, of the so-called seceded states. The contrary has not been demonstrated in any one of them. It is ventured to affirm this even of Virginia and Tennessee; for the result of an election, held in military camps, where the bayonets are all on one side of the question voted upon, can scarcely be considered as demonstrating popular sentiment. At such an election all that large class who are, at once, *for* the Union, and *against* coercion, would be coerced to vote against the Union.

"It may be affirmed, without extravagance, that the free institutions we enjoy have developed the powers, and improved the condition, of our whole people, beyond any example in the world. Of this we now have a striking and an impressive illustration. So large an army as the government has now on foot was never before known, without a soldier in it but who had taken his place there of his own free choice. But more than this: there are many single regiments whose members, one and another, possess full practical knowledge of all the arts, sciences, professions, and whatever else, whether useful or elegant, is known in the world; and there is scarcely one from which there could not be selected a president, a cabinet, a congress, and perhaps a court, abundantly competent to administer the government itself. Nor do I say this is not true also in the army of our late friends, now adversaries, in this contest; but if it is, so much the better reason why the government, which has conferred such benefits on both them and us, should not be broken up. Whoever, in any section, proposes to abandon such a government, would do well to consider in deference to what principle it is that he does it — whether better he is likely to get in its stead — whether the substitute will give, or be intended to give, so much of good to the people. There are some foreshadowings on this subject. Our adversaries have adopted some declarations of independence, in which, unlike the good old one penned by Jefferson, they omit the words 'all men are created equal.' Why? They have adopted a temporary national constitution, in the preamble of which, unlike our good old one signed by Washington, they omit 'We, the people,' and substitute 'We, the deputies of the sovereign and independent states.' Why? Why this deliberate pressing out of view the rights of men and the authority of the people?

"This is essentially a People's contest. On the side of the Union, it is a struggle for maintaining in the world that form and substance of government whose leading object is to elevate the condition of men; to lift artificial weights from all shoulders; to clear the paths of laudable pursuit for all; to afford all an unfettered start, and a fair chance in the race of life. Yielding to partial and temporary departures, from necessity, this is the leading object of the government for whose existence we contend.

"I am most happy to believe that the plain people understand and appreciate this. It is worthy of note, that while in this, the government's hour of trial, large numbers of those in the army and navy who have been favored with the offices have resigned, and proved false to the hand which had pampered them, not one common soldier, or common sailor, is known to have deserted his flag.

"Great honor is due to those officers who remained true despite the example of their treacherous associates; but the greatest honor, and most important fact of all, is the unanimous firmness of the common soldiers and common sailors. To the last man, so far as known, they have successfully resisted the traitorous efforts of those whose commands, but an hour before, they obeyed as absolute law. This is the patriotic instinct of plain people. They understand, without an argument, that the destroying the government which was made by Washington means no good to them.

"Our popular government has often been called an experiment. Two points in it our people have already settled — the successful *establishing* and the successful *administering* of it. One still remains — its successful *maintenance* against a formidable internal attempt to overthrow it. It is now for them to demonstrate to the world, that those who can fairly carry an election can also suppress a rebellion; that ballots are the rightful and peaceful successors of bullets; and that when ballots have fairly and constitutionally decided, there can be no successful appeal back to bullets; that there can be no successful appeal except to ballots themselves, at succeeding elections. Such will be a great lesson of peace; teaching men that what they cannot take by an election, neither can they take it by a war; teaching all the folly of being the beginners of a war.

"Lest there be some uneasiness, in the minds of candid men, as to what is to be the course of the government towards the southern states *after* the rebellion shall have been suppressed, the Executive deems it proper to say, it will be his purpose then, as ever, to be guided by the constitution and the laws; and that he probably will have no different understanding of the powers and duties of the federal government relatively to the rights of the states and the people, under the constitution, than that expressed in the inaugural address. He desires to preserve the government, that it may be administered for all, as it was administered by the men who made it. Loyal citizens everywhere have the right to claim this of their government, and the government has no right to withhold or neglect it. It is not perceived that

in giving it there is any coercion, any conquest, or any subjugation, in any just sense of those terms.

"The constitution provides, and all the states have accepted the provision, that 'The United States shall guarantee to every state in this Union a republican form of government.' But, if a state may lawfully go out of the Union, having done so, it may also discard the republican form of government; so that to prevent its going out is an indispensable *means* to the *end*, of maintaining the guarantee mentioned; and when an end is lawful and obligatory, the indispensable means to it are also lawful and obligatory.

"It was with the deepest regret that the Executive found the duty of employing the war-power in defence of the government forced upon him. He could not but perform this duty, or surrender the existence of the government. No compromise by public servants could, in this case, be a cure; not that compromises are not often proper, but that no popular government can long survive a marked precedent, that those who carry an election can only save the government from immediate destruction by giving up the main point upon which the people gave the election. The people themselves, and not their servants, can safely reverse their own deliberate decisions.

"As a private citizen, the Executive could not have consented that these institutions shall perish; much less could he, in betrayal of so vast and so sacred a trust as these free people had confided to him. He felt that he had no moral right to shrink, nor even to count the chances of his own life, in what might follow. In full view of his great responsibility, he has, so far, done what he deemed his duty. You will now, according to your own judgment, perform yours. He sincerely hopes that your views and your action may so accord with his, as to assure all faithful citizens, who have been disturbed in their rights, of a certain and speedy restoration of them, under the constitution and the laws.

"And having thus chosen our course, without guile, and with pure purpose, let us renew our trust in God, and go forward without fear, and with manly hearts.

"ABRAHAM LINCOLN.

"*July* 4, 1861."

By the report of the secretary of war, accompanying the President's message, it appeared that the federal forces then in the field numbered about two hundred and thirty-five thousand men, exclusive of regiments of volunteers for the war accepted but not yet in service, and of the new regiments of the regular army. Of these about eighty thousand were three months' volunteers, the term of whose service would generally expire in the latter part of July or early in August. But the new regiments of volunteers for the war, which were being organized, and the new regular army regiments, would nearly make up for the withdrawal of the three months' volunteers, who had so patriotically responded to the first call of the President.

Of the volunteer system and the character of the large army thus suddenly raised, the secretary wrote as follows : —

"I cannot forbear to speak favorably of the volunteer system, as a substitute for a cumbrous and dangerous standing army. It has, heretofore, by many been deemed unreliable and inefficient in a sudden emergency; but actual facts have proved the contrary. If it be urged that the enemies of order have gained some slight advantages at remote points, by reason of the absence of a sufficient regular force, the unexampled rapidity of concentration of volunteers already witnessed is an ample refutation of the argument. A government whose every citizen stands ready to march to its defence can never be overthrown; for none is so strong as that whose foundations rest immovably in the hearts of the people.

"The spectacle of more than a quarter of a million of citizens rushing to the field in defence of the constitution must ever take rank among the most extraordinary facts of history. Its interest is vastly heightened by the lavish outpouring, from states and individuals, of voluntary contributions of money, reaching an aggregate thus far of more than ten millions of dollars. But a few weeks since the men composing this great army were pursuing the avocations of peace. They gathered from the farm, from the workshop, from the factory, from the mine. The minister came from his pulpit, the merchant from his counting room, the professor and student from the college, the teacher and pupil from the common schools. Young men of fortunes left luxurious homes for the tent and the camp. Native and foreign born alike came forward with a kindred enthusiasm. That a well-disciplined, homogeneous, and efficient force should be formed out of such a seemingly heterogeneous mass, appears almost incredible. But what is the actual fact ? Experienced men, who have had ample opportunity to familiarize themselves with the condition of European armies, concede that, in point of *personnel*, this patriot army is fully equal to the finest regular troops of the Old World. A more intelligent body of men, or one actuated by purer motives, was never before marshalled in the field."

The equipment and subsistence of so large a force, with the limited means at the command of the government, was a difficult matter ; and it was no wonder that, through the inexperience or negligence of officers, and the delays consequent upon an incomplete system, many of the troops suffered some temporary hardships. Nor was it surprising that, in the immense and necessarily hurried contracts which were required for the support of the army, and to carry on war on so vast a scale, there should be found numerous instances of poor supplies unintentionally furnished and of wilful fraud. . That the country so engrossed in the pursuits of peace, and so unaccustomed to war, could so readily and successfully raise, equip, and supply such an army with all the munitions required, was the real marvel.

Among the measures taken for the promotion of the health and comfort of the troops was the appointment of a sanitary commission, to examine into the condition and wants of the army, and to coöperate with the medical department in providing for the care and comfort of the sick and wounded. This commission consisted of Henry W. Bellows, D. D.; Prof A. D. Bache, LL. D.; Prof Jeffries Wyman; Prof Walcott Gibbs, M. D.; W. H. Van Buren, M. D.; Samuel G. Howe, M. D.; R. C. Wood, surgeon United States army; George W. Cullum, United States army, and Alexander E. Shiras, United States army; all of them gentlemen who were distinguished for philanthropy, experience, or professional attainments. Serving without compensation, this commission devoted time and labor to the cause, and secured many reforms in the system of supplies for rations, as well as in equipments and camp equipage. But more than all, they directed the generous efforts of the patriotic people in furnishing for the troops additional clothing beyond that supplied by government, and for the sick and disabled the various necessaries and comforts which the government alone would have been entirely unable to supply. In connection with this department, Miss D. L. Dix, a lady who had achieved a wide reputation by her philanthropic labors in prisons and hospitals, was intrusted with the duty, which she volunteered to perform, of organizing the military hospitals and directing the employment of female nurses.

The report of the secretary of the navy, while it could not exhibit such a great increase of force as had been created for land service, showed that the navy department had not been idle. From twenty-four vessels of all kinds, carrying five hundred and fifty-five guns, which

were in commission on the 4th of March, the navy had been increased to eighty-two vessels in commission, carrying upwards of eleven hundred guns, and about thirteen thousand seamen. In addition to these, the several dock yards were busy with the construction of new steam-sloops, authorized by the preceding Congress, and with the fitting out of vessels purchased for the naval service, while contracts had been made with private parties for the construction of a fleet of steam gun-boats, and the department was still chartering and purchasing vessels to be used for gun-boats or armed transports.

Early in the session, Congress adopted a resolution to legislate only on subjects connected with the suppression of the rebellion; and the various measures brought before it were of that nature. Bills in relation to a volunteer force, for an increase of the navy, authorizing a loan of two hundred and fifty millions of dollars, increasing the duties on imports, levying an internal tax, to suppress insurrection, large appropriation bills, and other measures of detail in carrying out the purpose of organizing a large force for the suppression of the rebellion, were considered and passed by large votes, though not without some opposition. The ratification of the acts of the President met with strenuous opposition from certain men whose sympathies with the rebel states were scarcely disguised. This opposition manifested itself against all the measures intended to suppress the rebellion and to maintain the government by force against the attempts of traitors to overthrow it. Among those who were most forward in their opposition to these measures, and who showed a strong sympathy with rebellion, were Mr. Breckinridge, of Kentucky, and Mr. Polk, of Missouri, in the senate, and Mr. Burnett, of Kentucky, Mr. May, of Maryland, and some others of less note, in the house — men who would have had their states secede, if they could have effected it, and who now sat in Congress, as the members from Virginia and other seceded states had set there, the pretended supporters of the government, while, faithless to their duty and their oaths, they were laboring for its overthrow. Some of the members from Maryland strongly condemned the suspension of the habeas corpus, and on account of this opposed the approval of the acts of the President. There were also in both houses of Congress a few representatives from free states, who joined to a certain extent in this opposition, and either from party feeling, or worse motives, threw all possible obstacles in the way of the administration. A large majority, however, supported the President, ratified his acts for the maintenance of the government, strengthened his hands for the more vigorous prosecution of war against the rebels, and voted — what the loyal people were ready to give — money and forces without stint for this purpose. Among the most earnest and ablest supporters of the President's action was Andrew Johnson, the loyal senator from Tennessee, who, though politically opposed to the administration, and representing a state that had joined in the rebellion, gave the administration his cordial aid and approval, and labored in the senate most earnestly in behalf of the most vigorous measures for the suppression of the rebellion.

The bill authorizing the employment of volunteers provided for the acceptance of volunteers not exceeding half a million in number, and appropriated a very large sum for the equipment and maintenance of this force. The bill for the increase of the navy provided for the construction of a large additional number of steamers, including several iron-clad vessels, and for the purchase or charter of others, as the wants of the naval service might require. The various financial measures which were adopted, under the efficient and wise management of the able secretary of the treasury and the patriotism of the northern bankers, enabled

the government to obtain the large sums required to carry on the vast operations in which it was engaged. The act to suppress insurrection provided for the confiscation of the property of certain parties engaged in the rebellion, and for the freedom of their slaves. Most of the other measures adopted were for specific objects connected with the great general subject which engrossed the attention of Congress. These various measures of such vast importance, and involving such immense expenditures of money, were considered with unprecedented diligence and, notwithstanding the interruption and excitement of a disastrous battle, were disposed of in a month, and Congress adjourned on the 6th of August.

CHAPTER XXXVII.

Campaign in Western Virginia. — General McClellan takes command of the Federal Forces. — Advance of the Federal Army, and Retreat of the Rebels. — Action of the Rebel Government. — Proclamation of Governor Letcher. — Movement towards Beverly. — Battle of Rich Mountain. — Retreat of the Rebels. — General McClellan's Official Announcement of the Result. — Retreat of General Garnett. — Surrender of Colonel Pegram. — Pursuit of General Garnett's Force. — Battle of Carrick's Ford. — Rout of the Rebels. — Death of General Garnett. — Results of the Victory. — General McClellan's Despatch. — Success of the Campaign. — Movement of General Cox in the Kanawha Valley. — Skirmish at Barboursville. — Repulse at Scaryville. — Occupation of Charlestown. — General McClellan called to Washington.

RESUMING the narrative of military operations, we recur first to the campaign in Western Virginia. Major-General McClellan assumed command of the federal forces, in person, on the 20th of June, having previous to that time remained at Cincinnati, organizing his forces and directing the general movements. The entire force under his command numbered now about fifteen thousand; but they were necessarily divided, the advance into Virginia being from several different points. After the affair at Philippi there were occasional skirmishes, of no great importance, as the federal forces advanced, and the rebels, who as yet appeared in no great force, retired from town to town, with but little opposition. Guerrilla bands, however, carried on a petty warfare against the loyal people of the country, seizing property, destroying bridges, and in some cases wantonly taking life. The rebel governments of Virginia and the Confederate States, however, were making some preparation to resist the advance of the federal forces. Governor Letcher, in a proclamation to the people of North-western Virginia, appealed to them to submit to the will of the majority, who had declared for secession by an overwhelming vote, to join their brethren in Eastern Virginia, and " to drive the invader from their soil." He stated that he had sent a large force to their aid, but he relied " with the utmost confidence upon their own strong arms to rescue their firesides and altars from the pollution of a reckless and ruthless enemy." Governor Wise was appointed a brigadier-general, and sent into Western Virginia to organize the rebel forces; and considerable bodies of troops were gathered from the central counties, which were reënforced by several regiments of Confederate troops from other states.

Early in July, General McClellan moved his forces southward to Buckhannon and towards Beverly, in the vicinity of which a rebel force was collecting. Some skirmishes with small bands, of little consequence in their results, occurred along the march; but nothing of importance took place till the federal troops arrived near Beverly. At this place, two roads, one from Buckhannon, by which General McClellan advanced, and the other from Philippi, unite at an acute angle. Both these roads cross a mountain ridge, some miles north of Beverly, and at these points the rebel forces, under the command of General Garnett and Colonel Pegram, were posted in intrenched camps, surrounded by woods in all directions. Colonel Pegram was in immediate command at Rich

Mountain, on the Buckhannon road, and General Garnett at Laurel Hill, on the Philippi road. The position at Rich Mountain was very strong, and could not be carried by direct assault without great loss of life. General McClellan accordingly, on the 11th of July, despatched General Rosecrans with three regiments, to move along the mountain and get on the east side of the rebel position, so as to nearly surround them. After a long march, General Rosecrans came out upon a part of the rebel intrenchments at the top of the hill. The rebels had received information of the approach of the federal forces from this direction, and had a strong force ready to meet them. They fired upon the approaching column with several pieces of artillery; but the federal forces were soon formed in line of battle as well as the nature of the ground would admit, and, after firing a few volleys, they charged upon the battery and carried it. The contest was short but severe, and the rebels, unable to stand before the impetuous charge of the western troops, were soon utterly routed, and precipitately fled, leaving about one hundred and fifty dead and wounded on the field. The federal loss was about eleven killed and thirty-five wounded. A reënforcement, which was coming to the aid of the rebels, finding that they were routed, also retreated, and General Rosecrans remained in possession of the ground, capturing the cannon, many small arms, and the camp equipage.

In the mean time, General McClellan approached the lower and main position of the rebels, by cutting a road for his artillery through the woods. Night, however, came on before he was able to commence an attack. In the morning a white flag was discovered flying over the enemy's position, and it proved that he had hastily abandoned his camp, leaving all his equipage, several cannon, and many horses and wagons. Taking possession of these, General

McClellan pushed on rapidly to Beverly. The following are General McClellan's despatches, announcing the result of this contest : —

"HEADQUARTERS OF THE DEPARTMENT OF THE OHIO, } "RICH MOUNTAIN, VA., 9, A. M., *July* 12, 1861. }

"COLONEL E. D. TOWNSEND: We are in possession of all the enemy's works up to a point on the right of Beverly. I have taken all his guns, a very large amount of wagons, tents, &c., every thing he had, a large number of prisoners, many of whom were wounded, and several of them officers. They lost many killed. We have lost, in all, perhaps twenty killed and wounded, of whom all but two or three were in the column under Rosecrans, which turned the position. The mass of the enemy escaped through the woods, entirely disorganized. Among the prisoners is Dr. Taylor, formerly of the army. Colonel Pegram was in command.

"Colonel Rosecrans' column left camp yesterday morning, and marched some eight miles through the mountains, reaching the turnpike some two or three miles in the rear of the enemy, defeating an advanced post and taking two guns. I had a position ready for twelve guns near the main camp, and as the guns were moving up, I ascertained that the enemy had retreated. I am now pushing on to Beverly, a part of Colonel Rosecrans' troops being now within three miles of it. Our success is complete, and almost bloodless. I doubt whether Wise or Johnson will unite and overpower me. The behavior of the troops in the action and towards the prisoners was admirable.

"G. B. McCLELLAN,
"*Major-General commanding.*"

"BEVERLY, *July* 13.

"COLONEL E. D. TOWNSEND: The success of to-day is all that I could desire. We captured six brass cannon, of which one is rifled, and all the enemy's camp equipage and transportation, even to his cups. The number of tents will probably reach two hundred, and more than sixty wagons. Their killed and wounded will amount to one hundred and fifty, with at least one hundred prisoners; and more are coming in constantly. I know already of ten officers killed and prisoners. Their retreat was complete.

"I occupied Beverly by a rapid march. Garnet abandoned his camp early this morning, leaving much of his equipage. He came within a few miles of Beverly; but our rapid march turned him back in great confusion, and he is now retreating on the road to St. George. General Morris is to follow him up closely. I have telegraphed for the two Pennsylvania regiments at Cumberland to join General Hill at Bowlesburg. The general is concentrating all his troops at Bowlesburg, and will cut off Garnett's retreat near West Union, or, if possible, at St. George. I may say we have driven out some ten thousand troops, strongly intrenched, with the loss of eleven killed and thirty-five wounded.

"Previous returns here show Garnett's force to have been ten thousand men. They were Eastern Virginians, Georgians, Tennesseans, and I think, Carolinians. To-morrow I can give full details as to prisoners, &c. I trust that General Cox has, by this time, driven Wise out of the Kanawha Valley. In that case, I shall have accomplished the object of liberating Western Virginia. I hope the general in-chief will approve of my operations.

"G. B. McCLELLAN,
"*Major-General Department of Ohio.*"

General Garnett, who commanded in person at the rebel camp on Laurel Hill, also abandoned his camp and retreated towards Beverly; but the rapid march of General McClellan towards the same point induced him to change his course and march north-east towards St. George. General Morris, with his brigade, was immediately sent in pursuit, while the main body of the Union forces proceeded to Beverly.

Colonel Pegram, who abandoned the position

on Rich Mountain, finding himself unable to join General Garnett, and his retreat through Beverly cut off, after remaining in the woods for some time without food, sent to General McClellan a proposition to surrender as prisoners of war, expressing a hope that they would receive " such treatment as has been invariably shown to the northern prisoners by the south." In his reply, General McClellan said, " I will receive you and them with the kindness due to prisoners of war, but it is not in my power to relieve you or them from the liabilities incurred by taking arms against the United States." Accordingly, on the 13th, Colonel Pegram surrendered with his forces, numbering six hundred men. With those previously taken, the rebel prisoners now numbered nearly one thousand.

General Garnett, with his retreating forces, took a rugged road across the mountains; but he was followed rapidly by General Morris, whose advance came up with the enemy at Cheat River. The rebel general determined here to make a stand, and, by repulsing the pursuing forces, to make good his retreat. He selected an advantageous position on the river at Carricksford, where he crossed, on a high bluff which completely commanded the low and open ground on the side where the Union troops must approach. He concealed his force by the woods and shrubbery which bordered the bluff, and left his wagon train in the ford of the river, either for the purpose, as was afterwards supposed, of deceiving the pursuers and decoying them into a position where they would be directly under his fire, or because, with his disheartened men, he was unable to get safely across before the federal advance came up.

As the first regiment of the Union troops — the 14th Ohio — approached the river over the low ground mentioned, the rebels opened a fire of musketry upon them, followed quickly by a heavy artillery fire; but the aim was so poor that the regiment so greatly exposed suffered comparatively little, though taken by

surprise as they marched in column. Had the rebels been good marksmen, and had their leader been able to inspire them with his own courage and energy, they might have almost destroyed the advance federal force before the main body could come to reënforce them. But they were demoralized, and showed no determination or courage. The Ohio regiment immediately formed in line of battle, and returned the fire with much effect, although the enemy were protected by the bluff, or hidden from sight by the bushes upon its summit. Other regiments soon came up and joined in the battle.

Up the river a place was discovered where the bluff could be scaled, and an Indiana regiment, under Colonel Dumont, was sent to ford the river, scale the bluff, and attack the enemy on his flank. He had already overcome the obstacles, and reached the top of the bluff with a part of his command, and would soon have turned the flank of the enemy, — who had not yet discovered his movement, in consequence of the thick growth of laurel which hid his men from view, — when he was ordered to attempt to turn the left flank of the enemy, his superior officer not knowing that the obstacles had been overcome. Without questioning the order of his superior, the brave colonel led his men down the bluff again, and marched down the bed of the shallow river underneath the fire of the contending forces. Passing the wagon train, he led his regiment through a dense growth of laurel, and appeared most unexpectedly on the enemy's right flank. The rebels, who were hardly disposed, notwithstanding their advantage of position, to hold out against the federal force in their front, were panic-stricken at the appearance of this force on their flank, and fled in disorder. The Indiana regiment pursued the flying forces to the next ford, where General Garnett endeavored to rally his men. He was waving them back to resist their pursuers, when he was shot, and fell dead, a young Georgian soldier, the only one who remained with

34

him, falling by his side.* A portion of the rebel force rallied a little, and for a few minutes returned the fire of the federal troops; but they soon gave way again, and ran in confusion, pursued by the federal troops, until the latter halted from exhaustion.

The casualties of this battle were comparatively few, for the rebels were protected from the federal fire, while their own fire was far from being effective. The federal loss was four killed and eight wounded. The rebel loss was eleven killed and ten wounded, who were taken prisoners, while probably others, slightly wounded, escaped. The victory — and it was \ a substantial one — consisted in the utter rout of the rebel forces, so that they could not again be rallied. Numbers of prisoners, including many officers, were taken, and continued to be brought in for several days. Two stands of colors, a rifled cannon, and a large quantity of small arms, besides a train of forty wagons, were also captured. General McClellan announced the result to the government in the following despatch : —

"HUTTONVILLE, VA., July 15, 1861.
"COLONEL E. D. TOWNSEND, Assistant Adjutant-General;

"General Garnett and his forces have been routed, and his baggage and one gun taken. His army is completely demoralized. General Garnett was killed while attempting to rally his forces at Carricksford, near St. George. We have completely annihilated the enemy in Western Virginia. Our loss is but thirteen killed, and not more than forty wounded, while the enemy's loss is not far from two hundred killed ; and the number of prisoners we have taken will amount to at least one thousand. We have captured seven of the enemy's guns in all. A portion of General Garnett's forces retreated ; but I look for their capture by General Hill,

* General Garnett was a Virginian, who had been an officer in the United States army, and served with distinction in Mexico. He was more soldier than politician, but, when Virginia seceded, joined the rebels.

who is in hot pursuit. The troops that General Garnett had under his command are said to be the crack regiments of Eastern Virginia, aided by Georgians, Tennesseeans, and Carolinians. Our success is complete, and I firmly believe that secession is killed in this section of the country.

"GEORGE B. McCLELLAN,
"Major-General United States Army."

To his soldiers the general issued the following address : —

"SOLDIERS OF THE ARMY OF THE WEST:

"I am more than satisfied with you. You have annihilated two armies, commanded by educated and experienced soldiers, intrenched in mountain fastnesses, and fortified. You have taken five guns, twelve colors, and fifteen hundred stand of arms, and one thousand prisoners, including more than forty officers. One of the second commanders of the rebels is a prisoner, and the other lost his life on the field of battle. You have killed more than two hundred and fifty of the enemy, who have lost all their baggage and camp equipage. All this has been accomplished with a loss of twenty brave men killed and sixty wounded.

"You have proved that the Union men, fighting for the preservation of the government, are more than a match for misguided and erring brothers. More than this, you have shown mercy to the vanquished. You have made long and arduous marches, had insufficient food, and been exposed to the inclemency of the weather. I have not hesitated to demand this of you, feeling that I could rely on your endurance, patriotism, and courage. In the future I may have still greater demands to make upon you, still greater sacrifices for you to offer. It shall be my care to provide for you to the extent of my ability ; but I know now that by your valor and endurance you will accomplish all that is asked.

"Soldiers, I have confidence in you ; and I

trust you have learned to confide in me. Remember that discipline and subordination are qualities of equal value with courage. I am proud to say that you have gained the highest reward that American troops can receive — the thanks of Congress and the applause of your fellow-citizens.

"GEORGE B. McCLELLAN,
"*Major-General.*"

Huttonville, the place to which General McClellan moved from Beverly, was the rendezvous named in Governor Letcher's proclamation, summoning the people of Western Virginia to arms to repel the federal forces. It was now occupied by a victorious Union army; ten thousand rebel soldiers had been defeated and scattered, and the rebellion was virtually suppressed in North-western Virginia, there being no considerable force of rebels now within that section, except one in the valley of the Kanawha, against which another division of General McClellan's command, under General Cox, was operating.

General Cox had a sharp skirmish at Barboursville, where he drove out the rebel forces, and took possession of the place. At Scaryville, however, on the Kanawha, a part of his forces were repulsed in an attack made upon a body of rebels strongly posted. The Union force numbered about fifteen hundred men, and were sent out to capture a rebel camp at that place. The rebels, who were reported to number four thousand, with two pieces of artillery, occupied a hill, where they had intrenchments and some log houses pierced for musket firing. The federal troops were exposed to a severe fire as they approached the rebel position; but with their artillery they succeeded, after a time, in silencing that of the enemy, and driving the men from the log houses. It was probable that the rebels would have been defeated but for the failure of ammunition on the part of the federal troops, which compelled

them to retire, leaving their dead and wounded on the field. Several federal officers, belonging to regiments not engaged in the skirmish, who accidentally got within the rebel lines, were also captured. The rebels, however, gained no material advantage, and were compelled soon to retire before General Cox, who, on the 24th of July, occupied Charlestown, a town at the junction of the Kanawha and Elk Rivers. The enemy evacuated this place without a struggle, destroying the bridges and other property which might be useful to the pursuers, and retiring still farther eastward.

At this time General McClellan was appointed general-in-chief of the armies of the United States, and went to Washington, leaving General Rosecrans in command of the forces in Western Virginia. The campaign had rid the greater part of North-western Virginia of the rebel forces, afforded protection to the loyalists there, and given strength to the loyal government of the state. Here we leave, for the present, the narrative of the campaign in this section, to recur to the military operations in other fields.

CHAPTER XXXVIII.

Passage of General Patterson's Army over the Potomac. — Advance to Martinsburg and Bunker Hill. — Delay at Bunker Hill. — Reports of Rebel Strength at Winchester. — Movement to Charlestown. — Advance of the Army of North-Eastern Virginia. — Order for the Organization of the Army. — The Advance to Fairfax Court House. — Obstructions. — Entrance to Village of Fairfax Court House. — Progress to Centreville. — Reconnoisance at Bull Run. — Battle of Blackburn's Ford.

AFTER remaining near the line of the Upper Potomac for some time, General Patterson, with his forces, crossed the river at Williamsport on the 2d of July, and marched into Virginia. The rebel pickets soon gave signs of their presence in that vicinity, and near Haynesville there was a skirmish with the rebel forces that had been posted at Martinsburg. These forces, which were under the command of General

Jackson, were brought up, with four pieces of artillery, to resist the federal advance, and apparently with the expectation of driving the Union troops across the Potomac again ; for they had made preparations on the road by which they could harass a retreating force. The rebel troops, however, did not maintain their ground ; but after some skirmishing, in which the federal loss was three killed and several wounded, and the rebel loss somewhat larger, they retreated, and General Patterson's forces occupied their camp. The number of the rebels was stated, in General Patterson's despatch announcing the skirmish, to be ten thousand ; but it was probably not so large. They fell back to join the main body of their troops at Winchester, near which place their combined forces, under General Joseph E. Johnston, would apparently make a stand. They were said to number nearly twenty thousand men, including reënforcements just arrived, and to have upwards of twenty pieces of artillery. General Patterson's army advanced to Martinsburg, where they remained for a short time, waiting for his forces to be concentrated, neither army making any movement. On the 15th of July, General Patterson moved with his army, now numbering nearly twenty thousand men, towards Winchester, till he arrived at Bunker Hill, ten miles from Martinsburg, where the enemy at first had shown signs of taking position to resist the advance of the Union force. They had left that place, however, and only a skirmish with a part of their cavalry, which was put to flight without any loss on the part of the federal force, indicated that they were near.

At Bunker Hill General Patterson remained two days, his men expecting to move upon the rebels, who were supposed to be intrenched at Winchester. But scouts reported that the rebels had been largely reënforced, and, numbering from thirty-five to forty-two thousand men, were preparing for battle. This information induced the commanding general to call a

council of war ; and it was determined not to advance towards Winchester, nor yet to wait at Bunker Hill, but to withdraw to Charlestown, a town east of the position then held by the federal force, and nearer to Harper's Ferry. Accordingly, on the second day after reaching Bunker Hill, General Patterson's whole column marched to Charlestown, and part of it thence proceeded to Harper's Ferry, leaving the rebel forces either to pursue or to reënforce the army of Beauregard at Manassas.

In the mean time the army in front of Washington was organized, and preparations were made for an advance against the rebel forces collected at Manassas. This army had now reached sixty thousand or upwards in number, and there was a strong desire on the part of the people of the north that there should be a forward movement, and, before they had assembled a larger force, a blow should be struck at the rebels which should make them feel the power of the federal government. Such a movement was urged very strenuously by a portion of the press and by some of the members of Congress. Such advice was to be taken only when the military authorities were ready for a movement; and probably the desire of those who urged the forward movement was not to hasten an advance without due preparation, but to hurry the work of preparation, that the advance might be speedily made, before the term of the three months volunteers should expire, and the service of a large number of disciplined soldiers should be lost. Whether the movement was ordered before the military authorities considered the preparations complete, or against their advice, is a mooted point, which it is not easy to decide. But the order for an advance was finally given, and by authority of the President, who in military affairs, from the first, had almost entirely deferred to the opinions of General Scott.

On the 8th of July, an order was issued, by which the army was first organized into brigades and divisions. The regiments, as they arrived at Washington, had been sent into Virginia, to points where they were needed; in some cases they were attached to brigades, and in others they were independent. In very few cases were they organized and manœuvred as permanent brigades, or made acquainted with the movements of large bodies of troops.

The order alluded to organized the army into five divisions. . The first division was under Brigadier-General Daniel Tyler, of the Connectient volunteers, and consisted of four brigades, commanded by Colonel E. D. Keyes, of the regular army, Colonel William T. Sherman, also of the regular army, Brigadier-General Schenck, of the Ohio volunteers, and Colonel J. B. Richardson, of the Michigan volunteers. The second division was under command of Colonel David Hunter, of the regular army, and consisted of two brigades, commanded by Colonel Andrew Porter, of the regular army, and Colonel A. E. Burnside, of the Rhode Island volunteers. The third division, under command of Colonel S. P. Heintzelman, of the regular army, consisted of three brigades, commanded by Colonel W. B. Franklin, of the regular army, Colonel O. B. Wilcox, of the Michigan volunteers, and Colonel O. O. Howard, of the Maine volunteers. The fourth and fifth divisions constituted the reserve. The fourth was composed entirely of New Jersey troops, four regiments of three months' volunteers, and three regiments of three years' volunteers, all under the command of Brigadier-General Runyon, of New Jersey. The fifth, under command of Colonel D. S. Miles, of the regular army, consisted of two brigades, commanded by Colonel Blenker and Colonel Davies, of the New York volunteers.* The army, thus organized, numbered fifty thousand men or upwards, and with this force General McDowell, on the 16th of July,

* Most of the colonels above named were afterwards appointed brigadier-generals and major-generals, and nearly all of them assigned to important commands.   .

commenced the march for Fairfax and Manassas, his advance moving out on the evening of that day, and the main body following on the succeeding day. The troops marched in high spirits, excited with the prospect of meeting and defeating the rebel forces.

The army moved in four columns, which were to be concentrated at Fairfax Court House. Along the roads trees were cut down to oppose obstructions to the advance of the troops, and at different points some earthworks of little strength had been constructed, but were found abandoned. Within half a mile of Fairfax Court House a more extensive work was met with, consisting of an embankment extending half a mile, with embrasures for cannon. This also had been abandoned, and the guns, if there had been any, were removed. A rebel force of two or three thousand had been stationed at this village; but they retreated about two hours before the federal advance reached the place, leaving a quantity of fresh beef, flour, intrenching tools, and camp equipage behind them, with various other evidences of a hasty evacuation of the post. On the march the van of one of the columns had a very slight skirmish with rebel pickets, and a number of prisoners were captured; but there was no real show of resistance to the march of the federal forces, except such as was offered by the obstructions in the woods.

The entrance of the army into the village is described by those present as inspiriting in the highest degree. The long column came in marching to the national airs by the bands, and cheering loudly at the apparently easy victory before them, and heartily welcomed by the few Union people who remained. The troops bivouacked in and about the village, while a cavalry force dashed on in pursuit of the retreating foe. The day was excessively warm, and the pursuit was not long continued, the rebels being too far in advance to afford much prospect of overtaking them.

From Fairfax Court House the army moved on to Centreville, where the enemy had constructed intrenchments, and where it was supposed that he would dispute the progress of the federal forces. The troops were formed in line of battle; but instead of finding a rebel force to attack, they saw a Union flag raised above the intrenchments, and a solitary man advanced and announced that the rebels had retreated, taking with them their cannon and baggage. This continued retreat of the rebels, without a show of battle, made the march of the Union army appear like a pleasant excursion, and perhaps led the men to feel that its object was to be easily and speedily accomplished. Inexperienced in the stern realities of war, they did not meet with sufficient opposition to train them for an earnest conflict, and the facility of their progress rather unfitted than nerved them for a fierce battle such as was to ensue.

On the 18th of July, General Tyler advanced from Centreville with a part of his division, for the purpose of making reconnoissance in the direction which the retreating enemy had taken. As this column reached the crest of a hill sloping down to the stream called "Bull Run," at Blackburn's Ford, it was saluted with a shot from the enemy's artillery in position beyond the stream, and at a distance too great for the range of their guns. The firing was replied to by part of a battery of rifled cannon which accompanied the expedition, and skirmishers were sent forward into the woods which bordered the stream. Artillery was advanced to another position nearer the enemy, and infantry was also advanced to the woods. The skirmishers had failed to draw the fire of the enemy; but when the main body of the infantry reached the woods, full volleys of musketry were discharged at them by a large force of the rebels, who were concealed from the view of the federal soldiers. This fire was returned by them, however, aided by the artillery, which had been sent forward; but the enemy had the advantage in position as well as in numbers, and their fire was so severe that the twelfth New York regiment fell back in disorder, and the artillery which they had been ordered to support, as also a company of cavalry, all being on the left of the line, were withdrawn. The other troops engaged held their ground bravely, and Colonel Richardson, whose brigade formed the reconnoitring force, requested permission to charge through the woods with his other regiments, the first Massachusetts, and the second and third Michigan, feeling confident that he could drive the enemy from his position; but General Tyler, having accomplished his object in ascertaining the position of the enemy, ordered the troops to be withdrawn, and they subsequently returned to their camp near Centreville, though an effective fire of artillery was continued for some time at long range. This was a sharp skirmish, and assumed, indeed, the proportions of a battle, giving the first proof that the rebels were at last ready to oppose the federal forces. The loss of the latter was nineteen killed, thirty-eight wounded, and twenty-six missing; and the rebel loss, according to their official report, was fifteen killed and fifty-three wounded.

It was supposed that this reconnoissance would be followed immediately by an attack in force upon the rebel position; but the army rested for two days at Centreville before the advance was again made.

CHAPTER XXXIX.

Bull Run. — Position of the Rebel Army at Manassas. — Its Strength and Number of Rebel Troops. — Order for Advance of Federal Forces. — Plan of Attack. — Movement of the Divisions. — The Battle. — Successful Advance of Federal Troops. — Rebel Reenforcements. — Attack on the Right Flank of the Federal Forces. — Retreat, Disorder, and Rout. — Cavalry Charge on the Left Flank. — Panic and Flight of the Federal Troops. — Cause of the Panic. — Account of the Battle and Rout, by an Eye-witness.

THE reconnoissance and battle at Blackburn's Ford made it evident that the rebels had at length fallen back to their line of defence, and that here, on the banks of Bull Run, they would resist the farther advance of the federal army. The position of the rebel army was a strong one, and General Beauregard had strengthened its natural advantages and concentrated all the available forces of the rebels for its defence. The strength of this place and of the rebel force is thus described by one of their own writers a short time previous to the advance of the Union forces: "By nature, the position is one of the strongest that could have been found in the whole state. About half way between the eastern spur of the Blue Ridge and the Potomac, below Alexandria, it commands the whole country between, so perfectly that there is scarcely a possibility of its being turned. The right wing stretches off towards the head waters of the Occoquan, through a wooded country, which is easily made impassable by the felling of trees. The left is a rolling table-land, easily commanded from the successive elevations, till you reach a country so rough and so rugged that it is a defence to itself. The key to the whole position, in fact, is precisely that point which General Beauregard chose for his centre, and which he has fortified so strongly that, in the opinion of military men, five thousand men could there hold twenty thousand at bay. The position, in fact, is fortified, in part, by Nature herself. It is a succession of hills, nearly equidistant from each other, in front of which is a ravine so deep and so thickly wooded that it is passable only at two points, and those through gorges which fifty men can defend against a whole army.

"Of the fortifications superadded here by General Beauregard to those of nature, it is, of course, not proper for me to speak. The general reader, in fact, will have a sufficiently precise idea of them by conceiving a line of forts, some two miles in extent, zigzag in form, with angles, salients, bastions, casemates, and every thing that properly belongs to works of this kind. The strength and advantages of this position at Manassas are very much increased by the fact that fourteen miles farther on is a position of similar formation, while the country between is admirably adapted to the subsistence and intrenchment of troops in numbers as large as they can easily be manœuvred on the real battle field.

"As might be expected from the skill with which he has chosen his position and the system with which he encamps and moves his men, General Beauregard is very popular here. I doubt if Napoleon himself had more the undivided confidence of his army. By nature, as also from a wise policy, he is very reticent. Not an individual here knows his plans, or a single move of a regiment before it is made; and then only the colonel and his men know where it goes to. There is not a man here who can give any thing like a satisfactory answer how many men he has or where his exact lines are. For the distance of fourteen miles around you see tents every where, and from them you can make a rough estimate of his men; but how many more are encamped on the by-roads and in the forests none can tell. The new-comer, from what he sees at first glance, puts down the number at about thirty thousand men; those who have been here longest estimate his force at forty or fifty thousand, and

some even at sixty thousand strong. And there
is the same discrepancy as to the quantity of
his artillery."

The allusions to the strength of the rebel
forces at this point, though not explicit statements, are supported by much other similar
evidence from rebel sources, and are, probably,
a fair representation of the number of the army
under Beauregard, though in his report of the
battle of Bull Run that officer places the number of his forces much lower. The advantages
of the position are not overstated, according to
most military authorities; and the delay between
the time of the battle of Blackburn's Ford and
the advance of the federal forces from Centreville enabled the rebel general to concentrate
his forces and to receive that reënforcement
which finally turned the fortunes of the day so
much in his favor.

The orders for the advance of the federal
forces to attack the enemy's position were issued
on the 20th of July. General McDowell had
intended to move the troops forward several
miles on the evening of that day, so that the
march should be shorter on the morning of the
attack; but he deferred to the opinions of officers who had the greatest distance to go, and the
several columns did not move till early in the
morning of Sunday, the 21st. Reconnoissances
showed that the rebels had planted batteries at
points along the stream from Blackburn's Ford
to the ford at Sudley's Spring, and were in
strong force near the stone bridge by which
the Warrenton turnpike crossed it. General
McDowell's purpose was to turn the enemy's
position, drive him from the turnpike, and, reopening that road, advance to and destroy the
railroad leading into the valley of Virginia.
The army was ordered to advance in four columns; the first division, under General Tyler,
towards the stone bridge; the second division,
under Colonel Hunter, was to move to the
right after passing Cub Run, and to cross Bull
Run above the ford at Sudley's Spring; the

third division, under Colonel Heintzelman, was
to follow on the same road, but to cross at a
ford below Sudley's Spring; but no such ford was
found, and the division accordingly marched to
the ford crossed by Hunter's division; and the
fifth division, under Colonel Miles, with Richardson's brigade, was to advance towards Blackburn's Ford, and opening fire with artillery only,
to hold the position against any attack of the
enemy, and to form a reserve. The fourth
division, under General Runyon, was holding
the roads in the rear.

The several divisions moved towards their
appointed positions at an early hour in the
morning, and before dawn were well on their
way. But there were repeated obstructions and
delays; one division was waiting for another to
pass, and the advance was not made as if with
a unity of purpose, which lack was attributable,
in a great measure, to the recent organization
of the army and its want of familiarity with the
movements of brigades, as well as to the general inexperience of both officers and men.
General Tyler's division reached its position
at half past five o'clock, and was formed in line
of battle on each side of the turnpike. The
pickets of the enemy were driven in, and a few
shot were fired by the artillery at the rebel
forces on the other side of the stream. But
the ground was low, descending gradually towards the stream, and being much covered with
woods the view of the artillerists was obstructed.
This division remained in its position for a long
time, quietly waiting for the divisions of Hunter and Heintzelman to reach their position and
commence the attack on the enemy's left, after
crossing the run at Sudley's Spring. In the
mean time the batteries of Richardson's brigade,
which was attached to Miles's division, and was
advanced towards Blackburn's Ford, opened
a vigorous cannonade upon the enemy in that
direction. As soon as Hunter's column had
commenced the attack, the right of General
Tyler's division was advanced, and, crossing the

run, moved rapidly up the slope of a hill towards one of the enemy's positions, which they carried. The left brigade of the division also advanced, but was compelled to fall back before the fire of a battery which had been concealed by bushes, and it did not again advance so as to sustain the right. It was late in the forenoon when Hunter's and Heintzelman's divisions, having crossed the run, attacked the left wing of the enemy with great vigor. To this position the rebel general brought up his troops in great force, aware of the danger which threatened him if the federal army was successful here. But the Union forces advanced steadily, though slowly, compelling the rebels to retire from one strong position to another. They were not defeated or routed, however, except at one or two points, but generally withdrew in order to intrenchments and natural strongholds as advantageous as those they left, while the federal troops, exhausted by the severe labors of the march and the battle, gained little advantage by thus compelling the enemy to retire. The divisions of Tyler, Hunter, and Heintzelman continued to press forward, and it seemed that a junction of the two columns would soon be effected. But the advance of Tyler's right wing, and the neglect of the left wing to press the enemy and carry the position in front of it, had exposed the left of the federal lines; and the rebel general, seeing the weakness, advanced a body of fresh troops to attack at this point. These troops crossed the run and appeared upon the flank of the federal forces, threatening to cut off the line of retreat; but their advance was checked by the firmness of a part of the brigade remaining on that side of the run, and they were forced to retreat without following up the advantage which their position offered them.

It was now some hours after noon, and the troops on the right had been engaged in marching and fighting since an early hour in the morning. They had gained much, and had

driven the rebels southward across the Warrenton turnpike, but the strong positions of the enemy and the reënforcements which he was receiving rendered the result doubtful ; and at last a new body of reënforcements, from Johnston's army, which should have been kept employed by General Patterson's forces, attacked the right flank with such vigor that the exhausted troops who were exposed to the attack gave way, fell back, and then began to fly. The movement was rapidly communicated from battalion to battalion, and the men who had hitherto fought bravely, in some cases against as great odds as now threatened them, could not be made to rally, and seemed to think only of safety in flight. Soon after this disorder on the right, a panic was created in the rear, or, more properly, on the left of the federal line of battle, by a charge of rebel cavalry that had crossed Bull Run south of the stone bridge, and having turned the left flank, dashed in among the ambulances and wagon trains which had been advanced towards the stream. This charge created a panic among the teamsters and civilians, and caused the troops of this wing to imitate those on the other side of the run, so that the whole of the three divisions that were in the battle were at once entirely disorganized and routed. Meanwhile, the flying forces from the advanced positions of the battle field made their way towards Bull Run, some in the direction of the ford at Sudley's Spring, and others towards the stone bridge, leaving their dead and many wounded on the battle field. All was confusion, except among a part of the regular army who were ordered to protect the retreat. The roads were blocked, artillery carriages were broken down, and the pieces abandoned. The panic-stricken soldiers threw away their arms and all that would encumber their flight. At the crossing of the stream the confusion was increased, and more cannon were necessarily abandoned, for the enemy were following up their advantage, and were using their artillery

35

against the panic-stricken crowd. The tide was perfectly resistless, and when across the stream, and in a position where the rebels could have been stopped in a pursuit which they did not seem inclined to follow up, the flight continued. A part of the reserve of Miles's division was brought into position near Centreville, to protect the retreat; but the flying columns could not be rallied, and not even these solid lines, or those of Runyon's regiments, far back on the road to Fairfax, could stay the flight, and the rear guard itself finally made a rapid, though an orderly retreat. The flight and the retreat did not end till the troops reached their old camps in the vicinity of Washington.

A large number of civilians had come out from Washington, in carriages and on horseback, to witness the battle, which all had anticipated would result in a victory for the federal arms. These added to the confusion of the roads leading back to the capital, mingled as they were with artillery, wagons, and flying soldiers. The destruction of property was immense. Evidences of the panic were distributed all along the road; broken wagons, artillery carriages, caissons, provisions, clothing, arms and ammunition strewed the way. Wounded and weary soldiers sunk by the road-side, unable to proceed, and exposed to a drenching rain, which came on during the night. Fortunately the rebels did not know how terrible was the defeat and disorganization of the Union army, or they might have pursued with a force sufficient to overcome the rear guard, and to capture large numbers of prisoners and an immense amount of stores. They did not pursue that night even to Centreville, and by the next morning the fugitive soldiers were near the defences of Washington, leaving only the sick and wounded to be captured.

This disgraceful panic was attributed to various causes by parties present in different parts of the field; but the one here given is the one assigned in General McDowell's official report, and from all the evidence that can be gathered

appears to be the true one. On the right the attack of Johnston's heavy reënforcements caused the federal lines to break and fly in disorder, while very shortly after the cavalry charge on the left caused a panic which rendered it impossible to rally the flying troops.

But a brief outline of the battle and its results has been given in order to afford a general idea of the plan and the movement of the large divisions. The details and incidents of the conflict are hardly adapted to the purpose of this work, except so far as they are shown in the official reports which will be found in subsequent pages. But of the many descriptions of the battle which were written by those who witnessed it and the succeeding flight, we take extracts from one most general in its descriptions, and yet affording a vivid picture of the day's proceedings. The writer [*] accompanied General Tyler's division, from the advanced positions of which the general progress and effects of the entire engagement were apparent, though the particular movements of the other divisions could not be observed. After describing the advance of General Tyler's division to its first position, the account proceeds: —

" Our position was less commanding and less clear than that we had occupied on Thursday. We were still before the valley of Bull Run; but the descent from our side was more gradual, and we were surrounded by thick woods down almost to the ravine through which the stream flows. The enemy, on the contrary, had cleared away all obstructing foliage, and bared the earth in every direction over which they could bring their artillery upon us. Clumps of trees and bushes remained wherever their earthworks and other concealed defences could be advantageously planted among them. The ground on their side was vastly superior to ours. It rose in regular slopes to great heights, but was broken into knolls and terraces in numberless places, upon which strong earth-

---

[*] Correspondent of the New York Tribune.

works were successively planted, some openly, but the greater part concealed. The long interval between our first discharge of artillery and the positive attack afforded abundant opportunity to overlook the ground. In no spot did the enemy seem weak. Nature had supplied positions of defence which needed but little labor to render them desperately formidable. How thoroughly these advantages had been improved we know by the enormous efforts which were required to dislodge the troops, and by the obstinate opposition which they displayed before retiring from point to point.

" While our division waited, quiet and alert, General McDowell led the columns of Hunter and Heintzelman far around by the right, to the enemy's flank and rear. The march was long, and doubtless slow, for it was not until about eleven o'clock that we were able to discover indications of their having met the rebels. From Richardson's position, to the left, however, we heard, at eight o'clock, the commencement of vigorous cannonading. The deep, sullen sound from his distant batteries was all that broke the silence for nearly an hour. Then the hurrying of our officers up and down the hill, and through the woods, told us that our assault was about to open. The skirmishers had detected a thick and tangled abatis at the banks of the run, into which, before advancing, a few shells were thrown. As these burst, the rebels swarmed out from their hiding places, and took up their next fortified post beyond. General Schenck's brigade was moved forward at the left, but, before reaching the run, received the full fire of a battery masked with bushes, before which they retired to their first line. Again all operations were suspended by our division, and until eleven o'clock the contest was carried on by the artillery, which, indeed, at that hour resounded from every point of the field. The action by artillery must have extended over five or six miles, from Richardson's position at the extreme left around to Hunter's at the

right. The roar and rattle were incessant, and the air above the vast field soon became thick with smoke.

" Suddenly a line of troops was seen moving over the open hill-slope precisely in advance of us and within a mile — the least distance at which the rebel infantry had been seen. The third brigade, under Colonel Sherman, was now drawn from its shelter among the woods and led rapidly around by the right across the run, and towards one of the enemy's best positions. Brisk volleys of musketry were soon after heard; but the smoke hung like a veil before us, and it was impossible to discover by whom, or against whom, they were directed. A puff of wind afterwards cleared the view, and we saw the brigade still in firm line, and advancing with great speed. A few shots, and a round or two of artillery, next came from the right upon the second brigade, which had not yet moved forward, and which, as a whole, held its post squarely, although some squads broke and ran into the open road.

" At half past eleven o'clock, the cannonading was lighter from our side, and the attention of the enemy seemed to be distracted from us. We were then able to descry great volumes of smoke arising in front, in the precise spot at which Hunter's column should have arrived. This gloomy signal of the battle waved slowly to the left, assuring us that Hunter and Heintzelman were pushing forward, and driving the enemy before them. At the same time our right brigade disappeared over the eminence for which they had been contending, and the distant cheers, which evidently came from them, proved that the present triumph was their own. To sustain and reënforce them, the reserve brigade of Colonel Keyes was then brought down, and marched forward, in spite of a tremendous cannonade which opened upon them from the left, in the same line as that which Colonel Sherman had followed. The left brigade, under General Schenck, did not advance, but still remained on the ground where it had formed at the very outset. The result of this inaction was, that our left was, at the close of the battle, assailed and successfully turned; and although the enemy did not pursue this final triumph, it was not the fault of the commander of that brigade that great mischief was not done. Colonel Keyes soon vanished with his four regiments, and the second brigade was left isolated at the edge of the battle ground. Its best protection then was furnished by the thirty-two pound Parrot rifled cannon, which, some rods to the right, among the brushwood, was raking the road far ahead, and plunging shell among the strongholds which the enemy still maintained.

"At half past twelve o'clock the battle appeared to have reached its climax. Hunter's and Heintzelman's divisions were deep in the enemy's position, and our own force, excepting always the second brigade, was well at work. The discharges of artillery and musketry caused a continuous and unbroken roar, which sometimes swelled tumultuously to terrific crashes, but never lulled. On the heights before us, bodies of infantry were plainly seen driving with fury one against the other, and slowly pressing towards the left—another proof that our advance was resisted in vain. At one point, the rebels seemed determined to risk all rather than retreat. Many a regiment was brought to meet our onset, and all were swept back with the same impetuous charges. Prisoners who were subsequently brought in, admitted that some of our troops, especially the seventy-first New York regiment, literally mowed down and annihilated double their number. Two Alabama regiments, in succession, were cut right and left by the seventy-first. The flanking column was now fully discernible, and the junction of our forces was evidently not far distant. The gradual abandonment of their positions by the rebels could not be doubted. At some points they fled precipitately, but in most cases moved

regularly to the rear. It is probable that they only deserted one strong post for another even stronger, and that, however far we might have crushed them back, we should still have found them intrenched and fortified to the last—even to Manassas itself. But they had positively relinquished the entire line in which they had first arrayed themselves against Tyler's division, excepting one fortified elevation at the left, which could and should have been carried by the second brigade an hour before. How far the enemy had retreated before Hunter and Heintzelman I cannot say; but I am given to understand that they had forsaken all, excepting one powerful earthwork with lofty embankments, upon the highest ground of their field. It was this work, which, later in the day, was stormed by the Zouaves and other regiments, and which, in spite of a daring and intrepidity which our rebel prisoners speak of with amazement, resisted their charge. But other important works had been carried by the third and fourth brigades on our side, so that little appeared to remain for our victory but to perfect the union of the two columns, and to hold the ground we had won.

"The fire now slackened on both sides for several minutes. Although the movements of our own troops were mainly hidden, we could see a peculiar activity among the enemy at the spot where they had been most vehemently repulsed by Heintzelman. A long line of apparently fresh regiments was brought forward, and formed at the edge of a grove through which our men had penetrated. Four times we saw this line broken, and re-formed by its officers, who rode behind, and drove back with their swords those who fled. A fifth time it was shattered and re-formed, but could not be made to stand fast, and was led back to the fortified ground. This afforded us, who looked on from the lower battle field, a new ground for the conviction that the triumph would be with us.

"For nearly half an hour after this we were left in great uncertainty. The enemy languished, and our own movements were clogged by some mysterious obstacle. All that was done within our view was the leading forward of Schenck's brigade a few hundred rods on the open road. But as many of us, lookers-on, had long before passed ahead to Bull Run, and assured ourselves that the field was open for nearly a mile in advance, this was not regarded as of much importance. From Bull Run the aspect of the field was truly appalling. The enemy's dead lay strewn so thickly that they rested upon one another, the ground refusing space to many that had fallen. Few of our men had suffered here, although it seemed that farther on they lay in greater numbers. But the attention of those who gazed was quickly turned from these awful results of the battle to the imminent hazard of its renewal. Down towards our left, which had so long been exposed, a new line of troops moved with an alacrity that indicated entire freshness. As they swept around to the very woods upon which the second brigade rested, the artillery from the last intrenchments they held upon this field — that which should have been overrun betimes by our idle troops — opened with new vigor. Grape and round shot, most accurately aimed, struck the ground before, behind, and each side of General Schenck and the group of officers about him. The Ohio regiments were somewhat sheltered by a cleft in the road, but the New York second was more exposed. General Schenck was in great danger, to which, I am glad to say, he seemed perfectly insensible, riding always through the hottest of the fire, as if nothing more serious than a shower of paper pellets threatened him. . . .

"A few minutes later and the great peril of our division — that which should have been foreseen and provided against — was upon us. The enemy appeared upon the left flank, between us and our way of retreat. Why they failed, having once secured it, to pursue this enormous advantage, it is impossible to conjecture. I am inclined to believe that the coolness and precision of Colonel McCook, of the first Ohio regiment, saved us from this disaster. It is certain Colonel McCook displayed a firm resistance to the charge which menaced him, and that the enemy wavered, and then withdrew. But at this time the first proofs of the panic which had stricken the army were disclosed. From the distant hills our troops, disorganized, scattered, pallid with a terror which had no just cause, came pouring in among us, trampling down some, and spreading the contagion of their fear among all. It was even then a whirlwind which nothing could resist. The most reluctant of the officers were forced from the valley up the hill, in spite of themselves. Whoever had stood would have been trodden under foot by his own men. Near the top of the hill a like commotion was visible, but from a different cause. The rebel cavalry, having completely circumvented our left, had charged in among a crowd of wounded and stragglers, who surrounded a small building which had been used for our hospital. Nothing but the unexpected courage of a considerable number of unorganized men, many of them civilians, who seized the readiest weapons and repelled the enemy, saved that point from being occupied. . . .

"The secret of that panic will perhaps never be known. All essay to explain it, and all fail. Whether General McDowell did or did not give an order to retreat, I cannot say of my own knowledge. I am assured by one who was with him that he did, and by others that he also failed to preserve his self-control. If this be so, we shall know of it in time; but all we can now be sure of is the afflicting fact of our utter and absolute rout. How nearly one great object of the day had been accomplished may be understood when it is known that General Tyler and General McDowell had actually met. Many who came into the battle with Colonel Heintzelman and Colonel Hunter fled by the road over which General Tyler had advanced. In the race from a fancied danger, all divisions and all regiments were mingled. There was not even an attempt to cover the retreat of Tyler's division. With Heintzelman's it was better, Lieutenant Drummond's cavalry troop keeping firm line, and protecting the artillery until its abandonment was imperatively ordered. The extent of the disorder was unlimited. Regulars and volunteers shared it alike. A mere fraction of our artillery was saved. Whole batteries were left upon the field, and the cutting off of others was ordered when the guns had already been brought two miles or more from the battle ground, and were as safe as they would be in New York at this moment. A perfect frenzy was upon almost every man. Some cried piteously to be lifted behind those who rode on horses, and others sought to clamber into wagons, the occupants resisting them with bayonets. All sense of manhood seemed to be forgotten. I hope, and I am sure, there were exceptions, but I am speaking of the rule with the mass. Drivers of heavy wagons dashed down the steep road, reckless of the lives they endangered on the way. Even the sentiment of shame had gone. Some of the better men tried to withstand the rush, and cried out against the flying groups, calling them "cowards, poltroons, brutes," and reviling them for so degrading themselves, especially when no enemy was near. Insensible to the epithets, the runaways only looked relieved, and sought renewed assurance that their imagined pursuers were not upon them. Every impediment to flight was cast aside. Rifles, bayonets, pistols, haversacks, cartridge-boxes, canteens, blankets, belts, and overcoats lined the road. The provisions from the wagons were thrown out, and the tops broken away. All was lost to that American army, even its honor.

"The agony of this overwhelming disgrace can never be expressed in words, or understood by those who only hear the tale repeated. I believe there were men upon that field who turned their faces to the enemy, and marched to certain death, lest they should share the infamy which their fellows had invited and embraced. The suffering of a hundred deaths would have been as nothing compared with the torture under which the few brave soldiers writhed, who were swept along by that maniac hurricane of terror. But suddenly their spirits were revived by a sight which, so long as God lets them live, they will never cease to remember with pride and joy. Stretching far across the road, long before the hoped-for refuge of Centreville was reached, was a firm, unswerving line of men, to whom the sight of the thousands who dashed by them was only a wonder or a scorn. This was the German rifle regiment; and to see the manly bearing of their general, and feel the inspiration which his presence gave at that moment, was like relief to those who perish in a desert. At least, then, all was not lost, and we knew that, let our destiny turn that night as it should, there was one man who would hold and keep the fame of the nation unsullied to the end.

"I need not speak much in praise of the action of Blenker and the officers who served him so well. The events speak for them. Steady and watchful, he held his line throughout the evening, advancing his skirmishers at every token of attack, and spreading a sure protection over the multitudes who fled disordered through his columns. With three regiments he stood to fight against an outnumbering enemy already flushed with victory, and eager to complete its triumph. As the darkness increased, his post became more perilous and more honorable. At eleven o'clock the attack came upon the advance company of Colonel Stahl's Rifles, not in force, but from a body of cavalry whose successful passage would have been followed by a full force, and the consequent destruction of our broken host. The rebel cavalry was driven back, and never returned; and at two in the morning, the great body of our troops, having passed and found their road to safety, the command was given to retreat in order, and the brigade fell slowly and regularly back, with the same precision as if on parade, and as thoroughly at the will of their leader as if no danger had ever come near them. . . .

" Notwithstanding all that I had seen, it seemed incredible that our whole army should melt away in a night; and so I remained at Centreville, trusting that by the morning a sort of reorganization should have taken place, and that our front should still oppose the enemy. At seven o'clock I started towards the battlefield, but, on reaching a considerable acclivity, was amazed to find that no vestige of our troops remained, excepting a score or two of straggling fugitives who followed the tracks of those who had gone before. While returning to Centreville, a group of rebel cavalry passed, who looked inquiringly, but did not question. Their conversation turned upon the chances of cutting off the retreat at Fairfax Court House. . . . The road leading from Centreville to Germantown was filled with marks of the ruinous retreat. At the outskirts of the village thousands of dollars' worth of property lay wrecked and abandoned. In one field a quantity of powder had been thrown. . . . The destruction of property seemed to have increased at every mile. Baggage wagons were overturned, ambulances broken in pieces, weapons of every kind cast off. Horses lay dead and dying. Food was heaped about the wayside. Bags of corn and oats were trodden into the ground. Piles of clothing were scattered on all sides. In many places the discarded goods and equipments were ranged breast-high, and stood like monuments erected by our own hands to our own shame.

" At Fairfax I had hoped to find a rallying place, and could hardly believe that the flight had gone even beyond this. But the village was deserted, excepting by native prowlers, who were ransacking the emptied contents of our baggage wagons, and who scowled savagely enough at the fugitives who sought among them a temporary shelter from the storm. Beyond Fairfax the marks of destruction were less frequent, though the stream of the retreat grew even stronger. Along the main road the flying kept their way in something like a continuous line, dividing only at the turnpike which leads to Arlington, into which some diverged, while others moved on to Alexandria. Three miles from the Long Bridge I came upon the rear of Blenker's brigade, Stahl's German Rifles still holding the hindmost position, and the other two regiments, Steinwehr's and the Garibaldi Guard, moving in order before them. Still in advance of these was the De Kalb regiment, also intact. But beyond all was tumult again, and even to the city itself the wretched disorder and confusion had reached."

CHAPTER XL.

Official Report of General McDowell. — Reports of General Tyler, Colonel Porter, Colonel Heintzelman, and Colonel Miles. — Results of the Battle. — Demoralization of the Army. — Causes of the Defeat. — General Patterson and his Forces. — Beauregard's Report.

To complete the narrative of the battle of Bull Run, we give the following official report of General McDowell, and extracts from the reports of the several commanders of divisions : —

To Lieutenant-Colonel E. D. Townsend, Assistant Adjutant-General, Headquarters of the Army, Washington, D. C.

"HEADQUARTERS, DEPARTMENT NORTH-EASTERN "VIRGINIA,. ARLINGTON, VA., *August* 4, 1861.

" COLONEL : I have the honor to submit the following report of the battle of the 21st of July, near Manassas, Virginia. It has been delayed till this time for the inability of the subordinate commanders to get earlier a true account of the state of their commands.

" In my communication to you of the 26th

ultimo, I stated it as my intention to move that afternoon, and drive the enemy from the east side of Bull Run, so as to enable the engineers to make a sufficiently accurate reconnoissance to justify our future movements. Later in the day, they had obtained enough information of the passage across the stream to dispense with this reconnoissance, and it was decided to move without delay. It had been my intention to move the several columns out on the road a few miles on the evening of the 20th, so that they would have a shorter march in the morning; but I deferred to those who had the greatest distance to go, and who preferred starting early in the morning, and making but one move.

"On the evening of the 20th ult., my command was at or near Centreville. The enemy was at or near Manassas, distant from Centreville about seven miles to the south-west. Centreville is a village of a few houses, mostly on the west side of a ridge running nearly north and south. The road from Centreville to Manassas Junction was along this ridge, and crosses Bull Run about three miles from the former place. The Warrenton turnpike, which runs nearly east and west, goes over this ridge, through the village, and crosses Bull Run about four miles from it, Bull Run having a course between the crossing from north-west to south-east. The first division (Tyler's) was stationed on the north side of the Warrenton turnpike, and on the eastern slope of the Centreville ridge, two brigades on the same road, and a mile and a half in advance, to the west of the ridge, and one brigade on the road from Centreville to Manassas where it crosses Bull Run, at Blackburn's Ford, where General Tyler had the engagement of the 18th ult. The second division (Hunter's) was on the Warrenton turnpike, one mile east of Centreville. The third division (Heintzelman's) was on a road known as the Old Braddock road, which comes into Centreville from the south-east, about a mile and a half from the village. The fifth division (Miles's) was on the same road with the third division, and between it and Centreville. A map, which is herewith marked A, will show these positions better than I can describe them.

"On Friday night a train of subsistence arrived, and on Saturday its contents were ordered to be issued to the command, and the men required to have three days' rations in their haversacks. On Saturday orders were issued for the available force to march. As reported to you in my letter of the 19th ult., my personal reconnoissance of the roads to the south had shown that it was not practicable to carry out the original plan of turning the enemy's position on their right. The affair of the 18th, at Blackburn's Ford, showed he was too strong at that point for us to force a passage there without great loss, and if we did, that it would bring us in front of his strong position at Manassas, which was not desired. Our information was that the stone bridge over which the Warrenton road crossed Bull Run, to the west of Centreville, was defended by a battery in position, and the road on his side of the stream impeded by a heavy abatis. The alternative was, therefore, to turn the extreme left of his position. Reliable information was obtained of an undefended ford about three miles above the bridge, there being another ford between it and the bridge, which was defended. It was therefore determined to take the road to the upper ford, and after crossing, to get behind the forces guarding the lower ford and the bridge, and after occupying the Warrenton road east of the bridge, to send out a force to destroy the railroad at or near Gainesville, and thus break up the communication between the enemy's forces at Manassas and those in the valley of Virginia, before Winchester, which had been held in check by Major-General Patterson.

"Brigadier-General Tyler was directed to move, with three of his brigades, on the Warrenton road, and commence cannonading the

enemy's batteries, while Hunter's division, moving after him, should, after passing a little stream called Cub Run, turn to the right and north, and move around to the upper ford, and there turn south and get behind the enemy. Colonel Heintzelman's division was to follow Hunter's as far as the turning-off place to the lower ford, where he was to cross after the enemy should have been driven out by Hunter's division, the fifth division (Miles's) to be in reserve on the Centreville ridge.

"I had felt anxious about the road from Manassas by Blackburn's Ford to Centreville, along this ridge, fearing that whilst we should be in force to the front, and endeavoring to turn the enemy's position, we ourselves should be turned by him by this road; for if he should once obtain possession of this ridge, which overlooks all the country to the west to the foot of the spurs of the Blue Ridge, we should have been irretrievably cut off and destroyed. I had, therefore, directed this point to be held in force, and sent an engineer to extemporize some field works to strengthen the position.

"The fourth division (Runyon's) had not been brought to the front farther than to guard our communications by way of Vienna and the Orange and Alexandria Railroad. His advanced regiment was about seven miles in the rear of Centreville.

"The divisions were ordered to march at half past two o'clock, A. M., so as to arrive on the ground early in the day, and thus avoid the heat which is to be expected at this season. There was delay in the first division getting out of its camp on the road, and the other divisions were, in consequence, between two and three hours behind the time appointed — a great misfortune, as events turned out. The wood road leading from Warrenton turnpike to the upper ford was much longer than we counted upon, the general direction of the stream being oblique to the road, and we having the obtuse angle on our side.

36

"General Tyler commenced with his artillery at half past six, A. M.; but the enemy did not reply, and after some time it became a question whether he was in any force in our front, and if he did not intend himself to make an attack, and make it by Blackburn's Ford. After firing several times, and obtaining no response, I held one of Heintzelman's brigades in reserve, in case we should have to send any troops back to reenforce Miles's division. The other brigades moved forward as directed in the general orders. On reaching the ford at Sudley's Spring, I found part of the leading brigade of Hunter's division (Burnside's) had crossed; but the men were slow in getting over, stopping to drink. As at this time the clouds of dust from the direction of Manassas indicated the immediate approach of a large force, and fearing it might come down on the head of the column before the division could get over and sustain it, orders were sent back to the heads of regiments to break from the column and come forward separately as fast as possible. Orders were sent by an officer to the reserve brigade of Heintzelman's division to come by a nearer road across the fields, and an aid-de-camp was sent to Brigadier-General Tyler to direct him to press forward his attack, as large bodies of the enemy were passing in front of him to attack the division which had crossed over. The ground between the stream and the road leading from Sudley's Spring south, and over which Burnside's brigade marched, was, for about a mile from the ford, thickly wooded, whilst on the right hand of the road, for about the same distance, the country was divided between fields and woods. About a mile from the road the country on both sides of the road is open, and for nearly a mile farther large rolling fields extend down to the Warrenton turnpike, which crosses what became the field of battle through the valley of a small watercourse, a tributary of Bull Run.

"Shortly after the leading regiment of the

first brigade reaohed this open space, and whilst others and the second brigade were crossing to the front and right, the enemy opened his fire, beginning with artillery, and following it up with infantry. The leading brigade (Burnside's) had to sustain this shock for a short time without support, and did it well. The battalion of regular infantry was sent to sustain it, and shortly afterwards the other corps of Porter's brigade, and a regiment detached from Heintzelman's division to the left, forced the enemy back far enough to allow Sherman's and Keyes's brigades, of Tyler's division, to cross from their position on the Warrenton road. These drove the right of the enemy, understood to have been commanded by Beauregard, from the front of the field, and out of the detached woods, and down to the road, and across it up the slopes on the other side. While this was going on, Heintzelman's division was moving down the field to the stream and up the road beyond Beyond the Warrenton road, and to the left of the road, down which our troops had marched from Sudley's Spring, is a hill with a farm house on it. Behind this hill the enemy had, early in the day, some of his most annoying batteries planted. Across the road from this hill was another hill, or rather elevated ridge, or table of land. The hottest part of the contest was for the possession of this hill with a house on it. The force engaged here was Heintzelman's division, Wilcox's and Howard's brigades on the right, supported by part of Porter's brigade and the cavalry under Palmer, and Franklin's brigade of Heintzelman's division, Sherman's brigade of Tyler's division in the centre and up the road, whilst Keyes's brigade of Tyler's division was some of the left, attacking the batteries near the stone bridge. The Rhode Island battery of Burnside's brigade also participated in this attack by its fire from the north of the turnpike. The enemy was understood to have been commanded by J. E. Johnston. Rickett's battery, which did such effective ser-

vice, and played so brilliant a part in this contest, was, together with Griffin's battery, on the side of the hill, and became the object of the special attention of the enemy, who succeeded — our officers mistaking one of his regiments for one of our own, and allowing it to approach without firing upon it — in disabling the battery, and then attempted to take it. Three times was he repulsed by different corps in succession, and driven back, and the guns taken by hand, the horses being killed, and pulled away. The third time it was supposed by us all that the repulse was final, for he was driven entirely from the hill, and so far beyond it as not to be in sight; and all were certain the day was ours. He had before this been driven nearly a mile and a half, and was beyond the Warrenton road, which was entirely in our possession from the stone bridge westward, and our engineers were just completing the removal of the abatis across the road, to allow our reënforcement (Schenck's brigade and Ayers's battery) to join us.

" The enemy was evidently disheartened and broken. But we had been fighting since half past ten o'clock in the morning, and it was after three o'clock in the afternoon. The men had been up since two o'clock in the morning, and had made what to those unused to such things seemed a long march, before coming into action, though the longest distance gone over was not more than nine and a half miles; and though they had three days' provisions served out to them the day before, many, no doubt, did not eat them, or either threw them away on the march or during the battle, and were, therefore, without food. They had done much severe fighting. Some of the regiments which had been driven from the hill in the first two attempts of the enemy to keep possession of it, had become shaken, were unsteady, and had many men out of the ranks.

"It was at this time that the enemy's reënforcements came to his aid from the railroad train, understood to have just arrived from the valley with the residue of Johnston's army. They threw themselves in the woods on our right, and towards the rear of our right, and opened a fire of musketry on our men, which caused them to break and retire down the hillside. This soon degenerated into disorder, for which there was no remedy. Every effort was made to rally them, even beyond the reach of the enemy's fire, but in vain. The battalion of regular infantry alone moved up the hill opposite to the one with the house on it, and there maintained itself until our men could get down to and across the Warrenton turnpike, on the way back to the position we occupied in the morning. The plain was covered with the retreating troops, and they seemed to infect those with whom they came in contact. The retreat soon became a rout, and this soon degenerated still further into a panic.

"Finding this state of affairs was beyond the efforts of all those who had assisted so faithfully during the long and hard day's work in gaining almost the object of our wishes, and that nothing remained on the field but to recognize what we could no longer prevent, I gave the necessary orders to protect their withdrawal, begging the men to form in line, and offer the appearance, at least, of organization. They returned by the fords to the Warrenton road, protected, by my order, by Colonel Porter's force of regulars. Once on the road, and the different corps coming together in small parties, many without officers, they became intermingled, and all organization was lost.

"Orders had been sent back to Miles's division for a brigade to move forward and protect this retreat, and Colonel Blenker's brigade was detached for this purpose; and was ordered to go as far forward as the point where the road to the right left the main road.

"By referring to the general order, it will be seen that, while the operations were to go on in front, an attack was to be made at Blackburn's Ford by the brigade (Richardson's) stationed there. A reference to his report, and to that of Major Hunt, commanding the artillery, will show that this part of the plan was well and effectively carried out. It succeeded in deceiving the enemy for a considerable time, and in keeping in check a part of his force. The fire of the artillery at this point is represented as particularly destructive.

"At the time of our retreat, seeing great activity in this direction, much firing, and columns of dust, I became anxious for this place, fearing, if it were turned or forced, the whole stream of our retreating mass would be captured or destroyed. After providing for the protection of the retreat by Porter's and Blenker's brigades, I repaired to Richardson's, and found the whole force ordered to be stationed for the holding of the road from Manassas by Blackburn's Ford to Centreville, on the march, under the orders from the division commander, for Centreville. I immediately halted it, and ordered it to take up the best line of defence across the ridge that their position admitted of, and subsequently taking in person the command of this part of the army, I caused such disposition of the forces which had been added to by the first and second New Jersey and the De Kalb regiments, ordered up from Runyon's reserve, before going forward, as would best serve to check the enemy. The ridge being held in this way, the retreating current passed slowly through Centreville to the rear. The enemy followed us from the ford as far as Cub Run, and owing to the road becoming blocked up at the crossing, caused us much damage there, for the artillery could not pass, and several pieces and caissons had to be abandoned. In the panic, the horses hauling the caissons and ammunition were cut from their places by persons to escape with, and in this way much confusion was caused, the panic aggravated, and the road encumbered. Not only were pieces of artillery lost, but also many of the ambulances carrying the wounded.

"By sundown most of our men had gotten behind Centreville ridge, and it became a question whether we should or not endeavor to make a stand there. The condition of our artillery and its ammunition, and the want of food for the men who had generally abandoned· or thrown away all that had been issued the day before, and the utter disorganization, and consequent demoralization, of the mass of the army, seemed to all who were near enough to be consulted — division and brigade commanders and staff — to admit of no alternative but to fall back; the more so as the position at Blackburn's Ford was then in the possession of the enemy, and he was already turning our left. On sending the officers of the staff to the different camps, they found, as they reported to me, that our decision had been anticipated by the troops, most of those who had come in from the front being already on the road to the rear, the panic with which they came in still continuing and hurrying them along.

"At — o'clock, the rear guard (Blenker's brigade) moved, covering the retreat, which was effected during the night and next morning. The troops at Fairfax station, leaving by the cars, took with them the bulk of the supplies which had been sent there. My aid-de-camp, Major Wadsworth, staid at Fairfax Court House till late in the morning, to see that the stragglers and weary and worn-out soldiers were not left behind.

"I transmit herewith the reports of the several division and brigade commanders, to which I refer for the conduct of particular regiments and corps, and a consolidated return of the killed, wounded, and missing. From the latter it will be seen that our killed amounted to nineteen officers and four hundred and sixty-two non-commissioned officers and privates, and our wounded to sixty-four officers and nine hundred and forty-seven non-commissioned officers and privates. Many of the wounded will soon be able to join the ranks, and will leave our total of killed and disabled from further service under one thousand. The return of the missing is very inaccurate, the men supposed to be missing having fallen into other regiments and gone to Washington — many of the Zouaves to New York. In one brigade the number orginally reported at six hundred and sixteen, was yesterdy reduced to one hundred and seventy-four. These reductions are being made daily. In a few days a more correct return can be made.

"Of course nothing accurate is known of the loss of the enemy. An officer of their forces, coming from them with a flag of truce, admitted eighteen hundred killed and wounded ; and other information shows this to be much under the true number.

"The officer commanding the eleventh New York Zouaves, and Colonel Heintzelman, say that the returns of that regiment cannot be relied on, as many of those reported among the casualties have absented themselves since their return, and have gone to NewYork. Among the missing are reported many of our surgeons, who remained in attendance on our wounded, and were, against the rules of modern warfare, made prisoners.

"The issue of this hard-fought battle — in which certainly our troops lost no credit in their conflict on the field with an enemy ably commanded, superior in numbers, who had but a short distance to march, and who acted on his own ground, on the defensive, and always under cover, whilst our men were of necessity out in the open fields — should not prevent full credit being given to those officers and corps whose services merited success, if they did not attain it. . . .

"As my position may warrant, even if it does not call for, some explanation of the causes, as far as they can be seen, which led to the results herein stated, I trust it may not be out of place if I refer, in a few words, to the immediate ante-cedents of the battle. When I submitted to the general-in-chief, in compliance with his verbal instructions, the plan of operations and estimate of force required, the time I was to proceed to carry it into effect was fixed for the 8th July, Monday. Every facility possible was given me by the general-in-chief and heads of the administrative departments in making the necessary preparations. But the regiments, owing, I was told, to want of transportation, came over slowly. Many of them did not come across till eight or nine days after the time fixed upon, and went forward without my even seeing them, and without having been together before in a brigade. The sending reënforcements to General Patterson, by drawing off the wagons, was a further and unavoidable cause of delay. Notwithstanding the herculean efforts of the quartermaster-general, and his favoring me in every way, the wagons for ammunition, subsistence, &c., and the horses for the trains and the artillery, did not all arrive for more than a week after the time appointed to move. I was not even prepared as late as the 15th ultimo, and the desire I should move became great, and it was wished I should not, if possible, delay longer than Tuesday, the 16th ultimo. When I did set out, on the 16th, I was still deficient in wagons for subsistence. But I went forward, trusting to their being procured in time to follow me. The trains thus hurriedly gathered together, with horses, wagons, drivers, and wagon managers, all new and unused to each other, moved with difficulty and disorder, and was the cause of a day's delay in getting the provisions forward, making it necessary to make on Sunday the attack we should have made on Saturday.

"I could not, with every exertion, get forward with the troops earlier than we did: I wished to go to Centreville the second day, which would have taken us there on the 17th, and enabled us, so far as they were concerned, to go into action on the 19th, instead of the 21st; but when I went forward from Fairfax Court House, beyond Germantown, to urge them forward, I was told it was impossible for the men to march farther. They had only come from Vienna, about six miles, and it was not more than six and a half miles farther to Centreville — in all a march of twelve and a half miles; but the men were foot-weary, not so much, I was told, by the distance marched, as by the time they had been on foot, caused by the obstructions in the road and the slow pace we had to move to avoid ambuscades. The men were, moreover, unaccustomed to marching, their bodies not in condition for that kind of work, and not used to carrying even the load of light marching order.

"We crossed Bull Run with about eighteen thousand men of all arms, the fifth division (Miles's and Richardson's brigade) on the left, at Blackburn's Ford to Centreville, and Schenck's brigade, of Tyler's division, on the left of the road, near the stone bridge, not participating in the main action. The numbers opposed to us have been variously estimated. I may safely say, and avoid even the appearance of exaggeration, that the enemy brought up all he could which were not kept engaged elsewhere. He had notice of our coming on the 17th, and had from that time until the 21st to bring up whatever he had. It is known that in estimating the force to go against Manassas, I engaged not to have to do with the enemy's forces under Johnston, then kept in check in the valley by Major-General Patterson, or those kept engaged by Major-General Butler; and I know every effort was made by the general-in-chief that this should be done, and that even if Johnston joined Beauregard, it would not be because he could be followed by General Patterson, but from causes not necessary for me to refer to, if I knew them all. This was not done, and the enemy was free to assemble from every direction in numbers only limited by the amount of his railroad rolling stock and his supply of provisions. To the forces, therefore, we drove in from Fairfax Court House, Fairfax Station, Germantown, and Centreville, and those under Beauregard at Manassas, must be added those under Johnston from Winchester, and those brought up by Davis from Richmond to other places at the south, to which is to be added the levy *en masse* ordered by the Richmond authorities, which was ordered to assemble at Manassas. What all this amounted to, I cannot say; certainly much more than we attacked them with.

" I could not, as I have said, more early push on faster, nor could I delay. A large and the best part of my forces were three months' volunteers, whose term of service was about to expire, but who were sent forward as having long enough to serve for the purpose of the expedition. On the eve of the battle the fourth Pennsylvania regiment of volunteers and the battery of volunteer artillery of the New York eighth militia, whose term of service expired, insisted on their discharge. I wrote to the regiment, expressing a request for them to remain a short time, and the Hon. Secretary of War, who was at the time on the ground, tried to induce the battery to remain at least five days. But in vain. They insisted on their discharge that night. It was granted; and the next morning, when the army moved forward into battle, these troops moved to the rear to the sound of the enemy's cannon.

"In the next few days, day by day, I should have lost ten thousand of the best armed, drilled, officered, and disciplined troops in the army. In other words, every day which added to the strength of the enemy made us weaker.

" In conclusion, I desire to say, in reference to the events of the 21st ult., that the general order for the battle to which I referred was, with slight modifications, literally conformed to; that the corps were brought over Bull Run in the manner proposed, and put into action as before arranged; and that up to late in the after-

noon every movement ordered was carrying us successfully to the object we had proposed before starting — that of getting to the railroad leading from Manassas to the valley of Virginia, and going on it far enough to break up and destroy the communications and interviews between the forces under Beauregard and those under Johnston. And could we have fought a day or a few hours sooner, there is every thing to show how we could have continued successful, even against the odds with which we contended.

" I have the honor to be, very respectfully,

"Your most obedient servant,

"IRWIN McDOWELL,

"*Brigadier-General commanding.*"

GENERAL TYLER'S REPORT.

" HEADQUARTERS FIRST DIVISION DEPARTMENT N. E. VA.,
"WASHINGTON, *July* 27, 1861.

"GENERAL: In obedience to order No. 22, dated Centreville, July 20, Sherman's, Schenck's, and Keyes's brigades, of this division — Richardson's brigade having been left in front of Blackburn's Ford — moved at half past two, A. M., on the 21st inst., to threaten the passage of the Warrenton turnpike bridge, on Bull Run. I arrived in front of the bridge with Schenck's and Sherman's brigades, and Ayres's and Carlisle's batteries, about six, A. M., Keyes's brigade having been halted by your order to watch the road coming up from Manassas, and about two miles from the run. After examining the position, and posting Sherman's and Schenck's brigades and artillery, I fired the first gun at half past six, A. M., as agreed upon, to show that we were in position. As my orders were to threaten the passage of the bridge, I caused Schenck's brigade to be formed into line, its left resting in the direction of the bridge, and the battery which the enemy had established to sweep the bridge and its approach, so as to threaten both. Sherman's brigade was posted to the right of the Warrenton turnpike, so as to be in position to sustain Schenck, or to move across Bull Run in the direction of Hunter's column.

"The thirty-pounder gun attached to the Carlisle battery was posted on the Warrenton turnpike, with Ayres's battery considerably in its rear. Carlisle's battery was posted on the left of Sherman's brigade. In this position we awaited the appearance of Hunter's and Heintzelman's columns as ordered, until such time as the approach to the bridge should be carried, and the bridge rebuilt by Captain Alexander, of the engineers, who had on the spot the necessary structure for that purpose.

"Soon after getting into position we discovered that the enemy had a heavy battery, with infantry in support, commanding both the road and bridge approaches, on which both Ayers and Carlisle at different times tried the effect of their guns without success ; and, a careful examination of the banks of Bull Run satisfying me that they were impracticable for the purpose of artillery, these batteries had to remain comparatively useless until such time as Hunter's column might clear the approach by a movement on the opposite bank. During this period of waiting, the thirty-pounder was occasionally used with considerable effect against bodies of infantry and cavalry, which could be seen from time to time moving in the direction of Hunter's column, and out of the range of ordinary guns. Using a high tree as an observatory, we could constantly see the operations of Hunter's and Heintzelman's column from the time they crossed Bull Run ; and through one of my staff, Lieutenant O'Rourke, of the engineers, I was promptly notified as to any change in the progress of their columns up to the time when it appeared that the heads of both were arrested, and the enemy seemed to be moving heavy reënforcements to support their troops. At this time I ordered Colonel Sherman, with his brigade, to cross Bull Run, and to support the two columns already in action. Colonel Sherman, as appears by his reports, crossed the run without opposition, and after encountering a party of the enemy flying before Hunter's forces, found General McDowell, and received his orders to join in the pursuit. The subsequent operations of this brigade and its able commander having been under your own eye and directions, I shall not follow its movements any farther, but refer you to Colonel Sherman's report, which you will find herewith.

" So soon as it was discovered that Hunter's division had been arrested, I ordered up Keyes's brigade, which arrived just as the left of Sherman's was crossing the run, and having satisfied myself that the enemy had not the force nor the purpose to cross Bull Run, I ordered Keyes's brigade to follow Sherman, accompanying the move in person, as I saw it must necessarily place me on the left of our line, and in the best possible position, when we should have driven the enemy off, to join Schenck's brigade and the two batteries left on the opposite side. I ordered Colonel Keyes to incline the head of his column a little to the right of the line of march taken by Sherman's brigade, to avoid the fire of a battery which the enemy had opened. This movement sheltered the men to a considerable degree, and resulted in closing on the rear of Sherman's brigade ; and, on reaching the high ground, I ordered Colonel Keyes to form into line on the left of Sherman's brigade, which was done with great steadiness and regularity. After waiting a few moments, the line was ordered to advance, and came into conflict on its right with the enemy's cavalry and infantry ; which, after some severe struggles, it drove back, until the farther march of the brigade was arrested by a severe fire of artillery and infantry, sheltered by some buildings standing on the heights above the road leading to Bull Run. The charge was here ordered, and the second Maine and third Connecticut regiments, which were opposed to this part of the enemy's line, pressed forward to the top of the hill until they reached the buildings which were held by the enemy, drove them out, and for a moment had them in possession. At this point, finding the brigade under the fire of a strong force behind breastworks, the order was given to march by the left flank across an open field until the whole line was sheltered by the right bank of Bull Run, along which the march was conducted, with a view to turn the battery which the enemy had placed on the hill below the point at which the Warrenton turnpike crosses Bull Run. The march was conducted for a considerable distance below the stone bridge, causing the enemy to retire, and giving Captain Alexander an opportunity to pass the bridge, cut out the abatis which had been placed there, and prepared the way for Schenck's brigade and the two batteries to pass over. Before the contemplated movement could be made on the enemy's battery, it was removed and placed in a position to threaten our line; but before the correct range could be obtained, Colonel Keyes carried his brigade, by a flank movement, around the base of the hill, and was on the point of ascending it in time to get at the battery, when I discovered that our troops were on the retreat, and that, unless a rapid movement to the rear was made, we should be cut off; and through my aid, Lieutenant Upton, Colonel Keyes was ordered to file to the right and join the retreating column. The order was executed without the least confusion, and the brigade joined the retreating column in good order. When this junction was made, I left Keyes's brigade, and rode forward to ascertain the condition of Schenck's brigade and the artillery left this side of Bull Run, and on arriving there, found Ayers's battery and Lieutenant Haines's thirty-pounder waiting orders. I immediately ordered Lieutenant Haines to limber up and move forward as soon as possible. This was promptly done, and the piece moved on towards Centreville. I then went into the wood where the ammunition wagon of this piece had been placed, out of the reach of the fire,

and found that the driver had deserted, and taken away part of the horses, which made it impossible to move it. I then returned to Ayers's battery, which I found limbered up, and ordered it to move forward and cover the retreat, which was promptly done by its gallant officers; and when the cavalry charge was made, shortly afterwards, they repulsed it promptly and effectually. I then collected a guard, mainly from the second Maine regiment, and put it under the command of Colonel Jameson, with orders to sustain Captain Ayers during the retreat, which was done gallantly and successfully, until the battery reached Centreville. Before ordering Colonel Jameson to cover Ayers's battery, I passed to the rear to find General Schenck's brigade, intending, as it was fresh, to have it cover the retreat. I did not find it in the position in which I had left it, and supposed it had moved forward and joined the retreating column. I did not see General Schenck again until near Cub Run, where he appeared active in rallying his own or some other regiments. General Schenck reports that the two Ohio regiments left Bull Run after the cavalry charge, and arrived at Centreville in good order.

"In closing this report, it gives me great pleasure to express my admiration of the manner in which Colonel Keyes handled his brigade, completely covering it by every possible accident of the ground, while changing his positions, and leading it bravely and skilfully to the attack at the right moment, to which the brigade responded in every instance in a manner highly creditable to itself and satisfactory to its commanding officers. At no time during the conflict was this brigade disorganized, and it was the last off the field, and in good order.

"Colonel Keyes says, 'The gallantry with which the second Maine and third Connecticut regiments charged up the hill upon the enemy's artillery and infantry, was never, in my opinion, surpassed; and the conduct of Colonels Jame-

son and Chatfield, in this instance and throughout the day, merits the highest commendation.
Colonel Terry rendered great assistance by
his gallantry and excellent conduct. Lieutenant Hascall, acting assistant adjutant-general,
Lieutenants Walter and Ely, rendered gallant
and effective assistance.' It gives me pleasure
to be able to confirm the above from personal
observation, and to express my personal satisfaction with the conduct of this brigade. For
further particulars as to gallant conduct of individuals, I beg leave to refer you to the reports of commanders of brigades, hereunto
attached. Colonel Sherman speaks highly of
Colonel McCoon, of Wisconsin, and Lieutenants
Piper and McQuester — all on his personal staff.
"From my own personal staff I received, in
every instance, prompt and gallant assistance;
and my thanks are due to Captains Baird and
Merrill, Lieutenants Houston, Abbott, Upton,
O'Rourke, and Audenreid, for gallant conduct,
and the prompt and valuable assistance they
rendered me. Lieutenants Abbott and Upton
were both wounded, and each had a horse killed
under him, as also had Lieutenant O'Rourke.
"I enclose herewith a table of casualties,
showing our losses at Bull Run.
"I have the honor to be, with great respect,
"Your most obedient servant,
"DANIEL TYLER,
"Brigadier-General, commanding Division.
"To BRIGADIER-GENERAL McDOWELL,
COMMANDING DEPARTMENT NORTH-EASTERN VIRGINIA."

Colonel Hunter, commander of the second
division, was wounded early in the action, and the
command devolved on Colonel Andrew Porter,
whose report, with that of Colonel Burnside,
gives an account of the action of this division.

COLONEL PORTER'S REPORT.

"HEADQUARTERS FIRST BRIGADE, SECOND DIVISION,
"ARLINGTON, VA., July 25, 1861.

"CAPTAIN J. B. FRY, A. A. G.: . . . .
Owing to frequent delays in the march of
troops in front, the brigade did not reach Cen-

treville until thirty minutes past four o'clock,
A. M., and it was an hour after sunrise when
the head of it was turned to the right to commence the flank movement.

"The slow and intermittent movements of the
second brigade (Burnside's) were then followed
through the woods for four hours, which
brought the head of our division to Bull Run
and Sudley's Mills, where a halt of half an hour
took place, to rest and refresh the men and
horses. From the heights on this side of the
run a vast column of the enemy could be
plainly descried, at the distance of a mile or
more on our left, moving rapidly towards our
line of march in front. Some dispositions of
skirmishers were then directed to be made at
the head of the column by the division commander, in which Colonel Slocum, of the second
Rhode Island regiment, was observed to bear
an active part. The column moved forward,
however, before they were completed, and in
about thirty minutes emerged from the timber,
where the rattle of the musketry and occasional
crash of round shot, through the leaves and
branches of the trees in our vicinity, betokened
the opening of battle.

"The head of the brigade was immediately
turned slightly to the right, in order to gain
time and room for deployment on the right of
the second brigade. Griffin's battery found its
way through the timber to the fields beyond,
followed promptly by the marines, while the
twenty-seventh took direction more to the left,
and the fourteenth followed upon the trail
of the battery — all moving up at a double-
quick step.

"The enemy appeared drawn up in a long
line, extending along the Warrenton turnpike,
from a house and haystack upon our extreme
right to a house beyond the left of the division.
Behind that house there was a heavy masked
battery, which, with three others along his line
on the heights beyond, covered the ground upon
which we were advancing with all sorts of pro-

37

jectiles. A grove in front of his right wing afforded it shelter and protection, while the shrubbery along the road in the fences screened somewhat his left wing.

"Griffin advanced to within a thousand yards, and opened a deadly and unerring fire upon his batteries, which were soon silenced or driven away.

"Our right was rapidly developed ·by the marines, twenty-seventh, fourteenth, and eighth, with the cavalry in rear of the right; the enemy retreating in more precipitation than order as our line advanced. The second brigade (Burnside's) was at this time attacking the enemy's right with perhaps too hasty vigor.

"The enemy clung to the protecting wood with great tenacity, and the Rhode Island battery became so much endangered as to impel the commander of the second brigade to call for the assistance of the battalion of regulars. At this time I received the information, through Captain W. D. Whipple, A. A. G., that Colonel Hunter was seriously wounded, and had directed him to report to me as commander of the division, and in reply to the urgent request of Colonel Burnside, I detached the battalion of regulars to his assistance.

"For an account of its operations, I would respectfully beg a reference to the enclosed report of its commander, Major Sykes. The rebels soon came flying from the woods towards the right, and the twenty-seventh completed their rout by charging directly upon their centre in the face of a scorching fire, while the fourteenth and eighth moved down the turnpike to cut off the retiring foe, and to support the twenty-seventh, which had lost its gallant colonel, but was standing the brunt of the action, with its ranks thinning in the dreadful fire. Now the resistance of the enemy's left was so obstinate that the beaten right retired in safety.

"The head of Heintzelman's column at this moment appeared upon the field, and the eleventh and fifth Massachusetts regiments

moved forward to the support of our. centre while staff officers could be seen galloping rapidly in every direction, endeavoring to rally the broken eighth; but this laudable purpose was only partially attained, owing to the inefficiency of some of its field officers.

"The fourteenth, though it had broken, was soon rallied in rear of Griffin's battery, which soon took up a position farther to the front and right, from which his fire was delivered with such precision and rapidity as to compel the batteries of the enemy to retire in consternation far behind the brow of the hill in front.

"At this time my brigade occupied a line considerably in advance of that first occupied by the left wing of the enemy. The battery was pouring its withering fire into the batteries and columns of the enemy wherever they exposed themselves. The cavalry were engaged in feeling the left flank of the enemy's position, in doing which some important captures were made, one by Sergeant Socks, of the second dragoons, of a General George Stewart, of Baltimore. Our cavalry also emptied the saddles of a number of the mounted rebels.

"General Tyler's division was engaged with the enemy's right. The twenty-seventh was resting on the edge of the woods in the centre, covered by a hill, upon which lay the eleventh and fifth Massachusetts; occasionally delivering a scattering fire. The fourteenth was moving to the right flank; the eighth had lost its organization; the marines were moving up in fine style in rear of the fourteenth, and Captain Arnold was occupying a height in the middle ground with his battery. At this juncture there was a temporary lull in the firing from the rebels, who appeared only occasionally on the heights in irregular formations, but to serve as marks for Griffin's guns. The prestige of success had thus far attended the efforts of our inexperienced but gallant troops. The lines of the enemy had been forcibly shifted nearly a mile to their left and rear. The flags of eight regiments, though borne somewhat wearily, now pointed towards the hill, from which disordered masses of rebels had been seen hastily retiring. Griffin's and Rickett's batteries were ordered by the commanding general to the top of the hill on the right, supported with the "Fire Zouaves" and marines, while the fourteenth entered the skirt of wood on their right, to protect that flank; and a column, composed of the twenty-seventh New York, eleventh and fifth Massachusetts, second Minnesota, and sixty-ninth New York, moved up towards the left flank of the batteries; but so soon as they were in position, and before the flanking supports had reached theirs, a murderous fire of musketry and rifles, opened at pistol range, cut down every cannoneer and a large number of horses. The fire came from some infantry of the enemy, which had been mistaken for our own forces, an officer in the field having stated that it was a regiment sent by Colonel Heintzelman to support the batteries.

"The evanescent courage of the "Zouaves" prompted them to fire perhaps a hundred shots, when they broke and fled, leaving the batteries open to a charge of the enemy's cavalry, which took place immediately. The marines also, in spite of the exertions of their gallant officers, gave way in disorder. The fourteenth, on the right, and the column on the left, hesitatingly retired, with the exception of the sixty-ninth and thirty-eighth New York, who nobly stood, and returned the fire of the enemy for fifteen minutes. Soon the slopes behind us were swarming with our retreating and disorganized forces, while riderless horses and artillery teams ran furiously through the flying crowd.

"All further efforts were futile. The words, gestures, and threats of our officers were thrown away upon men who had lost all presence of mind, and only longed for absence of body. Some of our noblest and best officers lost their lives in trying to rally them. Upon our *first* *position* the twenty-seventh was the first to rally,

under the command of Major Bartlett, and around it the other regiments engaged soon collected their scattered fragments. The battalion of regulars, in the mean time, moved steadily across the field from the left to the right, and took up a position, where it held the entire forces of the rebels in check until our forces were somewhat rallied.

"The commanding general then ordered a retreat upon Centreville, at the same time directing me to cover it with the battalion of regulars, the cavalry, and a section of artillery. The rear guard, thus organized, followed our panic-stricken troops to Centreville, resisting the attacks of the rebel cavalry and artillery, and saving them from the inevitable destruction which awaited them, had not this body been interposed. . . .

"Very respectfully, your obedient servant,
"A. PORTER,
"*Colonel Sixteenth Reg., U. S. A., commanding.*"

COLONEL BURNSIDE'S REPORT.

"HEADQUARTERS SECOND BRIGADE, SECOND DIVISION.
"MAJOR-GENERAL McDOWELL'S COLUMN,
"WASHINGTON, *July* 24, 1861.

"SIR: I have the honor to report that the brigade under my command, in common with the rest of the division, left Washington at three, P. M., on Tuesday, July 15; encamped that night at Annandale; occupied Fairfax Court House, and encamped there on Wednesday; on Thursday, July 17, proceeded to Centreville, where we remained till Sunday morning, July 21, when the whole army took up the line of march to Bull Run.

"Nothing of moment occurred till the arrival of the division at the crossing of Bull Run, at half past nine o'clock, when intelligence was received that the enemy was in front with considerable force. The brigade was ordered to halt for a supply of water and temporary rest. Afterwards an advance movement was made, and Colonel Slocum, of the second Rhode Island regiment, was ordered to throw out skirmishers upon either flank and in front. These were soon confronted by the enemy's forces, and the head of the brigade found itself in presence of the foe. The second regiment Rhode Island volunteers was immediately sent forward with its battery of artillery, and the balance of the brigade was formed in a field to the right of the road. At this time, much to my sorrow, I met you returning from the field, severely wounded, and was requested to take charge of the formation of the division in the presence of the enemy. Finding that the second regiment Rhode Island volunteers was closely pressed by the enemy, I ordered the seventy-first regiment New York militia and the second regiment New Hampshire volunteers to advance, intending to hold the first Rhode Island volunteers in reserve; but owing to delay in the formation of the two former regiments, the first Rhode Island regiment was at once ordered on the field of action. Major Balch, in command, gallantly led the regiment into it, where it performed most effective service in assisting its comrades to repel the attack of the enemy's forces. The second Rhode Island regiment of volunteers had steadily borne the enemy's attack, and had bravely stood its ground, even compelling him to give way. At this time, Colonel Slocum fell, mortally wounded, and soon after Major Ballou was very severely injured by a cannon ball, that killed his horse and crushed one of his legs. The regiment, under the command of Lieutenant-Colonel Wheaton, continued gallantly to hold its position. Soon after, Colonel Martin, of the seventy-first regiment New York state militia, led his regiment into action, and planting the two howitzers belonging to the regiment upon the right of his line, worked them most effectively against the enemy's troops. The battery of the second Rhode Island regiment, on the knoll upon the extreme right, was used in silencing the heavy masked battery of the enemy in front, occasionally throwing in shot and shell upon the enemy's infantry, six regiments of which were attempting to force our position. Captain Reynolds, who was in command of this battery, served it with great coolness, precision, and skill. The second regiment of New Hampshire volunteers, under Colonel Marston, was now brought into the field, and rendered great service in defending the position. Colonel Marston was wounded early in the action, and Lieutenant-Colonel Fiske ably directed the advance of the regiment. Thus my whole brigade was brought into the engagement at the earliest possible moment, and succeeded in compelling the enemy to retire. We were wholly without support, bearing the brunt of the contest until relieved by Major Sykes, of the third infantry United States army, who formed his battalion most admirably in front of the enemy, and pouring in a destructive fire upon his lines, assisted in staggering him. At that moment, after the fight had continued an hour or more, Colonel Heintzelman's division was seen marching over the hill opposite our left flank, and, attacking the enemy at that point, the opposing force was soon dispersed. This point being gained, and the enemy retiring in confusion before the successful charge of Colonel Heintzelman's division, I withdrew my brigade into the woods in the rear of the line, for the purpose of supplying the troops with ammunition, which had become well nigh exhausted. The second regiment New Hampshire volunteers were sent forward to assist one of Colonel Heintzelman's brigades, at that time three quarters of a mile distant, and driving the enemy before them. The battery of the second Rhode Island volunteers changed its position into a field upon the right, and was brought to bear upon the force which Colonel Porter was engaging. The enemy's infantry having fallen back, two sections of Captain Reynolds's battery advanced, and succeeded in breaking the charge of the enemy's cavalry, which had now been brought into the engagement.

"It was nearly four o'clock, P. M., and the battle had continued for almost six hours since the time when the second brigade had been engaged, with every thing in favor of our troops, and promising decisive victory, when some of the regiments engaging the enemy upon the extreme right of our line, broke, and large numbers passed disorderly by my brigade, then drawn up in the position which they last held. The ammunition had been issued in part, when I was ordered to protect the retreat. The seventy-first regiment New York state militia was formed between the retreating columns and the enemy by Colonel Martin, and the second regiment Rhode Island volunteers by Lieutenant Colonel Wheaton. The first regiment Rhode Island volunteers moved out into the field at the bottom of the gorge near the ford, and remained for fifteen minutes, until a general retreat was ordered. The regiment then passed on to the top of the hill, where it was joined by the remainder of the brigade, and formed into column. Large bodies of stragglers were passing along the road, and it was found impossible to retain the order which otherwise would have been preserved. Yet the brigade succeeded in retiring in comparatively good condition, with Arnold's battery of artillery and Captain Armstrong's company of dragoons bringing up the rear. The retreat continued thus until the column was about emerging from the woods and entering upon the Warrenton turnpike, when the artillery and cavalry went to the front, and the enemy opened fire upon the retreating mass of men. Upon the bridge crossing Cub Run a shot took effect upon the horses of a team that was crossing. The wagon was overturned directly in the centre of the bridge, and the passage was completely obstructed. The enemy continued to play his artillery upon the train carriages,

ambulances, and artillery wagons that filled the road, and these were reduced to ruin. The artillery could not possibly pass, and five pieces of the Rhode Island battery, which had been safely brought off the field, were here lost. Captain Reynolds is deserving of praise for the skill with which he saved the lives of his men. The infantry, as the files reached the bridge, were furiously pelted with a shower of grape and other shot, and several persons were here killed or dangerously wounded. As was to be expected, the whole column was thrown into confusion, and could not be rallied again for a distance of two or three miles.

"The brigade reached Centreville at nine o'clock, P. M., and entered into the several camps that had been occupied the night before, where the brigade rested until ten o'clock, when, in pursuance of orders from the general commanding, the retreat was continued. The column reached Washington about nine o'clock, A. M., Monday morning, when the several regiments composing the brigade repaired to their respective encampments. . . .

"I have the honor to be, very respectfully, your obedient servant,

"A. E. BURNSIDE, *Colonel commanding.*
"To COLONEL HUNTER, COMMANDING SECOND DIVISION."

COLONEL HEINTZELMAN'S REPORT.

"HEADQUARTERS THIRD DIVISION, DEPARTMENT N. E. VA.,
"WASHINGTON, *July* 31, 1861.

"SIR: In obedience to instructions received on the 20th inst., the division under my command was under arms, in light marching order, with two days' cooked rations in their haversacks, and commenced the march at half past two, A. M., on the 21st, the brigade of Colonel Franklin leading, followed by those of Colonels Wilcox and Howard. At Centreville we found the road filled with troops, and were detained three hours to allow the divisions of General Tyler and Colonel Hunter to pass. I followed with my division immediately in the rear of the latter. Between two and three miles beyond Centreville we left the Warrenton turn-pike, turning into a country road on the right. Captain Wright accompanied the head of Colonel Hunter's column, with directions to stop at a road which turned in to the left to a ford across Bull Run, about half way between the point where we turned off from the turnpike and Sudley's Springs, at which latter point Colonel Hunter's division was to cross. No such road was found to exist; and about eleven, A. M., we found ourselves at Sudley's Springs, about ten miles from Centreville, with one brigade of Colonel Hunter's division still on our side of the run. Before reaching this point the battle had commenced. We could see the smoke rising on our left from two points, a mile or more apart. Two clouds of dust were seen, showing the advance of troops from the direction of Manassas. At Sudley's Springs, whilst waiting the passage of the troops of the division in our front, I ordered forward the first brigade to fill their canteens. Before this was accomplished, the leading regiments of Colonel Hunter's division became engaged. General McDowell, who, accompanied by his staff, had passed us a short time before, sent back Captain Wright, of the engineers, and Major McDowell, one of his aids, with orders to send forward two regiments to prevent the enemy from outflanking them. Captain Wright led forward the Minnesota regiment to the left of the road, which crossed the run at this point. Major McDowell led the eleventh Massachusetts up the road. I accompanied this regiment, leaving orders for the remainder of the division to follow, with the exception of Arnold's battery, which, supported by the first Michigan, was posted a little below the cross-ing of the run as a reserve. At a little more than a mile from the ford we came upon the battle field. Rickett's battery was posted on a hill, to the right of Hunter's division and to the right of the road. After firing some twenty minutes at a battery of the enemy, placed just

beyond the crest of a hill, on their entrance left, the distance being considered too great, it was moved forward to within about a thousand feet of the enemy's battery. Here the battery was exposed to a heavy fire of musketry, which soon disabled it. Franklin's brigade was posted on the right of a wood, near the centre of our line, and on ground rising towards the enemy's position. In the mean time, I sent orders for the Zouaves to move forward to support Rickett's battery on its right. As soon as they came up I led them forward against an Alabama regiment, partly concealed in a clump of small pines in an old field. At the first fire they broke, and the greater portion of them fled to the rear, keeping up a desultory firing over the heads of their comrades in front; at the same moment they were charged by a company of secession cavalry on their rear, who came by a road through two strips of woods on our extreme right. The fire of the Zouaves killed four and wounded one, dispersing them. The discomfiture of this cavalry was completed by a fire from Captain Collum's company of United States cavalry, which killed and wounded several men. Colonel Farnham, with some of his officers and men, behaved gallantly; but the regiment of Zouaves, as a regiment, did not appear again on the field. Many of the men joined other regiments, and did good service as skirmishers. I then led up the Minnesota regiment, which was also repulsed, but retired in tolerably good order. It did good service in the woods on our right flank, and was among the last to retire, moving off the field with the third United States infantry. Next was led forward the first Michigan, which was also repulsed, and retired in considerable confusion. They were rallied, and helped to hold the woods on our right. The Brooklyn fourteenth then appeared on the ground, coming forward in gallant style. I led them forward to the left, where the Alabama regiment had been posted in the early part of the action, but had now disappeared, but soon came in sight of the line of the enemy drawn up, beyond the clump of trees. Soon after the firing commenced, the regiment broke and ran. I considered it useless to attempt to rally them. The want of discipline in these regiments was so great, that the most of the men would run from fifty to several hundred yards to the rear, and continue to fire — fortunately for the braver ones — very high in the air, and compelling those in front to retreat. During this time, Reickell's battery had been taken and retaken three times by us, but was finally lost, most of the horses having been killed,— Captain Reickell being wounded, and First Lieutenant D. Ramsay killed. Lieutenant Kirby behaved very gallantly, and succeeded in carrying off one caisson. Before this time heavy reënforcements of the enemy were distinctly seen approaching by two roads, extending and outflanking us on the right. Colonel Stewart's brigade came on the field at this time, having been detained by the general as a reserve at the point where we left the turnpike. It took post on a hill on our right and rear, and for some time gallantly held the enemy in check. I had one company of cavalry attached to my division, which was joined during the engagement by the cavalry of Colonel Stanton's division. Major Palmer, who cannonaded them, was anxious to engage the enemy. The ground being unfavorable, I ordered them back out of range of fire. Finding it impossible to rally any of the regiments, we commenced our retreat about half past four, P. M. There was a fine position a short distance in the rear, where I hoped to make a stand with a section of Arnold's battery and the United States cavalry, if I could rally a few regiments of infantry. In this I utterly failed, and we continued our retreat on the road we had advanced on in the morning. I sent forward my staff officers to rally some troops beyond the run; but not a company would form. I stopped back a few moments at the hospital to see what arrange-

ments could be made to save the wounded. The few ambulances that were there were filled, and started to the rear. The church, which was used ~~ a hospital, with the wounded and some of the surgeons, soon after fell into the hands of the secession cavalry, that followed us closely. A company of cavalry crossed the rear, and seized an ambulance full of wounded. Captain Arnold gave them a couple of rounds of canister from his section of artillery, which sent them scampering away, and kept them at a respectful distance during the remainder of our retreat. At this point most of the stragglers were in advance of us. Having every reason to fear a vigorous pursuit from the enemy's fresh troops, I was desirous of forming a strong rear guard; but neither the efforts of the officers of the regular army, nor the coolness of the regular troops with me, could induce them to form a single company. We relied entirely for our protection on one section of artillery and a few companies of cavalry. Most of the road was favorable for infantry, but unfavorable for cavalry and artillery. About dusk, as we approached the Warrenton turnpike, we heard a firing of rifled cannon on our right, and learned that the enemy had established a battery enfilading the road. Captain Arnold, with his section of artillery, attempted to run the gantlet, and reached the bridge over Cub Run, about two miles from Centreville, but found it obstructed with broken vehicles, and was compelled to abandon his pieces, as they were under the fire of these rifled cannon. The cavalry turned to the left, and after passing through a strip of woods and some fields, struck a road which led them to some camps occupied by our troops in the morning, through which we regained the turnpike. At about eight, P. M., we reached the camps we had occupied in the morning. Had a brigade from the reserve advanced a short distance beyond Centreville, near one third of the artillery lost might have been saved, as it was abandoned at or near this crossing. Such a rout I never witnessed before. No efforts could induce a single regiment to form after the retreat had commenced.

"Our artillery was served admirably, and did much execution. Some of the volunteer regiments behaved very well, and much excuse can be made for those whó fled, as few of the enemy could at any time be seen. Raw troops cannot be expected to stand long against an unseen enemy. I have been unable to obtain any report from the Zouaves, as Colonel Farnham is still at hospital. Since the retreat, more than three fourths of the Zouaves have disappeared. . . .

"Very respectfully,
"S. P. HEINTZELMAN,
"*Colonel of the Seventeenth Infantry,*
"*commanding the First Division.*
"To Captain James B. Fry, Assistant Adjutant-General."

COLONEL MILES'S REPORT.

"Headquarters Fifth Division, }
"Camp near Alexandria, July 24, 1861. }

"SIR: . . . Pursuant to instructions, the brigades of Blenker or Davies, soon after daylight, were in readiness to march and take position, but were prevented from so doing by other divisions blocking up the road. I discovered, however, that Davies's brigade could be passed to the left and west, through fields, to Blackburn's Ford. Lieutenant Brinel, engineer officer, conducted the brigade, and as soon as possible it joined Colonel Ric¹ ..dson, before the crossing of this ford on ¹ .ll Run. Fire was then opened by Hunt's ba.tery, supported by Richardson's brigade on the right. Edwards's twenty-pounder rifled guns were posted on the left, about six hundred yards from Richardson's position, and sustained by a portion of Davies's brigade. Blenker's brigade took position at Centreville, and commenced throwing up intrenchments; one regiment being located at the former work of the enemy, one to the west of the town on the

Warrenton road, and two on the height towards Bull Run. With these last regiments were first placed Tidball's and Green's batteries — Green's afterwards being removed to Richardson's position, in consequence of notification being sent by that officer that about two thousand of the enemy were about to attack him, and that he required more artillery. I may here remark, that some difference existed in the order given Lieutenant Brinel and myself, in regard to the defensive works to be thrown up, and also as to the quantity of tools he was to receive — my orders being, by the lieutenant's advice, to intrench Centreville; his, from Major Barnard, to throw up works at Blackburn's Ford. No tools came forward but the small amount Lieutenant Brinel had of his own. These he took to Richardson's position, commenced a battery, and made several hundred yards of it. Blenker, with his pioneers, improved and extended the works at Centreville left by the enemy.

"It was soon reported that the fourth Pennsylvania regiment had left at its encampment a battery of field guns. For this, Colonel Blenker offered to organize a company of experienced European artillerists, which I accepted. The captain's name, I regret, I have forgotten, as I should recommend his having permanent command of the guns in question. He is an efficient officer. So soon as I completed my arrangements with Blenker, I visited Colonel Richardson — found him in proper position and effectively at work, Hunt's and Edwards's battery being in good position. There was no evidence of the enemy immediately about the ford until after the first opening of the fire, when he fled from barns and houses in the vicinity. Then, after ordering proper supports for the batteries, and placing a reserve force in position, I returned to Centreville, finding all quiet, and the troopers at work. Remaining here some time, I returned to Richardson, when it was surmised that there was no enemy at that place, and found the ammunition of the batteries rapidly diminishing. I ordered from the brigadier a few skirmishers to go forward and examine the ford, determined if I could cross to do so, and endeavor to cut the line of travel pursued by retreating and advancing detachments of the enemy. The line of skirmishers had barely entered the woods, when a large force of the enemy was discovered concealed by breastworks. He opened fire, which was handsomely returned. In this affair three of the sixteenth New York volunteers were wounded. The skirmishers report the force of the enemy greatly damaged by Green's battery. I made no other attempt on this ford, my orders being on no account to get into a general engagement. As I was again returning to Blenker's position, I received the notice to telegraph to Washington, which I found had been done by Lieutenant Wendell, topographical engineer in my staff, and was compelled by illness to remain at my headquarters. It was at this time the order was received to put two brigades on the Warrenton turnpike, at the bridge. I without delay sent a staff-officer to order forward Davies's brigade; but whilst this officer was executing my instructions, Davies sent word he wanted a reserve regiment forward; that the enemy, some three thousand, was attempting to turn his flank. The staff officer, therefore, properly suspended the giving of my order, and immediately reported the fact to me, and this caused me to advance but the one brigade (Blenker's) to the position on the Warrenton turnpike. Blenker's advance to that point was soon impeded by fugitives from the battle field. When these were passing my headquarters I endeavored to rally them, but my efforts were vain.

"The attack on Davies's position caused painful apprehension for the safety of the left flank of the army, and deeming it of the first importance that my division should occupy the strongest position, I sent instructions to Davies

and Richardson to have their brigades fall back on Centreville. Then followed Blenker's brigade to see if it was in position, when I was informed the commanding general had passed. I then returned to Centreville, and found Davies's and Richardson's brigades arriving, and commenced placing them in position — Richardson's brigade, with Green's battery, being placed about half a mile in advance of Centreville Heights, his line of battle facing Blackburn's Ford. In rear of Richardson I posted two regiments behind fences, as a support for the first line, and still farther in rear and on the heights I placed Hunt's and Edwards's batteries, two of Davies's regiments being in reserve to support them. I then followed Blenker, found Tidball's battery in admirable position, supported by the Garibaldi Guard; Blenker, with three regiments and the fourth Pennsylvania battery, being in advance. Having great confidence in his judgment and troops, I returned to Centreville Heights, to await events, when I found all my defensive arrangements changed. Not knowing who had done this, and seeing Colonel Richardson giving different positions to my troops, I asked by what authority he was acting, when he told me he had instructions from my superior officer. I soon thereafter met the commanding general, and complained of the change. The general's views were completed, and left me without further control of the division. At the time the attack was made on Davies's flank, the regiments of the brigade engaged performed their duty gallantly. The batteries of Hunt's and Edwards's opening fire did great damage to the advancing troops of the enemy, soon repulsing them. I am grieved that in this engagement a brave and accomplished young officer, Lieutenant Presby O'Craig, of the second regiment artillery, and who was attached to Hunt's battery, was almost instantly killed. Several of the New York volunteers were wounded; I have not the reports relative thereto.

"Blenker's brigade, whilst on the Warrenton road, was charged by cavalry; but by a prompt and skilful fire, emptied several saddles, and relieved themselves from further annoyance. This summary embraces the operations of my division up to the evening of the 21st. . . .

"In closing this report, I would make a personal allusion to my condition during the day. I had lost my rest the two nights previous; was sick, had eaten nothing during the day, and had it not been for the great responsibility resting on me, should have been in bed.

"I am, dear sir, respectfully,
            "Your obedient servant,
                    "D. J. MILES,
    "*Col Second Infantry, commanding Fifth Div.*"

"To Captain James B. Fry, Assistant Adjutant-General, Headquarters Department."

The result of the battle was a shameful defeat, which retarded the progress of the Union cause for months. The army which had been so promptly, and, as it was hoped, efficiently organized and put into the field to strike a heavy and an early blow at the rebellion, was broken, routed, and, for the time, utterly demoralized. The panic-stricken men, in many cases unrestrained by brave and efficient officers, fled back to their camps near the Potomac, into the intrenchments, across the river into Washington, and some of the New York Zouaves even to the city of New York. For days there were crowds of men about Washington, separated from their regiments, worn out by the severe labors of the battle and the more exhausting flight, and suffering for want of food and rest. Their arms and equipments had been thrown away; their courage and self-respect had vanished, for the want of organization and discipline. Even the regiments which had been kept together were worn down with fatigue, and demoralized by the hasty retreat.

Had the rebel army been prepared to follow up their advantage, and to advance immediately on Washington with a considerable force, the chances of a successful attack would have been greatly in their favor. But their forces were broken, too. They were, in truth, almost defeated before the reënforcements of Johnston turned the battle in their favor. They did not know how fearful was the panic in the Union army, and a few days' delay, necessary for their own reorganization, was sufficient also for such a disposition of the federal forces, as to render any attack on Washington more difficult. By stringent orders and activity on the part of some of the officers, the stragglers were gradually collected into their several regiments, and discipline was restored. The fortifications had been at once strengthened, and placed in charge of the strongest regiments, and very soon the fears for the capital, which had at first been entertained, were quieted, and the confidence both of the soldiers and of the people was restored.

The spirit of the loyal people of the north was, for a moment, disconcerted by this unfortunate result of the first attempt of their grand army to overthrow the rebellious forces; but it soon recovered, and aroused the government to renewed activity and energy. Confident in their superiority in numbers and resources, the people soon rallied from this defeat, demanded more vigorous action, and offered more generous supplies. At the same time there were, as usual among a people accustomed to discuss every thing, inquiries for the causes of the disaster, and various theories were suggested, and numerous charges were made, to account for what was so humiliating a result.

It was charged that members of Congress and other civilians had importuned the government to hasten the movement of the army towards Richmond, and that the government had yielded to their importunities and to the appeals of a portion of the press, and had ordered the advance contrary to the advice of the military authorities, and before adequate preparations were made. It is undoubtedly true, that leading men and influential journals urged a forward movement as early as possible; but there is no evidence that the government acted in response to such appeals, except so far as they were supported by sound and weighty argument, to which both civil and military authority could but give heed. A large army of volunteers for three months had been collected, and were now well disciplined and efficient; but their time of service would soon expire, and they would return to their homes, leaving their places to be filled by the new regiments, which could not for several months arrive at the same condition in discipline and efficiency. To wait for these new levies to be in a better condition than the forces then in the field, would cause a delay by which the rebels would equally profit, by increasing their numbers and discipline. There were reasons for believing that the forces they then had in the field could be scattered by the well-equipped army of the government, and there were reasons why a blow should be struck as soon as possible, for the sake of effect both at home and abroad. Such reasons, urged by civilians and military men, were of sufficient weight to justify and even to demand the advance before a large number of efficient and disciplined troops should be lost to the service. If there was want of preparation and organization of the army as a whole, it was because that work was not begun early enough or pushed with sufficient vigor, and because the inexperience of officers caused unnecessary delays. The regiments were not brigaded soon enough, or made familiar with brigade movements; nor were the men familiar even with the faces of their brigade commanders. Whether there had been sufficient time to perfect this organization may be a question; but certainly those who urged the advance for the reasons above stated should hardly be held responsible for any failure in this respect. The reasons were such as could not be put aside as un-

sound, nor is there any evidence that the military authorities did not admit their force.

The plan of battle adopted by General McDowell has been commended by military authority as a good one, with the exception, perhaps, that the reserve was not sufficiently strong or well posted. For a long time the tide of battle was in favor of the federal army. The men fought bravely, and drove the enemy from some of their strong positions; but they went into the battle greatly fatigued by a long march, to which they were unaccustomed, and they fought against an enemy who was fresh, and who also had the advantage of fighting on his own chosen ground. When, therefore, after a long struggle, in the heat of the day, the worn-out federal forces were attacked by the reënforcements brought by General Johnston, it is not strange that they gave way. Once broken, it was difficult, if not impossible, to rally forces who were no better disciplined, even had all the officers exerted themselves to that end. But officers as well as men joined in the retreat, in many instances without attempting to rally or organize their scattered commands. The panic which commenced among the non-combatants at sight of the retreating forces, and in consequence of the cavalry charge in the rear of Schenck's brigade, was soon communicated to the soldiers, so that all hope of rallying them and making another stand was out of the question. Thus what was only a repulse, so far as the enemy effected any thing, resulted in a complete rout.

The immediate cause of the repulse was the arrival of General Johnston's forces from Winchester. And it appeared that in making his plans, General McDowell had calculated upon such coöperation from General Patterson as should prevent reënforcements to the enemy from that quarter. In a previous chapter the movements of General Patterson have been narrated, and it was seen that, instead of attacking General Johnston, or so menacing him as to keep his forces at Winchester, General Patterson made a retrograde movement to Charlestown and Harper's Ferry, leaving Johnston to withdraw his army and reënforce Beauregard. In this movement General Patterson disregarded his orders and the evident object of his advance at this time into Virginia. General Scott informed General Patterson that General McDowell was about to attack Manassas, and instructed him to watch Johnston closely, and prevent him from reënforcing Beauregard. After the forward movement of General McDowell's army had commenced, General Scott advised General Patterson that the rebels were driven beyond Fairfax Court House, and ordered him to see that Johnston did not amuse him with a small force in front, while he reënforced Beauregard. General Patterson was further instructed, if Johnston commenced a retreat, to attack him; and if he did not attack and follow the retreating rebels, then to proceed by forced marches to reënforce General McDowell. These instructions, as has already been seen, were not followed; had they been, the result of the battle at Bull Run might have been far different, and the whole course of the war changed.

In justice to General Patterson, the reasons for his movements, viz., the superior force of the enemy, according to his information, and the expiration of the term of service of a large number of his troops who refused to stay beyond that term, should be stated. In a letter, written from Harper's Ferry, General Patterson said, "General Johnston retreated to Winchester, where he had thrown up extensive intrenchments, and had a large number of heavy guns. I could have turned his position and attacked him in the rear, but he had received large reënforcements from Mississippi, Alabama, and Georgia — a total force of over thirty-five thousand Confederate troops, and five thousand Virginia militia. My force is less than twenty

thousand — nineteen regiments, whose term of service was up, or will be within a week. All refused to stay one hour over their time but four, viz., two Indiana regiments, Frank Jarrett's, (the eleventh Pennsylvania,) and Owen's, (the twenty-fourth Pennsylvania.) Five regiments have gone home. Two more go to-day, and three more to-morrow. To avoid being cut off with the remainder, I fell back and occupied this place."

A writer, who was with General Patterson's forces, gives the following more particular explanations: —

"At the time the first advance into Virginia was ordered, General Johnston's force numbered over fourteen thousand men, and had attached to it a park of splendid artillery. General Patterson's command did not exceed eleven thousand men, and he had not over eight pieces of artillery, which latter were taken from him, compelling the return of our army to Maryland. The second advance was made by nine thousand men, and not over ten guns. General Patterson knew from information derived from scouts, deserters, &c., that Johnston's force exceeded his own, and the result of a battle with him was deemed by the general and army officers more than doubtful. Upon our arrival at Bunker Hill we had not one man more than eighteen thousand men. This calculation is based on the assumption that each regiment numbered seven hundred fighting men. This, however, is too liberal an estimate; and after deducting the sick and the camp guards, it will be seen that we could not have brought more than fourteen thousand men into the field. Our artillery numbered eighteen guns, all of small calibre, with the exception of four pieces. We had five companies of cavalry.

"Despatches from the war department showed that the advance of McDowell's column would commence Tuesday. On that day, General Patterson was at Bunker Hill, having driven

Johnston's cavalry into Winchester. That evening scouts brought information that Johnston's force had been under arms, anticipating an attack from us. They numbered from *thirty-five to forty-two thousand men*, and were drawn up in line one mile north of their intrenchments, wherein there were mounted *sixty-four guns*. This statement of the enemy's force has been since confirmed by all our accounts, by every deserter, and by Samuel Webster and John Staub, Esqrs., both well-known Union citizens of Martinsburg, the latter being a leading lawyer of the place, and a Union candidate in the spring for the legislature. Both gentlemen had been impressed in the secession force. Mr. Staub escaped in the confusion of the march from Winchester to Manassas.

"Immediately after the return of our scouts, a council of war was held, at which it was decided unanimously that the force should be moved to Charlestown.

"The reasons for so doing, as given, were, that a position at Charlestown would preclude the possibility of Johnston's going on the left of Beauregard and marching on Washington; again, that Patterson would be on the line of the railroad to Harper's Ferry, and could, therefore, better receive supplies and reënforcements; and, lastly, that in the case of the three months men refusing to remain ten days beyond their time, the army could fall back on Harper's Ferry."

In conclusion, we give the following abstract of Beauregard's report of the battle, as given in one of the Richmond journals.* This report was not made until several months after the battle, but why it was so long delayed does not appear.

"Beauregard opens with a statement of his position antecedent to the battle, and of the plan proposed by him to the government for

* The Richmond Dispatch.

the junction of the armies of the Shenandoah and Potomac, with a view to the relief of Maryland, and the capture of the city of Washington, which plan was rejected by the president. General Beauregard states that he telegraphed the war department, on the 13th of July, of the contemplated attack by General McDowell, urgently asking for a junction of General Johnston's forces with his own, and continued to make urgent requests for the same until the 17th of July, when the president consented to order General Johnston to his assistance. General Beauregard goes on to state that his plan of battle assigned to General Johnston an attack on the enemy on the left, at or near Centreville, while he himself would command in front; but the condition of the roads prevented this.

"It was then decided to receive the attack of the enemy behind Bull Run. After the engagement at Blackburn's Ford, on the 18th, General Beauregard was convinced that General McDowell's principal demonstration would be made on our left wing, and he then formed the idea of throwing forward a sufficient force, by converging roads, to attack the enemy's reserves at Centreville so soon as the main body of the latter became inextricably engaged on the left. Late in the day, finding that General Ewell, who was posted on the extreme right of our line, had not moved forward in accordance with the programme and the special order which had been sent him, General Beauregard despatched a courier to General Ewell to inquire the reason why the latter had failed to advance, and received a reply from General Ewell, stating that he had not received any such order. The enemy's attack having then become too strong on the left to warrant carrying out the original plan, as it would take three hours for General Ewell's brigade to reach Centreville, it became necessary to alter the plan, change front on the

left, and bring up our reserves to that part of
the field. This movement was superintended
in person by General Johnston, General Beauregard remaining to direct the movements in
front.

"At the time when General Kirby Smith and
General Early came up with their divisions, and
appeared on the right of the enemy, our forces
on the left occupied the chord of the arc of a
circle, of which the arc itself was occupied by
the enemy — the extremes of their line flanking
ours. The appearance of Smith's and Early's
brigades, and their charge on the enemy's right,
broke the lines of the latter, and threw them
into confusion, when shortly afterwards the
rout became complete.

"General Beauregard acknowledges the great
generosity of General Johnston in fully according to him (General Beauregard) the right to
carry out the plans he had formed with relation
to this campaign, in yielding the command of
the field after examining and cordially approving the plan of battle, and in the effective
coöperation which General Johnston so chival-
rously extended to him on that eventful day.

"He remarks that the retreat of our forces
from Fairfax, immediately previous to the engagement of the 18th, is the first instance on
record of volunteers retiring before an engagement, and with the object of giving battle in
another position. The number under his command on the 18th July is set down at seventeen thousand effective men, and on the 21st at
twenty-seven thousand, which includes sixty-
two hundred of Johnston's army, and seventeen hundred brought up by General Holmes
from Fredericksburg. The killed on our side,
in this ever-memorable battle, are stated in
the report to have been in number three
hundred and ninety-three, and the wounded
twelve hundred. The enemy's killed, wounded,
and prisoners are estimated by General Beauregard at forty-five hundred, which does not
include the missing.'

CHAPTER XLI.

THE campaign in South-western Missouri, the
movements for which have been alluded to in
a previous chapter, commenced early in July.
A considerable federal force, under the command of General Sweeny, had been sent in
that direction, and on the 4th of July were at
Springfield, the most considerable town of that
section of the state. Here General Sweeny
issued a proclamation, calling upon the loyal
citizens to aid in upholding the federal government, requiring the doubtful to take the oath
of allegiance, and all persons arrayed in arms
against the United States to disperse; and
preparations were made to enforce the last requirement against the secession forces which
were being collected in this vicinity. Jackson
and Price had brought their followers from
Booneville to this remote part of the state, and
had made great efforts to assemble troops under
the state law, to resist the authority of the
United States. These had assembled with such
arms and equipments as they could bring, a
portion belonging to the state, but the greater
part being private property — shot guns, rifles,
and various other weapons. While these efforts
were made in Missouri to array an army against
the federal authority, the "military board" of
Arkansas called for troops to resist invasion

from the north, and Ben McCulloch, former-ly famous as a Texas "ranger," and a com-missioner to Utah at the time of the Mormon war, now a brigadier-general of the rebel forces, appealed to the people of that state to join him in opposing the federal forces. "To defend your frontier," he said, "troops of Mis-souri are falling back upon you. If they are not sustained, your state will be invaded and your homes desolated." He accordingly called upon all men to arm themselves, and to ren-dezvous at Fayetteville, a town in the north-western part of the state, near Missouri. This force was collected to unite with the Missouri troops of Jackson and Price, for the purpose of driving back the federal forces, and securing Missouri for the Confederacy.

Jackson's troops were in Jasper county, in the south-western part of Missouri; and on the 5th of July they marched south, probably for the purpose of forming a junction with McCul-loch's forces before they could be attacked by the federal army. At Brier Forks, seven miles north of Carthage, the county seat of Jasper county, they were met by Colonel Sigel,[*] with less than fifteen hundred Union troops and eight pieces of artillery, who immediately pre-pared to give battle. The state troops were under the command of Generals Price and Rains, and were posted in a very advantageous position on a ridge in a prairie. They had five pieces of artillery, well supported by infantry, and a large body of cavalry on each flank, the whole numbering upwards of five thousand men. Colonel Sigel commenced the attack with ar-tillery, at half past ten o'clock in the forenoon; and his fire was so well directed, that in an hour the enemy's most effective gun was dismount-ed, and by noon his whole battery was nearly silenced. The fire of the artillery upon the infantry repeatedly caused them to give way in confusion; while, on the other hand, the fire

of the enemy's artillery was of little effect, their gunnery being wretched. Finding that they could not stand before the splendid ar-tillery of Colonel Sigel, and the effective fire of such of his infantry as was brought into action, the enemy sent a large force of cavalry to flank him and cut off his baggage train, which was about three miles in the rear, guarded by a small force. Fortunately, the ground was so open that Colonel Sigel could see the move-ment; and, anticipating the object, though the rebel forces were now giving way in their cen-tre, he gave the order to retreat, at the same time sending an order for his train to advance. The Union troops fell back in good order, and with the artillery to protect them, they made a rapid movement to reach the train before the enemy's cavalry could accomplish their purpose. The movement was successful, and the wagons were placed in the centre of the column, pro-tected on all sides by the artillery and infantry.

Failing in this attempt, the enemy, who had now, probably, ascertained the small number, as well as the bravery and excellence, of the Union troops, fell back to a position on some high bluffs overlooking a stream. There was but one road leading across this stream, and to move at all in the direction of Carthage it was necessary to cross the stream. To remain in the open prairie was to expose the federal troops to ultimate defeat and capture by the large force of the enemy. Finding his passage over the stream obstructed, Colonel Sigel or-dered his artillery to oblique right and left, following the movement with a part of his force. This manœuvre deceived the rebels, who evi-dently supposed that it was Sigel's purpose to effect a passage on their extreme sides; and, accordingly, a large force of cavalry advanced towards the right and left to resist the attempt. When this force, which was thus drawn away from the road in front, had advanced within five hundred yards of the federal troops, Colo-nel Sigel suddenly wheeled his artillery, and

---

[*] Franz Sigel, afterwards a major-general and commander of an army corps in Virginia.

poured into their ranks a terrific fire of canister. At the same time the infantry were ordered to advance rapidly across the bridge in their front. This sudden and damaging attack threw the rebel forces into confusion, and they were soon flying in all directions. They had no artillery to use against Colonel Sigel, and when once broken they made no attempt to rally. Colonel Sigel's force, with their train, accordingly passed the stream safely. The Union troops captured here about fifty prisoners, eighty-five horses, and a considerable number of arms, mostly shot guns.

Colonel Sigel now proceeded towards Carthage, seeing small bodies of the rebel forces along the road, at whom the infantry occasionally discharged a volley; but no attack was made. As the federal forces approached Carthage, that place was found to be in possession of the rebels; and as Colonel Sigel's ammunition had begun to fail, it was deemed necessary to retire to Sarcoxie, a place eight miles south-west of Carthage, from which a junction might be formed with the remainder of the south-western army, now being concentrated under the command of General Lyon. The road to Sarcoxie was on one side of Carthage, and led through thick woods, to reach which was Sigel's object, as the enemy's cavalry, of which his force was chiefly composed, could not follow him there. Aware of the advantage the federal commander would have if his force reached the woods, the enemy had taken a position on the road to dispute his advance in that direction. This led to the severest struggle of the day, the infantry on both sides being, for the first time, fairly engaged. The Union troops fought bravely, and the rebel troops showed more courage than in the preceding contests; but their arms were poor, and their cavalry was now of little use. After a contest of about two hours, Colonel Sigel got his force into the wood, and the enemy retreated to Carthage, baffled and beaten. The federal loss in the several contests was reported

as twenty-four killed and about fifty wounded, while the loss of the rebels in killed and wounded was thought to be nearly five hundred. It was not prudent to remain where so large a force of the enemy might cut him off from a junction with the other Union forces; and, notwithstanding the exhaustion of his men, Colonel Sigel continued his march to Sarcoxie, whence, after a day's rest, he proceeded to Mount Vernon, in Lawrence county, and thence to Springfield. A small guard which he left at Neosho, from which place he had moved to attack the rebels, was afterwards captured by a large force of Arkansas troops.

In this series of conflicts Colonel Sigel displayed great ability as a commander, and it was due to the admirable manner with which he handled his troops, as well as to their bravery, discipline, and effective arms, that he succeeded so well against an enemy of much greater numerical strength. Colonel Sigel, who is a German, with a thorough military education, had had experience in actual warfare in Baden, during the revolutionary period of 1848, and had successfully commanded a large army there.[*]

---

[*] A countryman of Colonel Sigel's, who served under him in Baden, has given the following sketch of his life : " Some years before the Baden revolution of 1842, which a year later culminated in open war, Sigel was a first lieutenant of artillery in the army of the government. A man of fine education and a close thinker, he had been but a short time in the army before he became aware that it required an entire remodelling, and he wrote a series of letters upon this subject, which was published in one of the most influential papers in Germany. The letters acquired a large circulation, and were read with great interest by military men throughout Germany and Prussia, and some years subsequently his reform was adopted in the army of the last-named kingdom.

" The notoriety of the letters at last became so great, that a search was made for the author ; and when it became known that a mere lieutenant had had the audacity to originate and advocate these reforms, the jealousy of the officials manifested itself by the imprisonment of the lieutenant and the withdrawal of his commission.

" A few years later, Herr Sigel, (not then even a lieutenant,) the revolution having broken out, was a general in the army of the revolution, and proved his right to that title in several minor conflicts, until, at the battle of Hemsbach, he showed himself far superior to General Mieroslawsky, who was in command ; and had he been the commander, instead of a subordinate, the battle

He inspired his soldiers with confidence and daring, and secured a discipline which made them the more effective. His ability as a commander, as displayed in this brief campaign, subsequently secured for him an appointment as a brigadier-general of volunteers, and he joined the army under General Lyon.

The several other bodies of federal troops which had been sent to South-western Missouri, now concentrated at Springfield, when General Lyon assumed command, and prepared, as well as the number of his forces and the arrival of his supplies would admit, to strike a blow at the rebel army. As the troops advanced to this point, there were several skirmishes with small bodies of the rebels, who were in all cases dispersed. Meanwhile numbers of Missourians were joining the forces under Price, and, though most of them were but poorly equipped, swelled his army to formidable dimensions. It was not till about the first of August that any movement of importance was made by General Lyon. In the mean time he had urgently requested reënforcements, in order to meet the enemy with something like equal numbers; but it had been impossible to send them, and the alternative was presented of withdrawing from this section of the state without a struggle, leaving the Union men there to the mercy of the rebel army, or with an inferior force to attempt to strike a blow which should cripple, if not repulse, the enemy, and secure a safer retreat. The latter course was determined upon, and General Lyon advanced beyond Springfield towards the position occupied by the rebels, and where, at "Dug Springs," near the town of Curran, on the 3d of August, they were discovered in some force. A scouting party of

cavalry, meeting with a regiment of rebel infantry, charged upon it and put it to flight, killing and wounding several. The charge was not ordered by General Lyon, and was supposed to have prevented the main body of this force of the rebels from attacking him — a movement which would inevitably have resulted in their complete rout.

General Lyon at once formed for battle upon discovering the enemy's position, and advanced to attack him. One column was ordered to enter a piece of woods for the purpose of flanking the rebel force, while a battery of artillery opened fire upon their front. The artillery, however, soon caused them to retreat without making any stand to encounter the infantry, and they fell back hastily to their main army. The federal troops encamped at Curran without meeting any resistance; but the next day, General Lyon, having discovered that the rebels were near in great force, and had a large body of mounted men, who might flank him and take Springfield, where his supplies were, determined to retire to that place to await the attack which there was reason to believe they would soon make, and hoping still for reënforcements. In a few days the rebels took up a position on Wilson's Creek, ten or twelve miles from Springfield, and General Lyon again advanced to make an attack himself, before he should be surrounded by overwhelming numbers.

On the evening of the 9th of August the federal forces moved out from Springfield. They numbered about five thousand five hundred; — two thousand home guards being left in the town, — and marched in two columns, the larger one, composed of the main body of the army, with ten pieces of artillery, being under the immediate command of General Lyon, and the other, which consisted of less than two thousand men, with six pieces of artillery, being under the command of General Sigel. The latter column moved in a southerly direction, with a view to pass around the extreme south-east-

would, without doubt, have resulted in the victory of the revolutionists.

"After the close of the revolution, General Sigel, who was made a refugee by the treachery of the government, fled to England, and afterwards came to the United States, as before stated. At twenty-eight he was a general; now he is about forty years of age, and is a colonel."

39

ern camp of the enemy, and attack him in the rear or on the flank, while General Lyon's column advanced more directly against his front; and the attack was to be made simultaneously by the two columns.

The rebel forces under Price, McCulloch, Mackintosh, and others, were encamped along the banks of Wilson's Creek, towards which the hills sloped gently, affording excellent camping grounds, which were overlooked by hills and ridges on the north, east, and west. Upon one of these ridges the rebels were first encountered by General Lyon's advance; but, after a brief contest, they were driven from their position, and the federal troops, gaining the summit of the ridge, commenced an artillery fire, while the infantry pushed on. From a second summit the rebels were driven in like manner, after a sharp contest. The action then became general, and continued with varying success; but the federal forces gradually gained ground by the valor with which they fought and the precision and effect with which their artillery was served. The rebels were driven back to their camps, and portions of them retreated in great disorder. In the midst of the contest, a body of rebel cavalry attempted to charge upon the federal flank and upon the rear, where the wounded were lying under a small guard; but the artillery was turned upon them, and scattered them in great disorder.

While the column under General Lyon thus attacked the enemy in front, General Sigel's column, after marching all night, had reached a position from which to attack them in the rear. The rebel outposts were driven in with scarcely any resistance, and General Sigel obtained possession of ground which commanded their camp. From this position he opened upon them so suddenly with artillery and musketry, that they were taken by surprise, and fled in alarm to a hill covered with brushwood, which afforded them an opportunity for concealment and rallying. General Sigel pursued them through their camp, in which they left a quantity of arms and equipments and a large number of horses. Without pausing to take possession of the booty, he followed the retreating rebels to the hill whither they had fled, and, forming his line of battle, commenced a vigorous attack. He was driving the enemy in the direction of General Lyon's forces, which were attacking with like vigor on their side. Being so hotly pressed on both sides, the rebel generals saw that their position was desperate unless they repulsed or cut through one or the other of the federal columns. Sigel's was the weaker force, and concentrating a strong body of troops, they made a desperate attack upon that, and succeeded in driving it back. The infantry supporting General Sigel's artillery were compelled to give way, and many of the horses having been shot, he was obliged to abandon five of his guns, which, however, were first spiked. The commander of the artillery succeeded in saving the other gun, by compelling some prisoners, whom he had previously taken, to draw it off. General Sigel, in falling back, took with him a considerable number of prisoners, and still continued the fight, and with a portion of his force obstinately resisted the overwhelming numbers of the enemy.

In the mean time General Lyon's force continued to advance, and drove the enemy through their camps in the opposite direction, when they set fire to their tents and baggage, to prevent them from falling into the hands of the federal troops. When they had succeeded in repulsing General Sigel's troops, the rebels rallied to oppose the other column more vigorously, and made several attempts to drive the federal troops from the position they had gained, but they were each time compelled to retire. In the midst of this conflict, after the repulse of General Sigel, General Lyon, who had previously received slight wounds, fell, mortally wounded, while leading an Iowa regiment to the charge against the enemy. He lived but a few minutes after his fall; but his troops, though losing a commander in whose ability and bravery they had the greatest confidence, did not waver, but, under the command of Major Sturges, continued the fight successfully.

After continuing from five o'clock in the morning until noon, the battle ceased. The rebel forces were too much dispirited to renew their attempts to drive back the successful Union troops; while the latter, wearied with the long and severe conflict, and being deficient in artillery ammunition, were not in condition to continue their attacks. Accordingly Major Sturges, after causing his wounded to be taken to Springfield, withdrew his forces in such a manner as to be able to repel any attack which might be made, should the enemy see fit to pursue. But the rebel army had suffered severely, and was in no condition, or its leaders were in no mood, to attempt a pursuit. Major Sturges's troops reached Springfield without further sight of the enemy, and General Sigel's force also arrived there without being followed.

The federal loss in this battle was between two and three hundred killed, and about nine hundred wounded and missing. The loss of the rebels was thought to be much larger. According to their own statements, their number of killed was two hundred and sixty-five, the number of wounded and missing not being stated. The federal forces engaged numbered scarcely five thousand five hundred, while, according to rolls and returns reported to have been found in the rebel camps, the entire force of the enemy was nearly or quite twenty thousand, of which number about fourteen thousand were well organized and equipped, and the greater part of these were probably brought into the battle.

Notwithstanding the rebels were so much crippled by this engagement that they were unable to follow the retreating federal forces, and did not advance even to Springfield for two or three days after the battle, they, nevertheless, claimed a great victory, which was announced by their generals in vain-glorious terms. But any advantage which they gained was because of the want of reënforcements to enable the federal army to continue the campaign, rather than the result of the battle.

In the death of General Lyon the country met with a serious loss. He was a thorough soldier, and was heartily enlisted in the cause of the Union. He belonged to a family which was somewhat distinguished for services in the revolutionary war, and was born July 14, 1819. Entering the Military Academy at West Point, in 1837, he graduated in 1841, the eleventh, in rank, of his class. Being commissioned as a lieutenant in the second regiment of infantry, his first service was in Florida. In the Mexican war he distinguished himself at Cerro Gordo and Contreras, and for his gallantry in the latter action received the brevet rank of captain. He also took part in the engagement on the entrance of the army into the city of Mexico, and received there a slight wound. After the Mexican war he served several years, as captain, in California, where he exhibited much ability and tact in dealing with the Indians. From California he was transferred to Kansas, where he espoused the free state cause. Early in 1861 he was placed in command of the St. Louis arsenal, in which position his actions have already been mentioned in previous pages of this work. His fidelity to the government was equalled by his energy, and in his whole administration of the duties of his command he proved himself vigilant, able, and brave; and he was regarded by all who knew him as one who would be one of the ablest leaders of the Union army. In his private character, as in his military career, he was worthy of all praise. His death was felt to be a national loss, and was sincerely mourned by all who were acquainted with his noble qualities. The body of the dead hero was safely brought from the field of battle, and was interred with military honors in his native place.

CHAPTER XLII.

Affairs in Northern Missouri. — Guerrilla Warfare and Bridge Burning. — Skirmishes. — Fight at Monroe. — Defeat of the Rebel Force. — Proclamation by General Hurlburt. — General Pope assigned to the Command in Northern Missouri. — Plan to suppress Guerrilla Warfare. — Its Success. — Civil Authority in Missouri. — State Convention. — Executive Offices declared vacant, and Legislature abolished. — H. R. Gamble elected Governor. — Address to the People — Proclamation of the Rebel Lieutenant-Governor. — Course of the new Government. — Proclamation by Governor Gamble. — General Fremont in Command of the Western Department.

WHILE the events just related were transpiring in South-western Missouri, the secessionists in the northern part of the state were resorting to guerrilla warfare, collecting in small bands, destroying the property, and in some cases, taking the lives, of loyal men, and burning the bridges, and otherwise interrupting communication along the great railroads. At some points they assembled considerable forces to resist or attack the federal forces which were sent to that part of the state for the protection of loyal citizens and the preservation of the railroad bridges. Skirmishing frequently took place between the small parties of the secessionists and the home guards formed by loyal citizens for their own protection, and occasionally detachments of the federal forces met parties of secessionists, but without any considerable engagement. One of the most important of these skirmishes at this time was at Monroe, a village and station on the Hannibal and St. Joseph railroad. A federal force, not exceeding six hundred men, under Colonel Smith, was stationed at this place, when a body of the rebels, said to number sixteen hundred or upwards, under General Harris, collected in the vicinity. Colonel Smith's force moved from the town July 10th, to attack a part of the rebel force, when another body of the rebels entered the town and destroyed the railroad buildings and cars. After some skirmishing, Colonel Smith, with his forces, retired to Mon-

roe, where he took up a position in a large academy building, and sent for reënforcements. The rebels advanced towards the town the next day, and with their superior numbers might have surrounded the place, and compelled a surrender of the federal force, had they made a determined attack. But they took up a position at too great a distance for an engagement with small arms, and opened an ineffectual artillery fire, which was returned by Colonel Smith with guns of longer range and more skilfully used. While this artillery contest continued without any loss to the federal troops, but, as it was supposed, with some effect against the rebels, reënforcements arrived and attacked the rebels in the rear. After a brief contest the enemy fled, the federal troops taking seventy-five prisoners, one gun, and a considerable number of horses. About twenty rebels were killed, and many others wounded, while the casualties on the federal side were only a small number wounded.

The northern and north-eastern portion of the state was so much disturbed by the action of the secessionists and the guerrilla bands which they organized, that General Hurlburt, who commanded the federal forces in Illinois and in North-eastern Missouri, issued a proclamation, calling upon the citizens to resume their usual avocations, in which they should be protected, and threatening the severest punishment, by military authority, of all those engaged in the system of assassination and arson with which these men waged war. Additional forces were also sent to that part of the state, and skirmishes continued with varying results. But the rebel warfare was of a character that could not successfully be met by troops alone, unless an immense army was distributed throughout that part of the state. Loyal people, and those whose sympathies were not very strong either way, dreaded the attacks of the rebel guerrilla parties more than they trusted to the federal troops for protection. To meet such a warfare, some of the people resorted to a similar course, and civil war, in its worst form, seemed about to ruin this portion of the state.

To put a stop to such occurrences, Brigadier-General Pope, who was assigned to the command of Northern Missouri, resorted to a new system of military restraint. General Hurlburt was assigned to the command of the forces on the line of the Hannibal and St. Joseph railroad, and Colonel Grant to the command of the forces on the line of the North Missouri railroad. These forces were posted at convenient stations along the railroads, in numbers sufficient to meet any rebel force that was likely to appear in that part of the state. The roads were then divided into districts, and the divisions placed under the protection of the leading citizens of the district, who were to be held responsible for the safety of the road ; and any neglect on their part, or connivance with marauding parties, resulting in injury, was declared to be an offence which should be severely punished. This plan was carried out, and generally with excellent success. Troops were posted in several counties along the railroad lines, and the county officers, or other prominent citizens, of each county, without regard to opinions, were appointed committees of safety, who were held responsible in the manner above named ; the military being held in readiness to respond to their call, should it be necessary, to suppress insurgent parties, or to protect property from guerrillas. The troops, when thus called for by the committees of safety, or required by their neglect, were quartered upon the people of the county. Under this system marauding parties soon became less numerous, and gradually peace was restored to that section of the state, secessionists as well as Union men finding that it was for their interest to remain quiet, and to discourage and repress all attempts to disturb the peace, or to destroy public or private property.

While the military measures which have been recounted were being taken for the suppression of the rebellion in Missouri, measures were also in progress to place the civil authority of the state on the side of the Union. Governor Jackson had fled from the capital, and subsequently convened the legislature, or those members of it who were in favor of secession, at Sarcoxie, in the south-western part of the state, where the rebel army was concentrated ; and he went himself to Richmond, to consult with the rebel government. The state was thus practically left without a government ; but the state convention, which had been called by the secession legislature for the purpose of taking the state out of the Union, and which at its meeting in March had declared against secession, still held over, having adjourned to a late period in the year. This body was now convened at the capital, where it assembled on the 22d of July. General Price had been the president of the convention at its former session ; but the office was declared vacant, and the vice-president, Mr. Wilson, a Union man, was elected presiding officer. A committee of seven was appointed to consider the extraordinary condition of affairs in the state, and to report what action should be taken. On the 25th of July the committee submitted their report with ordinances, declaring the offices of governor, lieutenant-governor, and secretary of state vacant, and providing for filling the vacancies; abolishing the existing legislature, and providing for the election of new members ; and repealing, in part, the military law and the law to suspend the distribution of the school fund. The several ordinances were adopted, though not without some strong opposition from secession members; and Judge H. R. Gamble, an earnest supporter of the Union, was forthwith elected governor, to serve until August, 1862. An address to the people of Missouri was also adopted, of which the following, exhibiting the aspect of affairs, and the reasons for the action of the convention, is the most material part : —

"To the People of the State of Missouri: —

"Your delegates assembled in convention propose to address you upon the present condition of affairs within our state.   ·

"Since the adjournment of this convention in March last, the most startling events have rushed upon us with such rapidity that the nation stands astonished at the condition of anarchy and strife to which, in so brief a period, it has been reduced.

"When the convention adjourned, although the muttering of the storm was heard, it seemed to be distant, and it was hoped that some quiet but powerful force might be applied, by a beneficent Providence, to avert its fury, and preserve our country from threatened ruin. That hope has not been realized. The storm, in all its fury, has burst upon the country — the armed hosts of different sections have met each other in bloody conflict, and the grave has already received the remains of thousands of slaughtered citizens. Reason, inflamed to madness, demands that the stream of blood shall flow broader and deeper; and the whole energies of a people, but a few months since prosperous and happy, are now directed to the collection of larger hosts, and the preparation of increased and more destructive engines of death.

"Your delegates enjoy the satisfaction of knowing that neither by their action, nor their failure to act, have they in any degree contributed to the ferocious war spirit which now prevails so generally over the whole land. We have sought peace; we have entreated .those who were about to engage in war to withhold their hands from the strife; and in this course we know that we but expressed the wishes and feelings of the state. Our entreaties have been unheeded; and now, while war is raging in other parts of our common country, we have felt that our first and highest duty is to preserve, if possible, our own state from its ravages. The danger is imminent, and demands prompt and decisive measures of prevention.

"We have assembled in Jefferson under circumstances widely different from those that existed when the convention adjourned its session at St. Louis.

"We find high officers of the state government engaged in actual hostilities with the forces of the United States, and blood has been spilt upon the soil of Missouri. Many of our citizens have yielded obedience to an ill-judged call of the governor, and have assembled in arms for the purpose of repelling the invasion of the state by armed bands of lawless invaders, as the troops of the United States are designated by the governor in his proclamation of the 17th day of June last.

"We find that troops from the state of Arkansas have come into Missouri for the purpose of sustaining the action of our governor in his contest with the United States, and this at the request of our executive.

"We find no person present, or likely soon to be present, at the seat of government, to exercise the ordinary functions of the executive department, or to maintain the internal peace of the state.

"We find that throughout the state there is imminent danger of civil war in its worst form, in which neighbor shall seek the life of neighbor, and bonds of society will be dissolved, and universal anarchy shall reign. If it be possible to find a remedy for existing evils, and to avert the threatened horrors of anarchy, it is manifestly the duty of your delegates, assembled in convention, to provide such a remedy; and, in order to determine upon the remedy, it is necessary to trace, very briefly, the origin and progress of the evils that now afflict the state.

"It is not necessary that any lengthy reference should be made to the action of those states which have seceded from the Union. We cannot remedy or recall that secession. They have acted for themselves, and must abide the consequences of their own action. So far as you have expressed your wishes, you have declared your determination not to leave the Union, and your wishes have been expressed by this convention.

"Any action of any officer of the state in conflict with your will, thus expressed, is an action in plain opposition to the principle of our government, which recognizes the people as the source of political power, and their will as the rule of conduct for all their officers. It would have been but a reasonable compliance with your will, that after you had, through this convention, expressed your determination to remain in the Union, your executive and legislative officers should not only have refrained from any opposition to your will, but should have exerted all their powers to carry your will into effect.

" We have been enabled to ascertain by some correspondence of different public officers, accidentally made public, that several of these officers not only entertained and expressed opinions and wishes against the continuance of Missouri in the Union, but actually engaged in schemes to withdraw her from the Union, contrary to your known wishes.

" After the adjournment of your convention, which had expressed your purpose to remain in the Union, Governor Claiborne F. Jackson, in a letter addressed to David Walker, president of the Arkansas convention, dated April 19, 1861, says, 'From the beginning, my own conviction has been that the interest, duty, and honor of every slaveholding state demand their separation from the non-slaveholding states.' Again, he says, 'I have been, from the beginning, in favor of decided and prompt action on the part of the southern states; but the majority of the people of Missouri, up to the present time, have differed with me.' Here we have the declaration of his opinion and wishes, and the open confession that a majority of the people did not agree with him.

" But he proceeds : 'What their future action [meaning the future action of the people] may

be, no man with certainty can predict or foretell; but my impression is, judging from the indications hourly occurring, that Missouri will be ready for secession in less than thirty days, and will secede if Arkansas will only get out of the way, and give her a free passage.'

" It will presently be seen, by an extract from another letter, what the governor means by being ready for secession; but it is very remarkable that he should undertake, not only to say that she would be ready to secede in thirty days, but further, that she will secede, when in fact your convention, at that time, stood adjourned to the 3d Monday of December next. His declaration that the state would secede, is made, doubtless, upon some plan of his own, independent of the convention.

" Nine days after this letter to the president of the Arkansas convention, he wrote another, addressed to J. W. Tucker, Esq., the editor of a secession newspaper in St. Louis. This letter is dated April 28, 1861. The writer says, 'I do not think Missouri should secede to-day or to-morrow, but I do not think it good policy that I should so openly declare. I want a little time to arm the state, and I am assuming every responsibility to do it with all possible despatch.'

" Again, he says, 'We should keep our own counsels. Every body in the state is in favor of arming the state; then let it be done. All are opposed to furnishing Mr. Lincoln with soldiers. Time will settle the balance. Nothing should be said about the time or the manner in which Missouri should go out. That she ought to go, and will go, at the proper time, I have no doubt. She ought to have gone last winter, when she could have seized the public arms and public property, and defended herself.'

" Here we have the fixed mind and purpose of the governor, that Missouri shall leave the Union. He wants time — a little time to arm the state. He thinks secrecy should be preserved by the parties with whom he acts in keeping their counsels. He suggests that nothing should be said about the time or the manner in which Missouri should go out; manifestly implying that the time and manner of going out, which he, and those with whom he acted, proposed to adopt, were some other time and manner than such as were to be fixed by the people through their convention. It was, no doubt, to be a time and manner to be fixed by the governor and the General Assembly, or by the governor and a military body to be provided with arms during the little time needed by the governor for that purpose.

"There have been no specific disclosures made to the public of the details of this plan; but the governor expresses his strong conviction that at the proper time the state will go out.

"This correspondence of the governor occurred at a time when there was no interference by soldiers of the United States with any of the citizens, or with the peace of the state. The event which produced exasperation through the state — the capture of Camp Jackson — did not take place until the 10th of May. Yet the evidence is conclusive that there was at the time of this correspondence a secret plan for taking Missouri out of the Union without any assent of the people through their convention.

"An address to the people of Missouri was issued by Thomas C. Reynolds, the lieutenant-governor, in which he declares that in Arkansas, Tennessee, and Virginia his efforts have been directed unceasingly, to the best of his limited ability, to the promotion of our interests, indissolubly connected with the vindication of our speedy union with the Confederate States. Here is the second executive officer of Missouri avowedly engaged in travelling through states which he must regard while Missouri continues in the Union as foreign states, and those states endeavoring, as he says, to promote the interest of our state.

"The mode of promoting our interests is disclosed in another passage of the address, in which he gives the people assurance that the people of the Confederate States, though engaged in a war with a powerful foe, would not hesitate still further to tax their energies and resources at the proper time, and on a proper occasion in aid of Missouri. The mode of promoting our interests, then, was by obtaining military aid, and this while Missouri continued in the Union. The result of the joint action of the first and second executive officers of the state has been, that a body of military forces of Arkansas has actually invaded Missouri, to carry out the schemes of your own officer, who ought to have conformed to your will, as you had made it known at elections, and had expressed it by your delegates in convention.

"Still further to execute the purpose of severing the connection of Missouri with the United States, the General Assembly was called, and when assembled sat in secret session, and enacted laws which had for their object the placing in the hands of the governor large sums of money, to be expended, in his discretion, for military purposes, and a law for the organization of a military force which was to be sustained by extraordinary taxation, and to be absolutely subject to the orders of the governor, to act against all opposers, including the United States. By these acts, schools are closed, and the demands of humanity for the support of lunatics are denied, and the money raised for the purposes of education and benevolence may swell the fund to be expended in war.

"Without referring more particularly to the provisions of these several acts, which are most extraordinary and extremely dangerous as precedents, it is sufficient to say that they display the same purpose to engage in a conflict with the general government, and to break the connection of Missouri with the United States, which had before been manifested by governor Jackson. The conduct of these officers of the legislative and executive departments has pro-

W. S. Rosecrans

duced evils and dangers of vast magnitude, and your delegates in convention have addressed themselves to the important and delicate duty of attempting to free the state from these evils.

"The high executive officers have fled from the government and from the state, leaving us without the officers to discharge the ordinary necessary executive functions. But, more than this, they are actually engaged in carrying on a war with the state, supported by troops from states in the Southern Confederacy; so that the state, while earnestly desirous to keep out of the war, has become the scene of conflict without any action of the people assuming such hostility. Any remedy for our present evil, to be adequate, must be one which shall vacate the offices held by the officers who have thus brought our trouble upon us.

"Your delegates desire that you shall by election fill these offices, by process of your own choice, and for this purpose they have directed, by ordinance, that an election shall be held on the first Monday in November. This time, rather than one nearer at hand, was selected, so as to conform to the spirit of the provision in the constitution, which requires three months' notice to be given of an election to fill a vacancy in the office of governor. But, in the mean time, much damage might happen to the state by keeping the present incumbents in office, not only by leaving necessary executive duties unperformed, while they prosecute their war measures, but by continuing and increasing the internal social strife which threatens the peace of the whole state.

"Your delegates judged it necessary that, in order to preserve the peace, and in order to arrest invasions of the state, these executive offices should be vacated at once, and be filled by persons selected by your delegates, until you could fill them by election. They have, therefore, made such selection as they trust will be

found to be judicious in preserving the peace of the state. The office of secretary of state has not been mentioned before, and it is sufficient to say that Benjamin F. Massey, the present incumbent, has abandoned the seat of government, and has followed the fortunes of the governor, taking with him the seal of state as an instrument of evil. He may be employed by the governor in action deeply injurious to the state; and he has been dealt with by your delegates in the same manner as the governor and lieutenant-governor.

"In regard to the members of the General Assembly, it is only necessary to say that by the enactment of the law called the "Military Bill," which violates the constitution, and places the entire military strength of the state at the almost unlimited control of the executive, and imposes onerous burdens upon the citizens for the support of an army, and by the passage of general appropriation acts which give to the executive the command of large funds to be expended at his discretion for military purposes, thus uniting the control of the purse and the sword in the same hands, they have displayed their willingness to sustain the war policy of the executive, and place the destinies of the state in the hands of the governor.

"The offices of the members of the General Assembly have, therefore, been vacated, and a new election ordered; so that you may have an opportunity of choosing such legislative representatives as may carry out your own views of policy.

"In order that the schemes of those who seek to take Missouri out of the Union may not further be aided by the late secret legislation of the General Assembly, your delegates have, by ordinance, amended the military law, and such other acts as were doubtless passed for the purpose of disturbing the relations of the state with the federal government.

"These are the measures adopted by your

delegates in convention for the purpose of restoring peace to our disturbed state, and enabling you to select officers for yourselves to declare and carry into effect your views of the true policy of the state. They are measures which seem to be imperatively demanded by the present alarming condition of public affairs, and your delegates have determined to submit them to you for your approval or disapproval, that they may have the authority of your sanction, if you find them to be adapted to secure the peace and welfare of the state."

But the deposed executive officers still claimed to exercise the functions of the offices to which they had been elected. Lieutenant-Governor Reynolds, who had been south to secure aid from the rebels, now returned, and issued a proclamation from New Madrid, in the south-eastern part of the state, claiming to exercise the executive authority in the absence of Governor Jackson. He denounced the national administration, and promised the aid of the Confederate States to overthrow the federal power in Missouri. His proclamation, however, was but the manifesto of an exile as well as a traitor, and had little effect, except upon those already committed to the rebellion.

Governor Gamble, and those elected with him, entered upon the duties of their offices on the 31st of July, and zealously exercised their legitimate powers to continue the state in the Union, and to restore peace within the borders of Missouri. The convention contributed further to the same end, and adopted ordinances to supply the place of necessary legislation, and to guard against secession in any form in which it might be attempted.

The following proclamation, issued by Governor Gamble, shows the spirit of the government as then established, which was, perhaps, as strongly on the side of the Union as the people would sustain. From that time a more unconditional and active Union sentiment seemed to increase in the state : —

"To the People of the State of Missouri : —

"Jefferson City, *August* 3, 1861.

" Your delegates, assembled in convention, have decided that in order to vindicate the sovereignty of the state, it was necessary to vacate the offices of governor, lieutenant-governor, secretary of state, and members of the General Assembly, and to order an election to take place on the first Monday of November next to fill those offices with persons of your own choice. They have chosen me to discharge the duties of chief magistrate until that election can take place.

" No argument will here be made in support of the action of the convention. An address has been issued to you by that body, in which are set forth the necessities for the action, and the power under which they have acted. I could give you no stronger expression of my deliberate judgment that their action was both constitutional and necessary, than is afforded by my acceptance of the office until the election can take place.

" The choice thus made of temporary or provisional governor will satisfy all that no countenance will be afforded to any scheme or to any conduct calculated in any degree to interfere with the institution of slavery existing in the state. To the very utmost extent of executive power that institution will be protected.

" The choice of temporary governor gives the further assurance to all that every effort will be made to stop the practices on the part of the military which have occasioned so much irritation throughout the state — such as arresting citizens who have neither taken up arms against the government, nor aided those who are in open hostility to it, and searching private houses without any reasonable ground to suspect the occupants of any improper conduct, and unnecessarily seizing or injuring private property. Such acts must be, and will be, discountenanced; and there is every reason to believe, from a general order recently issued by Lieutenant-

General Scott, and from the known disposition of Major-General Fremont, whose command embraces Missouri, that such oppressive conduct on the part of the military will in a short time be arrested.

"There exists in many parts of the state a most unfortunate and unnatural condition of feeling among our citizens, amounting to actual hostility, and leading often to scenes of violence and bloodshed; and even neighbors of the same race have come to regard each other as enemies. This feeling, too, has originated in questions of a political character, although the American mind has been accustomed to consider a difference upon such questions as affording no cause of hostility. Combinations have been formed for carrying out schemes of violence by one class against another, and by those holding one set of opinions against others holding a different set.

"Civil government in this state has no concern with men's opinions, except to protect all in their undisturbed enjoyment. It is only when they become the causes of acts that they bring those who entertain them into any responsibility to the law.

"While this freedom of opinion is the right of all, and while it is the duty of each to respect this right in others, it is plainly the duty of the government to suppress, as far as practicable, all combinations to violate this right, and all violence arising from a difference of opinion. Yet it is important that every well-disposed citizen should remember that the extreme and intemperate exercise of this right of expressing his opinions often leads to unnecessary discord and violence, and that refraining from the intemperate discussion of topics known to be exciting would be but a slight contribution made by each towards the preservation of the general peace. . . .

"The state has been invaded by troops from the State of Arkansas, and a large force, under General Pillow, of Tennessee, has landed upon the soil of Missouri, notwithstanding the congress of the Confederate States, in their act declaring war against the United States, expressly excepted Missouri as a state against which the war was not to be waged.

"General Pillow has issued a proclamation addressed to the people of Missouri, in which he declares that his army comes at the request of the governor of this state, and says they will help us to expel from our borders the population hostile to our rights and institutions, treating all such as enemies, if found under arms. It remains to be seen whether General Pillow, and other officers of the Confederate States, will continue their endeavor to make Missouri the theatre of war upon the invitation of Governor Jackson, or of any other person, when such invasion is contrary to the act of the Confederate States, and when the invitation given by the governor is withdrawn by the people. We have sought to avoid the ravaging our state in this war, and if the military officers of the Confederate States seek to turn the war upon us, upon the mere pretext that they are invited by a state officer to do so, when they know that no officer of the state has authority to give such invitation, then upon them be the consequences, for the sovereignty of Missouri must be protected.

"There should be, on the part of the people of Missouri, a paramount purpose to preserve the internal peace of their own state, whatever may be the condition of affairs in other states. Our first duties are at home. If there could be a general recognition of this principle, the duty of preserving peace would be less onerous upon the magistracy of the state. But all will admit that, however unpleasant it may be, the duty of preserving the peace must be discharged by those upon whom the law imposes it. The means furnished by law are ample, and must be employed."

In the mean time Major-General John C. Fremont assumed command of the western military department, and established his headquarters at St. Louis. The military operations under his command will be narrated in subsequent chapters.

CHAPTER XLIII.

Preparations to continue the War. — Major-General McClellan Commander of the Army of the Potomac. — Confidence of the People and the Government in him. — Defence of Washington, and Organization of the Army. — Order of General Scott for the Protection of Mount Vernon. — Movements of the Army in Western Virginia. — Advance of General Cox. — Governor Wise's Forces dispersed. — General Cox's Announcement of the Result. — Address of General Rosecrans to the loyal People. — Affairs in South-eastern Virginia. — Burning of Hampton by the Rebels under General Magruder. — Inhumanity of the Incendiaries. — Expedition to Hatteras Inlet. — General Wool in Command at Fortress Monroe. — Naval and Military Preparations. — Arrival at Hatteras Inlet. — Landing of Troops. — Naval Attack on the Forts. — Fort Clark abandoned. — Renewal of the Attack. — Surrender of Fort Hatteras. — Terms of Surrender. — Prisoners captured. — The Forts garrisoned. — General Butler's official Report.

THE federal government and the people of the loyal states, though disappointed, were not disheartened by the result of the battle at Bull Run. Congress authorized the acceptance of volunteers for the war, not exceeding five hundred thousand in number, and efforts were at once made to raise and organize this large force. Volunteers readily offered, and most of the states responded to the requisitions upon them for their respective quotas of the force to be raised. Criminations and recriminations, which were at first somewhat indulged in, gave place to united and well-directed efforts to furnish the men and means for the prosecution of the war to more successful results.

General McClellan, who was called from Western Virginia to take command of the army on the Potomac, was the youngest of the major-generals in the federal service, being at this time but thirty-five years of age. His father

was of Connecticut birth, but became an eminent physician in Philadelphia, where General McClellan was born. The latter was appointed a cadet in the Military Academy at West Point, where he graduated in 1846, at the age of twenty, one of the best scholars of his class. He acted as lieutenant in the Mexican war, and after its close attained to the rank of captain. He served in the engineers' corps, for which his talents and attainments especially qualified him, and afterwards in the cavalry. In 1855 he was appointed one of a military commission to visit Europe during the Crimean war, and subsequently prepared one part of the report of the commission in relation to the art of war, as shown in the Crimean campaign. After his return from Europe, he resigned his commission in the army, and became an officer of the Illinois Central Railroad, and subsequently of the Ohio and Mississippi Railroad. In the latter place he was engaged at the time the rebellion broke out, when he was appointed first a general officer of Ohio volunteers, and subsequently a major-general in the United States army. General McClellan was highly esteemed by General Scott, at whose suggestion, probably, he was appointed to the command of the most important of the federal armies.

The appointment of General McClellan gave general satisfaction to the people, with whom he at once became popular as the young hero who should lead their army to victory. In him they not only hoped to find, but believed they saw, all the military ability of Scott, combined with more youthful vigor and activity.* The government also reposed in him the greatest

----

* The confidence which was at once given to General McClellan by the people was somewhat remarkable; for he was taken wholly upon trust, not having then achieved any great deed either in his military or civil capacity. There were, however, certain elements in his character which inspired confidence and good will, and his capacity as an engineer was somewhat known, while the success of the army of Western Virginia, of which he was the commander, in a not very arduous campaign, gave éclat to his name.

confidence, and afforded every facility for him to organize and discipline the army committed to his charge. He arrived in Washington on the 25th of July, and soon entered upon his duties, though he did not formally take command of the army until some time after.

The first measures taken were to strengthen the defences of Washington, and so to dispose of the forces as to be best prepared for an aggressive movement on the part of the rebels. The small force remaining of Patterson's army, after the discharge of the three months' troops, were removed to the Maryland side of the Potomac, and were reënforced by a portion of the new regiments as they arrived. Major-General Nathaniel P. Banks was assigned to the command of this division of the army, which was now posted nearer to Washington, so as to be within supporting distance of that portion of the army on the Potomac north-west of Washington. The federal forces also occupied the Maryland shore of the Potomac below Washington, the lines being gradually extended towards the mouth of the river.

The new regiments of three years' volunteers soon made good the place of the three months' troops who had been discharged; and as the new levies were constantly arriving at or near the capital, the army soon grew to dimensions such as had hardly been anticipated when the war began. A systematic organization of the army into brigades and divisions was carried out, more strict discipline was enforced, and constant drill and camp duty made the soldiers more efficient. Meanwhile, the advance of the rebels towards Washington, and the accession to their army of large additional forces which occupied the strong positions in front of the whole federal line, made necessary a strong picket force, and constant watchfulness on the part of officers. Thus weeks and months passed away with various necessary but apparently unimportant movements, occasional alarms, and picket skirmishing, but scarcely any remarka-

ble event to vary the monotony of the daily report of "all quiet on the Potomac."

The position of the two armies was such that Mount Vernon, the home and burial place of Washington, was for a time in the disputed ground between them, and was subject to visits of pickets or reconnoitring parties of either force. It was charged by each side that the other had violated the sacred enclosure where repose the remains of "the Father of his Country." That this sacrilege might not be justly charged upon those who supported the Union which Washington had done so much to establish, General Scott issued the following order, which was strictly enforced and obeyed:—

"GENERAL ORDER, No. 13.

"GENERAL HEADQUARTERS OF THE ARMY, "WASHINGTON, July 31, 1861.

"It has been the prayer of every patriot that the tramp and din of civil war might at least spare the precincts within which repose the sacred remains of the Father of his Country. But this pious hope is disappointed. Mount Vernon, so recently consecrated anew to the immortal Washington, has already been overrun by bands of rebels, who, having trampled under foot the constitution of the United States, — the ark of our freedom and prosperity, — are prepared to trample on the ashes of him to whom we are all mainly indebted for these mighty blessings. Should the operations of war take the United States troops in that direction, the general-in-chief does not doubt that each and every man will approach with due reverence, and leave unimpaired, not only the tomb, but also the house, graves, and walks which were so loved by the greatest and best of men.

" WINFIELD SCOTT."

While matters remained thus quiet on the Potomac, there were some movements of the forces in other parts of Virginia. In Western Virginia, while the division of the "Army of Occupation," under the immediate command of

General Rosecrans, advanced southward slowly, the division under General Cox moved eastward from Charleston through the Kanawha valley, causing small bodies of the rebels, who were collected at different points, to disband or to retire to join the main rebel army in this part of the state, under the command of Governor Wise. The larger part of these forces, it was believed, disbanded without joining the main body, and retired to their homes, under the promise of protection from the federal commander. Many of them had taken up arms under the excitement caused by the appeals of Governor Wise and the rebel emissaries from Eastern Virginia, and were quite willing to lay them down upon the approach of the federal troops, when they saw that peace and quiet followed the army of occupation.

The main body of Wise's force was finally collected at Gauley Bridge, a strong position, where it was supposed that there might be a battle. But here, also, as farther down the valley, the rebels fled at the approach of the federal force, destroying the bridge over Gauley River, to prevent pursuit — a mode of escaping to which they had repeatedly resorted in their retreat up the valley. This final retreat, which occurred on the 29th of July, appeared to disorganize entirely the army under Wise, who was not among the last to retreat; and the rebel force, which was to "relieve Western Virginia from the invader," was driven out from that portion of the state, and the campaign, from which the rebels were promised so much, ended in utter failure, which was as good as a defeat. In a letter to Governor Pierpont, announcing the result of his campaign, General Cox said, —

"The Kanawha valley is now free from the rebel troops. Most of the forces raised by Wise in this valley left him between Charleston and this place. I had sent them assurances that if they laid down their arms they might go quietly to their homes; and many have done so, asserting that they were cheated into the rebel service. I regret to have to say that Wise, in his retreat, has burned a number of valuable bridges, and carried off most of the wagons and teams belonging to the people of the valley. All parties denounce him for his vandalism. I congratulate you on the success of this expedition."

Having substantially secured peace and quiet, for a time at least, to Western Virginia, General Rosecrans issued an address to the loyal people, in which, after describing the position of affairs in that part of the "Old Dominion," he declared the policy by which he sought to secure peace and to maintain the authority of the federal government. In this address he wrote, —

"You are the vast majority of the people. If the principle of self-government is to be respected, you have a right to stand in the position you have assumed, faithful to the constitution and laws of Virginia, as they were before the ordinance of secession.

"The Confederates have determined at all hazards to destroy the government which, for eighty years, has defended our rights, and given us a name among the nations. Contrary to your interests and your wishes, they have brought war upon your soil. Their tools and dupes told you you must vote for secession as the only means to insure peace; that unless you did so, hordes of abolitionists would overrun you, plunder your property, steal your slaves, seize upon your lands, and hang all those who opposed them.

"By these and other atrocious falsehoods they alarmed you, and led many honest and unsuspecting citizens to vote for secession. Neither threats, nor fabrications, nor intimidations sufficed to carry Western Virginia, against the interest and wishes of its people, into the arms of secession.

"Enraged that you dared to disobey their behests, Eastern Virginians, who had been accustomed to rule you and count your votes, and ambitious recreants from among yourselves, disappointed that you would not make good their promises, have conspired to tie you to the desperate fortunes of the Confederacy, or drive you from your homes.

"Between submission to them and subjugation or expulsion, they leave you no alternative. *You* say you do not wish to destroy the old government, under which you have lived so long and peacefully; *they* say you shall break it up. *You* say you wish to remain citizens of the United States; *they* reply you shall join the Southern Confederacy, to which the Richmond junta has transferred you; and to carry their will, their Jenkins, Wise, Jackson, and other conspirators proclaim upon your soil a relentless and neighborhood war; their misguided and unprincipled followers reëcho their cry, threatening fire and sword, hanging and expulsion, to all who oppose their arbitrary designs. They have set neighbor against neighbor, and friend against friend; they have introduced among you warfare only known among savages. In violation of the laws of nations and humanity, they have proclaimed that private citizens may and ought to make war.

"Under this bloody code, peaceful citizens, unarmed travellers, and single soldiers have been shot down, and even the wounded and defenceless have been killed; scalping their victims is all that is wanting to make their warfare like that which, seventy or eighty years ago, was waged by the Indians against the white race on this very ground. You have no alternative left you but to unite as one man in the defence of your homes, for the restoration of law and order, or be subjugated or expelled from the soil.

"I therefore earnestly exhort you to take the most prompt and vigorous measures to put a stop to neighborhood and private wars. You must remember that the laws are suspended in Eastern Virginia, which has transferred itself to the Southern Confederacy. The old consti-

tution and laws of Virginia are only in force in Western Virginia. These laws you must maintain.

"Let every citizen, without reference to past political opinions, unite with his neighbors to keep those laws in operation, and thus prevent the country from being desolated by plunder and violence, whether committed in the name of Secessionism or Unionism.

"I conjure all those who have hitherto advocated the doctrine of secessionism, as a political opinion, to consider that now its advocacy means war against the peace and interests of Western Virginia; it is an invitation to the Southern Confederates to come in and subdue you, and proclaims that there can be no law nor right until this is done.

"My mission among you is that of a fellow-citizen, charged by the government to expel the arbitrary force which domineered over you, to restore that law and order of which you have been robbed, and to maintain your right to govern yourselves under the constitution and laws of the United States.

"To put an end to the savage war waged by individuals, who, without warrant of military authority, lurk in the bushes and waylay messengers, or shoot sentries, I shall be obliged to hold the neighborhood in which these outrages are committed as responsible; and, unless they raise the hue and cry and pursue the offenders, deal with them as accessories to the crime.

"Unarmed and peaceful citizens shall be protected, the rights of private property respected, and only those who are found enemies of the government of the United States, and the peace of Western Virginia, will be disturbed. Of these I shall require absolute certainty that they will do no mischief.

"Put a stop to needless arrests and the spread of malicious reports. Let each town and district choose five of its most reliable and energetic citizens a committee of public safety, to act in concert with the civil and military authorities, and be responsible for the preservation of peace and good order.

"Citizens of Western Virginia, your fate is mainly in your own hands. If you allow yourselves to be trampled under foot by hordes of disturbers, plunderers, and murderers, your land will become a desolation. If you stand firm for law and order, and maintain your rights, you may dwell together peacefully and happily as in former days."

The rebel authorities, however, did not abandon Western Virginia, and additional forces were advanced in that direction, under General Floyd, the former secretary of war of President Buchanan. The result of this movement will be found in a subsequent chapter.

In South-eastern Virginia the general quiet which had prevailed in General Butler's department since the unsuccessful attack at Great Bethel, was broken by the destruction of the village of Hampton by the rebel forces under General Magruder. General Butler had fortified Hampton, and for a time had kept a force there for its defence; but having reason to fear an attack from the rebels while he had an insufficient force to hold this and the more important positions of his army, he had withdrawn all but a small guard, and it was consequently open to the attack of the enemy. General Magruder, with a force of six or seven thousand men, including cavalry and artillery, moved down the peninsula on the 7th of August, and took up a position about two and a half miles from Hampton, where he hoped to induce an attack from the federal forces at Newport News and at Hampton. Failing to draw out the federal troops, the rebels then moved nearer to Hampton, and again formed in line of battle. Here they remained till night, when a detachment entered the village, and while a part skirmished with the federal troops posted to defend the long bridge, which had been in part torn up and barricaded, another body set fire to the buildings in the village. But a few

whites and some two or three hundred negroes remained in the village. All who were found in the houses received but the briefest notice of the purpose of the incendiaries, and were allowed only time to save themselves, without removing any of their property. Among the incendiary force were some of the former residents of Hampton, and some of these set fire to their own dwellings. Houses of secessionists and Union men were alike remorselessly destroyed, and the rankest secessionist, equally with the loyal negro, was turned out of doors, several aged and sick persons being among the sufferers. Among the buildings destroyed was the ancient village church, a land-mark of the past, in which Washington had worshipped, which took fire accidentally, according to the rebel accounts. The reason for this destruction of property, even by those who were most deeply interested in it, was to prevent the federal force from occupying the dwellings or using them for the shelter of the numerous "contraband" negroes who were collecting within the Union lines. An attempt was made, in some of the rebel journals, to charge this act upon the federal troops; but the evidence was too clear to admit a doubt of the authors of the destruction.

Having accomplished this work of vandalism, General Magruder withdrew his forces to the neighborhood of Bethel, where he fortified his position. His force was too strong for the federal troops to risk a battle in the position chosen by the rebel general, though the four thousand men at Newport News would have been abundantly able, in their intrenched position, to have resisted an attack from the entire force of the enemy. The rebel general, however, was too prudent to venture such an attack; and having destroyed a village in which his own friends were most interested, he returned to act on the defensive, and made no other important demonstration.

One other affair of importance, not strictly

belonging to the operations in Eastern Virginia, but in which Fortress Monroe was the base, may be related in this connection, as the conclusion of the summer campaign. This was a joint military and naval expedition to Hatteras Inlet, a narrow passage through the sand bank which stretches along the coast of North Carolina like an outwork of the main shore. This inlet was the rendezvous of the rebel privateers, which were becoming quite numerous along the coast; and by passing through the intricate channel into Pamlico Sound, they were safe from storms, and were protected from pursuit by the shallow water, and by two forts erected on the northern side of the inlet. Information having been received of the position of the forts, and the strength and intentions of the rebel forces at this point, Commodore Stringham, the flag-officer of the Atlantic squadron, and General Butler, planned a joint expedition, which was undertaken with the approval of the government, to capture the forts, with the intention of destroying them and obstructing the inlet, so as to render it of little value to the rebels. The plan was already made, when Major-General John E. Wool, a veteran officer of the army, was ordered to take command of the department under General Butler, and the latter was assigned to the command of all the troops of the department outside of the fortress.

The expedition consisted of the flag-ship Minnesota, the Wabash, the Pawnee, the Monticello, and the Harriet Lane, war vessels, two steam transports, and the steam-tug Fanny. A number of surf boats were taken along, and a dismasted vessel, to be sunk in the channel of the inlet. The frigate Cumberland and the steamer Susquehanna were expected to join the expedition off the coast. The military part of the expedition, under General Butler, consisted of about nine hundred men, mostly New York volunteers; and the plan was to land this force, or a part of it, two or three miles north of the forts, while the ships of war should shell

the fortifications, and prepare the way for a decisive blow by the troops. The military force, however, did not play the important part which was anticipated for it.

The vessels arrived off Cape Hatteras on the afternoon of the 27th of August, and proceeding towards the inlet, prepared the surf boats for landing the troops the next morning. On the morning of the 28th, the troops were embarked in the surf boats, and the war vessels approached the forts for the purpose of covering the landing of the troops, which was to be effected at some distance north-east of the inlet. The landing of the troops, owing to the surf, was effected with much difficulty; and only a portion of them were safely put on shore, several of the boats being stove or swamped. In the mean time the war vessels approached the fortifications and commenced an attack, to which the rebels replied, though most of their shot fell short. The shells from the ships of war burst in and about the forts, and after a severe bombardment, the flags of both forts were hauled down. The rebel force in one of the batteries, Fort Clark, evacuated it, and hastened to the other fort; which movement being seen by the federal troops, they advanced, and taking possession of Fort Clark, hoisted the American flag, which was greeted with enthusiastic cheers by the crews of the vessels. As both flags had been hauled down, it was supposed that both forts were about to be surrendered; and accordingly the vessels of lighter draft were sent into the inlet, while the larger ships approached as near as the shoal water would allow. But the rebels were not yet disposed to surrender Fort Hatteras, and within the inlet were several steamers and vessels which had evidently brought reënforcements, the rebels having, without doubt, learned the destination of the expedition when it sailed from Hampton Roads. Fort Hatteras again opened fire upon the vessels, and the Monticello, which, being of light draft, was in an advanced position, was exposed to some danger. Several shot struck her, but without doing material damage. The ships returned the fire with effect until the approach of night and signs of squally weather rendered it necessary for them to haul off, the smaller vessels remaining where they could protect the troops.

The next morning, August 29, the attack was renewed with much vigor by the ships of war, and for a time the rebels made no response; but they at last returned the fire without effect. The battle thus continued several hours, the troops awaiting the result of the bombardment, and doing little except firing an occasional shot from some boat howitzers which were landed with them, and a six-pounder cannon that they had taken near Fort Clark. At last a white flag was raised over Fort Hatteras, and the vessels which appeared to have brought reenforcements were seen making off from the inlet.

As soon as communication was established with the shore, Captain Barron, formerly an officer of the United States navy, and now "flag-officer" in the rebel navy, and Colonel Martin and Major Andrews, commanding the rebel forces, stated that they had seven hundred troops in the fort and fifteen hundred more within call, and they proposed that if their officers should be permitted to retire with side arms and the men without arms, they would surrender the forts. General Butler, however, demanded an unconditional surrender as prisoners of war. After some parleying the terms were agreed to. The remainder of the federal land force was put on shore, the forts were taken possession of, and the rebel forces surrendered, and were taken on board the vessels as prisoners. In addition to the officers above named, many subordinate officers were captured, and between six and seven hundred rank and file. Several small vessels, with cargoes of some value, were also taken as prizes.

The object of the expedition, as before stated, had been to destroy the fortifications and obstruct the inlet; but upon examination of the forts and the position, General Butler saw that it would be an advantageous position to hold, and that a comparatively small force would be sufficient for the purpose. He accordingly, upon consultation with Commodore Stringham, determined to retain possession of the forts until he could report to the government and obtain further instructions. The forts were garrisoned and strengthened, and a part of the naval force remained to afford further protection. The other vessels, with a part of the troops and the prisoners, sailed for Hampton Roads and New York, and General Butler's course, being laid before the government by that able officer, was fully approved, and in subsequent movements proved to be a great advantage.

The report of Commodore Stringham gave in detail the movements of the several vessels under his command, and the operations by which the victory was achieved by that branch of the service. Of the report of General Butler, more comprehensive in its character, the following is the most material part: —

"We left Fortress Monroe on Monday, at one o'clock, P. M. The last ship of our fleet arrived off Hatteras Inlet about four o'clock Tuesday afternoon. Such preparations as were possible for the landing were made in the evening, and at daylight next morning dispositions were made for an attack upon the forts by the fleet, and for the landing of the troops.

"Owing to the previous prevalence of southwest gales, a heavy surf was breaking on the beach. Every effort was made to land the troops, and after about three hundred and fifteen were landed, including fifty-five marines from the fleet and the regulars, both the iron boats upon which we depended were swamped in the surf, and both flat-boats stove, and a brave attempt made by Lieutenant Crosby, of the United States army, (serving with the army as post-captain at Fortress Monroe,) who had volunteered to come down with the steam-tug Fanny, belonging to the army, to land in a boat from the war steamer Pawnee, resulted in the beaching of the boat, so that she could not be got off. It was impracticable to land more troops because of the rising wind and sea. Fortunately, a twelve-pound rifled boat gun, loaned us by the flag-ship, and a twelve-pound howitzer, were landed, the last slightly damaged. Our landing was completely covered by the shells of the Monticello and the Harriet Lane. I was on board the Harriet Lane, directing the disembarkation of the troops by means of signals, and was about landing with them at the time the boats were stove.

"We were induced to desist from further attempts at landing troops by the rising of the wind, and because, in the mean time, the fleet had opened fire upon the nearest fort, which was finally silenced, and its flag struck. No firing had opened upon our troops from the other fort, and its flag was also struck. Supposing this to be a signal of surrender, Colonel Weber advanced his troops, already landed, upon the beach. The Harriet Lane, Captain Faunce, by my direction, tried to cross the bar to get in the smooth water of the inlet, when fire was opened upon the Monticello (which had proceeded in advance of us) from the other fort. Several shots struck her, but without causing any casualties, as I am informed. So well convinced were the officers of both army and navy that the forts had surrendered at this time, that the Susquehanna had towed the frigate Cumberland to an offing. 'The fire was then reopened — as there was no signal from either — upon both forts. In the mean time, a few men from the 'Coast Guard' had advanced up the beach with Mr. Wiegel, (who was acting as volunteer aid, and whose gallantry and services I wish to commend,) and took possession of the smaller fort, which was found to have been abandoned by the enemy, and raised the American flag thereon. It had

become necessary, owing to the threatening appearance of the weather, that all the ships should make an offing, which was done with reluctance, from necessity, thus leaving the troops upon shore — a part in possession of the small fort, (about seven hundred yards from the larger one,) and the rest bivouacked upon the beach, near the place of landing, about two miles north of the forts. Early the next morning the Harriet Lane ran in shore for the purpose of covering any attack upon the troops. At the same time a large steamer was observed coming down the Sound, inside the land, with reënforcements for the enemy; but she was prevented from landing by Captain Johnson, of the 'Coast Guard,' who had placed the two guns from the ship, and a six-pounder captured from the enemy, in a small sand battery, and opened fire upon the rebel steamer.

"At eight o'clock the fleet opened fire again, the flag-ship being anchored as near as the water allowed, and the other ships coming gallantly into action. It was evident, after a few experiments, that our shot fell short. An increased length of fuse was telegraphed, and firing commenced with shells of fifteen seconds fuse. I had sent Mr. Fiske, acting aide-de-camp, on shore, for the purpose of gaining intelligence of the movements of the troops and of the enemy. I then went with the Fanny, for the purpose of effecting a landing of the remainder of the troops, when a white flag was run up from the fort. I then went with the Fanny over the bar into the inlet. At the same time the troops, under Colonel Weber, marched up the beach, and signal was made from the flag ship to cease firing. As the Fanny rounded in over the bar, the rebel steamer Winslow went up the channel, having a large number of secession troops on board, which she had not landed. We threw a shot at her from the Fanny, but she proved to be out of range. I then sent Lieutenant Crosby on shore to demand the meaning of the white flag. The boat soon returned, bringing Mr. Wiegel, with the following written communication from Samuel Barron, late captain in the United States navy :—

Memorandum.

'FORT HATTERAS, *August* 29, 1861.

'Flag-officer Samuel Barron, C. S. Navy, offers to surrender Fort Hatteras, with all the arms and munitions of war. The officers allowed to go out with side arms, and the men without arms to retire.

'S. BARRON,

Commanding Naval Defence,

'*Virginia and North Carolina.*'

And also a verbal communication, stating that he had in the fort six hundred and fifteen men, and a thousand more within an hour's call, but that he was anxious to spare the effusion of blood. To both the written and verbal communications I made the reply which follows, and sent it by Lieutenant Crosby :—

'*Memorandum.*

'Benjamin F. Butler, Major-General United States Army, commanding, in reply to the communication of Samuel Barron, commanding forces at Fort Hatteras, cannot admit the terms proposed. The terms offered are these : Full capitulation, the officers and men to be treated as prisoners of war. No other terms admissible.

'Commanding officers to meet on board flag-ship Minnesota, to arrange details.

'*August* 9, 1861.'

"After waiting three quarters of an hour, Lieutenant Crosby returned, bringing with him Captain Barron, Major Andrews, and Colonel Martin, of the rebel forces, who, on being received on board the tug Fanny, informed me that they had accepted the terms proposed in my memorandum, and had come to surrender themselves and their command as prisoners of war. I informed them that, as the expedition was a combined one from the army and navy, the surrender must be made on board the flag-ship to Flag-officer Stringham, as well as to myself. We went on board the Minnesota for that purpose. . . .

"I then landed, and took a formal surrender of the forts, with all the men and munitions of war, inspected the troops, to see that the arms had been properly surrendered, marched them out, and embarked them on board the Adelaide, and marched my own troops into the fort, and raised our flag upon it, amid the cheers of our men and a salute of thirteen guns, which had been shotted by the enemy. The embarkation of the wounded, which was conducted with great care and tenderness from a temporary wharf, erected for the purpose, took so long that night came on, and so dark that it was impossible for the pilots to take the Adelaide over the bar, thereby causing delay. I may mention in this connection that the Adelaide, in carrying in the troops, at the moment that my terms of capitulation were under consideration by the enemy, had grounded on the bar, but by the active and judicious exertions of Commander Stellwagen, after some delay, was got off. At the same time, the Harriet Lane, in attempting to enter the bar, had grounded, and remained fast; both were under the guns of the fort. This, to me, was a moment of the greatest anxiety. By these accidents, a valuable ship of war and a transport steamer, with a large portion of my troops, were within the power of the enemy. I had demanded the strongest terms, which he was considering. He might refuse, and, seeing our disadvantage, renew the action. But I determined to abate not a tittle of what I believed to be due to the dignity of the government; not even to give an official title to the officer in command of the rebels. Besides, my tug was in the inlet, and at least I could carry on the engagement with my two rifled six-pounders, well supplied with Sawyer's shell.

"Upon taking possession of Fort Hatteras, I found that it mounted ten guns, with four yet unmounted, and one large ten-inch columbiad, all ready for mounting. I append the official muster roll of Colonel Martin, furnished by him, of the officers and men captured by us.

"The position of the fort is an exceedingly strong one, nearly surrounded on all sides by water, and only to be approached by a marsh of five hundred yards circuitously over a long neck of sand, within half musket range, and over a causeway a few feet only in width, and which was commanded by two thirty-two pound guns, loaded with grape and canister, which were expended in our salute. It had a well-protected magazine and bomb-proof, capable of sheltering some three or four hundred men. The parapet was nearly of octagon form, enclosing about two thirds of an acre of ground, well covered, with sufficient traverses, and ramparts, and parapets, upon which our shells had made but little impression.

"The larger work, nearest this inlet, was known as Fort Hatteras. Fort Clark, which was about seven hundred yards northerly, is a square redoubt, mounting five guns and two six-pounders. The enemy had spiked these guns, but in a very inefficient manner, upon abandoning the fort the day before. I had all the troops on shore at the time of the surrender of the forts, but reëmbarked the regulars and marines. Finding it impossible to remain, without a delay of the fleet which could not be justified under the state of facts at Fortress Monroe, and owing to the threatening appearance of the weather, I disembarked the provisions, making, with the provisions captured, about five days' rations for the use of the troops.

"On consultation with Flag-officer Stringham and Commander Stellwagen, I determined to leave the troops and hold the fort, because of

the strength of the fortifications and its importance, and because, if again in the possession of the enemy, with a sufficient armament, of the very great difficulty of its capture, until I could get some further instructions from the government. Commodore Stringham directed the steamers Monticello and Pawnee to remain inside, and these, with the men in the forts, are sufficient to hold the position against any force which is likely, or indeed possible, to be sent against it. The importance of the point cannot be overrated. When the channel is buoyed out, any vessel may carry fifteen feet water over it with ease. Once inside, there is a safe harbor and anchorage in all weathers. From there the whole coast of Virginia and North Carolina, from Norfolk to Cape Lookout, is within our reach, by light draft vessels, which cannot possibly live at sea during the winter months. From it offensive operations may be made upon the whole coast of North Carolina to Bogue Inlet, extending many miles inland to Washington, Newbern, and Beaufort. In the language of the chief engineer of the rebels, Colonel Thompson, in an official report, 'it is the key of the Albemarle.' In my judgment it is a station second in importance only to Fortress Monroe on this coast. As a depot for coaling and supplies for the blockading squadron, it is invaluable. As a harbor for our coasting trade, or inlet from the winter storm, or from pirates, it is of the first importance. By holding it, Hatteras light may again send forth its cheering ray to the storm-beaten mariner, of which the worse than vandalism of the rebels deprives him. It has but one drawback — a want of good water; but that a condenser, like the one now in operation at Fortress Monroe, at a cost of a few hundred dollars, will relieve."

CHAPTER XLIV.

The Rebel Government. — The permanent Constitution of the Confederate States — The Cabinet. — Message of Jefferson Davis. — Measures adopted by the Rebel Congress. — Thanksgiving for the "Victory at Manassas."— Financial Schemes. — Adoption of Doctrines of International Law. — Commissioners to European Courts. — Admission of Missouri to the Confederacy. — Secret Sessions. — Coöperation of State Governments and People. — Slavery the Strength of the Rebellion. — Gigantic Proportions of the Rebellion. — Effect of the Battle of Bull Run.

AT this point we may leave the movements of the military forces to glance at the position of the rebel government and the seceded states, which assumed the character of nationality under the name of "Confederate States of America." The permanent constitution had early taken the place of the provisional constitution, and the provisional government assumed the powers of the permanent government, without change of men. The permanent constitution was ratified, eventually, by eleven states, in but one case being submitted to the vote of the people, but being adopted by the state conventions or legislatures, which bodies assumed all the powers that were necessary to carry out the purposes of .the secessionists. In all these states, except in the eastern part of Tennessee, all opposition to secession had been abandoned, the tyranny of the slave power crushing out all sentiments of loyalty to the Union, or all expression of such sentiments. In Eastern Tennessee the Union men were too numerous and too strong to be at once overwhelmed, and were subjected to the most violent persecution. Whatever of loyalty was felt in other states was suppressed through prudence, or was perverted to secession by the specious arguments of the leading rebels and the march of events. The seat of government was changed from Montgomery, Alabama, to Richmond, Virginia. Here the rebel government assumed still more audaciously the rights of nationality, and put forth energies worthy of a better cause to sus-

tain itself and to overthrow the national government, while it published to the world the grossest falsehoods and misrepresentations to justify itself, and to throw opprobrium upon the national administration. The cabinet of Jefferson Davis was constituted as follows : Secretary of State, Robert Toombs, of Georgia; Secretary of the Treasury, C. L. Memminger, of South Carolina ; Secretary of War, L. P. Walker, of Alabama ; Secretary of the Navy, Stephen R. Mallory, of Florida ; Postmaster, John H. Reagan, of Texas ; Attorney-General, Judah P. Benjamin, of Louisiana.*

The rebel Congress assembled at Richmond on the 20th of July, and the message of Jefferson Davis was transmitted to them on that day. That document, which, in some degree, shows the assumptions of the rebel government, and exhibits the misrepresentations to which it resorted to justify itself before the world, was as follows : —

"GENTLEMEN OF THE CONGRESS OF THE CONFEDERATE STATES OF AMERICA : —

" My message addressed to you at the commencement of the last session contained such full information of the state of the Confederacy as to render.it unnecessary that I should now do more than call your attention to such important facts as have occurred during the recess, and the matters connected with the public defence.

"I have again to congratulate you on the accession of new members to our Confederation of free and equally sovereign states. Our loved and honored brethren of North Carolina and Tennessee have consummated the action foreseen and provided for at your last session, and I have had the gratification of announcing, by proclamation, in conformity with law, that these states were admitted into the Confederacy. The people of Virginia, also, by a majority previously unknown in our history, have rati-

---

* Several changes occurred in this cabinet at an early period.

fied the action of her convention uniting her fortunes with ours. The states of Arkansas, North Carolina, and Virginia have likewise adopted the permanent constitution of the Confederate States, and no doubt is entertained of its adoption by Tennessee, at the election to be held early in next month.

"I deemed it advisable to direct the removal of the several executive departments, with their archives, to this city, to which you have removed the seat of government. Immediately after your adjournment, the aggressive movements of the enemy required prompt, energetic action. The accumulation of his forces on the Potomac sufficiently demonstrated that his efforts were to be directed against Virginia; and from no point could necessary measures for her defence and protection be so effectively decided as from her own capital. The rapid progress of events, for the last few weeks, has fully sufficed to lift the veil, behind which the true policy and purposes of the government of the United States had been previously concealed. Their odious features now stand fully revealed. The message of their President, and the action of their Congress during the present month, confess their intention of the subjugation of these states by a war, by which it is impossible to attain the proposed result, while its dire calamities, not to be avoided by us, will fall with double severity on themselves.

"Commencing in March last with the affectation of ignoring the secession of seven states, which first organized this government; persevering in April in the idle and absurd assumption of the existence of a riot, which was to be dispersed by a *posse comitatus;* continuing in successive months the false representation that these states intended an offensive war, in spite of conclusive evidence to the contrary, furnished as well by official action as by the very basis on which this government is constituted, — the President of the United States and his advisers succeeded in deceiving the people of those states into the belief that the purpose of this government was not peace at home, but conquest abroad; not defence of its own liberties, but subversion of those of the people of the United States. The series of manœuvres by which this impression was created, the art with which they were devised, and the perfidy with which they were executed, were already known to you; but you could scarcely have supposed that they would be openly avowed, and their success made the subject of boast and self-laudation in an executive message. Fortunately for truth and history, however, the President of the United States details, with minuteness, the attempt to reënforce Fort Pickens, in violation of an armistice of which he confessed to have been informed, but only by rumors, too vague and uncertain to fix the attention of the hostile expedition despatched to supply Fort Sumter, admitted to have been undertaken with the knowledge that its success was impossible. The sending of a notice to the governor of South Carolina of his intention to use force to accomplish his object, and then quoting from his inaugural address the assurance that 'there could be no conflict unless these states were the aggressors,' he proceeds to declare his conduct, as just related by himself, was the performance of a promise, so free from the power of ingenious sophistry as that the world should not be able to misunderstand it; and in defiance of his own statement that he gave notice of the approach of a hostile fleet, he charges these states with becoming the assailants of the United States, without a gun in sight, or in expectancy, to return their fire, save only a few in the fort. He is, indeed, fully justified in saying that the case is so free from the power of ingenious sophistry that the world will not be able to misunderstand it. Under cover of this unfounded pretence, that the Confederate States are the assailants, that high functionary, after expressing his concern that some foreign nations had so shaped their action as if they supposed the early destruction of the national Union probable, abandons all further disguise, and proposes to make this contest a short and decisive one, by placing at the control of the government for the work at least four hundred thousand men, and four hundred millions of dollars. The Congress, concurring in the doubt thus intimated as to the sufficiency of the force demanded, has increased it to half a million of men.

"These enormous preparations in men and money, for the conduct of the war, on a scale more grand than any which the new world ever witnessed, is a distinct avowal, in the eyes of civilized man, that the United States are engaged in a conflict with a great and powerful nation. They are at last compelled to abandon the pretence of being engaged in dispersing rioters and suppressing insurrections, and are driven to the acknowledgment that the ancient Union has been dissolved. They recognize the separate existence of these Confederate States, by an interdictive embargo and blockade of all commerce between them and the United States, not only by sea, but by land; not only in ships, but in cars; not only with those who bear arms, but with the entire population of the Confederate States. Finally, they have repudiated the foolish conceit that the inhabitants of this Confederacy are still citizens of the United States; for they are waging an indiscriminate war upon them all, with savage ferocity, unknown in modern civilization.

"In this war, rapine is the rule; private houses, in beautiful rural retreats, are bombarded and burned; grain crops in the field are consumed by the torch, and, when the torch is not convenient, careful labor is bestowed to render complete the destruction of every article of use or ornament remaining in private dwellings after their inhabitants have fled from the outrages of brute soldiery. In 1781, Great Britain, when invading the revolted colonies, took possession of every district and county near For-

tress Monroe, now occupied by the troops of the United States. The houses then inhabited by the people, after being respected and protected by avowed invaders, are now pillaged and destroyed by men who pretend that Virginians are their fellow-citizens. Mankind will shudder at the tales of the outrages committed on defenceless families by soldiers of the United States, now invading our homes; yet these outrages are prompted by inflamed passions and the madness of intoxication. But who shall depict the horror they entertain for the cool and deliberate malignancy which, under the pretext of suppressing insurrection, (said by themselves to be upheld by a minority only of our people,) makes special war on the sick, including children and women, by carefully devised measures to prevent them from obtaining the medicines necessary for their cure. The sacred claims of humanity, respected even during the fury of actual battle, by careful diversion of attack from hospitals containing wounded enemies, are outraged in cold blood by a government and people that pretend to desire a continuance of fraternal connections. All these outrages must remain unavenged, by the universal reprehension of mankind. In all cases where the actual perpetrators of wrongs escape capture, they admit of no retaliation. The humanity of our people would shrink instinctively from the bare idea of urging a like war upon the sick, the women, and the children of an enemy. But there are other savage practices which have been resorted to by the government of the United States, which do admit of repression by retaliation, and I have been driven to the necessity of enforcing the repression. The prisoners of war taken by the enemy on board the armed schooner Savannah, sailing under our commission, were, as I was credibly advised, treated like common felons, put in irons, confined in a jail usually appropriated to criminals of the worst dye, and threatened with punishment as such. I had made application for the exchange of these prisoners to the commanding officer of the enemy's squadron off Charleston, but that officer had already sent the prisoners to New York when application was made. I therefore deemed it my duty to renew the proposal for the exchange to the constitutional commander-in-chief of the army and navy of the United States, — the only officer having control of the prisoners. To this end, I despatched an officer to him under a flag of truce, and, in making the proposal, I informed President Lincoln of my resolute purpose to check all barbarities on prisoners of war by such severity of retaliation on prisoners held by us as should secure the abandonment of the practice. This communication was received and read by an officer in command of the United States forces, and a message was brought from him by the bearer of my communication, that a reply would be returned by President Lincoln as soon as possible. I earnestly hope this promised reply (which has not yet been received) will convey the assurance that prisoners of war will be treated, in this unhappy contest, with that regard for humanity which has made such conspicuous progress in the conduct of modern warfare. As measures of precaution, however, and until this promised reply is received, I still retain in close custody some officers captured from the enemy, whom it had been my pleasure previously to set at large on parole, and whose fate must necessarily depend on that of prisoners held by the enemy. I append a copy of my communication to the President and commander-in-chief of the army and navy of the United States, and of the report of the officer charged to deliver my communication. There are some other passages in the remarkable paper to which I have directed your attention, having reference to the peculiar relations which exist between this government and the states usually termed Border Slave States, which cannot properly be withheld from notice. The

hearts of our people are animated by sentiments towards the inhabitants of these states, which found expression in your enactment refusing to consider them enemies, or authorize hostilities against them. That a very large portion of the people of these states regard us as brethren; that, if unrestrained by the actual presence of large armies, subversion of civil authority, and declaration of martial law, some of them, at least, would joyfully unite with us; that they are, with almost entire unanimity, opposed to the prosecution of the war waged against us,— are facts of which daily-recurring events fully warrant the assertion that the President of the United States refuses to recognize in these our late sister states the right of refraining from attack upon us, and justifies his refusal by the assertion that the states have no other power than that reserved to them in the Union by the constitution. Now, one of them having ever been a state of the Union, this view of the constitutional relations between the states and the general government is a fitting introduction to another assertion of the message, that the Executive possesses power of suspending the writ of habeas corpus, and of delegating that power to military commanders at their discretion. And both these propositions claim a respect equal to that which is felt for the additional statement of opinion in the same paper, that it is proper, in order to execute the laws, that some single law, made in such extreme tenderness of citizens' liberty that practically it relieves more of the guilty than the innocent, should to a very limited extent be violated. We may well rejoice that we have forever severed our connection with a government that thus trampled on all principles of constitutional liberty, and with a people in whose presence such avowals could be hazarded.

The operations in the field will be greatly extended by reason of the policy which heretofore has been secretly entertained, and is now *avowed* and acted on, by them. The forces hitherto raised

42

provide amply for the defence of seven states which originally organized in the Confederacy, as is evidently the fact, since, with the exception of three fortified islands, whose defence is efficiently aided by a preponderating naval force, the enemy has been driven completely out of these stations; and now, at the expiration of five months from the formation of the government, not a single hostile foot presses their soil. These forces, however, must necessarily prove inadequate to repel invasion by the half million of men now proposed by the enemy, and a corresponding increase of our forces will become necessary. The recommendations for the raising of this additional force will be contained in the communication of the secretary of war, to which I need scarcely invite your earnest attention.

" In my message delivered in April last, I referred to the promise of the abundant crops with which we were cheered.. The grain crops, generally, have since been harvested, and the yield has proven to be the most abundant ever known in our history. Many believe the supply adequate to two years' consumption of our population. Cotton, sugar, tobacco, forming a surplus of the production of our agriculture, and furnishing the basis of our commercial interchange, present the most cheering promises ever known. Providence has smiled on the labor which extracts the teeming wealth of our soil in all parts of our Confederacy.

" It is the more gratifying to be able to give you this, because, in need of large and increased expenditure, in support of our army, elevated and purified by that sacred cause they maintain, our fellow-citizens, of every condition of life, exhibit most self-sacrificing devotion. They manifest a laudable pride of upholding their independence, unaided by any resources other than their own, and the immense wealth which a fertilizing and genial climate has accumulated in this Confederacy of agriculturists, could not be more strongly displayed than in

the large revenues which, with eagerness, they have contributed at the call of their country. In the single article of cotton, the subscriptions to the loan proposed by the government cannot fall short of fifty millions of dollars, and will probably exceed that sum; and scarcely an article required for the consumption of our army is provided otherwise than by subscription to the produce loan, so happily devised by your wisdom. The secretary of the treasury, in his report submitted to you, will give you the amplest details connected with that branch of the public service; but it is not alone in their prompt pecuniary contributions that the noble race of freemen who inhabit these states evidence how worthy they are of those liberties which they so well know how to defend. In numbers far exceeding those authorized by your laws, they have pressed the tender of their services against the enemy. Their attitude of calm and sublime devotion to their country; the cool and confident courage with which they are already preparing to meet the invasion, whatever proportions it may assume; the assurance that their sacrifices and their services will be renewed from year to year with unfailing purpose, until they have made good to the uttermost their rights to self-government; the generous and almost unequivocal confidence which they display in their government during the pending struggle,—all combine to present a spectacle such as the world has rarely, if ever, seen. To speak of subjugating such a people, so united and determined, is to speak in a language incomprehensible to them; to resist attack on their rights or their liberties is with them an instinct. Whether this war shall last one, or three, or five years, is a problem they leave to be solved by the enemy alone. It will last till the enemy shall have withdrawn from their borders; till their political rights, their altars, and their homes are freed from invasion. Then, and then only, will they rest from this struggle, to enjoy, in peace, the blessings which, with the favor of Providence, they have secured by the aid of their own strong hearts and steady arms.   "JEFFERSON DAVIS."

Among the acts adopted by the rebel Congress, one of the first was for a day of thanksgiving for "the victory at Manassas," which was expressed in the following language: —

"*Resolved*, That we recognize the hand of the Most High God, the King of kings and the Lord of lords, in the glorious victory with which he hath crowned our army at Manassas; and that the people of the Confederate States are invited, by appropriate services on the ensuing Sabbath, to offer up their united thanksgiving and praise for this mighty deliverance.

"*Resolved*, That, deeply deploring the necessity which has washed the soil of our country with the blood of so many of her noblest sons, we offer to their respective families and friends our warmest and most cordial sympathy, assuring them that the sacrifice made will be consecrated in the hearts of our people, and will there enshrine the names of the gallant dead as the champions of free and constitutional liberty."

Measures were taken to strengthen the rebel armies, and to provide ways and means for meeting the great expenditures incurred by carrying on the war. For the latter purpose the government issued a large amount of treasury notes; and a favorite measure was the pledge or contribution of cotton, to be stored by the government, and shipped, as occasion offered, to Europe, or retained till such time as the blockade should be raised, and then sold in the depleted markets of England and France. In the way of loans of money the rebel government had met with little success, and the expedient of contributing cotton had been resorted to in order to meet the deficiencies which were already becoming alarming in the rebel exchequer. This measure, though perhaps more successful than the ordinary loan, was hardly so much so as had been anticipated; while the impossibility of converting the cotton to any considerable extent, so long as the blockade continued, made it of little practical use to the government, except so far as it was the basis on which to issue "Confederate notes."

The Congress, assuming to represent a nation among the nations, adopted the doctrines of international law proposed by the Paris congress of 1856, except that relating to privateering, — a system upon which they relied to damage the northern states. Upon the same assumption Mr. Davis was authorized to appoint commissioners to courts in Europe, with more extensive powers than those already there possessed, who should attempt to secure the recognition of the Confederacy, and should represent it as a sovereign power. Measures of extraordinary severity against alien enemies and those who should indicate any sympathy for the Union cause were adopted, thus encouraging the persecutions with which the Unionists were pursued, and crushing out all show of opposition to secession and rebellion. An act was passed admitting Missouri to the Confederacy, recognizing the fugitive Governor Jackson and his compeers as the government of that state, and providing for the "protection" of the citizens of the state against "invasion" by the United States.

The sessions of the Richmond Congress were often secret, by which means they kept from the knowledge of the north some of their most important measures, and deprived the federal government of advantages which they themselves enjoyed by the open sessions and immediate publication of the action of the Congress of the United States. This secrecy, however, was not always agreeable to the people of the south, and loud protests were occasionally uttered by some of the southern papers against it. But the ruling spirits understood the methods by which their purposes were best to be obtained; and though the rule of close sessions was somewhat re-laxed, they did not hesitate to adhere to it whenever they considered it desirable.

The governments of the several states co-operated with the Confederate government in vigorous measures to increase the armies, strengthen fortifications, and otherwise to aid the rebel cause and injure the Union. The manufacture of arms and ordnance stores was encouraged as much as possible, though with-out affording any adequate supply. For the most part the rebel authorities depended upon the importation of these articles from Europe, which was effected by not infrequent evasions of the blockade, and by transportation over the Mexican boundary into Texas. The people appeared almost unanimously the ardent sup-porters of the rebellion, and submitted with apparent cheerfulness to many inconveniences and wants which they already experienced. Soldiers were not wanting, and while the able-bodied whites freely joined the army, the cul-tivation of the soil continued undiminished. The system of slavery was the strength of the rebellion, for the army of blacks on the planta-tions were maintaining the army of soldiers in their campaigns, and were also performing the severer labors of the camp and fortifications. Servile insurrections were scarcely feared, and the escape of slaves along the lines occupied by the federal forces was, as yet, a matter of little account.

Thus had the rebellion assumed gigantic proportions, and the seceded states presented a compact and strong confederacy, ruled by men bold, unscrupulous, defiant. The result of the battle of Bull Run, while it opened the eyes of the north to the strength and determination of the rebels, and in some degree to the real proportions of the rebellion, also made the rebels stronger and more confident of success. Those who had before lacked confidence be-came bold; and among the people, as well as the leaders, the cause gained infinitely in strength, and rebel generals and soldiers now looked only for victory.

CHAPTER XLV.

IN the history of a rebellion of such gigantic proportions and spread over so wide a territory, we are obliged to call the reader's attention somewhat abruptly from one field of operations to another, as the current events by their im-portance seem to demand. We now return to Missouri, and the administration of the military department of the west under General Fre-mont, whose appointment to that command has already been mentioned. General Fremont was in Europe when the rebellion broke out, and was appointed a major-general before he returned. While there he gave his influence and his services in behalf of his country, by enlightening public sentiment, and procuring arms of which, through the treachery of Secre-tary Floyd, the Union was much in need. His appointment was hailed with satisfaction by a large number of his personal and political friends, who had the greatest confidence in his ability and energy, as well as in his views of the rebellion and the measures required to suppress it. They were gratified that, after some delay, he was appointed to the important command of the western department, and anticipated some successful campaigns in that quarter, under his direction. But, from his former position as the candidate for the presidency, supported, in 1856, by the Republican party against Mr. Buchanan, there were not a few who were in some measure opposed to him, by the remembrance of former political associations. There were also some who were personally not well disposed towards him, and yet others who, upon a review of his career, doubted his capacity for a large command.

Under such circumstances General Fremont entered upon his duties, surrounded by much greater and more numerous difficulties than the commanders of armies nearer to the seat of government and more directly under the charge of the general-in-chief and the war department. Much of the burden of raising, organizing, and supplying the troops of his department was necessarily imposed upon him and his staff, while at the same time the difficulties of arming, equipping, and supplying these troops were much greater than at the east. The deficiency of good arms and equipments was especially felt, and caused great delays in preparing his regiments for the field. Such delays, though unavoidable, and diminished as much as possible by General Fremont's devotion of his private means and credit in aid of the government, created some complaint, especially at the time when General Lyon, in the face of a much greater numerical force of rebels, asked for reinforcements, which he much needed. General Fremont believed that he could not send forward the required reënforcements with safety to St. Louis and Eastern Missouri. His force, exclusive of the home guards, was not so large

as had been believed, and when he was nearly ready to send additional troops to the south-west, the exigencies of the service at the east, after the disaster at Bull Run, caused the government to order him to send east several regiments which were intended for the western service. Whether or not there were unnecessary delays in the preparation of his troops it is difficult to decide, amid the conflicting statements which were put forth. General Fremont, however, was not himself remiss in attention to his duties, and the delays occasioned by his subordinates, or the extravagance of his quartermaster's department, which were subsequently alleged and much discussed, were not altogether chargeable upon him.

After the battle of Wilson's Creek, in which the brave General Lyon fell, and the retreat of the federal forces from Springfield to Rolla, General Fremont increased his exertions to organize and equip an army to meet the rebel forces which were threatening an advance towards the state capital, and also upon St. Louis. The secessionists of Missouri, encouraged by what they called the success of the rebel army at Wilson's Creek, but what was really a repulse, though followed by the necessary retreat of the unequal federal force, were collecting in various parts of the state, forming guerrilla bands or organizing to join the army of Price, under the name of "state guards." To aid in suppressing these rebellious demonstrations, Governor Gamble issued a proclamation, calling for forty-two thousand volunteers from the militia, to serve for six months. These troops were organized as rapidly as they could be armed and equipped, and were so disposed as to aid the federal forces, but were not concentrated in any large body, or placed wholly under the direction of the commander of the department.

But General Fremont's attention was not confined to a campaign in Missouri. Operations in Kentucky and Tennessee were also receiving his attention, those states, and the movements from Cairo as a base, being under his command. Preparations were made for an advance down the Mississippi, and into Western Kentucky and Tennessee, against the rebel forces which had taken up strong positions there, and were threatening a movement towards St. Louis. To organize forces for this wide field of operations required great energy and much time; but the preparations progressed rapidly in spite of the difficulties alluded to.

While these preparations were being made, skirmishes and guerrilla fights became more frequent, and the spirit of secession, even among those who had not taken up arms, was every where becoming bold and dangerous. The late governor, Jackson, with the secession members of his legislature, assumed to be the legitimate government of the state, and were preparing to hold a session at Lexington, or even in Jefferson City, if the forces under Price could take that place and protect them in it. The tide of rebellion, which had receded for a time, was now rolling back again over the state.

In this condition of affairs, General Fremont, deeming it absolutely necessary to resort to the most stringent measures to suppress the rebellion, and to prevent secession sentiment from culminating every where, in open resistance to the federal authority, in which judgment he was supported by all truly loyal men in the state, issued the following proclamation : —

"HEADQUARTERS OF THE WESTERN DEPARTMENT, }
"ST. LOUIS, Saturday, *August* 31. }

" Circumstances, in my judgment, of sufficient urgency, render it necessary that the commanding general of this department should assume the administrative powers of the state. Its disorganized condition, the helplessness of the civil authority, the total insecurity of life, and the devastation of property by bands of murderers and marauders, who infest nearly every county in the state, and avail themselves of the public misfortunes and the vicinity of a hostile force to gratify private and neighborhood vengeance, and who find an enemy wherever they find plunder, finally demand the severest measures to repress the daily increasing crimes and outrages which are driving off the inhabitants and ruining the state. In this condition the public safety and the success of our arms require unity of purpose, without let or hinderance to the prompt administration of affairs.

" In order, therefore, to suppress disorders, to maintain as far as now practicable the public peace, and to give security and protection to the persons and property of loyal citizens, I do hereby extend and declare martial law throughout the state of Missouri. The lines of the army of occupation in this state are, for the present, declared to extend from Leavenworth, by way of the posts of Jefferson City, Rolla, and junction, to Cape Girardeau, on the Mississippi River.

" All persons who shall be taken with arms in their hands within these lines shall be tried by court martial, and, if found guilty, will be shot. The property, real and personal, of all persons in the State of Missouri, who shall take up arms against the United States, or who shall be directly proven to have taken an active part with their enemies in the field, is declared to be confiscated to the public use, and their slaves, if any they have, are hereby declared free men. All persons who shall be proven to have destroyed, after the publication of this order, railroad tracks, bridges, or telegraphs, shall suffer the extreme penalty of the law. All persons engaged in treasonable correspondence, in giving or procuring aid to the enemies of the United States, in disturbing the public tranquillity by creating and circulating false reports, or incendiary documents, are in their own interest warned that they are exposing themselves.

" All persons who have been led away from their allegiance are required to return to their homes forthwith : any such absence, without sufficient cause, will be held to be presumptive evidence against them.

"The object of this declaration is to place in the hands of the military authorities the power to give instantaneous effect to existing laws, and to supply such deficiencies as the conditions of war demand. But it is not intended to suspend the ordinary tribunals of the country where the law will be administered by the civil officers in the usual manner and with their customary authority, while the same can be peaceably exercised.

"The commanding general will labor vigilantly for the public welfare, and in his efforts for their safety hopes to obtain not only the acquiescence, but the active support, of the people of the country.

"J. C. FREMONT,
"Major-General commanding."

This proclamation occasioned a good deal of discussion, not only in the territory where martial law was declared, but throughout the country, and especially in the border states and in the seceded states. The loyal people of Missouri accepted it as a necessity, a relief from evils much greater than the inconveniences and restraint of martial law; and, for the most part, they approved of the stringency and completeness with which it carried out the principles of the recent legislation of Congress with regard to the confiscation of the property of rebels, including their slaves. But while the public opinion of the loyal people most interested in the matter was clearly in favor of the declaration of martial law, and of the confiscation of the property and the liberation of the slaves of rebels, in Kentucky the latter measure was deprecated among a portion of the Union men, and was strongly denounced by those who sympathized with the south every where. Earnest representations were made to the President by Mr. Holt, of Kentucky, and other citizens of the border slave states, for the purpose of inducing him to rescind or modify the order. The President, in consequence of these representa-

tions, privately requested General Fremont to modify that part of his order relating to the confiscation of the property and the liberation of the slaves of rebels, so that it should conform more exactly with the act of Congress. General Fremont, in reply, desired that the President should make an open order for such modification, and accordingly, the President wrote as follows: —

"WASHINGTON, D. C., *September* 11, 1861.
"TO MAJOR-GENERAL JOHN C. FREMONT.

"SIR: Yours of the 8th, in answer to mine of the 2d instant, was just received. Assured that you, upon the ground, could better judge of the necessities of your position than I could at this distance, on seeing your proclamation of August 30, I perceived no general objection to it; the particular clause, however, in relation to the confiscation of property and the liberation of slaves appeared to me to be objectionable in its non-conformity to the act of Congress, passed the 6th of last August, upon the same subjects, and hence I wrote you, expressing my wish that that clause should be modified accordingly. Your answer just received expresses the preference on your part that I should make an open order for the modification, which I very cheerfully do. It is therefore ordered that the said clause of said proclamation be so modified, held, and construed as to conform with, and not to transcend, the provisions on the same subject contained in the act of Congress entitled 'An Act to confiscate property used for insurrectionary purposes,' approved August 6, 1861, and that said act be published at length with this order. Your obedient servant,

"A. LINCOLN."

In this connection it may be observed that the rebels made complaint of another portion of the proclamation, and inquired of General Fremont if it was his purpose to shoot wounded men who might be taken prisoners. To this the general replied, —

"You have wholly misapprehended the meaning of the proclamation. Without undertaking to determine the condition of any man engaged in this rebellion, I desire it to be clearly understood that the proclamation is intended distinctly to recognize the usual rights of an open enemy in the field, and to be in all respects strictly conformable with the usages of war. It is hardly necessary for me to say that it was not prepared with any purpose to ignore the ordinary rights of humanity with respect to wounded men, or those who are humanely engaged in alleviating their sufferings."

Early in September the movements of the rebel forces were such as to require a concentration of the federal troops and active operations to defeat their purposes. There had been, as already stated, frequent skirmishes between detached bodies of federal troops and the rebel forces in various parts of the state. Now a large army was collected under General Price, who threatened the capital of the state, or at least to get possession of Lexington, a hundred and sixty miles farther up the river, where the rebel Governor Jackson and his legislature proposed to establish themselves, and had already been in session, and which place might form an advantageous base of future operations. A small federal force, composed chiefly of home guards, was stationed at Lexington, under Colonel Peabody, which had already had a skirmish with a body of rebels and repulsed them. To this place reënforcements were sent from Jefferson City, consisting of seven hundred cavalry, followed in a few days by a regiment called the "Irish Brigade," under Colonel Mulligan. These reënforcements made the force at Lexington a little more than twenty-six hundred men, of whom Colonel Mulligan now assumed command. At the same time several bodies of troops, under General Sturgis, were ordered to march towards Lexington from the north-western part of the state, and a body of Kansas troops, under General Lane, was expected to move from that state towards the same point.

Some slight fortifications had been constructed at Lexington when Colonel Mulligan arrived there. These he strengthened and extended as quickly as possible, an attack from the rebel forces being imminent. The position chosen for defence was about half a mile from the river, between the old and new towns of Lexington, which are about a mile apart. The work upon the intrenchments was unremitting, and by the 12th of September a part of them were completed; but an important work of defence on the west side, towards New Lexington, was yet weak. On that day the scouts, and advanced pickets who had been driven in, reported the approach of the rebels in force, and it was necessary to prepare at once to meet the assailants. Colonel Mulligan's artillery consisted of but six brass field pieces, and two mortars, which were of little use, as he had no shell. These he disposed of advantageously, and meeting the advance rebel force, which approached from the south, at some distance from his main position, he partially repulsed them with some loss. The next day, however, reënforcements of the rebels began to come up, and in such numbers that they were gradually enabled to surround the position occupied by Colonel Mulligan. The entire rebel force was stated to be more than thirty thousand, with thirteen pieces of artillery. Finding the capture of the place attended with some difficulty, notwithstanding their numbers, they collected large quantities of hemp, in bales, with which they formed breastworks, and advanced gradually under their protection, as in a regular siege, and were thus enabled to bring their guns to bear upon the weakest portion of the federal defences. These operations of the enemy were resisted by the federal forces as well as their small numbers would admit, by frequent skirmishes and occasional artillery shots. Colonel Mulligan and his men were determined to hold the place as long as possible: in the mean time, he despatched messengers for reënforcements, but all or a portion of them were captured by the rebels. So strong were the rebel forces, and so disposed, that any reënforcements, unless in large numbers, would probably have been captured or driven back, without being able to afford any aid to the beleaguered troops. They not only held positions on all sides of the federal troops on the south side of the river, but they also had possession of the river itself, and could prevent reënforcements from the north, whence it was expected General Sturgis would arrive. It was reported that on that side of the river the rebels actually compelled an Iowa regiment to retreat again towards St. Joseph.*

The rebel forces advanced in such numbers, and gained such strong positions, that the situation of the federal troops became desperate, and grew worse from day to day. The rebels threw shot and shell constantly within the federal lines, and among the horses and mules picketed in a somewhat exposed position, killing many animals, and creating the danger of a "stampede" of the whole number. On the 17th the rebel lines were so advanced that Colonel Mulligan's force was cut off from the river whence they obtained their supply of water. Fortunately, a heavy rain, at intervals, afforded some relief, though the troops were in so great want of water that they spread their blankets to collect the falling rain, and then wrung them over their camp kettles. This, with a small quantity obtained during a brief truce, was all that they had for more than two days. From the 16th to the 21st the fighting was continued almost incessantly, even the

nights bringing no cessation of the roar of artillery, while in the bright moonlight there were frequent sorties and skirmishes outside the works. Owing to the protection of the intrenchments and breastworks, however, the loss of life on either side was not great. Through all this time the federal troops, though worn down with fatigue, evinced great bravery, and a determination to hold out to the last, in the hope that reënforcements might come to their relief. The home guards, however, who were not so well disciplined, or inured to hardship, as some of the other troops, at last became disheartened, and on the 21st raised a white flag upon an outwork which they were defending, and where they were exposed to a severe fire. Colonel Mulligan immediately sent a detachment to take down the flag, and a desperate but unsuccessful charge was immediately after made upon the nearest rebel battery. The home guards then retired from their position to the inner line of intrenchments, and refused to fight longer. A white flag was again raised, this time from the centre of the fortifications, and the fire of the enemy soon slackened and ceased.

In this state of affairs Colonel Mulligan called a council of his officers, when it was decided to capitulate. Officers were despatched to meet those sent forward by General Price, and a surrender, as prisoners of war, was agreed upon; it being decided that the officers should be held, and the rank and file, after laying down their arms, should be permitted to march north, to a point on the Hannibal and St. Joseph Railroad. It was with much regret and dissatisfaction that Colonel Mulligan, and most of his officers and men, yielded to the necessity of a surrender; but to attempt to hold out longer, with his men exhausted by constant duty, and suffering for want of water, — a want more terrible to the weary men than the full ranks of the enemy, — and with an overwhelming force to contend against, would have resulted only in greater suf-

---

* This report probably arose from the fact that an Iowa regiment, under Colonel Scott, had a skirmish near Liberty, with a rebel force on its way to join Price, which is mentioned in the following pages.

fering and loss of life without any advantage. The terms of capitulation were carried out, and the rebel forces took possession of the town and the federal position, manifesting their joy at their not very glorious victory by disorderly carousals, in which some of the federal troops were outraged in a cowardly manner.

The loss on either side was small, considering the length of the contest, which was owing to the protection which each side had, the one from their intrenchments, and the other from the bales of hemp, which they moved before them in their advance. The federal loss was stated to be about three hundred killed and wounded. It was believed by the federal troops that the loss of the enemy was much greater; but General Price, in his report to Governor Jackson, states the rebel loss as twenty-five killed and seventy-five wounded.

The surrender of Colonel Mulligan's force, and the possession of Lexington, were great advantages to the rebels. Besides the prisoners and arms captured, they obtained a considerable amount of commissary stores, and many horses and wagons. A still more valuable prize was nearly a million of dollars in specie, which Colonel Mulligan had taken from the bank, and concealed, for safe keeping. In his official report, Price charged the federal officer with robbing the bank, and claimed that he had caused it to be restored; but it was subsequently asserted that the money was taken away when the rebels left the place. Another prize was the great seal of the state, which had been carried away from the capital by the disloyal secretary, and left at this place for further use.

While the unequal contest at Lexington was proceeding, a less important affair occurred at Blue Mills, near Liberty, a town farther up the Missouri, and near the western boundary of the state. A part of the third Iowa regiment, with a small number of home guards and a few artillerists with one cannon, numbering in all five hundred and seventy men, under the command of Lieutenant-Colonel Scott, were proceeding from Cameron, in the northern part of the state, to coöperate with a similar force, under Colonel Smith, which moved from St. Joseph, in the pursuit of a rebel force of about forty-five hundred men, which was marching from St. Joseph towards Lexington. Colonel Scott came up with the rebel force on the 17th, before he had effected a junction with Colonel Smith, to whom he had twice despatched messengers, informing him of his progress. After waiting a short time for some tidings of the latter's approach, Colonel Scott concluded to advance upon the enemy; and again sending word to Colonel Smith, he moved forward. His advance soon came upon the pickets of the rebels, who had turned back to attack the pursuers with their superior numbers, before a junction could be formed. The skirmish of pickets soon grew into a more serious conflict. The rebels attacked with a confidence of success, and Colonel Scott's artillerists were soon shot or scattered, so that the single piece of artillery was useless, and came near falling into the hands of the rebels. The infantry, however, bravely resisted the attack, though they were soon obliged to fall back towards Liberty. They retreated so slowly that the enemy, fearing reenforcements, did not follow up their advantage. Colonel Smith's force reached Liberty the same night, and the next morning it was proposed to attack the rebels; but it was found that they had left their position in the night, and had crossed the river. It was this engagement which probably gave rise to the report that an Iowa regiment, on its way to reënforce Colonel Mulligan at Lexington, had been turned back by a part of Price's force. Colonel Scott's force, however, was not marching to the relief of Lexington, though it appeared that a messenger had been despatched from St. Joseph, with orders to Colonel Smith to proceed with the united forces to Lexington. The messenger did not reach Colonel Smith, and he, therefore, did not continue his march beyond the point where Colonel Scott had met the enemy.

General Fremont was severely blamed by many for not promptly reënforcing Colonel Mulligan with sufficient forces to defeat the army of Price. It appears, however, that orders for such reënforcement had been sent to some of those forces the position of which would probably enable them to reach Lexington most readily. Whether there were other available troops in considerable numbers, which could safely be sent to reënforce Colonel Mulligan, is a disputed question. It will be remembered, however, that in consequence of the guerrilla warfare which the rebels were carrying on in Missouri, the federal troops were scattered in small bodies over a great extent of territory, while, on the other hand, the strong forces, perhaps more formidable than the army of Price, which were threatening an invasion from the south, rendered it prudent not to weaken too much the federal forces in the eastern and south-eastern part of the state.

But it was also stated that Colonel Mulligan was sent to Lexington to protect the bank and the loyal citizens there, who were subjected to the outrages of the secessionists, and to keep the state government of the rebels from assembling, and that it was not intended that he should undertake to hold the place against a large force; but upon the sudden approach of Price's army, he was induced by the loyal citizens to remain for their protection. Under such circumstances the necessity of reënforcements could not be seen until too late to move them a great distance. The following despatch from General Fremont, announcing the result of the attack on Lexington, indicates that the reënforcements were ordered, but did not reach the place in season to afford relief:—

"TO COLONEL E. D. TOWNSEND, ADJUTANT-GENERAL.

"I have a telegram from Brookfield that Lexington has fallen into Price's hands, he having cut off Colonel Mulligan's supply of water. Reënforcements, four thousand strong, under Sturgis, by capture of the ferry boats, had no means of crossing the river in time. Lane's force from the southward and Davis's from the south-east, — upwards of eleven thousand men in all, — could not get there in time. I am taking the field myself, and hope to destroy the enemy either before or after the junction of the forces under McCulloch. Please notify the President immediately.

"J. C. FREMONT."

CHAPTER XLVI.

GENERAL FREMONT, after nearly completing the organization of the army of the western department, and preparing an expedition down the Mississippi, which, in consequence of the preparations of the rebels, was deemed important, left St. Louis on the 27th of September, to assume command of the army then being concentrated to operate against Price, in Western, and McCulloch in South-western Missouri. The sudden appearance of Price, with his large body of " state troops," had compelled General Fremont to change his plans, which appear to have been to lead the expedition down the Mississippi. But it was necessary, before undertaking the latter movement, to check the progress of Price, and to render the state safe from invasion by McCulloch. After remaining near Jefferson City for some time, in order to concentrate his army, General Fremont moved west in pursuit of Price, who was already marching to the south-west, apparently for the purpose of forming a junction with the forces of McCulloch. His army was composed of five divisions, under Generals Hunter, Pope, Sigel, McKinstry, and Asboth, and numbered about thirty thousand men, including five thousand cavalry, with eighty-six pieces of excellent artillery. In addition to this force, Generals Sturgis and Lane were advancing from Kansas to join General Fremont at some point on the Osage, and a force then stationed at Rolla was to meet him near the same river. Lack of transportation and forage delayed the movement of the army; but about the middle of September the march was commenced, the several divisions moving by different routes towards the Osage. The rising waters rendered the fording of this river unsafe, and as there were no sufficient ferry boats to transport the army and trains quickly, there was a delay of several days for the construction of a bridge. This being completed, the army crossed the Osage and marched towards Springfield, near which it was anticipated that Price and McCulloch would unite their forces, and thus form an army of forty thousand men.

When about thirty miles from Springfield, a small body of cavalry, under Major White, was sent forward to make a reconnoissance in the direction of that town. Subsequently, a detachment of one hundred and sixty of the squadron of cavalry which acted as a body guard to General Fremont, under the command of Major Zagonyi,* was sent forward, with orders

to join the reconnoitring party, and then for the combined force, numbering about three hundred men, to attack the rebel garrison, supposed to be three or four hundred strong. When within two hours' march of the town, Major Zagonyi learned that a considerable rebel force, on its way to join Price's army, had arrived at Springfield, making the force there about two thousand strong. Sending back for reënforcements, Major Zagonyi, without waiting for them to arrive, determined to make a bold and perhaps imprudent dash into the rebel camp, and, by surprising them, in their confusion hoped to gain some slight advantage, which could be followed up by the reënforcements. A loyal farmer offered to conduct the small force by a circuitous route to the rear of the rebel position, and they accordingly made a wide *détour* for that purpose. In the mean time, Major White, the commander of the reconnoitring party, who was sick, and had stopped at a farm house to rest, rode forward with a half dozen men, to join the expedition; but being ignorant of the *détour*, proceeded by the direct road towards Springfield, and was taken prisoner. This circumstance, and the information of their scouts, put the rebels on their guard, and they were, therefore, preparing for action when Major Zagonyi reached a position from which he might make an attack. Of the brilliant and successful charge which followed, we make extracts from a most graphic description, written by a member of General Fremont's staff, who became acquainted with the facts upon the ground.†

"Making a *détour* of twelve miles, Zagonyi approached the position of the enemy. They were encamped half a mile west of Springfield, upon a hill which sloped to the east. Along the

* Major Zagonyi was a Hungarian by birth, who had been a cavalry officer under General Bem, in the Hungarian struggle for independence. He proposed to General Fremont to raise a picked company of cavalry for his body-guard, and such was the readiness to enlist in that service, that Major Zagonyi soon had three fine companies, and a fourth was raised and left in St. Louis

when General Fremont took the field. Under the command of their experienced and dashing commander, this body of cavalry soon became admirably trained, and evinced a spirit not surpassed by any similar force in the service.

† Major Dorsheimer, in the Atlantic Monthly.

northern side of their camp was a broad and well-travelled road; along the southern side a narrow lane ran down to a brook at the foot of the hill; the space between, about three hundred yards broad, was the field of battle. Along the west side of the field, separating it from the county fair-ground, was another lane, connecting the main road and the first-mentioned lane. The side of the hill was clear, but its summit, which was broad and flat, was covered with a rank growth of small timber, so dense as to be impervious to horse. . . .

"The foe was advised of the intended attack. When Major White was brought into their camp, they were preparing to defend their position. As appears from the confessions of prisoners, they had twenty-two hundred men, of whom four hundred were cavalry, the rest being infantry, armed with shot-guns, American rifles, and revolvers. Twelve hundred of their foot were posted along the edge of the wood upon the crest of the hill. The cavalry were stationed upon the extreme left, on top of a spur of the hill and in front of a patch of timber. Sharp-shooters were concealed behind the trees close to the fence alongside the lane, and a small number in some underbrush near the foot of the hill. Another detachment guarded their train, holding possession of the county fair-ground, which was surrounded by a high board-fence.

"This position was unassailable by cavalry from the road, the only point of attack being down the lane on the right; and the enemy were so disposed as to command this approach perfectly. The lane was a blind one, being closed, after passing the brook, by fences and ploughed land; it was, in fact, a *cul-de-sac*. If the infantry should stand, nothing could save the rash assailants. There are horsemen sufficient to sweep the little band before them, as helplessly as the withered forest leaves in the grasp of the autumn winds; there are deadly marksmen lying behind the trees upon the heights, and lurking in the long grass upon the lowlands; while a long line of foot stand upon the summit of the slope, who, only stepping a few paces back into the forest, may defy the boldest riders. Yet, down this narrow lane, leading into the very jaws of death, came the three hundred. . . .

"They pass the fair-ground. They are at the corner of the lane where the wood begins. It runs close to the fence on their left for a hundred yards, and beyond it they see white tents gleaming. They are half way past the forest, when, sharp and loud, a volley of musketry bursts upon the head of the column; horses stagger, riders reel and fall, but the troop presses forward undismayed. The farther corner of the wood is reached, and Zagonyi beholds the terrible array. Amazed, he involuntarily checks his horse. The rebels are not surprised. There to his left they stand crowning the height, foot and horse ready to ingulf him, if he shall be rash enough to go on. The road he is following declines rapidly. There is but one thing to do, — run the gantlet, gain the cover of the hill, and charge up the steep. These thoughts pass quicker than they can be told. He waves his sabre over his head, and shouting, "Forward! follow me! quick trot! gallop!" he dashes headlong down the stony road. The first company and most of the second follow. From the left a thousand muzzles belch forth a hissing flood of bullets; the poor fellows clutch wildly at the air and fall from their saddles, and maddened horses throw themselves against the fences. Their speed is not for an instant checked; farther down the hill they fly, like wasps driven by the leaden storm. Sharp volleys pour out of the underbrush at the left, clearing wide gaps through their ranks. They leap the brook, take down the fence, and draw up under the shelter of the hill. Zagonyi looks around him, and to his horror sees that only a fourth of his men are with him. He cries, 'They do not come, — we are lost!' and frantically waves his sabre.

" He has not long to wait. The delay of the rest of the guard was not from hesitation. When Captain Foley reached the lower corner of the wood and saw the enemy's line, he thought a flank attack might be advantageously made. He ordered some of his men to dismount and take down the fence. This was done under a severe fire. Several men fell, and he found the wood so dense that it could not be penetrated. Looking down the hill, he saw the flash of Zagonyi's sabre, and at once gave the order, 'Forward!' At the same time, Lieutenant Kennedy, a stalwart Kentuckian, shouted, 'Come on, boys! remember Old Kentucky!' and the third company of the guard, fire on every side of them, — from behind trees, from under the fences, — with thundering strides and loud cheers, poured down the slope and rushed to the side of Zagonyi. They have lost seventy dead and wounded men, and the carcasses of horses are strewn along the lane. . . .

" The remnant of the guard are now in the field under the hill, and from the shape of the ground, the rebel fire sweeps with the roar of a whirlwind over their heads. Here we will leave them for a moment, and trace the fortunes of the Prairie Scouts.*

" When Foley brought his troop to a halt, Captain Fairbanks, at the head of the first company of scouts, was at the point where the first volley of musketry had been received. The narrow lane was crowded by a dense mass of struggling horses, and filled with the tumult of battle. Captain Fairbanks says, — and he is corroborated by several of his men who were near, — that at this moment an officer of the guard rode up to him, and said, 'They are flying; take your men down that lane, and cut off their retreat,' — pointing to the lane at the

left. Captain Fairbanks was not able to identify the person who gave this order. It certainly did not come from Zagonyi, who was several hundred yards farther on. Captain Fairbanks executed the order, followed by the second company of Prairie Scouts, under Captain Kehoe. When this movement was made, Captain Naughton, with the third Irish dragoons, had not reached the corner of the lane. He came up at a gallop, and was about to follow Fairbanks, when he saw a guardsman, who pointed in the direction in which Zagonyi had gone. He took this for an order, and obeyed it. When he reached the gap in the fence, made by Foley, not seeing any thing of the guard, he supposed they had passed through at that place, and gallantly attempted to follow. Thirteen men fell in a few minutes. He was shot in the arm and dismounted. Lieutenant Connolly spurred into the underbrush, and received two balls through the lungs and one in the left shoulder. The dragoons, at the outset not more than fifty strong, were broken, and, dispirited by the loss of their officers, retired. A sergeant rallied a few, and brought them up to the gap again, and they were again driven back. Five of the boldest passed down the hill, joined Zagonyi, and were conspicuous by their valor during the rest of the day. Fairbanks and Kehoe, having gained the rear and left of the enemy's position, made two or three assaults upon detached parties of the foe, but did not join in the main attack.

" I now return to the guard. It is forming under the shelter of the hill. In front, with a gentle inclination, rises a grassy slope, broken by occasional tree-stumps. A line of fire upon the summit marks the position of the rebel infantry ; and nearer and on the top of a lower eminence to the right stand their horse. Up to this time no guardsman has struck a blow ; but blue coats and bay horses lie thick along the bloody lane. Their time has come. Lieutenant Maythenyi, with thirty men, is ordered

---
* The name given to Major White's squadron.

to attack the cavalry. With sabres flashing over their heads, the little band of heroes spring towards their tremendous foe. Right upon the centre they charge. The dense mass. opens, the blue coats force their way in, and the whole rebel squadron scatter, in disgraceful flight, through the cornfields in the rear. The bays follow them, sabring the fugitives. Days after, the enemy's horses lay thick among the uncut corn.

"Zagonyi holds his main body until May-thenyi disappears in the cloud of rebel cavalry; then his voice rises through the air, — 'In open order, — charge!' The line opens out to give play to their sword-arm, Steeds respond to the ardor of their riders; and, quick as thought, with thrilling cheers, the noble hearts rush into the leaden torrent which pours down the in-cline. With unabated fire the gallant fellows press through. Their fierce onset is not even checked. The foe do not wait for them, — they waver, break, and fly. The guardsmen spur into the midst of the rout, and their fast-falling swords work a terrible revenge. Some of the boldest of the southrons retreat into the woods, and continue a murderous fire from behind trees and thickets. Seven guard horses fall upon a space not more than twenty feet square. As his steed sinks under him, one of the officers is caught around the shoulders by a grape-vine, and hangs dangling in the air until he is cut down by his friends.

" The rebel foot are flying in furious haste from the field. Some take refuge in the fair-ground, some hurry into the cornfield; but the greater part run along the edge of the wood, swarm over the fence into the road, and hasten to the village. The guardsmen follow. Zagonyi leads them. . . .

"The conflict now rages through the vil-lage, in the public square, and along the streets. Up and down the guards ride in squads of three or four, and wherever they see a group of the enemy, charge upon and scatter them. It is

hand-to-hand. No one but has a share in the fray. . . .

" Meanwhile it has grown dark. The foe have left the village and the battle has ceased. The assembly is sounded, and the guard gathers in the Plaza. Not more than eighty mounted men appear; the rest are killed, wounded, or unhorsed."

It had been General Fremont's intention to concentrate the several divisions of his army on a wide prairie, some miles from Springfield, where he might review and manœuvre them briefly before moving against the enemy. But the affair at Springfield made it advisable to march at once to that place, to protect the wounded soldiers and the loyal inhabitants from an attack. The whole army was, accordingly, ordered to march to Springfield, and in the course of two or three days all the divisions, except General Hunter's, arrived there. In-formation was received that Price was moving from Neosho towards Springfield, for the pur-pose of giving battle, being impelled to do so by the short term of service of his troops and the advice of McCulloch, who was reported to have joined him. Fugitive Unionists came in from the direction of Neosho, reporting a very large force advancing from that direction, and it appeared to be certain that a battle was im-minent. The federal army was eager to meet the enemy, and preparations were being made for an advance to attack him, when orders were received from Washington, relieving General Fremont of his command, and directing him to transfer it to General Hunter.

The proclamation of General Fremont, de-claring martial law in Missouri, with its pro-visions in relation to confiscation and the liberation of the slaves of rebels, had caused a strong feeling against him, and, although modified by the President, continued to make for him enemies among those who sustained the institution of slavery. There was a vari-ety of other causes, some of them personal, some of them political, and others of a military nature, which had made enemies for the general. Among others, Hon. F. P. Blair, a member of Congress and a colonel of one of the Missouri regiments, made charges against the general, some of which were of a serious character.[*] The secretary of war and the adjutant-general visited St. Louis in consequence of these charges, to examine into the position of affairs in the western department. General Fremont had already started on his expedition, and the secretary and the adjutant-general visited his camp and briefly reviewed a portion of his army. They brought with them the order for the removal, but its issue was suspended till after their return. Whether upon their report of the position of affairs or for other reasons, the order was finally issued on the 24th of October, and sent forward from St. Louis to reach the army just as a battle was confidently expected.

The order caused not a little excitement in the army, the men composing which had great confidence in their commander, and were attached to him by reason of certain traits of character and his previous history. General Hunter had not yet arrived at Springfield, and his position was not known. General Fremont, however, at once prepared to comply with the orders, and waited only for the arrival of General Hunter, at the urgent advice of his general officers. A large number of officers waited upon the general, and urgently desired that he should carry out his plan and attack the enemy,

without waiting for the, as yet uncertain, arrival of his successor. The reasons urged for so doing were cogent, and General Fremont consented, if General Hunter did not arrive before midnight on that day, — November 3, — to act upon the request, and the orders for the several divisions to move on the following morning were accordingly issued. But the movement was destined not to take place. General Hunter arrived within the limited time, and General Fremont, explaining to him the position of affairs, resigned the command into his hands. The following are the orders of General Fremont upon relinquishing the command : —

"HEADQUARTERS WESTERN DEPARTMENT, }
"SPRINGFIELD, MO., *November* 2, 1861. }

"SOLDIERS OF THE MISSISSIPPI ARMY: Agreeably to orders received this day, I take leave of you. Although our army has been of sudden growth, we have grown up together, and I have become familiar with the brave and generous spirits which you bring to the defence of your country, and which makes me anticipate for you a brilliant career. Continue as you have begun, and give to my successor the same cordial and enthusiastic support with which you have encouraged me. Emulate the splendid example which you have already before you, and let me remain as I am, proud of the noble army which I have thus far labored to bring together.

"Soldiers, I regret to leave you. Most sincerely I thank you for the regard and confidence you have invariably shown me. I deeply regret that I shall not have the honor to lead you to the victory which you are just about to win; but I shall claim the right to share with you in the joy of every triumph, and trust always to be personally remembered by my companions in arms.

"JOHN C. FREMONT,
"*Major-General.*"

General Hunter did not carry out General Fremont's plan to advance against Price. By

---

[*] The charges against General Fremont were, that he neglected his duty by remaining at the east for three weeks after his appointment to the command of the western department; that he neglected and refused to reënforce General Lyon when urged to do so, and allowed him to be sacrificed, while he himself, with great pomp, proceeded to fortify Bird's Point; that he expended enormous sums of government money, through the hands of personal favorites, in erecting useless fortifications around St. Louis; that he affected an almost "regal state," and denied interviews to officers and civilians having important business with him; that he brought from California certain favorites, to whom he gave government contracts and offices, through which they received large sums of money; and that he suffered Colonel Mulligan to be sacrificed at Lexington; with others of a similar character.

Benj. F. Butler

many it was declared that there was no considerable rebel army to contend with, and that the advance of General Fremont's large army to the south-west was a movement against a mythical enemy. But the accounts from Springfield, at the time, indicated that the forces under Price were large, and that he did make a movement towards that town, probably with the expectation of meeting a smaller force than the concentrated federal army. The presence of Price near Neosho, and undoubtedly with a large force, was shown by the agreement entered into between him and General Fremont, in relation to exchange of prisoners, treatment of non-combatants, and expression of political opinions by citizens. The arrival of all the divisions of the army at Springfield probably caused a speedy retrograde movement of the rebels during the delay which succeeded the change of command. The agreement above named was, for good reasons, repudiated by General Hunter, who saw that it might be used successfully to promote the cause of rebellion, though entered into by General Fremont for the purpose of mitigating the evils of war.

The rebels having ceased, for the time being, to threaten any movement in force, and the guerrilla warfare being still continued in various parts of the state, the army collected by General Fremont was again separated and moved to different points, leaving South-western Missouri again exposed to the advance of the rebel army, and greatly discouraging the loyal people of that region.

In concluding the narrative of this comparatively fruitless campaign, it is but just to give a further extract from the writer whose description of the cavalry charge has been quoted, and who wrote from personal knowledge, whatever may have been his sympathy for General Fremont. Reviewing the record of General Fremont's command in the west, he says, —

"In bringing these papers to a close, the writer cannot refrain from expressing his re-gret that circumstances have prevented him from making that exposition of affairs in the western department which the country has long expected. While he was in the field, General Fremont permitted the attacks of his enemies to pass unheeded, because he held them unworthy to be intruded upon more important occupations, and he would not be diverted from the great objects he was pursuing; since his recall, considerations affecting the public service, and the desire not at this time to embarrass the government with personal matters, have sealed his lips. I will not now disregard his wishes by entering into any detailed discussion of the charges which have been made against him; but I cannot lay down my pen without bearing voluntary testimony to the fidelity, energy, and skill which he brought to his high office. It will be hard for any one who was not a constant witness of his career to appreciate the labor which he assumed and successfully performed. From the first to the last hour of the day, there was no idle moment. No time was given to pleasure — none even to needed relaxation. Often, long after the strength of his body was spent, the force of his will bound him to exhausting toil. No religious zealot ever gave himself to his devotions with more absorbing abandonment than General Fremont to his hard, and, as it has proved, most thankless task. Time will verify the statement, that, whether as respects thoroughness or economy, his administration of affairs at the west will compare favorably with the transactions of any other department of the government, military or civil, during the last nine months. . . .

"When General Fremont reached St. Louis, the federal militia were returning to their homes, and a confident foe pressed upon every salient point of an extended and difficult defensive position. Drawing his troops from a few sparsely settled and impoverished states, denied expected and needed assistance in money and material from the general government, he overcame every obstacle, and at the end of eight weeks led forth an army of thirty thousand men, with five thousand cavalry and eighty-six pieces of artillery. Officers of high rank declared that this force could not leave its encampments by reason of the lack of supplies and transportation; but he conveyed them one hundred and ninety miles by rail, marched them one hundred and thirty-five miles, crossing a broad and rapid river in five days, and in three months from his assumption of the command, and in one month after leaving St. Louis, placed them in presence of the enemy — not an incoherent mass, but a well-ordered and compact army, upon whose valor, steadiness, and discipline the fate of the nation might safely have been pledged.

"If General Fremont was not tried by the crowning test of the soldier — the battle field — it was not through fault of his. On the very eve of battle he was removed. His army was arrested in its triumphal progress, and compelled to a shameful retreat, abandoning the beautiful region it had wrested from the foe, and deserting the loyal people who trusted to its protection, and who, exiles from their homes, followed its retreating files — a mournful procession of broken-hearted men, weeping women, and suffering children. With an unscrupulousness which passes belief, the authors of this terrible disaster have denied the presence of the enemy at Springfield. The miserable wretches, once prosperous farmers upon the slopes of the Ozark Hills, who now wander mendicants through the streets of St. Louis, or crouch around the camp fires of Rolla and Sedalia, can tell whether Price was near Springfield or not.

"Forty-eight hours more must have given to General Fremont an engagement. What the result would have been no one who was there doubted. A victory such as the country has long desired and sorely needs — a decisive, complete, and overwhelming victory — was as certain as it is possible for the skill and valor of man to make certain any future event."

During General Fremont's campaign many skirmishes occurred, in various parts of the state, between detached bodies of federal troops and similar forces of the rebels, or guerrilla parties. Among the more important of these affairs were, a skirmish near Lebanon, October 13, in which two companies of United States cavalry routed about three hundred mounted rebels, and captured thirty prisoners; a skirmish near Frederickton, October 17, in which the federal forces attacked and routed the rebels; a more severe contest at Frederickton, October 21, when a large body of rebels, a portion of the force of Jefferson Thompson, a somewhat notorious rebel general, was defeated by about two thousand federal troops, after an engagement of two hours, in which the rebel commander, Colonel Lowe, was killed, and some of his scattered forces pursued a long distance. A more important engagement, which occurred at Belmont, in the south-eastern part of the state, opposite the rebel position at Columbus, Kentucky, belongs rather to the campaign in the latter state.

CHAPTER XLVII.

In Kentucky the close of the summer did not find the secessionists wholly hopeless of carrying that state over to the southern Confederacy. The great obstacle to an unconditional support of the Union and the government by the people of Kentucky, was the fatal delusion entertained by many, whose sympathies were not strongly enlisted on either side, that they might occupy a position of neutrality. This delusion was encouraged by secessionists as the means of finally securing the state; or, at least, of weakening by so much the power of the United States, and forming a barrier between the truly loyal states and those in open rebellion. For a long time the government had deferred to the apparent feeling of Kentucky; but the representations of truly loyal citizens of the state, as well as the evident purposes of the rebels, led to the occupation of Paducah, on the Ohio, and the organization of military forces in the northern and central parts of the state. Governor Magoffin, whose sympathies, as before seen, were evidently with the rebels, had encouraged the delusion of neutrality; and when the government at last formed camps within the limits of Kentucky, he addressed a letter to President Lincoln, complaining of the act, and requesting that the troops be withdrawn from the state. At the same time he sent a commissioner to Jefferson Davis, bearing a similar letter, in relation to the withdrawal of the rebel forces which had for a long time held positions within the limits of Kentucky. President Lincoln replied that, in organizing the troops in Kentucky, he had acted upon the urgent solicitation of many eminent Kentuckians, and in accordance with what he believed, upon careful inquiry, to be the desire of a large majority of the Union-loving people of the state; and that he did not find any reason to believe that they desired the removal of the troops. He concluded with the following pointed remark: "It is with regret I search for, and cannot find, in your not very short letter, any declaration or intimation that you entertain any desire for the preservation of the Federal Union." Jefferson Davis, knowing well what an advantage to the rebellion the neutrality of Kentucky would be, both in itself and as a means of eventually securing that state, acquiesced in the propriety of the governor's request, and agreed to withdraw the rebel forces if the United States troops were withdrawn, but only on that condition. A proposition to this effect was also communicated to Governor Magoffin by Bishop Polk, of Tennessee, who had been appointed a major-general in the rebel army.

The legislature of Kentucky were more loyal than the governor, and by their action thwarted the measures of the latter which encouraged secession. On the 11th of September they adopted a resolution, directing the governor to issue a proclamation ordering the rebel troops to leave the state, and refused to adopt a resolution requiring both federal and rebel troops to leave. Other resolutions were adopted, which declared that the peace and neutrality of Kentucky had been wantonly violated, and her soil invaded by the so-called "Southern Confederate" forces, requested the governor to call out the military to expel the invaders, invoked the assistance of the United States in so doing, requested General Anderson to enter upon his active duties as commander of the military district, and appealed to the people of Kentucky to assist in driving out the lawless invaders.

Thus instructed, the governor was obliged to act more directly than he had hitherto done. The state militia was called out by orders from General Crittenden; General Anderson assumed command of the military forces of the district, and commenced the organization of the troops, but was soon obliged to relinquish the post, on account of ill health. The position of Kentucky was at last taken; and although the idea of neutrality was still entertained, the action of the government, and the ready response of large numbers of loyal people, committed the state to the cause of the Union.

On the other hand, the secessionists of the state were not idle. Failing to control the government, they sought to lead away the people of the state, and when the legislature at last so openly declared against the rebellion, they as openly raised the standard of revolt, and called upon the people to resist the federal troops; and in so doing, they appealed to that desire of neutrality which had paralyzed the state. Among the leaders of the secessionists was General S. B. Buckner, who now received a commission from the rebel government, and was assigned to the command of the disloyal Kentuckians who should take up arms against the Union. He was a man of ability and great persuasive powers, and by his eloquence and popular manners misled a large number of young men in Kentucky to join the rebel army, and secured considerable material aid for the cause. Mr. Breckinridge, also, having at once put himself in close alliance with the rebel government after the adjournment of Congress, and being expelled from his home by the loyal people of his state, issued a manifesto, in which he endeavored, with specious arguments, and appeals as of a patriot martyr to an oppressed people, to seduce them into treason and rebellion, and declared that he exchanged, "with proud satisfaction, a term of six years in the Senate of the United States for the musket of a soldier."

The secessionists, however, found it not altogether safe to act up to their convictions, except in the southern and south-western part of the state, where they were near the seceded state of Tennessee, and virtually under the protection of the rebel armies. In this section the leading secessionists gathered for consultation and treason. They held a conference at Russellville, and adopted resolutions bidding "defiance both to the federal and state governments," denouncing both in unmeasured terms, and calling upon the people to join them in resisting the power of both. A convention was called, and measures taken to excite the people to rebellion, and to raise forces in each county. Among other resolutions was one requesting Governor Magoffin, whom they thus recognized as a traitor, to convene a legislature "outside of the lines of the Lincoln army," to be composed of such members then elected as would attend, or new ones elected for the purpose. The conference was not large, but was composed of determined and desperate men, who were ready to ruin their state if they could not drag it into the southern Confederacy. The "convention" was duly held, and was composed of members "appointed in any manner possible." It was, of course, composed of the leaders of secession, bent upon carrying out their own purposes, rather than any wishes of a constituency. They declared Kentucky absolved from all connection with the Union, and that the state government was betrayed by the legislature, and they accordingly established a "provisional government," of which a Mr. Johnson was the head, and the principal members of the convention were the subordinate executive officers and the "provisional council." This rebel junto, assuming to represent the state of Kentucky, appointed delegates to the Confederate Congress, among whom was Henry C. Burnett, who sat as a member from his state in the United States Congress at its recent extra session. These delegates were duly admitted to the Confederate Congress; and thus Kentucky was claimed by the rebels as one of the "Confederate States," although this movement was made only by a very small minority, who rebelled at once against the national and state governments.

These measures of the leading secessionists, in their self-constituted "provisional council," were sustained by actual revolt and organization of armed forces wherever there were sufficient numbers of those disposed to side with the southern Confederacy. In a short time considerable bodies of these armed rebels were collected in different parts of the state. This called for new activity on the part of the national and state governments, and additional troops from Indiana and Ohio were sent into the state, while the loyal Kentuckians also enlisted in the cause of the Union. Collisions soon followed, and the scenes which had so widely disturbed the peace of Missouri were reënacted, to some extent, in various parts of Kentucky, small bands of rebels carrying on a guerrilla warfare against the loyal people, and destroying their property. As the federal and state troops were moved forward, there were many skirmishes of more or less magnitude.

Among the more important of these engagements was one which occurred on the 21st of October, in Laurel County, in the south-eastern part of the state, where a rebel force, reported as upwards of six thousand men, under General Zollicoffer, made an attack upon "Camp Wild Cat," a position occupied by a portion of the federal forces under General Schœpf. A single Kentucky regiment had held this post for some days; but learning that an attack by the rebels was imminent, General Schœpf hurried forward two additional regiments and a battery of artillery, and these reënforcements arrived in season to participate in the engagement. The federal position was a strong one, on a hill, which the rebels twice attempted to carry; but they were repulsed each time, with some loss, and withdrew. The federal loss was four killed and twenty-one wounded; that of the rebels was unknown.

On the 23d of October a more decisive skirmish occurred at West Liberty, in the eastern part of the state, between a detachment of General Nelson's command and about seven hundred rebels. The latter were completely routed, with the loss of twenty-one killed, thirty-four prisoners, and a considerable number of horses, arms, and equipments. The federal force had none killed, and only two wounded. On the same day, another portion of General Nelson's command routed a body of rebels at Hazelgreen,

and took a number of prisoners. General Nelson's forces continued to advance, and the rebels to retire before him, until he reached Piketon, in the extreme eastern part of the state, where an engagement of more magnitude occurred. The federal forces advanced in two columns towards Piketon, with the view of cutting off and capturing the rebel force stationed there. One column, moving by the direct road, found many obstructions, and met with strong resistance; but they advanced steadily, compelling the enemy to retire: the other advanced by a circuitous march, and had but slight skirmishing. The main body of the rebels, however, was not captured, nor routed, but retreated during the night from Piketon. The rebel loss in killed, wounded, and missing, was variously stated from sixty to upwards of one hundred. The federal loss was nine killed and about forty wounded.* The operations of General Nelson, in a brief campaign of less than a month, drove the rebel forces, where they had collected in considerable numbers, from eastern Kentucky, and apparently restored peace to that section of the state.

While General Nelson was moving in eastern Kentucky, federal and state troops were also pushed forward towards the southern part of the state, where the rebels were concentrating forces and holding the railroads and thoroughfares leading to Tennessee. Although some slight skirmishes occurred here, too, there was no important engagement during the autumn. Movements were also made in the western part of the state, where the rebels had stronger

* The rebel commander, Colonel Williams, in his official report, states his loss to be ten killed, fifteen wounded, and forty missing, and that he at first believed that the federal loss was "but one hundred and fifty men," but he was satisfied from subsequent information,—"from spies, Union men, and escaped prisoners, and others who have examined their burial ground,"—that the loss was "over three hundred in killed, with the usual proportion of wounded." Such a loss would certainly have taken nearly half of the force engaged, and is a remarkable instance of the exaggeration with which an enemy's loss is sometimes computed.

forces and in more important positions. Advances were made from Paducah and Cairo towards Columbus, at which place the rebels were posted in considerable force, and which they were strongly fortifying, for the purpose of commanding the Mississippi, and preventing any expedition down the river against the seceded states. Here, as in eastern Kentucky, there were occasional skirmishes and some guerrilla fighting.

Connected with the campaign in western Kentucky was an expedition which moved from Cairo, on the 6th of November, down the Mississippi, to Belmont, a rebel post in Missouri, nearly opposite Columbus. The expedition consisted of about twenty-eight hundred men, under the immediate command of General McClernand, but accompanied by General Grant, commander of the forces at Cairo and vicinity, and was designed to prevent the enemy from sending troops into Missouri to cut off a federal force sent on another expedition. This force proceeded down the river in steamboats, and landed at Belmont under the protection of the gunboats Lexington and Tyler. The troops were immediately formed in line of battle, and attacked the rebels in their works. The rebel troops prepared to resist, and were speedily reënforced by additional troops from Columbus; but they were, after a sharp contest, driven from their positions and through their camps in great disorder. The federal troops captured many prisoners, twelve guns, and a large quantity of baggage, and burned the rebel camp. The stronger rebel post, Columbus, was held by a large force, and the federal success was hardly achieved when heavy additional reënforcements were sent across the river to aid the discomfited rebels at Belmont. These reënforcements made the rebel numbers much larger than the federal force. The battle was renewed just as the federal troops were about to retire; the rebels being commanded by Generals Pillow, Cheatham, and Russell, under direction of

General Polk, who went over with the last reënforcements. But notwithstanding their numbers they were several times repulsed. An attempt was made to cut off the retreat of the federal troops, while they were also pressed hard in front; but officers and men behaved with great bravery, and when the flank movement was observed, they cut their way through to their boats, and finally reëmbarked in good order, though a portion of the rebels continued to fire upon them till the boats steamed away.

The following is General Grant's official report : —

"CAIRO, *November* 12, 1861.

" On the evening of the 6th inst. I left this place with two thousand eight hundred and fifty men of all arms, to make a reconnoissance towards Columbus. The object of the expedition was to prevent the enemy from sending out reënforcements to Price's army in Missouri, and also from cutting off columns that I had been directed to send out from this place and Cape Girardeau, in pursuit of Jefferson Thompson. Knowing that Columbus was strongly garrisoned, I asked General Smith, commanding at Paducah, Kentucky, to make demonstrations in the same direction. He did so, by ordering a small force to Mayfield, and another in the direction of Columbus, not to approach nearer, however, than twelve or fifteen miles. I also sent a small force on the Kentucky side, with orders not to approach nearer than Ellicott's Mills, some twenty miles from Columbus. The expedition, under my immediate command, was stopped about nine miles below here on the Kentucky shore, and remained until morning. All this served to distract the enemy, and led him to think he was to be attacked in his strongly fortified position. At daylight we proceeded down the river to a point just out of range of the rebel guns, and debarked on the Missouri shore. From here the troops were marched by flank for about one mile toward Belmont, and then drawn up in line of battle, a battalion also having been left as a reserve near the transports. Two companies from each regiment, five skeletons in number, were then thrown out as skirmishers, to ascertain the position of the enemy. It was but a few moments before we met him, and a general engagement ensued.

" The balance of my forces, with the exception of the reserve, was then thrown forward, — all as skirmishers, — and the enemy driven foot by foot, and from tree to tree, back to their encampment on the river bank, a distance of two miles. Here they had strengthened their position by felling the timber for several hundred yards around their camp, and making a sort of abatis. Our men charged through this, driving the enemy over the bank into their transports in quick time, leaving us in possession of every thing not exceedingly portable. Belmont is on low ground, and every foot of it is commanded by the guns on the opposite shore, and of course could not be held for a single hour after the enemy became aware of the withdrawal of their troops. Having no wagons, I could not move any of the captured property ; consequently, I gave orders for its destruction. Their tents, blankets, &c., were set on fire, and we retired, taking their artillery with us, two pieces being drawn by hand ; and one other, drawn by an inefficient team, we spiked and left in the woods, bringing the two only to this place. Before getting fairly under way the enemy made · his appearance again, and attempted to surround us. Our troops were not in the least discouraged, but charged on the enemy again, and defeated him. Our loss was about eighty-four killed, one hundred and fifty wounded, — many of them slightly, — and about an equal number missing. Nearly all the missing were from the Iowa regiment, who behaved with great gallantry, and suffered more severely than any other of the troops.

" I have not been able to put in the reports from sub-commands, but will forward them as soon as received. All the troops behaved with much gallantry, much of which is attributed to the coolness and presence of mind of the officers, particularly the colonels. General McClernand was in the midst of danger throughout the engagement, and displayed both coolness and judgment. His horse was three times shot. My horse was also shot under me. To my staff, Captains Rawlins, Logan, and Hillyer, volunteer aids, and to Captains Hatch and Graham, I am much indebted for the assistance they gave. Colonel Webster, acting chief engineer, also accompanied me, and displayed highly soldier-like qualities. Colonel Dougherty, of the twenty-second Illinois volunteers, was three times wounded, and taken prisoner.

" The seventh Iowa regiment had their lieutenant-colonel killed, and the colonel and major were severely wounded. The reports to be forwarded will detail more fully the particulars of our loss. Surgeon Brinton was in the field during the entire engagement, and displayed great ability and efficiency in providing for the wounded and organizing the medical corps.

" The gunboats Tyler and Lexington, Captains Walker and Stemble, U. S. N., commanding, convoyed the expedition, and rendered most efficient service. Immediately upon our landing they engaged the enemy's batteries, and protected our transports throughout.

".For particulars, see accompanying report of Captain Walker.

" I am, sir, very respectfully,
" Your obedient servant,
" U. S. GRANT,
"*Brigadier-General commanding.*"

The following extracts from General McClernaud's report exhibit some of the details of the expedition. After stating the preliminary preparations and the rendezvous of the transports at an appointed time and place, General McClernand proceeds : —

" At that hour, preceded by the gunboats

Tyler and Lexington, and followed by the remainder of the transports, I proceeded down the river to the designated landing on the Missouri shore, about two and a half miles, in a direct line, from Columbus and Belmont.

"By half past eight o'clock the rest of the transports had arrived, and the whole force was disembarked, and, marching beyond a collection of cornfields in front of the landing, was formed for an advance movement, and awaited your order. Ordering Dollins's and Delano's cavalry to scour the woods along the road to Belmont, and report to me from time to time, the remainder of my command followed — the twenty-seventh in front, the thirtieth next — supported by a section of Taylor's battery, succeeded by the thirty-first, and the remainder of Taylor's battery, the seventh Iowa, (Colonel Lauman,) and the twenty-second Illinois, (Colonel Dougherty,) who had been assigned by you to that portion of the command.

"When the rear of the column had reached a road intersecting our line of march, about a mile and a half from the abatis surrounding the enemy's camp, the line of battle was formed on ground which I had previously selected. The twenty-seventh and thirtieth, having formed too far in advance, were recalled to the position first assigned them — the twenty-seventh on the right, and the thirtieth on the left. A section of Taylor's battery was disposed on the left of the thirtieth, and two hundred feet in rear of the line, the thirty-first in the centre, and the seventh Iowa and twenty-second Illinois forming the left wing, masking two sections of artillery.

"By this time Dollins's cavalry were skirmishing sharply with the enemy's pickets to the right, and in advance of our line, and the enemy had shifted the heavy fire of their batteries at Columbus from our gunboats to our advancing line, but without effect.

"With your permission I now ordered two companies from each regiment of my command to advance, instructing them to seek out and develop the position of the enemy, the twenty-second Illinois and seventh Iowa pushing forward similar parties at the same time.

"A sharp firing having immediately commenced between the skirmishing parties of the thirtieth and thirty-first and the enemy, I ordered forward another party to their support, rode forward, selected a new position, and ordered up the balance of my command — the twenty-seventh — to pass around the head of a pond, the thirtieth and thirty-first, with the artillery, crossing the dry bed of the same slough in their front.

"On their arrival, I reformed the line of battle in the same order as before. It was my expectation that the twenty-second Illinois and seventh Iowa would resume their former positions on the left wing, which would have perfected a line sufficient to enclose the enemy's camp on all sides accessible to us, thus enabling us to command the river above and below them, and prevent the crossing of reënforcements from Columbus, insuring his capture as well as defeat.

"The thirtieth and thirty-first and the artillery, moving forward, promptly relieved skirmishing parties, and soon became engaged with a heavy body of the enemy's infantry and cavalry. The struggle, which was continued for half an hour with great severity, threw our ranks into temporary disorder; but the men promptly rallied under the gallant example of Colonels Fouke and Logan, assisted by Major Berryman, acting assistant adjutant-general of my brigade; also by Captain Schwartz, acting chief of artillery, Captain Dresser, of the artillery, Lieutenant Babcock, of the second cavalry, and Lieutenant Eddy, of the twenty-ninth Illinois regiment, who had, upon my invitation, kindly joined my staff. Our men pressed vigorously upon the enemy and drove them back, their cavalry leaving that part of the field, and not appearing again until attacked by Captain Dollins, on the river bank below their encampment, and chased out of sight, near the close of the contest.

"Advancing about a quarter of a mile farther, this force again came up with the enemy, who by this time had been reënforced upon this part of the field, as I since learn, by three regiments and a company of cavalry. Thus strengthened, they attempted to turn our left flank; but, ordering Colonel Logan to extend the line of battle by a flank movement, and bringing up a section of Taylor's battery, commanded by First Lieutenant B. H. White, under the direction of Captain Schwartz, to cover the space thus made between the thirtieth and thirty-first, the attempt was frustrated.

"Having completed that disposition, we again opened a deadly fire from both infantry and artillery, and after a desperate resistance, drove the enemy back the third time, forcing them to seek cover among thick woods and brush, protected by the heavy guns at Columbus.

"In this struggle, while leading the charge, I received a ball in one of my holsters, which failed of harm by striking a pistol. Here Colonels Fouke and Logan urged on their men by the most energetic appeals; here Captain Dresser's horse was shot under him, while Captain Schwartz's horse was twice wounded; here the projectiles from the enemy's heavy guns at Columbus, and their artillery at Belmont, crashed through the woods over and among us; here, again, all my staff who were with me displayed the greatest intrepidity and activity; and here, too, many of our officers were killed or wounded; nor shall I omit to add that this gallant conduct was stimulated by your presence, and inspired by your example. Here your horse was killed under you.

"While this struggle was going on, a tremendous fire from the twenty-seventh, which had approached the abatis on the right and rear of the tents, was heard. About the same time the seventh and twenty-second, which had passed the rear of the thirtieth and thirty-first, hastened up, and, closing the space between them and the twenty-seventh, poured a deadly fire upon the enemy.

"A combined movement was now made upon three sides of the enemy's works, and, driving him across the abatis, we followed close upon his heels into the clear space around his camp. The twenty-seventh was the first seen by me entering upon this ground. I called the attention of the other regiments to their approach, and the whole line was quickened by eager and impatient emulation. In a few minutes our entire force was within the enclosure.

"Under the skilful direction of Captain Schwartz, Captain Taylor now brought up his battery within three hundred yards of the enemy's tents, and opened fire upon them. He fled with precipitation from the tents, and took shelter behind some buildings near the river, and in the woods above the camp, under cover of his batteries at Columbus.

"Near this battery I met Colonel Dougherty, who was leading the seventh and twenty-second through the open space towards the tents.

"At the same time our lines upon the right and left were pressing up to the line of fire from our battery, which now ceased firing, and our men rushed forward among the tents and towards some buildings near the river. Passing over to the right of the camp, I met with Colonel Buford, for the first time since his detour around the pond, and congratulated him upon the ardor of his men, to be the first to pass the enemy's works. . . .

"Having complete possession of the enemy's camp in full view of his formidable batteries at Columbus, I gave the word for three cheers for the Union, to which the brave men around me responded with the most enthusiastic applause.

"Several of the enemy's steamers being within range above and below, I ordered a section of Taylor's battery, under the direction of Captain

Schwartz, down near the river, and opened a fire upon them and upon Columbus itself, with what effect I could not learn. The enemy's tents were set on fire, destroying his camp equipage, about four thousand blankets, and his means of transportation. Such horses and other property as could be removed were seized, and four pieces of his artillery brought to the rear.

" The enemy at Columbus, seeing us in possession of his camp, directed upon us the fire of his heavy guns, but, ranging too high, inflicted no injury. Information came at the same time of the crossing of heavy bodies of troops above us, amounting, as I since learn, to five regiments, which, joining those which had fled in that direction, formed rapidly in our rear, with the design of cutting off our communication with our transports. To prevent this, and having fully accomplished the object of the expedition, I ordered Captain Taylor to reverse his guns and open fire upon the enemy in his new position, which was done with great spirit and effect, breaking his line and opening our way by the main road. Promptly responding to an order to that effect, Colonel Logan ordered his flag in front of his regiment, prepared to force his way in the same direction if necessary. Moving on, he was followed by the whole force, except the twenty-seventh and the cavalry companies of Captain Dollins and Delano. Determined to preserve my command unbroken, and to defeat the evident design of the enemy to divide it, I twice rode back across the field to bring up the twenty-seventh and Dollins's cavalry, and also despatched Major Brayman for the same purpose, but without accomplishing the object; they having sought, in returning, the same route by which they advanced in the morning.

" On passing into the woods, the thirtieth, the seventh, and twenty-second encountered a heavy fire on their right and left successively, which was returned with such vigor and effect as to drive back the superior force of the enemy

and silence his firing, but not until the seventh and twenty-second had been thrown into temporary disorder. Here Lieutenant-Colonel Wentz, of the seventh, and Captain Markley, of the thirtieth, with several privates, were killed ; and Colonel Dougherty, of the twenty-second, and Major McClurken, of the thirtieth, who was near me, were severely wounded. Here my body servant killed one of the enemy by a pistol shot.

" Driving the enemy back on either side, we moved on, occasionally exchanging shots with straggling parties, in the course of which my horse received another ball, being one of two fired at me from the corner of a field. Captain Schwartz was at my right when these shots were fired.

" At this stage of the contest, according to the admission of rebel officers, the enemy's forces had swelled, by frequent reënforcements from the other side of the river, to over thirteen regiments of infantry, and something less than two squadrons of cavalry ; excluding his artillery, four pieces of which were in our possession, and two of which, after being spiked, together with part of one of our caissons, were left on the way for want of animals to bring them off. The other two, with their horses and harness, were brought off.

" On reaching the landing, and not finding the detachments of the seventh and twenty-second, which you had left behind in the morning to guard the boats, I ordered Delano's cavalry, which was embarking, to the rear of the field to watch the enemy. Within an hour all our forces which had arrived were embarked, Captain Schwartz, Captain Hatch, assistant-quartermaster, and myself being the last to get on board. Suddenly the enemy, in strong force,— whose approach had been discovered by Lieutenant-Colonel John H. White, of the thirty-first, who was conspicuous through the day for his dauntless courage and conduct,—came within range of our musketry, when a terrible fire was opened upon him by the gunboats, as well as by Taylor's battery and the infantry.

" The engagement, thus renewed, was kept up with great spirit, and with a deadly effect upon the enemy, until the transports had passed beyond his reach. Exposed to the terrible fire of the gunboats and Taylor's battery, a great number of the enemy were killed and wounded in this the closing scene of a battle of six hours' duration.

" The twenty-seventh and Dollins's cavalry being yet behind, I ordered my transport to continue in the rear of the fleet, excepting the gunboats, and, after proceeding a short distance, landed, and directed the gunboats to return and await their appearance.

" At this moment Lieutenant H. A. Rust, adjutant of the twenty-seventh, hastened up and announced the approach of the twenty-seventh and Dollins's cavalry. Accompanied by Captains Schwartz and Hatch, I rode down the river bank, and met Colonel Buford with a part of his command. Inferring that my transport was waiting to receive him, I went farther down the river, and met Captain Dollins, whom I also instructed to embark, and still farther met the remainder of the twenty-seventh, which had halted on the bank where the gunboat Tyler was lying to, the Lexington lying still farther down. The rest of the boats having gone forward, Captain Walker, of the Tyler, at my request, promptly took the remainder of the twenty-seventh on board, Captain Stamble, of the Lexington, covering the embarkation.

" Having thus embarked all my command, I returned, with Captains Schwartz and Hatch, to my transports, and reëmbarked, reaching Cairo about midnight, after a day of almost unceasing marching and conflict.

" I cannot bestow too high commendation upon all whom I had the honor to command on that day. Supplied with inferior and defective arms, many of which could not be discharged, and others bursting in use, they fought an enemy in woods with which he was familiar, behind defensive works which he had been preparing for months, in the face of a battery at Belmont, and under his heavy guns at Columbus, and, although numbering three or four to our one, beat him, capturing several stands of his colors, destroying his camp, and carrying off a large amount of property, already mentioned. From his own semi-official account, his loss was six hundred killed, wounded, and missing, including among the killed and wounded a number of officers, and probably among the missing one hundred and fifty-five prisoners who were brought to this post."

The report of General Polk to the rebel government shows the odds against which the federal force had to contend when the battle was renewed. The force already in Belmont before the reënforcements were sent over, consisted of an Arkansas regiment, a battery of artillery, and a troop of cavalay, numbering, probably, at least a thousand men, in a fortified position. The following is General Polk's despatch : —

To General Headquarters, through General A. S. Johnston.

"Headquarters, First Division, Western Department,
"Columbus, Ky., *November* 7, 1861.

" The enemy came down on the opposite side of the river, to Belmont, to-day, about seven thousand five hundred strong, landed under cover of gunboats, and attacked Colonel Tappan's camp. I sent over three regiments, under General Pillow, to his relief, then, at intervals, three others, then General Cheatham.

" I then took over two others in person, to support a flank movement which I had directed. It was a hard-fought battle, lasting from half past ten A. M. to five P. M. They took Beltzhoover's battery, four pieces of which were recaptured. The enemy were thoroughly routed. We pursued them to their boats seven miles, then drove their boats before us. The road was strewn with their dead and wounded, guns, ammunition, and equipments. Our loss considerable; theirs heavy.

"L. POLK,
"*Major-General commanding.*"

The federal loss in this engagement was eighty-four killed and three hundred and forty wounded and missing, about one hundred and fifty of the wounded being brought from the field. The loss of the rebels must have been much greater; for, according to their official reports of four regiments, which included only about one third of their force, the number of killed was sixty-five, wounded one hundred and eighty-seven, missing one hundred and eight. The same ratio in the other regiments would make their loss upwards of one thousand. A semi-official account, as stated in General McClernand's report, made their loss about six hundred. Of these one hundred and fifty-five were taken prisoners, and the rebels held about the same number of federal prisoners.

No other important movement took place in this department for the present. Meanwhile preparations, commenced some time previously, were continued, for more formidable expeditions down the Mississippi and into Tennessee. Troops were collected at Cairo, Paducah, and at other places in Kentucky, where they could be readily concentrated, and at the same time be prepared for any offensive movement of the rebels. Gunboats, some of them iron-clad, were being constructed and equipped at St. Louis, Cairo, and on the Ohio River, for coöperation with the land forces. Two or three, already completed, had several times gone down the river to the vicinity of Columbus, and bombarded rebel batteries and camps with some effect. The sequel showed that these gunboats were important auxiliaries to army movements, and proved too formidable for the rebels to resist, although they, too, on the Mississippi, were constructing gunboats and "rams," on which they depended to hold the river.

CHAPTER XLVIII.

IN Western Virginia the flight of Wise, and the dispersion of many of his troops, did not put an end to the attempts of the rebels to subject that part of the "Old Dominion" to the control of the rebel government. In some of the more southern counties there were many secessionists, who were ready to join any force from the east both against the federal troops and against their loyal neighbors. Mr. Floyd, the treacherous secretary of war under President Buchanan, had been commissioned to organize forces for operations in Western Virginia at about the same time as Governor Wise; but the campaign of the latter was finished before the former came into the field. He then outranked Wise, and all the want of success which followed was attributed by the friends of the latter to the incompetency or cowardice of Floyd. The general direction of the rebel operations, however, was under General Lee.

Actual conflict between the federal and rebel

forces was recommenced on the 26th of August, at Summerville, in Nicholas County, on the Gauley River, about twenty-five miles from its junction with the Kanawha. The seventh Ohio regiment, Colonel Tyler, which was stationed here, was surrounded by a large body of rebels, who had made their dispositions and approach without the knowledge of the federal officers. Although surprised and evidently contending against superior numbers, the federal troops evinced steadiness and bravery, and succeeded in breaking through the surrounding forces. Colonel Tyler sent forward to a baggage train which was approaching Summerville, and turned it back towards Gauley Bridge, and then, with such of his regiment as had escaped, he retreated to the same place, losing about two hundred of the nine hundred under his command.

The federal troops were at this time distributed from the vicinity of Beverly to the Kanawha valley, the strongest forces being in the vicinity of Cheat Mountain. The movements of the rebels, however, required a more active campaign, and operations against the enemy were resumed. Having collected a sufficient force, General Rosecrans moved towards Summerville, from the north, to oppose Floyd, who, after Colonel Tyler was driven away, occupied the place, and subsequently posted his forces several miles farther south, in a position at once strong against an attack and dangerous to himself in case of disaster. The position was on a hill for the most part thickly wooded, except at the summit, where the approach by the roads could be easily commanded by artillery, while either flank was almost inaccessible; and in the rear was the Gauley River — a deep and rapid stream at this point. The descent to the river was steep, and in some places precipitous; and this, with the rapid current, presented an obstacle to the approach of an assailing force and the retreat of those holding the position. There was one road, however, descend-

ing to the river, where there was a ferry, called "Carnifex Ferry." Upon this hill Floyd had intrenched his force, and extended breastworks a long distance on either flank.

Having reached Summerville, General Rosecrans, on the 10th of September, advanced a part of his forces to make a reconnoissance and discover the enemy's position, and the strength of his intrenchments and forces, about which there were very conflicting and uncertain reports. The dense wood, which extended for a long distance from the rebel camp, entirely concealed their works from those approaching, and rendered a careful advance necessary. The force sent forward was the brigade of General Benham, supported afterwards by the brigade commanded by Colonel McCook, with six pieces of artillery. This force, being extended for a more effectual reconnoissance, advanced through the thick woods, and soon met the enemy's pickets, when skirmishing at once commenced. The advance of the rebels, consisting of one regiment, was driven in; but the main body and their fortifications were not discovered till the federal force reached the open ground near the top of the hill, within short range of their guns. The rebel artillery, as well as infantry, opened a severe fire upon the federal advance when it made its appearance, and caused it to fall back with loss into the woods, where it was again quickly rallied. Two attempts to carry the rebel battery by assault by single regiments were made, but the fire was too heavy for so small a number of troops, and they were again compelled to retire. In the mean time, one regiment moved to the left, to try the strength of the rebel lines on their right; and while the remainder of the brigade held its ground in front of the enemy, this regiment succeeded in turning the rebel right, and gaining a position from which an attack upon their weakest point could be made. But being unsupported, it could not follow up the advantage of its position before darkness caused a cessation of the contest. Before this advantage was known to General Benham, preparations were made for a charge by the brigade of Colonel McCook upon the principal battery of the rebels, and these troops were already moving for that purpose, when General Rosecrans, who had come up, countermanded the order, on account of the loss of life which it would occasion and the approach of night. Withdrawing the troops a little from their advanced position, behind ridges in front of the enemy, where they slept upon their arms, General Rosecrans awaited the morning for a renewal of the attack, confident of success.

But notwithstanding the strength of his position, General Floyd, it appeared, had no confidence that he could hold it. He sent to General Wise for reënforcements, but Wise could not send them ; and during the night he crossed the river in his rear, by means of the ferry and a temporary bridge, leaving a considerable quantity of arms, quartermaster's stores, and baggage, which he was unable to remove. The retreat of the rebels was not discovered by the federal forces until it had been successfully accomplished. The camp was then occupied, and a few prisoners captured ; but it was found impossible to follow the fugitives, as the bridge had been destroyed and the boats sunk, and the stream was too swift and deep for fording.

The following report of General Rosecrans, with extracts from the report of General Benham, exhibits more in detail the events of the engagement thus briefly sketched : —

REPORT OF GENERAL ROSECRANS.

"HEADQUARTERS, ARMY OF VIRGINIA, {
"CAMP SCOTT, Sept. 11, P. M. }

"COLONEL E. D. TOWNSEND.

"We yesterday marched seventeen and a half miles, reached the enemy's intrenched position, in front of Carnifex Ferry, driving his advance outposts and pickets before us. We found him occupying a strongly intrenched position, covered by a forest too dense to admit of its being seen at a distance of three hundred yards. His force was five regiments, besides the one driven in. He had, probably, sixteen pieces of artillery.

"At three o'clock we began a strong reconnoissance, which proceeded to such length, we were about to assault the position on the flank and front, when night coming on, and our troops being completely exhausted, I drew them out of the woods and posted them in the order of battle behind ridges immediately in front of the enemy's position, where they rested on their arms till morning.

"Shortly after daylight a runaway ' contraband ' came in, and reported that the enemy had crossed the Gauley during the night, by means of the ferry and a bridge which they had completed.

"Colonel Ewing was ordered to take possession of the camp, which he did about seven o'clock, capturing a few prisoners, two stand of colors, a considerable quantity of arms, with quartermaster's stores, messing and camp equipage.

"The enemy having destroyed the bridge across the Gauley, which here rushes through a deep gorge, and our troops being still much fatigued, and having no material for immediately repairing the bridge, it was thought prudent to encamp the troops, occupy the ferry and the captured camp, sending a few rifle cannon shots after the enemy to produce a moral effect.

"Our loss would probably amount to twenty killed and one hundred wounded. The enemy's loss had not been ascertained ; but from report it must have been considerable.

"W. S. ROSECRANS."

GENERAL BENHAM'S REPORT.

"HEADQUARTERS ARMY OF OCCUPATION, W. VA., {
"CAMP SCOTT, Sept. 3, 1861. }

"SIR: I have the honor to report as follows in relation to the operation of my brigade in the battle at the rebel intrenchments at Carnifex Ferry on the 10th instant. As previously stated to you, the head of my brigade started from the camp, eight miles north of Summerville, at about four A. M., reaching that place before eight A. M., in good order, and with the men eager for the continuance of the march towards the enemy, who, we there ascertained, were well intrenched and determined to resist us near Carnifex Ferry.

" After a halt of nearly two hours, about one mile short of the Cross Lanes, we moved rapidly forward towards the position of the enemy, until our arrival at the site of this camp, about one mile from their intrenchments, a little past two o'clock, when, after a reconnoissance by you, myself accompanying you, I was authorized to move forward with my brigade, ' using my best discretion in the case.' Upon receiving this order, and with the mass of my brigade well closed up, which had been accomplished during our reconnoissance, I moved carefully forward, with the tenth Ohio regiment leading, having our skirmishers well ahead, and at the flanks for nearly three fourths of a mile, when we discovered, through the opening of the woods on our left, their intrenchments in an open space on our left, beyond a deep and steep valley, and crowning the crest of the opposite hill.

" Having no engineer officer with my brigade, and no others, that I knew of, to replace one, I kept with the head of the regiment to avoid ambuscades, and to judge myself of their position and arrangements. After advancing about one fourth of a mile to the end of the woods, I halted the command, and could perceive that a heavy cross fire had been prepared for us at the open space at the debouche from the roads. Within some five minutes after this time, — nearly half past three o'clock — while carefully examining their earthworks on the road in front, and their intrenchments on our left, a tremendous fire of musketry was opened on us, which in a few minutes was followed by a discharge of grape and spelter canister from a

battery of some six pieces of artillery. This caused a break in the line for a few minutes, though for a few minutes only, for the men immediately returned to their ranks, under the lead of their officers, to their former position, where I retained them, as I was certain that the fire at us through the close woods was without direct aim, and because they were needed for the protection of our artillery, which I immediately ordered up; the two rifled guns of Captain Schneider, and Captain McMullen, with his four mountain howitzers, immediately followed, throwing their shells well into their intrenchments on our left.

" A further examination of their position convinced me that their weak part, and our true point of attack, was on their right flank, across the deep valley from our position; upon which orders were immediately sent to Colonel Smith, of the thirteenth regiment, and to Colonel Lowe, of the twelfth regiment, to advance and pass the valley on our left, under cover of the woods, to that attack. Neither of these regiments was to be found in their proper position on the road in my rear, as I expected. After a short time, Colonel Smith was met with on our right, where he had been drawn into the woods by the belief, from the sound of the firing, that the attack was upon our right. Upon the receipt of my order, however, Colonel Smith moved rapidly across the main road, down the ravine valley on our left, where he fortunately struck upon the most advantageous route, and thence he moved up the opposite hill, entirely past the right flank of the enemy. But as I had been unable to find the twelfth regiment to send forward to his support, though I have since learned that three companies, under Lieutenant-Colonel White, were near him, his movement became principally a reconnoissance, from which he soon after returned, reporting to me his opinion of the entire practicability of a successful attack upon the rebel intrenchments at that point, he having entirely passed by the breastwork on the right, approaching within one hundred yards of their line, pouring a fire into them, which, it is since satisfactorily ascertained, cleared that part of that breastwork of the enemy.

"As I was still unable to find the position of the twelfth regiment, which it has been reported to me had been ordered into the woods by the commanding general, I sent one of my staff to Colonel McCook, commanding the second brigade, to ask him to aid the thirteenth in this attack with his ninth regiment, to which request a reply was returned to me that there were other orders from the commanding general, as stated to my aid by acting Adjutant-General Captain Hartsuff.

"In this state of affairs I could only hold my position in front, with the tenth regiment protecting the artillery, which was endeavoring to silence the cannon of the enemy, which was to a considerable extent accomplished after the first fifteen or twenty minutes — their guns being at once removed to other positions, as was then also done with one half of Schneider's and McMullen's pieces, to enfilade the crest of the hill from the edge of the woods on our right, which gave a fair view of their battery at some three hundred and eighty yards' distance.

"At this time, or about one hour after the commencement of the action, Colonel Lytle, of the tenth, though not ordered by me, and while I was still endeavoring to obtain troops for the attack from our left, made a very gallant attempt to approach their battery through the cleared space in front of it, which of course failed, from the smallness of his force in that exposed situation — he being severely wounded and compelled to retire, with the loss of many men killed and wounded.

"Colonel Lowe, of the twelfth, also, at a subsequent period, made a similar attempt, and, as far as I can learn, without orders; in which, I regret to say, he fell, being instantly killed by a discharge of canister from the enemy.

"The above comprises the sum of the action of the portion of my brigade that was with me, until you arrived on the field and assumed the direction of affairs, some time after which arrival you also arranged for and directed the attack upon their right, with Colonel Smith's regiment, and a part of the twelfth and forty-seventh — Colonel Mohr. This attack, as having been first directed by myself, you will recollect, I offered to lead upon the enemy, recommending at the same time a simultaneous demonstration or attack by the ninth and twelfth regiments, under cover of the woods, from our right. The command moved forward, however, under the direction of Colonel Smith; but from the lateness of the hour it was compelled to return without attempting any thing, and the lateness of the hour seemed to forbid further operations for the day. . . .

"Very respectfully, your obd't servant,
"H. W. BENHAM,
"*Brigadier-General commanding First Brigade.*"

While General Rosecrans moved against the forces of Floyd, a larger body of rebels, under the command of General Robert E. Lee, threatened an attack upon the federal lines farther north, where General Reynolds held strong positions at Cheat Mountain and Elk Water. General Lee apparently attempted to get through Cheat Mountain Pass, with a view of attacking the federal forces in the rear, and gaining access to the open country west of the mountains, from which the rebel forces had been driven. Making a reconnoissance in force, the rebels approached secretly to within a short distance of the federal outposts, and on the 12th of September they met with detachments from two regiments, by whom they were repulsed, though greatly exceeding the federal force in numbers, the latter then falling back to the main body. At the same time another body of rebels advanced by another route, and succeeded in throwing a part of their force into the rear of Cheat Mountain. The federal position was a strong one, and the rugged nature of the country enabled a comparatively small body to hold in check superior numbers. While the federal force on Cheat Mountain held the rebels in check, reënforcements were sent from Elk Water and Cheat Mountain Pass, with orders to cut their way through the rebel forces if necessary. These reënforcements moved early on the morning of the 13th; but before they reached the mountain summit, the force there, numbering but three hundred men, had repulsed the enemy, compelling him to retire in haste, with the loss of a large quantity of clothing and equipments, which had been cast aside in making the attack.

While these movements were taking place at Cheat Mountain, General Lee advanced another portion of his forces towards Elk Water, about seven miles distant, by the shortest road, from the summit of the mountain; but a few shots from artillery compelled them to retire. On the 14th, however, they again approached Elk Water, and again retired before a moderate show of resistance. Another attempt was made upon the mountain also, and again the small garrison there repulsed the assailants. The next day a larger force of the enemy advanced upon the mountain, and attempted a flank movement; but the federal force were too strongly posted, and again succeeded in driving back superior numbers. Foiled in all his attempts to take the position or to advance into Western Virginia, the rebel general withdrew his forces. In these various engagements the federal loss was nine killed, a considerable number wounded, and about sixty prisoners, who belonged to the regiment on picket. Of the enemy it was supposed that nearly a hundred were killed and a proportionate number wounded, and twenty were taken prisoners. Among the killed was Colonel John A. Washington, the former proprietor of Mount Vernon, who was aid-de-camp to General Lee, and was shot while making a reconnoissance.

The following is the official report of General Reynolds: —

"HEADQUARTERS FIRST BRIGADE I. V. M.,
"ELK WATER, Sept. 17, 1861.

"GEORGE L. HARTSUFF, ASSISTANT ADJUTANT-GENERAL, DEPARTMENT OHIO.

"SIR: The operations of this brigade for the past few days may be summed up as follows: On the 12th instant, the enemy, nine thousand strong, with eight to twelve pieces of artillery, under command of General R. E. Lee, advanced on this position by the Huntersville Pike. Our advanced pickets — portions of the fifteenth Indiana and sixth Ohio — gradually fell back to our main picket station; two companies of the seventeenth Indiana, under Colonel Hascall, checking the enemy's advance at the Point Mountain Turnpike, and then falling back on the regiment which occupied a very advanced position on our right front, and which was now ordered in. The enemy threw into the woods on our left front three regiments, who made their way to the right and rear of Cheat Mountain, took a position on the road leading to Huttonville, broke the telegraph wire, and cut off our communication with Colonel Kimball's fourteenth Indiana cavalry on Cheat Summit. Simultaneously another force of the enemy, of about equal strength, advanced by the Staunton Pike on the front of Cheat Mountain, and threw two regiments to the right and rear of Cheat Mountain, which united with the three regiments from the other column of the enemy. (The two posts, Cheat Summit and Elk Water, are seven miles apart by a bridle path over the mountains, and eighteen miles by the wagon road, via Huttonville, Cheat Mountain Pass, the former headquarters of the brigade, being at the foot of the mountain, ten miles from the summit.) The enemy, advancing towards the pass by which he might possibly have obtained the rear or left of Elk Water, was met there by three companies of the thirteenth Indiana, ordered up for that purpose, and by one company of the fourteenth Indiana from the summit. These four companies engaged and gallantly held in check greatly superior numbers of the enemy, foiled him in his attempt to obtain the rear or left of Elk Water, and threw him into the rear and right of Cheat Mountain, the companies retiring to the pass at the foot of the mountains.

"The enemy, about five thousand strong, was closed in on Cheat Summit, and became engaged with detachments of the fourteenth Indiana, twenty-fourth and twenty-fifth Ohio, from the summit, in all only about three hundred, who, deployed in the wood, held in check and killed many of the enemy, who did not at any time succeed in getting sufficiently near the field redoubt to give Dunn's battery an opportunity of firing into him. So matters rested at dark on the 12th, with heavy forces in front, and in plain sight of both posts; communication cut off, and the supply train for the mountain, loaded with provisions which were needed, waiting for an opportunity to pass up the road. Determined to force a communication with Cheat, I ordered the thirteenth Indiana, under Colonel Sullivan, to cut their way, if necessary, by the mail road, and the greater part of the third Ohio and second Virginia, under Colonels Manon and Moss, respectively, to do the same by the path; the two commands starting at three o'clock A. M., on the 13th — the former from Cheat Mountain Pass, and the latter from Elk Water, so as to fall upon the enemy, if possible, simultaneously. Early on the 13th, the small force of about three hundred from the Summit engaged the enemy, and with such effect, that notwithstanding his greatly superior numbers, he retired in great haste and disorder, leaving large quantities of clothing and equipments on the ground; and our relieving forces, failing to catch the enemy, marched to the Summit, securing the provision train, and reopening our communication. While this was taking place on the mountain, and as yet unknown to us, the enemy, under Lee, ad-

vanced on Elk Water, apparently for a general attack. One rifled ten-pound Parrott gun, from Loomis's battery, was run to the front three fourths of a mile, and delivered a few shots at the enemy, doing fine execution, causing him to withdraw out of convenient range. Our relative positions remained unchanged until near dark, when we learned the result of the movement on the mountain, as above stated, and the enemy retired somewhat for the night.

"On the 14th, early, the enemy was again in position in front of Elk Water, and a few rounds, supported by a company of the fifteenth Indiana, were again administered, which caused him to withdraw as before. The forces that had been before repulsed from Cheat returned, and were again driven back by a comparatively small force from the mountain. The seventeenth Indiana was ordered up the path to open communication, and make way for another supply train; but, as before, found the little band from the Summit had already done the work. During the afternoon of the 14th the enemy withdrew from before Elk Water, and is now principally concentrated some ten miles from this post, at or near his main camp. On the 15th he appeared in stronger force than at any previous time, in front of Cheat, and attempted a flank movement by the left, but was driven back by the ever-vigilant and gallant garrison of the field redoubt on the Summit. To-day the enemy has also retired from the front of Cheat, but to what precise position I am not yet informed. . . .

"J. J. REYNOLDS,

"*Brigadier-General commanding First Brigade.*

"GEORGE S. ROSE, ASSISTANT ADJUTANT-GENERAL."

The rebel forces under Lee still threatened the federal lines; but their exact position and numbers, and their purposes, were matters of doubt. On the night of the 2d of October, General Reynolds accordingly started from Cheat Mountain with about five thousand troops and

twelve pieces of artillery, to make a reconnoissance of the rebel position on the Green
Brier range, about twelve miles south, where
they were reported to be intrenched. This
force drove in, after a sharp skirmish, the enemy's advanced regiments, and moved directly
upon the strong, fortified position which he held
on Buffalo Hill, when the batteries were brought
to bear upon the camp and works. The rebels
returned the fire, and for some time there was
a conflict of artillery, in which the rebels had
several guns disabled, and apparently lost a considerable number of men, while their own shots
were generally of little effect, owing to the
proximity of the attacking force and the protection of the trees. The infantry were not
content that the artillery should alone fight the
battle, and yielding to the request of the officers,
General Reynolds ordered a flank movement, by
which the infantry should make a demonstration,
and ascertain more particularly the strength
and location of the enemy, while the artillery
occupied his attention in front. The rebels,
however, observed the movement, and turned
their artillery upon the infantry, throwing one
of the regiments into confusion, and repulsing
them, though without much loss. In the mean
time it was evident that the rebels were receiving reënforcements, and General Reynolds,
having accomplished all that he anticipated,
by fixing the position and strength of the rebel
forces, ordered his troops to retire; and after a
four hours' battle, in which the federal loss was
eight killed and thirty-two wounded, and the
rebel loss was admitted to be much larger,
they returned in good order to their camp at
Cheat Mountain. The result was claimed as a
victory on the part of the rebels, though the
details of the battle, and the conduct of the
Union troops, and their orderly return to camp,
indicate nothing like a defeat. The following is General Reynolds's report of this movement:—

"HEADQUARTERS FIRST BRIGADE,
"ARMY OF OCCUPATION, WESTERN VIRGINIA,
"ELK WATER, Oct. 4, 1861.
"GEORGE L. HARTSUFF, Assistant Adjutant-General.

"SIR: On the night of the 2d of October, at
twelve o'clock, I started from the summit of
Cheat Mountain, to make an armed reconnoissance of the enemy's position on the Green Brier
River, twelve miles in advance. Our force consisted of Howe's battery, fourth regular artillery, Loomis's battery, Michigan volunteer artillery, part of Daum's battery, Virginia volunteer artillery, twenty-fourth, twenty-fifth, and
thirty-second Ohio regiments, seventh, ninth,
thirteenth, fourteenth, fifteenth, and seventeenth
Indiana regiments—the last four being reduced
by continuous hard service and sickness to about
half regiments—parts of Robinson's company
of Ohio, Greenfield's reserve, and Bracken's
Indiana cavalry; in all about five thousand.
Millroy's ninth Indiana drove in the enemy's
advanced pickets, and deployed to our right,
driving the enemy on that flank into his intrenchments. Kimball's fourteenth Indiana was
advanced directly to the enemy's front and
right, to drive his advanced regiments from a
position suitable for our artillery: this was
soon done in gallant style, and our batteries
promptly took their positions within about
seven hundred yards of the intrenchments, and
opened fire. Some of the enemy's guns were
visible, and others concealed. We disabled three
of his guns, made a thorough reconnoissance,
and, after having fully and successfully accomplished the object of the expedition, retired
leisurely and in good order to Cheat Mountain,
arriving at sundown, having marched twenty-
four miles, and been under the enemy's fire
four hours. The enemy's force was about nine
thousand, and we distinctly saw heavy reënforcements of infantry and artillery arrive,
while we were in front of the works.

"We took thirteen prisoners. The number

of killed and wounded could not be accurately ascertained; but from those actually counted in the field, and estimated in the trenches which could be seen from the heights, it is believed the number reached at least three hundred. Our loss was surprisingly small — eight killed and thirty-two wounded, most of them slightly; the proximity of our batteries to the intrenchments causing many shots to pass over us.

"Very respectfully, &c.,

"J. J. REYNOLDS,

"*Brigadier-General commanding.*

"GEORGE W. ROSE, ASSISTANT ADJUTANT-GENERAL."

Although the rebels claimed a victory in the affair on the Green Brier Mountain, they made no advance from that position, but, on the contrary, withdrew, after a time, to positions farther east, on the Alleghany range. Here, at a point some eight or ten miles beyond the scene of the battle of Green Brier, another engagement took place on the 13th of December. With about two thousand men, General Milroy moved from Cheat Mountain against this position of the rebels. Reaching the former rebel position, General Milroy divided his forces, with a view to attack the enemy on two sides simultaneously; but the road taken by one division was very bad, and much obstructed by fallen timber thrown across it by the rebels as a defence, and the march was so much impeded that this division did not reach a position for attack until the other division was retiring. The latter, which was under command of General Milroy in person, having reached the summit upon which the rebel camp was established, found it necessary to make an attack without waiting for the coöperation of the column that had moved to the right. The rebels had formed for battle when their pickets were driven in, and advanced to meet the federal force. They were speedily driven back, but soon rallied again, when they were again compelled to retire before the fire of their 'assailants. An attempt to turn the

flank of the small federal force also failed. But the ammunition of General Milroy's troops was nearly exhausted, and they were obliged to retire, nothing yet being heard from the other division. But General Milroy's troops had retired but a short time when this division commenced an attack on the right. The rebels, relieved from the attack of the first body, turned their strength against the new comers. The latter, however, skirmished successfully, and, when a rebel force came out of their works, drove them back by a well-directed fire. This part of the engagement continued for nearly four hours, without any decisive result, when the federal forces were withdrawn, carrying with them their dead and wounded. Had the attack been made simultaneously by the two divisions, as intended, the result would probably have been a decisive victory for the federal arms. As it was, the expedition failed of its purpose, though the federal troops were simply repulsed, not defeated. The rebels claimed a brilliant triumph, though their own accounts fail to make it appear. The federal loss was twenty killed, one hundred and seven wounded, and ten missing. The loss on the part of the rebels, according to their reports, was about the same.

Besides the engagements above described, detached bodies of troops belonging to the command of General Rosecrans, were moved to different points in the Kanawha valley, and had several skirmishes with the rebels, who had again collected forces in the valley. The most important of these engagements was one at Chapmanville, September 25, where a body of rebels were routed, with heavy loss, by a Kentucky regiment, under command of Colonel Enyart, and an Ohio regiment, under command of Colonel Piatt, each of which met the enemy separately, and compelled him to retire.

The troops of General Rosecrans were not idle, though no other important battle or movement occurred for the present. They were so disposed as to hold in check the rebel forces, and to press them gradually back from the slight advance they had made since the summer campaign. The roads were bad, and the movements of either side were greatly impeded by the difficulties of transportation. The tide of success, however, was in favor of the federal troops. On the 10th of November an advance was made against Floyd's forces in a strong position on Cotton Hill, near Gauley Bridge. General Cox's brigade crossed the river, and ascended the heights upon which the rebels were posted. After a slight resistance the latter abandoned their position, and retreated to other strongholds among the hills of that region. Preparations were made to pursue and attack them again as speedily as the bad roads would permit; but the active campaign in this part of Virginia was suddenly brought to a close by the sudden retreat of Floyd, who, on the 20th of November, broke up his camp near the Gauley River, burned a large number of tents, destroyed a quantity of camp equipage, and abandoned several wagons of ammunition and arms in his flight.

Floyd's forces were pursued some thirty miles by General Benham's troops, who had several skirmishes with the rear guard of the rebels. General Benham anticipated being able to entirely rout or capture the whole force at Raleigh; but while he was yet in pursuit, his brigade was transferred to General Schenck, and was ordered back.

A month later General Rosecrans issued an address to the army of Western Virginia, congratulating them upon their triumphs during the campaign then finished, and urging more perfect preparation for future operations. General Floyd, about the same time, issued an address to the troops under his command, expressing his admiration at the manner in which they had conducted a campaign of five months, and baffled the enemy. The success of General Floyd, however, was hardly acknowledged by

the rebel government; for he was relieved of command, and his forces were sent to Tennessee and Kentucky.

While the rebels made demonstrations against Western Virginia, they also organized a campaign in the mountainous region in the northern part of the state, from the region of Cheat River, where General Lee's forces moved against the federal forces at Cheat Mountain, to the vicinity of Harper's Ferry. The object was to get possession of and hold the Baltimore and Ohio Railroad, thus cutting off the most direct communication between Washington and the west, while they might also be able to turn the flank of the federal army of the Potomac, and even threaten incursions into Pennsylvania. Federal troops had moved forward along the railroad from Western Virginia, reopening communication which had been interrupted by the destruction of bridges, and guarding the more important places along the route. Slight skirmishes occurred at various points between small detachments of these troops and bands of disloyal inhabitants who were organized for guerrilla warfare or to join the rebel army. The increasing numbers of the rebel troops in this region rendered it necessary to add to the federal forces posted along the extended line which they held; but with such numbers as were sent no considerable force could be collected at one point.

The only engagements of any magnitude that occurred during the autumn, in this region, were at Romney, in Hampshire County, on the south branch of the Potomac. The first of these affairs took place on the 23d of September, when about one thousand men, including a small cavalry force, with one piece of artillery, advanced from New Creek towards Romney. At Mechanicsburg Gap, near Romney, they met a force of seven hundred rebels, whom they drove out of the gap, and then attacked the rebels posted in the town. The attack was sudden and vigorous, and the enemy, number-

ing about fourteen hundred men, retreated from the town to the neighboring mountains, with a loss of many killed and wounded. The federal troops did not attempt to hold the place, but retired to their former position.

The other engagement occurred on the 26th of October. General Kelley, with twenty-five hundred men, moved from New Creek towards Romney, on the west, and at the same time Colonel Johns, with seven hundred men, moved from Patterson's Creek to the north side of the town, to create a diversion in favor of General Kelley. At Mill Creek, about five miles from Romney, General Kelley's troops came upon the rebel outposts, and skirmishing commenced. The rebel force stationed here soon retreated, and General Kelley advanced to the Indian Mound Cemetery, where a larger body of the rebels made a stand, and opened fire with a rifled cannon, while at the same time other artillery, from high grounds on the east side of the river commanding the road taken by the federal troops, also commenced throwing shot at them. At the east end of the bridge the rebels had also thrown up intrenchments, from which they kept up a constant, though rather harmless, fire of musketry.

After responding briskly to the rebel fire with his three or four pieces of artillery, General Kelley, having ascertained the rebel position, ordered an assault upon battery and intrenchment. The cavalry dashed across the river, which was shallow and fordable, while the infantry charged rapidly over the bridge. This movement had hardly begun when the rebels abandoned their position and commenced a precipitate retreat through the town and towards Winchester. They were followed by the federal cavalry, who took many prisoners, while in the town General Kelley captured all their cannon, a quantity of small arms, many horses, tents, and a large amount of stores. The loss on either side was small, being one killed and five wounded on the federal side, and eight or

ten killed and fifteen wounded on the part of the rebels.

While General Kelley advanced on the west of the town, Colonel Johns approached through Springfield on the north. After a slight skirmish at Springfield, this force advanced to a bridge leading into Romney, where its passage was opposed by the rebels. An attempt to charge across the bridge was ineffectual, because of the removal of the planks from a part of it, which was not discovered till the federal troops were already upon the bridge, where they were exposed to a galling fire from the rebels on the other side. Colonel Johns, finding it impracticable to cross, and as his orders were simply to create a diversion in favor of General Kelley, which he had accomplished, now withdrew his troops. General Kelley had already succeeded in routing the enemy on his side, and the rebel force on the north of the town soon followed the fugitives towards Winchester.

The rebel forces, under General Jackson, continued to threaten the federal lines on the Upper Potomac and the forces that had advanced from the west; but though there were occasional slight skirmishes, and a constant oppression of all loyal persons who were within reach of the rebel forces, regular and irregular, no conflict or movement of importance occurred during this year.

CHAPTER XLIX.

The Army of the Potomac. — Its Position. — Reconnoissances and Skirmishes. — Occupation of Lewinsville. — Movement at Harper's Ferry, and successful Skirmish. — Battle of Ball's Bluff. — Object of a Movement towards Leesburg. — Feint at Edwards's Ferry, and Crossing at Harrison's Island. — Advance of the Massachusetts Fifteenth Regiment. — Skirmishing. —Advance of the Rebel Forces. — Severe Conflict. —Death of Colonel Baker. — The Federal Forces overcome. — Retreat. —Want of Transportation across the River. — Escape of the Soldiers. — Continued Attack of the Rebels. — Prisoners. — Colonels Lee and Coggswell. — Federal and Rebel Losses. — Report of General Stone. — Extracts from Report of Colonel

Devens. — Effect of the Defeat. — Inadequate Means of Crossing the River. — Extract from the Report of Colonel Hinks. — Colonel Baker.

WE now return to the army of the Potomac, which was posted in front of Washington from some distance below Alexandria to a point several miles beyond the chain bridge above Georgetown. Above that point, on the Maryland side of the river, were other federal forces, the pickets of which extended nearly to Harper's Ferry, while the principal body of these troops were stationed in the vicinity of Poolesville. In front of this line the rebels had collected a large army, which was posted in strong positions, constantly threatening an attack, and making movements which required vigilant watching and counter-movements on the part of the federal forces. Frequent skirmishes occurred between the pickets and reconnoitring and foraging parties of the two armies, with various success and more or less loss; but no engagement of any magnitude until a severe battle at Ball's Bluff, opposite Harrison's Island, in front of Poolesville. Previous to this the federal troops had made some advances and gained some of the strong positions held by the rebels. One of these movements was made October 10, from the chain bridge, towards Lewinsville, which place, with the neighboring eminences, was occupied by a strong force, without resistance on the part of the rebels, who retired at the approach of the federal troops. A few days after, a large rebel force advanced towards Lewinsville, probably for the purpose of reconnoitring; but a general attack was expected, and preparations were made to meet it, while great excitement prevailed at Washington in anticipation of a battle. The rebel force, however, after throwing a few artillery shot at long range, withdrew, and the federal position was strengthened.

On the Upper Potomac the skirmishes consisted principally of the firing of pickets and small parties across the river; but occasionally parties of either army crossed the river on foraging expeditions. One of these expeditions, worthy of mention, was an expedition, on the 15th of October, under command of Colonel Geary,* of Pennsylvania, who, with four hundred men, crossed the river at Harper's Ferry, and captured a large quantity of wheat, stored in a mill near that place. The rebels did not occupy Harper's Ferry, but were strongly posted on the neighboring heights and in the vicinity of Charlestown. On the return of the federal force the next day, an attack was made by a rebel force of cavalry, artillery, and infantry, while the batteries on the heights also commenced a heavy cannonading. After some skirmishing, Colonel Geary's force charged upon the battery on Bolivar Heights, and carried it, capturing one heavy piece of ordnance, and putting the rebels to flight. Being reënforced, he succeeded in compelling the whole rebel force to retire, and, as it appeared, with considerable loss, including several prisoners. The federal loss was four killed, eight wounded, and two taken prisoners. Having secured the wheat and destroyed an iron foundery used by the rebels for the casting of shot and shell, Colonel Geary's command recrossed the river without further attack.

The battle of Ball's Bluff occurred on the 21st of October. General McCall had occupied Drainesville, a village in Virginia, about midway between Washington and Leesburg, and General Stone, who commanded the forces near Poolesville, was directed to coöperate with reconnoissances from Drainesville by advancing a force towards Leesburg. Accordingly preparations were made to cross at Edwards's Ferry, in front of General Stone's position, and a feint of carrying out the movement was made, while a force of about twenty-one hundred men, consisting of detachments of the fifteenth and

* Afterwards brigadier-general.

twentieth Massachusetts regiments, first California, and Tammany regiments of New York, with sections of a Rhode Island and a regular battery of light artillery, were ordered to cross at Harrison's Island, some miles above. The latter force, with very limited means of transportation, crossed on the 21st, by small detachments and slowly, the fifteenth Massachusetts regiment, Colonel Devens,* being in the advance. The detachment from this regiment, having ascended the steep bluff which extended along the Virginia shore, advanced a mile or more towards Leesburg without meeting with the enemy, or seeing any signs of their presence in considerable numbers. While waiting here for reënforcements, a rebel force suddenly appeared, and skirmishing commenced, the federal troops retiring to a wood, and subsequently falling back towards the bluff. Here the twentieth Massachusetts regiment, Colonel Lee, had arrived, and Colonel Devens again advanced. While in his advanced position, a strong rebel force made an attack upon him, and compelled him to retire again to the position where the other Massachusetts regiment, with the California and Tammany regiments, were forming in line of battle. Colonel Baker, of the California regiment, by orders from General Stone, assumed command of the entire force, and prepared to meet the enemy. The latter came in numbers evidently greatly exceeding the federal troops, and advancing under the cover of woods, through which they threw out numerous skirmishers, they poured a heavy fire of artillery and musketry into the unprotected lines of Colonel Baker's force. The federal artillery responded briskly, but with some disadvantage, owing to the protection afforded to the rebels by the woods; but two or three pieces were soon nearly silenced by the loss of officers and men, and one piece was captured by being drawn up the bluff at the wrong point.

The infantry returned the enemy's volleys bravely, though it was soon evident that the rebels had in every way the advantage. Suddenly a conspicuous rebel officer, riding in front of his troops, beckoned to the federal soldiers as if daring them to advance. Colonel Baker, believing that the rebels were about to emerge from their cover and meet in open fight, ordered a charge, leading his own regiment himself; but they were met by a tremendous fire, as if reënforcements had arrived to aid the already overwhelming numbers of the rebels, and in this attack Colonel Baker fell, being instantly killed by a shot through the head. The federal force now wavered and fell back; but by the efforts of Colonel Coggswell, of the Tammany regiment, upon whom the command now devolved, they were rallied, and an attempt to cut a passage through to Edwards's Ferry, where troops had now been thrown across the river, was contemplated. This was soon found impracticable with so strong a force to oppose it, and the only thing that remained was to retreat down the bluff and recross the river to Harrison's Island. This movement was accordingly ordered, the enemy pursuing as soon as the retreat was evident. A few of the troops crossed in boats; but the large boat in which they had come over was too heavily laden, and was swamped, and a number of the men were drowned. Others, throwing their arms into the river, swam across, the rebels in the mean time firing upon them from the edge of the bluff, probably killing a few, or wounding them so that they were drowned. About five hundred were taken prisoners, including the wounded. Among the prisoners was Colonel Lee, of the twentieth Massachusetts, who declined to use a small boat which had been found, preferring to secure the safety of some of his wounded soldiers. Being unable to find other means of transportation, he was captured by a party of rebels, together with the major, adjutant, and assistant surgeon of his regiment. Colonel

---

* Afterwards brigadier-general.

Coggswell, who was wounded, also fell into the hands of the enemy. The federal loss in killed was about one hundred and fifty, and the wounded numbered at least two hundred and fifty. According to the report of the rebel commander, General Evans, he took seven hundred and ten prisoners, and his loss in killed and wounded was one hundred and fifty-three. The rebel force numbered about four thousand.

The details of this movement and battle are more minutely described in the following official reports : —

GENERAL STONE'S REPORT.

"HEADQUARTERS CORPS OF OBSERVATION,
"October 28, 1861.

"GENERAL: On the 20th inst., being advised from headquarters of General McCall's movements to Drainesville to reconnoitre and draw out the intentions of the enemy at Leesburg, I went to Edwards's Ferry, at one o'clock P. M., with General Gorman's brigade, seventh Michigan, two troops of the Van Alen cavalry, and the Putnam Rangers, while four companies of the fifteenth Massachusetts volunteers were sent to Harrison's Island, under Colonel Devens, who then had one company on the island, and Colonel Lee, with a battalion of the Massachusetts twentieth, a section of the Rhode Island battery and Tammany regiment, was sent to Conrad's Ferry. A section of Bunting's New York battery and Rickett's battery was already on duty, respectively at Edwards's and Conrad's Ferries.

"General McCall's movements had evidently attracted the attention of the enemy, a regiment of infantry having appeared from the direction of Leesburg, and taken shelter behind a hill about a mile and a half from our position at the ferry.

"General Gorman was ordered to deploy his forces in view of the enemy, and in so doing no movement of the enemy was excited. Three flat-boats were ordered, and at the same time, shell and spherical case-shot were thrown into the place of the enemy's concealment. This

47

was done to produce an impression that a crossing was to be made. The shelling at Edwards's Ferry, and launching of the boats, induced the quick retirement of the enemy's force seen there, and three boat loads of thirty-five men each, from the first Minnesota, crossed and recrossed the river, each trip occupying about six or seven minutes.

"While this was going on, the men evinced by their cheering that they were all ready and determined to fight gallantly when the opportunity was presented. At dusk, General Gorman's brigade and the seventh Michigan returned to camp, leaving the Tammany regiment and the companies of the fifteenth Massachusetts and artillery at Conrad's Ferry in position, awaiting the return of scouts. Meanwhile, General Stone remained at Edwards's Ferry. At ten o'clock P. M., Lieutenant Howe, quartermaster of the fifteenth Massachusetts, reported that scouts, under Captain Philbrick, had returned to the island, having been within one mile of Leesburg, and there discovering in the edge of a wood an encampment of thirty tents. No pickets were out any distance, and he approached to within twenty-five rods without being even challenged.

"Orders were then instantly sent to Colonel Devens to cross four companies to the Virginia shore, and march silently, under cover of the night, to the position of the camp referred to, to attack and destroy it at daybreak, pursue the enemy lodged there as far as would be prudent, and return immediately to the island, his return to be covered by a company of the Massachusetts twentieth, to be posted over the landing place. Colonel Devens was ordered to make close observation of the position, strength, and movements of the enemy, and in the event of there being no enemy there visible, to hold on, in a secure position, until he could be strengthened sufficiently to make a valuable reconnoissance.

"At this time orders were sent to Colonel

Baker to send the first California regiment to Conrad's Ferry, to arrive there at sunrise, and to have the remainder of his brigade ready to move early.

"Lieutenant-Colonel Ward, of the fifteenth Massachusetts, was also ordered to move with a battalion to the river bank opposite Harrison's Island by daybreak. Two mounted howitzers, in charge of Lieutenant French, of Rickett's battery, were ordered to the tow-path of the canal opposite Harrison's Island. Colonel Devens, in pursuance of his orders, crossed and proceeded to the point indicated, Colonel Lee remaining on the bluff, with one hundred men to cover his return. To distract attention from Colonel Devens's movements, and to make a reconnoissance in the direction of Leesburg from Edwards's Ferry, I directed General Gorman to throw across the river at that point two companies of the first Minnesota, under cover of a fire from Rickett's battery, and sent out a party of thirty-one Van Alen cavalry, under Major Mix, accompanied by Captain Charles Stewart, assistant adjutant-general, Captain Murphy, and Lieutenants Pierce and Gouraud, with orders to advance along the Leesburg road until they should come to the vicinity of a battery which was known to be on that road, and then turn to the left and examine the heights between that and Goose Creek, and see if any of the enemy were posted in the vicinity, find out their numbers as nearly as possible, their disposition, examine the country with reference to the passage of troops to the Leesburg and Georgetown turnpike, and return rapidly to cover behind the skirmishers of the Minnesota first. This reconnoissance was most gallantly conducted, and the party proceeded along the Leesburg road, nearly two miles from the ferry, and when near the position of the hidden battery, came suddenly upon a Mississippi regiment, about thirty-five yards distant, received its fire, and returned it with their pistols. The fire of the enemy killed one horse; but Lieutenant

Gouraud seized the dismounted man, and drawing him on his horse behind him, carried him unhurt from the field. One private of the fourth Virginia cavalry was brought off by the party a prisoner, who, being well mounted and armed, his mount replaced the one lost by the fire of the enemy.

"Meantime, on the right, Colonel Devens, having, in pursuance of his orders, arrived at the position designated to him as the site of the enemy's camp, found that the scouts had been deceived by the uncertain light, and mistaken openings in the trees for a row of tents. Colonel Devens found, however, a wood, in which he concealed his force, and proceeded to examine the space between that and Leesburg, sending back to report that thus far he could see no enemy. Immediately on receipt of this intelligence, brought me by Lieutenant Howe, who had accompanied both parties, I ordered a non-commissioned officer and ten cavalry to join Colonel Devens, for the purpose of scouring the country near him while engaged in the reconnoissance, and giving due notice of the approach of any force, and that Lieutenant-Colonel Ward, with his battalion of the fifteenth Massachusetts, should move on to Smoot's Mills, half a mile to the right of the crossing place of Colonel Devens, and see where, in a strong position, he could watch and protect the flank of Colonel Devens in his return, and secure a second crossing more favorable than the first, and connected by a good road with Leesburg. Captain Candy, assistant adjutant-general, and General Lander, accompanied the cavalry to serve with it. For some reason, never explained to me, neither of these orders was carried out. The cavalry were transferred to the Virginia shore, but were sent back without having left the shore to go inland; and thus Colonel Devens was deprived of the means of obtaining warning of any approach of the enemy.

"The battalion under Colonel Ward was detained on the bluff in the rear of Colonel

Devens, instead of being directed to the right. Colonel Baker, having arrived at Conrad's Ferry with the first California regiment at an early hour, proceeded to Edwards's Ferry, and reported to me in person, stating that his regiment was at the former place, and the three other regiments of his brigade ready to march. I directed him to Harrison's Island to assume command, and in full conversation explained to him the position as it then stood. I told him that General McCall had advanced his troops to Drainesville, and that I was extremely desirous of ascertaining the exact position and force of the enemy in our front, and exploring as far as it was safe on the right towards Leesburg, and on the left towards the Leesburg and Gum Spring road. I also informed Colonel Baker that General Gorman, opposite Edwards's Ferry, should be reënforced, and that I would make every effort to push Gorman's troops carefully forward to discover the best line from that ferry to the Leesburg and Gum Spring road, already mentioned; and the position of the breastworks and hidden battery, which prevented the movement of troops directly from left to right, was also pointed out to him.

"The means of transportation across, of the sufficiency of which he (Baker) was to be judge, was detailed, and authority given him to make use of the guns of a section each of Vaughan's and Bunting's batteries, together with French's mountain howitzers, all the troops of his brigade and the Tammany regiment, besides the nineteenth and part of the twentieth regiments of Massachusetts volunteers, and I left it to his discretion, after viewing the ground, to retire from the Virginia shore under the cover of his guns and the fire of the large infantry force, or to place our reënforcements in case he found it practicable and the position on the other side favorable. I stated that I wished no advance made, unless the enemy were of inferior force, and under no circumstances to pass beyond Leesburg, or a strong position between

it and Goose Creek, on the Gum Spring road, i. e., the Manassas road. Colonel Baker was cautioned in reference to passing artillery across the river; and I begged him, if he did do so, to see it well supported by good infantry. The general pointed out to him the position of some bluffs on this side of the river, from which artillery could act with effect on the other; and, leaving the matter of crossing more troops, or retiring what were already over, to his discretion, gave him entire control of operations on the right. This gallant and energetic officer left me about nine A. M., or half past nine, and galloped off quickly to his command.

"Reënforcements were rapidly thrown to the Virginia side by General Gorman at Edwards's Ferry, and his skirmishers and cavalry scouts advanced cautiously and steadily to the front and right, while the infantry lines were formed in such positions as to act rapidly and in concert, in case of an advance of the enemy, and shells were thrown by Lieutenant Woodruff's Parrott guns into the woods beyond our lines, as they gradually extended, care being taken to annoy the vicinity of the battery on the right. Messengers from Harrison's Island informed me, soon after the arrival of Colonel Baker opposite the island, that he was crossing his whole force as rapidly as possible, and that he had caused an additional flat-boat to be rafted from the canal into the river, and had provided a line to cross the boats more rapidly.

"In the morning a skirmish took place between two companies of the twentieth Massachusetts and about one hundred Mississippi riflemen, during which a body of the enemy's cavalry appeared. Colonel Devens then fell back in good order on Colonel Lee's position. Presently he again advanced, his men behaving admirably, fighting, retiring, and advancing in perfect order, and exhibiting every proof of high courage and good discipline. Had the cavalry scouting party, sent him in the morning, been with him then, he could have had timely warning of the approach of the superior force which afterwards overwhelmed his regiment. Thinking that Colonel Baker might be able to use more artillery, I despatched to him two additional pieces, supported by two companies of infantry, with directions to come into position below the place of crossing, and report to Colonel Baker. Colonel Baker suggested this himself, later in the day, just before the guns on their way arrived.

" After Colonel Devens's second advance, Colouel Baker went to the field in person; and it is a matter of regret to me that he left no record of what officers and men he charged with the care of the boats and insuring the regular passage of troops. If any were charged with this duty, it was not performed; for the reënforcements, as they arrived, found no one in command of the boats, and great delays were thus occasioned. Had one officer and a company remained at each landing, guarding the boats, their full capacity would have been made serviceable, and sufficient men would have been passed on to secure success. The forwarding of artillery before its supporting force of infantry, also impeded the rapid assembling of an imposing force on the Virginia shore. If the infantry force had first crossed, a difference of one thousand men would have been made in the infantry line at the time of attack, probably enough to have given us the victory.

" Between twelve and one P. M. the enemy appeared in force in front of Colonel Devens, and a sharp skirmish ensued, and was maintained for some time by the fifteenth Massachusetts, unsupported; and finding he would be outflanked, Colonel Devens retired a short distance, and took up a position near the wood, half a mile in front of Colonel Lee, where he remained until two o'clock, when he again fell back, with the approval of Colonel Baker, and took his place with the portions of the twentieth Massachusetts and first California, which had arrived. Colonel Baker now formed his line, and waited the attack of the enemy, which came upon him with great vigor about three P. M., and was well met by our troops, who, though pitched against much superior numbers,—three to one,—maintained their ground under a most destructive fire of the enemy. Colonel Coggswell reached the field amid the heaviest fire, and came gallantly into action, with a yell which wavered the enemy's line. Lieutenant Bramhall, of Bunting's battery, had succeeded, after extraordinary exertions and labor, in bringing up a piece of the Rhode Island battery, and Lieutenant French his two howitzers; but both officers, after well directed firing, were soon borne away wounded, and the pieces were hauled to the rear, so that they might not fall into the enemy's hands. At four P. M., Colonel Baker fell at the head of his column, pierced by a number of bullets, while cheering his men, and by his own example sustaining the obstinate resistance they were making. The command then devolved upon Colonel Lee, who prepared to commence throwing out forces to the rear; but it was soon found that Colonel Coggswell was the senior in rank, and he, taking the command, ordered preparation to be made for marching to the left, and cutting a way through to Edwards's Ferry. But just as the first dispositions were being effected, a rebel officer rode rapidly in front, and beckoned the Tammany regiment towards the enemy. It is not clear whether or not the Tammany men supposed this one of our officers; but they responded with a yell, and charged forward, carrying with them, in their advance, the rest of the line, which soon received a destructive fire from the enemy at close distance. The men were quickly recalled; but their new position frustrated the movement designed, and Colonel Coggswell gave the necessary order to retire. The enemy pursued to the edge of the bluff over the landing place, and poured in a heavy fire as our men were endeavoring to cross to the island. The retreat was rapid, but according to orders. The men formed near the river, maintaining for nearly half an hour the hopeless contest rather than surrender. The smaller boats had disappeared, no one knew where. The largest boat, rapidly and too heavily loaded, swamped some fifteen feet from the shore, and nothing was left to our soldiers but to swim, surrender, or die.

"With a devotion worthy of the cause they were serving, officers and men, while quarter was being offered to such as would lay down their arms, stripped themselves of their swords and muskets, and hurled them out into the river, to prevent their falling into the hands of the foe, and saved themselves as they could by swimming, floating on logs, and concealing themselves in the bushes of the forest, and endeavoring to make their way up and down the river bank to the place of crossing. The instances of personal gallantry of the highest order were so many, that it would be unjust to detail particular cases. Officers displayed for their men, and men for their officers, that beautiful devotion which is only to be found among true soldiers. While these scenes were being enacted on the right, I was preparing on the left for a rapid push forward to the road by which the enemy would retreat if driven, and entirely unsuspicious of the perilous condition of our troops. The additional artillery had already been sent, and when the messenger, who did not leave the field until after three o'clock, was questioned as to Colonel Baker's position, he informed me that the colonel, when he left, seemed to feel perfectly secure, and could doubtless hold his position in case he should not advance. The same statement was made by another messenger, half an hour later, and I watched anxiously for a sign of advance on the right, in order to push forward General Gorman. It was, as had been explained to Colonel Baker, impracticable to throw General Gorman's brigade directly to the right by reason of the battery in the woods, between which

we had never been able to reconnoitre. At four P. M., or thereabouts, I telegraphed to General Banks for a brigade of his division, intending it to occupy the ground on this side of the river near Harrison's Island, which would be abandoned in case of a rapid advance, and shortly after, as the fire slackened, a messenger was waited for, on whose tidings should be given orders either for the advance of General Gorman to cut off the retreat of the enemy, or for the disposition for the night in the position then held. At five P. M. Captain Candy arrived from the field, and announced the melancholy tidings of Colonel Baker's death; but with no intelligence of any further disaster. I immediately apprised General Banks of Colonel Baker's death, and I rode quickly to the right, to assume command. Before arriving opposite the island, men who had crossed the river plainly gave evidence of the disaster; and on reaching the same, I was satisfied of it by the conduct of the men then landing in boats.

"The reports made to me were, that the enemy's force was ten thousand men. This I considered, as it proved to be, an exaggeration. Orders were then given to hold the island, and establish a patrol on the tow-path from opposite the island to the line of pickets near the Monocacy, and I returned to the left, to secure the troops there from disaster, and make preparations for moving them as rapidly as possible.

"Orders arrived from General McClellan to hold the island on the Virginia shore at Edwards's Ferry at all risks, indicating at the same time that reënforcements would be sent; and immediately additional means of intrenching were forwarded, and General Gorman was furnished with particular directions to hold out against any and every force of the enemy.

"During that time, General Hamilton, with his brigade, was on the march from Darnestown. Before I left to go to the right, I issued orders to intercept him, and instructed him to repair to Conrad's Ferry, where orders awaited him to so dispose of his force as to give protection to Harrison's Island, and protect the line of the river. At three A. M. Major-General Banks arrived and took command.

"A report of division for the following days will be made out speedily. I cannot conclude without bearing testimony to the courage, good discipline, and conduct of all the troops of this division during the day. Those in action behaved like veterans, and those not brought into action showed that alacrity and steadiness in their movements which proved their anxiety to engage the foe in their country's cause. We mourn the loss of the brave departed dead on the field of honor, if not of success, and we miss the companionship of those of our comrades who have fallen into the hands of our enemies. But all feel that they have earned the title of soldier, and all await with increased confidence another measurement of strength with the foe.

"CHAS. P. STONE,
"*Brigadier-General commanding.*"

The following is an extract from the report of Colonel Devens : —

"At about ten o'clock, Quartermaster Howe returned, and stated that he had reported the skirmish of the morning, and that Colonel Baker would shortly arrive with his brigade, and take command. Between nine and eleven o'clock, I was joined by Lieutenant-Colonel Ward with the remainder of my regiment, making, in all, a force of six hundred and twenty-five men, with twenty-eight officers from my regiment, as reported to me by the adjutant, many of the men of the regiment being at this time on other duty. About twelve o'clock it was reported to me a force was gathering on my left, and about half past twelve o'clock a strong attack was made on my left by a body of infantry, concealed in the woods, and upon the skirmishers in front, by a body of cavalry. The fire of the enemy was resolutely returned by

the regiment, which maintained its ground with entire determination. Reënforcements not yet having arrived, and the attempt of the enemy to outflank us being very vigorous, I directed the regiment to retire about sixty paces into an open space in the wood, and prepared to receive any attack that might be made, while I called in my skirmishers. When this was done, I returned to the bluff, where Colonel Baker had already arrived. This was at a quarter past two P. M. He directed me to form my regiment at the right of the position he proposed to occupy — which was done by eight companies ; the centre and left being composed of a detachment of the twentieth Massachusetts, numbering about three hundred men, under command of Colonel Lee. A battalion of the California regiment, numbering about six hundred men, Lieutenant-Colonel Wistar commanding ; two howitzers, commanded by Lieutenant Pierce ; and a six-pounder, commanded by Lieutenant Bramhall, were planted in front, supported by company D, Captain Studley, and company F, Captain Sloan of the fifteenth Massachusetts. The enemy soon appeared in force, and after sharp skirmishing on the right, directed his attack upon our whole line, but more particularly upon our centre and left, where it was gallantly met by the Massachusetts twentieth and the California battalion. Skirmishing during all the action was very severe on the right ; but the skirmishers of the enemy were resolutely repulsed by our own, composed of companies A and I, Captains Rockwood and Joslin, of the Massachusetts fifteenth, and company —, of the twentieth Massachusetts, under the direction of Major Kimball, of the Massachusetts fifteenth.

"The action commenced about three o'clock P. M., and at about four P. M. I was ordered to detach two companies from the left of my regiment to the support of the left of the line, and to draw in proportionately the right flank — which was done, companies G and H, Captains Forehand and Philbrick, being detached for that purpose. By this time it had become painfully evident, by the volume and rapidity of the enemy's fire, and the persistency of his attacks, that he was in much larger force than we. The two howitzers were silent, and the six-pounder also. Their commanders came from the field wounded. Soon after I was called from the right of my regiment, there being at this time a comparative cessation of the enemy's fire to the centre of the line, and learned, for the first time, that Colonel Baker had been killed, and that Lieutenant-Colonel Ward, of the fifteenth Massachusetts, had been carried from the field severely wounded. Colonel Lee supposing it his duty to take command, I reported myself ready to execute his orders. He expressed his opinion that the only thing to be done was to retreat to the river, and that the battle was utterly lost. It soon appeared that Colonel Coggswell was entitled to the command, who expressed his determination to make the attempt to cut our way to Edwards's Ferry, and ordered me, as a preliminary movement, to form the fifteenth regiment in line towards the left. The fifteenth regiment accordingly moved across from the right to the left of the original line. Two or three companies of the Tammany New York regiment, just then arrived, formed also on its left: while endeavoring to make the necessary disposition to retreat, confusion was created by the appearance of an officer of the enemy's force in front of the Tammany regiment, who called on them to charge on the enemy, who were now in strong force along the wood occupied formerly by the fifteenth Massachusetts during the former portion of the action. The detachment of the Tammany regiment, probably mistaking this for an order from their own officers, rushed forward to the charge, and the Massachusetts fifteenth, supposing that an order had been given for the advance of the whole line, rushed with eagerness, but were promptly recalled by their officers, who had received no such order. The detachment

of the Tammany regiment were received by a shower of bullets, and suffered severely; in the disturbance caused by their repulse, the line was broken, but was promptly reformed. After this, however, although several volleys were given and returned, and the troops fought vigorously, it seemed impossible to preserve the order necessary for a combined military movement, and Colonel Coggswell reluctantly gave the order to retreat to the river bank. The troops descended the bluff, and reached the bank of the river, where there is a narrow plateau between the river and the ascent of the bluff, both the plateau and the bluff being heavily wooded. As I descended upon this plateau, in company with Colonel Coggswell, I saw the large boat upon which we depended as the means of crossing the river, swamped by the number of men who had rushed upon it. For the purpose of retarding as much as possible the approach of the enemy, by direction of Colonel Coggswell, I ordered the fifteenth regiment to deploy as skirmishers over the bank of the river, which order was executed, and several volleys were given and returned between them and others of our forces and the enemy, who were now pressing upon us in great numbers, and forcing down furious volleys on this plateau and into the river, to prevent any escape. It was impossible longer to continue to resist, and I should have had no doubt, if we had been contending with the troops of a foreign nation, in justice to the lives of men, it would have been our duty to surrender; but it was impossible to do this to rebels and traitors, and I had no hesitation in advising men to escape as they could, ordering them, in all cases, to throw their arms into the river rather than give them up to the enemy. This order was generally obeyed, although several of the men swam the river with their muskets on their backs, and others have returned to camp, bringing with them their muskets, who had remained on the Virginia shore for two nights, rather than to part with their weapons, in order to facilitate their escape. Having passed up along the line of that portion of the river occupied by my regiment, I returned to the lower end of it, and at dark myself swam the river by the aid of three of the soldiers of my regiment."

The sad defeat of our troops at Ball's Bluff created a deep feeling of regret, and not a little dismay, that the second battle upon the soil of Eastern Virginia should result as disastrously as the first. The cause of the disaster was freely canvassed, and it was variously attributed to the commanding officer of this division of the army and to the commander of the expedition who fell in the battle. It is perhaps difficult to decide upon whom the blame should rest; but it is evident that the want of adequate transportation across the river was the principal cause of the disaster, by preventing the rapid passage of the troops sent to support the advance of Colonel Devens, and especially by preventing the ready retreat of the defeated forces. Upon this point, Colonel Hinks, of the nineteenth Massachusetts regiment, who was in command at Harrison's Island at the time of the defeat, in his report thus speaks : —

"I cannot close this report with justice to our troops, who fought valiantly, without commenting upon the causes which led to their defeat and complete rout. The means of transportation, for advance in support, or for a retreat, *were criminally deficient* — especially when we consider the facility for creating proper means for such purposes at our disposal. The place for landing on the Virginia shore was most unfortunately selected, being at a point where the shore rose with great abruptness for a distance of some one hundred and fifty yards, at an angle of at least thirty-five degrees, and was entirely studded with trees, being perfectly impassable to artillery or infantry in line. At the summit, the surface is undulating, where the enemy were placed in force, *out of view*, and

cut down our troops with a murderous fire, which we could not return with any effect. The entire island was also commanded by the enemy's artillery and rifles. In fact, no more unfortunate position could have been forced upon us by the enemy for making an attack — much less selected by ourselves.

"Within a half mile upon either side of the points selected a landing could have been effected, where we could have been placed upon equal terms with the enemy, if it was necessary to effect a landing from the island. My judgment, however, cannot approve of that policy which multiplies the number of river crossings without any compensation in securing commanding positions thereby."

The death of Colonel Baker was a great loss to the country. By his ability and his surpassing eloquence he was just attaining to a commanding position in the United States Senate, as one of the leaders of the administration party, and a most earnest supporter of the government against the rebellion. Born in England, he came at a very early age, with his parents, to America, and, after living some years in Philadelphia, removed with them to the west. With a comparatively limited education, he improved his mind by constant study and reading, and early showed great talent in conversation and speaking. He pursued the study of the law, and practised in Illinois, where he first entered public life as a member of the legislature in 1837. Elected to Congress in 1844, he was achieving some distinction there, when the Mexican war broke out; and with a restless energy which characterized his whole life, he raised a regiment of volunteers, and entered the military service. He went to Mexico, and showed great gallantry at Cerro Gordo and in other engagements. After his return he was again elected to Congress from another district, and served there with success. In 1852 he went to California, and having won wealth and distinction, he subsequently removed to Oregon,

where he entered, with his accustomed earnestness, into political life. He was here elected to the Senate, and had served but a brief part of his term, — though long enough to take a foremost place as an orator, — when his restless spirit and his ardent patriotism led him to the more exciting service of a soldier. Declining the proffered appointment of brigadier-general, he raised a regiment in New York, called the "California regiment," in which many men who had sojourned in the Pacific states rallied eagerly around his standard. At the head of this regiment, leading them in a gallant but desperate charge, and impressed, it is said, with a foreboding of his end, he fell. With him fell other noble officers of less conspicuous position, and many brave men of the rank and file; while yet others were doomed to a long and cruel imprisonment.

CHAPTER L.

WHILE the large armies were organized, and various campaigns were made, as narrated in the preceding chapters, the navy department prepared and carried out naval operations upon an extended scale. The objects in view were, to blockade and close, as much as possible, the ports along the coast of the rebellious states, in extent nearly three thousand miles, to coöperate with land forces in expeditions against some

important points, and the pursuit of the rebel privateers which might escape from the blockaded ports, or be secretly fitted out for foreign ports. The vessels required for this various and extended service were constructed or purchased and fitted out as rapidly as possible. Congress, at the extra session, had made most liberal appropriations for this branch of the service, and authorized the construction of a large number of vessels adapted for service upon the coast and in the shallow waters of the southern harbors. But before these could be finished and fitted out, the navy department had created a large navy by fitting out all the available vessels belonging to the United States, completing those previously commenced, and purchasing a large number of sailing vessels and steamers.

After the capture of the forts at Hatteras Inlet, Commodore Stringham, at his own request, was relieved from his command of the Atlantic squadron, and the fleet was divided into two squadrons, one guarding the coast of Virginia and North Carolina, under the command of Commodore Goldsborough, and the other guarding the remainder of the south-eastern coast to the southern point of Florida, under the command of Commodore Dupont. In the Gulf was another large squadron, under the command of Commodore McKean, who succeeded Commodore Mervine.

Although the rebel states had little commerce of their own, there were numerous attempts to evade the blockade; and while not a few vessels succeeded in running in or out of the blockaded ports, probably a larger number was captured. Before the middle of November, more than one hundred and fifty vessels were taken as prizes. Many of these were small vessels, running to or from the West Indies; but some were large and valuable, and carried cargoes of contraband goods.

Besides blockading the ports in the usual manner by ships of war, the secretary of the

48

navy adopted another method, which it was hoped would be successful, and relieve the government from maintaining so large a number of vessels at some points along the coast. This plan was to sink old hulks, laden with stone, in the channels of the harbors, so as to prevent the passage of vessels of considerable size. A number of such hulks were sunk in Ocracoke Inlet, one of the numerous channels on the coast of North Carolina, which afforded opportunities for eluding the blockade and for the escape of privateers. A more elaborate attempt was subsequently made to effectually seal up Charleston harbor, by sinking a number of these stone-laden vessels upon the bar at the entrance of the harbor, and also to stop some of the channels opening into the Savannah River. For a while these obstructions appeared to answer their purpose; but the current, in course of time, seemed to remove them, or the stone settled so deeply into the sand, that the depth of water was but little diminished. This course produced, at first, great indignation in Charleston, where it was feared that the future commerce of the city would be essentially destroyed, and caused some excitement among the foreign sympathizers with the rebellion, who called upon the governments of France and England to protest against the unheard-of and barbarous mode of blockade, forgetting that an English admiral had practised upon this innovation nearly half a century before.

The rebel government had early proposed to issue letters of marque, under which all who were disposed to engage in the work might prey upon the extensive commerce of the northern states. There were few offers, however, to accept such authority from a power not recognized among the nations. But as fast as they were able, with few vessels and sailors at their command, privateers, or vessels directly in the service of the rebel government, were fitted out, not to oppose the navy of the United States, but to capture private property belonging to citizens of the northern states. These vessels were mostly of light draught, capable of running into harbors and inlets where the United States ships of war could not follow them. They succeeded in capturing many prizes, mostly vessels trading between northern ports and the West Indies.

The first privateer which succeeded in getting to sea, so as to commence operations, was the Savannah, a small schooner, armed with a heavy pivot gun. This vessel sailed from Charleston on the 2d of June, and on the next day captured a brig; but she had hardly made sure of her prize, when the United States brig Perry overhauled her, and after discovering her character by her suspicious movements, opened fire upon her. The rebel vessel returned the fire, but very soon, without any considerable show of resistance, made signals of surrender. The vessel was accordingly taken as a prize, and the rebel officers and crew were sent to New York, where they were subsequently tried for piracy. As soon as it was understood at the south that the rebel privateersmen were to be treated as pirates, Jefferson Davis sent to the President, under a flag of truce, a threat of retaliation upon an equal number of United States officers. As the privateersmen captured on board the Savannah, and others taken on board recaptured prizes, were kept in close confinement, and some of them were convicted of piracy, the threat was so far carried out as to confine several Union officers, under the most rigorous treatment, with the purpose of reeking vengeance upon them should the privateersmen be executed. The federal government, however, relaxed its policy in regard to the rebel prisoners, and the threatened retaliation was abandoned.

One of the most successful of these privateers, or rebel cruisers, was the brig "Jeff Davis," supposed to have been the former slaver Echo, which had brought a load of native Africans to the vicinity of Savannah. This vessel, having eluded the blockading squadron, captured a number of prizes in northern waters, taking two or three off Nantucket, and one even within two hundred miles of New York. One of these was retaken by the colored steward, who, watching his opportunity, killed the prize officer and two of his men, when near Charleston, and then, with the aid of a comrade, who was also left on board, and of two of the prize crew, navigated the vessel to New York.

The Jeff. Davis continued the work of capturing and destroying the vessels belonging to northern parties which were fallen in with. Several vessels were despatched after the piratical cruiser, and there was a chance of its being captured; when, in attempting to cross the bar at St. Augustine, Florida, on the 18th of August, to escape the pursuers, the vessel was wrecked, and became a total loss, the crew escaping in their boats.

A more formidable privateer was the steamer Sumter, which succeeded in running the blockade at the passes of the Mississippi, and sailing to the West Indian waters, where she commenced operations upon vessels belonging to northern owners. This vessel had belonged to the Mexican leader Miramon, and had been taken by a ship of war of the United States, near Vera Cruz, when it was considered that the movements of Miramon were hostile to the United States. Having been taken to New Orleans as a prize, she remained there at the commencement of the rebellion, and the rebel authorities took possession of her, and fitted her out to prey upon the private property of loyal merchants. She was commanded by Raphael Semmes, formerly an officer in the United States navy, and made her escape through the blockade, after long watching an opportunity, on the 7th of July. The United States steamer Brooklyn was blockading the Pass à l'Outre at this time, and a vessel having appeared in the offing, with the apparent purpose of running the blockade, the Brooklyn went in pursuit, and was led a chase of some fifteen miles away from her station. While the Brooklyn thus left the Pass unguarded, the Sumter steamed out with all speed, and the commander of the Brooklyn — although the Sumter was known to be waiting such an opportunity — very unwisely continued his chase of a vessel simply suspected of an attempt to enter the river. When the Sumter was fairly out of the Pass, the Brooklyn returned from the pursuit of the suspicious ship, and, when too late, gave chase to the privateer. After a short pursuit the chase was abandoned, and the Sumter went on her piratical cruise.

It was not long before the privateer reached the West Indies, and fell in with northern vessels, which were all captured, except those carrying cargoes on foreign account. Seven of these prizes were taken by the Sumter into the harbor of Cienfuegos, Cuba, with the view to having them condemned. The governor-general, however, held the vessels, and subsequently restored them to their proper crews and owners, when they were convoyed by a United States ship of war till beyond all probable danger. The Sumter continued to cruise about the waters of the West Indies, capturing other northern vessels, several of which were burned. War steamers were sent in pursuit, but did not succeed in finding the piratical cruiser. During the pursuit the Sumter put into the Dutch ports of Curaçoa and Surinam, the Brazilian port of Maranham, the French port of Martinique, and other places, in which she obtained coal or provisions, and her officers were treated with great attention and kindness. This good will was not extended to the officers of the United States vessels who came in pursuit of the pirate; but they were ordered off, in most cases, within twenty-four hours. The Sumter was treated with a similar show of "neutrality" at several ports into which she sailed; but every where there were numerous friends of the rebels, and the orders were evaded, or the officers succeeded in obtaining, by some means, the supplies and aid they wanted.

The United States steamer Powhattan had pursued the Sumter from place to place without succeeding in finding her, before being obliged to return for repairs. The Iroquois, subsequently, was more fortunate in tracking the rebel cruiser, and finally overhauled her in the harbor of St. Pierre, Martinique. But here the French authorities interposed the rules of international law for the benefit of the pirate, and the discomfiture of the national officers. A French ship of war afforded protection against any attack in violation of French neutrality, and the commander of the Iroquois was obliged, in order to avoid any cause of offence between his country and France, to sail out of the harbor before the Sumter, being determined not to wait twenty-four hours after the departure of the latter. Waiting outside the broad bay, beyond the jurisdiction of the French authorities, the commander of the Iroquois watched, as well as he could, the rebel vessel, whose officers were enjoying the hospitalities of the town. Every exertion appears to have been made by the officers and crew of the Iroquois to secure the capture of the Sumter; but in the darkness of the night, aided by the friendly authorities and people of the port, the privateer succeeded in escaping. The following extracts from the official report of the commander of the Iroquois, Commander James S. Palmer, show the difficulties attending the pursuit of the rebel vessel, and the sympathy and aid extended by the French authorities and residents at St. Pierre : —

"UNITED STATES STEAMER IROQUOIS,
"OFF ST. PIERRE, Martinique, *Nov.* 17, 1861.

"SIR : I addressed a letter to the department on the 11th inst., upon my arrival at St. Thomas. On the day following, in the midst of coaling, a mail steamer arrived, bringing information that the Sumter had just put in, on the 9th, to Port Royal, Martinique, in want of coals.

"I had been often led astray by false reports; but this seemed so positive that I instantly ceased coaling, got my engines together, and was off at two in the mid-watch for Martinique, arriving at St. Pierre in thirty-six hours. On turning into the harbor I discovered a suspicious steamer, which, as we approached, proved to be the Sumter, flying the secession flag, moored to the wharf, in the midst of this populous town, quietly coaling. The town and shipping in the harbor were instantly all excitement. I could not attack her in this position for humanity's sake, even were I disposed to be regardless of the neutrality of the port. I did not anchor, but cruised around the harbor within half gun-shot of her during the night.

"In the morning a French man-of-war arrived from Port Royal, the seat of government, only twelve miles distant. The Sumter had been there for the last two days. The government, it is true, had refused to give her any of its coals, but had allowed her to come around to St. Pierre, where she readily obtained them from some merchants, (English, I believe.)

"She evidently had been received with courtesy at the seat of government; and this farce of the non-recognition of the Confederate flag is played out of both France and England in the most flagrant manner.

"I now addressed a letter to the governor, assuming him to be ignorant of the character of the Sumter, a copy of which I enclose. I also enclose a translation of his reply. The department will observe that, from the generous disposition of the governor, the Sumter has the same privileges as this vessel.

"The captain of the French war steamer also addressed me a letter, saying he was directed by the governor to request me no longer to compromise the neutrality of the French waters by establishing a blockade within their jurisdiction, but to anchor, when every hospitality and facility should be afforded me, or to take my position without the distance of a marine league from shore. At the same time, that, while at anchor weigh it was contrary to the police regulations of the port to communicate with the shore.

"I consequently decided upon anchoring; which I had no sooner done than the French commander paid me a visit, offered me every civility and attention, saying that he did not doubt that all international law would be respected by me, and, in the course of conversation, quoting from Wheaton, reminded me that one belligerent could not depart until twenty-four hours after the other. I instantly got under weigh, with him on board, fearing that the Sumter should do so before me, as her steam was up.

"I have now accepted the alternative, and established myself at the mouth of the harbor, without the marine league, with much anxiety, lest, during the darkness of the night, under cover of the high land, the Sumter should be able to get off without my being aware of it.

"The majority of the town is in favor of the Sumter, and with the utmost vigilance, which all on board exert, she may yet escape, some night, for want of signals from the shore to give us notice of her departure. . . .

"P. S. November 18. I feel more and more convinced that the Sumter will yet escape me, in spite of all our vigilance and zeal, even admitting that I can outsteam her, which is a question.

"To blockade such a bay as this, which is almost an open roadstead, fifteen miles in width, the surrounding land very high and the water very bold, obliged, as we are by the neutrality laws, to blockade at three miles distance, it would require at least two more fast steamers, and a vessel of war of any description in port, to notify us by signal of her departure, to give any reasonable hope of preventing her escape.

"Even now, moonlight though it be, she may yet creep out under shadow of the land, and no one be able to perceive her, she being always able to observe my position, open to seawards. Though I have made arrangements to be in-formed by signal of her departure from shore, I fear I cannot depend upon the parties, so fearful are they of the authorities and of popular indignation."

"UNITED STATES STEAMSHIP IROQUOIS,
"ST. THOMAS, W. I., Nov. 25, 1861.

"SIR: As I expected, I have to report the escape of the Sumter, to the great dejection of us all, for never were officers and crew more zealous for a capture.

"At eight o'clock on the night of the 23d, the signal was faithfully made us from the shore, that the Sumter had shipped to the southward. Instantly we were off in pursuit, soon at full speed, rushing down to the southern part of the bay; but nothing was visible on the dark background.

"A small steamer, apparently one plying between St. Pierre and Port Royal, was off the point making signals, doubtless for the benefit of the Sumter. But we could see nothing of her, as we proceeded on, so dark was the shadow thrown by the high land. Still we went on, all searching the darkness in vain. So soon as I had opened Port Royal Point, and seen nothing on the now open horizon, I concluded that we had passed her, or that she had doubled on us and gone to the northward. I then turned, keeping close on the shore, looking into her former anchorage, thinking she might possibly have returned.

"No sign of her there. We continued on to the northward, but, when we opened the port, saw nothing of her this way. . . .

"I have the honor to be, very respectfully, your obedient servant,

"JAMES S. PALMER,
"Commander."

Subsequently the Sumter made her way to Europe, after capturing and destroying other American vessels. She put into Cadiz, whither she was followed by a United States cruiser; but under the rule of "neutrality" she was again permitted to escape, and went to Gibraltar. Here, for some months, she remained idle and out of repair, her commander, Semmes, having left her. Without funds to procure supplies, the privateer was unable to leave, and the crew gradually diminished by desertion. All this time she was closely watched by one or more United States cruisers, which were ready to pursue and capture her upon any attempt to leave. Finding the chances of escape and future depredations were far from flattering, the parties in control of the rebel vessel, in the latter part of the year 1862, disposed of her, professedly for a more peaceful employment, though the honesty and legality of the transfer were called in question by the commander of the federal cruiser.

Other rebel privateers were less successful than the Jeff Davis and Sumter, and, with the disappearance of the latter from the seas, northern commerce ceased to suffer. In the mean time several other vessels fitted out for such purposes were captured. The schooner Petrel, formerly a United States revenue cutter, was fitted out at Charleston, and upon her first expedition, on the 7th of August, mistaking the frigate St. Lawrence for a large merchant vessel, fired upon the expected prize. The St. Lawrence responded with a broadside, which speedily sunk the Petrel, the crew of which, with the exception of a few who were killed or drowned, were rescued by the boats of the frigate, and sent north as prisoners.

A more daring and brilliant exploit was the destruction of the privateer schooner Judah, at Pensacola, on the 14th of September. This vessel was being fitted out at the navy yard, evidently for privateering purposes, and Flag-officer Mervine, commanding the Gulf squadron, determined to destroy her, if possible, before she had an opportunity to evade the blockade. Accordingly, four boats, with about one hundred men, under the command of Lieutenant Russell, were sent into the harbor, at night, to

accomplish this purpose, and at the same time to spike a heavy cannon which was mounted in the navy yard. The forts and batteries about the harbor were still heavily garrisoned by the rebel troops, and nearly one thousand men were posted in and about the navy yard, and the federal ships of war were lying near Fort Pickens, a long distance from the navy yard, and where they could not afford protection to the boats. The expedition might, therefore, be considered a desperate one; but its audacity was, probably, the reason of its success. Such an attempt was not anticipated by the rebels, who were consequently taken somewhat by surprise. The boats, however, were discovered in season to prepare the men on the schooner for resistance, and to alarm the forces stationed in the navy yard. As the boats approached, a heavy volley of musketry was discharged at them; but the gallant crews rowed rapidly to the side of the privateer, and boarded her. A desperate resistance on deck was at first attempted; but the vessel was soon cleared of its rebel crew, and was then set on fire. In the mean time, one of the boats proceeded to a corner of the navy yard, where the heavy cannon was mounted, and the crew succeeded in spiking it without meeting with any resistance. When the boats left, the vessel was so thoroughly on fire, that the flames could not be extinguished with the means at the disposal of the rebels, and it was burned to the water's edge. The crew, driven from the vessel, rallied on the wharf, where they were joined by a detachment of soldiers, and continued to fire upon the assailants; but they were kept at some distance by the fire of the latter. The rebels continued to fire at the boats as they moved away, but with little effect, while they received in return several discharges of shrapnel from the boats' howitzers. The loss in this successful and gallant expedition was three killed and twelve wounded.

The privateer Beauregard, a small schooner,

armed with one rifled cannon, was captured, in the Bahama Channel, by the United States bark W. G. Anderson, on the 13th of November. This vessel had probably not succeeded in capturing any northern merchant vessels, although seven days out from Charleston. Being overtaken by the Anderson, the vessel was surrendered without resistance, and the crew were carried to Key West as prisoners.

No other rebel privateer or cruiser ventured to sea during this year, though there were constant rumors that they were fitting out in several of the southern ports, and several steamers were probably armed for attack on northern commerce, or resistance to federal cruisers, should either come in their way; but their principal object was to run the blockade with valuable cargoes, which object was, in too many instances, successfully accomplished.

While the chief duties of the vessels of the navy were to blockade the coast, and to capture such privateers as might get to sea, there were occasional engagements, mostly of little consequence, with some of the rebel fortifications. Several of these occurred in Hampton Roads, with the battery at Sewall's Point, and with other batteries up the James and York Rivers, as well as on the Potomac, where the rebels had industriously fortified commanding points so as at last completely to blockade the river. Most of these affairs, however, were without any practical result. On the coast of North Carolina there were also several engagements, of little importance, between federal gunboats and armed rebel steamers that occasionally made their appearance in the Sound. Attacks were also made upon several forts on this coast, and two or three small batteries were destroyed by boat expeditions from the ships of war. Near Hatteras Inlet the steamer Monticello shelled a land force of the rebels, and dispersed them apparently with much loss.

In the Gulf, besides the bombardment of Pensacola and the neighboring forts, the federal vessels had, during this year, but little to vary the monotony of blockading, except a slight engagement with a rebel steamer near Ship Island, the bombardment of Galveston, and the attack of a rebel "ram" on the ships lying in the Passes of the Mississippi. The bombardment of Galveston by the steamer South Carolina, Commander Alden, was induced by an attack from rebel batteries on a tender of the steamer, and subsequently on the steamer itself, and evident preparations for a contest on the part of the rebels. In replying to the shots from the rebel batteries, some of the shot and shell from the South Carolina were thrown into the city, causing great alarm and excitement. As soon as Commander Alden saw that he was causing more damage to the city than to the rebel batteries, he ceased firing, and withdrew. But the unintentional bombardment of the city called forth a "protest" from some of the foreign consuls at Galveston, which Commander Alden characterized as insulting, and entirely at variance with the facts. The commander made a spirited and apt reply to the interference of these officials in matters which belonged to the military authorities.

The affair at the Passes of the Mississippi occurred early in the morning of October 12. There had been rumors for some time that the rebels were constructing a formidable iron-clad "ram," with powerful engines, and a sharp iron beak, or prow, the purpose of which was to attack the federal vessels, and batter or cut holes through them below the water-line, while other rebel vessels joined in the conflict. The anticipated exploits of this vessel, which was called the Manassas, were loudly boasted of in the New Orleans journals; but the federal officers were not disposed to believe that the strange craft would accomplish what was threatened. Previous to the 12th there had been shots exchanged between the federal vessels and one or two armed steamers of the rebels, but without any result on either side. Early on the morning of the 12th the rebel fleet, consisting of the Manassas and several large armed steamers, came down the river towards the head of the Passes, where the United States steamers Richmond and Water Witch and the ships Preble and Vincennes were at anchor, with a vessel which was supplying the steamers with coal. With the rebel vessels were three large fire rafts, which were to be fired at a certain signal, and set adrift in the stream, to float down among the federal vessels, and set them on fire. The night was very dark, and the approach of the rebel vessels was not discovered till the Manassas, which took the lead, steamed at a rapid rate down the river directly at the federal ships. The Richmond was the farthest up the river, and the Manassas ran at full speed against her bow with the sharp beak alluded to, cutting a hole in her bottom, though not a very large one. An attempt was made to strike the Richmond again farther aft; but owing to some derangement in the machinery of the rebel ram, it was unable to strike another formidable blow. As soon as the strange assailant was discovered, the crew of the Richmond were beat to quarters, and the blow had no sooner been given than a broadside was discharged at the ram as it backed off. The shot, however, appeared to glance or fall harmless from the iron sheathing, and but for the derangement of the machinery alluded to, the ram would probably have caused further damage to the Richmond and the other federal vessels. Signals were made for the squadron to move down the Passes, and the vessels got under way as soon as possible. But the other rebel steamers now approached, and the fire rafts were lighted. The Richmond and Water Witch continued to fire at the ram, which had withdrawn after its assault upon the Richmond. The flames of the fire rafts illumined the river, which had before been shrouded in darkness, and the federal guns were turned upon the steamers up the river, which could now be indis-

tinctly seen. The length of the Richmond prevented her from being turned in the river with safety, and her broadside batteries could not be used advantageously. Her commander, Captain Pope, who was also in command of the squadron, deemed it prudent, therefore, to move down the Pass to its mouth. This was accordingly done, the rebel steamers and the fire rafts following. In crossing the bar the Vincennes grounded, and the Richmond fared no better. The Vincennes, being a sailing vessel, was entirely helpless in such a condition, and her commander, mistaking a signal on board of the Richmond, abandoned his ship, lighting a slow-match for the purpose of blowing it up. The rebel steamers here opened a heavy fire upon the federal vessels, and a brief engagement followed, in which the superiority of some of the rebel guns was manifested, though no material damage was done. After this contest, in which the rebels claimed, in their accounts, to have sunk the Vincennes, the rebel steamers withdrew up the river. The match fired on the Vincennes having gone out, the officers and crew returned to their vessel, and she was subsequently got afloat. The Richmond, though considerably damaged, was not so much so as to endanger her safety; and the other vessels were unharmed. But the affair was a mortifying discomfiture for the federal ships, which were thus disgracefully driven down the Pass; and it was loudly boasted by the rebels as a substantial triumph. The following is Captain Pope's official report: —

"UNITED STATES STEAMER RICHMOND, SOUTH-WEST ⎱
PASS OF MISSISSIPPI RIVER, Oct. 13, 1861. ⎰

"SIR: I have the honor to make the following report: At forty-five minutes past three A. M., October 12, 1861 while the watch on deck were employed in taking coal on board from the schooner Joseph H. Toone, a ram was discovered in close proximity to this ship. By the time the alarm could be given, she had struck the ship abreast of the port fore-channels, tearing the schooner from her fastenings, and forcing a hole through the ship's side. Passing aft, the ram endeavored to effect a breach in the stern, but failed. Three planks in the ship's side were stove in about two feet below the water-line, making a hole about five inches in circumference. At the first alarm, the crew promptly and coolly repaired to their quarters, and as the ram passed abreast of the ship the entire port battery was discharged at her, with what effect it is impossible to discover, owing to the darkness. A red light was shown as a signal of danger, and the squadron was under way in a very few minutes, having slipped their cables. I ordered the Preble and Vincennes to proceed down the South-west Pass while I covered their retreat, which they did at fifty minutes past four A. M.

"At this time three large fire rafts, stretching across the river, were rapidly nearing us, while several large steamers and a bark-rigged propeller were seen astern of them.

"The squadron proceeded down the river in the following order: first, the Preble, second, the Vincennes, third, the Richmond, fourth, the Water Witch, with the prize schooner Frolic in tow. When abreast of the Pilot Settlement, the pilot informed me that he did not consider it safe to venture to turn this ship in the river, but that he believed he could pass over the bar. I accordingly attempted to pass over the bar with the squadron; but in the passage the Vincennes and Richmond grounded, while the Preble went over clear. This occurred about eight o'clock; and the enemy, who were now down the river with the fire steamers, commenced firing at us, while we returned the fire from our port battery and rifled gun on the poop; our shot, however, falling short of the enemy, while their shell burst on all sides of us, and several passed directly over the ship.

"At half-past nine, Commander Handy of the

49

Vincennes, mistaking my signal to the ships outside the bar to get under way, for a signal to him to abandon his ship, came on board the Richmond, with all his officers and a large number of the crew, the remainder having gone on board the Water Witch. Captain Handy, before leaving his ship, had placed a lighted slow-match at the magazine. Having waited a reasonable time for an explosion, I directed Commander Handy to return to his ship, with his crew, to start his water, and, if necessary, at his own request, to throw overboard his small guns, for the purpose of lightening his ship, and to carry out his kedge with a cable to heave off by. At ten A. M. the enemy ceased firing, and withdrew up the river. During the engagement a shell entered our quarter-port, and one of the boats was stove by another shell. . . .

"I have succeeded in reducing the leak of this ship so that our small engines keep the ship free. This is only temporary, and the ship will have to go to some place and have three planks put in. I have received rifle guns, and placed the thirty-two-pounder on the forecastle and the twelve-pounder on the poop. Could I have possibly managed this ship in any other way than keeping her head up and down the river, I would have stopped at Pilot Town to give battle; but this was found too hazardous, owing to her extreme length. The attempt was made, but a broadside could not be brought to bear without running the ship ashore. I then concluded, as advised, to start for the bar, and trust to the chance of finding water enough to cross.

"In narrating the affair of the river, I omitted to state that the ram sunk one of our large cutters, and a shot from the enemy stove the gig.

"I am pleased to say that the Vincennes is afloat, and at anchor outside on my starboard quarter. Very respectfully,

"JOHN POPE, *Captain.*"

CHAPTER LI.

Naval and Military Expedition to Port Royal. — Preparations. — Extent of the Expedition. — Sailing of Fleet from Hampton Roads. — Stormy Weather. — Severe Gale. — The Fleet scattered. — Loss of Vessels. — Steamer Governor. — Critical Situation. — Rescue of Crew and Passengers. — The Winfield Scott. — Damage to Vessels. — Collection of the Fleet. — Arrival at the Rendezvous. — Passage over the Bar. — Port Royal and Beaufort. — Preparations for Attack. — Forts Walker and Beauregard. — The Plan of Attack. — The Battle. — Terrible Bombardment. — Movements of the Squadron. — Fort Walker evacuated. — The Union Flag raised on the Fort. — Fort Beauregard abandoned. — Occupation of Hilton Head. — Captures. — Rebel Force and Loss. — Loss on board the Fleet. — Results of the Victory. — Description of the Battle by an Eye-witness.

AFTER the capture of the forts at Hatteras Inlet, a more formidable combined naval and military expedition was contemplated, to operate at some more important point on the southern coast. It was intended that this expedition should be fitted out in September; but the great difficulties attending the organization of the military forces, preparation of transports, and collecting the necessary naval force, caused delays, and the expedition was not ready until the latter part of October. In the mean time a change of the destination of the expedition was made, and it was determined to take Port Royal harbor as a safe roadstead for the ships of war employed on the coast, and a base for future military operations. This, however, was not made known, and though it was generally supposed that the force was destined to some point in the vicinity of Charleston, South Carolina, from which it could operate upon that cradle of rebellion, yet the real destination was not known to the northern people until the announcement of its success was made.

The rendezvous of the naval vessels and transports was at Hampton Roads, and the collection of so many vessels and such considerable preparations would certainly have revealed to the rebels in their neighboring posts that a great expedition was in preparation, even if

there had not been, as at all times during the rebellion, spies who kept the enemy informed of all federal movements. It was reported that, a day or two before the sailing of the expedition, a clerk of one of the high officers of the fleet had fled, taking with him the charts and other papers which would reveal to the rebels the object of the expedition. But in this case the rebels did not seem to be aware of the exact point of attack, though they might reasonably have anticipated the general object of the expedition.

The naval force of this expedition, consisting of upwards of twenty-five armed vessels, of various size and armament, from the steam frigate Wabash, the flag-ship of the squadron, to the small steamer armed with one or two guns, was under the command of Flag-officer S. F. Dupont. The military force which was embarked on board of various transports, many of them steamers and ships of the largest size, was under the command of Brigadier-General T. W. Sherman, and numbered about twelve thousand men. The combined fleet of naval vessels and transports numbered fifty vessels — the largest squadron that had ever been collected under the United States flag. On the 28th of October Commodore Dupont despatched his coal vessels, twenty-five in number, (additional to the fleet just mentioned,) under convoy of the sloop of war Vandalia, to rendezvous off Savannah, with the view of misleading the enemy as to the true destination of the expedition. On the 29th the signal was given for the fleet to sail; and as the vessels moved out of the roads in their order, the scene was the most magnificent and inspiriting ever viewed in American waters, and demonstrated the power and resources of the Union, no less than did the grand armies collected upon the banks of the Potomac, and organizing in the west.

The weather had been unsettled, and had delayed several days the departure of the fleet; but on this morning there was a prospect of fair weather and favorable winds, which augured well for the speedy success of the expedition. But it was now the season for storms upon the southern coast, and off Hatteras the wind blew hard, and drove several vessels among the breakers, from which, however, they escaped without damage. On the 1st of November the wind had increased to a gale, and one of the most violent storms ever experienced upon that stormy coast succeeded. The fleet was utterly dispersed, and when the storm at last began to abate, only one vessel out of the whole number was visible from the deck of the flag-ship. At the commencement of the storm several of the smaller vessels had put back to Hampton Roads, and, probably thus escaped destruction. Several others, which were totally unfitted for any boisterous seas, were lost, or so disabled as to be saved with the greatest difficulty, and one or two were driven ashore on the coast of South Carolina, where the crews were captured and the vessels destroyed. These, however, were vessels carrying ordnance stores and supplies, and the naval vessels and transports, though some of them suffered severely, and were obliged to throw overboard their guns and heavy cargo, succeeded in riding through the terrible storm, except one steamer, the Governor. This vessel, on board of which was a battalion of marines, was for a long time in a most critical condition, and was kept afloat only by the unremitting labors of the crew and soldiers. Several vessels that came to the relief of the Governor, in answer to the signals of distress which were continually made, were unable to render any assistance to those on board the ill-fated steamer owing to the violence of the storm. The destruction of the vessel and the death of all on board seemed inevitable; but at last the frigate Sabine came to their assistance, and by the intrepid exertions of the officers and crew of that ship, continued for a long time, the crew and marines on the Governor were taken off, with the exception

of seven, who were lost in the attempt to board the Sabine. The arms of the marines were saved, but their equipments, clothing, and stores were all lost. It was but a short time after the living freight of the Governor was transferred to the Sabine that the former vessel went down.

The steamer Winfield Scott, an armed transport, which carried a part of the fiftieth Pennsylvania regiment, was also very nearly wrecked. This vessel suffered severely, and it became necessary to throw overboard the steamer's guns, the arms of the soldiers, and every thing except the rations, in order to keep the vessel from sinking. The armed steamer Bienville went to the assistance of the Winfield Scott, and as she came alongside, the engineers and a portion of the crew of the latter jumped on board, deserting their posts in the hour of danger. This action created a panic among the soldiers, and greatly increased the risk to the large number of persons remaining on board the damaged vessel. The captain of the Winfield Scott, however, by vigorous measures quieted the alarm, and having caused the recreant crew to be placed in irons, by great exertions, and the aid of the transport Vanderbilt, which also came to the rescue, the vessel was towed, in a greatly damaged condition, to the place of rendezvous.

Other vessels were more or less damaged by the terrible storm, but they succeeded in riding through it without serious loss; and as the storm abated they came in slowly to the place of rendezvous. It was a trying time for the commander of the fleet, who found his vessels thus scattered, and knew not how many were lost. Many of the transports were not built for sea-going vessels, and considering their character and the severity of the storm, there was too much reason to fear that many of them were utterly wrecked or helpless, and that, with the loss of many lives, the expedition was to prove a failure. But when the storm had passed, the vessels began to come in sight, and on the 4th of November the advance part of the fleet, numbering about twenty-five vessels, arrived off Port Royal bar. The masters of vessels which had become entirely separated from the flag-ships of the naval and military commanders had opened the sealed orders which were furnished to all in case of such accident, and had thus first learned the destination, or the rendezvous of the fleet. They came in slowly; but, as Commodore Dupont himself observed, there was reason for great thankfulness that the disasters had not been more numerous and distressing.

Finding the scattered vessels thus rejoining the expedition, measures were at once taken to carry out its object. By the aid of officers connected with the coast survey, the channel was soon surveyed, sounded, and buoyed, and the transports and gunboats of light draught passed over the bar, and anchored in the safe roadstead of Port Royal. This harbor or bay is by far the best on the Atlantic coast south of Hampton Roads. It is much superior to that of Charleston, admitting vessels of greater draught, and being quite as safe from the stormy winds; and had the people of South Carolina been imbued with the spirit of enterprise which characterizes the north, a city rivalling Charleston would long ago have been built here. But the early settlement of Beaufort,* which lies on one side of Port Royal Island, the largest of a group of many which are separated by channels of moderate breadth, was abandoned for various reasons, and the colonists settled at Charleston, which thus became the chief ₜₒwₙ of the colony; and association, aristocracy, and lack of enterprise contributed to preserve Charleston from a rival within the limits of South Carolina. The islands about

* Beaufort is about sixty miles by the road, and about thirty-five in a direct line, from Savannah, and about seventy by the road, and fifty in a direct line, from Charleston.

Port Royal, however, were found admirably adapted to the production of the finest quality of cotton; and they have been chiefly occupied for that purpose, while the town of Beaufort and its vicinity became a pleasant resort for wealthy residents of Charleston and a portion of the interior during the hot season.

Further soundings having been made, it was ascertained and reported that the flag-ship Wabash could safely pass the bar; and though some risk attended the passage of so large a vessel, it was safely accomplished on the 5th, and, followed by others of the larger vessels of war and transports, the flag-ship sailed into the roadstead loudly cheered by the crews and soldiers on board the vessels already there. Preparations were immediately made for an attack on the forts, by which the harbor or entrance to Broad Sound was defended. It was necessary, however, for the safety of the vessels, to place buoys at certain dangerous shoals, and the day was spent in such preparations. The next day a gale prevented the attack; but on the 7th, all things being ready, the signals were made for the vessels to move according to the orders already issued. The transports in the mean time were to remain in the roadstead, the military part of the expedition awaiting the reduction of the forts by the navy, it being impossible, from the position of the forts and the nature of the shore, to safely land a force to coöperate with the ships of war.

The forts to be reduced by the navy were two — one on Bay Point, on the north-east side of the entrance to Broad Sound, which was called Fort Beauregard, and the other on Hilton Head, on the south-western side, which was called Fort Walker. The latter was apparently the strongest and most important work, though a reconnoissance in force, which had drawn the fire of both, led to the belief that each mounted about twenty guns. They were well-constructed works, and evidently of sufficient strength to resist a formidable attack, and the result proved that Fort Walker contained twenty-three guns, most of them of large calibre, and several of them rifled, while Fort Beauregard mounted, including those in the outworks, eighteen guns, and had also two field pieces. · In addition to these forts for the defence of Port Royal, the rebels also had several armed steamers of small size, under the command of Captain Tatnall, formerly of the United States navy. These vessels were seen up the Sound, but they did not invite an engagement, the purpose of the commander being apparently to watch the result, and if any vessel of the federal fleet should be seriously damaged in the conflict with the forts, or become separated from the others, to join in the attack.

The plan adopted by Commodore Dupont was to reduce the fort on Hilton Head first, the distance being too great to engage both forts from a position midway between them. He formed his line of battle with vessels, of which the flag-ship Wabash took the lead, succeeded by the Susquehanna, three steam sloops of war and several gunboats following, one of them towing the sailing sloop of war Vandalia. In addition to this a flanking squadron of five gunboats was formed, which was to sail up the sound or harbor, and remain there to engage the rebel gunboats if they came within reach. The signal to move was made at eight o'clock on the morning of the 7th, and the vessels were soon under way in the order designated, keeping a course midway between the two forts. The action was commenced by a gun from Fort Walker, followed by another from Fort Beauregard. The Wabash replied with a part of her heavy batteries, and the Susquehanna immediately after responded; and as each of the squadron came so as to bring its guns to bear, they were discharged at the rebel batteries. Passing up the harbor about two miles and a half, the main squadron turned to the

west and south, while the flanking squadron passed on to its station to watch the rebel fleet. In going down the harbor, the main squadron passed nearer to Hilton Head, passing Fort Walker at a distance of less than six hundred yards. The attack now commenced in earnest. The Wabash poured in a tremendous and rapid fire from her heavy guns, and the Susquehanna and other vessels, as they reached the proper position, joined with no less spirit in the terrible cannonade. This attack, at so short a distance, and against the weakest flank of the fort, while at the same time a portion of the fire enfiladed the water faces of the work, showed the enemy the power with which he had to contend, while he did not at first succeed in bringing his guns to bear upon the vessels at so short a distance. Passing slowly down by Fort Walker with this severe and damaging fire, the squadron again turned, and, steaming nearer to Fort Beauregard than before, poured into that a similar storm of shot and shell, firing also, as it passed, at longer range against Fort Walker. Twice the squadron had passed up and down, sending its countless missiles of destruction with deafening and continuous roar into the devoted forts, when there were evident signs that the fire of the latter, especially Fort Walker, which had been hitherto kept up with spirit and some effect, had begun to slacken. The repeated experience by the defenders of Fort Walker of that terrible bombardment at short range was too severe for them to endure it again. Their flag had already been shot away, some of their guns had been dismounted, shell and shrapnel had dealt wounds and death amongst them, and before the third close attack could be made, they hastily evacuated the fort, and retreated, evidently in great disorder, over the island. The battle with Fort Walker was ended.

An officer with a flag of truce was sent on shore, but he found no one with whom to confer, and he soon raised the flag of the Union over the captured fort. The cheers and shouts of victory which arose from the crews of the ships of war and the soldiers on board the transports, who had watched the magnificent but terrible spectacle with breathless interest, must have sent dismay to the garrison of Fort Beauregard. That fort had not yet been subjected to the bombardment at short range, though a steady fire at long range, as the vessels passed, had been directed against it. It had not suffered as much as Fort Walker, and its garrison had not experienced the weight of metal thrown by the broadsides of the Wabash and Susquehanna, and the continuous discharges of the huge guns of the other vessels. But seeing that Fort Walker was lost, and hearing the shouts of victory which forewarned them of the futility of resistance, they were not long in following the example of their friends, and, hauling down their flag, hastily evacuated the fort. A squadron of gunboats sent to reconnoitre more closely after the evacuation of Fort Walker probably hastened their movements. In the mean time the rebel fleet that had shown itself uncertainly up the harbor steamed away up some of the numerous channels that open from Broad River.

A body of sailors and marines had been at once sent to take possession of the fort on Hilton Head, when its evacuation was discovered. They found abundant evidence of the effect of the bombardment, and the haste with which the rebels had retreated. Several of their dead were found in the fort, and there was reason to suppose that other bodies, as well as nearly or quite all their wounded, were carried away: only four prisoners were captured; large quantities of ammunition, tents, clothing, and stores, and some small arms, were found near the fort and on the road taken by the rebels in their retreat, and a mile from the works was a large camp, which the rebels had abandoned, leaving the tents standing, with much baggage and a quantity of small arms.

As soon as Hilton Head was evacuated, the transports moved up the harbor, and before night a brigade of troops landed and took possession of the fort. It was not till the next day that possession was taken of Fort Beauregard, which afforded ample evidence that it was abandoned with as much haste as Fort Walker had been.

The rebel forces in the two forts, and in position near them, were supposed to number twenty-five hundred or three thousand men; and the tents, baggage, and blankets captured indicated that this was about the force. They were under the command of General Drayton, of South Carolina; and it is a noteworthy incident that the steamer Pocahontas, which, having been delayed by the storm, came into the harbor in the midst of the battle and joined in the bombardment, was commanded by Commander Drayton, also a native of South Carolina, and brother of the rebel general.

The victory of Port Royal, which was a brilliant one for the navy, secured at once a safe and comfortable haven for the federal vessels in service along the southern coast, and a base for future military operations. To the rebels it was a severe blow and a great disappointment, while among the loyal people of the north it was hailed with delight, as a token of future successes.

Of the bombardment and victory, which we have so briefly described, the following account by an eye-witness will, perhaps, give the reader a clearer view : —

"At nine o'clock, the fleet was signalled from the Wabash to raise anchor, and in rather more than half an hour afterwards, all the vessels were in motion. They moved slowly towards the land, cautiously feeling the way with the sounding line, arranged in two columns, of which the first was led by the flag-ship, and the second by the Bienville. The first column comprised the Wabash, Susquehanna, Mohican, Seminole, Pawnee, Unadilla, Ottawa, Pembina, and Vandalia, in tow of the Isaac Smith. The gunboats Penguin, Augusta, Curlew, Seneca, and R. B. Forbes, followed in the track of the Bienville. Sufficient space was given each vessel, in order that the fire from one column might not interfere with the operation of the other.

"It was well understood that the commodore intended to fight at close quarters, and the fact intensified the interest every body felt in the approaching conflict. As the fleet moved majestically on towards the foe, the few minutes consumed in getting within range of the batteries seemed dreadfully long to the spectators, who watched in deep suspense for the commencement of the fight. At length, precisely at five minutes before ten o'clock, the Bay Point battery opened its fire upon the Wabash, and that at Hilton Head followed almost within a second. The ships were then nearly midway between the hostile guns, and scarcely within range. For a minute they made no reply; but presently the Wabash began. Then grandly she poured from both her massive sides a terrible rain of metal, which fell with frightful rapidity upon either shore. The other vessels were not slow in following her example, and the battle was fairly begun.

"From my point of observation on board the Atlantic, which had been taken as close to the combatants as was consistent with safety, in order that General Sherman might witness the proceedings, it was apparent that few of the shells, which at first were the only projectiles used, burst within the fortifications. The guns had too great an elevation, and their iron messengers went crashing among the tree-tops a mile or two beyond the batteries. The same was the case with the rebels, whose shot passed between the masts and above our vessels. The frigates and gunboats, each having delivered their fire, which mainly in this round was directed against Bay Point, passed within the bay, indifferent alike to the bursting shells, humming projectiles, and hot round shot which the rebels furiously discharged, breaking the water into foaming columns every where around them.

"It was, I believe, part of the plan of battle to engage the batteries alternately, and the vessels, preserving their relative positions, were to move in circles before the foe. This mode of procedure was decided upon, because current sets swiftly in the straits between the fortifications, which are about two miles and three quarters apart, and it was impossible, even had it been desirable, for the vessels to remain stationary long enough to silence one battery before attacking the other. Something occurred, however, to change these arrangements a little. It is true the larger vessels followed the Wabash, from first to last, in the prescribed way, and the Bienville, leading the second division, gallantly maintained the position which had been assigned to her throughout the entire action; but the gunboats, finding that they could bring a destructive enfilading fire to bear upon Hilton Head, by stationing themselves in a cove about a mile's distance to the left of the fortification, took that position, and performed most efficient service. The commodore, perceiving the good result of the manœuvre, permitted them to remain.

"The Wabash was brought as near Hilton Head battery as the depth of water permitted; while soundings were given and signals made during the whole time the ship was in action, as regularly as upon ordinary occasions.

"Within a distance of nine hundred yards from the rebel guns, the Wabash threw in her fiery messengers, while the other frigates, no farther away, participated in the deadly strife; and the gunboats, from their sheltered nook, raked the ramparts frightfully. Thus the fire of about fifty guns was concentrated every moment upon the enemy, who worked heroically, never wavering in his reply, except when the Wabash was using her batteries directly in front of him. Then it was too hot for flesh and blood to endure. Shells fell almost as rapidly as hail-drops within, and for a mile and a half beyond, the battery. As they struck and ploughed into the earth, a dense pillar of sand would shoot upward, totally obscuring the fortification, and driving the blinded gunners from their pieces.

"In describing their circuit and delivering their fire, the vessels consumed rather more than an hour for each round. Little more than half of this time, however, was spent in getting into position; for gliding slowly around, perhaps entering the bay beyond the fort half a mile, just far enough to permit the safe turning of his immense ship, the commodore brought her back, and repeated from his starboard battery, until the guns became too hot to handle, that devastating fire. What is true respecting the firing of the Wabash is also true respecting the Susquehanna, Bienville, Pawnee, Mohican, and the rest. Each vessel discharged her broadside at the shortest possible range, loading and firing again and again, with all the coolness and precision exercised in target practice, before she passed the battery.

"But the enemy was by no means inactive. He offered a stubborn and heroic resistance. Looking through a powerful telescope belonging to the engineer officers of the expedition, I saw, when the ships were approaching the battery the second time, two men wearing red shirts. They had been particularly active, and now sat at the muzzle of a gun, apparently exhausted, and waiting for more ammunition. This terrible fire from the fleet was falling all around them; but they moved not, and I doubted if they were alive. Finally they sprang up and loaded their piece—a shell at that instant burst near them, and they disappeared, doubtless blown into atoms. I heard frequently, during the hottest of the fight, most unqualified expressions of approval of the manner in which the rebels served their guns. That their marksmanship was good, the torn hulls and cut rig-ging of our vessels, rather than the number of killed on board, furnish full evidence.

"After the second round had been brilliantly fought on both sides, the Wabash gave a signal to the vessels which had been most actively engaged, to cease firing, and give refreshments to their men. Accordingly the steamers repaired to a point beyond reach of the batteries, and the poor sailors — nearly exhausted with their work — satisfied their hunger, and gratefully accepted a few moments' repose. Then it was that the gunboats did their most efficient cannonading. Their shell and round shot flew straight across the parapet of the fortification, driving the men from their guns, and making dreadful havoc. The little steam-tug Mercury, Master Commanding Martin, gallantly steamed into a shallow bay to the left of the fort, not more than half a mile distant, and presenting her diminutive figure to the rebel guns, opened upon them with her thirty-pounder Parrott, which was fired rapidly and with good effect. From her proximity to the fort, Captain Martin was probably the first to see that the rebels were preparing to evacuate the place. In rear of the fortification, extending about three fourths of a mile, is a broad meadow bounded by dense woods. Across this open space the enemy was carrying his dead and wounded, and wagons were hurriedly removing the equipage of the camp.

"The Mercury, steaming closer to the shore, found that the battery had been deserted, and immediately took the news to the flag-ship, which, by this time, with her sister vessels, was coming up like a destroying angel to renew the conflict. The commodore almost simultaneously received confirmation of the tidings from other sources, and, even while listening to the words of the messenger, the rebels struck their flag.

"The signal to cease firing was at once hoisted; and it being precisely a quarter to three o'clock, the bombardment had been nearly five hours in progress.

"The flag-ship lowered a boat and sent it ashore, carrying a flag of truce in the bow, and our own proud banner at the stern. Its mission was to inquire if the enemy had surrendered. Commander John Rodgers, a passenger on the Wabash, who had come down to join his vessel, the Flag, now blockading off Charleston, and had been acting during the fight as aid to Commodore Dupont, was assigned the duty of taking the flag ashore. Himself and crew were unarmed, but they found no one to receive them. He planted the American ensign upon the deserted ramparts, and took possession of the rebel soil of South Carolina in the majesty of the United States. Another and larger star-spangled banner was afterwards displayed upon the flag-staff of a building a few rods to the left, where the rebel standard had waved during the combat, and whence it had just been taken down.

"Commodore Tatnall and his gunboats disappeared in the early part of the engagement. He sent a few shots towards the fleet, but, as usual, his boats were not near enough to do us injury. Much regret was felt that neither of our fast steamers pursued and captured the commodore. He would have been an interesting prisoner. Among the papers found in the secessionist garrison was one from Mr. Tatnall, in which he promised emphatically to General Drayton, who commanded the rebel forces, that his gunboats should be brought down from Savannah, and that they should share the fate of the forts. The promise was kept, and the fate was shared — the latter much earlier than was necessary.

"Ten thousand eager eyes beheld our flag as it was planted upon the parapet; and who shall describe the enthusiasm with which the sight was greeted? Cheer followed cheer from the men-of-war, and were echoed by the transports in the distance. Tears of joyful pride filled many an eye; hands were cordially shaken,

50

heartfelt congratulations for the glorious victory were expressed. Some, in the exuberance of their exultation, danced wildly, and clapped their hands, until it seemed doubtful whether they would ever cease their antics. Nor was the ebullition of patriotic fervor at all decreased when the regimental bands, with earnest feeling, as if by a spontaneous impulse, all struck up 'The Star-Spangled Banner,' the majesty of which had been so signally vindicated."

CHAPTER LII.

Expedition to Port Royal, continued. — Official Reports. — Despatches of Commodore Dupont. — General Order, congratulating the Officers and Men of the Fleet. — Federal Loss and Damage of Vessels. — Report of General Sherman. — Proclamation of General Sherman to the People of South Carolina. — Occupation of Beaufort. — Advantages gained by the Expedition.

THE following are the despatches of Commodore Dupont, announcing the success of the expedition in gaining possession of Port Royal: —

"FLAG-SHIP WABASH, OFF HILTON HEAD,
"PORT ROYAL HARBOR, Nov. 6, 1861.

"SIR: The government having determined to seize and occupy one or more important points upon our southern coast, where our squadrons might find shelter, possess a depot, and afford protection to loyal citizens, committed to my discretion the selection from among those places which it thought available and desirable for these purposes.

"After mature deliberations, aided by the professional knowledge and great intelligence of the assistant secretary, Mr. Fox, and taking into consideration the magnitude to which the joint naval and military expedition had been extended, to which you have called my attention, I came to the conclusion that the original intentions of the department, if carried out, would fall short of the expectations of the country and of the capabilities of the fleet;

while Port Royal, I thought, would meet both in a high degree.

"I therefore submitted to General Sherman, commanding the military part of the expedition, this modification of our earliest matured plans, and had the satisfaction to receive his full concurrence; though he and the commanders of brigades very justly laid great stress on the necessity, if possible, of getting this frigate into the harbor of Port Royal.

"On Tuesday, the 29th of October, the fleet under my command left Hampton Roads, and, with the army transports, numbered fifty vessels. On the day previous I had despatched the coal vessels, twenty-five in all, under convoy of the Vandalia, Commander Haggerty, to rendezvous off Savannah, not wishing to give indications of the true point.

"The weather had been unsettled in Hampton Roads, though it promised well when we sailed. But off Cape Hatteras the wind blew hard; some ships got into the breakers, and two struck, without injury.

"On Friday, November 1, the rough weather soon increased into a gale, and we had to encounter one of great violence from the southeast, a portion of which approached to a hurricane. The fleet was utterly dispersed; and on Saturday morning one sail only was in sight from the deck of the Wabash. On the following day the weather moderated, and the steamers and ships began to reappear. Orders (not to be opened except in case of separation) were furnished to all the men-of-war by myself, and to the transports by Brigadier-General ˙Sherman.

"As the vessels rejoined, reports came in of disasters. I expected to hear of many; but, when the severity of the gale and the character of the vessels are considered, we have only cause for great thankfulness.

"In reference to the men-of-war, the Isaac Smith, a most efficient, well-armed vessel for the class, purchased, but not intended to en-

counter such a sea and wind, had to throw her formidable battery overboard to keep from foundering; but, thus relieved, Lieutenant Commanding Nicholson was enabled to go to the assistance of the chartered steamer Governor, then in a very dangerous condition, and on board of which was our fine battalion of marines, under Major Reynolds. They were finally rescued by Captain Ringold, of the frigate Sabine, under difficult circumstances; soon after which the Governor went down. I believe that seven of the marines were drowned by their own imprudence. Lieutenant Commanding Nicholson's conduct in the Isaac Smith has met my warmest commendations.

"The Peerless, transport, in a sinking condition, was met by the Mohican, Commander Gordon, and all the people on board — twenty-six in number — were saved, under very peculiar circumstances, in which service Lieutenant W. H. Miller was very favorably noticed by his commander.

"On passing Charleston, I sent in the Seneca, Lieutenant-Commanding Ammen, to direct Captain Lardner to join me with the Susquehanna, off Port Royal, without delay. On Monday, at eight o'clock in the morning, I anchored off the bar, with some twenty-five vessels in company, and many heaving in sight.

"The department is aware that all the aids to navigation had been removed, and the bar lies ten miles seaward, with no features on the shore line with sufficient prominence to˙ make any bearings reliable. But to the skill of Commander Davis, the fleet captain, and Mr. Boutelle, the able assistant of the coast ˙survey, in charge of the steamer Vixen, the channel was immediately found, sounded out, and buoyed. By three o'clock I received assurances from Captain Davis that I could send forward the lighter transports, — those under eighteen feet, — with all the gunboats, which was immediately done; and before dark they were securely anchored in the roadstead of Port Royal, South Carolina.

The gunboats almost immediately opened their batteries upon two or three rebel steamers, under Commodore Tatnall, instantly chasing him under the shelter of the batteries.

"In the morning, Commander John Rodgers, of the United States steamer Flag, temporarily on board this ship and acting on my staff, accompanied Brigadier-General Wright in the gunboat Ottawa, Lieutenant Commanding Stevens, and supported by the Seneca, Lieutenant Commanding Ammen, the Curlew, Acting Lieutenant Commanding Watmough, and the Isaac Smith, Lieutenant Commanding Nicholson, made a reconnoissance in force, which drew the fire of the batteries on Hilton Head and Bay Point, sufficiently to show that the fortifications were works of strength and scientifically constructed.

"In the evening of Monday, Captain Davis and Mr. Boutelle reported water enough for the Wabash to venture in. The responsibility of hazarding so noble a frigate was not a light one. Over a prolonged bar of more than two miles, there was but a foot or two of water to spare, and the fall and rise of the tide are such that if she had grounded she would have sustained most serious injury from straining, perhaps total loss. Too much, however, was at stake to hesitate, and the result was entirely successful.

"On the morning of Tuesday the Wabash crossed the bar, followed closely by the frigate Susquehanna, the Atlantic, Vanderbilt, and other transports of deep draught — and on running through that portion of the fleet already in, the safe passage of this great ship over the bar was hailed with gratifying cheers from the crowded vessels.

"We anchored, and immediately commenced preparing the ship for action; but the delay of planting the buoys, particularly on the Fishing Rip,— a dangerous shoal we had to avoid, — rendered the hour late before it was possible to move with the attacking squadron. In our anxiety to get the outline of the forts before dark, we stood in too near those shoals, and the

ship grounded. By the time she was gotten off it was too late, in my judgment, to proceed, and I made signals for the squadron to anchor out of gun shot from the enemy.

"To-day the wind blows a gale from the southward and westward, and the attack is unavoidably postponed.

"I have the honor to be, sir, respectfully, your obedient servant,

"S. F. DUPONT,

"*Flag-officer commanding South Atlantic*
"*Blockading Squadron.*"

"FLAG-SHIP WABASH, OFF HILTON HEAD,
"PORT ROYAL HARBOR, *Nov.* 8, 1861.
"HON. GIDEON WELLES, SECRETARY OF THE NAVY.

"SIR: I have the honor to inform you that yesterday I attacked the enemy's batteries on Bay Point and Hilton Head, (Forts Walker and Beauregard,) and succeeded in silencing them, after an engagement of four hours' duration, and driving away the squadron of rebel steamers under Commodore Tatnall. The reconnoissance of yesterday made us satisfied with the superiority of Fort Walker, and to that I directed my special efforts, engaging it at a distance of eight hundred, and afterwards at six hundred yards. But the plan of the attack brought the squadron sufficiently near Fort Beauregard to receive its fire, and the ships were frequently fighting the batteries on both sides at the same time.

"The action was begun, on my part, at twenty-six minutes after nine, and at half past two the American ensign was hoisted on the flagstaff of Fort Walker, and this morning at sunrise on that of Fort Beauregard.

"The defeat of the enemy terminated in utter rout and confusion. Their quarters and encampments were abandoned without an attempt to carry away either public or private property. The ground over which they fled was strewn with the arms of private soldiers, and the officers retired in too much haste to submit to the encumbrance of their swords.

"Landing my marines and a company of seamen, I took possession of the deserted ground, and held the fort on Hilton Head until the arrival of General Sherman, to whom I had the honor to transfer its occupation.

"We have captured forty-three pieces of cannon, most of them of the heaviest calibre and of the most improved design. The bearer of these despatches will have the honor to carry with him the captured flags, and two small brass field pieces, lately belonging to the state of South Carolina, which are sent home as suitable trophies of the success of the day. I enclose herewith a copy of the general order which is to be read in the field to-morrow morning at muster. A detailed account of this battle will be submitted hereafter.

"I have the honor to be, very respectfully, your obedient servant,

"S. F. DUPONT,

"*Flag-officer commanding South Atlantic*
"*Blockading Squadron.*"

"P. S. The bearer of despatches will carry with him the first American ensign raised upon the soil of South Carolina since the rebellion broke out.   S. F. D.

"GENERAL ORDER No. 2.

"FLAG-SHIP WABASH, HILTON HEAD, }
"PORT ROYAL BAY, *Nov.* 8, 1861. }

"It is the gratifying duty of the commander-in-chief to make a public acknowledgment of his entire commendation of the coolness, discipline, skill, and gallantry displayed by the officers and men under his command in the capture of the batteries at Hilton Head and Bay Point, after an action of four hours' duration. The flag-officer fully sympathizes with the officers and men of his squadron in the satisfaction they must feel at seeing the ensign of the United States flying once more in the state of South Carolina, which has been the chief promoter of the wicked and unprovoked rebellion they have been called upon to suppress.

"S. F. DUPONT,

"*Flag-officer commanding South Atlantic*
"*Blockading Squadron.*"

Commodore Dupont subsequently made a more detailed report, which did not contain any material facts not given in the foregoing despatches and the account in the preceding chapter. By other official reports it appeared that the loss on board the fleet was eight killed and twenty-three wounded. Most of the vessels directly engaged in the bombardment were more or less damaged by shot from the forts, but none of them received any serious injury. The loss of the rebels was unknown. Six of their dead were found in Fort Walker, and it was supposed that many others, as well as all their wounded, were removed. Notwithstanding the protection of their works, it is probable that the throwing of nearly two thousand shells and many solid shot into and about the forts, caused a considerable loss of men, as well as damage to their works.

After landing his troops and taking possession of the forts, General Sherman issued the following proclamation, which was conveyed, as best it could be, to such inhabitants as remained on Port Royal Island and the neighboring islands: —

"TO THE PEOPLE OF SOUTH CAROLINA: —

"In obedience to the orders of the President of these United States of America, I have landed on your shores with a small force of national troops. The dictates of a duty, which, under the constitution, I owe to a great sovereign state and to a proud and hospitable people, among whom I have passed some of the pleasantest days of my life, prompt me to proclaim that we have come among you with no feelings of personal animosity; no desire to harm your citizens, destroy your property, or interfere with any of your lawful laws, rights, or your social and local institutions, beyond what the causes herein briefly alluded to may render unavoidable.

"Citizens of South Carolina, the civilized world stands appalled at the course you are pursuing — appalled at the crime you are committing against your own mother — the best, the most enlightened, and heretofore the most prosperous of nations. You are in a state of active rebellion against the laws of your country. You have lawlessly seized upon the forts, arsenals, and other property belonging to our common country, and within your borders with this property you are in arms and waging a ruthless war against your constitutional government, and thus threatening the existence of a government which you are bound by the terms of the solemn compact to live under and faithfully support.

"In doing this you are not only undermining and preparing the way for totally ignoring your own political and social existence, but you are threatening the civilized world with the odious sentiment that self-government is impossible with civilized man.

"Fellow-citizens, I implore you to pause and reflect upon the tenor and consequences of your acts; of the awful sacrifices made by the devastation of your property; the shedding of fraternal blood in battle. The mourning and wailing of widows and orphans throughout our land are sufficient to deter you from further pursuing this unholy war. Then ponder, I beseech you, upon·the ultimate but not less certain result which its farther progress must necessarily and naturally entail upon your once happy and prosperous state. Indeed, can you pursue this fratricidal war, and continue to imbrue your hands in the loyal blood of your countrymen, your friends, your kinsmen, for no other object than to unlawfully disrupt the confederacy of a great people — a confederacy established by your own hands — in order to set up, were it possible, an independent government, under which you can never live in peace, prosperity, or quietness?

"Carolinians, we have come among you as loyal men, fully impressed with our constitutional obligations to the citizens of your state. These obligations shall be performed as far as in our power. But be not deceived. The obligation of suppressing armed combinations against the constitutional authorities is paramount to all others.

"If, in the performance of this duty, other minor but important obligations should be in any way neglected, it must be attributed to the necessities of the case, because rights dependent on the laws of the state must be necessarily subordinate to military exigencies created by insurrection and rebellion.

"T. W. SHERMAN,
"Brigadier-General commanding.

"HEADQUARTERS, G. C., PORT ROYAL, S. C., Nov. 8."

General Sherman, the commander of the land forces, which had acted the part of spectators rather than participants in the battle and the victory, sent the following despatch : —

"HEADQUARTERS EXPEDITION CORPS,
"PORT ROYAL, S. C., Nov. 8, 1861.
"ADJUTANT-GENERAL UNITED STATES ARMY, WASHINGTON.

"SIR: I have the honor to report that the force under my command embarked at Annapolis, Maryland, at Hampton Roads, Virginia, on the 22d ult. In consequence of the delay in the arrival of some of our transports and the unfavorable state of the weather, the fleet was unable to set out for the southern coast until the 29th, when, under the convoy of a naval squadron in command of Commodore Dupont, and after the most mature consideration of the objects of the expedition by that flag-officer and myself, it was agreed to reduce any works that might be found at Port Royal, South Carolina, and thus open the finest harbor on the coast that exists south of Hatteras. It was calculated to reach Port Royal in five days at most; but in consequence of adverse winds and a perilous storm on the day and night of the first of November, the fleet arrived at Port Royal bar not until the 4th, and then but in part, for it had been almost entirely dispersed by the gale, and the vessels have been straggling in up to this date. The transport steamers Union,

Belvidere, Osceola, and Peerless have not arrived. Two of them are known to be lost, and it is probable all are. It is gratifying, however, to say that none of the troop transports connected with the land forces were lost, though the Winfield Scott had to sacrifice her whole cargo, and the Roanoke a portion of her cargo, to save the lives of the regiments on board. The former will again be put to sea. The vessels connected with the naval portion of the fleet have also suffered much, and some have been lost. After a careful reconnoissance of Port Royal Bay, it was ascertained that the rebels had three field works of remarkable strength, strongly garrisoned, and covered by a fleet of three gunboats, under Captain Tatnall, late of the United States navy, besides strong land forces, which the rebels were concentrating from Charleston and Savannah. The troops of the rebels were afterwards ascertained to have been commanded by General Drayton.

" One of the first, and probably the strongest fort, was situated on Hilton Head, and the other two on Phillips' Island. It was deemed proper to first reduce the fort on Hilton Head, though to do this a greater or less fire might have to be met from the batteries on Bay Point. At the same time our original plan of coöperation of the land forces in this attack had to be set aside, in consequence of the loss during the voyage of a greater portion of our means of disembarkment, together with the fact that the only point where our troops should have landed was from five to six miles, measuring around the intervening shoal, from the anchoring place of our transports — altogether too great a distance for a successful debarkation, with our limited means. It was, therefore, agreed that the place should be reduced by the naval force alone. In consequence of the shattered condition of the fleet, and the delay in the arrival of vessels that were indispensable for the attack, it had to be postponed until the 7th instant.

" I was a mere spectator of the combat, and it is not my intention to render any report of this action. I deem it an imperative duty to say that the firing and manœuvring of our fleet against that of the rebels and their formidable land batteries, was a masterpiece of activity and professional skill that must have elicited the applause of the rebels themselves, as a tactical operation. I think that too much praise cannot be awarded to the science and skill exhibited by the flag-officer of the naval squadron and the officers connected with his ship. I deem the performance a masterly one, which ought to have been seen to be fully appreciated.

" After the works were reduced, I took possession of them with the land forces. The beautifully constructed work on Hilton Head was severely crippled, and many of the guns dismounted. Much slaughter had evidently been made there, many bodies having been buried in the fort, and some twenty or thirty were found some half a mile distant. The island, for many miles, was found strewed with army accoutrements and baggage of the rebels, which they threw away in their hasty retreat. We have also come into possession of about forty pieces of ordnance, most of which is of the heaviest calibre and the most approved models, and a large quantity of ammunition and camp equipage.

" It is my duty to report the valuable services of Mr. Boutelle, assistant in the coast survey, assisting with his accurate and extensive knowledge of this country. His services are invaluable to the army as well as to the navy, and I earnestly recommend that notice be taken of this very able and scientific officer by the war department.

" I am, very respectfully,
" Your obedient servant,
" T. W. SHERMAN,
" *Brigadier-General commanding.*"

The day after the capture of the forts, Commodore Dupont despatched two or three gunboats up the river to Beaufort, for the purpose of taking the light-boats, which had been removed by the rebels from the entrance to Port Royal Sound. These light-boats, however, were destroyed immediately after the evacuation of the forts. The islands on either side of the river, and the town of Beaufort, appeared to be abandoned by all except the negroes who had evaded the orders of their masters to leave when the forts were captured. Only one white person was found in Beaufort, and he seemed overcome with fear either of the federal forces or of the negroes. The negroes were wild with delight at the federal success, and were freely appropriating the property of the fugitive masters, and destroying much valuable furniture which was of no use to them. They seemed to feel that the day of their servitude was past, and that the victory of the Union fleet had at once driven off the rebel masters, and given them freedom and ownership in the abandoned property. Measures were taken, however, to prevent excesses; and in a short time the blacks settled down into quiet idleness, their wants for the present being amply supplied by what was left on the plantations and in the town. What was to be done with the large number of blacks who remained on Port Royal and the neighboring islands, and who came within the military lines of the army, soon became a question of much importance.

The possession of Port Royal harbor was a very great advantage gained, on account of the safe haven it afforded to vessels engaged in blockading the coast, and of its convenience for a depot of supplies. At the same time it gave to the government one of the ports the blockade of which had been evaded. It also afforded a base of future military operations, from which movements could be made towards the more important cities of Charleston and Savannah. Hilton Head soon became a great military post and naval station, full of activity and business; and without doubt the military occupation of this point was the foundation of a port which should soon completely overshadow the more ancient town of Beaufort.

The islands upon which the troops were landed, and the others of which they afterwards took possession, were mostly devoted to the culture of cotton, of which the finest quality, the "sea island," taking its name from these islands, has long been raised in large quantities. Considerable quantities of this cotton were found upon the plantations, though a great deal was destroyed upon the arrival of the federal force. The plantations were all deserted by their owners, who were, generally, among the most aristocratic of slaveholders and bitterest of secessionists. To make this valuable property useful to the government, and to give employment to the negroes abandoned by their masters, and now becoming dependent upon the military authorities, was a matter of much consequence; and measures, somewhat tardy and ill managed, were taken to secure a continuance of the culture of cotton, and at the same time to make the negroes support themselves.

CHAPTER LIII.

Important Naval Exploit. — Rebel Agents in Europe. — Mission of Messrs. Mason and Slidell. — They evade the Blockade, and arrive at Havana. — Their Reception. — They take Passage in the Trent for Europe. — Movements of Captain Wilkes in the San Jacinto. — Determination to capture the Rebel Envoys. — The Trent stopped and boarded. — Capture of Mason and Slidell, and their Secretaries. — Official Reports of Captain Wilkes and his Officers. — Prisoners carried to Fort Warren. — Excitement caused by the Act of Captain Wilkes. — Discussion, and Variety of Opinions. — Resentment towards England. — Excitement in England. — War threatened. — More moderate Action of the Government. — The Result. — Mr. Seward's Letter. — The Prisoners released. — Despatch of the French Government. — Mr. Seward's Reply. — The Question in Congress. — The Effects of the Settlement of the Question. — Delivery of the Prisoners on board an English Ship.

A naval exploit, of a different character, followed not long after the capture of Port Royal, and created an intense excitement, not only among the people of the loyal states and the rebels, but in England, whose neutral rights were affected, and in a less degree among the other nations of Europe. The rebels had early sent commissioners, or agents, to Europe, to procure arms, awaken sympathy, and secure recognition and encouragement from the leading governments. These commissioners were not, however, clothed with full powers as from an established government, and were not in any way officially recognized, though they may have received, unofficially, the notice and good wishes of those high in authority. The rebel government, soon after the meeting of the Congress of the seceded states, determined to send to France and England, as agents, men of more consideration, and clothed with greater powers, who, if they could secure a reception as such, should act as ministers plenipotentiary at the courts of those countries. Accordingly, John Slidell, of Louisiana, formerly United States senator from that state, was appointed envoy to France, and James M. Mason, of Virginia, who had also been United States senator, was appointed envoy to England. These men were well selected for their errands, being among the ablest and most earnest of the secessionists, while each was peculiarly adapted for his particular mission. The character and bearing, as well as the ability, of Mr. Mason, were generally considered such as would recommend him to the governing class in England, while great results were expected from the diplomacy of the wily and scheming Mr. Slidell at the French court.

It was known to the United States government that these agents were appointed, and awaited an opportunity of getting out of the blockaded states on their missions; and perhaps renewed vigilance was urged upon officers of the blockading fleet to prevent their escape. But after many rumors respecting them, the envoys, with their suites, succeeded in evading the blockade, and, escaping from Charleston in

the small steamer Theodora, sailed to Havana, where they arrived in the latter part of October. There they were received with marked attention by those who sympathized with the rebel cause, not the least prominent of whom was the British consul, who was officious in his attentions, though he undoubtedly represented his own feelings rather than the government whose agent he was. At Havana Messrs. Mason and Slidell took passage in the British mail steamer Trent for England, on the 7th of November.

Just after the arrival of the rebel envoys at Havana, the United States steamer San Jacinto, Captain Charles Wilkes, which had recently arrived in West India waters from the coast of Africa, and was in pursuit of the privateer Sumter, put into Cienfuegos, on the southern coast of Cuba, for coal. Learning that they had arrived at Havana in the Theodora, Captain Wilkes sailed as soon as possible for Havana, with the purpose of intercepting the Theodora on her return. For this, however, he was too late, the rebel steamer having already sailed. While at Havana Captain Wilkes learned that Messrs. Mason and Slidell, with their suites, had engaged passage on board the Trent, and he then determined that he would at least attempt the capture of these parties, who were going abroad on an errand so mischievous and traitorous to his country. In so doing, he believed that this act would be justified by international law, while he would be rendering an important service to his government. He accordingly left Havana on the 2d of November, and after running to Key West, proceeded to the "old Bahama Channel," and, at a point where it narrows to the width of about fifteen miles, he awaited the passage of the Trent on her way to St. Thomas.

On the 8th the Trent came in sight, and as she approached Captain Wilkes made the necessary preparations to carry out his purpose. When sufficiently near, a shot was fired from

E. V. Sumner

the San Jacinto across her bows; but the commander of the Trent, seeming to think that the display of the British flag was a sufficient answer to any demands of an American cruiser, kept his vessel on her course. A shell was then fired from the San Jacinto, which exploded at some distance ahead of the Trent. This had the effect of stopping the steamer in her course, and, hailing the commander, Captain Wilkes informed him that he would send an officer on board. Lieutenant Fairfax was accordingly sent with a boat's crew, armed, to ascertain if Messrs. Mason and Slidell were passengers on board the Trent, and, if so, to take them prisoners, and carry them to the San Jacinto.

Lieutenant Fairfax went on board the Trent, and demanded the papers and list of passengers. The captain refused to show them, when Lieutenant Fairfax said that he had information that Mr. Mason and Mr. Slidell, and Mr. McFarland and Mr. Eustis, their secretaries, were on board the Trent, and he must be satisfied on that point before he suffered the steamer to proceed. The parties named soon made their appearance; but they protested against going on board the San Jacinto, and the captain of the vessel interposed every possible obstacle to the execution of his orders by Lieutenant Fairfax. There were noisy demonstrations on the part of the officers of the Trent and many of the passengers. Not the least obnoxious of the persons who loudly opposed the United States officer, was the British mail officer, a retired officer of the English navy. Lieutenant Fairfax, finding that there was likely to be resistance, sent his boat back to the San Jacinto, to announce to Captain Wilkes that the rebel envoys were on board the steamer, but would not leave except by force. Another boat, with a small guard of marines and an armed crew, was accordingly sent to the support of Lieutenant Fairfax. The marines and armed sailors being brought on board the Trent, after some parley and violent protesta-

tions on the part of the principal parties sought, and of those who sympathized with them, the show of force by the United States officers induced a reluctant compliance with their demands. By applying nominal force to Mr. Mason, that gentleman was made a prisoner, and placed in one of the San Jacinto's boats. Mr. Slidell would not yield to so moderate a force; but after some further protests, in which Mr. Slidell's family — who were with him — joined, he was arrested, and conducted by two or three officers to the boat. The secretaries of the rebel emissaries followed their principals without resistance, and, the luggage of the whole party being also placed in one of the boats, they were taken on board the San Jacinto, and the Trent was permitted to resume her voyage.

While the American officers were performing their duty, — which, under the circumstances, was not a very agreeable one in the execution, however gratifying it might be in the result, — they were subjected to the insolence of a great part of the passengers and crew of the Trent. They were threatened with vengeance upon themselves and their country, and assailed with sneers and taunts. But they paid no attention to these attacks, and conducted with a forbearance and self-respect that could but elicit the respect of the petty assailants themselves. They entered into no altercations or angry disputes, to which they were tempted by the language and conduct of those on board the Trent; but, acting in a firm but dignified manner, they performed their duty successfully, and captured two of the most mischievous enemies of their country.

The following despatches of Captain Wilkes, with the reports of Lieutenant Fairfax and assistant-engineer Houston, describe more in detail this important capture, and the grounds upon which Captain Wilkes acted, in assuming the responsibility of so bold and important a transaction: —

"SIR: I have written to you, relative to the movements of this ship, from Cienfuegos, on the south coast of Cuba. There I learned that Messrs. Slidell and Mason had landed on Cuba, and had reached the Havana from Charleston. I took in some sixty tons of coal, and left with all despatch, on the 26th of October, to intercept the return of the Theodora; but on my arrival at the Havana, on the 31st, I found she had departed on her return, and that Messrs. Slidell and Mason, with their secretaries and families, were there, and would depart on the 7th of the month, in the English steamer Trent, for St. Thomas, on their way to England.

"I made up my mind to fill up with coal and leave the port as soon as possible, to await at a suitable position on the route of the steamer to St. Thomas, to intercept her and take ·them out.

"On the afternoon of the 2d I left the Havana, in continuation of my cruise after the Sumter on the north side of Cuba. The next day, when about to board a French brig, she ran into us on the starboard side at the main-chains, and carried away her bowsprit and fore-topmast, and suffered other damages. I enclose you herewith the reports of the officers who witnessed the accident. I do not feel that any blame is due to the officer in charge of this ship at the time the ship was run into; and the brig was so close when it was seen she would probably do so, that even with the power of steam, lying motionless as we were, we could not avoid it — it seemed as if designed.

"I at once took her in tow, and put an officer on board, with a party to repair her damages: this was effected before night; but I kept her in tow until we were up with the Havana, and ran within about eight miles of the light, the wind blowing directly fair for her to reach port.

"I then went over to Key West, in hopes of finding the Powhatan or some other steamer to accompany me to the Bahama Channel, to make it impossible for the steamer in which Messrs. Slidell and Mason were to embark to escape either in the night or day. The Powhatan had left but the day before, and I was therefore disappointed, and obliged to rely upon the vigilance of the officers and crew of this ship, and proceeded the next morning to the north side of the Island of Cuba, communicated with the Sagua la Grande on the 4th, hoping to receive a telegraphic communication from Mr. Shufelt, our consul general, giving me the time of the departure of the steamer.

"In this also I was disappointed, and ran to the eastward some ninety miles, where the old Bahama Channel contracts to the width of fifteen miles, some two hundred and forty miles from the Havana, and in sight of the Paredon del Grande lighthouse. There we cruised until the morning of the 8th, awaiting the steamer, believing that, if she left at the usual time, she must pass us about noon of the 8th, and we could not possibly miss her. At forty minutes past eleven A. M. on the 8th, her smoke was first seen; at twelve M. our position was to the westward of the entrance into the narrowest part of the channel, and about nine miles north-east from the lighthouse of Paredon del Grande, the nearest point of Cuba to us. We were all prepared for her, beat to quarters, and orders were given to Lieutenant D. M. Fairfax to have two boats manned and armed to board her and make Messrs. Slidell, Mason, Eustis, and McFarland prisoners, and send them immediately on board. The steamer approached and hoisted English colors; our ensign was hoisted, and a shot was fired across her bow; she maintained her speed, and showed no disposition to heave to; then a shell was fired across her bow, which brought her to. I hailed that I intended to send a boat on board, and Lieutenant Fairfax, with the second cutter of this ship, was despatched. He met with some difficulty, and remaining on board the steamer with a part of the boat's crew, sent her back to request more assistance ; the captain of the steamer having declined to show his papers and passenger list, a force became necessary to search her. Lieutenant James A. Greer was at once despatched in the third cutter, also manned and armed.

" Messrs. Slidell, Mason, Eustis, and McFarland were recognized and told they were required to go on board this ship. This they objected to until an overpowering force compelled them ; much persuasion was used, and a little force, and at about two o'clock they were brought on board this ship and received by me. Two other boats were then sent to expedite the removal of their baggage and some stores, when the steamer, which proved to be the Trent, was suffered to proceed on her route to the eastward, and at half past three P. M. we bore away to the northward and westward. The whole time employed was two hours and thirteen minutes.

" I enclose you the statements of such officers who boarded the Trent, relative to the facts, and also an extract from the log-book of this ship.

" It was my determination to have taken possession of the Trent, and sent her to Key West as a prize, for resisting the search and carrying these passengers, whose character and objects were well known to the captain ; but the reduced number of my officers and crew, and the large number of passengers on board, bound to Europe, who would be put to great inconvenience, decided me to allow them to proceed.

" Finding the families of Messrs. Slidell and Eustis on board, I tendered them the offer of my cabin for their accommodation to accompany their husbands ; this they declined, however, and proceeded in the Trent.

" Before closing this despatch I would bring to your notice the notorious action of her British Majesty's subjects, the consul general of Cuba and those on board the Trent, in doing every thing to aid and abet the escape of these four persons, and endeavoring to conceal their persons on board. No passports or papers of any description were in possession of them from the federal government ; and for this and other reasons which will readily occur to you, I made them my prisoners, and shall retain them on board here until I hear from you what disposition is to be made of them.

" I cannot close this report without bearing testimony to the admirable manner in which all the officers and men of this ship performed their duties, and the cordial manner in which they carried out my orders.

" To Lieutenant Fairfax I beg leave to call your particular attention for the praiseworthy manner in which he executed the delicate duties with which he was intrusted : it met and has received my warmest thanks.

" After leaving the north side of Cuba, I ran through the Santaren passage, and up the coast from off St. Augustine to Charleston, and regretted being too late to take a part in the expedition to Port Royal.

" I have the honor to be, very respectfully, your obedient servant,

" CHARLES WILKES, *Captain.*

"Hon. GIDEON WELLES, *Secretary of the Navy.*"

"UNITED STATES STEAMER SAN JACINTO, }
         AT SEA, *November* 12, 1861. }

" SIR : At twenty minutes past one P. M., on the 8th instant, I repaired alongside of the British mail packet in an armed cutter, accompanied by Mr. Houston, second assistant engineer, and Mr. Grace, the boatswain.

" I went on board the Trent alone, leaving the two officers in the boat with orders to await until it became necessary to show some force.

" I was shown up by the first officer to the quarter deck, where I met the captain, and informed him who I was, asking to see the passenger list. He declined letting me see it. I then told him that I had information of Mr. Mason, Mr. Slidell, Mr. Eustis, and Mr. McFarland having taken their passage at Havana in the packet to St. Thomas, and would satisfy myself whether they were on board before allowing the steamer to proceed. Mr. Slidell, evidently hearing his name mentioned, came up to me, and asked if I wanted to see him. Mr. Mason soon joined us, and then Mr. Eustis and Mr. McFarland, when I made known the object of my visit. The captain of the Trent opposed any thing like the search of his vessel, nor would he consent to show papers or passenger list. The four gentlemen above mentioned protested also against my arresting and sending them to the United States steamer near by. There was considerable noise among the passengers just about this time, and that led Mr. Houston and Mr. Grace to repair on board with some six or eight men, all armed. After several unsuccessful efforts to persuade Mr. Mason and Mr. Slidell to go with me peaceably, I called to Mr. Houston, and ordered him to return to the ship with the information that the four gentlemen named in your order of the 8th instant were on board, and force must be applied to take them out of the packet.

"About three minutes after there was still greater excitement on the quarter deck, which brought Mr. Grace with his armed party. I, however, deemed the presence of any armed men unnecessary, and only calculated to alarm the ladies present, and directed Mr. Grace to return to the lower deck, where he had been since first coming on board. It must have been less than half an hour after I boarded the Trent when the second armed cutter, under Lieutenant Green, came alongside, (only two armed boats being used.) He brought in the third cutter eight marines and four machinists, in addition to a crew of some twelve men. When the marines and some armed men had been formed just outside of the main deck cabin, where these four gentlemen had gone to pack up their baggage, I renewed my efforts to induce them to accompany me on board — still refusing to accompany me unless force was applied. I called in to my assistance four or five officers, and first taking hold of Mr. Mason's shoulder, with another officer on the opposite side, I went as far as the gangway of the steamer, and delivered him over to Lieutenant Greer, to be placed in the boat. I then returned for Mr. Slidell, who insisted that I must apply considerable force to get him to go with me; calling in at last three officers, he also was taken in charge, and handed over to Mr. Greer. Mr. McFarland and Mr. Eustis, after protesting, went quietly into the boat. They had been permitted to collect their baggage, but were sent in advance of it under charge of Lieutenant Greer. I gave my personal attention to the luggage, saw it put in a boat and sent in charge of an officer to the San Jacinto.

"When Mr. Slidell was taken prisoner, a great deal of noise was made by some of the passengers, which caused Lieutenant Greer to send the marines into the cabin. They were immediately ordered to return to their former position outside. I carried out my purpose without using any force beyond what appears in this report. The mail agent, who is a retired commander in the British navy, seemed to have a great deal to say as to the propriety of my course; but I purposely avoided all official intercourse with him. When I finally was leaving the steamer, he made some apology for his rude conduct, and expressed personally his approval of the manner in which I had carried out my orders. We parted company from the Trent at twenty minutes past three P. M.

"Very respectfully, your obedient servant,

"D. M. FAIRFAX,
"*Lieutenant and Executive Officer.*
"Captain CHARLES WILKES, U. S. N.,
"*Commanding San Jacinto.*"

"UNITED STATES STEAMER SAN JACINTO, ⎰
"AT SEA, *November* 13, 1861. ⎰

"SIR: In obedience to your order of the 11th instant, I respectfully report, —

"That upon going alongside of the English steamer Trent, on the 7th of this month, Lieutenant Fairfax went on board, ordering the boatswain and myself to remain in the boat. A few minutes after this my attention was attracted by persons speaking in a loud and excited manner upon the steamer's upper deck. While considering its meaning the noise was repeated, which decided me to join Lieutenant Fairfax immediately on board, and I found him surrounded by the officers of the ship and passengers, among whom I recognized Messrs. Mason, Slidell, and Eustis. The confusion at this time passes description. So soon, however, as he could be heard, the mail agent (who was a retired lieutenant or commander in the British navy) protested against the act of removing passengers from an English steamer. Lieutenant Fairfax requested Mr. Mason to go quietly to the San Jacinto; but that gentleman replied that he would "yield only to force;" whereupon I was ordered to our ship to report the presence of the above-named gentlemen, together with Mr. McFarland, and ask that the remainder of our force be sent to the Trent; after which I returned to her, and, entering the cabin, saw Mr. Fairfax endeavoring to enter Mr. Slidell's room, which was then prevented in a measure by the excitement which prevailed in and around that gentleman's quarters. The passengers (not including Mr. Mason, Slidell, Eustis, or McFarland) were disposed to give trouble: some of them went so far as to threaten, and, upon Lieutenant Greer being informed by me of this fact, he ordered the marines to clear the passage-way of the cabin: but as Mr. Slidell had now come out of his state room through the window, where we could get to him, the order to the marines was countermanded by Lieutenant Fairfax. Mr. Slidell

was removed to the boat by Mr. Grace and myself, and no more force was used than would show what would be done in case of necessity. Mr. Mason was taken in charge by Lieutenant Fairfax and Third Assistant Engineer Hall. The two secretaries walked into the boat by themselves.

"While we were on board the Trent many remarks were made reflecting discreditably upon us and the government of the United States. No one was more abusive than the mail agent, who took pains at the same time to inform us that he was the only person on board officially connected with her Britannic Majesty's government, who, he said, would, in consequence of this act, break the blockade of the Southern United States ports. Another person, supposed to be a passenger, was so violent that the captain ordered him to be locked up. A short time before leaving the steamer I was informed by one of her crew that the mail agent was advising the captain to arm the crew and passengers of his ship, which I immediately communicated to Lieutenant Greer. About half past three P. M. we returned to the San Jacinto.

"I am, respectfully, your obedient servant,
"J. B. HOUSTON,
"*Second Assistant Engineer*
"*U. S. Steamer San Jacinto.*
"Captain CHARLES WILKES, *Commanding.*"

"UNITED STATES STEAMER SAN JACINTO, ⎰
"AT SEA, *November* 16, 1861. ⎰

"SIR: In my despatch by Commander Taylor I confined myself to the reports of the movements of this ship, and the facts connected with the capture of Messrs. Mason, Slidell, Eustis, and McFarland, as I intended to write you particularly relative to the reasons which induced my action in making these prisoners.

"When I heard at Cienfuegos, on the south side of Cuba, of these commissioners having landed on the island of Cuba, and that they were at the Havana, and would depart in the

English steamer of the 7th November, I determined to intercept them, and carefully examined all the authorities on international law to which I had access, viz.: Kent, Wheaton, and Vattel, besides various decisions of Sir William Scott, and other judges of the Admiralty Court of Great Britain, which bore upon the rights of neutrals, and their responsibilities.

"The governments of Great Britain, France, and Spain, having issued proclamations that the Confederate States were viewed, considered, and treated as belligerents, and knowing that the ports of Great Britain, France, Spain, and Holland, in the West Indies, were open to their vessels, and that they were admitted to all the courtesies and protection vessels of the United States received, every aid and attention being given them, proved clearly that they acted upon this view and decision, and brought them within the international law of search, and under the responsibilities. I therefore felt no hesitation in boarding and searching all vessels of whatever nation I fell in with, and have done so.

"The question arose in my mind whether I had the right to capture the *persons* of these commissioners — whether *they* were amenable to capture. There was no doubt I had the right to capture vessels with *written* despatches; they are expressly referred to in all authorities, subjecting the vessel to seizure and condemnation if the captain of the vessel had the knowledge of their being on board; but these gentlemen were not despatches in the literal sense, and did not seem to come under that designation; and nowhere could I find a case in point.

"That they were commissioners I had ample proof from their own avowal, and bent on mischievous and traitorous errands against our country, to overthrow its institutions, and enter into treaties and alliances with foreign states, expressly forbidden by the constitution.

"They had been presented to the captain general of Cuba by her Britannic Majesty's consul general; but the captain general told me that he had not received them in that capacity, but as distinguished gentlemen and strangers.

"I then considered them as the *embodiment* of despatches; and as they had openly declared themselves as charged with all authority from the Confederate government to form treaties and alliances tending to the establishment of their independence, I became satisfied that their mission was adverse and criminal to the Union, and it therefore became my duty to arrest their progress and capture them if they had no passports or papers from the federal government, as provided for under the law of nations, viz.: 'That foreign ministers of a belligerent on board of neutral ships are required to possess papers from the other belligerent to permit them to pass free.'

"Report and assumption gave them the title of ministers to France and England; but inasmuch as they had not been received by either of these powers, I did not conceive they had immunity attached to their persons, and were but escaped conspirators, plotting and contriving to overthrow the government of the United States, and they were therefore not to be considered as having any claim to the immunities attached to the character they thought fit to assume.

"As respects the steamer in which they embarked, I ascertained in the Havana that she was a merchant vessel plying between Vera Cruz, the Havana, and St. Thomas, carrying the mail by contract.

"The agent of the vessel, the son of the British consul at Havana, was well aware of the character of these persons; that they engaged their passage and did embark in the vessel; his father had visited them, and introduced them as ministers of the Confederate States on their way to England and France.

"They went in the steamer with the knowledge and by the consent of the captain, who endeavored afterwards to conceal them by refusing to exhibit the passenger list and the papers of the vessel. There can be no doubt he knew they were carrying highly important despatches, and were endowed with instructions inimical to the United States. This rendered his vessel (a neutral) a good prize, and I determined to take possession of her, and, as I mentioned in my report, send her to Key West for adjudication, where, I am well satisfied, she would have been condemned for carrying these persons, and for resisting to be searched. The cargo was also liable, as all the shippers were knowing to the embarkation of these *live* despatches, and their traitorous motives and actions to the Union of the United States.

" I forbore to seize her, however, in consequence of my being so reduced in officers and crew, and the derangement it would cause innocent persons, there being a large number of passengers who would have been put to great loss and inconvenience, as well as disappointment, from the interruption it would have caused them in not being able to join the steamer from St. Thomas to Europe. I therefore concluded to sacrifice the interests of my officers and crew in the prize, and suffered the steamer to proceed, after the necessary detention to effect the transfer of these commissioners, considering I had obtained the important end I had in view, and which affected the interests of our country and interrupted the action of that of the confederates.

" I would add, that the conduct of her Britannic Majesty's subjects, both official and others, showed but little regard or obedience to her proclamation, by aiding and abetting the views, and endeavoring to conceal the persons, of these commissioners.

" I have pointed out sufficient reasons to show you that my action in this case was derived from a firm conviction that it became my duty to make these parties prisoners, and to bring them to the United States.

" Although, in my giving up this valuable prize, I have deprived the officers and crew of a well-earned reward, I am assured they are quite content to forego any advantages which might have accrued to them under the circumstances.

" I may add that, having assumed the responsibility, I am willing to abide the result.

" I am, very respectfully,
         " Your obedient servant,
                 " CHARLES WILKES, *Captain.*
" HON. GIDEON WELLES, SECRETARY OF THE NAVY."

Captain Wilkes proceeded at once to Hampton Roads with his prisoners, whom he treated with a courtesy which they freely acknowledged, and reported his action to the government. After a very brief delay, the San Jacinto was ordered to the Charlestown navy yard, and the rebel envoys were placed in Fort Warren, in Boston harbor, to await the action of the government.

The announcement of the capture of Messrs. Mason and Slidell, with their secretaries, produced an intense excitement through the loyal states; and although there were some misgivings as to the right of Captain Wilkes to make the capture as he did on board a neutral vessel, there was a general feeling of satisfaction at the result. In the popular mind this satisfaction was by no means diminished by the fact that the capture was made on board an English vessel and under the flag of England, whose professed neutrality had been constantly disregarded by English subjects. And when provincial threats were uttered, the people were ready to sustain Captain Wilkes and the government. The government, however, refrained from committing itself at once to an approval of the act, except that the secretary of the navy commended the prompt and decisive action of Captain Wilkes, which was a matter between the head of the department and a subordinate officer, for the encouragement of promptness and efficiency, rather than the assumption and ratification of the act. In the mean time international law applicable to such cases was thoroughly examined, and the question was fully discussed in the papers, until the public seemed perfectly content that the question which must arise between the British government and that of the United States should be settled upon the established principles of international law, whatever might be the result. There were, of course, many hasty and indiscreet opinions expressed, and in some instances the public press was not inclined to let the people forget England's shortcomings in her proclaimed neutrality, and the aid and comfort notoriously afforded to the rebels under the English flag. These did not allay the animosity excited by the taunts of the press and the public, which were freely hurled at the United States from England and all her provinces; and had not the people felt that the rebellion was taxing all the energies and resources of the north, a very decided war feeling would have been shown towards England.

But the feeling shown in the United States was by no means so great as that manifested in England and in some of the North American provinces, when the news of the seizure of the rebel envoys arrived there. Indignation meetings were held, belligerent resolutions were adopted, the public press — always too ready to complain of the north — denounced the act of Captain Wilkes as an insult to the British flag that must receive a summary punishment. The government was urged to send at once an overwhelming naval force to New York or Washington, to demand immediate reparation, and to summarily destroy those cities if refused. The friends and agents of rebellion fanned the flame which seemed to sweep through the people of England so suddenly, and for a time they had reason to hope, from the language of the people and the press, and the reported action of the British government, that they would soon have the powerful alliance which they most desired.

But in England, as in the United States, a calmer discussion followed, in some quarters, the first outbreak, and the blind rage of many Englishmen at the mere fact of the stopping a British vessel on the seas was soon seen to be quarrelling with one of the rights of a belligerent which Great Britain had asserted more frequently and strenuously than any other power. There was, however, but too much evidence that a large proportion of the ruling classes in England desired to humiliate the United States, and for that end were ready to take advantage of the unfortunate condition of the government of this country, which was using its whole power to suppress rebellion.

The British government did not accede to the demands of those most hostile to the United States; but, taking decided grounds that the act of Captain Wilkes was unwarranted by international law, it demanded, in moderate terms, the release of the captives, and their restoration to British protection. The character of this demand, the views of the United States government upon the question, and the grounds upon which the demand was acceded to, are fully set forth in the following reply from Mr. Seward to Lord Lyons. The previous policy of the United States, which England had hitherto in some measure combated, is also shown in Mr. Seward's able letter; and it will be seen that this demand on the part of Great Britain, and the release on the part of the United States, really committed the former to the principles for which the latter had long contended, and established a precedent in opposition to what had often been the practice of the British authorities.

Mr. Seward to Lord Lyons.

"DEPARTMENT OF STATE, }
"WASHINGTON, *December* 26, 1861. }

"MY LORD: Earl Russell's despatch of November the 30th, a copy of which you have left with me at my request, is of the following effect, namely:

"That a letter of Commander Williams, dated Royal Mail Contract Packet-boat Trent, at sea, November 9th, states that that vessel left Havana on the 7th of November, with her Majesty's mails for England, having on board numerous passengers. Shortly after noon, on the 8th of November, the United States war steamer San Jacinto, Captain Wilkes, not showing colors, was observed ahead. That steamer, on being neared by the Trent, at a quarter past one o'clock in the afternoon, fired a round shot from a pivot gun across her bows, and showed American colors. While the Trent was approaching slowly towards the San Jacinto, she discharged a shell across the Trent's bows, which exploded at half a cable's length before her. The Trent then stopped, and an officer, with a large armed guard of marines, boarded her. The officer said he had orders to arrest Messrs. Mason, Slidell, McFarland, and Eustis, and had sure information that they were passengers in the Trent. While some parley was going on upon this matter, Mr. Slidell stepped forward, and said to the American officer that the four persons he had named were standing before him. The commander of the Trent and Commander Williams protested against the act of taking those four passengers out of the Trent, they then being under the protection of the British flag. But the San Jacinto was at this time only two hundred yards distant, her ship's company at quarters, her ports open and tompions out, and so resistance was out of the question. The four persons before named were then forcibly taken out of the ship. A further demand was made that the commander of the Trent should proceed on board the San Jacinto; but he said he would not go unless forcibly compelled likewise, and this demand was not insisted upon.

"Upon this statement Earl Russell remarks, that it thus appears that certain individuals have been forcibly taken from on board a British vessel, the ship of a neutral power, while that vessel was pursuing a lawful and innocent voyage — an act of violence which was an affront to the British flag, and a violation of international law.

"Earl Russell next says, that her Majesty's government, bearing in mind the friendly relations which have long subsisted between Great Britain and the United States, are willing to believe that the naval officer who committed this aggression was not acting in compliance with any authority from his government; or that, if he conceived himself to be so authorized, he greatly misunderstood the instructions which he had received.

"Earl Russell argues that the United States must be fully aware that the British government could not allow such an affront to the national honor to pass without full reparation; and they are willing to believe that it could not be the deliberate intention of the government of the United States unnecessarily to force into discussion between the two governments a question of so grave a character, and with regard to which the whole British nation would be sure to entertain such unanimity of feeling.

"Earl Russell, resting upon the statement and the argument which I have thus recited, closes with saying that her Majesty's government trust that when this matter shall have been brought under the consideration of the government of the United States, it will, of its own accord, offer to the British government such redress as alone could satisfy the British nation, namely, the liberation of the four prisoners taken from the Trent, and their delivery to your lordship, in order that they may again be placed under British protection, and a suitable apology for the aggression which has been committed. Earl Russell finally instructs you to propose those terms to me, if I should not first offer them on the part of the government.

"This despatch has been submitted to the President.

"The British government has rightly conjectured, what it is now my duty to state, that

Captain Wilkes, in conceiving and executing the proceeding in question, acted upon his own suggestions of duty, without any direction or instruction, or even foreknowledge of it, on the part of this government. No directions had been given to him, or any other naval officer, to arrest the four persons named, or any of them, on the Trent or on any other British vessel, or on any other neutral vessel, at the place where it occurred or elsewhere. The British government will justly infer from these facts, that the United States not only have had no purpose, but even no thought, of forcing into discussion the question which has arisen, or any other which could affect in any way the sensibilities of the British nation.

" It is true that a round shot was fired by the San Jacinto from her pivot gun when the Trent was distantly approaching. But, as the facts have been reported to this government, the shot was, nevertheless, intentionally fired in a direction so obviously divergent from the course of the Trent, as to be quite as harmless as a blank shot, while it should be regarded as a signal.

" So, also, we learn that the Trent was not approaching the San Jacinto slowly when the shell was fired across her bows; but, on the contrary, the Trent was, or seemed to be, moving under a full head of steam, as if with a purpose to pass the San Jacinto.

" We are informed also that the boarding officer (Lieutenant Fairfax) did not board the Trent with a large armed guard, but he left his marines in his boat when he entered the Trent. He stated his instructions from Captain Wilkes to search for the four persons named, in a respectful and courteous, though decided manner, and he asked the captain of the Trent to show his passenger list, which was refused. The lieutenant, as we are informed, did not employ absolute force in transferring the passengers; but he used just so much as was necessary to satisfy the parties concerned that refusal or resistance would be unavailing.

" So, also, we are informed that the captain of the Trent was not at any time, or in any way, required to go on board the San Jacinto.

" These modifications of the case, as presented by Commander Williams, are based upon our official reports.

" I have now to remind your lordship of some facts, which doubtlessly were omitted by Earl Russell, with the very proper and becoming motive of allowing them to be brought into the case, on the part of the United States, in the way most satisfactory to this government. These facts are, that at the time the transaction occurred an insurrection was existing in the United States, which this government was engaged in suppressing, by the employment of land and naval forces; that in regard to this domestic strife the United States considered Great Britain as a friendly power, while she had assumed for herself the attitude of a neutral; and that Spain was considered in the same light, and had assumed the same attitude as Great Britain.

" It had been settled by correspondence that the United States and Great Britain mutually recognized as applicable to this local strife these two articles of the declaration made by the congress of Paris in 1856, namely, that the neutral or friendly flag should cover enemy's goods not contraband of war, and that neutral goods not contraband of war are not liable to capture under an enemy's flag. These exceptions of contraband from favor were a negative acceptance by the parties of the rule hitherto every where recognized as a part of the law of nations, that whatever is contraband is liable to capture and confiscation in all cases.

" James M. Mason and E. J. McFarland are citizens of the United States, and residents of Virginia. John Slidell and George Eustis are citizens of the United States, and residents of Louisiana. It was well known at Havana, when these parties embarked in the Trent, that James M. Mason was proceeding to England in the affected character of a minister plenipotentiary to the court of St. James, under a pretended commission from Jefferson Davis, who had assumed to be president of the insurrectionary party in the United States, and E. J. McFarland was going with him in a like unreal character of secretary of legation to the pretended mission. John Slidell, in similar circumstances, was going to Paris as a pretended minister to the Emperor of the French, and George Eustis was the chosen secretary of legation for that simulated mission. The fact that these persons had assumed such characters has been since avowed by the same Jefferson Davis, in a pretended message to an unlawful and insurrectionary congress. It was, as we think, rightly presumed that these ministers bore pretended credentials and instructions, and such papers are in the law known as despatches. We are informed by our consul at Paris that these despatches, having escaped the search of the Trent, were actually conveyed and delivered to emissaries of the insurrection in England. Although it is not essential, yet it is proper to state, as I do also upon information and belief, that the owner and agent, and all the officers of the Trent, including Commander Williams, had knowledge of the assumed characters and purposes of the persons before named when they embarked on that vessel.

"Your lordship will now perceive that the case before us, instead of presenting a merely flagrant act of violence on the part of Captain Wilkes, as might well be inferred from the incomplete statement of it that went up to the British government, was undertaken as a simple legal and customary belligerent proceeding by Captain Wilkes to arrest and capture a neutral vessel engaged in carrying contraband of war for the use and benefit of the insurgents.

"The question before us is, whether this proceeding was authorized by, and conducted according to, the law of nations. It involves the following inquiries : —

"1. Were the persons named, and their supposed despatches, contraband of war ?

"2. Might Captain Wilkes lawfully stop and search the Trent for these contraband persons and despatches ?

"3. Did he exercise that right in a lawful and proper manner ?

"4. Having found the contraband persons on board and in presumed possession of the contraband despatches, had he a right to capture the persons ?

"5. Did he exercise that right of capture in the manner allowed and recognized by the law of nations ?

"If all these inquiries shall be resolved in the affirmative, the British government will have no claim for reparation.

"I address myself to the first inquiry, namely : Were the four persons mentioned, and their supposed despatches, contraband ?

"Maritime law so generally deals, as its professors say, *in rem*, that is, with property, and so seldom with persons, that it seems a straining of the term 'contraband' to apply it to them. But persons, as well as property, may become contraband, since the word means broadly, 'contrary to proclamation, prohibited, illegal, unlawful.'

"All writers and judges pronounce naval or military persons in the service of the enemy contraband. Vattel says, war allows us to cut off from an enemy all his resources, and to hinder him from sending ministers to solicit assistance. And Sir William Scott says, you may stop the ambassador of your enemy on his passage. Despatches are not less clearly contraband, and the bearers, or couriers, who undertake to carry them, fall under the same condemnation.

"A subtlety might be raised whether pretended ministers of a usurping power, not recognized as legal by either the belligerent or the neutral, could be held to be contraband.

But it would disappear on being subjected to what is the true test in all cases, namely, the spirit of the law. Sir William Scott, speaking of civil magistrates who are arrested and detained as contraband, says, —

"'It appears to me on principle to be but reasonable that when it is of sufficient importance to the enemy that such persons shall be sent out on the public service at the public expense, it should afford equal ground of forfeiture against the vessel that may be let out for a purpose so intimately connected with the hostile operations.'

"I trust that I have shown that the four persons who were taken from the Trent by Captain Wilkes, and their despatches, were contraband of war.

"The second inquiry is, whether Captain Wilkes had a right, by the law of nations, to detain and search the Trent.

"The Trent, though she carried mails, was a contract or merchant vessel — a common carrier for hire. Maritime law knows only three classes of vessels — vessels of war, revenue vessels, and merchant vessels. The Trent falls within the latter class. Whatever disputes have existed concerning a right of visitation or search in time of peace, none, it is supposed, has existed in modern times about the right of a belligerent in time of war to capture contraband in neutral and even friendly merchant vessels, and of the right of visitation and search, in order to determine whether they are neutral, and are documented as such according to the law of nations.

"I assume in the present case what, as I read British authorities, is regarded by Great Britain herself as true maritime law: That the circumstance that the Trent was proceeding from a neutral port to another neutral port does not modify the right of the belligerent captor.

"The third question is, whether Captain Wilkes exercised the right of search in a lawful and proper manner.

"If any doubt hung over this point, as the case was presented in the statement of it adopted by the British government, I think it must have already passed away before the modifications of that statement which I have already submitted.

"I proceed to the fourth inquiry, namely: Having found the suspected contraband of war on board the Trent, had Captain Wilkes a right to capture the same?

"Such a capture is the chief, if not the only recognized, object of the permitted visitation and search. The principle of the law is, that the belligerent exposed to danger may prevent the contraband persons or things from applying themselves, or being applied, to the hostile uses or purposes designed. The law is so very liberal in this respect, that when contraband is found on board a neutral vessel, not only is the contraband forfeited, but the vessel which is the vehicle of its passage or transportation, being tainted, also becomes contraband, and is subjected to capture and confiscation.

"Only the fifth question remains, namely: Did Captain Wilkes exercise the right of capturing the contraband in conformity with the law of nations?

"It is just here that the difficulties of the case begin. What is the manner which the law of nations prescribes for disposing of the contrabaud when you have found and seized it on board of the neutral vessel? The answer would be easily found if the question were what you shall do with the contraband vessel. You must take or send her into a convenient port, and subject her to a judicial prosecution there in admiralty, which will try and decide the questions of belligerency, neutrality, contraband, and capture. So, again, you would promptly find the same answer if the question were, What is the manner of proceeding prescribed by the law of nations in regard to the contraband, if it be property, or things of material or pecuniary value?

"But the question here concerns the mode of procedure in regard, not to the vessel that was carrying the contraband, nor yet to contraband things which worked the forfeiture of the vessel, but to contraband persons.

"The books of law are dumb. Yet the question is as important as it is difficult. First, the belligerent captor has a right to prevent the contraband officer, soldier, sailor, minister, messenger, or courier from proceeding in his unlawful voyage and reaching the destined scene of his injurious service. But, on the other hand, the person captured may be innocent — that is, he may not be contraband. He, therefore, has a right to a fair trial of the accusation against him. The neutral state that has taken him under its flag is bound to protect him if he is not contraband, and is, therefore, entitled to be satisfied upon that important question. The faith of that state is pledged to his safety, if innocent, as its justice is pledged to his surrender if he is really contraband. Here are conflicting claims, involving personal liberty, life, honor, and duty. Here are conflicting national claims, involving welfare, safety, honor, and empire. They require a tribunal and a trial. The captors and the captured are equals; the neutral and the belligerent state are equals.

"While the law authorities were found silent, it was suggested at an early day by this government that you should take the captured persons into a convenient port, and institute judicial proceedings there to try the controversy. But only courts of admiralty have jurisdiction in maritime cases, and these courts have formulas to try only claims to contraband chattels, but none to try claims concerning contraband persons. The courts can entertain no proceedings and render no judgment in favor of or against the alleged contraband men.

"It was replied, all this was true; but you can reach in those courts a decision which will have the moral weight of a judicial one by a circuitous proceeding. Convey the suspected men, together with the suspected vessel, into port, and try there the question whether the vessel is contraband. You can prove it to be so by proving the suspected men to be contraband, and the court must then determine the vessel to be contraband. If the men are not contraband the vessel will escape condemnation. Still, there is no judgment for or against the captured persons. But it was assumed that there would result from the determination of the court concerning the vessel a legal certainty concerning the character of the men.

"This course of proceeding seemed open to many objections. It elevates the incidental inferior private interest into the proper place of the main paramount public one, and possibly it may make the fortunes, the safety, or the existence of a nation depend on the accidents of a merely personal and pecuniary litigation. Moreover, when the judgment of the prize court upon the lawfulness of the capture of the vessel is rendered, it really concludes nothing, and binds neither the belligerent state nor the neutral upon the great question of the disposition to be made of the captured contraband persons. That question is still to be really determined, if at all, by diplomatic arrangement or by war.

"One may well express his surprise when told that the law of nations has furnished no more reasonable, practical, and perfect mode than this of determining questions of such grave import between sovereign powers. The regret we may feel on the occasion is, nevertheless, modified by the reflection that the difficulty is not altogether anomalous. Similar and equal deficiencies are found in every system of municipal law, especially in the system which exists in the greater portions of Great Britain and the United States. The title to personal property can hardly ever be resolved by a court, without resorting to the fiction that the claimant has lost and the possessor has found it, and the title to real estate is disputed by real litigants under the names of imaginary persons. It must be confessed, however, that while all aggrieved nations demand, and all impartial ones concede, the need of some form of judicial process in determining the characters of contraband persons, no other form than the illogical and circuitons one thus described exists, nor has any other yet been suggested. Practically, therefore, the choice is between that judicial remedy or no judicial remedy whatever.

"If there be no judicial remedy, the result is, that the question must be determined by the captor himself, on the deck of the prize vessel. Very grave objections arise against such a course. The captor is armed, the neutral is unarmed. The captor is interested, prejudiced, and perhaps violent; the neutral, if truly neutral, is disinterested, subdued, and helpless. The tribunal is irresponsible, while its judgment is carried into instant execution. The captured party is compelled to submit, though bound by no legal, moral, or treaty obligation to acquiesce. Reparation is distant and problematical, and depends at last on the justice, magnanimity, or weakness of the state in whose behalf and by whose authority the capture was made. Out of these disputes reprisals and wars necessarily arise, and these are so frequent and destructive that it may well be doubted whether this form of remedy is not a greater social evil than all that could follow if the belligerent right of search were universally renounced and abolished forever. But carry the case one step farther. What if the state that has made the capture unreasonably refuse to hear the complaint of the neutral, or to redress it? In that case, the very act of capture would be an act of war — of war begun without notice, and possibly entirely without provocation.

"I think all unprejudiced minds will agree that, imperfect as the existing judicial remedy may be supposed to be, it would be, as a general practice, better to follow it than to adopt the summary one of leaving the decision with the captor, and relying upon diplomatic debates to review his decision. Practically, it is a question of choice between law, with its imperfections and delays, and war, with its evils and desolations. Nor is it ever to be forgotten that neutrality, honestly and justly preserved, is always the harbinger of peace, and therefore is the common interest of nations, which is only saying that it is the interest of humanity itself.

"At the same time it is not to be denied that it may sometimes happen that the judicial remedy will become impossible, as by the shipwreck of the prize vessel, or other circumstances which excuse the captor from sending or taking her into port for confiscation. In such a case, the right of the captor to the custody of the captured persons, and to dispose of them, if they are really contraband, so as to defeat their unlawful purposes, cannot reasonably be denied. What rule shall be applied in such a case? Clearly, the captor ought to be required to show that the failure of the judicial remedy results from circumstances beyond his control, and without his fault. Otherwise, he would be allowed to derive advantage from a wrongful act of his own.

"In the present case, Captain Wilkes, after capturing the contraband persons and making prize of the Trent in what seems to be a perfectly lawful manner, instead of sending her into port, released her from the capture, and permitted her to proceed with her whole cargo upon her voyage. He thus effectually prevented the judicial examination which might otherwise have occurred.

"If, now, the capture of the contraband persons and the capture of the contraband vessel are to be regarded, not as two separate or distinct transactions under the law of nations, but as one transaction, one capture only, then it follows that the capture in this case was left unfinished, or was abandoned. Whether the United States have a right to retain the chief public benefits of it, namely, the custody of the captured persons on proving them to be contraband, will depend upon the preliminary question whether the leaving of the transaction unfinished was necessary, or whether it was unnecessary, and therefore voluntary. If it was necessary, Great Britain, as we suppose, must, of course, waive the defect, and the consequent failure of the judicial remedy. On the other hand, it is not seen how the United States can insist upon her waiver of that judicial remedy, if the defect of the capture resulted from an act of Captain Wilkes, which would be a fault on their own side.

"Captain Wilkes has presented to this government his reasons for releasing the Trent. 'I forbore to seize her,' he says, 'in consequence of my being so reduced in officers and crew, and the derangement it would cause innocent persons, there being a large number of passengers who would have been put to great loss and inconvenience, as well as disappointment, from the interruption it would have caused them in not being able to join the steamer from St. Thomas to Europe. I therefore concluded to sacrifice the interest of my officers and crew in the prize, and suffered her to proceed after the detention necessary to effect the transfer of those commissioners, considering I had obtained the important end I had in view, and which affected the interest of our country and interrupted the action of that of the Confederates.'

"I shall consider, first, how these reasons ought to affect the action of this government; and, secondly, how they ought to be expected to affect the action of Great Britain.

"The reasons are satisfactory to this government, so far as Captain Wilkes is concerned. It could not desire that the San Jacinto, her officers and crew, should be exposed to danger and loss by weakening their number to detach a prize crew to go on board the Trent. Still less could it disavow the humane motive of preventing inconveniences, losses, and perhaps disasters, to the several hundred innocent pas-

sengers found on board the prize vessel. Nor could this government perceive any ground for questioning the fact that these reasons, though apparently incongruous, did operate in the mind of Captain Wilkes, and determine him to release the Trent. Human actions generally proceed upon mingled, and sometimes conflicting motives. He measured the sacrifices which this decision would cost. It manifestly, however, did not occur to him that beyond the sacrifice of the private interests (as he calls them) of his officers and crew, there might also possibly be a sacrifice even of the chief and public object of his capture, namely, the right of his government to the custody and disposition of the captured persons. This government cannot censure him for this oversight. It confesses that the whole subject came unforeseen upon the government, as doubtless it did upon him. Its present convictions on the point in question are the result of deliberate examination and deduction now made, and not of any impressions previously formed.

"Nevertheless, the question now is, not whether Captain Wilkes is justified to his government in what he did, but what is the present view of the government as to the effect of what he has done. Assuming now, for argument's sake only, that the release of the Trent, if voluntary, involved a waiver of the claim of the government to hold the captured persons, the United States could in that case have no hesitation in saying that the act which has thus already been approved by the government must be allowed to draw its legal consequence after it. It is of the very nature of a gift or a charity that the giver cannot, after the exercise of his benevolence is past, recall or modify its benefits.

"We are thus brought directly to the question whether we are entitled to regard the release of the Trent as involuntary, or whether we are obliged to consider that it was voluntary. Clearly the release would have been involuntary had it been made solely upon the first ground assigned for it by Captain Wilkes, namely, a want of a sufficient force to send the prize vessel into port for adjudication. It is not the duty of a captor to hazard his own vessel in order to secure a judicial examination to the captured party. No large prize crew, however, is legally necessary, for it is the duty of the captured party to acquiesce, and go willingly before the tribunal to whose jurisdiction it appeals. If the captured party indicate purposes to employ means of resistance which the captor cannot with probable safety to himself overcome, he may properly leave the vessel to go forward; and neither she nor the state she represents can ever afterwards justly object that the captor deprived her of the judicial remedy to which she was entitled.

"But the second reason assigned by Captain Wilkes for releasing the Trent differs from the first. At best, therefore, it must be held that Captain Wilkes, as he explains himself, acted from combined sentiments of prudence and generosity, and so that the release of the prize vessel was not strictly necessary or involuntary.

"Secondly. How ought we to expect these explanations by Captain Wilkes of his reasons for leaving the capture incomplete to affect the action of the British government?

"The observation upon this point which first occurs is, that Captain Wilkes's explanations were not made to the authorities of the captured vessel. If made known to them, they might have approved and taken the release upon the condition of waiving a judicial investigation of the whole transaction, or they might have refused to accept the release upon that condition.

"But the case is one not with them, but with the British government. If we claim that Great Britain ought not to insist that a judicial trial has been lost because we voluntarily released the offending vessel out of consideration for her innocent passengers, I do not see how

she is to be bound to acquiesce in the decision which was thus made by us without necessity on our part, and without knowledge of conditions or consent on her own. The question between Great Britain and ourselves thus stated would be a question not of right and of law, but of favor to be conceded by her to us in return for favors shown by us to her, of the value of which favors on both sides we ourselves shall be the judge. Of course the United States could have no thought of raising such a question in any case.

"I trust that I have shown to the satisfaction of the British government, by a very simple and natural statement of the facts, and analysis of the law applicable to them, that this government has neither meditated, nor practised, nor approved any deliberate wrong in the transaction to which they have called its attention; and, on the contrary, that what has happened has been simply an inadvertency, consisting in a departure, by the naval officer, free from any wrongful motive, from a rule uncertainly established, and probably by the several parties concerned either imperfectly understood or entirely unknown. For this error the British government has a right to expect the same reparation that we, as an independent state, should expect from Great Britain or from any other friendly nation in a similar case.

"I have not been unaware that, in examining this question, I have fallen into an argument for what seems to be the British side of it against my own country. But I am relieved from all embarrassment on that subject. I had hardly fallen into that line of argument when I discovered that I was really defending and maintaining, not an exclusively British interest, but an old, honored, and cherished American cause, not upon British authorities, but upon principles that constitute a large portion of the distinctive policy by which the United States have developed the resources of a continent, and thus becoming a considerable maritime power, have won the respect and confidence of many nations. These principles were laid down for us in 1804, by James Madison, when secretary of state in the administration of Thomas Jefferson, in instructions given to James Monroe, our minister to England. Although the case before him concerned a description of persons different from those who are incidentally the subjects of the present discussion, the ground, he assumed then was the same I now occupy, and the arguments by which he sustained himself upon it, have been an inspiration to me in preparing this reply.

" 'Whenever,' he says, 'property found in a neutral vessel is supposed to be liable, on any ground, to capture and condemnation, the rule in all cases is, that the question shall not be decided by the captor, but be carried before a legal tribunal, where a regular trial may be had, and where the captor himself is liable to damages for an abuse of his power. Can it be reasonable, then, or just, that a belligerent commander who is thus restricted, and thus responsible in a case of mere property of trivial amount, should be permitted, without recurring to any tribunal whatever, to examine the crew of a neutral vessel, to decide the important question of their respective allegiances, and to carry that decision into execution by forcing every individual he may choose into a service abhorrent to his feelings, cutting him off from his most tender connections, exposing his mind and his person to the most humiliating discipline, and his life itself to the greatest danger? Reason, justice, and humanity unite in protesting against so extravagant a proceeding.'

"If I decide this case in favor of my own government, I must disavow its most cherished principles, and reverse and forever abandon its essential policy. The country cannot afford the sacrifice. If I maintain those principles, and adhere to that policy, I must surrender the case itself. It will be seen, therefore, that this government could not deny the justice of the claim

presented to us in this respect upon its merits. We are asked to do to the British nation just what we have always insisted all nations ought to do to us.

" The claim of the British government is not made in a discourteous manner. This government, since its first organization, has never used more guarded language in a similar case.

" In coming to my conclusion I have not forgotten that, if the safety of this Union required the detention of the captured persons, it would be the right and duty of this government to detain them. But the effectual check and waning proportions of the existing insurrection, as well as the comparative unimportance of the captured persons themselves, when dispassionately weighed, happily forbid me from resorting to that defence.

" Nor am I unaware that American citizens are not in any case to be unnecessarily surrendered for any purpose into the keeping of a foreign state. Only the captured persons, however, or others who are interested in them, could justly raise a question on that ground.

" Nor have I been tempted at all by suggestions that cases might be found in history where Great Britain refused to yield to other nations, and even to ourselves, claims like that which is now before us. Those cases occurred when Great Britain, as well as the United States, was the home of generations, which, with all their peculiar interests and passions, have passed away. She could in no other way so effectually disavow any such injury as we think she does by assuming now as her own the ground upon which we then stood. It would tell little for our own claims to the character of a just and magnanimous people if we should so far consent to be guided by the law of retaliation as to lift up buried injuries from their graves to oppose against what national consistency and the national conscience compel us to regard as a claim intrinsically right.

" Putting behind me all suggestions of this

kind, I prefer to express my satisfaction that, by the adjustment of the present case upon principles confessedly American, and yet, as I trust, mutually satisfactory to both of the nations concerned, a question is finally and rightly settled between them, which, heretofore exhausting not only all forms of peaceful discussion, but also the arbitrament of war itself, for more than half a century alienated the two countries from each other, and perplexed with fears and apprehensions all other nations.

"The four persons in question are now held in military custody at Fort Warren, in the state of Massachusetts. They will be cheerfully liberated. Your lordship will please indicate a time and place for receiving them.

"I avail myself of this occasion to offer to your lordship a renewed assurance of my very high consideration.

"WILLIAM H. SEWARD.

"The Right Hon. LORD LYONS, &c., &c., &c."

The French government also interposed its advice in the question by a despatch from M. Thouvenel, the Minister of Foreign Affairs, to M. Mercier, the French Minister at Washington, which was communicated to the federal government. In that despatch M. Thouvenel wrote: —

"The Trent was not destined to a point belonging to one of the belligerents. She was carrying to a neutral country her cargo and her passengers; and, moreover, it was in a neutral port that they were taken. If it were admissible that, under such conditions, the neutral flag does not completely cover the persons and merchandise it carries, its immunity would be nothing more than an idle word; at any moment the commerce and the navigation of third powers would have to suffer from their innocent and even their indirect relations with the one or the other of the belligerents. These last would no longer find themselves as having only the right to exact from the neutral entire

impartiality, and to interdict all intermeddling on his part in acts of hostility. They would impose on his freedom of commerce and navigation restrictions which modern international law has refused to admit as legitimate; and we should, in a word, fall back upon vexatious practices, against which, in other epochs, no power has more earnestly protested than the United States.

"If the cabinet of Washington would only look on the two persons arrested as rebels, whom it is always lawful to seize, the question, to place it on other ground, could not be solved, however, in a sense in favor of the commander of the San Jacinto. There would be, in such case, misapprehension of the principle which makes a vessel a portion of the territory of the nation whose flag it bears, and violation of that immunity which prohibits a foreign sovereign, by consequence, from the exercise of his jurisdiction. It certainly is not necessary to recall to mind with what energy, under every circumstance, the government of the United States has maintained this immunity, and the right of asylum which is the consequence of it."

To this Mr. Seward replied, that "M. Thouvenel has not been in error in supposing, first, that the government of the United States has not acted in any spirit of disregard of the rights or of the sensibilities of the British nation, and that he is equally just in assuming that the United States would consistently vindicate, by their practice on this occasion, the character they have so long maintained as an advocate of the most liberal principles concerning the rights of neutral states in maritime war."

The capture of the rebel envoys, and the questions which arose in consequence, gave rise to much debate in Congress. Some very belligerent speeches were made, and a determination was generally expressed not to submit to any arrogant demands on the part of England, nor yet to precipitate a war with that power.

As usual in such assemblies, some opinions were expressed hastily, evincing patriotism rather than a thorough understanding of the case and of international law. Among those, however, who spoke with a full appreciation of the facts, and a thorough knowledge of international law and the principles upon which the American government had hitherto insisted, was Senator Sumner, of Massachusetts, who was chairman of the committee on foreign affairs in the Senate. Mr. Sumner made an able and exhaustive speech, taking the ground which Mr. Seward maintained in his reply to Lord Lyons, but supporting it with convincing argument and precedents drawn from the history of the government, and showing conclusively that the release of the prisoners was but maintaining the principles for which the United States had always contended.

The settlement of this question was a great relief to those who believed the relations between England and the United States to be in a very critical condition, and to many, also, who, perhaps inconsiderately, were disposed to resist, at any cost, an arrogant demand on the part of England. The English government had presented the demand in as moderate and inoffensive a way as it could well be made and be a demand. By this course American pride was not touched, nor the bitter resentment and hostility kindled which would have followed any arrogant or threatening course. That a more imperious demand would have followed, if the question had not been settled as it was, is altogether probable, and hostile feelings in both countries would then have become so inflamed that war might but too easily have been the result. But, fortunately, the governments acted with more moderation and wisdom than were shown by portions of the people of either country.

It was, indeed, distasteful to the people of the United States, and in some degree humiliating, to give up these rebel emissaries, who had been so opportunely captured at the commencement of their voyage; but it was a source of satisfaction to know that the question was settled upon principles of public law for which the United States had always contended, and that, throwing out of the case the particular individuals concerned, the conclusion was a triumph for the government of the United States. To the rebels, and to those of the English who were really unfriendly to the United States, the settlement of the question was a disappointment, as it destroyed their hopes of a war between the United States and England, in which they were confident that against such odds the former would be overwhelmed.

Messrs. Mason and Slidell, with their secretaries, were released; but their disappointment and detention from their missions, in which they would by this time have been industriously aiding the rebellion, received no other compensation. For more than a month they were confined in Fort Warren, not deprived of comforts, but under military guard, and experiencing the inclemency of a New England winter rather than the pleasures of London and Paris. The arrangements for their release were made by Mr. Seward and Lord Lyons, and it was agreed that the released prisoners should be put on board her Majesty's ship Rinaldo, in Provincetown harbor, at the extremity of Cape Cod. They were accordingly transported to that point in a small steamer, and were duly placed, without ceremony, or, as far as appeared, any special mark of respect, once more under "the protection of the British flag."

It was feared that the capture and imprisonment of the rebel emissaries might add to their influence when they at last arrived at their destination; but while there were parties in England and France who perhaps extended to them a more cordial sympathy on account of their alleged misfortunes, the question between the governments had been so promptly and gracefully settled, that there was all the more reason on the part of the English or French governments for not recognizing or receiving them in any official capacity.

CHAPTER LIV.

Fort Pickens. — Rebel Preparations to reduce it. — Long Delay of the Attack. — Reenforcement and Strengthening of the Fort. — Wilson's Zouaves. — Federal Operations. — Destruction of the Dry Dock. — Night Attack upon the Island of Santa Rosa. — Sudden Assault upon the Zouaves. — Burning of their Tents. — Resistance to the Rebels. — Disorder among the Assailants. — Their Retreat and Loss. — Official Report of Colonel Brown. — Results of the Attack. — Bombardment of the Rebel Fortifications by Fort Pickens and Ships of war. — Response of the Rebels. — Effects of their Fire. — Action by the Ships of War. — The Rebel Batteries silenced. — Cessation of the Cannonade for the Night. — The Conflict renewed. — The Town of Warrington destroyed by Fire. — Results of the Bombardment. — Casualties. — Official Report of Colonel Brown.

In the early stages of the rebellion, Fort Pickens, which was the only southern fort commanding the entrance to a port, except Sumter, that had not been taken possession of by the secessionists without opposition, was an object of solicitude on the part of the government, and its possession was considered a matter of paramount importance by the rebels. The unsuccessful measures taken to secure it, and which were foiled by the prompt action of Lieutenant Slemmer, have been narrated in a former chapter. As soon as Sumter had fallen, and the war had thus been commenced, a determination was avowed by the rebels to take Fort Pickens in like manner. Large numbers of troops were collected at Pensacola and vicinity. Forts Barrancas and McRae, old fortifications belonging to the United States, were strengthened and furnished with heavy armaments, and new batteries were constructed at different points along the shore of the main land, to command the harbor and bear upon Fort Pickens.* These operations were under the com-

mand of General Bragg, formerly an officer of the United States, and great confidence was expressed by the rebels that they would be able to reduce Fort Pickens and compel its surrender. For months the preparations continued, and the rebel troops began to grow discontented at the long delay of the promised attack. But, unlike Sumter, Fort Pickens could not be almost surrounded by batteries, and none were sufficiently near to insure a breach.

Meanwhile Fort Pickens was also strengthened. The garrison had been largely reenforced by regular troops, under the command of Colonel Harvey Brown. The guns were all mounted, and large quantities of ammunition supplied. The interior of the fort was so prepared as to afford protection from shells that might be thrown into it, and the barbette guns were protected by sand bags. Outside of the fort some new batteries were constructed, and all the works were put into a complete state for defence. In addition to the garrison of the fort, the sixth regiment of New York volunteers, — a regiment raised in the city of New York under peculiar auspices,* and containing many lawless and desperate men — was sent to the Island of Santa Rosa, on which Fort Pickens is constructed, and encamped about a mile from the fort, where they held a position protected, in part, by intrenchments. A naval force of several vessels was, most of the time, at hand,

---

* Fort Pickens is on the western end of Santa Rosa Island, a long and narrow sandy island, that extends along the front of Pensacola Bay. It commands the entrance to the bay, and on the opposite side of the entrance, on a point connected with the main land, is Fort McRae. Above the entrance the main shore curves, and extends towards the east for several miles. On this shore, facing the channel, is the old Spanish fort Barrancas. Farther east, near the point where the shore runs again to the north, is the navy yard. From the navy yard to Fort McRae, — a distance of about four miles, — the rebels constructed numerous batteries, distant from Fort Pickens from about a mile and a quarter to a mile and three quarters, and embracing about one third of a circle.

* This regiment was enlisted immediately after the attack on the Massachusetts troops in Baltimore, April 19, 1861, and with the avowed purpose of marching through Baltimore. It was recruited among the "roughs" and men of desperate habits and character, and probably on account of its composition was sent to this distant post.

to aid in the defence of the fort or in an attack upon the rebel works.

The attack on Fort Pickens, so long expected by its garrison, and so earnestly desired by the over-confident rebels, was still delayed, General Bragg evidently not sharing in the confidence of success which was expressed by the rebel journals. In the mean time two or three enterprises were successfully carried out by the federal forces, which, though of no great importance in themselves, annoyed the enemy, and encouraged the garrison and naval forces. One of these — the destruction of the privateer Judah, at the navy yard wharf, by an expedition from the Colorado — has been mentioned in a previous chapter. Another, which was accomplished by a few men from the garrison of Fort Pickens, was the destruction of the floating dry dock belonging to the navy yard.

This dock, which was a large and costly work, had, early in the summer, been removed from the navy yard and sunk in the channel opposite. Subsequently, a plan was formed to raise it, and, floating it down to a position opposite Fort McRae, to sink it in the channel, where it would completely obstruct the entrance of large vessels into the bay. Colonel Brown, having received information of the intentions of the rebels, and observing the preparations, determined to prevent the movement. Accordingly, on the night of the 2d of September, he sent Lieutenant Shipley, with a few picked men, in a boat, to destroy the dock, which was now afloat. Reaching the dock without being discovered, they at once boarded it, finding, to their surprise, no sentinels upon it. They soon disposed of the combustible materials which they had brought, and placed shells in the boilers, and then, applying the torch, rowed safely back to the fort. The flames soon spread over the structure ; the shells exploded, destroying the boilers and the adjacent parts of the work ; and to save the dock from entire destruction was beyond the ability of the rebels. It burned

through the night, and was so far destroyed as to be utterly useless even for obstructing the channel. It was supposed that the burning of the dry dock would be the signal for a general attack from the rebel batteries upon the fort, and preparations were made to respond to the bombardment. But, though there was an alarm in the rebel forts and camps, not a gun was discharged, and the expected and even much desired attack was not made.

The monotonous quiet which prevailed about the fort was not again disturbed, except by the destruction of the privateer Judah by the naval expedition, until the 9th of October, when the rebels made a night attack upon the forces on the island outside of the fort. A force of twelve or fifteen hundred* rebels, under the command of General Anderson, landed on the island of Santa Rosa, about four miles from Fort Pickens, and three miles from the camp of the New York sixth regiment, or " Wilson's Zouaves," as they were more familiarly called. Approaching the federal position cautiously, the rebel force killed several of the picket guards, and drove in the others. They then made a sudden attack upon the Zouaves, who were hastily drawn up to meet them, and threw them into confusion, in the midst of which the assailants succeeded in setting fire to a part of the tents. The Zouaves were soon rallied, and, with a small force of regulars who were stationed nearer the fort, successfully resisted the attack of what was evidently a superior force. The rebels soon fell into disorder, and failed to carry out the plan which they had apparently contemplated. Their disorder soon led to a retreat, which was hastened by the more determined attack of the federal troops, who soon began to press after them. They reached their boats, in which they embarked, under a brisk fire of the Zouaves and regulars, leaving fourteen killed and seven wounded upon the island, and twenty-seven

* Variously stated in their own accounts from twelve hundred to eighteen hundred men.

others prisoners. Many others were supposed to be killed or wounded while in the boats, exposed to the fire of the federal troops, and a number of the wounded were safely taken from the island. The federal loss was fourteen killed, twenty-nine wounded, and twenty-four taken prisoners. The rebel accounts of the affair, while claiming that the expedition was completely successful, admitted that their retreat was hasty, and that their loss was severe.

The following official report of Colonel Brown describes more particularly the attack and its results : —

"HEADQUARTERS DEPARTMENT OF FLORIDA, }
"FORT PICKENS, October 11, 1861. }

"COLONEL: I briefly reported to you on the 9th instant that the rebels had landed on this island, partially destroyed the camp of the sixth regiment New York volunteers, and had been driven off by our troops. I now report in more detail the results of the attack. For the better understanding of the several movements, it may be well to state that the enemy landed about four miles from this fort. The place may be recognized on the map by three ponds and a mound — that the island there is about three fourths of a mile wide ; that a short distance below it narrows to some two hundred yards, then widens again, and at the camp the distance across is about five eighths of a mile ; that a succession of three or four sand ridges run on the sea side, parallel to the coast, along the island ; and low, swampy ground, interspersed with sand hillocks, some bushes, and a few trees, extend along the harbor side, both shores being sandy beach. Wilson's camp is near the sea-coast, and a short mile from the fort. The two batteries spoken of in this report, and to which he retreated, — batteries Lincoln and Totten, — are, the first on the harbor, and the other on the Gulf side, about four hundred yards from Fort Pickens.

"About two o'clock on the morning of the 9th instant I was awakened by the officer of the day, who reported that a picket, driven in, had reported the landing of sixty men on the point. Having little confidence in the correctness of the report, I directed that no alarm should be made ; and shortly after he reported that the alarm was false.

"About half past three o'clock he again reported that volleys of musketry were heard at the camp of the sixth New York volunteers. I immediately ordered the roll to be beaten, Major Vogdes to take two companies and proceed to the spot, and Major Arnold to man the guns on the ramparts on the space. About half an hour after this time the firing was heavy, and the light of the burning camp was seen ; and I sent a staff-officer to communicate with Major Vogdes, who returned very soon, and said that he had fallen in with a large body of the enemy on the inside shore, and could not find the major.

"I immediately ordered Major Arnold to proceed to support Major Vogdes with two companies, and at the same time sent an order to Colonel Wilson to advance and attack the enemy. I also despatched a staff officer on board the steamer McClellan, with orders for him to take position opposite the landing place and open on the enemy ; unfortunately at the same time directing him to go to the Potomac, lying near, and ask for some men to assist him, in case landing was necessary. Captain Powell directed him to tow his ship to the scene of action, which so delayed him that he did not arrive until after the enemy had vacated. Captain Powell acted from the best motives, and, under ordinary circumstances, from correct principles. But the result was unfortunate ; as the McClellan could have driven the rebel steamers away, and we must have made prisoners of most of the invaders.

"At the request of Major Arnold, late in the morning, I sent forward a light field gun, which, however, did not reach him until the affair was over.

"As I propose only briefly to allude to the volunteers, I respectfully refer you to the official report of the colonel of the regiment. The picket of this regiment and the guards sustained its principal, if not entire loss, and behaved well. Captain Daly's company, on duty with the regulars, did good service, and the captain is spoken of by Major Arnold in terms of high approbation. He had two men killed. Captain Bailey's company was at a battery, and not called out. He was performing his appropriate duty during the fight.

"Major Vogdes, with companies A, first artillery, and E, third infantry, proceeded beyond the Spanish fort, about a mile from this fort, when, from the obscurity of the night, he found himself and command completely intermingled with the enemy. He was immediately recognized, and made prisoner; the command devolving on Captain Hildt, of the third infantry, who disengaged his command from their perilous position, and opened a heavy fire on the enemy, and finally, with great gallantry, forced them to retreat, (he being ably supported by Lieutenant Seely, my assistant adjutant-general, who volunteered for the occasion,) with a loss of eleven killed.

"Major Arnold at this moment came up, and, the enemy retreating, followed on. During this time Major Tower and Lieutenant Jackson, whom I had successively sent on to push forward the Zouaves, succeeded in getting some collected; and Colonel Wilson also advanced, the enemy precipitately retreating. Major Arnold, with Captain Robertson and Lieutenant Shipley's companies, promptly followed, and attacked, as they were embarking, the other companies arriving up successively. Captain Robertson opened a heavy fire, at short musket range, on the crowded masses, and Lieutenant Shipley, some fifteen minutes later, joined him, and their fire must have been very effective.

"This was continued so long as they were within range. When they had got beyond it, the gallant major ordered them to cease firing, and to give them three cheers, to which no response was made. During the time of this occurrence, Major Tower came up with two small companies of Zouaves, and subsequently Colonel Wilson with a portion of his regiment.

"When it is considered that less than two hundred regulars, with some fifty volunteers, pursued five times their number four miles, and expelled them, under a heavy fire, from the island they had desecrated, it will, I trust, be considered an evidence of their having gallantly performed their duty.

"The plan of attack of the enemy was judicious, and, if executed with ordinary ability, might have been attended with serious loss. But he failed in all save the burning of one half of the tents of the sixth regiment, which, being covered with bushes, were very combustible, and in rifling the trunks of the officers. He did not reach within five hundred yards of either of the batteries, the guns of which he was to spike; nor within a mile of the fort he was to enter pell-mell with the fugitives retreating before his victorious arms. I have now in my possession nine spikes taken from the bodies of the dead, designed for our guns.

"Our loss is — of regulars, four killed, twenty wounded, most very slightly, and eight missing, among whom is Major Vogdes; of the sixth regiment New York volunteers, ten killed, nine wounded, and sixteen missing. The enemy lost, as known to us, fourteen killed, including one captain; seven wounded, including one lieutenant, (two since dead;) and five officers and twenty-two enlisted men prisoners; and as he was known to have carried off some of his dead, and probably most of his wounded, those in our hands being all severely so, and unable to be removed, and as the heaviest loss is supposed to have been in the boats, at the reëmbarkation, it was probably three times as great, in killed and wounded, as I have named. . . .

" I estimated the force of the enemy at twelve or fifteen hundred, having closely observed them through a fine telescope as they retreated. Their two large steamers, and a large barge of equal size, and five or six launches, were all crowded with troops; and the almost unanimous estimate of the officers is fifteen hundred, from personal observation.

" I am, colonel, very respectfully, yours,
                         " HARVEY BROWN,
                          " Colonel commanding.
" Colonel E. D. TOWNSEND, A. A. G.

" P. S. I have seen a Pensacola paper, which gives their loss as follows: killed, twenty-one; wounded, thirty-eight; prisoners, twenty-one; which, probably, is not one fourth their actual loss. General Anderson is severely wounded."

The report of Colonel Wilson, alluded to in Colonel Brown's report, gave a detailed, and, probably, a somewhat exaggerated account of the part taken by the regiment of Zouaves in the affair, which, according to this report, was a very sanguinary conflict. After they recovered from their surprise, the Zouaves appear to have behaved with bravery, though some of them fought without much regard to order and discipline. The combined force of regulars and Zouaves was very much inferior to the enemy in numbers, and in the end succeeded in driving off the rebels, who failed to accomplish much, except the destruction of a part of the camp of the volunteers. Had the steamer McClellan proceeded to a position opposite the landing place of the rebels, as ordered, instead of stopping to tow the Potomac, the rout of the enemy would have been complete, and probably a large number of prisoners would have been taken. But the delay prevented the accomplishment of Colonel Brown's purpose, and the rebels succeeded in escaping without a very serious loss.

After the night attack on Santa Rosa Island, affairs at Fort Pickens again resumed the quiet that had previously prevailed. The rebels still delayed the attack so long threatened, and no event of importance occurred until the 22d of November, when Colonel Brown, who was now fully prepared for such an attack, opened fire, with the coöperation of the naval force, upon the rebel forts and the navy yard, and initiated a general bombardment.

Having made the necessary arrangements with Flag-officer McKean, Colonel Brown commenced the attack at about ten o'clock on the morning of the 22d. Two or three steamers, which had run daily between Pensacola and the navy yard, had already run down to the latter place, and were there exposed to the guns of Fort Pickens at long range. The first fire was directed at these and the batteries at the navy yard, and one of the boats was soon seriously damaged; but another succeeded in steaming away with but slight injury. Immediately after the first gun from Fort Pickens, the other batteries on the island also opened fire, and all the guns of the fort that bore upon the rebel fortifications and the navy yard soon joined in the roar, and sent their shot and shell in quick succession against those positions of the enemy.

In half an hour the rebel batteries began to reply, and very soon they were nearly all in play, from the navy yard to the extreme point south of Fort McRae; several batteries, which had previously been masked, joining in the bombardment, and the whole numbering fourteen, besides Forts McRae and Barrancas. But though the rebels had some very heavy guns, a portion of which were rifled, their inability speedily to reduce the fort by means of their batteries, so deliberately erected, was soon manifest. Their shot and shell had but little damaging effect upon the solid walls, though battering them in many places; and such precautions had been taken to protect the interior of the fort and the men from injury by the explosion of shells, that but one man was killed and four others were wounded during the whole bombardment. The barbette guns were also well protected; only one gun — and that a casemate gun — was partially dismounted during the whole bombardment, and the same shot which effected this occasioned the casualties just mentioned.

The first gun from the fort was a signal for the ships of war to sail in towards the entrance of the bay, and join in the bombardment. The only vessels that were available for the purpose were the Niagara and the Richmond. These vessels steamed in as near to Fort McRae as the depth of water would apparently admit, and opened their guns upon that fort and the neighboring batteries. The distance was too great for the guns of the ships to have their full effect, and only the shots from their heaviest and rifled guns caused certain damage. But, sending out a boat to sound, Captain McKean found that he could lay his ships somewhat nearer, and he accordingly advanced to a position where the depth of water under the keel of the Niagara was but little more than a foot. The Richmond, which was of less draught and lighter armament, went farther in towards Fort McRae. Here the vessels continued the bombardment with more effect, and received a full share of attention from the enemy. The latter, however, did not succeed in striking either of the ships until the bombardment had continued several hours, when the Richmond was struck by a solid shot, which killed one man and wounded several, and damaged the vessel considerably. The Niagara was afterwards struck several times, but sustained no damage to impair the efficiency of the vessel, and lost none of the crew.

The continued fire from the ships of war and Fort Pickens, with its auxiliary batteries, apparently had more effect upon the rebel works, and, long before it was suspended by the approach of night, the guns of Fort McRae and adjacent batteries had ceased to reply. This result might not have been altogether the effect of the bombardment, though the fort and garrison, without doubt, suffered from it; but the caving in of a magazine at Fort McRae occasioned a loss of life and limb, and probably temporarily limited the supply of ammunition. Whatever may have been the cause, the fire of all the rebel fortifications, long before the federal batteries were silent, had begun to slacken, and at last almost entirely ceased. At nightfall the ships of war steamed out to a safe anchorage, and the thunders of the bombardment were succeeded by the stillness of an undisturbed night at Fort Pickens, and on the main land by the steady labor of the rebels to repair and extend their works.

The next morning Colonel Brown resumed the bombardment, firing with more deliberation, and probably more effect, than the first day. During the night the wind had changed to the north, and, blowing freshly down the bay and off shore, reduced the depth of the water, and made it so rough that it was impossible for the ships of war to approach as near the rebel works as on the previous day. The Richmond, the guns of which were of too short range, did not attempt to join in the attack. The Niagara steamed in as far as possible, and for some time continued to fire at Fort McRae and the nearer batteries; but it was found that most of her shots fell short, while the rebels returned her fire from a heavy rifled gun of long range, which threatened serious damage without any prospect of silencing it. The Niagara was accordingly withdrawn, and the bombardment was continued by Fort Pickens and the batteries on Santa Rosa. Fort McRae did not respond to the fire this day, and the rebel guns were distributed along the shore in small batteries, some of which were protected by woods, rendering it more difficult to disable or silence them. The steady fire of the federal force was not without effect upon these rebel batteries, and the hot shot and shell, thrown at the navy

54

yard and adjacent buildings occupied by the rebels, at last set fire to some of the houses in the town of Warrington. The flames spread from building to building until the greater part of the town was destroyed, and some of the structures in the navy yard were materially injured. The cannonading continued occasionally until midnight, when Colonel Brown ceased firing, and the rebel batteries also became silent. The following day was Sunday, and its quiet was not disturbed, Colonel Brown having determined not to renew the conflict unless compelled to do so by a rebel attack. He had damaged the enemy's works and destroyed a large amount of property, while he had at the same time drawn the fire of the rebel batteries, and tested the strength of his own position. While he felt assured that the enemy could not easily take or damage Fort Pickens, he had no inducement to continue the bombardment; for, however successful he might be, with the coöperation of the navy, in silencing the guns, or destroying the works of the rebels, he had no force with which to maintain the advantage thus gained. Nor were the rebels disposed to renew a contest which was more damaging to them than to the beleaguered fort, and, whatever further preparations they projected with reference to a future attack, they did not prosecute the work with much vigor.

The rebels claimed that their works suffered but little. It was evident, however, that the damage was greater than they admitted. The loss of life was, probably, small ; being but seven or eight killed, and ten or twelve wounded, the greater part of whom were killed or wounded by the falling in of a magazine at Fort McRae. The federal loss in the fort was one killed and four wounded ; on board the ships of war, one man was killed and seven slightly wounded. After the bombardment, during which the garrison had so wonderfully escaped greater injury from the missiles of the enemy, an accident occurred by which a much greater loss was suffered. Colonel Brown had ordered all the shot and shell which had been thrown into the fort to be collected, in order that the men might not tamper with the shells that had not exploded. This work was being performed, when one of the men attempted to empty a shell by knocking it against another, while a number of his comrades were standing about him. This careless act caused an explosion of the shell, which was followed by another, instantly killing five men and wounding seven others. In the batteries outside the fort the enemy's shot caused little damage, and no loss of life.

Colonel Brown's official report of the bombardment is as follows : —

"HEADQUARTERS DEPARTMENT OF FLORIDA,
"FORT PICKENS, *November* 25, 1861.

"GENERAL : That Fort Pickens has been beleaguered by the rebels for the last nine months, and that it was daily threatened with the fate of Sumter, is a fact notorious to the whole world. Since its occupancy by Lieutenant Slemmer, the rebels have been surrounding it with batteries, and daily arming them with the heaviest and most efficient guns known to our service, — guns stolen from the United States, — until they considered this fort as virtually their own, its occupancy being only a question of time.

"I have been in command since the 16th of April, and during the whole of that time their force has averaged, so far as I can learn, from eight to ten times the number of mine. The position in which I have thus been placed has been sufficiently trying, and I have, at three separate times, intended to free myself from it, by opening my batteries on them; but imperious circumstances, over which I had no control, has, unexpectedly, in each instance, prevented.

"Affairs were in this state on the morning of the 9th of October, when the enemy, fifteen hundred strong, attacked by surprise a portion of my command, on an intensely dark night. They were defeated, and driven from the island with great loss, by less than two hundred regulars and fifty volunteers — all the efficient force I had disposable for the purpose. An insult so gross to the flag of my country could not by me be passed unnoticed, and I designed immediately to take appropriate notice of it; but, as I said before, circumstances over which I had no control prevented. I make these prefatory remarks to explain why I have now opened my batteries on the enemy, when, from the smallness of my forces, — about one sixth of his, thirteen hundred to eight thousand, — I have not the means of producing any decisive results, and as evidence of my having accomplished what I designed — the punishing the perpetrators of an insult on my country's flag.

"Having invited Flag-officer McKean to cooperate with me in attacking the rebels, and to which he gave a ready and cordial assent, I, on the morning of the 22d, opened my batteries on the enemy ; to which, in the course of half an hour, he responded from his numerous forts and batteries, extending from the navy yard to Fort McRae, a distance of about four miles, the whole nearly equidistant from this fort, and on which line he has two forts, — McRae and Barrancas, — and fourteen separate batteries, containing from one to four guns, many of them being ten inch columbiads, and some twelve and thirteen inch sea-coast mortars, the distance varying from two thousand one hundred to two thousand nine hundred yards from this fort. At the same time of my opening, Flag-officer McKean, in the Niagara, and Captain Ellison, in the Richmond, took position as near to Fort McRae as the depth of water would permit; but which, unfortunately, was not sufficiently deep to give full effect to their powerful batteries. They, however, kept up a spirited fire on the fort and adjacent batteries during the whole day. My fire was incessant from the time of opening until it was too dark to see, at the rate of a shot for each gun every fifteen or twenty minutes, the fire of the enemy being

somewhat slower. By noon, the guns of Fort McRae were all silenced but one, and three hours before sunset this fort and the adjoining battery ceased fire. I directed the guns of batteries Lincoln, Cameron, and Totten principally on the batteries adjacent to the navy yard, those of battery Scott to Fort McRae and the lighthouse batteries, and those of the fort to all. We reduced very perceptibly the fire of Barrancas, entirely silenced that in the navy yard, and in one or two of the other batteries, the efficiency of our fire, at the close of the day, not being the least impaired.

"The next morning I again opened about the same hour, the navy, unfortunately, owing to a reduction in the depth of water, caused by a change of wind, not being able to get so near as yesterday; consequently the distance was too great to be effectual. My fire this day was less rapid, and I think more efficient, than that of yesterday. Fort McRae, so effectually silenced yesterday, did not fire again to-day. We silenced entirely one or two guns, and had one of ours disabled by a shot coming through the embrasure.

"About three o'clock fire was communicated to one of the houses in Warrington, and shortly afterwards to the church steeple, the church and the whole village being immediately in rear of some of the rebel batteries, they apparently having placed them purposely directly in front of the largest and most valuable buildings. The fire rapidly communicated to other buildings along the street, until probably two thirds of it was consumed ; and about the same time fire was discovered issuing from the back part of the navy yard, probably in Wolcott, a village to the north and immediately adjoining the yard, as Warrington does on the west. Finally, it penetrated to the yard, and as it continued to burn brightly all night, I concluded that either in it or in Wolcott many buildings were destroyed. Very heavy damage was also done to the buildings of the yard by the ava-

lanche of shot, shell, and splinters showered unceasingly on them for two days; and being nearly
fire-proof, being built of brick and covered with
slate, I could not succeed in firing them, my
hot shot nor shells not having any power of
igniting them.

"The steamer Time, which was at the wharf
at the time, was abandoned on the first day,
and exposed to our fire, which probably entirely
disabled her. The fire was again continued till
dark, and with mortars occasionally, until two
o'clock the next morning, when the combat
ceased.

"This fort, at its conclusion, though it has
received a great many shot and shell, is in every
respect, save the disabling of one gun-carriage
and the loss of service of six men, as efficient
as it was at the commencement of the combat;
but the ends I proposed in commencing having
been attained, except one, which I find to be
impracticable with my present means, I do not
deem it advisable further to continue it, unless
the enemy think it proper to do so, when I
shall meet him with alacrity.

"The attack on 'Billy Wilson's' camp, the
attempted attack on my batteries, and the insult to our glorious flag, have been fully and
fearfully avenged. I have no means of knowing the loss of the enemy, and have no disposition to guess at it. The firing on his batteries
was very heavy, well directed, and continuous
for two days, and could hardly fail of having
important results.

"Our loss would have been heavy, but for the
foresight which, with great labor, caused us to
erect elaborate means of protection, and which
saved many lives. I lost one private killed, one
sergeant, one corporal, and four men (privates)
wounded, only one severely. . . .

"In closing, I tender to Flag-officer McKean
and Captain Ellison, of the navy, and to their
officers and crews, my best thanks for their able
coöperation, which would have had the happiest
results but for the unfortunate fact that great

draught of water prevented their sufficiently
near approach to the works of the rebels.

"I am, general, very respectfully, your obedient servant,   HARVEY BROWN,
                                    "Colonel commanding.
"Brigadier-General L. THOMAS,
    "Adjutant-General U. S. Army, Washington, D. C."

CHAPTER LV.

Retirement of General Scott. — Confidence of the People in his
Military Knowledge and Experience. — Letter to the Secretary of War. — Action of the Cabinet. — Order of the President. — Reply of the Secretary of War. — Effect of the Retirement upon the People. — Visit to Europe.

IN closing our record of the campaigns of
1861, we should not pass unnoticed the retirement of Lieutenant-General Scott from his
position as general-in-chief of the army of the
United States. Long the most distinguished
soldier of the country, the loyal people had
naturally regarded him with great respect and
admiration, and they reposed the highest confidence in his military knowledge and skill to
conduct the war into which the country was
plunged by secession. The safety of the capital and the peaceful inauguration of President
Lincoln were generally attributed, in a great
measure, to his prudence and foresight, and his
loyal determination to maintain the constitutional government. Upon his experience both
the government and the country had relied for
the organization into armies of the immense
numbers of troops which had been called from
among the people, and for the planning and
conduct of campaigns against the rebels.

But General Scott was now advanced in
years, and had become too infirm for active
military duties; and though his mind was un-
dimmed, and he gave all its energies to his
duties, so far as they could be performed in his
office, when the army increased and the duties
became more arduous, it was evident that a
younger and more active man was necessary to

have the immediate command. For this reason, General McClellan had been called to the
command of the army of the Potomac, after
the disaster at Bull Run. General Scott, however, still remained general-in-chief of the entire army, and, while relieved of a part of his
burdens, continued to supervise the general
organization of the army and the plans of the
several campaigns. In this position he continued to serve the country until the last of
October, when he asked to be placed upon the
retired list, in the following letter: —

"HEADQUARTERS OF THE ARMY,
"WASHINGTON, D. C., October 31, 1861.

"SIR: For more than three years I have been
unable, from a hurt, to mount a horse or walk
more than a few paces at a time, and that with
much pain. Other and new infirmities, dropsy
and vertigo, admonish me that a repose of mind
and body, with the appliances of surgery and
medicine, are necessary to add a little more to
a life already protracted much beyond the usual
span of man.

"It is under such circumstances, made doubly
painful by the unnatural and unjust rebellion
now raging in the southern states of our so
late prosperous and happy Union, that I am
compelled to request that my name be placed
on the list of army officers retired from active
service.

"As this request is founded on an absolute
right granted by a recent act of Congress, I am
entirely at liberty to say that it is with deep
regret that I withdraw myself, in these momentous times, from the orders of a President
who has treated me with distinguished kindness and courtesy — whom I know, upon much
personal intercourse, to be patriotic without
sectional partialities, or prejudices, to be highly
conscientious in the performance of every duty,
and of unrivalled activity and perseverance.

"And to you, Mr. Secretary, whom I now
officially address for the last time, I beg to
acknowledge my many obligations for the uni-

form high consideration I have received at your
hands, and have the honor to remain, sir,
"With high respect, your obedient servant,
"WINFIELD SCOTT.
"Hon. S. CAMERON, Secretary of War."

A special cabinet council was held to consider this resignation of General Scott, and it
was determined, in consideration of his reasons
for tendering it, that it should be accepted.
The President, with his cabinet, waited upon
the old soldier, and announced to him that his
request to be placed upon the retired list was
acceded to, in the following order, which was
also promulgated to the army and to the country: —

"On the 1st day of November, A. D. 1861,
upon his own application to the President of
the United States, Brevet Lieutenant-General
Winfield Scott is ordered to be placed, and
hereby is placed, upon the list of retired officers
of the army of the United States, without
reduction in his current pay, subsistence, or
allowances.

"The American people will hear with sad-
ness and deep emotion, that General Scott has
withdrawn from the active control of the army,
while the President and the unanimous cabinet
express their own and the nation's sympathy
in his personal affliction, and their profound
sense of the important public services rendered
by him to his country during his long and brilliant career, among which will ever be gratefully distinguished his faithful devotion to the
constitution, the Union, and the flag, when
assailed by a parricidal rebellion.
"ABRAHAM LINCOLN."

The reply of the Secretary of War to General Scott's letter was as follows: —

"WAR DEPARTMENT, WASHINGTON, Nov. 1, 1861.

"GENERAL: It was my duty to lay before the
President your letter of yesterday, asking to be
relieved, under the recent act of Congress.

"In separating from you, I cannot refrain from expressing my deep regret that your health, shattered by long service and repeated wounds, received in your country's defence, should render it necessary for you to retire from your high position at this momentous period of our history.

"Although you are not to remain in active service, I yet hope that while I continue in charge of the department over which I now preside, I shall at times be permitted to avail myself of the benefits of your counsels and sage experience. It has been my good fortune to enjoy a personal acquaintance with you for over thirty years, and the pleasant relations of that long time have been greatly strengthened by your cordial and entire coöperation in all the great questions which have occupied the department and convulsed the country for the last six months.

"In parting from you I can only express the hope that a merciful Providence, which has protected you amidst so many trials, will improve your health and continue your life long after the people of the country shall have been restored to their former happiness and prosperity.

"I am, general, very sincerely, your friend and servant,   SIMON CAMERON,
                                        "Secretary of War.
"To Lieutenant-General WINFIELD SCOTT, present."

The retirement of General Scott was regarded as an event of no small consequence by the loyal people. His military experience and fame had secured the utmost confidence of the people, and many believed that the success of the Union cause must depend very much upon him. Some things had, perhaps, occurred to diminish this confidence and belief, and the want of more youthful vigor was generally acknowledged. General McClellan, who was immediately appointed to succeed General Scott as general-in-chief, had already been hailed by the people as the future hero and organizer of victories, and they felt that he would be a worthy successor of the veteran chief   Nevertheless, there was a general regret that the experienced soldier and hero of many victories already won, could not continue to serve the country in its extreme peril.*

Soon after his retirement, General Scott visited Europe, his wife being ill in Paris. It was believed that his presence there contributed to the preservation of amicable relations between France and England and the United States. His early and unexpected return was supposed to have some diplomatic import in connection with the 'Trent affair; but it did not transpire that he came upon such an errand, a natural desire to be at home at so momentous a period being a sufficient reason for his return.

---

* It was generally supposed that there were reasons besides his age and infirmities which induced General Scott to retire at this time. It is quite probable that he was not satisfied with his position. Surrounded by much younger and more active men, he could not but feel his age and infirmities the more keenly, while he may also have felt that he was a relic of the past, glorious though it might be, and that the younger men of the present were jostling him in their haste. A letter which has but recently (February, 1863) been made public, shows what may have been, in part, the reasons which prompted his resignation. This letter was addressed to the Secretary of War, early in October, 1861, and complained that subordinate officers, referring especially to General McClellan, treated him with disrespect, by communicating directly with the government, instead of through him as general-in-chief, in violation of military etiquette and positive orders. It also complained of direct disobedience of orders on the part of General McClellan. Such conduct naturally wounded the feelings of one who had been so long the commander of the armies, and offended his sense of military propriety and subordination, and its continuance, in spite of his remonstrance, probably led to his retirement.

CHAPTER LVI.

Review of the Progress of the Rebellion and the Efforts to suppress it. — Position of Affairs at the Time of Meeting of Congress. — President Lincoln's Message. — Report of the Secretary of War. — The Navy. — The Character of Congress.

WE have narrated the principal events of the rebellion, and the military and naval operations, down to the time for the annual session of Congress. During the seven and a half months since the commencement of actual hostilities, the people of all sections of the country had been called from the pursuits of profound peace to the realization of war on a gigantic scale. The magnitude and strength of the rebellion were made manifest in the large armies organized by the rebel government, and the determination of a large part of the people in the seceded states, under the influence of their leaders, to achieve what they were pleased to call their independence, and to establish a southern Confederacy for the perpetuation and intrenchment of slavery. The national government, ill prepared for such an insurrection, or for warlike operations, had met the emergency with . vigor, and the loyal people had responded to its call with a spirit that could hardly be expected in a nation so wholly unaccustomed to war, and so confirmed in the habits and pursuits of peace.

Although the government had accomplished little, as yet, towards the actual suppression of the rebellion, and had met with some sad reverses, much had been done to consolidate the loyal states, and call out their military resources, and to place limits to the rebellion much within the extent contemplated by its leaders. Maryland, by the efforts of the loyal part of her people, supported by the government, had disappointed the hopes of the rebels, and was secured to the Union. The people of Western Virginia had risen against the fraudulent attempt to transfer them to the rebel Confeder-

acy, and the federal troops had mainly driven the rebel forces from a large part of the Old Dominion west of the Alleghanies. Kentucky had somewhat tardily taken position on the side of loyalty and the Union, and the rebel forces, which were being organized among her recreant sons, had been scattered and driven beyond her borders; and though rebel armies still held some strong positions within her territory, large forces of her own loyal sons, supported by the hardy soldiers of the north-west, were preparing to drive out the invaders. The government of Missouri had been rescued from the hands of traitors, and the state saved from secession; and though the scene of many unhappy conflicts, the tide of success had, in the main, been with the Union forces, which held the more important points in the greater part of the state, and no considerable army of the rebels maintained a threatening position within its borders. Besides this, the Union forces had taken possession of important points on the coast of North and South Carolina, which should be the bases of future operations, while the rebel ports were more or less closely sealed by the blockade, which shut out the supplies upon which the people and the armies so much depended.

Such was the general condition of the war when Congress assembled for the regular session in December. At that session President Lincoln transmitted a message, of which the following are the material portions relating to the rebellion: —

" FELLOW-CITIZENS OF THE SENATE AND
HOUSE OF REPRESENTATIVES :

"In the midst of unprecedented political troubles, we have cause of great gratitude to God for unusual good health and most abundant harvests.

"You will not be surprised to learn that, in the peculiar exigencies of the times, our intercourse with foreign nations has been attended with profound solicitude, chiefly turning upon our own domestic affairs.

"A disloyal portion of the American people have, during the whole year, been engaged in an attempt to divide and destroy the Union. A nation which endures factious domestic division is exposed to disrespect abroad ; and one party, if not both, is sure, sooner or later, to invoke foreign intervention.

"Nations thus tempted to interfere are not always able to resist the counsels of seeming expediency and ungenerous ambition, although measures adopted under such influences seldom fail to be unfortunate and injurious to those adopting them.

"The disloyal citizens of the United States who have offered the ruin of our country, in return for the aid and comfort which they have invoked abroad, have received less patronage and encouragement than they probably expected. If it were just to suppose, as the insurgents have seemed to assume, that foreign nations, in this case, discarding all moral, social, and treaty obligations, would act solely, and selfishly, for the most speedy restoration of commerce, including, especially, the acquisition of cotton, those nations appear, as yet, not to have seen their way to their object more directly or clearly, through the destruction, than through the preservation, of the Union. If we could dare to believe that foreign nations are actuated by no higher principle than this, I am quite sure a sound argument could be made to show them that they can reach their aim more readily, and easily, by aiding to crush this rebellion, than by giving encouragement to it.

"The principal lever relied on by the insurgents for exciting foreign nations to hostility against us, as already intimated, is the embarrassment of commerce. Those nations, however, not improbably, saw, from the first, that it was the Union which made as well our foreign as our domestic commerce. They can scarcely have failed to perceive that the effort

for disunion produces the existing difficulty, and that one strong nation promises more durable peace, and a more extensive, valuable, and reliable commerce, than can the same nation broken into hostile fragments.

"It is not my purpose to review our discussions with foreign states ; because, whatever might be their wishes or dispositions, the integrity of our country and the stability of our government mainly depend, not upon them, but on the loyalty, virtue, patriotism, and intelligence of the American people. The correspondence itself, with the usual reservations, is herewith submitted.

"I venture to hope it will appear that we have practised prudence and liberality towards foreign powers, averting causes of irritation, and with firmness maintaining our own rights and honor.

"Since, however, it is apparent that here, as in every other state, foreign dangers necessarily attend domestic difficulties, I recommend that adequate and ample measures be adopted for maintaining the public defences on every side. While, under this general recommendation, provision for defending our sea coast line readily occurs to the mind, I also, in the same connection, ask the attention of Congress to our great lakes and rivers. It is believed that some fortifications and depots of arms and munitions, with harbor and navigation improvements, all at well selected points upon these, would be of great importance to the national defence and preservation. I ask attention to the views of the secretary of war, expressed in his report, upon the same general subject. . . .

"The operations of the treasury during the period which has elapsed since your adjournment have been conducted with signal success. The patriotism of the people has placed at the disposal of the government the large means demanded by the public exigencies. Much of the national loan has been taken by citizens of the industrial classes, whose confidence in their country's faith, and zeal for their country's deliverance from present peril, have induced them to contribute to the support of the government the whole of their limited acquisitions. This fact imposes peculiar obligations to economy in disbursement and energy in action.

"The revenue from all sources, including loans, for the financial year ending on the 30th June, 1861, was eighty-six million eight hundred and thirty-five thousand nine hundred dollars and twenty-seven cents, and the expenditures for the same period, including payments on account of the public debt, were eighty-four million five hundred and seventy-eight thousand eight hundred and thirty-four dollars and forty-seven cents; leaving a balance in the treasury, on the 1st July, of two million two hundred and fifty-seven thousand sixty-five dollars and eighty cents. For the first quarter of the financial year, ending on the 30th September, 1861, the receipts from all sources, including the balance of 1st of July, were one hundred and two million five hundred and thirty-two thousand five hundred and nine dollars and twenty-seven cents, and the expenses ninety-eight million two hundred and thirty-nine thousand seven hundred and thirty-three dollars and nine cents; leaving a balance, on the 1st of October, 1861, of four million two hundred and ninety-two thousand seven hundred and seventy-six dollars and eighteen cents.

"Estimates for the remaining three quarters of the year, and for the financial year 1863, together with his views of ways and means for meeting the demands contemplated by them, will be submitted to Congress by the secretary of the treasury. It is gratifying to know that the expenditures made necessary by the rebellion are not beyond the resources of the loyal people, and to believe that the same patriotism which has thus far sustained the government will continue to sustain it till peace and union shall again bless the land.

"I respectfully refer to the report of the secretary of war for information respecting the numerical strength of the army, and for recommendations having in view an increase of its efficiency and the well being of the various branches of the service intrusted to his care. It is gratifying to know that the patriotism of the people has proved equal to the occasion, and that the number of troops tendered greatly exceeds the force which Congress authorized me to call into the field.

"I refer with pleasure to those portions of his report which make allusion to the creditable degree of discipline already attained by our troops, and to the excellent sanitary condition of the entire army.

"The recommendation of the secretary for an organization of the militia upon a uniform basis is a subject of vital importance to the future safety of the country, and is commended to the serious attention of Congress.

"The large addition to the regular army, in connection with the defection that has so considerably diminished the number of its officers, gives peculiar importance to his recommendation for increasing the corps of cadets to the greatest capacity of the Military Academy.

"By mere omission, I presume, Congress has failed to provide chaplains for hospitals occupied by volunteers. This subject was brought to my notice, and I was induced to draw up the form of a letter, one copy of which, properly addressed, has been delivered to each of the persons, and at the dates respectively named and stated, in a schedule, containing also the form of the letter, marked A, and herewith transmitted.

"These gentlemen, I understand, entered upon the duties designated at the times respectively stated in the schedule, and have labored faithfully therein ever since. I therefore recommend that they be compensated at the same rate as chaplains in the army. I further suggest that general provision be made for chaplains to serve at hospitals, as well as with regiments.

"The report of the secretary of the navy presents in detail the operations of that branch of the service, the activity and energy which have characterized its administration, and the results of measures to increase its efficiency and power. Such have been the additions, by construction and purchase, that it may almost be said a navy has been created and brought into service since our difficulties commenced.

"Besides blockading our extensive coast, squadrons larger than ever before assembled under our flag have been put afloat, and performed deeds which have increased our naval renown.

"One of the unavoidable consequences of the present insurrection is the entire suppression, in many places, of all the ordinary means of administering civil justice by the officers, and in the forms of existing law. This is the case, in whole or in part, in all the insurgent states; and as our armies advance upon and take possession of parts of those states, the practical evil becomes more apparent. There are no courts nor officers to whom the citizens of other states may apply for the enforcement of their lawful claims against citizens of the insurgent states; and there is a vast amount of debt constituting such claims. Some have estimated it as high as two hundred million dollars, due, in large part, from insurgents in open rebellion, to loyal citizens, who are, even now, making great sacrifices in the discharge of their patriotic duty to support the government.

"Under these circumstances, I have been urgently solicited to establish, by military power, courts to administer summary justice in such cases. I have thus far declined to do it, not because I had any doubt that the end proposed — the collection of the debts — was just and right in itself, but because I have been unwilling to go beyond the pressure of neces-

sity in the usual exercise of power. But the powers of Congress, I suppose, are equal to the anomalous occasion, and therefore I refer the whole matter to Congress, with the hope that a plan may be devised for the administration of justice in all such parts of the insurgent states and territories as may be under the control of this government, whether by a voluntary return to allegiance and order, or by the power of our arms. This, however, not to be a permanent institution, but a temporary substitute, and to cease as soon as the ordinary courts can be reëstablished in peace.

"It is important that some more convenient means should be provided, if possible, for the adjustment of claims against the government, especially in view of their increased number by reason of the war. It is as much the duty of government to render prompt justice against itself, in favor of citizens, as it is to administer the same, between private individuals. The investigation and adjudication of claims, in their nature belong to the judicial department; besides, it is apparent that the attention of Congress will be more than usually engaged, for some time to come, with great national questions. It was intended, by the organization of the Court of Claims, mainly to remove this branch of business from the halls of Congress; but while the court has proved to be an effective and valuable means of investigation, it in great degree fails to effect the object of its creation, for want of power to make its judgments final.

"Fully aware of the delicacy, not to say the danger, of the subject, I commend to your careful consideration whether this power of making judgments final may not properly be given to the court, reserving the right of appeal on questions of law to the Supreme Court, with such other provisions as experience may have shown to be necessary.   .   .   .

"The present insurrection shows, I think, that the extension of this district across the Potomac River, at the time of establishing the capital here, was eminently wise, and consequently that the relinquishment of that portion of it which lies within the State of Virginia was unwise and dangerous. I submit for your consideration the expediency of regaining that part of the district, and the restoration of the original boundaries thereof, through negotiations with the State of Virginia. . . .

"The relations of the government with the Indian tribes have been greatly disturbed by the insurrection, especially in the southern superintendency and in that of New Mexico. The Indian country south of Kansas is in the possession of insurgents from Texas and Arkansas. The agents of the United States appointed since the 4th of March for this superintendency have been unable to reach their posts, while the most of those who were in office before that time have espoused• the insurrectionary cause, and assume to exercise the powers of agents by virtue of commissions from the insurrectionists. It has been stated in the public press that a portion of those Indians have been organized as a military force, and are attached to the army of the insurgents. Although the government has no official information upon this subject, letters have been written to the commissioner of Indian affairs by several prominent chiefs, giving assurance of their loyalty to the United States, and expressing a wish for the presence of federal troops to protect them. It is believed that upon the repossession of the country by the federal forces the Indians will readily cease all hostile demonstrations, and resume their former relations to the government. . . .

"Under and by virtue of the act of Congress entitled 'An act to confiscate property used for insurrectionary purposes,' approved August 6, 1861, the legal claims of certain persons to the labor and service of certain other persons have become forfeited; and numbers of the latter, thus liberated, are already dependent on the United States, and must be provided for in some way.

Besides this, it is not impossible that some of the states will pass similar enactments for their own benefit respectively, and by operation of which persons of the same class will be thrown upon them for disposal. In such case I recommend that Congress provide for accepting such persons from such states, according to some mode of valuation, in lieu, *pro tanto*, of direct taxes, or upon some other plan to be agreed on with such states respectively; that such persons, on such acceptance by the general government, be at once deemed free; and that, in any event, steps be taken for colonizing both classes (or the one first mentioned if the other shall not be brought into existence) at some place, or places, in a climate congenial to them. It might be well to consider, too, whether free colored people already in the United States could not, so far as individuals may desire, be included in such colonization.

"To carry out the plan of colonization may involve the acquiring of territory, and also the appropriation of money beyond that to be expended in the territorial acquisition. Having practised the acquisition of territory for nearly sixty years, the question of constitutional power to do so is no longer an open one with us. The power was questioned at first by Mr. Jefferson, who, however, in the purchase of Louisiana, yielded his scruples on the plea of great expediency. If it be said that the only legitimate object of acquiring territory is to furnish homes for white men, this measure effects that object; for the emigration of colored men leaves additional room for white men remaining or coming here. Mr. Jefferson, however, placed the importance of procuring Louisiana more on political and commercial grounds than on providing room for population.

"On this whole proposition, including the appropriation of money with the acquisition of territory, does not the expediency amount to absolute necessity — that without which the government itself cannot be perpetuated?

"The war continues. In considering the policy to be adopted for suppressing the insurrection, I have been anxious and careful that the inevitable conflict for this purpose shall not degenerate into a violent and remorseless revolutionary struggle. I have, therefore, in every case, thought it proper to keep the integrity of the Union prominent as the primary object of the contest on our part, leaving all questions which are not of vital military importance to the more deliberate action of the legislature.

"In the exercise of my best discretion I have adhered to the blockade of the ports held by the insurgents, instead of putting in force, by proclamation, the law of Congress enacted at the late session for closing those ports.

"So, also, obeying the dictates of prudence, as well as the obligations of law, instead of transcending, I have adhered to the act of Congress to confiscate property used for insurrectionary purposes. If a new law upon the same subject should be proposed, its propriety will be duly considered. The Union must be preserved; and hence, all indispensable means must be employed. We should not be in haste to determine that radical and extreme measures, which may reach the loyal as well as the disloyal, are indispensable.

"The inaugural address at the beginning of the administration, and the message to Congress at the late special session, were both mainly devoted to the domestic controversy out of which the insurrection and consequent war have sprung. Nothing now occurs to add or subtract, to or from, the principles or general purposes stated and expressed in those documents.

"The last ray of hope for preserving the Union peaceably expired at the assault upon Fort Sumter; and a general review of what has occurred since may not be unprofitable. What was painfully uncertain then is much better defined and more distinct now; and the progress of events is plainly in the right direction.

The insurgents confidently claimed a strong support from the north of Mason and Dixon's line; and the friends of the Union were not free from apprehension on the point. This, however, was soon settled definitely, and on the right side. South of the line, noble little Delaware led off right from the first. Maryland was made to *seem* against the Union. Our soldiers were assaulted, bridges were burned, and railroads torn up, within her limits; and we were many days, at one time, without the ability to bring a single regiment over her soil to the capital. Now, her bridges and railroads are repaired and open to the government; she already gives seven regiments to the cause of the Union, and none to the enemy; and her people, at a regular election, have sustained the Union by a larger majority and a larger aggregate vote than they ever before gave to any candidate, or any question. Kentucky, too, for some time in doubt, is now decidedly, and, I think, unchangeably, ranged on the side of the Union. Missouri is comparatively quiet; and, I believe, cannot again be overrun by the insurrectionists. These three states of Maryland, Kentucky, and Missouri, neither of which would promise a single soldier at first, have now an aggregate of not less than forty thousand in the field for the Union; while, of their citizens, certainly not more than a third of that number, and they of doubtful whereabouts, and doubtful existence, are in arms against it. After a somewhat bloody struggle of months, winter closes on the Union people of Western Virginia, leaving them masters of their own country.

"An insurgent force of about fifteen hundred, for months dominating the narrow peninsular region constituting the counties of Accomac and Northampton, and known as eastern shore of Virginia, together with some contiguous parts of Maryland, have laid down their arms; and the people there have renewed their allegiance to, and accepted the protection of, the old flag. This leaves no armed insurrectionist north of the Potomac, or east of the Chesapeake.

"Also, we have obtained a footing at each of the isolated points, on the southern coast, of Hatteras, Port Royal, Tybee Island, near Savannah, and Ship Island; and we likewise have some general accounts of popular movements, in behalf of the Union, in North Carolina and Tennessee.

" These things demonstrate that the cause of the Union is advancing steadily and certainly southward.

"Since your last adjournment, Lieutenant-General Scott has retired from the head of the army. During his long life, the nation has not been unmindful of his merit; yet, on calling to mind how faithfully, ably, and brilliantly he has served the country, from a time far back in our history, when few of the now living had been born, and thenceforward continually, I cannot but think we are still his debtors. I submit, therefore, for your consideration, what further mark of recognition is due to him, and to ourselves, as a grateful people.

"With the retirement of General Scott came the executive duty of appointing, in his stead, a general-in-chief of the army. It is a fortunate circumstance that neither in counsel nor country was there, so far as I know, any difference of opinion as to the proper person to be selected. The retiring chief repeatedly expressed his judgment in favor of General McClellan for the position; and in this the nation seemed to give a unanimous concurrence. The designation of General McClellan is, therefore, in considerable degree, the selection of the country, as well as of the Executive; and hence there is better reason to hope there will be given him the confidence and cordial support thus, by fair implication, promised, and without which he cannot, with so full efficiency, serve the country.

"It has been said that one bad general is better than two good ones; and the saying is true, if taken to mean no more than that an army is better directed by a single mind, though inferior, than by two superior ones at variance and cross-purposes with each other.

"And the same is true in all joint operations wherein those engaged *can* have none but a common end in view, and *can* differ only as to the choice of means. In a storm at sea, no one on board *can* wish the ship to sink; and, yet, not unfrequently, all go down together, because too many will direct, and no single mind can be allowed to control.

" It continues to develop that the insurrection is largely, if not exclusively, a war upon the first principle of popular government — the rights of the people. Conclusive evidence of this is found in the most grave and maturely considered public documents, as well as in the general tone of the insurgents. In those documents we find the abridgment of the existing right of suffrage, and the denial to the people of all right to participate in the selection of public officers, except the legislative, boldly advocated, with labored arguments to prove that large control of the people in government is the source of all political evil. Monarchy itself is sometimes hinted at as a possible refuge from the power of the people.

" In my present position, I could scarcely be justified were I to omit raising a warning voice against this approach of returning despotism.

" It is not needed, nor fitting here, that a general argument should be made in favor of popular institutions; but there is one point, with its connections, not so hackneyed as most others, to which I ask a brief attention. It is the effort to place *capital* on an equal footing with, if not above *labor*, in the structure of government. It is assumed that labor is available only in connection with capital; that nobody labors unless somebody else, owning capital, somehow, by the use of it, induces him to labor. This assumed, it is next considered whether it is best that capital shall *hire* laborers, and thus induce them to work by their own consent, or *buy* them, and drive them to it without their consent. Having proceeded so far, it is naturally concluded that all laborers are either *hired* laborers, or what we call slaves. And further, it is assumed that whoever is once a hired laborer is fixed in that condition for life.

"Now, there is no such relation between capital and labor as assumed; nor is there any such thing as a free man being fixed for life in the condition of a hired laborer. Both these assumptions are false, and all inferences from them are groundless.

"Labor is prior to, and independent of, capital. Capital is only the fruit of labor, and could never have existed if labor had not first existed. Labor is the superior of capital, and deserves much the higher consideration. Capital has its rights, which are as worthy of protection as any other rights. Nor is it denied that there is, and probably always will be, a relation between labor and capital, producing mutual benefits. The error is in assuming that the whole labor of community exists within that relation. A few men own capital, and that few avoid labor themselves, and, with their capital, hire or buy another few to labor for them. A large majority belong to neither class — neither work for others, nor have others working for them. In most of the southern states, a majority of the whole people, of all colors, are neither slaves nor masters; while in the northern, a large majority are neither hirers nor hired. Men with their families — wives, sons, and daughters — work for themselves, on their farms, in their houses, and in their shops, taking the whole product to themselves, and asking no favors of capital on the one hand, nor of hired laborers or slaves on the other. It is not forgotten that a considerable number of persons mingle their own labor with capital; that is, they labor with their own hands, and also buy or hire others to labor for them; but this is only a mixed, and not a distinct class. No principle stated is disturbed by the existence of this mixed class.

"Again: as has already been said, there is not, of necessity, any such thing as the free hired laborer being fixed to that condition for life. Many independent men every where in these states, a few years back in their lives, were hired laborers. The prudent, penniless beginner in the world labors for wages a while, saves a surplus with which to buy tools or land for himself; then labors on his own account another while, and at length hires another new beginner to help him. This is the just, and generous, and prosperous system, which opens the way to all — gives hope to all, and consequently energy, and progress, and improvement of condition to all. No men living are more worthy to be trusted than those who toil up from poverty — none less inclined to take, or touch, aught which they have not honestly earned. Let them beware of surrendering a political power which they already possess, and which, if surrendered, will surely be used to close the door of advancement against such as they, and to fix new disabilities and burdens upon them, till all of liberty shall be lost.

"From the first taking of our national census to the last are seventy years; and we find our population, at the end of the period, eight times as great as it was at the beginning. The increase of those other things which men deem desirable, has been even greater. We thus have, at one view, what the popular principle, applied to government, through the machinery of the states and the Union, has produced in a given time; and also what, if firmly maintained, it promises for the future. There are already among us those who, if the Union be preserved, will live to see it contain two hundred and fifty millions. The struggle *of* to-day is not altogether *for* to-day — it is for a vast future also. With a reliance on Providence all the more firm and earnest, let us proceed in the great task which events have devolved upon us.

"ABRAHAM LINCOLN.

"WASHINGTON, *December 3, 1861.*"

By the report of the secretary of war it appeared that the estimated number of troops in the service of the United States was, of volunteers six hundred and forty thousand six hundred and thirty-seven, and of regulars twenty thousand three hundred and thirty-four, making an aggregate of six hundred and sixty thousand nine hundred and seventy-one men. In relation to the organization of this immense army, the secretary said, —

"Congress, during its extra session, authorized the army to be increased by the acceptance of a volunteer force of five hundred thousand men, and made an appropriation of five hundred millions of dollars for its support. A call for the troops was immediately made; but so numerous were the offers that it was found difficult to discriminate in the choice, where the patriotism of the people demanded that there should be no restriction upon enlistments. Every portion of the loyal states desired to swell the army, and every community was anxious that it should be represented in a cause that appealed to the noblest impulses of our people.

"So thoroughly aroused was the national heart, that I have no doubt this force would have been swollen to a million, had not the department felt compelled to restrict it, in the absence of authority from the representatives of the people to increase the limited number. It will be for Congress to decide whether the army shall be further augmented, with a view to a more speedy termination of the war, or whether it shall be confined to the strength already fixed by law. In the latter case, with the object of reducing the volunteer force to five hundred thousand, I propose, with the consent of Congress, to consolidate such of the regiments as may from time to time fall below the regulation standard. The adoption of this measure will decrease the number of officers, and proportionably diminish the expenses of the army.

"It is said of Napoleon, by Jomini, that, in the campaign of 1815, that great general, on the 1st of April, had a regular army of two hundred thousand men. On the 1st of June he had increased this force to four hundred and fourteen thousand. 'The like proportion,' adds Jomini, 'had he thought proper to inaugurate a vast system of defence, would have raised it to seven hundred thousand men by the 1st of September.' At the commencement of this rebellion, inaugurated by the attack upon Fort Sumter, the entire military force at the disposal of this government was sixteen thousand and six regulars, principally employed in the west to hold in check marauding Indians. In April, seventy-five thousand volunteers were called upon to enlist for three months' service, and responded with such alacrity that seventy-seven thousand eight hundred and seventy-five were immediately obtained. Under the authority of the act of Congress of July 22, 1861, the states were asked to furnish five hundred thousand volunteers, to serve for three years, or during the war; and by the act approved the 29th of the same month, the addition of twenty-five thousand men to the regular army of the United States was authorized. The result is, that we have now an army of upwards of six hundred thousand men. If we add to this the number of the discharged three months' volunteers, the aggregate force furnished to the government since April last exceeds seven hundred thousand men.

"We have here an evidence of the wonderful strength of our institutions. Without conscriptions, levies, drafts, or other extraordinary expedients, we have raised a greater force than that which, gathered by Napoleon with the aid of all these appliances, was considered an evidence of his wonderful genius and energy, and of the military spirit of the French nation. Here every man has an interest in the government, and rushes to its defence when dangers beset it."

In another part of his report the secretary advised the thorough organization of the militia of the country, as a means of raising speedily, in case of necessity, large armies for defence, and even for aggression. Upon this point the secretary said, —

"In my last report I called attention to the fact that legislation was necessary for the reorganization, upon a uniform basis, of the militia of the country. Some general plan should be provided by Congress in aid of the states, by which our militia can be organized, armed, and disciplined, and made effective at any moment for immediate service. If thoroughly trained in time of peace, when occasion demands, it may be converted into a vast army, confident in its discipline and unconquerable in its patriotism. In the absence of any general system of organization, upwards of seven hundred thousand men have already been brought into the field ; and, in view of the alacrity and enthusiasm that have been displayed, I do not hesitate to express the belief that no combination of events can arise in which this country will not be able not only to protect itself, but, contrary to its policy, which is peace with all the world, to enter upon aggressive operations against any power that may intermeddle with our domestic affairs."

Of the extent of the territory embraced by the rebellion, and in relation to the disaster at Bull Run, the report spoke as follows : —

"The conspiracy against the government extended over an area of seven hundred and thirty-three thousand one hundred and forty-four square miles, possessing a coast line of three thousand five hundred and twenty-three miles, and a shore line of twenty-five thousand four hundred and fourteen miles, with an interior boundary line of seven thousand and thirty-one miles in length. This conspiracy stripped us of arms and ammunitions, and scattered our navy to the most distant quarters of the globe. The effort to restore the Union, which the government entered on in April last, was the most gigantic endeavor in the history of civil war. The interval of seven months has been spent in preparation.

"The history of this rebellion, in common with all others, for obvious causes, records the first successes in favor of the insurgents. The disaster of Bull Run was but the natural consequence of the premature advance of our brave but undisciplined troops, which the impatience of the country demanded. The betrayal also of our movements by traitors in our midst, enabled the rebels to choose and intrench their position, and by a reënforcement in great strength, at the moment of victory, to snatch it from our grasp. This reverse, however, gave no discouragement to our gallant people ; they have crowded into our ranks, and although large numbers have been necessarily rejected, a mighty army in invincible array stands eager to precipitate itself upon the foe. The check that we have received upon the Potomac has, therefore, but postponed the campaign for a few months. The other successes of the rebels, though dearly won, were mere affairs with no important or permanent advantages. The possession of Western Virginia and the occupation of Hatteras and Beaufort have nobly redeemed our transient reverses."

The report of the secretary of the navy gave a detailed account of the increase of that branch of the service, from the feeble and scattered naval force which he found at his control when the rebellion commenced, to the large fleet which was brought so rapidly into the service. The number of vessels in actual service, or nearly completed and equipped, was two hundred and sixty-four, a large proportion of which were steamers ; the whole carrying twenty-five hundred and fifty-seven guns, and not less than twenty-two thousand seamen.

The rebellion imposed upon Congress the necessity of legislating on a great variety of important subjects. A large majority of both houses were political supporters of the administration, and at this time the greater part of its political opponents gave a cordial support to most of its measures for the suppression of the rebellion. There were a few, indeed, who were opposed to the war, or to "coercive measures," as they were called, towards the seceded states. But in the general hearty loyalty of all parties these men could do but little besides making themselves conspicuous as opponents of the war in which the patriotic sympathies of the whole people were enlisted. The business of Congress, therefore, proceeded with more order and diligence than had been the custom for many years while the men who were now in rebellion occupied seats in the Capitol.

CHAPTER LVII.

Approach of Winter. — Military Preparations. — General Halleck in the Western Department. — His Orders. — Skirmishes. — General Pope's Movements. — Attack on a Rebel Camp at Milford. — Capture of the Rebel Force. — General Pope's Report. — South-eastern Missouri and Kentucky. — Partisan Conflicts. — Bitter Enmity and Warfare. — Army of the Potomac. — Skirmishes. — Affair at Drainesville. — Success of the Federal Troops. — Defeat of the Rebels. — General Ord's Report. — Winter on the Potomac. — Bad Roads. — Delay in Army Movements. — Winter Quarters. — Position of the Rebel Army. — Blockade of the Potomac.

As winter came on, active military operations were materially interfered with by the inclemency of the weather, and the difficulty of moving troops on account of the condition of the roads. The federal forces, however, were not altogether idle, and while preparations were made for more active campaigns in the spring, there were numerous skirmishes and movements, both at the west and in Virginia, most of which resulted favorably to the cause of the Union. General Halleck, a man of great intellectual power and military knowledge, was now

in command of the western department, and pushed forward the preparations for a grand movement towards the south when the season should permit, while he at the same time did not neglect to advance the federal forces to such positions as should hold the rebels in check. He also issued some important orders in relation to disloyal inhabitants in Missouri. One of these compelled such disloyal parties to contribute to the support of loyal refugees, who had been deprived of their property and driven from their homes by the rebel forces in the south-western part of the state. Another ordered the severest penalties to be inflicted upon rebel marauders and guerrillas, who preyed upon the property of loyal citizens, destroyed bridges, and committed other offences, without belonging to the organized forces of the rebels. Other orders issued by General Halleck, looking to a restoration of slaves to their owners, and prohibiting the harboring of them within the federal lines, gave less satisfaction; but his general administration strengthened the Union cause, and vigorously advanced the preparations for future campaigns.

Numerous skirmishes occurred in various parts of his department, but most of them were of little importance in themselves, or in their consequences upon the campaign. One of the most successful movements was a surprise of a rebel camp at Milford, in western Missouri, a part of General Pope's forces. A slight skirmish ensued when the federal troops first advanced upon the rebel position, but the approach was so well managed that the rebels found themselves almost surrounded before they could make any effectual resistance, and they were compelled to surrender. The number of prisoners taken by this movement was thirteen hundred, with a large number of small arms, and ammunition and supplies. Similar successes, of less importance, by General Pope's forces, materially weakened the rebels, by discouraging those who sympathized with their cause. General Pope's official report gives the following account of his advance and successful operations : —

"HEADQUARTERS DISTRICT CENTRAL MISSOURI, }
" OTTERVILLE, Dec. 23, 1861. }

"CAPTAIN: I have the honor to state that, having replaced by troops from Lamine the garrison of Sedalia, I marched from that place on Sunday the 15th instant, with a column of infantry, cavalry, and artillery, numbering about four thousand men. The first brigade was commanded by Colonel J. C. Davis, Indiana volunteers ; the second by Colonel F. Steele, Eighth Iowa regiment. The object of the movement was to interpose between Price's army on the Osage and the recruits, escort, and supplies on their way south from the Mississippi River. This body of the enemy was represented to be between four and six thousand strong, with a large train of supplies.

"I encamped on the 15th, eleven miles southwest of Sedalia. That the enemy might be thoroughly misled as to the destination of the expedition, it was given out that the movement was upon Warsaw, and the troops pursued the road to that place several miles beyond Sedalia. I threw forward on Clinton four companies of the first Missouri cavalry, under Major Hubbard, with orders to watch any movement from Osceola, to prevent any reconnoissance of our main column, and to intercept any messengers to the enemy at Osceola. On the 16th I pushed forward by forced march twenty-seven miles, and, with my whole force, occupied at sunset a position between the direct road from Warrensburg to Clinton, and the road by Chilhowee, which latter is the road heretofore pursued by returning soldiers and by recruits. Shortly after sunset, the advance, consisting of four companies of Iowa cavalry, under Major Torrence, captured the enemy's pickets at Chilhowee, and learned that he was encamped in force (about twenty-two hundred) six miles north of that town.

"After resting the horses and men for a couple of hours, I threw forward ten companies of cavalry, and a section of artillery, under Lieutenant-Colonel Brown, seventh Missouri regiment, in pursuit, and followed with my whole force, posting the main body between Warrensburg and Rose Hill, to support the pursuing column. I, at the same time, reënforced Major Hubbard with two companies of Merrill's Horse, and directed him, in order to secure our flank in the pursuit, to push forward, as far as possible, towards Osceola. This officer executed his duty with distinguished ability and vigor, driving back and capturing the pickets, and one entire company of the enemy's cavalry, with tents, baggage, and wagons. One of the pickets and two wagons were captured within the lines of Rains's division, encamped north of the Osage River.

"The column under Lieutenant-Colonel Brown continued the pursuit vigorously all night of the 16th, all day of the 17th, and part of the night of the same day, his advance guard consisting of Foster's company of Ohio cavalry, and a detachment of thirty men of the fourth regular cavalry, occupying Johnstown in the course of the night. The enemy began to scatter as soon as the pursuit grew close, disappearing in every direction in the bushes, and by every by-path, driving their wagons into farm-yards remote from the road, and throwing out their loads. As these wagons were all two-horse wagons of the country, and had been in fact taken by force from the farm-houses, it was impossible to identify them. When our pursuit reached Johnstown, about midnight on the 17th, the enemy, reduced to about five hundred, scattered completely, one portion fleeing precipitately toward Butler, and the other toward Papinsville.

"The main body of my command moved slowly towards Warrensburg, awaiting the return of the force under Lieutenant-Colonel Brown, which proceeded from Johnstown to scour the country south of Grand River to the neighborhood of Clinton. In these operations sixteen wagons, loaded with tents and supplies, and one hundred and fifty prisoners, were captured. The enemy's force was thoroughly dispersed.

"On the morning of the 18th, Lieutenant-Colonel Brown's force rejoined the command. Knowing that there must still be a large force of the enemy north of us, I moved forward slowly, on the 18th, towards Warrensburg, and, when near that town, the spies and scouts I had sent out before marching from Sedalia, in the direction of Lexington, Waverly, and Arrow Rock, reported to me that a large force was moving from the two latter places, and would encamp that night at the mouth of Clear Creek, just south of Milford.

"I posted the main body of my command between Warrensburg and Knob Noster, to close all outlet to the south between those two points, and despatched seven companies of cavalry, (five of the Ohio first and two of the fourth regular cavalry,) afterward reënforced by another company of regular cavalry, and a section of artillery, all under command of Colonel J. C. Davis, Indiana volunteers, to march on the town of Milford, so as to turn the enemy's left and rear, and intercept his retreat to the north-east, at the same time directing Major Marshall, with Merrill's regiment of horse, to march from Warrensburg on the same point, turning the enemy's right and rear, and forming junction with Colonel Davis.

"The main body of my command occupied a point four miles south, and ready to advance at a moment's notice, or to intercept the enemy's retreat south. Colonel Davis marched promptly and vigorously with the forces under his command, and at a late hour in the afternoon came upon the enemy encamped in the wooded bottom-land on the west side of Blackwater, opposite the mouth of Clear Creek. His pickets were immediately driven in across the stream, which was deep, miry, and impassable, except by a long, narrow bridge, which the enemy occupied in force, as is believed, under Colonel Magoffin.

"Colonel Davis brought forward his force, and directed that the bridge be carried by assault. The two companies of the fourth regular cavalry being in advance, under the command, respectively, of Lieutenant Gordon and Lieutenant Amory, were designated for that service, and were supported by the five companies of the first Iowa cavalry. Lieutenant Gordon, of the fourth cavalry, led the charge in person, with the utmost gallantry and vigor, carried the bridge in fine style, and immediately formed his company on the opposite side. He was promptly followed by the other companies. The force of the enemy posted at the bridge retreated precipitately over a narrow open space, into the woods, where his whole force was posted. The two companies of the fourth cavalry formed in line at once, advanced upon the enemy, and were received with a volley of small arms, muskets, rifles, and shot guns. One man was killed and eight wounded by this discharge. With one exception, all belonged to company D, fourth cavalry, Lieutenant Gordon.

"Lieutenant Gordon himself received several balls through the cap. Our forces still continuing to press forward, and the enemy finding his retreat south and west cut off, and that he was in presence of a large force, and at best could only prolong the contest a short time, surrendered at discretion. His force, reported by colonel commanding, consisted of parts of two regiments of infantry and three companies of cavalry, numbering in all thirteen hundred men, among whom there were three colonels, (Robinson, Alexander, and Magoffin,) one lieutenant-colonel, (Robinson,) one major, (Harris,) and fifty-one commissioned company officers. About five hundred horses and mules, seventy-three wagons heavily loaded with powder, lead, tents, subsistence stores, and supplies of various kinds, fell into our hands, as also a thousand stand of arms.

"The whole force captured, with their train, were marched into the camp of the main body, reaching there about midnight. Many arms were thrown away by the enemy, in the bushes and creek, when he surrendered, and have not yet been found. . . .

"I am, captain, your obedient servant,
"JOHN POPE,
"*Brigadier-General commanding.*
"To Captain J. C. KELTON, A. A. G.,
"*Department of the Missouri.*"

Skirmishes and small engagements occurred, also, in south-eastern Missouri and in Kentucky, besides the affairs recorded in previous pages. The success was various, but for the most part the advantage was on the side of the federal troops. None of these engagements, however, were of much importance, except so far as they kept in check movements by which the rebels might have gained considerable advantages. Through the greater part of both Missouri and Kentucky there were partisan conflicts. The people were divided in their allegiance, and in some places a bitter and relentless warfare was waged by those who enlisted in the rebel cause upon their loyal neighbors, when the latter were in a minority. It would be but natural if such a warfare, which was originated by the disloyal, should sometimes be waged in retaliation by Union men, as in some places it undoubtedly was. But the persecution, robbery, and slaughter by the rebel partisans and guerrilla parties infinitely exceeded all the acts of this kind which could justly be charged upon loyal men. The orders of General Halleck were directed to the suppression of such internecine warfare, and stringent measures succeeded in some measure in restoring peace to a large part of these states, by overawing or compelling the departure of those who were disposed to aid the rebel cause. In the mean time the preparations for a grand advance at the west into the rebellious states were prosecuted with vigor, and on a scale that promised good results.

Along the line of the army of the Potomac, though there were occasional slight skirmishes between small advanced parties and pickets, no affair of importance occurred during the month of December, except an engagement at Drainesville, between a large foraging party of the federal army and about an equal force of the rebels, which took place on the 20th of that month. The federal troops were under the command of Brigadier-General Ord, and consisted of that officer's brigade, a regiment of rifles, a battery of light artillery, and two squadrons of cavalry, all of the "Pennsylvania Reserves," under Major-General McCall. This force was sent forward for the purpose of driving back the enemy's pickets to a greater distance from the federal lines and to procure forage. Near Drainesville, a small village on the road leading from Washington to Leesburg, a rebel force of four or five regiments, with artillery and cavalry, under command of General Stuart, was also moving out upon a foraging expedition. General Ord entered Drainesville with a part of his force, driving out and scattering the rebel cavalry picket which was stationed there. He then awaited the collection of forage, disposing of his forces as they came up so as to protect the foraging party. While thus engaged, the rebel forces of General Stuart advanced to make an attack. After some skirmishing between the flanking companies and rebels concealed in the woods, the attack was commenced more in earnest by the rebel artillery, which was served with little effect, and was responded to by General Ord's artillery from a position in which it could enfilade the road where the enemy's guns and a part of his infantry were posted. Soon the infantry on both sides were advanced, and a considerable part of them became engaged. The rebels made a determined attack upon one flank of the federal troops, but they were met with spirit, and were driven back with loss. One of General Ord's regiments was ordered to charge upon and take the rebel battery; but to do this they were obliged to advance through a thick wood, and when they emerged in the vicinity of the position which had been occupied by the rebel artillery, the latter had retreated, and the entire force of the enemy were soon rapidly retiring, a portion of it in great confusion. The retreating forces were followed but a short distance; sufficient, however, to make certain a very decided success on the part of the Union troops. The loss of the enemy greatly exceeded that of the federal force, and the arms and equipments which they left upon the field, as well as the considerable number of wounded, whom they did not even attempt to carry with them, showed the haste in which they had retired. General McCall arrived upon the field near the close of the engagement, and when the success was secured he ordered the federal force to retire, deeming it imprudent to remain with such a force in a place to which the rebels could in a short time bring up heavy reënforcements to their discomfited comrades. Accordingly General Ord's command retired to their camp, taking with them the forage they had collected, the wounded prisoners, and their own dead and wounded. The following is the principal part of General Ord's official report:—

"CAMP PIERPONT, VA., *Dec.* 21, 1861.

"SIR: I have to report that, in obedience to the enclosed order, I, at six A. M. yesterday, started towards Dickey's and Henderson's, about three miles this side of Drainesville, on the Leesburg pike, with my brigade, the first rifles, Lieutenant-Colonel Kane, Easton's battery, and two squadrons of cavalry. I likewise heard that it was probable there was a respectable picket of cavalry in Drainesville, and that the pickets supposed by you to be near the river, behind Dickey's, had left. I then determined to send three companies of the tenth, and twenty cavalry, with the foraging party to Gunnell's, between the pike and the river, and with the remainder of the force proceed to Drainesville, satisfied that, though I might be exceeding the letter of my instructions, should I find the enemy and pick up a few, you would not object. This I did, though Colonel McCalmont, hearing that there was a large force on our left, remained with his part of a regiment, and that detained the two regiments behind him, (I had sent for them;) but was obliged to enter Drainesville with my artillery and cavalry, and a small advanced guard only on the road, the first rifles and Colonel Jackson's regiment flanking this column in the woods on the right and left. The cavalry picket in town fled, scattered, and remained in small squads, watching.

"While waiting in Drainesville for the regiments in the rear to come up, I posted my artillery and cavalry, and Jackson's regiment of infantry, and a couple of companies of the first rifles, so as to cover the approaches, and sent for Colonel Kane's regiment to occupy the road in our then rear, my front being towards Centreville. This I did, because, from the occasional appearance of a few mounted men on a slope behind some woods in a hollow to my left and front, and a broad mass of smoke in that neighborhood, I felt pretty sure that there was a force there preparing some mischief As soon as Colonel McCalmont came up with his regiment, the tenth, followed by Lieutenant-Colonel Penrose, the sixth, and Colonel Taggart with the twelfth, and while preparing to resist any attack and to cover my foraging party, I learned that the enemy, in force, had approached on the south side of the Leesburg pike, with field pieces and infantry, and had driven in my pickets, wounding two men. Thinking they would attack on *both* sides of the turnpike as I returned eastward, I ordered (to meet this expected attack) Colonel McCalmont's regiment on the left or river side of the road in the woods, left in front, and if the enemy showed himself on that side, to bring his regiment forward into line. Colonel Jackson's regiment, of which and its gallant colonel I cannot speak in too high terms, I ordered to flank the road in the same way on the right of the road in the woods, and do the same if the enemy showed on that side. Between these flanking regiments I ordered the Kane rifles to meet the enemy (behind us) in the road, the cavalry to follow, and the artillery I took with me to post them and answer the enemy's artillery, which had opened fire on our (their) right, (the *south*,) directing the rear guard to cover the column of the sixth and twelfth regiments infantry in the road from cavalry. The artillery went at a run past the station I selected for them, capsizing one of their pieces. I brought them back, told the captain where to post his guns, and then went to remove the cavalry, then exposed in the road swept by the enemy, (whose attack was from a thickly wooded hill on our right flank, the south.) Their force, I saw, was a very bold one, very well posted, and the artillery was only about five hundred yards off, with a large force of infantry on both its flanks and in front, covered and surrounded by woods and thickets. Moving east with the cavalry, which was of no use here, I came to a place in the road, covered toward the enemy by a high bluff and dense thickets, which thickets I intended to occupy with infantry. Here I left the cavalry, surrounded by dense forests, wherein they could neither fight nor be hurt.

"As I had at first thought the enemy would attack on both sides of the road, and moved my infantry to meet such an attack, and as their attack was confined to the right, it became necessary to change my front. As neither McCalmont nor Jackson had had time to come into line under first orders, when I discovered this, and was moving by the flank, and as, before I placed the artillery and cavalry, I had seen the rifles closely engaging the enemy by a flank movement, covering themselves by some

houses and fences, my right, in meeting the attack, thus became the village of Drainesville, my left the gorge and woods occupied by my cavalry on the Leesburg pike. After securing the cavalry, I found, by carefully observing the enemy's fire and battery, that their guns were in a road which could be enfiladed. I ordered Captain Easton to right the capsized gun, and bring it to the spot from which this road could be raked; removed two other guns to this spot, gave the gunners the distance and elevation, observed the result, and finding, after a round or two, that the enemy's fire slackened, and the gunners were raking the road beautifully, without being discomposed by the enemy's fire, I told them "to keep at that," and determined to push the infantry forward. I found them (except the Kane rifles, the ninth, Jackson's, and the tenth, the McCalmont regiment, which were as above stated) in the ditches, under fences, and covering themselves as best they might. I started them forward, Kane at the head of his regiment leading. His and Jackson's regiments required no urging. McCalmont's regiment was kept in excellent order by its colonel, (than whom a better officer is not found in my brigade,) and acted as a reserve. I put them in the woods — pushed and exhorted them up the hill, having directed the battery to cease firing, and proceeding with my infantry with the bayonet. About this time, between three and four o'clock, (the action began at half-past two,) General McCall, I was informed, arrived on the field. As I was very busy urging the men forward, and they required all my attention to keep them to their work, I did not at once report; but when we reached the ground occupied by the enemy's battery, I reported to him. He was so kind as to direct me to continue the pursuit in the same order, and to continue my dispositions, which I did. The enemy were pursued fully half a mile further, but they had left the neighborhood in great haste, leaving their arms, a portion of their dead and wounded, clothing, ten horses, and a quantity of artillery equipments, with two caissons and a limber, scattered along the road towards Centreville, and in the woods on both sides. . . .

"The enemy left twenty-one of their most desperately wounded on the field, who were taken up, carried to houses, and their wounds dressed by our surgeons, but they will nearly all die. Their dead left on the field is variously estimated from fifty to seventy-five. Our artillery did terrible havoc, exploding one ammunition wagon, and some of their men whom we brought in say the slaughter was terrible. Several dead lay around the exploded caisson, three of whose blackened corpses were headless. The prisoners further state that Colonel Taylor was doubtless killed; two of their officers were left on the ground, and how many were carried off it is difficult to say. After the affair, we built our bivouac fires in Drainesville. Thus, sir, we, on returning to camp, had marched twenty-four miles, beaten the enemy, loaded our wagons with forage, bringing in twelve mules, our killed, (seven,) and wounded, (sixty,) among whom are four captains. . . .

"The prisoners report that the brigade engaged against us was composed of the Kentucky rifles, an Alabama, a South Carolina, and a Virginia regiment, with a six-gun battery, all under the command of General Stuart.

"I must not forget the prompt manner in which General Reynolds came up from Difficult Creek, some four miles off, as soon as he heard the cannonading. He arrived too late, it is true, to take part in the affair, but the certainty that he would come with his brigade, insured a victory, and stimulated our men to earn it.

"With respect, sir, your obedient servant,

"E. O. C. ORD,
"*Brigadier-General Volunteers.*

"Col. H. J. BIDDLE,
"*Assistant Adjutant General, McCall's Division.*"

As the winter season advanced, the roads became in many places impracticable for artillery and heavy trains, and though a movement of the great army which had been collected and organized on the Potomac was for a long time confidently expected by the people, it became evident at last that the season for an effective campaign was passed. This was a great disappointment to the loyal people, who desired that a crushing blow should be struck at once, and not a little discontent was manifested on account of the delay, which was variously attributed to the government and to the commanding general. The army did not nominally go into winter quarters, and this kept alive for a long time the expectation that a movement would be made. The soldiers, however, suffered from the exposure in their tents, until they were permitted by various expedients to render them more comfortable. Some of the troops had huts which proved a better shelter than the tents. Others contrived, by walls of turf over which the tents were raised, to make more comfortable quarters. Various expedients and inventions were also resorted to by which the huts and tents could be warmed by fire. With abundant supplies the health of the army continued good, notwithstanding what was considered its great exposure to the cold and storms; and the soldiers were moreover contented and confident of victory whenever they should be led to battle by their commander.

Meanwhile the rebel army, the main body of which was posted near Manassas, prepared their winter quarters in a similar manner, though with a more evident purpose of a continuance in their position through the inclement season. They were not so well provided with tents as the Union troops, and constructed a large number of huts, in which they were quartered. Their advance posts and pickets continued to be thrown forward towards the federal lines, and they boasted that the position of their army was such that it could be concentrated in a short time to resist successfully any attack that might be made by the federal forces. The rebels, however, did not appear disposed at this time to assume the offensive, and there is reason to believe that had the army of the Potomac, strong in numbers and enthusiasm, been led against the enemy before the winter rendered an advance impossible, it would have found the rebels unprepared to resist the attack and would have achieved a great victory. But the policy of the federal government, or of the commanding general, appeared to be delay for the preparation of other armies and expeditions, and the perfection of the soldiers in discipline and drill.

Since the 22d of October, the Potomac had been effectually blockaded by the rebel batteries, erected upon all the commanding points on the Virginia side below Alexandria. No vessels, except occasionally by stealth, could pass up or down the river, and the immense supplies required for the federal army were necessarily transported by railroad. The horses consequently suffered frequently for the want of forage. The naval forces on the Potomac were ready and anxious to attack and silence the various rebel batteries, if a sufficient land force should coöperate and hold the positions thus gained. But the proposition was not received with favor by those who controlled the movements of the army, the position of the enemy along the banks of the river being considered of little value, in a military view, though for the time being a serious inconvenience in the transportation of supplies. Accordingly no attempt was made to dislodge the enemy from these positions, and Washington was effectually blockaded from direct communication with the sea. Such was the general position of affairs at the end of the year 1861.

The year closed with disappointment, both to the people of the loyal states and to the insurgents. Though much had really been gained by the federal government since the commencement of hostilities, the loyal people had expected that some early decisive blow would be struck, which should show the power of the government and lead to submission and peace. The course of events had dispelled that idea, so generally entertained at first, and the loyal people, convinced that they must show an overwhelming force, and a determination to use it to crush rebellion, furnished with patriotism and spirit the men and means required. They asked only that the forces thus supplied should be used promptly and effectually. When the year closed with immense armies in the field, and large fleets upon the sea, and all apparently idle, it was quite natural that there should be some feeling of disappointment and dissatisfaction. Such a feeling was manifested, however, only by an earnest call for activity and efficiency on the part of the government and its officers.

On the other hand the rebels, more impulsive than the people of the north, and more in earnest, had also expected, by some sudden blows, to sever the Union and achieve their independence. Their success at Bull Run encouraged this idea, and among the people of the south there was great disappointment that the army, which they then believed invincible, did not move at once on Washington, and end the war by a decisive victory. The leaders of the rebellion saw the necessity of a different policy. With delay, intervention on the part of foreign powers, the hope of which had been entertained from the outset, became an element of eventual success, which was invariably counted upon. The capture of Mason and Slidell, and their forcible removal from a British vessel, it was confidently expected would not only secure the intervention of the British government, but in the form of active hostilities, which would certainly ruin the United States. When the difficulties which arose out of that capture were amicably settled, and the

Natl. P. Banks

expectation of an immediate alliance with Great Britain was disappointed, a general feeling of depression and discontent seemed to pervade the rebel states. The success of the federal arms in the latter part of the year, in most places where they had been advanced, served to increase the discontent and disappointment, which was freely expressed in some of the leading rebel papers. But a determination to resist the federal authority, and a continuance of the Union, was every where avowed, and all possible preparations were made to meet the forces which they saw the north was organizing for the maintenance of the national government and the Union.

CHAPTER LVIII.

Opening of the Year 1862. — Continued Inactivity. — Alleged Causes of Delay. — Resignation of Mr. Cameron. — Appointment of Hon. Edwin M. Stanton Secretary of War. — Popular Opinion of the Appointment. — Continuance of Skirmishes in Missouri and Kentucky. — Battle of Mill Springs. — Federal and Rebel Forces. — Attack by the Rebels, and Repulse. — Death of General Zollicoffer. — Retreat of the Rebels. — Pursuit by Federal Forces, and Preparations to attack the Rebel Intrenchments. — Flight of the Rebels at Night. — Capture of Arms, etc. — General Thomas's Report. — Effect of the Victory.

THE year 1862 opened with almost entire inactivity in the army of the Potomac, and no prospect of any immediate movement of importance. Though the armies were being strengthened, and several expeditions were in preparation, the delay of an advance in some direction with strong forces had greatly disappointed the people of the north, and with the opening of a new year there was a renewed demand for a more vigorous prosecution of the war. The delay was not attributed altogether to the elements, and the difficulties of moving troops and supplies over almost impassable roads, but was ascribed also to the inefficiency of the war department, and by some to the excessive caution,

or unwillingness to move, of the commanding general. Concerning the head of the war department, there had been various indefinite complaints, which had created a distrust of that official, and a change was demanded. Before the middle of January the change was made. Mr. Cameron, secretary of war, resigned, and Hon. Edwin M. Stanton, of Pennsylvania, was appointed his successor. Mr. Stanton was a democrat in politics, and had been attorney-general under Mr. Buchanan, during a short period before the close of his administration. He was known to be thoroughly in favor of putting down the rebellion, and as a vigorous, energetic man. Mr. Holt, who had been secretary of war under Mr. Buchanan after the traitors left his cabinet, would have been preferred by a majority of the people; but the appointment of Mr. Stanton gave general satisfaction, and especially to that part of the people who had sympathized with him politically; and it was hailed as a token of the more perfect union of all parties at the north, for the maintenance of the Union, and the suppression of the rebellion. More activity and vigor were soon infused into the war department, and, by degrees, into military operations, inspiring a general confidence that the immense preparations which were being made would, as soon as the season permitted, result in success.

During the month of January there were few movements, except the departure of an expedition to North Carolina, and a portion of another for the Gulf, which will be noticed in subsequent pages. In Missouri and Kentucky, however, skirmishes continued between some of the advance forces which were sent forward to scatter the gathering bands of rebels, and something was in this way accomplished to prevent these states being overrun by rebel forces. Kentucky was now seriously threatened by the forces of the seceded states and her own recreant sons. But the Union army there and at Cairo was constantly augmenting and preparing for a campaign that should relieve the state from serious invasion. In the mean time some of the federal troops were advanced to positions in which they could hold the rebel forces in check. This led to some encounters between the opposing forces, the most important of which was the battle of Mill Springs, or Logan's Cross Roads.*

Brigadier-General George H. Thomas had been ordered to advance with his brigade, supported by some other forces, to Logan's Cross Roads, for the purpose of holding in check the rebel forces under Generals Crittenden and Zollicoffer, who were about ten miles south of that point, in an intrenched camp on the banks of the Cumberland River. The roads were in a very bad condition, but General Thomas reached the Cross Roads on the 17th of January with a part of his command, others of his troops coming up the next day. His whole force at this time consisted of four regiments of infantry, sections of three batteries of artillery, and a small force of cavalry. Another brigade of three regiments of Tennesseans from General Schoepf's command was ordered to join him, to remain till his whole command arrived. These, however, did not, for some reason, take a very active part in the battle, the tide being already turned in favor of the federal forces when they came upon the field.

On the 19th of January, before General Thomas's whole force had arrived, and he had time to intrench his position, the enemy advanced from their camp to make an attack. Generals Crittenden and Zollicoffer had, in their intrenched camp and vicinity, nine or ten regiments of infantry, several batteries of artillery, and a considerable force of cavalry. They marched to the attack with eight regiments of infantry, six pieces of artillery, and two battalions of cavalry.

The federal pickets were driven in quite

* Called also the battle of Fishing Creek.

early in the morning, and the long roll soon called the regiments into line, though a serious attack on the part of the enemy was not anticipated. The tenth Indiana regiment first met the advancing forces, and held them in check till supported by other troops with artillery, but the rebels nearly flanked this small federal force which was first brought into action, and but for the opportune arrival of other regiments would have achieved a decided advantage. The rebels brought up their forces with great spirit and a determination to drive the federal troops from their position, but they were received with a hot fire, which compelled them to fall back, and after repeated unsuccessful attempts, charges by some of the federal regiments caused them at last to give way in confusion, and soon to retreat. In the midst of the most determined advance on the part of the rebels, General Zollicoffer was killed by Colonel Fry, of the fourth Kentucky regiment, while in advance of his forces. The fall of the general, in whom they appeared to have most confidence, probably had a dispiriting effect upon some of the rebel soldiers, and they soon after gave way before the severe fire, which was succeeded by an impetuous charge of the federal troops.

The retreat of the rebels, when they had given way, was hurried and disorderly. The federal troops, as soon as they received a new supply of ammunition, marched in pursuit, and late in the afternoon reached a position in front of the rebel intrenchments. They were immediately formed in line of battle, and the intrenchments were vigorously cannonaded with the field artillery. Several guns were placed so as to command the ferry across the Cumberland River, and shots were fired to deter the enemy from attempting to cross, and in the mean time preparations were made for an assault upon the fortifications the next morning. Three or four regiments arrived to reenforce General Thomas in the afternoon and evening, and there was no doubt of a successful assault and complete victory. But the rebel commander succeeded in escaping with his forces by crossing the ferry in the night, to the south side of the river, abandoning his artillery, a quantity of small arms, ammunition, and camp equipage, and a large number of horses, mules, and wagons. Having crossed the river he destroyed the ferry boats so as to prevent pursuit, and the federal forces were obliged to be content with the decided victory they had achieved, though disappointed in the expectation of capturing a large number of prisoners.

The following is General Thomas's official report of the battle: —

> "HEADQUARTERS FIRST DIVISION,
> DEPARTMENT OF THE OHIO,
> SOMERSET, KY., *January* 31, 1862.

"CAPTAIN: I have the honor to report that in carrying out the instructions of the General commanding the department, contained in his communications of the 29th of December, I reached Logan's Cross Roads, about ten miles north of the intrenched camp of the enemy, on the Cumberland River, on the 17th inst., with a portion of the second and third brigades, Kinney's battery of artillery, and a battalion of Wolford's cavalry. The fourth and tenth Kentucky, fourteenth Ohio, and the eighteenth United States infantry, being still in the rear, detained by the almost impassible condition of the roads, I determined to halt at this point to await their arrival, and to communicate with General Schoepf

"The tenth Indiana, Wolford's cavalry, and Kinney's battery took position on the road leading to the enemy's camp. The ninth Ohio and second Minnesota (part of Colonel McCook's brigade) encamped three fourths of a mile to the right, on the Robertsport road.

"Strong pickets were thrown out in the direction of the enemy, beyond where the Somerset and Mill Springs road comes into the main road from my camp to Mill Springs, and a picket of cavalry some distance in advance of the infantry.

"General Schoepf visited me on the day of my arrival, and, after consultation, I directed him to send to my camp Standart's battery, the twelfth Kentucky, and the first and second Tennessee regiments, to remain until the arrival of the regiments in the rear.

"Having received information, on the evening of the 17th, that a large train of wagons, with its escort, was encamped on the Robertsport and Danville road, about six miles from Colonel Stedman's camp, I sent an order to him to send his wagons forward, under a strong guard, and to march with his regiment, (the fourteenth Ohio,) and the tenth Kentucky, (Colonel Harlan,) with one day's rations in their haversacks, to the point where the enemy were said to be encamped, and either capture or disperse them.

"Nothing of importance occurred, from the time of my arrival until the morning of the 19th, except a picket skirmish on the 17th. The fourth Kentucky, the battalion of Michigan engineers, and Wetmore's battery, joined on the 18th. About five and a half o'clock, on the morning of the 19th, the pickets from Wolford's cavalry, encountered the enemy advancing on our camp; retired slowly, and reported their advance to Colonel M. D. Manson, commanding the second brigade. He immediately formed his regiment, (the tenth Indiana,) and took a position on the road, to await the attack, ordering the fourth Kentucky, (Colonel S. S. Fry,) to support him, and then informed me in person that the enemy were advancing in force, and what disposition he had made to resist them. I directed him to join his brigade immediately, and hold the enemy in check until I could order up the other troops, which were ordered to form immediately, and were marching to the field in ten minutes afterward.

"The battalion of Michigan engineers, and Company A, of the thirty-eighth Ohio, Captain

Greenwood, were ordered to remain as guard to the camp.

"Upon my arrival on the field soon afterward, I found the tenth Indiana formed in front of their encampment, apparently awaiting orders, and ordered them forward to the support of the fourth Kentucky, which was the only whole regiment then engaged.

"I then rode forward myself to see the enemy's position, so that I could determine what disposition to make of my troops as they arrived. On reaching the position held by the fourth Kentucky, tenth Indiana, and Wolford's cavalry, at a point where the roads fork, leading to Somerset, I found the enemy advancing through a cornfield, and evidently endeavoring to gain the left of the fourth Kentucky regiment, which was maintaining its position in a most determined manner. I directed one of my aids to ride back, and order up a section of artillery, and the Tennessee brigade to advance on the enemy's right, and sent orders for Colonel McCook to advance, with his two regiments, (the ninth Ohio and second Minnesota,) to the support of the fourth Kentucky and tenth Indiana.

"A section of Kinney's battery took a position on the edge of the field, to the left of the fourth Kentucky, and opened an efficient fire on a regiment of Alabamians, which was advancing on the fourth Kentucky.

"Soon afterwards, the second Minnesota, (H. P. Van Cleve,) the colonel reporting to me for instructions, I directed him to take the position of the fourth Kentucky and tenth Indiana, which regiments were nearly out of ammunition. The ninth Ohio, under the immediate command of Major Kaemmerling, came into position, on the right of the road, at the same time.

"Immediately after the regiments had gained their position, the enemy opened a most determined and galling fire, which was returned by our troops, in the same spirit, and, for nearly half an hour, the contest was maintained, on both sides, in the most obstinate manner. At this time, the twelfth Kentucky (Colonel W. A. Hoskins) and the Tennessee brigade reached the field, to the left of the Minnesota regiment, and opened fire on the right flank of the enemy, who then began to fall back. The second Minnesota kept up a most galling fire in front, and the ninth Ohio charged the enemy on the right, with bayonets fixed, turned their flank, and drove them from the field, the whole line giving way, and retreating in the utmost disorder and confusion.

"As soon as the regiments could be formed, and refill their cartridge-boxes, I ordered the whole force to advance. A few miles in the rear of the battle-field, a small force of cavalry was drawn up near the road, but a few shots from our artillery, (a section of Standart's battery,) dispersed them, and none of the enemy were seen again until we arrived in front of their intrenchments; as we approached their intrenchments the division was deployed in line of battle, and steadily advanced to the summit of the hill at Moulden's.

"From this point I directed their intrenchments to be cannonaded, which was done, until dark, by Standart's and Wetmore's batteries. Kinney's battery was placed in position on the extreme left, at Russell's house, from which point he was directed to fire on their ferry, to deter them from attempting to cross. On the following morning, Captain Wetmore's battery was ordered to Russell's house, and assisted, with his Parrott guns, in firing upon the ferry.

"Colonel Manson's brigade took position on the left, near Kinney's battery, and every preparation was made to assault their intrenchments on the following morning.

"The fourteenth Ohio, Colonel Stedman, and the tenth Kentucky, Colonel Harlan, having joined from detached service, soon after the repulse of the evening, continued with their brigade in the pursuit, although they could not get up in time to join in the fight. General Schoepf also joined me, on the evening of the 19th, with the seventeenth, thirty-first, and thirty-eighth Ohio. His entire brigade entered with the other troops.

"On reaching the intrenchments, we found the enemy had abandoned every thing, and retired during the night. Twelve pieces of artillery, with their caissons packed with ammunition, one battery wagon and two forges, a large amount of ammunition, a large number of small arms, (mostly the old flint-lock muskets,) one hundred and fifty or sixty wagons, and upwards of one thousand horses and mules; a large amount of commissary stores, intrenching tools, and camp and garrison equipage, fell into our hands. A correct list of all the captured property will be forwarded as soon as it can be made up and the property secured.

"The steam and ferry-boats having been burned by the enemy, in their retreat, it was found impossible to cross the river and pursue them; besides, their command was completely demoralized, and retreated with great haste, and in all directions, making their capture, in any numbers, quite doubtful, if pursued. There is no doubt but what the moral effect produced by their complete dispersion, will have a more desired effect, in reëstablishing Union sentiment, than though they had been captured.

"It affords me much pleasure, to be able to testify to the uniform steadiness and good conduct of both officers and men, during the battle, and I respectfully refer to the accompanying reports of the different commanders, for the names of those officers and men whose good conduct was particularly noticed by them. . .

"A number of flags were taken on the field of battle, and in the intrenchments. They will be forwarded to headquarters as soon as collected together.

"The enemy's loss, as far as known, is as follows: Brigadier-General Zollicoffer, Lieutenant Baillie Peyton, and one hundred and ninety officers and non-commissioned officers and privates killed.

"Lieutenant-Colonel W. B. Carter, twentieth Tennessee, Lieutenant J. W. Allen, fifteenth Mississippi, Lieutenant Allan Morse, sixteenth Alabama, and five officers of the medical staff, and eighty-one non-commissioned officers and privates taken prisoners.

"Lieutenant J. E. Patterson, twentieth Tennessee, and A. J. Knapp, fifteenth Mississippi, and sixty-six non-commissioned officers and privates wounded. Making one hundred and ninety-two killed, eighty-nine prisoners not wounded and sixty-two wounded. A total of killed, wounded, and prisoners, of three hundred and forty-nine.

"Our loss is as follows: One commissioned officer and thirty-eight men were killed, and fourteen officers, including Lieutenant Burt, United States infantry, A. D. C., and one hundred and ninety-four men, commissioned officers and privates, wounded.

"A complete list of our killed and wounded, and of the prisoners, is herewith attached.

"I am, sir, very respectfully, your obedient servant.

"General GEORGE H. THOMAS,
"*Brigadier-General U. S. V., commanding.*
"Captain JAMES B. FRY, A. A. G., *Chief of Staff,*
Headquarters Department of the Ohio, Louisville, Ky.

The rebel forces were greatly demoralized by their defeat, and there were charges of treachery against General Crittenden, though there was probably little foundation for them. It was an unexpected check to the rebel advance into the richer counties of Kentucky, and it was an equally great encouragement to the loyal troops and people after a long period of apparent inactivity and want of success.

CHAPTER LIX.

New Military and Naval Expeditions. — Expedition to the Coast of North Carolina. — Preparations and Departure, and Arrival at Hatteras Inlet. — Marine Disasters. — Delay at Hatteras Inlet. — Departure of the Expedition to Roanoke Island. — Entrance into Croatan Sound. — Rebel Gunboats. — Naval Engagement and Bombardment of Rebel Forts. — Landing of Troops. — Advance against the Rebel Positions. — Movement through Swamps and " Impenetrable " Thickets. — The Battle. — The Rebel Position flanked. — Charge upon the Battery. — Flight of the Rebels. — The advance of the Federal Troops. — Flag of Truce and Surrender. — Complete Success of the Expedition. — Official Despatches. — Expedition of Gunboats to Elizabeth City. — Engagement with Rebel Gunboats and Battery. — Defeat of the Rebels and Destruction of their Gunboats. — Official Despatches.

THE government, having determined not to confine military operations to an advance from the north against the rebels, but to make attacks upon some of the most vulnerable and important points on the southern coast, after the capture of the islands at Port Royal entrance, made preparations for two more important expeditions. One of these was organized under Brigadier-General A. E. Burnside of Rhode Island, to effect a landing and gain possession of important positions on the coast of North Carolina, and the other, under Major-General Butler, was designed for operations on the Gulf coast.

General Burnside's forces were collected at Annapolis, Maryland, and were composed chiefly of new regiments just recruited, a large proportion of them being from New England, and they numbered about twenty thousand men. A naval force of twenty-four steam gunboats, of small size, which were under the command of Flag-Officer L. M. Goldsborough, of the North Atlantic blockading fleet, was prepared to coöperate with the land forces. Most of the gunboats had sailed separately from Hampton Roads during the week previous to the sailing of the transports carrying the military forces, to rendezvous at Hatteras Inlet. The land forces embarked at Annapolis, and after lying a short time in Hampton Roads, the large fleet of transports sailed thence on the 13th of January, also for Hatteras Inlet. The expedition, like that for Port Royal, experienced the stormy weather for which the dangerous coast of North Carolina is noted in the winter season, and when the transports arrived off Hatteras Inlet, the heavy swell of the sea and the high wind rendered it exceedingly dangerous for the larger vessels to attempt an entrance through the narrow and shallow cut in the great sand barrier into the sound beyond. Several of the transports, though chartered under an order that they should not exceed a certain draught, were found to be of too deep draught to admit a safe passage over the bar and through the inlet; and in the storm a large number of soldiers were exposed for a time to imminent danger, and the success of the expedition was in some degree imperilled, or at least greatly delayed. One transport, the steamer " City of New York," grounded among the breakers, and though the crew and passengers, after long exposure within sight of the fleet inside the bar, were saved, the vessel and most of her cargo were lost. Several other vessels grounded upon the shoals, and were seriously damaged, but were more fortunate than the City of New York.

After arriving inside of Hatteras Inlet the expedition was delayed three weeks, waiting for ordnance stores and other preparations for active operations in the sound. In the mean time measures were taken to ascertain the position of the rebels, through spies and the slaves, who here, as elsewhere, came off in considerable numbers to the federal fleet. It was ascertained that the rebels were fortified on Roanoke Island, lying between Roanoke Sound on the east, and Croatan Sound on the west, and north of Pamlico Sound, in which the fleet lay. Several armed steamers, and other vessels of small size, were seen in the distance, and it was understood that the rebels had a naval force in these waters under Commander Lynch, formerly of the United States navy, which might prove quite formidable in conjunction with the land batteries. The squadron under Commodore Goldsborough, however, though composed of small vessels adapted for the shallow waters of the sound, was sufficient to meet any naval force which the rebels could possibly bring against him, and to contribute also to the reduction of the fortifications.

All things being at last prepared, the fleet sailed from Hatteras Inlet on the 5th of February, the gunboats in advance, followed by the transports, the whole numbering sixty-five vessels, and presenting a spectacle such as never before had been seen in the waters of North Carolina. A fleet of nearly fifty vessels was still left at Hatteras Inlet, and a considerable force was added to the garrison of the forts at the inlet, or remained on board some of the vessels. The expedition proceeded slowly up the sound, anchoring the first night about ten miles from Roanoke Island. A storm the next day prevented a further advance, navigation at the entrance to Croatan Sound being difficult, and the weather very thick.

On the 7th, however, the gunboats being prepared for action, moved towards the narrow entrance, scarcely more than two hundred feet in width, which is called Roanoke Inlet. It was expected that the rebels had erected batteries to command this narrow and difficult channel, but the fleet passed through without opposition or obstruction. As they sailed up Croatan Sound, six or seven of the rebel gunboats were seen near the shore, as if under cover of the shore batteries. As soon as the federal gunboats came within long range, fire was opened upon the rebel boats, and continued as the fleet moved slowly up the sound, the enemy's vessels soon retiring to the north, as if to draw the attacking boats under the fire of the batteries

erected near the northern end of Roanoke Island. A line of piles and sunken vessels obstructed the main channel opposite the point where the batteries were erected, with a view to prevent the passage of the fleet, and to detain them under the fire of the forts. The rebel boats, by another channel, passed these obstructions, but the federal boats, instead of attempting to pursue them, directed their fire at the batteries, the principal of which was called Fort Barton, and was a strong and well constructed work, and armed with heavy guns. After bombarding the forts for some time, the fire of the latter, which had been ineffective, began to slacken, and it was supposed that the enemy's guns would soon be silenced. But after a short interval the fire from the batteries was renewed with vigor, and with more precision than previously, and the rebel gunboats again approached to join in the engagement, or possibly to flank the federal gunboats, and attack the transports below. Flag-Officer Goldsborough prevented such a movement, if contemplated, by detaching some of his boats to intercept it. At this time the engagement was quite general and spirited. Fire had already been communicated to the rebel barracks, and the fort was enveloped in flames and smoke, but its guns were served with none the less spirit. The largest and best of the enemy's gunboats was also disabled, and being run ashore, was set on fire by the crew and destroyed.

Shortly after, the fire of the rebel batteries nearly ceased, and the transports having all passed through Roanoke Inlet into the sound, measures were taken for landing the troops for an assault. But when several of the federal gunboats were withdrawn from their advanced position in order to cover the debarkation, the rebel boats and batteries renewed the contest. The landing of the troops, however, was not delayed, and was very successfully made at a cove called Ashby's Harbor, a point about two miles south of Fort Barton. The landing commenced just at nightfall on the 7th, and before the next morning nearly the whole division had been put on shore.

On the morning of the 8th, a few shots were exchanged between the federal gunboats and the rebel batteries, but the rebel gunboats had all disappeared in the night, and did not again make their appearance. The land forces were early prepared for an advance upon the rebel positions, which General Burnside had pretty definitely ascertained. The force was divided into three columns; the centre, composed of the twenty-fifth, twenty-third, and twenty-seventh Massachusetts, and tenth Connecticut regiments, was commanded by Brigadier-General Foster; the left flanking column, consisting of the twenty-first Massachusetts, fifty-first New York, ninth New Jersey, and fifty-first Pennsylvania regiments, was commanded by Brigadier-General Reno; and the right flanking column, formed by the fourth and part of the fifth Rhode Island, and ninth New York regiments, was commanded by Brigadier-General Parke. With the centre was a battery of six twelve-pounder boat howitzers from the navy. The approach to the rebel position was through a swamp, covered with a thick growth of wood, and rendered almost impassable by the dense underwood. Upon a narrow cart road through this swamp the rebels had constructed a field work, which completely commanded that road, and for the protection of their flanks they relied upon the swamps and thickets which they considered impenetrable. The federal troops, however, did not find the swamps and bushes an insurmountable obstacle; but while the centre column moved along the road, the flanking columns struck boldly into the swamp, and by perseverance and determination, advanced so as to support the central column, and eventually to flank and surprise the enemy. For some distance in front of the rebel battery, the woods had been cut down, so that their guns could have fair play upon an attacking force, and imme- diately in front was a pond, or natural moat, which added to the strength of the work against a direct assault.

Early in the march the central column met with the rebel pickets, and skirmishers annoyed the troops, but fell back before their steady advance. The battery of howitzers, which headed General Foster's column, having reached a curve in the road, from which the rebel works were seen directly across the clearing, opened fire upon them, and continued a vigorous cannonade until the ammunition was exhausted. In the mean time the infantry of the several columns was brought up, the flanking columns had penetrated the swampy thickets, and the centre was soon engaged in a musketry conflict with a body of the enemy thrown out to flank them. These rebel troops were soon compelled to retreat before the federal forces, whose steady advance neither the musketry nor artillery of the enemy appeared to prevent. For a time there was quite a fierce contest, the advantage of protection and position being greatly in favor of the rebels. But as the centre advanced, and forced back the rebel force sent to flank them, the flanking columns of Generals Reno and Parke succeeded in overcoming all obstacles to their advance, and the forces of the former surprised the rebels by a sudden charge from the swamp on which they had relied for protection. An assault from a portion of General Parke's force was made about the same time, and before the advance of the three columns, where they had looked for but one, the rebels fled from their works precipitately.

The federal troops soon followed the retreating rebels, supposing that they had retired to a stronger position behind more formidable batteries. But the battle was over, and the victory was won. A very slight resistance was made by the pickets of one of the rebel camps, and then the force, a North Carolina regiment, surrendered unconditionally to General Reno.

Soon after, General Foster's force approached another camp of the rebel forces, and was met by a flag of truce, the officer who accompanied it asking what terms would be granted. An unconditional surrender was demanded; and while the rebels yet delayed to reply to this demand, General Foster advanced his troops to enforce it. He was met by Colonel Shaw, the commander of the rebel forces, who surrendered his whole command, and the forts of Roanoke Island. The number of rebel troops thus surrendered was about twenty-five hundred; the batteries captured numbered more than thirty guns, many of large calibre, and rifled; their camps were composed of comfortable wooden barracks, and the camp equipage and stores were very considerable. This success was accomplished not without severe labor and indomitable energy on the part of the federal troops, as well as an unequal exposure to the fire of the enemy, by which their loss greatly exceeded that of the rebels. The entire loss of the latter was but about forty in killed and wounded, while the federal loss was about thirty-five killed and nearly two hundred wounded and missing. On board the fleet during the bombardment and the fight with the rebel gunboats, the loss in killed and wounded was about thirty. The following are the brief despatches of General Burnside and Flag-Officer Goldsborough, announcing the victory which they had achieved: —

"HEADQUARTERS DEPARTMENT OF NORTH CAROLINA, }
"ROANOKE ISLAND, Feb. 10, 1862. }

"MAJOR-GENERAL GEORGE B. McCLELLAN, COMMANDING U. S. ARMY, WASHINGTON: I have the honor to report that a combined attack upon this island was commenced on the morning of the 7th by the naval and military forces of this expedition, which has resulted in the capture of six forts, forty guns, over two thousand prisoners, and upwards of three thousand small

58

arms. Among the prisoners are Colonel Shaw, commander of the island, and O. Jennings Wise, commander of the Wise Legion. The latter was mortally wounded, and has since died. The whole work was finished on the afternoon of the 8th, after a hard day's fighting, by a brilliant charge in the centre of the island, and a rapid pursuit of the enemy to the north end of the island, resulting in the capture of the prisoners mentioned above. We have had no time to count them, but the number is estimated at nearly three thousand.

"Our men fought bravely, and have endured most manfully the hardships incident to fighting through swamps and dense thickets. It is impossible to give the details of the engagement, or to mention meritorious officers and men in the short time allowed for writing this report, the naval vessel carrying it starting immediately for Hampton Roads, and the report of the brigadier-generals not yet having been handed in. It is enough to say that the officers and men of both arms of the service have fought gallantly, and the plans agreed upon before leaving Hatteras were carried out.

"I will be excused for saying in reference to the action, that I owe every thing to Generals Foster, Reno, and Parke, as more full details will show. I am sorry to report the loss of about thirty-five killed and about two hundred wounded, ten of them probably mortally. Among the killed are Colonel Russell of the tenth Connecticut, and Lieutenant-Colonel Victor De Monteuil of the D'Epineuil Zouaves. Both of them fought most gallantly. I regret exceedingly not being able to send a full report of the killed and wounded, but will send a despatch in a day or two with full returns.

"I beg leave to enclose a copy of a general order issued by me on the 9th.

"I am most happy to say that I have just received a message from Commodore Goldsborough, stating that the expedition of his gun-boats against Elizabeth City and the rebel fleet has been entirely successful. He will, of course, send his returns to his department.

"I have the honor to be, General,
            "Your obedient servant,
    "A. E. BURNSIDE, *Brigadier-General,*
"*Commanding Departmant of North Carolina.*"

"UNITED STATES FLAG SHIP PHILADELPHIA, ⎬
        "OFF ROANOKE ISLAND, Feb. 9. ⎭

"Roanoke Island is ours. Its military authorities struck to us yesterday. Their means of defence were truly formidable, and were used with a determination worthy of a better cause. They consisted of two elaborately constructed works, mounting twenty-two heavy guns, three being one hundred pounders, rifled, and other batteries mounting twenty guns, a large proportion of these, also, being of heavy calibre, and some rifled, eight steamers of two guns each, and each with a rifled gun with a diameter of a thirty-two pounder.

"We encountered prolonged obstructions of sunken vessels and piles to thwart our advance.

"A body of men numbering scarcely less than five thousand are now our prisoners.

"Fighting commenced on the morning of the 7th, at seven o'clock, and continued until dark. It was resumed next morning early, lasting until well into the afternoon, when by a bold charge of our army the rebel flag was made to succumb, and our own was hoisted every where on the island. No attack could have been more completely executed, and it was carried out precisely in accordance with the arrangements made before the expedition left Hatteras. Detailed accounts of the naval operations will be forwarded hereafter.

"I submit herewith a general order to be read on the quarter-deck of each vessel.

        "Respectfully,   J. M. GOLDSBOROUGH.
"To Hon. GIDEON WELLES."

The day after the victory at Roanoke Island a naval expedition, consisting of fourteen small steamers, was despatched by Flag-officer Goldsborough in pursuit of the rebel gunboats, which it was supposed had gone to Elizabeth City, a town at the head of one of the arms of Albemarle Sound, and connected with Norfolk by the canal through the Dismal Swamp. On the morning of the 10th of February, this flotilla, which was under Commander S. C. Rowan, sailed up the arm or river towards Elizabeth City, and soon discovered several rebel gunboats, to which chase was immediately given. As the pursuers approached the city, where the river narrows, a battery of four guns was discovered, while another gun in the city completely commanded the channel. The federal commander did not hesitate, but engaged at once the rebel gunboats and batteries, closing in upon them gradually, and sending a storm of shot and shell from his little squadron. In twenty minutes from the time of opening fire a rebel schooner struck her colors, and a signal was made from the battery for the crews of the rebel steamers to abandon their vessels. They were immediately run close to the shore and set on fire, and though the federal gunboats were soon near them, only one was saved from destruction, and captured. The battery was abandoned at the same time as the boats, and the fugitive rebels then set fire to many buildings in the town, wantonly destroying much valuable private property. The success of the expedition was complete, the greater part of the rebel naval force in the waters of North Carolina having been destroyed or captured. This was accomplished with the loss of but two killed and twelve wounded, and with but little damage to the federal vessels. Flag-officer Goldsborough announced this success in the following despatch, enclosing the brief report of Commander Rowan: —

"SIR: Just as I closed my despatch to you yesterday, I received reliable information that the rebel steamers which escaped had gone to Elizabeth City. I immediately ordered Commander Rowan to take thirteen of our steamers and go in pursuit; also to deploy up the North River, a link of the Albemarle and Chesapeake Canal. He dashed off with a whole heart at his work, and the way he has already accomplished the first part of it his preliminary report will inform you. I have decided to send the Stars and Stripes to Hampton Roads tomorrow for ammunition. Mr. Van Brunt, my secretary, will deliver the despatches and two rebel flags to you.

"J. M. GOLDSBOROUGH."

"To Hon. GIDEON WELLES, *Secretary of the Navy.*"

"STEAMER DELAWARE, ⎱
"OFF ELIZABETH CITY, *Feb.* 10. ⎰

"I have the happiness to report that I met the enemy off this place at nine o'clock this morning. After a very sharp engagement we succeeded in destroying and capturing his entire naval force, and silencing and destroying his battery on Cobb's Point. The only vessel saved from destruction is the steamer Ellis, Captain Cook, who is wounded, and with the other prisoners.

"I am happy to say that our casualties are few. Two or three were killed and about the same number wounded. I send the steamer Ellis to you under command of Acting Master Chase, whom I hope you will confirm in the command.

"The conduct of the gallant men I have the honor to command is worthy of all praise.

"I am happy to say that none of our vessels were severely injured.

"I shall leave a small force here and visit the canals, to take a look into other places, before I return.

"Your obedient servant,

"J. C. ROWAN."

CHAPTER LX.

Active Military Operations. — Policy of the Administration. — Order of the President. — Movements at the West. — Rebel Position at Columbus and •Bowling Green. — Movement against Fort Henry. — Military Dispositions. — Advance of the Gunboats. — The attack and the Battle. — The Fort surrendered. — Report of Flag-Officer Foote. — Expedition up the Tennessee. — Destruction of Rebel Boats and Property. — Federal Gunboats at Florence, Alabama. — Union Sentiment among the People. — Lieutenant Phelps's official Report of the Expedition.

SOON after the departure of General Burnside's expedition to North Carolina there were indications that active movements were to be made in other quarters, and that in the spring there would be an advance against the rebels from all directions. The people, hardly yet realizing the · magnitude of the work before them, had become more and more impatient of the long comparative inactivity, and demanded every where an aggressive policy. The sailing of General Burnside's expedition encouraged the belief that the long delay and the extensive preparations were ended, and even before the first success of this expedition had cheered the hearts of the loyal people, a campaign more stirring, if not more important, had opened at the west.

The administration had determined to respond to the call of the people for a vigorous prosecution of the war, and the accession of Mr. Stanton to the war department was followed by a more active and energetic conduct of military affairs. A general plan of operations was adopted, and in the latter part of January the President, for the purpose of carrying it into effect, issued the following order:

"EXECUTIVE MANSION, ⎱
"WASHINGTON, *January* 22, 1862. ⎰

"Ordered, that the 22d day of February, 1862, be the day for the general movement of the land and naval forces of the United States against the insurgent forces; that especially the army at and about Fortress Monroe, the army of the Potomac, the army of Western Virginia, the army near Munfordsville, Kentucky, the army and flotilla at Cairo, and a naval force in the Gulf of Mexico, be ready for a movement on that day; and that all the other forces, both land and naval, with their respective commanders, obey existing orders for the time, and be ready to obey additional orders when duly given; that the heads of departments, and especially the Secretaries of War and the Navy, with all their subordinates, and the General-in-Chief, with all other subordinates of the land and naval forces, will severally be held to their strict and full responsibilities for the prompt execution of this order.

"ABRAHAM LINCOLN."

At the West, at least, the preparations for active operations were already in an advanced state, and before the time named in the President's order the army and flotilla at Cairo, the army at Munfordsville, and the army in Missouri, were ready for the campaign. The position and movements of the rebel forces, against whom these armies were to act, made it necessary to open the campaign at an early day. The army in the vicinity of Cairo belonged to the department of General Halleck, but was under the immediate command of Major-General U. S. Grant, and the flotilla was commanded by Flag-Officer A. H. Foote, under whose direction and vigorous management this formidable branch of the service had been prepared. The army near Munfordsville was under the command of Major-General D. C. Buell. The strong positions of the rebels in Kentucky were at Bowling Green, where they posted in formidable works, at Columbus on the Mississippi River, a position of great strength by nature and elaborately fortified, at Fort Donelson on the Cumberland River, and at Fort Henry on the Tennessee River. The army of General Buell was to operate against the enemy near Bowling Green, and the forces of General Grant, with the gunboats under Flag-Officer Foote, were to move against the rebel positions in Western Kentucky. .

The rebel position at Columbus, which commanded the Mississippi, and until reduced would prevent any movement down that river, was a very strong one, and presented obstacles which it would be difficult to overcome in a direct attack upon the place. The gunboats had several times approached Columbus and exchanged shots with the forts at long range, and with several rebel gunboats which were stationed in the vicinity. A reconnoisance in force had also been made by the army, but if a direct attack upon the stronghold was contemplated, a strategical movement which should more easily accomplish the object, the opening of the Mississippi at this point, was finally determined upon. This was an advance against Forts Henry and Donelson, by which the federal army could reach the rear of the rebel forces at Columbus, so that they would be compelled to evacuate that position or be exposed to a more disadvantageous attack, their communication with the heavier forces at Bowling Green being cut off.

The first movement was up the Tennessee River against Fort Henry, which was constructed on the right bank of that river, about seventy miles from the Ohio and near the northern boundary of Tennessee. It was erected to protect the railroad which crosses the river a few miles above, by which the rebels kept open their communications between their forces in Western Kentucky and their base in Tennessee. The fort was a well constructed earthwork, mounted with twenty guns and several mortars, and though not protected by bomb proofs, was considered by the rebel officers as sufficiently strong for its purpose. It was not, however, calculated to withstand a bombardment from the heavily armed gunboats of the federal flotilla, and it would seem that the rebel officers had hardly contemplated such an attack. Two or three light-armed steamers, which they had upon the river, they evidently supposed would be sufficient, in conjunction with the fort, to repel any federal force which should be sent in this direction. They were not then aware of the efficiency of the flotilla which had been prepared by the federal government, several of the boats of which were partially iron clad, and all of them well armed.

The movement was kept a secret more successfully than some previous federal expeditions, and the real point of attack for which the preparations were being made did not appear to the enemy until the attacking force was well on its way. On the 3d of February a force of ten thousand men was embarked on board of transports at Cairo and Paducah, and under convoy of four iron clad gunboats and three others, proceeded up the Tennessee River. On the 5th the transports remained at a point about ten miles below Fort Henry, while a portion of the gunboats proceeded up the river slowly, shelling the woods as they went, in order to discover any concealed battery or camp of the rebels. The fire of the fort was at length drawn upon the boats, and the rebel position and the range of their guns were ascertained. The transports then proceeded to a point about four miles from the fort, where the troops disembarked and encamped for the night. On the morning of the 6th the land forces were divided into three columns, one being sent to take possession of the roads leading east to Fort Donelson and Dover, in order to intercept reënforcements and to cut off the retreat of the garrison of Fort Henry and the forces in the camp near by; another to the west side of the river to take possession of the heights commanding the fort on that side; while the third was to be prepared for an assault on the enemy's works, or to join the column first named, as occasion might require. The time assigned for the movement of the several divisions was a comparatively late hour, all the troops not having arrived at the point of landing when the orders of General Grant were issued. The land forces, in consequence of this, did not take any part in the conflict of the day or share in the honor of the victory.

The gunboats moved up the river at the appointed time, and soon opened fire upon the fort, gradually approaching until they reached within six hundred yards of the rebel works. The guns of the fort were well manned, and replied to the fire from the gunboats rapidly and with some effect. A ball struck the boilers of the gunboat Essex, disabling the engine, and severely scalding the commander and a large number of the crew. The Essex was consequently obliged to drop down the river, while the other three armored boats continued the attack, supported at some distance by the wooden gunboats. The boats were repeatedly struck by the shots from the fort, but sustained no material damage or loss of men, the shots falling almost harmless from the iron clad casemates. On the other hand the shot and shell from the boats, which were discharged with great rapidity and precision, evidently had a very damaging effect upon the fort. Its embankment was ploughed up, the sand bags and gabions with which its guns were protected were knocked in pieces, several of its guns were dismounted or damaged, and the shells bursting over the garrison, who were unprotected by casemates, spread wounds and consternation among them. In an intrenched camp outside the fort a considerable part of the rebel force was posted. Some of the shot and shells from the boats falling in the midst of these troops, they scattered and fled, leaving their arms and equipments. The troops in the fort, however, were held to their work by the determination of their officers and by the guard stationed to prevent their escape. The defence of the fort was continued till there were but four guns which could be brought to bear upon the flotilla, and as the fire of the latter became more and more damaging as the boats came within three or four hundred yards, the rebel commander, General Tilghman, considered a further contest useless, and the flag was lowered. The firing immediately ceased, and in one hour and a quarter from the commencement of the bombardment the victory was won by the flotilla, the federal land forces not yet having reached the positions to which they were ordered, on account of the bad condition of the roads and the high water of the streams. A boat was sent ashore, and the national flag was soon raised over the captured fort, amid the most enthusiastic cheers of the crews of the gunboats. After a brief parley General Tilghman surrendered, with the garrison, to Flag-Officer Foote, all his other troops, except a few stragglers afterwards picked up, having escaped. When the troops of General Grant at last arrived at the fort, the works and the prisoners were transferred to him, and dispositions were at once made to hold the post, the loss of which was a serious damage to the rebels, and opened a passage through their line of fortifications to the rear of some of their important positions.

The following is the official report of Flag-Officer Foote in relation to this engagement and victory : —

"Cairo, Ill., Feb. 7, 1862.

"Sir: I have the honor to report that on the 6th inst., at 12½ o'clock, P. M., I made an attack on Fort Henry, on the Tennessee River, with the iron clad gunboats Cincinnati, Commander Stembel, the flag-ship, the Essex, Commander Porter, the Carondolet, Commander Walker, and the St. Louis, Lieutenant Spaulding ; also taking with me the three old gunboats Conestoga, Lieutenant-Commanding Phelps, the Tyler, Lieutenant-Commanding Gwin, and the Lexington, Lieutenant-Commanding Shirk, as a second division, in command of Lieutenant-Commanding Phelps, which took a position astern and in shore of the armed boats, doing good execution there in the action, while the armed boats were placed in the first order of steaming, approaching the fort in a parallel line.

"The fire was opened at seventeen hundred yards distance from the flag-ship, which was followed by the other gunboats, and responded to by the fort. As we approached the fort, slow steaming till we reached within six hundred yards of the rebel batteries, the fire from both gunboats and fort increased in rapidity and accuracy of range. At twenty minutes before the flag was struck, the Essex unfortunately received a shot in her boilers, which resulted in the wounding and scalding of twenty-nine officers and men, including Commander Porter, as will be seen in the enclosed list of casualties. The Essex then necessarily dropped out of the line astern, entirely disabled, and unable to continue the fight in which she had so gallantly participated until the sad catastrophe.

"The firing continued with unabated rapidity and effect upon the three gunboats as they continued still to approach the fort with their destructive fire, until the rebel flag was hauled down, after a very severe and closely contested action of one hour and fifteen minutes.

"A boat containing the adjutant-general and the captain of engineers came alongside after the flag was lowered, and reported that General Lloyd Tilghman, the commander of the fort, wished to communicate with the flag-officer, when I despatched Commander Stembel and Lieutenant-Commanding Phelps, with orders to hoist the American flag where the secession ensign had been flying, and to inform General Tilghman that I would see him on board the flag-ship. He came on board soon after the Union had been substituted for the rebel flag on the fort, and possession taken of it. I received the general and his staff and some sixty or seventy men as prisoners, and a hospital ship containing sixty invalids, together with the fort and its effects, mounting twenty guns, mostly of heavy calibre, with barracks and tents capable of accommodating fifteen thousand men, and sundry articles which, as I turned the fort and its effects over to General Grant, commanding the army, on his arrival in an hour after we had made the capture, he will be enabled to give the government a more correct statement of them than I am enabled to communicate from the short time I had possession of the fort.

"The plan of attack, so far as the army reaching the rear of the fort to make a demonstration simultaneously with the navy, was frustrated by the excessively muddy roads and the high stage of water, preventing the arrival of our troops until sometime after I had taken possession of the fort.

"On securing the prisoners and making the necessary preliminary arrangements, I despatched Lieutenant-Commanding Phelps with his division up the Tennessee River, as I had previously directed, and as will be seen in the enclosed orders to him, to remove the rails and so far render the bridge of the railroad for transportation and communication between Bowling Green and Columbus useless, and afterwards to pursue the rebel gunboats and secure their capture if possible. This being accomplished, and the army in possession of the fort, and my services being indispensable at Cairo, I left Fort Henry in the evening of the same day, with the Cincinnati, Essex, and St. Louis, and arrived here this morning.

"The armed gunboats resisted effectually the shot of the enemy when striking the casemate. The Cincinnati, flag-ship, received thirty-one shots, the Essex fifteen, and the Carondolet six, killing one and wounding nine in the Cincinnati, and one in the Essex, while the casualties in the latter from steam amounted to twenty-eight in number. The Carondolet and St. Louis met with no casualties. The steamers were admirably handled by the officers, presenting only their bow guns to the enemy, to avoid the exposure of the vulnerable parts of their vessels.

"Lieutenant-Commanding Phelps, with his division, also executed my orders very effectually, and promptly proceeded up the river in their further execution after the capture of the fort. In fact, all the officers and men gallantly performed their duty, and considering the little experience they have had under fire, far more than realized my expectations.

"Fort Henry was defended with the most determined gallantry by General Tilghman, worthy of a better cause, who, from his own account, went into action with eleven guns of heavy calibre bearing upon our boats, which fought until seven of the number were dismantled or otherwise rendered useless.

"I have the honor to be, very respectfully,
"Your obedient servant,
"A. H. FOOTE, *Flag-Officer.*
"To Hon. GIDEON WELLS, *Secretary of the Navy, Washington, D. C.*"

General Grant in his official report to General Halleck, stated that he believed the rebel forces must have commenced a retreat from their camp the night previous to the attack on Fort Henry, or early in the morning of that day. The probability, however, is, that they hastily fled when they found that the attack was too powerful for the fort to withstand. General Grant's purpose was, had he not felt it an imperative necessity to attack the fort that day, to have invested the fort completely before opening the attack, so as to secure the capture of the whole rebel force. But it was not probable that the result would have been different, or the victory more decisive or advantageous to the federal cause.

Fort Henry having been taken, Flag-Officer Foote sent three of his gunboats up the river for the purpose of destroying the railroad bridge on the line of rebel communication, and the rebel steamers, and to make a reconnois-sance into the state of Tennessee. These boats, under command of Lieutenant Phelps, accomplished the object for which they were despatched very successfully. Having passed and destroyed the railroad bridge, with some camp equipage in the vicinity, Lieutenant Phelps gave chase to several steamers loaded with military stores, and after a pursuit of some hours compelled the crews to abandon and burn them. One of the boats had on board several submarine batteries or "torpedoes," intended to be sunk in the river for the destruction of the federal boats, and another was loaded with a large quantity of powder and other ordnance stores. These caused a fearful explosion, which completely destroyed the boats and a dwelling house near by, while the woods upon the banks of the river for a long distance were cut and torn as if by a heavy cannonade. Proceeding up the river the expedition destroyed other boats, one of which was being prepared for a gunboat, and continned its course as far as Florence, Alabama, the head of navigation, where the rebels destroyed other of their boats upon the approach of the federal gunboats. Every where along the banks of the river they found loyal Union men, who hailed with joy the flag of their country, and numbers expressed a desire to join the federal forces. The most gratifying result of the expedition was the discovery of so strong and so general a sentiment of loyalty among the people in this portion of the revolted states. The following report of Lieutenant Phelps gives an interesting account of the expedition, and of the development of this loyal sentiment:

"UNITED STATES GUNBOAT CONESTOGA,
"TENNESSEE RIVER, Feb. 10, 1862.

"SIR: Soon after the surrender of Fort Henry on the 6th instant, I proceeded, in obedience to your order, up the Tennessee River with

the Tyler, Lieutenant-Commanding Gwin, Lexington, Lieutenant-Commanding Shirk, and this vessel, forming a division of the flotilla, and arrived after dark at the railroad crossing, twenty-five miles above the fort, having on the way destroyed a small amount of camp equipage abandoned by the flying rebels. The draw of the bridge was found closed and the machinery for turning it disabled. About half a mile above were several rebel transport steamers escaping up stream.

"A party was landed, and in one hour I had the satisfaction to see the draw open. The Tyler, being the slowest of the gunboats, Lieutenant-Commanding Gwin landed a force to destroy a portion of the railroad track, and to secure such military stores as might be found, while I directed Lieutenant-Commanding Shirk to follow me with all speed in chase of the fleeing boats. In five hours this boat succeeded in forcing the rebels to abandon and burn those of their boats loaded with military stores. The first one fired (Samuel Orr) had on board a quantity of submarine batteries, which very soon exploded. The second one was freighted with powder, cannon, shot, grape, balls, &c. Fearing an explosion from the fired boats — there were two together — I had stopped at a distance of one thousand yards; but even there our skylights were broken by the concussion, the light upper deck was raised bodily, doors were forced open, and locks and fastenings every where broken.

"The whole river for half a mile round about was completely "beaten up" by. the falling fragments, and the shower of shot, grape, balls, &c. The house of a reported Union man was blown to pieces, and it is suspected there was design in landing the boats in front of the doomed house. The Lexington having fallen behind, and being without a pilot on board, I concluded to wait for both of the boats to come up. Joined by them we proceeded up the river. Lieutenant-Commanding Gwin had destroyed some of the trestle work of the end of the bridge, burning with them lots of camp equipage. J. N. Brown, formerly a lieutenant in the navy, now signing himself C. S. N., had fled with such precipitation as to leave his papers behind. These Lieutenant-Commanding Gwin brought away, and I send them to you, as they give an official history of the rebel floating preparations on the Mississippi, Cumberland, and Tennessee. Lieutenant Brown had charge of the construction of gunboats.

"At night on the 7th we arrived at a landing in Hardin county, Tennessee, known as Cerro Gordo, where we found the steamer Eastport being converted into a gunboat. Armed boat crews were immediately sent on board, and search made for means of destruction that might have been devised. She had been scuttled, and the suction pipes broken. These leaks were soon stopped. A number of rifle shots were fired at our vessels, but a couple of shells dispersed the rebels. On examination I found that there were large quantities of timber and lumber prepared for fitting up the Eastport; that the vessel itself — some two hundred and eighty feet long — was in excellent condition and already half finished; considerable of the plating designed for her was lying on the bank, and every thing at hand to complete her. I therefore directed Lieutenant-Commanding Gwin to remain with the Tyler to guard the prize and to load the lumber, &c., while the Lexington and Conestoga should proceed still higher up.

"Soon after daylight on the 8th we passed Eastport, Mississippi, and at Chickasaw, further up near the state line, seized two steamers, the Sallie Wood and Muscle — the former laid up and the latter freighted with iron — destined for Richmond and for rebel use. We then proceeded on up the river, entering the state of Alabama, and ascending to Florence at the foot of the Muscle Shoals. On coming in sight of the town three steamers were discovered, which

were immediately set on fire by the rebels. Some shots were fired from the opposite side of the river below. A force was landed, and considerable quantities of supplies marked 'Fort Henry,' were secured from the burning wrecks. Some had been landed and stored. These I seized, putting such as we could bring away on our vessels, and destroying the remainder. No flats or other craft could be found. I found, also, more of the iron and plating intended for the Eastport.

"A deputation of citizens of Florence waited upon me, first desiring that they might be made able to quiet the fears of their wives and daughters with assurances from me that they would not be molested ; and secondly, praying that I would not destroy their railroad bridge. As for the first, I told them we were neither ruffians nor savages, and that we were there to protect them from violence and to enforce the law ; and with reference to the second, that if the bridge were away we could ascend no higher, and that it could possess no military importance, so far as I saw, as it simply connected Florence itself with the railroad on the south bank of the river.

"We had seized three of their steamers, one the half-finished gunboat, and had forced the rebels to burn six others loaded with supplies, and their loss, with that of the freight, is a heavy blow to the enemy. Two boats are still known to be on the Tennessee, and are doubtless hidden in some of the creeks, where we shall be able to find them when there is time for the search. We returned on the night of the 8th to where the Eastport lay. The crew of the Tyler had already gotten on board of the prize an immense amount of lumber, &c. The crews of the three boats set to work to finish the undertaking, and we have brought away probably two hundred and fifty thousand feet of the best quality of ship and building lumber, all the iron, machinery, spikes, plating, nails, &c., belonging to the rebel gunboats, and

I caused the mill to be destroyed where the lumber had been sawed.

"Lieutenant-Commanding Gwin had in our absence enlisted some twenty-five Tennesseeans, who gave information of the encampment of Colonel Drew's rebel regiment at Savannah, Tennessee. A portion of the six or seven hundred men were known to be "pressed" men, and all were badly armed. After consultation with Lieutenants-Commanding Gwin and Shirk, I determined to make a land attack upon the encampment. Lieutenant-Commanding Shirk, with thirty riflemen, came on board the Conestoga, leaving his vessel to guard the Eastport, and accompanied by the Tyler we proceeded up to that place, prepared to land one hundred and thirty riflemen and a twelve-pounder rifle howitzer. Lieutenant-Commander Gwin took command of this force when landed, but had the mortification to find the camp deserted.

"The rebels had fled at one o'clock in the night, leaving considerable quantities of arms, clothing, shoes, camp utensils, provisions, implements, &c., all of which were secured or destroyed, and their winter quarters of log huts were burned. I seized also a large mail bag, and send you the letters giving military information. The gunboats were then dropped down to a point where arms, gathered under the rebel "press law," had been stored, and an armed party under Second-Master Goudy, of the Tyler, succeeded in seizing about seventy rifles and fowling pieces. Returning to Cerro Gordo we took the Eastport, Sallie Wood, and Muscle in tow, and came down the river to the railroad crossing. The Muscle sprang a leak, and all efforts failing to prevent her sinking, we were forced to abandon her, and with her a considerable quantity of fine lumber. We are having trouble in getting through the draw of the bridge here.

"I now come to the, to me, most interesting portion of this report — one which has already become lengthy; but I must trust you will find some excuse for this in the fact that it embraces a history of labors and movements, day and night, from the 6th to the 10th of the month, all of which details I deem it proper to give you. We have met with the most gratifying proofs of loyalty every where across Tennessee and in the portions of Mississippi and Alabama we visited. Most affecting instances greeted us almost hourly. Men, women, and children several times gathered in crowds of hundreds, shouted their welcome, and hailed their national flag with an enthusiasm there was no mistaking; it was genuine and heartfelt. Those people braved every thing to go to the river bank, where a sight of their flag might once more be enjoyed, and they have experienced, as they related, every possible form of persecution. Tears flowed freely down the cheeks of men as well as of women, and there were those who had fought under the stars and stripes at Moultrie who in this manner testified to their joy.

"This display of feeling and sense of gladness at our success, and the hopes it created in the breasts of so many people in the heart of the confederacy, astonished us not a little, and I assure you, sir, I would not have failed to witness it for any consideration. I trust it has given us all a higher sense of the sacred character of our present duties. I was assured at Savannah that of the several hundred troops there, more than one half, had we gone to the attack in time, would have hailed us as deliverers, and gladly enlisted with the national force.

"In Tennessee the people generally, in their enthusiasm, braved secessionists, and spoke their views freely, but in Mississippi and Alabama what was said was guarded. 'If we dared express ourselves freely, you would hear such a shout greeting your coming as you never heard.' 'We know there are many Unionists among us, but a reign of terror makes us afraid of our shadows.' We were told, too, 'Bring us a small, organized force, with arms and ammunition for us, and we can maintain our position, and put down rebellion in our midst.' There were, it is true, whole communities who, on our approach, fled to the woods, but these were where there was less of the loyal element, and where the fleeing steamers in advance had spread tales of our coming with firebrands, burning, destroying, ravishing, and plundering.

" The crews of these vessels have had a very laborious time, but have evinced a spirit in the work highly creditable to them. Lieutenants-Commanding Gwin and Shirk have been untiring, and I owe to them and to their officers many obligations for our entire success.

" I am, respectfully, your obedient servant,
"S. L. PHELPS,
" *Lieutenant-commanding, U. S. N.*
" Flag-Officer A. H. FOOTE, U. S. N.,
" *Commanding Naval Forces Western Waters.*"

CHAPTER LXI.

AFTER the capture of Fort Henry, additional federal forces were sent to that point, and General Grant made preparations to move against the stronger and more important rebel position

at Fort Donelson, near the small town of Dover, on the Cumberland River, and about twelve miles east of Fort Henry. Before his entire command had arrived at the latter place, General Grant ordered a part of it, about eight thousand men, who were on the way up the Tennessee River in transports, to return down the river, and then proceed up the Cumberland, convoyed by the gunboats, to a point a few miles below Fort Donelson. With about fifteen thousand men and some sixteen batteries of artillery, he then marched from Fort Henry, on the 12th of February, across the country, to attack the rebel stronghold, arranging his plans so that the troops sent by the boats should land at about the same time that he brought the others into position for the intended attack. The weather was mild and pleasant, and the roads were in excellent condition for the season, so that the several columns in which the army moved made good progress, and met with no obstacles or inconveniences to dampen the ardor and confidence of victory with which they entered upon the campaign.

Fort Donelson was a position of great strength. As the key to the Cumberland River, by which, during the high stages of the water, the federal forces and the gunboats, which had already created a salutary fear among the rebels of the west, could advance into the heart of Tennessee, the rebel generals had expended much labor and skill in attempting to make it impregnable. At a slight bend in the river, a short distance below Dover, they had constructed two water batteries nearly down to the water's edge, one of which was mounted with nine heavy guns and the other with three, all of which commanded the river for a long distance. These guns were protected by breastworks of great thickness, and were in such a favorable position that they were considered by the rebel officers as capable of preventing the advance of any gunboats or transports that might attempt to ascend the river. Back of these batteries the banks of the river rise rather abruptly, and, a mile below the village of Dover, form a bluff or hill about one hundred feet above the water, on which Fort Donelson itself was constructed. It was an irregular earthwork, which enclosed nearly a hundred acres. It contained only a very few heavy guns, but as the work was designed to protect a land force which should occupy this position, it could be defended by field artillery, both within the intrenchments, in the outworks, and upon the natural ridges, by which the surface west of the fort is broken. Immediately around the fort the timber was cleared so as to expose any storming party to the unobstructed fire of the rebel guns. Beyond this clearing were woods, which at the west of the fort had been cut down in some places and formed into formidable abatis. These abatis rendered an advance upon that side exceedingly difficult and dangerous, but were also found an obstruction to the movement of the rebels themselves. Still beyond the abatis, and nearly a mile from the fort, rifle pits, with occasional breastworks, extended along the top of high ridges almost entirely around the position, from the river bank above the village nearly to the river again a mile below the fort.

Within these works there were about eighteen thousand rebel troops, under command of Generals Floyd, Pillow, Buckner, and Bushrod Johnson, well supplied with field artillery in addition to the heavy guns of the fort and batteries. Upon the surrender of Fort Henry reënforcements had been hurried from Bowling Green to assist in defending and holding this point of vital importance for the safety of rebellion in Tennessee, and, if occasion offered, to recapture Fort Henry. With this force it was confidently expected that any federal force which could be brought against the position would be repulsed and defeated. The event, however, proved that the plans of the federal commander, and the numbers and bravery of his troops, were too formidable for the strength of the rebel position, the skill of their officers, or the courage and dash of their soldiers.

The country west of the fort, through which the army of General Grant advanced, is undulating and thickly wooded, the hills varying in height from one hundred to three hundred feet, and separated by narrow valleys and ravines. Through this country, which was carefully examined by the advance, General Grant's forces approached the fort to a point where it was necessary to form for the attack, about two miles from the fort. The enemy's pickets had already been met as the columns advanced, and compelled to retire, but the nature of the ground afforded opportunities for them to annoy seriously the federal troops as they moved forward from one ridge to another. As the several brigades arrived at the front, they were moved to the right and left, until the whole army was disposed in a line, the extremities of which were to be gradually advanced towards the river, thus investing the rebel position. The right wing, which extended towards the river on the south of the fort, was commanded by General McClernand, and the left, which was towards the western and north-western sides of the fortifications, was under the command of General Smith. The evening of the day on which the troops had moved from Fort Henry saw this general disposition of them made, the officers in command of the two wings being instructed to place the artillery in position, and to advance their forces the next morning towards the river, on the south and north of the fort. In this position the federal troops lay upon their arms during the night. They had brought no tents and camp equipage, and were obliged to content themselves with cold rations and the cover of a blanket only. This night was mild and pleasant, and in the anticipation of a sharp battle on the morrow, and the hopes of victory, discomforts like these were of little account. Subsequent nights, however, when warm weather was succeeded by a snow storm and piercing cold, the brave troops suffered intensely.

The morning of the 13th was clear and pleasant, and with the dawn the skirmishers were sent forward into the valley and ravines before the rebel intrenchments, and the artillery, which had been posted on the hills, opened a slow fire upon the distant camp of the enemy, and upon such points as appeared to be held by rebel troops. The response of the rebel artillery gradually revealed the position of their batteries and the extent of their works, which were found to be more formidable than the federal officers had anticipated. But the plan determined upon was carried out. On the right the brigades of General McClernand were moved forward in a series of reconnoissances, in which, with only slight skirmishes, the enemy retired from some of his advanced positions, and this wing was extended well towards the river above Dover. In the mean time a body of sharpshooters, who had been sent forward as skirmishers, had greatly annoyed the rebels whenever they showed themselves above their rifle pits and breastworks, and had effectually silenced a battery which had commanded a road by which the federal troops advanced. General Smith, on the left, had advanced his brigades in a similar manner, and by noon the line of his forces was so far extended as nearly to complete the investment of the rebel position, and to be within easy reach of the division which was to come up the Cumberland and land below the fort.

In the afternoon of this day General McClernand ordered an assault upon a redoubt erected upon a high hill, which formed a part of the ridge along which the rebel outworks were constructed. From its commanding position, and the more open country in front of it, the battery in this redoubt had annoyed the federal troops as they advanced over the brow of a hill, unprotected by woods, and to carry this position would not only save further loss or interruption of that kind, but would give the federal forces one of the most advantageous positions for further movements against the enemy. Three regiments of Illinois troops, under command of Colonel Morrison, were detailed for this assault, and they advanced gallantly to the work in spite of a galling fire of musketry and artillery from the enemy. They had nearly reached the breastworks when Colonel Morrison fell, and his own regiment fell into some confusion. The others advanced, however, but found it impossible to pass through the abatis immediately in front of the works, and after a few discharges of musketry they were forced to retire, with considerable loss. The federal artillery prevented any pursuit by the rebel force, which had been concentrated at this point upon the indications of an assault. On the left wing the rebels were more bold, and made a sortie upon an Indiana regiment, which had got into an exposed position. This regiment resisted bravely until reënforced, when the enemy was in turn driven back.

In the mean time the division of federal troops, which proceeded up the Cumberland River, and was expected to arrive at the landing place below Fort Donelson on the night of the 12th, had not made its appearance. This delay caused some uneasiness, as the extensive circuit necessary to invest the fort required a larger number of troops, and the coöperation of the gunboats was desired to divide the attention of the enemy, and to weaken his batteries if they could not even destroy his works. But in the afternoon of the 13th the Carondelet, an iron-clad gunboat, which had sailed in advance of the other vessels, arrived below the fort, and her commander immediately proceeded to make a reconnoissance. Taking a position somewhat protected by a slight promontory jutting out from the bank of the river, the Carondelet opened fire upon the water batteries of the fort. These batteries replied with all their guns, making a very unequal contest for the gunboat, but the latter was damaged by only one shot, which wounded several men, and after discharging a hundred shots, some of which seriously damaged the batteries, withdrew to await the arrival of the other gunboats.

This closed the operations of Thursday, the 13th. The federal forces had gradually advanced and extended their lines, and though they had gained no decided advantage in a contest with the enemy, they had obtained positions from which future movements could be advantageously made. The night of the 13th was cold and stormy. The weather had thus far been very mild and pleasant, but towards evening on this day the air grew cold and rain commenced falling, which was succeeded by a severe snow storm. The federal troops lay upon their arms in the positions to which they had been brought during the day, without tents or shelter save such as the leafless trees afforded. Many of them during the warm weather of the morning had laid aside their overcoats and blankets, which were now left in the rear, and suffered intensely from exposure to the cold and storm. During the night the rebels made a sortie against one of the positions of the right wing, attempting to capture a battery which had during the afternoon seriously troubled them. The federal troops, however, notwithstanding their fatigue and suffering from cold, met the assailants and drove them back.

On the morning of the 14th the earth was covered with snow and ice, and the air was unusually cold for that part of the country. The unfavorable condition of the ground, and the discomfort of the troops, were sufficient to delay immediate operations, while the landing of the reënforcements from the transports, which had arrived during the night, rendered it expedient to wait till they had joined the main army, and the attack could thus be made more formidable. There was therefore no demonstration of hostilities by the land forces, beyond some slight skirmishing of the sharpshooters in the advance, and an occasional discharge of artillery. On the river, however, the gunboats, which had come up with the transports, made a combined attack upon the fortifications. The attack was made, as at Fort Henry, by four iron-clad gunboats in advance, and three wooden gunboats at a safer distance, the flotilla being under the command of Flag-Officer Foote. A heavy bombardment ensued, in which the guns of the fort and of the water batteries replied to the rapid fire of the boats. The cannonade for a time was terrific, as it echoed among the hills along the banks of the river, and in apparent fierceness greatly exceeded that at Fort Henry, but with less effect against the fortifications than in the attack on that work. Fort Donelson was too high for the guns of the boats to be used against it very successfully while in motion, but the shots were thrown at it with great perseverance and with some apparent effect, as some of its guns ceased to respond. Against the water batteries a heavier fire was directed, with the prospect of soon silencing them. As the boats continued the engagement they slowly approached the fortifications, and they had already got within about four hundred yards, and could soon have used grape shot to drive the rebel gunners from their works, when a shot disabled the steering apparatus of the Louisville, and a chance shot from one of the wooden boats in the rear destroyed her rudder, so that she became unmanageable, and as she swung round in the current received further damage from the rebel guns. This mischance deranged the plans for the attack, and the gunboats soon withdrew in order to repair damages, after an engagement of two hours, during which the Louisville lost six killed and eight or ten wounded, and a few were wounded on the other boats. The damage to the vessels, except the Louisville, was inconsiderable, and the officers and men were anxious to renew the attack, confident that they would be successful.

The night following was exceedingly cold, and the troops again suffered intensely. But the dispositions were made for the battle on the morrow, which it was hoped would be decisive, and, notwithstanding their sufferings, the soldiers were ready and eager to enter the conflict. The morning was cold and cheerless, and gave promise of a stormy day. The chilled troops had hardly partaken of their cold rations when the gray dawn revealed the fact that the rebels also had been making a new disposition of their forces, and had concentrated a number of their batteries, and massed a large number of troops upon the extreme right of the federal lines. This movement was made with a view to drive back the right wing of the federal army, so as to open a passage by which the rebel forces could be withdrawn in case the attack should be successful at other points. As soon as it was sufficiently light these batteries opened a heavy fire upon Ogleby's brigade of five regiments, which held the advance at this point, and immediately afterwards a force of eight or ten thousand infantry, as estimated by the federal officers, with a considerable cavalry force, advanced from the rebel works against the brigade. The sally was unexpected, and the rebel troops advanced with great impetuosity and determination. Their numbers seemed overwhelming, but the brave soldiers of Illinois, who composed the brigade, notwithstanding they were not adequately supported by artillery, stood their ground, and for a time held in check the greatly superior numbers of the enemy, driving a portion of them back to their intrenchments. The rebel general, however, determined to make a desperate attempt here, and rapidly bringing up his troops, he forced back the gallant federal brigade, whose ammunition had been exhausted. Another brigade, under the command of Colonel W. H. L. Wal-

lace, then met the advancing enemy, and the fierce contest continued till this brigade, and still other troops, were driven back by the rebels in their powerful and determined attack. There was, however, no rout, and in most of the regiments but little confusion. The federal troops fell back slowly, contesting every inch of ground, as the rebel General Pillow in his official report acknowledged, and it was only when the rebels swept on with continued success, and their ammunition was exhausted, that their retreat became at all hasty. The loss on both sides was large, and the rebels succeeded in capturing a battery of six guns and several hundred prisoners. The commander of the battery was unable, through loss of horses and the condition of the ground, to drag his guns away, and the prisoners who were captured were the wounded, and such as persistently stood their ground till they were actually surrounded by the enemy.

But the rebel battalions which were advancing with so much success, elated with what they fancied was a victory, were at last stopped in their progress by some strongly posted and very skilfully managed batteries, supported by fresher troops. The fire from this artillery was rapid and effective, and with the musketry of its supporting force compelled the rebels, in their turn, to retire. They held, however, the position which had been occupied in the morning by the federal troops on the right, and the battle for a time subsided, having continued from dawn till nearly noon.

General Grant had gone in the morning to the extreme left of his forces, on the river below the fort, to confer with Flag-Officer Foote, and this conflict had taken place during his absence. He had ascertained that a combined naval and military attack could not be made for two or three days, but he found upon his return that such delay, under existing circumstances, would either strengthen the rebels and demoralize his own forces, or would enable the rebel force to escape by the ground where they had relieved themselves from investment. He must at least retrieve the lost ground, and again complete the investment of the rebel works. Accordingly preparations were at once made to regain, before night, all that had been lost since the morning.

On the left General Smith had successfully disposed of his forces, and awaited the order for an attack upon his side. His troops had not yet been seriously engaged, with the exception of a small portion of them, and they were eager to take part in the battle which had raged on their right. An attack on his side would create a diversion in favor of the right wing, and render it more easy to regain the lost positions. The attack was accordingly ordered, and with two brigades of troops from Illinois, Indiana, Iowa, and Missouri, he advanced against the enemy's position. The ridges upon which the rebels were posted in front of General Smith's division were steep, and in some places precipitous, and to storm them was a difficult task in the face of a determined foe. But selecting three regiments for a storming party, the main body of his division was moved to occupy the attention of the enemy on the right, and when the latter had commenced a demonstration against the works in their front General Smith himself led the storming party up the steep ascent. They were met by a fierce fire of musketry and artillery, which opened gaps in their ranks; but closing up as fast as their comrades fell, the soldiers followed their commander with enthusiasm and daring. In excellent order they reached the top of the ridge, and opening with a volley, they then charged upon the rebel force with a shout of victory, and drove them back from their rifle pits and intrenchments in dismay. The position being thus gained, the storming party was at once supported by the other troops with artillery, and the line was held in such force that the rebels could

scarcely hope to dislodge them. The afternoon was now far advanced, and though the troops were eager to press forward, it was not deemed expedient to continue the attack until the right wing should also advance. The outer line of the enemy's intrenchments had been carried, and the federal troops were in a position from which, with increased numbers, they could successfully storm the interior works on the morrow.

While these movements were taking place on the left, preparations were made for an attack from the federal right, in order to regain the ground lost in the morning, and to again complete the investment of the rebel works. To General Lew. Wallace this work was intrusted, and, with a part of his own brigade and several other regiments which had not been seriously engaged in the battle of the morning, he advanced towards the positions still held by a strong force of the enemy, though a part of the numbers which had driven back the federal line in the morning had been withdrawn. Just as General Wallace's troops were about to commence the attack, the success of General Smith on the left was announced, and with an enthusiastic shout they dashed forward. Commencing the engagement with volleys at long range, they moved rapidly forward in spite of the storm of shells and grape hurled at them by the rebel artillery. As soon as the regiments which were in advance had approached sufficiently near the rebel lines, they ceased firing and made a gallant charge, before which the enemy gave way and retired in confusion. Followed close by a strong support, the advance brigade pressed forward, driving the rebel regiments before them into their inner line of intrenchments, recapturing the battery abandoned in the morning, regaining the lost ground, and even a more advanced position. Here, too, as on the left, the officers and men elated with their success, were eager to continue the fight, and to storm the enemy's

Lew. Wallace,

stronghold. But night was at hand, and confident that his troops were now in positions where they could keep the rebel forces in their fortifications, General Grant determined to give them rest, and to delay an assault until the next morning. Another night the troops lay upon their arms without shelter; but they were now confident of victory, and determined to avenge their fallen comrades whose bodies were found where they had fallen in the battle of the morning, and they were only anxious for the morrow, which should see their triumph, and end their privations.

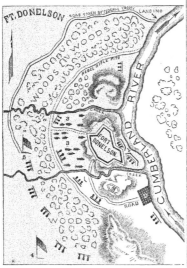

1. Water Batteries.
2. Breastworks.
3. Abatis.
4. General McClernand's Division.
5. General Smith's Division.
D. Village of Dover.

In the rebel intrenchments discouragement had succeeded the triumph of the morning. They had made a desperate and successful effort to relieve their position of investment, and open a passage for retreat. But before they could avail themselves of their hard-earned success, they were again driven back, and again encompassed, as they supposed by a greatly increased federal force, which was in a position, and ready, to make a final assault with overwhelming numbers. Their condition is thus described by General Pillow: "We had fought this battle to open the way for our army and relieve us from investment, which would necessarily reduce us and the position by famine. We had occupied the whole day to accomplish our object, and before we could prepare to leave, after taking in the wounded and the dead, the enemy had thrown around us again in the night an immense force of fresh troops, and re-occupied his original position in the line of investment, thus cutting off our retreat."

Under these circumstances the rebel generals held a council to determine what should be done. The impossibility of holding the works appears to have been admitted by all these officers, but they did not agree upon the course which should be pursued. General Buckner, who was in command of the position opposite General Smith's forces, confessed that he could not hold it against the assault which would be made at dawn, and as there were not boats by which they could transport their troops up the river, he saw no other course than to surrender on such terms as could be obtained. Generals Floyd and Pillow were both the superiors of General Buckner in command; but though they professed to be opposed to a surrender, they did not exercise their right to order any different course. They could not but feel that a surrender was necessary either at once, or after a vain, and perhaps bloody struggle, but they were not willing to share in the disgrace, nor the direct responsibility of such an act. Accordingly, they went through the forms of transferring the command from Floyd to Pillow, and from Pillow to Buckner, who was willing to act according to the necessity of the case, and who, at least, exhibited more honor and humanity than his superiors, by standing with his subordinate officers and men, saving them from further sacrifice, and sharing with them the disgrace of a surrender. General Floyd, with a part of his own troops, succeeded in retreating, by means of a transport, up the Cumberland in the night, taking with him two hundred federal prisoners who had been captured the morning previous. General Pillow with his staff also escaped, and General Buckner was left in command, to perform the unpleasant duty of capitulating. In relation to this unusual course of action on the part of the superior officers, General Pillow, in his official report to the rebel government, wrote as follows: —

"In this condition the general officers held a consultation to determine what we should do. General Buckner gave it as his decided opinion that he could not hold his position one half hour against an assault of the enemy, and said the enemy would attack him next morning at daylight. The proposition was then made by the undersigned to again fight our way through the enemy's line, and cut our way out. General Buckner said his command was so worn out, and cut to pieces, and demoralized, that he could not make another fight; that it would cost the command three quarters of its present number to cut its way through, and it was wrong to sacrifice three quarters of a command to save a quarter; that no officer had a right to cause such a sacrifice. General Floyd and Major Gilman I understood to concur in this opinion.

"I then expressed the opinion that we could hold out another day, and in that time we could get steamboats and set the command over the river, and probably save a large portion of it. To this General Buckner replied that the enemy would certainly attack him at daylight, and that he could not hold his position half an hour.

"The alternative of these propositions was a surrender of their position and command. General Floyd said that he would neither surrender the command, nor would he surrender himself a prisoner. I had taken the same position. General Buckner said he was satisfied nothing else could be done, and that, therefore, he would surrender if placed in command. General Floyd said he would turn over the command to him if he could be allowed to withdraw his command. To this General Buckner consented. Thereupon General Floyd turned the command over to me. I passed it instantly to General Buckner, saying I would neither surrender the command nor myself a prisoner. I directed Colonel Forrest to cut his way out. Under these circumstances General Buckner accepted the command, and sent a flag of truce to the enemy for an armistice of six hours, to negotiate for terms of capitulation. Before this flag and communication were delivered, I retired from the garrison."

It may be observed, in this connection, that the reports of Generals Pillow and Floyd were considered very unsatisfactory by the rebel government, and their conduct of affairs generally for the defence of Fort Donelson, as well as their extraordinary action in transferring the command for the purposes of capitulating, were severely condemned by Mr. Davis, in his message transmitting the reports to the rebel congress.

When the morning of Sunday, the 16th of February, dawned, the federal troops who were ready for, and were eagerly expecting the order for an assault upon the enemy's works, but to their surprise a white flag was raised over the fort, and already a messenger had come from General Buckner, with a communication for General Grant, proposing an armistice for the purpose of arranging the terms of capitulation. General Grant replied that no terms other than an unconditional and immediate surrender could be accepted, and that he proposed to move immediately upon the rebel works. General Buckner accepted these terms, which he considered " ungenerous and unchivalrous," and the federal troops were soon moved forward to take possession of the fort, over which the national flag was raised, amid the shouts of victory from the federal troops. The rebel forces laid down their arms and surrendered as prisoners of war, and the most important and decisive victory of the war, thus far, was consummated by the capture of nearly thirteen thousand prisoners, and the possession of a most important stronghold of the rebels. About fourteen thousand stand of small arms were taken, and upwards of forty pieces of artillery, the greater part of which consisted of field batteries. This important victory was not won without a heavy loss on both sides. The federal loss was about two hundred and forty killed, one thousand and seventy-five wounded, and two hundred missing. The rebel loss was two hundred and thirty killed, and upwards of one thousand wounded. According to some rebel reports the forces in the fort numbered about fourteen thousand, though by other authority they were placed as high as eighteen thousand. The position and strength of the works were such that this force could maintain themselves against a much larger number of assailants. It was both the superior numbers, essential in such an engagement, and the valor of the federal troops, that achieved the victory.

CHAPTER LXII.

Official Reports of the Capture of Fort Donelson. — Report of General Grant. — Report of Colonel W. H. L. Wallace. — Report of General Lew. Wallace. — Report of Colonel Lauman. — General Grant's Order. — General Lew. Wallace's Order. — General McClernand's Order. — Flag-Officer Foote's Report.

THE following official reports of the engage-

ments before Fort Donelson, and its capture, embrace the operations in the different parts of the field : —

GENERAL GRANT'S REPORT.

"HEADQUARTERS ARMY IN THE FIELD, FORT DONELSON, *February* 16, 1862.

"GENERAL : I am pleased to announce to you the unconditional surrender, this morning, of Fort Donelson, with twelve to fifteen thousand prisoners, at least forty pieces of artillery, and a large amount of stores, horses, mules, and other public property.

"I left Fort Henry on the twelfth instant, with a force of about fifteen thousand men, divided into two divisions, under the command of Generals McClernand and Smith. Six regiments were sent around by water the day before, convoyed by a gunboat, or rather started one day later than one of the gunboats, with instructions not to pass it.

"The troops made the march in good order, the head of the column arriving within two miles of the fort at twelve o'clock, M. At this point the enemy's pickets were met and driven in.

"The fortifications of the enemy were from this point gradually approached and surrounded, with occasional skirmishing on the line. The following day, owing to the nonarrival of the gunboats and reënforcements sent by water, no attack was made; but the investment was extended on the flanks of the enemy, and drawn closer to his works, with skirmishing all day. The evening of the 13th, the gunboats and reënforcements arrived. On the 14th a gallant attack was made by Flag-Officer Foote upon the enemy's works, with his fleet. The engagement lasted, probably, one hour and a half, and bade fair to result favorably to the cause of the Union, when two unlucky shots disabled two of the armored gunboats, so that they were carried back by the current. The remaining two were very much disabled also, having received a number of heavy shots about the pilot-house and other parts of the vessels. After these mishaps, I concluded to make the investment of Fort Donelson as perfect as possible, and partially fortify, and await repairs to the gunboats. This plan was frustrated, however, by the enemy making a most vigorous attack upon our right wing, commanded by General J. A. McClernand, with a portion of the force under General Lew. Wallace. The enemy were repulsed after a closely contested battle of several hours, in which our loss was heavy. The officers, and particularly field officers, suffered out of proportion. I have not the means yet of determining our loss even approximately, but it cannot fall far short of one thousand two hundred killed, wounded, and missing. Of the latter, I understand through General Buckner, about two hundred and fifty were taken prisoners. I shall retain enough of the enemy to exchange for them, as they were immediately shipped off, and not left for recapture.

"About the close of this action the ammunition in the cartridge-boxes gave out, which, with the loss of many of the field officers, produced great confusion in the ranks. Seeing that the enemy did not take advantage of this fact, I ordered a charge upon the left — enemy's right — with the division under General C. F. Smith, which was most brilliantly executed, and gave to our arms full assurance of victory. The battle lasted until dark, giving us possession of part of their intrenchments. An attack was ordered upon their other flank, after the charge by General Smith was commenced, by the divisions under Generals McClernand and Wallace, which, notwithstanding the hours of exposure to a heavy fire in the fore part of the day, was gallantly made, and the enemy further repulsed. At the points thus gained, night having come on, all the troops encamped for the night, feeling that a complete victory would crown their labors at an early hour in the morning. This morning, at a very early hour, General S. B. Buckner

sent a message to our camp, under a flag of truce, proposing an armistice, &c. A copy of the correspondence which ensued is herewith accompanied.

"I cannot mention individuals who specially distinguished themselves, but leave that to division and brigade officers, whose reports will be forwarded as soon as received. To division commanders, however, Generals McClernand, Smith, and Wallace, I must do the justice to say, that each of them were with their commands in the midst of danger, and were always ready to execute all orders, no matter what the exposure to themselves.

"At the hour the attack was made on General McClernand's command I was absent, having received a note from Flag-Officer Foote, requesting me to come and see him, he being unable to call.

"My personal staff — Colonel J. D. Webster, Chief of Staff; Colonel J. Riggin, Jr., volunteer Aid; Captain J. A. Rawlins, A. A. General; Captains C. B. Lagow and W. S. Hillyer, Aids, and Lieutenant-Colonel V. B. McPherson, Chief Engineer — all are deserving of personal mention for their gallantry and services.

"For full details, and reports and particulars, reference is made to the reports of the engineer, medical director, and commanders of brigades and divisions, to follow.

"I am, General, very respectfully,
        "Your obedient servant,
            "U. S. GRANT, *Brigadier-General.*
"General G. W. CULLUM,
        "*Chief of Staff Department of Missouri.*"

REPORT OF GENERAL W. H. L. WALLACE.

"HEADQUARTERS, SECOND BRIGADE, FIRST DIVISION,
        UNITED STATES ADVANCE FORCES,
FORT DONELSON, TENN., *February* 17, 1862. }

"SIR: I have the honor to submit the following report of the operations of my brigade, from the time of leaving Fort Henry, on the 11th instant, up to the 16th instant, when the federal forces entered this fortification. . .

"About noon of the 11th instant, while in camp at Fort Henry, I received orders from General McClernand to put the infantry and artillery of my brigade on the march, and move out three or four miles on the telegraph road towards this place. At four o'clock P. M., the forces designated marched out, and encamped on the road, four miles from Fort Henry. At sunrise on the next day, (the 12th instant,) I was joined by Colonel Dickey's cavalry, and marched with my whole command, by the telegraph road, towards Fort Donelson, keeping up frequent communication with Colonel Oglesby's first brigade, which was moving at the same time by the right road, Colonel Dickey's cavalry reconnoitring the country as the column marched. Soon after noon I came within sight of the enemy's encampments on the opposite side of the creek, about a mile in advance. Having caused the road to be reconnoitred, and finding the creek impassable on account of back water from the Cumberland, I moved to the right, up the creek, and effected a junction with Colonel Oglesby's brigade in the low grounds west of Fort Donelson, when heavy wooded hills intervened between us and the enemy's position. Colonel Dickey's cavalry was again thrown forward, and occupied the heights, and thoroughly scouted and reconnoitred the grounds in front. Colonel Oglesby's brigade moved up the railroad to the south of Fort Donelson, while I threw my brigade, by its front, into the heights, dragging the artillery up the steep, wooded hills. After further reconnoitring, the brigade advanced and occupied a ridge south of the centre of the enemy's fortifications, with its right resting on the left of Colonel Oglesby's brigade. Some slight skirmishing occurred here, and after resting in this position for an hour or more, and further reconnoitring, in accordance with the orders of General McClernand, I moved the brigade by the right flank, following Colonel Oglesby's brigade across the valley towards the left of the enemy's position. By this time it was dark, and Colonel Oglesby's brigade being involved in ground which had not been reconnoitred, and which was very hilly, and covered with a dense growth of underbrush, I was ordered by the general commanding the division to return to the position on the west of the valley, which I did, moving by the left flank, when my brigade rested for the night. At daylight, on the morning of the 13th, the enemy opened fire with his artillery from the inside redoubt. Soon afterwards, by order of General McClernand, I marched the eleventh, twentieth, forty-fifth regiments, and Taylor's battery, to the right across the valley, leaving McAllister's battery, supported by the forty-eighth Illinois infantry, on the ridge west of the valley, and ordered Colonel Dickey's cavalry to move in rear, with detachments thrown towards the right, to reconnoitre the Cumberland and Dover. Reaching the high grounds east of the valley, Taylor's battery was put in position on the road leading up to Dover, where the left of the enemy's lines rested behind earthworks — intrenchments strengthened by strong abatis in front. The whole force continued to move steadily to the right, Colonel Oglesby's brigade heading the artillery of his brigade and Taylor's battery on the road, while the infantry was in rear of and near to the road. Along this road the artillery advanced, taking successive positions to the right, and keeping up a constant cannonade on the enemy's works on the right and in the middle redoubt across the valley. The open space afforded a fine opportunity for artillery practice at a long range, and the fire of Taylor's, Schwartz's, and Dresser's guns, warmly returned by those of the enemy in the middle redoubt and the works on the left, presented a rare example of the use of that arm of the service.

"About noon I was ordered by General McClernand to detach the forty-eighth regiment, (Colonel Hayne,) to operate with the seventeenth Illinois, (Major Smith commanding,) and the forty-ninth Illinois, (Colonel Morrison,) of the third brigade, in making an assault on the enemy's middle redoubt, on the hill west of the valley, supported by the fire of McAllister's guns.

"This force was under the command of Colonel Hayne, as senior colonel. They formed in line and advanced in fine order across the intervening ravines, and mounted the steep heights upon which these works are situated in the most gallant manner, and under a heavy fire of musketry from the enemy, posted in the lines of the earthwork. They advanced up the hill, delivering their fire with coolness and precision. The line not being long enough to envelop the works, by order of General McClernand, I detached the forty-fifth Illinois (Colonel Smith) to their support on the right. This regiment advanced in beautiful order down the slope, across the valley, and up the opposite steep, with skirmishers deployed in front, and were soon warmly engaged. These operations had given the enemy time to reenforce their position with strong bodies of infantry from his reserves in the rear, and field artillery, which opened a destructive fire on the advancing line. The roll of musketry showed the enemy in powerful force behind his earthwork; notwithstanding, our forces charged gallantly up the heights to the very foot of the works, which were rendered impassable by the sharp, strong points of brushwood in which it was built. All the regiments engaged in this daring attempt suffered more or less from the enemy's fire. In the mean time the enemy began to show in strength in his intrenchments in front of Colonel Oglesby's brigade. Schwartz's battery was advanced along the road to within three hundred yards of the works, but being without canister range, they were withdrawn by General McClernand's order, and directed Captain Taylor to throw forward two sections of his battery to that position. The position being beyond the reach of my lines, the infantry support was to be furnished from Colonel Oglesby's brigade, which was immediately in the rear. These sections took their positions under the most galling fire of rifles and musketry from the enemy's lines. The ground was covered with brush, and some time was required to put the army in position, and during this time the enemy's fire was very galling, and Taylor's men suffered somewhat from its effects. As soon as his position was gained, however, the rapid and well directed fire of the sections soon silenced the enemy. The coolness and daring of the officers and men of these sections, directed by Captain Taylor in person, are worthy of high praise.

"The forty-eighth, forty-fifth, forty-ninth and seventeenth regiments having been ordered to retire from the hill where they had so gallantly assaulted the enemy's works, the forty-fifth and forty-eighth resumed their position in my line, and Colonel Morrison, commanding the seventeenth and forty-ninth, having been wounded in this assault, these regiments were temporarily attached to my brigade, and acted under my orders during the subsequent operations, until noon of the 15th.

"The night of the 13th was one of great suffering and hardships to the whole command. We lay within point-blank musket and rifle range of the enemy's breastworks; and at dark a storm of rain, soon turning to snow, and accompanied by severe blasts, beat upon the unprotected ranks. The pickets of the enemy were out in strong force, and a constant firing between his pickets and our own was kept up during the night. The spirits of the men, animated and encouraged by the conduct of their officers, never flagged, notwithstanding they were without tents or fire, and were exposed to the storm and assailed by the enemy's shot.

"During the night it was evident that the

enemy were receiving large reënforcements, and when morning broke on the 14th, it showed that they had been busy during the night in erecting new works in commanding positions, and mounting them with guns. McAllister's battery was ordered from the other side of the valley, and put into position on the road. During this day my brigade occupied a position a little in the rear of the road, and under cover of the hill; the right resting on the left of Colonel Oglesby's line, and being within three or four hundred yards of the salient angle of the enemy's works on his left. We lay in this position most of the day, the order of the regiments from right to left being as follows: Eleventh, twentieth, forty-eighth, forty-fifth, forty-ninth, and seventeenth. Taylor's battery was posted at the intervals between the seventeenth and forty-ninth. McAllister's guns were distributed along the point; Dickey's cavalry were in the rear and on the right, to observe the enemy and guard the flank. Under instructions from General McClernand, to commence the construction of a small earthwork on the road to cover three or four guns, Mr. Frecellion, of the forty-ninth, had charge of the work, which was completed during the night, and two of McAllister's guns and a ten-pound rifle gun of the first Mississippi artillery, were placed on it the next morning. During the whole of the 14th a rambling and irregular fire of sharpshooters was kept up, varied by occasional discharges of artillery. The enemy's shells and round shot fell at times thickly within the lines, but the casualties were few.

"At daybreak on the morning of the 15th, the enemy threw a heavy force of infantry and cavalry, supported by field artillery and his batteries within the work, out of his intrenchments, and commenced a vigorous assault upon the right of the whole line.

"The attack was commenced and continued with great spirit, and gradually drove back our extreme right. About seven o'clock A. M., the eleventh and twentieth Illinois, on my right, became engaged with a heavy force of the enemy's infantry. They charged up the hill and gained the road in front of my position, but the moment the rebel flag appeared above the hill, a storm of shot from the eleventh and twentieth drove them back in confusion. Again a new and fresh line of infantry appeared, and I ordered the whole line, except the seventeenth and the left wing of the forty-ninth, to advance and occupy the hill. The forty-ninth advanced boldly and in order to the brow of the hill, where they were exposed, uncovered, not only to the fire of the enemy's infantry, but to a raking of the enemy's batteries of artillery across the valley. They opened their fire, supported by Taylor's battery and two of McAllister's guns, (one having been disabled by a shot from the enemy's cannon,) and for some time the conflict was strong and fierce. But at length the strong masses of the enemy's infantry gave way before the steady, well-directed, and continued fire of the right of my line. They fell back, however, only to give place to another line of fresh troops, who advanced to the support, and who were also compelled by the steady, unflinching valor of our men, to give way.

"In the mean time there were indications that the enemy were gaining some advantage on the right of the whole line. Reënforcements, consisting of Kentucky and Indiana troops, had been sent forward past my position to support the right, but notwithstanding this, it became evident to me from the sounds coming from the direction of the enemy's shot, which began to rake my line from the rear of my right, that the right of the line was giving way. My orders being peremptory to hold that position of the line occupied by my brigade to the last extremity, I sent one of my aids to General McClernand with information of the state of affairs, and to express my fears that my right flank would be completely turned, unless reënforcements should be speedily sent to that quarter. Finding that no reënforcements were within reach, and General McClernand having left me to my discretion if I found my position untenable, and seeing that the enemy steadily advanced on my right flank, and was speedily gaining my rear, many of the corps having exhausted their ammunition, I gave orders to move the whole brigade to the rear up the road, with a view of forming a new line of battle. Before this order was given, all our troops on the right of my brigade had fallen back, except the thirty-first Illinois, Colonel John A. Logan, who occupied the left of Colonel Oglesby's brigade. Immediately adjoining the thirty-first, and on the right of my line, was the eleventh Illinois, Lieutenant-Colonel T. E. G. Ransom, commanding. When the order to retire was given, it failed to reach Lieutenant-Colonel Ransom, who, with the eleventh regiment, was gallantly supporting the thirty-first against a fierce onslaught on their right. Rapidly as the gaps were opened in the ranks of the enemy, they were as promptly closed to the right, and the shortway point alone showed the destructiveness of that fire. Soon the thirty-first, their ammunition having failed, retired, and the eleventh took their place, changing front to the rear under a most galling fire, with all the coolness and precision of veterans.

"In the mean time the order to retire was being executed in good · order by the other regiments in the brigade. The character of the ground rendered it impossible for me to see the whole line at once. When the eleventh changed their front, they were exposed to a fire in front and on both flanks, and the enemy's cavalry charging upon their flank, they were thrown into some confusion and retired, but steadily and in comparatively good order. After falling back some half a mile, I halted the brigade, and as rapidly as possible procured a supply of ammunition, and formed a second

line of battle. At this point Colonel Ross, of the nineteenth Illinois, arrived on the field and took command of the seventeenth and forty-ninth regiments, and we were reënforced by some troops of General Lew. Wallace's division, and with their aid, and with the assistance of Taylor's battery and some pieces of Dresser's and Willard's batteries, the · advance of the enemy was checked, and he was driven within his intrenchments, leaving a large number of his dead and wounded on the field. . .

"In order to a due appreciation of the courage, endurance, and fortitude of the men by whom this victory has been won, it must be, borne in mind that they marched from Fort Henry without transportation, or tents, or rations, except what they carried, and that they were exposed for three days and nights without tents, and almost without fires, being so near the enemy's lines as to render fires imprudent; that the weather was extremely severe — two nights they were thus exposed, accompanied with driving snow-storms and severe cold; that during the whole three days, they were under fire, and compelled to bivouac in line of battle, with their arms in their hands. Added to this, most of them had never seen a battle, and but few had ever heard a hostile shot. Under all the circumstances, it is certainly a great matter of congratulation that so long and fierce a conflict, against an intrenched enemy, fighting on a position well known to him and unknown to us, and so greatly superior in artillery, has resulted so gloriously for our arms.

"Very respectfully, Your obedient servant,

"W. H. L. WALLACE,
" Colonel commanding Second Brigade, First Div."
<small>" Major M. BRAYMAN, *Assistant Adjutant-General First Division.*"</small>

REPORT OF GENERAL LEW. WALLACE.

<small>" HEADQUARTERS THIRD DIVISION U. S. FORCES,
DISTRICT OF WEST TENNESSEE,
FORT HENRY, *February* 20, 1862.</small>

"SIR: A report of the action of my division

before Fort Donelson has been delayed from various causes. I submit it to the general as speedily as possible. . . .

" The position of the third division was in the centre of the line of attack, General Mc-Clernand being on the right, and General Smith on the left. My orders, received from General Grant, were to hold my position and prevent the enemy from escaping in that direction — in other words, to remain there and repel any sally from the fort. Under the orders, I had no authority to take the offensive.

" The line established for my command was on the cone of a high ridge, thickly wooded to the front and rear, and traversed by a road which made the way of communication from the right to the left of our army. The right of my division, when posted, was within good supporting distance from General McClernand, and not more than five hundred yards from the enemy's outworks; indeed, my whole line was within easy cannon shot from them.

" The evening of the 14th (Friday) was quiet, broken at intervals by guns from the rebels. At night, pickets were sent to the front along the line, which was retired somewhat behind the ridge, to enable the men in safety to build fires for their bivouacs. They lay down, as best they could, on beds of ice and snow, a strong cold wind making their condition still more disagreeable.

" The morning of the 15th my division formed line early, called up by the sound of battle raging on the extreme right, supposed at first to be General McClernand attacking. The firing was very heavy and continuous, being musketry and artillery mixed. About eight o'clock came a message from General McClernand, asking assistance. It was hurried to headquarters, but General Grant was, at that time, on board one of the gunboats, arranging, as was understood, an attack from the river side. Before it was heard from, a second message reached me from General McClernand, stating,

61

substantially, that the enemy had turned his flank, and were endangering his whole command. Upon this, Colonel Cruft was instantly ordered to move his brigade on to the right, and report to General McClernand. Imperfectly directed by a guide, the colonel's command was carried to the extreme right of the engaged lines, where it was attacked by a largely superior force, and, after the retreat or retirement of the division he was sent to support, for a time bore the brunt of the battle. After a varied struggle, charging and receiving charges, the enemy quit him, when he fell back in position nearer to support, his ranks in good order and unbroken, except where soldiers of other regiments plunged through them in hurried retreat. In this way, a portion of Colonel Shackelford's regiment, (twenty-fifth Kentucky,) and about twenty of the thirty-first Indiana, with their commanding officers, became separated from their colors.

" Soon fugitives from the battle came crowding up the hill, in rear of my own line, bringing unmistakable signs of disaster. Captain Rawlins was conversing with me at the time, when a mounted officer galloped down the road, shouting, " We are cut to pieces ! " The effect was very perceptible. To prevent a panic among the regiments of my third brigade, I ordered Colonel Thayer to move on by the right flank. He promptly obeyed. Going in advance of the movements myself, I met portions of regiments of General McClernand's division coming back in excellent order, conducted by their brigade commanders, Colonels Wallace, Oglesby and McArthur, and all calling for more ammunition, want of which was the cause of their misfortune. Colonel Wallace, whose coolness under the circumstances was astonishing, informed me that the enemy were following, and would shortly attack. The crisis was come ; there was no time to await orders ; my third brigade had to be thrust between our retiring forces and the advancing foe. Accordingly I conducted Colonel Thayer's command up the road, where the ridge dips towards the rebel works; directed the colonel to form a new line of battle at a right angle with the old one; sent for company A, Chicago light artillery, and despatched a messenger to inform General Smith of the state of affairs, and ask him for assistance. The head of Colonel Thayer's column filed right, double-quick. Lieutenant Wood, commanding the artillery company sent for, galloped up with a portion of his battery, and posted his pieces so as to sweep approach by the road in front; a line of reserve was also formed at convenient distance in the rear of the first line, consisting of the seventy-sixth Ohio, and forty-sixth and fifty-seventh Illinois.

"The new front thus formed covered the retiring regiments, helpless from lack of ammunition, but which coolly halted not far off, some of them actually within reach of the enemy's musketry, to refill their cartridge-boxes. And, as formed, my new front consisted of Wood's battery across the road; on the right of the battery, the first Nebraska and fifty-eighth Illinois; left of the battery, a detached company of the thirty-second Illinois, Captain Davison, and the fifty-eighth Ohio, its left obliquely retired.

Scarcely had this formation been made when the enemy attacked, coming up the road, and through the shrubs and trees on both sides of it, and making the battery and the first Nebraska the principal points of attack. They met this storm, no man flinching, and their fire was terrible. To say they did well is not enough — their conduct was splendid. They alone repelled the charge. Colonel Cruft, as was afterwards ascertained, from his position saw the enemy retire to their works pell-mell, and in confusion. Too much praise cannot be given Lieutenant Wood and his company, and Lieutenant-Colonel McCord and his sturdy regiment. *That was the last sally from Fort Donelson.*

"This assault on my position was unquestionably a bold attempt to follow up the success gained by the enemy in their attack on our right. Fortunately, it was repelled. Time was thus obtained to look up Colonel Cruft's brigade, which, after considerable trouble, was found in position to the right of my new line, whither it had fallen back. Riding down its front, I found the regiment in perfect order, having done their duty nobly, but with severe loss, and eager for another engagement. The deployment of a line of skirmishers, readily united them with Colonel Thayer's brigade, and once more placed my command in readiness for orders.

"About three o'clock, General Grant rode up the hill, and ordered an advance and attack on the enemy's left, while General Smith attacked their right. At General McClernand's request I undertook the proposed assault. Examining the ground forming the position to be assailed, (which was almost exactly the ground lost in the morning,) I quickly arranged my column of attack. At the head were placed the eighth Missouri, Colonel M. L. Smith, and the eleventh Indiana, Colonel George McGinniss, the two regiments making a brigade, under Colonel Smith. Colonel Cruft's brigade completed the column. As a support, two Ohio regiments, under Colonel Ross, were moved up and well advanced on the left flank of the assailing force, but held in reserve.

"Well aware of the desperate character of the enterprise, I informed the regiments of it as they moved on, and they answered with cheers, and cries of "Forward! forward!" and I gave the word.

"My directions as to the mode of attack were general: merely to form columns of regiments, march up the hill which was the point of assault, and deploy as occasion should require. Colonel Smith observed that form, attacking with the eighth Missouri in front. Colonel Cruft, however, formed his line of battle at the foot of the hill, extending his regiment around to the right. And now began the most desperate, yet, in my opinion, the most skilfully executed performance of the battle.

"It is at least three hundred steps from the base to the top of the hill. The ascent is much broken by out-cropping ledges of rock, and, for the most part, impeded by dense underbrush. Smith's place of attack was clear, but rough and stony. Cruft's was through the trees and brush. The enemy's lines were distinctly visible on the hillside. Evidently they were ready.

"Colonel Smith began the fight without waiting for the first brigade. A line of skirmishers from the eighth Missouri sprang out and dashed up, taking intervals as they went, until they covered the head of the column. A lively fire opened on them from the rebel pickets, who retired, obstinately contesting the ground. In several instances, assailant and assailed sought cover behind the same tree. Four rebel prisoners were taken in this way, of whom two were killed by a shell from their own battery, while being taken to the rear.

"Meantime, the regiments slowly followed the skirmishers. About quarter the way up, they received the first volley from the hill-top, around which it ran, a long line of fire, disclosing somewhat of the strength of the enemy. Instantly, under orders of Colonel Smith, both his regiments lay down. The skirmishers were the chief victims. George B. Swarthout, captain of company H, eighth Missouri, was killed, gallantly fighting, far in advance. Soon as the fury of the fire abated, both regiments rose and marched on; and in that way they at length closed upon the enemy, falling when the volleys grew hottest, dashing on when they slackened or ceased. Meanwhile, their own firing was constant and deadly. Meanwhile, also, Colonel Cruft's line was marching up in support and to the right of Colonel Smith.

The woods through which he moved seemed actually to crackle with musketry. Finally, the eighth and eleventh cleared the hill, driving the rebel regiments at least three quarters of a mile before them, and halting within one hundred and fifty yards of the intrenchments, behind which the enemy took refuge. This was about five o'clock, and concluded the day's fighting. In my opinion, it also brought forth the surrender.

"While the fighting was in progress, an order reached me through Colonel Webster, to retire my column, as a new plan of operations was in contemplation for the next day. If carried out, the order would have compelled me to give up the hill so hardly recaptured. Satisfied that the general did not know of our success when he issued the direction, I assumed the responsibilty of disobeying it, and held the battle ground that night.

"Wearied as they were, few slept; for the night was bitter cold, and they had carried the lost field of the morning's action, thickly strewn with the dead and wounded of McClernand's regiments. The number of Illinoisans there found, mournfully attested the desperation of their battle, and how firmly they had fought it. All night, and till far in the morning, my soldiers, generous as they were gallant, were engaged ministering to and removing their own wounded and the wounded of the first division, not forgetting those of the enemy.

"Next morning, about daybreak, Lieutenant Ware, my aide-de-camp, conducted Colonel Thayer's brigade to the foot of the hill. Lieutenant Wood's battery was ordered to the same point, my intention being to storm the intrenchments about breakfast time. While making disposition for that purpose, a white flag made its appearance. The result was, that I rode to General Buckner's quarters, sending Lieutenant Ross, with Major Rogers, of the third Mississippi (rebel) regiment, to inform

General Grant that the place was surrendered, and my troops in possession of the town and all the works on the right. . . .

"Sincerely hoping the general may prove as fortunate in every battle he may have occasion to fight, I beg leave to congratulate him on his success in this one, and subscribe myself,

"Most respectfully,

"His very obedient servant,

"LEWIS WALLACE,

"*General Third Division.*

"Captain JOHN A. RAWLINS, *Assistant Adjutant-General United States Forces, District of West Tennessee.*"

REPORT OF COLONEL LAUMAN.

"HEADQUARTERS FOURTH BRIGADE,
SECOND DIVISION UNITED STATES ARMY,
FORT DONELSON, *February* 18, 1862.

"GENERAL: I have the honor to report the following movements of the fourth brigade, second division.

"We left Fort Henry on the morning of the 12th instant, arriving near Fort Donelson the same evening. Immediately on our arrival, I received your order to move the seventh Iowa infantry to the front to support a battery of Major Cavender's twenty-pounder rifled Parrott guns, which were placed in a position to command a portion of the rebel works. I obtained permission from you to associate the regiment of Birge's sharpshooters in the movement, and placed the two regiments in position, where they remained during the night.

"In accordance with order, on the morning of Thursday, the 13th instant, I moved the left wing of my brigade, consisting of the fourteenth Iowa, Colonel Shaw, and twenty-fifth Indiana, Colonel Veatch, from their encampment towards the enemy, who were intrenched about a mile distant therefrom.

"The advance was made steadily, and in as good order as the nature of the ground would admit of, until we reached the ravine at the base of the hill on which were the enemy's fortifications. Here we halted until the line could be formed, when the fifteenth Indiana, under Colonel Veatch, moved steadily up the hill towards the intrenchments, under a most galling fire of musketry and grape, until their onward progress was obstructed by the fallen timber and brushwood. Having, however, succeeded in obtaining an advantageous position, they held it unflinchingly for more than two hours, and until ordered to fall back out of the range of the enemy's fire. The loss of this regiment in killed and wounded was very severe. The fourteenth Iowa advanced at the same time, and took position on the right and across a ravine, and did good execution. Whilst these two regiments were taking the above positions, the seventh Iowa infantry, under Lieutenant-Colonel Parrott, came up in fine style and took position in the centre, between the twenty-fifth Indiana and the fourteenth Iowa.

"The first regiment of sharpshooters, western division, Lieutenant-Colonel B. S. Compton, were posted on the hill to the extreme right, except a detachment of about sixty, who were deployed as skirmishers, and rendered most effective service in that capacity, and proving by their deadly aim that they are a most valuable arm of the service. We held this position until night, when we fell back to the position occupied in the morning. On the following day, we remained in camp, skirmishing with the rebels during the day and night.

"On Saturday, the 15th instant, at about two o'clock, I received your order to advance with my whole brigade, and assault the heights on the left of the position attacked on the previous Thursday. The brigade was promptly in motion, in the following order: —

"The second Iowa, Colonel Tuttle, led the advance, followed by the fifty-second Indiana, (temporarily attached to my brigade,) who were ordered to support them. This regiment was followed closely by the twenty-fifth Indiana, the seventh Iowa, and the fourteenth

Iowa. The sharpshooters were previously deployed as skirmishers on our extreme right and left. Colonel Tuttle led the left wing of his regiment in line of battle up the hill, supported by the right wing, advancing at a distance of about one hundred and fifty yards in the rear. So soon as he came within range of the enemy's fire, he led his men forward, without firing a gun, up to and charged into the rebel works, driving the enemy before him, and planting his colors on their fortifications. He was closely followed by the other regiments in the order of advance above named. The enemy were closely pursued, and driven behind their inner works. Night coming on, we held the position we had gained, and remained under arms until morning, intending at the dawn of day to recommence the attack. In this engagement the second Iowa suffered terribly. Captains Slaymaker and Cloutman fell just as they entered the enemy's fortifications. Cloutman was instantly killed, and Slaymaker died gallantly shouting to his men to go forward and consummate the work.

"In the morning, as day dawned, we were attracted to the inner fortifications by the sound of a bugle, and saw the rebels displaying a white flag. I instantly despatched Lieutenant-Colonel Parrott to ascertain the intent of it, who reported that an officer wished to see me. I repaired to the spot, and received from him offers of capitulation, which I at once forwarded to you. The result is well known. . . .

"With sentiments of high regard, I remain respectfully, your obedient servant,

"J. G. LAUMAN, *Colonel,*
" *Commanding Fourth Brigade, Second Division.*
"To Brigadier-General C. F. SMITH,
" *Commanding Second Division.*"

The following orders congratulating the soldiers on their brilliant victory, were subsequently issued by Generals Grant, Wallace, and McClernand:—

GENERAL GRANT'S ORDER.

" HEADQUARTERS DISTRICT OF WEST TENNESSEE, }
FORT DONELSON, *February* 17, 1862. }

"The general commanding takes great pleasure in congratulating the troops of this command for the triumph over rebellion gained by their valor on the 13th, 14th, and 15th instants.

"For four successive nights, without shelter, during the most inclement weather known in this latitude, they faced an enemy in large force, in a position chosen by himself. Though strongly fortified by nature, all the additional safeguards suggested by science were added. Without a murmur this was borne, prepared at all times to receive an attack, and with continuous skirmishing by day, resulting ultimately in forcing the enemy to surrender without conditions.

"The victory achieved is not only great in the effect it will have in breaking down the rebellion, but has secured the greatest number of prisoners of war ever taken in any battle on this continent.

"Fort Donelson will hereafter be marked in capitals on the map of our united country, and the men who fought the battle will live in the memory of a grateful people.

"By order U. S. GRANT,
" *Brigadier-General commanding.*"

GENERAL WALLACE'S ORDER.

" HEADQUARTERS THIRD DIVISION, }
DISTRICT OF WEST TENNESSEE, *February* 23, 1862. }
"SOLDIERS OF THE THIRD DIVISION:

"It was my good fortune to command you at the capture of Fort Donelson. Sickness has kept me from thanking you for the patience, endurance, courage, and discipline you showed on that occasion. The country, ringing with the glory of that victory, thanks you, and its thanks are indeed precious.

"You were last to arrive before the fort; but it will be long before your deeds are forgotten. When your gallant comrades of the first division, having fired their last cartridge, fell back upon your support, you did not fail them; you received them as their heroism deserved; you encircled them with your ranks, and drove back the foe that presumed to follow them.

"And to you, and two gallant regiments from the second division, is due the honor of the last fight — the evening battle of Saturday — the reconquest, by storm, of the bloody hill on the right — the finishing blow to a victory which has already purged Kentucky of treason, and restored Tennessee to the confederacy of our fathers. All honor to you.

"LEW. WALLACE,
"*General Third Division.*"

GENERAL McCLERNAND'S FIELD ORDER.

"HEADQUARTERS FIRST DIVISION,
FORT DONELSON, *February* 18, 1862.

"OFFICERS AND MEN OF THE FIRST DIVISION OF THE ADVANCE FORCES:

"You have continually led the way in the valley of the Lower Mississippi, the Tennessee and the Cumberland. You have carried the flag of the Union further south than any other land forces, marching from the interior towards the seaboard.

"Being the first division to enter Fort Henry, you also pursued the enemy for miles, capturing from him, in his flight, six field pieces, many of his standards and flags, a number of prisoners, and a great quantity of military stores.

"Following the enemy to this place, you were the first to encounter him outside of his intrenchments, and drive him within them.

"Pursuing your advantage, the next day, being on the right, you advanced upon his lines, in the face of his works and batteries, and for the time silenced them.

"The next day, skirmishing all along his left, you daringly charged upon his redoubts, under a deadly fire of grape and canister, and were only prevented from taking them by natural obstacles, and the accumulated masses which were hurried forward to defend them.

"The next day you extended your right in the face of newly-erected batteries, quite to the Cumberland, thus investing his works for nearly two miles.

"The next day, after standing under arms for two days and nights, amid driving storms of snow and rain, and pinched by hunger, the enemy advanced in force to open the way to his escape. By his own confession, formed in a column of ten successive regiments, he concentrated his attack upon a single point. You repulsed him repeatedly, from seven o'clock to eleven o'clock A. M., often driving back his formidable odds.

"Thus, after three days' fighting, when your ammunition was exhausted, you fell back until it came up, and re-formed a second line in his face.

"Supported by fresh troops, under the lead of a brave and able officer, the enemy was again driven back, and by a combined advance from all sides, was finally defeated. His unconditional surrender the next day consummated the victory.

"Undiverted by any other attack, for near four hours from any other part of our lines, the enemy was left to concentrate his attack with superior numbers upon yours. Thus, while you were engaged for a longer time than any other of our forces, you were subjected to much greater loss.

"The battle field testifies to your valor and constancy. Even the magnanimity of the enemy accords to you an unsurpassed heroism, and an enviable and brilliant share in the hardest fought battle and most decisive victory ever fought and won on the American continent.

"Your trophies speak for themselves; they consist of many thousand prisoners, forty pieces of cannon, and extensive magazines of all kinds of ordnance, quartermasters' and commissary stores.

"The death knell of rebellion is sounded, an army has been annihilated, and the way to Nashville and Memphis is opened. This momentous fact should, as it will, encourage you to persevere in the path of glory. It must alleviate your distress for your brave comrades who have fallen or been wounded. It will mitigate the grief of bereaved wives and mourning parents and kindred. It will be your claim to a place in the affections of your countrymen, and upon a blazoned page of history.

"By order of Brigadier-General McClernand, commanding.   A. SCHWARTZ,
"*Captain and Acting Chief of Staff.*"

The report of Flag-Officer Foote relative to the engagement of the gunboats is as follows: —

"U. S. FLAG-SHIP ST. LOUIS, NEAR FORT DONELSON, }
VIA PADUCAH, *February* 15, 1862. }

"I made an attack on Fort Donelson yesterday, at three o'clock P. M., with four iron-clad gunboats and two wooden ones, and after one hour and a quarter severe fighting, the latter part of the day within less than four hundred yards of the fort, the wheel of this vessel and the tiller of the Louisville were shot away, rendering the two boats unmanageable. They then drifted down the river. The two remaining boats were also greatly damaged between wind and water. This vessel alone received fifty-nine shots, and the others about half that number each. There were fifty-four killed and wounded in this attack, which we have reason to suppose would, in fifteen minutes more, could the action have been continued, have resulted in the capture of the fort bearing upon us, as the enemy was running from his batteries when the two gunboats helplessly drifted down the river from disabled steering apparatus, as the relieving tackles could not steer the vessels in the strong current. The fleeing enemy returned to the river battery guns, from which they had been driven, and again hotly poured

fire upon us. The enemy must have brought over twenty guns to bear upon our gunboats from the water battery and the main fort on the hill, while we could only return the fire with twelve boat guns from the four boats. One rifled gun aboard the Carondelet burst during the action.

The officers and men, in this hotly contested but unequal fight, behaved with the greatest gallantry and determination, all deploring the accident which rendered two of our gunboats helpless in the narrow river and swift current. On consultation with General Grant and my own officers — as my services here, until we can repair damages by bringing up a competent force from Cairo to attack the fort, are much less required than they are at Cairo — I shall proceed to that place.

"I have sent the Tyler to the Tennessee River, to render the railroad bridge impassable.
"A. H. FOOTE, *Flag Officer*,
"*Commanding Naval Force Western Division.*
"To the Hon. GIDEON WELLES, *Secretary of the Navy.*"

CHAPTER LXIII.

Advance of General Buell's Army to Bowling Green. — Rebel Obstructions. — Rapid Advance of Federal Troops. — Destruction of Bridges and Property by the Rebels. — Arrival opposite Bowling Green. — Retreat of the Rebel Forces. — Effect of the Capture of Fort Donelson. — Sudden Alarm at Nashville. — Arrival of Floyd and Pillow. — Withdrawal of the State Government to Memphis. — Excitement among the People. — Distribution of Stores. — Wanton Destruction of costly Bridges. — Capture of Clarksville. — Arrival of Federal Troops opposite Nashville. — Interview of the Mayor and Citizens with General Buell, and Surrender of the City. — Condition of Affairs in Nashville. — Arrival of the Forces of Generals Grant and Buell. — Evacuation of Columbus by the Rebels. — Expedition down the Mississippi, and Occupation of the Rebel Strongholds. — Report of General Cullom.

WHILE General Grant was operating against Fort Donelson, part of General Buell's army advanced towards Bowling Green, which was held by a large force of the rebels, and was so strongly fortified that they boasted it was impregnable. The advance division was that of Brigadier-General O. M. Mitchell,* which left camp at Bacon Creek on the 11th of February, and moved towards the rebel stronghold. The troops made an easy march, over good roads, the first day, but after a day's delay they were pushed forward more rapidly. They soon began to meet with obstructions interposed by the advance force of the rebels, who retreated before the federal army, destroying bridges, buildings, and a large number of cattle and horses, as well as much property which they could not remove. A storm of rain and snow also rendered the march more difficult, but the federal troops continued to move rapidly, and notwithstanding the bad condition of the roads, and the obstructions made by the retreating enemy, they accomplished a march of more than forty miles in thirty hours.

It was supposed that the rebels, after withdrawing their advance forces, would make a stand at Bowling Green, and would even fight on the side of the river opposite that place. A force of cavalry and artillery were accordingly sent forward, supported closely by infantry, the brigade being under the command of General Turchin. They found no rebel force, however, to oppose their march to the river. The artillery being placed in position, some shells were thrown into the town on the opposite side of the river, and two or three regiments of the rebels hurried to the railroad and left the town. The bridges had been destroyed, and the river was not fordable, so that the federal troops could not cross, and the enemy had ample time to escape. They had begun their retreat some days previous, and had removed a large quantity of army stores; but much property which they could not remove they had destroyed by fire, and had also burned the public buildings and others, the flames of which were not ex-

* Previously well known as an astronomer, and for many years in charge of the Observatory at Cincinnati.

tinguished when the federal forces arrived within sight of the town.

After some delay, a portion of the troops were transported across the river in a small boat, and when a sufficient force had crossed they advanced into the town, meeting with no resistance, and glad, in the falling snow and chilly atmosphere, to feel the warmth of the rebel fires. The transportation of the army across the river was so slow, that some fears were entertained that the rebel forces might return, and with overwhelming numbers repulse the three or four regiments which crossed the first day. But their retreat was too hurried for them to plan and carry out any such movement, and a day or two longer gave ample strength to the federal forces to hold the position.

The capture of Fort Donelson, and the advance of General Buell's army, rendered the rebel position at Columbus untenable, opened Middle Tennessee to the federal forces, which also threatened to drive the rebel armies from Western Tennessee. Nashville was at once exposed to capture, and when the true condition of affairs was known there the greatest alarm and excitement ensued. Up to the 16th of February, the day of the surrender of Fort Donelson, it was believed, on the reports sent from that post, that the federal troops were not only repulsed, but were driven before the pursuing rebel forces. The exaggerated accounts of rebel valor and success, and of the national losses, confirmed the public of Nashville in the belief not only of the safety of that city, but that the federal armies were driven out of Tennessee, and that Kentucky might soon be secured to the confederacy. The first intimation which they had of a disaster was the arrival of Floyd and Pillow, with the forces which had escaped from Fort Donelson. It was Sunday, and the churches were instantly vacated by the excited and alarmed people. The stories of the atrocities of federal troops had been so persistently told by the rebel leaders and press, that a large portion of the public believed that the advance of the federal armies would be characterized by rapine and destruction.

Governor Harris issued a proclamation to the people of Tennessee, calling them to arms, and convened the legislature, to act as best they could, in view of the " invasion" of the state. That body met, but it could scarcely make provision for so grave and unexpected a contingency, and its only action was to adjourn to Memphis, whither the state government was at once transferred, with such of the archives as were necessary for the maintenance of the forms and insignia of power. Special trains hurried away the executive and legislative bodies, and such citizens as were disposed to leave, and had the means for so doing.

In the afternoon the panic was increased by the arrival of General Johnston's forces from Bowling Green, coming in a somewhat hasty retreat, and in no manner to encourage the faint-hearted citizens that the capital of Tennessee would be obstinately defended by the valor of the southern soldiers. Passing through the city, they encamped beyond its limits, and made little or no disposition to meet the enemy, who was said to be advancing, and to be even then at Clarksville, which was already captured by the dreaded gunboats. Orders were given to distribute among the people the public stores which could not be carried away by the heavily laden trains. Some progress was made in the execution of this order, when it was discovered that the federal forces were not in such close proximity as had been reported, and the distribution was suspended. The rebel army, however, moved south, for the purpose of concentrating at some point, where, with heavy forces, they could withstand the federal advance.

General Floyd was left in command at Nashville, but with a force sufficient only to retard

the progress of the federal troops by the destruction of bridges rather than to resist them by an engagement, and to remove the rebel stores. When it was found that the federal advance was not so close as at first apprehended, an attempt was made to collect the stores which had been distributed among the people, and large quantities were transported from the city to Memphis and other points south. But with fresh rumors of the federal advance distribution was resumed, and was continued for several days, the mob having complete control of affairs till the arrival of the federal troops. In spite of the remonstrances of the more considerate citizens, the wire bridge across the Cumberland, and the railroad bridge, both costly structures, and of great importance to the city, were destroyed by the military authorities. This was a foolish act of vandalism, for the federal forces were in part approaching by the river, with the gunboats, whose power was so much dreaded, and their command of transportation would render the want of the bridges of little comparative consequence. But there, as elsewhere, the rebel leaders paid little regard to the wishes or interests of the people, if they could in any degree injure or annoy the national forces. Two valuable steamers, which were being prepared for gunboats, were also destroyed, and much other property, estimated to amount to several millions, was either destroyed or abandoned to those who would take it, although much might have been preserved for the use of the rebel army but for the panic, which was shared alike by citizens and the military. The rebel commander and his associates were scarcely equal to the task assigned them, but, demoralized by the defeat at Fort Donelson, they sought only to dispose, in the quickest manner, of every thing that could be used by their enemy, and then to escape themselves.

It was, however, a week after the arrival of Floyd and Johnston, with their retreating forces, when the federal troops actually approached

Nashville. The gunboats, after the capture of Fort Donelson, had moved up the river as far as Clarksville, meeting along the banks of the river with various demonstrations of loyalty. There were some defensive works at Clarksville, but they were not occupied, and a large part of the citizens had fled from the town, anticipating its destruction by the gunboats. The place was occupied without resistance, and the people assured of protection. Commodore Foote then returned for additional gunboats, and some mortar boats, thinking that some of the strong positions on the banks of the river might be held by the rebel forces.

In the mean time a portion of General Buell's army moved directly towards Nashville, while another division went to Clarksville, from which place they went up the river in transports. Of the former division the advance guard reached Edgefield, a small town opposite Nashville, on Sunday, the 23d of February. No attempt, however, was made to cross the river and enter the city, and no movement was made until the arrival of General Buell, and the division of General Nelson, which came from Clarksville on transports the next day. A committee of citizens, headed by the mayor, then waited upon the general, and after an interview, in which they received assurances that the liberty and property of all peaceably disposed citizens should be respected, they surrendered the city.

The federal troops entered the city and took strong positions to guard against a surprise. A considerable number of guns were found, but they were either spiked or otherwise rendered useless, and all the army stores of the rebels which had not been carried away had already been taken possession of by the mob. Several steamers were captured, but beyond these little of value was taken by the federal forces. The people of Nashville were generally hearty sympathizers with the rebel cause, and manifested a sullen and gloomy spirit

towards the Union troops. They were fully impressed with the belief that the federal army had come to destroy their property, and to steal their slaves, as they had constantly been taught by their leaders and newspapers. The experience of a few days, however, proved to them that they were quite as safe from outrage as they were when under the protection of the rebel troops. There were a few men who were still loyal to the government, and who heartily rejoiced to be able again to express their Union sentiments, which for so long a period they had been obliged to suppress or disguise. A few small national flags, which had been secretly treasured as memorials of the Union, were gladly hung out by their owners to welcome the national troops.

The forces of General Buell and General Grant gradually came up, and were posted in convenient positions in the suburbs of the city, their further advance depending upon the positions taken by the rebel troops. Some skirmishes occurred between the federal pickets and guerrilla parties of the enemy in the vicinity of Nashville, but it was soon evident that no considerable body of the rebel army was near the city. They had retired towards Memphis, in the south-western part of the state, and to the northern line of Alabama and Mississippi, where, by their railroad facilities, they had a better line of defence.

As before observed, the fall of Fort Donelson, and the advance of the federal troops to Nashville, rendered the rebel position at Columbus untenable, and the strong works which had been constructed there to command the Mississippi, were now of little use, as communication with the south could easily be cut off, and the place invested, if necessary, so as to insure its fall. The rebel military authorities, therefore, at once gave orders for its evacuation, and after destroying the property and ordnance that could not be removed, the greater part of the rebel force withdrew. A reconnoissance by

Commodore Foote, after returning from Clarks-ville, hastened the complete evacuation of the stronghold. On the 3d of March, Commodore Foote, with six gunboats, accompanied by three transports, carrying upwards of two thousand troops, again went down the river, to drive out any force which might yet be remaining at the post. It was found, however, that the rebels had entirely evacuated the works, and a small body of federal troops, which had been sent forward by land to reconnoitre, were already in possession. The works were found to be more formidable than they had been supposed to be. The fortifications extended over an area of more than four miles, and were of great strength on all sides, being designed to resist any force attacking on the south and east, as well as on the north sides. Many of the heavy guns had been thrown into the river, and others, which could not easily be removed, were spiked. A large quantity of ordnance stores were left, and a heavy chain cable, which was designed to be stretched across the Mississippi, to ob-struct the passage of federal gunboats, was left broken on the shore. The quarters of the troops and quantities of provisions had been burned, and there were numerous evidences that the rebels had finally evacuated the place in haste. General Cullom, chief of staff to Gen-eral Halleck, who accompanied the expedition, made the following report of its success : —

GENERAL CULLOM'S REPORT.

COLUMBUS, KY., *March* 4, 1862.

" Columbus, the Gibraltar of the West, is ours, and Kentucky is free, thanks to the brilliant strategy of the campaign, by which the enemy's centre was pierced at Forts Henry and Donel-son, his wings isolated from each other and turned, compelling thus the evacuation of his stronghold of Bowling Green first, and now Columbus.

" The flotilla, under Flag-Officer Foote, con-sisted of six gunboats, commanded by Captains Dove, Walke, Stemble, Paulding, Thompson, and Shirk, and four mortar boats, in charge of Captain Phelps, United States navy, assisted by Lieutenant Ford, advance corps United States army, and three transports, conveying Colonel Buford's twenty-seventh Illinois regiment, and a battalion of the fifty-fourth and seventy-fourth Ohio, and fifty-fifth Illinois, commanded by Majors Andrews and Sanger, the whole brigade being under Brigadier-General Sherman, who rendered the most valuable and efficient assist-ance.

" On arriving at Columbus it was difficult to say whether the fortifications were occupied by our own cavalry, or a scout from Paducah, or by the enemy. Every preparation was made for opening fire and landing the infantry, when General Sherman and Captain Phelps, with thirty soldiers, made a dashing reconnoissance with a tug, steaming directly under the water batteries. Satisfied that our troops had posses-sion, they landed, ascended to the summit of the bluff, and together planted the stars and stripes, amid the heartiest cheers of our brave tars and soldiers.

" Though rising from a sick bed to go upon the expedition, I could not resist landing to examine the works, which are of immense strength, consisting of tiers upon tiers of bat-teries on the river front, and a strong parapet and ditch, crossed by a thick abatis, on the land side. The fortifications appear to have been evacuated hastily, considering the quan-tities of ordnance and ordnance stores, and number of anchors, and the remnant of the chain which was once stretched over the river, and a large supply of torpedoes remaining. Desolation was visible every where ; huts, tents, and barricades presenting but their blackened remains, though the town was spared. I dis-covered what appeared a large magazine, smoking from both extremities. I ordered the train to be immediately cut. A garrison was left in the work of nearly two thousand infantry, and four hundred cavalry, which I will strengthen immediately.

"GEORGE W. CULLOM,

"*Brigadier-General, Chief of Staff.*

"To Major-General McCLELLAN."

Having obtained these decided advantages in Tennessee, the government adopted measures designed to hold the state, and to develop the loyal sentiment which still existed there. Honorable Andrew Johnson, United States senator from that state, and the only one from a seceded state who remained loyal and maintained his position in the senate, was appointed a brigadier-general, for the purpose of organizing a Union force in the state, and to act as military governor until a loyal civil government should be established. Mr. Johnson had already shown himself one of the truest patriots in the country, and one of the strongest opponents of secession, and the aristocratic principles on which the new confederacy was, in fact, founded. Popular among a large portion of his fellow-citizens, of great determination, and a firm believer in democratic institutions, he was considered especially fit for the duties now assigned him, and he entered upon them with a full knowledge of the position of affairs, the character of the rebellion, and the difficulties which surrounded him.

CHAPTER LXIV.

Army Movements in Missouri. — Position of General Price. — Advance of Federal Forces, and Retreat of General Price. — Movement of General Curtis into Arkansas. — Expeditions against Rebel Detachments. — Approach of a large Rebel Force. — Retreat of General Sigel, with Part of his Force, to the main Army. — Movements of the Rebel Army under Van Dorn. — The Rebel Commander's Strategy. — Advance upon the Federal Position from the West and North. — Battle between General Sigel's Forces and the Rebels on the West. — Repulse and Retreat of the Rebels. — Battle in Front of the Federal Position, and Retreat of the Rebels. — Severe Con-

flict with the Rebel Forces at the North, in the Rear of the Federal Position. — The Federal Troops driven back. — Want of Reenforcements. — The Battle terminated by Night. — Arrival of General Sigel's Forces. — Change of Federal Front. — Preparations for a Renewal of the Battle. — Position of the two Armies. — Commencement of the Conflict. — Heavy Fire of Artillery. — Advance of General Sigel's Divisions. — Effective Artillery. — Fierce Conflict, and Rebel Right Driven Back. — Waving of the Rebel Line. — Federal Charge and Rebel Flight. — Pursuit by General Sigel's Troops. — Rebel Losses. — Death of Generals McCulloch and McIntosh. — Rebel and Indian Atrocities. — General Curtis's Report. — Effects of the Victory.

WHILE the armies of Generals Grant and Buell were advancing in Kentucky and Tennessee, other Union forces, under General Curtis, were moving to south-western Missouri, again to oppose the rebel army collected there by the rebel governor, Jackson, and General Price. The latter had organized a considerable force among the disloyal people of Missouri, and forces raised in Texas and Arkansas were ready to coöperate with him, the design being to wrest the state, or as much of it as possible, from the authority of the federal government, and to complete the secession, which a traitorous executive had promulgated and attempted to consummate. His headquarters were at Springfield, and he had there, and in the vicinity, a force variously estimated from six to twelve thousand troops, with many pieces of artillery.

In the latter part of January the army of General Curtis was, in part, concentrated at Rolla, which place had been held since the withdrawal of General Hunter, after General Fremont's brief campaign, and early in February an advance was made towards Springfield. General Price, expecting the rebel forces of General Van Dorn and General McCulloch, which were in Arkansas, to move to his support, and that their combined forces would be sufficiently strong to overwhelm the federal army, remained in Springfield till the advance of the federal column drove in his pickets. Finding that his friends did not come to his support, and unwilling to risk any battle alone, or to oppose seriously the federal advance, Price evacuated Springfield, and hastily retreated southward to Arkansas. He left behind several hundred of his troops, sick, who were taken prisoners, and a quantity of stores and wagons. The federal troops advanced towards the town, expecting to meet with resistance, but they entered the place February 14, with scarcely a skirmish, the rebels being already in full retreat. General Curtis sent a part of his forces in pursuit, which, having overtaken the rebel rear, a series of skirmishes and small engagements ensued for several days, greatly annoying the rebels, and hastening their flight, though the loss was not severe on either side.

General Curtis remained a short time at Springfield, bringing up the several divisions of his army, and establishing a base from which he could operate against any forces of the enemy in south-western Missouri or northern Arkansas. In the mean time the federal troops were gradually advanced along the mail route, from Springfield towards Fayetteville, in the north-western part of Arkansas, and on the first of March were on the borders of the latter state, a portion being as far as Bentonville. Expeditions were then sent in various directions to cut off and capture detached bodies of the rebel troops, reported to be at different points. The rebel detachments, however, succeeded in avoiding the federal troops, some bodies of which at last found themselves unexpectedly in the vicinity of a large force of the rebels, and were compelled to fall back to the main body of the federal army. General Curtis was at once apprised of the vicinity and apparent approach of the rebel army, and at once concentrated his forces at Sugar Creek, a short distance south of a place called Pea Ridge, where there was a good position for defence. General Sigel, with a portion of his command, was at Bentonville, and when marching to join

General Curtis, his rear guard was attacked by a heavy force of the rebels, who attempted to cut them off. The general sent forward his baggage train, and remaining himself with the rear guard, which consisted of only one regiment and a part of another, with his artillery, by his energy and skill he cut his way through the superior force of the rebels, held them in check while his trains moved on, and effected his retreat in the most brilliant and successful manner, joining the remainder of his command and the other forces of General Curtis before the enemy could reach them, and in the contest sustaining comparatively a small loss.

The rebel army, which was now evidently approaching for an attack upon the federal forces, was composed of nearly thirty thousand men, under the chief command of General Van Dorn, formerly an officer in the United States army. Under General Van Dorn were General McCulloch, with a large body of Texans, General Price, with his Missouri troops, and a body of Indians and whites, under General Albert Pike, who, being formerly United States Indian agent, had used his position and influence to enlist the Creeks, Cherokees, and other Indians against the government. The position which the main body of the rebel army had occupied was on the Boston Mountains, about thirty miles from General Curtis's camp, near Pea Ridge. From this position they moved on the morning of March 5, taking with them four days' rations, and leaving their baggage in camp. Van Dorn's plan was to march north, so as to reach the rear of the federal army, cut them off from retreat to Springfield, and while he made a feint upon their front, to fall upon their rear with the main body of his army. Knowing the position of the rebel army, General Curtis expected an attack from that direction upon his front, and he accordingly threw up some earthworks, and constructed other defences, which should strengthen his position against what he had reason to believe was a superior force to his own. But Van Dorn, knowing the country well, had adopted the plan above named, both on account of the advantages which the nature of the ground gave him in an attack from the north, and for the purpose of a surprise of the federal army. In order to carry out his strategy, while with his main body he moved north, he left a body of troops to make a feint against the front of the federal forces, and another for a like movement on their right flank.

General Sigel reached the extreme right of the federal position, and formed a junction with the other forces of General Curtis on the night of March 6. The rebels had followed, and taken position on the flank of the federal army, as above stated, and the next morning the scouts reported a strong body of the rebel army posted on the hills west of the federal position, and on its right. Another force was reported to have appeared at the north, in the rear, and subsequently a smaller body was seen in front. The indications were that the force on the right was the largest, and General Sigel, with two divisions, was sent to dislodge the enemy from their position, while Colonel Carr, commanding one division, was sent to the north, and another division, under Colonel Jefferson C. Davis, prepared to meet the forces in front.

About three miles from camp one of General Sigel's divisions encountered what was supposed to be a small body of rebels, posted on the edge of a wood. An attack with artillery was made, and after a few rounds a cavalry force was ordered to charge, but the rebels were found to be too strong in numbers and position, and the cavalry fell back in confusion. The rebels followed up the advantage they gained by the repulse of the federal cavalry, and, making a charge, captured the three pieces of artillery which had been brought to bear upon them. The advantage thus gained, however, was of short duration, for General

Osterhaus, commanding the division, brought up his infantry, which, by a succession of volleys, followed by a gallant charge, drove back the enemy and recaptured the guns. The other forces of General Sigel coming up, a heavy fire of artillery ensued, by which the rebels were finally dislodged from their position. They retreated towards the north, for the purpose of joining the main body of their army, and possibly for the purpose of dividing and weakening the federal forces. The retreating enemy were followed for several miles, the artillery opening upon them whenever an opportunity offered. General Sigel then abandoned the pursuit, and returned to the position from which he had marched in the morning.

The conflict between General Sigel's troops and the enemy on the right had hardly commenced, when the rebel force in front advanced to offer battle. Colonel Davis, who commanded at this point, moved out against them, and a sharp conflict took place, in which the enemy was driven back in some confusion, and retired by a circuitous route, to join their army in the rear.

In the mean time Colonel Carr's division had moved about two miles to the north, to meet the rebels who had made their appearance in that direction, as it was supposed, in not very large numbers. The enemy was found to be posted on a wooded ridge, somewhat abrupt on the side towards the federal troops, and naturally a favorable position. The division of Colonel Carr having formed in line of battle upon a gentle declivity, sloping towards the enemy's position, a fire of artillery was opened upon the rebel lines with some effect. They replied with artillery, which was, also, well aimed, and the explosion of two limber boxes by their shells appeared to be a signal for them to pour in a heavy fire of musketry, which was followed by a charge upon the federal battery, in which they succeeded in capturing one of the guns. But the infantry supporting the battery soon drove them back, with severe loss, and they retired to their position on the ridge. The conflict continued about an hour, without any result, except to show that the enemy was here in strong force, and was preparing to make an attack, with large numbers, upon the federal lines. Colonel Carr accordingly withdrew his force to a better position, a short distance in his rear. The battle was immediately renewed, and the rebel troops made several ineffectual charges, being repeatedly driven back by the well-directed fire of the federal infantry. They succeeded, at last, in capturing another gun, though not without severe loss on their part. Many of the rebels were armed with double-barrelled shot guns, loaded, in many cases, with buckshot as well as balls, and in their charges their fire, at short range, though not so fatal as that of musketry, was more effective in wounding and disabling their opponents.

The battle continued for hours, and it being evident that his division was contending against greatly superior numbers, Colonel Carr sent repeatedly to headquarters for reënforcements. But it was impossible for General Curtis to send the desired aid, for the troops of General Sigel and Colonel Davis were out in pursuit of the enemy with whom they had been fighting, and the force at his disposal was only sufficient to protect his camp. Colonel Carr's division, however, held out bravely, and disputed the ground inch by inch as they were compelled to retire. Late in the afternoon they received a reënforcement of two regiments of infantry and a battery from General Sigel's command, which enabled them to maintain their position till night came to relieve the brave but exhausted troops. They lay upon their arms, receiving refreshments from the camp, and preparing for a desperate struggle on the morrow. The lines of the two armies were but a few hundred yards apart, and it was necessary to observe the greatest caution to be prepared for a sudden attack, and to guard against revealing any movement to the enemy. General Sigel's and Colonel Davis's forces having returned, General Curtis at once changed the front of his army, to meet what was evidently the entire forces of the rebels. They had been held in check by a greatly inferior force, and the well-conceived plan of Van Dorn had not been successfully carried out as he had anticipated. It was now too late for him to meet a divided federal force, and though the latter had lost the advantage of the defences prepared to oppose an enemy approaching from the south, the army was during the night concentrated, and by a change of front, ready to meet the attack, intended to be overwhelming.

It was an anxious and sleepless night in the federal camp. The enemy was in greater strength than had been anticipated, and had obtained an advantageous position from which to make an attack. But officers and men were determined to do their utmost to repulse, and, if possible, to defeat the rebels. The wounded were, as far as possible, brought in and placed in the care of the surgeons, rations were distributed, and overcoats and blankets carried to the men who rested on their arms in front, while every disposition was made to meet the foe on the morrow. The rebels also made preparations for the battle, and were posted in some very strong positions, a part of their force, with several batteries of artillery, occupying an eminence of gentle declivity towards the north, but precipitous on the side towards the federal troops. On the right and left of this eminence other troops and batteries were placed, a strong force of infantry and artillery being posted on the rebel right, near the western base of the hill, at the edge of a piece of woods. The main body of the federal army occupied some open and nearly level land, where, under the command of General Sigel, it was formed in line of battle. It was evident that to win the victory it would be necessary to dislodge the enemy from their strong position on the hill, and the dispositions were made for that purpose.

Early in the morning skirmishing commenced along the centre and right of the federal lines, and soon after eight o'clock the battle opened in earnest by a fierce cannonading on both sides. The federal artillery was the most effective and skilfully managed, and its shot did great execution on the rebel lines. General Sigel's divisions, under Colonel Carr and Colonel Davis, on the federal left, moved steadily forward, with admirably managed artillery and solid ranks of infantry, until they reached the position occupied by the advance of the enemy, on the edge of the timber land. Here a charge was made upon a rebel battery, which had annoyed the advancing columns, and it was speedily captured. One by one the other rebel guns in this part of the field were silenced, and their right, after a fierce encounter in the woods, was driven back. This decided advantage, together with the heavy cannonade that from other parts of the federal line for two hours had poured a fearful storm of shot and shell among them, seemed to dishearten the rebel soldiers if not their officers. Some of their infantry broke and fled, and their guns began to be withdrawn from the advantageous position on the brow of the hill. The wavering of the rebel line was a signal for a charge by the federal troops, who were accordingly pushed forward for that purpose. The rebels, however, did not any where stand to meet the charge, but hastily withdrew their guns, and at once commenced a precipitate and disorderly retreat, even before the entire line of the federal forces had advanced to support their comrades who led the charge.

Of General Sigel's brilliant and successful movements, an officer of the regular army wrote as follows:—

"General Sigel, having learned the exact position of the enemy's batteries, commenced to form his line of battle by changing his front so as to face the right flank of the enemy's position. Probably no movement during the war has shown more skill in the disposition of forces, or caused as great destruction to the party attacked, with so little loss to the attacking party. He first ordered the twenty-fifth Illinois, under the command of Colonel Coler, to take a position along a fence, in open view of the enemy's batteries, which at once opened fire upon them. Immediately a battery of six of our guns (several of them twelve-pounders, rifled) were thrown into line, one hundred paces in the rear of our advanced infantry, on a rise of ground. The twelfth Missouri then wheeled into line, with the twenty fifth Illinois on their left, and another battery of guns was similarly disposed a short distance behind them. Then another regiment and another battery wheeled into position, until thirty pieces of artillery, each about fifteen or twenty paces from the other, were in a continuous line, with infantry lying down in front. Each piece opened fire as it came in position. The fire of the entire line was directed so as to silence battery after battery of the enemy.

"Such a terrible fire no human courage could stand. The crowded ranks of the enemy were decimated, their horses shot at their guns, large trees literally demolished, but the rebels stood bravely to their post. For two hours and ten minutes did Sigel's iron hail fall thick as autumn leaves, furious as the avalanche, deadly as the simoom. One by one the rebel pieces ceased to play. Onward crept our infantry; onward came Sigel, and his terrible guns. Shorter and shorter became the range. No charge of theirs could face that iron hail, or dare to venture on that compact line of bayonets. They turned and fled. Again Sigel advanced his line, making another partial change of front. Then came the order to charge the enemy in the woods, and those brave boys, who had lain for hours with the hail and shot of the enemy falling upon them,

U. S. Grant.

and the cannon of Sigel playing over them, rose up and dressed their ranks as if it were but an evening parade, and as the 'forward' was given, the twenty-fifth Illinois moved in compact line, supported on the left by the twelfth Missouri, acting as skirmishers, and on the right by the twenty-second Indiana. As they passed into the dense brush, they were met by a terrible volley. This was answered by one as terrible and far more deadly. Volley followed volley, yet on and on went that line of determined men. Steadily they pushed the rebel force until they gained more open ground. Here the confederate forces broke in confusion and fled. The day was ours, and the battle of Pea Ridge was added to the already long list of triumphs clustering around the old starry flag."

General Sigel, with his forces, went in pursuit of the panic-stricken rebels, and followed them for ten or twelve miles, capturing a large number of wagons with supplies and ammunition, nearly a thousand stand of arms, and a few prisoners. The flight of the enemy was too rapid for the weary federal troops and horses to overtake and capture the whole force, or any considerable body, and the pursuit was accordingly abandoned, and the federal troops returned to their camp. The rebel forces had divided in their flight, a portion going east, and others in different directions, towards the Boston Mountains. The federal cavalry, for several days, scoured the country about the battle field, but found no considerable body of the rebels, though in all directions numbers of wounded and stragglers.

In the battle of March 7, the loss of the rebels opposed to General Sigel's divisions was very heavy, and among the officers killed were Generals McCulloch and McIntosh. They left a large number of dead and wounded on the field from which they were driven, and along the route by which they moved to join Van Dorn. In the last day's battle their loss was

63

again very severe, from the terrible storm of shot and shell poured into their lines by the well-trained artillery of the federal army, and the effective fire of musketry. In their flight they left along the road ample evidences of their heavy loss, as well as of the haste of their retreat, in which they were compelled to abandon their dead and wounded. Their entire loss could hardly be estimated, the dead and wounded were scattered over so wide an extent of country, but it was apparently much greater than that of the federal army, which was reported to be from ten to twelve hundred killed, wounded, and missing. Their army suffered still more from demoralization than by casualties, a large part of it being scattered or rendered utterly useless.

It was charged upon the rebels that when they obtained an advantage against the federal troops, they inhumanly shot down and bayoneted the wounded and helpless, and there was but too good reason to believe that some of the Indians who composed a portion of the rebel army, resorted to their savage custom of scalping the dead and wounded of the federal soldiers who fell within their reach. This savage warfare occasioned some correspondence between General Curtis and General Van Dorn, when the latter subsequently sent a flag of truce to the federal lines. General Van Dorn discredited and virtually disowned the atrocity, and in return charged inhumanity upon the Germans, which appeared, however, not to be well established.

The following is General Curtis's brief report of the battle : —

OFFICIAL REPORT OF GENERAL CURTIS.

"HEADQUARTERS ARMY OF THE SOUTH-WEST, }
"PEA RIDGE, ARKANSAS, March 9. }

"GENERAL: On Thursday, the 6th inst., the enemy commenced an attack on my right, assailing and following the rear guard of a detachment, under General Sigel, to my main lines on Sugar Creek Hollow, but ceased firing when he met my reënforcement, at about four P. M. During the night I became convinced he had moved on so as to attack my right or rear. Therefore, early on the 7th, I ordered a change of front to right, on my right, which, thus becoming my left, still rested on Sugar Creek Hollow. This brought my line across Pea Ridge, with my new right resting on the head of Cross Timber Hollow, which is the head of Big Sugar Creek. I also ordered an immediate advance of cavalry and light artillery, under Colonel Osterhaus, with orders to attack and break what I supposed would be the reënforced line of the enemy.

" This movement was in progress, when the enemy, at eleven A. M., commenced an attack on my right. The fight continued mainly at these points during the day, the enemy having gained a point, hotly contested by Colonel Carr, at Cross Timber Hollow, but were entirely repulsed with the fall of their commander, McCulloch, in the centre, by the forces of Colonel Davis.

" The plan of attack on the centre was gallantly carried forward by Colonel Osterhaus, who was immediately sustained and superseded by Colonel Davis's entire division, supported also by General Sigel's command, which had remained till near the close of the day on the left. Colonel Carr's division held the right, under a galling and continuous fire, all day.

" In the evening, the fire having entirely ceased on the centre, and there having been none on the left, I reënforced the right by a portion of the second division, under General Asboth. Before the day closed I was convinced that the enemy had concentrated his main force on the right. I therefore commenced another change of front, forward, so as to face the enemy, where he had deployed on my right flank in strong position. The change had been only partially effected, but was fully in progress, when, at sunrise on the 8th, my right and centre renewed the firing, which was immediately answered by the enemy, with renewed energy, all along the whole extent of the line. My left, under Sigel, moved close to the hills occupied by the enemy, driving him from the heights, and advancing steadily towards the head of the Hollows. I immediately ordered the centre and right wing forward, the right turning the left of the enemy and cross-firing on his centre. This final position enclosed the enemy in the arc of a circle. A charge of infantry, extending throughout the whole line, completely routed the whole rebel force, which retired in great confusion, but rather safely, through a deep and impassable defile of cross timber.

" Our loss is heavy; the enemy's can never be ascertained, for the dead are scattered over a large field, and their wounded, too, may, many of them, be lost and perish. The foe is scattered in all directions, but I think his main force has returned to the Boston Mountains. Sigel follows towards Keitsville, while my cavalry is pursuing him towards the mountains, scouring the country, bringing in prisoners, and trying to find the rebel Major-General Van Dorn, who had command of the entire force.

" I have not as yet the statements of the dead and wounded, so as to justify a report, but I will refer you to a despatch I will forward very soon. Officers and soldiers have displayed such unusual gallantry, that I hardly dare to make distinctions. I must, however, name the commanders of divisions. General Sigel gallantly carried the heights, and drove back the left wing of the enemy. Asboth, who is wounded in the arm, in his gallant effort to reënforce the right. Colonel and Acting Brigadier-General Davis, who commanded the centre, where McCulloch fell on the 7th, and pressed forward the centre on the 8th. Colonel and Acting Brigadier-General Carr is also wounded in the arm, and was under the continuous fire of the enemy during the two hardest days of the struggle. Illinois, Indiana, Iowa, Ohio, and Missouri may proudly share the honors of the victory which their gallant heroes won over the combined forces of Van Dorn, Price, and McCulloch, at Pea Ridge, in the Ozark Mountains of Arkansas.

"I have the honor to be, general,
"Your obedient servant,
"SAMUEL R. CURTIS,
"Brigadier-General.
"Major-General HALLECK."

This brilliant victory put an end, for the time being, to the rebel scheme for invading Missouri, and securing that state to the confederacy. Following the successes already achieved by the federal armies in Kentucky and Tennessee, it was a discouraging blow to the rebellion, and a decided advantage to the Union cause, especially in Missouri, where the public mind, both of the loyal citizens and those inclined to disloyalty, became more settled in the conviction that the federal power would be successfully maintained in that state.

CHAPTER LXV.

The Army of the Potomac. — Orders for its Advance. — The President's Plan. — General McClellan's Plan. — Army Corps. — New Military Departments. — Retreat of the Rebel Army. — Advance of Federal Troops to Manassas. — Backward Movement to Alexandria. — Address of General McClellan to the Army. — Movement to Fortress Monroe. — The Defences of Washington. — Troops left for the Protection of Washington. — Difference of Opinion relative to the Number necessary. — General McDowell's Corps detained. — Departure of the other Forces for Fortress Monroe.

WHILE the events recorded in the preceding chapter were transpiring at the west, the army of the Potomac still remained in front of Washington, and no movement was made towards the enemy. This army, exclusive of the forces under General Dix in Baltimore and vicinity, numbered about one hundred and eighty thousand men. It was well armed, and supplied with the best artillery, and during the months through which the greater part of it had been in the field, it had become generally well disciplined. On this large and well appointed army the loyal people relied for brilliant service, and it was hoped that it might deal a blow against the rebellion which should render its subsequent suppression a comparatively easy task. While, therefore, victory was crowning the federal arms in the campaigns which had opened according to the order of the President, there was some impatience among the people at the delay in the movements of this, the largest and most carefully organized army in the field. But great confidence was felt by the public generally in the commanding general and in the new secretary of war, although there were occasional rumors of disagreement between these two officers.

Besides the general order of the President, mentioned in a previous chapter, in which February 22d was assigned for an advance of the several armies, the President issued a special order on the 31st of January, "that all the disposable force of the army of the Potomac, after providing safely for the defence of Washington, be formed into an expedition for the immediate object of seizing and occupying upon the railroad south-westward of what is known as Manassas Junction; all details to be in the discretion of the general-in-chief, and the expedition to move before or on the 22d day of February." The ultimate object was an advance in that direction upon Richmond, the fall of which, as the seat of the rebel government, and the overthrow of the rebel army which had been collected in Virginia, were generally deemed as matters of the utmost importance, in which was involved the fate of the rebellion.

General McClellan objected to this movement, and proposed, as one which would more surely result in success, an advance by the way of the Rappahannock, the troops being transported down Chesapeake Bay and up that river to Urbanna. He also suggested an advance from Fortress Monroe up the peninsula between the York and James Rivers, as better than the direct movement proposed by the President. The question was submitted to a council of war, composed of several of the superior general officers of the army, in which, after some discussion, the movement by way of the Rappahannock received the approval of a majority of the officers. Several of the ablest and most experienced officers, however, favored the direct advance proposed by the President.* But the army still remained in its old position for some time subsequent to this decision, and no movement was made for an advance by either route.

For the more complete organization of so large an army, and to render it more efficient in the field, it was deemed necessary to divide it into army corps. The President, accordingly, in March, before any movement was made, issued an order for the organization of army corps, each consisting of two or more divisions. General McDowell was appointed to the command of the first army corps; General Sumner to that of the second; General Heintzelman to that of the third, and General Keyes to that of the fourth. The troops under General Banks, in the vicinity of Harper's Ferry, were also organized as a fifth army corps, under command of General Banks. General McClellan assumed command of the whole of these forces; and upon taking the field, was relieved from the command of all the other military departments which had previously been under him as general-in-chief. These other military departments were established anew, the several departments west of a line

drawn north and south through Knoxville, Tennessee, being consolidated as the department of the Mississippi, under the command of General Halleck, a new department between the department of the Mississippi and the department of the Potomac being established, and called the mountain department, to which General Fremont was assigned. Subsequently that portion of Virginia and Maryland lying between the mountain department and the Blue Ridge was made a separate department, called the department of the Shenandoah, under the command of General Banks, who, with his forces, was thereby detached from the army of the Potomac.

Early in March the rebels suddenly abandoned their batteries on the Potomac, the navigation of which they had so long obstructed, and fell back to the position occupied by their main army. In a few days it was rumored that the entire rebel army had fallen back from its position at Manassas, and had withdrawn to the south side of the Rappahannock. Some adventurous civilians proved the truth of 'the rumor before any reconnoissance by the army had discovered the fact. But the federal army was now ready to move, and an advance was immediately made towards Manassas, it being supposed by some that the enemy were yet in the vicinity of their old position. The works at Manassas were found to be somewhat formidable, and there were indications that the rebel army in Virginia was large; but, according to good military authority, the position was by no means impregnable, or the rebel forces probably sufficient to withstand an attack by the large federal force that could have been brought against them. The rebels were soon discovered to have fallen back upon the Rappahannock and Rapid Ann, where they could hold a stronger line of defence. But an advance in this direction had been decided against by General McClellan and a majority of the officers who were consulted; and after making this movement to Manassas, which was in the nature of a feint, the army was marched back again to the Potomac for transportation to a new base. The plan of advance for which General McClellan had before expressed a preference, by way of the Rappahannock, was now relinquished, and a council of the commanders of army corps decided in favor of a movement by way of the peninsula between the York and James Rivers, which had also been suggested by General McClellan as more advantageous than a direct advance.

The army had moved forward with great enthusiasm, and appeared eager to meet the enemy. The brilliant victories and general success of their brethren at the west, inspired the soldiers with a desire to achieve equal success, and to strike even a more severe blow against the rebellion. The retreat of the enemy was a great disappointment to the army, and the orders for a backward movement would have, without doubt, in some degree a demoralizing effect if no explanation were given. It was on the eve of the backward movement that General McClellan, in whom the army had the fullest confidence, issued the following address, which was calculated to relieve the disappointment, and to account for a movement the object of which could not be avowed: —

"HEADQUARTERS ARMY OF THE POTOMAC, }
FAIRFAX COURT HOUSE, VA., *March* 14. }

"SOLDIERS OF THE ARMY OF THE POTOMAC: For a long time I have kept you inactive, but not without a purpose. You were to be disciplined, armed, and instructed. The formidable artillery you now have, had to be created. Other armies were to move and accomplish certain results. I have held you back that you might give the death blow to the rebellion that has distracted our once happy country. The patience you have shown, and your confidence in your general, are worthy of a dozen victories. These preliminary results are now accomplished. I feel that the patient labors of many months

have produced their fruit. The army of the Potomac is now a real army, magnificent in material, admirable in discipline and instruction, and excellently equipped and armed. Your commanders are all that I could wish. The moment for action has arrived, and I know that I can trust in you to save our country.

"As I ride through your ranks, I see in your faces the sure prestige of victory. I feel that you will do whatever I ask of you. The period of inaction has passed. I will bring you now face to face with the rebels, and only pray that God may defend the right. In whatever direction you may move, however strange my actions may appear to you, ever bear in mind that my fate is linked with yours, and that all I do is to bring you where I know you wish to be — on the decisive battle field. It is my business to place you there. I am to watch over you as a parent over his children; and you know that your general loves you from the depths of his heart. It shall be my care — it has ever been — to gain success with the least possible loss; but I know that, if it is necessary, you will follow me to your graves for our righteous cause. God smiles upon us. Victory attends us. Yet I would not have you think that our aim is to be obtained without a manly struggle. I will not disguise it from you, that you have brave foes to encounter; foemen well worthy of the steel that you will use so well. I shall demand of you great, heroic exertions, rapid and long marches, desperate combats and privations, perhaps. We will share all these together; and when this sad war is over, we will all return to our homes, and feel that we can ask no higher honor than the proud consciousness that we belonged to the army of the Potomac.

"GEO. B. McCLELLAN,
"*Major-General commanding*."

The army was marched back to Alexandria, where they were to embark, and waited some time for transports, which had not yet been provided in sufficient numbers, the movement down the Potomac and Chesapeake Bay apparently not having been definitely determined upon in season to provide them. It was necessary in changing the operations of the army to a new base at a distance from Washington, and not between that city and the enemy, that a sufficient force should be left for its protection. It was agreed by all military authority, that a considerable force was required for this purpose; but the number of troops to be left was a question upon which there was some difference of opinion. In this state of affairs, the President, in approving of the movement decided upon by the general officers, stipulated only that a sufficient force should be left in front of Washington to render the capital safe, and to prevent the enemy from re-occupying his old position and line of communication. General McClellan desired to have as large a force as possible for his movement upon the peninsula; and considering the danger of an advance by the rebels against Washington as inconsiderable, was disposed to leave a force which by some of the most experienced officers was not considered adequate, and by the President was deemed altogether insufficient, according to the understood opinions of the generals comprising the council of war above mentioned. The forces in and about Washington were under the command of General Wadsworth, who also reported the number which was left at his disposal as inadequate for the important trust committed to his charge. Adjutant-General Thomas, and General Hitchcock, an old and experienced officer, concurred in this opinion. This state of affairs led the President to detain the army corps of General McDowell, which was the last one to embark. But exclusive of this corps, according to the official reports, the number of troops which moved down to the peninsula was upwards of one hundred thousand, while the advance of this corps to a position between Washington and the rebel

capital might not only serve to protect the seat of government from a daring rebel movement, but would enable it to coöperate with the army of General McClellan.

The first division of the army sailed from Alexandria on the 22d of March, and arrived at Fortress Monroe on the 23d. The transportation continued till April 2d, when the greater part of the army had arrived at Old Point, and being landed, soon commenced a movement towards Yorktown. Before entering upon a narrative of the peninsula campaign, some events which occurred previously to any important operations by General McClellan's army should be recorded.

CHAPTER LXVI.

Naval Preparations of the Rebels. — The United States Vessels sunk at Norfolk. — The steamer Merrimac raised and ironplated. — Contradictory Reports of the Experiment. — Danger to United States Wooden Vessels and Northern Ports. — Advent of the Merrimac in Hampton Roads. — The frigates Cumberland and Congress at Newport News. — Appearance of the Merrimac. — Preparations on board the Frigates for Defence. — Attack by the Merrimac on the Cumberland. — Invulnerability of the Merrimac. — She strikes the Cumberland with her " Ram." — The Cumberland disabled and sunk. — Desperate and gallant Defence. — Scenes on board the sinking Vessel. — Attack on the Congress. — Spirited Defence. — Death of Captain Smith. — The Flag hauled down. — Unsuccessful Attempt to take the Crew Prisoners. — The Congress burned. — Heavy Losses. — Movements of the Ships of War near Fortress Monroe. — The Minnesota aground. — Attack by the Merrimac. — Withdrawal of the Rebel Vessels. — Arrival of the Iron-clad Monitor. — Her Appearance. — Preparations to meet the Merrimac. — Reappearance of the Rebel Vessels. — Battle between the Merrimac and the Monitor. — The Merrimac injured and compelled to retire. — The Monitor uninjured. — Lieutenant Worden. — Effects of the Rebel Fire. — The Success of the Monitor, and Relief to the Public Mind. — Official Reports.

AFTER the abandonment of the Norfolk navy yard by the federal officers at the commencement of the rebellion, the rebels early took measures to avail themselves of the means thus acquired, for the creation of a naval force. They had a few small steamers and other vessels, which were speedily armed, but were by no means formidable; and as the federal fleet in Hampton Roads soon became strong, they scarcely ventured to show themselves within long range of the ships of war and forts. The vessels which had been sunk at Norfolk, with the exception of the steamer Merrimac, were old and of little value for the purposes of modern warfare. The Merrimac, which was needlessly, if not treacherously abandoned, although set on fire before she sunk, was not damaged beyond repair, and as she was one of the finest steam frigates in the United States navy, was a valuable acquisition to the rebels if she could be raised. They soon attempted to avail themselves of this valuable prize; and after many delays and frequent reported failures, they succeeded in raising the steamer, and at once commenced preparations to transform her into a more formidable war vessel than any in the United States navy. The most common reports of their proceedings represented that the vessel was badly damaged, and would prove worthless; that the work of repair and alteration was slow, and, when it was certain that she was to be heavily iron-plated, that the experiment was proving a failure even before completion. These reports were generally credited by the naval authorities, though the government took precautions to prepare to some extent for so formidable a war vessel, should the rebels partially succeed in their efforts.

The work, however, went on as rapidly and successfully as the means at the command of the rebels permitted, and early in the year (1862) it was reported that the Merrimac — called by the rebels the "Virginia" — was nearly or quite ready for a trip down the river to Hampton Roads. Then again followed reports of the impossibility of the vessel passing down the river, on account of the deep draught caused by her armor and armament, and that she was unmanageable for the same reason.

The frequent recurrence of such reports caused the naval authorities and the northern public to believe that the vessel, from which the rebels had threatened so much, and which had caused no little trepidation among those interested in the commercial marine of the north, would after all prove a failure. Whether the rebels encouraged these reports or not, it at last became evident that their work was not altogether a failure; and about the 1st of March the appearance of the Merrimac was almost daily looked for in Hampton Roads. Some of the naval officers, still wanting confidence in iron armor for vessels, doubted the ability of the Merrimac to do much damage, or to prove an unequal foe to the heavily armed wooden vessels. The advent of the vessel was, however, looked for with fear and anxiety, as well as curiosity. If she was as formidable and invulnerable as had been represented, and had sufficient motive and steering power to be well controlled, she might, indeed, prove not only a terrible antagonist for the naval vessels opposed to her, but a scourge to northern ports and commerce.

On Saturday, the 8th of March, the Merrimac, as the vessel was generally still named, sailed from Norfolk, accompanied by the armed steamers Jamestown and Yorktown, and several tugboats. The approach of the rebel vessels was first discovered on board the federal fleet and in the forts at about noon, and as the appearance of the principal rebel vessel indicated that it was none other than the Merrimac, preparations were made for the expected attack. The frigates Cumberland and Congress, both sailing vessels, had been for some time anchored off Newport News Point, for the protection of the federal troops there from an attack by water. They were, therefore, some six miles or more above Fortress Monroe and the other large vessels of the federal fleet. Coming out from the Elizabeth River, the Merrimac and her consorts steamed directly across the

Roads towards these two frigates, the intention of the rebel officers being to destroy these vessels, which were practically blockading James River, and which being without steam power, would be comparatively helpless against the manœuvres of the Merrimac. For the destruction of these vessels the rebel crew were promised large shares of prize money.

The appearance of the Merrimac was grim and mysterious. Covered by an iron-plated roof, the sides of which rose from the water, with no signs of life on board, but moving silently under a dense cloud of smoke issuing from her huge smoke-stack, she was at once an object of wonder and alarm. Her heavy guns protruded through narrow ports which closed with iron shutters, and at her bow was a huge "ram," or extended prow of iron, designed to cut through the sides of wooden vessels below the water line. With such formidable offensive and defensive armor the strange vessel moved steadily towards the object of attack.

As the rebel "monster" approached, preparations were made on board the Cumberland and Congress to resist the attack. The former, which was the first object of attack, was swung across the channel, so as to bring a broadside to bear upon the Merrimac; and when the iron-clad was about a mile distant, the Cumberland commenced firing some of her heavy guns. The shot which struck the Merrimac glanced off her mailed sides without effect, and she continued to approach, regardless of the Cumberland's broadside, which was discharged when within suitable range. Firing a few shot at the Congress as she passed, the apparently invulnerable assailant steamed directly towards the Cumberland, and struck that vessel with her formidable ram near the bow, crashing through the wooden walls with irresistible force, and making a large hole, through which the water poured into the hold with fearful rapidity. Then backing off, the rebel vessel discharged her heavy guns at the ill-fated frigate

while preparing for another assault with her ram. A second blow cut another hole in the bottom of the Cumberland, which had already begun to settle in the water, and the continued fire of the Merrimac's guns at short range did fearful execution upon the frigate's crew. But though contending under such fearful disadvantages, the federal officers and crew, with noble heroism, continued to fight, and poured a storm of shot and shell upon the Merrimac, which would have nearly destroyed an ordinary vessel, but which fell almost harmless from the iron armor. One or two of the Cumberland's shots took effect in the ports of the Merrimac, disabling one gun, and wounding several men.

As the vessel began to sink rapidly the scene on board the Cumberland was fearful. The decks were strewn with the dead and wounded, and the fragments of the vessel and disabled gun carriages; but the gallant men who yet survived unharmed remained at the guns, and continued firing till the rapid settling of the ship caused the order to be given for them to save themselves. Attempts had already been made to remove a part of the wounded; but before many could be brought up from the cockpit it was filled with water. Several brave fellows, also, who remained in one of the magazines to pass up the ammunition as long as possible, were at last prevented from escape by the sudden rush of the water. When there was no longer any use in remaining at the guns, the men serving them sought their own safety, several of the guns being discharged just before they sunk beneath the surface of the water. After a most noble, but utterly unequal contest, of about three quarters of an hour, the Cumberland went down, with her flag still flying; and as her masts rose above the surface of the water, it waved over the spot illustrated by the most signal yet hopeless bravery and devotion to duty.

The fate of the Cumberland being sealed, the Merrimac was directed towards the Congress.

The officers of that vessel seeing the danger of remaining within the reach of the iron ram of the Merrimac, had made sail, and attempted to run into shoal water, where the iron-clad could not follow. The latter, however, safely encased in armor which defied the shot of her antagonist, with her heavy guns, discharged at short range, could make fearful work upon a wooden vessel. She sailed slowly about the Congress, not venturing to strike with the iron beak, but firing her guns with a precision which made almost every shot destructive; first raking the frigate fore and aft, and then moving slowly back and forth within one hundred yards, pouring broadside after broadside into her wooden sides, assisted also by the other rebel vessels at longer range. The fire was returned by the Congress with spirit and determination. Every gun that could be brought to bear upon the rebel vessel was rapidly discharged; but the shot had little apparent effect upon the iron armor, which left no vulnerable point. One shot, however, disabled one of the rebel guns, and it was believed that others had caused more or less injury to the armor of the Merrimac. The Congress was several times set on fire, but the flames were soon extinguished. Some of her guns were disabled, until at last only two could be brought to bear upon the Merrimac; the other rebel vessels were firing some damaging shots, and the loss of men in the unequal fight was becoming serious. Lieutenant Joseph B. Smith, the commanding officer, a brave and persistent man, was killed, and the command devolving upon Lieutenant Pendergrast, after consultation with his officers, he considered it wisest to spare a further loss of life, and he accordingly hauled down the national flag, and raised a white flag in its place. The Merrimac soon ceased firing, and a rebel tug proceeded to the Congress with officers to take charge of what they considered their prize, and to make prisoners of the crew. The federal officers refused to go on board the tug, trusting to the nearness of the shore for escape. A portion of the men, however, through mistake or alarm, went on board the tug, when it was driven off by the fire of troops on shore. The Merrimac then again opened fire upon the Congress, notwithstanding the white flag was flying, but it was not long continued, and the iron-clad moved away, as if for an attack on vessels below. The smaller rebel vessels did not again approach, and the surviving officers and crew of the Congress abandoned the vessel, which was now on fire, and safely reached the shore. The fire spread through the ship slowly but surely, and before midnight reached the magazines, when, with a terrible explosion, the Congress was blown up.

The Cumberland and Congress were fine specimens of their class, the old sailing frigate; but as the event too conclusively showed, they were in no way equal to a contest with steam, and iron-armor, and improved ordnance combined. But the bravery with which they were defended, especially the Cumberland, was worthy of the fame achieved by the American navy in its former palmiest days. The loss was very heavy on board each of these vessels, being nearly a third of those on board the Cumberland, and a fourth of those on board the Congress. The gallantry of officers and crews was justly honored with the heartiest praise and thanks, although it had proved so unavailing.

When the Merrimac and attendant vessels first appeared in the upper Roads, and it was evident that they were out on an errand of mischief, the steam frigates Roanoke and Minnesota, and sailing frigate St. Lawrence, and other vessels lying in the lower Roads and near Fortress Monroe, were signalled to prepare for action, and move up to meet the enemy. The Roanoke, whose machinery was out of repair, and the St. Lawrence were towed by tugboats, and before reaching any considerable distance got aground, and were unable to do more than to respond with an ineffectual fire to the shots from Sewall's Point. The Minnesota proceeded farther up the Roads, but when within a mile and a half of Newport News got aground, and all efforts to force the vessel over the shoal, or to get her into deeper water, were fruitless. The Minnesota was thus placed in a most dangerous position, where she would be exposed to the attack of the Merrimac, and would .be in a comparatively helpless condition. Tow-boats sent to the assistance of the Minnesota, were unable to render any service, and it seemed probable that the rebel vessels, having accomplished their work at Newport News, would soon come down to continue their successful operations. But the officers and men of the Minnesota were prepared to make a strong resistance, and the little gunboat Dragon, which had attempted to get the frigate afloat, lay by to render any assistance possible.

Leaving the Congress, as before stated, the Merrimac steamed slowly down the Roads, towards the Minnesota, but either for fear of getting aground, or, as was afterwards suggested, because they desired to capture rather than destroy the Minnesota, the rebel officers did not approach within a mile of the frigate. The rebel vessels — the Jamestown and another, accompanying the Merrimac — took positions, and opened fire upon the Minnesota. The shots from the Merrimac were poorly aimed, and but one struck the frigate ; but some rifled guns on the other steamers caused some damage and loss of life. A few shells, thrown from one of the heavy guns of the Minnesota, drove these vessels away, one of them apparently damaged and set on fire by the explosion of a shell. At nightfall the Merrimac also withdrew towards Sewall's Point, much to the relief of those who, knowing the fate of the Cumberland and Congress, had expected to see the Minnesota destroyed with scarcely more delay.

The achievements of the Merrimac had naturally created great alarm in Hampton Roads, and although the destructive monster had retired for a time, it seemed but too probable that the rebels, thus encouraged, would make renewed and greater efforts to destroy the federal vessels one by one, while only some accident, or singular good fortune on the part of a federal gun, could prevent the threatened destruction. Gloomy forebodings were, therefore, indulged in by many during this night of suspense, while on the part of the officers and crew of the Minnesota there was only a determination to resist to the last. But in the night came a protection for the federal ships and national honor.

The iron-clad battery " Monitor," constructed by Captain J. Ericsson, of New York, upon a plan devised and matured by himself, arrived at Hampton Roads on the evening of the 8th, and was soon sent up the Roads to assist the Minnesota against an attack from the Merrimac. This vessel, of comparatively small size, was strongly built and heavily plated with iron, sitting very low in the water, and having the appearance of a raft, rather than of a well-constructed vessel. Midway from stem to stern rose an iron revolving turret, in which were two heavy guns, which composed the entire armament of the vessel. These guns, protruding through narrow ports, which were closed except when the guns were run out, revolved with the turret, and were discharged as soon as brought to bear upon the object of attack. A small iron pilot house and the heavy smokestack were all that broke the surface of the broad iron deck, which was itself but little above the surface of the water. Singular in its appearance, and somewhat insignificant compared with the more ponderous Merrimac, the Monitor appeared as if it must be but a feeble antagonist for the formidable rebel iron-clad. The sequel, however, proved that it was the least vulnerable and the more efficient of the two. Taking a position in the night behind the Minnesota, the coming of daylight and the rebel vessels was anxiously awaited.

The next morning the Merrimac, with the other rebel vessels, steamed out from the vicinity of Sewall's Point in the direction of the Minnesota. As the rebel fleet approached, the Monitor, which had been lying under the shadow of the Minnesota with steam up, started out upon a reconnoissance, and proceeded to meet the rebel vessels. The latter continued their course, entirely ignorant of the character of the singular craft which now made its appearance in these waters for the first time. The wooden steamers kept on with the Merrimac until a shell from one of the Monitor's guns apparently disabled one of them, and kept them afterwards at a safer distance, where they could fire only at long range.

The Merrimac, however, continued her course, and a battle between the iron-clads soon commenced in earnest. They approached each other to a distance not exceeding forty or fifty yards, and sometimes to within as many feet, and during the four hours' contest which ensued, they were not at any time more than two hundred yards apart. The firing from each vessel was rapid, the Merrimac sometimes discharging a broadside at the Monitor, while the latter, from her two eleven-inch guns, as the turret revolved, threw her immense shot at her antagonist. Upon each vessel the shot rattled like gigantic hail, glancing or falling off, for the most part, harmless. In the mean time each was moving about as if to obtain some advantage; the Monitor apparently endeavoring to obtain a position from which she could throw her shot at the stern of the Merrimac, which was supposed to be the most vulnerable part, and the Merrimac attempting to run down the Monitor with her iron beak. During these movements the Merrimac got aground for a short time, and the Monitor, sailing about her, continued to fire her heavy missiles, two or three of which apparently took effect. Succeeding in getting afloat again, the Merrimac again attempted to run down her antagonist,

and this time succeeded in striking the Monitor amidship. The shock careened the Monitor a little and threw her out of her course, but caused no serious damage. The Merrimac, however, had been considerably damaged by the fire of the Monitor, and because of these injuries began to retire from the contest. It appeared that she leaked considerably, and according to the testimony of parties on board of her who subsequently deserted, the engineer had reported serious damage by two or three shots from the Monitor. The latter, which was uninjured to any extent, followed the rebel vessels for some distance; but finally abandoned the pursuit, the Merrimac with her attendant vessels making for the Elizabeth River, and thence up to Norfolk, where it was soon ascertained she was undergoing considerable repairs.

To the Monitor, in this long conflict of four hours, but little damage was done, and there were no casualties on board, except to her brave and enterprising commander, Lieutenant Worden. While looking through a narrow aperture in the little iron pilot house of his vessel, just as the Merrimac was withdrawing, worsted, from the conflict, a shell burst upon the outside of this house close to the aperture, and minute scales of iron were forced through it, severely injuring the face and eyes of Lieutenant Worden. The wound was painful and dangerous, and following a great prostration of strength, caused by a long imprisonment at the hands of the rebels, the young officer who had dared so much in an untried experiment, was for a long time a sufferer, and his sight nearly despaired of. Universal sympathy and gratitude was felt towards him by the loyal people, who heartily rejoiced when he was at last restored to the service he had honored.

The contest had not been confined entirely to the two iron-clads. The Merrimac, finding that the Monitor was as invulnerable as herself, had discharged her guns more frequently at the Minnesota, and that vessel had replied with occasional shot during the whole period of the battle, but evidently with little or no effect upon the Merrimac. A shot from the latter had struck the boiler of the small gunboat Dragon, which lay near the Minnesota, causing an explosion of steam, which slightly damaged the vessel and scalded some of the men. Beyond this no serious damage was done to the federal vessels, and · the wooden vessels of the rebels kept at so great a distance that they were scarcely exposed to the fire of the former.

The relief afforded by the result of this day's battle to the minds of the loyal persons in Hampton Roads and at Fortress Monroe, and indeed throughout the north, can hardly be expressed. The formidable rebel iron-clad, so much dreaded after the destruction of the Cumberland and Congress, had found more than a match in the little Monitor, and the success of this vessel was an honor to its ingenious inventor as well as a subject for congratulation among the loyal people. The efficiency of iron-clad ships of war had never before been practically tested, and both the achievements of the Merrimac against wooden vessels and her encounter with the Monitor, were regarded with much interest in Europe as well as the United States. The invulnerability of Ericsson's vessel and its successful operation, induced the government to order at once the construction of others upon the same plan, the result of the conflict demonstrating, in some degree, the superiority of this mode of construction over the ordinary plan of plating vessels which had been adopted in Europe.

The following are among the official reports of the events above described. Commander Radford, of the Cumberland, was serving as a member of a court of inquiry on board the Roanoke at the time of the appearance of the Merrimac, and although he made every effort to reach his ship, he did not arrive at her station until she had sunk. The Cumberland was, therefore, at the time, under the command of Lieutenant George M. Morris, who made the following report: —

LIEUTENANT MORRIS'S REPORT.

"NEWPORT NEWS, VA., March 9, 1862.

"SIR: Yesterday morning, at nine A. M., I discovered two steamers at anchor off Smithfield Point, on the left hand or western side of the river, distant about twelve miles. At twelve meridian, I discovered three vessels under steam, standing down the Elizabeth River, towards Sewall's Point. I beat to quarters, double-breeched the guns on the main deck, and cleared ship for action.

"At one P. M., the enemy hove in sight, gradually nearing us. The iron-clad steamer Merrimac, accompanied by two steam gunboats, passed ahead of the Congress frigate and steered down towards us. We opened fire on her. She stood on and struck us under the starboard fore-channels. She delivered her fire at the same time. The destruction was great. We returned the fire with solid shot with alacrity.

" At thirty minutes past three the water had gained upon us, notwithstanding the pumps were kept actively employed, to a degree that the forward magazine being drowned, we had to take powder from the after magazine for the ten-inch gun. At thirty-five minutes past three the water had risen to the main hatchway, and the ship cantered to port, and we delivered a parting fire — each man trying to save himself by jumping overboard.

"Timely notice was given, and all the wounded who could walk were ordered out of the cockpit; but those of the wounded who had been carried into the sick bay and on the berth deck were so mangled that it was impossible to save them.

"It is impossible for me to individualize. Alike, the officers and men all behaved in the most gallant manner. Lieutenant Selfridge and Master Stuyvesant were in command of the gun-deck divisions, and they did all that noble and gallant officers could do. Acting Masters Randall and Kennison, who had charge each of a pivot-gun, showed the most perfect coolness, and did all they could to save our noble ship; but, I am sorry to say, without avail. Among the last to leave the ship were Sergeant Martin and Assistant-Surgeon Kershaw, who did all they could for the wounded promptly and faithfully.

"The loss we sustained I can not yet inform you of, but it has been very great. The warrant and steerage officers could not have been more prompt and active than they were at their different stations. Chaplain Lenhart is missing. Master's mate John Harrington was killed. I should judge we have lost upwards of one hundred men. I can only say, in conclusion, that all did their duty, and we sank with the American flag flying at the peak.

"I am, sir, &c.,

"Geo. M. Morris,

"*Lieutenant and Executive Officer.*

Lieutenant Pendergrast, upon whom devolved the command of the Congress after the death of Lieutenant Smith, reported that after learning the death of his superior officer, he took command. "Seeing that our men were being killed without the prospect of any relief from the Minnesota, which vessel had run ashore in attempting to get up to us from Hampton Roads, not being able to get a single gun to bear upon the enemy, and the ship being on fire in several places, upon consultation with Commander William Smith, we deemed it proper to haul down our colors, without any further loss of life on our part. We were soon boarded by an officer of the Merrimac, who said he would take charge of the ship. He left shortly afterwards, and a small tug came alongside, whose captain demanded that we should surrender and get out of the ship, as he intended to burn her immediately. A sharp fire with muskets and artillery was maintained from our troops ashore upon the tug, having the effect of driving her off The Merrimac again opened upon us, although we had a peak to show that we were out of action. After having fired several shells into us, she left us, and engaged the Minnesota and the shore batteries."

Captain John Marston, commanding the Roanoke, was the senior officer of the fleet, and acting flag-officer. His report is as follows: —

"United States Steamer Roanoke,
Hampton Roads, *March* 9, 1862.

"Sir: I have the honor to inform you that yesterday, at one o'clock, one of the look-out vessels reported by signal that the enemy was coming out. I immediately ordered the Minnesota to get under way, and as soon as two tugs appointed to tow this ship came alongside I slipped our cable.

"The Merrimac was soon discovered passing out by Sewall's Point, standing up towards Newport News, accompanied by several small gunboats. Every exertion was made by us to get all the speed on the Roanoke that the two tugs were capable of giving her, but in consequence of our bad steerage we did not get ahead as rapidly as we desired to.

"The Merrimac went up and immediately attacked the Congress and Cumberland, but particularly the latter ship, which was hid from us by the land. When about seven or eight miles from Fortress Monroe the Minnesota grounded. We continued to stand on, and when we came in sight of the Cumberland we saw that she had careened over, apparently full of water.

"The enemy, who had been joined by two or three steamers from James River, now devoted themselves exclusively to the Congress; but she being aground, could bring but five guns to bear on them, and at ten minutes before four o'clock we had the mortification of seeing her haul down her flag. I continued to stand on until we found ourselves in three and a half fathoms of water, and was on the ground astern.

"Finding that we could go no further, I ordered one of the tugs to tow us round, and as soon as the Roanoke's head was pointed down the bay, and I found she was afloat again, I directed the tugs to go to the assistance of the Minnesota, under the hope that, with the assistance of the two others which had accompanied her, they would be able to get her off; but up to the time that I now write they have not succeeded in doing so.

"At five o'clock the frigate St. Lawrence, in tow of the Cambridge, passed us, and not long after she also grounded; but by the aid of the Cambridge she was got afloat again, and being unable to render any assistance to the Minnesota, came down the harbor.

"In passing the batteries at Sewall's Point, both going and returning, the rebels opened fire upon us, which was returned from our pivot guns; but the range was too great for them, while the enemy's shots fell far beyond us. One shot went through our foresail, cutting away two of our shrouds, and several shells burst over and near the ship, scattering their fragments on the deck. Between seven and eight o'clock we discovered that the rebels had set fire to the Congress, and she continued to burn until one o'clock, when she blew up. This was a melancholy satisfaction to me; for as she had fallen into the hands of the enemy, it was far better to have her destroyed than that she should be employed against us at some future day.

"It was the impression of some of my officers that the rebels hoisted the French flag.

"I heard that the Monitor had arrived, and soon after Lieutenant-Commanding Worden came on board, and I immediately ordered him to go up to the Minnesota, hoping she would be able to keep off an attack on the Minnesota until he had got her afloat again.

"This morning the Merrimac renewed the attack on the Minnesota, but she found, no doubt greatly to her surprise, a new opponent in the Monitor.

"The contest has been going on during most of the day between these two armored vessels, and most beautifully has the little Monitor sustained herself, showing herself capable of great endurance.

"I have not received any official accounts of the loss of the Congress and Cumberland, but no doubt shall do so, when they will be transmitted to you.

"I should do injustice to this military department did I not inform you that every assistance was freely tendered to us, sending five of their tugs to the relief of the Minnesota, and offering all the aid in their power.

"I would also beg leave to say that Captain Poor, of the ordnance department, kindly volunteered to do duty temporarily on board this ship, and from whom I have received much assistance.

"I am, very respectfully,

"Your obedient servant,

"JOHN MARSTON,

"*Captain and Senior Officer.*

" To Hon. GIDEON WELLES, *Secretary of the Navy.*"

Captain Van Brunt, who commanded the Minnesota, and participated in the general engagement, and who, from his position, had an opportunity of witnessing the contest between the Merrimac and Monitor, made the following report: —

REPORT OF CAPTAIN VAN BRUNT.

" UNITED STATES STEAMER MINNESOTA, }
March 10, 1862. {

"SIR: On Saturday, the eighth instant, at forty-five minutes after twelve o'clock P. M., three small steamers, in appearance, were discovered rounding Sewall's Point, and as soon as they came into full broadside view, I was convinced that one was the iron-plated steam-battery Merrimac, from the large size of her smoke-pipe. They were heading for Newport News, and I, in obedience to a signal from the senior officer present, Captain John Marston, immediately called all hands, slipped my cables, and got under way for that point, to engage her. While rapidly passing Sewall's Point, the rebels there opened fire upon us from a rifle-battery, one shot from which going through and crippling my mainmast. I returned the fire with my broadside-guns and forecastle-pivot. We ran without further difficulty within about one and a' half miles of Newport News, and there, unfortunately, grounded. The tide was running ebb, and although in the channel there was not sufficient water for this ship, which draws twenty-three feet, I knew the bottom was soft and lumpy, and endeavored to force the ship over, but found it impossible so to do. At this time it was reported to me that the Merrimac had passed the frigate Congress and run into the sloop of war Cumberland, and in fifteen minutes after, I saw the latter going down by the head. The Merrimac then hauled off, taking a position, and about half past two o'clock P. M., engaged the Congress, throwing shot and shell into her with terrific effect, while the shot from the Congress glanced from her iron-plated sloping sides, without doing any apparent injury. At half past three o'clock P. M., the Congress was compelled to haul down her colors. Of the extent of her loss and injury, you will be informed from the official report of her commander.

"At four o'clock P. M., the Merrimac, Jamestown, and Patrick Henry, bore down upon my vessel. Very fortunately, the iron battery drew too much water to come within a mile of us. She took a position on my starboard bow, but did not fire with accuracy, and only one shot passed through the ship's bow. The other two steamers took their position on my port bow and stern, and their fire did most damage in killing and wounding men, inasmuch as they fired with rifled guns; but with the heavy gun that I could bring to bear upon them, I drove them off, one of them apparently in a crippled state. I fired upon the Merrimac with my ten-inch pivot-gun, without any apparent effect, and at seven o'clock P. M., she too hauled off, and all three vessels steamed towards Norfolk.

"The tremendous firing of my broadside guns had crowded me further upon the mud bank, into which the ship seemed to have made for herself a cradle. From ten P. M., when the tide commenced to run flood, until four A. M., I had all hands at work, with steamtugs and hawsers, endeavoring to haul the ship off the bank, but without avail; and as the tide had then fallen considerably, I suspended further proceedings at that time.

"At two A. M., the iron-battery Monitor, Commander John L. Worden, which had arrived the previous evening at Hampton Roads, came alongside and reported for duty, and then all on board felt that we had a friend that would stand by us in our hour of trial.

"At six A. M., the enemy again appeared, coming down from Craney Island, and I beat to quarters; but they ran past my ship, and were heading for Fortress Monroe, and the retreat was beaten, to allow my men to get something to eat. The Merrimac ran down near the Rip Raps, and then turned into the channel through which I had come. Again all hands were called to quarters, and opened upon her with my stern guns, and made signal to the Monitor to attack the enemy. She immediately ran down in my wake, right within the range of the Merrimac, completely covering my ship, as far as was possible with her diminutive dimensions, and, much to my astonishment, laid herself right alongside of the Merrimac, and the contrast was that of a pygmy to a giant. Gun after gun was fired by the Monitor, which was returned with whole broadsides from the rebels, with no more effect, apparently, than so many pebble stones thrown by a child. After a while they commenced manœuvring, and we could see the little battery point her bow for the rebels, with the intention, as I thought, of sending a shot through her bow porthole; then she would shoot by her, and rake her through her stern. In the mean time the rebels were pouring broadside after broadside, but almost all her shot flew over the little submerged propeller; and when they struck the bomb-proof tower, the shot glanced off without producing any effect, clearly establishing the fact that wooden vessels cannot contend successfully with iron-clad ones, for never before was any thing like it dreamed of by the greatest enthusiast in maritime warfare. The Merrimac finding that she could make nothing of the Monitor, turned her attention once more to mê in the morning. She had put one eleven-inch shot under my counter, near the water-line, and now, on her second approach, I opened upon her with all my broadside guns and ten-inch pivot — a broadside which would have blown out of water any timber-built ship in the world. She returned my fire with her rifled bow-gun, with a shell which passed through the chief engineer's state room, through the engineer's mess room amidships, and burst in the boatswain's room, tearing four rooms all into one, in its passage exploding two charges of powder, which set the ship on fire, but it was promptly extinguished by a party headed by my first lieutenant. Her second went through the boiler of the tugboat Dragon, exploding it, and causing some consternation on board my ship for the moment, until the matter was explained. This time I had concentrated upon her an incessant fire from my gun-deck, spar-deck, and forecastle pivot-guns, and was informed by my marine officer, who was stationed on the poop, that at least fifty solid shot struck her on her slanting side, without producing any apparent effect. By the time she had fired her third shell, the little Monitor had come down upon her, placing herself between us, and compelled her to change her position, in doing which she grounded, and

again I poured into her all the guns which could be brought to bear upon her. As soon as she got off, she stood down the bay, the little battery chasing her with all speed, when suddenly the Merrimac turned around, and ran full speed into her antagonist. For a moment I was anxious, but instantly I saw a shot plunge into the iron roof of the Merrimac, which surely must have damaged her, for some time after the rebels concentrated their whole battery upon the tower and pilot house of the Monitor, and soon after the latter stood down for Fortress Monroe, and we thought it probable she had exhausted her supply of ammunition, or sustained some injury. Soon after the Merrimac and the two other steamers headed for my ship, and I then felt to the fullest extent my condition. I was hard and immovable aground, and they could take position under my stern and rake me. I had expended most of my solid shot, and my ship was badly crippled, and my officers and men were worn out with fatigue; but even in this extreme dilemma I determined never to give up the ship to the rebels, and after consulting my officers, I ordered every preparation to be made to destroy the ship, after all hope was gone to save her. On ascending the poop deck, I observed that the enemy's vessels had changed their course, and were heading for Craney Island; then I determined to lighten the ship by throwing overboard my eight-inch guns, hoisting out provisions, starting water, &c. At two P. M., I proceeded to make another attempt to save the ship, by the use of a number of powerful tugs and the steamer S. R. Spaulding — kindly sent to my assistance by Captain Talmadge, Quartermaster at Fortress Monroe — and succeeded in dragging her half a mile distant, and then she was again immovable, the tide having fallen. At two A. M., this morning I succeeded in getting the ship once more afloat, and am now at anchor opposite Fortress Monroe.

"It gives me great pleasure to say, that during the whole of these trying scenes the officers and men conducted themselves with great courage and coolness.

"I have the honor to be your very obedient servant, G. J. VAN BRUNT,

"*Captain U. S. Navy, com. Frigate Minnesota.*

' Hon. GIDEON WELLES, Secretary of the Navy, Washington, D. C."

CHAPTER LXVII.

Federal Movement in North Carolina. — Expedition against Newbern. — Debarkation of Troops. — March towards Newbern. — Bivouac near the Rebel Lines. — Rebel Fortifications and Troops. — The Advance for Attack. — The Battle. — Gallantry of Federal Troops. — Fortifications stormed. — Successful Assaults by the three Brigades. — The Works carried. — Flight of the Rebels. — Movements of the Gunboats. — Batteries and Obstructions. — The Obstacles overcome. — The Gunboats at Newbern. — Burning of the Railroad Bridge and Houses in Newbern. — The Town occupied. — Federal Military Authority. — Official Reports.

IN North Carolina, after the capture of Roanoke Island and the destruction of the rebel flotilla at Elizabeth City, as narrated in a previous chapter,* no new movement was made for upwards of a month. In the mean time reconnoissances were made, and General Burnside, while receiving additional troops and supplies, and making the necessary preparations for an advance, had obtained information respecting the rebel position and the waters and coast of the state. Early in March preparations were made for an immediate movement against Newbern, situated at the confluence of the Neuse and Trent Rivers, a town of some commercial importance, but of much more consequence as a strategic point in the military occupation of the state.

General Burnside embarked parts of three brigades, under Generals Foster, Reno, and Parke, on board his transports on the 11th of March, and on the 12th sailed from Hatteras Inlet, where his vessels had been directed to

rendezvous, in company with a small flotilla of gunboats, under the command of Commodore Rowan. The vessels arrived the same night at the point for debarkation at the mouth of Slocum's Creek, about eighteen miles below Newbern, and early the next morning the troops commenced landing and moving up the bank of the river. The debarkation, owing to the shoal water, was necessarily slow and tedious; but in the course of the day the whole force was landed, and the advance had moved on some twelve miles towards Newbern. With the troops, which were entirely of infantry, were eight howitzers from the gunboats and transports. These were drawn and manned by sailors, but were under the command of the military. A heavy rain had made the progress of the troops very difficult, and it required a large number of soldiers to aid in dragging the artillery through the mud. As the column moved the gunboats sailed up the river, shelling the woods in its advance, to compel any rebel force there to retire, or to reveal their position. On the march some formidable but unfinished fortifications were found, which a few weeks later might have added more serious obstacles to the success of the expedition. There were signs of hasty retreat from these points, but no rebel forces were discovered, and at night the advance of the federal troops bivouacked within a mile and a half of the enemy's stronghold, the rebel pickets then first being met. After their wet and toilsome march, the federal soldiers found only the moist ground on which to rest, and their blankets to protect them from the rain; but they were full of enthusiasm and confidence, and by their bivouac fires they cheerfully bore their hardships, in anticipation of a victory on the morrow.

Although the lower or outer fortifications had not been completed, the approaches to Newbern were defended by extensive works, consisting of a line of water batteries on the river, which were connected with field works, mounted with heavy cannon, and rifle pits and redoubts, reaching some three miles from the town. They had mounted upwards of forty heavy guns, and had also three field batteries, while according to subsequent reports, there were eight regiments of infantry and about five hundred cavalry, in addition to the light artillery, to defend the works and the town. To attack so strongly fortified a position, held by so considerable a force, was a formidable undertaking for an army no larger than General Burnside's, and having only eight guns of comparatively light calibre; but the attempt was to be made, in the fullest confidence of success.

Early in the morning of the 14th the whole division was ordered to advance in three columns. General Foster's brigade, on the right, moved by the main road to attack the enemy's left; General Reno's brigade moved along the railroad, which ran near the river directly towards Newbern, to engage the enemy's right; while General Parke's brigade followed for some distance the route taken by General Foster's, for the purpose of attacking the rebel front, and to support either of the other brigades. The several brigades moved forward promptly and with the steadiness of veterans. General Reno's troops, on the railroad, were the first to meet with the enemy. A railroad train, which had apparently brought reënforcements from Newbern, was discovered on the track in their front, and men were engaged in unloading a heavy rifled gun, when the sudden advance of General Reno's force drove the rebels hastily into their intrenchments, and the train moved back towards the town. Finding his advance troops close upon the formidable earthworks of the enemy, General Reno formed his brigade in line of battle in the woods, which extended on either side of the railroad, and opened fire with musketry upon the rebels occupying the main fortifications and the rifle pits on the left.

In the mean time General Foster's brigade had advanced along the carriage road through the woods, which for the most part covered the country, until they came to the clearing in front of the rebel position. Here General Foster soon disposed of his troops in line of battle, and commenced the attack on the enemy's left. General Parke's brigade, which had also advanced by the same road, was brought into position between General Foster's and General Reno's, and thus the line of battle was completed along the whole front of the rebel works. The naval artillery was placed in position in the centre, and was worked with the greatest gallantry by the officers and men in charge.

The federal troops had hardly formed in line of battle and opened fire upon the enemy, when the latter replied with their numerous pieces of artillery and heavy volleys of musketry, which took serious effect upon the unprotected Union troops. They fought, however, like veterans, and pressed forward in spite of the damaging fire, and notwithstanding the nature of the ground, which was in many places such as to give great advantage to the enemy. The right wing of General Reno's brigade, a part of the twenty-first Massachusetts, pressed forward by the railroad, and succeeded in entering the rebel breastworks, where they charged upon the rebel battery of artillery, and drove the men from their pieces. The national colors were planted within the works, and could this regiment have been immediately supported, the battle here would have been quickly decided. But the rebels immediately brought up two regiments to meet the four companies which entered the works, and the latter were compelled to retire. But the success with which they had met encouraged the federal soldiers to renewed efforts, and a report of the condition of affairs behind the rebel breastworks induced Colonel Rodman, of the fourth Rhode Island, which was next in line to the twenty-first Massachusetts, without the orders of General Parke, in whose brigade he was, to charge upon the battery. His regiment moved quickly and firmly forward, and succeeded in entering the breastwork on the flank of the battery. Here it was speedily formed, and charged upon the gunners, driving them, completely routed, from their pieces, and capturing the whole battery. Being soon supported by the other regiments of General Parke's brigade, the rebels fled from this part of the field with precipitation, leaving the federal troops in undisputed possession of the ground, and the arms which they had so gallantly captured.

Almost simultaneously with the assault in the centre, the extreme right of General Foster's brigade, the twenty-fourth Massachusetts, which had pressed forward under a galling fire and very great disadvantages of ground, planted their colors upon the parapet of the rebel fortifications in their front, and this gallant regiment, followed by the whole brigade, poured into the rebel works. The rebel forces fled in dismay, abandoning all that encumbered their flight.

Quickly following this success was a charge by General Reno's brigade, which had contended against a series of forts and rifle pits for several hours, and had suffered severely in the contest. Bringing up a regiment held in reserve, General Reno ordered a charge by the whole brigade; and in the face of the heavy fire of the rebels, which had not abated in this part of their works, and in spite of the abatis and other obstacles which met them on the acclivity up which they moved, the troops advanced quickly and steadily, carrying the works immediately before them in a gallant manner. At the same time a supporting charge, by a part of General Parke's brigade within the intrenchments, completed the rebel rout and the federal victory. The whole line of works had been carried, and almost as if by the same order the troops in the several brigades had stormed the enemy's position along its whole front, and won a speedy victory.

While the army marched from the place of debarkation and attacked the rebels by land, the gunboat flotilla proceeded up the river to attack the batteries constructed for defence from a naval attack. The first day two batteries, some miles below Newbern, were encountered. The first, mounting four guns, was speedily silenced by the fire of the gunboats, the rebel garrison abandoning their guns in haste after the discharge of a few shot. The next mounted twelve or fifteen guns, but the rebel force in the work appeared to be terror-stricken at the approach of the gunboats, and a few shots sufficed to drive them precipitately from their guns and to seek safety in flight. A small cavalry force was also compelled to beat a hasty retreat by the shells thrown among them by the gunboats. The national flag was raised over the captured forts, and the flotilla came to anchor for the night.

On the 14th, when the attack by General Burnside's forces was made, the gunboats again moved up the river. About six miles below Newbern they came upon some formidable obstructions, which were evidently expected by the rebels to prevent any nearer approach by the navy to the town. The river was at this point divided by a shoal into two channels, one of which was obstructed by the sinking of numerous vessels in such a manner as to present an impassable barrier, and in the other were sunk heavy spars pointed down the river, the ends of which were armed with sharpened iron, so as to run through the bows or sides of a vessel moving up the river. There were also several torpedoes sunk in this channel, designed to explode by the contact of a vessel with timbers projecting from them. A battery was constructed on the bank to command the river at this point, and to rake the approaching vessels while detained by the obstructions. Commodore Rowan, after briefly examining the obstructions, ordered the gunboats to follow the flag-ship Delaware, and boldly pressed through the dangerous channel without serious injury to any of the vessels. During the passage of the gunboats through the obstructions a brisk fire was kept up by the battery, but without much effect upon the flotilla, and a few well-directed shot from the gunboats soon silenced the guns and drove the men from the works.

Having passed the barrier which was so confidently expected to prevent the federal gunboats from ascending the river, still another fort opposed the advance of the flotilla. But this, too, after a short engagement, was abandoned by the rebels, who were now flying from all their works before the assault of the federal troops and the approach of the ever dreaded gunboats. Proceeding up the river to the town, a few shot and shell were thrown at the rebels, who were seen hurrying away in trains upon the railroad.

The rebel force having safely crossed the river into the town of Newbern, the railroad bridge was burned, whether by accident or for the purpose of preventing pursuit by the victorious national troops, did not appear. General Burnside ordered his forces forward, expecting at first to meet with another line of defence. Their progress, however, was altogether unobstructed by any rebel force, and they marched to the river, which they were unable immediately to cross, on account of the burning of the railroad bridge and the destruction of the draw in the bridge of the common road. The gunboats having arrived at this point, after a brief delay, a part of the troops were transported across the river, but the rebel force had retreated beyond the town, which had been fired in several places by the flying soldiers or frightened citizens. Measures were at once taken to extinguish the flames and to quiet the alarm of the comparatively few people who remained in the town. The federal troops were so posted as to hold their position against attack, and Newbern was soon quietly under the military rule of the United States. Many of the peo-ple were induced to return to their homes and occupations, and from the strict discipline of the federal troops, and the firm but moderate rule of General Foster, who was appointed military governor, they found quite as much safety, unless openly demonstrative of their sympathy with rebellion, as they had enjoyed under the rebel authorities, and much greater prospect of prosperity.

The following are the official reports of General Burnside and Commodore Rowan:—

GENERAL BURNSIDE'S REPORT.

"HEADQUARTERS DEPARTMENT OF NORTH CAROLINA, }
          NEWBERN, March 16, 1862. }

"GENERAL: I have the honor to report that, after embarking the troops with which I intended to attack Newbern, in conjunction with the naval force on the morning of the 11th, a rendezvous was made at Hatteras Inlet. Flag-Officer Goldsborough having been ordered to Hampton Roads, the naval fleet was left in command of Commander Rowan. Early on the morning of the 12th, the entire force started for Newbern, and that night anchored off the mouth of Slocum's Creek, some eighteen miles from Newbern, where I had decided to make a landing. The landing commenced by seven o'clock the next morning, under cover of the naval fleet, and was effected with the greatest enthusiasm by the troops. Many, too impatient for the boats, leaped into the water, and waded, waist deep, to the shore, and then, after a toilsome march through the mud, the head of the column marched within a mile and a half of the enemy's stronghold, at eight P. M., a distance of twelve miles from the point of landing, where we bivouacked for the night, the rear of the column coming up with the boat-howitzers about three o'clock next morning, the detention being caused by the shocking condition of the roads, consequent upon the heavy rain that had fallen during that day and the whole of the night, the men often wading knee deep in mud, and requiring a whole regiment to drag the eight pieces which had been landed from the navy and our own vessels.

"By signals agreed upon, the naval vessels, with the armed vessels of my force, were informed of our progress, and were thereby enabled to assist us much in our march by shelling the road in advance.

"At daylight, on the morning of the 14th, I ordered an advance of the entire division, which will be understood by the enclosed pencil sketch. General Foster's brigade was ordered up the main country road, to attack the enemy's left; General Reno up the railroad, to attack their right, and General Parke to follow General Foster, and attack the enemy in front, with instructions to support either or both brigades.

"I must defer, for want of time, a detailed account of the action. It is enough to say that, after an engagement of four hours, we succeeded in carrying a continuous line of field works of over a mile in length, protected on the river bank by a battery of thirteen heavy guns, and on the opposite bank by a line of redoubts of over half a mile in length, for riflemen and field pieces, in the midst of swamps and dense forests, which line of works was defended by eight regiments of infantry, five hundred cavalry, and three batteries of field artillery, of six guns each. The position was finally carried by a most gallant charge of our men, which enabled us to gain the rear of all the batteries between this point and Newbern, which was done by a rapid advance of the entire force up the main road and the railroad, the naval fleet meantime pushing its way up the river, throwing their shots into the forts and in front of us.

"The enemy, after retreating in great confusion, throwing away blankets, knapsacks, arms, &c., across the railroad bridge and country road, burned the former, and destroyed the draw of the latter, thus preventing further pursuit, and causing detention in occupying the town by our military force; but the naval force had arrived at the wharves, and commanded it by their guns. I at once advanced General Foster's brigade, to take possession of the town, by means of the naval vessels, which Commander Rowan had kindly volunteered for the purpose. The city was set on fire by the retreating rebels in many places; but, owing to the exertions of the naval officers, the remaining citizens were induced to aid in extinguishing the flames, so that but little harm has been done. Many of the citizens are now returning, and we are now in quiet possession of the city. We have captured the printing press, and shall at once issue a daily sheet. By this victory our combined force have captured eight batteries, containing forty-six heavy guns, and three batteries of light artillery, of six guns each, making in all sixty-four guns; two steamboats, a number of sailing vessels, wagons, horses, a large quantity of ammunition, commissary and quartermaster's stores, forage, the entire camp equipage of the rebel troops, a large quantity of rosin, turpentine, cotton, &c., and over two hundred prisoners.

"Our loss, thus far ascertained, will amount to ninety-one killed, and four hundred and sixty-six wounded, many of them mortally. Among these are some of our most gallant officers and men. The rebel loss is severe, but not so great as our own, they being effectually covered by their works.

"Too much praise cannot be awarded to the officers and men for their untiring exertion, and unceasing patience, in accomplishing this work. The effecting of the landing, and the approach to within a mile and a half of the enemy's works on the 13th, I consider as great a victory as the engagement of the 14th.

"Owing to the difficult nature of the landing, our men were forced to wade ashore waist deep, march through mud to a point twelve miles distant, bivouac on low, marshy ground, in a rain storm, for the night, engage the enemy at daylight in the morning, fighting them for four hours, amid a dense fog, that prevented them from seeing the position of the enemy, and finally advancing rapidly over bad roads upon the city. In the midst of all this, not a complaint was heard; the men were only eager to accomplish their work. Every brigade, and in fact every regiment, and I can almost say every officer and man of the force landed, was in the engagement.

"The men are all in good spirits, and, under the circumstances, are in good health.

"I beg to say to the general commanding that I have under my command a division that can be relied upon in any emergency.

"A more detailed report will be forwarded as soon as I receive the brigade returns. The brigadier-generals, having been in the midst of their regiments whilst under fire, will be able to give me minute accounts. I beg to say to the general commanding the army, that I have endeavored to carry out the very minute instructions given me by him before leaving Annapolis, and thus far events have been singularly coincident with his anticipations; I only hope that we may in future be able to carry out in detail the remaining plans of the campaign. The only thing I have to regret, is the delay caused by the elements.

"I desire again to bear testimony to the gallantry of our naval fleet, and to express my thanks to Commander Rowan, and the officers under him, for their hearty and cheerful coöperation in this movement. Their assistance was timely and of great service in the accomplishment of our undertaking.

"I omitted to mention that there was a large arrival of reënforcements of the enemy in Newbern during the engagement, which retreated with the remainder of the army by the cars and the country roads.

"I have the honor, general, to be

"Your obedient servant,

"A. E. BURNSIDE,

"*Brig.-Gen. com'g Department of North Carolina.*

"General L. THOMAS, *Adjutant-General United States Army.*"

COMMODORE ROWAN'S REPORT.

"UNITED STATES FLAG-STEAMER PHILADELPHIA, ⎱
OFF NEWBERN, N. C., *March* 16. ⎰

"SIR: I have the honor to report the capture of all the rebel batteries upon the Neuse River, the complete defeat and rout of the enemy's forces in this vicinity, and the occupation of the city of Newbern by the combined forces of the army and navy of the United States on yesterday, Friday, at noon. The incidents of the expedition, briefly stated, are these:

"The fleet under my command, and that of the army, left Hatteras Inlet at half past seven on Wednesday morning, the 12th instant, and arrived, without accident or delay, on the point selected for disembarking the troops, and within sight of the city of Newbern, at sunset on the evening of the same day, where we anchored for the night.

"On Thursday morning I hoisted my pennant on board the steamer Delaware.

"At half past eight A. M., our gunboats commenced shelling the woods in the vicinity of the proposed place of landing, taking stations at intervals along the shore, to protect the advance of the troops.

"At half past nine A. M, the troops commenced landing, and at the same time six naval boat-howitzers, with their crews, under the command of Lieutenant R. S. McCook, of the Stars and Stripes, were put on shore to assist the attack. The army commenced to move up the beach at about half past eleven A. M., the debarkation of troops still continuing. In the mean time our vessels were slowly moving up, throwing shell in the wood beyond.

"At a quarter past four P. M., the first of the enemy's batteries opened fire on the foremost of our gunboats, which was returned by them at long range. The troops were now all disembarked, and steadily advancing without resistance. At sundown the firing was discontinued, and the fleet came to anchor in position to cover the troops on shore.

"At half past six A. M., on Friday, the 14th instant, we heard a continuous firing of heavy guns and musketry inland, and immediately commenced throwing our shells in advance of the position supposed to be held by our troops. The fleet steadily moved up, and gradually closed in towards the batteries. The lower fortifications were discovered to have been abandoned by the enemy. A boat was despatched to it, and the stars and stripes planted on the ramparts.

"As we advanced, the upper batteries opened fire upon us. The fire was returned with effect, the magazine of one exploding.

"Having proceeded in an extended line as far as the obstructions in the river would permit, the signal was made to follow the movements of the flag-ship, and the whole fleet advanced in order, concentrating our fire on Fort Thompson, mounting thirteen guns, on which rested the enemy's land defences. The army having with great gallantry driven them out of those defences, the forts were abandoned.

"Several of our vessels were slightly injured in passing the barricades of piles and torpedoes which had been placed in the river.

"The upper battery having been evacuated on the approach of the combined forces, it was abandoned, and subsequently blew up.

"We now steamed rapidly up to the city. The enemy had fled, and the place remained in our possession.

"Upon our approach, several points of the city were fired by the enemy where stores had been accumulated. Two small batteries, constructed of cotton bales, and mounting two guns each, were also fired by them. Two small steamers were captured, another having been burnt. A large raft, composed of barrels of pitch and bales of cotton, which had been prepared to send down upon the fleet, was fired, and floating against the railroad bridge, set it on fire, and destroyed it. In addition to the prizes, a quantity of cotton, pitch, tar, a gun-

boat, and another vessel on the stocks, several schooners afloat, and an immense quantity of arms and munitions of war, fell into our hands.

"At about four P. M., I sent several of our vessels to the right bank of the Trent River, to carry General Foster's brigade to occupy the city of Newbern.

"I am, respectfully,

"S. C. ROWAN,

"Com. U. S. Naval Forces in Pamlico Sound.
"Flag-Officer L. M. GOLDSBOROUGH, commanding
North Atlantic Blockading Squadron, &c."

CHAPTER LXVIII.

Movement of General Banks's Corps. — Advance to Winchester. — Reconnoissance in Force. — Rebel Force of General Jackson. — Strategy of General Shields. — Departure of a Part of General Banks's Forces. — Advance of the Rebels. — Skirmishes. — General Shields wounded. — Peparations to meet the Enemy. — Attack by the Rebels. — The Battle. — Repulse of the Rebels on the Federal left. — Formidable Attack on the Federal right. — Counter Movements. — Federal Charge. — The Rebels routed. — The Pursuit. — Results of the Battle. — Official Reports.

THE force under General Banks, which had been posted on the Upper Potomac, advanced, when the army of the Potomac moved, from Harper's Ferry towards Winchester, in the valley of the Shenandoah, thence to form a junction with the federal forces near Manassas, and establish a more perfect protection for Washington. After some skirmishes with rebel cavalry, the greater part of General Banks's forces reached the vicinity of Winchester. From this point a reconnoissance in force was made by the division under command of General Shields, in the direction of Mount Jackson, with the view of ascertaining whether any considerable force of the enemy was in that part of the valley, and, if necessary, to give battle before a portion of General Banks's command was moved to Centreville, near Bull Run. This reconnoissance was made on the 18th and 19th of March, and resulted in the discovery of a large force of rebels, under the command of General Jackson,* strongly posted, and in communication with other forces at Luray and Washington, farther up the valley.

Not deeming it expedient to attack the rebel force in so strong a position, General Shields sought to draw Jackson from it, and separate him from his supports. To effect this, he fell back upon Winchester on the 20th of March, in such a manner as to give the impression of a hasty retreat. The movement, however, apparently failed to deceive the wary Jackson, who did not follow to attack the retreating federal force, and after a day's delay, preparations were made for the march of the division which was to go to Centreville, the greater part of which moved on the 22d. General Shields's division being so posted as to conceal its real strength, the rebel scouts and citizens of Winchester were under the impression that only a few regiments remained to garrison the place. This impression was speedily communicated to Jackson, and the rebel force immediately advanced from its position towards Winchester. In the afternoon of the day on which the last of the troops destined for Centreville moved from the town, the rebel cavalry, under Colonel Ashby, drove in the federal pickets, when General Shields threw a few regiments between the advancing enemy and Winchester to repulse them. This was done in a manner to deceive the enemy into the belief that the whole of the garrison was thrown out for the defence of their post, but the object was accomplished, and the enemy held in check till the federal troops could be properly disposed to meet the attack. In a skirmish which followed General Shields was wounded in the arm and shoulder by a fragment of a shell, and so much injured that he was unable to keep the field. He showed, however, a true soldier's courage, and vigorous-

ly continued his preparations to repulse the enemy.

A reconnoissance on the following morning discovered no rebel force except Ashby's cavalry, and it was concluded by the federal officers that Jackson did not intend to make any serious attack. General Banks and staff accordingly left for Washington, thence to join his division at Centreville. General Shields, however, held his troops in position, ready to meet the enemy, one brigade being strongly posted in advance, about two miles from the town, and the others ready to support it and to meet any attack upon the federal flanks. The precautions of General Shields were wisely taken; for early in the forenoon it became evident that a considerable force of the enemy, in addition to Ashby's cavalry, was in front, and was approaching so much under cover of the woods that it was impossible to estimate the number. Colonel Kimball, who commanded in the field, opened fire with a portion of his artillery, with the view of unmasking the enemy's position and line of approach, and soon it was evident that Jackson's whole force was coming to attack. The rebel artillery responded, as they brought up battery after battery to strong positions, and opened fire along their whole line. The artillery fire on both sides continued with little effect for several hours, the rebels gradually approaching and bringing up their supports. They soon advanced a column of infantry and cavalry on the left flank of the federal force, but an active body of skirmishers, supported by several pieces of artillery and a brigade of infantry, was advanced to meet it, and after a brisk fire and a determined resistance, the rebel column was repulsed.

Having failed in this attempt, the rebel general moved the greater portion of this force from his right to the support of his left and centre, and then made a more formidable attack upon the federal right. He concentrated a large portion of his artillery upon this part of the

* Familiarly known as "Stonewall" Jackson, because he had declared at the battle of Bull Run that the brigade under his command would stand as firm as a stone wall.

Engraved by H. Wright Smith from a Photograph

Geo. G. Meade

field, advantageously posted, and then moved a heavy column upon the federal position. The federal batteries posted on the right wing, though well served, were found entirely inadequate to check the advance of this column, which approached steadily, as if with a determination to overwhelm the federal force opposing it, turn the right flank, and with this advantage soon utterly defeat the federal army. General Shields directed the movements of the day from his couch, notwithstanding his wound, and when the advance of this formidable rebel force was reported to him, he at once issued orders to meet the emergency, and even before the rebel infantry could commence the attack, a counter movement was made, and the attack was opened by the federal troops. The brigade under General Tyler was ordered to advance and carry the enemy's batteries, and turn his left flank if possible. This brigade moved with great spirit to their work. They drove the rebel skirmishers hastily back, and steadily advanced till they approached a stone wall, behind which the rebels were securely posted, and poured upon them a destructive fire. The brigade wavered but for a moment. Several regiments were already coming rapidly up to their support, and soon the whole force charged upon the rebel position, and drove the enemy from their shelter. They fought with spirit, but soon fell back in great disorder through the woods to their supports. Here they rallied, and formed a new line of resistance; but the federal troops, encouraged by their success, advanced with great enthusiasm, and by a steady and destructive' fire again drove the rebels from their position, and soon the whole force of the enemy were in full retreat, leaving their killed and wounded on the field. Night, and the exhaustion of the federal troops, prevented pursuit; and the rebels, after retreating about five miles, took up a position for the night.

It seemed evident to General Shields that

Jackson would not have ventured this battle so far from the main body of the rebel army unless he had expected reënforcements, and fearing that these might be brought up in such numbers as to lead to a renewal of the rebel attack in overwhelming force, General Shields made preparation for such a turn. He brought together all the troops at his command, and despatched a messenger for the last brigade which had left for Centreville to march at once to Winchester during the night, (an order which General Banks, hearing the cannonade, had already anticipated;) and he also prepared to follow up his success, and if possible to harass and drive the rebel forces before their reënforcements could arrive. Early on the following morning the federal artillery opened fire in the direction of the enemy, and the troops moved forward again in pursuit. No reënforcements had arrived to enable Jackson to again resume the offensive, and he accordingly retreated before the advance of the federal force, of which General Banks, who had returned from Harper's Ferry, now assumed the command. The retreat was at first orderly, but the defeat of the previous day, and the constant pressure of the pursuing force, demoralized the rebel troops, and their retreat was soon accelerated into disorderly flight. The federal force followed as far as Woodstock, but there the pursuit ended, in consequence of the exhaustion of the men, and the apparently complete rout of the rebels.

The federal success was decided and important at this juncture, while the movement of Jackson indicated the necessity of retaining a considerable force in the valley of the Shenandoah. The force with which Jackson moved towards Winchester was composed of eleven regiments and an Irish battalion of infantry, a very efficient body of cavalry, under Colonel Ashby, with thirty-six pieces of artillery. The whole force numbered about eleven thousand men, of whom fifteen hundred were cavalry.

66

The federal force left with General Shields, after the movement of a part of the army corps to Centreville, numbered about six thousand infantry, seven hundred and fifty cavalry, with twenty-four pieces of artillery. The federal loss was about one hundred killed, and upwards of two hundred wounded, while the rebel loss was much greater, the number of killed being estimated at three hundred, and one hundred and fifty of their wounded were left on the field, in addition to a large number who were taken with them in their retreat. About two hundred prisoners were also captured, and the rebels abandoned two pieces of artillery and a large number of small arms.

The following official reports of General Shields and of Colonel Kimball, who commanded in the field, give a more detailed account of the battle, of which the general features and movements are given above : —

OFFICIAL REPORT OF GENERAL SHIELDS.

"HEADQUARTERS SHIELDS'S DIVISION, {
WINCHESTER, VA., *March* 29, 1862. {

"SIR: I have the honor to report that during my reconnoissance of the 18th and 19th instants, in the direction of Mount Jackson, I ascertained that the enemy under Jackson was strongly posted near that place, and in direct communication with a force at Luray and another at Washington. It became important, therefore, to draw him from his position and supporting force if possible. To endeavor to effect this, I fell back to Winchester on the 20th, giving the movement all the appearance of a retreat. The last brigade of the first division of Banks's *corps d'armée*, General Williams commanding, took its departure for Centreville by way of Berryville, on the morning of the 22d, leaving only Shields's division and the Michigan cavalry in Winchester. Ashby's cavalry, observing this movement from a distance, came to the conclusion that Winchester was being evacuated, and signalized Jackson to that effect. We saw their signal fires and di-

vined their import. On the 22d, about five o'clock P. M., they attacked and drove in our pickets. By order of General Banks, I put my command under arms, and pushed forward one brigade and two batteries of artillery to drive back the enemy, but, to keep him deceived as to our strength, only let him see two regiments of infantry, a small body of cavalry, and part of the artillery. While directing one of our batteries to its position I was struck by the fragment of a shell, which fractured my arm above the elbow, bruised my shoulder, and injured my side. The enemy being driven from his position, we withdrew to Winchester. The injuries I had received completely prostrated me, but were not such as to prevent me from making the required dispositions for the ensuing day. Under cover of the night, I pushed forward Kimball's brigade nearly three miles on the Strasburg road. Daum's artillery was posted in a strong position to support his brigade if attacked. Sullivan's brigade was posted in the rear of Kimball's, and within supporting distance of it, covering all the approaches to the town by Cedar Creek, Front Royal, Berryville, and Romney roads. This brigade and Broadhead's cavalry were held in reserve, so as to support our force in front at any point where it might be attacked. These dispositions being made I rested for the night, knowing that all the approaches by which the enemy might penetrate to this place were effectually guarded.

"I deem it necessary in this place to give a brief description of these approaches, as well as of the field, which next day became the scene of one of the bloodiest battles of the war. Winchester is approached from the south by three principal roads — the Cedar Creek road on the west, the Valley Turnpike road leading to Strasburg in the centre, and the Front Royal road on the east. There is a little village, called Kernstown, on the Valley road, about three and a half miles from Winchester. On the west side of this road, about half a mile north of Kernstown, is a ridge of ground which commands the approach by the turnpike and a part of the surrounding country. This ridge was the key-point of our position. Here Colonel Kimball, the senior officer in command on the field, took his station. Along this ridge Lieutenant-Colonel Daum, chief of artillery, posted three of his batteries, keeping one of his batteries in reserve some distance in the rear. Part of our infantry was first placed in position in the rear and within supporting distance of these batteries, well sheltered in the windings and sinuosities of the ridge. The main body of the enemy on the ridge was posted in order of battle about half a mile beyond Kernstown, his line extending from the Cedar Creek road to a little ravine near the Front Royal road, a distance of about two miles. This ground had been so skilfully selected that, while it afforded facilities for manœuvring, it was completely masked by high and wooded ground in front. These woods he filled with skirmishers, supported by a battery on each flank; and so adroitly had this movement been conducted, and so skilfully had he concealed himself, that at eight o'clock A. M., on the 23d, nothing was visible but the same force under Ashby which had been repulsed the previous evening. Not being able to reconnoitre the front in person, I despatched an experienced officer, Colonel John T. Mason, of the fourth Ohio volunteers, about nine o'clock A. M., to the front, to perform that duty, and to report to me, as promptly as possible, every circumstance that might indicate the presence of the enemy. About an hour after Colonel Mason returned, and reported to me that he had carefully reconnoitred the country in front and on both flanks, and found no indications of any hostile force except that of Ashby's.

"I communicated this information to Major-General Banks, who was then with me, and after consulting together, we both concluded that Jackson could not be tempted to hazard himself so far away from his main support. Having both come to this conclusion, General Banks took his departure for Washington, being already under orders to that effect. The officers of his staff, however, remained behind, intending to leave for Centreville in the afternoon. Although I began to conclude that Jackson was nowhere in the vicinity, knowing the crafty enemy we have to deal with I took care not to omit a single precaution. Between eleven and twelve o'clock A. M., a message from Colonel Kimball informed me that another battery on the enemy's right had opened on our position, and that there were some indications of a considerable force of infantry in the woods in that quarter. On receiving this information I pushed forward Sullivan's brigade, which was placed, by order of Colonel Kimball, in a position to oppose the advance of the enemy's right wing. The action opened with a fire of artillery on both sides, but at too great a distance to be very effective. The initiative was taken by the enemy. He pushed forward a few more guns to his right, supported by a considerable force of infantry and cavalry, with the apparent intention of enfilading our position and turning our left flank. An active body of skirmishers, consisting of the eighth Ohio, Colonel Carroll, and three companies of the sixty-seventh Ohio, was immediately thrown forward on both sides of the Valley road to resist the enemy's advance. These skirmishers were admirably supported by four pieces of artillery under Captain Jeuks, and Sullivan's gallant brigade. This united force repulsed the enemy at all points, and gave him such a check that no further demonstration was made upon that flank during the remainder of the day. The attempt against our left flank having thus failed, the enemy withdrew the greater part of his force to the right, and formed it into a reserve to support his left flank in a forward movement. Ho then added his original reserve and two batteries to his main body, and then, advancing with this combined column, under shelter of the bridge on his left, on which other batteries had been previously posted, seemed evidently determined to turn our right flank or overthrow it. Our batteries on the opposite ridge, though admirably managed by their experienced chief, Lieutenant-Colonel Daum, were soon found insufficient to check, or even retard, the advance of such a formidable body. At this stage of the combat a messenger arrived from Colonel Kimball, informing me of the state of the field, and requesting direction as to the employment of the infantry. I saw there was not a moment to lose, and gave positive orders that all the disposable infantry should be immediately thrown forward on our right to carry the enemy's batteries, and to assail and turn his left flank, and hurl it back on the centre. Colonel Kimball carried out these orders with promptitude and ability. He intrusted this movement to Tyler's splendid brigade, which, under its fearless leader, Colonel Tyler, marched forward with alacrity and enthusiastic joy to the performance of the most perilous duty of the day. The enemy's skirmishers were driven before it and fell back upon the main body, strongly posted behind a high and solid stone wall, situated on an elevated ground. Here the struggle became desperate, and for a short time doubtful; but Tyler's brigade being soon joined on the left by the fifth Ohio, thirteenth Indiana, and sixty-second Ohio, of Sullivan's brigade, and the fourteenth Indiana, eighty-fourth Pennsylvania, seven companies of the sixty-seventh Ohio, and three companies of the eighth Ohio, of Kimball's brigade, this united force dashed upon the enemy with a cheer and yell that rose high up above the roar of battle, and though the rebels fought desperately, as their piles of dead attest, they were forced back through the woods by a fire as destructive as ever fell upon a retreating foe. Jackson, with his supposed invincible stone-wall brigade and the accompanying brigades, much to their mortification and discomfiture, were

compelled to fall back in disorder upon their reserve. Here they took up a new position for a final stand, and made an attempt for a few minutes to retrieve the fortunes of the day; but again rained down upon them the same close and destructive fire. Again cheer upon cheer rang in their ears. A few minutes only did they stand up against it, when they turned dismayed and fled in disorder, leaving us in possession of the field, the killed and wounded, three hundred prisoners, two guns, four caissons, and a thousand stand of small arms. Night alone saved him from total destruction. The enemy retreated above five miles, and, judging from his camp fires, took up a new position for the night. Our troops, wearied and exhausted with the fatigues of the day, threw themselves down to rest on the field.

"Though the battle had been won, still I could not have believed that Jackson would have hazarded a decisive engagement at such a distance from the main body without expecting reënforcements. So, to be prepared for such a contingency, I set to work during the night to bring together all the troops within my reach. I sent an express after Williams's division, requesting the rear brigade, about twenty miles distant, to march all night and join me in the morning. I swept the posts and route in my rear of almost all their guards, hurrying them forward by forced marches, to be with me at daylight. I gave positive orders also to the forces in the field to open fire on the enemy as soon as the light of day would enable them to point their guns, and to pursue him without respite, and compel him to abandon his guns and baggage or cut him to pieces. These orders were implicitly obeyed as far as possible. It now appears that I had rightly divined the intentions of our crafty antagonist. On the morning of the 23d, a reënforcement from Luray, of five thousand, reached Front Royal, on their way to join Jackson. This reënforcement was being followed by another body of ten thousand from Sperryville; but recent rains having rendered the Shenandoah River impassable, they found themselves compelled to fall back, without being able to effect the proposed junction. At daylight, on the morning of the 24th, our artillery again opened on the enemy. He entered upon his retreat in very good order, considering what he had suffered. General Banks, hearing of our engagement on his way to Washington, halted at Harper's Ferry, and with remarkable promptitude and sagacity, ordered back Wiliams's whole division, so that my express found the rear brigade already en route to join us. The general himself returned here forthwith, and after making me a hasty visit, assumed command of the forces in pursuit of the enemy. The pursuit was kept up with vigor, energy, and activity, until they reached Woodstock, where the enemy's retreat became flight, and the pursuit was abandoned because of the utter exhaustion of our troops.

"The killed and wounded in this engagement cannot even yet be accurately ascertained. Indeed, my command has been so overworked, that it has had but little time to ascertain any thing. The killed, as reported, are one hundred and three, and among them we have to deplore the loss of the brave Colonel Murray, of the eighty-fourth Pennsylvania volunteers, who fell at the head of his regiment while gallantly leading it in the face of the enemy. The wounded are four hundred and forty-one, many of them slightly, and the missing are twenty-four. The enemy's loss is more difficult to ascertain than our own. Two hundred and seventy were found dead on the battle field. Forty were buried by the inhabitants of the adjacent village, and by a calculation made by the number of graves found on both sides of the valley road between here and Strasburg, their loss in killed must have been about five hundred, and in wounded one thousand. The proportion between the killed and wounded of the enemy shows the closeness and terrible destructiveness of our

fire — nearly half the wounds being fatal. The enemy admit a loss of between one thousand and one thousand five hundred killed and wounded. Our force in infantry, cavalry, and artillery did not exceed seven thousand. That of the enemy must have exceeded eleven thousand. Jackson, who commanded on the field, had, in addition to his own stone-wall brigade, Smith's, Garnett's, and Longstreet's brigades. Generals Smith and Garnett were here in person. The following regiments were known to have been present, and from each of them were made prisoners on the field: the second, fourth, fifth, twenty-first, twenty-third, twenty-seventh, twenty-eighth, thirty-third, thirty-seventh, and forty-second Virginia; first regiment provisional army, and an Irish battalion. None from the reserve were made prisioners. Their force in infantry must have been nine thousand. The cavalry of the united brigades amounted to one thousand five hundred. Their artillery consisted of thirty-six pieces. We had six thousand infantry, and a cavalry force of seven hundred and fifty, and twenty-four pieces of artillery.

"I cannot conclude this report without expressing thanks and gratitude to officers and soldiers of my command for their valuable conduct on this trying day. It was worthy of the great country whose national existence they have pledged their lives to preserve. Special thanks are due to Colonel Kimball, commanding first brigade, and senior officer in the field. His conduct was brave, judicious, and efficient. He executed my orders, in every instance, with vigor and fidelity, and exhibited wisdom and sagacity in the various movements that were necessarily intrusted to his direction. Colonel Tyler, commanding third brigade, has won my admiration by his fearless intrepidity. His brigade is worthy of such an intrepid leader. This brigade, and the regiments accompanying it, achieved the decisive success of the day. They drove the forces of the enemy before them on the left flank, and by hurling this flank back upon the reserve, consummated this glorious action. High praise is due to Colonel Sullivan, commanding second brigade, for the manner in which he contributed to the first repulse of the enemy in the morning. To him and Colonel Carroll of the eighth Ohio volunteers, who commanded the skirmishers, is the credit due of forcing back the right wing of the enemy, and of intimidating and holding him in check on our left during the rest of the day. The chief of artillery, Lietenant-Colonel Daum, deserves high commendation for the skilful manner in which he managed his batteries during the engagement. This skilful management prevented the enemy, doubtless, from using effectually his formidable artillery. The cavalry performed its duty with spirit in this engagement, and, with its gallant officers, exhibited activity which paralyzed the movements of the enemy. The commanders of regiments are also entitled to especial mention, but sufficient justice cannot be done them in this report. I must, therefore, refer you on this head to the report of the brigade commanders. The officers of my staff have my thanks for the fidelity with which they discharged the trying duties that devolved upon them. They had to penetrate the thickest of the fight to bring me intelligence of the state of the field, and performed their perilous duty throughout the day with cheerful alacrity. It affords me pleasure, as it is my duty, to recommend all the officers whose names I have specially mentioned, to the consideration of the government.

"I have the honor to be,

"Your obedient servant,

•   "JAS. SHIELDS,

"Brigadier-General commanding.

"To Major-General BANKS."

REPORT OF ACTING BRIGADIER-GENERAL KIMBALL.

"HEADQUARTERS SHIELDS'S DIVISION, ⎞
CAMP NEAR STRASBURG, VA., March 26, 1862. ⎠

"SIR: I have the honor to submit the following report of the battle which was fought near Winchester, Virginia, on Sunday, the 23d instant, between the forces composing this division, which I had the honor to command, and the rebel forces under General Jackson.

"Early in the morning of the 23d the enemy commenced the attack, advancing from Kernstown, and occupying a position with their batteries on the heights to the right of the road, and the wood in the plain to the left of the road, with cavalry, infantry, and one battery. I at once advanced the eighth Ohio, Colonel Carroll, with four companies, taking the left, and Lieutenant-Colonel Sawyer, with three companies, taking the right of the turnpike road. Colonel Carroll advanced steadily, coming up with two companies of the sixty-seventh Ohio, who had been out as pickets, and uniting them with his command, drove one of the enemy's batteries, which had opened a heavy fire upon him, and after a sharp skirmish, routing five companies of the infantry which were posted behind a stone wall, and supported by cavalry, holding this position during the whole day, thus frustrating the attempt of the enemy to turn our left. The right of the eighth Ohio remained in front until about four o'clock P. M., when they were recalled to support one of our batteries on the heights. The sixty-seventh Ohio was thrown on a hill to our right, to support Jenks's battery, which had been advanced to a position commanding the village of Kernstown and the wood on the right.

"The fourteenth Indiana was sent forward to support Clark's battery, which advanced along the road. The eighty-fourth Pennsylvania was thrown over the hills to the right, to prevent a flank movement of the enemy. The second brigade, commanded by Colonel Sullivan, composed of the thirteenth Indiana, fifth Ohio, sixty-second Ohio, and thirty-ninth Illinois, were sent to the left, supporting Carroll's skirmishers, a section of Davis's battery, and Robinson's . first Ohio battery, and to prevent an attempt which was made to turn that flank. We had succeeded in driving the enemy from both flanks and the front until four o'clock P. M., when Jackson, with the whole of his infantry, supported by artillery and cavalry, took possession of the hillside on the right, and planted his batteries in a commanding position, and opened a heavy and well-directed fire upon our batteries and their supports, attracting our attention whilst he attempted to gain our right flank with his infantry. At this juncture, I ordered the third brigade, Colonel E. B. Tyler, seventh Ohio, commanding, composed of the seventh and twenty-ninth Ohio, first Virginia, seventh Indiana, and one hundred and tenth Pennsylvania, to move to the right, to gain the flank of the enemy, and charge them through the woods to their batteries posted on the hill. They moved forward steadily and gallantly, opening a galling fire on the enemy's infantry.

"The right wing of the eighth Ohio, the fourteenth and thirteenth Indiana, sixty-seventh and fifth Ohio, and eighty-fourth Pennsylvania, were sent forward to support Tyler's brigade, each one in its turn moving forward gallantly, sustaining a heavy fire from both the enemy's batteries and his musketry. Soon all the regiments above named were pouring forth a well-directed fire, which was promptly answered by the enemy, and after a hotly-contested action of two hours, just as night closed in, the enemy gave way, and were soon completely routed, leaving their dead and wounded on the field, together with two pieces of their artillery and four caissons. Our forces retained possession of the field, and bivouacked for the night. The batteries, under their chief, Lieutenant-Colonel Daum, were well posted and admirably served during the whole action.

"I respectfully refer you to the several accompanying reports for the details of the engagement. I regret to report the loss of the gallant Colonel Murray, of the eighty-fourth Pennsylvania, who fell while bravely leading forward his men amidst a fearful storm of shot and shell. When all have done so well, both officers and men, and achieved so much, it would be seemingly invidious to particularize any individual officer, yet I can say, without doing injustice to others, that Colonel Tyler deserves the highest commendations for the gallant manner in which he led his brigade during the conflict, and the gallant Carroll, Harrow, Foster, Lewis, Patrick, Thoburne, Sawyer, Buckley, Cheek, and Creighton deserve well of their country. Colonel Sullivan, Candy's brigade, on the left, was not attacked in force. His batteries and skirmishers engaged the enemy, and prevented the turning of that flank; and he, too, merits the highest commendation.

"NATHAN KIMBALL,
"*Colonel commanding Shields's Division.*
"Major H. G. ARMSTRONG, *A. A. A. General.*"

CHAPTER LXIX.

Rebel Fortifications on the Mississippi. — Advantages of the Possession of the River. — Necessity for opening the River, and Preparations therefor. — Gunboats. — Island No. Ten. — Military Expedition to New Madrid. — Operations of General Pope. — Evacuation of New Madrid by the Rebels. — Advantage gained by the Federal Forces. — Movement of the Gunboats. — Bombardment of the Rebel Forts. — Slow Progress. — Construction of a Canal by General Pope's Forces for Passage of Transports. — Success of the Work. — Passage of Gunboats by the Island. — Attack on the Forts below New Madrid, and crossing of General Pope's Forces. — Evacuation of Rebel Fortifications. — Retreat of Rebels interrupted. — Their Confusion and Disorganization. — Capture of the Rebel Army. — Surrender of Island No. Ten. — Prisoners and Material captured. — The Result and its Advantages. — Official Report.

BY the occupation of the outlet of the Mississippi River, and the seizure and fortification of strong points upon its banks, nearly up to the Ohio, the rebels secured a most important means of communication through the southwestern states, and inflicted a serious damage upon the north-west by closing the natural channel by which its immense products found passage to the markets of the world. The fortifications at Columbus and other points had effectually closed the river to the hitherto unrestricted navigation of the numerous steamers of the north-western states, and a vast amount of northern property had been detained within the limits of secession, and confiscated or stolen. The possession of many valuable river boats gave the rebels great facilities for the transportation of troops and supplies, and for a time enabled them, with extemporized gunboats, to threaten the comparatively unprotected cities upon the banks of the Mississippi and Ohio, and to interfere with the military preparations of the federal government.

To the north-western states it was of the utmost importance that the Mississippi should be opened to their commerce, while in a military view its possession was a great advantage and source of strength to the rebels, and its loss to them would prove a blow that would seriously weaken if not completely overthrow the rebel power in the south-west. It was, therefore, early felt to be necessary that the federal government should open the Mississippi, and maintain its free navigation to the loyal north-western states, while from its banks the rebellion should be pressed back into the interior, where it could not be sustained. Preparations were accordingly made for an expedition down the river, and to this General Fremont, during his command in the western department, gave much attention.

There were, however, various obstacles to the early success of the purposed plans. The rebels had not been content with taking the states which had, in form at least, voluntarily seceded, but intent upon having all the slave states, they had invaded Kentucky and Missouri, and occupied important points in such force that it became necessary first to protect the loyal people of those states, and to drive the rebel forces beyond their limits. Other preparations and expeditions interfered with the accomplishment of the grand movement which had long been in contemplation. There is reason to believe, too, that the early plans for an expedition to open the Mississippi were almost exclusively of a military character. But it became evident that gunboats might play an important part in the expedition. General Fremont made some attempt to supply these important auxiliaries, but his efforts in this direction met with some disfavor. Several gunboats, however, were soon after constructed, and their successful service in affairs of minor importance led to the construction of others of an improved and more formidable character. The beginning of the year 1862 saw, therefore, a very large and powerful fleet of gunboats, several of which were wholly or partially iron-clad, and most of them heavily armed. In addition to these was a fleet of mortar-boats or rafts, each carrying a mortar of the largest size. The value of the gunboats was realized in the reduction of Fort Henry and in the expeditions up the Cumberland and Tennessee Rivers, and they would, doubtless, have played an important part in the reduction of Columbus, had not that point been evacuated without attack.

But though the rebels had retired from their position at Columbus, which was not tenable after the fall of Forts Henry and Donelson and the advance of the federal forces into Tennessee, they held other points which were equally strong in natural position and the fortifications constructed upon them, and which secured to them the exclusive navigation of the Mississippi so long as they held them, and prevented the passage of the federal gunboats. The first, and at this time the most important of these positions, was at New Madrid and Island No. Ten;[*] this island being about forty-five miles, by the river, below Columbus, and New Madrid lying five miles farther down on the Missouri side of the river.

* The islands in the Mississippi, below the confluence of the Ohio, are designated by numbers.

Having driven the rebel forces essentially from Kentucky, and forced them to abandon their stronghold at Columbus, the federal authorities prepared to continue the progress of the Union forces down the Mississippi. A fleet of eight gunboats and a number of mortar rafts, with numerous despatch and ammunition boats and transports, were collected at Cairo, under the command of Commodore Foote, in whose skill and bravery the government and people had the most perfect confidence. But while the naval preparations were yet in progress, a military expedition, under command of General Pope, had moved from St. Louis towards New Madrid by land. They had several skirmishes on the march, and arriving before this town on the 3d of March, General Pope found it occupied by a considerable force of infantry and artillery, and protected by fortifications which commanded the approaches to the town, while several steamboats, carrying from four to eight heavy guns each, lay in the river, and owing to' the high stage of the water, were sufficiently high to throw their shot over the surrounding country. This force, well intrenched, and supported by such formidable batteries as the gunboats presented, rendered the position too strong for an assault. The fortifications might have been carried by such assault, indeed, but the gunboats which commanded them would have driven the federal troops speedily out. General Pope, accordingly, without exposing his force to the danger of a conflict which would have proved so useless, annoyed the enemy as much as possible with his light guns and infantry, while he sent to Cairo for heavy ordnance with which to contend on more equal terms with the rebel batteries. In the mean time he also sent a part of his force to Point Pleasant, about twelve miles below New Madrid, with a field battery of Parrott guns, to take up a position there, and construct rifle pits and sunken batteries, by which they could command the river and prevent the passage of gunboats or transports. This work was successfully accomplished after a slight opposition on the part of some boats lying near the point. The rifle pits were constructed, the guns placed in position, and the forces so disposed that subsequent attempts made by the rebel gunboats to dislodge them were unavailing, and the river was quite effectually closed to transports or even gunboats.

The heavy guns for which General Pope had sent arrived at his position on the 12th, and at night were mounted in redoubts speedily constructed upon ground from which the enemy's pickets had been driven. The next morning fire was opened from these heavy guns upon the enemy's works, and especially upon the gunboats. Both the land batteries and gunboats of the rebels replied with a furious cannonade ; but while General Pope's forces and batteries suffered but little from their fire, he succeeded in disabling some of the boats and damaging the works of the enemy. At the same time he was threatening an assault on another side, and pushing forward his trenches with a view to advance his heavy batteries near the banks of the river, and thus be able more effectually to silence or destroy the gunboats. The work was pushed on vigorously through the night, during the greater part of which a severe thunder storm prevailed, and the programme of the commanding general would, without doubt, have been successfully carried out had not the rebels, without further coercion, evacuated their fortifications and beat a precipitate retreat.

At daylight it was announced that the rebel fortifications were abandoned, and upon examination it appeared that the report was true. The federal troops were at once put in motion, and soon entered the works of the enemy. Every thing here indicated that the rebels had evacuated their position in great haste, leaving all their artillery, a large quantity of ammunition, and a great variety of public stores and

67

private property. A large amount of this property was hastily thrown into the river, but in such a position that guns and other articles of value were easily recovered. The artillery was nearly all spiked, but so indifferently that a short time sufficed to restore the greater part of it to use, and the guns were turned upon the river face of the works to bear upon any of the rebel gunboats that should attempt to come down the river from Island No. Ten. The gunboats and transports which lay in the river had disappeared, some of them having probably gone up to the island, while possibly others had succeeded in passing the batteries at Point Pleasant and escaped down the river. Most of the rebel troops, it was found, had been transported across the river, and had landed upon the Tennessee shore, to move, as best they might, away from the threatening federal forces. The artillery captured amounted to thirty-three pieces, many of them heavy siege guns. The small arms were generally of an inferior quality, but quite numerous, and there was a large amount of ammunition, which the rebels apparently made no attempt to carry away or destroy.

The capture of the rebel fortifications at New Madrid was an important success, for the federal forces now held a position, strongly fortified, below the rebel works at Island No. Ten, and prevented any reënforcements or supplies reaching that place by water, and the land on the Tennessee side was of such a character as to render it very difficult to transport supplies or move considerable bodies of troops. It appeared certain, therefore, that the island must soon surrender or be evacuated if the federal gunboats and troops should come down the river and make an attack. The place, however, was strongly fortified and well supplied, and it was considered of so much importance by the rebels, as the key to the Mississippi, that it was not likely to be speedily surrendered. They, moreover, considered the posi-

tion impregnable. So long as the rebels held the island it seemed impossible for the federal gunboats or transports to pass down the river, and the capture of New Madrid would prove of comparatively little importance if this obstruction remained. But, as already stated, the position had now become a critical one, with the only valuable means of communication cut off, and the reduction of the place was but a question of time.

On the 14th of March the flotilla of gunboats and mortars, under Commodore Foote, together with a number of transports and supply boats, sailed from Cairo and proceeded down the Mississippi to operate against Island No. Ten. There was some anxiety felt for the situation of General Pope's forces, and it was considered necessary, in order to secure his safety, that the fleet should wait no longer. With few delays it proceeded down the river to the vicinity of the bend where the waters turn again towards the north, some five or six miles above the celebrated island. At this point the boats anchored or made fast to the shore, and a reconnoissance was made. It was discovered that the rebels had established batteries on the Tennessee side of the river, commanding the approach to the bend, and still others commanding the bend, and near the latter an extensive camp was seen, showing the presence of a large body of troops. These batteries were in part upon higher land than Island No. Ten, and owing to the bend in the river, were thought by the federal officers to be more formidable obstacles to the passage of the boats than the works on the island. It was at least evident that these fortifications, whether the main works or not, must be disposed of before operations could be commenced by the gunboats against the island, except at long range, across the point of land around which the river bends. Fire was opened upon the nearest batteries by one or two of the gunboats, to which the rebels responded, indicating the position of their guns. Some of the mortar boats were then placed in position near the shore, and out of the reach of the rebel shots, and the crews commenced practice with their huge pieces of ordnance, throwing enormous shells into the vicinity of the rebel works. In the mean time some of the transports had landed troops on the Missouri shore, and preparations were made for more serious and vigorous operations.

From this time a continual bombardment of the rebel works and camps was kept up from the gunboats and mortars the greater part of the time during two weeks. The first or upper battery of the enemy was silenced, and a small party of soldiers succeeded in spiking the guns. But notwithstanding the expenditure of shot and shell, and the skill and courage of the naval officers, little progress appeared to be made towards the reduction or surrender of the position. The military force which accompanied Commodore Foote was not sufficiently large to operate against the enemy, and the swampy nature of the point which lay between them and the island was altogether unfavorable for military operations or the construction of batteries. The success of the movement against this real stronghold of the rebels, except by storming the garrison, soon appeared somewhat doubtful. General Pope's position at New Madrid and Point Pleasant prevented the rebels from receiving reënforcements or new supplies by water, and the chances of getting them through the swamps which enclosed them on the south were very small. But they had large supplies on hand, and a regular siege would prove a tedious process, and might seriously retard other operations already commenced.

Upon the evacuation of New Madrid, the rebels had constructed batteries along the Tennessee shore from the vicinity of Island No. Ten to Tiptonville, their lowest landing place, which was now blockaded by General Pope's

Point Pleasant batteries. They feared an attack upon the rear of their position, to coöperate with the gunboat attack in front. But General Pope had no means of crossing the river. The rebels had escaped with their boats which lay at New Madrid, and there was no federal boat in the Mississippi below Island No. Ten. General Pope informed Commodore Foote of his operations to blockade the river below the rebel position, and desired, if possible, that a gunboat might run by the rebel works, and then transport his troops across the river in such force as should prevent the retreat of the rebels, and soon compel them to surrender. But this was considered too dangerous an experiment, and was not then attempted. At this juncture, General Hamilton, who commanded a brigade of General Pope's forces, suggested the possibility of excavating a canal through the tongue of land on the Missouri shore, so as to pass gunboats and transport steamers from above the island to a point below, in communication with General Pope's forces. A regiment of engineers under Colonel Bissell were sent to perform this work, if found practicable, and Colonel Bissell's energy and skill soon discovered a feasible passage through the swamps and bayous, upon which his troops, with other men from the forces above the island, were immediately set at work to excavate and clear a channel or canal for a distance of twelve miles. It was a work of great difficulty, inasmuch as it was necessary, for a great part of the distance, to saw off the trunks of large trees several feet below the surface of the water. It was intended to have the canal sufficiently deep for the passage of gunboats; but the difficulties to be overcome, and the longer time which would be required, caused that purpose to be abandoned, and it was only made navigable for transports which were of lighter draught.

While this work was in progress, General Pope, knowing that it would be impracticable, without the protection of gunboats, to cross his army in the face of the batteries which the rebels had constructed along the river bank from Island No. Ten as far as the high land extended, and believing that the gunboats above the island could not pass down to his aid, constructed a floating battery of great strength, and armed with heavy guns, which should serve the purpose of a gunboat in silencing some of the enemy's guns, or covering the passage of his troops. This was ready for use when the canal was finished, and the transports succeeded in passing through; but its use was superseded by the access of more serviceable vessels.

The canal was completed on the 4th of April, and the transports and barges were brought through to its outlet, near New Madrid. The same night Commodore Foote, determined to coöperate with General Pope, if possible, sent one of his gunboats, the Carondelet, a wooden vessel without armor, under command of Captain Walke, to attempt a passage by the enemy's batteries. The attempt was entirely successful, the boat running the gantlet of the rebel guns without injury. With this gunboat Captain Walke ran down the river, shelling the enemy's batteries from the point opposite New Madrid to the lowest one, nearly opposite Point Pleasant. The last one he succeeded in silencing, and a small infantry force, being landed, spiked the guns. The next night Commodore Foote sent down the Pittsburg, an iron-clad gunboat, which also passed the rebel works without injury. With the two gunboats to cover the passage of his troops, General Pope brought his transports from the canal, embarked a division under General Paine, and prepared to cross as soon as the rebel batteries near the point selected for landing should be silenced. The gunboats and the heavy batteries on the opposite side of the river accomplished this part of the work in a few hours, and the troops were immedi-

ately transported across the river and landed without opposition. Indeed, as soon as the crossing commenced, the rebels apparently abandoned their shore batteries and began to retreat. The federal troops were hurried forward, to intercept the retreat or flight of the enemy, to Tiptonville, the lowest point of dry land above named, nearly opposite Point Pleasant. To this place it was found that the greater part of the rebel force was hastily moving, in the hope of escaping down the river by boats. The federal forces, however, succeeded in turning them back; and they were consequently detained upon what was little better than an island, the swamps and bayous on the south-east being scarcely more passable than the river itself. The leading division under General Paine was promptly supported by the greater part of General Pope's forces, and the escape of the rebels was wholly cut off. One or two attempts to resist the federal troops were at first made, but they were feeble and ineffectual; and finally, the rebels, retreating from the different points which they had occupied, met in great confusion in the night, and were so disorganized that they were easily and speedily driven back into the swamps by the advancing federal troops. Here they were soon forced to surrender, only a few escaping through the forests and swamps into the interior of Tennessee.

The garrison on Island No. Ten was at this time a small one; and finding that they had been deserted by their friends on the main land, and knowing that General Pope's forces had crossed the river so as to be able to attack their position in the rear, they surrendered to Commodore Foote, who had continued a slow bombardment during the preparations and movements of General Pope, and was now prepared to coöperate with him by a closer and more vigorous attack. Previous to the surrender, a formidable floating battery, mounting sixteen heavy guns, which had been partially disabled by the federal shots in the first engagement in which it was used, was turned adrift, and stranded on the shore below New Madrid. The batteries on the island and along the Tennessee shore were strong earthworks, supplied with a large number of heavy guns. But guns, ammunition, and stores were all abandoned by the rebels in their precipitate flight, without destruction or material injury. Four steamers afloat, and two which had been sunk, were captured, together with a gunboat, which was also sunk. The supply of ammunition captured was very large, indicating the expectation of the rebel authorities that the position would be desperately defended.

The number of prisoners captured by General Pope and surrendered to Commodore Foote was about seven thousand, of whom there were three general and two hundred and seventy-three other commissioned officers. The artillery numbered one hundred and twenty-three pieces, a large proportion of which were of the most approved patterns. Seven thousand stand of small arms were also captured, and the supplies of almost all kinds, as well as the transportation, showed a liberal provision for the forces which were expected to hold this important post.

For the federal cause this was another gratifying and important success. It opened the Mississippi for a long distance, and removed another of the obstructions which the rebels had raised to the progress of northern arms, and to the free navigation of this natural highway to the sea, so important to the northwestern states. This success was due chiefly to the energy and vigorous measures of General Pope, and the engineering skill of Colonel Bissell, who opened the passage for transports through the swamps and upland of the Missouri shore, and to the energy and determination of the troops. This point was, indeed, justly regarded by the rebels as the key to the passage down the river. No other position throughout the course of the river possessed greater natural advantages, in some respects, or was at that time more strongly fortified, than Island No. Ten and the adjacent shore. Fort Pillow and Memphis were of little account when Island No. Ten was lost; and Vicksburg, which afterwards proved so long impregnable, was then but moderately defended by fortifications. Two of the rebel strongholds on the river, Columbus and Island No. Ten, were lost, and the great river was open for progress into the heart of the rebel territory. It was a happy augury of further and early successes by the combined naval and military forces of the United States, and was hailed with great satisfaction by the loyal people of the northwestern states.

The following are the official reports of the operations at New Madrid and Island No. Ten:—

GENERAL POPE'S OFFICIAL REPORT OF THE CAPTURE OF NEW MADRID.

"HEADQUARTERS DISTRICT OF THE MISSISSIPPI, }
NEW MADRID, *March* 14, 1862. }

"GENERAL: I have the honor to submit, for the information of the general commanding the department, the following report of the operations which resulted in the capture of this place.

"I arrived before this town with the forces under my command on Monday, the third instant. I found the place occupied by five regiments of infantry and several companies of artillery. One bastioned earthwork, mounting fourteen heavy guns, about half a mile below the town, and another irregular work at the upper end of the town, mounting seven pieces of heavy artillery, together with lines of intrenchments between them, constituted the defensive works. Six gunboats, carrying from four to eight heavy guns each, were anchored along the shore, between the upper and lower redoubts.

"The country is perfectly level for miles around the place, and as the river was so high that the guns of the gunboats looked directly over the banks, the approaches to the town for seven miles were commanded by direct and cross fire from at least sixty guns of heavy calibre.

"It would not have been difficult to carry the intrenchments, but it would have been attended with heavy loss, and we should not have been able to hold the place half an hour, exposed to the destructive fire of the gunboats. As there seemed no immediate hope of the appearance of our own gunboats, it became necessary to bring down a few heavy guns by land to operate against those of the enemy. They were accordingly sent for, and, meantime, forced reconnoissances were pushed over the whole ground, and into several parts of the town. Some brisk skirmishes resulted, in which the enemy invariably retreated precipitately. It was found impossible to induce them to trust any considerable force of their infantry outside of their intrenchments. As soon as I found that it would be necessary to await the arrival of our heavy guns, I determined to occupy some point on the river below, and establish our small guns, if possible, in such a position as to blockade the river, so far as transports were concerned, and to cut off supplies and reënforcements for the enemy from below.

"Point Pleasant, twelve miles below, was selected, as being in a rich agricultural region, and being the terminus of the plank-road from the interior of Arkansas. I accordingly threw forward Colonel Plummer, eleventh Missouri, to that point, with three regiments of infantry, three companies of cavalry, and a field battery of ten-pound Parrott and rifled guns, with orders to make a lodgment on the river bank, to line the bank with rifle pits for a thousand men, and to establish his artillery in sunk batteries of single pieces between the rifle pits. This arrangement was made to present as small a mark as possible to the shells of the

gunboats, and to render futile the use of round shot from their heavy guns. Colonel Plummer marched with all speed, and, after some cannonading from gunboats which he found there, succeeded in making a lodgment, constructing his batteries and rifle pits, and occupying them in sufficient force to maintain them against any open assault.

"After persistent and repeated cannonading from the gunboats, the enemy found it impossible to dislodge him, and he maintained obstinately his position, and the blockade of the river to transports, during the whole of our operations. Meantime the enemy continued every day to reënforce New Madrid from Island No. Ten, until, on the 12th, they had nine thousand infantry, besides a considerable force of artillery, and nine gunboats. The fleet was commanded by Commodore Hollins, the land forces by Generals McCown, Stewart, and Gantt. On the 11th the siege guns were delivered to Colonel Bissell's engineer regiment, who had been sent to Cairo for the purpose. They were at once shipped to Sikeston, reached here at sunset on the 12th, were placed in battery during the same night, within eight hundred yards of the enemy's main work, so as to command that and the river above it, and opened fire at daylight, on the 13th, just thirty-four hours after they were received at Cairo. One brigade, consisting of the tenth and sixteenth Illinois, under Colonel Morgan, of the tenth, was detailed to cover the construction of the battery, and to work in the trenches. They were supported by Stanley's division, consisting of the twenty-seventh and thirty-ninth Ohio, under Colonel Groesbeck, and the forty-third and sixty-third Ohio, under Colonel Smith. Captain Mower, first United States infantry, with companies A and H of his regiment, was placed in charge of the siege guns.

"The enemy's pickets and grand guards were driven in by Colonel Morgan, from the ground selected for the battery, without firing a shot, although the enemy fired several volleys of musketry. The work was prosecuted in silence and with the utmost rapidity, until, at three o'clock A. M., two small redoubts, connected by a curtain, and mounting the four heavy guns which had been sent me, were completed, together with rifle pits in front and on the flanks for two regiments of infantry. Our batteries opened as soon as the day dawned, and were replied to in front and on the flanks by the whole of the enemy's heavy artillery on land and water. As our supply of ammunition for heavy artillery was very limited, I directed Captain Mower to fire only occasionally at the enemy's land batteries, and to concentrate all his fire upon the gunboats. Our guns were served by Captain Mower with vigor and skill, and in a few hours disabled several of the gunboats, and dismounted three of the heavy guns in the enemy's main work. Shortly after our batteries opened, one of the twenty-four pound guns was struck in the muzzle by a round shot from the enemy's batteries and disabled.

"The cannonading was continued furiously all day by the gunboats and land batteries of the enemy, but without producing any impression upon us. Meantime, during the whole day, our trenches were being extended and advanced, as it was my purpose to push forward our heavy batteries in the course of the night to the bank of the river. While the cannonading was thus going on on our right, I instructed General Paine to make demonstrations against intrenchments on our left, and supported his movements by Palmer's division. The enemy's pickets and grand guards were driven into his intrenchments, and the skirmishers forced their way close to the main ditch.

"A furious thunder storm began to rage about eleven o'clock that night, and continued almost without interruption until morning.

Just before daylight, General Stanley was relieved in his trenches, with his division, by General Hamilton. A few minutes after daylight, a flag of truce approached our batteries, with information that the enemy had evacuated his works. Small parties were at once advanced by General Hamilton to ascertain whether such was the fact, and Captain Mower, first United States infantry, with companies A and H of that regiment, was sent forward to plant the United States flag over the abandoned works.

"A brief examination of them showed how hasty and precipitate had been the flight of the enemy. Their dead were found unburied, their suppers untouched standing on the tables, candles burning in the tents, and every other evidence of a disgraceful panic. Private baggage of officers and knapsacks of men were left behind. Neither provision nor ammunition was carried off. Some attempt was made to carry ammunition, as boxes without number were found on the bank of the river where the steamers had been landed.

"It is almost impossible to give any exact account of the immense quantities of property and supplies left in our hands. All their artillery, field batteries and siege guns, amounting to thirty-three pieces, magazines full of fixed ammunition of the best character, several thousand stand of inferior small arms, with hundreds of boxes of musket cartridges, tents for an army of ten thousand men, horses, mules, wagons, intrenching tools, &c., are among the spoils. Nothing except the men escaped, and they with only what they wore. They landed on the opposite side of the river, and are scattered in the wide bottoms. I immediately advanced Hamilton's division into the place, and had the guns of the enemy turned upon the river, which they completely command.

"The flight of the enemy was so hasty that they abandoned their pickets, and gave no intimation to the forces at Island No. Ten.· The consequence is, that one gunboat and ten large steamers, which were there, are cut off from below, and must either be destroyed or fall into our hands. Island No. Ten must necessarily be evacuated, as it can neither be reënforced nor supplied from below.

"During the operations here, the whole of the forces were at different times brought under the fire of the enemy, and behaved themselves with great gallantry and coolness. It seems proper, however, that I should make special mention of those more directly concerned in the final operations against the place.

"The tenth and sixteenth Illinois, commanded respectively by Colonels Morgan and J. R. Smith, were detailed as guards to the proposed trenches and to aid in constructing them. They marched from camp at sunset on the 12th, and drove in the pickets and grand guards of the enemy, as they were ordered, at shouldered arms and without returning a shot; covered the front of the intrenching parties, and occupied the trenches and rifle pits during the whole day and night of the 13th, under furious and incessant cannonading from sixty pieces of heavy artillery. At the earnest request of their colonels, their regimental flags were kept flying over our trenches, though they offered a conspicuous mark to the enemy. The coolness, courage, and cheerfulness of these troops, exposed for two nights and a day to the furious fire of the enemy at short range, and to the severe storm which raged during the whole night of the 13th, are beyond all praise, and delighted and astonished every officer who witnessed it. The division of General Stanley, consisting of the twenty-seventh, thirty-ninth, forty-third, and sixty-third Ohio regiments, supported the battery from two o'clock A. M., on the 13th, to daylight on the 14th, exposed to the full fury of the cannonade without being able to return a shot, and to

the severe storm of that night, and displayed coolness, courage, and fortitude worthy of all praise. In fact, the conduct of all the troops of this command so far exceeded my expectations, that I was astonished and delighted, and feel very safe in predicting for them a brilliant career in arms.　.　.　.

"Our whole loss during the operation was fifty-one killed and wounded. A detailed list will be transmitted as soon as it can be made. The enemy's loss cannot be ascertained. A number of his dead were left unburied, and over a hundred new graves attested that he must have suffered severely.

"I am, general, respectfully,
"Your obedient servant,
"JOHN POPE,
"*Brigadier-General commanding.*"

"Brigadier-General G. W. CULLUM, *Chief of Staff and of Engineers, Dep't. of the Mississippi, St. Louis.*"

GENERAL POPE'S OFFICIAL REPORT OF THE CAPTURE OF ISLAND NO. TEN.

"HEADQUARTERS ARMY OF THE MISSISSIPPI, FIVE ⎱
MILES FROM CORINTH, MISS., *April* 30, 1862. ⎰

"GENERAL: I have the honor to submit the following report of the operations which resulted in the capture of Island No. Ten, and the batteries on the main shore, together with the whole of the land forces of the enemy in that vicinity. A brief sketch of the topography of the immediate neighborhood seems essential to a full understanding of the operations of the army.

"Island No. Ten lies at the bottom of a great bend of the Mississippi, immediately north of it being a long, narrow promontory on the Missouri shore. The river from Island No. Ten flows north-west to New Madrid, where it again makes a great bend to the south as far as Tiptonville, otherwise called Merriweather's Landing, so that opposite New Madrid also is a long, narrow promontory. From Island No. Eight, about four miles above Island No. Ten, the distance across the land to New Madrid is six miles, while by river it is fifteen. So like-wise the distance over land from Island No. Ten to Tiptonville is five miles, while by water it is twenty-seven.

"Commencing at Hickman, a great swamp, which afterwards becomes Reelfoot Lake, extends along the left bank of the Mississippi, and discharges its waters into the river forty miles below Tiptonville, leaving the whole peninsula opposite New Madrid between it and the river. This peninsula, therefore, is itself an island, having the Mississippi on three sides, and Reelfoot Lake and the great swamps which border it on the other. A good road leads from Island No. Ten along the west bank of Reelfoot Lake to Tiptonville. The only means of supply, therefore, for the forces at and around Island No. Ten, on this peninsula, was by the river. When the river was blockaded at New Madrid, supplies and reënforcements were landed at Tiptonville, and conveyed across the neck of the peninsula by land. There was no communication with the interior, except by a small flatboat, which plied across Reelfoot Lake, a distance of two miles, and that through an opening cut through cypress swamps for the purpose. Supplies and reënforcements, or escape, to any considerable extent, were therefore impracticable on the land side.

"One mile below Tiptonville begin the great swamps along the Mississippi, on both sides, and no dry ground is to be found, except in occasional spots, for about sixty miles below. By intercepting the navigation of the river below Tiptonville, and commanding by heavy artillery the lowest point of dry ground near that place, the enemy would be at once cut off from his resources, and prevented from escaping.

"Immediately after the reduction of New Madrid, this subject engaged my attention. The roads along the river, in the direction of Point Pleasant, followed a narrow strip of dry land between the swamps and the river, and

were very miry and difficult. With much labor the heavy guns captured from the enemy at New Madrid were dragged by hand and established in battery at several prominent points along the river, the lower battery being placed immediately opposite the lowest point of dry ground below Tiptonville. This extended my lines seventeen miles along the river. A week was thus passed in severe labor. The enemy, perceiving the consequence of establishing these batteries, attempted in every way by his gunboats to prevent their construction. They were, therefore, in every case established in the night. As soon as daylight unmasked our lowest battery, the enemy saw at once that we must either be dislodged or all reliable communication with his forces would be cut off. Five gunboats, therefore, at once advanced against the battery, which consisted of two twenty-four pound siege guns and two ten-pound Parrotts, manned by a detachment of the first United States infantry under Lieutenant Bates, and supported by General Palmer's division, encamped one and a half miles in the rear. Rifle pits for five hundred sharp-shooters were dug on the flanks of the battery close to the river bank, and were constantly occupied. The gunboats ran up within three hundred yards, and a furious cannonade was kept up for an hour and a half, when they were repulsed, with the loss of one gunboat sunk, several badly damaged, and many men shot down at their guns by our sharpshooters from the rifle pits. Our loss was one man killed. From that time no attempt against the battery was made, and all communication from below with the forces near Island No. Ten was cut off. One of the gunboats would occasionally, during a dark night, steal up close along the opposite shore to Tiptonville, but always at such great risk that it was seldom undertaken. Neither supplies nor men could be taken up or carried off in this way.

"Such was the condition of affairs on the

16th of March. The object for which the land forces had been moved on New Madrid was accomplished in the capture of that place and the blockade of the river to any supplies and reënforcements for the enemy at and around Island No. Ten.

"Meantime the flotilla had been firing at long range, both from the gun and mortar boats, at the batteries of the enemy in and opposite the island, for seven consecutive days, without any apparent effect, and without any advance whatever towards their reduction. This result was doubtless due to the defective construction of the boats.

"On the 16th of March I received your despatch directing me, if possible, to construct a road through the swamps to a point on the Missouri shore opposite Island No. Ten, and transfer a portion of my force, sufficient to erect batteries at that point, to assist in the artillery practice on the enemy's batteries. I accordingly despatched Colonel J. W. Bissell's engineer regiment to examine the country with this view, directing him at the same time, if he found it impracticable to build a road through the swamps and overflow of the river, to ascertain whether it were possible to dig or cut a canal across the peninsula from some point above Island No. Ten to New Madrid, in order that steam transports might be brought to me, which would enable my command to cross the river. The idea of the canal was suggested to me by General Schuyler Hamilton, in a conversation upon the necessity of crossing the river and assailing the enemy's batteries, near Island No. Ten, in the rear.

"On the 17th of March I suggested to Commodore Foote, by letter, that he should run the enemy's batteries with one of his gunboats, and thus enable me to cross the river with my command — assuring him that by this means I could throw into the rear of the enemy men enough to deal with any force he might have. This request the com-modore declined on the ground of impracticability.

"Colonel Bissell having reported a road impracticable, but that a route could be found for a channel sufficient for small steamers, I immediately directed him to commence the canal, with the whole regiment, and to call on Colonel Buford, commanding the land forces temporarily on duty with the flotilla, — which had been placed under my command, — for any assistance in men or material necessary for the work. Supplies of such .articles as were needed, and four steamers of light draught, were sent for to Cairo, and the work begun. It was my purpose to make the canal deep enough for the gunboats; but it was not found practicable to do so within any reasonable period. The work performed by Colonel Bissell and his regiment of engineers was beyond measure difficult, and its completion was delayed much beyond my expectations. The canal is twelve miles long, six miles of which are through very heavy timber. An avenue fifty feet wide was made through it, by sawing off trees of large size four and a half feet under water. For nineteen days the work was prosecuted with untiring energy and determination, under exposures and privations very unusual even in the history of warfare. It was completed on the 4th of April, and will long remain a monument of enterprise and skill.

"During all this time the flotilla had kept up its fire upon the batteries of the enemy, but without making any progress towards their reduction. It had by this time become very apparent that the capture of Island No. Ten could not be made unless the land forces could be thrown across the river, and their works carried from the rear; but during this long delay, the enemy, anticipating such a movement, had erected batteries along the shore from Island No. Ten entirely round to Tiptonville, at every point where troops could be landed. The difficulty of crossing the river in force had, therefore, been greatly increased; and what would have been a comparatively safe undertaking three weeks before had become one full of peril.

"It is not necessary to state to you that the passage of a great river lined with batteries, and in the face of the enemy, is one of the most difficult and hazardous operations of war, and cannot be justified except in a case of urgent necessity. Such a case seemed presented for my action.

"Without this movement, operations against Island No. Ten must have been abandoned, and the land forces at least withdrawn. It is but justice to say, that, although the full peril of the moment was thoroughly understood by my whole command, there was not an officer or a man who was not anxious to be placed in the advance.

"There seemed little hope of any assistance from the gunboats. I therefore had several heavy coal barges brought into the upper end of the canal, which, during the progress of the work, were made into floating batteries.

"Each battery consisted of three heavy barges lashed together, and bolted with iron. The middle barge was bulkheaded all around, so as to give four feet of thickness of solid timber both at the sides and on the ends. The heavy guns, three in number, were mounted on it, and protected by traverses of sand-bags. It also carried eighty sharpshooters. The barges outside of it had a first layer in the bottom of empty water-tight barrels, securely lashed, then layers of dry cotton-wood rails and cotton bales packed close. They were then floored over at the top to keep every thing in its place, so that a shot penetrating the outer barges must pass through twenty feet of rails and cotton before reaching the middle one, which carried the men and the guns. The arrangement of water barrels and cotton bales was made in order that, even if penetrated frequently by the enemy's shot,

and filled with water, the outer barges could not sink.

"It was my purpose, when all was ready, to tow one or two of these batteries over the river to a point opposite New Madrid, where swamps prevented any access to the river, and where the enemy, therefore, had been unable to establish his batteries. When near the shore, the floating batteries, with their crews, were to be cut loose from the steamer, and allowed to float down the river to the point selected for landing the troops. As soon as they arrived within a short range of it, they were to cast out their anchors so as to hold the barges firmly, and open fire upon the enemy's batteries.

"I think that these batteries would have accomplished their purpose, and my whole force volunteered to man them. They were well provided with small boats, to be kept out of danger, and, even if the worst happened, and the batteries were sunk by the enemy's fire, the men would meet with no worse fate than capture.

"On the 5th of April the steamers and barges were brought near to the mouth of the bayou which discharges into the Mississippi at New Madrid, but were kept carefully out of sight of the river, while our floating batteries were being completed. The enemy, as we afterwards learned, had received positive advices of the construction of the canal, but were unable to believe that such a work was practicable. The first assurance they had of its completion was the appearance of the four steamers loaded with troops, on the morning of the 7th of April.

"On the 4th Commodore Foote allowed one of the gunboats to run the batteries at Island No. Ten, and Captain Walke, U. S. N., who had volunteered, — as appears from the commodore's order to him, — came through that night with the gunboat Carondelet. Although many shots were fired at him as he passed the batteries, his boat was not once struck. He informed me of his arrival early on the 5th.

"On the morning of the 6th, I sent General Granger, Colonel Smith of the forty-third Ohio, and Captain L. H. Marshall of my staff, to make a reconnoissance of the river below, and requested Captain Walke to take them on board the Carondelet, and run down the river to ascertain precisely the character of the banks and the position and number of the enemy's batteries.

"The whole day was spent in this reconnoissance, the Carondelet steaming down the river in the midst of a heavy fire from the enemy's batteries along the shore. The whole bank, for fifteen miles, was lined with heavy guns at intervals; in no case, I think, exceeding one mile. Intrenchments for infantry were also thrown up along the shore, between the batteries.

"On his return up the river, Captain Walke silenced the enemy's battery opposite Point Pleasant, and a small infantry force, under Captain L. H. Marshall, landed and spiked the guns. On the night of the 6th, at my urgent request, Commodore Foote ordered the Pittsburg also to run down to New Madrid. She arrived at daylight, having, like the Carondelet, come through without being touched. I directed Captain Walke to proceed down the river at daylight on the 7th, with the two gunboats, and, if possible, silence the batteries near Watson's Landing, the point which had been selected to land the troops; and at the same time I brought the four steamers into the river, and embarked Paine's division, which consisted of the tenth, sixteenth, twenty-second, and fifty-first Illinois regiments, with Houghtaling's battery of artillery. The land batteries of thirty-two pounders, under Captain Williams, first United States infantry, which I had established some days before, opposite the point where the troops were to land, were ordered to open their fire upon the enemy's batteries opposite as soon as it was possible to see them.

"A heavy storm commenced on the night of the 6th, and continued, with short intermissions, for several days. The morning of the 7th was very dark, and the rain fell heavily until midday. As soon as it was fairly light, our heavy batteries on the land opened their fire vigorously upon the batteries of the enemy, and the two gunboats ran down the river and joined in the action. I cannot speak too highly of the conduct of Captain Walke during the whole of these operations. Prompt, gallant, and cheerful, he performed the hazardous service assigned him with signal skill and success. About twelve o'clock M. he signalled me that the batteries near our place of landing were silenced, and the steamers containing Paine's division moved out from the landing and began to cross the river, preceded by the gunboats.

"The whole force designed to cross had been drawn up along the river bank, and saluted the passing steamers with shouts of exultation. As soon as we began to cross the river, the enemy commenced to vacate his positions along the banks and the batteries on the Tennessee shore, opposite Island No. Ten. His whole force was in motion towards Tiptonville, with the exception of the few artillerists on the island, who, in the haste of the retreat, had been abandoned. As Paine's division was passing opposite the point I occupied on the shore, one of my spies, who had crossed on the gunboats from the silenced battery, informed me of this hurried retreat of the enemy. I signalled General Paine to stop his boats, and sent him the information, with orders to land as rapidly as possible on the opposite shore, and push forward to Tiptonville, to which point the enemy's forces were tending from every direction. I sent no force to occupy the deserted batteries opposite Island No. Ten, as it was my first purpose to capture the whole army of the enemy.

"At eight or nine o'clock that night, (the 7th.) the small party abandoned on the island, finding themselves deserted, and fearing an attack in the rear from our land forces, which they knew had crossed the river in the morning, sent a message to Commodore Foote, surrendering to him. The divisions were pushed forward to Tiptonville as fast as they were landed, Paine leading. The enemy attempted to make a stand several times near that place, but Paine did not once deploy his columns. By midnight all our forces were across the river, and pushing forward rapidly to Tiptonville. The enemy retreating before Paine, and from Island No. Ten, met at Tiptonville during the night in great confusion, and were driven back into the swamps by the advance of our forces, until, at four o'clock A. M. on the 8th, finding themselves completely cut off, and being apparently unable to resist, they laid down their arms and surrendered at discretion. They were so scattered and confused that it was several days before any thing like an accurate account of their number could be made.

"Meantime I had directed Colonel W. L. Elliott, of the second Iowa cavalry, who had crossed the river after dark, to proceed as soon as day dawned to take possession of the enemy's abandoned works on the Tennessee shore, opposite Island No. Ten, and to save the steamers if he possibly could. He reached there before sunrise that morning, (the 8th,) and took possession of the encampments, the immense quantity of stores and supplies, and of all the enemy's batteries on the main land. He also brought in almost two hundred prisoners. After posting his guards and taking possession of the steamers not sunk or injured, he remained until the forces landed. As Colonel Buford was in command of these forces, Colonel Elliott turned over to his infantry force the prisoners, batteries, and captured property, for safe keeping, and proceeded to cross the country in the direction of Tiptonville, along Reelfoot Lake, as directed.

"It is almost impossible to give a correct account of the immense quantity of artillery, ammunition, and supplies of every description which fell into our hands.

"Three generals, two hundred and seventy-three field and company officers, six thousand seven hundred prisoners, one hundred and twenty-three pieces of heavy artillery, all of the very best character and of the latest patterns, seven thousand stand of small arms, several wharf-boat loads of provisions, an immense quantity of ammunition of all kinds, many hundred horses and mules, with wagons and harness, &c., &c.; are among the spoils. Very few if any of the enemy escaped, and only by wading and swimming through the swamps. The conduct of the troops was splendid throughout, as the results of this operation and its whole progress very plainly exhibit. We have crossed the great river, the banks of which were lined with batteries and defended by seven thousand men; we have pursued and captured the whole force of the enemy and all his supplies and material of war, and have again recrossed and occupied the camp at New Madrid, without losing a man or meeting with an accident. Such results bespeak efficiency, good conduct, high discipline, and soldierly deportment of the best character, far better than they can be exhibited in pitched battles or the storming of fortified places. Patience, willing labor, endurance of hardship and privation for long periods, cheerful and prompt obedience, order and discipline, bravery and spirit, are the qualities which these operations have developed in the forces under my command, and which assure for them a brilliant and successful career in arms. It is difficult to express the feeling which such conduct has occasioned me, fortunate enough to be the commander of such troops There are few material obstacles within the range of warfare which a man of courage and spirit would hesitate to encounter with such a force. . . .

" Our success was complete and overwhelming, and it gives me profound satisfaction to report that it was accomplished without loss of life.

" JOHN POPE,
" *Major-General commanding.*"

COMMODORE FOOTE'S OFFICIAL REPORT.

"FLAG-SHIP BENTON, ISLAND NO. TEN,
April 8, 1862.

" I have the honor to inform the department that since I sent the telegram last night, announcing the surrender to me of Island No. Ten, possession has been taken both of the island and works upon the Tennessee shore by the gunboats and the troops under General Buford. Seventeen officers and three hundred and sixty-eight privates, besides one hundred sick and one hundred men employed on board transports in our hands, are unconditional prisoners of war. I have caused a hasty examination of the forts, &c., captured. There are eleven earthworks, seventy heavy cannon, ranging from thirty-two to one hundred pounders, rifled. The magazines are well supplied with powder, and there are large quantities of shot, shell, and other munitions of war; also great quantities of provisions.

" Four steamers afloat have fallen into our hands, and two others, with the rebel gunboat Grampus, are sunk, but can be easily raised. The floating battery of sixteen heavy guns, turned adrift by the rebels, is said to be lying on the Missouri shore below New Madrid.

" The enemy upon the main land appear to have fled with great precipitation after dark last night, leaving in many cases half-prepared meals in their quarters. There seems to have been no concert of action between the rebels upon the island and those occupied on the shore; but the latter fled, leaving the former

to their fate. These works were erected with the highest engineering skill, and are of great strength, and with their natural advantages would have been impregnable if defended by men fighting in a better cause.

" A combined attack of naval and land forces would have taken the place this afternoon or to-morrow morning, had not the rebels so hastily abandoned their stronghold; to mature the plans of attack having absolutely required twenty-three days' preparation.

" General Pope is momentarily expected to arrive with his army at this point, he having successfully crossed the river yesterday under a heavy fire, which, no doubt, led to the hasty abandonment of the works last night.

" I am unofficially informed that the two gunboats, which so gallantly ran the fire of the rebel batteries a few nights since, yesterday attacked and reduced the fort of the enemy opposite, dismounting eight guns.

" The following is a copy of the order of General McCall in assuming command of the rebel forces, 5th instant: —

"'SOLDIERS: We are strangers, commander and commanded, to each other. Let me tell you who I am. I am a general made by Beauregard — a general selected by Beauregard and Bragg for this command, when they knew it was in peril.

"'They have known me for twenty years. Together we have stood on the fields of Mexico. You have given them your confidence; now give it to me when I have earned it.

"'Soldiers: the Mississippi valley is intrusted to your courage, to your discipline, to your patience. Exhibit the vigilance and coolness of last night, and hold it.

"'W. D. McCALL.'

" I regret that the painful condition of my feet still requires me to use crutches, and which prevented me from making a personal examination of the works. I was, therefore, compelled to delegate Lieutenant-commanding Phelps, of the Benton.

"A. H. FOOTE, *Flag-Officer.*

"To Hon. GIDEON WELLES."

CHAPTER LXX.

Advance of the Federal Forces in Tennessee. — General Grant's Army. — Rebel Movements under General Beauregard. — Concentration of Rebel Forces. — Position of General Grant's Army. — Aggressive Movement by the Rebels. — Battle of Shiloh, or Pittsburg Landing. — Sudden Attack upon the Federal Camps. — Divisions of General Prentiss, General Sherman, and General McClernand driven back. — Occupation of the Federal Camps by the Rebels. — Desperate Condition of the Federal Troops. — Continued Advance of the Rebel Forces. — Hurlbut's and Wallace's Divisions. — The Federal Troops driven near the River. — Fire of Gunboats. — Approach of Night, and Failure of the Rebels to complete their Victory. — Losses and Condition of General Grant's Army. — Arrival of General Buell's Army and Lew. Wallace's Division. — Preparations for Renewal of the Battle. — Attack by the Federal Forces. — Severe Conflict. — The Enemy driven from his Position. — Rebel Defeat and Retreat. — The Result. — Official Reports.

SHORTLY after the capture of Fort Donelson and the occupation of Nashville the federal forces made a further advance into the rebel territory. General Grant's army, which had occupied different points in Western Kentucky, was concentrated, and reënforced by a number of new regiments, moved up the Tennessee River in transports to Pittsburg Landing, a point near the southern line of Tennessee. Here and at Crump's Landing, about six miles below, the forces debarked and established themselves in camps, awaiting the advance and cooperation of the army under General Buell. The latter gradually collected his forces from Eastern Kentucky, and prepared to move from Nashville to Columbia, and thence to coöperate with General Grant against the rebel forces which were concentrating near the boundary line of Tennessee and Mississippi.

The main part of the army of General Grant had been encamped near Pittsburg Landing for about three weeks before there were any signs of a conflict or of active operations. A few expeditions, not very formidable or effective, had been sent out to interrupt the rebel communications by the destruction of railroads; but while a severe blow in this way might have been struck, and the concentration of the rebel forces thus materially delayed, no considerable damage was done to the railroads, and but slight interruption to the rebel movements was caused. And although the federal forces had thus far advanced for an aggressive campaign, the necessary preparations for keeping their communications open and obtaining supplies, or some other cause, brought the aggressive movement to a stand, and the delay enabled the rebels to assume the offensive, and to attempt to drive out those whom they called invaders. This attempt on the part of the rebels was well conceived, and the movement was carried out with such promptness and spirit that it came near being successful.

In view of the movements which were expected to take place on the Mississippi, the rebel authorities had sent General Beauregard, whose skill as an engineer is admitted, to inspect and to command the defences which had been constructed on the banks of the river and elsewhere. Whatever he imagined or advised the strength of these works to be, it seemed probable that before the combined attack of the land and naval forces they must sooner or later yield. But now the armies that had moved down through Kentucky into Tennessee were in advance of the expedition down the river, and unless they were repulsed, the fortifications on the river would be of as little account as was Columbus after the fall of Forts Henry and Donelson. The rebel general saw the necessity of this, and prepared with spirit and promptness to defeat the purposes of General Grant. He called upon the governors of the neighboring states to furnish additional troops, while he concentrated all the available forces of his own command, and received large reënforcements from Mobile and Pensacola, under General Bragg. To these forces was also added those under the command of General A. S. Johnston, then the general-in-chief of the rebel army, which were in South-eastern Tennessee. These rebel forces were rapidly concentrated, considering the moderate facilities for their movement, while greater activity on the part of the federal forces, such as has since been exhibited under similar circumstances, might have greatly interrupted, if not wholly defeated, the rebel plans. As it was, General Beauregard concentrated an army of sixty thousand men, or upwards, at Corinth, in the northern part of the state of Mississippi, only about twenty miles from the federal position at Pittsburg Landing. He knew, through his scouts and the information so easily obtained from his friends in Tennessee within the federal lines, that General Buell's forces were moving so as to form a junction with General Grant, and that their combined armies could easily drive him from his position at Corinth; and he therefore determined to advance at once against General Grant, and by his superior numbers completely overwhelm him before General Buell could render him any assistance. The army of the latter, not so large as General Grant's, could then be speedily defeated, and the federal forces thus be driven from Tennessee. To carry out his plans, General Beauregard moved his whole army from Corinth on the 4th and 5th of April, and advanced towards the federal camps.

The position occupied by the federal forces was on an undulating table land on the west side of the Tennessee, elevated some eighty or one hundred feet above the river, and lying between Lick Creek on the south and Snake Creek on the north. Near the river the ground is broken by some deep ravines, and towards Lick Creek rises into hills of considerable height, which have a gradual slope on the north, but are steep and abrupt on the side of the creek. Much of the country was covered with woods, through most of which troops could move without difficulty; but there were occasional thickets of underbrush, and in some places were cultivated fields of considerable extent. Upon one of the roads leading from Pittsburg Landing towards Corinth was a little church called Shiloh Church, from which the region took its name among the people of the vicinity.

General Grant's forces were encamped from two to five miles out from Pittsburg Landing. They were composed of five divisions, of which Brigadier-General Sherman's was in the most advanced position, and extended along a front of about four miles, one brigade under Colonel Stuart occupying the extreme left of the federal line, and another nearly the extreme right. Close to General Sherman's line were the divisions of Brigadier-General Prentiss' and Major-General McClernand, partially filling the gaps left between the brigades of General Sherman's division. General Prentiss's division was on the left, next to Colonel Stuart's brigade, and General Sherman's was on the right of Prentiss, and a little more in the rear. These three divisions formed the front of General Grant's army, and back of them, within a mile of the Landing, were the division of General Hurlbut on the left and the division of General W. H. Wallace on the right. At Crump's Landing, some six miles below, was the division of General Lew. Wallace.

This position of the army was on some accounts a good one, affording excellent camping grounds, and offering some advantages for defence in case of attack. But the disposition of the forces has been severely criticised. The extended line of the advance, showing gaps of which an enemy could easily take advantage and which were not covered by the supporting line, and the separation of the brigades of General Sherman's division, were serious defects in

the occupation of the ground, and were the immediate causes of the disasters which followed. While the ground also offered opportunities for works of defence, and the position could thus have been greatly strengthened by redoubts, even if of slight construction, by rifle pits, and in some places by formidable abatis, the troops were encamped here for three weeks, and no measures for such defence were taken. There was, for some days at least, reason to suppose that an attack might be made by the rebels, whose movements were but partially known, and General Grant expected such an attack, while General Sherman declared that the position he occupied was dangerous. Yet nothing was done to strengthen the position, to occupy more favorable ground, or to make a more thorough disposition of the troops for meeting the anticipated attack. And it would seem that, notwithstanding the expectations and declarations of the generals, the additional precautions of stronger and more advanced pickets, and more extensive scouting, were not observed. Yet the officers highest in command were esteemed able and comparatively experienced, and since that time have proved themselves among the most competent and skilful generals; and it is difficult to believe that with any real expectations of attack they should neglect to adopt such common precautions, unless they entirely underrated the rebel forces.

The rebel army numbered sixty thousand men, and was composed of three grand divisions, under the command of Generals Beauregard, Bragg, and Hardee, General Johnston, as general-in-chief, having command of the whole army, though the plan of attack and disposition of the forces were Beauregard's. These forces arrived at a position a comparatively short distance from the federal pickets, on the evening of Saturday, the 5th of April, and the several divisions were disposed for an attack early on the following morning. Shortly after

dawn the pickets of General Prentiss's division were driven in, and immediately afterwards a part of General Sherman's pickets were also compelled to fall back before the advancing enemy. The attack was unexpected, and the federal camps were but just astir, and as unprepared as if no enemy were within striking distance. When the pickets, after a few shots (which, from the too frequent and causeless occurrence of such reports, at first created little alarm), rushed into the camps, the troops were yet in confusion. Arms and accoutrements had hardly been seized, ammunition was but ill-supplied, and, roused by the sudden alarm, the soldiers, in haste and confusion, were just rushing to form the regimental lines. The advance of the enemy was close upon the heels of the pickets, and before the federal lines could be formed the rebel artillery had already commenced throwing shot and shell into the camps. Not yet in line and under the control of their officers, nor feeling the confidence which discipline and organization inspire, many of the soldiers fled in alarm. A great part of them were new troops, who had never before been under fire or exposed to attack, and were therefore less prompt to rally to meet the enemy who came so suddenly. But though their ranks were thinned by the flight of the cowardly, and soon by the fall of numbers before the fierce fire of the rebels, most of the regiments made a spirited resistance, as soon as they could rally and form for the purpose. The rebels, however, came sweeping on in such strong and compact columns, that the federal troops were obliged at once to abandon their camps, leaving in some cases men not yet out of their tents to be taken prisoners, and not a few wounded and dead, who had fallen even before they had taken their arms.

Falling rapidly back through the woods in the rear of their camp, the broken regiments of General Sherman's division were finally

69

formed behind a ridge which afforded them some protection, and succeeded in checking for a time the advance of the enemy. General Sherman himself, and many of his officers, showed great courage and determination in rallying the troops; they exposed themselves freely to the dangers of the field, encouraged their men by their presence and gallantry, and demanded only that the soldiers should follow where they led. By their spirited efforts the division was saved from utter destruction, and the rebels were for a time held in check, and thus prevented from carrying out their plan of completing the ruin or capture of General Grant's army by that day's battle. But General Sherman's troops were compelled to retire before the greater numbers and more compact masses of the rebels, who pressed on, flushed with success. The shattered brigades of this division fell back, still fighting, but in some disorder, till they came to the position occupied by General McClernand's division, the greater part of which was posted in the rear of General Sherman's camps. General Sherman had resisted the rebel advance with great energy, and, inspired by his example, his troops repeatedly manifested a valor which might have repulsed the enemy, but for his superior numbers. The retreat of his brigades brought General McClernand's troops to the front. A portion of the latter had, indeed, been brought into action earlier to support the left of General Sherman's line, which was being pressed more rapidly back; but the whole of General Sherman's line was now driven back, and falling behind General McClernand's troops, the latter were soon engaged with the advancing enemy.

Meanwhile General Prentiss's division was attacked by the enemy quite as vigorously as General Sherman's. Most of his troops rallied to the battle call, and were formed in line; but unfortunately they were formed in an open field, while the rebels advanced under the cover of a thicket in front. Notwithstanding this, the troops held their ground bravely for a time, and would have repulsed the enemy but for the overwhelming numbers which he threw against the federal lines. The other federal divisions were not in position to cover the gaps on either side of General Prentiss, and to protect his flanks, and the enemy, while pushing him fiercely in front, closed in upon each side. Thus situated, the division fell back more and more rapidly, and their resistance became more faint and irregular. A part of the division, under the immediate command of General Prentiss, standing its ground more firmly than the others, became separated. These troops held their position some time longer, but they were at last surrounded by the rebels, so that they were obliged to surrender. Three regiments, or what remained of them, and a division commander were thus made prisoners. The remainder of the division was now far in the rear, and so shattered that it was virtually defeated, and presented no front to the enemy.

When General Sherman's division fell back, pressed by the rebel forces, General McClernand was obliged to bring his whole division into action. But the defeat of General Prentiss's division, and the retiring of General Sherman's, exposed the flanks of General McClernand's line. The rebels were prompt to avail themselves of the advantage thus gained, and they advanced in large numbers through the federal camps, to turn McClernand's right. Artillery was promptly placed in position to meet this movement, and played upon the rebel columns with great slaughter. But they advanced in spite of this severe fire, and additional forces coming up, they pressed upon the federal lines with a fierce fire of musketry, and in some places with desperate charges. The federal troops fought well, and several times repulsed the enemy; but they were again and again driven further back with heavy losses. Many officers fell, the regiments were greatly weakened by the loss of men, and a number of pieces of artillery were either abandoned for want of horses to draw them off, or were captured in the charges of the enemy. The rebel numbers and their determined spirit were too much for the federal troops to withstand, and McClernand's division, with Sherman's shattered brigades, were driven back to the position occupied by General Hurlbut's division, which was scarcely a mile out from the river.

While these events were transpiring more directly in the front or centre of the federal position, one brigade of General Sherman's division, under Colonel Stuart, which was posted on the extreme left of the federal line, was engaged with the enemy by itself. While the conflict with General Prentiss's division was going on this brigade was not attacked, but when that division met with disaster, a column of rebel troops suddenly made its appearance in front of Colonel Stuart's force. The regiment in advance fell back to its supports, and the advancing column turned towards the retreating troops of General Prentiss. But shortly after a battery of rebel artillery opened upon them from the bluffs along Lick Creek, and under cover of this fire the rebel infantry advanced rapidly upon them. For a few minutes the brigade met the enemy with a steady fire of musketry and the section of a battery; but it was very soon evident that its position, exposed to the shells from the rebel batteries and a destructive fire from the advancing infantry, was untenable, and it was withdrawn in good order to the next wooded ridge. Here an attack was threatened by a body of rebel cavalry which had gained its flank, but the disposition of his forces by Colonel Stuart and the nature of the ground kept the cavalry from making a charge. The rebel infantry, however, soon advanced, and a portion of them came in from the pursuit of General Prentiss's troops, upon the right of the federal brigade. Thus it was hard pressed, and was in fact driven from

ridge to ridge, till at last, much broken and discouraged, it retired behind the lines of General W. H. L. Wallace's troops, a part of which had been thrown forward in this direction to support it.

It was hardly noon when the entire line of federal troops was thus driven back upon their reserves. The camps of three divisions, with all their equipage and a quantity of supplies, were in the possession of the rebels. In the camps were a considerable number of the federal sick and wounded, some of whom suffered anew from the shot of their own friends, discharged at the enemy as he occupied or marched through the grounds. The ranks of the several divisions had been thinned by the fall of many brave men, and the flight of a larger number of the timid and undisciplined. All along the river bank near Pittsburg Landing were hundreds and even thousands of men who should have been in the front fighting the enemy, but were, instead, crouching under the bluff. Some of them had come there early in the day, saying that their regiments were cut to pieces and the federal troops utterly defeated; others had straggled in later with as fearful tales, until the fugitives could be numbered almost by regiments. For many of them it was their first engagement, and the suddenness of the attack, and the lax discipline of most of the regiments, produced this unfortunate thinning of the federal ranks, against which no precaution had been, or perhaps could be, taken. But while there was this large number of the timid and demoralized, the greater part of the troops had fought bravely, though at great disadvantage and against superior numbers. They had repeatedly, for a time, repulsed the rebel forces; but the latter were well handled, and fresh troops were pressed on with so much vigor that it was impossible to withstand them. Each commander of division, and in some cases even brigade commanders, had thus far fought the battle as best they might, without much concert, and no general direction of a superior, but with spirit and ability. And now they had been driven back, with forces shattered and in confusion, within a mile of the Landing. The losses had already been heavy. Besides the fall of many brave officers and men upon the obstinately contested portions of the field, a large part of the field artillery of the three divisions had been lost, and the army thus materially weakened in this most important arm as well as in numbers. The condition of the federal troops was, therefore, not a little critical, and even desperate, for so early an hour in the day.

General Grant, who was on the river and some miles away from the battle field, did not arrive until most of these disasters had occurred. But his arrival and assuming direction of the disposition of the troops, with the knowledge that General Lew. Wallace's division was moving from Crump's Landing, and that General Buell's advance was near the river and rapidly approaching, gave a less discouraging aspect to affairs, and nerved officers and men to a more determined resistance. As the shattered divisions which had been in front fell back to the positions now occupied and bravely defended by the divisions of Generals Hurlbut and W. H. L. Wallace, the officers again rallied their men, and the regiments were quickly reorganized, formed again in line of battle, and posted as supports to the forces which were in their turn receiving the brunt of the rebel attack. Parts of these two divisions had been, early in the day, advanced to the support of those in front, and had been long engaged with the enemy. But the whole federal line was now forced back, even beyond the camping ground of General Hurlbut's division. Here, where more favorable ground was found, a most determined stand was taken. The line was now composed of General Hurlbut's and General W. H. L. Wallace's divisions, with detached parts of the divisions which had been driven

from the front, General Hurlbut having command of the left and General Wallace of the right. As the rebels pressed on, they were almost every where met with such a terrible fire of artillery and musketry that their lines wavered and were repulsed. In several instances gallant charges were made by the federal troops upon some bodies of the rebel forces, as they wavered under this fire, and they were driven back in confusion. But they were quickly rallied and supported, and returned to the attack in such numbers, that the Union soldiers, though they fought bravely, were gradually pressed back from the ground they had thus gained.

For five or six hours this last position of the federal forces was gallantly maintained, with an occasional temporary advance. The rebel troops were brought up repeatedly, to be driven back with great loss, but again to return to the onset, under the direction of officers who evinced the fiercest determination to achieve a complete victory. They were handled with ability, and quickly supported by their reserves wherever they were repulsed. Numbers of troops, comparatively fresh, were thus repeatedly thrown upon the federal lines, even the reserves of which were wearied with a long and unequal contest. The rebels pressed so desperately upon General Hurlbut's division that at last it was compelled to yield the ground it had so long held, and this part of the line retired in good order, nearly half a mile farther towards the Landing. The enemy advanced as the federal troops retired, and occupied and passed through the camps of General Hurlbut's division. They were not able, however, to drive the federal troops, who withdrew steadily, with artillery so posted as to keep the enemy in check.

The troops under General Wallace still held their ground, and had several times driven the enemy back with heavy loss. They were eager to remain in their position, even after the troops on their left had retired, and were confident that they could keep the rebels in check. But the falling back of General Hurlbut's division exposed their flank, and enabled the rebel officers to concentrate their forces upon this gallant division and the troops which were co-operating with them. It would, therefore, have been rash to have continued the contest under such circumstances, and this division also was ordered to fall back. At this time General Wallace, who had given evidence of the greatest bravery and marked ability as an officer, received a mortal wound, and was borne from the field. The troops, however, were not disorganized by the fall of their general, in whom they had the greatest confidence, but retired in good order, the artillery playing upon the enemy with great effect whenever the nature of the ground admitted it.

The greater part of the army was now within half a mile of Pittsburg Landing, occupying a position immediately about the camps of General Wallace's division. They were crowded into a rather narrow compass for effective operations, and a further repulse would drive them to the river bank, where, in a confused mass, they would be utterly unable to contend against a pursuing enemy, and equally unable to escape across the river. All that could now be done would be to keep the rebel forces back until night should put an end to the battle. General Grant and his officers were not discouraged. They were confident that for an hour or two longer they could keep the enemy at bay, until darkness should prevent his further movements; while before another morning General Lew. Wallace's division, which should already have arrived, would come up from Crump's Landing, and General Buell's forces, which were known to be near, would arrive, and these fresh troops would drive the enemy back from his advanced position, and wrest from him the victory which he might fancy was already won. Disposition of the troops was immediately made for the

desperate resistance which would be necessary if the rebels continued their attacks.

After the last retreat there was a lull in the storm of battle. The enemy did not immediately press forward, and for a brief period there was some doubt whether he intended to continue the conflict and attempt to crush the federal army that night, or await the morning and reënforcemets, in the belief that they had ample time before General Buell could arrive. This delay on the part of the enemy was improved for the better disposition of the federal troops and the posting of the artillery where it could operate most effectively. It soon became evident that the rebel officers were only preparing for another, and, as they hoped, a final and successful attack. They brought up their freshest troops, and advanced them as much as possible under the cover of the woods and undergrowth. Suddenly, with a heavy volley of musketry from the woods, they recommenced the battle, but it was at too great a distance to be effective. The attack was made on the federal left and centre, and anticipating that this would be the point of attack, Colonel Webster, General Grant's chief of staff, and an able artillery officer, placed the guns which he could collect in position to sweep the rebel lines. The enemy's musketry fire was a signal for these guns to open, and as the rebel lines emerged from the woods, they were met by a storm of shot and shell against which they could not advance. The rebel artillery responded, attempting to silence the guns that played so severely upon their infantry, but in this they did not succeed; and though the rattle of musketry in each army was continuous, the rebel infantry did not advance much, nor obtain any advantage in position. The rebel troops were pressed forward with desperate energy, and finding the centre of the federal lines so strong, a movement was made more to the left. Night was approaching, and the victory must be speedily won, if won at all, that day. Heavy columns were, therefore, pushed forward, but in moving against the left of the federal lines they approached the river, and were suddenly met by an unexpected fire.

Two of the gunboats had moved up the river towards Lick Creek, and had been ready to aid the land forces with their heavy guns whenever an opportunity offered. General Hurlbut had communicated with the commander of the gunboats, and these were now lying opposite a ravine, extending from the river for some distance through the bluff. At a given signal, when the federal troops were out of range, the gunboats opened fire, directing the shots up the ravine directly into the rebel lines. With rapid and accurate fire the gunboats drove back the advancing columns of the enemy, while the artillery of the army continued to hold them in check in front. The federal troops, encouraged by the aid of the gunboats and the effect of their field artillery, were ready to meet the enemy more firmly than ever should he advance. But the heavy shot and shell from the gunboats, and the continuous fire of the land artillery, among which were two or three large siege guns, were too much for him to face, and night came on at last without any further advance of his forces. The fire of artillery was continued till it was evident that the rebel forces were withdrawn, disappointed in obtaining the victory which they might well have thought was within their grasp.

This last repulse settled the fortunes of the battle. The enemy had failed to accomplish his object of defeating General Grant's army before it could be reenforced by General Buell. His only chance of ultimate success was in achieving it on the day of the attack. General Buell's troops were already arriving on the other side of the river, and General Lew. Wallace's division was approaching from Crump's Landing. The latter had moved about noon, but had taken a road which led too far to the right, so that it would have been unable to have joined the other divisions of General Grant's army, and might have been thoroughly routed by superior forces of the enemy. The error was seasonably discovered to save the division from defeat, but the retracing of some weary miles of its march delayed it so much that it did not reach the battle field in season to take part in the conflict. An hour after the battle ceased, however, this division had arrived and taken position on the extreme right, near the camp of General W. H. L. Wallace's division. General Nelson's division of General Buell's army had arrived on the other bank of the river, nearly opposite to Lick Creek, and during the night was ferried across, taking position on the extreme left. As two other divisions of General Buell's army — General Crittenden's and General McCook's — arrived, they were assigned a position on General Nelson's right. General Grant's divisions were reorganized, and filled the space between General McCook's and General Lew. Wallace's divisions. Thus a new and more extended line of battle was formed, strong in all its parts, and composed in a great measure of troops that had not yet been engaged, while many of them were the veterans of other fields.

It was late in the night before these dispositions of the troops were determined upon and carried into effect, and all of General Buell's troops were not brought over to their positions till the next morning. But at last the wearied soldiers in the front lay down upon their arms, awaiting the renewal of the conflict, which they now felt confident would ultimately result in victory. The commanding generals continued their conferences till the plans of the morrow's work were completed and the orders issued for their execution. Through the night the gunboats fired occasionally up the ravine, where they had checked the rebel columns, the shells bursting far away in the woods, in which the enemy was supposed to lie. But no movement was made by the rebel forces, except to withdraw from the position thus rendered dangerous to them, and to prepare for the renewal of the battle, in which they perhaps had some reason to suspect that they would meet with a reënforced enemy. The falling back beyond the reach of the shots from the gunboats was, in effect, a yielding of all the ground they had gained in the later conflicts of the day. They still held, however, the greater part of the field which had first been occupied by the federal army; and, as events proved, were preparing for an attack upon the right of the federal army, where they would be less exposed to the fire of the gunboats.

It had been determined by the Union generals to assume the offensive, and to make an attack early in the morning. Accordingly, soon after daybreak, on Monday, April 7, the federal troops were put in motion, and the several divisions were advanced in line of battle towards the enemy. It was supposed that the latter would also renew the battle at dawn, but the withdrawal of their advance had considerably increased the distance between the armies, and some time elapsed before the opposing forces were brought within fighting distance. Shortly before seven o'clock the battle was commenced by the artillery of General Wallace's division, which opened upon certain rebel batteries strongly posted, and threatening to prevent his advance. General Wallace had ascertained the situation of these batteries the night before, and selected the positions from which his own artillery should open upon them. He had selected them well; and the rebel artillery, after a brief duel, during which a body of infantry made a rapid advance through the low land in their front, as if for an assault, withdrew, and opened the way for the advance of General Wallace's division. This advance was made as soon as General Sherman's division, which was the next on the left, had come up. so as to hold that part of the field and pro-

teet General Wallace's flank. As the division arrived upon the crest of the ridge where the rebel batteries had been posted, the movements and designs of the rebels were revealed. A strong column was seen moving rapidly at a distance and on a line parallel to General Wallace's line of battle, and it was evident that the enemy had abandoned his plan of battle of the previous day, and instead of attacking the federal left and centre, where the gunboats might enter into the contest, was massing his forces with the intention of turning the right. General Wallace's artillery opened quickly upon this column of the enemy, and the rebel batteries almost as quickly replied. But the rebel movements were to be met by something more than artillery fire at long range. They were taking dangerous positions on the right, and General Wallace was not slow in sending batteries, strongly supported by infantry, to meet them. Here a spirited fire of artillery, mingled with scattering shots of skirmishers, for some time ensued, while the division waited for General Sherman to come into position. At last General Sherman's division came up, and after bravely facing a severe storm of musketry and grape, his right brigade succeeded in gaining a position which flanked a part of the rebel artillery, and compelled it to retire in haste. This opened the way for a further advance, and enabled General Wallace to reënforce the batteries and supporting brigade, which were now being hotly pressed and more fiercely threatened on the extreme right. The troops sent forward to this point were in time to check the rebel movement, and soon the rebel batteries were silenced by the deadly fire of the daring skirmishers, or the well-served guns of the federal batteries. Again the whole division pressed forward, and meeting now the rebel infantry face to face, a fierce fire of musketry followed. After a sharp conflict the rebel infantry fell back, and thus gradually the rebels were pressed back from the positions to which they had advanced in the morning. The advantages gained were secured only by hard fighting, and not with uniform success. At one time the right of General Sherman's division was broken and repulsed, but the line being quickly re-formed by new regiments promptly brought up, the position was maintained, and soon the enemy was again driven back. From line to line on which the rebels contested the field the right wing of the federal army thus advanced, and the rebel forces retired until late in the afternoon, when their entire left wing joined in the retreat which had already commenced on their right.

While the divisions of Generals Wallace and Sherman were thus engaged in a severe contest with the rebels on the right, General Nelson's division, comprising the left of the federal army, moved forward from its position near the river and in the vicinity of Lick Creek. Its advance was over that portion of the country where Colonel Stuart's brigade had operated the day before, and the position of General Prentiss's division, and it flanked the line which the enemy had occupied after their last successes on the previous evening. But the rebel forces having been withdrawn from the range of the heavy guns of the boats and massed towards the federal right and centre, General Nelson's division did not meet with the enemy until some time after the battle had commenced on the right. When they were found, they were not at first in sufficient numbers to resist the advance of the federal troops, and retired before the skirmishers, who were thrown out a long distance in front of the main body of the division. But as General Nelson gradually pressed them back over the ground where they had the day before achieved their successes, and through a part of the federal camps which they had for a time occupied, they at last rallied on their reserves under cover of the woods, and met the advancing line of Union troops with a heavy fire of artillery and musketry. Thus far

the advance had been so easy, and the enemy had fallen back with so little resistance, that the federal troops had begun to anticipate an easy victory, and they were not prepared for this sudden stand and the vigorous onset with which the rebels now met them. For a time they wavered and fell back, and the enemy rapidly advanced ; but General Nelson's artillery opened a rapid and severe fire, which checked but did not repulse him. Rebel skirmishers picked off the artillerists so that some of the pieces were scarcely manned, and infantry advanced to charge upon and capture guns, the horses and men of which had suffered so much that they could not be removed. But the federal infantry was promptly brought up, and saved the pieces. Infantry and artillery now joined in the battle, which raged for nearly two hours upon this ground with varying fortune. A rebel battery was charged and captured by one of General Nelson's brigades ; but being exposed to a damaging cross-fire, and attacked by a heavy force of infantry, the brigade was forced to abandon its prize and retire. In turn a portion of the federal line was sorely pressed for a time. The rebels fought here with desperate energy, but the Union troops manifested at least an equal gallantry, and these were comparatively veteran troops. They went bravely into the work before them, and under their steady fire the enemy at last faltered. It was a signal which did not escape the notice of the federal general, and his division being advanced rapidly, the rebel troops fell back, with an occasional stand to check their pursuers, till at last they began a steady retreat. It was scarcely three o'clock in the afternoon when this part of the field was won. The rebels had been driven back with heavy loss over all the ground which he had gained on the previous day, and the camps of Generals Prentiss and Sherman had been regained. With these advantages came the recapture of several guns lost the previous day, the capture of many wounded prisoners, and the rescue of many of the federal wounded who had been left on the field the day before.

On the right of General Nelson's division was that under the command of General Crittenden, which moved at the same time as the former, and met the enemy at about the same time. Both these divisions and that of General McCook, which was on the right of General Crittenden's, were under the command of General Buell, who assumed direction of their operations. Their movements, therefore, and the conflicts in which they were engaged, though narrated separately, were but parts of one general battle, in which they were all engaged, and in which they coöperated with the divisions still further to the right, including General Wallace's, which were under the direction of General Grant.

General Crittenden's troops at first met with little more resistance than General Nelson's, but when the rebels at last rallied to repel the advance, they were as strong in front of General Crittenden as they were in front of General Nelson. The former had vigorously attacked and carried a rebel battery which was well supported, after a sharp but short engagement. This success, however, had hardly been accomplished, when the rebel onset which so suddenly checked General Nelson's advance, extended to this part of the field, and a heavy force of the enemy was thrown against General Crittenden's line. For a time the conflict raged fiercely about the captured guns, but at last the federal troops were compelled to retire and abandon their prize, the guns, however, first being rendered useless. General Crittenden's brigades, though compelled to withdraw, were immediately formed in a new line of battle, and held the position bravely against the desperate attacks of the rebels. After a long contest they began to gain advantage, and when the enemy was driven in General Nelson's front, his troops

70

yielded here too, and the retreat soon extended to this part of his line.

Upon General Crittenden's right, General McCook's division of brave and veteran soldiers was brought into action, meeting the enemy in strong force. General McCook moved his troops with great ability, and though they were not engaged in so many severe conflicts as the divisions on their left, they accomplished as important results with much smaller loss. The enemy was compelled to fall back before the advance of this division, and though at times some of his batteries were hotly pressed, they were saved by the rapid and gallant movements of his infantry. As one of his brigades, under General Rousseau, was drawn off from an attack in which they had compelled the enemy to retire, the rebel forces were pushed rapidly forward again, their general hoping to take the retiring troops at disadvantage. Another brigade, however, was at hand, and charging across an open field, they drove back the rebel forces before their impetuous advance. The battle now raged fiercely in this part of the field also, and some desperate attempts were made to flank the division, but all such attempts were successfully met and defeated. The enemy made his last determined stand on this part of the field in some woods beyond the camps of General Sherman's division, but General McCook's reserves were brought up, and soon the rebels fell back and joined in the retreat which had become general throughout their right wing.

Though the rebel right was thus driven back, and at last forced to retreat, on their left, where the rebel general had massed troops in the change of his plan, the battle raged longer. On the right of General McCook were the divisions of Generals McClernand and Hurlbut, which, like that of General Sherman further to the right, were a part of General Grant's army that had suffered so severely in the unequal contest of the day before. These divisions had been reorganized as well as the brief time allowed, and the manner in which the men, notwithstanding their jaded condition, moved forward, showed that they were far from being conquered or demoralized. The field of their operations was on the left of General Sherman, whose movements and success have already been mentioned. Like the other divisions, they met strong bodies of the enemy, whose movements were in concert with those in front of Generals Wallace and Sherman. There were some desperate conflicts, in which ground was alternately gained and lost. But the Union troops, now conscious of their strength, fought with a spirit of determination and generous rivalry with the men of General Buell's army, and after long and repeated contests, the shouts of victory, which had begun on their left, were taken up by these divisions as the enemy gave way. The withdrawal of the rebel forces was at first covered by a desperate resistance, but their retreat was soon manifest, and gradually extended to the extreme left of their line, where the result has already been recorded.

The want of a sufficient cavalry force and the exhausted condition of the men, who had thus been engaged for many hours, as well as the heavy losses, prevented a long pursuit of the retreating rebels. A portion of the troops, however, were sent forward to make sure of the rebel movement. This advance revealed that the enemy had at last retreated in haste, though in good order. They had left, however, nearly all the material that they had captured the previous day, and a large number of their killed and wounded upon the field. A still further advance of federal troops on the following day proved that the rebel forces had almost wholly disappeared. Most of the rebel cavalry, with some artillery, remained in their rear to cover the retreat, and a portion of General Sherman's troops had a short skirmish with a part of this force, and after a slight

reverse in the beginning of the engagement, drove the enemy beyond his camp, capturing some prisoners. The rebel forces, with the exception of this rear guard, had been withdrawn to Corinth, from which place they had marched, confident of a complete victory over the Union armies. They had met with success at first, but their movement was too late, and they had been driven back discomfited, with a heavy loss and a discouraging failure.

Of the forces engaged in the battle of Pittsburg Landing, or Shiloh, as it is more appropriately called, it was estimated by the most careful authorities that the rebel army numbered on the first day of the battle nearly sixty thousand, while General Grant's army did not exceed forty thousand effective men. During the night, it was supposed, the rebels received reënforcements to the number of five or six thousand men, and the forces brought in on the Union side by General Buell consisted of three divisions, numbering not more than twenty thousand. It was, therefore, to their superior numbers, well handled, that the rebels owed their successes on the first day, while on the second day the opposing forces were nearly equal, and the result was due to the courage of the federal troops and the energy and skill of the officers. The enemy believed, indeed, that the united armies of Generals Grant and Buell greatly exceeded their own, and the idea that they were contending against superior numbers and a host of fresh men, undoubtedly dampened the ardor of both officers and men, while on the other hand the federal troops believed that with the combined armies they were invincible.

The losses were very large on both sides. The official report of General Beauregard placed the rebel loss at one thousand seven hundred and twenty-eight killed, eight thousand and twelve wounded, and nine hundred and fifty-nine missing; and it is not improbable that the actual loss exceeded this number.

The exact loss on the part of the federal forces cannot be stated. General Grant's first report estimated the number of killed at fifteen hundred, and thirty-five hundred wounded. But the loss proved to be much greater than this, and probably reached eighteen or nineteen hundred killed, upwards of seven thousand wounded, and nearly four thousand missing and prisoners.* This would make the aggregate federal loss between twelve and thirteen thousand. It was generally believed by the Union officers, who judged by the number of rebel dead and wounded left upon the field, that the enemy's loss in killed and wounded considerably exceeded their own.

The result of the battle of Shiloh, while it was a defeat of the purposes of the rebel general, was not a decisive victory for the federal troops. It could be called but little else than a drawn battle. The federal army was not in a condition to follow up its success of the second day, but it had driven back, in a crippled condition, the rebel forces, and was itself in a condition to be reorganized and rendered efficient in a short time, and in a position to receive speedily all necessary reënforcements. The delay required for these preparations, however, enabled the rebels to fortify their position at Corinth, and thus to render the work of the federal generals more difficult. Before any advance was made, General Halleck, the commander of the department, assumed command of the combined armies of Generals Grant and Buell, and directed the operations which will be mentioned in a subsequent chapter.

---

* The official reports of some of the divisions give the following losses : —

Hurlbut's division, 313 killed, 1449 wounded, 223 missing.
W. H. L. Wallace's " 226 "   1033   "   1164   "
Sherman's   "   318 "   1275   "   441   "
Buell's three   "   263 "   1816   "   88   "

The losses in McClernand's, Lew. Wallace's, and Prentiss's divisions are not found stated exactly in the reports. Prentiss's division was driven back early the first day, with the loss of many prisoners. Its subsequent loss may be included in that of other divisions. General Wallace's was engaged only the second day, as were also General Buell's forces.

From the numerous reports of the federal officers, the following are selected as giving a general view of the operations in the different parts of the field : —

GENERAL GRANT'S OFFICIAL REPORT.

"HEADQUARTERS DISTRICT WESTERN TENNESSEE, }
PITTSBURG, April 9, 1862. }

"CAPTAIN: It becomes my duty again to report another battle fought between two great armies, one contending for the maintenance of the best government ever devised, and the other for its destruction. It is pleasant to record the success of the army contending for the former principle.

"On Sunday morning our pickets were attacked and driven in by the enemy. Immediately the five divisions stationed at this place were drawn up in line of battle to meet them.

"The battle soon waxed warm on the left and centre, varying at times to all parts of the line. There was the most continuous firing of musketry and artillery ever heard on this continent, kept up until nightfall.

"The enemy having forced the centre line to fall back nearly half way from their camps to the Landing, at a late hour in the afternoon a desperate effort was made by the enemy to turn our left and get possession of the Landing, transports, &c.

"This point was guarded by the gunboats Tyler and Lexington, Captains Gwin and Shirk commanding, with four twenty-four pounder Parrott guns, and a battery of rifled guns.

"As there is a deep and impassable ravine for artillery or cavalry, and very difficult for infantry at this point, no troops were stationed here except the necessary artillerists and a small infantry force for their support. Just at this moment the advance of Major-General Buell's column and a part of the division of General Nelson arrived, the two generals named both being present. An advance was immediately made upon the point of attack, and the enemy was soon driven back.

"In this repulse, much is due to the presence of the gunboats Tyler and Lexington, and their able commanders, Captains Gwin and Shirk.

"During the night the divisions under Generals Crittenden and McCook arrived.

"General Lew. Wallace, at Camp Landing, six miles below, was ordered, at an early hour in the morning, to hold his division in readiness to move in any direction it might be ordered. At eleven o'clock, the order was delivered to move it up to Pittsburg, but owing to its being led by a circuitous route, did not arrive in time to take part in Sunday's action.

"During the night all was quiet, and, feeling that a great moral advantage would be gained by becoming the attacking party, an advance was ordered as soon as day dawned. The result was the gradual repulse of the enemy at all points of the line, from nine until probably five o'clock in the afternoon, when it became evident the enemy was retreating.

"Before the close of the action the advance of General T. J. Wood's division arrived in time to take part in the action.

"My force was too much fatigued, from two days' hard fighting and exposure in the open air to a drenching rain during the intervening night, to pursue immediately.

"Night closed in cloudy and with a heavy rain, making the roads impracticable for artillery by the next morning.

"General Sherman, however, followed the enemy, finding that the main part of the army had retreated in good order.

"Hospitals, with the enemy's wounded, were found all along the road as far as pursuit was made. Dead bodies of the enemy and many graves were also found. I enclose herewith a report of General Sherman, which will explain more fully the result of the pursuit, and of the part taken by each separate command.

"I cannot take special notice in this report, but will do so more fully when the reports of the division commanders are handed in.

"General Buell, commanding in the field with a distinct army long under his command, and which did such efficient service, commanded by himself in person on the field, will be much better able to notice those of his command who particularly distinguished themselves than I possibly can.

"I feel it a duty, however, to a gallant and able officer, Brigadier-General W. T. Sherman, to make special mention. He not only was with his command during the entire two days of the action, but displayed great judgment and skill in the management of his men ; although severely wounded in the hand on the first day, his place was never vacant. He was again wounded, and had three horses killed under him. In making this mention of a gallant officer, no disparagement is intended to other division commanders or major-generals, Jno. A. McClernand and Lewis Wallace, and Brigadier-Generals Hurlbut, Prentiss, and W. H. L. Wallace, all of whom maintained their places with credit to themselves and the cause. General Prentiss was taken prisoner on the first day's action, and General W. H. L. Wallace was severely, and probably mortally, wounded. His Assistant Adjutant-General, Captain William McMichael, is missing, and was probably taken prisoner. My personal staff are all deserving of particular mention, they having been engaged during the entire two days in carrying orders to every part of the field. It consists of Colonel J. D. Webster, Chief of Staff; Lieutenant-Colonel J. B. McPherson, Chief of Engineers, assisted by Lieutenants W. L. B. Jenny and Wm. Kossac; Captain J. A. Rawlings, Assistant Adjutant-General ; W. S. Hilger, W. R. Rawley, and C. B. Lagon, Aids-de-Camp ; Colonel G. Pride, Volunteer Aid, and Captain J. P. Hawkins, Chief Commissary, who acccompanied me upon the field. The medical department, under direction of Surgeon Hewitt, Medical

Director, showed great energy in providing for the wounded and in getting them from the field, regardless of danger.

" Colonel Webster was placed in special charge of all the artillery, and was constantly upon the field. He displayed, as always heretofore, both skill and bravery. At least in one instance he was the means of placing an entire regiment in position of doing most valuable service, and where it would not have been but for his exertions. Lieutenant-Colonel McPherson, attached to my staff as Chief of Engineers, deserves more than a passing notice for his activity and courage. All the grounds beyond our camps for miles have been reconnoitred by him, and the plans, carefully prepared under his supervision, give the most accurate information of the nature of the approaches to our lines. During the two days' battle he was constantly in the saddle, leading the troops as they arrived to points where their services were required. During the engagement he had one horse shot under him.

" The country will have to mourn the loss of many brave men who fell at the battle of Pittsburg, or Shiloh, more properly.

" The exact loss in killed and wounded will be known in a day or two.

" At present I can only give it approximately at one thousand five hundred killed and three thousand five hundred wounded.

" The loss of artillery was great, many pieces being disabled by the enemy's shots, and some losing all their horses and many men. There were probably not less than two hundred horses killed.

" The loss of the enemy in killed and left upon the field was greater than ours. In the wounded an estimate cannot be made, as many of them must have been sent to Corinth and other points.

" The enemy suffered terribly from demoralization and desertion.

" A flag of truce was sent in to-day from General Beauregard. I enclose herewith a copy of the correspondence.

" I am, respectfully,
" Your obedient servant,
" U. S. GRANT,
" *Major-General commanding*

" Captain N. H. McLEAN, A. A. G., *Department of Mississippi, St. Louis.*"

GENERAL SHERMAN'S REPORT.

" HEADQUARTERS FIFTH DIVISION,
CAMP SHILOH, *April 10, 1862.*

" SIR: I had the honor to report that on Friday, the 4th instant, the enemy's cavalry drove in our pickets, posted about a mile and a half in advance of my centre, on the main Corinth road, capturing one first lieutenant and seven men; that I caused a pursuit by the cavalry of my division, driving them back about five miles, and killing many. On Saturday, the enemy's cavalry was again very bold, coming well down to our front; yet I did not believe he designed any thing but a strong demonstration. On Sunday morning, early, the 6th instant, the enemy drove our advance-guard back on the main body, when I ordered under arms all my division, and sent word to General McClernand, asking him to support my left; to General Prentiss, giving him notice that the enemy was in our front in force, and to General Hurlbut, asking him to support General Prentiss. At this time, seven A. M, my division was arranged as follows: —

" First brigade, composed of the sixth Iowa, Colonel J. A. McDowell; fortieth Illinois, Colonel Hicks; forty-sixth Ohio, Colonel Worthington; and the Morton battery, Captain Behr, on the extreme right, guarding the bridge on the Purdy road, over Owl Creek.

" Second brigade, composed of the fifty-fifth Illinois, Colonel D. Stuart; fifty-fourth Ohio, Colonel T. Kilby Smith; and the seventy-first Ohio, Colonel Mason, on the extreme left, guarding the ford over Lick Creek.

" Third brigade, composed of the seventy-seventh Ohio, Colonel Hildebrand ; fifty-third Ohio, Colonel Appler; and the fifty-seventh Ohio, Colonel Mungen, on the left of the Corinth road, its right resting on Shiloh meeting-house.

"Fourth brigade, composed of the seventy-second Ohio, Colonel Buckland ; forty-eighth Ohio, Colonel Sullivan ; and seventieth Ohio, Colonel Cockerill, on the right of the Corinth road, its left resting on Shiloh meeting-house.

"Two batteries of artillery, Taylor's and Waterhouse's, were posted, the former at Shiloh, and the latter on a ridge to the left, with a front fire over open ground between Mungen's and Appler's regiments. The cavalry, eight companies of the fourth Illinois, under Colonel Dickey, were posted in a large open field to the left and rear of Shiloh meeting-house, which I regarded as the centre of my position. Shortly after seven A. M., with my entire staff, I rode along a portion of our front, and when in the open field before Appler's regiment, the enemy's pickets opened a brisk fire on my party, killing my orderly, Thomas D. Holliday, of company H, second Illinois cavalry. The fire came from the bushes which line a small stream that rises in the field in front of Appler's camp, and flows to the north along my whole front. This valley afforded the enemy cover, but our men were so posted as to have a good fire at him as he crossed the valley and ascended the rising ground on our side.

"About eight A. M. I saw the glistening bayonets of heavy masses of infantry to our left front, in the woods beyond the small stream alluded to, and became satisfied, for the first time, that the enemy designed a determined attack on our whole camp. All the regiments of my division were then in line of battle, at their proper posts. I rode to Colonel Appler, and ordered him to hold his ground at all hazards, as he held the left flank of our first line of battle, and I informed him that he had a good

battery on his right and strong support in his rear. General McClernand had promptly and energetically responded to my request, and had sent me three regiments, which were posted to protect Waterhouse's battery and the left flank of my line. The battle began by the enemy opening a battery in the woods to our front, and throwing shell into our camp.

"Taylor's and Waterhouse's batteries promptly responded, and I then observed heavy battalions of infantry passing obliquely to the left across the open field in Appler's front ; also other columns advancing directly upon my division. Our infantry and artillery opened along the whole line, and the battle became general. Other heavy masses of the enemy's forces kept passing across the field to our left, and directing their course on General Prentiss. I saw at once that the enemy designed to pass my left flank, and fall upon Generals McClernand and Prentiss, whose line of camps was almost parallel with the Tennessee River, and about two miles back from it. Very soon the sound of musketry and artillery announced that General Prentiss was engaged, and about nine A. M. I judged that he was falling back. About this time Appler's regiment broke in disorder, followed by Mungen's regiment, and the enemy pressed forward on Waterhouse's battery, thereby exposed. The three Illinois regiments in immediate support of this battery stood for some time, but the enemy's advance was vigorous, and the fire so severe, that when Colonel Raith, of the forty-third Illinois, received a severe wound, and fell from his horse, his regiment and the others manifested disorder, and the enemy got possession of three guns of this (Waterhouse's) battery. Although our left was thus turned, and the enemy was pressing our whole line, I deemed Shiloh so important, that I remained by it, and renewed my orders to Colonels McDowell and Buckland to hold their ground ; and we did hold these positions until about ten o'clock A. M., when the enemy had got his artillery to the rear of our left flank, and some change became absolutely necessary. Two regiments of Hildebrand's brigade (Appler's and Mungen's) had already disappeared to the rear, and Hildebrand's own regiment was in disorder. I therefore gave orders for Taylor's battery, still at Shiloh, to fall back as far as the Purdy and Hamburg road, and for McDowell and Buckland to adopt that road as their new line. I rode across the angle, and met Behr's battery at the cross-roads, and ordered it immediately to come into battery, action right. Captain Behr gave the order, but he was almost instantly shot from his horse, when drivers and gunners fled in disorder, carrying off the caissons, and abandoning five out of six guns without firing a shot. The enemy pressed on, gaining this battery, and we were again forced to choose a line of defence. Hildebrand's brigade had substantially disappeared from the field, though he himself bravely remained. McDowell's and Buckland's brigades maintained their organization, and were conducted by my aids so as to join on General McClernand's right, thus abandoning my original camps and line. This was about half past ten A. M., at which time the enemy had made a furious attack on General McClernand's whole front. He struggled most determinedly, but finding him pressed, I moved McDowell's brigade directly against the left flank of the enemy, forced him back some distance, and directed the men to avail themselves of every cover — trees, fallen timber, and a wooded valley to our right. We held this position for four long hours, sometimes gaining and at other times losing ground, General McClernand and myself acting in perfect concert, and struggling to maintain this line. While we were so hardly pressed, two Iowa regiments approached from the rear, but could not be brought up to the severe fire that was raging in our front, and General Grant, who visited us on that ground, will remember our situation about three P. M.; but about four P. M. it was evident that Hurlbut's line had been driven back to the river, and knowing that General Wallace was coming with reënforcements from Crump's Landing, General McClernand and I, on consultation, selected a new line of defence, with its right covering a bridge by which General Wallace had to approach. We fell back as well as we could, gathering, in addition to our own, such scattered forces as we could find, and formed the new line. During this change the enemy's cavalry charged us, but were handsomely repulsed by an Illinois regiment, whose number I did not learn at that time or since.

"The fifth Ohio cavalry, which had come up, rendered good service in holding the enemy in check for some time; and Major Taylor also came up with a new battery, and got into position just in time to get a good flank fire upon the enemy's column as he pressed on General McClernand's right, checking his advance, when General McClernand's division made a fine charge on the enemy, and drove him back into the ravines to our front and right. I had a clear field about two hundred yards wide in my immediate front, and contented myself with keeping the enemy's infantry at that distance during the day. In this position we rested for the night. My command had become decidedly of a mixed character. Buckland's brigade was the only one that retained organization. Colonel Hildebrand was personally there, but his brigade was not. Colonel McDowell had been severely injured by a fall of his horse, and had gone to the river, and the three regiments of his brigade were not in line.

"The thirteenth Missouri, Colonel Crafts J. Wright, had reported to me on the field, and fought well, retaining its regimental organization, and it formed a part of my line during Sunday night and all Monday. Other fragments of regiments and companies had also fallen into my division, and acted with it during the remainder of the battle.

"Generals Grant and Buell visited me in our bivouac that evening, and from them I learned the situation of affairs on other parts of the field. General Wallace arrived from Crump's Landing shortly after dark, and formed his line to my right and rear. It rained hard during the night, but our men were in good spirits and lay on their arms, being satisfied with such bread and meat as could be gathered at the neighboring camps, and determined to redeem on Monday the losses of Sunday. At daybreak of Monday I received General Grant's orders to advance and recapture our original camps. I despatched several members of my staff to bring up all the men they could find, and especially the brigade of Colonel Stuart, which had been separated from the division all the day before; and at the appointed time the division, or rather, what remained of it, with the thirteenth Missouri and other fragments moved forward, and occupied the ground on the extreme right of General McClernand's camp, where we attracted the fire of a battery located near Colonel McDowell's former headquarters. Here I remained patiently awaiting for the sound of General Buell's advance upon the main Corinth road. About ten A. M., the firing in this direction, and its steady approach, satisfied me, and General Wallace being on our right, flanked with his well-conducted division, I led the head of my column to General McClernand's right, formed the line of battle facing south, with Buckland's brigade directly across the ridge, and Stuart's brigade on its right, in the woods, and thus advanced steadily and slowly, under a heavy fire of musketry and artillery. Taylor had just got to me from the rear, where he had gone for ammunition, and brought up three guns, which I ordered into position to advance by hand-firing. These guns belonged to company A, Chicago light artillery, commanded by Lieutenant P. P. Wood, and did most excellent service. Under cover of their fire, we advanced till we reached the point where the Corinth road crosses the line of General McClernand's camp; and here I saw, for the first time, the well-ordered and compact Kentucky forces of General Buell, whose soldierly movement at once gave confidence to our newer and less disciplined forces. Here I saw Willich's regiment advance upon a point of water-oaks and thicket, behind which I knew the enemy was in great strength, and enter it in beautiful style. Then arose the severest musketry fire I ever heard, and lasted some twenty minutes, when this splendid regiment had to fall back. This green point of timber is about five hundred yards east of Shiloh meeting-house, and it was evident here was to be the struggle. The enemy could also be seen forming his lines to the south. General McClernand sending to me for artillery, I detached to him the three guns of Wood's battery, with which he speedily drove them back; and seeing some others to the rear, I sent one of my staff to bring them forward, when, by almost Providential decree, they proved to be two twenty-four pounder howitzers belonging to McAllister's battery, and served as well as guns ever could be. This was about two P. M. The enemy had one battery close by Shiloh, and another near the Hamburg road, both pouring grape and canister upon any column of troops that advanced upon the green point of water-oaks. Willich's regiment had been repulsed; but a whole brigade of McCook's division advanced, beautifully deployed, and entered this dreaded wood. I ordered my second brigade, then commanded by Colonel T. Kilby Smith, (Colonel Stuart being wounded,) to form on its right, and my fourth brigade, Colonel Buckland, on its right, all to advance abreast with this Kentucky brigade before mentioned, which I afterwards found to be Rousseau's brigade of McCook's division. I gave personal direction to the twenty-four pounder guns, whose well-directed fire first silenced the enemy's guns to the left, and afterwards at the Shiloh meeting-house. Rousseau's brigade moved in splendid order steadily to the front, sweeping every thing before it, and at four P. M. we stood upon the ground of our original front line, and the enemy was in full retreat. I directed my several brigades to resume at once their original camps. I am now ordered by General Grant to give personal credit where I think it is due, and censure where I think it merited. I concede that General McCook's splendid division from Kentucky drove back the enemy along the Corinth road, which was the great centre of the field of battle, and where Beauregard commanded in person, supported by Bragg's, Polk's, and Breckinridge's divisions. I think Johnston was killed, by exposing himself in front of their troops at the time of their attack on Buckland's brigade on Sunday morning, although in this I may be mistaken.

"My division was made up of regiments perfectly new, all having received their muskets for the first time at Paducah. None of them had ever been under fire, or beheld heavy columns of an enemy bearing down on them, as this did on last Sunday. To expect of them the coolness and steadiness of older troops would be wrong. They knew not the value of combination and organization. When individual fear seized them, the first impulse was to get away. My third brigade did break much too soon, and I am not yet advised where they were during Sunday afternoon and Monday morning. Colonel Hildebrand, its commander, was as cool as any man I ever saw, and no one could have made stronger efforts to hold his men to their places than he did. He kept his own regiment, with individual exceptions, in hand an hour after Appler's and Mungen's regiments had left their proper field of action. Colonel Buckland managed his brigade well. I commend him to your notice as a cool, intelligent, and judicious gentleman, needing only confidence and experience to make a good commander. His subordinates, Colonels Sulli-

71

van and Cockerill, behaved with great gallantry, the former receiving a severe wound on Sunday, and yet commanding and holding his regiment well in hand all day ; and on Monday, until his right arm was broken by a shot, Cockerill held a larger proportion of his men than any colonel in my division, and was with me from first to last. Colonel J. A. McDowell, commanding the first brigade, held his ground on Sunday till I ordered him to fall back, which he did in line of battle, and when ordered he conducted the attack on the enemy's left in good style. In falling back to the next position he was thrown from his horse and injured, and his brigade was not in position on Monday morning. His subordinates, Colonels Hicks and Worthington, displayed great personal courage. Colonel Hicks led his regiment in the attack on Sunday, and received a wound which is feared may prove fatal. He is a brave and gallant gentleman, and deserves well of his country. Lieutenant-Colonel Walcott, of the Ohio forty-sixth, was severely wounded on Sunday, and has been disabled ever since. My second brigade, Colonel Stuart, was detached near two miles from my headquarters. He had to fight his own battle on Sunday against superior numbers, as the enemy interposed between him and General Prentiss early in the day. Colonel Stuart was wounded severely, and yet reported for duty on Monday morning, but was compelled to leave during the day, when the command devolved on Colonel T. Kilby Smith, who was always in the thickest of the fight, and led the brigade handsomely. I have not yet received Colonel Stuart's report of the operations of his brigade during the time he was detached, and must therefore forbear to mention names. Lieutenant-Colonel Kyle, of the seventy-first, was mortally wounded on Sunday, but the regiment itself I did not see, as only a small fragment of it was with the brigade when it joined the division on Monday morning.

"Several times during the battle cartridges gave out but General Grant had thoughtfully kept a supply coming from the rear. When I appealed to regiments to stand fast although out of cartridges, I did so because to retire a regiment for any cause has a bad effect on others. I commend the fortieth Illinois and thirteenth Missouri for thus holding their ground under heavy fire, although their cartridge-boxes were empty. Great credit is due the fragments of men of the disordered regiments who kept in the advance. I observed and noticed them, but until the brigadiers and colonels make their reports, I cannot venture to name individuals, but will in due season notice all who kept in our front, as well as those who preferred to keep back near the steamboat landing. I will also send a full list of the killed, wounded, and missing, by name, rank, company, and regiment. At present I submit the result in figures : —

" Officers, killed, 16 ; wounded, 45 ; missing, 6. Soldiers, killed, 302 ; wounded, 1230 ; missing, 435. Aggregate loss in the division, 2034.

" The enemy captured seven of our guns on Sunday, but on Monday we recovered seven — not the identical guns we had lost, but enough in number to balance the amount. At the time of recovering our camps, our men were so fatigued that we could not follow the retreating masses of the enemy ; but on the following day, I followed up with Buckland's and Hildebrand's brigades for six miles, the result of which I have already reported. . . . .

" I am, &c., your obedient servant,
                        " W. T. SHERMAN.
" Captain J. A. RAWLINS, *Assist. Adjt.-General to General Grant.*"

GENERAL HURLBUT'S REPORT.

          " HEADQUARTERS FOURTH DIVISION,   }
          ARMY OF WEST TENNESSEE, *April* 12, 1862. }

" SIR : I have the honor to report, in brief, the part taken by my division in the battle of the 6th and 7th April.

" On Sunday morning, April 6, about half past seven A. M., I received a message from Brigadier-General Sherman, that he was attacked in force, and heavily upon his left.

" I immediately ordered Colonel J. C. Veatch, commanding the second brigade, to proceed to the left of General Sherman. This brigade, consisting of the twenty-fifth Indiana, fourteenth, fifteenth and forty-sixth Illinois, was in march in ten minutes, arrived on General Sherman's line rapidly, and went into action. I must refer to Colonel Veatch's report for the particulars of that day.

" Receiving in a few moments a pressing request for aid from Brigadier-General Prentiss, I took command in person of the first and third brigades, respectively commanded by Colonel N. G. Williams, of the third Iowa, and Brigadier-General J. G. Laumann.

" The first brigade consisted of the third Iowa, forty-first Illinois, twenty-eighth Illinois, and thirty-second Illinois.

" The third brigade, of the thirty-first Indiana, forty-fourth Indiana, seventeenth Kentucky, and twenty-fifth Kentucky. In addition, I took with me the first and second battalions of the fifth Ohio cavalry ; Mann's light battery, four pieces, commanded by First-Lieutenant E. Brotzmann ; Ross's battery, second Michigan, and Meyer's battery, thirteenth Ohio.

" As we drew near the rear and left of General Prentiss's line, his regiments, in broken masses, drifted through my advance, that gallant officer making every effort to rally them.

" I formed my line of battle — the first brigade thrown to the front on the southerly side of a large open field, the third brigade continuing the line with an obtuse angle around the other side of the field, and extending some distance into the brush and timber. Mann's battery was placed in the angle of the lines, Ross's battery some distance to the left, and the thirteenth Ohio battery on the right and somewhat advanced in cover of the timber, so as to concentrate the fire upon the open ground in front, and waited for the attack.

"A single shot from the enemy's batteries struck in Meyer's thirteenth Ohio battery, when officers and men, with a common impulse of disgraceful cowardice, abandoned the entire battery — horses, caissons, and guns — and fled, and I saw them no more until Tuesday. I called for volunteers from the artillery, the call was answered, and ten gallant men from Mann's battery and Ross's battery brought in the horses, which were wild, and spiked the guns.

"The attack commenced on the third brigade through the thick timber, and was met and repelled by a steady and continuous fire, which rolled the enemy back in confusion after some half hour of struggle, leaving many dead and wounded. The glimmer of bayonets on the left and front of the first brigade showed a large force of the enemy gathering, and an attack was soon made on the forty-first Illinois and twenty-eighth, on the left of the brigade, and the thirty-second Illinois and third Iowa on the right. At the same time a strong force of very steady and gallant troops formed in columns, doubled on the centre, and advanced over the open field in front. They were allowed to approach within four hundred yards, when fire was opened from Mann's and Ross's batteries, and from the two right regiments of the first brigade, and seventeenth and twenty-fifth Kentucky, which were thrown forward slightly, so as to flank the column. Under this withering fire they vainly attempted to deploy, but soon broke and fell back under cover, leaving not less than one hundred and fifty dead and wounded as evidence how our troops maintained their position. The attack on the left was also repulsed, but as the ground was covered with brush the loss could not be judged.

"General Prentiss having succeeded in rallying a considerable portion of his command, I permitted him to pass to the front of the right of my third brigade, where they redeemed their honor by maintaining that line for some time while ammunition was supplied to my regiments. A series of attacks upon the right and left of my line were readily repelled, until I was compelled to order Ross's battery to the rear, on account of its loss in men and horses. During all this time Mann's battery maintained its fire steadily, effectively, and with great rapidity, under the excellent handling of Lieutenant E. Brotzmann.

"For five hours these brigades maintained their position under repeated and heavy attacks, and endeavord with their thin ranks to hold the space between Stuart's and McClernaud's, and did check every attempt to penetrate the lines.

"When, about three o'clock, Colonel Stuart, on my left, sent me word that he was driven in, and that I would be flanked on the left in a few moments, it was necessary for me to decide at once to abandon either the right or left. I considered that General Prentiss could, with the left of General McClernand's troops, probably hold the right, and sent him notice to reach out towards the right, and drop back steadily parallel with my first brigade, while I rapidly moved General Laumann from the right to the left, and called up two twenty-pounder pieces of Major Cavender's battalion to check the advance of the enemy upon the first brigade. These pieces were taken into action by Dr. Corvine, the surgeon of the battalion, and Lieutenant Edwards, and effectually checked the enemy for half an hour, giving me time to draw off my crippled artillery, and to form a new front with the third brigade. In a few minutes two Texan regiments crossed the ridge separating my line from Stuart's former one, while other troops also advanced.

"Willard's battery was thrown into position, under command of Lieutenant Wood, and opened with great effect on the Lone Star flags, until their line of fire was obstructed by the charge of the third brigade, which, after delivering its fire with great steadiness, charged full up the hill, and drove the enemy three hundred or four hundred yards. Perceiving that a heavy force was closing on the left between my line and the river, while heavy fire continued on the right and front, I ordered the line to fall back. The retreat was made quietly and steadily, and in good order. I had hoped to make a stand on the line of my camp, but masses of the enemy were pressing rapidly on each flank, while their light artillery was closing rapidly in the rear. On reaching the twenty-four pounder siege guns in battery, near the river, I again succeeded in forming line of battle in rear of the guns, and by direction of Major-General Grant I assumed command of all troops that came up. Broken regiments and disordered battalions came into line gradually upon my division.

"Major Cavender posted six of his twenty-pound pieces on my right, and I sent my Aid to establish the light artillery — all that could be found — on my left. Many officers and men unknown to me, and whom I never desire to know, fled in confusion through the line. Many gallant soldiers and brave officers rallied steadily on the new line. I passed to the right, and found myself in communication with General Sherman, and received his instructions. In a short time the enemy appeared on the crest of the ridge, led by the eighteenth Louisiana, but were cut to pieces by the steady and murderous fire of the artillery. Dr. Corvine again took charge of one of the heavy twenty-four-pounders, and the line of fire of that gun was the one upon which the other pieces concentrated. General Sherman's artillery also was rapidly engaged, and after an artillery contest of some duration the enemy fell back.

"Captain Gwin, U. S. N., had called upon me by one of his officers to mark the place the gunboats might take to open their fire. I advised him to take position on the left of my camp ground, and open fire as soon as our fire was within that line. He did so, and from my own observation and the statement of prisoners, his fire was most effectual in stopping the advance of the enemy on Sunday afternoon and night. About dusk the firing ceased. I advanced my division one hundred yards to the front, threw out pickets, and officers and men bivouacked in a heavy storm of rain. About twelve P. M. General Nelson's leading columns passed my line and went to the front, and I called in my advanced guard. The remnant of my division was reunited, Colonel Veatch with the second brigade having joined me about half past four P. M.

"It appears from his report, which I desire may be taken as part of mine, that soon after arriving on the field of battle in the morning, the line of troops in front broke and fled through the lines of the fifteenth and forty-sixth Illinois, without firing a shot, and left the fifteenth exposed to a terrible fire, which they gallantly returned. Lieutenant-Colonel Ellis and Major Goddard were killed here early in the action, and the regiment fell back. The same misfortune, from the yielding of the front line, threw the forty-sixth Illinois into confusion, and although the fire was returned by the forty-sixth with great spirit, the opposing force drove back this unsupported regiment, Colonel Davis in person bringing off the colors, in which gallant act he was severely wounded.

"The twenty-fifth Indiana and fourteenth Illinois changed front and held their ground on the new alignment until ordered to form on the left of General McClernand's command. The fifteenth and forty-sixth were separated from the brigade, but fell into line with General McClernand's right.

"The battle was sustained in this position — the left resting near my headquarters until the left wing was driven in. The second brigade fell back towards the river, and was soon followed by the first and third, and reunited at the heavy guns. This closes the history of

Sunday's battle, so far as this division is concerned.

"On Monday, about eight o'clock A. M., my division was formed in line close to the river bank, and I obtained a few crackers for my men. About nine A. M., I was ordered by General Grant to move up to the support of General McClernand, then engaged near his own camp with the first brigade and Mann's battery. I moved forward under the direction of Captain Rowley, Aid-de-Camp, and formed line on the left of General McClernand, with whom that brigade and battery remained during the entire day, taking their full share of the varied fortunes of that division in the gallant charges and the desperate resistance which checkered the field. I am under great obligations to General McClernand for the honorable mention he has personally given to my troops, and have no doubt that his official report shows the same, and as they fought under his immediate eye, and as he was in chief command, I leave this to him.

"The second and third brigades went into action elsewhere, and again I am compelled to refer to the reports of their immediate commanders, only saying that the second brigade led the charge ordered by General Grant, until recalled by Major-General Buell, and that the third brigade was deeply and fiercely engaged on the right of General McClernand, successfully stopping a movement to flank his right, and holding their ground until the firing ceased. About one o'clock of that day, (Monday,) General McCook having closed up with General McClernand, and the enemy demonstrating in great force on the left, I went, by the request of General McClernand, to the rear of his line, to bring up fresh troops, and was engaged in pressing them forward until the steady advance of General Buell on the extreme left, the firmness of the centre, and the closing in from the right of Generals Sherman and Wallace, determined the success of the day, when I called

in my exhausted brigades, and led them to their camps. The ground was such on Sunday that I was unable to use cavalry. Colonel Taylor's fifth Ohio cavalry was drawn up in order of battle until near one o'clock, in the hope that some opening might offer for the use of this arm. None appearing, I ordered the command withdrawn from the reach of shot.

"They were not in action again until the afternoon of Monday, when they were ordered to the front, but returned to their camps. Their subsequent conduct will be no doubt reported by the officer who conducted the special expedition of which they made part. On Sunday the cavalry lost one man killed, six wounded, and eight horses, before they were withdrawn. The greater portion of Ross's battery was captured on Sunday in the ravine near my camp.

"For the officers and men of my division I am at a loss for proper words to express my appreciation of their courage and steadiness; where all did their duty so well, I fear to do injustice by specially naming any. The fearful list of killed and wounded officers in my division shows the amount of exposure which they met, while the returns of loss among the privates who fell, unnamed, but heroic, without the hope of special mention, shows distinctly that the rank and file were animated by a true devotion and as firm a courage as their officers. . . . .

"Very respectfully,

"Your obedient servant,

"A. S. HURLBUT,

"*Brigadier-General commanding Fourth Division.*

"Captain JOHN A. RAWLINS, *Assistant Adjutant-General.*"

COLONEL TUTTLE'S REPORT.

"HEADQUARTERS FIRST BRIGADE, SECOND DIVISION,
PITTSBURG, TENN., *April* 10, 1862.

"GENERAL: I have the honor to report the part taken by the first brigade in the action of the 6th and 7th instants, as well as such other regiments and corps as were under my command during the engagement. On the morning of the 6th, I proceeded with my brigade, consisting of the second, seventh, twelfth, and fourteenth Iowa infantry, under the direction of Brigadier-General W. H. L. Wallace, and formed line on the left of his division. We had been in line but a few moments when the enemy made their appearance and attacked my left wing, (twelfth and fourteenth Iowa,) who gallantly stood their ground, and compelled the assailants to retire in confusion. They again formed under cover of a battery, and renewed the attack upon my whole line, but were repulsed as before. A third and fourth time they dashed upon us, but were each time baffled and completely routed. We held our position about six hours, when it became evident that our forces on each side of us had given way, so as to give the enemy an opportunity of turning both our flanks. At this critical juncture, General Wallace gave orders for my whole brigade to fall back, which was done in good order. The second and seventh regiments retired through a severe fire from both flanks and re-formed, while the twelfth and fourteenth, who were delayed by their endeavors to save a battery which had been placed in their rear, were completely cut off and surrounded, and were compelled to surrender.

"In passing through the cross fire General Wallace fell mortally wounded, and as you were reported wounded, and Captain McMichael informing me that I was the ranking officer, I assumed command of the division, and rallied what was left of my brigade, and was joined by the thirteenth Iowa, Colonel Crocker; ninth Illinois, Colonel Mersey; twelfth Illinois, Lieutenant-Colonel Chottain, and several other fragments of regiments, and formed in line on the road, and held the enemy in check until the line was formed that resisted the last charge just before dark of that day. On Monday morning I collected all of the division that could be found, and such other detached regi-

ments as volunteered to join me, and formed them in column by battalion, closed in mass, as a reserve for General Buell, and followed up his attack until we arrived near the position we had occupied on Sunday, where I deployed into line, in rear of his forces, and held my command subject to his orders. The second Iowa and second Illinois were called on at one time. The second was sent to General Nelson's division, and was ordered by him to charge bayonets across a field on the enemy, who were in the woods beyond, which they did in the most gallant manner, the enemy giving way before they reached them. The seventh Iowa, under orders from General Crittenden, charged and captured one of the enemy's batteries, while the thirteenth Iowa rendered General McCook valuable service near the close of the engagement. . . . . .

"Very respectfully, your obedient servant,

"J. M. TUTTLE,
"*Colonel commanding First Brigade,*
Second Division.
" Brigadier-General J. McARTHUR, *Comm'g Second Division.*"

REPORT OF MAJOR-GENERAL LEW. WALLACE.

"HEADQUARTERS THIRD DIVISION U. S. FORCES,
DISTRICT OF WEST TENNESSEE,
PITTSBURG LANDING, *April* 12, 1862.

"SIR: Sunday morning, 6th instant, my brigades, three in number, were encamped, the first at Crump's Landing, the second two miles from that Landing, and the third at Adamsville, two miles and a half further on the road to Purdy.

"The eleventh Indiana, Colonel George F. McGinnis; eighth Missouri, Lieutenant-Colonel James Peckham; and twenty-fourth Indiana, Colonel Alvin P. Hovey, composed the first brigade, Colonel Morgan L. Smith commanding.

"The first Nebraska, Lieutenant-Colonel W. D. McCord; twenty-third Indiana, Colonel W. L. Sanderson; fifty-eighth Ohio, Colonel V. Bausenwein; and fifty-sixth Ohio, Colonel P. Kinney, composed the second brigade, Colonel John M. Thayer commanding.

"The third brigade consisted of the twentieth Ohio, Lieutenant-Colonel M. F. Force; seventy-sixth Ohio, Colonel Charles R. Woods; seventy-eighth Ohio, Colonel M. D. Leggett; and the sixty-eighth Ohio, Colonel S. H. Steadman, Colonel Charles Whittlesey commanding.

"To my division were attached Lieutenant Thurber's Missouri battery and Captain Thompson's Indiana battery, also the third battalion fifth Ohio cavalry, Major C. T. Hayes, and the third battalion eleventh Illinois cavalry, Major James F. Johnson.

"Hearing heavy and continuous cannonading in the direction of Pittsburg Landing, early Sunday morning, I inferred a general battle, and in anticipation of an order from General Grant to join him at that place, had the equipage of the several brigades loaded in wagons, for instant removal to my first camp at the river. The first and third brigades were also ordered to concentrate at the camp of the second, from which proceeded the nearest and most practicable road to the scene of battle.

"At half past eleven o'clock the anticipated order arrived, directing me to come up and take position on the right of the army, and form my line of battle at a right angle with the river. As it also directed me to leave a force to prevent surprise at Crump's Landing, the fifty-sixth and sixty-eighth Ohio regiments were detached for that purpose, with one gun from Lieutenant Thurber's battery.

"Selecting a road that led directly to the right of the lines, as they were established around Pittsburg Landing on Sunday morning, my column started immediately, the distance being about six miles. The cannonading, distinctly audible, quickened the steps of the men. Snake Creek, difficult of passage at all times, on account of its steep banks and swampy bottom, ran between me and the point of junction. A short distance from it Captains Raw-

lins and Rowley, attached to General Grant's staff, overtook me. From them I learned that our lines had been beaten back; that the right, to which I was proceeding, was then fighting close to the river, and that the road pursued would take me in the enemy's rear, where, in the unfortunate condition of the battle, my command was in danger of being entirely cut off. It seemed, on their representations, most prudent to carry the column across to what is called the "river road," which, following the windings of the Tennessee bottom, crossed Snake Creek by a good bridge close to Pittsburg Landing. This movement occasioned a countermarch, which delayed my junction with the main army until a little after nightfall.

"About one o'clock at night my brigades and batteries were disposed, forming the extreme right wing, and ready for battle. Shortly after daybreak Captain Thompson opened fire on a rebel battery posted on a bluff opposite my first brigade, and across a deep and prolonged hollow, threaded by a creek, and densely wooded on both sides. From its position, and that of its infantry supports, lining the whole length of the bluff, it was apparent that crossing the hollow would be at heavy loss, unless the battery was first driven off. Thurber was accordingly posted to assist Thompson by a cross fire, and at the same time sweep the hiding-places of the enemy on the brow of the hill. This had the desired effect. After a few shells from Thurber the enemy fell back, but not until Thompson had dismounted one of their rifled guns. During this affair General Grant came up, and gave me my direction of attack, which was forward at a right angle with the river, with which my line at the time ran almost parallel.

"The battery and its supports having been driven from the opposite bluff, my command was pushed forward, the brigades in echelon, the first in front, and the whole preceded by skirmishers. The hollow was crossed, and the hill gained almost without opposition. As General Sherman's division, next on my left, had not made its appearance to support my advance, a halt was ordered for it to come up. "I was then at the edge of an oblong field that extended in a direction parallel with the river. On its right was a narrow strip of woods, and beyond that lay another cleared field, square, and very large. Back of both fields, to the north, was a range of bluffs, overlooking the swampy low grounds of Snake Creek, heavily timbered, broken by ravines, and extending in a course diagonal with that of my movement. An examination satisfied me that the low grounds afforded absolute protection to my right flank, being impassable for a column of attack. The enemy's left had rested upon the bluffs, and as it had been driven back that flank was now exposed. I resolved to attempt to turn it. For that purpose it became necessary for me to change front by a left half-wheel of the whole division. While the movement was in progress across a road through the woods at the southern end of the field we were resting by, I discovered a heavy body of rebels going rapidly to reënforce their left, which was still retiring, covered by skirmishers, with whom mine were engaged. Thompson's battery was ordered up, and shelled the passing column with excellent effect, but while so engaged was opened upon by a full battery, planted in the field just beyond the strip of woods on the right. He promptly turned his guns on the new enemy. A fine artillery duel ensued, very honorable to Thompson and his company. His ammunition giving out in the midst of it, I ordered him to retire, and Lieutenant Thurber to take his place. Thurber obeyed with such alacrity that there was scarcely an intermission in the fire, which continued so long and with such warmth as to provoke an attempt on the part of the rebels to charge the position. Discovering the in-

tention, the first brigade was brought across the field to occupy the strip of woods in front of Thurber. The cavalry made the first dash at the battery, but the skirmishers of the eighth Missouri poured an unexpected fire into them, and they retired pell-mell. Next the infantry attempted a charge. The first brigade easily repelled them. All this time my whole division was under a furious cannonade, but being well masked behind the bluff, or resting in the hollows of the wood, the regiment suffered but little.

"General Sherman now moved forward a handsome line of battle to engage the enemy posted in front of his command. Simultaneously mine was ordered to advance, the first brigade leading. Emerging from the woods, it entered the second field I have mentioned, speedily followed by the second brigade, when both marched in face of the enemy aligned as regularly as if on parade.

"Having changed front as stated, my movement was now diagonal to the direction originally started on, though the order was still in echelon, with the centre regiment of each brigade dropped behind its place in line as a reserve. While thus advancing, Colonel Whittlesey, as appears from his report, in some way lost his position, but soon recovered it.

"The position of the enemy was now directly in front, in the edge of the woods, fronting and on the right of the open field my command was so gallantly crossing. The ground to be passed getting at them dipped gradually to the centre of the field, which is there intersected by a small run well fringed with willows. Clearing an abrupt bank beyond the branch, the surface ascends to the edge of the woods held by the enemy, and is without obstruction, but marked by frequent swells that afforded protection to the advancing lines, and was the secret of my small loss. Over the branch, up the bank, across the rising ground, moved the steady first brigade; on its right,

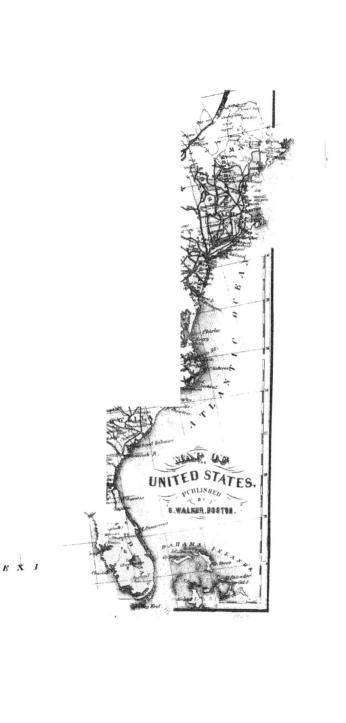

MAP OF THE UNITED STATES, PUBLISHED BY S. WALKER, BOSTON.

E X I

with equal alacrity, marched the second, the whole in view, their banners gayly decking the scene. The skirmishers in action all the way cleared the rise and grouped themselves behind the ground swells, within seventy-five yards of the rebel lines; as the regiments approached them, suddenly a sheet of musketry blazed from the woods, and a battery opened upon them. About the same instant, the right of Sherman's division fell hastily back. To save my flank I was compelled to order a halt. In a short time Sherman repulsed the enemy, and recovered his lost ground. My skirmishers, meanwhile, clung to their hillocks, sharp shooting at the battery. Again the brigades advanced, their bayonets fixed for a charge, but pressed by Sherman, and so threatened in front, the enemy removed their guns and fell back from the edge of the woods. In the advance Lieutenant-Colonel John Gerber was killed, and it is but justice to say of him, " no man died that day with more glory, yet many died, and there was much glory." Captain McGriffin and Lieutenant Southwick of the same regiment also fell — gallant spirits, deserving honorable recollection. Many soldiers, equally brave, perished, or were wounded in the same field.

"It was now noon, and the enemy having fallen so far back, the idea of flanking them further had to be given up. Not wishing to interfere with General Sherman's line of operations, but relying upon him to support me on the left, my front was again changed, the movement beginning with the first brigade taking the course of attack precisely as it had been in the outset. While the manœuvre was being effected, a squadron of rebel cavalry galloped from the woods on the right to charge the flank temporarily exposed. Colonel Thayer threw forward the twenty-third Indiana, which, aided by an oblique fire from a company of the first Nebraska, repelled the assailants with loss.

"Scarcely had the front been changed, when

the supporting force on the left again gave way, closely followed by the masses of the enemy. My position at this time became critical, as isolation from the rest of the army seemed imminent. The reserves were resorted to. Colonel Woods, with his regiment, was ordered into line on the left. The remnant of a Michigan regiment sent me by General McClernand was despatched to the left of Woods. Thurber galloped up, and was posted to cover a retreat, should such a misfortune become necessary. Before these dispositions could be effected, the eleventh Indiana, already engaged with superior numbers in its front, was attacked on its left flank, but backward wheeling three companies of his endangered wing, Colonel McGinnis gallantly held his ground. Fortunately, before the enemy could avail themselves of their advantage by the necessary change of front, some fresh troops dashed against them, and once more drove them back. For this favor my acknowledgments are especially due to Colonel August Willich and his famous regiment.

"Pending this struggle, Colonel Thayer pushed on his command and entered the woods, assaulting the rebels simultaneously with Colonel Smith. Here the fifty-eighth Ohio and twenty-third Indiana proved themselves fit comrades in battle with the noble first Nebraska. Here also the seventy-sixth Ohio won a brilliant fame. The first Nebraska fired away its last cartridge. In the heat of the action, at a word, the seventy-sixth Ohio rushed in and took its place. Off to the right, meanwhile, arose the music of the twentieth and seventy-eighth Ohio, fighting gallantly in support of Thurber, to whom the sound of rebel cannon seemed a challenge — no sooner heard than accepted.

"From the time the wood was entered, "Forward!" was the only order, and step by step, from tree to tree, position to position, the rebel lines went back, never stopping again — in-

72

fantry, horses and artillery — all went back. The firing was grand and terrific. Before us was the Crescent regiment of New Orleans; shelling us on the right was the Washington artillery of Manassas renown, whose last stand was in front of Colonel Whittlesey's command. To and fro, now in my front, then in Sherman's, rode General Beauregard, inciting his troops and fighting for his fading prestige of invincibility. The desperation of the struggle may be easily imagined. While this was in progress, far along the lines to the left the contest was raging with equal obstinacy. As indicated by the sounds, however, the enemy seemed retiring every where. Cheer after cheer rang through the woods, and each man felt the day was ours.

"About four o'clock the enemy to my front broke into rout and ran through the camps occupied by General Sherman on Sunday morning. Their own camp had been established about two miles beyond. There, without halting, they fired tents, stores, &c. Throwing out the wounded, they piled their wagons full of arms, (Springfield muskets and Enfield rifles,) ingloriously thrown away by some of our troops the day before, and hurried on. After following them until nearly nightfall, I brought my division back to Owl Creek and bivouacked it.

"The conduct of Colonel M. L. Smith and Colonel John M. Thayer, commanding brigades, was beyond the praise of words; Colonel Whittlesey's was not behind them. To them all belong the brightest honors of victory.

"The gratitude of the whole country is due Colonel Geo. F. McGinnis, Lieutenant-Colonel James Peckham, Colonel Alvin P. Hovey, Lieutenant-Colonel W. D. McCord, Colonel W. L. Sanderson, Colonel Valentine Bausenwein, Lieutenant-Colonel M. F. Force, Col. Charles R. Woods, Colonel M. D. Leggett, and their field, staff, and company officers. Aside from the courage they all displayed, one point in their conduct is especially to be noted and imitated.

I mean the skill each one showed in avoiding unnecessary exposure of his soldiers. They are proud of what the division achieved, and, like myself, they are equally proud that it was all done with so little loss of their brave men.

"Of my regiments I find it impossible to say enough; excepting the twenty-third and twenty-fourth Indiana and twentieth Ohio, all had participated in the battle of Donelson. But this was a greater than Donelson, and consequently a more terrible ordeal in which to test what may be a thing of glory or shame — the courage of an untried regiment. How well they all behaved I sum up in the boast — not a man, officer or soldier, flinched; none but the wounded went to the Landing. Ohio, Indiana, Missouri, and Nebraska will be proud of the steadfast third division, and so am I.

"Captain Thompson and Lieutenant Thurber and their officers and men have already been spoken of.

"My acknowledgments are again given the gallant gentlemen of my staff — Captain Fred. Knefler and Lieutenants Ross and Ware. To them I add Captain E. T. Wallace, of the eleventh Indiana volunteers, acting Aid. The courage and judgment of all of them were many times severely tried.

"After the battle, General Nelson took pleasure in honorably mentioning two of my orderlies; one of them, Thomas W. Simpson, of company I, fourth United States cavalry. I again call attention to his gallantry, as deserving reward. Along with him I place Albert Kaufman, a sergeant in the same company, who was of great service to me, and has every quality that goes to make a practical officer.

"Finally, it is so rare to find one of his grade in the constant and full performance of his peculiar duties, that, as a matter of justice, a passing tribute is due the Rev. John D. Rogers, chaplain of the twenty-third Indiana. After the battle he was unwearied in his attention to the wounded, and 'that the resting-places of the dead of his regiment might not be forgotten, he collected their bodies and buried them tenderly, and with prayer and every religious rite; and in this, as far as my knowledge goes, he was as singular as he was Christian.

"Herewith you will find a statement of the dead and wounded of my division.

"Very respectfully, sir,

"Your obedient servant,

"LEW. WALLACE,

"*Commanding Third Division.*

"Captain JOHN A. RAWLINS, *A. A. General.*"

REPORT OF GENERAL BUELL.

"HEADQUARTERS ARMY OF THE OHIO, }
FIELD OF SHILOH, *April* 15, 1862. }

"SIR: The rear divisions of the army under my command, which had been delayed a considerable time in rebuilding the Duck River bridge, left Columbia on the 2d instant. I left the evening of that day, and arrived at Savannah on the evening of the 5th. General Nelson, with his division, which formed the advance, arrived the same day. The other divisions marched with intervals of about six miles. On the morning of the sixth, firing of musketry and cannon was heard in the direction of this place. Apprehending that a serious engagement had commenced, I went to General Grant's headquarters to get information as to the means of reaching the battle-field with the division that had arrived. At the same time orders were despatched to the divisions in rear to leave their trains, and push forward by forced marches. I learned that General Grant had just started, leaving orders for General Nelson to march to the river, opposite Pittsburg Landing, to be ferried across. An examination of the roads up the river, discovered it to be impracticable for artillery, and General Nelson was directed to leave his, to be carried forward by steamers.

"The impression existed at Savannah that the firing was merely an affair of outposts, the same thing having occurred for two or three previous days; but as it continued, I determined to go to the scene of action, and accordingly started with my chief of staff, Colonel Fry, on a steamer, which I ordered to get under steam. As we proceeded up the river, groups of soldiers were seen upon the west bank, and it soon became evident that they were stragglers from the engaged army. The groups increased in size and frequency, until, as we approached the Landing, they numbered whole companies, and almost regiments; and at the Landing the banks swarmed with a confused mass of men of various regiments. There could not have been less than four thousand or five thousand. Late in the day it became much greater. Finding General Grant at the Landing, I requested him to send steamers to Savannah to bring up General Crittenden's division, which had arrived during the morning, and then went ashore with him. The throng of disorganized and demoralized troops increased continually by fresh fugitives from the battle, which steadily drew nearer the Landing, and with these were intermingled great numbers of teams, all striving to get as near as possible to the river. With few exceptions, all efforts to form the troops, and move them forward to the fight, utterly failed. In the mean time the enemy had made such progress against our troops, that his artillery and musketry began to play into the vital part of the position, and some persons were killed on the bank at the very Landing. General Nelson arrived with Colonel Ammen's brigade at this opportune moment. It was immediately posted to meet the attack at that point, and with a battery of artillery, which happened to be on the ground, and was brought into action, opened fire on the enemy, and repulsed him. The action of the gunboats also contributed very much to that result. The attack at that point was not renewed. Night having come on, the firing ceased on both sides. In the mean time the remainder of General Nelson's division crossed, and General Crittenden's arrived from Savannah by steamers. After examining the ground —as well as was possible at night—in front of the line on which General Grant's troops had formed, and as far to the right as General Sherman's division, I directed Nelson's and Crittenden's divisions to form in front of that line, and move forward as soon as it was light in the morning. During the night and early the following morning, Captain Bartlett's Ohio battery, Captains Mendenhall and Terrell's regular batteries arrived. General McCook, by a forced march, arrived at Savannah during the night of the 6th, and reached the field of battle early in the morning of the 7th. I knew that the other divisions could not arrive in time for the action that day. . . . .

"Soon after five o'clock on the morning of the 7th, General Nelson's and General Crittenden's divisions, the only ones yet arrived on the ground, moved promptly forward to meet the enemy. Nelson's division, marching in line of battle, soon came upon his pickets, drove them in, and at about six o'clock received the fire of his artillery. The division was here halted, then Mendenhall's battery brought into action, to reply while Crittenden's division was being put into position on the right of Nelson's. Bartlett's battery was posted in the centre of Crittenden's division, in a commanding position, opposite which the enemy was discovered to be in force. By this time McCook's division arrived on the ground, and was immediately formed on the right of Crittenden's. Skirmishers were thrown to the front, and a strong body of them to guard our left flank, which, though somewhat protected by rough grounds, it was supposed the enemy might attempt to turn, and in fact did, but· was repulsed with great loss. Each brigade furnished its own reserve, and in addition Boyle's brigade of Crittenden's division, though it formed at first in the line, was kept somewhat back when the

line advanced, to be used as occasion might require. I found upon the ground parts of about two regiments, perhaps one thousand men, and subsequently a similar fragment came up of General Grant's force. The first I directed to act with General McCook's attack, and the second one was similarly employed on the left. I sent other straggling troops of General Grant's force immediately on General McCook's right, as some firing had already commenced there. I had no direct knowledge of the disposition of the remainder of General Grant's force, nor is it my province to speak of them. I regret that I am unable to name those that came under my direction in the way I had stated, for they rendered willing and efficient service during the day.

"The force under my command occupied a line of about a mile and a half. In front of Nelson's division was an open field, partially screened to his right by a skirt of woods, which extended through the enemy's line, with a thick undergrowth in front of the left brigade of Crittenden's division; then an open field in front of Crittenden's right and McCook's left, and in front of McCook's right, woods again with a dense undergrowth. The ground, mainly level in front of Nelson's, formed a hollow in front of Crittenden's, and fell into a small creek, which empties into Owl Creek, in front of McCook's. What I afterwards learned was the Hamburg road, which crosses Lick Creek a mile from its mouth, passed perpendicularly through the line of battle near Nelson's left. On a line slightly oblique to us, and beyond the open field, the enemy was formed, with a battery in front of Nelson's left; a battery commanding the woods in front of Crittenden's left, and flanking the field in front of Nelson; a battery commanding the same woods and the field in front of Crittenden's right and McCook's left, and a battery in front of McCook's right. A short distance in rear of the enemy's left, on high open ground, were the encampments of

McClernand's and Sherman's divisions, which the enemy held.

"While my troops were getting into position on the right, the artillery fire was kept up between Mendenhall's battery and the enemy's second battery with some effect. Bartlett's battery, put in position before the enemy's third battery, opened fire on that part of the line, and when, very soon after, our line advanced, with strong bodies of skirmishers in front, the action became general, and continued with severity during the greater part of the day, and until the enemy was driven from the field.

"The obliquity of our line upon the left being thrown forward, brought Nelson's division first into action, and it became very hotly engaged at an early hour. A charge of the nineteenth brigade, from Nelson's right, by its commander, Colonel Hazen, reached the enemy's second battery, but the brigade sustained a heavy loss by a cross fire of the enemy's batteries, and was unable to maintain its advantage against the heavy infantry force that came forward to oppose it. The enemy recovered the battery, and followed up his advantage by throwing a heavy force of infantry into the woods in front of Crittenden's left. The left brigade of that division, Colonel W. S. Smith commanding, advanced into the woods, repulsed the enemy handsomely, and took several prisoners. In the mean time, Captain Terrell's battery, which had just landed, reached the field, and was advanced into action near the left of Nelson's division, which was very heavily pressed by the great numbers of the enemy. It belonged properly to McCook's division. It took position near the Hamburg road, in the open ground in front of the enemy's right, and at once began to act with decided effect upon the tide of battle in that quarter. The enemy's right battery was silenced.

"Ammen's brigade, which was on the left, advanced in good order upon the enemy's right, but was checked for some time by his endeavor to turn our left flank, and by his strong centre attack in front. Captain Terrell, who in the mean time had taken an advanced position, was compelled to retire, leaving one caisson, of which every horse was killed or disabled. It was very soon recovered. Having been reënforced by a regiment from General Boyle's brigade, Nelson's division again moved forward, and forced the enemy to abandon entirely his position. This success flanked the enemy at his second and third batteries, from which he was soon driven, with the loss of several pieces of artillery by the concentrated fire of Terrell's and Mendenhall's batteries, and an attack from Crittenden's division in front. The enemy made a second stand some eight hundred yards in rear of this position, and opened fire with his artillery. Mendenhall's battery was thrown forward, silenced the battery, and it was captured by Crittenden's division, the enemy retreating from it. In the mean time the division of General McCook on the right, which became engaged somewhat later in the morning than the divisions on the left, had made steady progress until it drove the enemy's left from the hotly contested field. The action was commenced in this division by General Rousseau's brigade, which drove the enemy in front of it from his first position, and captured a battery. The line of attack of this division caused a considerable widening of the space between it and Crittenden's right. It was also outflanked on its right by the line of the enemy, who made repeated strong attacks on its flanks, but was always gallantly repulsed. The enemy made his last decided stand in front of this division, in the woods beyond Sherman's camp.

"Two brigades of General Wood's division arrived just at the close of the battle; but only one, that of Colonel Wagner, in time to participate actively in the pursuit, which it continued for about a mile, and until halted by my order. Its skirmishers became engaged for a few minutes with skirmishers covering the enemy's rear-guard, which made a momentary stand. It was also fired upon by the enemy's artillery on its right flank, but without effect. It was well conducted by its commanders, and showed great steadiness.

"The pursuit was continued no further that day. I was without cavalry, and the different corps had become a good deal scattered in a pursuit in a country which secreted the enemy's movements, and of the roads of which I knew practically nothing. In the beginning of the pursuit, thinking that the enemy had retired principally by the Hamburg road, I had ordered Nelson's division to follow as far as Lick Creek on that road, from which I afterwards learned the direct Corinth road was separated by a difficult ravine, which empties into Lick Creek. I therefore occupied myself with examining the ground, getting the different divisions into position, which was not effected until some time after dark.

"The following day, in pursuance of the directions of General Grant, General Wood was sent forward with two of his brigades, which arrived the previous evening, and a battery of artillery, to discover the position of the enemy, and to press him if he should be found in retreat. General Sherman, with about the same force from General Grant's army, was on the same service, and had a spirited skirmish with the enemy's cavalry, driving it back. The main force was found to have retreated beyond Lick Creek, and our troops returned at night.

"There were no idlers in the battle of the 7th. Every portion of the army did its work. The batteries of Captains Terrell and Mendenhall were splendidly handled and served; that of Captain Bartlett was served with great spirit and gallantry, though with less decisive results. . . . .

"The loss of the force under my command is two hundred and sixty-three killed, one thousand eight hundred and sixteen wounded,

eighty-eight missing. Total, two thousand one hundred and sixty-seven. The trophies are twenty pieces of artillery, a greater number of caissons, and a considerable number of small arms. Many of the cannon were recaptured from the loss of the previous day. Several stands of colors were also recaptured.

"The troops which did not arrive in time for the battle, General Thomas's and General Wood's divisions, (a portion of the latter, as I have previously stated, took part in the pursuit, and the remainder in the evening,) are entitled to the highest praise for the untiring energy with which they pressed forward night and day to share the danger of their comrades. General Thomas's division had already, under his command, made its name honorable by one of the most memorable victories of the war — Mill Springs — on which the tide of success seemed to turn steadily in favor of the Union.

"Very respectfully, your ob't servant,
"D. C. BUELL,
"*Major-General commanding Army of the Ohio.*
"Captain N. H. McLAIN, *Assistant-Adjutant General, Department of the Mississippi.*"

The following extract from the report of Beauregard, gives the rebel account of the battle and its result as viewed by him : —

"Thirty minutes after five o'clock A. M., our lines and columns were in motion, all animated evidently by a promising spirit. The front line was engaged at once, but advanced steadily, followed in due order with equal resolution and steadiness by the other lines, which were brought successively into action with rare skill, judgment, and gallantry, by the several corps commanders, as the enemy made a stand, with his masses rallied for the struggle for his encampments. Like an Alpine avalanche our troops moved forward, despite the determined resistance of the enemy, until after six o'clock P. M., when we were in possession of all encampments between Owl and Lick Creeks but one. Nearly all of his field artillery, about thirty flags, colors, and standards, over three thousand prisoners, including a division commander (General Prentiss) and several brigade commanders, thousands of small arms, an immense supply of subsistence, forage, and munitions of war, and a large amount of means of transportation—all the substantial fruits of a complete victory—such indeed, as rarely have followed the most successful battles; for never was an army so well provided as that of the enemy.

"The remnant of his army had been driven in utter disorder to the immediate vicinity of Pittsburg, under the shelter of the heavy guns of his iron-clad gunboats, and we remained undisputed masters of his well-selected, admirably-provided cantonments, after over twelve hours of obstinate conflict with his forces, who had been beaten from them and the contiguous covert, but only by a sustained onset of all the men we could bring into action.

"Our loss was heavy, as will appear from the accompanying return, marked 'B.' Our commander-in-chief, General A. S. Johnston, fell mortally wounded, and died on the field at half past two P. M., after having shown the highest qualities of the commander, and a personal intrepidity that inspired all around him, and gave resistless impulsion to his columns at critical moments.

"The chief command then devolved upon me, though at the time I was greatly prostrated, and suffering from the prolonged sickness with which I had been afflicted since early in February. The responsibility was one which, in my physical condition, I would have gladly avoided, though cast upon me when our forces were successfully pushing the enemy back upon the Tennessee River, and though supported on the immediate field by such corps commanders as Major-Generals Polk, Bragg, and Hardee, and Brigadier-General Breckinridge commanding the reserve.

"It was after six o'clock P. M., as before said,

when the enemy's last position was carried, and his forces finally broke and sought refuge behind a commanding eminence covering the Pittsburg Landing, not more than half a mile distant, and under the guns of the gunboats, which opened on our eager columns a fierce and annoying fire with shot and shell of the heaviest description. Darkness was close at hand. Officers and men were exhausted by a combat of over twelve hours without food, and jaded by the march of the preceding day through mud and water. It was therefore impossible to collect the rich and opportune spoils of war scattered broadcast on the field left in our possession, and impracticable to make any effective dispositions for their removal to the rear.

"I accordingly established my headquarters at the church at Shiloh, in the enemy's encampment, with Major-General Bragg, and directed our troops to sleep on their arms, in such positions, in advance and rear, as corps commanders should determine, hoping, from news received by a special despatch, that delay had been encountered by General Buell in his march from Columbia, and that his main forces therefore could not reach the field of battle in time to save General Grant's shattered fugitive forces from capture or destruction on the following day.

"During the night the rain fell in torrents, adding to the discomfort and harassed condition of the men; the enemy, moreover, had broken their rest by a discharge, at measured intervals, of heavy shells, thrown from the gunboats; therefore, on the following morning, the troops under my command were not in condition to cope with an equal force of fresh troops, armed and equipped like our adversary, in the immediate possession of his depots, and sheltered by such an auxiliary as the enemy's gunboats.

"About six o'clock on the morning of the 7th of April, however, a hot fire of musketry and artillery opened from the enemy's quarter on our advanced line, assured me of the junction of his forces, and soon the battle raged with a fury which satisfied me I was attacked by a largely superior force. But from the onset our troops, notwithstanding their fatigue and losses from the battle of the day before, exhibited the most cheering, veteran-like steadiness. On the right and centre the enemy was repulsed in every attempt he made with his heavy column in that quarter of the field; on the left, however, and nearest to the point of arrival of his reënforcements, he drove forward line after line of his fresh troops, which were met with a resolution and courage of which our country may be proudly hopeful. Again and again our troops were brought to the charge, invariably to win the position at issue, invariably to drive back their foe. But hour by hour thus opposed to an enemy constantly reënforced, our ranks were perceptibly thinned under the unceasing, withering fire of the enemy, and by twelve meridian, eighteen hours of hard fighting had sensibly exhausted a large number; my last reserves had necessarily been disposed of, and the enemy was evidently receiving fresh reënforcements after each repulse; accordingly, about one P. M., I determined to withdraw from so unequal a conflict, securing such of the results of the victory of the day before as were practicable.

"Officers of my staff were immediately despatched with the necessary orders to make the best disposition for a deliberate, orderly withdrawal from the field, and to collect and post a reserve to meet the enemy, should he attempt to push after us. In this connection I will mention particularly my adjutant-general, Colonel Jordan, who was of much assistance to me on this occasion, as he had already been on the field of battle on that and the preceding day.

"About two o'clock P. M., the lines in advance, which had repulsed the enemy in their last fierce assault on our left and centre, received the orders to retire; this was done with uncommon steadiness, and the enemy made no attempt to follow."

CHAPTER LXXI.

Operations on the Southern Coast. — Reconnoissances.— Rebel Designs. — Military and Naval Expedition. — Reconnoissances towards Savannah. — Warsaw Sound and Wilmington Narrows. — Expedition along the Coast of Georgia and Florida. — Occupation of Fernandina and St. Mary's. — Occupation of Brunswick. — Occupation of St. Augustine and Jacksonville. — General Success of the Expeditions. —Operations against Fort Pulaski. — General Gillmore. — Construction of Batteries. — Difficulties of the Work. — Completion of the Batteries. — Demand for Surrender. — The Bombardment. — Rifle Guns and Mortars. — Breaching of the Fort. — Preparations for an Assault. — Surrender of the Fort. — The Result. — Official Reports.

IN the chronicles of a rebellion so vast in its proportions, and spreading over so wide an extent of country as this which was aimed at the destruction of the American Union, it is necessary that the reader's attention should be called frequently from one part of the country to another, as we follow the events which at this period transpired so rapidly at the different and widely separated points of interest. So numerous are these events, indeed, that we are obliged to pass over or refer only in general terms to many, which though of interest and of local consequence at the time they transpired, are comparatively unimportant in the general progress of the war, and to confine our narrative chiefly to the leading movements and expeditions. From the important movements at the west recounted in the preceding chapters, we return to operations upon the coast which were in progress at the same time.

After the capture of Port Royal harbor and the adjacent islands, numerous reconnoitring excursions were made in different directions, by small expeditions from the naval force, but no movement of considerable magnitude was made, and no advance of the land forces was attempted. The strength of the army here would not admit of any important movement, as against Charleston or Savannah, for the maintenance of this position as a base for future operations and a naval station was of the greatest importance, and the military force was not much more than sufficient for this purpose. On the other hand, the rebels were not only preparing to resist any advance towards either of the two cities, against which Port Royal was so convenient a base for operations, but stoutly showed a disposition to hem in the federal forces, and even to recover some of their lost ground. They established batteries on the Coosaw River, near Port Royal Ferry, and collected a body of troops there, which could be thrown against any one of several points held by the federal forces, and probably with success.

To prevent the accomplishment of such designs on the part of the rebels, a joint naval and military expedition was organized to drive them from their position. The naval force consisted of several small gunboats and some launches with boat howitzers, under Commander C. R. P. Rodgers, and the military consisted of five regiments, under command of General I. I. Stevens. This expedition moved on the 31st of December, 1861, and the troops were landed at two or three points, under cover of the gunboats, early on the morning of the 1st of January. All the preliminary movements were prompt and successful, the troops advanced with some slight skirmishing, and the positions of the enemy being discovered, they were shelled by the gunboats. A rebel ambuscade, by which they designed to capture one of the federal detachments by a superior force, was revealed by negroes, and the shells of the gunboats soon drove the rebel force, with some loss, from its concealed position. Without further contest the rebels retired, and upon approaching their fortifications, it was discovered that these had already been abandoned and

most of the guns removed. The works were destroyed, and such disposition of the federal forces was made as to prevent the reconstruction of them. But no such attempt was made, and the rebel force withdrew several miles into the interior.

Soon after the occupation of Port Royal, reconnoissances were made on the islands and through the narrow and intricate channels at the south of Hilton Head, as far as the Savannah River and Warsaw Sound. Batteries were discovered at various points, some unfinished, some abandoned, and others armed and occupied. A force had been landed on Tybee Island, on the south side of the entrance to Savannah River, but the island was not held by any considerable body of troops. The city of Savannah is situated on the river of the same name, about fifteen miles from its mouth. Its chief defences were Fort Pulaski, near the mouth of the river, and Fort Jackson, about five miles below the city. Earthworks were also erected at several points on the river, and obstructions sunk in the channel, to aid in protecting the city from federal expeditions. Its most formidable protection, however, was Fort Pulaski, and in the months of December and January several reconnoissances were made for the purpose of discovering some passage into the Savannah River above its mouth. Two or three of these were of the most daring character, but were conducted with so much skill and caution that they were entirely successful. One of these expeditions, under Lieutenant J. H. Wilson, of the corps of Topographical Engineers, who had been employed from the first occupation of Hilton Head in surveying and making charts of the neighboring islands and waters, with the aid of some negroes familiar with the intricate channels, had discovered a passage through several creeks, and thence by an artificial cut, called "Wall's Cut," into Savannah, on the north side, above Fort Pulaski. The cut was obstructed, and the passage

73

was difficult even for small vessels, but the discovery was important, as it might lead to the cutting off of Fort Pulaski, and through that to occupation of Savannah. Another expedition was accordingly sent out by General Sherman to remove the obstructions and prepare the way for further movements. This expedition was also successful, though its work was accomplished under great risks and difficulties, the land being low and open on all sides, and the obstructions being near the Savannah River, where vessels and boats were frequently passing. The work, however, was prosecuted at night, all sportsmen or negroes who came near by chance were taken into custody, and no rebel pickets made their appearance.

This work having been accomplished and its success ascertained by naval officers, after some delay an expedition of small gunboats was sent to prove the feasibility of the passage. But the operations of the Union forces had been discovered by the rebels before the expedition moved, and they took measures to frustrate the plans of the federal officers. The expedition was not abandoned, however; but, somewhat reduced, moved in concert with another which was sent to Warsaw Sound, south of the Savannah River. By the assistance of negroes, who in all explorations proved here, as in other parts of the rebel territory, the most valuable of friends, a passage was found leading from Warsaw Sound up in the rear of Fort Pulaski, and entering the Savannah River a short distance above the fort. This passage is called "Wilmington Narrows," and appeared to be free from rebel batteries and obstructions so far as it was explored. To explore fully this passage, and ascertain the advantages which it might offer for further operations, six or seven small gunboats, under command of Captain C. H. Davis, with transports carrying a military force, under General Wright, was despatched the latter part of January.

The expedition sailed up Warsaw Sound and thence into Wilmington Narrows, through which it moved past the rear of Fort Pulaski, without eliciting a shot from that work. The rebels were, indeed, taken by surprise at the appearance of federal gunboats in those waters, and the fortress was not prepared to open upon an enemy on that side. Proceeding some distance above Fort Pulaski, the expedition at last came to obstructions in the shape of heavy piles across the channel, which prevented further progress, and the passage into Savannah River. Anchoring at this point, the neighboring creeks and islands were fully explored, without meeting an enemy, though the traces of troops were found. Before night a rebel fleet of four or five gunboats, with barges laden with supplies for Fort Pulaski, were seen moving down the Savannah River, and anchored at the mouth of the creek connecting Wilmington Narrows with the river. It was supposed that the rebel gunboats would make an attack, but the night passed quietly, the work of surveying the adjacent waters and islands being diligently prosecuted by the federal officers. The next morning the rebel gunboats moved down the Savannah with barges laden with supplies for Fort Pulaski. Wilmington Narrows are separated from the river by a low, marshy island, over which the vessels in either channel are in plain view except at low water, and within range of rifled ordnance. As the rebel boats came down the river, fire was opened upon them from Captain Davis's gunboats, and also from the gunboats of the other expedition, under Captain Rodgers, which had reached a similar position on the north side of the river, by the passage before mentioned. The result of this fire, which was replied to by the rebels, was that one of the rebel boats was somewhat damaged and was compelled to return up the river, while the others, with little or no injury, proceeded to the fort. On their return at a later hour, the fire was resumed, but the water was low, and the shots were without effect on either side. After a thorough reconnoissance, in which the practicability of the passage for gunboats was proved, the expedition returned to Port Royal. It had thrown Savannah into a state of great excitement, the inhabitants anticipating that an immediate attack was to be made, and the appearance of federal gunboats above their most important defence creating great alarm. But though the practicability of passing gunboats through these passages was proved, for want of sufficient military force, or for some other reason, no attempt was made to follow the reconnoissance with more formidable and effective operations; while on the other hand, the rebels proceeded to strengthen their weak points, and to guard against the success of such an expedition in the future.

One of the objects of the expedition to Port Royal was to take and keep under control the entire sea coast of Georgia, with portions of that of the adjoining states of South Carolina and Florida, and thus more effectually stop the commerce carried on by means of the numerous creeks and channels by which small vessels could reach the ports of those states and easily evade a blockade. Much of this work in the vicinity of Port Royal was speedily accomplished by the action of Flag-Officer Dupont, with the coöperation of the military authorities, the gunboats being stationed in the inlets, and a military force holding possession of a few important points. In the latter part of February an expedition was prepared for a more important movement to the coast of Florida. Nearly twenty gunboats, mostly of light draft, composed the naval part of this expedition, and six transports carried a brigade of troops under General Wright, as the military part. The fleet sailed from Port Royal on the last day of February, and entered Cumberland Sound on the 2d of March, Commodore Dupont's intention being to reach Fernandina through this sound, and thus avoid encountering Fort Clinch and other formidable works at the main entrance to the harbor. But before moving through the sound it was reported by negroes that the rebels had abandoned the forts at the main entrance, and the fleet was divided, some of the smaller boats proceeding through the sound while the others sailed out and entered the main channel. The report proved true, the forts, which were strong and capable of great resistance, being found abandoned and some of the guns removed. As the gunboats came near the town, the rebels were evacuating it in haste, the inhabitants as well as military being seen departing. A few musket shots were fired from the town, but no resistance was offered. A steamboat laden with army supplies and passengers was captured, the forts were occupied, and the military took possession of the town, which was deserted by the greater part of its inhabitants, by the order, as it was stated, of the rebel military authorities. The town of St. Mary's, in the same harbor, was also occupied, and found deserted in a great measure like Fernandina. The rebels had constructed strong earthworks in addition to Fort Clinch, for the defence of this harbor, and the fortifications were of such a character and so well situated that it was a matter of surprise that they were abandoned without any attempt at defence. But here, as elsewhere, there appeared to be a dread of the gunboats, and the rumors of the approaching expedition had created a panic which gave to the federal forces a bloodless victory. The abandonment, in a similar manner, of strong works on St. Simon's Island, about midway on the coast of Georgia, and the only other important military post on that coast south of the Savannah River, virtually gave to Flag-Officer Dupont the control of the entire coast of Georgia, and enabled him to say in his official despatch that the instructions of the navy department had now been carried out.

The occupation of Fernandina was followed by other operations of the fleet with the coöperation of the land forces upon the coast of Georgia and Northern Florida. One of these was an expedition of three gunboats to Brunswick, Georgia, which met with equal success with that sent to Fernandina. The forts were found to be evacuated by the rebel troops, though they had been constructed with great engineering skill, and had been occupied by a considerable force. The town was found to be almost wholly deserted, and the flag of the Union was raised without opposition. An attempt was made to reach Darien, on the Altamaha River, through a passage from St. Simon's Sound, but the boats met with obstructions which prevented them from reaching the river. It was learned, however, that Darien was also evacuated, and it appeared that along the whole coast exposed to visits from the gunboats the rebels were disposed to retire without resistance.

St. Augustine, Florida, was also visited by a portion of the fleet. A white flag was found flying on one of the bastions of Fort Marion, a strong fortification constructed by the United States for the protection of the harbor. Communication being held with the people of the town, they were found generally ready to acknowledge the authority of the federal government — the only opposition coming from the women, who here, as elsewhere at the south, were very bitter. The town and fort were surrendered by the mayor, in whose charge the public property was then placed, and he, with the other municipal authorities, were held responsible for its safety and the peaceable conduct of the people.

Jacksonville, in the same state, was occupied about the same time, and a military force was landed here. The rebel forces had disappeared, but large fires were burning in the neighborhood, said to have been set by the rebel military, or the more malignant of the citizens, for the destruction of the property of those who were supposed to be favorable to the Union.

The great majority of the people apparently welcomed the arrival of the Union forces, and manifested a desire to return to their allegiance. They showed much greater fear of the rebel troops and partisans than of the federal gunboats and troops. In these operations, as in others of less importance, the people remaining in the towns were treated with kindness, private property was respected, and the advantages of remaining under the flag of the Union was felt and acknowledged by the majority of the people. Secession and rebellion seemed to have little attraction for them, and it was only by the tyranny of the rebel leaders and military that they were compelled to support those heresies. It was, perhaps, the indifference of the people to the cause that induced the rebel authorities to abandon, so generally as they did at this time, the greater part of north-eastern Florida and a part of the coast of Georgia.

While these expeditions were in progress, the more important work of obtaining possession of the water approaches to Savannah, and perhaps of operating against that city, was in preparation. For some months the federal military force had been at Port Royal, and established there a base for future movements, but nothing had been done beyond the expeditions above mentioned to reëstablish the authority of the United States. The capture of Charleston, or Savannah, or both, was supposed to be the real object of the expedition to Port Royal, but no steps were for a long time taken which would indicate that this work was to be attempted. The long delay, however, had been improved in obtaining a more accurate knowledge of the country, the intricate water passages between the numerous islands that skirt the coast, and the means by which this important work might be accomplished should it be undertaken. And at last it was determined to attempt the reduction of Fort Pulaski by batteries to be constructed on Tybee Island. The engineers had declared that this was possible, but no steps were taken to carry out the plan suggested by them till March. A portion of Tybee Island had been for some time occupied by federal troops, who had indeed control of the entire island. This force was strengthened, and the work of constructing batteries, to be mounted with siege guns of the heaviest calibre and improved rifled ordnance, was commenced, Brigadier-General Gillmore having charge of the operations. General Gillmore went out with the expedition as a captain in the engineer corps. An able and energetic officer, he advised and planned the attempt thus to reduce Fort Pulaski. Though the work was at first considered almost impracticable by his superiors, orders were at last issued for the siege operations, and they were placed under the immediate charge of General Gillmore who was promoted for the purpose of taking the command. General H. W. Benham commanded the district, and was the immediate superior of General Gillmore.

It was an undertaking which required not only great skill in engineering, but a great deal of energy on the part of the commanding officer and his subordinates, and a vast amount of labor by the soldiers. But the necessary material being provided, the work proceeded with energy and success. Eleven batteries were constructed upon Tybee Island, varying in distance from Fort Pulaski from three thousand four hundred yards to one thousand six hundred and eighty-five yards. Seven of these were in full sight from the fort and exposed to its fire, but the work was prosecuted mostly at night till the embankments afforded sufficient protection. To reach the batteries most distant from the landing place, it was necessary to cross a marshy piece of ground, and over this, in order to transport ordnance, General Gillmore was obliged to construct a causeway nearly a mile in length, which, from its exposed position, it was also necessary to construct in the night. All the heavy guns and other material were landed upon a beach exposed to the sea, and remarkable for its heavy surf This was a work of great labor, but still more severe labor was required to transport the ordnance stores to the batteries, the most advanced of which were two and a half miles from the beach. This work was performed by the men under cover of the night, and the difficulty attending it may be conceived from the fact that two hundred and fifty men were barely sufficient to draw a single one of the heavy mortars. The nature of the ground added to the difficulties and the severe labor of the men; but skill, ingenuity, and indomitable perseverance overcame all obstacles. The rebel garrison, in the mean time, did something to annoy the federal troops, and to prevent the progress of their work; but the rebel officers did not believe that, with all their labor, the federal forces could materially injure the strong fort which they held, or gain any advantage by such movements.

The most distant of the batteries were nearly east of the fort, and from that point the works extended along the shore of the island a mile and a half to a point south-east of the fort. They were armed with heavy mortars, columbiads, and several thirty and twenty-four pounder rifle guns, whose merits were here to be first practically tested in bombarding a fortification. The work on the several batteries was completed, the guns mounted, and the large supplies of ammunition necessary for a continued bombardment were furnished by the 9th of April, and on that day General Gillmore issued his orders for opening the bombardment on the following day, giving specific instructions for the management of the guns and the general conduct of the bombardment, which evinced a perfect confidence in the success of his operations. Just previous to the completion of the siege works, Major-General Hunter was assigned to the command of the Department of the South, which embraced all the territory occupied by the federal forces on the Atlantic coast in the states of South Carolina, Georgia, and Florida, superseding General Sherman. General Hunter, with his staff, were present at Tybee Island, but left the opera-tions against Fort Pulaski in the hands of General Gillmore, and General Benham, who, as commander of the district, heartily coöperated with General Gillmore in carrying out his plans.

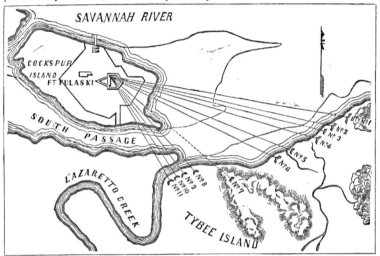

No. 1. Battery Stanton.　No. 3. Battery Lyon.　No. 5. Battery Burnside.　No. 7. Battery Halleck.　No. 9. Battery Sigel.　No. 11. Battery Totten.
" 2. Battery Grant.　" 4. Battery Lincoln.　" 6. Battery Sherman.　" 8. Battery Scott.　" 10. Battery McClellan.

Previous to opening the bombardment, General Hunter demanded the immediate surrender of the fort. "This demand," he wrote, "is made with a view to avoiding, if possible, the effusion of blood which must result from the bombardment and attack now in readiness to be opened. The number, calibre, and completeness of the batteries surrounding you, leave no doubt as to the result in case of refusal; and as the defence, however obstinate, must eventually succumb to the assailing force at my disposal, it is hoped you will see fit to avert the useless waste of life." The rebel commander, however, refused to comply with the demand, replying briefly, and with spirit, that he was there to defend the fort, not to surrender it.

The surrender of the fort being thus refused, fire was opened from the batteries at about half past seven o'clock on the morning of the 10th of April, according to the orders previously issued. The bombardment continued through the day without intermission, the batteries being served with great efficiency, with one or two exceptions, though the men were but little trained in the use of the heavy guns. The rebel garrison responded with spirit and a well directed fire, which, however, did but little damage to the Union forces, in consequence of the ample protection which had been provided by the engineering skill of General Gillmore and his assistants. More than three thousand projectiles were thrown from the federal batteries during the day, but it was found that shells from the heavy mortars, even when they fell within the fort, did not produce the effect which had been anticipated, and several of the large columbiads were early in the day dismounted by their own recoil in consequence of defective carriages. The most effective fire was from the breaching batteries of rifled guns, which were now, for the first time, tested in actual use against a strong fortification. These, though not all served with the requisite skill, had effected a breach in the south-east angle of the fort, which promised, by a continuance of the fire, to become practicable for an assault.

During the night a continuous but slow fire was kept up from the batteries, for the purpose of fatiguing the garrison of the fort, and the next morning the bombardment was resumed with great vigor, one of the breaching batteries, which had been the least efficiently served the previous day, being now manned by a detachment of sailors from the fleet. The fire from both parties was more accurate than on the first day, but the shots told with greatest effect upon the fort. The breach which had been commenced on the day previous was soon extended, and the adjacent embrasures were also enlarged by the well-directed shots of the breaching batteries. The parapet was battered down, and several of the guns in the fort were dismounted or rendered useless. By noon a considerable portion of the wall, where first breached, fell into the ditch, and the ruin began to extend to the adjacent casemates, under the severe blows of the shot from the rifled guns. These shot now passed through the casemates to the opposite angle of the fort, where the principal magazine was located. The breaches were becoming so large that preparations were made for a storming party, the bombardment in the mean time being continued as effectively as ever. But while these preparations were in progress a white flag was raised upon the fort, and the rebel flag was lowered, in token of surrender. The rebel garrison had defended the fort with spirit till it was so badly breached that a part of it was scarcely defensible, while a number of their guns were rendered useless, and the federal shot and shell were endangering the magazine. A short time longer, even if the magazine should not be reached by a federal shell, would render the breaches so extensive that the work could hardly be held against an assault, and the officers in command accordingly determined to cease from a vain defence.

With the appearance of the signal of submission on the fort the fire from the federal batteries ceased, and General Gillmore, who was entitled to the chief credit of the success of the operations against the work, was sent by General Benham to accept the surrender. With two of his aids, General Gillmore proceeded in a small boat to Cockspur Island, on which Fort Pulaski was situated, and being met by a rebel officer, was conducted to the fort. Here an interview of an hour was held between the general and Colonel Olmstead, the rebel commandant, in which the terms of the capitulation were discussed. The result was that the fort, with all its armament and ordnance stores, together with small arms, should be given up to the federal officers, and the garrison, consisting of three hundred and sixty men, should surrender as prisoners of war. The officers and men were allowed to retain their private property, except arms, and the sick and wounded were to be sent within the rebel lines. Major Halpine, of General Hunter's staff, who, with other federal officers, arrived during the conference of General Gillmore with the rebel commander, received the swords of the rebel officers, the fort, with its contents, was surrendered in due form, and the flag of the Union was again raised over its walls. The surrender took place on the 11th of April, the anniversary of the opening of the fire of the rebels upon Fort Sumter, a circumstance which was not forgotten by the captors.

The condition of Fort Pulaski showed how terrible had been the fire from the federal batteries. Its interior exhibited a greater amount of damage than the breaches in its walls would indicate. It seemed, indeed, but a mass of ruins, into which a practicable breach would admit an assailing party; but in spite of the sad condition of the fort, and the dismounting of seven of its available guns, Colonel Olmstead declared that it was his purpose to hold out till night, had not the principal magazine been exposed to the shot and shell which were thrown so continuously and with so much accuracy from the federal batteries. He had defended the fort bravely, but it could not withstand the shot from the rifled ordnance and the storm of shells which exploded within it; and when the danger of an explosion of the magazine was added to the chances of an assault, his discretion induced a surrender.

The success of the bombardment had not disappointed the expectations of General Gillmore, and had astonished not only the rebel garrison, but many of the federal officers, who were not prepared for this revolution in siege operations which had been effected by the use of rifled guns. It gave an impulse to the ordnance departments of both army and navy to supply liberally the improved artillery, and it caused not a little excitement, not to say consternation, in Europe, whose governments were now, for a second time, startled by the overthrow of their established theories and experience in offensive and defensive warfare.

While the final preparations were being made for the bombardment of Fort Pulaski from Tybee Island, another expedition, under Brigadier-General Viele, had proceeded through the passages on the north side of the Savannah River, to islands above the fort, and on the opposite side of the river, for the purpose of cutting off communication between the fort and Savannah, and of establishing batteries to operate against the gorge of the fort. The difficulties of this expedition were such that it was not considered expedient to construct the batteries till those on Tybee Island were completed. But on the night before the opening of the bombardment two batteries were thrown up, and guns were nearly ready to be mounted, when the fort surrendered. Otherwise these batteries might also have played an important part in the reduction of the rebel stronghold.

The following are among the official reports of the operations against Fort Pulaski : —

REPORT OF MAJOR-GENERAL HUNTER.

"HEADQUARTERS DEPARTMENT OF THE SOUTH, FORT PULASKI, COCKSPUR ISLAND, GA., *April* 13, 1862.

"SIR: The flag of our country waves over Fort Pulaski. I summoned the garrison to surrender, at sunrise, on the morning of the 10th instant. Immediately on receiving their refusal, at eight A. M. we opened fire, the bombardment continuing, without intermission, for thirty hours. At the end of eighteen hours' firing, the fort was breached in the south-east angle, and at the moment of surrender, two o'clock P. M., on the 11th instant, we had commenced preparations for storming.

"The whole armament of the fort, forty-seven guns, a great supply of fixed ammunition, forty thousand pounds of powder, and large quantities of commissary stores, have fallen into our hands; also three hundred and sixty prisoners, of whom the officers will be sent north by the first opportunity that offers.

"The result of this bombardment must cause, I am convinced, a change in the construction of fortifications as radical as that foreshadowed in naval architecture by the conflict between the Monitor and Merrimac. No works of stone or brick can resist the impact of rifled artillery of heavy calibre.

"Too much praise cannot be given to Captain Q. A. Gillmore, United States Engineers, (Acting Brigadier-General,) the officer immediately in charge of our works on Tybee Island, for his industry, skill, and patriotic zeal. Great credit is also due to his assistants, Lieutenant J. H. Wilson, United States Topographical Engineers, and Lieutenant Horace Porter, of the Ordnance Department. I have also to gratefully acknowledge the services of Captain C. R. P. Rodgers, United States Navy, who, with one hundred of his men, from the Wabash, under the command of Lieutenant Irwin, did nobly at the guns.

"Our gallant volunteers, under the scientific direction of Captain Gillmore, displayed admirable energy and perseverance in the construction of the earthworks on Tybee Island; and nothing could be finer or more impressive than the steadiness, activity, skill, and courage with which they worked their guns in battery.

"When I receive the reports of the officers more immediately in command, Brigadier-General H. W. Benham, and Acting Brigadier-General Gillmore, a statement more in detail will be immediately forwarded; but I cannot close without expressing my thanks to both these officers, and the hope that Acting Brigadier-General Gillmore may be confirmed in the position of brigadier-general, to which, in this bombardment, he has established such deserving claims.

"I am happy to state that our loss was but one man killed, the earthworks of our batteries affording secure protection against the heaviest fire of the enemy. The loss of the enemy has been stated as three severely wounded.

"I have the honor to be, sir, most respectfully, your very obedient servant,

"DAVID HUNTER,

"*Major-General commanding Dep't of the South.*

"Hon. E. M. STANTON, *Secretary of War, Washington.*"

74

REPORT OF BRIGADIER-GENERAL BENHAM.

"HEADQUARTERS FIRST DIVISION,
NORTHERN DISTRICT, DEP'T OF THE SOUTH,
FORT PULASKI, COCKSPUR ISLAND, GA., *April* 12, 1862.

"SIR: I have the honor to report the conclusion of the operations of the siege of Fort Pulaski, in Savannah River, Georgia, which have resulted in the capture of that fortress and its armament, and the unconditional surrender of the effective force of the garrison, amounting to three hundred and sixty-one, of whom twenty-four were officers, besides about eighteen who were sick or wounded.

"This siege is, as I would remark, the first trial, at least on our side the Atlantic, of the modern heavy and rifled projectiles against forts erected and supposed to be sufficiently strong, prior to these inventions, almost equalling, as it would appear, the revolution accomplished in naval warfare by the iron-clad vessels recently constructed.

"These operations, with the cordial assistance and coöperation of the naval forces, under Flag-Officer S. F. Dupont, have been accomplished by a portion of the troops of my division, for the most part under the immediate direction of Captain Q. A. Gillmore, Corps of Engineers, Acting Brigadier-General, and Chief Engineer of the siege, to whose report, a copy of which is respectfully forwarded herewith, I have the honor to refer you for the detail of the operations.

"Immediately after our arrival in this department, as you are aware, I visited Tybee Island, (on the 31st ult.,) and carefully inspected the works being erected there for the direct attack upon this fort, which had been well advanced by General Gillmore, under the direction of that faithful and judicious officer, Brigadier-General T. W. Sherman, my predecessor in this district. These works consisted of eleven batteries, prepared for thirty-five to thirty-seven pieces of heavy ordnance, extending along an oblique line of about one and a half miles in length, opposite the south-east face of the fort, the extremities of this line being at distances, respectively, of about one and two miles from the fort. They were placed with great skill and judgment, and constructed properly, and with as much strength and regularity as the circumstances of the case would permit; and the care and forethought of the engineer in providing for the proper supply of ordnance, and other stores that might be needed, is worthy of especial mention, the whole arrangement at Tybee Island meeting my entire approval.

"Desiring, however, if possible, to obtain a concentric fire upon the work, I endeavored to arrange with General Viele (commanding at Dawfuskie Island) to accomplish this object, directing him, upon the 6th instant, to place a battery on Long Island to attack the gorge of the fort on the west; and after a second visit to him on the 9th, to construct another (if practicable, and the distance was not too great) upon Turtle Island, on the north, the object being mainly the moral effect of an encircling fire, rather than the expectation of any serious effect upon the walls at that distance. From some cause, however, the heavy ordnance for these batteries did not arrive in time, and the lighter pieces most available, and placed in position on Long Island, served rather as a diversion than for any serious demonstration upon the work.

"The main attack upon the fort, as you are aware, commenced on the morning of the 10th instant, at about half past seven o'clock, and immediately after the refusal of its commander to surrender, according to your summons, previously sent. Being present yourself, at or between our batteries, for the greater portion of the day, during the contest between these batteries and the fort, you are, of course, personally aware of the great efficiency with which these batteries were served, and of the successful commencement of the breach at the southeast angle of the fort on that day. You are also aware of the efficient and accurate firing of the guns at the fort, directed as they were with great precision, not only at our batteries, but even at the individual persons passing between them or otherwise exposed. The firing on our part, though delayed at first by the necessity of obtaining the proper range, was kept up with such vigor that over three thousand projectiles, varying in size from the thirteen-inch mortar shell to the thirty-pound Parrott shot, were thrown at the fort during the first day.

"At evening, as it was necessary to guard against the possibility of attack from the Wilmington marshes, a force of some two regiments was stationed upon the ridges of land adjacent, one immediately in rear of the upper batteries, and one on a ridge running towards Tybee River; and to give General Gillmore an opportunity for the rest which he required, I arranged with him to remain myself at the batteries, in general charge of the forces, during the first half of the night, directing, at the same time, that the shells should be thrown at the fort every ten or fifteen minutes during the night, for the purpose of fatiguing the garrison. This shell practice, especially during the early part of the night, while the moon was up, was reported to be most successful, or fully as accurate as by daylight.

"As a principal battery, of one James and five Parrott guns, near the fort, appeared not to have been as successfully served as was possible during the day, and as a detachment of one hundred seamen from the navy, under Lieutenant Irwin, had been kindly furnished to us by Flag-Officer Dupont, (at the suggestion of Captain C. R. P. Rodgers,) which had unfortunately reached us too late for the first assignment to the batteries, I directed that a portion of this battery should be placed in the hands of this command, and the remainder with suitable men, to be under Captain Turner, A. C. S., late of the first artillery, U. S. A., and now Chief Commissary of your staff, and the

James and three of the Parrott guns were assigned to the naval detachment accordingly.

"At about seven, on the evening of the 11th, the fire opened with great vigor and accuracy, the certainty as to direction and distance being greatly beyond that of the previous day, especially on the part of the enemy, there being scarcely any exposure of our force that did not draw a close shot, while the embrasures and parapets of our batteries were most accurately reached.

"At about ten to eleven A. M. I visited the batteries, finding each of them most efficiently served, especially the small mortar-batteries nearest the fort, the batteries just referred to, in charge of the navy and Captain Turner, and the columbiad batteries under Captain Pelouze. I found that an embrasure at the breached point, which was much enlarged on the previous day, was now opened to fully the size of the recess arch, or some eight or ten feet square, and the adjacent embrasures were rapidly being brought to a similar condition. At about noon the whole mask and parapet-wall of the casemate first injured fell into the ditch, raising a ramp quite visible to us, and soon after the corresponding parts of the adjacent casemates began to fall, the Parrott and James shot passing quite through, as we could see the heavy timber blindage in rear of the casemates, to the rear of the magazine, on the opposite (northwest) angle of the fort.

"In this state of things I felt sure that we would soon be called to peel off the whole scarp wall from the front of the casemates of the south-east front, making a breach greatly larger than the small garrison could defend, with, probably, another smaller breach upon the opposite side; and I at once determined that, if the resistance was continued, it would be best, and entirely practicable, to storm the fort successfully within thirty to forty hours. And I had given directions to General Gillmore to have suitable scaling-ladders prepared for the purpose, and was arranging for the proper forces, boats, &c., when, at about two P. M., we discovered a white flag thrown up, and the rebel flag, after telling out to the wind for a few minutes at *half-mast*, came slowly to the ground.

"I then directed my Assistant Adjutant-General, Captain A. B. Ely, to leave for the fort; but finding soon after your own Adjutant-General, Major Halpine, at the batteries, I commissioned him (accompanied by Captain Ely) to proceed there with the terms I proposed — simply those of your own first note, demanding the surrender of the garrison, and all the armament and weapons; no other modification to be allowed than that they should have as favorable terms as are given by our government in this war. General Gillmore reaching the upper batteries soon after, and appearing to desire it, and as his services most eminently merited that his wishes should be gratified, I authorized him to pass over to accept the surrender of the fort; and the terms assented to by him, are essentially those dictated by me, excepting, perhaps, those relating to the disabled men, who would otherwise have been a burden to us. And by the return of these, I have endeavored to provide, by a letter from Colonel Olmstead, the rebel commander, for the receiving of a like number of men of the forty-sixth New York regiment, captured from Tybee about two weeks since. . . .

"I would respectfully recommend in relation to the commander of the garrison of the fort, Colonel Charles H. Olmstead, whose gallant conduct as an enemy, and whose courtesy as a gentleman, are entitled to all consideration, that should you deem it proper, the courtesy of the return of his own sword should be extended to him. His defence, I would remark, was continued until almost the latest limit possible; for a few hours more of our fire would, to all appearance, have sufficed for the destruction of the magazine and a larger portion of the fort, while another day would have unavoidably placed the garrison at the mercy of a storming column from our command.

"I have the honor to be, sir, very respectfully, your obedient servant,

"H. W. BENHAM,

"*Brigadier-General commanding Northern*

"*District, Department of the South.*

"Major-General DAVID HUNTER, *commanding Department of the South.*"

GENERAL GILLMORE'S REPORT.

"HEADQUARTERS, FORT PULASKI, GA.,)
April 12, 1862. $

"SIR : I have the honor to report that several batteries established on Tybee Island, to operate against Fort Pulaski, opened fire on the morning of the 10th inst., at a quarter past eight o'clock, commencing with the thirteen-inch mortars.

"When the range of these pieces had been approximately obtained, by the use of signals, the other batteries opened in the order previously prescribed in "General Orders, No. 17," from these headquarters, hereunto appended, as part of this report, so that by half past nine o'clock all our batteries—eleven in number—had commenced their work.

"The breaching batteries opened at half past nine o'clock. With the exception of four ten-inch columbiads, dismounted at the outset by their own recoil, in consequence of their having been supplied pintles, and from very serious defects in the wrought-iron chapis, which will be noticed more fully in my detailed report, all the pieces were served through the day.

"With few exceptions, strict regard was paid to the instructions laid down in the order regulating the rapidity and direction of the fire. At dark all the pieces ceased firing, except the thirteen-inch mortars, one ten-inch mortar, and one thirty-pound Parrott, which were served through the night at intervals of twenty minutes for each piece.

"The only plainly perceptible result of this cannonade of ten and a half hours' duration, the breaching batteries having been served but nine and a half hours, was the commencement of a breach in the easterly half of the *pancoupé* connecting the south and south-east faces, and in that portion of the south-east face spanned by the two casemates adjacent to the *pancoupé*. The breach had been ordered in this portion of the scarp so as to take in reverse, through the opening, the magazine located in the angle formed by the gorge and north face.

"Two of the barbette guns of the fort have been disabled, and three casemate guns silenced. The enemy served both tiers of guns briskly throughout the day, but without injury to the materiel or personnel of our batteries.

"The result from the mortar-batteries was not at all satisfactory, notwithstanding the care and skill with which the pieces were served.

"On the morning of the 11th our batteries again opened a little after sunrise, with decided effect, the fort returning a heavy and well-directed fire from its barbette and casemate guns. The breach was rapidly enlarged. At the expiration of three hours the entire casemate next the *pancoupé* had been opened, and by eleven o'clock the one adjacent to it was in a similar condition. Directions were then given to train the guns upon the third embrasure, upon which the breaching batteries were operating with effect, when the fort hoisted the white flag. This occurred at two o'clock P.M.

"The formalities of visiting the fort, receiving the surrender, and occupying it with our troops, consumed the balance of the afternoon and evening.

"I cannot indulge in detail, however interesting and instructive, in this hasty and preliminary report; but the pleasing duty of acknowledging the services of the officers and men under my command, during the laborious and fatiguing preliminaries for opening fire, as well as during the action, I do not feel at liberty to defer.

"The labor of landing the heaviest ordnance, with large supplies of ordnance stores, upon an open and exposed beach, remarkable for its heavy surf, taking advantage of the tide day and night; the transportation of these articles to the advanced batteries under cover of night; the erection of seven of the eleven batteries in plain view of Fort Pulaski, and under its fire; the construction, upon marshy ground, in the night-time exclusively, of nearly one mile of causeway, resting on fascines and brushwood; the difficult task of hauling the guns, carriages, and chapis to their positions, in the dark, over a narrow road, bordered by marsh, by the labor of the men alone, (the advance being two and a half miles from the landing;) the indomitable perseverance and cheerful deportment of the officers and men under the frequent discouragement of breaking down and miring in the swamp, are services to the cause and country which I do not feel at liberty to leave unrecorded. An idea of the immense labor expended in transporting the ordnance can be gained from the fact that two hundred and fifty men could hardly move a thirteen-inch mortar, loaded, on a sling-cart. Another circumstance deserving especial mention, is, that twenty-two of the thirty-six pieces comprised in the batteries were served during the action by the troops who had performed the fatiguing labors to which I have referred above. They received all their instructions in gunnery, at such odd times as they could be spared from other duty, during the week preceding the action. . . . .

"I will close this preliminary report by some general deductions from absolute results, without going into details or reasons.

"1. Mortars (even thirteen-inch sea-coast) are unavailable for the reduction of works of small area like Fort Pulaski. They cannot be fired with sufficient accuracy to crush the casemate arches. They might, after a long time, tire out any ordinary garrison.

2. "Good rifled guns, properly served, can breach rapidly at one thousand six hundred and fifty yards distance.

"A few heavy round shot, to bring down the masses loosened by the rifled projectiles, are of good service.

"I would not hesitate to attempt a practicable breach in a brick scarf at two thousand yards distance, with guns of my own selection.

3. "No better piece for 'breaching can be desired than the forty-two pounder James. The grooves, however, must be kept clean.

"Parrott guns, throwing as much metal as the James, would be equally good, supposing them to fire as accurately as the Parrott thirty-pounder.

"I append to this report a map, giving the position of our several batteries, and the orders issued, assigning the detachments to the batteries, and regulating the direction and rapidity of the firing.

"Very respectfully, your obedient servant,
"Q. A. GILMORE,
"Brigadier-General Vols., commanding U. S.
Forces, Tybee and Cockspur Islands, Ga.

"Lieutenant A. B. ELY, Acting Assistant Adjutant-General, Northern District, Department of the South."

CHAPTER LXXII.

Expedition to the Gulf. — Ship Island. — Arrival of the Vanguard of the Expedition. — Proclamation of General Phelps. — General Butler. — Naval and Military Preparations. — New Orleans and its Defences. — Forts Jackson and St. Philip. — Obstructions and Fire-Rafts. — Federal Preparations. — Mortar Flotilla. — Movement up the River. — Preliminary Surveys. — Trial of Mortars. — Rebel Fire-Raft. — Commencement of the Bombardment. — Its Effects. — Continuation of the Bombardment. — Removal of Obstructions. — Preparation of the Squadron to pass the Forts. — Chain-clad Ships. — The advance of the Squadron. — Rebel Resistance. — Heavy Cannonade. — Passage of the Squadron above the Forts. — Severe Conflict. — The Varuna. — Destruction of Rebel Steamers. — Complete Success of the Squadron. — Passage up the River. — Arrival of General Butler and his Command. — Military Movements. — Attempt to land Troops in the Rear of Fort St. Philip. — Condition of the Garrisons. — Surrender of the Forts. — Advance of General Butler to New Orleans. —

SOON after the occupation of Hatteras Inlet, on the coast of North Carolina, in August, 1861, General Butler had received instructions to recruit troops in New England, and to organize an expedition, composed principally of those troops, for operations in the Gulf of Mexico. General Butler entered upon his work with the zeal and energy which he had constantly displayed in his military career, and before the last of November the van of his expedition sailed from Boston, and other forces were nearly ready to follow. The first brigade was under Brigadier-General J. W. Phelps, of Vermont, who assumed command at Hampton Roads, and proceeded with a part of his force, numbering about two thousand men, to the Gulf The immediate destination of this expedition was Ship Island, off the coast of Mississippi, about midway between Mobile and New Orleans. This island had been taken possession of by a naval force in the September preceding, and its fortifications, constructed chiefly by the rebels, who had abandoned it in fear of a naval attack, were held by sailors and marines. It was considered, from its position, a good base from which to operate against either New Orleans or Mobile directly, or to occupy the neighboring mainland, and thence to move as expediency required.

General Phelps arrived at Ship Island on the 3d of December, and landing his troops, encamped them there, and awaited the arrival of other forces of the expedition. In the mean time he issued a proclamation to the people of the neighboring country, addressed to the "loyal citizens," in which, after a calm discussion of the slavery question, he declared that his command came as the advocates and defenders of "free labor and working-men's rights." This proclamation appeared to have little effect, other than to excite the slaveholders more

bitterly against the north, while among the northern people it caused considerable discussion, finding many advocates as well as opponents. It was disclaimed by General Butler, the commander of the expedition, and was virtually disapproved by the government by its subsequent action. It was, indeed, not especially military in its character, but it contained much truth, expressed in a somewhat peculiar manner, and was the declaration of an earnest man as well as able soldier.

Two or three reconnoissances by small forces on the main land were made from Ship Island, but nothing of importance was accomplished, while the troops there waited for the arrival of the other forces of the expedition. The latter arrived slowly, and General Butler himself left Boston the latter part of February with a part of his command. After being nearly wrecked on Frying-Pan Shoals, off the coast of South Carolina, and consequently delayed some time at Port Royal, General Butler arrived at Ship Island about the middle of March. A new military department was created, called the Department of the Gulf, comprising all the coast of the Gulf of Mexico west of Pensacola, and General Butler was appointed the commander. In the mean time the government had been augmenting the naval forces in the Gulf, and a strong squadron, called the Western Gulf Blockading Squadron, under Flag-Officer D. G. Farragut, was prepared to coöperate with General Butler in any decided movement against the rebels. This fleet was not idle, but while the Mississippi and all harbors of any importance were vigilantly blockaded, reconnoissances were made to Lake Borgne and to the entrance of Lake Pontchartrain by some of the smaller vessels, and occasionally an engagement, at long range and of little consequence, took place between them and rebel armed steamers.

The rebels anticipated an attempt to capture either Mobile or New Orleans, and made preparations to defeat it. The latter city, which was rightly supposed to be the chief object of attack, was thought well protected by the formidable Forts Jackson and St. Philip, on the Mississippi, constructed by the United States, and now made more complete by the rebels, and by fortifications which commanded the approaches by Lake Borgne and Lake Pontchartain. A considerable number of steamers were also armed, and several formidable iron-cased rams were constructed, while obstructions were placed in the river to add to the difficulties of navigation. With these means of defence, the rebels believed that they could surely keep the federal fleet from ascending the river, while the difficulties of any other approach where the military forces could not be supported by formidable war vessels, seemed to render the city safe from capture.

Forts Jackson and St. Philip, upon which the defence of New Orleans chiefly depended, were strong works, constructed by the United States. The former, an extensive fortification on the right bank of the river, was not completed when the rebellion commenced, but it had been greatly improved by the rebels, and a heavy armament had been mounted, most of the guns having been sent to the fort by the traitor Floyd, while secretary of war, in anticipation of the conflict between the north and the south. The fort was capable of mounting more than a hundred guns, but was not fully armed. Fort St. Philip, a work of less importance and magnitude, on the opposite side of the river and a little higher up, was built on the site of an old Spanish fort of the same name. This also had been strengthened and more fully armed, and with its water batteries could mount about one hundred guns. The two forts commanded the river with a large number of guns. But in addition to these fortifications the rebels had constructed outworks and water batteries, which added to the strength of the position. The river was obstructed by rafts and hulks, bear-ing heavy chains, stretching from bank to bank, and by other ingenious contrivances, which rendered the removal of the chain a difficult matter. There were also a number of rafts and flat boats, loaded with combustibles, to be fired and set adrift in the current, in order that they might be carried among the federal vessels and destroy them by fire. Above the obstructions were the armed steamers, intended to coöperate with the forts in resisting the advance of the fleet. With all these preparations, which had been elaborately made, the rebels believed that the city could not be reached by the federal forces, and against these defences the naval expedition was to operate before the land forces would be brought into requisition.

But the means of attack provided by the government were commensurate with the work to be attempted. In addition to the fleet of steamers, with their formidable armaments, which Flag-Officer Farragut had under his command, a fleet of small sailing vessels, carrying heavy mortars, had been quietly despatched to the passes of the Mississippi, under the command of Captain David D. Porter, and were ready to join in the bombardment of the rebel fortifications. Waiting for the completion of the naval preparations, General Butler's command, numbering, when all had arrived, ten or twelve thousand men, remained at Ship Island, in rather narrow limits for so large a force, impatiently waiting for some movement against the rebels. The naval officers, however, knew the difficulties before them, and were determined to make ample preparation for their work.

It was the 12th of April before the preparations were completed so far as to commence the movement. On that day, Flag-Officer Farragut's squadron and Captain Porter's mortar fleet commenced moving up the river, to be placed in position for bombarding Forts Jackson and St. Philip. Each of these vessels had been painted with a coat of mud, and the masts and rigging were covered with branches; to render them less conspicuous objects for the aim of the rebel artillerists. But before the bombardment could be commenced, it was necessary to survey the river in order to ascertain the bearings and distances of certain points, the position and nature of the rebel obstructions, and the character of the defences. This was a work which required skill and daring; but in three days, in spite of rebel artillery and rifles, it was quite thoroughly accomplished by officers of the coast survey, and charts were made for the use of the squadron.

The preliminary surveys and other necessary preparations having been made, on the evening of the 16th of April fire was opened upon Fort Jackson, for the purpose of trying the range of the mortars, but it was not till two days afterwards that the bombardment of the forts commenced in earnest. At a distance of thirty-eight hundred yards from the fort the huge mortars hurled their monstrous shells high in the air, to drop and burst in and about the work, while the vessels which carried them lay in such a position, or were so disguised, as to be comparatively safe from the rebel artillery. The trial was satisfactory to Captain Porter, and accordingly the arrangements for opening the bombardment were perfected, and on the 18th of April the work of reducing the forts was commenced by the entire mortar fleet. In the mean time, however, the rebels finding the river below them filled with so large a fleet, and so formidable an attack threatened, sought to destroy some of the numerous vessels which appeared crowded together, by sending down some of their fire-rafts, hoping thus to disorganize the naval force, and derange the plans of attack. But the naval officers had seen these fire-rafts before, and ample preparations were made to prevent them from accomplishing the work designed. Boats, with crews properly armed to contend with such an enemy, pulled away from the fleet, and met the raft some

distance above the anchorage ground, and a steamer grappling it, towed it down the river, so as to keep it clear of all vessels, the fire being at the same time extinguished by streams of water thrown from the steamer and the exertions of the crews of the small boats, who vigorously attacked the flaming foe. The success with which this danger was overcome dispelled all great fear of this method of attack among the federal officers and men, and the force detailed to meet the fire-rafts was soon perfectly organized and trained to the work, which promised and proved to be quite an important one.

When the mortar boats were being towed to their position on the morning of the 18th, the rebels opened fire upon them from the forts, but without effecting any damage. One division of the mortars was placed in position on the west side of the river, and another on the east side, and at an early hour the bombardment commenced, the shot being directed against Fort Jackson. Fort St. Philip was to be left for the fleet of Flag-Officer Farragut to dispose of after the reduction or silence of Fort Jackson. Several gunboats, attached to the mortar flotilla, steamed up the river nearer to the forts, and joined with some effect in the bombardment, succeeding in silencing for a time the barbette guns, and thus protecting the mortar boats, some of which, on the east side of the river, had been struck by the rebel shot. The steamers Iroquois and Owasco were conspicuous in this engagement, being greatly exposed to the rebel shot, but handled with skill and bravery by the officers and crews. The mortars kept up a constant fire during the day, and though from the inexperience of the gunners many of the shells were thrown without effect, the result was not unsatisfactory. The citadel of Fort Jackson was struck several times and nearly destroyed, two or three barbette guns were dismounted, several rebel soldiers killed or wounded, and fire was com-

MAJ. GEN. P. KEARNEY.

municated to some wooden structure and cotton bales, used for strengthening the works, which apparently caused an extensive conflagration. It was thought possible that a continuation of the bombardment during the night might, in consequence of this conflagration, have caused an evacuation of the fort. The bombardment, however, was suspended at dark, and the mortar boats were removed to a safer anchorage down the river.

The next morning the bombardment was resumed by the mortar flotilla, and from that time till the morning of the 24th, was continued without cessation. The huge shells were constantly showered into and around the forts, causing much damage and endangering life, but failing to break through the casemates or to render the works untenable. The gunboats were also continually engaged in bombarding the forts or throwing shot at some rebel steamer that ventured within sight. These vessels moved up the river much nearer to the forts than the mortar boats, and drew upon themselves the fire of the rebel batteries, escaping by their constant change of position, however, any serious damage. To the fierce bombardment to which they were subjected the rebels replied quite vigorously the greater part of the time, and with very effective guns, skilfully served. Their officers were quite confident that the forts could not be taken, and they boasted that they would never surrender; and, in spite of the heavy bombardment, the works did not appear to be damaged or weakened sufficiently to render them less formidable to the passage of the fleet.

In the mean time the fleet was waiting a reduction of the forts or a diminution of their fire to make the passage, but the slow progress made by the bombardment rendered the officers and crews impatient of the delay, and Flag-Officer Farragut determined to make the attempt to pass the forts without waiting for the desired result. It was first necessary, however, to remove the obstructions in the river, and this was successfully accomplished by the officers and men of the gunboat Itasca, who, by persevering efforts, unshackled the chains which connected the hulks moored across the river, and the latter being removed, a wide passage was opened, which was quite sufficient for the entrance of the squadron. This work was not accomplished without great risk, and in effecting it the Itasca was carried by the current towards the eastern shore, where she grounded, and for nearly two hours lay exposed to the shot from both forts, but without being struck.

The want of iron-clad steamers to contend against the formidable fortifications and the "rams" of the rebels, made it necessary that Flag-Officer Farragut's squadron should be prepared as thoroughly as possible for the terrible ordeal which it was to undergo. No pains were spared to render the vessels invincible, and, as far as possible, invulnerable in the most exposed parts. Various means were devised and carried into execution to protect them, not only from shot and shell, but from the "rams" and fire-rafts with which it was understood the rebels were abundantly supplied. Several of the larger ships, including the sloops of war Richmond, Brooklyn, and Pensacola, had their engines and boilers protected by a novel kind of armor improvised for the occasion, which consisted of chains hung upon the outside and bound together with strong cordage. Other vessels had their engines protected by chains, logs, and bales of bagging closely packed about them inside the ship. Sand-bags and other devices were also used to protect the bows of some of the ships, as well as the engines and boilers. These preparations had been perfected during the several days' bombardment, and with his vessels thus equipped as no other squadron had previously been, Flag-Officer Farragut determined to attempt the passage of the forts at night, and to fight

75

his way through against forts, gunboats, rams, and fire-rafts. It was a daring movement, and its complete success proved that the navy, under such a leader, was able and ready to perform its share in the war.

The squadron consisted of seventeen sloops of war and gunboats, all of which were steamers, carrying upwards of two hundred guns. The vessels were formed in three divisions or lines; the first, under command of Captain Bailey comprised the Cayuga, Pensacola, Mississippi, Oneida, Varuna, Katahdin, Kineo, and Wissahickon. The second, under Flag-Officer Farragut himself, comprised the steam sloops Hartford, Brooklyn, and Richmond. The third, under Commander Bell, was composed of the Scioto, Iroquois, Pinola, Winona, Itasca, and Kennebec. While this formidable squadron moved up the river, the gunboats attached to the mortar flotilla steamed up sufficiently to enfilade the water batteries, which were the most formidable obstacle to the passage of the fleet, the mortars, in the mean time, keeping up their constant fire upon the forts. The movement was made on the night of the 23d of April, but it was not till three o'clock on the morning of the 24th that the squadron was fairly under way. The intention was to pass the forts in the darkness of the night, before the rising of the moon, but the moon was just appearing above the horizon when the fleet moved. The river, however, was still dark, and the state of the atmosphere was such as to render it the more difficult to distinguish objects on the water; and when the firing commenced, the smoke settled heavily over the river and enveloped the vessels. To this obscurity the success of the movement was in a great measure due, for had the squadron attempted to pass the forts by daylight, it is hardly possible that it would have escaped without great loss of men and probably of vessels.

As soon as the movement commenced, the mortar boats resumed fire upon the forts more heavily than ever before, the shells being thrown with the greatest possible rapidity. The gunboats attached to the mortar flotilla also opened their enfilading fire upon the water batteries of the enemy, and the bombardment was heavier and more persistent than at any time since its commencement. Under cover of this fire the squadron moved up the river, and passed through the opening in the barrier of chains and hulks which the Itasca had effected the previous night. The fleet advanced in three lines, by divisions, one ship following another, Flag-Officer Farragut's division on the western side of the river, Captain Bailey's on the eastern, and Commander Bell's in the middle.

Captain Bailey's division on the eastern side was the first to feel the enemy's fire. His flag-ship had scarcely passed through the opening in the barrier when both forts opened upon her, and the other vessels, as they advanced. On account of the too great elevation of the rebel guns, however, the greater part of the shot passed over the vessels and through the rigging. But some of them were struck several times in the hull, and the wisdom of the precautions taken for the safety of the machinery was abundantly proved, the chain armor and other defences affording, in this case, ample protection to the vital parts of the steamers. The vessels steamed on under the fire of the enemy for some distance without making any reply, but as they approached Fort St Philip, Captain Bailey ran his flag-ship, the Cayuga, in close to the fort, and poured broadsides of grape and canister upon them, driving the rebel soldiers from their guns, which were almost wholly *en barbette*. The other vessels of the division followed close behind the Cayuga, and each delivered broadsides of grape and canister as they passed, with such effect that the fire of the fort was for the time completely silenced. This division thus passed the forts without serious damage, though each of the vessels had been struck in some part, and slightly injured. The crews had manifested the greatest bravery, and were eager for a conflict in which they could show their skill and courage. The passage of the forts brought them suddenly into such a conflict, the result of which was a most brilliant victory.

While Captain Bailey advanced on the eastern side of the river, Flag-Officer Farragut, with his three noble vessels, the most formidable of the fleet, moved up on the western side towards Fort Jackson. When a mile and a quarter from that work the enemy opened upon him a heavy fire, which was better aimed than that directed against Captain Bailey's vessels. The flag-ship Hartford continued her course directly towards the fort, in spite of the shot which frequently struck her, and responded to the fire with a few of her guns. When within half a mile of the fort the vessel sheered off, and poured her heavy broadsides of grape and canister into the fort so effectually that the gunners were driven under cover, and none but the casemate guns continued the fire. These, however, were trained upon the Hartford the more effectively, as the flashes of her broadsides indicated through the smoke and fog the position of the vessel, and she was struck many times, and suffered some loss of men. But she passed the forts without being, to any extent, disabled, and was followed by the Richmond, which was manœuvred in the same manner, and continued the shower of small shot upon the fort, by which the fire of the barbette guns was silenced. The Brooklyn was unfortunately detained by coming in contact with the hulks, but having been extricated from these obstructions, she proceeded on her course, and, contending against rebel ram, fire-raft, and gunboat, while still under the fire of Fort Jackson, succeeded in joining her consorts after a severer, if not more glorious, contest than they had experienced. The Brooklyn first encountered the famous "ram" Manassas,

which had been a terror to the fleet since the vessels were driven by it from the passes of the Mississippi. This vessel came dashing against the side of the Brooklyn, first discharging her heavy gun when within a few feet of the latter. The shot, however, lodged in the sand bags which protected the engine, and the chain armor effectually warded off the iron beak intended to cut through the vessel's side. The ram, thus entirely unsuccessful, soon moved off, to meet with still greater failure; for, making a dash at the Mississippi, that vessel prepared for the encounter by a similar movement, and the Manassas, avoiding the blow, made for the shore, where she was soon disabled by the guns of the Mississippi, and, being deserted by her crew, drifted inoffensively down the river. Having got clear of the ram, the Brooklyn fell in with a large rebel steamer, which opened fire upon her, but this vessel was quickly disposed of by a broadside from the Brooklyn at short range, which set her on fire, and thus completely destroyed her.

In the mean time the middle division, under Commander Bell, proceeded on its course, and though not discernible from the forts, owing to the too great elevation of the rebel guns, received the shock of the heavy fire directed at the side divisions. Two of the vessels, the Itasca and Winona, were early disabled, the former receiving a shot in the boiler, and both floated helplessly down the river. The Kennebec became entangled in the cables connecting the barrier of hulks; and when, after a long delay, she was extricated, she was far in the rear, and so enveloped in smoke that the officers were uncertain as to their course, and the vessel soon after returned to her anchorage. With his other three vessels Commander Bell advanced on his course, under the heavy fire of both forts, and succeeded in passing them, though not without some damage and the loss of a number of men.

The federal vessels had hardly passed the

forts when they encountered a new enemy in the fleet of rebel gunboats which lay in order of battle just above Fort St. Philip. As soon as the federal vessels appeared above the forts the rebel steamers commenced the attack. Captain Bailey, in the Cayuga, was the first to receive this attack. He found himself in the midst of them before he was aware that he was to meet such an enemy. The rebel steamers dashed at the Cayuga with the intention of running her down, at the same time discharging their guns. By skilful manœuvring the Cayuga avoided any severe blow, and the brave officers and crew were not slow in meeting the danger by opening a rapid fire from her heavy guns, the solid shot from which speedily disposed of three of the assailants before the other vessels of the squadron came up. The Varuna and Oneida, however, soon followed the lead of the Cayuga, their crews eager to join in the conflict, and they too were speedily engaged with the enemy. A severe naval battle ensued, which was soon brought to a close by the entire and remarkable success of the federal vessels; not, however, till the Varuna was so disabled that she sank. This steamer, under command of Captain Boggs, had followed the Cayuga, and came suddenly into the midst of the rebel vessels, both gunboats and transports. Her brave commander, nothing daunted, pressed his vessel forward, discharging her guns at the rebel vessels on either side. This well-delivered fire exploded the boiler of one boat, which appeared crowded with troops, and disabled and set on fire three others, one of which was a gunboat. The Varuna was then attacked by a steamer with an iron-clad bow, which attempted to pierce her sides with a sharp prow. This vessel succeeded in striking the Varuna two or three blows, which did slight damage; but the latter soon partially disabled her assailant by throwing shot and shell into the after part of the vessel, so that she soon dropped out of action. But

this attack was followed by a more successful one by another similar iron-clad steamer, which struck the Varuna two or three damaging blows, causing her to leak rapidly. The gallant officers and crew of the Varuna, however, met the danger with skill and bravery. Never was vessel more ably and bravely managed. By pressing forward, the assailant was drawn around so as to expose the vulnerable parts, and a rapid fire of eight-inch shell soon set the too successful "ram" in flames. The Varuna, however, was filling with water and rapidly sinking. Captain Boggs immediately ran towards the river bank, the guns of his devoted vessel still throwing their shot and shell at the rebel vessels within range; and it was not till the water had risen to the gun-trucks that the firing ceased. The dead and wounded were then removed, and the brave commander and his crew left the vessel which they had so nobly defended, and with such heavy loss to the enemy.

While Captain Bailey's vessels were thus engaged, a part of the rebel fleet had passed down and met the vessels of Flag-Officer Farragut. When the Hartford had passed Fort Jackson, and had arrived opposite Fort St. Philip, where he was firing broadsides of grape and canister, a large fire-raft suddenly blazed up in close proximity to the ship, and it was discovered that the raft was being pushed forward against the Hartford by an iron-clad "ram." In the attempt to avoid this dangerous enemy the Hartford was run upon a bank, and the raft came alongside. In a moment the ship was all ablaze on this side, but the fire department was so thoroughly organized that it soon extinguished the flames, and the vessel was backed off from the shoal, the guns meanwhile being trained upon the forts and upon one or two of the rebel steamers which came within range. It was a moment of intense excitement and interest when the flag-ship was thus threatened with destruction. The conflict was at its height. The forts were firing with great vigor at the federal vessels, all of which had not yet passed by; the battle was raging between Captain Bailey's division and the rebel gunboats a little farther up the river; and the mortar boats and steamers below continued their heavy bombardment. The roar of the cannonade was terrific; the river was lighted up by the flames of the burning rebel vessels and the constant flashes of guns and exploding shells. It was impossible to tell which side was gaining the advantage, and so difficult, amid the smoke and murky atmosphere, to distinguish friend from foe, that there was a constant fear on board the federal vessels that they would fire into each other. Each vessel was fighting its own battle, and nearly all of them engaged both forts and rebel steamers. The duration of this severe conflict, however, was short. The noise of the battle soon diminished, the forts were passed, and the rebel boats had disappeared. Ship after ship of the federal fleet came up, and cheers resounded over the river for the passage of the forts, and the victory which had been achieved, in the short space of an hour and a half from the time of leaving the anchorage below.

A greater naval success was never achieved than this running the gantlet of Forts Jackson and St. Philip with their outlying batteries, and the complete and quick destruction of the rebel fleet, with comparatively so small a loss. The fire of more than a hundred guns in the forts had been encountered and safely passed. "Ram" and fire-raft had been met and overcome, and well-armed gunboats had been engaged, and captured or destroyed. In accomplishing this the federal vessels had suffered some damage, but none had been lost or disabled except the Varuna, which had fought so noble a fight, and had, indeed, achieved a splendid victory before she went down. The loss of men on board all the vessels was thirty killed, and one hundred and nineteen wounded.

On the other hand, the rebels had lost all; for, though the forts had not been reduced, or materially damaged, they no longer barred the passage to New Orleans, and must speedily be surrendered; eleven rebel steamers, the whole flotilla which was to resist the federal squadron, were destroyed, and the loss of men must have been large. Only one rebel vessel of any consequence had escaped, and that was a large and unwieldy iron-clad floating battery, which had successfully resisted the federal shot, but was incomplete and useless for want of motive power. Two or three smaller armed steamers had also escaped destruction, but they were of little account for defence, and were entirely subject to the fate of the forts.

While most of the vessels came to anchor above the scene of the conflict, and were delayed to repair damages, to bury the dead and provide for the wounded, Captain Bailey, in the Cayuga, steamed farther up the river, notwithstanding his ship had been considerably damaged. About five miles above the forts, at the quarantine station, a rebel camp was discovered, and in the gray dawn the rebel soldiers were seen hastily leaving it. The flight of the troops was stopped, and the position and a small force were surrendered. The other vessels were soon repaired, and the other arrangements being completed, the squadron, with the exception of two gunboats which were left at the quarantine ground to coöperate with a contemplated military movement in the rear of the forts, before noon resumed its movement up the river.

General Butler had anxiously watched the naval movement, and awaited its result to determine the course to be taken by the military forces. The morning revealed the rebel flag flying defiantly over the forts, but it was certain that a portion of the fleet had passed in comparative safety, for the national flag could be discovered flying from their masts as they lay far above the forts. The evidences of rebel disaster which had floated down the stream in the shape of burning vessels, and the disabled ram Manassas, confirmed the belief that the squadron had succeeded in all but the reduction of the forts, which, indeed, had hardly been anticipated. Captain Porter, determining to ascertain the condition of the forts, sent a summons for a surrender. This was promptly refused, and indications of some movement were reported, which was supposed to be a formidable attack by gunboats and the iron-clad battery, which was known to be uninjured, upon the fleet, now reduced by the passage of its most effective vessels above the forts. The mortar vessels, for safety from such an attack, were sent down the river to the head of the passes, and for several days the forts were undisturbed by gunboat or mortar, the garrisons improving the respite to repair damages and place the works in as complete a state of defence as before the bombardment.

The opportunity and necessity for carrying out a military movement previously conceived, seemed to have arrived. General Butler, whose troops to the number of nine thousand were impatiently waiting in the passes of the river for an order to advance, was prompt to act, and at once sent a part of his force to Sable Island, in the Gulf, twelve miles in the rear of Fort St. Philip, the other part remaining in the river ready to coöperate, or to advance up the river should the forts surrender. From Sable Island a portion of the expeditionary corps were, with great difficulty, transported through the shallow bayous to the banks of the Mississippi, where a small force was posted on each side of the river, supported by the gunboats left by Flag-Officer Farragut. In order to land a more effective force with artillery, additional means of transportation were required; but before these were procured, events rendered them unnecessary. The condition of the forts was, in fact, hopeless for the rebels. Though well supplied, perhaps, with provisions, they were now effectually cut off from the city, where the federal squadron had already arrived, and the posting of troops in the river above indicated an attack in the rear, or a siege of which there could be but one result. The rebel soldiers, at least, regarded any farther defence useless, however defiant the officers may have been, and a part of the garrison of Fort Jackson mutinied, spiked some of the guns, and, leaving the fort at night, gave themselves up to the federal picket on the western side of the river, two hundred and fifty men surrendering to a mere handful. The next morning the officers also deemed it prudent to capitulate; and a conference with Captain Porter resulted in the surrender of the forts. The iron-clad battery, before referred to, was set on fire by her officers and cast adrift in the current, evidently with the hope that her flames or the explosion of her magazine might cause disaster to the national vessels. The explosion, however, fortunately took place before the hulk reached the anchorage ground of the fleet. The forts were taken possession of by the naval authorities, and immediately garrisoned by a military force sent up by General Williams. Fort Jackson had been considerably damaged by the bombardment, during which more than eighteen hundred shells had fallen within the work. It appeared to be much shattered, and was considered by the garrison to be weak and unsafe, but a subsequent examination showed that its strength for defence against an assault was not greatly diminished; while Fort St. Philip exhibited but little evidence of injury. The former work was found to be mounted with about eighty guns, and the latter with about forty.

At the time of the surrender of the forts, General Butler was with Flag-Officer Farragut, at New Orleans, whither he had gone to arrange with that officer for some light-draught steamers, and in relation to future movements. On his return he found the flag of the Union flying over both forts, and the river open for the advance of his forces to New Orleans, where there was need of their speedy arrival. The troops at Sable Island were ordered back by way of the passes, and after leaving sufficient garrisons at the forts, those already in the river were transported to New Orleans. Their arrival was hailed with much satisfaction by the naval officers, for the condition of affairs in the city was such that it was impossible to secure any advantage without the aid of troops to take charge of the public property and hold the mob in subjection.

Flag-Officer Farragut had steamed up the river with his squadron, expecting to find his advance contested by batteries erected on its banks. No show of resistance, however, was manifested, but, on the contrary, the Union flag was discovered flying over several houses, and in some places the negroes hailed the squadron with cheers. The squadron came to anchor on the night of the 24th, about eighteen miles below the city. Up the river was seen the light of fires, supposed at first to be fire-rafts sent down for the destruction of the fleet, but which proved to be ships laden with cotton, ready to run the blockade. Proceeding in the morning, the first attempt to dispute or retard the progress of the ships was experienced at Chalmette, about three miles below the city, where batteries had been erected on each side of the river. From these batteries fire was opened upon the ships as they advanced, but as soon as the latter reached a position from which they could reply, a few broadsides dispersed the rebel gunners, and the squadron passed on without further molestation. At noon the squadron came to anchor before the city.

When the passage of the forts by the federal fleet was announced, the greatest excitement spread through New Orleans. Gold and valuables were hurried from the city, or placed under the protection of the foreign consuls. The mob raged, and threatened more fearful things than could possibly be anticipated from the advancing enemy. Fierce secessionists demanded the destruction of cotton and sugar (which were supposed to be particularly desired by the northern forces), and even of the city itself. Only a small number of rebel troops was in the city; and as this force could afford no protection against the squadron, and the army which would soon follow, it was withdrawn from the city, which was given into the hands of the municipal authorities. It was a dangerous time for the orderly and property-holding people of New Orleans, for the withdrawal of the military power left no protection from the lawless mob, which was ready to avail itself of circumstances to plunder and destroy. The municipal authorities called upon the European brigade, a body of citizen soldiers composed of foreigners resident in the city, to preserve order, and such protection as the city had until the arrival of General Butler and his forces, was afforded by this legion. The defence against the federal forces was the presence of the women and children; for whatever might be the epithets which rebel hatred applied to the northern soldiers, they knew well that the city would not be bombarded while the helpless non-combatants were in it. The insane order was issued by the rebel military commander, on the approach of the fleet, to burn all the cotton in the city, and to destroy the sugar and molasses. This order was quite thoroughly carried out, and when the fleet arrived the cotton was burning all along the levee, and numbers of steamboats in the river were in flames. Other property was destroyed also, and the mob aiding in the work of destruction did not neglect the opportunity for plunder. The amount of property thus foolishly destroyed was immense. Fifteen thousand bales of cotton on the levee, and ten or twelve ships laden with that product, were burned. A large number of steamboats that could not be removed, a half-finished floating battery of formidable dimensions, dry docks, immense piles of steamboat wood and coal, lumber, and other property, were also consigned to the flames; while stores of sugar, molasses, and provisions were destroyed or distributed among the mob.

This condition of affairs had existed for two days in the "Crescent City" when the Union fleet came to anchor before it. On the levee, notwithstanding a heavy rain, a vast crowd collected to witness the movements of the "invaders," as the national forces were generally considered; an excited crowd, that manifested the intensest hatred for the flag of the Union and its loyal defenders, and punished, with summary vengeance, any demonstration among the people of joy or welcome to that flag. Shortly after the arrival of the fleet, Flag-Officer Farragut despatched his second in command, Captain Bailey, with two or three other officers, to demand of the mayor a surrender of the city, and that the national flag should be raised over the public buildings. The officers, without any guard, proceeded to the levee in their boat, and landed amid noisy demonstrations of animosity on the part of the mob. They were not assailed, however, by more than words, for though the mob might speedily have executed their threats, they had a wholesome dread of the guns which frowned upon them from the open ports of all the vessels. The messengers were conducted to the mayor, followed by the excited crowd, and made the demand for which they were sent. The mayor replied that, not being a military commander, he had no authority to surrender the city. General Lovell, the rebel commander, who was still in the city, was accordingly sent for, and he also refused to surrender the city, and declared he had removed his forces in order to avoid a bombardment, though he still intended to resist the federal forces. Without accomplishing any thing satisfactory, Captain Bailey and his companions returned to the

fleet, being accompanied to their boat by General Lovell, whose presence protected them from the still more infuriated mob. It had been determined that the demand made by the federal commander should be submitted to the city council. Delay and hesitation on the part of the city authorities followed, but after some deliberation the city council at length decided that the mayor should return an answer to the demand for a surrender substantially like that which he had already given, and declining to raise the national flag in place of the "confederate" emblem. The reply was accordingly thus communicated to Flag-Officer Farragut, who immediately determined that the Union flag should be raised over at least one of the public buildings. A party was sent from the Pensacola, which lay off the Mint, to raise the flag upon that edifice. This being done, the people were notified that at any attempt to remove the flag the guns of the Pensacola would open upon the building No guard, however, was left to protect the flag, and the threat was not sufficient to deter all from the attempt. A party of four men succeeded in hauling down the flag, with which the mob marched in triumph through the city, and then tore it into shreds. The excitement on board the federal vessels at this act was intense, and but for the timely removal of the priming wafers, by which the guns are discharged, more than one broadside probably would have carried death and destruction into the city, through the impulsive movement of the men who sprang to the guns at the alarm.

Flag-Officer Farragut shared in the indignation of his men, but his position was a difficult one. The city lay at the mercy of his guns, but the women and children were practically placed as a defensive barrier between them and the rebel mob. He had triumphed over the military and naval force with which the rebels had undertaken to hold New Orleans, but civil functionaries, and an unorganized mob protected by this barrier, defied him. General Butler, who was present at this time, advised a threat of bombardment, and a demand for the immediate removal of the women and children. This advice was partially followed; but the threat, though contingent on the continued resistance of the people, was misconstrued, and occasioned the interference of the commander of a French ship of war which was in the river. The charge of inhumanity was brought against the federal commander, though the safety of the city lay in the keeping of its civil authorities and the people, and under no circumstances would he have carried out the threat until the removal of the women and children had been effected. Under the threat the national flag was again raised over the Mint and over the Custom House, where it remained undisturbed, protected by a small force of marines.

From his difficult position the Flag-Officer was, after two or three days of perplexing trial, happily relieved, by the arrival, on the 1st of May, of the advance of General Butler's troops. Without delay these troops were disembarked and marched to the Custom House and Mint. The populace were indignant and abusive, but they dared not offer any opposition, and the forces were promptly posted. Captain Farragut notified the city authorities that they must thereafter negotiate with the commander of the army; and, leaving a sufficient force of his squadron, he subsequently moved up the Mississippi, to coöperate with Commodore Foote, whose squadron was operating from above, in again opening its majestic tide to the flag which had so long and prosperously floated over it.

Of the official reports in relation to the capture of Forts Jackson and St. Philip, and the movement to New Orleans, the following describe the more important events:—

REPORT OF FLAG-OFFICER FARRAGUT.

"UNITED STATES FLAG-SHIP HARTFORD,
AT ANCHOR OFF CITY OF NEW ORLEANS, April 29.

"SIR : I am happy to announce to you that our flag waves over both Forts Jackson and St. Philip, and at New Orleans over the Custom House.

"I am taking every means to secure the occupatiou by General Butler of all the forts along the coast. Berwick's Bay and Fort Pike have been abandoned ; in fact there is a general stampede, and I shall endeavor to follow it up. I am bringing up the troops as fast as possible.

"We have destroyed all the forts above the city, four in number, which we understood to be all the impediments between this and Memphis.

"I am, very respectfully,

"Your obedient servant,

"D. G. FARRAGUT,

" Flag-Officer Western Gulf Block'g Squadron

"Hon. GIDEON WELLES, Secretary of the Navy."

REPORT OF COMMODORE PORTER.

" UNITED STATES STEAMER HARRIET LANE,
MISSISSIPPI RIVER, April 25, 1862.

"SIR : I have the honor to inform you that Flag-Officer Farragut, with the fleet, passed Forts Jackson and St. Philip on the morning of the 24th, and should be in New Orleans by this time, as he can meet with no obstacles such as he has already passed, the way being comparatively open before him.

"We commenced the bombardment of Fort Jackson on the 18th, and continued it without intermission until the squadron made preparations to move.

"The squadron was formed in three lines to pass the forts. Captain Bailey's division, composed of the following vessels, leading to the attack of Fort St. Philip : Cayuga, Pensacola, Mississippi, Oneida, Varuna, Katahdin. Kineo, Wissahickon ; Flag-Officer Farragut leading the following, (second line:) Hartford, Brooklyn, Richmond ; and Commander Bell leading the third division, composed of the following vessels : Scioto, Iroquois, Pinola, Winona, Itasca, and Kennebec.

"The steamers belonging to the mortar flotilla, one of them towing the Portsmouth, were to enfilade the water-battery commanding the approaches. Mortar-steamers Harriet Lane, Westfield, Owasco, Clifton, and Marine — the Jackson towing the Portsmouth.

"The vessels were rather late in getting under way and into line, and did not get fairly started until half-past three A. M., and the unusual bustle apprised the garrison that something was going on.

"In an hour and ten minutes after the vessels had weighed anchor they had passed the forts under a most terrific fire, which they returned with interest.

"The mortar-fleet rained down shells on Fort Jackson, to try and keep the men from the guns, whilst the steamers of the mortar-fleet poured in shrapnel upon the water-battery commanding the approach, at a short distance, keeping them comparatively quiet.

"When the last vessel of ours could be seen among the fire and smoke to pass the battery, signal was made to the mortars to cease firing, and the flotilla steamers were directed to retire from a contest that would soon become un-equal.

"It was now daylight, and the fleet having passed along, the forts began to pay their attention to our little squadron of steamers, the Portsmouth, which was being towed up, and three of the gunboats which failed to pass through. These latter became entangled in some wrecks and chains placed in the river to obstruct, and which were only partially re-moved. One of these vessels (the Winona) got through as far as Fort St. Philip, but having all the guns bearing on her she sensibly retired. The Itasca was fairly riddled, and had a shot through her boiler, and the Kennebec escaped unhurt.

"I am disposed to think that our squadron received but little damage, considering the unequal contest — one hundred and forty-two guns on board ship opposed to one hundred on shore, placed in a most commanding position. For twenty minutes after the ships passed, the forts fired very feebly on the vessels that remained outside ; so much so, that the Ports-mouth was enabled to drop with the current out of gun-shot, though the shot fell pretty freely about her at last. I think the fire from the ships must have been very destructive of life.

"The last we saw of our vessels, they were standing up the river. Some explosion took place, which made us feel rather uneasy, but which may have been the rebel gunboats. We could see that our squadron had not destroyed all the enemy's vessels at the fort, for three or four of them were moving about in all direc-tions, evidently in a state of excitement.

"Before the fleet got out of sight it was reported to me that the celebrated ram Manas-sas was coming out to attack us ; and sure enough there she was, apparently steaming along shore, ready to pounce upon the appar-ently defenceless mortar-vessels. Two of our steamers and some of the mortar-vessels opened fire on her, but I soon discovered that the Manassas could harm no one again, and I ordered the vessels to save their shot. She was beginning to emit smoke from her ports or holes, and was discovered to be on fire and sinking. Her pipes were all twisted and riddled with shot, and her hull was also well cut up. She had evidently been used up by the squad-ron as they passed along. I tried to save her as a curiosity, by getting a hawser around her and securing her to the bank, but just after doing so she faintly exploded. Her only gun went off, and emitting flames through her bow port, like some huge animal, she gave a plunge and disappeared under the water.

"Next came a steamer on fire, which ap-peared to be a vessel of war belonging to the rebels, and after her two others, all burning and floating down the stream. Fires seemed to be raging all along the " up river," and we supposed that our squadron were burning and destroying the vessels as they passed along. It appears, however, that the McRae, one or two river boats, and their celebrated floating battery, (brought down the night before,) were left unhurt, and were still flying the confederate flag.

" The matter of the floating battery becomes a very serious affair, as they are all hard at work at Fort Jackson mounting heavy rifled guns on it, which are no farther use to them in the fort. She mounts sixteen guns, is almost as formidable a vessel as the Merrimac, perfectly shot-proof, and has four powerful engines in her. I shall at all events take such steps as will prevent her from destroying any thing, and we may still hold her in check with the steamers, though they are rather fragile for such a service. This is one of the ill effects of leaving an enemy in the rear. I suppose that the ships fired on her as they passed through, but that her mail resisted the shot. She had steam on this morning, and was moving about quite lively. I tried to put some mortar-shell through her roof, but without effect, as she moved off.

" The forts are now cut off from all communication with New Orleans, as I presume that Flag-Officer Farragut has cut the wires.

" I have sent the Miami round with General Butler to the back of Fort St. Philip, to try and throw in troops at the quarantine, five miles along the forts, and at the same time open communication that way with the Flag-Officer, and supply him with ammunition.

" I am also going to send part of the mortar-fleet to the back of Fort Jackson, to cut off the escape of the garrison by that way, and stop supplies. A deserter, who can be relied on, informs us that they have plenty of provisions for two months, plenty of ammunition, and plenty of discomforts. Our shell set the citadel

on fire the first afternoon we opened. It burned fiercely for seven hours, but I thought it a fire-raft behind the fort, as they continually send them down on us, but without any effect.

" But few casualties occurred to vessels on this side of the forts. The Harriet Lane lost but one man killed, and one, I fear, mortally wounded; the Winona lost three killed and three wounded ; and the Itasca, with fourteen shot through her, had but few men hurt.

" These forts can hold out still for some time ; and I would suggest that the Monitor and Mystic, if they can be spared, be sent here without a moment's delay, to settle the question.

" The mortar-fleet have been very much exposed, and under a heavy fire for six days, during which time they kept the shells going without intermission. One of them, the Maria I. Carlton, was suuk by a shot passing down through her magazine, and then through her bottom.

" The flotilla lost but one man killed and six wounded. The bearing of the officers and men was worthy of the highest praise. They never once flagged during a period of six days ; never had an accident to one of the vessels by firing, and when shell and shot were flying thick above them showed not the least desire to have the vessels moved to a place of safety. The incidents of the bombardment will be mentioned in my detailed report. I merely write this hurried letter to apprise the Department of the state of affairs, and shall send it off at once via Havana.

" The sight of this night attack was awfully grand. The river was lit up with rafts filled with pine knots, and the ships seemed to be fighting literally amidst flames and smoke. Where we were the fire of the enemy was high, and comparatively harmless.

" I am in hopes that the ships above fared as well as we did. Though amid such a terrific fire, it was gratifying to see that not a ship wavered, but stood steady on her course ; and

I am in hopes (and I see no reason to doubt it) that they now have possession of New Orleans.

"I am, with great respect,

"Your obedient servant,

"DAVID D. PORTER,

"Commanding Flotilla.

"Hon. GIDEON WELLES, Secretary of Navy."

COMMODORE PORTER'S SECOND REPORT.

"U. S. SHIP HARRIET LANE, April 29, 1862.

"SIR : The morning after the ships passed the forts, I sent a demand to Colonel Higgins for a surrender of the forts, which was declined. On the 27th I sent Lieutenant-Colonel Higgins a communication, herewith enclosed, asking again for the surrender. His answer is enclosed. On the 28th I received a communication from him, stating that he would surrender the forts, and I came up and took possession, drew up articles of capitulation, and hoisted the American flag over the forts.

"These men have defended these forts with a bravery worthy of a better cause. I treated them with all the consideration that circumstances would admit. The three steamers remaining were under the command of Commander J. K. Mitchell. The officer of the fort acknowledged no connection with them, and wished in no way to be considered responsible for their acts. While I had a flag of truce up they were employed in towing the iron floating battery of sixteen guns (a most formidable affair) to a place above the forts, and, while drawing up the articles of capitulation in the cabin of the Harriet Lane, it was reported to me that they had set fire to the battery and turned it adrift upon us. I asked the general if it had powder on board or guns loaded. He replied that he would not undertake to say what the navy officers would do ; he seemed to have a great contempt for them. I told him, ' we could stand the fire and blow up if he could,' and went on with the conference, after directing the officers to look out for their ships. While drifting down on us, the guns, getting heated, exploded, throwing the shot above the river. A few moments after, the battery exploded with a terrific noise, throwing fragments all over the river, and wounding one of their own men in Fort St. Philip, and immediately disappeared under water. Had she blown up near the vessels, she would have destroyed the whole of them.

"When I had finished taking possession of the forts, I got under way in the Harriet Lane and started for the steamers, one of which was still flying the confederate flag. I fired a shot over her and they surrendered. There was on board of them a number of naval officers and two companies of marine artillery. I made them surrender unconditionally, and for their infamous conduct in trying to blow us up while under a flag of truce, I conveyed them to close confinement as prisoners of war, and think they should be sent to the north, and kept in close confinement there until the war is over, or they should be tried for their infamous conduct. I have a great deal to do here, and will send you all papers when I am able to arrange them.

I turned over the forts to General Phelps. Fort Jackson is a perfect ruin. I am told that over eighteen hundred shells fell in and burst over the centre of the fort. The practice was beautiful. The next fort we go at we will settle sooner, as this has been hard to get at.

"The naval officers sunk one gunboat while the capitulation was going on, but I have one of the other steamers at work, and hope soon to have the other. I find that we are to be the hewers of wood and drawers of water ; but, as the soldiers have nothing here in the shape of motive power, we will do all we can.

"I should have demanded an unconditional surrender, but with such a force in your rear it was desirable to get possession of these forts as soon as possible. The officers turned over every thing in good order, except the walls and buildings, which are terribly shattered by the mortars.

"Very respectfully,   D. D. PORTER,
                    "*Commanding Flotilla.*
"Flag-Officer D. G. FARRAGUT."

REPORT OF CAPTAIN BAILEY.

"UNITED STATES GUNBOAT CAYUGA, ⎱
OFF NEW ORLEANS, *April 25*, 1862. ⎰

"FLAG-OFFICER: Your boldly conceived and splendidly executed plan of battle having resulted in perfect success, leaves me time to make up the report of my division.

"You will find in Lieutenant-Commanding Harrison's report an accurate outline of the noble part taken by the Cayuga, under his command, and bearing my division flag.

"We led off at two A. M., in accordance with your signal, and steered directly up stream, edging a little to starboard, in order to give room for your division. I was followed by the Pensacola in fine style, the remainder of my division following in regular and compact order. We were scarcely above the boom when we were discovered, and Jackson and St. Philip opened upon us. We could bring no gun to bear, but steered directly on. We were struck from stem to stern. At length we were close up with St. Philip, when we opened with grape and canister. Scarcely were we above the line of fire, when we found ourselves attacked by the rebel fleet of gunboats. This was hot, but more congenial work. Two large steamers now attempted to board at our starboard bow; the other astern; a third on our starboard beam. The eleven-inch Dahlgren being trained on this fellow, we fired at a range of thirty yards. The effect was very destructive. She immediately steered in shore, run aground, and sunk. The Parrott gun on the forecastle drove off the one on the bow, while we prepared to repel boarders, so close was our remaining enemy about this time. Boggs and Lee came dashing in, and made a finish of the rebel boats, eleven in all.

"In the gray of the morning we discovered a camp, with the rebel flag flying; opened with canister at five A. M.; received the sword and flag of Colonel Szymanski, and his command of fire companies, arms, and camp equipage.

"While engaged at this point, observed the Varuna in conflict with a number of gunboats. She had been butted by one of them and sunk, but, with his forward guns still above water, he was bravely maintaining the fight, driving off his enemies, and saving his crew. Informing Captain Lee, of the Oneida, who had also been engaged with the enemy, of the Varuna's situation, he instantly steamed up, and made a finish of the rebel boats.

"The remainder of the fleet now came up. The Mississippi had been detained below with the Manassas and another iron-clad. After this every thing passed under your observation.

"I must, in conclusion, express the pleasure which I experience in witnessing the seaman-like manner in which all the ships were handled. The reports of divisional captains will inform you of the particular part borne by each ship.

"Respectfully, your obedient servant,
                    "T. BAILEY,
    "*Captain Commanding Division of the Red.*
"To Flag-Officer D. G. FARRAGUT, *Commander-in-Chief, etc.*"

GENERAL REPORT OF CAPTAIN BAILEY.

"UNITED STATES GUNBOAT CAYUGA, ⎱
AT SEA, *May* 7, 1862. ⎰

"SIR: Having found it impossible to get the Colorado over the bars of the Mississippi, I sent up a large portion of her guns and crew, filling up deficiencies of both in the different vessels, and with my aid, Acting Midshipman Higginson, steward and boat's crew, followed up myself, hoisting, by authority of the Flag-Officer, my Red, distinguishing flag as second in command, first on the Oneida, Commander Lee, and afterwards on the Cayuga.

"That brave, resolute, and indefatigable officer, Commodore D. D. Porter, was at work with his mortar-fleet, throwing shells at and into Fort Jackson, while General Butler, with a division of his army, in transports, was waiting a favorable moment to land.

"After the mortar-fleet had been playing upon the forts for six days and nights, without perceptibly diminishing their fire, and one or two changes in programme, Flag-Officer Farragut formed the ships into two columns, 'line ahead,' — the column of the Red, under my orders, being formed on the right, and consisted of the Cayuga, Lieutenant-Commanding Harrison, bearing my flag, and leading the Pensacola, Captain Morris; the Mississippi, Commander M. Smith; Oneida, Commander S. P. Lee; Varuna, Commander C. L. Boggs; Katahdin, Lieutenant-Commanding Preble; Kineo, Lieutenant-Commanding Ransom, and the Wissahickon, Lieutenant-Commanding A. W. Smith.

"The column of the Blue was formed on the left, heading up the river, and consisted of the flag-ship Hartford, Commander R. Wainwright, and bearing the flag of the Commander-in-Chief Farragut; the Brooklyn, Captain T. T. Craven; the Richmond, Commander Alden; the Scioto, bearing the divisional flag of the fleet, Captain H. H. Bell, followed by the Iroquois, Itasca, Winona, and Kennebec.

"At two A. M., on the morning of the 24th, the signal 'to advance' was thrown out from the flag-ship. The Cayuga immediately weighed anchor and led on the column. We were discovered at the boom, and a little beyond both forts opened their fire. When close up with St. Philip, we opened with grape and canister, still steering on. After passing this line of fire, we encountered the 'Montgomery flotilla,' consisting of eighteen gunboats, including the ram Manassas, and iron battery Louisiana of twenty guns. This was a moment of anxiety, and no supporting ship was in sight. By skilful steering, however, we avoided their attempts to butt and board, and had succeeded in forcing the surrender of three, when the

Varuna, Captain Boggs, and Oneida, Captain Lee, were discovered near at hand. The gallant exploits of these ships will be made known by their commanders.

"At early dawn discovered a rebel camp on the right bank of the river. Ordering Lieutenant-Commanding N. B. Harrison to anchor close along, I hailed and ordered the colonel to pile up his arms on the river bank and come on board. This proved to be the Chalmetto regiment, commanded by Colonel Szymanski. The regimental flag, tents, and camp equipage were captured.

"On the morning of the 25th, still leading and considerably ahead of the line, the Chalmetto batteries, situated three miles below the city, opened a cross-fire on the Cayuga. To this we responded with our two guns. At the end of twenty minutes the flag-ship ranged up ahead, and silenced the enemy's guns.

"From this point no other obstacles were encountered except burning steamers, cotton ships, fire-rafts, and the like.

"Immediately after anchoring in front of the city, I was ordered on shore by the flag-officer to demand the surrender of the city, and that the flag should be hoisted on the Post Office, Custom House, and Mint. What passed at this interview will be better stated in the flag-officer's report.

"On the 26th I went with the flag-officer some seven miles above the city, where we found the defences abandoned, the guns spiked, and gun-carriages burning. These defences were erected to prevent the downward passage of Captain Foote. On the 27th a large boom, situated above these defences, was destroyed by Captain S. Phillips Lee.

"On the 28th General Butler landed above Fort St. Philip, under the guns of the Mississippi and Kineo. This landing of the army above, together with the passage of the fleet, appears to have put the finishing touch to the demoralization of their garrison (three hundred having mutinied in Fort Jackson). Both forts surrendered to Commodore Porter, who was near at hand with the vessels of his flotilla.

"As I left the river General Butler had garrisoned Forts Jackson and St. Philip, and his transports, with troops, were on the way to occupy New Orleans.

"I cannot too strongly express my admiration of the cool and able management of all the vessels of my line by their respective captains.

"After we had passed the forts it was a contest between iron hearts in wooden vessels and iron-clads with iron beaks, and the 'iron hearts' won.

"On the 29th the Cayuga, Lieutenant-Commanding Harrison, was selected to bring me home a bearer of despatches to the government.

"I have the honor to be, very respectfully,
"Your obedient servant,
"THEODORUS BAILEY, *Captain.*
"Hon. GIDEON WELLES, *Secretary of the Navy.*"

REPORT OF COMMANDER BOGGS.

"UNITED STATES STEAMER BROOKLYN, ?
OFF NEW ORLEANS, *April* 29, 1862. ?

"SIR: I have the honor to report that after passing the batteries with the steamer Varuna under my command, on the morning of the 24th, finding my vessel amid a nest of rebel steamers, I started ahead, delivering her fire, both starboard and port, at every one that she passed.

"The first vessel on her starboard beam that received her fire appeared to be crowded with troops. Her boiler was exploded, and she drifted to the shore. In like manner three other vessels, one of them a gunboat, were driven ashore in flames, and afterwards blew up.

"At six A. M. the Varuna was attacked by the Morgan, iron-clad about the bow, commanded by Beverly Kennon, an ex-naval officer. This vessel raked us along the port gangway, killing four and wounding nine of the crew, butting the Varuna on the quarter and again on the starboard side. I managed to get three eight-inch shell into her abaft her armor, as also several shot from the after rifled gun, when she dropped out of action partially disabled.

"While still engaged with her, another rebel steamer, iron-clad, with a prow under water, struck us in the port gangway, doing considerable damage. Our shot glanced from her bow. She backed off for another blow, and struck again in the same place, crushing in the side ; but by going ahead fast the concussion drew her bow around, and I was able, with the port guns, to give her, while close alongside, five eight-inch shells abaft her armor. This settled her, and drove her ashore in flames.

"Finding the Varuna sinking, I ran her into the bank, let go the anchor, and tied up to the trees.

"During all this time the guns were actively at work crippling the Morgan, which was making feeble efforts to get up steam. The fire was kept up until the water was over the gun-trucks, when I turned my attention to getting the wounded and crew out of the vessel. The Oneida, Captain Lee, seeing the condition of the Varuna, had rushed to her assistance, but I waved her on, and the Morgan surrendered to her, the vessel being in flames. I have since learned that over fifty of her crew were killed and wounded, and she was set on fire by her commander, who burnt his wounded with his vessel.

"I cannot award too much praise to the officers and crew of the Varuna for the noble manner in which they supported me, and their coolness under such exciting circumstances, particularly when extinguishing fire, having been set on fire twice during the action by shells.

"In fifteen minutes from the time the Varuna was struck she was on the bottom, with only her top-gallant forecastle out of water. The officers and crew lost every thing they possessed, no one thinking of leaving his station until driven thence by the water. I trust the attention of the department will be called to their loss, and compensation made to those who have lost their all.

"The crew were taken off by the different vessels of the fleet as fast as they arrived, and are now distributed through the squadron. The wounded have been sent to the Pensacola.

"I would particularly commend to the notice of the department Oscar Peck, second-class boy, and powder-boy of the after rifle, whose coolness and intrepidity attracted the attention of all hands. A fit reward for such services would be an appointment to the Naval School.

"The marines, although new recruits, more than maintained the reputation of that corps. Their galling fire cleared the Morgan's rifled gun, and prevented a repetition of her murderous fire. Four of the marines were wounded, one, I fear, mortally.

"So soon as the crew were saved, I reported to you in person, and within an hour left in the only remaining boat belonging to the Varuna, with your despatches for General Butler, returning with him yesterday afternoon

"Very respectfully,

"CHARLES BOGGS,

"*Commander U. S. Navy.*

"Flag-Officer DAVID G. FARRAGUT, *Commanding W. G. B. Squadron.*"

REPORT OF GENERAL BUTLER.

"HEADQUARTERS DEPARTMENT OF THE GULF, }
FORTS JACKSON AND PHILIP, *April* 29, 1862. }

"SIR: I have the honor to report that, in obedience to my instructions, I remained on the Mississippi River, with the troops named in my former despatch, awaiting the action of the fleet engaged in the bombardment of the Forts Jackson and St. Philip.

"Failing to reduce them after six days of incessant fire, Flag-Officer Farragut determined to attempt their passage with his whole fleet, except that part thereof under the immediate command of Captain Porter, known as the mortar-fleet.

"On the morning of the 24th instant the fleet got under way, and twelve vessels, including the four sloops of war, ran the gantlet of fire of the forts, and were safely above. Of the gallantry, courage, and conduct of this heroic action, unprecedented in naval warfare, considering the character of the works and the river, too much cannot be said. Of its casualties, and the details of its performance, the flag-officer will give an account to the proper department. I witnessed this daring exploit from a point about eight hundred yards from Fort Jackson, and unwittingly under its fire, and the sublimity of the scene can never be exceeded.

"The fleet pressed on up the river to New Orleans, leaving two gunboats to protect the quarantine station, five miles above.

"In case the forts were not reduced and a portion of the fleet got by them, it had been arranged between the flag-officer and myself that I should make a landing from the Gulf side, in the rear of the forts at the quarantine, and from thence attempt Fort St. Philip by storm and assault, while the bombardment was continued by the fleet.

"I immediately went to Sable Island with my transports, twelve miles in the rear of Fort St. Philip, the nearest point at which a sufficient depth of water could be found for them. Captain Porter put at my disposal the Miami, drawing seven and one half feet, being the lightest draught vessel in the fleet, to take the troops from the ship as far in as the water would allow. We were delayed twenty-four hours by her running ashore at Pass a l'Outre. The twenty-sixth regiment Massachusetts volunteers, Colonel Jones, were then put on board her, and carried within six miles of the fort, where she again grounded.

"Captain Everett, of the sixth Massachusetts battery, having very fully reconnoitred the waters and bayous in that vicinity, and foresee-ing the necessity, I had collected and brought with me some thirty boats, into which the troops were again transshipped, and conveyed by a most fatiguing and laborious row some four and a half miles farther, there being within one mile of the steamer only two and a half feet of water.

"A large portion of this passage was against a heavy current, through a bayou. At the entrance of Mameel's Canal, a mile and a half from the point of landing, rowing became im-possible, as well from the narrowness of the canal as the strength of the current, which ran like a mill-race. Through this the boats could only be impelled by dragging them singly, with the men up to their waists in water.

"It is due to this fine regiment, and to a portion of the fourth Wisconsin volunteers and twenty-first Indiana, who landed under this hardship without a murmur, that their labors should be made known to the department, as well as to account for the slowness of our operations.

"The enemy evidently considered this mode of attack impossible, as they had taken no measures to oppose it, which might very easily have been successfully done.

"We occupied at once both sides of the river, thus effectually cutting them off from all sup-plies, information, or succor, while we made our dispositions for the assault.

"Meantime Captain Porter had sent into the bayou, in the rear of Fort Jackson, two schoon-ers of his mortar-fleet, to prevent the escape of the enemy from the fort in that direction.

"In the hurry and darkness of the passage of the forts, the flag-officer had overlooked three of the enemy's gunboats and the iron-clad battery Louisiana, which were at anchor under the walls of the fort. Supposing that all the rebel boats had been destroyed, (and a dozen or more had been,) he passed on to the city, leaving these in his rear. The iron steam-

battery being very formidable, Captain Porter deemed it prudent to withdraw his mortar-fleet some miles below, where he could have room to manœuvre it if attacked by the iron monster, and the bombardment ceased.

"I had got Brigadier-General Phelps in the river below with two regiments to make demonstrations in that direction if it became possible.

"In the night of the 27th, learning that the fleet had got the city under its guns, I left Brigadier-General Williams in charge of the landing of the troops, and went up the river to the flag-ship to procure light draught transportation. That night the larger portion (about two hundred and fifty) of the garrison of Fort Jackson mutinied, spiked the guns bear-ing up the river, came up and surrendered themselves to my pickets, declaring that, as we had got in their rear, resistance was useless, and they would not be sacrificed. No bomb had been thrown at them for three days, nor had they fired a shot at us from either fort. They averred that they had been impressed, and would fight no longer.

"On the 28th the officers of Forts Jackson and St. Philip surrendered to Captain Porter, he having means of water transportation to them. While he was negotiating, however, with the officers of the forts under a white flag, the rebel naval officers put all their muni-tions of war on the Louisiana, set her on fire and adrift upon the Harriet Lane, but when opposite Fort St. Philip she blew up, killing one of their own men by the fragments which fell into that fort.

"I have taken possession of the forts, and find them substantially as defensible as before the bombardment — St. Philip precisely so, it being quite uninjured. They are fully provisioned, well supplied with ammunition, and the rav-ages of the shells have been defensibly repaired by the labors of the rebels. I will cause Lieu-tenant Wietzel, of the engineers, to make a

77

detailed report of their condition to the department.

" I have left the twenty-sixth regiment Massachusetts volunteers in garrison, and am now going up the river to occupy the city with my troops, and make further demonstrations in the rear of the enemy now at Corinth.

" The rebels have abandoned all their defensive works in and around New Orleans, including Forts Pike and Wood, on Lake Pontchartrain, and Fort Livingston from Barataria Bay. They have retired in the direction of Corinth, beyond Manchac Pass, and abandoned every thing up the river as far as Donaldsonville, some seventy miles beyond New Orleans.

" I propose to so far depart from the letter of my instructions as to endeavor to persuade the flag-officer to pass up the river as far as the mouth of Red River, if possible, so as to cut off their supplies, and make there a landing and a demonstration in their rear as a diversion in favor of General Buell, if a decisive battle is not fought before such movement is possible.

" Mobile is ours whenever we choose, and we can better wait.

" I find the city under the dominion of the mob. They have insulted our flag — torn it down with indignity. This outrage will be punished in such manner as in my judgment will caution both the perpetrators and abettors of the act, so that they shall fear the *stripes* if they do not reverence the *stars* of our banner.

" I send a marked copy of a New Orleans paper containing an applauding account of the outrage.

" Trusting my action may meet the approbation of the department,

" I am, most respectfully,
    " Your obedient servant,
        " BENJAMIN F. BUTLER,
        " *Major-General commanding.*
' Hon. E. M. STANTON, *Secretary of War.*"

CHAPTER LXXIII.

THE administration of affairs in New Orleans by General Butler, is one of the most remarkable passages in the history of the rebellion ; and his success, notwithstanding the difficulties with which he had to contend, stamped him as peculiarly adapted for the work assigned him. The difficulties of his position met him at the outset, and continued until he showed the rebellious, whether citizen or foreigner, that the government of the United States, through him as its representative, was their master.

The intense hatred entertained by the earnest secessionists and rebels towards the national government and the people of the north, can find scarcely a parallel in modern history, when its sudden growth and want of cause is considered. The manner and degree in which it has been demonstrated, since first aroused by the discovery that secession could not arrogantly and insolently triumph, has scarcely ever been equalled in malignancy by any people towards the most cruel enemy. Whether this be attributed to the warm passion of southern natures, or to the peculiarities of their social system and education, the fact of this bitter hatred, ever manifested in all possible ways, and in the most cruel or most insolent manner, according as circumstances might permit, cannot be denied. In New Orleans there was a sufficient number of secession leaders, bold and unscrupulous in their action, to carry the city and state into rebellion in spite of the probable Union majority. The first steps being taken, a large majority even of those who would have preferred the Union, accepted secession and the southern confederacy as accomplished facts, and became imbued to a greater or less extent with the feelings of bitter hostility which characterized the leaders of the rebellion. Those who still adhered to the Union were few, and necessarily undemonstrative. But the mob, the numbers of unscrupulous and depraved or of ignorant and unthinking men that can be found in a city like New Orleans, had been controlled and swayed by the violent rebels, and was, perhaps, at the time of the arrival of Commodore Farragut and General Butler, a fair illustration of the dominant sentiment of the city. It was insolent, malignant, and threatening in its manifestations of hatred to the national cause and its defenders; but it was cowardly, and needed only a firm and uncompromising exercise of power to hold it in subjection. General Butler knew well the nature of a mob, and the surest way of subduing it. He soon showed that he had the nerve to do as experience and reason taught him must be done, and he succeeded. Behind the mob were its instigators and supporters, and these were a more troublesome class; but General Butler, understanding men and the character of the rebellion, soon determined what course to take in relation to this class, and, in proportion as his work was permitted to stand, he succeeded here too. The mob and its instigators being disposed of, those who still adhered to the Union could declare themselves, and the majority of those who accepted accomplished facts might be found on the side of the national authority thus reëstablished with a firm hand.

As soon as the advance of his army was posted in New Orleans, General Butler prepared a proclamation to the people, setting forth the purposes of his occupation of the city, and the principles which would govern his administration of affairs as commander of the department. This proclamation was sent to the office of the *True Delta* newspaper to be put in print, but the proprietor refused to print it. It was not difficult, however, to find in any considerable body of northern troops men skilled in almost any branch of the mechanic arts, and after a short period a file of soldiers was sent to the printing office, and taking possession of the establishment, they soon had the document printed. In the mean time General Butler had taken possession of the deserted St. Charles Hotel, and established his headquarters there. He then sent for the mayor of the city to visit him. That officer at first refused, but being warned that such refusal would complicate matters, he deemed it expedient to comply with a demand which was so peremptory. Accordingly, with Mr. Soulé, formerly a United States senator and envoy to Spain, and with other friends, he went to the General's headquarters. While there, the mob assembled about the building in large numbers and under great excitement. A regiment of troops was on duty there, and cannon were planted so as to sweep the street. But the mob was greatly excited, and apparently mistook the quiet demeanor of the troops for fear or a lack of spirit, and the outcries and threats soon so increased that an assault from the mob seemed inevitable. General Butler being informed of this state of affairs, gave orders for the officer in command to open upon the mob with artillery, if it could not be restrained by the show of force. This order alarmed the mayor and his friends, and they addressed the excited populace from the building, and counselled them to retire. The addresses of the mayor and his friends, with the report that the advice would be enforced at the mouth of the cannon unless quietly complied with, had the desired effect.

This interview with the mayor did not result in any understanding by which the administration of municipal affairs should be continued. The city authorities were contumacious, but General Butler was not disposed to be trifled with, and soon gave them to understand that the government of the United States was supreme, that the city was under martial law, and that they must yield to his authority as representative of that government. But while he maintained the authority of the national government, he desired that the city authorities should exercise ordinary municipal functions for the quiet and health of the city. The proposition was finally accepted by the city council, who saw the uselessness of a refusal. It was soon discovered by them, as by all who came in contact with the general, that he was in earnest, — as much so as even the most determined of their own rebel leaders, — and that he was not to be trifled with. They did not, however, carry out the agreement with much vigor or good faith, so that many of the municipal duties which they should have performed were more promptly assumed and discharged by the military authorities. It was evident that they were so hostile to the Union that they preferred to obstruct rather than aid in the measures for the good order, health, and welfare of the city. The mayor especially manifested such a disposition, and, vacillating between submission and opposition to General Butler's orders and policy, as he was in his presence, or absent and under the influence of others, he at last so exasperated the general that the latter sent him to Fort Jackson, and appointed General Shepley, military commandant, to act in his place.

The proclamation was forthwith promulgated,* a provost marshal and provost judge

appointed, and stringent orders issued for the safety and good conduct of the troops and the peace and quiet of the city. As other troops

* The following were among the provisions of this proclamation : —

"All persons in arms against the United States are required to surrender themselves, with their arms, equipments, and munitions of war. The body known as the European Legion, not being understood to be in arms against the United States, but organized to protect the lives and property of the citizens, are invited to still coöperate with the forces of the United States to that end, and, so acting, will not be included in the terms of this order, but will report to these headquarters.

"All ensigns, flags, devices, tending to uphold any authority whatever, save the flags of the United States and those of foreign consulates, must not be exhibited, but suppressed. The American ensign, the emblem of the United States, must be treated with the utmost deference and respect by all persons, under pain of severe punishment.

"All persons well disposed towards the government of the United States, who shall renew the oath of allegiance, will receive a safeguard of protection to their persons and property from the army of the United States, and the violation of such safeguard will be punishable with death. All persons still holding allegiance to the confederate states will be deemed rebels against the government of the United States, and regarded and treated as enemies thereof. All foreigners, not naturalized, and claiming allegiance to their respective governments, and not having made oath of allegiance to the government of the confederate states, will be protected in their persons and property, as heretofore, under the laws of the United States. All persons who may have heretofore given adherence to the supposed government of the confederate states, or been in their service, who shall lay down or deliver up their arms, return to peaceful occupations, and preserve quiet and order, holding no farther correspondence, nor giving aid and comfort to enemies of the United States, will not be disturbed in their persons or property, except so far under the orders of the commanding general as the exigencies of the public service may render necessary."

"Sufficient force will be kept in the city to preserve order and maintain the laws. The killing of American soldiers by any disorderly person or mob, is simply assassination and murder, and not war, and will be so regarded and punished. The owner of any house in which such murder shall be committed will be held responsible therefor, and the house be liable to be destroyed by the military authority. All disorders, disturbances of the peace, and crimes of an aggravated nature, interfering with the forces or laws of the United States, will be referred to a military court for trial and punishment. Other misdemeanors will be subject to the municipal authority, if it desires to act."

"The circulation of confederate bonds, evidences of debt (except notes in the similitude of bank notes) issued by the confederate states, or scrip, or any trade in the same, is forbidden. It has been represented to the commanding general, by the civil authorities, that these confederate notes, in the form of bank notes, in a great measure, are the only substitutes for money which the people have been allowed to have, and that great distress would ensue among the poorer classes if the circulation of such notes should be suppressed. Such circulation, therefore, arrived, they were posted on the opposite side of the river, and in a camp above the city, only a comparatively small force remaining within the city, at the suggestion of some of the citizens, who alleged that the danger of collision would be increased by the presence of a large army. But a sufficient force was retained for the protection of headquarters and the public buildings, and any movement of mob or organized rebel force could speedily be met by the troops quartered outside of the city. The occupation of the city was thus thoroughly effected.

The vigorous measures adopted by General Butler, and the arrangement entered into for the administration of ordinary municipal affairs by

will be permitted so long as any one will be inconsiderate enough to receive them, until farther orders.

"No publication of newspapers, pamphlets, or handbills, giving accounts of the movements of the soldiers of the United States within this department, reflecting in any way upon the United States, intended in any way to influence the public mind against the United States, will be permitted, and all articles on war news, editorial comments, or correspondence making comments upon the movements of the armies of the United States, must be submitted to the examination of an officer, who will be detailed for that purpose from these headquarters. The transmission of all communications by telegraph will be under the charge of an officer detailed from these headquarters.

"The armies of the United States came here not to destroy, but to restore order out of chaos, to uphold the government and the laws in the place of the 'passage' of men. To this end, therefore, the efforts of all well-disposed are invited, to have every species of disorder quelled.

"If any soldier of the United States should so far forget his duty or his flag as to commit outrage upon any person or property, the commanding general requests his name to be instantly reported to the provost guard, so that he may be punished, and his wrongful act redressed. The municipal authority, so far as the police of the city and environs are concerned, is to extend as before indicated, until suspended.

"All assemblages of persons in the streets, either by day or night, tend to disaster, and are forbidden. The various companies composing the fire department of New Orleans will be permitted to retain their organizations, and are to report to the provost marshal, so that they may be known, and not interfered with in their duties.

"And, finally, it may be sufficient to add, without farther enumeration, that all the requirements of martial law will be imposed so long as, in the judgment of the United States authorities, it may be necessary; and while it is desired by these authorities to exercise this government mildly, and after the usages of the past, it must not be supposed that it will not be rigorously and firmly administered as the occasion calls for it."

the city government, promised to secure quiet to the city, and in a few days it was "as tranquil and peaceable as in the most quiet times." But the military authorities soon found that they had much to do besides the administration of martial law. The first thing that pressed upon their attention was the short supply of provisions, and the exorbitant prices (in confederate currency, the only one in use) at which they were held. The poor were unable to obtain sufficient food, the supply of which was rapidly diminished, with scarcely any accession. The trade of the city with the interior was entirely stopped, and the markets were cut off from their usual sources of supply. The suffering soon became very great, and demanded prompt and decisive action. General Butler at once took measures to relieve the necessities of the poor, and to secure, as far as possible, a supply of food for the markets, by granting permits and passes, under certain restrictions, for that purpose. These permits were but too frequently abused, by being used for conveying information and even supplies to the rebels. Even while the poor were starving, provisions were sent out of the city to the rebel army. On the other hand, to relieve the immediate wants of the poor, General Butler gave a thousand dollars from his private purse, and from the army supplies, which were as yet limited, distributed food to such extent as was expedient; the "invaders," as the northern army was termed by the rebels, thus proving themselves more charitable and generous than the wealthy citizens, whose means were freely given to aid rebellion, but were denied to the suffering poor of the city.

The means at the command of the general were, however, insufficient to meet the wants of the people, and the supplies brought in under permits were limited, while the permits were abused by faithless rebels. The city authorities neglected their duty in respect to making provision for the poor, and manifested a disposition to thwart rather than aid the measures adopted by the commanding general. In this state of affairs General Butler issued the following order, which showed his democratic sympathies and his thorough understanding of the character of the rebellion:—

"NEW ORLEANS, *May* 9, 1862.

"The deplorable state of destitution and hunger of the mechanics and working classes of this city has been brought to the knowledge of the commanding general.

"He has yielded to every suggestion made by the city government, and ordered every method of furnishing food to the people of New Orleans that government desired. No relief by those officials has yet been afforded. This hunger does not pinch the wealthy and influential, the leaders of the rebellion, who have gotten up this war, and are now endeavoring to prosecute it, without regard to the starving poor, the workingman, his wife, and child. Unmindful of their suffering fellow-citizens at home, they have caused or suffered provisions to be carried out of the city for confederate service since the occupation by the United States forces.

"Lafayette Square, their home of affluence, was made the depot of stores and munitions of war for the rebel armies, and not of provisions for their poor neighbors. Striking hands with the vile, the gambler, the idler, and the ruffian, they have destroyed the sugar and cotton which might have been exchanged for food for the industrious and good, and regrated the price of that which is left, by discrediting the very currency they had furnished, while they eloped with the specie ; as well that stolen from the United States, as from the banks, the property of the good people of New Orleans, thus leaving them to ruin and starvation.

"Fugitives from justice, many of them, and others, their associates, staying because too puerile and insignificant to be objects of punishment by the clement government of the United States.

"They have betrayed their country :

"They have been false to every trust:

"They have shown themselves incapable of defending the state they had seized upon, although they have forced every poor man's child into their service as soldiers for that purpose, while they made their sons and nephews officers:

"They cannot protect those whom they have ruined, but have left them to the mercies and assassinations of a chronic mob:

"They will not feed those whom they are starving:

"Mostly without property themselves, they have plundered, stolen, and destroyed the means of those who had property, leaving children penniless and old age hopeless.

"MEN OF LOUISIANA, WORKINGMEN, PROPERTY-HOLDERS, MERCHANTS, AND CITIZENS OF THE UNITED STATES, of whatever nation you may have had birth, how long will you uphold these flagrant wrongs, and, by inaction, suffer yourselves to be made the serfs of these leaders ?

"The United States have sent land and naval forces here to fight and subdue rebellious armies in array against her authority. We find, substantially, only fugitive masses, runaway property-burners, a whiskey-drinking mob, and starving citizens with their wives and children. It is our duty to call back the first, to punish the second, root out the third, feed and protect the last.

"Ready only for war, we had not prepared ourselves to feed the hungry and relieve the distressed with provisions. But to the extent possible, within the power of the commanding general, it shall be done.

"He has captured a quantity of beef and sugar intended for the rebels in the field. A thousand barrels of these stores will be distributed among the deserving poor of this city, from whom the rebels had plundered it; even although some of the food will go to supply the craving wants of the wives and children of those now herding at 'Camp Moore' and elsewhere, in arms against the United States.

"Captain John Clark, acting chief commissary of subsistence, will be charged with the execution of this order, and will give public notice of the place and manner of distribution, which will be arranged, as far as possible, so that the unworthy and dissolute will not share its benefits."

Later in the season General Butler issued another order for the relief of the poor, which was characteristic of his administration, and the justice of which can hardly be questioned. This was an order assessing certain parties who had subscribed a large sum for the defence of New Orleans against the national forces, or who had advised the planters not to send their cotton to the city. The order startled those whose names were borne upon the subscription roll, but by this time it was universally understood that the orders of the general were to be obeyed without question, and with a bad grace the parties assessed paid the tax, which yielded more than three hundred and forty thousand dollars for the benefit of the poor.

Another of the early measures of importance adopted by General Butler was the cleansing of the city, and the establishment of stringent sanitary regulations. When the troops first arrived in the city, they were greeted with prophecies of the ravages of the yellow fever, and it was confidently expected that this scourge of New Orleans would prevail to an alarming extent, and sweep away the northern soldiers more fearfully than the bloodiest battle. In their hearts the more bitter rebels hoped and prayed for this terrible ally, even though the inhabitants of the city should furnish the larger part of the victims. General Butler and his officers knew and appreciated the danger which threatened the unacclimated, and they knew, also, that the only way to meet and avert it was by wholesome and strict sanitary regula-

tions, and the removal of nuisances and causes of sickness, which had accumulated to an unusual extent. Prompt to act, and experienced in the more thorough sanitary systems of northern cities, they at once, before the fatal epidemic was likely to make its appearance, adopted measures to prevent its introduction and spread. A large number of men were employed in cleaning the streets and unoccupied lands, dredging canals, filling up pools, and removing all refuse matter which would occasion disease ; and all this in a far more thorough manner than had usually been the practice in New Orleans. These laborers were paid from the fund raised by the assessment upon the disloyal parties above named, which was thus most judiciously employed in preserving the health of the city and relieving the wants of the poor.

Besides taking these precautionary measures in the city, and requiring the strictest observance of the sanitary regulations, General Butler enforced a quarantine of all vessels arriving from infected ports, of such duration and under such regulations in all cases as should insure safety from disease. The enforcement of this quarantine, which applied only to vessels from ports where the yellow fever existed, occasioned not a little complaint, and numerous protests and claims for damages, in which charges of favoritism were freely made. These charges, however, were not well substantiated, and the wisdom of the measure was abundantly proved by the entire absence of the fatal disease from the city during the season when it was confidently expected and predicted that it would prevail to an alarming extent. Notwithstanding the complaints, the quarantine was strictly enforced, and the action of the commanding general was sustained by the government. The entire success of these sanitary measures elicited the encomiums of all who desired that the city should not be visited by the much dreaded scourge, and was acknowledged by those who had even hoped that the Union army might be swept away by the disease.

The energetic and thoroughly earnest administration of General Butler, in which he showed little leniency towards the aiders and abettors of rebellion, created a strong feeling among them against him. He was, indeed, met by this class upon his arrival with the fiercest maledictions, and some of his orders were of a nature to increase their hatred. This hostility, however, was entertained only by the bitter sympathizers with rebellion, for upon these only did the hand of martial law weigh heavily. Those disposed to be loyal soon discovered that the military power was exercised, for the most part, for their protection and welfare. Among those who at first manifested the greatest aversion and the most bitter hostility towards the officers and men of the federal army, were many of the women even among those who held a high social position. They indicated their feelings in the most insulting manner whenever and wherever they met a federal officer or soldier. The latter were under the strictest discipline required to avoid all manifestations of resentment, or any acts which should lead to disturbance, and they were consequently obliged to endure the insults and taunts with which the female rebels continually annoyed them and degraded themselves. But it was hardly in human nature to endure with patience these constant and ever-increasing insults from the inhabitants of a conquered city. Officers and men, while observing the strict discipline which was required of them, chafed under the insolence to which they were constantly subjected, and there was danger of resentment, collisions, street broils, and the rising of the mob which would have deluged the city with blood. It was necessary, if possible, to put a stop to such action on the part of those who, relying upon their sex for safety, wholly disregarded the general order which required respectful conduct on the part of the

inhabitants of the city towards the military; and when at length the thing was past endurance, General Butler issued an order * which had the desired effect, but which was wilfully misconstrued by the rebels, to arouse anew the spirit of hatred among the southern people, and to excite the indignation of foreign nations. The order was undoubtedly intended to carry with it a sting which should be felt by those at whom it was aimed, but it gave to the soldiery no license, and never was construed by officer or soldier as giving them a right to do more than show the contempt which such conduct merited, or to subject the guilty to the penalty awarded by the local laws to the class of persons in which they were thus comprehended. On the other hand it was only necessary for those rebellious women to abstain from their offensive practices, in order to avoid the danger which it was pretended they had reason to fear. The order had the effect to put an end to the more insolent and intolerable demonstrations on the part of the female rebels, without a single arrest, but it was used throughout the rebel states, and wherever the rebels found sympathy, to attach infamy to the name of General Butler. Results, however, proved the propriety of the order and the worthiness of the northern soldiers.

There were afterwards, however, several instances of peculiar and aggravated offence on the part of females which met with stern punishment. One of these was the case of a Mrs.

---

* The following is the order referred to : —

"HEADQUARTERS DEPARTMENT OF THE GULF, }
NEW ORLEANS, May 15, 1862. }

"GENERAL ORDER No. 28.

"As the officers and soldiers of the United States have been subject to repeated insults from the women (calling themselves ladies) of New Orleans, in return for the most scrupulous non-interference and courtesy on our part, it is ordered that hereafter when any female shall, by word, gesture, or movement, insult or show contempt for any officer or soldier of the United States, she shall be regarded and held liable to be treated as a woman of the town plying her avocation.

"By command of   MAJOR-GENERAL BUTLER.

"GEO. C. STRONG, A. A. G., *Chief of Staff.*"

Phillips, who had been previously sent from Washington within the rebel lines for treasonable sympathies and practices. On the occasion of the funeral of a brave young federal officer, Lieutenant DeKay, some of the rebellious residents of New Orleans were guilty of many of the grossest indecencies to outrage the feelings of the Union officers and men and to insult the memory of the deceased. Among others Mrs. Phillips made herself conspicuous in these improprieties and insults, and General Butler, in order to make an example which should produce a good effect, sent her to Ship Island, where she was confined, until released at the suggestion of the government. Several men who were engaged in the same insulting proceedings were punished in a similar manner. A prompt and stern exercise of the military power was important at this time, for the disasters to the federal arms in Virginia had excited the rebellious inhabitants of New Orleans with joy, and the belief that the days of federal occupation were numbered, and it was necessary to nip in the bud any demonstrations which would lead to greater troubles.

Another instance of the stern exercise of power, which occurred just previous to the issue of the order in relation to women, was the execution of Mumford, a person of dissolute character, who boasted himself the hero of the act of tearing down the Union flag from the Mint when raised thereon by Flag-Officer Farragut. The offence under the circumstances was of a serious nature, for it endangered the lives of all the inhabitants of the city, and it was a flagrant insult to the authority of the United States, which could not be tolerated without affording excuse for its repetition under still more aggravated circumstances. But the course of Mumford, in boasting of his act and his threats of repeating it, in defiance of the federal authority, as well as the distinction which was awarded him by the rebel sympathizers, called for prompt punishment. He was

arrested, tried, and condemned to death by a military tribunal, and though the penalty may seem severe for the offence, it must be remembered that this was war on the part of the offender and on the part of the military authorities, and that the safety of the army and of Union citizens, as well as the establishment of the authority of the government, required the sternest exercise of martial law. General Butler approved the sentence, and it was carried into execution. The execution struck terror into the hearts of many who were disposed to trifle with the federal power, and it is quite probable that in its general results it was the means of saving life, by repressing the mad spirit of rebellion and defiance which might have led to outbreaks and resistance.

This act, and others such as have been named above, made General Butler feared by the enemies of the government, and every where among them he was execrated, and his name branded with the most opprobrious epithets. But while he was charged with tyranny, cruelty, and bloodthirstiness, there is reason to believe that the approval of the sentence of death cost him a severe struggle, and it was acquiesced in because he saw no other course for him to pursue with fidelity to the cause in which he was so earnestly enlisted. It was well for New Orleans and the Union cause that in this and other cases he was not too tender. But his severity was not visited wholly upon the enemies of the Union, and General Butler proved by subsequent acts that he meted out the stern justice of martial law to those who offended against the stringent regulations which he established for the protection alike of friend and foe. At a time when searches were being made for concealed property of the rebel government, and for arms and supplies intended for the rebel army, several men were arrested, charged with making search without authority, and appropriating the property of the unfortunate parties whom they visited. The authorized searches were made under the most stringent regulations, and by trustworthy officers. These parties, who had been connected with the transports or with the army, for the sake of plunder undertook to visit and search certain dwelling houses, conducting themselves in a courteous manner, but appropriating, under the pretence of seizing in behalf of the United States, whatever valuable property they could remove. By means of the admirable detective police which had been established by the provost marshal these plunderers were discovered, and after a thorough examination by the commanding general, they were found guilty and sentenced to be hung. It is certain that in causing this sentence to be executed General Butler suffered intense mental agony, but he firmly adhered to what he considered his duty to the army, to the people of New Orleans, and to his country, and the unfortunate parties suffered the extreme penalty to which they were condemned. General Butler thus extorted, even from his enemies, the admission of his impartial justice, and the work of plunderers was effectually stopped.

On the other hand, there were many instances of mercy shown to those condemned for the violation of martial law. Several rebel soldiers, who were paroled prisoners, violated their parole, and organized for the purpose of passing the federal pickets and joining the rebel army again. The punishment for such an offence is usually death, and these prisoners having been detected in their designs and tried by a military commission, were condemned to suffer that penalty. The sentence was approved by the commanding general, but there were numerous intercessions from Union citizens and his own officers in behalf of the unfortunate men, who were the dupes of others, and he reprieved them and sent them to Ship Island. So in a conspiracy against his own life, the proof of which was sufficient to lead to the arrest of several infamous persons, the general, content with frustrating their scheme, required only that they should leave the city.

General Butler's administration was certainly stern and uncompromising towards the rebels, and all who sympathized with them, and his experience and observation taught him that the life of the rebellion was in the aristocracy based upon slavery and wealth. His democratic sympathies led him to protect and favor the poor, while he sought to punish and humble the proud and rebellious aristocrat. For this he had many opportunities, which were improved by himself and his subordinates, from furnishing food and remunerative employment, to the protection of the poor tenant from the extortion and wrong of the landlord, or of the unfortunate slave from the cruelty of master or mistress.

One of the greatest and most annoying difficulties with which General Butler was obliged to contend was the action of the foreign consuls, who, from the first arrival of the federal forces, omitted no opportunity to interfere with and oppose the orders issued by the commanding general. There was a large foreign population in New Orleans, of all classes, and nowhere in the United States have the foreign residents occupied so influential a position. Some of these were naturalized citizens of the United States; others had been long residents in the city, but had not been naturalized, though their interests were wholly identified with their place of residence; and still others were more recent comers, who were not yet entitled to the privileges of citizenship. A large proportion of this foreign population sympathized with the rebellion; many had enlisted in the rebel army, and the wealthy had used their influence and contributed largely from their means to promote the rebel cause. The foreign consuls were no exception to the rule which seems to have governed the sympathies of their respective fellow-countrymen, but were in some instances among the ardent supporters of secession and the aiders and abettors of treason and rebellion.

The Prussian consul had raised a military force, and had entered the rebel service with it. Other consuls, while they had not taken so open and bold a step, had favored the rebel cause in more or less substantial ways; and when the city came to be occupied by the federal troops, they were not backward in manifesting their sympathies, under the plea of maintaining the rights of neutrals.

In the administration of martial law it was impossible that many orders for the safety of the city, or the maintenance of the federal authority, should not bear upon the resident foreigner as well as citizen. In a place like New Orleans, where a large number of the foreigners had shown their sympathy, or even identified themselves, with the rebel cause, it was natural and just that general orders aimed at rebels, covert and open, should apply to and reach them as well as the native traitor. But all such orders at once met the indignant protest of the foreign consuls, who demanded exemption from them for all who claimed to be subjects of their respective governments. And the number who claimed to be such subjects of foreign powers was very large, and embraced many who had, by all the means in their power, aided the rebellion. Men whose interests and social life had been for years identified with New Orleans; native-born members of foreign families, which had long ago taken up their abode in the city with no idea of returning to their country; men who had enjoyed the privileges of citizens, and held office in the state or city governments; such were those who claimed the protection of the consuls to screen them from a forfeiture of their rights or property on account of their complicity with treason and rebellion. The readiness of most of the consuls to take up the cause of these men, and the manner in which they entered their protests, proved that they too were in sympathy with traitors to the government to which they were accredited.

There were numerous orders and regulations to which the consuls objected, and had the objections been made for the purpose of protecting the rights of honest neutrals only, they would have been just and proper. But there were too many instances in which the consular interference was invoked and offered in behalf of the proved enemies of the United States government. A few of the cases may be cited, to show the obstacles with which General Butler had to contend, and the firmness with which he maintained the authority of his government.

The British Guard, a part of the European Brigade, which had been used to maintain order in the city just before the arrival of the federal troops, when that brigade was disbanded, voted to send their arms and equipments to General Beauregard, and carried the vote into effect. When this came to the knowledge of General Butler, he ordered the members of this company to leave New Orleans within twenty-four hours. The acting British consul interfered in a manner displeasing to the commanding general, and without effect. The violation of neutrality by this open aid to the enemies of the power now established in New Orleans could not be tolerated, and the order was enforced. All but two of the company left the city, and those two were promptly sent to Fort Jackson. The consul complained to the British minister, who presented the case to the government, and after some diplomatic correspondence, it was recommended to General Butler to release the two prisoners, which was done after a detention of several weeks.

The case of Charles Heidsieck, in which the French consul interfered, was disposed of with similar firmness on the part of General Butler, and leniency on the part of the government. This person, a native and subject of France, being in the southern states on business, had espoused the rebel cause, and after the occupation of New Orleans, was detected in carrying letters and despatches between the rebels in Mobile and New Orleans, disguised as a bar-tender on board of a boat carrying, by special permit, provisions from the former to the latter city. He was arrested as a spy and sent to Fort Jackson, and in due time would have been tried. The French consul, finding that he could not prevail against the determination of General Butler, presented the case to the government, through the French minister at Washington. After several months' imprisonment, during which the matter was the subject of diplomacy, Heidsieck was released by order of the government, upon his parole not to visit the rebel states. He demanded reparation for his confinement, but this insolent demand was not heeded. The leniency shown by the government in these and other cases was perhaps wise. The secretary of state was disposed to conciliate foreign powers, or at least to have no cause of quarrel with them while the rebellion continued, if possible to avoid it without humiliation. In this view the action of the government may have been politic, but its effect upon the rebels of New Orleans and their alien abettors was to render the task of the federal general much more difficult.

The action of General Butler which excited the greatest indignation among the foreign consuls, was the seizure of eight hundred thousand dollars in silver, in charge of the consul of the Netherlands; the manner of the seizure, and the force used against the consul's person, being the alleged chief cause of offence. General Butler had reason to believe, from evidence which had been placed in his possession, that this silver had been secretly removed from the Citizens' Bank to the Dutch consulate, to be used for the benefit of the rebel government in Europe, in fraud of the creditors of the bank, or as the actual property of that government, received for its treasury notes. He sent officers to demand its surrender until the case could be investigated and adjudicated. The consul pro-

tested, with great vehemence, against this violation of his consular rights and privileges; but the officers obeyed their orders, and after much trouble, and forcibly taking the key to the consular vault from his person, the silver was discovered, contained in a large number of boxes, marked " Hope & Co.," the style of a large banking house in Amsterdam. Other effects, unquestionably the property of the bank, were found, which could not have been honestly placed under the protection of the Dutch consul, and plates of " confederate " treasury notes were also discovered in the same safe-keeping. The property discovered, and all the circumstances connected with the discovery, afforded additional evidence of a fraudulent use of the consular flag, and justification of the seizure. The further investigations of General Butler proved that he was right. But the violation of the " rights " of the Dutch consul called forth a protest from the other consuls, in which they complained somewhat bitterly of the indignity and ill usage to which he had been subjected. To this General Butler made a characteristic reply, in which he justified the seizure upon the proofs in his possession, and gave the consuls to understand " that in order to be respected, the consul, his office, and the use of his flag, must each and all be respectable."

The seizure of the silver in the possession of the Dutch consul was followed by the sequestration of another large sum which had been deposited with the French consul, to be used for the payment, on the part of the rebel government, for certain clothing and munitions imported for it by a French house. A large quantity of sugar, which was with good reason supposed to be pledged to support the credit of the rebel government, was also seized, and three of the foreign consuls protested against the seizure, on the ground that the transactions in relation to these sugars were strictly mercantile. General Butler, however, had evidence besides the mere superficial statement and appearance of the affair, and held the sugar for further investigation. Various other seizures, of arms and other supplies, intended for the rebel government, or to be sold to it, or of other proceeds of cotton run through the blockade, in part on account of the rebel government, were made from time to time, and called forth complaints and protests from the foreign consuls, because the parties engaged in the transactions were subjects of foreign powers. But General Butler, brushing away mere outside appearances and pretences, looked at the purpose and result of such transactions, and finding these to be aid and comfort to the rebels, he determined to stop them if in his power. The enforcement of the confiscation act of Congress, in anticipation of the operation of which much property was transferred by the rebel residents of New Orleans to foreigners or loyal citizens, called forth further complaints from the consuls, as did also the quarantine regulations.

An order requiring that all citizens and foreign born persons who had resided in the country five years, and had claimed or received no "protection" from their government, should take the oath of allegiance to the United States before receiving any favor, protection, privilege, passport, or other benefit from the United States authorities (except protection from personal violence, which was extended to all), and requiring that foreigners, who had protections from their governments, before receiving like favors should take an oath not to give aid and comfort, directly or indirectly, to the enemies of the United States, was the cause of another joint protest on the part of the consuls. To this General Butler replied with caustic severity and sound argument; but he modified the oath required of all foreigners, by substituting one in form like that previously taken by all the officers of the foreign legion in support of the rebel government. Against that oath no protests had been made to the rebel authorities by

foreign consul or subject, although stronger and more direct than that one first required by General Butler; and when it was adopted by the latter, with the simple substitution of United States for " Confederate States," the outwitted consuls and their rebel friends were obliged to submit with what grace they were able. Similar difficulties arose upon a necessary order for disarming the people, which was enforced against citizen and foreigner alike, except where the parties were of undisputed loyalty.

These various subjects of complaint were duly referred by the consuls to the ministers of their respective governments at Washington, with such representations as should show the strongest possible case of aggression and wrong on the part of General Butler. The complaints were carried by the ministers to the government through the secretary of state, and voluminous correspondence followed. The government had not yet adopted a firm and decided policy with regard to the rebellion. Conciliation and leniency, which had been spurned by the rebels, and proven by experience to be unavailing, were not abandoned, even towards the most malignant rebel districts. Towards foreign powers, the relations with which were in the main conducted with great ability by Mr. Seward, there was a disposition to preserve the most friendly conduct, and to avoid the slightest cause of complaint. The wisdom of such a general policy with regard to foreign powers, in the existing condition of domestic affairs, can hardly be disputed, but that it was carried to the extreme limit consistent with national dignity, is also true. In the case of the consul of the Netherlands, after much correspondence, the course pursued by General Butler was virtually condemned, and the consul was requested to resume his functions. Other cases were disposed of in a similar spirit of conciliation and deference to the demands of the foreign ministers, and in addition to this a military governor of Louisiana was appointed, nominally, though not practically, to supersede General Butler in the administration of affairs, and Mr. Reverdy Johnson, of Maryland, prominent as one of the most " conservative" supporters of the government, was sent to New Orleans, as a special commissioner, to investigate the subjects of complaint, and to determine the various claims set up by resident foreigners.

Mr. Johnson, apparently acting under instructions from the state department, entered upon his duties with an evident disposition to conciliation and leniency. The cases brought before him were investigated without reference so much to the evidence in the possession of the military authorities as to the statements of the claimants, and general principles applied to the facts, as represented by the parties interested. Upon such statements of fact and general principles the decisions of the commissioner were correct, but the facts suppressed by the claimants, which controlled each particular case and showed the complicity of alleged neutrals with the rebels, do not appear to have been investigated or to have had much weight. Subsequent events proved, as in the case of the silver sequestrated while in the possession of the French consul, that the military authorities had good reason to doubt the neutrality of consuls and the parties whom they represented. The silver seized at the Dutch consulate, as well as that sequestrated while in the possession of the French consul, because there was good reason to believe that it was to be used for the benefit of the rebel government, was restored to the claimants. The sugar seized on the reasonable ground that it was to support the rebel credit abroad, was also delivered to the claimants. The proceeds of cotton exported in violation of the blockade, a part of which was for the direct aid of the rebellion, was given up on technical grounds. All these and similar decisions were made, not with the view of punishing traitors and crushing the rebellion, which was the stern purpose of General Butler, but for the purpose of removing all causes of complaint which might compromise the friendly relations with foreign powers, and perhaps of conciliating men who might possibly, by such a course, abandon their sympathies with the rebel cause. The result of Mr. Johnson's mission was not favorable to the Union cause, or to the strength of the military authority in New Orleans. The earlier decisions induced many, who had otherwise submitted to the decrees of martial law, to present their claims to Mr. Johnson, who, in many cases, decided in favor of the claimants, while others were reserved to be presented to the government at Washington.

The natural consequence of all this, without intention on the part of the government, was to weaken General Butler's authority and influence, and really to endanger the national cause in New Orleans. Rebels, and their foreign sympathizers and aiders, believing that the commanding general was not sustained by his government, were the more unwilling to submit to his orders and regulations, and the quicker to resent alleged violations of neutral rights, and to appeal from him to the government. With a man of less firmness and determination than General Butler the result might have been almost fatal to the national cause. But his earnestness was not dampened, nor the rigor of his measures abated, and in all matters where his military authority could not be disputed or appealed from, he maintained the power of the United States, and held rebels in subjection with an iron hand. Meanwhile the Union sentiment extended and grew stronger, and the general found that he was supported by a large number of loyal residents, who, in proportion to the strength of their loyalty, approved his measures.

Next to the foreign consuls, the banks were, perhaps, for a time the most troublesome parties with whom the national authorities had to deal. The currency had at the outset demanded the attention of General Butler. It was found in a deplorable condition. " Confederate " notes composing the principal part of it, and these depreciated to less than half their nominal value, while the smaller currency consisted of omnibus tickets and notes or checks issued by drinking-house keepers and other individuals, *ad libitum.* General Butler determined to put an end to the circulation of the " confederate " notes; but on the representations of Mr. Soulé and others, that there being no other sufficient currency the poor would be the greatest sufferers by such a measure, the temporary circulation of these notes was allowed. The banks had profited by the depreciation of the " confederate " notes, both before and after the occupation of the city by the federal forces, buying them at their depreciated value, and issuing them at par in the place of their own notes, which had almost entirely disappeared. All the specie of the banks, which had not been placed under the protection of foreign consuls, had been transferred to other places within the rebel lines, where it was seized by the rebel government, under the pretext of protecting it from falling into the hands of the federal forces. An attempt by the banks to recover it, under the promise of protection given by General Butler, failed, the rebel government refusing to restore it. The banks were, therefore, compelled to do business on the basis of this coin, which was beyond their reach, or to suspend operations entirely. Under the circumstances the former was the smaller evil, and the banks, with two or three exceptions, continued their business.

General Butler found that the temporary circulation of the "confederate" notes was operating more for the advantage of the rebel government and its sympathizers than for the relief of the people of New Orleans. So long as the notes of the rebel government were circulated, its authority was represented and respected, and it was no part of General Butler's policy to recognize or tolerate in any way the

rebel authority. He accordingly issued an order, prohibiting "all circulation of, or trade in, confederate notes or bills," on and after the 27th day of May, and declaring void all transfers of property, made after that date, in consideration of such notes or bills. The order produced great agitation among the bankers and others who were freely using the rebel currency; but they had come to know that the orders of General Butler would be enforced, and had not then learned that his government would not sustain him in all his measures. They immediately prepared to carry out the order, with such evasions as they could practice. They called upon all those who had deposited "confederate" notes to draw their money in these notes before the day prescribed, or the deposit would be at the risk of the depositor. This action of the banks caused as great an excitement among the traders and others as General Butler's order had among the bankers, and was designed to transfer, as much as possible, all losses or inconveniences from the banks to the merchants and traders. The effect was bad, and the conduct of the banks unjust and offensive. As soon as this was perceived, General Butler issued an order, which, after reciting the reprehensible course of banks, directed that no more "confederate" notes should be paid out to depositors or creditors, but that all such should be paid in current bills of the city banks, United States notes, or in gold and silver. The order also regulated the issue of bank notes, and was designed, generally, to restore a safe and convenient currency to the community, while it abolished the representation of rebel authority, and destroyed the baleful influence of rebel financiers. The order at once produced a good effect among the people, by increasing confidence in the national authority; and in its operation, in spite of the attempts to evade and thwart it, it proved a great benefit to the community. In all his orders and correspondence with contumacious bank officers in relation to the currency, General Butler manifested great promptness and knowledge of business and of human nature, as well as a firm and undeviating purpose to suppress rebellion and punish rebels.

Another order, which affected the banks as well as agents and officers of the rebel government, was one for the surrender of all property belonging to the rebel government. In some of the banks there were sums of money standing to the credit of the rebel government or its agents, which were declared now to belong to the United States; and though the bank which acknowledged the largest deposits of this kind endeavored to evade the full force of the order, it was enforced like all others, and General Butler thus secured a considerable sum for the United States before it could be transferred beyond his reach.

Prompt and vigorous in action, as General Butler was, an uncompromising enemy of rebellion, and troubled with no tenderness towards his enemies and those of his country, it could hardly be expected that his administration would be conciliatory towards rebel sympathizers under his almost absolute control, or that it could be without fault in some of its various departments. It was, undoubtedly, sometimes exceedingly harsh and severe upon known or suspected rebels, and he resorted, perhaps, in some cases, to extreme measures. But his whole policy was directed to the maintenance of the national authority and the crushing of rebellion. He made the rebels fear and obey him, and so sternly was his administration felt by them, that by his acts, and those falsely ascribed to him, he seems to have inspired an almost universal hatred among the people of the rebel states, and secured an impotent proclamation of outlawry from the rebel president. While he showed little mercy to rebels, especially those of wealth and social position, he did much for the benefit of the masses of the people and the protection of those disposed to be loyal. By his prompt and vigorous measures he supplied food to the suffering people; he gave employment and support to the poor; he restored a sound currency; he secured good order and safety to life and property, such as the community had not for years enjoyed; he adopted a system of sanitary measures which preserved the city from pestilence, and will stand as an example for future years; he administered justice to the poor, not infrequently retribution to the oppressor or swindler, and he afforded protection to the oppressed, both bond and free. In many respects, by ability, education, and temperament, General Butler was peculiarly fitted to deal with the southern rebels, and the national cause was greatly indebted to him for its successful maintenance in New Orleans. But questions of policy, foreign and domestic, which it was thought could not be disposed of by the vigorous measures of General Butler, prevented the full effect even of his unquestioned acts, and led eventually to a change in the command of the department.

CHAPTER LXXIV.

As stated in a previous chapter,* after the battle of Shiloh, General Halleck assumed the

---

* Chapter LXX.

command of the combined armies of Generals Grant and Buell, and at once took the field. The army was reorganized to some extent, — Generals Grant and Buell retaining command of their respective forces, — and, reënforced by the division of General Pope, which arrived from New Madrid, and added about twenty-five thousand men to the federal forces. With this and other unimportant reënforcements, the army of General Halleck numbered about one hundred and eight thousand men. It was near the end of April before the preparations were completed for an advance, and then it was commenced with certainty, but with great deliberation and caution. Day by day some slight progress was made by the advance of a division a few miles, and the extension of outposts. Bridges, which had been destroyed by the rebels, were rebuilt; old roads were repaired and new constructed, and numerous obstructions were removed, so as to render the movement of artillery and the transportation of subsistence more sure and easy. In the mean time expeditions were sent out to reconnoitre, and to sever the enemy's communications when possible. Occasional skirmishes took place between these parties and the rebel forces, whose presence in all directions indicated a large rebel force at Corinth and in its vicinity, and an activity which was likely to result in severe battle.

The rebel position at Corinth was a strong one for defence, as well as on account of railroad communication, the Memphis and Charleston railroad running through it from east to west, and the Mobile and Ohio railroad from north to south. The fortifications extended nearly fifteen miles, strong batteries being constructed at points commanding every road and all possible approaches. A sluggish stream flowed along their whole front through a ravine much below the works, and between this and the fortifications a dense timber was cut down at all accessible points, so as to form an abatis impassable for cavalry or artillery.

The rebel force was increased after the battle of Shiloh by troops from New Orleans and Pensacola, when those places were occupied by the federal forces, and by others called out by the governor of Mississippi, so that the army under Beauregard was supposed to be fully equal in numbers to that under General Halleck. The strength of their position and fortifications would enable the rebels to repulse a much larger attacking army, and they were encouraged by their leaders to believe that in the impending battle they would utterly defeat the federal forces, and drive them back, at least, into Tennessee.

The country between the rebel position and the Tennessee, through which the federal army advanced, is broken into long ridges and hills, with numerous valleys more or less abrupt, and swampy bottoms, and much of it was covered with a dense forest, which had been felled in many places, to form obstructions to the advance of the army. The movement of the army over this ground was difficult and necessarily slow, and the caution with which the commanding general advanced, keeping his forces well together, and throwing up breastworks at each halting-place, rendered the progress still more slow. On the 3d of May the main body of the army was within eight miles of Corinth, but from this point the advance was made even more slowly and with still greater caution. Movements were now made with the view of cutting off the retreat of the rebels, by destroying their railroad communications, and then by drawing in the federal lines more closely about them, practically to besiege them in their fortifications, and, by a vigorous attack, compel a surrender. These movements were made from the right wing, now commanded by General Thomas, and from the left wing, commanded by General Pope, who occupied the most advanced position in the federal lines.

The most important of these preliminary operations was a reconnoissance to Farming-

ton, about five miles east of Corinth, by a portion of General Pope's command, and at the
same time an expedition to the Charleston and
Memphis railroad, for the destruction of bridges
and interruption of communications. The force
sent by General Pope to Farmington discovered
the rebels to the number of four or five thousand, posted there in a strong position, and
manifesting at first a determination to resist
the advance of the federal troops. After sharp
skirmishing through woods and swamps with
the enemy's pickets, a heavy fire of artillery
was opened upon the main body of his forces,
and they were soon driven away. The federal
force took possession of the village and the
positions previously occupied by the rebels,
having gained a decided advantage with but
small loss, while the loss of the enemy, though
not large, was comparatively much greater.
In the mean time the expedition sent farther
south to the railroad had destroyed two bridges,
and otherwise interrupted communication.

The reconnoissances from the federal army
indicated a determination on the part of the
rebels to resist, at every point, the farther advance of the federal army, and a few days after
the occupation of Farmington, on the 9th of
May, they assumed the offensive, by attacking,
in strong force, the federal brigade which had
been advanced a little beyond that place, and
was separated from the remainder of the division
by a creek. From the rebel accounts it appears that the intention was to flank General
Pope's forces, and by getting a large force in
his rear while the attack was made in front, to
capture the greater part of his troops posted in
the vicinity of Farmington. This purpose, however, if contemplated, utterly failed of accomplishment. The federal brigade, which was in
the advance, maintained its position for several
hours, though the conflict was, for much of that
time, scarcely more than a skirmish. When
it began to be pressed by evidently superior
numbers, and General Pope found that he could

not sustain it except by crossing the creek with
his whole force, the brigade was ordered to retire, and to fall back to the main position of
the division a short distance east of Farmington. To have crossed the creek with his whole
force might have brought on a general engagement, which was contrary to the desire and
orders of General Halleck. The loss of the
federal force in this affair was about one hundred and fifty in killed, wounded, and missing, and the loss of the enemy was about the
same. The rebels occupied their former position at Farmington for a few days, as a result
of their not very decided success, and may
have gained some knowledge of the strength
and position of General Pope's command; but
the advantage was not very encouraging, and
they soon abandoned Farmington, and the
federal line was again advanced.

The enemy probably discovered by this
movement that General Halleck's army was so
disposed as to prevent a successful flank attack,
and he may have learned also that its slow
progress was not to be attributed to timidity,
as in their inflated addresses to their soldiers
the rebel leaders declared, so much as to the
caution of a general who was determined to
achieve success by the application of military
science to all his plans and movements. The
federal army had been advanced but a few miles
at a time, and then along its whole front breastworks or redoubts of timber and earth were
constructed, as a protection against an attack
by the enemy before a farther advance, and as
a line of safety in case of a reverse on a more
advanced field. Every thing that was necessary
to facilitate the movement of artillery and supplies was attended to at each stage of progress,
and the heavy guns, as well as the light batteries, were every where in available position
for offensive or defensive purposes.

Whether the character of General Halleck's
movements were fully known or not to the
rebel generals, it appears that soon after the

movement at Farmington, while they continued to strengthen their position by fortifications, and to encourage their men by grandiloquent promises of a speedy victory, they must have contemplated, if not made preparations for, a withdrawal from Corinth, by the removal of supplies and ammunition. By the 21st of May the federal lines had advanced to within three miles of Corinth, and the skirmishing of pickets became almost constant along the whole front, and was continued up to the time of the final advance, showing that the enemy was prepared for an attack, and ready to resist at all points. This condition of affairs continued a week, while General Halleck was deliberately making his dispositions for a final advance, and so perfecting his plans and getting his forces in hand that success might be insured. Before making his final advance and attack, General Halleck despatched a cavalry force to destroy the railroad leading south from Corinth, the travel upon which had not yet been interrupted. This force proceeded to Booneville, about twenty-four miles south of Corinth, where a large amount of stores, arms, and ammunition was found and destroyed, a considerable number of sick rebel soldiers were paroled, and railroad communication was temporarily interrupted by the destruction of engines, cars, and depot, and the removal of rails.

While this cavalry force was absent, and before it had accomplished its work, on the 28th of May, three strong reconnoitring columns were advanced by General Halleck from the right, centre, and left of his lines, to feel of the enemy and unmask his batteries. The country was here very thickly wooded, and the federal forces advanced slowly, as it were feeling their way. The rebel pickets resisted the advance at all points, and sharp skirmishing ensued, especially on the left of the federal line. The result was an advance of the federal forces with their artillery to positions from which fire could be opened the next morning upon the rebel intrenchments, the position of which had been ascertained. The movements were made with the same caution and care as before; the enemy's pickets being driven back, the advance parties constructed works on which the siege and field guns were mounted, the supports were brought up, and assaulting parties were organized. These preparations were not completed till the 29th, and they were opposed not only by the pickets and advanced force of the enemy, but by a heavy fire from the rebel batteries. This opposition was kept up with much vigor by the rebels until nine o'clock on the morning of the 29th, when their musketry firing almost entirely ceased, though a gradually diminished fire from their batteries was kept up till the close of that day. During the succeeding night a number of heavy explosions were heard in the enemy's works, which were supposed to be the destruction of his magazines. In the latter part of the night several buildings in the village of Corinth were discovered to be in flames by those in the front of the federal lines, and it was correctly surmised that the rebels were evacuating their position.

On the morning of the 30th of May it was apparent that there was no force to resist the federal advance, for which preparations were made at an early hour. Some of the federal officers, seeing that there was no enemy in front, and impatient to discover his movement, rode forward in advance of the troops, and passing through his strong and well constructed works without meeting any rebels, entered the town at half past six o'clock. Here they discovered that the enemy had indeed gone, and had destroyed vast quantities of supplies and ammunition which he was unable to remove. One large storehouse of provisions remained undamaged, but much larger quantities had been destroyed, while others had, without doubt, been removed. An examination of the rebel works showed that they had succeeded in removing all their ordnance, and what ammunition had been left was mostly in a damaged and useless condition. That the work of evacuation had been completed in haste was evident, but it was also certain that the movement had been going on for several days, and preparations for it had probably commenced more than a week previous. As in all such movements, the final operations were effected amid much confusion, causing a serious loss of material, and a demoralization of men scarcely better than a defeat in the field.

The following despatches of General Halleck, announcing the final movements of the army and their result, show how unexpected to him was the evacuation:—

"Headquarters Department of Mississippi,
Camp on Corinth Road, May 28, 1862.

"Three strong reconnoitring columns advanced this morning on the right, centre, and left, to feel the enemy and unmask his batteries. The enemy hotly contested his ground at each point, but was driven back with considerable loss. The column on the left encountered the strongest opposition. Our loss was twenty-five killed and wounded. The enemy left thirty dead on the field. The losses at other points are not yet ascertained. Some five or six officers and a number of privates were captured. The fighting will probably be renewed to-morrow morning at daybreak. The whole country is so thickly wooded that we are compelled to feel our way.

"H. W. Halleck, *Major-General.*
"Hon. E. M. Stanton, *Secretary of War.*"

"Near Corinth, May 30, 1862.

"General Pope's heavy batteries opened upon the enemy's intrenchments yesterday, about ten A. M., and soon drove the rebels from their advanced battery.

"Major-General Sherman established another battery yesterday afternoon within one thousand yards of their works, and skirmishing parties advanced at daybreak this morning.

"Three of our divisions are already in the

enemy's advanced works, about three quarters of a mile from Corinth, which is in flames.

"The enemy has fallen back of the Mobile railroad.

"H. W. Halleck, *Major-General.*
"Hon. E. M. Stanton, *Secretary of War.*"

"Near Corinth. May 30, 1862.

"Our advanced guard are in Corinth. There are conflicting accounts as to the enemy's movements. They are believed to be in strong force on our left flank, some four or five miles south of Corinth, near the Mobile and Ohio railroad.

"H. W. Halleck, *Major-General.*
"Hon. E. M. Stanton, *Secretary of War.*"

"Headquarters Camp near Corinth, May 30, 1862.

"The enemy's position and works in front of Corinth were unexpectedly strong. He cannot occupy a stronger position in his flight.

"This morning he destroyed an immense amount of public and private property, stores, provisions, wagons, tents, &c.

"For miles out of town the roads are filled with arms, haversacks, &c., thrown away by his flying troops.

"A large number of prisoners and deserters have been captured, and are estimated by General Pope at two thousand.

"General Beauregard evidently distrusts his army, or he would have defended so strong a position. His troops are generally much discouraged and demoralized. In all their engagements for the last few days their resistance has been weak.

"H. W. Halleck, *Major-General.*
"Hon. E. M. Stanton, *Secretary of War.*"

The advance of General Pope's forces entered the town shortly before seven o'clock, just as the last of the rebel cavalry, detailed for some work of destruction, galloped out on the other side. One company of cavalry, General Pope's escort, pushed after the retreating rebels, and had a brisk skirmish, in which several were killed and captured; but a few miles out, further pursuit was stopped by the burning of a bridge over a swampy creek, which it was difficult to cross otherwise. There seems to have been some unexplained delay in sending forward a sufficient force of cavalry and light artillery in pursuit of the retreating rebels. As other bodies of the federal army were advanced, however, a considerable number of stragglers were captured in the woods and along the roads, many of them having been on picket duty, and not informed of the proposed evacuation. Later in the day, a brigade of cavalry and a battery of artillery, under General Granger, were sent out by General Pope from Farmington, to pursue the enemy and to annoy and cut off his rear guard. This force, just at night, came up with the rebel rear guard at Tuscumbia Creek, eight miles south of Corinth, and on the following day drove them from their position. The pursuit was afterwards resumed, and near Booneville, the advance of General Granger's force came in sight of the rebels, and pursued them closely to within one mile of that town. This was two days after the cavalry force sent by General Halleck to cut the railroad had visited this place, as previously mentioned. That force had reached Booneville before the main body of the rebel army, and its operations had created great alarm among the rebels, and had so disconcerted their generals that a part of their army was moved in another direction. General Granger's whole force having come up, he entered Booneville, and thence pursued the rebel forces on several roads, skirmishing sharply most of the day, and capturing a few prisoners. The pursuit was continued, though not very sharply, till the 10th of June, when it terminated in the occupation of Baldwin and Guntown, the rebels having been driven from two or three positions, where they had made a show of resistance. The pursuit resulted in the capture of not a very large number of prisoners, but revealed the loss of supplies

and baggage, and a considerable number of small arms and equipments thrown away by the demoralized stragglers of the retreating army. The main body of the rebel army fell back to Tupelo, and the campaign in this section was ended for the season.

The following letter from General Granger, called forth by a statement of Beauregard, denying certain reports of the federal success which had been officially announced, gives a report of the operations of the cavalry force under his command: —

"HEADQUARTERS, CAVALRY DIVISION,
ARMY OF THE MISSISSIPPI, July 4, 1862.

"I have read, with mingled feelings of surprise and regret, a communication signed by G. T. Beauregard, addressed to the Mobile News of the 19th ultimo; surprise, that facts so patent, and so easily susceptible of proof, should be denied by him; and regret, that so weak, wicked, and unholy a cause as is this cursed rebellion should have rendered utterly false and unscrupulous a man whom, for fifteen years, I have always associated with all that was chivalric, high-minded, and honorable.

"The pursuit from Corinth I led with one brigade of my cavalry and a battery, leaving Farmington at noon on the 30th day of May. On the evening of the same day I came upon the rear guard of the enemy, whom I found strongly posted in the bottom of Tuscumbia Creek, eight miles south of Corinth. The next day this rear guard was driven out, and on Sunday, the 1st June, the pursuit recommenced. We passed Rienzi only two hours behind the retreating army, and found the bridges between Rienzi and Booneville so recently fired that the timbers were nearly all saved. My advanced guard came up with the enemy late in the afternoon of the 1st June, about four miles from Booneville, and chased them within one mile of the town, when it was halted by my order, on account of the lateness of the hour. At five o'clock on the morning of the 2d June I entered Booneville, and during all of that day my cavalry was constantly skirmishing with the enemy on every road leading southward and westward from Booneville to Twenty-mile Creek.

"On the next day I made a reconnoissance in force towards Baldwin, driving the enemy across Twenty-mile Creek; and on the 4th another reconnoissance was made by Colonel Elliott, via Blackland, with similar results. On the 10th, Baldwin and Guntown were occupied by my troops, which was as far as the pursuit has been carried.

"Booneville is twenty-four miles by the railroad from Corinth, and Twenty-mile Creek is eleven miles farther. By the highway the distance from Corinth to Twenty-mile Creek is reckoned by the inhabitants at thirty-nine miles.

"The facts of the 'farmer's story' are these. I met at Rienzi, on Sunday, the 1st June, the citizen whose house Beauregard occupied while there, and his statement to me was that Beauregard was much excited and utterly surprised at the explosion of the ordnance in the burning cars, fired by Colonel Elliott at Booneville, that he pronounced it to be at Corinth, and that he violently swore at a report that reached him, that the explosions were at Booneville. That he sent all over town to ascertain the author of the rumor, and while engaged in this search a messenger arrived direct from Booneville confirming the report that 'the Yankees were there.' Whereat, Beauregard altered his route and galloped away immediately, taking the roundabout way of Blackland to Baldwin. This statement was made in the presence of several officers, and was entirely voluntary and unasked for.

"Colonel Elliott arrived at Booneville on the 30th of May, at two o'clock A. M. He remained secreted in the woods east of the railroad until daylight, when he moved down upon the town, and was met by a body of about two hundred rebel cavalry, who incontinently fled at a volley from Captain Campbell's second Michigan revolving rifles. This was the only resistance Colonel Elliott encountered. He found in the town about eight hundred well soldiers and two thousand sick and convalescent; but none were inclined to oppose him. On the contrary, at least five hundred wished to go back with him as prisoners, but it was impossible for him to take them.

"The two thousand sick and convalescent found by Colonel Elliott were in the most shocking condition. The living and the putrid dead were lying side by side together, festering in the sun, on platforms, on the track, and on the ground, just where they had been driven off the cars by their inhuman and savage comrades. No surgeon, no nurses were attending them. They had had no water or food for one or two days, and a more horrible scene could scarcely be imagined.

"Colonel Elliott set his own men to removing them to places of safety, and they were all so removed before he set fire to the depot and cars, as can be proved by hundreds.

"General Beauregard states that the burning of two or more cars is not enough to make him frantic. The exact number of the cars destroyed by Colonel Elliott is as follows:—

"Five cars loaded with small arms.

"Five cars loaded with loose ammunition.

"Five ears loaded with fixed ammunition.

"Six cars loaded with officers' baggage.

"Five cars loaded with clothing, subsistence, stores, harness, saddles, &c.

"Making a total of twenty-six cars, besides three pieces of artillery and one locomotive.

"This, of course, does not include the depot and platform, which were filled with provisions and stores of every description.

"The nine men of Colonel Elliott's command taken prisoners were a party who had taken a hand-car and gone up the track a mile or two to destroy a water-tank. It is presumed they were surprised by some skulkers who were afraid to approach Booneville while Colonel Elliott was there.

"The charge of burning up five sick men in the depot and handing down Colonel Elliott's name to infamy, I must confess is only in character with General Beauregard's previous statements. He knows better. He knows it is false. The rebellion, in which he is a prominent leader, must have imbued him with more credulity than reason; a spirit of malicious exaggeration has taken the place of truth. To convict himself of inhumanity, treachery, and deception in almost every word, act, and deed, he has only to take the combined and concurrent testimony of thousands of his own subalterns and men, especially those who have fallen into our hands as prisoners and the large numbers who have deserted his sinking cause.

"G. GRANGER, *Brigadier-General.*
"Hon. E. M. STANTON, *Secretary of War.*"

The result of the movement against the rebel army at Corinth hardly answered the hopes and expectations of the government and the country. It was hoped that with so large and well-appointed an army, and under a commander who was reported to be a master of military science, and was aided by generals of known ability and bravery, the rebel army might be wholly defeated, a large part of it captured, and the prestige of its general destroyed among his own followers. On the other hand, it was anticipated, or feared by many, that the slow and cautious movements of General Halleck would result in finding the enemy gone when the time for the final attack should come. The latter were not wrong in their conjectures. The slowness but certainty with which the federal army advanced, and the completeness of all its movements, seem to have convinced the rebel leaders that its final success would be certain, and at the same time afforded them opportunity to escape. So far as they were compelled to abandon a chosen position, im-

portant as a strategic point in that campaign, before the capture of Memphis, it was virtually a defeat to them and a gratifying success for the federal general. So far as the rebel army was demoralized by a hasty evacuation of a carefully and laboriously fortified position, a wholesale destruction of supplies, and a sudden retreat before the very presence of its opponents, and all in the face of the vainglorious orders and promises of its leaders, it was a ruinous defeat to the rebels and a great advantage to the Union cause. But notwithstanding these disadvantages, the rebel army had escaped with comparatively little loss, and could be used for other movements, while on the other hand the federal army could not make a farther advance until the Mississippi should be opened and its base of supplies changed. The balance of advantages was, however, decidedly on the side of the federal cause, and was so felt to be by the enemy.

When General Buell's army left Nashville, one division, under General O. M. Mitchell, moved in the direction of Murfreesboro' instead of towards the Tennessee River. The rebel troops which had retreated in this direction retired before the advance of General Mitchell's division, and went to join the forces of Beauregard at Corinth. Accordingly, there was no considerable body of troops to oppose the federal advance, and apparently a movement in this direction was not anticipated by the rebel leaders. General Mitchell was not slow in availing himself of this condition of affairs, and moved from Murfreesboro' on the 4th of April, towards Alabama, crossing the state line on the 8th, and reaching that night the vicinity of Huntsville, through which passes the Memphis and Charleston railroad, connecting the Mississippi with the east.

About ten miles from Huntsville the vanguard of the division bivouacked, awaiting the coming up of the artillery and main body of the infantry. Before morning the forces were concentrated and moved towards the town, fully prepared to attack any force which might resist their progress. A few miles from the town the shrill whistle of a locomotive announced the approach of a railroad train, which was promptly brought to a stand by one or two shots from the light artillery. Capturing the train and a number of prisoners, the forces moved rapidly forward to Huntsville, which they entered before the people had left their beds. The clatter of troops and rattle of artillery soon startled the residents from their slumbers, and great was their consternation when they learned that the federal forces had reached their town so far inland, and protected, as they supposed, by the strategic positions of the rebel troops. Any fears which they might have entertained of ill treatment and plunder by the federal soldiers were soon quieted by the good order and discipline which characterized the troops, and the stringent orders of the officers.

Troops were at once despatched to take possession of the railroad and all public or military property; and it was soon found that the occupation of the place, though not at the cost of a battle, or even a skirmish, was a most important advantage gained, and a corresponding damage to the rebels. At the railroad depot were found seventeen locomotives, and a large number of cars, some of which contained supplies for the rebel army; and at a foundery were several cannon and some small arms. These, with other similar property, were seized, and the railroad was promptly used to extend the advantage already gained. Trains of cars with troops were despatched east and west, and before night General Mitchell had possession of one hundred miles of the railroad, extending from Stevenson on the east to Decatur on the west, and had captured, besides other engines and cars, the entire camp equipage of a regiment. From Decatur a force was advanced to Tuscumbia, and communication opened with the combined armies of Generals Grant and Buell, soon after

the battle of Shiloh. The rebel communications were thus completely interrupted in this direction, and the capture of so large a number of locomotives and cars was a serious loss to the means of transportation possessed by the rebels, though a considerable number, both of engines and cars, had been run down from the railroads in Tennessee and Kentucky, as the rebel forces retired. All this work was accomplished, and the advantages gained, without the loss of a man. The success was announced by General Mitchell in the following orders, expressing his thanks to his soldiers:—

"HEADQUARTERS THIRD DIVISION,
CAMP TAYLOR, HUNTSVILLE, *April* 16, 1862.
"GENERAL ORDER No. 93.

"SOLDIERS: Your march upon Bowling Green won the thanks and confidence of our commanding general. With engines and cars captured from the enemy, our advance guard precipitated itself upon Nashville. It was now made your duty to seize and destroy the Memphis and Charleston Railway, the great military road of the enemy. With a supply-train only sufficient to feed you at a distance of two days' march from your depot, you undertook the herculean task of rebuilding twelve hundred feet of heavy bridging, which by your untiring energy was accomplished in ten days.

"Thus, by a railway of your own construction, your depot of supplies was removed from Nashville to Shelbyville, nearly sixty miles, in the direction of the object of your attack. The blow now became practicable. Marching with a celerity such as to outstrip any messenger who might have attempted to announce your coming, you fell upon Huntsville, taking your enemy completely by surprise, and capturing not only his great military road, but all his machine shops, engines, and rolling stock.

"Thus providing yourselves with ample transportation, you have struck blow after blow with a rapidity unparalleled. Stevenson fell, sixty miles to the east of Huntsville. Decatur and

Tuscumbia have been in like manner seized, and are now occupied. In three days you have extended your front of operations more than one hundred and twenty miles, and your morning gun at Tuscumbia may now be heard by your comrades on the battle-field made glorious by their victory before Corinth.

" A communication of these facts to headquarters has not only won the thanks of our commanding general, but those of the department of war, which I announce to you with proud satisfaction.

" Accept the thanks of your commander, and let your future deeds demonstrate that you can surpass yourselves. By order of

" O. M. MITCHELL,
" *Brigadier-General commanding.*
" W. P. PRENTICE, A. A. G."

General Mitchell, in consequence of his success, was raised to the rank of major-general, and his division was constituted an independent command. But to hold this great extent of railroad his force was not sufficient, and the extension of his lines rendered his situation far from safe should the rebels concentrate any force upon one point. The importance of this line of communication was too great for them to permit him to hold it without opposition, and they soon began to gather in some force, and to threaten him. At this time, however, it was impossible to send him reënforcements without weakening some other point perhaps as important as this. General Mitchell was, therefore, obliged to concentrate his forces before the threatened movements of the rebels, who collected in the vicinity of Tuscumbia, and kept up a constant skirmishing, and interrupted the transportation of supplies. On the 24th of April, his force abandoned Tuscumbia, and fell back to Decatur, where a fine bridge across the Tennessee was destroyed, to prevent pursuit by the rebels, who pressed forward as they discovered the retreat. The bridge was

scarcely destroyed when a rebel cavalry force appeared on the other side, but their pursuit was here effectually interrupted. From Decatur the federal troops were also withdrawn, and concentrated at Huntsville, and operations were now directed to the places east of that point. An expedition to Bridgeport secured control of the bridge at that place, and there being no bridge across the Tennessee below that since the destruction of the one at Decatur, with the river in his front and between him and any force of the enemy which he had to fear, General Mitchell's position was now safe. Moreover, the communication between the extremes of his lines was by railroad, which was in his possession, and he could the more readily concentrate his force if occasion required.

Had Gen. Mitchell's force been larger, he might have accomplished more important results by penetrating farther into Alabama and into Georgia, destroying the rebel communication by railroad, and seizing some important points, as well as capturing much war material very essential to the enemy. Whether he would have been able to have held the ground thus occupied, without a very large army after the evacuation of Corinth, is a question not so easily decided.

Subsequently to the operations recorded above, General Mitchell advanced upon Chattanooga, and compelled the rebel forces in East Tennessee to retire. Considerable heavy skirmishing ensued upon this movement, and on the 6th of June General Negley with a part of the division attacked the rebels in Chattanooga with artillery across the river. The rebels in considerable force the next day made an attack, but were repulsed. The difficulty of procuring supplies, and the want of a larger force, however, compelled the federal general to abandon any further attempt in this direction; and soon after, when General Buell's army moved from Corinth to the line of the Tennessee, this division was again incorporated into his army, and General Mitchell was ordered to take command of the department of the south.

CHAPTER LXXV.

ON the 12th of April, a few days after the capture of Island Number Ten,* the flotilla of gunboats under Commodore Foote, with the mortar boats and a number of transports carrying a large part of General Pope's forces, moved down the Mississippi for operations against the next rebel stronghold, which was Fort Wright or Pillow, on the first Chickasaw Bluffs, about seventy miles above Memphis, and relied upon as a defence to that place. A few miles below Fort Pillow was Fort Randolph; and both of these works were so advantageously located and so well constructed that they were confidently relied upon by the rebels to resist successfully the federal progress down the river, and were believed by the federal officers to be very difficult to reduce, the passage down the river

* See Chapter LXIX.

without their reduction being still more difficult. The gunboats moved in line of battle and prepared to encounter the rebel gunboats, of which there were supposed to be several quite formidable, or batteries posted on shore. As the fleet descended the river, three or four steamboats, supposed to be armed, were seen in the distance; but they retired as the federal boats advanced, without offering any resistance. Two days after leaving New Madrid the fleet came to anchor at Plum Point, about three and a half miles from Fort Pillow, and operations were at once commenced against that stronghold. The mortar boats were moored to the Arkansas shore at a distance of about three quarters of a mile from the fort in a direct line, and on the 17th of April opened fire upon the batteries and gunboats of the enemy. The rebel batteries replied vigorously, but without much effect, and the shells from the mortars, though soon accurately thrown, promised no speedy result.

The height of the river, and the nature of the ground below the bluffs on which the rebel works were constructed, prevented any coöperation of the land forces; and it only remained for the mortars to keep up a constant fire, which must cause more or less damage to the enemy, until a lower stage of the water should permit the commencement of military operations, or the rebel forces should at length be wearied out. The land forces, however, were destined to take no part in the reduction or capture of the fort, for after the battle of Shiloh, General Pope, with his force of nearly twenty-five thousand men, which had been destined for operations on the Mississippi, was ordered to join the army under General Halleck, then moving against Corinth. The departure of the land forces appeared to put an end to the operations which were expected to open the mighty river to New Orleans; but the naval part of the expedition remained to prevent any hostile movements by the rebel gunboats, or any attempt to reoccupy points farther up the river; and a slow bombardment of the fort was continued, though with but little hope of accomplishing any favorable results. Soon after the withdrawal of the land forces, Commodore Foote, anticipating no immediate movement of importance, obtained leave of absence, and was succeeded in ·the command of the flotilla by Captain Charles H. Davis.

Up to the 10th of May there was little to vary the monotony of the slow bombardment of the fort. The rebel gunboats occasionally made their appearance at a distance, but made no demonstration within range of the guns of the federal vessels. The rebels, however, were in the mean time increasing their naval strength, or awaiting a favorable opportunity for attacking the federal boats at a disadvantage. On the day above named, their preparations being completed, or the desired opportunity, as they believed, having arrived, the rebel flotilla moved up the river for an attack upon the federal vessels. This flotilla consisted of eight boats, several of which were partially iron-clad and fitted with sharp iron bows, or "rams." The federal gunboats were seven in number, and were moored on each side of the river, three on the eastern side and four on the western side. The mortar boats, which were simply flat-boats, depended upon the gunboats both for locomotion and protection, and were a source of weakness rather than of strength in case of an attack at close quarters. Four of the federal vessels were partially iron-clad; the others had no armor, but the engines and boilers were protected by bales of cotton and heavy timbers. Some of the mortar boats had been moored for their daily work of bombarding the fort, and the foremost of the rebel gunboats apparently aimed at first capturing these persistent annoyers. As the rebel boats approached, and were yet at a distance, one of the mortar boats opened the conflict with its heavy mortar, the elevation of the piece and the charge being reduced to meet

the circumstances. Though the shot did not appear to take effect, the gallantry of the commander and crew of this boat, which was the most exposed to attack, in thus defending it with such a ponderous and unwieldy piece of ordnance, received the commendation of the flag officer and all who saw it.

The rebel flotilla was led by an iron-clad ram, which, as it approached the position of the federal vessels, made for the Cincinnati, which was the most advanced of the gunboats. It was some time before the Cincinnati was cut loose and got under headway into the stream, and the rebel ram had by that time approached to within a comparatively short distance, the stern guns of the former having been discharged in vain against the iron armor of the ram. As soon as the Cincinnati was fairly under way she discharged her broadside guns, but with no better result. The ram kept on, and, making for the federal vessel under all steam, struck her on the quarter with great force, and did considerable damage, though it did not disable her. In return, the Cincinnati discharged a full broadside at the ram at short range, but apparently without inflicting any serious damage; for the latter immediately prepared for another attack. Both vessels were now manœuvred with skill, the one attempting to strike with its iron prow, and the other to avoid the blow, while at the same time firing rapidly upon her antagonist. Finally, as the ram approached, Commander Stembel, of the Cincinnati, ordered out the small arms, cutlasses, and boarding pikes, with the determination of joining in a desperate hand-to-hand encounter, should the ram again strike and seriously injure his vessel. These preparations were scarcely made, when the vessels struck, and at the same moment the broadside of the Cincinnati was discharged directly into her antagonist. Amid the uproar and confusion of the moment, Commander Stembel shot the rebel pilot, and was himself immediately after wounded. The rebel vessel was evidently damaged, and drifted down the stream without any attempt to renew the conflict. The Cincinnati, though much damaged and leaking fast, was not disabled, and for a time continued in the fight, discharging her guns at the other rebel vessels within range, and placing one *hors du combat*, until, becoming partially unmanageable in consequence of settling in the water, she was run upon a shoal, where she soon sunk.*

In the mean time the other federal gunboats became engaged with other rebel vessels, and a general battle raged. The Mound City was struck by a ram, but not seriously damaged, and continued to throw her heavy shot and shell at her antagonist, which was soon forced to retire. In the general conflict three of the enemy's vessels were disabled, two by the explosion of boilers, or steam-chests, which were struck by shot from the federal vessels. The engagement lasted rather more than half an hour, and for a part of that time it appeared to be a severe contest, which must necessarily cause a great loss of life. The result, however, was, that none were killed on board the federal vessels, and but three were wounded, one of whom was Commander Stembel. The official statement of the rebel loss was two killed and one wounded. The Cincinnati was the only federal boat that was seriously damaged. On the part of the rebels it was evident that several of their boats were more or less disabled, as they floated helplessly down the stream ; and the result was

certainly such as not to encourage them to seek again an engagement with the federal gunboats. The rebel commander, however, reported that the boats were recalled by him because the federal vessels were taking positions where the water was too shallow for his own to reach them, while they also carried a greater number of guns, and of much heavier calibre. His somewhat inconsistent statement at least proves that he felt that his vessels were not a match for their antagonists, notwithstanding he reported serious damage to the latter.

The following is the official despatch of Captain Davis, announcing the engagement and its results : —

OFFICIAL REPORT OF CAPTAIN DAVIS.

"UNITED STATES FLAG-STEAMER BENTON, }
OFF FORT PILLOW, *May* 11, 1862. {

" SIR : I have the honor to inform the department that yesterday morning, a little after seven o'clock, the rebel squadron, consisting of eight iron-clad steamers, — four of them, I believe, fitted as rams, — came round the point at the bend above Fort Pillow, and steamed gallantly up the river, fully prepared for a regular engagement.

" The vessels of this squadron were lying at the time tied up to the bank of the river, — three on the eastern and four on the western side, — and (as they were transferred to me by Flag-officer Foote) ready for action. Most of the vessels were prompt in obeying the signal to follow the motions of the commander-in-chief.

" The leading vessels of the rebel squadron made directly for mortar-boat No. 16, which was for a moment unprotected. Acting Master Gregory and his crew behaved with great spirit during the action ; he fired his mortar eleven times at the enemy, reducing the charge and diminishing the elevation.

" Commander Stembel, in the gunboat Cincinnati, which was the leading vessel in the line on that side of the river, followed immediately by Commander Kilty, in the Mound City,

---

* It was related at the time by newspaper correspondents who were with the federal flotilla, that after the retirement of the first rebel ram from the engagement with the Cincinnati, the latter was attacked by the "Mallory," another ram of slower and more clumsy movement, and for some time by skilful manœuvres evaded a collision. But as the ram was about to be more successful in the attempt to strike the Cincinnati. the St. Louis bore down rapidly upon the rebel vessel, and striking her amidships, cut into her so that she sunk at once, carrying down most of the crew, a few only escaping by jumping on board the St. Louis. No mention of this, however, is made in the official despatches either of Captain Davis, the federal flag officer, or of the rebel commander. The report of the blowing up of two of the rebel boats by the explosion of shells in their magazines appears equally unsupported by the official despatches.

hastened to the support of the mortar-boats, and both were repeatedly struck by the enemy's rams, at the same time that they disabled the enemy and drove him away. The two leading vessels of the enemy's line were successively encountered by this ship. The boiler or steam-chest of one of them was exploded by our shot, and both of them were disabled. They, as well as the first vessel encountered by the Cincinnati, drifted down the river.

"Commander Walke informs me that he fired a fifty-pound rifle-shot through the boilers of the third of the enemy's gunboats, of the western line, and rendered her for the time being helpless.

"The action lasted during the better part of an hour, and took place at the closest quarters. The enemy finally retreated with haste below the guns of Fort Pillow.

"I have to call the especial attention of the department to the gallantry and good conduct exhibited by Commanders Stembel and Kilty, and Lieutenant-commanding S. L. Phelps. I regret to say that Commander Stembel, Fourth Master Reynolds, and one of the seamen of the Cincinnati, and one of the Mound City, were severely wounded. The other accidents of the day were slight.

"I have the honor to be,

"Your most obedient servant,

"C. H. Davis,

"*Captain commanding Mississippi Flotilla, pro tem.*

"Hon. Gideon Welles, *Secretary of the Navy.*"

After this engagement affairs remained quiet until early in June, except that an occasional bombardment of the fort was kept up from the mortar-boats. No further demonstration was made by the rebel gunboats, and the Union flotilla could not hope to make any progress without the coöperation of a large land force. In the mean time, however, the naval part of the expedition was kept prepared for any active operations, and a fleet of several "rams," fitted

out by the war department, and under the command of a military officer, Colonel Ellett, had arrived, and was ready to coöperate. These "rams" were swift, stern-wheel river steamers, fitted with sharp iron prows, and protected about the machinery with iron or cotton bales; the sides were pierced with loopholes for rifles, which, in the hands of sharpshooters, were the only armament. They were lighter and swifter than the rebel rams, and were expected to prove useful for rapid movements, should such be required, as well as effective in the peculiar use for which they were intended. The commander of this fleet, Colonel Ellett, was a brave and dashing officer, and was supported with like spirit by his brother, Lieutenant-Colonel Ellett, and son, as well as by those who had charge of the management of the boats. The arrival of these rams under the command of an army officer, and independent of the naval authorities, caused some jealousy between them; but, fortunately, it assumed the form of rivalry, and did not interfere with the activity or success of either.

The tenure of Fort Pillow and Memphis by the rebels depended upon the issue of the operations at Corinth; and when Beauregard was compelled to retreat from that position, the evacuation of these places followed as a matter of course. The transfer, therefore, of General Pope's forces to the main army before Corinth did not deprive the naval expedition of all military coöperation, and may not, in view of the slow progress made by General Halleck, have seriously retarded the progress of the expedition. Fort Pillow and Fort Randolph, about twelve miles below, were evacuated on the night of the 4th of June, a few days after the retreat from Corinth; and as soon as the preparations could be completed. The greater part of the forces which had for some time occupied Fort Pillow, after the abandonment of Columbus, had been called to reënforce Beauregard at Corinth, when General Pope went to the Tennessee, and the garrison had, for some days previous to the evacuation, been only sufficient to keep up a show of occupation by responding to the federal fire. Although such a movement might have been suspected by the Union officers, whose reconnoissances had been more frequent for a few days, and preparations were made for a military movement under certain contingencies, it did not appear that their suspicions were confirmed until the movement was accomplished. Early in the evening of the 4th of June there were indications of extensive conflagrations in the direction of the fort and beyond, and it became quite certain that the rebels were burning their barracks and storehouses preparatory to an entire abandonment of the position. At the same time the discharge of some of their heavy guns, which sent shot and shell in the direction of the federal vessels, seemed to indicate that the garrison was still ready to resist the advance of the Union flotilla. It appeared afterwards, however, that the rebels had loaded and pointed these guns, and had then set the carriages on fire, by which means they were discharged when the garrison had already left. An advance of the flotilla, or any detachment, was not considered expedient until the next morning; but early on that day the whole fleet got under way, preceded by the rams, and moved down the river to a point opposite the fort.

Lieutenant-Colonel Ellett, with a few men in a yawl, immediately landed, and were followed by Colonel Fitch, commanding an Indiana brigade, and a part of his force. An examination of the rebel works showed that by position and natural advantages, as well as great engineering skill and labor, they were exceedingly strong, and could for a long time have resisted any attempt to take them. They consisted of an immense system of earthworks, extending several miles, and prepared for numerous guns, a large number of which, com-

manding all the land approaches as well as the river, appeared to have been mounted. The rebels, however, had removed the greater part of the guns, and had attempted to render others useless by bursting or spiking them, and burning the carriages. All the barracks and other buildings had been burned, and there were evidences of the destruction of other property which could not be removed. Some very large guns and mortars were found, a portion of which were not seriously damaged; but beyond these there was little left that could be of value to the captors. The works themselves were of little use to the federal forces, the rebels having now almost entirely abandoned West Tennessee. The Union flag was raised over the deserted and useless fort, and, a small force being left to guard it, the fleet proceeded down the river to Fort Randolph, a less important work, twelve miles below, which was also evacuated at the same time as Fort Pillow.

The following is the official despatch of Colonel Ellett, whose activity seems to have placed him in advance of the naval flotilla: —

COLONEL ELLETT'S REPORT.

"OPPOSITE RANDOLPH, BELOW FORT PILLOW, June 5, 1862.

"To my mortification the enemy evacuated Fort Pillow last night. They carried away or destroyed every thing valuable. Early this morning Lieutenant-Colonel Ellett and a few men in a yawl went ashore, followed immediately by Colonel Fitch ashore and a party of his command. The gunboats then came down and anchored across the channel.

"I proceeded with three rams twelve miles below the fort to a point opposite Randolph, and sent Lieutenant-Colonel Ellett ashore with a flag of truce to demand the surrender of the place. Their forces had all left in two of their gunboats only an hour or two before we approached. The people seemed to respect the flag which Lieutenant-Colonel Ellett planted.

The guns had been dismantled, and some piles of cotton were burning.

"I shall leave Lieutenant-Colonel Ellett here in the advance, and return immediately to Fort Pillow to bring on my entire force. The people attribute the suddenness of the evacuation to the attempt made night before last to sink one of their gunboats at Fort Pillow. Randolph, like Pillow, is weak, and could not have held out long against a vigorous attack. The people express a desire for the restoration of the old order of things, though still professing to be secessionists.

"CHARLES ELLETT, Jr.,
"Colonel commanding Ram Flotilla.
"Hon. E. M. STANTON, Secretary of War."

From Randolph the combined forces moved at once towards Memphis, which was now protected by no work of importance, and the only obstacle anticipated was the rebel flotilla of gunboats. On the passage down, a large rebel transport was captured by one of the tug tenders of the gunboats, this being the only important event which transpired on the way. On the 5th of June the fleet arrived within two miles of Memphis without meeting any opposition, and anchored for the night. During the night a rebel tug approached the anchorage, as was supposed on a reconnoitring expedition, and getting aground so that she could not be got off, was set on fire by her crew and destroyed. Early on the morning of the 6th, the gunboats were signalized to prepare for action, and to drop down the river. The Mound City having been left at Port Pillow to convoy the transports, the fleet consisted of only five vessels, the Benton (flag-ship), the Louisville, the Carondelet, the Cairo, and the St. Louis.

The arrival of the fleet above the city was evidently known in Memphis, for the bluffs were covered with the people who had come out to witness its coming and the naval battle which was about to take place between it and the rebel gunboats. The latter, eight in number, were opposite the city, and as the federal boats came slowly down were formed in line of battle to meet them, the rebel officers apparently being determined that the engagement should, for some reason, take place in front of the city. The rebel flag-ship, the "Little Rebel," fired the first gun, to which the Benton soon replied; and very shortly the other vessels on both sides followed, and the engagement became general, though not yet at close quarters. The federal boats, though fewer in number, carried more guns, and of heavier metal, and soon showed that they were not engaged in an unequal conflict. Before their shot, however, began to take effect upon their antagonists, which were yet at a distance, four rams, commanded by Colonel Ellett, came down the river at full speed, and two of them, passing the gunboats, steamed directly for the enemy. The gunboats continued their fire, avoiding the range of the rams, and the rebels replied vigorously. Hidden partially by the smoke of the battle, the rams dashed on, and were near the enemy's vessels before they were discovered. The ram Queen of the West was in the advance, followed closely by the Monarch. As the former approached the rebel vessels she received a shot, which caused but little damage, and did not deter her bold commander from his work. Dashing at the rebel gunboat Beauregard, she struck her a blow which would have proved very damaging but for the skilful movement of the latter. Pressing on, the Queen next struck with full force the General Lovell, as the latter was turning, and cut through in such a manner as to be for a few moments firmly fixed in her side. As soon as the ram became disengaged, the rebel gunboat sunk in deep water, and a part of her crew were carried down. This assault, however, so damaged the Queen, that she was obliged to retire from the contest, Colonel Ellett having also been wounded by a splinter. The Monarch had pushed on with such force and speed that she passed through the rebel fleet, striking one of them a damaging blow. Then promptly returning to the conflict, she was in turn attacked by the Beauregard; but her pilot skilfully evaded the blow, and the Beauregard went crashing into the side of one of her own consorts, the General Price, and inflicted so severe an injury that the disabled boat was run upon the Arkansas shore and abandoned. Again attacking the Beauregard, before she was free from the General Price, the Monarch cut through her sides. At the same moment a shot from one of the gunboats exploded the boiler of the Beauregard, and the double injury caused her soon to sink. Many of the rebel crew were scalded, and others were thrown violently into the water; but in this case, as in that of the General Lovell, boats were promptly sent from the federal vessels to rescue the suffering and drowning men. The ram Switzerland, through a misapprehension of the signals, remained in the rear, and failed to participate in the engagement. The Lancaster was accidentally backed ashore and disabled, so that she also was prevented from joining in the battle and doing the service which was expected.

In the mean time the federal gunboats had also come down, and were engaging the enemy at close quarters, their heavy shot taking effect in spite of the iron armor of the rebel boats. The loss of two of their boats had already caused the rebel officers to turn their vessels down the river, though they still kept up their fire. The battle had thus passed along the whole front of the city, and the result was no longer doubtful to the thousands who witnessed the exciting spectacle. Success was wholly on the side of the Union fleet. The rebel flagship was soon so badly damaged by shot, that she also was run upon the Arkansas shore, and the officers and crew escaped, although one of the rams had closely followed her. Four of the rebel gunboats being thus disposed of, includ-

ing the flag-ship, the others sought safety in flight. But they were pursued by the federal gunboats and rams, and three of them were badly damaged, and being run ashore, were abandoned by their crews. One only, the Van Dorn, which was laden with a large quantity of property belonging to the rebel government, escaped. She was pursued by two of the rams for many miles, but they did not succeed in capturing or destroying her.

The battle lasted but little more than an hour, and the victory thus speedily achieved by the federal fleet was won without the loss of a single life, or the cost of even any serious wound. The vessels were scarcely injured, except the rams, as already mentioned, and the fleet at the close of the action was ready to meet another even stronger force of the enemy. The rebel defeat was complete. Seven of their eight gunboats were destroyed or captured, and their loss of officers and men was estimated at one hundred and fifty killed by shot, scalded, or drowned, and about one hundred prisoners. It was a fatal blow to the naval operations of the rebels on the Mississippi, and, with the previous victory of Flag-officer Farragut below New Orleans, swept away the greater part of the navy which they had organized for the defence and control of the river. In addition to the gunboats, five steamers were captured as prizes at the landing in Memphis; but the greater part of the enemy's ordnance stores and supplies had already been removed.

While the battle was yet in progress below the city, Colonel Ellett, who had been obliged to withdraw his ram, the Queen, from the contest, and was in the rear of the fleet, was informed that a white flag had been raised in the city. He accordingly sent his son, with an army officer and a small guard on shore, under a flag of truce, bearing a note to the mayor, to the effect that, understanding that the city had surrendered, he sent the party to raise the United States flag upon the Custom House and

Geo H Thomas.

the Court House. The mayor replied that the civil authorities of the city were not advised of its surrender, but that they had no forces to oppose the raising of the flags. Upon receiving this reply the small party proceeded to raise the flags as directed, and accomplished their purpose, although they were several times fired upon and stoned by the mob. The better portion of the people, however, reprobated this conduct of the mob, and the party returned in safety, notwithstanding the violent threats of the populace.

The gunboats having returned from the pursuit of the rebel vessels, Flag-officer Davis sent a small party ashore with a note to the mayor, requesting the surrender of the city. To this the mayor replied, that the civil authorities had no means of defence, and by the force of circumstances the city was in the hands of Captain Davis and his forces. The rebel general, Jeff. Thompson, with the rear guard of his forces, had left the city by railroad during the battle, and neither military force nor arms appeared to have been left. Subsequently, the transports having brought down the brigade of Colonel Fitch, that officer took military possession of the city, and at once put it under martial law, receiving the coöperation of the mayor in closing drinking houses and preserving peace and quiet. No resistance was made or threatened to the movements of the federal troops, and though strong indignation and hatred was expressed by the more intense rebels, there was evidently a pretty strong Union sentiment among a portion of the people, and but little disinclination to a change of military rule on the part of a large number. Military discipline and martial law were strictly enforced, and the people of Memphis were obliged to admit, that under the rule of the federal forces the city was far more orderly and quiet than it had been during the presence of the rebel troops.

The following are the official reports of Captain Davis and Colonel Ellett: —

REPORT OF COMMANDER DAVIS.

"UNITED STATES FLAG-STEAMER BENTON,
MEMPHIS, June 6, 1862.

"SIR: In my despatch of yesterday, dated at Fort Pillow, I had the honor to inform the department that I was about moving to this place with the men-of-war and transports. I got under way from Fort Pillow at noon, leaving the Pittsburg, Lieutenant-commanding Egbert Thompson, to coöperate with a detachment of Colonel Fitch's command, in holding possession of Fort Pillow and securing public property at that place; and also the Mound City, Commander A. H. Kilty, to convoy the transports containing the troops, not then ready to move.

"On the way down, I came suddenly, at a bend of the river, upon the rebel transport-steamer Sovereign, which turned immediately to escape from us. I sent forward Lieutenant Joshua Bishop, with a body of small-armed men in a light tug, by whom she was captured. She is a valuable prize.

"The gunboats anchored at eight o'clock P. M, at the lower end of Island Number 45, about a mile and a half above the city of Memphis; the mortar-boats, tow-boats, ordnance, commissary, and other vessels of the fleet tied up at Island Number 44 for the night.

"At daylight this morning the enemy's fleet, consisting of the rebel rams and gunboats, now numbering eight vessels, were discovered lying at the levee. They dropped below Railroad Point, and returning again, arranged themselves in front of the city.

"At twenty minutes past four the flotilla, consisting of the following five vessels, — the flag-ship Benton, Lieutenant-commanding S. L. Phelps; the Louisville, Commander B. M. Dove; the Carondelet, Commander Henry Walke; the

Cairo, Lieutenant-commanding N. C. Bryant; and the St. Louis, Lieutenant-commanding Wilson McGunnegle, got under way by signal, and dropped down the river.

"The rebels, still lying in front of the town, opened fire, with the intention of exposing the city to injury from our shot. The fire was returned on our part, with due care in this regard. While the engagement was going on in this manner, two vessels of the ram fleet, under command of Colonel Ellett, the Queen of the West and Monarch, steamed rapidly by us, and ran boldly into the enemy's line. Several conflicts had taken place between the rams before the flotilla, led by the Benton, moving at a slower rate, could arrive at the closest quarters. In the mean time, however, the firing from our gunboats was continuous and exceedingly well directed. The General Beauregard and the Little Rebel were struck in the boilers and blown up.

"The ram Queen of the West, which Colonel Ellett commanded in person, encountered, with full power, the rebel steamer General Lovell and sunk her, but in doing so sustained some serious damage.

"Up to this time the rebel fleet had maintained its position and used its guns with great spirit; these disasters, however, compelled the remaining vessels to resort to their superiority in speed as the only means of safety. A running fight took place, which lasted nearly an hour, and carried us ten miles below the city. It ended in the capture or destruction of four or five of the remaining vessels of the enemy; one only, supposed to be the Van Dorn, having escaped. Two of the rams, the Monarch and Lancaster Number 3, pursued her, without success; they brought back, however, another prize. . . . .

"I have not received such information as will enable me to make an approximate statement of the number of killed, wounded, and prisoners on the part of the enemy. One of the vessels going down in deep water, carried a part of her crew with her; another, the General Beauregard, having been blown up with steam, many of her crew were frightfully scalded. I doubt whether it will ever be in my power to furnish an accurate statement of these results of the engagement.

"The attack made by the two rams under Colonel Ellett, which took place before the flotilla closed in with the enemy, was bold and successful.

"Captain Maynardier, commanding the mortar-fleet, accompanied the squadron in a tug, and took possession of the Beauregard, and made her crew prisoners. He captured also other prisoners during the action, and received many persons of the rebel fleet, who returned and delivered themselves up after their vessels had been deserted. It is with pleasure that I call the attention of the department to his personal zeal and activity, the more conspicuous because displayed while the mortar-boats under his command could take no part in the action.

"The officers and men of the flotilla performed their duty. Three men only of the flotilla were wounded, and those slightly; but one ship was struck by shot.

"I transmit herewith copies of my correspondence with the mayor of Memphis, leading to the surrender of the city.

"At eleven o'clock A. M. Colonel Fitch, commanding the Indiana brigade, arrived and took military possession of the place.

"There are several prizes here, among them four large river-steamers, which will be brought at once into the service of the government.

"I have the honor to be, very respectfully, your most obedient servant,

"C. H. DAVIS, *Flag-Officer,*
"*Commanding Western Flotilla,*
"*Mississippi River, pro tem.*

"Hon. GIDEON WELLES, *Secretary of the Navy.*"

DESPATCHES FROM COLONEL ELLETT.

"OPPOSITE MEMPHIS, *June* 6, 1862.

" The rebel gunboats made a stand early this morning opposite Memphis, and opened a vigorous fire upon our gunboats, which was returned with equal spirit.

" I ordered the Queen, my flag-ship, to pass between the gunboats, and run down ahead of them upon the two rams of the enemy, which first boldly stood their ground. Colonel Ellett, in the Monarch, of which Captain Dryden is First Master, followed gallantly. The rebel rams endeavored to back down-stream, and then to turn and run, but the movement was fatal to them. The Queen struck one of them fairly, and for a few minutes was fast to the wreck. After separating, the rebel steamer sunk. My steamer, the Queen, was then herself struck by another rebel steamer, and disabled, but though damaged, can be saved. A pistol-shot wound in the leg deprived me of the power to witness the remainder of the fight. The Monarch also passed ahead of our gunboats, and went most gallantly into action. She first struck the rebel boat that struck my flag-ship, and sunk the rebel. She was then struck by one of the rebel rams, but not injured. She then pushed on, and struck the Beauregard, and burst in her side. Simultaneously the Beauregard was struck in the boiler, by a shot from one of our gunboats. The Monarch then pushed at the gunboat Little Rebel, the rebel flag-ship, and having but little headway, pushed her before her, the rebel commodore and crew escaping. The Monarch then, finding the Beauregard sinking, took her in tow until she sunk in shoal water. Then, in compliance with the request of Colonel Davis, Lieutenant-Colonel Ellett despatched the Monarch and the Switzerland in pursuit of the remaining gunboat and some transports which had escaped the gunboats, and two of my rams have gone below.

" I cannot too much praise the conduct of the pilots and engineers and military guard of the Monarch and the Queen, the brave conduct of Captain Dryden, or the heroic conduct of Lieutenant-Colonel Ellett. I will name all parties in special report.

" I am myself the only person in my fleet who was disabled.

" CHARLES ELLETT, JR.,
" *Colonel commanding Ram-Fleet.*
"HON. E. M. STANTON, Secretary of War."

"OPPOSITE MEMPHIS, *June* 6, 1862.

" It is proper and due to the brave men on the Queen and the Monarch to say to you briefly, that two of the rebel steamers were sunk outright and immediately by the shock of my two rams. One, with a large amount of cotton on board, was disabled by an accidental collision with the Queen, and secured by her crew. After I was personally disabled, another rebel boat, which was also hit by a shot from the gunboats, was sunk by the Monarch, and towed into shoal water by that boat. Still another, also injured by the fire of our gunboats, was pushed into shore and secured by the Monarch. Of the gunboats, I can only say that they bore themselves, as our navy always does, bravely and well.

" CHARLES ELLETT, JR.,
" *Colonel commanding Ram-Fleet.*
"HON. E. M. STANTON, *Secretary of War.*"

"OPPOSITE MEMPHIS, *June* 10, 1862.

" There are several facts touching the naval engagement of the 6th instant, at this place, which I wish to place on record. Approaching Memphis, the gunboats were in advance. I had received no notice that a fight was expected, but was informed on landing within sight of Memphis, that the enemy's gunboats had retreated down the river.

" My first intimation of the presence of the enemy was a shot which passed over my boat. I had four of my most powerful rams in advance and ready for any emergency.

" The others were towing the barges. On

advancing to the attack, I expected, of course, to be followed by the Monarch, the Lancaster, and the Switzerland.

"The Monarch came in gallantly. Some of the officers of the Lancaster, which now held the next place in line, became excited and confused, but the engineers behaved well.

"The pilot erred in the signals, and backed the boat ashore and disabled her rudder.

"The captain of the Switzerland construed the general signal order to keep half a mile in the rear of the Lancaster to mean that he was to keep half a mile behind her in the engagement, and therefore failed to participate.

"Hence the whole brunt of the fight fell upon the Queen and Monarch. Had either the Lancaster or Switzerland followed me as the Monarch did, the rebel gunboat Van Dorn would not have escaped, and my flag-ship would not have been disabled.

"Three of the rebel rams and gunboats, which were struck by my two rams, sunk outright, and were lost.

"Another, called the General Price, was but slightly injured, and I am now raising her, and purpose to send her to my fleet.

"Respectfully,

"(Signed)   CHAS. ELLETT, JR.,

"*Colonel commanding Ram-Fleet.*

"Hon. E. M. STANTON, *Secretary of War.*"

A few days after the occupation of Memphis, four gunboats and three transports, carrying a regiment of troops, were sent on an expedition to White River, to open communication with General Curtis, whose forces were in the vicinity of Batesville, in Arkansas. After the battle of Pea Ridge, General Curtis had remained in north-western Arkansas, waiting for reënforcements, and watching the movements of the rebel army, which was supposed to be concentrating, under Price, for a new invasion of Missouri. To meet such a movement, General Curtis moved towards Spring-

field, against which it was reported that the rebels were already advancing. The rebel invasion did not take place, however, and General Curtis again moved into Arkansas, at a more easterly point, and marched, by way of Salem, to Batesville, on White River, and the most important town in north-eastern Arkansas. From Batesville General Curtis was advancing upon Little Rock, the capital of the state, and had arrived within fifty miles of that place, when an order was received from General Halleck (who made every other movement in his department subordinate to his own operations) to send ten regiments, by a forced march, to Cape Girardeau, and thence to Corinth. This reduction of his forces rendered it inexpedient for General Curtis to continue his movement towards Little Rock, and he accordingly fell back to Batesville. Here the want of transportation and the scarcity of supplies in the vicinity, caused not a little suffering among the troops; while the distance from his base, and his position in a hostile country, with his communications-cut, and the rebel forces concentrating to oppose him, rendered the situation of his army critical, and excited much apprehension.

To open communication with, and relieve General Curtis, by way of White River, was the object of the expedition, and it was thought to be of sufficient strength to meet and overcome any force or obstructions which would be found on the river. The expedition proceeded without meeting any opposition, till it arrived in the vicinity of St. Charles. At this point a reconnoissance revealed the fact that the enemy had erected batteries, and were apparently disposed to dispute the further progress of the Union boats. The woods were so dense, however, that the position of the rebel batteries could not be discovered, and the gunboats advanced cautiously, shelling the banks on either side of the river. This fire elicited a response from the batteries, and as the boats turned a bend in the river, the position of the batteries was revealed, the first being but about five hundred yards distant. This battery, mounted four twelve-pounder Parrott guns, and another a little higher up and nearer the river, mounted three forty-two pounders. As the gunboats came in view of the batteries, a sharp cannonade opened on both sides, the Mound City passing on towards the upper battery. The engagement had lasted about half an hour, without any injury to the federal vessels, but with some effect upon the lower battery, which was nearly silenced, when a forty-two pound shot struck the Mound City, killing several men, and piercing the steam-drum. Instantly the hot steam rushed out and filled the whole vessel, scalding a large number of men, who were confined at the guns between the decks, and whose shrieks of agony are described as being heart-rending. Many were suffocated at once, but others succeeded in throwing themselves through the ports into the river. Fifty or sixty men were soon struggling in the water, many of them more or less severely scalded.

As soon as the misfortune was seen on board the other boats, assistance was immediately sent; but before the suffering men in the river could be rescued, they were fired upon by the rebels with small arms, and several of them were killed or wounded. The guns of the lower battery were also fired upon the boats which went to the rescue. This barbarous act, worthy of the execration of mankind, and in such contrast with the humane action of the federal officers and crews at Memphis, when a similar affair occurred on board one of the rebel boats, it appeared was perpetrated by the orders of the officer commanding the rebel forces, a Captain Fry, formerly a lieutenant in the United States navy. Of one hundred and seventy-five men, composing the officers and crew of the Mound City, but twenty-five escaped without injury; upwards of eighty were killed instant-

ly, or subsequently died by being scalded, and about thirty were killed in the river by the enemy's shots, or were drowned.

This calamity might have proved fatal to the expedition, or at least resulted in a complete repulse, but for the movement of the military force under Colonel Fitch, which had previously been landed about two and a half miles below the batteries. This force had advanced towards the batteries, and had driven in the rebel pickets, when the fatal shot struck the Mound City. Having disposed his forces for an attack, Colonel Fitch signalled his movement to the gunboats, and before the rebels had ceased their barbarous fire upon the helpless men in the river, he charged upon the batteries, delivering a deadly fire as he advanced, and driving the gunners from their pieces at the point of the bayonet. From the batteries a part of the troops proceeded to the low land, where the rebel infantry were firing upon the crew of the Mound City, and drove them quickly away, scattering in all directions. The federal soldiers were exasperated by the barbarity of the rebels, and gave no quarter. Many of the enemy were killed or wounded, and about thirty were taken prisoners, including Captain Fry. The number of the rebel force was not known, but it was not large, and consisted of the crew of a rebel gunboat, commanded by Captain Fry, and a small force of infantry which he had brought together to aid him.

The following are the official reports of Captain Davis and Colonel Fitch concerning this engagement:—

REPORT OF CAPTAIN DAVIS.

"UNITED STATES FLAG-STEAMER BENTON,
MEMPHIS, June 19, 1862.

"SIR: The Conestoga, Lieutenant-commanding G. W. Blodgett, arrived here to-day from White River.

"She brings information of the capture of two batteries at St. Charles, eighty miles from the mouth; the first of which mounted four Parrott guns, and the second three forty-two-pounder rifled guns.

" Three guns, it is understood, were taken from the gunboat Mariposa, which, after being dismounted, was sunk.

" There is now but one gunboat remaining in White River, the Pontchartrain, mounting three or five guns, and having her machinery protected by iron and cotton.

" The enemy has attempted to block up the river by driving piles and by sinking boats, but no serious obstructions have yet been discovered.

" The Conestoga will return to White River to-night with reënforcements, accompanied by an additional transport laden with commissary stores.

" The victory at St. Charles, which has probably given us the command of White River, and secured our communication with General Curtis, would be unalloyed with regret but for the fatal accident to the steam-drum and heater of the Mound City, mentioned in my telegraph despatch.

" Of the crew, consisting of one hundred and seventy-five officers and men, eighty-two have already died, forty-three were killed in the water or drowned, twenty-five are severely wounded, and are now on board the hospital boat. Among the latter is Captain Kilty. They promise to do well. Three officers and twenty-two men escaped uninjured.

" After the explosion took place the wounded men were shot by the enemy while in the water, and the boats of the Conestoga, Lexington, and St. Louis, which went to the assistance of the scalded and drowning men of the Mound City, were fired into both with great guns and muskets, and were disabled — one of them forced on shore to prevent sinking.

" The forts were commanded by Lieutenant Joseph Fry, late of the United States navy, who is now a prisoner and wounded.

" The department and the country will contrast these barbarities of a savage enemy with the humane efforts made by our own people to rescue the wounded and disabled under similar circumstances in the engagement of the 6th instant.

" Several poor fellows, who expired shortly after the engagement, expressed their willingness to die when they were told that the victory was ours.

" I have the honor to be, very respectfully, your obedient servant,

" C. H. DAVIS,
" *Flag-Officer commanding Western Flotilla.*
" Hon. GIDEON WELLES, *Secretary of the Navy.*"

REPORT OF COLONEL FITCH.

" ST. CHARLES, WHITE RIVER, ARK., *June* 17, 1862.

" On arriving eight miles below here last evening, we ascertained that the enemy had two batteries here, supported by a force — number unknown — of infantry.

" A combined attack was made at seven o'clock A. M. to-day. The regiment under my command (forty-sixth Indiana) landed two and a half miles below the battery, and skirmishers were thrown out. who drove in the enemy's pickets.

" The gunboats then moved up and opened on their batteries. A rifled shot from one of the batteries penetrated the steam-drum of the Mound City, disabling, by scalding, most of her crew.

" Apprehensive that some similar accident might happen to the other gunboats, and thus leave my small force without their support, I signalled the gunboats to cease firing, and we would storm the battery. They ceased at exactly the right moment, and my men carried the battery gallantly. The infantry were driven from the support of the guns, the gunners shot at their posts, their commanding officer Fry (formerly of the United States navy) wounded and captured, and eight brass and iron guns, with ammunition, captured.

"The enemy's loss is unknown. We have buried seven or eight of their dead, and other dead and wounded are being brought in.

"The casualties among my own command are small, the only real loss being from the escaping steam in the Mound City. She will probably be repaired and ready to proceed with us up the river to-morrow.

"A full report will be made as early as possible.   Very respectfully,

"G. N. FITCH,

"Colonel commanding Forty-sixth Indiana Vols.

"Hon. E. M. STANTON, Secretary of War."

The disaster to the Mound City delayed the further progress of the expedition, but did not wholly defeat it. One of the gunboats and a transport were sent back to Memphis with the wounded, and to procure a new crew for the unfortunate vessel and additional supplies. The Mound City was not so seriously injured but that a few days sufficed to repair the damages, and upon the return of the boats from Memphis, the expedition was soon ready to proceed. It was found, however, from the low stage of the water, that the boats could not reach Batesville, and the expedition failed to open communication with General Curtis.

Subsequently, supplies were sent to General Curtis from Missouri, much to the relief of his army. The advance upon Little Rock was abandoned for the time, and on the 24th of June the entire army of General Curtis, with rations for twenty days, left Batesville, and marched to Helena, on the Mississippi River, a distance of one hundred and seventy-five miles. The long and difficult march through a wild and unsettled country, was rendered more difficult and fatiguing by a comparatively small force of rebels, who obstructed the roads by felling trees, attacking exposed trains, and in every possible way annoying the federal troops. Several skirmishes took place with this rebel force, in which it was driven off with loss. The advance of General Curtis's

force arrived at Helena on the 12th of July, and the entire army soon followed. Here it remained for some months, except that a part of the force made a reconnoissance towards the Arkansas River, it being reported that Price was moving in that quarter, to cross the Mississippi. Upon this expedition a large number of ferry-boats and others were destroyed, and the enemy's means of crossing the river in force seriously crippled.

CHAPTER LXXVI.

Brief Review of the Results of the Campaign in the West.

WE have now narrated the principal events and operations of the spring campaign in 1862, at the west. Before resuming the account of the war in Virginia, which absorbed the interest and hopes of the nation more than the broader fields and more extended operations at the west, we may briefly review this campaign and its results.

In the far west there had been several skirmishes and battles, which have not been recorded in detail, because they were so disconnected from the other fields of operations, and were comparatively unimportant in their effect upon the general course of the war. The federal troops on the frontiers of Texas, who had not followed their traitorous officers in joining the rebellion, had fallen back to New Mexico, and the scattered companies had been concentrated to resist a force of Texans who had invaded New Mexico, with the determination of holding it as a territory of the "Confederate States." These troops, under Colonel Canby, with some volunteers from the loyal people of the territory, numbering all together some fifteen hundred, had several spirited engagements with the Texans, with various but not very decisive results. The federal troops gradually fell back to Fort Craig and Fort

Union, the two most important military posts in New Mexico, and the latter containing a large amount of public property. These positions were held until reënforced by troops from Colorado and Kansas, some of whom had moved with remarkable celerity through the intervening wilderness and desert. The purposes of the Texans were thus foiled, and New Mexico was not conquered or betrayed into the hands of the rebels.

In Missouri, the federal army, under General Curtis, had advanced to the south-west, driving out the rebel forces of Price and his associates, and freeing the state of rebels, except guerilla bands, and small bodies of the state troops organized by the rebel governor, Jackson. Following the retiring rebels into Arkansas, General Curtis had defeated them at the battle of Pea Ridge so severely, that for a time all thought of again invading Missouri must have been abandoned. Then moving again into Arkansas, General Curtis was about to advance upon Little Rock, the capital of the state, and would probably have succeeded in his purpose, but for the necessity of diminishing his force. But Missouri had been cleared of the rebel army, and its territory as well as its government was now secured to the Union. The successful movement of General Curtis from Northern Arkansas to the Mississippi, was a disappointment to the rebels scarcely less dispiriting than his previous operations.

In Kentucky, the armies of Grant and Buell, with repeated victories, had driven out the rebel forces, which had extended from the Mississippi to the Alleghanies, and had given the loyal sentiment of the state an opportunity to control its destinies. Advancing into Tennessee, victories had been won at Fort Henry, Fort Donelson, and Shiloh, and the rebel army forced back into Mississippi. Middle and West Tennessee were rid of the rebel army, and another state was substantially wrested from the rebel confederacy.

The Mississippi River had been effectually opened from above as far as Vicksburg, and already there was a fair prospect that its entire course would, before long, be once more free to the commerce of the great North-west. From the Gulf to New Orleans it was also again under the national flag, and the federal gunboats had passed up towards Vicksburg. New Orleans, by far the most important city of the rebellious states, was occupied by Union troops; the federal power was firmly reëstablished there, and a base secured for important future operations.

All these important advantages had been gained since the order of the President for a general advance of the Union armies. The success which had thus far attended the movements of the armies in the west justified the order; and had like success followed the movements of the army in the east, well might the loyal people hope for the suppression of the rebellion at no very distant day.

THE SOUTHERN REBELLION
JAN'T 1863
EMANCIPATION

CHAPTER LXXVI.

THE War in Virginia. — Army of the Potomac. — Reconnoissance up the Peninsula. — Yorktown. — — Intrenchments and Siege Operations. — Skirmishes and Reconnoissances. — Engagement, April 16. — Assault on a Rebel Battery, April 26. — Charge of a Massachusetts Company. — The Redoubt taken and destroyed. — Continuance of Siege Operations. — Description by the Prince de Joinville. — Rebel Strategy. — Completion of the Federal Works. — Evacuation of their Fortifications by the Rebels. — Occupation of Yorktown by Federal Troops. — Condition of Rebel Works. — Deliberate Withdrawal of the Rebels. — Mines and Torpedoes. — Guns captured. — General McClellan's Despatches. — The Result.

In a former chapter,* the movements of the Army of the Potomac were narrated down to the time of its arrival in the vicinity of Fortress Monroe, the greater part of it having reached that point by the 2d of April, 1862, at

------

* Chapter LXV.

which date General McClellan arrived there and assumed command. Previous to this, General Heintzelman ordered a reconnoissance towards Yorktown, and found indications of only a small force of rebels on the peninsula between the James and York Rivers. General Heintzelman believed that he could force the

enemy's line, isolate the rebel forces at Yorktown so as to prevent reënforcements, and
open a road to Richmond. General McClellan,
however, was anxious that the enemy should
not in any way be informed of the direction
in which his army would move, and General
Heintzelman withdrew his troops and awaited
the general advance. On the 4th of April
the advance was commenced, and the army
was soon in the vicinity of Yorktown. York
River, to that point, was held by the federal
gunboats, but the James River was not yet
opened, and the dreaded Merrimack seemed to
prevent a movement in that quarter.

At this time the rebel forces on the peninsula numbered from eight to twelve thousand men, who had held the position since the
engagement at "Big Bethel" the year previous.
Yorktown was defended by some considerable
earthworks, and the rebel line of defence, which
extended from Yorktown by the Warwick River or Creek to James River, was naturally a
position of some strength, but with the rebel
forces then there it could not have withstood
a determined attack by an army as large and
efficient as that of General McClellan. That
army numbered upwards of one hundred thousand men, the greater part of whom had already
advanced to the vicinity of Yorktown, and its
artillery, the most of which was at hand, consisted of three hundred and forty guns, of
approved pattern, some of them being one hundred and two hundred pounder rifled siege
guns. In most respects the army was thoroughly organized and equipped, and the men full
of enthusiasm and confidence in their leader
and their cause. With such an army, and abundance of materiel, General McClellan, as subsequent events proved, by a persistent attack
at first, could have overcome the obstacles at
Yorktown, defeated the rebel forces there, and
moved at once against Richmond. But there
was some reason to suppose that a knowledge
of the federal movements, which was always

possessed by the rebel leaders, had led them
already to mass large forces at Yorktown, or its
immediate vicinity, to resist the federal advance.
The inability of the navy to coöperate with
the army in an attack on Yorktown, for want of
vessels, and to open the James River for fear
of the Merrimack, also led to a necessary modification of the original plan of the campaign.
General McClellan, therefore, after feeling the
enemy's lines, decided upon a cautious system
of operations, and instead of assaulting the rebel
works, or attempting to turn them, entered upon
a siege, by which, with skilful engineering, his
great superiority in artillery would eventually
compel a surrender of the rebel position.*

The siege works were laid out with skill by
General Barnard, chief of engineers, and were
pushed forward with great vigor by the patient
labor of the men and officers, although they
were anxious for more dashing and exciting
operations. The work of the besiegers called
out corresponding action on the part of the
rebels. Their fortifications were enlarged and
strengthened; new works were constructed;

* Colonel Freemantle, an English officer, who spent several
months in the rebel states and with the rebel armies, in his
"Three Months in the South," mentions an interview with General Magruder, in which the latter spoke of the satisfaction with
which he had seen General McClellan, "with his magnificent
army, begin to break ground before earthworks defended only
by eight thousand men."

General McClellan, in his official report, puts the number of
Magruder's forces at fifteen thousand, but the testimony of rebel
prisoners and deserters confirmed the statement that, at the commencement of the siege, the rebel force did not exceed eight
thousand men. General McClellan also states that the withdrawal of McDowell's corps, and the withholding of the forces at
Fortress Monroe, so diminished his army, that an attempt to turn
the enemy's position was out of his power, and he could only
attack in front, which he decided he would do by siege.

As to the number of men in General McClellan's command,
there has been some controversy. General McClellan, in a despatch of April 7, stated that when all his forces joined him, he
should have eighty-five thousand men. The official returns of
about the same date gave about one hundred and eight thousand,
and on the last of April the official returns gave more than one
hundred and twelve thousand on the peninsula present for duty.
The effective force was, probably, above one hundred thousand
men.

the water of the Warwick River was made an ally, by means of dikes and sluices, and the reënforcements which it had been supposed were already there when the federal army first advanced, were brought up in sufficient numbers for the purposes of the rebel leaders, and the position daily became more difficult to take. It was impossible, however, for the rebels to hold the place against the skill and materiel with which General McClellan was operating, and the surrender, under the circumstances, was rightly deemed only a question of time. As the federal batteries, one after another, were completed and mounted with the heavy siege guns, they still remained almost wholly silent, awaiting the completion of the whole system of works. Had a portion of these batteries opened upon the rebel works as they were ready, the evacuation of Yorktown, in the opinion of able artillery officers, would have been hastened. But the commanding general's purpose was to open the bombardment on all sides at once, and thus speedily reduce the enemy's works, when strong assaulting parties would complete the victory, and secure the defeat and capture of the rebel forces.

The siege was not wholly without excitement, for there were daily skirmishes between the pickets of the opposing forces, and advanced lines of sharpshooters caused not a little damage and annoyance to the rebel artillerymen. There were also occasional trials of the range of the siege artillery as it was mounted, and some more decided attacks by field batteries, to prevent the construction of new fortifications, or the occupation of important positions by the rebels, who also were not idle in making similar efforts against the movements of the besiegers. Much of the time, too, a heavy bombardment was kept up from the rebel works upon the points where the federal troops were engaged in the construction of batteries.

Some of the skirmishes resulting from reconnoissances, or the advance of the federal line for the construction of a new battery, were quite brisk engagements, which at an earlier stage of the war would have been deemed considerable battles. One of the most important of these occurred on the 16th of April, near Lee's Mills, a strongly defended rebel position on the Warwick Creek, the capture of which might have hastened the evacuation or surrender of Yorktown. At this point the rebels had an earthwork, opposite to which the federal forces had also constructed a considerable work, which was mounted with field batteries. Between the two was an open field, skirted on the north by woods, in which skirmishers were advanced on either side, and Warwick Creek also flowed between the two. Four light batteries opened fire on the federal side, and by their well-directed shots soon drove the rebels from their guns. A detachment of four companies from a Vermont regiment were ordered forward through the woods, to assault the enemy's works. These troops pushed bravely forward against scattering shots of musketry, and had crossed the creek, when the rebels opened upon them a heavy fire of musketry and rifles. Finding the force in front was too strong, the troops were recalled; but as they were recrossing the creek, the rebels opened a sluice above them, and they were suddenly nearly overwhelmed by the flood of waters. They struggled through, however, under the protection of the batteries, which, with the sharpshooters, kept the rebels within their entrenchments, and prevented an attack under disadvantages which would have been disastrous to the federal force. They succeeded in bringing away nearly all their killed and wounded, who numbered about one hundred and fifty out of a force of but little more than three hundred. A more determined and powerful attack on this point at this time, was not deemed expedient, and no further attempt was made to assault any of the principal works of the enemy.

Another more successful affair was an assault upon and capture of a redoubt which the rebels had constructed in advance of their main line of fortifications. This occurred on the 26th of April, and was participated in by detachments of the first and eleventh Massachusetts regiments. The assault was made by one company [*] of the first regiment, the others being deployed as skirmishers, or held in reserve, the troops of the eleventh being posted as supports to the artillery. The assailants advanced boldly towards the redoubt, in spite of a brisk fire of musketry, which greeted them when their movement was discovered. Reserving their fire till they reached the ditch in front of the redoubt, they then discharged their pieces at the rebels, and charged quickly across the ditch, up the embankment, and over the parapet, to find the enemy flying from their work. But though the rebels fled, the assailants captured fourteen prisoners. The other troops were advanced, when the redoubt was thus gallantly taken, and though the rebels opened fire from their main batteries, the work was soon essentially destroyed, and the captors retired in admirable order. The loss was three killed and sixteen wounded, one of them mortally. The loss to the rebels was fourteen prisoners and several killed and wounded, besides the destruction of their redoubt.

In the mean time the siege operations continued, and the work is described by the Prince de Joinville,[†] who was an officer of General McClellan's staff, as follows : —

"Ten thousand laborers were unceasingly employed cutting through the woods and forming roads, trenches, and batteries. It was a curious spectacle. A straight arm of the sea,

fringed by a thick and strong vegetation, mixed with trees of all kinds, living and dead, entangled with withes and moss, approached in a serpentine form to the front of the attack. The first parallel was made. The wood which surrounded us was an admirable protection. This arm of the sea was covered with bridges. Roads were cut along its margin in the midst of tulips, flowers of Judea, and azaleas in full bloom. From this natural parallel others were formed by the hands of man, and we rapidly approached the place. The defenders opened a terrific fire on those works that they could see, as well as upon those which they supposed were in progress. Shells whistled on every side through the large trees, cutting down branches, frightening horses, but otherwise doing very little harm. Nobody cared about it. In the evening, when all the laborers returned in good order, with their rifles on their backs, and their shovels on their shoulders, the fire became more furious, as if the enemy had marked the hour of their return. We went to this cannonade as to a show ; and when, on a beautiful night in spring-time, the troops gayly marched along to this martial music through the flowering woods ; when the balloon, with which we made our reconnoissances, was floating in the air, we seemed to be spectators at a fête, and for a moment were made to forget the miseries of war.

"The siege, however, still went on. Powerful artillery, with great difficulty, had been brought up ; one hundred and even two hundred-pounder rifled cannon and thirteen-inch mortars were ready to batter the place. Fourteen batteries were constructed, armed, and appointed. If our fire had not yet been opened, it was because it was designed to open all our batteries together along the whole line ; and for this reason we waited until nothing was wanting to complete our preparations. We could not, however, resist the desire to try the two hundred-pounders. These enormous pieces were handled with incredible ease. Four men sufficed to load and aim them, without any more difficulty than in the working of our old twenty-four-pounders. At a distance of three miles their fire was admirably precise. One day one of these immense pieces had a kind of duel with a rifled piece of somewhat smaller calibre, in position on the bastions at Yorktown. The curious among us mounted on the parapet to see where the missiles might fall, and while they communicated their observations to one another, the sentry on the lookout would announce when the enemy was about to fire in turn; but the distance was so great that, between the discharge and the arrival of the projectile, every body had time to descend without any hurry, and to place himself under the shelter of the parapet. Such, however, was the precision, that we were sure to see the enormous projectile passing over the very spot where the group of observers had been standing but a moment before; then it would bound along and tear up the earth some fifty or sixty yards off, and its inflammable composition would burst with a loud explosion, throwing into the air a cloud of dust as high as the water jets of St. Cloud.

"It was evident that with the powerful means at our disposal, the capture of Yorktown was but a work of time. Shattered beneath the tremendous fire which was about to be opened upon it, without casemates to cover their soldiers, without any other defence than outworks and palisades, the place had not even the chance of opposing a lengthened resistance. Every thing was ready for the final blow. Not only was a terrific bombardment about to be opened upon the town, not only were the most select troops set apart to follow up this bombardment by a grand assault, but the steam transports only awaited a sign to push immediately up the York River, and to land Franklin's troops at the upper part of the stream, on the line of retreat of the confederate army. A part of these troops were also to remain on board the transports. They would have taken but a few hours to traverse by water the distance it would have taken the enemy's army two days at least to march by land. Driven from the lines of Yorktown by a powerful attack, pursued, sword in hand, intercepted on the route by fresh troops, that army would have been in a most critical position, and the federals would have obtained what they so much desired — an astonishing military success."

This contemplated military success, however, did not follow. The rebel officers undoubtedly were well informed of the progress of the federal works, and of the artillery which would open upon them when the batteries were completed, and force them to surrender or evacuate the position. They had already gained much by the delay of the siege, and the works for the defence of Richmond were well advanced. To await the terrible storm of the bombardment would but insure a loss of life, without any advantage; to remain to the latest moment, with a show of determined resistance, and then to withdraw safely, would be successful strategy and a gain to their cause. This course, probably contemplated by some from the first, was determined upon in due season, and promptly carried into effect.

The federal batteries and parallels were so far completed that preparations were made to open fire upon the rebel works, and it was determined to commence the bombardment on the 5th or 6th of May. Forces were organized to follow up the bombardment by assault at the proper time, and General Franklin's division, which was still on board transports in York River, was to proceed, with other troops, up the river to West Point, some miles above Yorktown, to intercept the rebels, or make an attack upon their flank as they were driven from Yorktown. The attack was eagerly looked for by the officers and men of the army, and awaited with some impatience, by the people. But on the night of the 3d of May, the light of a fire was seen within the rebel lines, and a heavy explosion took place towards morning. This unusual occurrence indicated that the rebels were making some movement, though they occasionally fired a shot from some of their batteries, which had been more active than ever on the 3d, until a late hour in the night. As morning dawned, the entire silence of the enemy's batteries, and the disappearance of pickets and sentinels on the works, indicated that their fortifications had been abandoned. A closer examination of the rebel lines confirmed the suspicion, and a small force was sent forward, which entered one of the principal forts without opposition, and raised the national flag upon the ramparts.

A sufficient force to guard against surprise was immediately sent forward to hold the abandoned fortifications, occupy the town, and secure such trophies as the enemy left. The works were pronounced exceedingly strong, well planned and constructed, and in their condition when abandoned could have been held against an attacking force of much superior numbers to that defending them. A large number of the heavy guns with which the works were mounted had been left behind, spiked, but not injured, and appeared to have been abandoned at last in some haste, probably because they had been used up to the latest moment. Considerable ammunition for these guns was at hand, and the magazines were subsequently found well supplied. There were quantities of hospital stores discovered, a few tents standing, but no commissary or quartermaster's stores. The general appearance of the position, so recently occupied by the rebels, indicated that they had deliberately removed their stores and every thing of value, except the guns and ammunition which had been actively used to conceal their movements. All the sick and wounded had been removed, and Yorktown itself was

deserted, except by some negroes and a few deserters, who had concealed themselves when the rebel army left. Another indication of the deliberation of their movement, as well as of their barbarous warfare, was the planting of percussion shells and torpedoes in the ground, in such positions that they would be exploded by the tread of the Union soldiers when they entered the works and the town. A number of federal soldiers were killed in this way, and many others wounded; and so dangerous were these mines, that careful search was made for them, and some of the rebel prisoners were justly employed in the work of discovering and removing them.

The number of guns captured, including those at Gloucester, on the north side of York River, opposite Yorktown, which was also strongly fortified and formed a part of the rebel position, and was abandoned at the same time, was seventy-three, of various calibre and quality. The field artillery, and probably some of the more valuable heavy guns, had all been removed. These, combined with the guns which were left, made a large number, and would have offered a formidable resistance to any attack. That a large part of them had been mounted since the federal army had commenced its movement against Yorktown, there could be little doubt, as the rebels had not been idle in strengthening their position while the besiegers were at work. This armament, however, would have been of but little avail against the greater number and more effective guns which General McClellan had planted against them, when all the latter should have been brought into use and rained their terrible storm of shot and shell upon the rebel works. But without calling into use this formidable artillery, the guns of the rebels were abandoned, their works evacuated, and their position occupied by the besiegers. The success had been achieved, too, without great loss of life, and this was indeed its great glory.

The following are the brief despatches by telegraph, in which General McClellan announced the results of his operations : —

"HEADQUARTERS OF THE ARMY OF THE POTOMAC, }
May 4, 9 A. M. }

"We have the ramparts. Have guns, ammunition, camp equipage, &c. We hold the entire line of his works, which the engineers report as being very strong. I have thrown all my cavalry and horse-artillery in pursuit, supported by infantry. I move Franklin's division, and as much more as I can transport by water, up to West Point to-day. No time shall be lost. The gunboats have gone up York River. I omitted to state that Gloucester is also in our possession. I shall push the enemy to the wall.

"G. B. McCLELLAN, *Major-General*.
' Hon. E. M. STANTON, *Secretary of War.*"

"HEADQUARTERS, ARMY OF THE POTOMAC }
May 5, 11.30 A. M. }

"An inspection just made, shows that the rebels abandoned in their works at Yorktown, two three-inch rifled cannon, two four and a half-inch rifled cannon, sixteen thirty-two pounders, six forty-two pounders, nineteen eight-inch columbiads, four nine-inch Dahlgrens, one ten-inch columbiad, one ten-inch mortar, and one eight-inch siege howitzer, with carriages and implements complete, each piece supplied with seventy-six rounds of ammunition. On the ramparts there are also four magazines, which have not yet been examined. This does not include the guns left at Gloucester Point and their other works to our left.

"G. B. McCLELLAN, *Major-General.*
" Hon. E. M. STANTON, *Secretary of War.*"

In some respects the result at Yorktown was a great military success. for the rebels had been compelled to retire from their strong position, abandon materiel of which they had no abundance, and open the way to Richmond ; but the delay of the siege had undoubtedly strength-

ened them for future operations in the defence of Richmond, and enabled them to set on foot a diversion to weaken the federal army, which otherwise might have been pressing them before their capital. Nor was it that kind of success which inspires an army with enthusiasm and confidence, like a more dearly bought victory in the field. The severe labor of the soldiers, though not vain, had not brought the victorious results which they had expected, — a defeated enemy, captured prisoners, arms and stores, and all the evidences of undisputed success. The enemy had gone intact, and they were yet to meet him, the battle being postponed, not won. To the officers and men the result was not, therefore, wholly satisfactory, and some of them were much chagrined.

CHAPTER LXXVII.

Advance from Yorktown and Pursuit of the Rebels. — Difficult Roads. — Movements of Cavalry. — Advance of General Hooker's and General Smith's Divisions. — Arrival in Front of Rebel Position. — Attack postponed. — Preparations for Battle. — Movement of General Hooker's Division. — Attack on the Rebel Works. — Successful Opening of the Battle. — Rebel Repulse. — Rally of the Rebels. — Severe Conflict. — Rebel Reënforcements. — Want of Reenforcements by General Hooker. — Efforts of General Kearney to reach the Front. — Critical State of Affairs. — Loss of Artillery. — Failure of Ammunition. — Order for falling back. — Bravery of the Federal Troops. — Arrival of General Kearney's Division. — Attack by the Reënforcements. — The Rebels driven beyond their Intrenchments. — Movements on the Federal Right. Advance of General Hancock's Brigade. — Occupation of Rebel Works. — Attack by the Rebels. — Strategy of General Hancock. — Resistance and Bayonet Charge by his Brigade. — The Enemy driven back. — The gallant Charge. — Retreat of Rebels by Night. — Their Purpose accomplished. — Difficulty of Pursuit. — Occupation of Williamsburg. — Advance of a Cavalry Force, and its Return. — Limited Captures. — Extract from General McClellan's Report. — Reports of General Hooker and General Kearney.

WHEN it was found that the rebel forces had wholly withdrawn from Yorktown, preparations were made for pursuit. The greater part of the cavalry, with light artillery, under the command of General Stoneman, were at once advanced on the roads leading from Yorktown and Lee's Mills towards Williamsburg and Richmond. A large force of infantry followed a few hours afterwards, to support the cavalry and artillery, the forces consisting of the army corps of Generals Heintzelman and Keyes, and General Sumner, the second in rank in the army, was assigned to take charge of the movement. At the same time the division of General Franklin, with other forces, moved up the York River in transports to West Point, where they were to debark and make a movement to intercept the retreat of the rebel forces. This latter movement, it would appear from the attention given to it by the commanding general, was expected to be the most important in its purpose and its results; and while the direct advance might press the rear guard of the retreating rebels, the forces by way of West Point would fall upon their flank, and between the two the rebel army would be utterly defeated. But the rebel plan of campaign was as well defined as that of the federal general, and with their knowledge of the country they were better able to carry it out.

Recent rains had rendered the roads muddy and almost impassable. The advance of cavalry and artillery had so cut them up, that it was with great difficulty that the infantry could march and the artillery and ammunition trains be moved. But in spite of the difficulties, the advance divisions, General Hooker's and General Smith's, pushed forward as rapidly as they could. In the mean time the cavalry had skirmished with a rear guard of rebel cavalry, supported by a battery of artillery, and compelled them to retreat towards the James River.. A few prisoners were captured, but in consequence of the infantry not reaching the point where they were expected, the rebel force effected their escape. Soon after the cavalry came upon the line of the rebel fortifications near Williamsburg. These fortifications extended nearly across the

peninsula, and were strong earthworks, capable, from their position and thoroughness of construction, of resisting a powerful attack, if defended with pertinacity by a considerable force. After passing one redoubt, which was undefended, an attack by the cavalry and light artillery upon a second earthwork resulted in a repulse with some loss, and the cavalry fell back to await the arrival of the infantry and other batteries of artillery, not, however, without some gallant fighting by a part of the cavalry, who repulsed a rebel cavalry force, which in turn had made a fierce attack as the federal force withdrew.

As the columns of General Hooker and General Smith advanced, some confusion occurred, on account of the latter changing his route, the road by which he advanced being found seriously obstructed. As the head of General Hooker's column came out upon the main road in the afternoon, it encountered the column of General Smith, and was delayed several hours for the latter to pass. Then following on, General Hooker's division advanced, and by order of General Heintzelman, turned into a cross road, and thence moved out on the Lee's Mill road, thus changing positions with General Smith's division, which had been assigned to the left, while General Hooker's was to have moved to the right. It was late in the afternoon when General Smith's division arrived at General Stoneman's position, and having been deployed, General Sumner, who had arrived upon the ground, ordered an attack upon the enemy in front. The lines, however, were thrown into some confusion while moving through the dense forest, and darkness coming on, the order for attack was countermanded, and the troops bivouacked for the night. A heavy rain commenced falling, and continued through the night and the next day. Weary and wet, the soldiers lay down without shelter, and awaited the coming of the next day, which promised to be one of severe conflict and carnage. In the mean time General Hooker's division moved on for several hours after dark, till it approached the principal position of the enemy, Fort Magruder, when his soldiers also, worn out by their long and difficult march, bivouacked for the remainder of the night.

The next day (May 5) dawned rainy and cheerless, and as the troops arose from their wet and comfortless couches, there was little to encourage them or to awake that enthusiasm which carries the soldier successfully through the battle. But the work was before them, and they prepared bravely to do their duty. General Hooker, having reconnoitred the enemy's position, disposed his forces, and by half past seven o'clock commenced moving forward for an attack. Skirmishing had already commenced between the pickets of the opposing armies, and every thing now indicated that the rebels intended to make a final stand here, or to resist the further progress of the federal army until they had made other dispositions for the protection of Richmond. General Hooker's division made a circuit to the left, through the woods, towards James River, and came into position before some smaller works of the enemy and the large work called Fort Magruder, or Fort Page. The artillery was posted on the edge of the woods, in an open field, and commenced the battle by a vigorous cannonade. The infantry, in the mean while, remained under cover of the thicket, secure from the fire of the heavy rebel guns, which opened from the several works in front. The fire of General Hooker's artillery, after a time, prepared the way for an assault by the infantry, and they were accordingly ordered forward, and charged gallantly at the enemy in the smaller works, which were feebly defended, and speedily abandoned as the Union troops advanced. Falling back from one position to another, the rebels at last rallied behind and about Fort Magruder, and it soon became apparent that they were disposing a large force in that vicinity, to re-sist the federal attack and perhaps to assume the offensive.

The battle soon became severe, the enemy bringing up infantry to oppose the federal infantry, while they kept up a heavy fire from the guns of the fort. The rain fell fast, and the ground was in such a condition that it was with great difficulty that artillery could be moved; but in spite of obstacles, the pieces were boldly pushed forward, and did effective service. The fire of musketry was rapid, and as the rebel troops advanced to drive the federal forces back from the positions already gained, they suffered severely, and were compelled again and again to retire. But their numbers increased by reënforcements much more than they were diminished by the federal fire, and they boldly persisted in their efforts. The federal troops as bravely held their ground, though their losses were heavy, and they were exhausted by marching and fighting. But it was evident that they could not accomplish the work assigned them, even if they could hold their ground, without assistance. General Hooker sent for reenforcements, and General Heintzelman sent repeatedly to General Sumner for other troops to hurry forward. But for some reason, although a large part of the army, as it was stated at the time, was within an hour's ride, the needed reenforcements did not arrive. The troops which were nearest to the front do not appear to have been ordered forward at all, but General Kearney's division, which was in the rear, was early in the day ordered to support General Hooker's.[*] By great effort, General Kearney succeeded in passing the intervening troops, and at last reaching the front, much to the joy of General Heintzelman, who, learning that he

---

[*] General Sumner subsequently stated that his own corps was in the rear, and when applied to for reenforcements he had at hand but three thousand infantry and a body of cavalry, who could not be used with effect in this battle. By what order other troops, not far distant, were prevented from being moved forward, does not appear.

was coming, had sent messenger after messenger to hurry him forward. The terrible condition of the roads, and the obstruction of other troops, had delayed him, but he had pressed forward with great energy, and arrived in time to save the brave division of General Hooker.

In the mean time affairs were becoming critical with the latter division. It was opposed by superior numbers, and the rebels continued their efforts to drive it back. But all their attempts were unavailing, and the Union troops held on bravely till their ammunition began to fail. Even then they took what cartridges they could find upon the dead or disabled, and, fixing bayonets, stood ready to meet the enemy with bristling steel. At this juncture, in one of their attacks, the rebels succeeded in capturing a battery of artillery, which could not be withdrawn in consequence of the loss of men and horses. They were, however, compelled to abandon three of the pieces, by the vigorous fire of other batteries and a portion of the infantry whose ammunition was not yet exhausted. But they were encouraged by their success, and prepared for still more determined efforts. It seemed useless for troops who had suffered so severely as a part of this gallant division, to attempt longer, without ammunition, to hold their advanced position against superior numbers. The ammunition train was far back on the almost impassable roads, and the hoped for reënforcements did not arrive. Under these circumstances, the order to fall back was reluctantly given to one of the brigades. The movement, so dangerous in the face of an advancing enemy, caused a wavering and breaking of a part of the line, which might have resulted in disaster, but for the efforts of officers and the noble bearing of some regiments, who, with fixed bayonets, prepared to meet the assault. The wavering troops rallied, and went back to their position, and notwithstanding the rebel fire was more severe than ever, the ground was still maintained. It was

the last chance for the enemy to succeed. General Kearney's division had arrived, and welcomed by the cheers of those in the rear, was moving to the front, where it was hailed with still wilder shouts.

General Kearney's troops arrived just in time to save General Hooker's division from defeat. The advance brigade, commanded by General Berry, was rapidly moved forward, and by their heavy volleys of musketry drove back the enemy, who was sorely pressing the weary troops of General Hooker, and was on the point of capturing another battery. Following up their heavy fire with a charge, the newly arrived troops drove the rebels back to their works. Another charge drove them from the redoubt, which was held in spite of several attempts to retake them. The other brigades of General Kearney came up, and General Hooker was able to withdraw his troops, who had contended so bravely and under such disadvantages. The tide of battle was rolled back beyond the enemy's first position; with additional troops, General Heintzelman formed a new line of battle, and as night closed in the rebel forces had retired behind the fortifications, which they still held.

Of the arrival of General Kearney's division, a writer who was on the field, gives the following graphic description : —

"It was now that death passed fastest through our ranks. Officers fell thickly, and men went to earth in heaps. Ten minutes more would have ruined us — for demi-gods could not have sustained such an inequality as eight thousand to twenty-five thousand. Ten minutes more would have saved the rebellion, and caused the recognition of the revolted states. Ten minutes more would have crushed military reputation, and driven a political party out of power, and its administrators perhaps out of life. But now, Brigadier Berry, of the stout state of Maine, — wading through the mud and rain at such speed that he actually overtook and passed three other brigades, — came in sight. Heintzelman shouted with gratitude. He ran to the nearest band, and ordered it to meet the coming regiments with 'Yankee Doodle,' and to give them marching time into the field with the 'Starspangled Banner.' A wild 'hurrah' went up from the army; and, with a yell that was electric, three regiments of Berry's brigade went to the front, formed a line nearly half a mile long, and commenced a volley-firing that no troops on earth could stand before; then, at the double-quick, dashed with the bayonet, at the rebel array, and sent them flying from the field into their earthworks, pursued them into the largest of them, and drove them out behind with the pure steel, and then invited them to retake it. The attempt was repeatedly made, and repeatedly repulsed."

While the events above narrated were transpiring on the left, a more successful movement was made at the right, by a part of General Smith's division. This division was posted mainly in the centre, fronting the enemy's position, but one brigade, under General Hancock, was sent to the right, across a causeway or dam, to take possession of a redoubt which seemed to be feebly, if at all, defended. General Hancock moved his brigade rapidly to the position indicated, though a determined enemy might have successfully resisted his passage of the causeway. It appeared, however, that there was no considerable rebel force near that point at the time, and General Hancock's troops soon occupied the redoubt, which was found undefended. From this point he advanced to another of the enemy's works, which was also deserted. Beyond this was another redoubt, occupied by rebel forces, and commanding the open ground between it and Fort Magruder; but to take this work, and thus advance towards the position of General Hooker and on the flank of the force which was opposing him, required more troops. General Hancock sent for reënforcements, and orders were twice given

for other brigades of General Smith's division to join him, but before they could be carried into effect they were countermanded, General Sumner fearing that he should weaken his centre too much by the movement. General Hancock was, therefore, obliged to remain in his position without attempting a further advance.

But the rebel generals were not disposed to wait for an attack. Seeing his somewhat isolated position, and his hesitation to advance, late in the afternoon they brought a large force against him. General McClellan had at this time arrived at the front from Yorktown, and understanding the position of affairs, ordered two brigades to reënforce General Hancock. These troops were at once pushed forward, but before they could reach General Hancock's position, the enemy made their attack upon him with superior numbers. The ground which he had gained was too important to be relinquished without a struggle, but the attacking force was too large for any thing like an equal contest. General Hancock, however, was ready with resources, and disposing his troops advantageously, he fell back slowly, as if retreating before the advancing enemy. The rebels, observing the movement, came on with exultation at their supposed success, and hoping perhaps to rout the federal force and capture many prisoners. But suddenly General Hancock's forces halted and faced the foe, his artillery wheeled and opened a rapid and effective fire, and the entire force of infantry poured upon the enemy a terrific volley of musketry. This sudden and unexpected fire checked the eager advance of the rebels, and threw their ranks into some confusion, though they continued to approach in more irregular lines. Succeeding volleys thinned their ranks; and as they again wavered, General Hancock ordered a bayonet charge, which was made with an enthusiastic shout, and with such firmness and steadiness, that the rebels turned and fled to their intrenchments. It was a gallant charge, and achieved the victory in this part of the field, for the rebels did not again attempt to move from their works, and night coming on, the fire of artillery was soon suspended.

General Hancock's brigade had accomplished much with but a very small loss, and won this last glory of the day before General Smith's other brigades, though hurred forward, could reach the field. The general's skill and bravery received the highest commendation from his superiors, and the bayonet charge of his brigade was described as one of the most brilliant engagements of the war. Circumstances, and the neglect of the enemy to defend the first points of attack, had given to this brigade a success which their gallant charge maintained and deserved; but the hard struggle had been on the left, in General Hooker's division, which, though for a time less successful, had at greater sacrifice bravely maintained an unequal contest till reënforcements beat the enemy back.

The next morning the rebel forces had disappeared. Their works were abandoned, and the town of Williamsburg was evacuated by all save a large number of their wounded. They had partially, if not wholly, accomplished their purpose, by retarding the advance of the federal army till their trains were safely far towards Richmond, and their main force could be concentrated there. The engagement near Williamsburg was at first but the skirmishing of their rear guard with the federal advance cavalry force, but finding that they were able, with comparative ease, to check that, they sent back reënforcements to hold, for a time longer, the line of works at Williamsburg against such force as should follow the cavalry. Even after General Hooker's forces had opened the battle, reënforcements came back from Williamsburg, the rebel generals hoping to inflict a severe repulse upon the comparatively small federal force which was making the attack. They had succeeded in retarding for more than a day the federal army; and while the soldiers of the latter slept upon their arms, and expected a renewal of the battle at dawn, they had quietly and safely withdrawn. Events proved that they had gained more, perhaps, than they had anticipated, for General McClellan considered it impossible to continue the pursuit at once, in consequence of the bad state of the roads and the exhausted condition and wants of the troops which had been engaged. Many of them were without rations and ammunition, and the supply trains, delayed by the movement of troops and almost impassable roads, had not come up. General McClellan, moreover, had decided to make West Point his depot for supplies, as affording greater facilities for transportation, and a large part of the army was already sent to that place, from which a movement could at once be made to intercept or pursue the enemy.

The rebel works and the town of Williamsburg were soon entered by the federal forces. Several guns and caissons, which the rebels had not been able to remove, were found, and a quantity of small arms was collected from the various works and roads, but the capture of materiel was unimportant. All supplies had been removed, and the retreat was made in an orderly manner. A cavalry force, under Colonel Averill, was sent forward to overtake and annoy the enemy's rear guard; but the condition of the roads, and a want of supplies, prevented a long or vigorous pursuit. This force found a number of guns abandoned in the deep mud of the road, and picked up a considerable number of stragglers, but succeeded in accomplishing nothing more, and returning to Williamsburg, awaited a general advance of the army.

The following extract from General McClellan's Report on the Organization and Campaigns of the Army of the Potomac, embraces the principal part of his account of the battle of Williamsburg : —

" The roads leading from the lower part of

the Peninsula to Williamsburg, one along the York River (the Yorktown road), and the other along the James (the Lee's Mill road), unite between the heads of the tributary streams a short distance in front of Fort Magruder, by which they are commanded, and debouch from the woods just before uniting. A branch from the James River road leaves it about one and three fourths of a mile below Fort Magruder, and unites with the road from Allen's landing to Williamsburg, which crosses the tributary of College Creek over a dam at the outlet of the pond, and passes just in rear of the line of works, being commanded by the three redoubts on the right of the line, at about the same distance from Fort Magruder. A branch leaves the York River road and crosses the tributary of Queen's Creek on a dam, and passing over the position and through the works in its rear, finally enters Williamsburg. This road is commanded by redoubts on the left of the line of the works.

"General Stoneman debouched from the woods with his advance guard (consisting of a part of the first United States cavalry, and one section of Gibson's battery, under the command of General Cook), and the enemy immediately opened on him with several field-pieces from Fort Magruder, having the correct range, and doing some execution. Gibson's battery was brought into position as rapidly as the deep mud would permit, and returned the fire ; while the sixth United States cavalry was sent to feel the enemy's left. This regiment passed one redoubt, which it found unoccupied, and appeared in the rear of a second, when a strong cavalry force, with infantry and artillery, came down upon it, whereupon the regiment was withdrawn. The rear squadron, under command of Captain Saunders, repelled a charge of the enemy's cavalry in the most gallant manner. In the mean time the enemy was being reënforced by infantry, and the artillery fire becoming very hot, General Stoneman, hav-

ing no infantry to carry the works, ordered the withdrawal of the battery. This was accomplished, with the exception of one piece, which could not be extricated from the mud. The enemy attempted to prevent the movement, but their charges were met by the first United States cavalry, under command of Lieutenant-colonel Grier, and they were driven back, losing several officers and one stand of colors. General Stoneman then took a defensive position, a short distance in the rear of the first, to await the arrival of the infantry.

"The advance of General Smith's column reached Skiff's Creek about half past eleven o'clock, and found the bridge over that stream in flames, and the road impassable. A practicable route to the Yorktown road having been discovered, the division, by order of General Sumner, moved on by that road, and reached General Stoneman's position about half past five o'clock. General Sumner, arriving with it, assumed command.

"Generals Heintzelman and Keyes also arrived. During the afternoon of the 4th, near the Halfway House, the head of General Hooker's column encountered Smith's division filing into the road, and was obliged to halt between three and four hours until it had passed. General Hooker then followed on, and at Cheesecake Church turned off, by General Heintzelman's direction, taking a cross-road, and moved out on the Lee's Mill road, thus changing places with General Smith. Marching part of the night, he came in sight of Fort Magruder early in the morning of the 5th.

"General Smith's division having been deployed, General Sumner ordered an attack on the works in his front ; but the lines having been thrown into confusion while moving through the dense forest, and darkness coming on, the attempt for that night was abandoned. The troops bivouacked in the woods, and a heavy rain began, which continued until the morning of the 6th, making the roads, already in very bad condition, almost impassable. During the morning of the 5th General Sumner reconnoitred the position in his front, and at eleven o'clock ordered Hancock's brigade, of Smith's division, to take possession of a work on the enemy's left, which had been found to be unoccupied. The remainder of Smith's division occupied the woods in front without being actually engaged.

"The divisions of Couch and Casey had received orders during the night to march at daylight; but on account of the terrible condition of the roads, and other impediments, were not able to reach the field until after one o'clock P. M., at which time the first brigade of Couch's division arrived, and was posted in the centre, on Hooker's right. The other two brigades came up during the afternoon, followed by Casey's division.

"In the mean time General Hooker, having reconnoitred the enemy's position, began the attack at half past seven A. M., and for a while silenced the guns of Fort Magruder, and cleared the ground in his front; but the enemy being continually reënforced, until their strength greatly exceeded his, made attack after attack, endeavoring to turn his left.

"For several hours his division struggled gallantly against the superior numbers of the enemy. Five guns of Webber's battery were lost, and between three and four o'clock his ammunition began to give out. The loss had been heavy, and the exhaustion of the troops was very great. At this time the division of General Kearney came up, who, at nine A. M., had received orders to reënforce Hooker, and who had succeeded, by the greatest exertions, in passing Casey's troops, and pushing on to the front through the deep mud. General Kearney at once gallantly attacked, and thereby prevented the loss of another battery, and drove the enemy back at every point, enabling General Hooker to extricate himself from his position, and withdraw his wearied troops. Peck's brigade, of Couch's division, as has been

mentioned before, was, immediately on its arrival, ordered by General Sumner to deploy on Hooker's right. This was promptly done, and the attacks of the enemy at that point were repulsed. General Peck held his position until late in the afternoon, when he was relieved by the other two brigades of Couch's division, and they were in quiet possession of the ground when night closed the contest. The vigorous action of these troops relieved General Hooker considerably. General Emory had been left with his command, on the night of the 4th, to guard the branch of the Lee's Mill road which leads to Allen's farm; and on the morning of the 5th it was ascertained that by this route the enemy's right could be turned. A request for infantry for this purpose was made to General Heintzelman, who, late in the afternoon, sent four regiments and two batteries of Kearney's division — the first disposable troops he had — and directed General Emory to make the attack. With these reënforcements his force amounted to about three thousand men and three batteries. General Emory, on account of want of knowledge of the ground, and the lateness of the hour, did not succeed in this movement. It involved some risks, but, if successful, might have produced important results.

"At eleven A. M., as before mentioned, General Smith received orders from General Sumner to send one brigade across a dam on our right, to occupy a redoubt on the left of the enemy's line. Hancock's brigade was selected for this purpose. He crossed the dam, took possession of the first redoubt, and afterwards, finding the second one vacated, he occupied that also, and sent for reënforcements to enable him to advance further and take the next redoubt, which commanded the plain between his position and Fort Magruder, and would have enabled him to take in reverse and cut the communication of the troops engaged with Generals Hooker and Kearney.

"The enemy soon began to show himself in

strength before him, and as his rear and right flank were somewhat exposed, he repeated his request for reënforcements. General Smith was twice ordered to join him, with the rest of his division, but each time the order was countermanded at the moment of execution, General Sumner not being willing to weaken the centre. At length, in reply to General Hancock's repeated messages for more troops, General Sumner sent him an order to fall back to his first position, the execution of which General Hancock deferred as long as possible, being unwilling to give up the advantage already gained, and fearing to expose his command by such a movement.

"During the progress of these events, I had remained at Yorktown, to complete the preparations for the departure of General Franklin's and other troops to West Point by water, and to make the necessary arrangements with the naval commander for his coöperation. .

"By pushing General Franklin, well supported by water, to the right bank of the Pamunkey, opposite West Point, it was hoped to force the enemy to abandon whatever works he might have on the Peninsula below that point, or be cut off. It was of paramount importance that the arrangements to this end should be promptly made at an early hour of the morning. I had sent two of my aids (Lieutenant-Colonel Sweitzer and Major Hammerstein) to observe the operations in front, with instructions to report to me every thing of importance that might occur. I received no information from them leading me to suppose that there was any thing occurring of more importance than a simple affair of a rear guard, until about one o'clock P. M., when a despatch arrived from one of them, that every thing was not progressing favorably. This was confirmed a few minutes later by the reports of Governor Sprague and Major Hammerstein, who came directly from the scene of action.

"Completing the necessary arrangements,

I returned to my camp without delay, rode rapidly to the front, a distance of some fourteen miles, through roads much obstructed by troops and wagons, and reached the field between four and five P. M., in time to take a rapid survey of the ground. I soon learned that there was no direct communication between our centre and the left under General Heintzelman ; the centre was chiefly in the nearer edge of the woods, situated between us and the enemy. As heavy firing was heard in the direction of General Hancock's command, I immediately ordered General Smith to proceed with his two remaining brigades, to support that part of the line. General Naglee, with his brigade, received similar orders. I then directed our centre to advance to the further edge of the woods mentioned above, which was done, and I attempted to open direct communication with General Heintzelman, but was prevented by the marshy state of the ground in the direction in which the attempt was made.

"Before Generals Smith and Naglee could reach the field of General Hancock's operations, although they moved with great rapidity, he had been confronted by a superior force. Feigning to retreat slowly, he awaited their onset, and then turned upon them, and after some terrific volleys of musketry, he charged them with the bayonet, routing and dispersing their whole force, killing, wounding, and capturing five hundred to six hundred men, he himself losing only thirty-one men.

"This was one of the most brilliant engagements of the war, and General Hancock merits the highest praise for the soldierly qualities displayed, and his perfect appreciation of the vital importance of his position.

"Night put an end to the operations here, and all the troops who had been engaged in this contest slept on the muddy field, without shelter, and many without food.

"Notwithstanding the report I received from General Heintzelman, during the night, that

General Hooker's division had suffered so much that it could not be relied on next day, and that Kearney's could not do more than hold its own without reenforcements — being satisfied that the result of Hancock's engagement was to give us possession of the decisive point of the battle-field during the night, I countermanded the order for the advance of the divisions of Sedgwick and Richardson, and directed them to return to Yorktown, to proceed to West Point by water.

" Our loss during the day, the greater part of which was sustained by Hooker's division, was as follows : —

" Killed, four hundred and fifty-six; wounded, one thousand four hundred; missing, three hundred and seventy-two; total, two thousand two hundred and twenty-eight.

· " On the next morning we found the enemy's position abandoned, and occupied Fort Magruder and the town of Williamsburg, which was filled with the enemy's wounded, to whose assistance eighteen of their surgeons were sent by General J. E. Johnston, the officer in command. Several guns and caissons, which the enemy could not carry off on account of the mud, were secured. Colonel Averill was sent forward at once with a strong cavalry force, to endeavor to overtake the enemy's rear guard. He found several guns abandoned, and picked up a large number of stragglers, but the condition of the roads and the state of the supplies forced him to return, after advancing a few miles.

" It is my opinion that the enemy opposed us here with only a portion of his army. When our cavalry first appeared there was nothing but the enemy's rear guard at Williamsburg. Other troops were brought back during the night and the next day to hold the works as long as possible, in order to gain time for the trains, &c., already well on the way to Richmond, to make their escape. Our troops were greatly exhausted by the laborious march through the mud from their position in front of Yorktown, and by the protracted battle through which they had just passed. Many of them were out of rations and ammunition, and one division, in its anxiety to make a prompt movement, had marched with empty haversacks. The supply trains had been forced out of the roads on the 4th and 5th, to allow the troops and artillery to pass to the front, and the roads were now in such a state after thirty-six hours' continuous rain, that it was almost impossible to pass empty wagons over them. General Hooker's division had suffered so severely that it was in no condition to follow the enemy, even if the roads had been good. Under these circumstances, an immediate ·pursuit was impossible. Steps were at once taken to care for and remove the wounded, and to bring up provisions, amunition, and forage."

The following are the official reports of Generals Hooker and Kearney, which describe the principal events in the engagement : —

GENERAL HOOKER'S OFFICIAL REPORT.

" HEADQUARTERS HOOKER'S DIVISION, THIRD ARMY CORPS, ₎
        WILLIAMSBURG, VA., *May* 10, 1862. ₎

" I have the honor to report that under the instructions received through the Headquarters Third Army Corps, dated .May 4th, ' to support Stoneman, and aid him in cutting off the retreat of the enemy,' my division marched from its camp before Yorktown about noon that day.

" We marched towards Williamsburg. After advancing five or six miles on this road, I learned that Brigadier-General Stoneman had fallen upon the rear of the enemy's retreating column, and was there awaiting the arrival of an infantry force to attack them.

" This was five or six miles in advance of me, and immediately I left my command and gallopped to the front, in order to see what disposition it would be necessary to make of my force on its arrival. While here, I was in-

BEAUTIFULLY ILLUSTRATED

HISTORY OF THE UNITED STATES,

AND

BIOGRAPHIES OF THE SIGNERS OF THE DECLARATION OF INDEPENDENCE.

·THE American people have always received with favor works on the History of their country, and none perhaps has had a wider circulation, or been more generally approved, than this of which the publisher now offers a new and improved edition, *brought down to the adminis. tration of President Buchanan.*

A testimonial to a former edition, signed by DANIEL WEBSTER, GEORGE P. MARSH, MOSES H. GRINNELL, and others, thus speaks of the author and his work : "His spirited and impartial narrative, exhibiting an unusual degree of industry, candor, and carefulness ; his manly and philosophical views of the physical, social, and political aspects of our Republic ; and the completeness of the sketch he presents of American society, in its widely various features, — all combine to invest it with a standard character." And it recommends the History "as a *standard work,* remarkable for the clearness with which it is written, and for the impartiality with which many vexed questions, so interesting to us as Americans, are treated."

The present edition will offer to the reader a *complete record* of our national annals, and will show the progress and condition of the country as exhibited by the census of 1860.

The Biographies of the Signers of the Declaration of Independence are a valuable addition to the History, which it is believed must prove highly acceptable to all who reverence that great instrument and the patriots who pledged "their lives, their fortunes, and their sacred honors" to its support.

The work will be beautifully illustrated with fine steel engravings and wood cuts, executed expressly for it, from pictures by eminent artists, and original designs by Hammatt Billings. It will also contain a map of the United States, engraved expressly for the work ; and the publisher can safely say that no serial publication of equal value and beauty, has ever before been offered to the American public at so low a price.

CONDITIONS OF PUBLICATION.

THE work will be published in parts, each containing two fine steel engravings, engraved expressly for this work, also numerous highly finished wood cuts will be given in the course of publication.

Each part will be furnished to subscribers at twenty-five cents, payable on delivery.

The work is expected to be completed in thirty parts; but should the number exceed thirty-two, all over that number will be furnished to subscribers *gratis.*

☞ *No subscription will be taken for less than one entire copy.*

☞ The Southern Rebellion has given a new interest to the History of the United States, by calling attention to the origin and progress of the Union, and especially to those past events and acts which serve to explain, in some degree, the present state of affairs. The publisher is therefore induced to continue the History through this most important era of the nation's existence, and thus to make a complete History of the country, from the earliest period down to the close of Rebellion. With this object, a new volume will be issued, commencing with Mr. Buchanan's Administration, illustrated with the finest engravings, and giving a narrative of events, compiled from official documents and other authentic sources. Specimen parts are now ready.